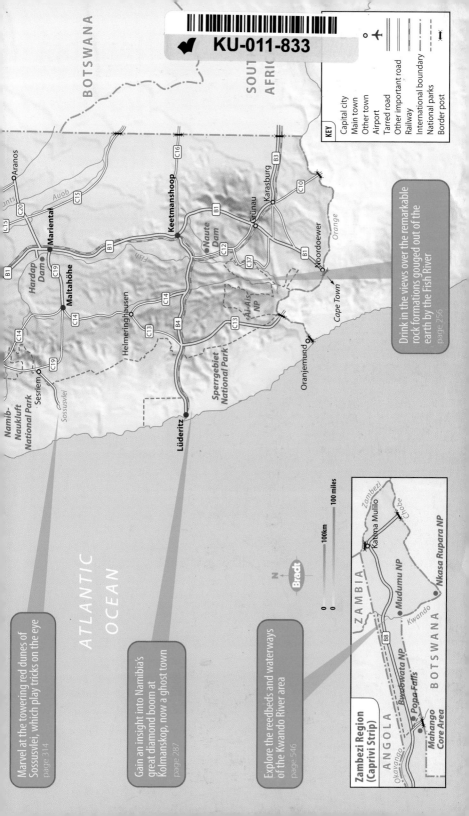

KU-011-833

KEY

○ Capital city
● Main town
○ Other town
✈ Airport
— Tarred road
— Other important road
— Railway
—·— International boundary
–––– National parks
⋉ Border post

BOTSWANA

BOTSWANA

SOUTH AFRICA

Aranos

Auob

Mariental

C20

C15

C19

C14

C14

C14

C14

C13

C13

C3

C19

Sesriem

Sossusvlei

Namib-Naukluft National Park

Hardap Dam

Maltahöhe

Helmeringhausen

Keetmanshoop

Naute Dam

Grünau

Karasburg

C16

B1

B1

C2

C37

C10

B3

B1

Noordoewer

Orange

Cape Town

Oranjemund

B4

C13

Ai-Ais NP

Sperrgebiet National Park

Lüderitz

Fish

ATLANTIC OCEAN

Drink in the views over the remarkable rock formations gouged out of the earth by the Fish River
page 256

Marvel at the towering red dunes of Sossusvlei, which play tricks on the eye
page 314

Gain an insight into Namibia's great diamond boom at Kolmanskop, now a ghost town
page 287

Explore the reedbeds and waterways of the Kwando River area
page 546

N

Bradt

0   100km
0   100 miles

Zambezi Region (Caprivi Strip)

ANGOLA

ZAMBIA

ZAMBIA

BOTSWANA

Okavango

Bwabwata NP

Popa Falls

Mahango Core Area

B8

Kwando

Mudumu NP

Nkasa Rupara NP

Katima Mulilo

Zambezi

Zambezi

Chobe

Namibia Don't miss...

Around Sossusvlei
This is the Namib Desert at its most dramatic — towering ochre dunes and gracefully curving ridges
(ET) page 306

Culture
The Himba live almost entirely in their traditional areas in remote Kaokoland (ET) page 88

Fish River Canyon

At 161km long, up to 27km wide, and almost 550m at its deepest, the Fish River Canyon is arguably second in size only to Arizona's Grand Canyon (SS) page 256

Wildlife

Cheetah do exceptionally well in Namibia, which is said to have about 40% of Africa's population (IT/DT) page 24

Rock art

Many of the engravings at Twyfelfontein are of animals and their spoor, or geometric motifs – which have been suggested as maps to water sources (AVZ) page 406

Namibia in colour

above   At Epupa the river widens to accommodate a few islands, before plunging into a geological fault (GDP/S) page 425

left   The ghost town of Kolmanskop is gradually being buried by the surrounding dunes (SS) page 287

below   Sculpted dunes tower over the wreck of the *Shawnee* south of Walvis Bay (SS) page 370

above Even in the driest areas of Namibia, underground rivers sustain stately camelthorn trees (*Vachellia erioloba*) (CH/I/FLPA) page 9

below left The quivertree, or kokerboom, is specially adapted to survive in extremely arid conditions (AVZ) page 246

below right Research suggests that Namibia's famous welwitschia plants can live for over 1,000 years (AVZ) page 408

top   Southern Namibia in flower after rain (PS) page 10

above left Nara melons provide water for thirsty desert inhabitants such as the brown hyena (SS) page 362

above right Sometimes known as the edelweiss of the desert, the low-growing *Helichrysum roseo-nivum* enlivens the desert soil (SS)

below *Euphorbia virosa* is one of several poisonous plants that thrive in Namibia's arid conditions (CSB/MP/FLPA)

AUTHOR

Chris McIntyre went to Africa in 1987, after reading physics at Queen's College, Oxford. He taught with VSO in Zimbabwe for almost three years and travelled around extensively, mostly with a backpack. In 1990 he co-authored the UK's first guide to Namibia and Botswana, published by Bradt, before spending three years as a shipbroker in London.

Since then, Chris has concentrated on what he enjoys most: Africa. He wrote the first guidebook to Zambia for Bradt in 1996, the first edition of this Namibia guide in 1998, then a first Botswana guide in 2003; he also co-authors guides to Tanzania and Zanzibar. While keeping these guidebooks up to date, his day job is managing director of Expert Africa – a specialist tour operator which organises high-quality trips throughout Africa for individual travellers from around the world, including a very wide range of trips to Namibia. This also includes the Wild about Africa programme of trips guided by top professional guides.

In his spare time, Chris maintains a keen interest in development and conservation issues, acting as adviser to various NGOs and projects associated with Africa. He is a Fellow of the Royal Geographical Society and contributes photographs and articles to various publications. Now based in Dockenfield, Surrey, Chris and his wife, Susan, still regularly travel and research in Africa.

Chris can usually be contacted by email on **e** chris.mcintyre@expert.africa.com.

Call the author

I am Chris McIntyre, the author of this book, and I run *Expert Africa*. My small team of Namibia specialists and I can help you plan your perfect holiday to Namibia.

Few people know Namibia's camps, lodges and safari destinations as well as we do; our advice is unbiased, our approach is responsible and award-winning, and our aim is simple: to ensure that you have the best possible guidance as you plan your trip.

Visit *expert.africa* for thousands of unedited reviews on Namibia's lodges written by our recent travellers – plus detailed inspection reports, candid slide-shows, amazing satellite maps and much more.

Call us. We'll understand your needs in order to create an amazing trip to suit you perfectly. We focus on fly-in trips, privately guided safaris and self-drive holidays to Namibia's better lodges and camps.

tel: +44 (0)203 405 6666
info@expert.africa
www.expert.africa

Est. 1994

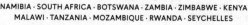

EXPERT·AFRICA

PUBLISHER'S FOREWORD

The first Bradt travel guide was written in 1974 by George and Hilary Bradt on a river barge floating down the Amazon. Over the following years, Bradt earned a highly respected reputation as a ground-breaking publisher: its guidebooks were often the first to cover those destinations, and its authors were ahead of the game in promoting responsible travel. Now, 45 years since the company was founded, Bradt has more than 200 books on its list, ranging from full-country and regional guides to wildlife titles and travel literature. And the pioneering spirit still burns strong. Whether focusing on countries overlooked by other publishers or areas a little more 'mainstream', Bradt seeks out those hidden corners and champions the road less travelled.

Sixth edition August 2019
First published 1998

Bradt Travel Guides Ltd
31a High Street, Chesham, Buckinghamshire, HP5 1BW, England
www.bradtguides.com
Print edition published in the USA by The Globe Pequot Press Inc, PO Box 480, Guilford, Connecticut
06437-0480

ISBN: 978 1 78477 637 4

British Library Cataloguing in Publication Data
A catalogue record for this book is available from the British Library

Photographs Ariadne Van Zandbergen (www.africaimagelibrary.com) (AVZ); Alamy Stock Photos: Inge Johnsson (IJ/A); Dreamstime.com: Itacud (IT/D); Expert Africa: Grootberg Lodge (GL/EA), Mowani Mountain Camp (MMC/EA), Tom Morris (TM/EA), Natural Selection (NS/EA); John Flashman (JF); Flickr: Ralph Apenldoorn (RA/F), John Dale (JD/F), Randall Knox (RK/F); FLPA (www.flpa.co.uk): Peter Davey (PD/FLPA), Christian Heinrich/Image Broker (CH/I/FLPA), Jelger Herder, Buitenbeeld/Minden Pictures (JHB/MP/FLPA), Malcolm Schuyl (MS/FLPA), Chris Stenger/ Buitenbeeld/Minden Pictures (CSB/MP/FLPA); Getty Images: Martin Harvey (MH/G); Tricia Hayne (TH); Chris McIntyre (CM); Jeanne Meintjes (JM); Anna Moores (AM); Tom Morris (TM); Claire Scott (CS); Serondela Lodge: Lauren Adriaanse (LA/SL); Tanya Sharapova (TS); Shutterstock.com: AZ Outdoor Photography (AZOP/S), Stacey Ann Alberts (SAA/S), Bobby Bradley (BB/S), EcoPrint (EP/S), FRDMR (F/S), Paula French (PF/S), Jiri Haureljuk (JH/S), Vladislav T Jirousek (VTJ/S), kavram (k/S), Ian Kennedy (IK/S), The Law of Adventure (LA/S), Felix Lipov (FL/S), LouieLea (LL/S); Dawie Nolte (DN/S), Gunter Nuyts (GN/S), JT Platt (JTP/S), Grobler du Preez (GDP/S), Prisma Nova Photography (PNP/S), Ondrej Prosicky (OP/S), Marina Snelling (MS/S), Mogens Trolle (MT/S), Silvia Truessel (ST/S), View Apart (VA/S), Claude Weiss (CW/S), Cathie Withers-Clarke (CWC/S); SuperStock (SS); Piet Swiegers (PS); Emma Thomson (ET)
Front cover A cheetah walks across a dune (MH/G)
Back cover Quiver tree (SS); Himba woman (PNP/S)
Title page The red dunes of Sossusvlei (SS); swallow-tailed bee eater (SS); Windhoek's *Unknown Soldier* monument (SS)

Illustrations Annabel Milne, Carole Vincer
Maps David McCutcheon FBCart.S
Typeset by Ian Spick, Bradt Travel Guides Ltd and www.dataworks.co.in
Production managed by Jellyfish Print Solutions; printed in India
Digital conversion by www.dataworks.co.in

MAJOR CONTRIBUTORS

In preparing this edition, Chris was assisted by a number of experienced Africa travellers and writers, many within the team at Expert Africa. With decades of previous Namibia and wider Africa experience between them, they travelled the length and breadth of the country, from the far reaches of the Zambezi Region (formerly the Caprivi Strip), down to the Orange River in the country's deep south, and east from Swakopmund and Lüderitz across Etosha and the central highlands to the Kalahari and the Botswana border.

So this book, just as much as previous editions, has been a team effort; many have devoted their energy to it. Largest among the contributions to this edition have been from the following:

Tricia and Bob Hayne worked extensively on this and three previous editions, as well as on many other guidebooks. Formerly editorial director of Bradt Travel Guides, Tricia is now a freelance travel writer with a focus on hiking and southern Africa.

Richard Ball studied zoology at university before becoming a guide in Botswana. His passion for wildlife and for Botswana led him to join Expert Africa in 2016, and he is now expanding his knowledge to include Namibia. Richard contributed to the Lüderitz and southern Kalahari chapters.

Amanda Bond has been regularly drawn back to Africa since her first visit in 2004. After graduating with a degree in geography, Amanda returned to Africa to manage lodges in Zanzibar and South Africa. Now at Expert Africa, she helped to update the northern areas of the country, from Etosha to the far northeast.

Josh Flatman first visited South Africa while studying for a degree in conservation biology and ecology. Following a masters in biosciences, and various wildlife conservation and research projects, he volunteered and travelled in Namibia for three months. He now works for Expert Africa and helped to update the sections on southern, southwestern and eastern Namibia.

Tracy Lederer taught in the UK for 15 years, spending her holidays travelling. A backpacking trip around Zimbabwe, Zambia and Malawi kindled a love of Africa. Having joined Expert Africa in 2004 she now specialises in South Africa, Botswana and Namibia, amongst others, and for this edition helped to update Etosha and the former Caprivi Strip.

Tom Morris first visited southern Africa in 2009, and since then has travelled the region extensively. He joined Expert Africa in 2015, where his original focus on Namibia and Zimbabwe has been extended to include Botswana. For this edition, Tom helped to update the sections covering central, southern, southwestern, far northwestern and eastern Namibia, and much more besides.

Freddie Sutton's passion for travel and wildlife led him to Africa as the perfect continent for combining these interests. With a degree in zoology he worked as a research assistant in the Udzungwa Mountains, and now is one of the team at Expert Africa. For this edition he updated sections on Swakopmund, Damaraland, Etosha and Namib-Naukluft National Park.

Richard Trillo is Kenya destination manager at Expert Africa and is a specialist in African travel, with an MA in East African ethnography, Swahili literature and African linguistics. For many years he was director of communications at Rough Guides and he is the author of, among others, *The Rough Guide to Kenya*. For this edition he updated Damaraland and Etosha.

However, this guide has been built very much on the solid foundations laid by contributions for the previous editions. Foremost among these are Africa expert and fellow author, Philip Briggs, who kindly allowed me to build on his original text to create the *Namibia Wildlife Guide*; Purba Choudhury, arts, press and PR professional, who researched and wrote the original arts and crafts section; David Else, expert author and old Africa hand, who kindly gave route descriptions for the Naukluft hiking section; Sue Grainger, traveller and writer, who wrote much original material for the Kaokoveld chapter, and commented on more besides; Jonathan Hughes, ecologist, who wrote most of the boxes on survival in the Namib, and gave other valuable critiques; and Emma Thomson, Sue Watt, Martha Young and Angela Griffin for their invaluable work on the fourth and fifth editions. Finally, and by no means least, is the contribution to this sixth edition from Chantal Pinto and Sabina Hekandjo in Windhoek, helped by Edna Mohrmann, who patiently and painstakingly checked so many facts for the Windhoek and Ovamboland chapters, and more, to ensure that this edition is as up to date as possible.

AUTHOR'S STORY

I first visited Namibia in 1989, as the South African administration started to relinquish its grip and the country prepared for independence. By then I had lived in Zimbabwe for several years and travelled widely. Namibia was rumoured to be wonderful; but nobody seemed to know any details. The world knew South West Africa (Namibia) only as a troubled place from news bulletins, nothing more.

So I hired a VW Golf and drove from Namibia's northeastern tip to its southern border in 12 days. Overseas tourism simply didn't exist then. Sesriem had one campsite with just 11 pitches for tents; the Fish River Canyon was deserted. The trip was terribly rushed, but Namibia captivated me. The scale of its wilderness was enchanting, and travelling was remarkably easy.

Six months later I returned to explore – and to research the first English guidebook to the country. While I was there, Namibia's independence arrived, putting the country's troubles into the past. Optimism was tangible, justified by democracy, an implausibly reliable infrastructure and rich mineral resources. I delved a little deeper into its magic and remained entranced. It was this that inspired me to start a travel company, originally focusing on Namibia, and I'm very grateful to be able to keep in close contact with a country that I still love.

Acknowledgements

This sixth edition couldn't have been written without the help of many people who have not yet been mentioned – some who helped with previous editions, and some with this one. Many names I have forgotten, others I never knew. I hope those who aren't named here will forgive me, but some who stand out for their help and input include: the entire Wilderness Safaris team; the community at the remarkable Torra Conservancy; Arno and Estelle Oosthuysen; Dirk Maes at Pelican Point Lodge; Jeanne Meintjes of Eco Marine Kayaks; Naude from Pelican Point Kayaking; Russell from Erongo; Donna, Tristan and the Okonjima team; and, as ever, Kate and Bruno Nebe – without whom Namibia just wouldn't be the same.

The team at Expert Africa sends hundreds of travellers to Namibia every year, and many of these have helped me with their personal perspectives on the country – through both discussions and some very extensive and detailed feedback reports which they've kindly posted to our website. Meanwhile, back in the office, Maruska, Megan and the rest of the Namibia team have always been on hand to help with much information and experience. (The support of John, Noel and Dudley with this writing is always appreciated.)

Immense gratitude, as always, to those who worked on producing the book, particularly Claire Strange and David McCutcheon, whose hard work made this book possible. That which is good and correct owes much to their care and attention, while errors and omissions remain my own.

Contents

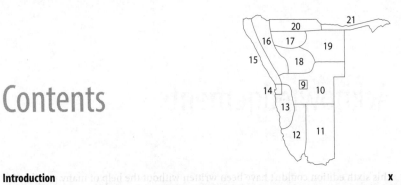

KEY TO SYMBOLS

═══	Tarred road (regional)	✝	Church/cathedral
▄▄▄	Railway (passenger/freight)	❀	Garden
----------	Footpath/walking trail	▶	Golf course
··········	Featured footpath/trek	⚲	Lighthouse
✈ ✦	Airport (international/domestic)	⌂	Cave/rock shelter
✦	Airstrip (light aircraft)	⚓	Wreck site
→	Direction of traffic/route	✕	Birdwatching
⛽	Filling station/garage	◢	Fishing site
🅿	Car park	⚬	Archaeological/historic site
🚌	Bus station etc	▲	Summit (height in metres)
ℹ ⓘ	Tourist information office/kiosk	≫	Steep gradient/mountain pass
♨	Museum/art gallery	⤬⤬	Park gate/barrier
⚑	Statue/monument	⤬⤬	Border post
$	Bank/bureau de change	⊕	GPS location
✉	Post office	○	Waterhole/spring
⊞	Hospital/clinic etc		Salt lake/pan
✚	Pharmacy/dentist		Marsh
ⓔ	Internet café		National park/protected area
⌂	Hotel/inn etc		Urban park
⚠	Campsite		Market
✕	Restaurant		Shopping centre/mall

LIST OF MAPS

FEEDBACK REQUEST AND UPDATES WEBSITE

At Bradt Travel Guides we're aware that guidebooks start to go out of date on the day they're published – and that you, our readers, are out there in the field doing research of your own. You'll find out before us when a fine new family-run hotel opens or a favourite restaurant changes hands and goes downhill. So why not write and tell us about your experiences? Contact us on ☏01753 893444 or e info@bradtguides.com. We will forward emails to the author, who may post updates on the Bradt website at www.bradtupdates.com/namibia. Alternatively, you can add a review of the book to www.bradtguides.com or Amazon.

Introduction

Namibia has no idyllic sandy beaches, no warm tropical waters or big brassy hotels. However, it does have huge tracts of pristine wilderness, home to some stunning wildlife. Glance around. The Namib Desert has plants and animals found nowhere else on earth. Here is the world's oldest desert, where endemic wildlife has evolved to survive – like the contorted *Welwitschia mirabilis* that lives for millennia, the elusive golden mole and the unique fog-basking beetles.

Namibia's population has always been tiny, a sprinkling of settlements founded by different peoples: some ancient, some colonial. Around these outposts, vast open areas remain protected as national parks, supplemented by conservancies where scattered local communities protect the wildlife in their own areas. Namibia has little industry or pollution, so you look up at the clearest stars you'll ever see.

Best of all, Namibia's wilderness is still easy to explore independently. Choose back roads here and you can drive for hours through endless plains, huge mountain massifs and spectacular canyons without seeing a soul. Even in Etosha, one of Africa's top game parks, driving around is easy, and you can stop beside the waterholes for as long as you like. As animals wander all around, you just sip a cold drink and focus your camera.

Namibia's not an ideal country for backpacking. However, if you can afford to hire a car, then the country is your oyster – and it's not expensive. Good food, wine, beer and cheap camping make the cost of staying in Namibia lower than anywhere else in southern Africa. With just a little more cash to spare, and advanced bookings, you'll find Namibia's lodges, camps and guest farms cost a fraction of the price of similar places elsewhere in the region. Here you can afford comfort and expert guides who will help you discover their own areas, instructing you in everything from tracking black rhino to understanding the native flora.

In the last 30 years I've been lucky enough to make dozens of trips back to Namibia. I've watched tourism gradually develop and change – and on the whole it's done so positively. While there are more visitors now, these are exploring more destinations within Namibia, so the country still seems empty. There are many new lodges and guest farms, but these are spread widely and most remain small, offering personal attention and unique attractions. Namibia is still not a mass-market destination, and there's no sign that it will be.

The contribution to the economy made by visitors is increasing, and the government recognises its importance – which is vital if the wild areas that attract visitors are to be conserved. Even more importantly, the people living in those remote, rural areas are also benefiting from tourism. The Kaokoveld, in particular, is home to some thriving community projects – successes that are rare in most parts of Africa. Elsewhere, new conservancies are sprouting up, where neighbouring farms join forces and return wild game to their land, replacing domestic animals.

Just as Namibia is evolving, so are the ways to travel. At first, flying around was strictly the preserve of those who could afford to charter their own plane. They knew that Namibia's landscapes are often most spectacular from the air, and that flying around gives a whole new perspective on the country. Now it has become more accessible, with tour operators tailor-making fly-in trips around the country, and charging per seat, not per plane. These hops between lodges remain more costly than driving, but they are breathtaking, and allow easy access to even the remotest corners of the Skeleton Coast and Kaokoveld.

So Namibia and trips there are changing. Travel there is also changing on a personal level: since the last edition of this book was published, I have taken my children (now aged six and nine) there several times. Every time I go, I am again surprised at the ease of travel in Namibia, and seeing it through their eyes I'm reminded just how remarkable this country is.

AUTHOR'S FAVOURITES Finding genuinely characterful accommodation or that unmissable off-the-beaten-track café can be difficult, so the authors and updaters have chosen a few of their favourite places throughout the country to point you in the right direction. These 'author's favourites' are marked with a ✳.

MAPS
Keys and symbols All town maps include alphabetical keys covering the locations of those places to stay, eat or drink that are featured in the book. On regional maps, lodges are marked directly on the map. Please note that maps may not show all hotels and restaurants in the area: other establishments may be located in towns shown on the map.

Grids and grid references Several maps use grid lines to allow easy location of sites. Map grid references are listed in square brackets after the name of the place or sight of interest in the text, with page number followed by grid number, eg: [176 A1].

ACCOMMODATION LISTINGS Where a small group of lodges or hotels come under the same umbrella organisation within a similar area, these have been grouped together. For ease of recognition, the typography used for the 'parent' lodge is as for other lodges, but subsidiaries within the group are noted in small capital letters, with a grey symbol. For example, see Okonjima (page 464):

🏠 **Okonjima**
🏠 PLAINS CAMP
🏠 BUSH CAMP
🏠 OKONJIMA VILLA
⛺ OMBOROKO CAMPSITE

PRICE CODES Throughout this guide we have used price codes to indicate the cost of those places to stay and eat listed in the guide. For a key to these price codes, see page 116 for accommodation and page 118 for restaurants.

DATUM FOR GPS CO-ORDINATES For GPS co-ordinates given in this guide, note that the datum used is WSG 84 – and you must set your receiver accordingly before copying in any of these co-ordinates.

All GPS co-ordinates in this book have been expressed as degrees, minutes, and decimal fractions of a minute.

WEBSITES Although all third-party websites were working at the time of going to print, some may cease to function during this edition's lifetime. If a website doesn't work, you might want to check back at another time as they often function intermittently. Alternatively, you can let us know of any website issues by emailing info@bradtguides.com.

Part One

GENERAL INFORMATION

NAMIBIA AT A GLANCE

Location Southwest Africa, astride the Tropic of Capricorn and beside the South Atlantic Ocean. Its main borders are with South Africa, Botswana and Angola, though it also adjoins Zambia.

Size 824,292km^2

Climate Subtropical desert climate

Status Republic

Population 2,533,794 (2017 UN data estimate)

Population growth per year 2.1% (2015–20, UN data estimate)

Population density 3.1 per km^2 (2016 UN data estimate)

Life expectancy at birth 64 years (2016 World Bank estimate)

Capital Windhoek, population 368,000 (2016 UN data estimate)

Other main towns Swakopmund, Walvis Bay, Rundu, Oshakati, Katima Mulilo

Economy Major earners: mining, including uranium, diamonds and other minerals; agriculture; tourism

GDP US$5,588 per capita (2014 UN data estimate)

GDP growth rate 4.5% (2014 UN data estimate)

Currency Namibian dollar (N$), equivalent to (and interchangeable with) South African rand

Rate of exchange £1 = N$18.19; US$1 = N$14.37, €1 = N$16.05 (May 2019)

Language English (official), Afrikaans, German, several ethnic languages (most in Bantu and Khoisan language groups)

Religion Christianity; traditional beliefs

International telephone code +264

Time GMT +2

Electricity 220 volts, plugs with three round pins, as in South Africa

Weights and measures Metric

Flag Diagonal red stripe bordered by narrow white stripes separates two triangles: one green; one blue with a yellow sun motif.

Public holidays New Year's Day (1 January), Independence Day (21 March), Good Friday, Easter Monday, Workers' Day (1 May), Cassinga Day (4 May), Africa Day (25 May), Ascension Day (40 days after Easter Sunday), Heroes' Day (26 August), Human Rights Day (10 December), Christmas Day (25 December), Family Day (26 December)

Tourist information www.namibiatourism.com.na

1

The Natural Environment

PHYSICAL ENVIRONMENT

The Republic of Namibia is located in southwest Africa, astride the Tropic of Capricorn and beside the South Atlantic Ocean. Its main borders are with South Africa, Botswana and Angola, though it also adjoins Zambia. Covering about 824,292km², the country is much larger than Kenya, and more than twice the size of Zimbabwe. In Western terms, Namibia is almost twice the size of California, or more than twice the size of Germany.

CLIMATE Most of Namibia is classified as an arid to semi-arid region (the line being crossed from semi-arid to arid when evaporation exceeds rainfall). Most of it has a subtropical 'desert' climate, characterised by a wide range in temperature (from day to night and from summer to winter), and by low rainfall and humidity. The northern strip follows the same pattern, but has a more moderate, less dry climate. Note that although the terms 'summer' (November to April) and 'winter' (May to October) are sometimes used, they are not as applicable as, say, in a European maritime climate.

Temperatures range widely from very hot to very cold, depending on the height of the land above sea level and the month. From April to September, in the 'dry season', it is generally cool, pleasant, clear and dry. Temperatures average around 25°C during the day, but nights are much colder. Frost is possible in the higher areas and the deserts. October and November are still within the 'dry season' but then the temperatures are higher, especially in the lower-lying and more northerly areas.

Most of Namibia's rain falls in the summer, from around December to March, and it can be heavy and prolonged in the northern regions of Ovamboland and the Zambezi Region. The further south or west you go, the drier it becomes, with many southern regions of the Kalahari and the whole of the coastal Namib Desert receiving no rainfall at all some years. In this 'rainy' season temperatures occasionally reach above 40°C, and sometimes you may find it humid in the north.

THE FOSSIL DESERT

Though the Namib is one of the world's oldest deserts, many insist that the Kalahari doesn't qualify for the title 'desert' as it receives much more than 100mm of rain per year. However, the sand sheet that covers the Kalahari results in virtually no surface water, and evidence suggests that it may once have been much more arid than it is now. So although it is commonly called a desert, a better description of it would be 'a fossil desert'.

3

CLIMATE STATISTICS: WINDHOEK

The average maximum and minimum temperatures for Windhoek are typical of central Namibia, although as elsewhere in the world, things are changing. Nevertheless, Windhoek's temperatures are less extreme than you might expect in the highlands, or in the Kalahari or Namib deserts, where the mercury will often dip below freezing at night in July and August, and may well approach 40°C during the day during October and November. Conversely in coastal areas, you can expect temperatures to be generally lower both day and night, especially if the mist comes in. Similarly, rainfall in the capital is far higher than in desert areas, but lower than you might expect along the country's northern boundary, including the Kavango and Zambezi regions, and in parts of the central highlands.

	Temp °C max	Temp °C min	Temp °F max	Rainfall min	mm
January	31	18	88	65	85
February	29	17	84	63	91
March	28	16	82	61	69
April	26	14	80	58	35
May	24	10	75	50	6
June	21	7	70	45	2
July	22	7	72	45	0
August	24	9	75	48	1
September	28	12	82	54	5
October	29	15	84	59	13
November	30	16	87	61	29
December	32	17	90	63	31

Weather The beginning of the year, in **January** and **February**, is midsummer. Then it's hot and fairly damp with average maximum temperatures around 25–35°C and average minima around 10–20°C (depending exactly where you are). These averages, however, hide peaks of well over 45°C in the desert.

While prolonged rain may occur on occasion, on a typical day during the rains, the sky will start blue and by early afternoon the clouds will appear. In the late afternoon there will be an hour's torrential rain on some days. Such tropical storms are spectacular; everything feels terrifically fresh afterwards, though you wouldn't want to be caught outside. By the early evening the sky will usually begin to clear again.

The frequency of the rains decreases, and they cease around **March** or **April**. From then the heat is waning and the land gradually cools and dries out. As the skies clear, the nights quickly become cooler, accentuating the temperature difference with the bright, hot days. **May** is a lovely month: there is minimal chance of rain, nights are not yet too cold, and many of the summer's plants are still lush and green.

By **June** the nights are cold, approaching freezing in desert areas where night game drives can be bitter. **July** and **August** are winter, when the average maximum temperatures are around 15–25°C and the average minima around 0–10°C. That said, you may still find yourself wearing shorts and a T-shirt during the day, and getting sunburnt if you are not careful. Clouds will be a rare sight for the next few months.

September is another super month, dry and clear, yet not too hot. By then most green vegetation is fading as the heat begins to build. Everything is dry. All through **October** the heat mounts, and by **November** it is very hot during the day. However, the humidity is still exceedingly low, so even the high temperatures feel quite pleasant.

By November the air seems pregnant with anticipation. Everything is dry, awaiting the rains. Though the clouds often build up in the afternoon, they won't usually deliver until at least **December**. When (and if) the rains do arrive, they are a huge relief, dropping the temperatures at a stroke, clearing the air and reviving the vegetation. Despite all this, the traditional seasons are no longer as reliable as they once were. In 2009, for example, the rains in the north started in mid-October, unseasonably early; climate change is a reality in Namibia, too.

The coastal strip Temperatures on the Namibian coast follow a similar overall pattern, though it may seem very different from one day to the next. Here the climate is largely determined by the interaction between warm dry winds from inland and the cold Benguela Current. The sea is too cold for much evaporation to take place and, consequently, rain-bearing clouds don't form over the coast. Most of the coast is classified as desert – rainfall is an extremely low 15mm per annum on average, and in some years there may be none.

However, hot air from the interior mixes regularly with cold sea air to produce a moist fog that penetrates up to 60km inland. This happens regardless of season, and has done for millennia. It is this periodic morning fog that provides the desert's only dependable source of moisture, and the Namib's endemic flora and fauna have evolved to take advantage of it.

GEOLOGY Geologically, Namibia forms part of an extremely old region, with Precambrian granitic and metamorphic rocks dating back over two billion years. These shield or 'basement' rocks are usually covered by more recent sedimentary rocks, mostly deposited during the Mesozoic era (65–235 million years ago).

KIMBERLITE (DIAMOND) PIPES

Diamond is a crystalline form of ordinary carbon created under conditions of extreme pressure and temperature. In nature, such conditions are only found deep below the earth's surface in the lower crust or upper mantle. Under certain circumstances in the past (usually associated with tectonic activity) the rock matrix in which diamonds occurred was subjected to such great pressure that it became fluid and welled up to the earth's surface in a volcanic pipe of fluidised material. The situation is similar to a conventional volcanic eruption, except that instead of basaltic magma being erupted through fissures in the crust, the volcanic material is a peculiar rock called kimberlite. This contains a wide assortment of minerals (including diamond) in addition to large chunks of other rocks that have been caught up in the process.

The pipes are correctly termed kimberlite pipes, and occur throughout southern Africa, from the Cape to the Democratic Republic of Congo. However, only a small proportion of those discovered have proved to contain diamonds in sufficient abundance to be profitably worked. Namibia's diamonds derive not from primary kimberlite pipes, but from secondary diamond deposits – areas where diamonds have been washed down and deposited by old rivers, which have eroded kimberlite pipes in the interior on their way.

Tectonic activity or movement in the earth's crust over the last 100 million years or so created a number of rifts through which magma was able to reach the surface (see box, page 5) and resulted in the uplifting of most of the area above sea level.

TOPOGRAPHY The topography of Namibia can be divided into four regions. At 2,000m, the highest land is the central plateau that runs roughly from north to south, from south of Keetmanshoop to north of Otjiwarongo. This is hilly, verdant country where most of Namibia's best farmland is concentrated.

To the west of this plateau, the land falls off in a dramatic escarpment down to the Namib Desert, one of the world's oldest deserts, which stretches for 1,600km beside the Atlantic Ocean. The escarpment, and the incisions that have been cut through it by river action over the years, provides some of Namibia's most spectacular scenery. Below, the Namib is a flat coastal plain whose profile is broken only by shifting dunes and the odd towering inselberg (page 297).

East of the central plateau, the land slopes off much more gradually, merging into the great sand sheet of the Kalahari Desert. A plateau standing at about 1,000m, stretching from Namibia into Botswana and even beyond, this is rolling country with vegetated sand dunes.

DESERTS – BY DEFINITION

'Desert' is an arbitrary term whose meaning is widely disputed, even among experts. Some refer to Noy-Meir's definition of a 'water-controlled ecosystem with infrequent, discrete and largely unpredictable water inputs'. Others are quantitative, defining a desert as receiving an average of less than 100mm of rain per annum. In practice, any arid habitat can be called a desert – and the Namib is certainly very arid.

Antarctica has close to zero precipitation, and most of the water there is frozen, so, strictly speaking, the whole continent is a desert. However, the normal usage of 'desert' refers to dry places which are also hot. These cover 5% of the land on Earth, and are to be found in two neat rings around the globe, straddling the lines of the tropics of Capricorn and Cancer.

The uniform distribution of deserts is due to the pattern of sunlight landing on the planet. Sunlight intensity is highest at the Equator, which is directly underneath the sun for most of the year. With all this light energy, water evaporates more vigorously at this latitude. As the water rises in the atmosphere, it condenses and falls on to the equatorial rainforests. The dry air remaining in the upper atmosphere journeys away from the Equator towards the tropics. Here it descends to ground level, waterless. What water there is at ground level is then picked up and exported by low-altitude winds travelling back towards the Equator to complete the cycle – hence the desert.

This desiccating climate creates a habitat that challenges life. Levels of solar radiation are enormous; air temperatures can soar during the day and, without insulating cloud cover, plunge below freezing at night; the ground is almost too hot to touch; strong winds are common and, where there is sand, sandstorms scour the land. Worst of all, water becomes a luxury. Since all living things are built from water-packed cells, there could hardly be a more uninhabitable environment on Earth. It is a credit to evolution that deserts are often inhabited by a wealth of organisms with sophisticated adaptations to survive in these conditions.

Sand dunes

Barchan or crescentric dunes These arise wherever sand-laden wind deposits sand on the windward (upwind) slopes of a random patch on the ground. The mound grows in height until a 'slip-face' is established by sand avalanching down on the sheltered leeward (downwind) side. The resulting dune is therefore in a state of constant (if slow) movement – sand is continuously being deposited and blown up the shallow windward slope and then falling down the steep leeward slope. This slow movement, or migration, is more rapid at the edges of the dune (where there is less wind resistance) than in the centre, which results in the characteristic 'tails' of a mature barchan.

Fairly constant winds from the same direction are essential for the growth and stability of barchan dunes, which can migrate from anything up to 6m a year for high dunes to 15m a year for smaller dunes. Probably Namibia's best examples of barchan dunes occur in the Skeleton Coast, where some of the dune crests are highlighted by a purple dusting of garnet sand. You'll see them 'marching' across the road near where the C39 turns from the main C34 coastal road.

Seif dunes Where the prevailing wind is interrupted by crosswinds driving in sand from the sides, a long seif or longitudinal dune is formed, instead of a swarm of barchans. The shape of seif dunes is that of a long ridge with high crests, parallel to the direction of the prevailing wind. They commonly occur in long parallel ranges, such as those south of the Kuiseb River which show up so clearly on satellite photographs.

Star dunes When the winds blow from several different directions, a tall pyramidal structure or star dune is formed, with three or more arms or ridges that radiate away from the top. Several dunes of this type are to be found in the Namib Desert around Sossusvlei.

Sand sheets Sand sheets occur when the land is vegetated with grass and scrub, or is covered with rocks and pebbles. Then the force of the wind is broken and it becomes less homogenous. In such situations poorly developed seif dunes or irregular barchans form, and may often join together to some extent, making an undulating sand sheet. From this platform of coarser sand, more erratic dunes often rise.

Sand sheets, in one form or another, are the most common dune formation in southern Africa, since the 'textbook' conditions needed to form perfect barchan or seif dunes are rare. However, the principles remain the same and 'imperfect' dunes of barchan or seif origin are widespread throughout the Kalahari and Namib deserts.

FLORA AND FAUNA

For more detailed coverage of Namibia's wildlife, see Chapter 2, *page 19.*
Despite its aridity, Namibia is full of fascinating wildlife. Its national parks and concession areas have protected their flora and fauna effectively and offer some superb big game, far from the tourist hordes of more conventional safari countries. Namibia has been the most successful country in the world at protecting its black rhino population, and has Africa's largest population of cheetahs.

Because the Namib is one of the world's oldest deserts, the extraordinary way that plants, animals and even human populations have adapted and evolved in order to survive here is fascinating. There are many endemic species: animals and plants not found anywhere else. From beetles and birds to big game like the famous 'desert elephants' and strange welwitschia plants – Namibia has unique and varied wildlife.

VEGETATION TYPES As with animals, each species of plant has its favourite conditions. External factors determine where each species thrives, and where it will perish. These include temperature, light, water, soil type, nutrients, and which other species of plants and animals live in the same area. Species with similar needs are often found together, in communities which are characteristic of that particular environment. Namibia has a number of such communities, or typical 'vegetation types', within its borders – each of which is distinct from the others. East of the desert, some of the more common include the following:

Mopane woodland

The dominant tree here is the remarkably adaptable mopane (*Colophospermum mopane*), which is sometimes known as the butterfly tree because of the shape of its leaves. It is very tolerant of poorly drained or alkaline soils and those with a high clay content. This tolerance results in the mopane having a wide range of distribution throughout southern Africa; in Namibia it occurs mainly in the higher, slightly wetter areas including Etosha, the northern Kunene, Caprivi and the Kalahari.

Mopane trees can attain a height of 25m, especially if growing on rich, alluvial soils. However, shorter trees are more common in areas that are poor in nutrients, or have suffered from extensive fire damage. Stunted mopane will form a low scrub, perhaps only 5m tall. All mopane trees are semi-deciduous. The leaves turn beautiful shades of yellow and red before falling between August and October, depending on their proximity to water (the closer the water, the later the leaves fall), then fresh new leaves start unfurling from late October.

Ground cover in mopane woodland is usually sparse – just thin grasses, herbs and the occasional bush. The trees themselves are an important source of food for game, as the leaves have a high nutritional value – rich in protein and phosphorus – which is favoured by browsers and is retained even after they have fallen from the trees. Mopane forests support large populations of rodents, including bush or tree squirrels (*Peraxerus cepapi*), which are so typical of these areas that they are known as 'mopane squirrels'.

Savannah

This all-encompassing category refers to those areas of dry, thorny woodland that occur when trees and shrubs have invaded open grassland, often because of some disturbance like cultivation, fire or overgrazing. It could be subdivided further into 'thorntree', 'bush' and 'mixed tree and shrub' savannah.

Some form of savannah covers much of the Namibian Highlands. Here, the dominant families of trees and bushes are the acacia, terminalia (bearing single-winged seeds) and combretum (bearing seeds with four or five wings), but many others are also present.

Teak forest

In a few areas of the Kalahari (including some within Khaudum National Park), the Zambezi teak (*Baikaea plurijuga*), forms dry semi-evergreen forests on a base of Kalahari sand. This species is not fire-resistant, so these stands occur only where slash-and-burn cultivation methods have never been used. Below the tall teak is normally a dense, deciduous thicket of vegetation, interspersed with sparse grasses and herbs in the shadier spots of the forest floor.

Moist evergreen forest

In areas of high rainfall, or near main rivers and swamps where a tree's roots will have permanent access to water, dense evergreen forest is found. This lush vegetation contains many species and is characterised by having three levels: a canopy of tall trees, a sublevel of smaller trees and bushes, and a variety of ground-

A TREE BY ANY OTHER NAME...

Picture an image of the African savannah and you could well be conjuring up a broad grassy plain with a lone acacia breaking the horizon. Such is the iconic nature of this tree in the African landscape that discussions over changing the species name from *Acacia* have proved long and heated. In the end, though, the scientists have prevailed. With a view to differentiating the erstwhile African acacias from the native acacias of Australia, the former have now been reclassified as *Vachellia* or *Senegalia* (those with hooked thorns) spp – respectively differentiating trees with straight thorns from those with hooked thorns.

For the purposes of this guidebook, I have continued to use 'acacia' in a generic sense, but where I refer to individual species, I have corrected their names, as follows:

Brandberg acacia (*Senegalia montis-usti*)
camelthorn (*Vachellia erioloba*)
candle-pod acacia (*Vachellia hebeclada*)
Kalahari sand acacia or bastard umbrella thorn (*Vachellia luederitzii*)
umbrella thorn (*Vachellia tortilis*)
blackthorn (*Senegalia mellifera*)
bladethorn (*Senegalia fleckii*)
bluethorn (*Senegalia erubescens*)
knobthorn (*Senegalia nigrescens*)
monkey thorn (*Senegalia galpinii*)

Such recategorisation is not new, of course; these discussions are going on all the time. The anaboom or winterthorn was reclassified from *Acacia albida to Faidherbia albida* some years ago, and another species name that has shifted allegiance more recently is the *Lonchocarpus*, which is now known as *Philenoptera*:

Kalahari appleleaf (*Philenoptera nelsii* rather than *Lonchocarpus nelsii*)
raintree (*Philenoptera violacea* rather than *Lonchocarpus capassa*)

level vegetation. In effect, the environment is so good for plants that they have adapted to exploit the light from every sunbeam. In Namibia, this occurs only as riparian forest (sometimes called riverine forest), which lines the country's major rivers.

Vlei A 'vlei' is a shallow grass depression, or small valley, that is either permanently or seasonally wet – though Namibia's vleis are drier than the areas that one would call vleis in countries further east. These open, verdant dips in the landscape usually support no bushes or trees. In higher valleys among hills, they sometimes form the sources of streams and rivers. Because of their dampness, they are rich in species of grasses, herbs and flowering plants. Their margins are usually thickly vegetated by grasses, herbs and smaller shrubs.

Floodplain Floodplains are the low-lying grasslands on the edges of rivers, streams, lakes and swamps that are seasonally inundated by floods. Namibia has only a few floodplains, in the Caprivi area. The best examples are probably beside

WHERE TO FIND LIFE? The Namib Desert receives its stingy allotment of water in two ways. Its eastern edges, near the escarpment, get rare showers of rain. There you will find inselbergs (page 297), which can store the water for a time and support permanent communities of perennial plants and resident animals. At the coast, the desert's western edge, the annual rainfall is even lower (less than 5mm at Walvis Bay), and there most organisms rely on the fogs which regularly roll in from the sea. However, in the middle of the desert where neither the rain nor fog reach, there is very little life indeed.

SURVIVING IN THE NAMIB: BY ESCAPING Many of the Namib's species can only survive at all if they either escape or retreat from the extremes. An 'escape' is an extended period of absence from the desert community, such as a suspension of the life cycle, aestivation (the desert equivalent of hibernation) or by actually migrating out of the desert.

Many of the Namib's plants stop their life cycle for particularly harsh periods, leaving behind dormant seeds able to withstand temperatures of up to 100°C and remain viable for years. Growth is eventually triggered by a threshold amount of rainfall, leading to the phenomenon of the 'desert bloom', where a carpet of flowers covers the ground. These plants, called ephemerals, must then complete their life cycles in a matter of days before the water disappears. A blooming desert obviously requires its pollinators, so various insect species also conduct ephemeral life cycles, switching them on and off as rainfall dictates.

On the great plains of the Namib, a different community waits for rain in any slight depression. When it arrives, and the depression fills, an explosion of activity occurs and pond life comes to the desert. Algae, shrimps and tadpoles fill the ponds for their short lives, employing rapid development techniques to mature swiftly to adulthood.

Large-scale migrations are not common in the Namib, but springbok do trek between arid regions, following any rain, and the Namib's largest mammal, the oryx, also moves in a predictable pattern. After rainfall, they move into the Namib's dune sea, looking for the ephemeral grasses. When these vanish, they travel to the dry Kuiseb River bed to compete with the resident baboons for acacia pods and water. Here they excavate waterholes, which they maintain from year to year.

SURVIVING IN THE NAMIB: BY RETREATING A 'retreat' is a short-term escape, typically a matter of hours. This has a serious disadvantage: it results in what ecologists call a 'time crunch', where time for foraging and social activity is greatly reduced. It follows that retreating animals must be very efficient at foraging.

Most species retreat to some extent. The Namib's beetles, reptiles, birds and mammals disappear into burrows and nests during the hottest periods of the

the Okavango in Mahango, and near the Chobe and Zambezi rivers in the Impalila area. These contain no trees or bushes, just a low carpet of grass species that can tolerate being submerged for part of the year.

Pan Though not an environment for rich vegetation, a pan is a shallow, seasonal pool of water with no permanent streams leading into or from it. The bush is full of small pans in the rainy season, most of which will dry up soon after the rains day. One of the most visible is the social weaver bird, which builds enormous communal nests that insulate the birds during cold nights, and provide a handy retreat during the heat of the day.

In order to extend the time spent on the surface, and minimise this time crunch, one Namib resident, the sand-diving lizard, has developed the remarkable behaviour of 'dancing' on the surface. By lifting its legs at intervals (never all at once!), it manages to reduce its body temperature and stay out for a few extra minutes of activity.

SPECIALISED PLANTS   Although some form of escape or retreat is practical for most animal species, plants do not have the same luxury. They cannot move quickly and therefore have to become tolerant.

Most of the Namib's plants have very deep root systems, to acquire what little ground water is available, and adaptations to reduce water loss. Their leaves are usually small and often covered in hairs or a waxy coating. These designs all reduce water loss by evaporation. Smaller leaves mean less surface area, hairs trap still air adjacent to the leaf and waxy coatings don't allow moisture to pass through. The swollen, waxy leaves of succulents are filled with water, and hence must be protected from thirsty grazers. They usually employ toxins, or spines, but in the Namib there are also the extraordinary geophytes, plants – such as lithops – which camouflage themselves as stones.

Added to the problem of desiccation is that of overheating. Most desert plants are orientated to minimise heating, by having their narrowest edge facing the sun. Some geophytes go one better by growing almost entirely underground.

ANIMAL ADAPTATIONS   Water, the ultimate limitation of the desert, is of key importance to the Namib's animals. Without exception, all of the animal species here tolerate extreme levels of desiccation, and some employ interesting techniques. The male Namaqua sandgrouse travels miles to find water each day. When successful, he paddles in it, allowing his breast feathers to absorb water like a sponge. Laden with this cargo he travels back to the nest to feed the thirsty young and his partner. Springbok and oryx have kidneys that are so efficient at absorbing water that a pellet form of urine is produced.

The African ground squirrel faces away from the sun at all times, and uses its tail as a parasol while it forages. Perhaps most peculiar to the Namib are the dune beetles, which inhabit the crests of the desert's taller sand dunes. They are early risers when there is fog about, and sit motionless for hours in order to allow it to condense on their bodies. Periodically they perform a spectacular dance to move the precious water along their bodies and into their mouths.

cease. The Etosha and Nyae Nyae pans are just much larger versions, which attract considerable numbers of migrant birds when full.

DESERT FLORA   Weighty tomes have been written on the flora of the Namib Desert, with its endemic plants and multitude of subtly different vegetation zones. One of the easiest to read is Dr Mary Seely's excellent book *The Namib Desert* (page 574), which is widely sold in Namibia. This is well worth buying when you arrive, as it will increase your understanding and enjoyment of the desert immensely.

Distance from the coast and altitude are crucial to note when looking at the Namib's flora, as both are factors in determining how much moisture a plant receives by way of the fog. This is maximised at an altitude of about 300–600m above sea level, and extends up to about 60km inland. Thus the communities of vegetation can differ widely over very small distances: the plains full of delicate lichens in one place, but empty a kilometre away. Adaptations to the extremes are all around: wax-covered leaves to reduce transpiration, hollow stems to store water, low growth to avoid the wind, slow growth to take advantage of the infrequent moisture.

The species differ too widely to describe here, but are mentioned in the relevant chapters. Many will become familiar to even a casual observer; none could forget the prehistoric welwitschia (*Welwitschia mirabilis*), the kokerbooms silhouetted on rocky mountainsides, or the strange halfmen (*Pachypodium namaquensis*) seen in the far south.

CONSERVATION

A great deal has been written about conservation in Africa, much of it oversimplistic and intentionally emotive. As an informed visitor you are in the unique position of being able to see some of the issues at first hand, and to appreciate the perspectives of local people. So abandon your preconceptions, and start by appreciating the complexities of the issues involved. Here I shall try to develop a few ideas, touched on only briefly elsewhere in the book, which are common to most current thinking on conservation.

First, *conservation* must be taken within its widest sense if it is to have meaning. Saving animals is of minimal use if the whole environment is degraded, so best practice in modern conservation is to aim to conserve the flora and fauna of environment and ecosystems, not just the odd isolated species or individual animal.

Observe that land is regarded as an asset by most societies, in Africa as it is elsewhere. (In common with most hunter-gatherer groups worldwide, the Bushmen used to be perhaps a notable exception to this.) To 'save' the land for the animals and to use it merely for the recreation of a few privileged foreign tourists – while the local people remain in poverty – is a recipe for huge social problems. Local people in Namibia have hunted game for food for centuries. They have always killed those animals that threatened them or ruined their crops. If we now try to proclaim animals in a populated area as protected, without addressing the concerns of the people, then our efforts will fail.

The only pragmatic way to conserve Namibia's wild areas is to see the *conservation* of animals and the environment as inseparably linked to the *development* of the local people. In the long term one will not work without the other. Conservation without development leads to resentful local people who will happily, and frequently, shoot, trap and kill animals. Development without conservation will simply repeat the mistakes that most developed countries have already made: it will lay waste a beautiful land, and kill off its natural heritage. Look at the tiny areas of natural vegetation which survive undisturbed in the UK, the USA or Japan, to see how unsuccessful they have been at long-term conservation over the last 500 years.

As an aside, the local people in Namibia – and other developing countries – are sometimes wrongly accused of being the only agents of degradation. Observe the volume of tropical hardwoods imported by the industrialised countries to see that the West plays no small part in this.

In conserving some of Namibia's natural areas, and helping its people to develop, the international community has a vital role to play. It could use its aid projects to encourage the Namibian government to practise sustainable long-term strategies, rather than grasping for the short-term fixes which politicians seem universally to prefer. But such strategies must have the backing of the people themselves, or they will fall apart when foreign funding eventually wanes.

Most Namibians are more concerned about where they live, what they can eat, and how they will survive, than they are about the lives of small, obscure species of antelope that taste good when roasted. To get backing from the local communities, it is not enough for a conservation strategy to be compatible with development: it must actually promote it and help the local people to improve their own standard of living. If that situation can be reached, then rural populations can be mobilised behind long-term conservation initiatives.

Governments are the same. As one of Zambia's famous conservationists once commented, 'governments won't conserve an impala just because it is pretty'. But they will work to save it *if* they can see that it is worth more to them alive than dead.

The best strategies tried so far on the continent attempt to find lucrative and sustainable ways to use the land. They then plough much of the revenue back into the surrounding local communities. Once the people see revenue from conservation being used to help them improve their lives – to build houses, clinics and schools, and to offer paid employment – then such schemes stand a chance of getting their backing and support. It can take a while…

PROTECTED AREAS Over 40% of Namibia's land falls under private or state protection. There are very few countries in Africa where land is being returned to a more natural state, with fewer livestock and more indigenous game, and so Namibia is a great success story.

National parks and game reserves The country's 20 national parks, game reserves and other state-protected areas cover over 140,000km², or around 17% of Namibia's total land area. All are designated for photographic visitors, and no hunting is allowed.

/Ai-/Ais Richtersveld Transfrontier Park	**Mangetti National Park**
Bwabwata National Park (formerly Caprivi	**Mudumu National Park**
Game Park; now incorporating the former	**Namib-Naukluft National Park**
Mahango National Park)	**National Botanic Garden (Windhoek)**
Cape Cross Seal Reserve	**Naute Recreation Resort**
Daan Viljoen Game Park	**Nkasa Rupara National Park** (formerly Mamili
Dorob National Park (formerly National West	National Park)
Coast Tourist Recreational Area)	**Popa Falls Game Park**
Etosha National Park	**Skeleton Coast Park**
Gross Barmen Hot Springs	**Sperrgebiet National Park**
Hardap Game Reserve	**Von Bach Recreation Resort**
Khaudum National Park	**Waterberg Plateau Park**

The first national park to be gazetted was Etosha in 1907, with one of the most recent, the Sperrgebiet National Park south of Lüderitz, proclaimed in 2009. Then in 2010, the last section of Namibia's 1,570km coastline, previously the National West Coast Tourist Recreational Area, was afforded national park status as Dorob National Park. As a result, formal protection of the entire Namibian coastal strip now stretches from the country's northern border on the Kunene River right down to the Orange River in the south.

Government protection also extends to the sea, with the proclamation in 2009 of the Namibian Islands' Marine Protected Area. Stretching along 400km of coastline, from Meob Bay in the Namib-Naukluft National Park to Chamais Bay in the Sperrgebiet National Park, it is designed to protect the small islands and islets that provide refuge for seals and seabirds, as well as the surrounding waters which are breeding grounds for both whales and dolphins.

Private protected areas Many private farms and reserves now have game on their land, and have adopted a similar policy to that of the national parks, encouraging photographic tourists to visit as a means of supporting wildlife conservation. Others, however, style themselves as 'hunting farms'. These attract mainly overseas hunters (primarily from Germany and the USA), who pay handsomely for the privilege. The livelihood of these farms depends on hunting, and so they generally practise it sustainably.

Conservancies In 1995 the Namibian cabinet passed a landmark policy on wildlife management, utilisation and tourism in communal areas (areas occupied by subsistence farmers rather than large-scale commercial ranches). Many interested groups, including the IRDNC (see box, opposite) were closely involved with the formulation of this policy, which encouraged the linking of 'conservation with rural development by enabling communal farmers to derive financial income from the sustainable use of wildlife and from tourism'. It also aimed to 'provide an incentive to the rural people to conserve wildlife and other natural resources, through shared decision-making and financial benefit'.

Put simply, this gave a framework for local communities to take charge of the wildlife in their own areas for sustainable utilisation – with decisions made by the local communities, for the community.

The visitor travelling through the more isolated areas of Namibia will frequently come across signs demarcating the boundaries of these communal conservancies. One of the first was the Torra Conservancy in southern Damaraland, which is home to Damaraland Camp. By 2018, 86 communal conservancies had been registered, covering an area of more than 163,000km^2 and impacting on the lives of almost 190,000 local people. Through Conservancy Safaris Namibia (page 421) visitors have a real opportunity to learn about the individual conservancies at first hand.

Entirely separate are private conservancies, created by commercial farmers who have joined forces with neighbouring farms to protect the environment – and the wildlife – within their boundaries. Among these are the NamibRand Nature Reserve and the Erongo Mountain Nature Conservancy.

TOURISM Namibia lies far from Africa's 'original' big-game safari areas of East Africa, Kenya and Tanzania, and from the newer destinations of Zimbabwe and Zambia. Aside from Etosha, and the national parks of the Kavango and Zambezi regions in the far northeast, Namibia doesn't have the density of game that visitors would expect for such a trip, or the warm tropical shores that they would expect for a beach holiday (anyone who has been to Lüderitz will surely agree). Thus the country doesn't generally attract first-time visitors who simply want to tick off game, or see game and lie on a beach – a combination that accounts for much volume in the travel business. Therefore few cheap charter planes arrive in Namibia,

IRDNC

Integrated Rural Development and Nature Conservation (*www.irdnc. org.na*) is a small organisation founded by Garth Owen-Smith, a Namibian nature conservator, and Dr Margaret Jacobsohn, a Namibian anthropologist who worked for years among the Himba people. Since the mid 1980s their goal has been to ensure the sustainable social, economic and ecological development of Namibia's communal areas, and the founders have received several international environmental prizes. Typical of their low-key approach, they emphasise that they have always worked as part of a team with the government, various NGOs, community groups and like-minded organisations in the private sector. (Namibia's Save the Rhino Trust is another notable player in much of this work; see box, page 414.)

The IRDNC was one of the pioneers of the **Community Game Guard** scheme set up in 1983 in the Kaokoveld, now the Kunene Region. In its simplest form, a community game guard is appointed from each community, and is paid to ensure that no member of the community hunts any animal that they are not allowed to hunt. Originally called the Auxiliary Game Guard scheme, it was behind the phenomenal recovery of the desert-adapted populations of elephant and black rhino in the area.

Later, the organisation helped to set up some of the **community campsites** in the same region. It facilitated important projects to return money from lodges to local communities at Lianshulu and Etendeka, and was also involved with setting up the joint venture between the community and Wilderness Safaris that is behind Damaraland Camp. More recently, IRDNC has been involved in the establishment of **conservancy-owned safaris**, helping to test the concept and to facilitate conservancy involvement. These are now operated under the umbrella of **Conservancy Safaris Namibia** (*www.kcs-namibia.com.na*).

The IRDNC currently works with more than 40 conservancies in the Kunene and Zambezi regions, which in turn employ several community workers.

and there is still only a small number of large hotels, most of which aim more for businesspeople than tourists.

The main area of growth in Namibia's tourism is in individual self-drive trips and small-group tours and, most recently, in fly-in safaris. These are perfect for the small lodges and guest farms, and have encouraged many small-scale tourist ventures to develop and thrive – utilising not only the few famous national parks, but also old cattle ranches and otherwise unproductive sections of desert.

In the long term, this is a huge advantage for the country. With tourism continuing to grow slowly but steadily, it is hoped that Namibia will avoid the boom-then-bust experience of wildlife-rich countries like Kenya. Every month, new small camps, lodges and guest farms open for visitors; most try hard to retain that feeling of 'wilderness' which is so rare in more densely populated countries, and much sought after by visitors. Namibia has so much space and spectacular scenery that, provided the developments remain small-scale and responsible, it should have a very long and profitable career in tourism ahead.

Perhaps Namibia's most promising attributes in this field are its successes in linking tourism with community-development projects. Tourism is a vital source of revenue for many of these projects and, if it helps to provide employment and bring foreign exchange into the country, the politicians in turn have a solid reason to support environmental conservation.

Community campsites

Tourists who are camping would do well to seek out community campsites, which aim to enable local communities to benefit directly from passing tourists. The community sets up a campsite, then the money generated goes into a central community fund – and the whole community decides how that revenue is spent. In addition, once tourists have stopped to camp, members of the community have a chance to earn money by guiding them on local walks, and selling curios or firewood, or whatever else seems appropriate in the area. Even travellers on a lower budget can thus have a direct impact on some of Namibia's smaller, rural communities.

There are several community campsites in the Kunene Region, and an increasing number in the Zambezi Region (formerly the Caprivi). Many of the most successful ventures are run under the auspices of NACSO (*www.nacso.org. na*) – the Namibian Association of CBNRM (Community-Based Natural Resource Management) Support Organisations. NACSO has essentially taken up the role of the former NACOBTA, which was a non-profit organisation working with communities seeking to develop tourism initiatives at local level. A partner of NACSO, Community Conservation Namibia (*www.namibiawildlifesafaris.com*) offers helpful profiles and contact information for many community campsites across Namibia, though they cannot assist with making reservations.

Lodges

A few operators have really excellent, forward-thinking ways of helping their local communities. The success of Etendeka and then Damaraland Camp in this context opened up the possibility for other ventures along similar lines, with more recent initiatives including Doro !Nawas, Grootberg and Spitzkoppen Lodge. Some others make a form of 'charity' donation to local communities, but otherwise only involve local people as workers. While this is valuable, much more is needed. Local people must gain greater and more direct benefits from tourism if conservation is going to be successful in Africa, and Namibia is no exception.

If you're staying in lodges, asking the right questions can go a long way towards encouraging Namibia's operators to place development initiatives higher on their list of priorities. For example, how much of the lodge's revenue goes directly back to the local community? How do the local people benefit directly from the visitors staying at *this* camp? How much of a say do they have about what goes on in the area where *these* safaris are operated? If enough visitors did this, it would make a big difference.

'PHOTOGRAPHIC' V HUNTING VISITORS

It matters little to the Namibian people, or ultimately to the wildlife in general terms, whether visitors come to shoot the animals with a camera or with a gun – as long as any hunting is done on a sustainable basis (ie: that only a few of the oldest 'trophy' animals are shot each year, and the size and genetic diversity of the animal population remains largely unaffected). Big-game hunting, where visiting hunters pay large amounts to kill trophy animals, is a practical source of revenue for many 'hunting farms' that accept guests. Some also accept non-hunters or 'photographic' guests.

Although many find hunting distasteful, it does benefit the Namibian economy greatly, and encourages farms to cultivate natural wildlife rather than introduced livestock. Until there are enough photographic guests to fill all the guest farms used for hunters, pragmatic conservationists will encourage the hunters.

Photographers may claim the moral high ground, but should remember that hunters pay far more for their privileges. Hunting operations generate large revenues from few guests, who demand minimal infrastructure and so cause little impact on the land. Photographic operations need more visitors to generate the same revenue, and so may have greater negative effects on the country. In practice, there is room for both types of visitor in Namibia: the photographer and the hunter. The main challenge in allowing sustainable hunting is in implementing the regulations designed to keep it sustainable, a challenge that has effectively defeated many African countries.

POACHING Namibia is not alone in trying to stem the rising tide of large-scale poaching throughout sub-Saharan Africa. Rhino horn, elephant ivory and pangolin scales, so-called essential ingredients for Chinese and Vietnamese medicine, change hands for extraordinary amounts of money, tempting the unscrupulous and bringing suffering and misery to animals, owners and rangers alike. In South Africa alone, more than a thousand rhinos are being killed each year, and the so-called industry is now spilling over the borders into Namibia. The government has scaled up anti-poaching measures, but they are dealing with highly organised and well-armed criminal syndicates who will seemingly stop at nothing to secure their prize.

WHICH BINOCULARS ARE BEST FOR ME?

James Lowen

You're probably well aware that binoculars are a fabulous tool for getting close to nature. But choosing the right pair can be daunting – particularly if you are thinking of upgrading. This guide aims to help.

BUYING BINOCULARS: THE BASICS Three guiding principles may help. First, what's right for me may not be for you. Binoculars are a personal thing, so never buy without testing. Second, prepare for trade-offs between weight, performance, practicality and price. Third, buy the best you can afford. You get what you pay for. My Swarovski 'bins', bought in 2004, remain as brilliant as on day one.

Binoculars are described in off-putting jargon. Their names include two numbers, the magnification factor and objective lens diameter (in mm). An 8x56 binocular magnifies objects by eight times through a 56mm-wide lens. Larger numbers usually mean heavier, more cumbersome binoculars. I advise sticking to the ranges 7–10 (magnification) and 30–56 (lens). The ratio between the numbers influences how much light the binocular lets in – and thus how bright the image. The larger the ratio, generally, the better low-light performance. I favour a ratio of 1:4 (eg: 8x32) or 1:5 (eg: 8x42), but up to 1:7 (eg: 8x56) may enhance use in shady forests or at twilight.

Numbers aside, binoculars are either 'roof-prisms' (H-shaped, slimline) or 'porro-prisms' (M-shaped, chunky). For tight budgets, porro-prisms arguably offer better value. Although pricier, roof-prisms tend to be better quality, easier to handle and more compact. They get my vote.

TESTING BINOCULARS: WHAT TO LOOK FOR Pick them up: is the weight evenly distributed? Can you hold them steady? Spectacle-wearers need eyecups that roll or slide so that the binocular offers 14–17mm of 'eye relief'. Now look through the optics. You want a wide field of view – but no need to go overboard. Ensure the image is sharp, ideally right to the edge of vision. How close can you focus? If you anticipate watching insects, choose a pair that focuses on your feet. Check that colours look natural – with no blue or yellow cast. Finally, examine a backlit object: if it is fringed yellow or purple, choose another pair.

WHAT MAKES BINOCULARS REALLY GOOD? Consider each candidate binocular's finer characteristics, which sort wheat from chaff across years of service. 'Fully multi-coated' lenses and prisms are recommended; they maximise light transmission, contrast and clarity. Look for an image so sharp it sears your eyes. Extra-low dispersion (ED) or high-density (HD) lenses correct colour fringing. Depth-of-field is important: you want to minimise time spent refocusing. Durability is key: seek high-strength but ideally lightweight housing. Weatherproofing keeps out dust and water. Finally, if things go wrong, you want the manufacturer to stand by its product, with excellent after-sales service and a 10-year warranty. There's a reason why my Swarovskis go on… and on…

2

Namibia Wildlife Guide

This wildlife guide is designed in a manner that should allow you to name most large mammals that you see in Namibia, and to introduce you to the most widely seen marine creatures, reptiles, amphibians and birds that inhabit this surprisingly diverse country.

There are times, of course, when you may be presented with a series of animal tracks rather than the animal itself. A good guide can make these come alive, helping you to make sense of what you see in the bush. Showing you, for example, that cats' tracks have three lobes at the bottom, whereas dog and hyena tracks feature only two; pointing out the cheetah's claws, usually absent from other cat tracks; or the direction in which an elephant's walking from small scuff marks around its track. To aid your interpretation, we have included in this guide an illustrated section on some of Namibia's more common signs and tracks (page 565); the more you learn, the more you'll enjoy about the bush.

For more detailed coverage of wildlife found in Namibia, see Bradt's *Southern African Wildlife: A Visitor's Guide* by Mike Unwin. Get 10% off at www.bradtguides.com/shop.

LAND MAMMALS

Namibia's large mammals are typical of the savannah areas of southern Africa, though those that rely on daily water are restricted in their distributions. With modern game capture and relocation techniques, some species, including waterbuck and lechwe, now occur far from their natural ranges. A number of native South African species,

including bontebok, blesbok and black wildebeest, have also been introduced to private ranches in Namibia. Thus what you may see in a given area may be different from what 'occurs naturally'.

The large predators are all here in Namibia. **Lion** are locally common, but largely confined to the parks, the arid northwest and the Caprivi Area/Zambezi Region away from dense human habitation. **Leopard** are common throughout the country, and the central highlands provide just the kind of rocky habitat that they love. They are, however, rarely seen naturally. **Cheetah** do exceptionally well in Namibia, mainly because commercial farmers eradicated lion and hyena (the natural enemies of cheetah) relatively easily, and allow smaller antelope, the cheetah's natural prey, to coexist with cattle.

Wild dog have their last Namibian strongholds in the wild areas in and around Khaudum and the Zambezi Region, but are seldom seen elsewhere. The social **spotted hyena** is common in the north and northwest of the country, though far less so in the Namib's central desert areas and the Naukluft Mountains. Much more common and widespread is the solitary, secretive **brown hyena**, which scavenges among seal colonies by the coast, though is rarely seen.

Buffalo occur in protected national parks in the Caprivi/Zambezi Region, and have been reintroduced to Bushmanland and Waterberg from South Africa, but are not found elsewhere in Namibia. **Elephant** occur widely in the north, in Khaudum, the Caprivi/Zambezi Region and Etosha. A separate population of desert-adapted elephants has its stronghold in the Kunene Region. **Black rhino** occur in similar areas, but poaching now effectively limits them to some of the national parks, mainly Etosha, and areas of the Kunene Region. **White rhino** have been reintroduced to Waterberg and Etosha.

Giraffe are fairly widespread and can be seen from the Namib-Naukluft National Park all the way up to the Kunene River, but are most common in Etosha.

Antelope are well represented, with springbok, gemsbok and kudu being numerically dominant depending on the area. The rare endemic **black-faced impala** is a subspecies found only in northwestern Namibia and southern Angola, and can be seen in Etosha.

Roan antelope are found in the Caprivi/Zambezi Region, Waterberg and with luck in Etosha. **Sable** occur only in the Zambezi Region, with excellent numbers often seen on the Okavango's floodplains on the edge of Mahango. In the Zambezi Region's wetter areas there are also **red lechwe**, **reedbuck** and the odd **sitatunga**.

Red hartebeest are widespread in the east, though common nowhere. **Blue wildebeest** are found only in Etosha. **Eland** occur in Etosha and the Kalahari, while **kudu** seem the most adaptable of the large antelope, occurring everywhere apart from the coastal desert strip.

Among the smaller antelope, **common duiker** are widespread everywhere apart from the desert, as are **steenbok**. **Klipspringer** occur throughout Namibia's mountains. Namibia's smallest antelope, the **Damara dik-dik** can be found in most rocky areas north and west of Windhoek, and Etosha, particularly around Namutoni.

In the section below, less common land mammal species are featured under the heading *Similar species* beneath the animal to which they are most closely allied, or bear the strongest resemblance.

CATS AND DOGS
Lion (*Panthera leo*) Shoulder height 100–120cm; weight 150–220kg. Africa's largest predator, the lion is the animal that everybody hopes to see on safari. It is a sociable creature, living in prides of five to ten animals and defending a territory of

20–200km². Lions often hunt at night, and their favoured prey is large or medium-sized antelope such as wildebeest and impala. Most of the hunting is done by females, but dominant males normally feed first after a kill. Rivalry between males is intense and takeover battles are frequently fought to the death, so two or more males often form a coalition. Young males are forced out of their home pride at three years of age, and male cubs are usually killed after a successful takeover.

When not feeding or fighting, lions are remarkably indolent – they spend up to 23 hours of any given day at rest – so the anticipation of a lion sighting is often more exciting than the real thing. Lions naturally occur in any habitat, except desert or rainforest. They once ranged across much of the Old World, but these days they are all but restricted to the larger conservation areas in sub-Saharan Africa (one remnant population exists in India).

In Namibia, lions are increasingly visible in the Kaokoveld, even venturing down river valleys as far as the Skeleton Coast; in the Caprivi, where they often commute from Botswana; and in the central highlands, on a few specific game farms. However, Etosha is certainly the most reliable place to see them in the wild.

Leopard (*Panthera pardus*) Shoulder height 70cm; weight 60–80kg. The powerful leopard is the most solitary and secretive of Africa's big cats. It hunts at night, using stealth and power, often getting to within 5m of its intended prey before pouncing.

If there are hyenas and lions around then leopards habitually move their kills up into trees to safeguard them. The leopard can be distinguished from the cheetah by its rosette-like spots, lack of black 'tear marks' and more compact, low-slung, powerful build.

The leopard is the most common of Africa's large felines, yet hard to observe in the wild. In fact there are many records of individuals living for years undetected in close proximity to humans. These cats occur everywhere apart from the desert, though they favour habitats with plenty of cover, like riverine woodlands and rocky kopjes. Namibia's central highlands are perfect for leopard, where they are resident on almost all the farms. At some lodges, like Okonjima, the leopard are radio collared, allowing them to be tracked by vehicle. Others encourage sightings by offering them food.

Cheetah (*Acynonix jubatus*) Shoulder height 70–80cm; weight 50–60kg. This remarkable spotted cat has a greyhound-like build, and is capable of running at up to 100km/h in bursts, making it the world's fastest land animal. Despite superficial similarities, you can easily tell a cheetah from a leopard by the former's simple spots, disproportionately small head, streamlined build, diagnostic black tearmarks, and preference for relatively open habitats. It is often seen pacing the plains restlessly, either on its own or in a small family group consisting of a mother and her offspring or a coalition of young males. A diurnal hunter, the cheetah favours the cooler hours of the day to hunt smaller antelope, like steenbok and duiker, and small mammals like scrub hares. Namibia probably has Africa's highest cheetah population – estimated at around 2,500, or 25% of the world's population. This is largely due to the eradication of lion and spotted hyena from large areas of commercial farmland, where cheetah are not usually regarded (by enlightened farmers) as a threat to cattle.

Cheetah are found in all of Namibia's major parks. Etosha is the best of these in which to see them, although there's probably a higher density on many farms in the central highlands and the east side of the country. Cheetah can be domesticated to some extent, and in the past it wasn't uncommon to find guest farms with caged animals. Now this is thankfully rare, although rescued cheetah can be readily seen at Okonjima, where those that cannot be released are cared for and others prepared for release back into the wild.

Similar species The **serval** (*Leptailurus serval*) is smaller than a cheetah (shoulder height 55cm) but has a similar build and black-on-gold spots giving way to streaking near the head. Seldom seen, it is widespread and quite common in moist grassland, reed-beds and riverine habitats throughout Africa, including Ovamboland, Etosha, Bushmanland and the Zambezi Region (formerly the Caprivi Strip). It preys primarily on rodents, but may also take birds, reptiles and sometimes even the young of small antelope.

Caracal (*Caracal caracal*) Shoulder height 45cm; weight 15–20kg. The caracal resembles a lynx, with its short tail and tufted ears. Uniform tan in colour, it is a solitary hunter, feeding on birds, small antelope and young livestock. Found throughout the subcontinent, it thrives in Namibia's relatively arid savannah habitats, and occurs everywhere except the far western coastal strip of the Namib. It is largely nocturnal and rarely seen.

Caracal

Similar species The smaller **African wild cat** (*F. lybica*) ranges from the Mediterranean to the Cape of Good Hope, and is similar in appearance to the domestic tabby cat. I once saw a wild cat in Sossusvlei, during the day, but they are more commonly seen on spotlit night drives. The African wild cat has an unspotted torso, which should preclude confusion with the even smaller **small spotted cat** (*F. nigripes*), a relatively rare resident of southeastern Namibia, which has a more distinctively marked coat. Both species are generally solitary and nocturnal, often utilising burrows or termite mounds as daytime shelters. They prey upon reptiles, amphibians and birds as well as small mammals.

African wild cat

African wild dog (*Lycaon pictus*) Shoulder height 70cm; weight 25kg. Also known as the African painted wolf, the wild dog is distinguished from other African dogs by its large size and mottled black, brown and cream coat. Highly sociable, living in packs of up to 20 animals, wild dogs are ferocious hunters that literally tear apart their prey on the run. The most endangered of Africa's great predators, they are now threatened with extinction. This is the result of relentless persecution by farmers, who often view the dogs as dangerous vermin, and their susceptibility to diseases spread by domestic dogs. Wild dogs are now extinct in many areas, and they are common nowhere. The global population is estimated to be just 3,000–5,500, and is concentrated in Tanzania, Zambia, Zimbabwe, Botswana, South Africa and Namibia.

Wild dogs prefer open savannah with only sparse tree cover, if any, and packs have enormous territories, typically covering 400km² or more. They travel huge distances in search of prey and so few parks are large enough to contain them. In Namibia, wild dogs are sometimes seen in Khaudum or on the Caprivi Strip. Botswana's nearby parks of Chobe and Moremi are one of their main strongholds, and so they certainly move across the border. Attempts to reintroduce them into Etosha have so far failed.

Black-backed jackal (*Canis mesomelas*)
Shoulder height 35–45cm; weight 8–12kg. The black-backed jackal is an opportunistic feeder capable of adapting to most habitats. Most often seen singly or in pairs at dusk or dawn, it is ochre in colour with a prominent black saddle flecked by a varying amount of white or gold. It is probably the most frequently observed small predator in Africa south of the Zambezi, and its eerie wailing call is a characteristic sound of the bush at night. It is found throughout Namibia, excluding the Zambezi Region, and is particularly common in Etosha, where it is frequently seen inside the restcamps at night, scavenging for scraps.

Black-backed jackal

Similar species The similar **side-striped jackal** (*C. adustus*) is more cryptic in colour, and has an indistinct pale vertical stripe on each flank and a white-tipped tail. Nowhere very common, in Namibia it is found in the Zambezi Region (erstwhile Caprivi Strip) and occasionally Khaudum or Ovamboland.

Side-striped jackal

Bat-eared fox (*Otocyon megalotis*) Shoulder height 30–35cm; weight 3–5kg. This endearing small, silvery-grey insectivore is unmistakable with its huge ears and black eye-mask. It is mostly nocturnal, but can sometimes be seen in pairs or small family groups during the cooler hours of the day, usually in dry open country. It digs well, and when foraging will often 'listen' to the ground (its ears operating like satellite dishes) while wandering around, before stopping to dig with its forepaws. As well as termites, bat-eared foxes will eat lizards, gerbils, small birds, scorpions and beetle larvae. They are relatively common throughout Namibia, anywhere that the harvester termite is found, although they are most frequently seen in the southern Kalahari. Intu Africa Kalahari Game Reserve seems to have a particularly high density of them.

Bat-eared fox

Similar species The **Cape fox** (*Vulpes chama*) is an infrequently seen dry-country predator which occurs throughout Namibia, but is absent from the Caprivi Strip. This species lacks the prominent ears and mask of the bat-eared fox, and its coat is a uniform sandy grey colour. I once had a Cape fox

Cape fox

approach me cautiously, after dusk, while camping at Bloedkoppie in the northern section of the Namib-Naukluft National Park, but have never seen another.

Spotted hyena (*Crocuta crocuta*)

Shoulder height 85cm; weight 70kg. Hyenas are characterised by their bulky build, sloping back, rough brownish coat, powerful jaws and doglike expression. Contrary to popular myth, spotted hyenas are not exclusively scavengers; they are also adept hunters which hunt in groups and kill animals as large as wildebeests. Nor are they hermaphroditic, an ancient belief that stems from the false scrotum and penis covering the female hyena's vagina. Sociable animals, hyenas live in loosely structured clans of about ten animals, led by females who are stronger and larger than males, based in a communal den.

Hyenas utilise their kills far better than most predators, digesting the bones, skin and even teeth of antelope. This results in the distinctive white colour of their faeces – which is an easily identified sign of them living in an area.

The spotted hyena is the largest and most common hyena, identified by its light brown, blotchily spotted coat. It is found in the wetter areas of northern Namibia, most of the national parks and reserves devoted to game, and occasionally in eastern parts of the Namib Desert. Although mainly nocturnal, spotted hyenas can often be seen around dusk and dawn in the protected parks of Etosha and the Caprivi Strip, and the wilder areas of the Kaokoveld and Bushmanland. Their distinctive, whooping calls are a spine-chilling sound of the African night.

Brown hyena (*Hyaena brunnea*)

Shoulder height 70–80cm; weight 35–45kg. The secretive brown hyena has a shaggy, unmarked dark brown coat – not unlike a large, long-haired German shepherd dog – and distinctive pointed ears. In contrast to the spotted hyena, brown hyenas tend to scavenge rather than hunt, and are generally solitary while doing so. They occur throughout the Kalahari and are the dominant carnivore in the drier areas of the Namib. There is a particularly high density of them

along the beaches, especially around seal colonies. Because of this, the local name for them is *strandwolf*, or beach wolf.

Brown hyenas forage for whatever they can find, from small birds and mammals to the remains of kills and even marine organisms cast up upon the beaches. During drier, leaner periods they will eat vegetable as well as animal matter, and can go without water for long periods by eating nara melons.

Aardwolf

IK/S

Chacma baboon

JF

Vervet monkey

Lesser bushbaby

PD/FLPA

Aardwolf (*Proteles cristatus*) Shoulder height 45–50cm; weight 7–11kg. With a tawny brown coat and dark, vertical stripes, this insectivorous hyena is not much bigger than a jackal and occurs in low numbers in most parts of Namibia. It is active mainly at night, gathering harvester termites, its principal food, with its wide, sticky tongue. These termites live underground (not in castle-like termite mounds) and come out at night to cut grass, which they drag back down with them. Thus open grassland or lightly wooded areas form the typical habitat for aardwolves, which can sometimes be spotted around dusk or dawn, or on very overcast days, especially during the colder months. They seem to be thriving in Namibia's central ranchland, giving you as good a chance of glimpsing one as anywhere in Africa.

PRIMATES

Chacma baboon (*Papio cynocaphalus ursinus*) Shoulder height 50–75cm; weight 25–45kg. This powerful terrestrial primate, distinguished from any other monkey by its much larger size, inverted U-shaped tail and distinctive doglike head, is fascinating to watch from a behavioural perspective. It lives in large troops which maintain a complex, rigid social structure characterised by a matriarchal lineage and plenty of inter-troop movement by males seeking social dominance. Omnivorous and at home in almost any habitat, the baboon is the most widespread primate in Africa, frequently seen in most game reserves.

The chacma baboon is one of five species found in Africa and the only one that occurs in Namibia. With a highly organised defence system, the only predator that seriously threatens them is the leopard, which will try to pick them off at night, while they are roosting in trees or cliffs. Look out for baboons in less populated areas across the country.

Vervet monkey (*Cercopithecus aethiops*) Length (excluding tail) 40–55cm; weight 4–6kg. Also known as the green or grivet monkey, the vervet is probably the world's most numerous monkey and certainly the most common and widespread representative of the *Cercopithecus* guenons, a taxonomically controversial genus associated with African forests. An atypical guenon in that it inhabits savannah and woodland rather than true forest, the vervet spends a high proportion of its time on the ground. In Namibia, it is found only around the narrow belts of woodland beside the Orange and Kunene rivers, and in the lush areas of Mahango and the Caprivi Strip.

The vervet's light grey coat, black face and white forehead band are distinctive – as are the male's garish blue genitals. The only animal that is even remotely similar is the baboon, which is much larger and heavier.

Vervets live in troops averaging about 25 animals. They are active during the day and roost in trees at night. They eat mainly fruit and vegetables, though are opportunistic and will take insects and young birds, and even raid tents at campsites (usually where ill-informed visitors have previously tempted them into human contact by offering food).

Lesser bushbaby (*Galago senegalensis*) Length (without tail) 17cm; weight 150g. The lesser bushbaby is the most widespread and common member of a group of small and generally indistinguishable nocturnal primates, distantly related to the lemurs of Madagascar. In Namibia they occur throughout the north, from northern Kaokoland and Etosha to Khaudum and the Caprivi Strip.

More often heard than seen, the lesser bushbaby is nocturnal but can sometimes be picked out by tracing a cry to a tree and shining a torch into the branches; its eyes reflect as two red dots. These eyes have adapted to function in what we would describe as total darkness.

Bushbabies feed on insects – some of which are caught in the air by jumping – and also on sap from trees, especially acacia gum. They inhabit wooded areas, and prefer acacia trees or riverine forests. I remember being startled while lighting a braai at Halali restcamp, in Etosha, by a small family of bushbabies. They raced through the trees above us, bouncing from branch to branch while chattering and screaming – the noise out of all proportion to their size.

LARGE ANTELOPE

Sable antelope (*Hippotragus niger*) Shoulder height 135cm; weight 230kg. The striking male sable is jet black with a distinct white face, underbelly and rump, and long decurved horns – a strong contender for the title of Africa's most beautiful antelope. The female is chestnut brown and has shorter horns, while the young are a lighter red-brown colour. Sable are found throughout the wetter areas of southern and east Africa. In Namibia, a thriving herd frequents the floodplain beside the Okavango River in the Mahango Core Area of Bwabwata National Park, and there are other groups further east in the Zambezi Region's other parks.

Sable are normally seen in small herds: either bachelor herds of males, or breeding herds of females and young which are often accompanied by the dominant male in that territory. The breeding females drop their calves around February or March, the calf remaining hidden away from the herd for its first few weeks. Sable are mostly grazers though they will browse, especially when grazing is scarce. They need to drink at least every other day, and seem especially fond of low-lying dewy vleis in wetter areas.

Roan antelope (*Hippotragus equinus*) Shoulder height 120–150cm; weight 250–300kg. This handsome, horselike antelope is uniform fawn-grey with a pale belly, short decurved horns and a light mane. It could be mistaken for the female sable antelope, but this has a richer, chestnut-brown coat and a well-defined white belly. The roan is a relatively rare antelope; common almost nowhere in Africa (Malawi's Nyika Plateau being one obvious exception). In Namibia, small groups are found in Etosha, Waterberg, Khaudum and the Caprivi.

Oryx

Roan need lots of space if they are to thrive and breed; they don't generally do well where game densities are high. On game farms they are highly prized and thus among the most expensive antelope. They need access to drinking water, but are adapted to subsist on relatively high plateaus with poor soils.

Oryx or gemsbok (*Oryx gazella*) Shoulder height 120cm; weight 230kg. This is the quintessential desert antelope; unmistakable with its ash-grey coat, bold black facial marks and flank strip, and unique long, straight horns. Of the three species of oryx in Africa, the gemsbok is the largest and most striking. It occurs throughout the Kalahari and Namib and is widespread all over Namibia, from the coast to the interior highlands.

As you might expect, gemsbok are very adaptable. They range widely and are found in areas of dunes, alkaline pans, open savannah and even woodlands. Along with the much smaller springbok, they can sometimes even be seen tracking across flat desert plains with only dust-devils and mirages for company. Gemsbok can endure extremes of temperature, helped by specially adapted blood capillaries in their nasal passages that can cool their blood before it reaches their brains. Thus although their body temperature can rise by up to 6°C, their brains remain cool and they survive. They do not need drinking water and will eat wild melons and dig for roots, bulbs and tubers when grazing or browsing becomes difficult.

Waterbuck (*Kobus ellipsiprymnus*) Shoulder height 130cm; weight 250–270kg. The waterbuck is easily recognised by its shaggy brown coat and the male's large lyre-shaped horns. The common race of southern Africa and areas east of the Rift Valley has a distinctive white ring around its rump, while the defassa race of the Rift Valley and areas further west has a full white rump. In Namibia, waterbuck are very uncommon, only occasionally seen on the eastern fringes of the Caprivi Strip – or on the occasional game farm to which they have been introduced. They need to drink very regularly, so usually stay within a few kilometres of water, where they like

Blue wildebeest

JF

to graze on short, nutritious grasses. At night they may take cover in adjacent woodlands. It is often asserted that waterbuck flesh is oily and smelly, which may discourage predators.

Blue wildebeest (*Connochaetes taurinus*) Shoulder height 130–150cm; weight 180–250kg. This ungainly antelope, also called the brindled gnu, is easily identified by its dark coat and bovine appearance. The superficially similar buffalo is far more heavily built. Where they have enough space, blue wildebeest can form immense herds – as perhaps a million do for their annual migration from Tanzania's Serengeti Plains into Kenya's Masai Mara. In Namibia they naturally occur in the north of the country, including Etosha, and east into the Caprivi Strip (Zambezi Region). They are also found in the Kalahari, Khaudum and the country's far eastern borders. They are adaptable grazers, but prefer short grass plains and need access to drinking water. They have been introduced on to several game ranches.

Similar species The **black wildebeest** (*C. gnou*), endemic to South Africa's central highveld, now numbers a mere 4,000. It is seen most easily in South Africa's Golden Gate National Park, though has also been introduced into several private game areas in Namibia. It differs from the blue wildebeest in having a white tail, a defined black-on-white mane, and horns that resemble racing-bike handlebars, curving down and back up again.

Red hartebeest

LA/S

Red hartebeest (*Alcelaphus buselaphus*) Shoulder height 125cm; weight 120–150kg. Hartebeests are ungainly antelopes, readily identified by the combination of high shoulders, a sloping back, a glossy, red-brown coat and smallish horns in both sexes. Numerous subspecies are recognised, all of which are generally

Tsessebe

seen in small family groups in reasonably open country. Though once hartebeest were once found from the Mediterranean to the Cape, only isolated populations still survive. The only one native to Namibia is the red hartebeest, which is found throughout the arid eastern side of the country, and north into Etosha and Ovamboland. It has been introduced on to the NamibRand Nature Reserve but is absent from the Caprivi Strip, and common nowhere. Hartebeests are almost exclusively grazers; they like access to water though will eat melons, tubers and rhizomes when water is scarce. Etosha's waterholes, especially those in areas of sparse mopane woodland, probably offer your best chance to see hartebeest in Namibia.

Similar species The **tsessebe** (*Damaliscus lunatus*) is basically a darker version of the hartebeest with striking yellow lower legs and more open horns that slant backwards. (Related subspecies are known as *topi* in east Africa.) Widespread but thinly and patchily distributed, the tsessebe occurs occasionally in the Caprivi

Bontebok

Strip (though it is common in Botswana's Okavango Delta). Its favourite habitat is open grassland, where it is a selective grazer, eating the newer, more nutritious grasses. The tsessebe is one of the fastest antelope species, and jumps very well.

Bontebok (*Damaliscus dorcas dorcas*) Shoulder height 85–95cm; weight 60–70kg. Though endemic to the fynbos areas of the Western Cape in South Africa, bontebok have been introduced into many private reserves in Namibia. They look like particularly striking small hartebeest, with a distinctive white face, chestnut back, black flanks and white belly and rump. Bontebok were hunted close to extinction in the early 20th century, and now they are largely found in private protected areas, such as the grounds of Mokuti Lodge or the NamibRand Nature Reserve.

33

Kudu

Similar species The duller but more common **blesbok** (*D. d. phillipsi*) is, in essence, the highveld race of bontebok native to eastern South Africa. That, too, has occasionally been introduced on to the odd private reserve in Namibia.

Greater kudu (*Tragelaphus strepsiceros*) Shoulder height 140–155cm; weight 180–250kg. The greater kudu – often known simply as 'kudu' – is, in Namibia, the most frequently observed of the *Tragelaphus* or spiral-horned antelopes. All species in this genus are characterised by twisted or spiral horns in the male and vertical white stripes on the flanks of both sexes. They are generally associated with wooded habitats, where their stripes act as camouflage.

The greater kudu is very large, with a grey-brown coat and up to ten stripes on each side. The male has magnificent double-spiralled corkscrew horns. Occurring throughout southern Africa, and in smaller numbers in parts of East Africa, kudu are widespread and common, though not in dense forests or open grasslands. In Namibia they are absent only from the Namib Desert – though they are found in the river valleys and are very common on farmland, where their selective browsing does not compete with the indiscriminate grazing of the cattle.

Eland (*Taurotragus oryx*) Shoulder height 150–175cm; weight 450–900kg. Africa's largest antelope, the eland is light brown in colour, sometimes with a few faint white vertical stripes. Its somewhat bovine appearance is accentuated by relatively short horns and a large dewlap. It was once widely distributed in east and southern Africa, but in Namibia is now found only in isolated Kalahari areas, Etosha and Waterberg. There is a particularly good population of eland on Mundulea Reserve. Small herds frequent grasslands and light woodlands, often fleeing at the slightest provocation. (They have long been hunted for their excellent meat, so perhaps this is not surprising.)

Eland

Bushbuck

Eland are opportunist browsers and grazers, eating high-protein fruit, berries, seed pods and leaves, as well as green grass after the rains, and roots and tubers when times are lean. They run slowly, though can trot for great distances and jump exceedingly well.

MEDIUM AND SMALL ANTELOPE

Bushbuck (*Tragelaphus scriptus*) Shoulder height 70–80cm; weight 30–45kg. This attractive antelope, a member of the same genus as the kudu, is widespread throughout Africa and shows great regional variation in its colouring. It occurs in forest and riverine woodland, where it is normally seen singly or in pairs. The male is dark brown or chestnut, while the much smaller female is generally a pale reddish brown. The male has relatively small, straight horns and both sexes are marked with white spots and sometimes stripes, though the stripes are often indistinct.

Bushbuck tend to be secretive and very skittish, except where used to people, when they can become very tame. They depend on cover and camouflage to avoid predators, and are often found in the thick vegetation along river banks. They will freeze if disturbed, before dashing off into the undergrowth. Bushbuck are both browsers and grazers, choosing the more succulent grass shoots, fruit and flowers. In Namibia they have a very limited distribution around the Okavango River in the Mahango Core Area of Bwabwata National Park, and beside the Chobe and Kwando rivers on the eastern side of the Caprivi Strip.

Impala

Impala (*Aepyceros melampus*) Shoulder height 90cm; weight 45kg. This slender, handsome antelope is superficially similar to the springbok, but in fact belongs to its own separate genus. Chestnut in colour, and lighter underneath than above, the impala has diagnostic black-and-white stripes running down its rump and tail, and the male has large lyre-shaped horns. One of the most widespread and successful antelope species in east and southern Africa, the impala is normally seen in large herds in wooded savannah habitats. It is the most common antelope in the Zambezi Region (Caprivi Strip), and throughout much of the country further east, although it is absent from much of Namibia.

A separate subspecies, the near-endemic **black-faced impala** (*A. m. petersi*), occurs in Etosha, the Kunene Region and southern Angola. Slightly larger and heavier than the normal impala, it is distinguished by bolder black markings on its face, including a prominent one down the front of its nose. The total population of black-faced impalas is about a thousand individuals, but with a few days spent in Etosha you have a surprisingly good chance of spotting some. (Sadly, the presence of both the common impala and the black-faced impala within Etosha has led to hybridising and thus the dilution of the gene pool for the black-faced subspecies.)

As you mght expect of such a successful species, impalas both graze and browse, depending on the level of protein available.

Springbok (*Antidorcas marsupilis*)

Shoulder height 60cm; weight 20–25kg. Springbok are graceful, relatively small antelope – members of the gazelle family – which generally occur in large herds. They have finely marked short coats: fawn-brown upper parts, a white face and a white belly, separated from the flanks by a dark brown band. Springbok occur throughout Namibia; they are often the most common small antelope. They occur by the thousand in Etosha – and I've also seen them from the Kalahari to the dunes at Sossusvlei.

Springbok favour dry, open country, preferring open plains or savannah, and avoiding thick woodlands and mountains. They can subsist without water for long periods, if there is moisture in the plants they graze or browse.

Reedbuck (*Redunca arundinum*)

Shoulder height 80–90cm; weight 45–65kg. Sometimes referred to as the southern reedbuck (as distinct from mountain and Bohor reedbucks, found further east), these slim, medium-sized antelope are uniformly fawn in colour, and lighter below than above. They are generally found in reed-beds and tall grasslands, often beside rivers, and are easily identified by their loud, whistling alarm call and distinctive bounding running style. In Namibia they occur only on the Caprivi Strip and a few riverine areas in the far north.

Klipspringer (*Oreotragus oreotragus*) Shoulder height 60cm; weight 13kg. The klipspringer is a strongly built little antelope, normally seen in pairs, and easily identified by its dark, bristly grey-yellow coat, slightly speckled appearance and unique habitat preference. Klipspringer means 'rockjumper' in Afrikaans and it is an apt name for an antelope that occurs exclusively in mountainous areas and rocky outcrops, where its uniquely adapted tip-toe hooves allow it to run with great agility over cliff faces and boulders.

This antelope is common throughout Namibia, wherever rocky hills or kopjes are found – which means most of the central highlands and western escarpment, but not in the far north or the Caprivi Strip. Klipspringers are mainly browsers, though they do eat a little new grass. When spotted they will freeze, or bound at great speed across the steepest of slopes.

Red lechwe (*Kobus leche*) Shoulder height 90–100cm; weight 80–100kg. Often known simply as 'lechwe', this sturdy antelope has a reddish coat, a noticeably high rump and beautiful lyre-shaped horns. It is usually found only in moist, open environments, and in Namibia occurs only beside the great rivers of the Caprivi Strip.

Lechwe need dry land on which to rest, but otherwise will spend much of their time grazing on grasses and sedges, standing in water if necessary. Their hooves are splayed, adapted to bounding through their muddy environment when fleeing from the lion, hyena and wild dog that hunt them.

Sitatunga (*Tragelaphus spekei*) Shoulder height 85–90cm; weight 105–115kg. This semi-aquatic antelope is a widespread but infrequently observed inhabitant of west and central African swamps from the Okavango in Botswana to the Sudd in Sudan. In Namibia it occurs in the Okavango River beside Mahango, and in protected areas of the Kwando–Linyanti–Chobe–Zambezi river system where there are extensive papyrus reed-beds. Because of its preferred habitat, the sitatunga is very elusive and seldom seen, even in areas where it is relatively common.

Steenbok (*Raphicerus cempestris*) Shoulder height 50cm; weight 11kg. This fawn-coloured, delicate-looking little antelope has red-brown upper parts and clear white underparts, and the male has short straight horns. It is an abundant species in Namibia, where a small antelope glimpsed dashing away across farmland is most likely to be a steenbok. Like most other small antelopes, the steenbok is normally encountered singly or in pairs and tends to 'freeze' when disturbed, before taking flight.

Similar species Sharpe's grysbok (*R. sharpei*) is similar in size and appearance, though it has a distinctive white-flecked coat. It occurs alongside the steenbok in the far eastern reaches of the Zambei Region (Caprivi Strip), but is almost entirely nocturnal in its habits and so very seldom seen. The **oribi** (*Ourebia ourebi*) is a widespread but very uncommon antelope, which is usually found only in large, open stretches of grassland. It looks much like a steenbok but stands about 10cm higher at the shoulder and has an altogether more upright bearing. In Namibia you have a chance of seeing these only on the Caprivi Strip, and you'll need to look hard.

Damara dik-dik (*Madoqua kirkii damarensis*) Shoulder height 30–40cm; weight 4–6kg. Namibia's smallest antelope occurs in the central-north of the country, including Etosha and the Kunene. A subspecies of Kirk's dik-dik, which occurs in east Africa, this is an attractive and dainty animal, easily distinguished from the steenbok by its smaller size and distinctive twitchy nose. It is adapted to arid areas and prefers a mixture of bushes and spare grassland cover. Damara dik-diks are common in Etosha and on the Waterberg Plateau, and will often sit motionless beside the road while you pass by without noticing. They are active during the cooler hours of the day as well as the night, and are almost exclusively browsers.

Common duiker (*Sylvicapra grimmia*) Shoulder height 50cm; weight 20kg. This stocky little antelope resembles a larger, more robust steenbok, and is the only member of the (large) duiker family to occur outside forests. Generally grey in colour, the common duiker can most easily be separated from other small antelopes by the black tuft of hair that sticks up between its horns. It occurs throughout Namibia, everywhere except the Namib Desert. Common duikers frequent most habitats except for true forest and very open country, and are tolerant of nearby human settlements. They are opportunist feeders, taking fruit, seeds and leaves, as well as crops, and even small reptiles and amphibians.

TM

OTHER LARGE HERBIVORES

African elephant (*Loxodonta africana*) Shoulder height 2.3–3.4m; weight, up to 6,000kg (males), 3,500kg (females). The world's largest land animal, the African elephant is intelligent, social and often very entertaining to watch. Female elephants live in close-knit clans in which the eldest plays matriarch over her sisters, daughters and younger offspring. Mother–daughter bonds are strong and may last for up to 50 years. Males generally leave the family group at around 12 years to roam singly or form bachelor herds. Under normal circumstances, elephants range widely in search of food and water, but when concentrated populations are forced to live in conservation areas their habit of uprooting trees can cause serious environmental damage. Elephants are widespread and common in habitats ranging from desert to savannah woodland. In Namibia they are common in the Zambezi Region (Caprivi Strip) and Etosha, and in Kalahari areas around Khaudum.

Read about the history of Etosha, and you'll realise that the park used to cover much of the present Kaokoveld. Until about 50 years ago, Etosha's elephants used to migrate, spending the wetter parts of the year in the northern Kunene Region and the drier months nearer to Etosha's permanent waterholes. Etosha's boundary fence has stopped that. However, the herds still tend to head to the hills of western Etosha during the rains, returning to the pan several months later as the bush dries out. Every year a few break out of the park's fences.

The elephants that frequent the river valleys of the Kaokoveld, though, are commonly

DNS

59

known as 'desert elephants' – though desert-adapted might be a more accurate term. These family groups have learnt where the rivers and waterholes are, probably from their elders, and can navigate through the Kaokoveld's mountains and dunes to find water. This ancestral knowledge, passed down the generations, is easily lost, although in recent years various conservation/development schemes have been so successful that these 'desert-adapted' elephants are now thriving.

After several decades of persecution by humans, these elephants are now (understandably) noted for their aggression. Even visitors in sturdy vehicles should treat them with exceptional respect (see box, page 144).

Black rhinoceros (*Diceros bicornis*) Shoulder height 160cm; weight 1,000kg. This imposing and rather temperamental creature is the smaller of Africa's two rhino species. It has been poached to extinction in most of its former range, but still occurs in *very* low numbers in many southern African reserves; Namibia offers one of its best chances of long-term survival, though as a deterrent against poaching, most of the rhino in the areas worst affected have been dehorned.

Black rhinos exploit a wide range of habitats, from dense woodlands and bush, through to the very open hillsides of the Kaokoveld. Also known as the hook-lipped rhino, from the distinctive shape of its mouth, this species is adapted to browsing: unlike the white rhino, it can raise its head to shoulder height to pluck twigs and foliage from trees. Over its range it utilises hundreds of different plants, though local populations are often more specific in their diet: in the Kaokoveld, for example, *Euphorbia damarana* is a great favourite.

Black rhinos are generally solitary animals and can survive without drinking for 4–5 days. However, they will drink daily if they can, and individuals often meet

Black rhinoceros

White rhinoceros

TM

at waterholes – as delighted visitors to the floodlit waterholes at Okaukuejo and Halali will often see. They are strongly territorial and have very regular patterns of movement, which makes them an easy target for poachers. Black rhinos can be very aggressive when disturbed and will charge with minimal provocation. Their hearing and sense of smell is acute, while their eyesight is poor (so they often miss if you keep a low profile and don't move). Rhino-tracking trips are possible in several areas of the Kunene Region, most easily at Desert Rhino Camp.

White rhinoceros (*Ceratotherium simum*) Shoulder height 180cm; weight 1,500–2,300kg (males exceptionally up to 3,600kg). The white rhino is in fact no paler in colour than the black rhino: the 'white' derives from the Afrikaans *weit* (wide) and refers to its broad, square mouth, an ideal shape for cropping grass. This is the best way to tell the two rhino species apart, since the mouth of the black rhino, a browser in most parts of its range, is more rounded with a hooked upper lip. (Note that there is *no colour difference at all* between these two species of rhino; 'white' and 'black' are not literal descriptions.)

In fact, the white rhino can be split into two subspecies (or possibly species, according to the latest research). The northern white rhino occurred naturally in Uganda, southern Chad, southwestern Sudan, the eastern part of Central African Republic, and northeastern Democratic Republic of the Congo. Sadly, however, this race has been hunted to extinction in the wild, and the only two known remaining individuals, both female, are in a reserve in Kenya.

The southern white rhino naturally occurred in a band across southern Africa, but was similarly poached to the verge of extinction in the 1970s and 1980s. By protecting populations in Umfolozi and Hluhluwe parks in South Africa, conservationists effectively saved the species and have since helped to repopulate many of southern Africa's parks. White rhino were reintroduced to Waterberg and back into Etosha – where they seem to frequent the areas between Namutoni and Springbokfontein waterhole – but poaching remains a constant threat. Unlike their smaller cousins, white rhino are generally placid grazing animals and are rarely aggressive. They prefer open grassy plains and are often seen in small groups.

43

Hippopotamus

Cape buffalo

Plains zebra

Hartmann's mountain zebra

46

Hippopotamus (*Hippopotamus amphibius*) Shoulder height 150cm; weight up to 2,000kg. Characteristic of Africa's large rivers and lakes, this large, lumbering animal spends most of the day submerged but emerges at night to graze. Strongly territorial, herds of ten or more animals are presided over by a dominant male who will readily defend his patriarchy to the death. Hippos are abundant in most protected rivers and water bodies, and hippos are still quite common outside of reserves, where they are widely credited with killing more people than any other African mammal.

In Namibia they occur only in the great rivers of the Caprivi Strip or Zambezi Region, and occasionally in the Kunene River, at the north end of the Kaokoveld. Otherwise you won't generally see them.

Cape buffalo (*Syncerus caffer*) Shoulder height 140cm; weight 700kg. Frequently and erroneously referred to as a water buffalo (an Asian species), the Cape, or African, buffalo is a distinctive, highly social oxlike animal that lives as part of a herd. It prefers well-watered savannah, though also occurs in forested areas. Common and widespread in protected areas across sub-Saharan Africa, in Namibia it is limited to the Caprivi Strip, largely by the absence of sufficient water elsewhere.

Buffalo are primarily grazers and need regular access to water, where they swim readily. They smell and hear well, and old bulls have a reputation for charging at the slightest provocation. Lion often follow herds of buffalo, their favourite prey.

Giraffe (*Giraffa camelopardis*) Shoulder height 250–350cm; weight 1,000–1,400kg. The world's tallest and longest-necked land animal, a fully grown giraffe can measure up to 5.5m high. Quite unmistakable, the giraffe lives in loosely structured herds of up to 15, though herd members often disperse and are then seen singly or in smaller groups. Formerly distributed throughout east and southern Africa, the 'southern' subspecies of these great browsers (*G. c. giraffa*) is found in the north of Namibia, from northern Damaraland and Kaokoland to the Caprivi. Etosha has a thriving population, many of which are very relaxed around cars and allow visitors in vehicles to approach very closely.

Plains zebra (*Equus quagga*) Shoulder height 130cm; weight 300–340kg. Also known as the common zebra, this attractive striped horse is abundant and widespread throughout most of east and southern Africa, where it is often seen in large herds alongside wildebeest. It is common in most conservation areas from northern South Africa, Namibia and Botswana all the way up to the southeast of Ethiopia. Different subspecies of plains zebra are recognised across Africa. The one found in Namibia is Burchell's zebra, and is distinguished by having paler brownish 'shadow stripes' between the bold black stripes that are present in all races.

Hartmann's mountain zebra (*E. grevyi hartmannae*) Shoulder height 150cm; weight 250–350kg. The slightly taller Hartmann's mountain zebra is confined to Namibia's western escarpment and the plains nearby. It is very closely related to the Cape mountain zebra, which occurs in South Africa. Both species of mountain zebra have a slightly lighter frame than the plains zebra, their underparts are not striped, the striping on their legs extends all the way to their hooves, and they have a dewlap, which the plains zebras lack. They occur from the conservation area around the Fish River Canyon to the Hartmann Valley in the Kaokoveld, and have been introduced on to several private reserves away from the escarpment area.

Warthog (*Phacochoerus africanus*) Shoulder height 60–70cm; weight up to 100kg. This widespread and often conspicuously abundant resident of the African savannah is grey in colour with a thin covering of hairs, wartlike bumps on its face, and rather large upward curving tusks. Africa's only diurnal swine, the warthog is often seen in family groups, trotting around with its tail raised stiffly (a diagnostic trait) and a determinedly nonchalant air. Warthogs occur everywhere in Namibia apart from the far south and the western desert areas, although I have often seen them grazing, on bended knee, where the C36 cuts through the Namib-Naukluft National Park.

Similar species Bulkier, hairier and more brown, the **bushpig** (*Potomochoerus larvatus*) is only known to occur in Namibia in the Caprivi Strip. It is very rarely seen due to its nocturnal habits and preference for dense vegetation.

SMALL MAMMALS
African civet (*Civettictis civetta*) Shoulder height 40cm; weight 10–15kg. This bulky, long-haired creature of the African night is primarily carnivorous, feeding on small animals and carrion, but will also eat fruit. It has a similarly coloured coat to a leopard, which is densely blotched with large black spots that become stripes towards the head and tail. Civets are widespread and common in many habitats, but very rarely seen. In Namibia, they are restricted to the far north.

African civet

Large-spotted genet

Similar species The **small-spotted genet** (*Genetta genetta*) and **large-spotted genet** (*G. tigrina*) belong to the Viverridae, the same family as the African civet, but are smaller, more slender, longer tailed and generally more feline in appearance (though they are *not* cats). Both have a grey to gold-brown coat marked with black spots and a long ringed tail. Most likely to be seen on nocturnal game drives or scavenging around game-reserve lodges, the large-spotted genet is gold-brown with very large spots and a black-tipped tail, whereas the small-spotted genet is greyer with rather small spots and a pale-tipped tail. Exact identification is a job for experts. The small-spotted genet is found all over Namibia, while the large-spotted genet is restricted to the Caprivi Strip and the area adjacent to the Okavango River.

Banded mongoose (*Mungos mungo*)

Shoulder height 20cm; weight around 1kg. The banded mongoose is probably the most commonly observed member of a group of small, slender, terrestrial carnivores. Uniform dark grey-brown except for a dozen black stripes across its back, it is a diurnal mongoose occurring in playful family groups, or troops, in most habitats north and east of Okahandja. This species feeds on insects, scorpions, amphibians, reptiles and even carrion and birds' eggs, and can move across the veld at quite a pace.

Banded mongoose

Similar species Another eight or so mongoose species occur in Namibia; some are social and gather in troops, others solitary. Several are too scarce and nocturnal to be seen by casual visitors. Of the rest, the water or **marsh mongoose** (*Atilax paludinosus*) is large, normally solitary and has a very scruffy brown coat; it is widespread along the Caprivi Strip (Zambezi Region) , the Kunene and the Orange. The **white-tailed mongoose** (*Ichneumia albicauda*) is another mongoose that is widespread in the Caprivi. It is a solitary, large grey-brown mongoose, easily identified by its bushy white tail.

Slender mongoose

The **slender mongoose** (*Galerella sanguinea*) is also widespread and solitary, but is diurnal and much smaller (barely squirrel-sized). It has a uniform brown or reddish coat and a black-tipped tail, which it often holds aloft. It is replaced in the far south of Namibia by the **small grey mongoose** (*G. pulveruntela*), similar in size but grey with white flecks on its coat.

The **yellow mongoose** (*Cynitis penicillata*) is a small, sociable mongoose with a tawny or yellow coat, and is commonly found across most of Namibia. It normally forages alone and is easily identified by its white tail tip.

Dwarf mongoose

Finally, the **dwarf mongoose** (*Helogate parvula*) is a diminutive (shoulder height 7cm), highly sociable, light brown mongoose often seen in the vicinity of the termite mounds where it lives.

Meerkat or suricate (*Suricata suricatta*)

Shoulder height 25–35cm; weight 650–950g. Found throughout the Kaokoveld and southern Namibia, meerkats are only absent from the driest western areas of the Namib (although I have had one confirmed report of them being seen on the Skeleton Coast) and the wetter parts of northeast Namibia. These small animals belong to the mongoose family. Sandy-

Meerkat

to silvery-grey in colour, with dark bands running across their backs. They are exclusively diurnal and have a distinctive habit of sitting upright on their hind legs. They do this when they first emerge in the morning, to sun themselves, and also throughout the day.

Living in complex social groups, meerkats are usually seen scratching around for insects, beetles and small reptiles in dry, open, grassy areas. While the rest forage, one or two of the group will use the highest mound around as a sentry post – looking out for predators using their remarkable eyesight. Meerkats' social behaviour is very complex: they squeak constantly to communicate and even use different alarm calls for different types of predators. Because of their photogenic poses and fascinating social behaviour, they have been the subject of several successful television documentaries filmed in the southern Kalahari. Good sightings of meerkat are often made from Bagatelle in the Kalahari.

Honey badger

Honey badger (*Mellivora capensis*) Shoulder height 30cm; weight 12kg. Also known as the ratel, the honey badger is black with a puppyish face and grey-white back. It is an opportunistic feeder best known for its reputedly symbiotic relationship with a bird called the honeyguide which leads it to a beehive, waits for it to tear it open, then feeds on the scraps, including wax. The honey badger is among the most widespread of African carnivores, and also among the most powerful for its size. It occurs all over Namibia, but is thinly distributed and rarely seen – except where habituated individuals turn up on cue to scavenge or be fed at safari camps. (Okonjima's nightly feeding session used to get occasional visits from honey badgers.)

Similar species Several other mustelids occur in the region, including the **striped polecat** (*Ictonyx striatus*), a common but rarely seen nocturnal creature with black underparts and a bushy white back, and the similar but much scarcer **striped weasel** (*Poecilogale albincha*). The **Cape clawless otter** (*Aonyx capensis*) is a brown freshwater mustelid with a white collar, which is found in the Caprivi area, the Kunene and the Orange River. The smaller **spotted-necked otter** (*Lutra maculicollis*) is darker with light white spots on its throat, and is restricted to the Caprivi and Okavango River.

Aardvark (*Orycteropus afer*) Shoulder height 60cm; weight up to 70kg. This singularly bizarre nocturnal insectivore is unmistakable, with its long snout, huge

Aardvark
RK/F

ears and powerful legs, adapted to dig up the nests of termites, on which it feeds. Aardvarks occur throughout southern Africa, except the driest western areas of the Namib. Though their distinctive three-toed tracks are often seen, and they are not uncommon animals, sightings of them are rare.

Aardvarks prefer areas of grassland and sparse scrub, rather than dense woodlands, and Namibia's ranchland suits them well – although their excavations into roads and dam walls are not appreciated by farmers.

Pangolin (*Manis temmincki*) Total length 70–100cm; weight 8–15kg. Sharing the aardvark's diet of termites and ants, pangolins are another very unusual nocturnal insectivore – with distinctive armour plating and a tendency to roll up into a ball when disturbed. Sometimes known as Temminck's pangolin, or scaly anteater, these strange animals walk on their hind legs, using their tail and front legs for

balance. They occur in eastern and northern Namibia, but not in the Namib Desert, and are both nocturnal and rare – so sightings are exceedingly unusual.

Pangolin
JF

In some areas, such as Zimbabwe, local custom is to make a present of any pangolin found to the paramount chief (often taken to mean the president), which has caused great damage to their population – though a far greater threat nowadays is from poaching for the traditional medicine market in the Far East.

Porcupine (*Hystrix africaeaustralis*) Total length 80–100cm; weight 15–25kg. This is the largest rodent found in the region, and occurs all over southern Africa, except for the western reaches of the Namib Desert. It easily identified by its black-and-white-striped quills, generally black hair, and shambling gait. If heard in the dark, then the rustle of its foraging is amplified by the slight rattle of its quills. These drop off fairly regularly, and are often found in the bush.

Porcupine
SH/S

The porcupine's diet is varied, and they are fairly opportunistic when it comes to food.

Roots and tubers are favourites, as is the bark of certain trees. They will also eat meat and small reptiles or birds if they have the chance.

Similar species Also spiky, the **southern African hedgehog** (*Atelerix frontalis*) is found in north-central areas, including the Kaokoveld and Ovamboland. This species is much smaller than the porcupine (about 20cm long), but is also omnivorous. It is not common.

Rock hyrax

Rock hyrax (*Procavia capensis*) Shoulder height 20–30cm; weight 4kg. Rodent-like in appearance, hyraxes (also known as dassies) are, in fact, among the closest living relatives of elephants. They are generally seen sunning themselves in rocky habitats, and may become tame when habituated to people. They are often seen sunning themselves in rocky habitats, and become tame when used to people.

Hyraxes are social animals, living in large groups, and largely herbivorous, eating leaves, grasses and fruits. Wherever you see lots of dassies, watch out for black eagles and other raptors which prey extensively on them

Scrub hare (*Lepus saxatilis*) Shoulder height 45–60cm; weight 1–4.5kg. This is the largest and commonest African hare or rabbit, occurring everywhere in Namibia except the far west and south. In some areas a short walk at dusk or after nightfall might reveal three or four scrub hares. They tend to freeze when disturbed.

Springhare

Springhare (*Pedetes capensis*) Shoulder height 30cm; weight 3kg. Despite the name, the springhare is not actually a hare but a nocturnal rodent. With two very strong hind legs and a long, black-tipped tail, it bounds along like a kangaroo, feeding on grasses, roots and seeds. Springhares are found throughout Namibia, although less so in coastal desert regions.

Ground squirrel

Ground squirrel (*Xerus inauris*) Shoulder height 20–30cm; weight 400–700g. This terrestrial rodent is common in most arid parts of Namibia, except the far west of the desert. It is grey to grey-brown with a prominent white eye ring and silver-black tail. Within its range, it might be confused with the meerkat, which also spends much time on its hind legs. Unlike the meerkat, ground squirrels have a characteristic squirrel mannerism of holding food in their forepaws.

The ground squirrel is a social animal; large groups share one communal burrow. It can often be spotted searching for vegetation, seeds, roots and small insects, while holding its tail aloft as a sunshade.

Bush squirrel (*Paraxerus cepapi*) Total length 35cm; weight 100–250g. This common rodent is a uniform grey or buff colour, with a long tail that is furry but not bushy. It's widely distributed all over southern and east Africa, and occurs where there are moist woodland habitats in Namibia. Bush squirrels are so numerous in mopane woodlands that it can be difficult to avoid seeing them – hence its other common names, the mopane or tree squirrel.

Bush squirrel

Bush squirrels live alone, in pairs or in small groups, usually nesting in a drey of dry leaves, in a hole in a tree. They are diurnal and venture to the ground to feed on seeds, fruit, nuts, vegetable matter and small insects. When alarmed they often bolt up the nearest tree, keeping on the side of the trunk away from the threat, out of sight as much as possible. If they can find a safe vantage point with a view of the threat, then they'll sometimes make a loud scolding alarm call.

REPTILES AND AMPHIBIANS

Namibia's numerous ecosystems are home to around 250 species of reptile, from the Nile crocodile to tiny lizards and skinks.

NILE CROCODILE (*Crocodylus niloticus*) Length 3.5–5m, exceptionally up to 6m; weight up to 1,000kg. Few visitors to Namibia will have the opportunity to see this antediluvian creature, which is largely confined to the Kunene and Kavango rivers along the country's northern boundary. With its powerful serrated tail, horny plated skin and up to 100 peg-like teeth crammed into a long, sinister smile, the Nile crocodile is the stuff of nightmares and action movies. Contrary to the more lurid myths, crocodiles generally avoid people (understandably, given the slaughter they have suffered). Yet while they will not usually launch themselves into boats or come galloping after you on land, humans are still potential prey for a big one, and tragedies do occasionally occur. When in crocodile country, it is sensible to keep your distance from the water's edge.

Nile crocodile

Crocodiles can live up to 100, but reach sexual maturity at 12–15 years. They inhabit lakes, rivers and swamps. Whereas youngsters are boldly marked in black and green, adults are generally a muddy grey-brown colour – usually lighter in rivers than in lagoons. Theirs is an amphibious life: basking on land, jaws agape to lose heat, or cruising the waters, raised eyes and nostrils allowing them to see and breathe undetected. As well as eating fish such as bream and barbel, adult crocs will ambush mammals up to the size of buffalo, grabbing them with an explosive sideways lunge from the water, before dragging them under to drown. Large numbers of crocodiles gather to scavenge big carcasses, churning up the water as they thrash and spin to dislodge chunks of flesh. They will even leave the water to steal a nearby lion kill.

LIZARDS The largest of the lizard species in Namibia are the monitor lizards, which can grow to over 2m in length, but there are also numerous skinks, sand lizards, geckos, chameleons and agamas. With the arguable exception of the monitor lizards, which could in theory inflict a nasty bite if cornered, all are harmless to humans.

The **water monitor** (*Varanus niloticus*) is regularly observed on the banks of the Kavango River, where you may hear them splash before seeing them. Size alone might make it possible to fleetingly mistake a monitor for a small crocodile, but their more colourful yellow-dappled skin and smaller head precludes sustained confusion. They, and the less frequently seen **rock or white-throated monitor** (*Varanus albigularis*) are predatory, feeding on anything from birds' eggs to smaller reptiles and mammals, and occasional carrion.

Also very common are various **agama** species, often seen basking prominently on rocks. These are distinguished from other lizards by their relatively large size (20–25cm), their prominent heads and their colourful, almost plastic-looking, scaling. This ranges from blue and purple to orange or red, depending on the species, with the head usually a different colour from the body. **Skinks**, too, are widespread: small, long-tailed lizards, usually quite dark and with thin black stripes running from head to tail.

Adapting to desert conditions has been perfected by the endemic **shovel-snouted lizard** (*Zeros anchietae*), which races across the sand, lifting diagonally opposed feet in the air in a weird dance to avoid being burnt on the hot sand. Here you'll also find the strangely beautiful **Namib sand gecko** (*Pachydactylus rangei*), its bug eyes particularly entrancing against the iridescent colours of its translucent skin.

In their natural habitat, **chameleons** have excellent camouflage, as the light coming off the surrounding vegetation is picked up by cells in their skin which then replicate that colour. On the roads, however, the same does not apply. Chameleons tend to freeze when faced with an approaching vehicle, and then the bright green of the flap-necked chameleon (*Chamaeleo dilepis*) is a real giveaway. Do, though, keep a watchful eye for the sand-coloured endemic Namaqua chameleon (*Chamaeleo namaquensis*) which blends almost seamlessly into the gravel.

Rock monitor lizard

SS

Rock agama

Shovel-snouted lizard

Sand gecko

Flap-necked chameleon

Horned adder

SNAKES Namibia may have more than 90 species of snake, but only 11 are considered capable of delivering a lethal bite to humans – and of these, most are rarely seen unless actively sought. The most likely non-venomous snake to be seen is Africa's largest, the **rock python** (*Python sebae*), which has gold-on-black mottled skin and can grow to 5m or more. Pythons kill their prey – small antelopes, large rodents and similar animals – by strangulation, wrapping their muscular bodies around it until it cannot breathe, then swallowing it whole and dozing off for a couple of months while it is digested. Few are large or bold enough to tackle an adult human, but many could kill a small child.

One of the most commonly encountered venomous snakes is the **puff adder** (*Bitis arietans*), a large, thick-set resident that feeds mainly on rodents. Although it does not have the most powerful venom among Africa's dangerous snakes, it accounts for more serious bites than any other. This is due to a combination of factors, including its abundance, large size and aggressive disposition, and its habit of basking quietly by footpaths. When threatened, it will coil its body into a defensive S shape and make a loud puffing noise by releasing air slowly.

The S-shape is notable for another reason in **Peringuey's sidewinder** (*Bitis peringueyi*), a desert snake that, as the name implies, moves sidewise, leaving a clear S-shaped trail in the sand. **Horned adders** (*Bitis caudalis*) – distinctive for their small horns – frequent this environment, too, as does the **Namaqua dwarf adder** (*Bitis schneideri*), which averages just 18–25cm long.

Other venomous species, such as black mambas (*Dendroaspis polylepis*), boomslangs (*Dispholidus typus*) and various cobras (spitting, Cape and Anchieta's or Angolan), are seldom seen and usually flee or go into cover way before you have a chance to see them.

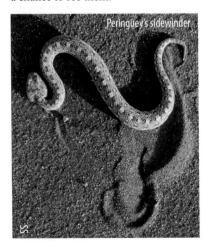

Peringuey's sidewinder

Namaqua dwarf adder

Leopard tortoise

Marsh terrapin

JF

JF

TORTOISES AND TERRAPINS Tortoises and terrapins are unique in being protected by a prototypal suit of armour formed by their heavy exoskeleton. Of Namibia's seven species (the only country with more is South Africa), the most common is the **leopard tortoise** (*Stigmochelys pardalis*), which is named for its gold-and-black mottled shell, and can weigh up to 30kg. Three species of tent tortoise include the **Kalahari tent tortoise** (*Psammobates oculifer*) which, as its name suggests, is found largely in the Kalahari regions of central Namibia. The other two hail from Bushmanland and Namaqualand, and are named accordingly.

Terrapins are essentially the freshwater equivalent of turtles. Somewhat flatter in shape than tortoises, they generally have a plainer brown shell. They might be seen sunning on rocks close to water or peering out from roadside puddles. Hinged, side-neck and soft-shelled terrapins are all in residence where water is plentiful, particularly along the country's northern boundary, or in manmade lakes such as Gross Barmen.

FROGS Many of Namibia's 50 species of frogs, such as the **giant African bullfrog** (*Pyxicephalus adspersus*) in Etosha and the **desert rain frog** (*Breviceps macrops*) in the Sperrgebiet, spend their lives underground, awaiting the rains before they emerge to breed. If you're on the river in the Zambezi Region, particularly in a mokoro (dugout canoe), keep a close eye on the reeds for the tiny **painted reed frog**. Up to about 40mm long, adults have extremely variable colours and patterns, from clear stripes through to dots, patches and vermiculations – and from bright green and yellow through to red and dark brown. Given the huge colour variability in these frogs, a precise identification will challenge many herpetologists, but the Angolan painted reed frog (*Hyperolius parallelus*) and the painted reed frog (*Hyperolius marmoratus*) are two key candidates. Listen at night beside water: that distinctive chorus of gentle individual notes, as if from tiny bells, is the frogs calling.

Giant African bullfrog

MS/FLPA

Painted reed frog

JHB/MP/FLPA

Cape fur seal

MARINE LIFE

Cooled by the Benguela Current, the waters of the Atlantic are teeming with wildlife. For most visitors, it's the creatures that brave the shores that are of greatest interest. Readily seen year round are dolphins – both the bottlenose and Heaviside's – as are colonies of Cape fur seals. Towards the end of the year, leatherback turtles appear, along with migrating humpback, southern right, Minke and even killer whales. There's also the chance of spotting the impressive giant or ocean sunfish (*Mola mola*), which can weigh in at up to 1,000kg.

CAPE FUR SEAL (*Arctocephalus pusillus pusillus*) Also known as the South African fur seal. Length 1.8–2.3m; weight: female 75–120kg, male 200–360kg. Ranging from southern Angola to South Africa, Cape fur seals are indigenous to the region. They fall into the category of eared seals or sealions, distinguished from seals by their visible ears and ability to move around on land by raising their bodies on their front flippers. Readily seen, heard and smelled in all their noisy, smelly glory at Cape Cross (see box, page 382), they are found right along the Namibian coast, including Walvis Bay – where they regularly cavort around the tourist boats and kayaks (page 361).

BOTTLENOSE DOLPHIN (*Tursiops truncatus*) Length up to 13.5m; weight 150–400kg; males much larger than females. The sociable bottlenose dolphin is regularly spotted in small groups along the Namibian coast. When conditions are right, it sometimes comes right in to the lagoon at Walvis Bay to feed on easy pickings of fish and squid.

HEAVISIDE'S DOLPHIN (*Cephalorhynchus heavisidii*) Also known as the Benguela dolphin, South African dolphin. Length up to 1.7m; weight 60–70g. Heaviside's is smaller than the bottlenose dolphin, and not quite as sociable. Restricted to the Atlantic coast of Namibia and South Africa, it was named after a certain Captain Haviside, master of an East Indiaman, who brought a specimen back from a voyage in the early 19th century. It is distinctive for its black, white and grey coloration, along with a blunt nose and triangular dorsal fin, and is often seen by visitors on boat trips from Walvis Bay and Lüderitz.

AFRICAN PENGUIN (*Spheniscus demersus*) Also known as the black-footed penguin, jackass penguin Height 60–70 cm; weight 3.7–4g. Always busy, always on the move, African penguins in their patterned black-and-white suits can seem like the comedians of the coast. Their range is restricted to western South Africa and Namibia, where they are readily seen on boat trips to Halifax Island from Lüderitz.

Bottlenose dolphin

Heaviside's dolphin

African penguin

Much of Namibia is very dry, and thus hasn't the variation in resident birds that you might find in lusher environments – yet even then the bird count tops 600 species. Many of those dry-country birds have restricted distributions, and so are endemic, or close to being so. Further, where Namibia's drier interior borders a wetter area, as within the Mahango Core Area of Bwabwata National Park, or along the Kunene and Okavango rivers to the north, the species count shoots up.

Inevitably the rains from December to around April see an explosion in the availability of most birds' food: seeds, fruits and insects. Hence this is the prime time for birds to breed, even if it is also the most difficult time to visit the more remote areas of the country.

ENDEMICS For serious birders, the region's endemic species are a real draw. The perfect place to start is Etosha, home to the bare-cheeked babbler, violet woodhoopoe, white-tailed shrike, Carp's black tit, Rüppell's parrot, rockrunner, Monteiro's hornbill and Hartlaub's spurfowl. To the west, the coastal desert harbours Gray's, Barlow's and – behind Walvis Bay and Swakopmund – dune larks, along with Rüppell's korhaan, while on the coast itself, the tiny Damara tern may occasionally be spotted among its larger cousins. For the Damara hornbill, Herero chat and Cinderella waxbill, you'll need to head for the Kunene, with the last of these restricted to a narrow band along the Kunene River.

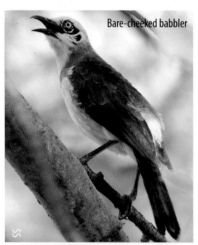
Bare-cheeked babbler

Hartlaub's spurfowl

Monteiro's hornbill

Ruppell's korhaan

Blue waxbill

CWCS

Lilac-breasted roller

TM

Rosy-faced lovebirds

TM

Swallow-tailed bee-eater

TH

MIGRANTS In addition to its residents, Namibia receives many migrants. In September and October the Palaearctic migrants appear (ie: those that come from the northern hemisphere – normally Europe), and they remain until around April or May. This is also the peak time to see the intra-African migrants, which come from further north in Africa.

The coastal wetland sites, most notably around Walvis Bay and Sandwich Harbour, receive visits from many migrating species, as well as seabird species that aren't normally seen in the interior of southern Africa. So trips including the coast, as well as the country's interior and riverine borders, make Namibia an excellent and varied destination for birders.

BIRDING HIGHLIGHTS Top in the popularity stakes among visitors is the lilac-breasted roller. Although readily visible except in coastal areas and the Namib Desert, it is no less dazzling for being relatively common. Similarly widespread – and eye-catching – are the swallow-tailed bee-eater and the yellow-billed hornbill, whose huge bill has earned it the nick name of 'flying banana' among safari guides.

Colour is strikingly apparent in the fertile environment of the central highlands and acacia woodlands, too. Cape and golden-breasted buntings, eye-catching rosy-faced lovebirds and a whole host of waxbills, firefinches and pytilias swoop down to feed at ground level, with the spectrum further enhanced by the vivid crimson-breasted boubou, or shrike.

Mountains and plains Namibia's plains are stalked by the larger species, from the ostrich and kori bustard to secretary birds and korhaans. Sociable weavers are ever present, readily identified by their huge communal nests that can eventually bring down the host tree. Often seen posing on telegraph poles is the pale chanting goshawk, while lording it over all are martial, tawny and a variety of snake eagles including the closely related bateleur. And then there are the vultures, mostly lappet-faced and white-backed, now endangered as a result of feeding on animals that have been given drugs such as diclofenac, which can prove fatal to the birds.

Ostrich

Brown snake eagle

White-backed vulture

Bateleur eagle

Rivers and lakes Along the permanent rivers, tiny malachite kingfishers flash their jewel-like plumage, in contrast with the more sober-coloured giant kingfisher, which tends to watch for prey from the trees. Perched much higher, look out for the distinct dark brown and white of the African fish eagle, Namibia's national bird. Towards the end of the dry season a flash of crimson and turquoise signals the return of the carmine bee-eaters to nest in the sandy riverbanks of the Kwando and Okavango rivers.

Any area of water will attract its share of water-loving geese, herons, storks, ducks and lapwings, along with avocets, black-winged stilts and many more besides. But if you're after flamingos (see box, overleaf) or pelicans, your best bet is to head for Walvis Bay from about September onwards.

For more detail on the birdlife of Namibia's individual habitats, see the entries in the individual chapters.

Malachite kingfisher

Black-winged stilt

Blacksmith's lapwing

White pelican

Goliath heron

Of the world's half-dozen or so species of flamingo, two are found in Namibia: the greater (*Phoenicopterus roseus*) and the lesser (*P. minor*). Both species have wide distributions – from southern Africa north into east Africa and the Red Sea – and are highly nomadic. The best way to tell the two species apart is by their beaks: that of the greater flamingo is almost white, while the lesser flamingo has a uniformly dark beak. Looking from further away, the body of the greater flamingo appears white, while that of the lesser looks smaller and pinker.

Flamingos are usually found wading in large areas of shallow saline water, where they filter-feed by holding their specially adapted beaks upside down. The lesser flamingo walks or swims while swinging its head from side to side, mainly taking blue-green algae from the surface. The larger, greater flamingo holds its head submerged while filtering out small organisms (detritus and algae), even stirring the mud with its feet to help the process. Both species are gregarious; flocks can number millions of birds, although hundreds are more common.

Only occasionally do flamingos breed in southern Africa, choosing Etosha Pan or perhaps Botswana's Makgadikgadi Pans. When the conditions are right (usually March to June, following heavy rains) both species build low mud cones in the water and lay one or (rarely) two eggs in a small hollow on the top. These are then incubated by both parents for about a month until they hatch, and after a further week the young birds flock together and start to forage with their parents. Some ten weeks later the young can fly and fend for themselves.

During their first few months, the young are very susceptible to the shallow water drying out. In 1969, a rescue operation was mounted when Etosha Pan dried out. Thousands of chicks were moved to nearby Fischer's Pan, which was still covered in water.

Namibia's best places for flamingos are usually the lagoons at Walvis Bay and Sandwich Harbour – unless you hear that Etosha or Nyae Nyae are full of water. Then, by the time you arrive, the flamingos will probably have beaten you there.

3

History, Politics and Economy

HISTORY

PREHISTORY
Namibia's earliest inhabitants Palaeontologists looking for evidence of the first ancestors of the human race have excavated a number of sites in southern Africa. The earliest remains yet identified are Stone Age tools dated at about 200,000 years old, which have been recovered in gravel deposits around what is now the Victoria Falls. It is thought that these probably belong to *Homo erectus*, whose hand-axes have been dated in Tanzania to half a million years old. These were hunter-gatherer people, who could use fire, make tools, and had probably developed some simple speech.

Experts divide the Stone Age into the middle, early and late periods. The transition from early to middle Stone Age technology – which is indicated by a larger range of stone tools, often adapted for particular uses, and signs that these people had a greater mastery of their environment – was probably in progress around 125,000 years ago in southern Africa. The late Stone Age is characterised by people who used composite tools, those made of wood and/or bone and/or stone used together, and by the presence of a revolutionary invention: the bow and arrow. This first probably appeared about 15,000 years ago, by which time the original Namibians were already roaming the plains of Damaraland and painting on the rocks at Twyfelfontein.

Africa's Iron Age Around 3000BC, late Stone Age hunter-gatherer groups in Ethiopia, and elsewhere in North and West Africa, started to keep domestic animals, sow seeds and harvest the produce: they became the world's first farmers.

By around 1000BC these new pastoral practices had spread south into the equatorial forests of what is now Congo, to around Lake Victoria, and into the northern area of the Great Rift Valley, in northern Tanzania. However, agriculture did not spread south into the rest of central/southern Africa immediately. Only when the technology, and the tools, of iron-working became known did the practices start their relentless expansion southward.

The spread of agriculture and Iron Age culture seems to have been rapid, brought south by Bantu-speaking Africans who were taller and heavier than the existing Khoisan-speaking inhabitants of southern Africa.

BANTU COLONISATION
Khoisan coexistence By around the time of Christ, the hunter-gatherers in Namibia seem to have been joined by pastoralists, the Khoi-khoi (or Nama people), who used a similar language involving clicks. Both belong to the Khoisan language family, as distinct from the Bantu-language family. These were pastoralists who combined keeping sheep, goats and cattle with foraging.

These stock animals are not native to southern Africa and it seems likely that some Khoisan hunters and gatherers acquired stock, and the expertise to keep them, from early Bantu tribes in the Zimbabwe area. As the Bantu spread south, into the relatively fertile Natal area, the Khoisan pastoralists spread west, across the Kalahari into Namibia. Their traditional gathering knowledge, and ability to survive on existing plant foods, meant that they didn't depend entirely on their stock. Hence they could expand across areas of poor grazing which would have defeated the less flexible Bantu.

By around the 9th century another group, the Damara, are recognised as living in Namibia and speaking a Khoisan language. They cultivated more than the Nama, and hence were more settled. Their precise origin is hotly debated, as they have many features common to people of Bantu origin and yet speak a Khoisan language.

The first Bantu people By the 16th century the first of the Bantu-speaking peoples, the Herero, arrived from the east. Oral tradition suggests that they came south from East Africa's great lakes to Zambia, across Angola, arriving at the Kunene River around 1550. However they got here, they settled with their cattle in the north of the country and the plains of the Kaokoveld. (Note that the Himba people living in the Kaokoveld today are a subgroup of the Herero, speaking the same language.)

Where the Herero settled, the existing people clearly had to change. Some intermarried with the incoming groups; some may even have been enslaved by the newcomers. A few could shift their lifestyles to take advantage of new opportunities created by the Herero, and an unfortunate fourth group (the Bushmen of the time) started to become marginalised, remaining in areas with less agricultural potential. This was the start of a poor relationship between the cattle-herding Herero and the Bushmen.

These iron-working, cattle-herding Herero people were very successful and, as they thrived, so they began to expand their herds southward and into central Namibia.

The early explorers Meanwhile, in the 15th century, trade between Europe and the East opened up sea routes along the Namibian coast and around the Cape of Good Hope. The first Europeans recorded as stepping on Namibian soil were the Portuguese in 1485. Diego Cão stopped briefly at Cape Cross on the Skeleton Coast and erected a limestone cross. On 8 December 1487, Bartolomeu Dias reached Walvis Bay and then continued south to what is now Lüderitz. However, the coast was so totally barren and uninviting that, even though the Portuguese had already settled in Angola, and the Dutch in the Cape, little interest was shown in Namibia.

It was only in the latter half of the 18th century, when British, French and American whalers began to make use of the ports of Lüderitz and Walvis Bay, that the Dutch authorities in the Cape decided in 1793 to take possession of Walvis Bay – the only good deepwater port on the coast. A few years later, France invaded Holland, prompting England to seize control of the Cape Colony and, with it, Walvis Bay.

Even then, little was known about the interior. It wasn't until the middle of the 19th century that explorers, missionaries and traders started to venture inland, with Francis Galton and Charles John Andersson leading the way.

Oorlam incursions By the second half of the 18th century, the Dutch settlers in the Cape of South Africa were not only expanding rapidly into the interior, but they were also effectively waging war on any of the indigenous people who stood in their way. In *Africa: A Biography of the Continent*, John Reader (page 574) comments:

THE OORLAM PEOPLE

Originating from the Cape, the Oorlam people were a variety of different groups, all speaking Khoisan languages, who left the Cape because of European expansion there. Some were outlaws, others wanted space far from the Europeans. Many broke away from fixed Nama settlements to join roving Oorlam bands. Under the leadership of *kapteins*, these groups would hunt, trade and steal for survival.

Khoisan resistance hardened as the frontier advanced during the 18th century. [The] Government [of the Cape's] edicts empowered [commando groups of settlers]... to wage war against all the region's Khoisan, who were now to be regarded as vermin. Slaughter was widespread. Official records show that commandos killed 503 Khoisan in 1774 alone, and 2,480 between 1786 and 1795. The number of killings that passed unrecorded can only be guessed at.

By 1793 the settler population in the Cape totalled 13,830 people, who between them owned 14,747 slaves.

With this pressure from the south, it is no wonder that mobile, dispossessed bands of Khoisan, known as Oorlam groups, pressed northward over the Orange River and into southern Namibia. They often had guns and horses, and had learned some of the Europeans' ways. However, they still spoke a Khoisan language and were of the same origins as the Nama pastoralists who had already settled in southern Namibia.

At that time, these Nama peoples seem to have settled into a life of relatively peaceful, pastoral coexistence. Thus the arrival of a few Oorlam groups was not a problem. However, around the start of the 19th century more Oorlams came, putting more pressure on the land, and soon regular skirmishes were a feature of the area.

In 1840 the increasingly unsettled situation was calmed by an agreement between the two paramount chiefs: Oaseb of the Nama, and Jonker Afrikaner of the Oorlam people. There was already much intermingling of the two groups, and so accommodating each other made sense – especially given the expansion of Herero groups further north.

The deal split the lands of southern Namibia between the various Nama and Oorlam groups, while giving the land between the Kuiseb and the Swakop rivers to the Oorlams. Further, Jonker Afrikaner was given rights over the people north of the Kuiseb, up to Waterberg.

Nama–Herero conflict By around the middle of the 18th century, the Herero people had expanded beyond Kaokoland, spreading at least as far south as the Swakop River. Their expansion south was now effectively blocked by Oorlam groups, led by Jonker Afrikaner, who won several decisive battles against Herero people around 1835 – resulting in his Afrikaner followers stealing many Herero cattle, and becoming the dominant power in central Namibia. From 1840, Jonker Afrikaner and his Oorlam followers created a buffer zone between the Hereros expanding from the north, and the relatively stable Nama groups in the south.

EUROPEAN COLONISATION

The missionaries In the early 1800s, missionaries were gradually moving into southern Namibia. The London Missionary Society and the German Rhenish and

Finnish Lutheran Mission societies were all represented. These were important for several reasons. First, they tended to settle in one place, which became the nucleus around which the local Nama people would permanently settle. Often the missionaries would introduce the local people to different ways of cultivation: a further influence to settle in permanent villages, which gradually became larger.

Secondly, they acted as a focal point for traders, who would navigate through the territory from one mission to the next. This effectively set up Namibia's first trade routes – routes that soon became conduits for the local Nama groups to obtain European goods, from guns and ammunition to alcohol. It seems that the missionaries sometimes provided firearms directly to the local people for protection. While understandable, the net effect was that the whole area became a more dangerous place.

In 1811, Reverend Heinrich Schmelen founded Bethanie, and more missions followed. By December 1842, Rhenish missionaries were established where Windhoek now stands, surrounded by about 1,000 of Jonker Afrikaner's followers. The settlement soon started trading with the coast, and within a few years there was a steady supply of guns arriving.

Nama conflict In 1861 Jonker Afrikaner died while returning from a raid he had mounted on the Ovambo people (a group of Bantu origin who had settled in the far north of the country and displaced some of the Hereros). Jonker's death left a power vacuum in central Namibia.

There were many skirmishes for control during the rest of the 1860s, and much politicking and switching of alliances between the rival Nama groups (some of Oorlam descent). The main protagonists included the Witboois from around Gibeon, the Afrikaners based in Windhoek, the Swartboois, the Bondelswarts, the Topnaar and the Red Nation.

The traders By around 1850 many hunters and traders were penetrating Namibia's interior, in search of adventure and profit – usually in the form of ivory and ostrich feathers. Among these, Charles John Andersson was particularly important, both for his own role in shaping events, and also for the clear documentation that he left behind, including the fascinating books *Lake Ngami* and *The River Okavango* (page 573) – chronicling his great journeys of the late 1850s.

In 1860 Andersson bought up the assets of a mining company, and set up a centre for trading at Otjimbingwe, a very strategic position on the Swakop River, halfway between Walvis Bay and Windhoek. (Now it is at the crossroads of the D1953 and the D1976.) In the early 1860s he traded with the Nama groups in the area, and started to open up routes into the Herero lands further north and east. However, after losing cattle to a Nama raid in 1861, he recruited hunters (some the contemporary equivalent of mercenaries) to expand his operations and protect his interests.

In 1863 the eldest son of Jonker Afrikaner led a foolish raid on Otjimbingwe. He was defeated and killed by Andersson's men, adding to the leadership crisis among the Nama groups. By 1864 Andersson had formed an alliance with the paramount Herero chief, Kamaherero, and together they led a large army into battle with the Afrikaner Namas at Windhoek. This was indecisive, but did clearly mark the end of Nama domination of central Namibia, as well as inflicting a wound on Andersson from which he never fully recovered.

The peace of 1870 During the late 1860s the centre of Namibia was often in a state of conflict. The Hereros under Kamaherero were vying for control with the various Nama clans, as Charles Andersson and his traders became increasingly important by forming and breaking alliances with them all.

After several defeats, the Nama *kaptein* Jan Jonker led an army of Afrikaners to Okahandja in 1870 to make peace with Kamaherero. This was brokered by the German Wesleyan missionary Hugo Hahn – who had arrived in Windhoek in 1844, but been replaced swiftly after Jonker Afrikaner had complained about him, and requested his replacement by his missionary superiors.

This treaty effectively subdued the Afrikaners, and Hahn also included a provision for the Basters, who had migrated recently from the Cape, to settle at Rehoboth. The Afrikaners were forced to abandon Windhoek, and Herero groups occupied the area. Thus the Basters around Rehoboth effectively became the buffer between the Herero groups to the north, and the Namas to the south.

The 1870s was a relatively peaceful era, which enabled the missionaries and, especially, the various traders to extend their influence throughout the centre of the country. This most affected the Nama groups in the south, who began to trade more and more with the Cape. Guns, alcohol, coffee, sugar, beads, materials and much else flowed in. To finance these imports, local Nama chiefs and *kapteins* charged traders and hunters to cross their territory, and granted them licences to exploit the wildlife.

The Hereros, too, traded: but mainly for guns. Their social system valued cattle most highly, and so breeding bigger herds meant more to them than the new Western goods. Thus they emerged into the 1880s stronger than before, while the power of many of the Nama groups had waned.

THE SCRAMBLE FOR AFRICA In the last few decades of the 19th century the Portuguese, the British, the French, and Leopold II of Belgium were starting to embark on the famous 'Scramble for Africa'. Germany had long eschewed the creation of colonies, and Bismarck is widely quoted as stating: 'So long as I am Chancellor we shan't pursue a colonial policy.'

However, in March 1878 the English government of South Africa's Cape formally annexed an enclave around Walvis Bay. (The British had been asked earlier by missionaries to help instil order in the heartland of Namibia, but they didn't feel that it was worth the effort.)

In late 1883 a German merchant called Adolf Lüderitz started to buy land on the coast. He established the town named Lüderitzbucht – usually referred to now as Lüderitz – and began trading with the local Nama groups. (It was news of this act that was said to have finally prompted Britain to make Bechuanaland a protectorate.)

Faced with much internal pressure, Bismarck reversed his policy in May 1884. He dispatched a gunboat to Lüderitz and in July claimed Togo and Cameroon as colonies. By August Britain had agreed to Germany's claims on Lüderitz, from which sprang the German colony of South West Africa. Lüderitz itself was bought out a few years later by the newly formed German Colonial Company for South West Africa, and shortly after that the administration of the area was transferred directly to Germany's control.

In May 1884, Portugal proposed an international conference to address the territorial conflicts of the colonial powers in the Congo. This was convened in Berlin, with no Africans present, and over the next few years the colonial powers parcelled Africa up and split it between them. Among many territorial dealings, mostly involving pen-and-ruler decisions on the map of Africa, a clearly defined border between Britain's new protectorate of Bechuanaland and Germany's South West Africa was established in 1890 – and Britain ceded a narrow corridor of land to Germany. This was subsequently named after the German Chancellor, Count von Caprivi, as the Caprivi Strip.

German South West Africa After a decade of relative peace, the 1880s brought problems to central Namibia again, with fighting between the Hereros, the Basters, and various Nama groups, notably the Afrikaners and the Swartboois. However, with German annexation in 1884 a new power had arrived. For the first five years, the official German presence in South West Africa was limited to a few officials stationed at Otjimbingwe. However, they had begun the standard colonial tactic of exploiting small conflicts by encouraging the local leaders to sign 'protection' treaties with Germany.

The Hereros, under Chief Maharero, signed in 1885, after which the German Commissioner Göring wrote to Hendrik Witbooi – the leader of the Witbooi Namas who occupied territory from Gibeon to Gobabis – insisting that he desist from attacking the Hereros, who were now under German protection. Witbooi wrote to Maharero, to dissuade him from making a 'pact with the devil' – he was, perhaps, ahead of his time in seeing this German move as an opening gambit in their bid for total control of Namibia.

In 1889 the first 21 German soldiers, Schutztruppe, arrived. More followed in 1890, by which time they had established a fort in Windhoek. That same year Maharero died, which enabled the German authorities to increase their influence in the internal politics of succession which brought Samuel Maharero to be paramount chief of the Herero. By 1892 the first contingent of settlers (over 50 people) had made their homes in Windhoek.

A fair trade? The 1890s and early 1900s saw a gradual erosion of the power and wealth of all Namibia's existing main groups in favour of the Germans. Gradually traders and adventurers bought more and more land from both the Nama and the Herero, aided by credit-in-advance agreements. A rinderpest outbreak in 1897 decimated the Herero's herds, and land sales were the obvious way to repay their debts. Gradually the Herero lost their lands and tension grew. The Rhenish Missionary Society saw the evil, and pressurised the German government to create areas where the Herero *could not* sell their land. Small enclaves were thus established, but these didn't address the wider issues.

THE 20TH CENTURY

Namibian war of resistance 1904–07 As land was progressively bought up, or sometimes simply taken from the local inhabitants by colonists, various skirmishes and small uprisings developed. The largest started in October 1903 with the Bondelswarts near Warmbad, which distracted most of the German Schutztruppe in the south. See page 573 for details of Mark Cocker's excellent *Rivers of Blood, Rivers of Gold* which gives a full account of this war.

The Herero nation had become increasingly unhappy about its loss of land, and in January 1904 Samuel Maharero ordered a Herero uprising against the German colonial forces. Initially he was clear to exclude as targets Boer and English settlers and German women and children. Simultaneously he appealed to Hendrik Witbooi, and other Nama leaders, to join the battle – they, however, stayed out of the fight.

At first the Hereros had success in taking many German farms and smaller outposts, and in severing the railway line between Swakopmund and Windhoek. However, later in 1904, the German General Leutwein was replaced by von Trotha – who had a reputation for brutal oppression after his time in East Africa. Backed by domestic German opinion demanding a swift resolution, von Trotha led a large German force including heavy artillery against the Hereros. By August 1904 the Hereros were pushed back to their stronghold of Waterberg, with its permanent waterholes, and von Trotha proposed that the only solution to the problem was to eliminate or expel the Hereros as a nation. On 11 August, over 3,500 Herero warriors and their families assembled expecting peace negotiations, but instead were attacked by 1,500 German soldiers. In what would become known as the Battle of Waterberg it is estimated that 3,000–5,000 Hereros were killed. Those who survived fled east into the desert, and von Trotha set up guard to prevent their return. Immediately following the battle, any Herero that the German troops caught up with was put to death, including women and children. In October 1904, von Trotha stated that the Hereros were no longer German subjects, ordering them to leave Namibia or face death on their capture. This is cited in the UN Whitaker Report on Genocide as one of the earliest examples of genocide in the 20th century. However, in late 1904, following a change of orders, Herero prisoners were sent to concentration camps. Shark Island in Lüderitz is a notorious example, where captured prisoners were made to work as slave labour. Conditions at these camps were very poor, and death rates were high.

Thereafter, somewhat too late to be effective, Hendrik Witbooi's people also revolted against the Germans, and wrote encouraging the other Nama groups to do the same. The Red Nation, Topnaar, Swartbooi and Bondelswarts joined in attacking the Germans, though the last were largely incapacitated after their battles the previous year. The Basters stayed out of the fight.

For several years these Nama groups waged an effective guerrilla campaign against the colonial forces, using the waterless sands of the Kalahari as a haven in which the German troops were ineffective. However, in 1905 Hendrik Witbooi was killed, and January 1907 saw the last fighters sue for peace.

German consolidation With South West Africa under stable German control, there was an influx of German settler families and the colony began to develop rapidly. The settlers were given large plots of the country's most productive lands, the railway network was expanded, and many of the towns began to grow. The non-European Namibians were increasingly marginalised, and simply used as a source of labour.

The building of the railway to Lüderitz led to the discovery of diamonds around there in 1908, and the resulting boom encouraged an influx of prospectors and German opportunists. By that time the mine at Tsumeb was already thriving, and moving its copper produce south on the newly built railway.

The German settlers thrived until the declaration of World War I. Between 1907 and 1914 they were granted self-rule from Germany, a number of the main towns were declared municipalities, and many of Namibia's existing civic buildings were constructed.

World War I At the onset of World War I, Britain encouraged South Africa to push north and wrest South West Africa from the Germans. In July 1915, the German colonial troops surrendered to South African forces at Khorab, where a memorial now marks the spot. At the end of the war, Namibia became a League of Nations 'trust territory', assigned to the Union of South Africa as 'a sacred trust in the name of civilisation' to 'promote to the utmost the material and moral well-being of its inhabitants'. At the same time, the Caprivi Strip was incorporated back into Bechuanaland (now Botswana) – only to be returned 20 years later.

THE FINAL COLONISTS
South African rule After overcoming their initial differences, new colonists from South Africa and the existing German colonists soon discovered a common

interest – the unabashed exploitation of the native population whose well-being they were supposed to be protecting.

Gradually more and more of the land in central Namibia was given to settler families, now often Boers from South Africa rather than Germans from Europe. The native population was restricted to various 'native areas' – usually poor land which couldn't be easily farmed by the settlers: Bushmanland and Hereroland in the Kalahari, Damaraland and Kaokoland bordering on the Namib. Much of the rest of the black population was confined to a strip of land in the north, as far from South Africa as possible, to serve as a reservoir of cheap labour for the mines – which South Africa was developing to extract the country's mineral wealth.

In 1947, after World War II, South Africa formally announced to the United Nations its intention to annex the territory. The UN, which had inherited responsibility for the League of Nations trust territories, opposed the plan, arguing that 'the African inhabitants of South West Africa have not yet achieved political autonomy'. Until 1961, the UN insisted on this point. Year after year it was systematically ignored by South Africa's regime.

The struggle for independence Between 1961 and 1968, the UN tried to annul the trusteeship and establish Namibia's independence. Legal pressure, however, was ineffective and some of the Namibian people led by the South West African People's Organisation (SWAPO) chose to fight for their freedom with arms. The first clashes occurred on 26 August 1966.

In 1968, the UN finally declared the South African occupation of the country as illegal and changed its name to Namibia. Efforts by the majority of the UN General Assembly to enforce this condemnation with economic sanctions were routinely vetoed by the Western powers of the UN Security Council – they had vested interests in the multi-national companies in Namibia and would stand to lose from the implementation of sanctions.

The independence of Angola in 1975 affected Namibia's struggle for freedom, by providing SWAPO guerrillas with a friendly rearguard. As a consequence the guerrilla war was stepped up, resulting in increased political pressure on South Africa. But strong internal economic factors also played heavily in the political arena. Right up to independence, the status quo preserved internal inequalities and privileges. Black Africans (approaching 90% of the population) consumed only 12.8% of the gross domestic product (GDP). Meanwhile the inhabitants of European origin (10% of the population) received 81.5% of the GDP. Three-quarters of agricultural production was in the hands of white farmers. Although average income per capita was (and remains) one of the highest in Africa, whites earned on average over 17 times more than blacks. The white population clearly feared they had a great deal to lose if a majority government came to power and addressed itself to these racially based inequalities.

However, external South African economic factors had perhaps the greatest effect in blocking Namibian independence. South African and multi-national companies dominated the Namibian economy and carried massive political influence. Prior to independence, the Consolidated Diamond Mines Company (a subsidiary of Anglo-American) contributed in taxes 40% of South Africa's administrative budget in Namibia. Multi-nationals benefited from extremely generous facilities granted to them by the South African administration in Namibia. According to one estimate, the independence of Namibia would represent costs for South Africa of US$240 million in lost exports, and additional outlays of US$144 million to import foreign products.

In South Africa the official government view stressed the danger that a SWAPO government might present to Namibia's minority tribes (since SWAPO membership is drawn almost exclusively from the Ovambo ethnic group), while taking few serious steps towards a negotiated settlement for Namibian independence.

On the military side, South Africa stepped up its campaign against SWAPO, even striking at bases in southern Angola. It also supported Jonas Savimbi's UNITA (National Union for the Total Independence of Angola) forces in their struggle against the Soviet/Cuban-backed MPLA (Popular Movement for the Liberation of Angola) government in Luanda. Meanwhile, Cuban troops poured into Angola and aggravated the situation further by threatening the South African forces in Namibia.

Resolution 435 On the diplomatic front, the UN Security Council put forward a proposal (Resolution 435) in 1978, calling for, among other things, the cessation of hostilities, the return of refugees, the repeal of discriminatory legislation and the holding of UN-supervised elections. South Africa blocked this by tying any such agreement to the withdrawal of Cuban troops from Angola, and demanding guarantees that its investments in Namibia would not be affected. SWAPO refused to agree to special benefits for the European population and other minority groups, nor would it accept predetermined limitations to constitutional change following independence.

By 1987, all the states involved in the conflict were showing clear signs of wanting an end to hostilities. After 14 years of uninterrupted war, Angola's economy was on the brink of collapse. (The war is calculated to have cost the country US$13 billion.) On the other side, South Africa's permanent harassment of Angola, and military occupation of Namibia, were costing the regime dearly, both economically and diplomatically.

In December 1988, after prolonged US-mediated negotiations, an agreement was reached between South Africa, Angola and Cuba for a phased withdrawal of Cuban troops from Angola to be linked to the withdrawal of South African troops from Namibia and the implementation of Resolution 435.

INDEPENDENCE The independence process began on 1 April 1989, and was achieved with the help of the United Nations Transition Assistance Group (UNTAG). This consisted of some 7,000 people from 110 countries who worked from nearly 200 locations within the country to ensure free and fair elections and as smooth a transition period to independence as was possible.

In November 1989, 710,000 Namibians (a 97% turnout) voted in the members of the National Assembly that would draft the country's first constitution. SWAPO won decisively, but without the two-thirds majority it needed to write the nation's constitution single-handedly, thereby allaying the fears of Namibia's minorities. The 72 elected members (68 men and four women) of the Constituent Assembly, representing between them seven different political parties, soon reached agreement on a constitution for the new Namibia, which was subsequently hailed as one of the world's most democratic. Finally, at 00.20 on 21 March 1990, I watched as the Namibian flag replaced South Africa's over Windhoek, witnessed by Pérez de Cuéllar, the UN Secretary-General, F W de Klerk, the South African President, and Sam Nujoma, Namibia's first president.

The country's mood was peaceful and, on the day, ecstatic. There was a tremendous feeling of optimism, as (arguably) Africa's last colonial territory had earned its independence – after sustained diplomatic pressure and a bitter liberation struggle that stretched back to the turn of the century.

POLITICS SINCE INDEPENDENCE Since the start there has been every indication that Namibia would stand by its constitution and develop into a peaceful and prosperous state. Walvis Bay, previously disputed by South Africa, was transferred to Windhoek's control on 28 February 1994, and Namibia's relations with neighbouring countries remain good.

An important part of post-independence politics in Namibia is the redistribution of land. These reforms have taken place relatively peacefully and at a fairly slow pace, with land purchased for redistribution based on mutual agreement between buyer and seller. Periodically, with political pressures and upcoming elections, there is talk of increasing the rate of land redistribution. However, unless the constitution is amended to facilitate this change, the land reform programme will continue at its current pace.

In December 1994, general elections for the National Assembly returned SWAPO to power, with 53 out of 72 seats, and extended Sam Nujoma's presidency for a further five years. The main opposition among the remaining six parties was the Democratic Turnhalle Alliance (DTA).

Under the terms of the constitution, the president may serve only two terms in office. Despite that, Sam Nujoma went on to serve a third term, prompting concerns that the carefully crafted constitution was being pushed to one side. It wasn't until 2004 that Nujoma made way for his chosen successor, Hifikepunye Pohamba, while himself remaining head of the party. Five years later, in November 2009, SWAPO was again returned to power with over 74% of the vote, and Pohamba's position as president was consolidated. However, the role of opposition switched to the Rally for Democracy and Progress (RDP), with 11% of the vote and just eight seats, overtaking the DTA, which is still haunted by the stigma of its co-operation with the former South African regime.

Like Nujoma, who has since retired from politics, Pohamba was a founding member of SWAPO and was head of the party until the 2014 presidential election. As a leader, he was generally considered to be both liberal and honest, committed to continuing the party's policies and to governing by consensus.

NAMIBIA'S THIRD PRESIDENT TAKES OFFICE By the time of the 2014 elections, Pohamba had reached his two-term limit, and with SWAPO gaining both 87% of the presidential vote, and 80% of the national assembly vote, the office of president moved in March 2015 to Hage G Geingob. Geingob was Namibia's first prime minister following independence in 1990, a position that he held until 2002. He then briefly had a ministerial role, as well as working with an African policy group based in Washington, then in 2007 he was elected vice-president of SWAPO, becoming prime minister once again in 2012. His role as president is also significant in that he is a Herero, making him the first non-Ovambo leader of SWAPO, and of Namibia. Already he is making inroads, gaining a reputation as a progressive and no-nonsense leader who gets things done. Controversial plans announced by SWAPO in the run up to the 2014 election for a gender-equality quota, referred to as a 'zebra system', in parliament have been implemented, with women accounting for 46% of MPs by 2018.

In the background, the role of largest opposition party switched once again following the election from the RDP back to the DTA, who won three and five seats respectively. The next election is set to take place in November 2019.

GOVERNMENT AND ADMINISTRATION

The Republic of Namibia's modern constitution, adopted on independence in 1990, was hailed as one of the world's most democratic. Its entrenched Bill of Rights provides for freedom of speech, press, assembly, association and religion. It also set up a bicameral Westminster-style parliament, with a strong executive and independent judiciary. General elections for the first house, the National Assembly, are held every five years. The constitution limits the president to a maximum of two terms of office – although Sam Nujoma's third term in office stretched this to breaking point in 1999.

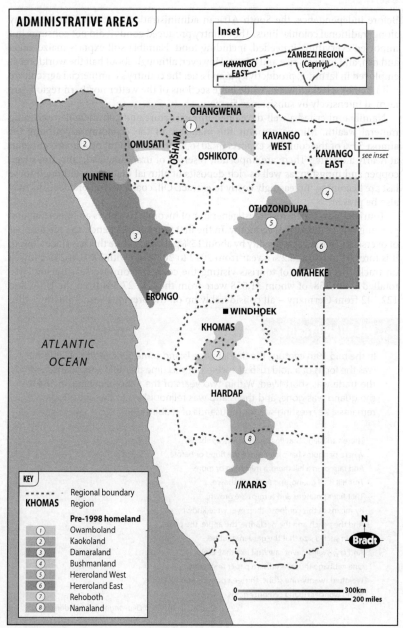

ADMINISTRATIVE AREAS

Inset

KAVANGO
EAST

ZAMBEZI REGION
(Caprivi)

see inset

OHANGWENA
①

OMUSATI

OSHANA

KAVANGO
WEST

KAVANGO
EAST

②

OSHIKOTO

KUNENE

④

OTJOZONDJUPA

③

⑤

⑥

OMAHEKE

ERONGO

■ WINDHOEK

KHOMAS

ATLANTIC
OCEAN

⑦

HARDAP

⑧

//KARAS

N

Bradt

KEY

- - - - - Regional boundary
KHOMAS   Region

Pre-1998 homeland
① Owamboland
② Kaokoland
③ Damaraland
④ Bushmanland
⑤ Hereroland West
⑥ Hereroland East
⑦ Rehoboth
⑧ Namaland

0 ———————— 300km
0 ———————— 200 miles

For administrative purposes, the country is divided into 14 regions, replacing the homeland territories that prevailed from 1963 until 1998. The 26 members of the second house, the National Council, are drawn from the regional councils, which are elected every six years.

ECONOMY

Before independence, the South African administration controlled the economy along traditional colonial lines. The country produced goods it did not consume but imported everything it needed, including food. Namibia still exports maize, meat and fish, and imports rice and wheat. However, although about half the workforce is employed in farming, productivity is an issue: the country's commercial agriculture is limited by a lack of water, while large sections of the wetter northern regions are farmed intensively by subsistence farmers.

Namibia inherited a well-developed infrastructure and considerable remaining mineral wealth. Mining remains the mainstay of the economy, accounting for almost 37% of the country's exports in 2016, with agricultural products coming in at nearly a quarter. There are important reserves of uranium, lead, zinc, tin, silver, copper and tungsten, as well as rich deposits of alluvial diamonds, although these last are becoming increasingly costly to extract. Oil, coal and iron ore deposits may also be present.

Tourism, now the third-largest generator of income, also plays an important and growing role in the formal economy. In the first years of independence, the number of overseas visitors grew steadily by about 15% per year. While this has since slowed, it is forecast to rise at 5.2% a year from 2012 to 2020 and with 5.9% in 2016, is well on track. The number of tourists visiting the country from overseas during 2016 totalled 1,469,258, of whom 31,558 were from the UK, 27,264 from the USA, and 122,142 from Germany – all considerably up on the previous year. Tourism is also

THE GUANO TRADE

In the mid 19th century, the tiny Ichaboe Island some 50km north of Lüderitz was the focus of a gold rush of sorts – but this time the 'gold' was guano, and the trade was short-lived. Within two years of the mine's opening, in 1843, the guano was gone, and the island was relinquished to the birds. Today, it remains a key nesting site for thousands of seabirds.

There's an island that lies on West Africa's shore,
Where penguins have lived since the flood or before,
And raised up a hill there, a mile high or more.
This hill is all guano, and lately 'tis shown,
That finer potatoes and turnips are grown,
By means of this compost, than ever were known;
And the peach and the nectarine, the apple, the pear,
Attain such a size that the gardeners stare,
And cry, 'Well! I never saw fruit like that 'ere!'
One cabbage thus reared, as a paper maintains,
Weighed twenty-one stone, thirteen pounds and six grains,
So no wonder Guano celebrity gains.

Quoted in *The River Okavango* by C J Andersson

a powerful earner of foreign exchange, a substantial employer, and a vital support for numerous community-development schemes. Namibia's main attractions for visitors are stunning scenery, pristine wilderness areas and first-class wildlife. As long as the country remains safe and its wilderness areas are maintained, then its potential for quality tourism is unrivalled in Africa.

Economically, Namibia remains dependent on South Africa for around 16% of its exports – albeit a significant reduction since the early years of independence – and almost two-thirds of imports. Realistically, the economy is likely to stay closely involved with that of South Africa, especially while Namibia continues to peg its currency to the value of the South African rand. The country's other main trading partners are Switzerland, the European Union, Botswana and Zambia. What these figures don't indicate, however, is the level of foreign involvement in Namibian mines, in particular from China, whose investment reached US$76 billion in 2018 and whose 'soft loans' are frequently repaid in mining rights; China now owns most of the country's uranium mines.

Despite these positive factors, Namibia is experiencing an economic downturn, with unemployment hitting 37.3% in 2017, and youth unemployment topping 43%. Around 13% of the population still subsists on US$1.90 per day or less – a gap which must be closed if the country is to have a secure and prosperous future.

FOLLOW BRADT

For the latest news, special offers and competitions, subscribe to the Bradt newsletter via the website www.bradtguides.com and follow Bradt on:

 BradtTravelGuides
 @BradtGuides
 @bradtguides
 bradtguides
 bradtguides

4

People and Culture

POPULATION OVERVIEW

At the time of the 2011 census, Namibia's population stood at 2,113,077, an increase of around 15.4% over the previous decade, representing a growth rate of around 1.5% per year. By 2017, the population stood at an estimated 2,533,794 (World Bank).

The effect of HIV/AIDS on the Namibian population has been devastating. In 2007, 15.3% of adults were affected, with 5,100 related deaths and 66,000 more orphans. The latest UN AIDS estimates from 2017 suggest that HIV prevalence has fallen to 12.1%, with the number of deaths due to AIDS during the year also falling, to 2,700, with 34,000 children orphaned as a result. Life expectancy, which plummeted to just 45 years in 2004, and rose only slightly to 51 in 2007, had by 2014 returned to 63 years, edging up to 64 in 2016 – just one year short of the turn-of-the-century average.

While the population is densest in the north (near the Angolan border), where rainfall is heaviest, and in the capital, Windhoek, the overall density is exceptionally low: less than three people per square kilometre. At the time of the 2011 census, just over a third of Namibia's people were under 15 years of age, while only 7% were over 60. Around 87.5% of the population were black African in origin, and the remaining 12.5% were mostly of European or mixed race.

Of course, statistics say nothing of the charm of many Namibians. If you venture into the rural areas you will often find that Namibians are curious about you. Chat to them openly and you will find most to be delightful. They will be pleased to help you where they can, and as keen to help you learn about them and their country as they are interested in your lifestyle and what brings you to their country.

ETHNIC GROUPS

When the colonial powers carved up Africa, the divisions between the countries bore virtually no resemblance to the traditional areas of the various ethnic groups, many of which therefore ended up split between two or more countries. As you will see, there are cultural differences between the groups in different parts of Namibia, but they are only a little more pronounced than those between the states of the USA, or the regions of the (relatively tiny) UK.

There continues to be a great deal of intermarriage and mixing of these various peoples and cultures – perhaps more so than there has ever been, because of the efficiency of modern transport systems. Generally, there is very little friction between these communities (whose boundaries, as we have said, are indistinct) and Namibia's various peoples live peacefully together.

In Namibia, which is typical of any large African country, historians identify numerous ethnic groups. The main ones, detailed on the next page, are arranged alphabetically. Apart from Afrikaans, their languages fall into two main families: Khoisan and Bantu. The population sizes given are based on surveys done during the 1980s, and adjusted according to estimated average growth rates since then.

BASTERS These Afrikaans-speaking people are descendants of indigenous Nama – or Hottentot – women and the Dutch settlers who first arrived at the Cape in the early 17th century. The original 'coloured' or 'bastard' children found themselves rejected by both the white and the black communities in the Cape, so keeping together they relocated themselves further north away from the colonialists. Proudly calling themselves 'Basters', they set up farming communities and developed their own distinct social and cultural structures.

During the 1860s, white settlers began to push into these areas so, to avoid confrontation, the Basters crossed the Orange River in 1868 and moved northward once again. Trying to keep out of the way of the warring Hereros and Namas, they founded Rehoboth in 1871 and set up their own system of government under a *kaptein* (headman) and a *volksraad* (legislative council). Their support of the German colonial troops during the tribal uprisings brought them later protection and privileges.

Demands for self-rule and independence were repressed until the Rehoboth Gebiet was granted the status of an independent state in the 1970s. This move by the South African administration was made with the aim of reinforcing racial divisions among the non-whites – rather like in the South African 'independent homelands'.

SOCIAL GROUPS OR 'TRIBES'

4

The people of Africa are often viewed, from abroad, as belonging to a multitude of culturally and linguistically distinct 'tribes' – which are often portrayed as being at odds with each other. While there is certainly an enormous variety of different ethnic groups in Africa, most are closely related to their neighbours in terms of language, beliefs and way of life. Modern historians eschew the simplistic tags of 'tribes', noting that such groupings change with time.

Sometimes the word tribe is used to describe a group of people who all speak the same language; it may be used to mean those who follow a particular leader or to refer to all the inhabitants of a certain area at a given time. In any case, 'tribe' is a vague word that is used differently for different purposes. The term 'clan' (blood relations) is a smaller, more precisely defined unit – though rather too precise for our broad discussions here.

Certainly groups of people or clans who share similar languages and cultural beliefs do band together and often, in time, develop 'tribal' identities. However, it is wrong to then extrapolate and assume that their ancestors will have had the same groupings and allegiances centuries ago.

In Africa, as elsewhere in the world, history is recorded by the winners. Here the winners, the ruling class, may be the descendants of a small group of intruders who achieved dominance over a larger, long-established community. Over the years, the history of that ruling class (the winners) usually becomes regarded as the history of the whole community, or tribe. Two 'tribes' have thus become one, with one history – which will reflect the origins of that small group of intruders, and not the ancestors of the majority of the current tribe.

Today, Namibia's Basters still have a strong sense of identity and make up around 2% of the population. Most still live and work as stock or crop farmers in the good cattle-grazing land around Rehoboth. Their traditional crafts include products like *karosses* (blankets), rugs, wall-hangings and cushion covers made of cured skins.

BUSHMEN/SAN There is not another social/language group on this planet which has been studied, written about, filmed and researched more than the Bushmen, or San, of the Kalahari, although they currently comprise only about 3% of Namibia's population. Despite this, or indeed because of it, popular conceptions about them, fed by their image in the media, are often strikingly out of step with the realities. Thus they warrant the extended section devoted to them here.

The aim of these next few pages is to try to explain some of the roots of the misconceptions, to look at some of the realities, and to make you think. Although I have spent a lot of time with Bushmen in the Kalahari, it is difficult to separate fact from oft-repeated, glossy fiction. If parts of this discussion seem disparate, it's a reflection of this difficulty.

Recent scientific observations on the Khoisan
Our view of the Bushmen is partly informed by some basic anthropological, linguistic and genetic research, which is worth outlining to set the scene. Most of this research applies to the Khoisan, comprising the various peoples of the Khoi and the Bushmen. All have relatively light golden-brown skin, almond-shaped eyes and high cheekbones. Their stature is generally small and slight, and they are now found across southern Africa.

Anthropology The first fossil records that we have of our human ancestors date back to at least about 60,000 years ago in East Africa. These are likely to have been the ancestors of everyone living today.

Archaeological finds from parts of the Kalahari show that human beings have lived here for at least 40,000 years. These are generally agreed to have been the ancestors of the modern Khoisan peoples living in Botswana today.

Language research Of the world's 20 linguistic families, four are very different from the rest. All these four are African families – and they include the Khoisan and the Niger–Congo (Bantu) languages. This is among the evidence that has led linguists to believe that human language evolved in Africa, and further analysis has suggested that this was probably among the ancestors of the Khoisan.

The Khoisan languages are distinguished by their wide repertoire of clicking sounds. Don't mistake these for simple: they are very sophisticated. It was observed by Dunbar (page 573) that, 'From the phonetic point of view these [the Khoisan languages] are the world's most complex languages. To speak one of them fluently is to exploit human phonetic ability to the full.'

At some point the Khoisan languages diverged from a common ancestor, and today three distinct groups exist: the northern, central and southern. Languages gradually evolve and change as different groups of people split up and move to new areas, isolated from their old contacts. Thus the evolution of each language is specific to each group.

According to Michael Main (page 574), the northern group are San and today they live west of the Okavango and north of Ghanzi, with representatives found as far afield as Angola. The southern group are also San, who live in the area between Kang and Bokspits in Botswana. The central group are the Khoi (or Khoe), who live in central Botswana, extending north to the eastern Okavango and Kasane, and west into Namibia, where they are known as the Nama.

Each of these three Khoisan language groups has many dialects. These have some similarities, but they are not closely related, and some are different to the point where there is no mutual understanding. Certain dialects are so restricted that only a small family group speaks them; it was reported recently that one San language died out completely with the death of the last speaker.

This huge number of dialects, and variation in languages, reflects the relative isolation of the various speakers, most of whom now live in small family groups as the Kalahari's arid environment cannot sustain large groups of people living together in one place as hunter-gatherers.

In Namibia, the three main Bushmen language groups are the Haixom in the northern districts of Otavi, Tsumeb and Grootfontein; the !Kung in Bushmanland; and the Mbarankwengo in west Caprivi. See also page 502 for more information on languages that use clicks.

Genetic discoveries Most genetically normal men have an X and a Y chromosome, while women have two X chromosomes. Unlike the other 22 pairs of (non-sex) chromosomes that each human has, there is no opportunity for the Y chromosome to 'swap' or 'share' its DNA with any other chromosome. Thus all the information in a man's Y chromosome will usually be passed on, without change, to all of his sons.

However, very rarely a single 'letter' in the Y chromosome will be altered as it's being passed on, thus causing a permanent change in the chromosome's genetic sequence. This will then be the start of a new lineage of slightly different Y chromosomes, which will be inherited by all future male descendants.

In November 2000, Professor Ronald Davis and a team of Stanford researchers (page 573) claimed to have traced back this lineage to a single individual man, and that a small group of East Africans (Sudanese and Ethiopians) and Khoisan are the closest present-day relatives of this original man. That is, their genetic make-up is closest to his. (It's a scientific 'proof' of the biblical Adam, if you like.)

This is still a very contentious finding, with subsequent researchers suggesting at least ten original male sources ('Adams') – and so although this is interesting, the jury remains out on the precise details of all these findings. If you're interested in the latest on this, then you'll find a lot about it on the web – start searching with keywords: 'Khoisan Y chromosome'.

Historical and current views of the Bushmen
Despite much evidence and research, our views of the Bushmen seem to have changed relatively little since both the Bantu groups and the first Europeans arrived in southern Africa.

The settlers' view Since the first Bantu farmers started migrating south through East Africa, the range of territory occupied by the foragers, whose Stone Age technology had dominated the continent, began to condense. By the time the first white settlers appeared in the Cape, the Khoisan people were already restricted to Africa's southwestern corners and the Kalahari.

All over the world, farmers occupy clearly demarcated areas of land, whereas foragers will move more and often leave less trace of their presence. In Africa, this made it easier for farmers, first black then white, to ignore any traditional land rights that belonged to foraging people.

Faced with the loss of territory for hunting and gathering, the foragers – who, by this time were already being called 'Bushmen' – made enemies of the farmers by killing cattle. They waged a guerrilla war, shooting poison arrows at parties of men who set out to massacre them. They were feared and loathed by the settlers, who, however, captured and valued their children as servants.

Some of the Khoisan retreated north from the Cape – like the ancestors of Namibia's Nama people. Others were forced to labour on the settlers' farms, or were thrown into prison for hunting animals or birds which had been their traditional prey, but which were now designated property of the Crown.

This story is told by Robert J Gordon in *The Bushman Myth: The Making of a Namibian Underclass* (page 573). He shows that throughout history the hunter-gathering Bushmen have been at odds with populations of settlers who divided up and 'owned' the land in the form of farms. The European settlers proved to be their most determined enemy, embarking on a programme of legislation and massacre. Many Bushmen died in prison, with many more shot as 'vermin'.

Thus the onslaught of farmers on the hunter-gatherers accelerated between the 1800s and the mid 1900s. This helped to ensure that hunter-gathering as a lifestyle continued to be practical only in marginal areas that couldn't be economically farmed – like the Kalahari. Archaeological evidence suggests that hunter-gatherer peoples have lived for about 60,000 years at sites like the Tsodilo Hills in Botswana.

Western views Though settlers in the Cape interacted with Khoisan people, so did Europe and the US, in a very limited way. Throughout the 1800s and early 1900s a succession of Khoisan people were effectively enslaved and brought to Europe and the US for exhibition. Sometimes this was under the guise of anthropology, but usually it didn't claim to be anything more than entertainment.

One of the first was the 'Hottentot Venus' – a woman who was probably of Khoisan extraction who was exhibited around London and Paris from 1810 to 1815, as an erotic curiosity for aristocrats.

A string of others followed. For example, the six Khoisan people exhibited at the Coney Island Pleasure Resort, beside New York, and later in London in the 1880s and billed as the 'missing link between apes and men', and the 'wild dancing Bushman' known as Franz brought to England around 1913 by Paddy Hepston (see Parsons's piece in *Botswana Notes & Records*, page 574).

In the 1950s a researcher from Harvard, John Marshall, came to the Kalahari to study the !Kung San. He described a peaceful people living in harmony with nature, amid a land that provided all their needs. The groups had a deep spirituality and no real hierarchy: it seemed like the picture of a modern Eden (especially when viewed through post-war eyes). Marshall was a natural cameraman and made a film that follows the hunt of a giraffe by four men over a five-day period. It swiftly became a classic, both in and outside of anthropological circles.

Further research agreed, with researchers noting a great surfeit of protein in the diet of the !Kung San and low birth rates akin to modern industrial societies.

Again the Bushmen were seen as photogenic and sources of good copy and good images. Their lives were portrayed in romantic, spiritual terms in the book and film *The Lost World of the Kalahari* by Laurens van der Post (page 576). This documentary really ignited the worldwide interest in the Bushmen and led to subsequent films such as *The Gods Must Be Crazy*. All the images conveyed an idyllic view of the Bushmen as untainted by contact with the modern world.

The reality The reality was much less rosy than the first researchers thought. Some of their major misconceptions have been outlined particularly clearly in chapter 13 of John Reader's *Africa: A Biography of the Continent* (page 574). He points out that far from an ideal diet, the nutrition of the Bushmen was often critically limited, lacking vitamins and fatty acids associated with a lack of animal fat in their diet. Far from a stable population with a low birth rate, it seems likely that there had been a decline in the birth rate in the last few generations. The likely cause for this was periods of inadequate nourishment during the year when they lost weight from lack of food, stress and the great exertions of their lifestyle.

In fact, it seems likely that the San, whom we now see as foragers, are people who, over the last two millennia, have become relegated to an underclass by the relentless advance of the black and white farmers who did not recognise their original rights to their traditional land.

The Bushmen and the modern media
Though scientific thought has moved on since the 1950s, much of the media has not. The Bushmen are still perceived to be hot news.

The outpost of Tsumkwe is the centre for many of the Bushmen communities in Namibia. It's a tiny crossroads with a school and a handful of buildings, in a remote corner of northeastern Namibia. Despite its isolation, by 2001 this desert outpost was hosting no fewer than 22 film crews per year. Yes, really; that's an average of almost two full-scale film crews each month – not counting a whole host of other print journalists and photographers. These numbers are probably even greater now.

Talk to virtually any of the directors and you'll realise that they arrive with very clear ideas about the images that they want to capture. They all think they're one of the first, they think they're original, and they want to return home with images which match their preconceived ideas about the Bushmen as 'the last primitive hunter-gatherers'.

As an example, you'll often see pictures in the media of Bushmen hunters in traditional dress walking across a hot, barren salt-pan. When asked to do these shoots the Bushman's usual comment is, 'Why? There's no point. We'd never go looking for anything there.' But the shots look spectacular and win prizes… so the photographers keep asking for them. From the Bushmen's perspective, they get paid for the shots, so why not pose for the camera? I'd do the same!

Thus our current image of the San is really one that *we* are constantly recreating. It's the one that we expect. But it doesn't necessarily conform to any reality. So on reflection, popular thinking hasn't moved on much from Marshall's first film in the 1950s.

CAPRIVIAN The Caprivi people, whose language is of the Bantu family, live in the fertile, swampy land between the Chobe and Zambezi rivers – at the eastern end of the Caprivi Strip. The agricultural potential of the area is one of the highest in Namibia, but this potential has been largely unrealised. Before the war with Angola, and the heavy involvement of South African troops (which brought roads and infrastructure), the whole of the Kavango and Caprivi (now Zambezi) region was one of the least developed in Namibia.

Like the Kavango and the Ovambo, the Caprivians farm a variety of crops, raise livestock, and fish. They make up about 4% of Namibia's population, and most can be considered as members of one of five main groups: the Masubia and Mafwe groups, and the smaller Mayeyi, Matotela and Mbukushu. Their traditional crafts include baskets (extensively used for fish traps and carrying grain), wooden masks and stools, drums, pottery, leather goods and stone carvings.

Looking at the current lifestyle of the Bushmen who remain in the more remote areas of the Kalahari, it's difficult not to lapse into a romantic view of ignoring present realities. There are too many cultural aspects to cover here, so instead I've just picked out a few that you may encounter.

NOMADS OF THE KALAHARI Perhaps the first idea to dispel is that the Bushmen are nomads. They're not. Bushmen family groups have clearly defined territories, called a *n!ore* (in the Ju/'hoansi language), within which they forage. This is usually centred on a place where there is water, and contains food resources sufficient for the basic subsistence of the group.

Groups recognise rights to the *n!ore*, which is passed on from father to first-born son. Any visiting people would ask permission to remain in these. Researchers have mapped these areas, even in places like the Central Kalahari.

SOCIAL SYSTEM The survival of the Bushmen in the harsh environment of the Kalahari is evidence of the supreme adaptability of humans. It reflects their detailed knowledge of their environment, which provides them not only with food, but with materials for shelter and medicine in the form of plants.

Another very important factor in their survival is the social system by which the Bushmen live. Social interaction is governed by unwritten rules that bind the people in friendship and harmony, which must be maintained. One such mechanism is the obligation to distribute the meat from a large kill. Another is the obligation to lend such few things as are individually possessed, thereby incurring a debt of obligation from the borrower.

The San also practise exogamy, which means they have an obligation to marry outside the group. This creates social bonds between groups. Such ties bind the society inextricably together, as does the system of gift exchange between separate groups.

Owing to environmental constraints a group will consist of between 80 and 120 people, living and moving together. In times of shortage the groups will be much smaller, sometimes consisting of only immediate family – parents, grandparents and children. They must be able to carry everything they possess. Their huts are light constructions of grass, and they have few possessions.

Because no-one owns property, no-one is richer or has more status than another. A group of Bushmen has a nominal leader, who might be a senior member of the group, an expert hunter, or the person who owns the water rights. The whole group takes decisions affecting them, often after vociferous discussions.

HUNTER-GATHERERS Any hunter-gatherer lifestyle entails a dependence on, and extensive knowledge of, the environment and the resident fauna and flora found

DAMARA Along with the Nama and the Bushmen, or San, the Damara are presumed to be the original inhabitants of Namibia, speaking a similar 'Khoi' click language (Khoisan family). Like the Nama, the Damara were primarily hunting people who owned few cattle or goats. Traditionally enemies of the Nama and Herero, they supported the German colonial forces at Waterberg against the Herero uprisings and were rewarded for their loyalty by an 'enlarged' homeland from the German authorities: Damaraland, the area adjacent to the Skeleton Coast (now the southern part of the there. In the Kalahari, water is the greatest need and the Bushmen know which roots and tubers provide liquid to quench thirst. They create sip wells in the desert, digging a hole, filled with soft grass, then using a reed to suck water into the hole, and send it bubbling up the reed to fill an ostrich egg. Water-filled ostrich eggs are also buried at specific locations within the group's 'area'. When necessary the Bushmen will strain the liquid from the rumen of a herbivore and drink that.

Researchers have observed that any hunting is done by the men. When living a basic hunting and gathering lifestyle, with little external input, hunting provides only about 20% of their food. The remaining 80% is provided largely by the women, helped by the children, who forage and gather wild food from the bush. By age 12 a child might know about 200 plant species, and an adult more than 300.

HUNTING The Bushmen in the Kalahari are practised hunters, using many different techniques to capture the game. Their main weapons are a very light bow, and an arrow made of reed, in three sections. The arrowhead is usually poisoned, using one of a number of poisons obtained from specific plants, snakes and beetles. (Though most Bushmen know how to hunt with bows and arrows, the actual practice is increasingly uncommon when it's not done to earn money from observing visitors.)

All the hunters may be involved in the capture of large game, which carries with it certain obligations. The whole group shares in the kill and each member is entitled to a certain portion of the meat.

There are different methods for hunting small game, which only the hunter's family would usually share. One method for catching spring hares involves long (sometimes 4m), flexible poles made of thin sticks, with a duiker's horn (or more usually now a metal hook) fastened to the end. These are rammed into the hare's hole, impaling the animal, which is then pulled or dug out.

TRANCE DANCING Entertainment for the Bushmen, when things are good, usually involves dancing. During some dances, which may often have overtones of ritual or religion, the dancers may fall into a trance and collapse.

These trances are induced by a deliberate breathing technique, with a clear physiological explanation. Dances normally take place in the evening, around a fire. Then the women, children and old people will sit around and clap, while some of the younger men will dance around the circle in an energetic, rhythmic dance. Often this is all that happens, and after a while the excitement dies down and everyone goes to sleep.

However, on fairly rare occasions, the dancers will go into a trance. After several hours of constant exertion, they will shorten their breathing. This creates an oxygen deficiency, which leads to the heart pumping more strongly to compensate. Blood pressure to the brain increases; the dancer loses consciousness and collapses.

Kunene Region). Of the Damara today, only a quarter manage to survive in this area – the rest work on commercial farms, in mines or as labourers in the towns. They make up about 7% of Namibia's population, sharing their language with the Namas. Damara women share the same Victorian style of dress as the Herero and Nama women.

Traditionally Damara people were thought of as miners, smelters, copper traders, stock farmers and tobacco growers, until the end of the 19th century when they moved to Damaraland and started practising agriculture.

Their traditional crafts include leather goods, glass and metal beadwork, wooden bowls and buckets, clay pipes and bowls, and more recently 'township art' such as wire cars.

HERERO In 1904, the Hereros and the Namas staged a massive uprising against the German colonial troops in South West Africa. It ended in a bloody massacre of over half the total Herero population at the Battle of Waterberg (page 73).

The few Herero that survived fled into the Kalahari, some crossing into what is now Botswana. In 2001, the Herero People's Reparation Corporation, based in Washington, sued the German government and two companies for £2.6 billion. The case was fiercely contested, and was finally dismissed in its entirety.

Today, the Herero constitute the third-largest ethnic group in Namibia, after the Ovambo and Kavango – over 7% of the present population. Their language is Bantu-based. In Botswana, they are a minority group inhabiting Ngamiland, south and west of the Okavango Delta.

Traditionally pastoralists, the Herero prefer raising cattle to growing crops – prestige and influence are dependent on the number of cattle possessed. Today, the majority of Namibian Herero use their cattle-handling skills on commercial farms.

Herero women wear very distinctive long, flowing Victorian gowns and headdresses. Multiple layers of petticoats made from over 12m of material give a voluminous look (two women walking side-by-side occupy the whole pavement!). Missionaries, who were appalled by the Herero's semi-nakedness, introduced this style of dress in the 1800s. Now the Herero continue to wear these heavy garments and it has become their traditional dress – though they will admit just how hot it is if asked.

Traditional Herero crafts include skin and leather products, basketry, jewellery and ornaments, and dolls in traditional Victorian-style dress, which are a very popular curio for visitors.

HIMBA The Himba people share a common ethnic origin and language with the Hereros, having split from the main Herero group on the Namibia–Botswana border and moved west to present-day Kaokoland in the northern Kunene in search of available land. The place they found, however, is mountainous, sparsely vegetated and very arid. Cattle are central to their way of life, with the size of the herd an indication of wealth and prestige – but overgrazing of the poor soils is a major problem. Thus these people are semi-nomadic, moving with their cattle in search of suitable pasture.

The Himba are a minority group in Namibia (numbering less than 1% of the population), and live almost entirely in their traditional areas in remote Kaokoland. Their society is traditionally polygamous, with men having up to eight wives.

Of all Namibia's ethnic groups, the Himba – or at least, Himba women and children – are probably the most photographed. Himba women adorn their skin and hair – and often that of their children – with deep-red ochre powder mixed with fat, both for protection against insects and the sun, and for cleanliness; water for washing is a rarity. Their striking appearance is further enhanced by elaborate headdresses and jewellery, much of it symbolic, while their clothes are limited to a simple goatskin skirt, and – for warmth – a rough blanket. As in many traditional societies, the men tend the cattle, so are usually absent during the day, leaving the bulk of the work to the women.

Traditional Himba crafts include work in skin and leather (headdresses, girdles and aprons), jewellery (copper-wire neckbands and bracelets), musical instruments, wooden neck rests, basketry and pottery.

KAVANGO The Kavango people share their name with the Okavango River, which forms part of the northern border of Namibia with Angola. Not surprisingly, they have based their traditional agricultural and fishing existence on the fertile land and good water supply afforded by this environment.

Many of the Kavango, who used to live on the northern side of the Okavango River in Angola, came south of the river into Namibia during the 1970s, 1980s and early 1990s. They fled from the civil war between South African-backed UNITA rebels and the Soviet/Cuban-backed MPLA regime. As a consequence, the Kavango population in Namibia more than doubled in size during the 1970s, and now forms the second-largest ethnic group in the country, making up almost 10% of the population.

Closely related to the Ovambos, and with a Bantu-based language, the Kavango people are traditionally fishermen, and crop and stock farmers. Their craftwork includes woodcarving (bowls, spoons, mortars, masks, boxes and furniture), basketry, pottery, jewellery (grass bracelets and copper-bead necklaces), mats, spears, daggers, pipes, musical instruments and headdresses.

NAMA The Nama, or Hottentot, people are perhaps the closest in origin to the Bushmen or San, traditionally sharing a similar type of 'click' or Khoisan language, the same light-coloured yellow skin, and a hunter-gatherer way of life. One of the first peoples in Namibia, their tribal areas were traditionally communal property, as indeed was any item unless it was actually made by an individual. Basic differences in the perception of ownership of land and hunting grounds led in the past to frequent conflicts with the Herero people. The 60,000 or so Nama today, making up about 5% of Namibia's population, live mostly in the area that was Namaland, north of Keetmanshoop in the south of Namibia. Nama women share the same Victorian traditional dress as the Herero and Damara women.

The Nama people are traditionally stock farmers, and work mainly on commercial farms. Their crafts include leatherwork (aprons and collecting bags), *karosses* (mantle of animal skins) and mats, musical instruments (eg: reed flutes), jewellery, clay pots and tortoiseshell powder containers.

OVAMBO By far the largest group in Namibia, the Ovambo people (sometimes called Owambo) make up just over half the population. Their language, Oshivambo (sometimes known as Ambo or Vambo), is Bantu-based. Most of the Ovambo belong to one of eight tribes: the Kwanyama, Ndongo, Kwambi, Ngandjera, Mbalantu, Kwaluudhi, Nkolokadhi and Eunda. Typically, they are traders and businessmen. The great majority still live in their traditional area of Ovamboland in the remote far north of the country, along the border with Angola. This area receives one of the highest rainfalls in the country, and supports a range of traditional crops as well as allowing good grazing for their extensive cattle herds.

Before independence, the existence of half a million indigenous Namibians on the border with (socialist) Angola seriously perturbed the South African administration. By investing money into the region, the administration hoped to establish a buffer against Angola to protect the areas in the interior. The policy backfired – Ovamboland became the heartland of SWAPO during the struggle for independence. The consequent harassment by the South African Defence Force, and a rapid population increase (exacerbated by a large influx of refugees from Angola), left the area overpressurised and undeveloped, a situation that is now being addressed, with substantial investment being sunk into the region.

Traditional Ovambo craftwork includes basketry, pottery, jewellery, wooden combs, wood and iron spears, arrows and richly decorated daggers, musical

Comments here are intended to be a general guide, just a few examples of how to travel more sensitively. They should not be viewed as blueprints for perfect Namibian etiquette. Cultural sensitivity is really a state of mind, not a checklist of behaviour – so here we can only hope to give the sensitive traveller a few pointers in the right direction.

When we travel, we are all in danger of leaving negative impressions with local people whom we meet: by snapping that picture quickly, while the subject is not looking; by dressing scantily, offending local sensitivities; or by just brushing aside the feelings of local people, with the high-handed superiority of a rich Westerner. These things are easy to do, in the click of a shutter, or flash of a large dollar bill.

However, you will get the most representative view of Namibia if you cause as little disturbance to the local people as possible. You will never blend in perfectly when you travel – your mere presence there, as an observer, will always change the local events slightly. However, if you try to fit in and show respect for local culture and attitudes, then you may manage to leave positive feelings behind you.

One of the easiest, and most important, ways to do this is with **greetings**. African societies are rarely as rushed as Western ones. When you first talk to someone, you should greet him or her leisurely. So, for example, if you enter a shop and want some help, do not just ask outright, 'Where can I find…?' That would be rude. Instead you will have a better reception (and better chance of good advice) by saying:

Traveller: 'Good afternoon.'
Namibian: 'Good afternoon.'
Traveller: 'How are you?'
Namibian: 'I am fine, how are you?'
Traveller: 'I am fine, thank you.' (Pause) 'Do you know where I can find…?'

This approach goes for anyone – always greet them first. For a better reception still, learn these phrases of greeting in the local language. English-speakers are often lazy about learning languages, and, while most Namibians understand English, a greeting given in an appropriate local language will be received with delight. It implies that you are making an effort to learn a little of their language and culture, which is always appreciated.

instruments, fertility dolls, and ivory buttons (*ekipa*) – worn by women and conveying their status and indicating their husband's/family's wealth.

OTHER NAMIBIANS
Coloured Namibians The term 'coloured' is generally used in southern Africa to describe people of mixed (black–white) origin. These coloured people maintain a strong sense of identity and separateness from either blacks or whites – though they generally speak either Afrikaans or English (or frequently both) rather than an ethnic 'African' language. They are very different in culture from any of Namibia's ethnic groups, white or black.

Most coloureds in Namibia live in the urban areas – Windhoek, Keetmanshoop and Lüderitz. Those in Walvis Bay are mainly fishermen, and some in the south are stock farmers. Their traditional crafts centre mainly on musical instruments, like drums and guitars.

Very rarely in the town or city you may be approached by someone who doesn't greet you, but tries immediately to sell you something, or hassle you in some way. These people have learned that foreigners aren't used to greetings, so have adapted their approach accordingly. An effective way to dodge their attentions is to reply to their questions with a formal greeting, and then politely, but firmly, refuse their offer. This is surprisingly effective.

Another part of the normal greeting ritual is **handshaking**. As elsewhere, you would not normally shake a shop-owner's hand, but you would shake hands with someone to whom you are introduced. Get some practice when you arrive, as there is a gentle, three-part handshake used in southern Africa which is easily learnt – but not easily taught in a book.

Your **clothing** is an area that can easily give offence. Skimpy, revealing clothing is frowned upon by most Namibians, especially when worn by women. Shorts are fine for the bush or the beach, but dress conservatively and avoid short shorts, especially in the more rural areas. Respectable locals will wear long trousers (men) or long skirts (women).

Photography is a tricky business. Most Namibians will be only too happy to be photographed – provided you ask their permission first. Sign language is fine for this question: just point at your camera, shrug your shoulders, and look quizzical. The problem is that then everyone will smile for you, producing the type of 'posed' photograph which you may not want. However, stay around and chat for 5 or 10 minutes more, and people will get used to your presence, stop posing and you will get more natural shots (a camera with a quiet shutter is a help). Note that care is needed near government buildings, army bases and similar sites of strategic importance. You must ask permission before snapping photographs or you risk people taking offence.

The specific examples above can teach only so much; they are general by their very nature. But wherever you find yourself, if you are polite and considerate to the Namibians you meet, then you will rarely encounter any cultural problems. Watch how they behave and, if you have any doubts about how you should act, then ask someone quietly. They will seldom tell you outright that you are being rude, but they will usually give you good advice on how to make your behaviour more acceptable.

White Namibians The first whites to settle in Namibia were the Germans who set up trading businesses around the port of Lüderitz in 1884. Within a few years, Namibia formally became a German colony, and German settlers began to arrive in ever-increasing numbers. Meanwhile, white farmers of Dutch origin (the Boers, who first settled on the African continent at the Cape in 1652), were moving northward in search of land free from British interference, following the cession of the Dutch Cape Colony to the British government in 1806. After World War I, when control of German Namibia was transferred to South Africa, Boers (Afrikaners) moved into Namibia, and soon significantly outnumbered the German settlers.

The first Namibians of European descent came as missionaries, traders and hunters, though they are now found throughout the economy. They live mainly in urban, central and southern parts of the country – though they also own and run most of the commercial farming operations. Virtually all of the tourism industry is

LGBT TRAVELLERS

The majority of Namibians that you'll meet on your travels are friendly towards visitors, irrespective of their gender and sexual orientation. Staff in the tourism industry, and especially in the more remote camps, lodges and hotels, are used to dealing with a wide range of guests from a variety of backgrounds, and acceptance is the norm. Rooms are generally configured with double or single beds, as requested, without fuss.

Visitors to the more cosmopolitan cities, such as Swakopmund and Windhoek, are likely to meet similarly liberal views, but in rural communities these tend to be very conservative. Here, the assumption is often that people are born heterosexual, and that other sexual behaviour is somehow wrong. Although same-sex friends will often wander around hand-in-hand without a second thought, such behaviour has no sexual or relationship connotations. Even among heterosexual couples, public displays of affection or overtly sexual behaviour are strongly frowned upon, and any indication of an LGBT relationship would certainly be regarded as taboo in such an environment.

This conservative attitude remains enshrined in laws inherited by Namibia, which prohibits some sexual relations between men. We understand that there have been no prosecutions under this law since independence. However, we would always advise travellers to tread with caution to avoid any potential problem.

managed by white Namibians. Perhaps a legacy of colonialism, they are normally among the more affluent members of society.

The crafts currently produced by the whites include leatherwork (shoes, handbags, belts), German Christmas and Easter decorations, needlework (including embroidery, patchwork and clothing), printed T-shirts, costume jewellery, greetings cards and various classical European art forms.

There is also a significant 'expat' community in Namibia. Typically they stay for two or three years, working on short-term contracts, often for either multi-national companies or aid agencies, but some then choose to take up residence. Most are highly skilled individuals who come to share their knowledge with Namibian colleagues – often teaching skills that are in short supply in Namibia.

LANGUAGE

Namibia's variety of languages reflects the diversity of its peoples – black and white. Following independence, one of the new government's first actions was to make English Namibia's only official language (removing Afrikaans and German). This step sought to unite Namibia's peoples and languages under one common tongue ('the language of the liberation struggle'), leaving behind the colonial overtones of Afrikaans and German. This choice is also helping with international relations and education, as English-language materials are the most easily available.

While English is taught throughout the education system, Afrikaans is still the lingua franca among many of the older generation, and in rural areas Afrikaans tends to be more widely used than English (which may not be spoken at all) – despite the widespread enthusiasm felt for the latter. Virtually all black Namibians also speak one or more African languages, and many will speak several. Many white Namibians (especially those in the commercial farming communities of the central region) regard German as their first language, though they will normally understand English and Afrikaans as well.

Among the indigenous languages there are two basic language groups which bear no relation to each other: Bantu (eg: Ovambo, Herero) and Khoisan (eg: Bushmen, Nama). Linguistics experts have identified at least 28 different languages and numerous dialects among the indigenous population. Although these different language groupings do loosely correspond to what might be described as Namibia's 'tribes', the distinctions are blurred by the natural linguistic ability of most Namibians. Thus, ethnic groupings provide only a rough guide to the many languages and dialects of Namibia's people.

RELIGION

Some 85–90% of the population follows a Christian religion. Dutch Reformed, Roman Catholic, Lutheran, Methodist and Presbyterian churches are all common. However, most black Namibians will also subscribe to some traditional African religious practices and beliefs. Among these are ancestor worship, practised by the Herero and Himba, whose traditional homesteads incorporate a holy fire through which they can communicate with the dead.

EDUCATION

Since independence, the government has poured resources into an expansion of the education system, with primary education free since 2013. As a result, some 98% of children are enrolled in primary school, although that figure falls to just 57% with the move to secondary education. Adult literacy is estimated by UNESCO at about 76%.

There are small primary schools in the most rural of areas, some of them mobile to cater for a semi-nomadic population, while large secondary schools are established in the regional centres. Children in secondary school study for the IGCSE (International General Certificate of Secondary Education) and then move on to the HIGCSE. Lessons are taught almost exclusively in English, although some indigenous languages may also be taught. The state-run University of Namibia, established immediately after independence, is based in Windhoek, with 11 satellite campuses nationwide.

CULTURE

Namibia boasts some of the world's oldest rock paintings and engravings, which have been attributed to ancestors of the Bushmen. The scenes are naturalistic depictions of animals, people, hunting, battles and social rituals. Local geology determined the colour usage in the paintings. Some are monochrome pictures in red, but many are multicoloured, using ground-up earth pigments mixed with animal fat to produce 'paints' of red, brown, yellow, blue, violet, grey, black and white. Rock engravings have also been found, often in areas where there is an absence of smooth, sheltered rock surfaces to paint on. Some of the best examples of paintings and engravings are in the Brandberg, Twyfelfontein and Erongo areas.

However, there is more to Namibian creativity than rock paintings and engravings. Traditional arts and crafts include basketry, woodcarving, leatherwork, beadwork, pottery, music-making and dancing. More contemporary arts and crafts encompass textile weaving and embroidery, sculptures, printmaking and theatre.

4

The annual Bank Windhoek Arts Festival (*www.bankwindhoekarts.com.na*) draws together every aspect of the arts, from music, dance and drama to the visual arts and even creative writing. Events are held primarily in Windhoek, but participants are selected from across the country.

For up-to-date information on cultural events, buy a copy of *The Namibian* and read its 'Arts and Entertainment' section.

CRAFTS AND VISUAL ARTS

Basketry Baskets are typically woven by women and are part of the crafts tradition of the northern Namibian peoples – Caprivi, Himba, Herero, Kavango and Ovambo.

Most baskets are made from strips of makalani palm leaves coiled into a shape that is determined by its purpose: flat, plate shapes for winnowing baskets, large bowl-shaped baskets for carrying things, small closed baskets with lids and bottle shapes for storing liquids. Symbolic geometric patterns are woven into a basket as it is being made, using strips of palm leaves dyed in dark browns, purples and yellows.

Recently, baskets have been made using strips of recycled plastic bags to wind around the palm-leaf strips or grasses.

Woodcarving The northern Namibian peoples – Bushmen, Caprivians, Damara, Himba, Kavango and Ovambo – have a tradition of woodcarving, which is usually practised by men. Wooden objects are carved using adzes, axes and knives; lathe-turned work is not traditional. Carving, incising and burning techniques are used to decorate the wood. A wide range of woodcarving is produced: sculptural headrests, musical instruments such as drums and thumb pianos; masks, walking sticks, toys, animal figurines, bows, arrows and quivers; domestic utensils including oval and round bowls and buckets as well as household furniture.

Leatherwork Leatherwork is practised by all the peoples of Namibia. The leather-workers are usually women, though men also participate if large, heavy skins are being tanned or dyed. The skins of cattle, sheep and game are tanned and dyed using vegetable materials, animal fat and sometimes red ochre. The goods crafted include carrying skins and bags, tobacco pouches, *karosses* (to be used as rugs or blankets) and traditional clothing – headdresses, girdles/aprons and sandals as well as more contemporary fashion accessories like shoes, boots, handbags, belts and jackets.

Beadwork Beadwork is traditionally the domain of the Bushman and Himba peoples. The Bushmen make beads from ostrich-egg shells, porcupine quills, seeds, nuts and branches, and also use commercially produced glass beads. The Himba people use iron beads and shells. In both peoples, men tend to make the beads and the women weave and string them into artefacts. These include necklaces, bracelets, armlets, anklets and headbands. The Bushmen also use beadwork to decorate their leatherwork bags, pouches and clothing – a particularly striking traditional design being the multicoloured circular 'owl's-eye'.

In addition to beadwork, the Himba people make a traditional iron-bead and leather head ornament (*oruvanda*) that all women wear, and belts (*epanda*), worn only by mothers.

Pottery Namibia's more renowned potters are women from the Caprivi, Kavango and Ovambo peoples. Traditionally, geometric patterns of various colours decorate

KARAKULS, SWAKARA AND NAKARA

Karakuls are central Asian sheep, the young of which have long been prized for their pelts. In 1902, a German fur trader called Paul Thorer shipped 69 of these from Uzbekistan to Germany in the hope of breeding them there. The damper European climes did not suit them, but in 1907 12 of those animals were shipped out to German South West Africa – as Namibia's climate was thought to be similar to that of the dry central Asian areas from where they had come.

They did well, and two years later 278 more animals were brought out from Asia. Later, the South Africans continued the work started by the Germans, when they took over as the reigning colonial power in Namibia. An experimental farm was started near Windhoek, to investigate the farming and breeding of karakuls.

Over the next 50 or 60 years Namibia gradually became one of the three main producers of karakul fur, or 'Persian lamb' as it is often known. Early on, selective breeding in Namibia had developed white pelts, which were not produced in either the USSR or Afghanistan – the competing countries. Then Namibia marketed its fur under the trade name of Swakara, for South West African karakul. Now, one firm markets these as Nakara, for Namibian karakul (page 197).

The trade grew rapidly, and as early as 1937 the country exported over a million pelts for over £1,200,000. At its peak in 1976, about 2.8 million pelts earned some 50 million rand and the nickname 'black gold' was coined. Then the antifur campaigns of the late 1970s and 1980s slashed the demand for fur, and the prices paid for pelts.

When the market crashed, the biggest single source of income for many farmers in southern Namibia was removed. Given that the fur came only from the slaughter of very young lambs (it is said to be at its softest when they are 36 hours old), it's not surprising that people felt unhappy about buying it. However, these are tough sheep, well suited to Namibia's extremes of temperatures and semi-desert climate, and finding new markets was important. Initially, the production of hand-woven karakul carpets served to increase the demand for the wool of adults, and now the market for pelts has stabilised, too, with interest coming from countries as diverse as Japan, Russia and Italy.

the vessels of different shapes and uses. Contemporary potters are experimenting with decoration by textures and a variety of sculptural motifs.

Textiles Nama women traditionally used patchwork techniques when making dresses and shawls. Now these women utilise their sewing skills in the art of embroidery and appliqué, making table and bed linens, cushion covers and wall-hangings depicting Namibian animals and village scenes.

Another, rather more recent textile craft is the hand-weaving of pure karakul wool into wall-hangings and rugs. The designs are usually geometric patterns or Namibian landscapes, though almost any design can be commissioned, and colours can be matched to your own décor.

Painting, sculpture and prints The work of contemporary Namibian artists, sculptors and printmakers is on display (and often available for sale) in the many galleries in urban areas. The country's biggest permanent collection is at the

National Art Gallery of Namibia (page 203), which has over 560 works of art dating from 1864 to the present day. Among the earlier works are many landscapes and paintings of wild animals. Modern-day artists can compete for the Bank Windhoek Triennal, which was inaugurated in 2007 as part of the Bank Windhoek Arts Festival. Contemporary Namibian visual arts are exhibited in Windhoek at John Muafangejo Art Centre and the Centre for Visual and Performing Arts (page 204). There's also Namibian Jewellers and Arts Gallery in Swakopmund (page 343).

PERFORMING ARTS

Dance Traditional dancing in Namibia is a participatory activity at community gatherings and events like weddings. Hence, a visitor is unlikely to witness any, unless invited by a Namibian. Occasionally, public performances of traditional dancing are to be seen at local arts festivals, or even in traditional villages such as Lizauli (page 551). In Bushmanland, in villages surrounding Tsumkwe, traditional Bushmen dances are performed for tourists – usually for a fee. This is generally a relaxed, uncontrived affair.

Performances of European dance, including ballet, take place at either the National Theatre of Namibia or at the Franco-Namibian Cultural Centre (page 193).

Music Most of the Namibian peoples have a music-making tradition – singing, and playing drums, bows, thumb pianos and harps. The Namas also have a tradition of religious singing in four-part harmony, a cappella. One group that has taken this to a wider audience is the University of Namibia Choir, which has gained an enviable reputation for performing a range of traditional music in both Namibian and European languages.

Pre-independence colonial influences have resulted in many Namibian musicians performing in the Western tradition. Concerts are regularly performed in Windhoek by the Namibia National Symphony Orchestra, National Youth Choir and touring foreign musicians in the main auditorium of the National Theatre of Namibia. Out of Windhoek, the national tour circuit includes large venues in Swakopmund, Walvis Bay and Okahandja.

Theatre and film Namibian theatre companies come and go, as elsewhere, but there is no shortage of venues for performances – at least in the capital (page 193).

The best of Namibian theatre (and other arts and crafts) can be seen at the annual Bank Windhoek Arts Festival (page 94).

SPORT

Athletics aficionados will be familiar with the name of Frankie Fredericks, the Namibian 200m sprinter. Slightly overshadowed by Michael Johnson, he nevertheless brought home a string of international medals, the last of which was in the 2002 Commonwealth Games, which marked the finale of an international career that spanned well over a decade.

More recently, Namibia has gone football crazy, spurred on by the 2010 Football World Cup held in South Africa. Rugby, too, is increasingly popular; Namibia has competed in five world cups since 1999, and has qualified for the 2019 event in Japan. Other sports played in schools include hockey, netball and basketball. The opportunity to take part in endurance sports is here, too, though the Namib Desert Challenge – a gruelling 220km, five-day event around Sossusvlei – is definitely not for the faint-hearted.

5

Planning and Preparation

In the three decades or so since independence, Namibia has seen tourist facilities develop substantially. While the original restcamps, developed for South African visitors driving their own vehicles, are still thriving, there has been a real boom in lodges and bushcamps, and once-marginal farms have gained a new role as guest farms. Such small, individual places cater largely for overseas visitors, rather than the local market, and costs are relatively high. They don't suit large tours or high-volume tour operators, who use only the bigger hotels for their groups. While the number of such hotels is gradually increasing in places like Swakopmund, Namibia still works best for self-drive trips and fly-in safaris by independent visitors who actively seek out the smaller establishments.

At the more economic end of the spectrum, there is also a significant number of first-time visitors travelling around Namibia on small-group camping trips, led by a driver/guide. This arrangement can offer great flexibility, and a real taste of the country at pretty low cost. Often people who first visit with a group like this will then return for their own individual self-drive trip – or even fly-in safari.

And then there are those who really want to get under the country's skin and are fairly self-sufficient. For them, the small network of community campsites – often run in conjunction with local companies – offers exceptional opportunities for independent exploration at leisure.

Namibia is fortunate: its roads are good, its attractions well signposted, and its national parks well managed. In addition, despite its phenomenal growth, tourism is still on a small scale, a fraction of that found in, say, South Africa or Tanzania. So the feeling of wilderness has not been lost; in many corners of the country you will still feel like the only visitors.

WHEN TO VISIT

Although much of Namibia can seem deserted, individual places can often be very busy, especially around Easter and from July to the end of October.

Many of the lodges and restcamps in and around Etosha, Damaraland and the Namib-Naukluft area are fully booked for the peak season as early as 12–18 months ahead, so advanced booking is essential at these times – and increasingly year round. Outside of the peak months, though, there are times when you'll find the lodges quieter and may even have some of the attractions to yourself.

Avoid coming during the Namibian school holidays if possible. These are generally around 25 April–25 May, 15 August–5 September and 5 December–15 January. Then many places will be busy with local visitors, especially the less expensive restcamps and the national parks.

While there really are neither any 'bad' nor any 'ideal' times to visit Namibia, there are times when some aspects of the country are at their best. See the *Climate* section (page 3), for a more detailed discussion of the weather – perhaps the biggest influence on your decision. Then consider your own specific requirements, which might include some of the following.

PHOTOGRAPHY For photography, Namibia is a stunning country in any month. Even with the simplest of camera equipment you can get truly spectacular results. My favourite time for photography is April to June. Then the dust has been washed out of the air by the rains, the vegetation is still green, and yet the sky is clear blue with only a few wispy white clouds.

WILDLIFE VIEWING The latter parts of the dry season, between July and late October, are certainly the best time to see big game. Then, as the small bush pools dry up and the green vegetation shrivels, the animals move closer to the springs or the waterholes and rivers.

During and after the rains, you won't see much wildlife partly because the lush vegetation hides the animals, and partly because most of them will have moved away from the waterholes (where they are most easily located) and gone deeper into the bush. However, many of the animals you do see will have young, as food (animal or vegetable) is at its most plentiful then.

BIRDWATCHING The last few months of the year witness the arrival of the summer migrant birds from the north, anticipating the coming of the rains. Further, if the rains are good the natural pans in Etosha and Bushmanland will fill with aquatic species, including huge numbers of flamingos. This is an amazing spectacle (see box, page 64). However, bear in mind that Namibia's ordinary feathered residents can be seen more easily during the dry season, when there is less vegetation to hide them.

WALKING Daytime temperatures can top 40°C in October and November, and heavy rainstorms are likely during the first two or three months of the year. Hence walkers should try to come between about May and September, when the temperatures are at their coolest, and the chances of rain are minimised. Note that most of the long trails in the national parks are closed between November and March, and sometimes for longer.

DRIVING AROUND Driving usually presents few problems at any time of year. However, visitors in the first three months of the year and occasionally even slightly either side of these may find roads blocked by flooding rivers. These usually subside within a matter of hours, and certainly within a day or so, but do provide an extra hazard. A 4x4 may be useful at these times, although it is always worth considering an alternative and probably safer route; see also the advice on fording rivers, page 146. Those mounting 4x4 expeditions to the more remote corners of the country should certainly avoid these months, when large tracts of Bushmanland and Kaokoland, for example, become totally impassable in any vehicle.

For detailed coverage of driving in Namibia, see *Chapter 7*. For suggested itineraries, see page 147.

HIGHLIGHTS

NAMIBIA'S TRADITIONAL CULTURES Get to know people of a radically different cultural background in one of Namibia's more remote areas. Visit a Himba village in the Kunene Region and see how these semi-nomadic desert-dwelling people live, or spend time in a traditional Bushman village, learning in detail about their hunter-gatherer culture.

ZAMBEZI REGION This narrow stretch of land in the northeast of Namibia, still widely known as the Caprivi Strip, offers a great contrast to the rest of the country and some exciting birdlife. Watered by a generous annual rainfall, it's a lush environment, with chances to see wildlife not found elsewhere in Namibia; among others, look out for crocodile, hippo and buffalo.

ETOSHA NATIONAL PARK One of Africa's best game reserves, Etosha National Park protects a vast shallow bowl of silvery sand more than three times the size of Greater London, along with its surrounding bush. It excels during the dry season when huge herds of animals can be seen amid some of the most startling safari scenery in Africa.

SKELETON COAST Although it is difficult to visit the northern Skeleton Coast, accessing Namibia's coastline anywhere will give you a feel for just how wild and windy it can be. Expect barren and desolate landscapes and large colonies of Cape fur seals. The occasional remaining shipwreck serves as a reminder of the treacherous fogs and strong currents found offshore.

TWYFELFONTEIN The slopes of Twyfelfontein, amid the flat-topped red-granite mountains typical of Damaraland, conceal one of the continent's greatest concentrations of rock art. At first sight, it seems like any other hillside strewn with rocks, but the boulders that litter these slopes are dotted with thousands of paintings and ancient engravings, classified by UNESCO as a World Heritage Site.

SOSSUSVLEI The classic desert scenery around Sesriem and Sossusvlei is the stuff that postcards are made of – enormous apricot dunes with gracefully curving ridges, invariably pictured in the sharp light of dawn with a photogenic oryx or feathery acacia adjacent. Climb the dunes at sunrise to catch the best light for your photos.

KOLMANSKOP This ghost town, once the principal town of the local diamond industry, was abandoned over 45 years ago and now gives a fascinating insight into the area's great diamond boom. Many of the buildings are left exactly as they were deserted, and now the surrounding dunes are gradually burying them.

FISH RIVER CANYON The Fish River Canyon is the largest canyon in Africa, and among the largest in the world: approaching from the north is like driving across Mars. The vast rocky landscape breaks up into a series of spectacular cliffs, formed by the Fish River as it meanders between boulders over half a kilometre below. Its size is impressive: 161km long, up to 27km wide and almost 550m at its deepest.

HOW TO TRAVEL AND BUDGETING

Obviously your style of travel around Namibia depends on your budget, though more expensive doesn't always guarantee a better trip.

BACKPACKING Backpacking around Namibia is very limiting. You need private transport to see most of the national parks, and will be missing out on a lot if you don't have it. However, if you can splash out on a few days' car hire here, and a couple of guided trips from a hostel there, you might get by on £30/US$45 per day for the rest of your time.

SELF-DRIVE TRIPS The best way to see the country is certainly to have your own vehicle. Whether you opt to use camps, lodges and restcamps, to bring your own camping kit or to hire an equipped vehicle with everything you'll need, it is then merely a matter of style. The questions of what, how and where to hire a vehicle, and how much it will cost, are extensively covered in *Chapter 7*.

If you have a tight budget, a much better bet than backpacking would be to find four people to share the car, and camp everywhere. Then you could keep costs to around £60/US$80 per person per day.

For a less basic self-drive trip, with two people sharing the car and staying in a variety of small lodges and restcamps, expect a cost of about £90–150/US$120–200

NOTES FOR TRAVELLERS WITH LIMITED MOBILITY

@gordonrattray; updated by Endeavour Safaris

A vast land of sand, strewn with rocks and pitted by rivers and ravines sounds inadvisable for people who have trouble walking, and downright impossible for wheelchair users. Surprisingly, the opposite is true. Namibia is one of Africa's most accessible destinations, with decent infrastructure, facilities catering to most needs and operators ranging from 'ready and efficient' to 'experienced and specialised'.

Granted, depending on your needs, a lot of research and effort may be necessary to get the best from your trip, but Namibians love a challenge and, as other travellers have shown, almost anything is possible.

ACCOMMODATION Namibia has (for Africa) an unusually high proportion of accessible accommodation. In Etosha, most of the NWR lodges and restcamps (page 441) have varying degrees of accessibility, from wider doorways and extra space in the rooms to full adaptation of the bathrooms including as toilets with handrails, and pull-down seats in the showers. This awareness is echoed throughout the country – albeit on a lesser scale. Most lodge proprietors are easily contactable by email, so you can discuss your requirements beforehand.

TRANSPORT

By air If you need assistance then let the airline know in advance and arrive early for your departure. During the flight, anyone who uses a pressure-relieving wheelchair cushion should consider using it instead of (or on top of) the fitted seat cushion.

Windhoek's Hosea Kutako International Airport has wheelchairs, an aisle chair and staff to assist with transfers. It also has roomy, step-free toilets for both sexes with grab rails. More provincial airports won't guarantee such 'luxuries', but if needed, aisle chairs can usually be ordered.

By road Unless you choose a specialised operator, most tour companies use 4x4s and minibuses, which are higher than normal cars, usually making entry more difficult. Similarly, buses and minibuses have no facilities for wheelchairs, and getting off and on can be a hectic affair. But that does not necessarily mean these options are to be discounted; drivers, guides and fellow passengers are each per day. If you choose more expensive lodges, with guided activities included, then this might rise to about £250–450/US$325–600 or even more – but should guarantee a first-class trip.

GROUP TOURS Another option is to take a scheduled, guided group tour around the country. These suit single travellers as they provide ready-made companions, those who may not feel confident driving, and those who really do want the input of a guide for their trip – often without spending too much money. In either case, provided that you are happy to spend your whole holiday with the same group of people, such a trip might be ideal. Guided trips with larger groups are generally less expensive than self-drive trips which follow the same itinerary and use the same accommodation, and taking a guided trip that includes some nights camping can help to bring costs down substantially.

usually prepared to assist. Do remember, however, that they are not trained in these skills so you must thoroughly explain your needs and stay in control of the situation.

It may be worth taking an assistant for the guide with you on a tour, enabling the guide to focus on the traditional aspects of guiding, and the assistant to help as required with a wheelchair or other access needs.

HEALTH Namibian hospitals and pharmacies in urban areas are usually well equipped, but those in rural regions can be basic, so if possible, take all essential medication and equipment with you. It is advisable to pack this in your hand luggage during flights in case your main bags don't arrive immediately. Doctors will know about 'everyday' illnesses, but you must understand and be able to explain your own particular medical requirements. Depending on the season it can also be hot; if this is a problem for you then try to book accommodation and vehicles with fans or air conditioning. A plant-spray bottle is a useful cooling aid.

SECURITY For anyone following the usual security precautions (page 131) the chances of robbery are greatly reduced. In fact, as a person with a disability I often feel more 'noticed' when in public places, and therefore a less attractive target for thieves. But the opposite may also apply, so do stay aware of where your bags are and who is around you, especially when transferring to another car or similar activities.

SPECIALIST OPERATOR
Endeavour Safaris ✆+267 686 0887; m +267 7230 9099; e info@endeavour-safaris.com; www.endeavour-safaris.com. Specialists in accessible travel for people with disabilities.

FURTHER INFORMATION
www.gov.uk/guidance/foreign-travel-for-disabled-people The UK's gov.uk website: general information about travelling for people with disabilities.
www.globalaccessnews.com Searchable database of disability travel information.
www.rollingrains.com Searchable website advocating disability travel.
www.youreable.com UK-based general resource for disability information, with an active forum.

Generally, the smaller the vehicle used and the group size, the better and the more expensive the trip becomes. On a cheaper trip, expect participatory camping, with a group size of 12–15+ people, for around £130/US$170 per day, based on a 12-day itinerary. For something less basic, using smaller vehicles with fewer people, and staying in luxury mobile camps, a trip of one to two weeks will cost around £1,800/US$2,340 a day, per person sharing, including all meals and activities. Several operators run guided accommodated trips for those who do not fancy camping but like the idea of a small-group trip. These cost around £200–250/US$260–325 per person per night, depending on the quality of the lodges used.

PRIVATE GUIDED TRIPS If money is not so restricted, and especially if you're travelling in your own small group with four or more people (eg: a family trip), consider a private guided trip. Your group would then have its own vehicle and guide for the whole trip. You might sleep in existing lodges and camps, or use camping kits supplied by your guide – or might even stay at luxury private tented camps set up just for you. The choice will be yours when you arrange the trip. This isn't a cheap way to travel, especially for smaller groups, but can be well worth the price tag. As an example, two people might expect to pay around £440/US$575 per person per night, whereas for a group of six people that cost would fall to around £300/US$390. Other factors that will affect costs are the standard of accommodation and style of camping.

FLY-IN TRIPS Finally, if your budget is very flexible (and especially if your time is very limited), then consider doing some or all of your trip as a fly-in safari. Small private charter flights can be arranged to many of the smaller lodges and guest farms; it's a very easy way to travel. It is also the only way to get to some of the more inaccessible corners, like the northern section of the Skeleton Coast.

A very popular combination is to fly down to the Sesriem area for three or four nights, hop up to Swakopmund or back to Windhoek, and then pick up a hire car to drive yourself north to Damaraland and Etosha.

Expect to pay upwards of about £500/US$650 per person per night for a full fly-in trip, and note that your choice of lodge will be restricted to those that can arrange all your activities for you.

ORGANISING YOUR TRIP

Most visitors who come to Namibia for a holiday use the country's guest farms, lodges and restcamps – often combining them into a self-drive tour around the country. Such trips are quite complex, as you will be using numerous hotels, camps and lodges in your own particular sequence. Many of these places are small (and so easily filled), and organise their own logistics with military precision. Finding space at short notice is becoming increasingly difficult.

To arrange everything, it's best to use a reliable, independent tour operator based in your own country. Although many operators sell trips to Namibia, few really know the country well. Insist on dealing directly with someone who does. Namibia changes so fast that detailed local knowledge is vital in putting together a trip that runs smoothly and suits you. Make sure that whoever you book with is fully bonded, so that your money is protected if they go broke; and, ideally, pay with a credit card. Never book a trip from someone who doesn't know Namibia personally: you are asking for problems.

Trips around Namibia are not cheap, though they are currently cheaper (and also better value in many cases) than in neighbouring countries such as Botswana and

Zambia. Expect to pay around the same to an operator as you would have to pay directly: from about £650–2,000/US$850–2,600 per person per week, including car rental, but excluding airfares. At this price you can expect a good level of service while you are considering the options and booking the trip. If you don't get it, go elsewhere.

Booking directly with Namibian safari operators or agencies is possible, but telephone communication can be more difficult and you will have no recourse if anything goes wrong. European and US operators usually work on commission for the trips that they sell, which is deducted from the basic cost that the visitor pays. Thus you should end up paying about the same whether you book through an overseas operator or talk directly to someone in Namibia.

TOURIST INFORMATION AND NATIONAL PARKS

TOURIST OFFICE The national tourist board, Namibia Tourism (\ *+264 (0)61 290 6000;* e *info@namibiatourism.com.na; www.namibiatourism.com.na*), based in Windhoek, is worth contacting for information before your trip. They have overseas representation in the UK, Germany and China.

China Shanghai c/o Oriental Gateway Consultancy, 3/F, #2150, Jinxuxiu Rd 200127; \ +86 21 5059 6888; e zhuzheng0312@yahoo.com

Germany Schiller Strasse 42–44, D-60313 Frankfurt am Main; \ +49 69 133 7360; e info@ namibia-tourism.com

UK c/o Hills Balfour Synergy, Colechurch Hse, 1 London Bridge Walk, London SE1 2SX; \ +44 (0)20 7367 0962; e namibia@hbportfolio.co.uk

NATIONAL PARKS The Ministry of Environment and Tourism (**MET**; *www.met. gov.na*) is the government department responsible for the national parks, but most parks' accommodation is run by Namibia Wildlife Resorts (**NWR**; *Central Reservations: P Bag 13196, Windhoek;* \ *061 285 7200;* e *reservations@nwr.com. na; www.nwr.com.na*). While both might appear to be reasonably well organised, bureaucracy and red tape can cause difficulties and delays.

Reservations for accommodation must be made in advance, either online or through the NWR offices in Windhoek or Swakopmund; you can, theoretically, book by phone too – but postal applications are not worth the hassle. Advance payment, which can be made by credit card to the reservations office, is required. Alternatively, book in advance through a tour operator that understands the system.

Entry permits for most parks are available at the gates, provided that you're there before they close and that there is space left. The exceptions are permits for the restricted areas of the Namib-Naukluft, such as the Welwitschia Plains, and for the Sperrgebiet National Park, which must be bought in advance from the MET's office in Windhoek, Swakopmund or Lüderitz.

Entrance to the major national parks – Etosha, Namib-Naukluft (Sesriem entrance), Waterberg, Ai-Ais Transfrontier and the Skeleton Coast – is currently N$80 per person per day (under 16s free), plus N$10 per vehicle. At other parks, the entrance fee is N$40 per person, but the vehicle fee remains N$10. That said, it is anticipated that these fees will rise, possibly quite significantly, during the life of this edition. Note that accommodation fees do not include park entrance fees; both are payable.

If you have booked accommodation in advance through the NWR, it's worth confirming this just before your trip. Despite the best of intentions, there have been occasions when visitors have arrived to find prebooked accommodation closed for reasons such as flooding or a presidential visit, so it's wise to be cautious. It is also essential that you take your NWR reservation number with you to prove you have a booking.

TOUR OPERATORS

As Namibia has become better known, many overseas tour operators have seized the opportunity to put together programmes without knowing what they're doing. Often they are just selling tours that someone in Namibia has designed and marketed. Few have spent much time in the country themselves, and fewer still can give detailed first-hand guidance on all of the country, let alone a wide range of guest farms, camps and lodges.

Don't be talked into thinking that there are only a handful of places to visit and a few camps to stay in. There are many, all individual and different. Ask about ones mentioned in these chapters; a good operator will know the vast majority of them and be able to describe them to you.

Here I must, as the author, admit a personal interest in the tour-operating business: I organise and run the African operations of the UK-based operator Expert Africa (see below), including Wild about Africa (see opposite). Together we are the leading operator to Namibia for English-speaking travellers from Europe and America – with the widest choice of Namibian lodges and camps available anywhere. In Namibia, Expert Africa concentrates on flexible self-drive trips and fly-in safaris; starting at about £1,000/US$1,300 per person for 11 nights, including car hire, accommodation and some meals – but excluding international flights (typically £1,100 return from the UK). Wild about Africa focuses on guided small-group trips, starting at around £2,200/US$2,860. Booking with a tour operator will often cost you the same as or less than if you contact Namibia's camps directly – plus you have independent advice, financial protection, and arrangements made for you by experts.

For a fair comparison, tour operators that feature Namibia include:

UK

Aardvark Safaris +44 (0)1980 849160; e mail@aardvarksafaris.com; www. aardvarksafaris.co.uk. Small, upmarket operator featuring much of Africa & Madagascar.

Abercrombie & Kent +44 (0)1242 386460; e info@abercrombiekent.co.uk; www. abercrombiekent.co.uk. Long-established, large & posh operator worldwide, with a wide choice of Africa trips – which include its own lodges.

Africa Explorer +44 (0)20 8987 8742; e john@ africa-explorer.co.uk; www.africa-explorer.co.uk; see ad, page xii. Tiny but knowledgeable company, run by the jovial John Haycock.

Africa Travel +44 (0)20 7843 3500; e info@ africatravel.co.uk; www.africatravel.co.uk. Featuring east & southern Africa.

Audley Travel +44 (0)1993 227950; e africa@ audleytravel.com; www.audleytravel.com. Tailor-made operator with worldwide coverage including Namibia.

Cazenove & Loyd +44 (0)20 7384 2332; www.cazloyd.com. Old-school, established tailor-made specialists to east/southern Africa, Asia, Indian Ocean, & Central/South America.

Cox & Kings +44 (0)20 3553 7925; e sales@ coxandkings.co.uk; www.coxandkings.co.uk. Old company renowned for India, now also featuring Latin America, Indian Ocean, Middle East, China, Asia & Africa, including some Namibian trips.

Expert Africa +44 (0)20 3405 6666; e info@ expertafrica.com; www.expertafrica.com; see ad, pages i and 134. Started trips to Namibia in 1992, & now has the most comprehensive programme to the country, run by Chris McIntyre – this book's author.

Explore! +44 (0)1252 888543; e sales@ explore.co.uk; www.explore.co.uk. A relatively large company specialising in escorted small-group tours & tailor-made trips throughout the world.

Gane & Marshall +44 (0)1822 600600; e info@ ganeandmarshall.com; www.ganeandmarshall.

com; see ad, page xii. Tailor-made trips to East & southern Africa & the Indian Ocean.

Hartley's Safaris ☏+44 (0)1673 861600; e info@hartleysgroup.com; www.hartleys-safaris.co.uk. Old-school, established tailor-made specialists to East/southern Africa.

Intrepid ☏+44 (0)808 274 5111; e ask@intrepidtravel.com; www.intrepidtravel.com. Offers a wide range of group trips worldwide, including southern Africa.

Journeys Discovering Africa ☏0800 088 5470, +1 888 428 2772 (USA); e enquiries@journeysdiscoveringafrica.com; www.journeysdiscoveringafrica.com; see ad, 4th colour section. UK company with well-established operations in Uganda & Rwanda now offering trips to southern Africa, inc Namibia & Botswana.

Okavango Tours & Safaris m +44 (0)7721 387738; e info@okavango.com; www.okavango.com. Small, long-established specialists to East/southern Africa, Madagascar & the Indian Ocean islands.

Original Travel ☏+44 (0)20 7978 7333; e ask@originaltravel.co.uk; www.originaltravel.co.uk. Bespoke worldwide operator now incorporating Tim Best's Africa programme.

Rainbow Tours ☏+44 (0)20 3733 6544; e info@rainbowtours.co.uk; www.rainbowtours.co.uk; see ad, inside back cover. Established operator with destinations that include southern, East & West Africa & Madagascar.

Safari Consultants ☏+44 (0)1787 888590; e info@safariconsultantuk.com; www.safari-consultants.co.uk. Old-school tailor-made specialists to East, central & southern Africa, including Namibia, & the Indian Ocean islands.

Safari Drive ☏+44 (0)1488 71140; e info@safaridrive.com; www.safaridrive.com; see ad, 4th colour section. Self-drive expeditions using very well-equipped Land Rovers in East & southern Africa, & Argentina.

Scott Dunn ☏+44 (0)20 3733 5209; e enquiries@scottdunn.com; www.scottdunn.com. Worldwide luxury operator featuring Asia, Latin America, ski chalets, Mediterranean villas & Africa, including Namibia.

Steppes Travel ☏+44 (0)1285 601776; e enquiry@steppestravel.co.uk; www.steppestravel.co.uk. Founded as Art of Travel, this posh tailor-made specialist now has worldwide coverage, including Namibia.

Ultimate Travel Company ☏+44 (0)20 3553 3982; e enquiry@theultimatetravelcompany.co.uk; www.theultimatetravelcompany.co.uk. Wide-ranging operator including central, East & southern Africa.

Wild about Africa ☏+44 (0)20 3405 6655; e enquiries@wildabout.africa; www.wildabout.africa. Sister company of Expert Africa with small-group trips in Namibia, Victoria Falls & parts of Botswana, from luxury camping trips to privately guided expeditions.

Wildlife Worldwide ☏+44 (0)1962 302086; e reservations@wildlifeworldwide.com; www.wildlifeworldwide.com. Wide-ranging small operator with tailor-made & tour programmes across the globe, including options that feature Namibia.

Zambezi Safari & Travel ☏+44 (0)1752 878858; e info@zambezi.com; www.zambezi.com. Tailor-made specialist to a range of East, central & southern African destinations.

Overland specialists

Dragoman ☏+44 (0)1728 861133; e info@dragoman.co.uk; www.dragoman.co.uk. Overland truck & small-group tours worldwide, including Africa.

Exodus ☏+44 (0)20 3811 4258; e sales@exodus.co.uk; www.exodus.co.uk. Overland truck & set tours worldwide, including 8 Namibia-only options.

FRANCE

Makila Voyages ☏+33(0)1 42 96 80 00; e info@makila.fr; www.makila.fr. Tailor-made trips worldwide, with a focus on southern Africa.

USA

Africa Adventure Company ☏+1 800 882 9453; e safari@africanadventure.com; www.africa-adventure.com. One of the older Africa travel companies in the USA, run by the irrepressible Mark Nolting.

SOUTH AFRICA

Drifters ☏+27 (0)11 888 1020; e drifters@drifters.co.za; www.drifters.co.za. Established specialists in overland trips.

Jenman African Safaris ☏+27 (0)871 284 5010; e info@jenmansafaris.com; www.jenmansafaris.com; see ad, 4th colour section

Pulse Africa ☏+27 (0)11 325 2290; e info@pulseafrica.com; www.pulseafrica.com; see ad, page 122. Tailor-made trips to East & southern Africa & Indian Ocean islands.

Currently all visitors require a passport which is valid for at least six months after they are due to leave, a completely blank page for Namibian immigration to stamp, and an onward ticket of some sort. In practice, the third requirement is rarely even considered if you look neat, respectable and fairly affluent.

At present, British, Irish and US citizens can enter Namibia without a visa for 90 days or less for a holiday or private visit, as can nationals of other countries that include Angola, Australia, Austria, Belgium, Botswana, Brazil, Canada, Denmark, Finland, France, Germany, Hong Kong, Iceland, Italy, Japan, Kenya, Lesotho, Liechtenstein, Luxembourg, Macau, Malawi, Malaysia, Mauritius, Mozambique, the Netherlands, New Zealand, Norway, Portugal, Russian Federation, Singapore, South Africa, Spain, Swaziland, Sweden, Switzerland, Tanzania, Zambia and Zimbabwe.

That said, it is *always* best to check with your local Namibian embassy or high commission before you travel. If you have difficulties in your home country, contact the Ministry of Home Affairs and Immigration in Windhoek (*Cohen Bldg, Kasino St, P Bag 13200, Windhoek;* ✆*061 292 2111; www.mha.gov.na*).

The 90-day tourist visa can be extended by application in Windhoek. You will then probably be required to show proof of the 'means to leave', like an onward air ticket, a credit card, or sufficient funds of your own. The current cost of a tourist or business visa is N$500 plus handling fees.

TRAVELLING TO NAMIBIA WITH CHILDREN In Namibia, as in Botswana and South Africa, parents travelling to, or through, the country are required by law to provide a full birth certificate for each accompanying child under the age of 18. This applies even when both biological parents or the legal guardians are present. The regulations on this are complex and controversial, even if the reasons for their implementation (to curb child trafficking and exploitation) are commendable.

If a child is travelling with only one parent named on the birth certificate, or with neither biological parent, things become even more complex and there has been a spate of passengers being denied boarding on flights or entry on arrival. Thus if you are planning to travel with a minor, we strongly suggest that you check the latest information on this with your nearest Namibian high commission or embassy, well in advance of your departure date.

IMPORTS AND EXPORTS

Since Namibia is a member of the Southern African Customs Union (SACU), there are few import and export restrictions between Namibia and either Botswana or South Africa. If you wish to export animal products, including skins or legally culled ivory, make sure you obtain a certificate confirming the origin of every item bought. Remember: even with such a certificate, the international CITES convention prohibits the movement of some things across international borders. Do consider the ethics of buying any animal products that might be covered by CITES.

Visitors can reclaim the VAT on any purchases for export at Hosea Kotako Airport in Windhoek against commission of 1% of the VAT claimed, with a minimum charge of N$15.

EMBASSIES AND HIGH COMMISSIONS

A list of the foreign embassies in Windhoek can be found on page 198. Namibia's diplomatic representatives overseas include the following:

Ⓔ Angola (embassy) Rua dos Coquiros 37, Luanda; +244 239 5483/4730; e embnam@netangola.com

Ⓔ Austria (embassy) Zuckerkandlgasse 2, 1190 Vienna; +43 1 402 9371; e nam.emb.vienna@speed.at; www.embnamibia.at

Ⓔ Belgium (embassy) Av de Tervuren 454, BE 1150 Brussels; +32 2 771 1410; e info@namibiaembassy.be; www.namibiaembassy.be

Ⓔ Botswana (high commission) 186 Morara CI, Gaborone; +267 390 2181; e namibhc@botsnet.bw

Ⓔ Brazil (embassy) SHIS QI 09, Conjunto 08, Casa 11, Lago Sul Brasilia-DF; +55 61 3248 6274/7621; e info@embassyofnamibia.org.br; www.embassyofnamibia.org.br

Ⓔ China (embassy) 2-9-2 Ta Yuan, Diplomatic Office Bldg, Beijing 100600; +86 10 6532 2211/4810; e namemb@eastnet.com.cn

Ⓔ DRC (embassy) 138 Bd du 30 Juin, Kinshasa/Gombe; +243 81 555 9840/1; e namembassy@namembdrc.org; http://namembdrc.org/

Ⓔ Cuba (embassy) Calle 36 No 504, Miramar, Havana City; +53 7 204 1428/30; e namembassycuba@hotmail.com; www.namembassycuba.co.cu

Ⓔ Egypt (embassy) Villa 59 Rd 13, Maadi, Cairo; +20 2 235 89649; e namembcai@link.net

Ⓔ Ethiopia (embassy) Bole Rd W, 17 Kebel 19, Hse 002, Addis Ababa; +251 116 611966; e nam.emb@ethionet.et

Ⓔ France (embassy) 42 rue Boileau, Paris 75016; +33 1 44 17 32 65; e info@embassyofnamibia.fr; www.embassyofnamibia.fr

Ⓔ Germany (embassy) Reichsstrasse 17, 14052 Berlin; +49 30 254 0950; e info@namibia-botschaft.de; www.namibia-botschaft.de

Ⓔ India (high commission) D-6/24 Vasant Vihar, New Delhi 110 057; +91 11 261 40389; e nam@nhcdelhi.com

Ⓔ Japan (embassy) Amerex Bldg, 3-5-7 Azabudai, Minato-Ku, Tokyo 106-0041; +81 3 6426 5460; e embassy@namibiatokyo.or.jp; http://namibiatokyo.or.jp

Ⓔ Malaysia (high commission) Suite 15-01, Level 15, Menara HLA, No 3 Jalan Kia Peng, 50450 Kuala Lumpur; +60 3 216 46520; e secretary@namhckl.com.my; http://namhckl.com.my

Ⓔ Nigeria (high commission) 16 T Y Danjuma St, Asokoro, Abuja; +234 905 386 2451; e info@namibiahc.com.ng; www.namibiahc.com.ng

Ⓔ Russian Federation (embassy) 2nd Kazachy Lane, Hse No 7, Moscow; +7 495 230 3275; e namembrf@online.ru

Ⓔ South Africa (high commission) 186 Blackwood St, Arcadia, Pretoria; +27 12 481 9100; e secretary@namibia.org.za; www.namibia.org.za

Ⓔ Sweden, Norway, Denmark, Iceland (embassy) Luntmakargatan 88, 11351 Stockholm; +46 8 442 9800; e info@embassyofnamibia.se; www.embassyofnamibia.se

Ⓔ Tanzania (high commission) 3 Rufiji St, Masaki, Msasani Peninsula, Dar es Salaam; +255 22 260 1903; e namhcdar@gmail.com; www.namibiahc.or.tz

Ⓔ UK (high commission) 6 Chandos St, London W1G 9LU; +44 20 7636 6244; e info@namibiahc.org.uk; www.namibiahc.org.uk

Ⓔ USA (embassy) 1605 New Hampshire Av NW, Washington, DC 20009; +1 202 986 0540; e info@namibianembassyusa.org; www.namibianembassyusa.org

Ⓔ Zambia (high commission) 30A Mutende Rd, Woodlands, Lusaka; +260 0211 211407/8; e namibia@coppernet.zm

Ⓔ Zimbabwe (high commission) Lot 1 of 7A, Borrowdale Estates, 69 Borrowdale Rd, Harare; +263 4 885841; e namhighcom@africaonline.co.zw

GETTING THERE AND AWAY

BY AIR

From Europe Several reliable airlines fly to southern Africa from Europe, with onward connections to Windhoek. Most fly overnight, so you can fall asleep on the plane in London and wake in the southern hemisphere ready for the short connecting flight to Windhoek. The time difference between western Europe and Namibia is minimal, so there's no jet lag.

Air Namibia's (SW; *www.airnamibia.com.na*) only direct flight to Windhoek from Europe is from Frankfurt, which connects easily with London. Flights depart in the evening in both directions, arriving early the following morning. Air Namibia also operates connecting flights to/from Johannesburg and Cape Town to link up with most of their intercontinental flights to/from Windhoek.

For many European travellers, the best choice is to fly via Johannesburg. There's a whole host of other options here, from many European airports. British Airways (BA; *www.britishairways.com*) and South African Airways (SA; *www.flysaa.com*) have daily overnight services from London, and both operate add-on connections to Windhoek, run by their subsidiaries. Virgin (VS; *www.virgin-atlantic.com*) also services the Johannesburg route, though they do not have an add on to Windhoek so passengers have to use another airline.

For a standard fare, expect to pay from around £800/US$1,040 return if booked direct with the airline, though the occasional special offer can reduce this quite substantially. Prices rise significantly for departures during Easter, July and August, and peak from mid-December to mid-January, when you can expect to pay upward of £1,600/US$2,080. The quietest periods are mid-April to the end of June, and November.

Other airlines with routes to Namibia from Europe include Qatar, KLM Royal Dutch Airlines and Ethiopian Airlines, as well as a few predominantly German charter companies. These are often cheaper than the more established flights above but generally do not offer daily departures in either direction. To add to the mix, some of the budget airlines based in South Africa, such as Kulula, Mango and Fast Jet, have rapidly expanding regional networks, with Kulula already offering flights to Namibia.

Finding cheap tickets, and the right flights, is an art in itself. Your first stop should probably be to research the possibilities and costs on some of the large online travel agents (OTAs) – companies like Kayak (*www.kayak.co.uk*), Skyscanner (*www.skyscanner.net*) and Expedia (*www.expedia.co.uk*). That should tell you what routes and flights are available, and give you a broad idea of their costs. You might also want to look at these same flights on the websites of the airlines concerned, and perhaps a local flight specialist if there is one.

If you plan to hire a car and arrange accommodation in advance, then also speak to a specialist tour operator (page 104) *before* you book your flights. They will usually quote one cost for your whole trip – flights, car and accommodation. The best operators will usually be cheaper than booking the various components directly, and be able to guide you so that organising your trip becomes a lot less hassle. However, if you're on a very tight budget and want to fly in and backpack around, then go straight to an OTA.

From the Americas South African Airways operates direct flights between New York and Johannesburg, code-sharing with United (*www.united.com*), with numerous onward flights to Windhoek. Delta (*www.delta.com*) has direct flights between Atlanta and Johannesburg. Alternatively, many travellers from the US fly via Europe, either joining the Air Namibia flight from Frankfurt, or taking a flight to Johannesburg, then connecting through to Windhoek. As in Europe, start your research online.

Given the duration of these flights, travellers often include a few days in Europe as they transit. However, do allow a day or so in London between the flights, as your flights will not technically 'connect' – and if one is late you don't want to miss the other.

Travellers from Central and South America might use the Atlanta, Middle East or European gateways, or the direct flights between São Paulo and Johannesburg, run daily by South African Airways.

From elsewhere There are direct flights to Johannesburg from most of the major centres in the Far East, including Hong Kong (with South African Airways or Cathay Pacific) and Singapore (Singapore Airlines). From the Middle East, Qatar Airways has direct flights from Doha to Windhoek and Johannesburg. From Australasia, the best route is probably one of the flights from Perth or Sydney to Johannesburg, with South African Airways or Qantas, connecting to Windhoek. It may also be worth considering the services offered by South African Airlines, Ethiopian Airlines and KLM.

OVERLAND Entering over one of Namibia's land borders is equally easy – whether by car or by bus – as there are fast and direct links on good tarred roads with South Africa, Botswana and Zambia.

Namibia's few remaining passenger trains cover only internal routes, but those wishing to cross the border in style would do well to consider Rovos Rail's Namibia safari (*www.rovos.com/journeys/namibia-safari*); for details, see page 151.

Border crossings Namibia's borders are generally hassle-free and efficient. If you are crossing with a hired car, then remember to let the car-hire company know as they will need to provide you with the right paperwork before you set off. Opening hours at the borders – listed clockwise – are as follows.

With Angola

Ruacana – near the hydro-electric station	08.00–18.00
Omahenene – north of the C46 between Outapi and Ruacana	08.00–18.00
Oshikango – on the B1 north	08.00–18.00
Rundu – cross the river to go north	08.00–18.00

With Zambia

Wenela – just north of Katima Mulilo	06.00–18.00

With Botswana

Impalila Island – over the river from Kasane	07.30–16.30
Ngoma Bridge – on the B8 between Caprivi/Zambezi and Kasane	07.00–18.00
Mohembo – on the C48, on the southern side of Mahango	06.00–18.00
Dobe – between Tsumkwe and Nokaneng	08.00–18.00
Buitepos – on the B6 Gobabis–Ghanzi road	07.00–midnight

With South Africa

Mata-Mata – on C15, bordering Kgalagadi Transfrontier Park	08.00–16.30
Klein Menasse – on C16 Aroab–Rietfontein road	08.00–22.00
Hohlweg – on D622 southeast of Aroab	08.00–16.30
Ariamsvlei – on B3 Karasburg–Upington road	24 hours
Velloosdrif – on C10 southeast of Karasburg	08.00–22.00
Noordoewer – on B1 Windhoek–Cape Town road	24 hours
Sendelingsdrift – ferry across the Orange River within Ai-Ais Richtersveld Transfrontier Park	08.00–16.30
Oranjemund – bridge over the Orange River	06.00–22.00

By rail and coach For details of rail and coach services across the border from South Africa and Zimbabwe, see *Chapter 7*.

WHAT TO TAKE

This is difficult advice to give, as it depends upon how you travel and your own personality. If you intend to do a lot of hitching or backpacking, then you should plan carefully what you take in an attempt to keep things as light as possible. If you have a vehicle for your whole trip, then weight and bulk will not be such an issue.

CLOTHING During the day you will usually want light, loose-fitting clothing. Cotton (or a cotton-rich mix) is cooler and more absorbent than synthetic fibres. For men, shorts (long ones) are fine, but long trousers are more socially acceptable in towns and especially in rural settlements and villages. For women, knee-length or long skirts, long shorts, or loose trousers are best. Namibia has a generally conservative dress code, and revealing or scruffy clothing isn't generally respected or appreciated. If you're spending time on safari, try to keep to neutral colours: green, khaki and dust-brown are the norm.

For the evenings, especially for chilly rides in the back of safari vehicles and during rainstorms, you will need something warm. This is particularly important in the winter months (July to October), when night-time temperatures can dip below freezing, especially in desert areas. If possible, dress in layers, taking along a light sweater or fleece and a long-sleeved jacket, or a tracksuit, a light but waterproof anorak, and maybe a down jacket in winter. Note that some excellent cotton safari wear is produced and sold locally; try the department stores in Windhoek or the shops at Johannesburg Airport.

Finally, don't forget a squashable sunhat. Cotton is perfect. Bring one for safety's sake, even if you hate hats, as it will greatly reduce the chance of your getting sunstroke when out walking.

OTHER USEFUL ITEMS See page 156 for information on recommended types of camping equipment to take. In addition, below I have outlined a few of my own favourites and essentials, just to jog your memory:

- sunblock and lipsalve – vital for protection from the sun
- sunglasses – essential – ideally dark with a high UV absorption
- insect repellent, especially if travelling to the north or during the rains
- binoculars – essential for watching wildlife and birds
- camera – a long lens is vital for good wildlife shots
- 'Leatherman' multi-purpose tool
- electrical insulating tape – remarkably useful for general repairs
- basic sewing kit, with at least some really strong thread for repairs
- cheap waterproof watch (leave expensive ones, and jewellery, at home)
- couple of paperback novels
- CDs to play in hire cars
- large plastic 'bin-liner' (garbage) bags, for protecting your luggage from dust
- simple medical kit
- magnifying glass, for looking at some of the smaller attractions
- a couple of cheap walkie-talkies if travelling in convoy
- torch (flashlight) – LED Lenser torches are particularly good and worth the investment

Useful extras, especially for backpackers and those staying in budget accommodation, might include:

- concentrated, biodegradable washing powder or liquid
- long-life candles – African candles are often soft, and burn quickly
- nylon 'paracord' – at least 20m for emergencies and washing lines
- good compass and a whistle
- more comprehensive medical kit (page 124)
- universal plug

MAPS AND NAVIGATION A reasonable selection of maps is available in Europe and the USA from specialised outlets. The Michelin map of East and southern Africa (sheet 995) sets the standard for the whole subcontinent, but is not really detailed enough for Namibia. Better maps are those published by Map Studio and Globetrotter, which both contain town plans. For online maps, it is worth taking a look at www.map-of-namibia.com, an offshoot of the exhaustive website www.namibia-1on1.com. Imported maps are obtainable in Britain from Stanfords at 7 Mercer Walk, Covent Garden, London, WC2H 9FA (✆020 7836 1321; www.stanfords.co.uk) or in the USA from East View Geospatial (✆+1 952 252 1205; www.geospatial.com). Another useful source is one of the bookshops at Johannesburg Airport.

Many overland travellers with a GPS (see box, page 112) would be lost (sometimes quite literally) without Tracks4Africa (www.tracks4africa.co.za), a digital mapping software package that covers the whole continent – or you can download the regional maps separately. That said, it is only compatible with Garmin devices, and while the Tracks4Africa mobile app is often useful, it isn't as good at the real thing, being decidedly hit and miss in certain areas. A good alternative is the free maps.me app. I wouldn't recommend that travellers rely on Google maps: it's not (yet?) the right tool for driving in the bush. For all of these, you should certainly download any apps and maps that you want before you leave home, so you can use your device offline. Data roaming is prohibitively expensive, and even using a local SIM would leave you with a significant phone bill.

An excellent range of detailed, albeit very old, 'Ordnance Survey' type maps of Namibia is available cheaply in Windhoek from the Surveyor General's office (page 172). If you are planning a 4x4 expedition, then you may need to buy some of these before you head out into the bush. However, for most normal visitors on self-drive or guided trips, these maps are *far* too detailed and unwieldy to use. Much better is the TASA map, with a street plan of Windhoek, which is perfectly adequate for self-drive trips on Namibia's roads. It is available from some of the better specialist tour operators, as well as fairly widely in shops and fuel stations in Namibia.

ELECTRICITY Sockets usually supply alternating current at 220/240V and 50Hz. These are the same as South African sockets (the very old standard British design) with three round pins. Adaptors for these are usually easiest to find in Jo'burg Airport or Windhoek; you may struggle to find them elsewhere.

PHOTOGRAPHY AND OPTICS Away from centres such as Windhoek and Swakopmund, optical equipment isn't widely available in Namibia – so bring everything that you will need with you. If you're shooting film, and especially if you have a specific film that you want to use, bring a large stock with you.

GPS SYSTEMS

If you are heading into one of the more remote parks in your own vehicle, then you really should invest in a hand-held GPS (global positioning system). These can fix your latitude, longitude and elevation to within about 10m, using a network of American military satellites that constantly pass in the skies overhead. They will work anywhere on the globe.

Although many smartphones incorporate GPS receivers, don't be fooled into thinking that they're anywhere near as good as a dedicated GPS unit in the more rural areas – they're not.

WHAT TO BUY Commercial hand-held GPS units cost from around £80/US$150 in Europe or the USA. As is usual with high-tech equipment, their prices are falling and their features are expanding as time progresses.

I have been using a variety of Garmin GPS receivers for years now. The early ones ate batteries at a great rate and often took ages to 'fix' my position; more recent models not only have endless new functions and far better displays, but also use fewer batteries, fix positions much more quickly, and usually even work when sitting on the car's dashboard. Whatever make you buy, you don't need a top-of-the-range machine.

WHAT A GPS CAN DO A GPS should enable you to store 'waypoints' and build a simple electronic picture of an area, as well as working out basic latitude, longitude and elevation. So, for example, you can store the position of your campsite and the nearest road, making it much easier to be reasonably sure of navigating back without simply retracing your steps.

It will also enable you to programme in points, using the co-ordinates given throughout this book and by some of the maps listed on page 111, and use these for navigation. Thus you should be able to get an idea of whether you're going in the right direction, and how far away your destination is.

Namibia's scenery and wildlife are a big draw for photographers, but the country's harsh environment creates its own problems. Pictures taken around dawn and dusk will have the richest, deepest colours, whilst those taken in the middle of the day, when the sun is high, will seem pale and washed-out by comparison. Beware in particular of deep shadows and high contrast; a camera cannot capture the range of colours and shades that our eyes can. By restricting your photography to mornings, evenings and simple shots you will get better pictures and encounter fewer problems.

To mitigate the problems of dust, bring plenty of lens-cleaning cloths, and a blow-brush, and take great care not to get dust into the back of your camera, especially when changing lenses.

For tips on photography from wildlife experts Jonathan and Angela Scott, see the Bradt website: www.bradtguides.com/articles/phototips.

Camera insurance Most travel insurance policies are poor at covering valuables, including cameras. If you are taking valuable camera equipment abroad, then include it in your house insurance policy, or cover it separately with a specialist.

Binoculars A good pair of binoculars is essential if you're planning to incorporate a safari, or any birding, into your trip. They will bring you far more enjoyment than

When you return home, if you have a fast internet connection then knowing the GPS co-ordinates for a place will enable you to see satellite images of the place using programmes like Google Maps and Google Earth. See Expert Africa's website (*www.expertafrica.com*) for a demonstration of the satellite images of lodges that are possible.

WHAT A GPS CAN'T DO First, a GPS isn't a compass and, when you're standing still, it can't tell you which direction is which. It can only tell you a direction if you're moving. (That said, some of the more expensive GPS units do now incorporate electronic compasses that can do just this!)

Secondly, it can give you a distance and a bearing for where you might want to go but it can't tell you how to get there. You'll still need to find a track. You should NEVER just set out across the bush following a bearing; that's a recipe for disaster.

Finally, it can't replace a good navigator. You still need to be able to navigate and think to use a GPS effectively. If you're clueless on navigation then driving around any unfamiliar place, including Namibia, you may get you into a mess, with or without a GPS.

ACCESSORIES Most GPS units use quite a lot of battery power, so bring plenty of spare batteries with you. Also get hold of a cigarette lighter adaptor for your GPS when you buy it. This will enable you to power it from the car while you're driving, and thus save batteries.

WARNING Although a GPS may help you to recognise your minor errors before they are amplified into major problems, note that such a gadget is no substitute for good map work and navigation. They're great fun to use, but shouldn't be relied upon as a sole means of navigation. You MUST always have a back-up plan – and an understanding of where you are – or you will be unable to cope if your GPS fails.

a camera, as they make the difference between merely seeing an animal or bird at a distance, and being able to observe its markings, movements and moods closely. Do bring one pair per person; one between two is just not enough.

There are two styles: the small 'compact' binoculars, perhaps 10–12cm long, which account for most popular modern sales, and the larger, heavier styles, double or triple that size, which have been manufactured for years. For more on these, see box, page 18. The cheapest cost from around about £40/US$60, but to get a decent level of quality spend at least £200/US$300. In a different league entirely are top-of-the range binoculars manufactured by Swarovski and Leica. You will be able to see the difference when you use them.

MONEY

The Namibian dollar (N$) is divided into 100 cents. This is freely convertible in Namibia; there's no black market and no customs regulations applicable to moving it across borders. It is currently tied to the South African rand (R) so that N$1 = R1. Rand can be used freely in Namibia – nobody even notices. It is, however, often difficult to change Namibian dollars once you leave Namibia. Even in South Africa, you must change the dollars at a bank, and may be charged a small premium for doing so.

It is not possible to get Namibian dollars outside of Namibia. Exchange your currency for South African rand, and use that instead. You can get Namibian dollars out of local cash machines. Try to use up any Namibian change while you're still there; you won't be able to exchange it once you're home.

If the rand plummets in the future, then the government in Windhoek could take full control of its currency and allow it to float free from the rand. Namibia's economy is probably strong enough to make this a very positive move. Check the latest situation with one of the bigger banks before you leave.

For most of the late 1990s the rand slowly but steadily devalued, slipping from about £1 = R6 in 1996 to £1 = R12 in 2001. Then in late 2001 it tumbled down to almost £1 = R20, only to recover back to £1 = R12 in 2003. It remained around the £1 = R11–12 until 2012, but since then has been devaluing steadily. In May 2019, the rates of exchange were:

£1	= N$18.19
US$1	= N$14.37
€1	= N$16.05

Despite the volatility, travel in Namibia for the Western visitor remains largely good value compared with the rest of the region.

Prices in Namibia are subject to VAT at 15%.

HOW TO TAKE YOUR MONEY The best system is always to have some cash Namibian dollars (or rand – remember they are interchangeable) with you, while conserving these by using credit cards where you can. You can gradually withdraw more money from your credit or debit cards as your trip progresses. However, it's important to remember that there are long distances between towns and lodges, so be sure to assess your needs thoroughly in advance, and always make sure that your Namibian dollars will last until you can get to a bank or reliable ATM.

Cash in the form of Namibian dollars or South African rand is essential for buying fuel (credit cards are not always accepted) as well as for small items, and in remote areas. It is also useful for tipping when staying at lodges.

The major **credit cards** (Visa and Mastercard) are widely accepted by lodges, hotels, restaurants and shops, but American Express and Diners Club cards are often not accepted. Even the smaller towns now have ATMs, either as part of a bank, or inside a supermarket, and withdrawing cash by this means is usually no harder than at home. That said, Visa cards are easier to use than most. Whether you are using a debit card or a credit card, you should enter 'credit card account' and not 'bank account' when an ATM asks you where you want your money to come from. It is advisable to take at least two cards, and to notify your bank of your travel plans in advance of departure, in case of any attempted fraud while you're travelling.

The use of **travellers' cheques** has decreased substantially. You may find some banks still exchanging travellers' cheques, but don't rely on them. Cash and cards are much more reliable and the norm, so you will be fine with these.

For details of changing money, see opposite.

BANKS Namibia's major banks are FNB, Standard, Bank Windhoek and Nedbank, and most town-centre branches have ATMs. Note that FNB has close links with Barclays in the UK, and is best for Visa transactions, but if you're using Mastercard, then Standard is generally a better bet. That said, it's wise to take at least two cards, and to accept that the ATMs can be a bit hit and miss.

Changing money at any of the commercial banks is as easy and quick as it is in Europe – at least in the major towns. Away from these, you may come across problems with banking systems going down, or banks running short of cash, so it's best to allow for this when in Windhoek or Swakopmund. Normal banking hours are 09.00–15.30 weekdays and sometimes 09.00–11.00 Saturdays, depending upon the town; in major centres a few branches open seven days a week. Banks will in theory give cash advances on credit cards, though the clearance required for a cash advance may take 30 minutes or so and it doesn't always go through. Note that you may need to take a passport, even just to change currency. Be aware, too, that at the end of the month, when many employees are paid, queues at the bank can be several hours long.

BUDGETING Namibia genuinely offers something to suit travellers of every budget, with accommodation ranging from backpackers' hostels to luxurious lodges, with everything in-between. For an indication of budgeting for various styles of trip, see page 99.

TIPPING Tipping is a very difficult and contentious topic that is worth thinking about carefully; thoughtlessly tipping too much is just as bad as tipping too little.

Always ask locally what's appropriate; suitable levels of tipping vary significantly, so my guidance here can only be general. Helpers with baggage might expect a couple of Namibian dollars for their assistance. Restaurants will often add an automatic service charge to the bill, in which case an additional tip is not usually given. If they do not do this, then 10% would certainly be appreciated if the service was good.

At upmarket lodges, tipping is not obligatory, despite the destructive assumptions of some visitors that it is. If a guide has given you really good service, then a tip of about N$100 (£5/US$7) per guest per day would be a generous reflection of this. If the service hasn't been that good, then don't tip. Always tip at the end of your stay, not at the end of each day/activity, which can lead to the guides only trying hard when they know there's a tip at the end of the morning. Such camps aren't pleasant to visit and this isn't the way to encourage top-quality guiding. Give what you feel is appropriate in one lump sum, though before you do this find out if tips go into one box for all of the camp staff, or if the guides are treated differently. Then ensure that your tip reflects this – with perhaps as much again divided between the rest of the staff.

ACCOMMODATION

HOTELS, PENSIONS, LODGES AND CAMPS Namibia's hotels are without exception fairly clean and safe. Unless you choose a really run-down old-style hotel in one of the smaller towns, you're unlikely to find anywhere that's dirty. Generally you'll get what you pay for, with the level of choice outside Windhoek and Swakopmund improving year on year. All places in this guide have en-suite shower or bathroom unless otherwise stated.

Establishments are licensed as hotels, lodges, restcamps, etc, according to their facilities, though the distinction between a hotel and a lodge depends on its location – a hotel must fall within a municipal area; a lodge will be outside. Similarly, a guest farm must be a working farm, otherwise it will be classified as a lodge. They are also graded by stars, from one to five, but the system is more a guide to their facilities and size than the quality or service. A 'T' alongside the star rating indicates that the place has been judged suitable for tourists, while the number of 'Y's reflects the type of licence to serve alcohol (three 'Y's being a full licence).

Most bush camps and lodges are of a high standard, though their prices – and atmosphere – vary widely. Price is a guide to quality here, though not a reliable one. Often the places that have better marketing (ie: you've heard of them) cost more than their less famous neighbours that are equally good.

GUEST FARMS These are private, working farms that host small numbers of guests, usually arranged in advance. They are often very personal and you'll eat all your meals with the hosts and be taken on excursions by them during the day. Although many focus on German-speaking visitors, those mentioned here also welcome English-speaking guests (and will often make enormous efforts to make you feel at home).

Most guest farms have some game animals on their land and conduct their own game drives. One or two have interesting rock formations, or cave paintings to visit. Those listed in this guide usually encourage mainly 'photographic' visitors – those with a general interest in the place and its wildlife. Others that concentrate on hunters coming to shoot trophy animals have generally not been included. However, a few accept both hunters and 'photographic' guests, though the two rarely meet. If you don't hunt, but choose to stay at these places, ensure either that you are comfortable with hunting per se, or that there are no hunters on the farm while you are there. Arguments over dinner are surprisingly common.

Their prices vary, but are rarely less than N$1,000 per person per night – and usually nearer N$2,000. They usually include half board and sometimes a trip around the farm.

CAMPING Wherever you are in Namibia, you can usually find a campsite nearby. Even in remote areas, there may be a community campsite (see box, opposite) although, if you're far from any settlements, nobody bothers if you just sleep by the road.

The campsites that are dotted all over the country generally have good ablution blocks, which vary from a concrete shed with toilets and cold shower, to an

---

ACCOMMODATION PRICES AND PRICE CODES

Prices in this guide were correct at the time of research, but inevitably many will rise during the life of the guide. The price codes are intended both as a quick reference, and to give an enduring indication of how the cost of a night's stay at one establishment is likely to compare with others.

The price codes are typically based on the establishment's high-season rate for a double room with breakfast (B&B), but at the higher end may well include dinner, bed and breakfast (DBB), full board (FB), or even full board, drinks and activities (FBA). Thus while the symbols are designed as an indication of costs, they should be seen in the context of the rates that are given alongside for most lodges, along with an indication of what is included where it differs from B&B. Do note that single supplements may apply, averaging 20–30%, but often significantly higher.

$$$$$$$	N$12,000+ (US$800+)
$$$$$$	N$6,000–12,000 (US$400–800)
$$$$$	N$3,000–6,000 (US$200–400)
$$$$	N$1,500–3,000 (US$100–200)
$$$	N$750–1,500 (US$50–100)
$$	N$300–750 (US$20–50)
$	up to N$300 (up to US$20)

COMMUNITY CAMPSITES

With the backing of the government and the IRDNC (see box, page 15), several communities have opened small campsites, many under the auspices of NACSO (*www.nacso.org.na*) – the Namibian Association of CBNRM (Community-Based Natural Resource Management) Support Organisations.

Supporting these communities, by staying there and paying for their crafts, and by using their skills as guides to the local area, is a practical way in which visitors can help some of the poorest of rural people to raise both money and pride.

Many of these sites have only rudimentary facilities and simple ablutions, while others are more elaborate – but in almost all you will need a self-contained 4x4 with your own food and supplies.

immaculately fitted-out set of changing rooms with toilets and hot showers. The more organised ones will also have facilities for washing clothes, barbecue stands and electric points.

Prices nowadays are usually per person rather than per pitch, although at NWR sites in Etosha and Waterberg there is still a site fee as well. Rates vary widely, from around N\$110 per person per night at a community campsite, to N\$300 or more. There is sometimes an extra charge for a vehicle.

CHILDREN Many of Namibia's hotels, lodges and camps offer special rates for children, which can range from discounts to free accommodation to those sharing a room with their parents. Some go out of their way to cater for children, too, perhaps with a family room that has loft accommodation. Conversely, a few venues are not suitable for youngsters. It's always worth checking for the availability of any 'family rooms' when making your initial enquiries, as well as ensuring that your chosen location is suitable for children. However, don't expect anywhere to be completely free of risks for children; they will always need to be supervised to some extent.

EATING AND DRINKING

FOOD Traditional Namibian cuisine is rarely served for visitors, so the food at restaurants tends to be European in style, with a bias towards German dishes and seafood. It is at least as hygienically prepared as in Europe, so don't worry about stomach upsets.

Namibia is a very meat-orientated society, and many menu options will feature steaks from one animal or another. If you eat fish and seafood you'll be fine; menus often feature white fish such as kingklip and kabeljou, as well as lobster in coastal areas. Otherwise, most restaurants offer a small vegetarian selection, and lodge chefs will usually go out of their way to prepare vegetarian dishes if given notice.

Travellers with special dietary requirements, for example coeliacs, should be sure to notify the various hotels and lodges well in advance. While restaurant options have improved in recent years, the situation is patchy, so do bring gluten-free breads and snacks if you are likely to be away from the main centres.

In the larger supermarkets you'll find meat, fresh fruit and vegetables (though the more remote the areas you visit, the smaller your choice), and plenty of canned foods, pasta, rice, bread, etc. Most of this is imported from South Africa, and you'll probably be familiar with some of the brand names.

Traditional foodstuffs eaten in a Namibian home may include the following:

eedingu	dried meat
eendunga	fruit of the makalane palm, rather like a rusk
kapana	bread
mealiepap	form of porridge, most common in South Africa
omanugu	also known as mopane worms (*Imbrassia belina*) – these are fried caterpillars, often cooked with chilli and onion
ombindi	spinach
oshifima	dough-like staple made from millet
oshifima ne vanda	millet with meat

DRINK

Alcohol Because of a strong German brewing tradition, Namibia's lagers are good, the Hansa and Windhoek draughts being particular favourites. In cans or bottles, Windhoek lager and Tafel – from around N$30 – provide a welcome change from brands such as Castle that dominate the rest of the subcontinent, and now the occasional craft brewery is putting in an appearance too.

Although wine served in restaurants is mainly South African, an increasing number of drinkable wines are being produced in Namibia. The top South African wines match the best that California or Australia have to offer, and at generally lower prices. You can get a bottle of palatable wine in a restaurant from around N$175.

Soft drinks Canned soft drinks, from Diet Coke to sparkling apple juice, are available ice cold from just about anywhere – which is fortunate, considering the amount that you'll need to drink in this climate. They cost about N$10 each, and can be kept cold in insulating polystyrene boxes made to hold six cans. These cheap containers are invaluable if you are on a self-drive trip, and not taking a large coolbox. They are available from some camping stores such as Cymot for about N$50.

In an Ovambo home you may be offered *oshikundu*, a refreshing breakfast drink made from fermented millet and water.

Water The water in Namibia's main towns is generally safe to drink, though it may taste a little metallic if it has been piped for miles. Natural sources should usually be purified, though water from underground springs and dry river-beds seldom causes any problems. (See page 126 for more detailed comments.)

PUBLIC HOLIDAYS

During Namibia's public holidays the towns shut down, though the national parks and other attractions just carry on regardless.

New Year's Day	1 January
Independence Day	21 March
Good Friday	variable
Easter Monday	variable
Workers' Day	1 May
Cassinga Day	4 May
Africa Day	25 May
Ascension Day	40 days after Easter Sunday
Heroes' Day	26 August
Human Rights Day	10 December
Christmas Day	25 December
Family Day	26 December

SHOPPING

With the exception of supermarkets and convenience stores at fuel stations, shops are typically open from 08.30 to 17.00 Monday to Friday, and on Saturday mornings. In the larger towns, supermarkets often stay open all day Saturday and Sunday, but this is by no means always the case. In general, Namibia's towns become ghostlike at weekends – so if you're self-catering, do make sure that you plan ahead.

ARTS AND CRAFTS To access the whole range of Namibian regional arts and crafts in one place, visit the Namibia Craft Centre (page 196) in Windhoek. Outside of the capital, many towns have street markets selling curios, and numerous lodges showcase local arts and crafts, albeit sometimes at rather inflated prices. At grass-roots level, the number of local communities that have set up small-scale craft projects is growing, bringing employment and attracting revenue back to where both are needed. Many of these are within the fold of the Namibian Association of CBNRM (Community-Based Natural Resource Management) support organisations (*www.nacso.org.na*), and are well worth seeking out.

Many professional artists choose to sell their work at street markets rather than pay a gallery commission on any items sold, so high-quality arts and crafts can often be found by the roadside and on the pavements. In Kavango and Caprivi/Zambezi, you'll find good **woodcarvings** of various sizes sold on small stalls by the side of the road. However, the best selection is at the two huge street markets on either side of Okahandja (page 215). There are also some good buys to be had from street stalls in Windhoek, while for more unusual work, try Tikoloshe in Omaruru (page 458).

Bushman crafts are best bought either locally in the Tsumkwe area or at the Tsumeb Arts and Crafts Centre (page 489). Authentic **Himba crafts** are easiest to find in Kaokoland, where you will often be offered crafts by local villagers.

The best examples of **basketwork** are found in the northern arts and crafts co-operatives, which include the craft shop at Khorixas (page 403); Tsumeb Arts and Crafts Centre (page 489); Mashi Crafts, beside the B8 in Kongola (page 547); and the outdoor craft market in Katima Mulilo (page 558).

Swakopmund has several shops sellings crafted **leatherwork**. One of the best selections of **pottery** is found at the Katima Mulilo craft market (page 558).

Karakul rugs can be found at the Namibia Craft Centre, but specialists are Swakopmund's Karakulia and African Kirikara Arts and Crafts (page 343) and Kiripotib near Dordabis (page 227). For more on crafts, see page 94.

CRYSTALS AND GEMSTONES With rich deposits of natural minerals, Namibia can be a good place for the enthusiast to buy crystals and gems – but don't expect many bargains, as the industry is far too organised. For the amateur, the desert roses (gypsum crystals incorporating a lot of sand and creating forms like flowers) are unusual and often cheap, while iridescent tiger's eye is rare elsewhere and very attractive. If you're really interested, forget the agates on sale and look for the unusual crystals. In Windhoek, the House of Gems (page 196) and The Diamond Works (page 196) are a must, and Gallery 116 in Omaruru (page 457) has a fascinating collection. There are also Swakopmund's Stonetique (page 343) and Kristall Galerie (page 346).

MEDIA AND COMMUNICATIONS

POST The postal service, Namib Post, is efficient and reasonably reliable. A postcard or airmail letter to Europe or the USA costs N$8.50; delivery to Europe takes about a fortnight. For larger items, sending them by sea is much cheaper, but it may take up to three months and isn't recommended for fragile items. Philatelists might like to note that Namibia's stamps feature numerous designs, often focusing on wildlife.

Post offices are normally open 08.00–16.30 Monday–Friday, and those in towns also 08.00–noon Saturdays.

TELEPHONE AND FAX Dialling into Namibia, the country code is 264. Dialling out, the international access code is 00. In both cases, omit the first 0 of the area code. If you can find one that's working, you can dial internationally, without going through the operator, from any public phone box, provided you've a phonecard, or Telecard. These are available from post offices and several shops, including some supermarkets.

Almost all areas have direct-dial numbers, preceded by three-digit area codes like 061, 063 and 064, but the more recent 083 code – from a private operator rather than Namtel – could also precede a landline number. Mobile numbers usually start with 081.

Note that 'a/h' written next to a phone number means 'after hours' – ie: a number where the person is reachable in the evenings and at weekends. Often this is included for emergency contact, not for casual enquiries.

Mobile and satellite phones Mobiles work in much of Namibia, though not in the more remote areas of the country. If you plan to use your own mobile phone without a Namibian SIM card, contact your service provider to make sure you are set for global roaming including Namibia. However, unless you plan to use it only for emergencies, it's far cheaper to buy a local SIM card on arrival in Namibia and use this for the duration of your trip. Alternatively, mobile phones can be rented from various locations, including Windhoek International and Walvis Bay airports.

The main Namibian service provider, MTC, provides excellent coverage in almost all towns and in some (but not all) remote areas. Their MTC Traveller SIM card costs N$19.95, including N$19 airtime, with top-up cards of varying values available. If you plan to visit the more remote regions independently, it may be worth considering taking a satellite phone for emergencies.

INTERNET Internet access continues to grow, with relatively extensive coverage, and even 4G in major towns. That said, services are not always up to standard, so don't expect swift responses to all emails sent to Namibia. There are plenty of internet cafés in major towns, and most hotels and backpackers' lodges have internet facilities too – many with Wi-Fi access – though these can be unreliable.

THE PRESS There are no official press restrictions in Namibia, and generally there's a healthy level of debate and criticism in some of the media, although that's not to say that important issues don't sometimes escape public scrutiny because of powerful pressures on editors. In short, it's just like back home!

There is a choice of about seven commercial newspapers, which are easiest to obtain in the larger cities. Getting them elsewhere often means that you will be a few days out of date. *The Namibian* (*www.namibian.com.na*) has the widest circulation and is probably the best during the week, and the *Windhoek Observer* (*www.observer.com.na*) on Sunday is also good. Others include the daily *Namibia Economist* (*www.economist.com.na*) and the online state-owned *New Era* (*www.neweralive.na*), as well as a couple published in Afrikaans and German.

Aimed at the tourist are various colour magazines, including *Flamingo*, the in-flight magazine of Air Namibia (available online at *www.airnamibia.com/category/flamingo-magazine*), and the monthly *Namibia Tourismus* (*www.tourismus.com.na*), with articles in both English and German on travel, wildlife and conservation.

RADIO AND TELEVISION The government-sponsored Namibian Broadcasting Corporation (NBC; *www.nbc.na*) accounts for one public television channel and several radio stations. They broadcast radio in six languages from Windhoek, and in three from transmitters in the north of the country.

Among the commercial radio stations, which are primarily music-based, are Radio Wave, Kudu FM, Energy 100FM and Radio 99, a well as the German Hitradio Namibia and the Afrikaans Kosmos 94.1. Frequencies vary around the country, but can be difficult to receive away from Windhoek and the larger centres.

On television, satellite channels offer a variety of international news, sport and movies – the same the world over. By far the most common is the South African-based M-Net TV, which is installed in many of the larger hotels.

TRAVELLING POSITIVELY

Visitors spending significant amounts of money on their trip to Namibia are usually, by their mere presence, making some financial contribution to development and conservation in Namibia. Should you wish to do more, there are numerous organisations working to improve the lot of Namibia's most disadvantaged. Among the most worthwhile are the following, any of which would be delighted to suggest a worthwhile home for your donation – where every cent of your money will be put to good use, without causing any damage to the people that you are trying to help:

IRDNC (see box, page 15)
The Nyae Nyae Conservancy (page 500)
Save the Rhino Trust (see box, page 414)

There are also countless individual projects worthy of support. Seek out your own, or consider the **Bernhard Nordkamp Centre** in Windhoek (see box, page 174).

Volunteering Namibia hasn't been slow to take advantage of the upsurge in volunteering holidays. If working with animals appeals, consider contacting the Rare & Endangered Species Trust (REST; page 474), who have a volunteer programme, or the charitable foundation N/a'an ku sê (*https://naankuse.com*), who aim to rehabilitate orphaned and injured animals that are either released back into the wild or, when this isn't possible, remain on their sanctuary for study and education. The foundation also works with San Bushmen, providing them with education and schooling, and operates both N/a'an ku sê and Kanaan lodges (pages 186 and 291). On a smaller scale, there's the Bernhard Nordkamp Centre for children (see box, page 174).

Meanwhile, there are many pitfalls for unwary volunteers, so be sure to do your homework – especially if you are trying to get involved with a local community. An excellent place to start is www.ethicalvolunteering.org, which also has a downloadable pamphlet entitled *The Ethical Volunteering Guide*. Some of the many issues to consider include:

- For every bona fide organisation, there will be others who are willing to take your cash without delivering on their side of the deal.
- Try to be realistic about what your skills are; they will probably define what you can usefully contribute. Namibian communities don't need unskilled hobbyists; they need professionals. To teach skills properly takes years of volunteering, not weeks. (How long did *you* take to learn those skills?) So, for example, if you're not a qualified teacher or builder in your home country, then don't expect to be let loose to do any teaching or building in Namibia.
- Most volunteers will learn much more than the members of the communities that they come to 'help'; be aware of this when you describe who is helping whom.
- Make sure that what you are doing isn't effectively taking away a job from a local person.

Time in Namibia will do you lots of good; make sure it's not to the detriment of your hosts.

6

Health and Safety

with Dr Felicity Nicholson and Dr Jane Wilson-Howarth

There are always pitfalls when writing about health and safety for the uninitiated visitor. It is all too easy to become paranoid about exotic diseases that you may catch, and all too easy to start distrusting everybody you meet as a potential thief – falling into an unfounded us-and-them attitude towards the people of the country you are visiting.

As a comparison, imagine an equivalent section in a guidebook to a Western country – there would be a list of possible diseases and advice on the risk of theft and mugging. Many Western cities are very dangerous, but with time we learn how to assess the risks, accepting almost subconsciously what we can and cannot do.

It is important to strike the right balance: to avoid being excessively cautious or too relaxed about your health and your safety. With experience, you will find the balance that best fits you and the country you are visiting.

HEALTH

BEFORE YOU GO Sensible preparation will go a long way to ensuring your trip goes smoothly. Particularly for first-time visitors to Africa, this includes a visit to a **travel clinic** to discuss matters such as vaccinations and malaria prevention.

To help travellers prepare for a trip, the Bradt website carries a section on health in Africa (*www.bradtguides.com/africahealth*). While this elaborates on the information below, the following summary points are worth emphasising:

- **Insurance** Don't travel without comprehensive medical travel insurance that will fly you home in an emergency.
- **Immunisations** Having a full set of immunisations takes time, normally at least six weeks, although some protection can be had by visiting your doctor as late as a few days before you travel. No immunisations are required by law for entry into Namibia, unless you are coming from an area where **yellow fever** is endemic. In that case, a vaccination certificate is mandatory. To be valid the vaccination must be obtained at least ten days before entering the country. It is wise to be up to date on **tetanus**, **polio** and **diphtheria** (now given as an all-in-one vaccine, Revaxis, that lasts for ten years), hepatitis A and typhoid. Immunisations against hepatitis B and rabies may also be recommended. Immunisation against cholera is not usually required for trips to Namibia. Vaccination against **rabies** is now recommended for all visitors as there is an international shortage of rabies immunoglobulin (RIG), which is essential if you have not had three doses of vaccine before you travel. Experts differ over whether a BCG vaccination against **tuberculosis** (TB) is useful in adults: discuss this with your travel clinic.

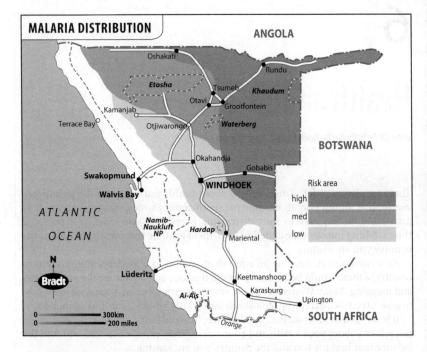

MALARIA DISTRIBUTION

ANGOLA

Oshakati

Etosha

Tsumeb

Rundu

Khaudum

Otavi

Kamanjab

Grootfontein

Terrace Bay

Otjiwarongo

Waterberg

BOTSWANA

Okahandja

Gobabis

Swakopmund

WINDHOEK

Walvis Bay

Risk area

ATLANTIC

high

OCEAN

Namib-Naukluft NP

Hardap

med

low

Mariental

N

Bradt

Lüderitz

Keetmanshoop

Karasburg

Ai-Ais

Upington

0 ——— 300km
0 ——— 200 miles

Orange

SOUTH AFRICA

- **Malaria** There is no vaccine against malaria, but preventative drugs are available, including mefloquine, atovaquone/proguanil (Malarone) and the antibiotic doxycycline. Malarone and doxycycline need only be started two days before entering Namibia, but mefloquine should be started two to three weeks before. Doxycycline and mefloquine need to be taken for four weeks after the trip and Malarone for seven days. It is as important to complete the course as it is to take it before and during the trip. The most suitable drug varies depending on the individual and the country they are visiting, so visit your GP or a specialist travel clinic for medical advice. If you will be spending a long time in Africa, and expect to visit remote areas, be aware that no preventative drug is 100% effective, so carry a cure too. It is also worth noting that no homeopathic prophylactic for malaria exists, nor can any traveller acquire effective resistance to malaria. Those who don't make use of preventative drugs risk their life in a manner that is both foolish and unnecessary.

- **First-aid kit** Anybody travelling away from major centres should carry a personal first-aid kit. Contents might include:

  – a good drying antiseptic (eg: iodine or potassium permanganate)
  – Band-Aids/plasters
  – suncream
  – insect repellent
  – paracetamol or other painkiller
  – antifungal cream (eg: Canesten)
  – ciprofloxacin or norfloxacin (for severe diarrhoea)
  – antibiotic eye drops
  – tweezers
  – condoms or femidoms

    – a digital thermometer
    – a needle-and-syringe kit with accompanying letter from a health-care
      professional.

- **Deep vein thrombosis (DVT)** Prolonged immobility on long-haul flights can
  result in DVT, which can be dangerous if the clot travels to the lungs to cause
  pulmonary embolus. The risk increases with age, and is higher in obese or
  pregnant travellers, heavy smokers, those taller than 6ft/1.8m or shorter than
  5ft/1.5m, and anybody with a history of clots, recent major operation or
  varicose veins surgery, cancer, a stroke or heart disease. If any of these criteria
  apply, consult a doctor before you travel.
- **Prescription drugs/devices** Bring any drugs or devices relating to known
  medical conditions with you. That applies to those who are on medication prior
  to departure, and those who are, for instance, allergic to bee stings, or prone
  to attacks of asthma. Always check with the country website to identify any
  restricted medications. Carry a copy of your prescription and a letter from your
  GP explaining why you need the medication.

TRAVEL CLINICS AND HEALTH INFORMATION A full list of current travel clinic
websites worldwide is available on www.istm.org. For other journey preparation
information, consult www.travelhealthpro.org.uk (UK) or www.wwwnc.cdc.gov/
travel (USA). Information about various medications may be found on www.
netdoctor.co.uk/travel. All advice found online should be used in conjunction with
expert advice received prior to or during travel.

IN NAMIBIA Although Namibia's doctor/patient ratio is one of the best in Africa,
health provision remains patchy, especially outside urban centres.

Hospitals, dentists and pharmacies
Namibia's main **hospitals** are good and
will treat you first and ask for money later. However, with comprehensive medical
insurance as part of your travel cover, it is probably better to go to one of the **private
clinics**. The main ones are in Windhoek and Otjiwarongo, and these are capable of
serious surgery and a good quality of care. There are also private medical facilities
in Swakopmund, Tsumeb and Walvis Bay.

If you've a serious problem outside of Windhoek, then contact **International SOS**
(✆ +27 11 541 1300; www.internationalsos.com), which organises medical evacuations
from anywhere. They do insure individual travellers, but many lodges are members,
covering you while you are staying there, and it may be that your insurers overseas
would ultimately pick up the International SOS bills if their services were needed.

Pharmacies in the main towns stock a good range of medicine, though often not
in familiar brands. Bring with you a repeat prescription for anything you may lose
or run out of.

Staying healthy
Namibia is probably the healthiest country in sub-Saharan Africa
for visitors. It has a generally low population density and a very dry climate, which
means there are comparatively few problems likely to affect visitors. The risks are
further minimised if you are staying in good hotels, lodges, camps and guest farms,
where standards of hygiene are generally at least as good as you will find at home.

The major dangers in Namibia are car accidents caused by driving too fast on
gravel roads, and sunburn. Both can also be very serious, yet both are within the
power of the visitor to avoid.

The following advice is applicable to travelling anywhere, including Namibia.

Food and storage Throughout the world, most health problems encountered by travellers are contracted by eating contaminated food or drinking unclean water. If you are staying in safari camps or lodges, or eating in restaurants, then you are unlikely to have problems in Namibia.

However, if you are backpacking and cooking for yourself, or relying on local food, then you need to take more care. Tins, packets and fresh green vegetables (when you can find them) are least likely to cause problems – provided that clean water has been used in preparing the meal. In Namibia's hot climate, keeping meat or animal products unrefrigerated for more than a few hours is asking for trouble.

Water and purification Tap water in Namibia's major towns and borehole water used in many more remote locations is perfectly safe to drink. However, even the mildest of the local microbes may cause slight upset stomachs for an overseas visitor. Two-litre bottles of mineral water are available from most supermarkets; these are perfect if you're in a car.

If you need to purify water for yourself in the bush, then first filter out any suspended solids, perhaps by passing the water through a piece of closely woven cloth or something similar. Then bring it to the boil, or sterilise it chemically with chlorine dioxide tablets (iodine is not considered to be safe to use any more). Boiling is much more effective, provided that you have the fuel available. By far the easiest solution is to use a filter bottle such as Aquapure, which filters out all microbes and minerals. It is very cost-effective and means that you can even drink river water if you need to.

Medical problems

Malaria Malaria is the most dangerous disease in Africa, and the greatest risk to the traveller. It occurs in northern, and occasionally central, Namibia (see map, page 124), so it is essential that you take all possible precautions against it (see box, opposite). Broadly, antimalarial tablets are recommended for the northern third of the country from November to June, and for the Okavango and Kunene rivers and the Zambezi Region (Caprivi Strip) all year round.

Since no malaria prophylactic is 100% effective, one should take all reasonable precautions against being bitten by the nocturnal *Anopheles* mosquitoes that transmit the disease. Malaria usually manifests within two weeks of transmission, but it can be as little as seven days and anything up to a year. Any fever occurring after seven days should be considered as malaria until proven otherwise. Symptoms typically include a rapid rise in temperature (over 38°C), and any combination of a headache, flu-like aches and pains, a general sense of disorientation, and possibly even nausea and diarrhoea. The earlier malaria is detected, the better it usually responds to treatment. So if you display possible symptoms, get to a doctor or clinic immediately (in the UK, go to accident and emergency and say that you have been to Africa). A simple test, available at even the most rural clinic in Africa, is usually adequate to determine whether you have malaria. You need three negative tests to be sure it is not the disease. And while experts differ on the question of self-diagnosis and self-treatment, the reality is that if you think you have malaria and are not within easy reach of a doctor, it would be wisest to start treatment.

Travellers' diarrhoea Many visitors to unfamiliar destinations suffer a dose of travellers' diarrhoea, usually as result of imbibing contaminated food or water. Rule

AVOIDING MOSQUITO AND INSECT BITES

The *Anopheles* mosquitoes that spread malaria are active at dusk and after dark. Most bites can thus be avoided by covering up at night. This means donning a long-sleeved shirt, trousers and socks from around 30 minutes before dusk until you retire to bed, and applying a DEET-based insect repellent to any exposed flesh. It is best to sleep under a net, or in an air-conditioned room, though burning a mosquito coil and/or sleeping under a fan will also reduce (though not entirely eliminate) bites. Travel clinics usually sell a good range of nets and repellents, as well as Permethrin treatment kits, which will render even the tattiest net a lot more protective, and helps prevent mosquitoes from biting through a net when you roll against it. These measures will also do much to reduce exposure to other nocturnal biters. Bear in mind, too, that most flying insects are attracted to light: leaving a lamp standing near a tent opening or a light on in a poorly screened hotel room will greatly increase the insect presence in your sleeping quarters. It is also advisable to think about avoiding bites when walking in the countryside by day, especially in wetland habitats, which often teem with diurnal mosquitoes. Wear a long loose shirt and trousers, preferably 100% cotton, as well as proper walking or hiking shoes with heavy socks (the ankle is particularly vulnerable to bites), and apply a DEET-based insect repellent to any exposed skin.

one in avoiding diarrhoea and other sanitation-related diseases is to wash your hands regularly, particularly before snacks and meals. As for what food you can safely eat, a useful maxim is: PEEL IT, BOIL IT, COOK IT OR FORGET IT. This means that fruit you have washed and peeled yourself should be safe, as should hot cooked foods. However, raw foods, cold cooked foods, salads, fruit salads prepared by others, ice cream and ice are all risky. It is rarer to get sick from drinking contaminated water but it happens, so stick to bottled water, which is widely available. If you suffer a bout of diarrhoea, it is dehydration that makes you feel awful, so drink lots of water and other clear fluids. These can be infused with sachets of oral rehydration salts, though any dilute mixture of sugar and salt in water will do you good, for instance a bottled soda with a pinch of salt. If diarrhoea persists beyond a couple of days, it is possible it is a symptom of a more serious sanitation-related illness (typhoid, cholera, hepatitis, dysentery, worms, etc), so get to a doctor. If the diarrhoea is greasy and bulky, and is accompanied by sulphurous (eggy) burps, one likely cause is giardia, which is best treated with tinidazole (four x 500mg in one dose, repeated seven days later if symptoms persist). Cirprofloxacin (500mg), one tablet repeated 10–12 hours later will work for travellers' diarrhoea in most cases. Alternatively, 4 x 250mg of azithromycin taken as one dose can also be used. The latter is also useful in cases of bacillary dysentery where you are unable to access medical help quickly.

Rifaximin is a newer treatment for simple travellers' diarrhoea which is not absorbed into the body so is less likely to cause side effects associated with taking antibiotics. It can only be used in those aged 18 and over but is a useful addition to a medical pack for those who are particularly susceptible to travellers' diarrhoea or for those travelling more remotely. A three-day course is needed and is only available on prescription.

Bilharzia Also known as schistosomiasis, bilharzia is an unpleasant parasitic disease transmitted by freshwater snails most often associated with reedy shores where there is lots of water weed. It cannot be caught in hotel swimming pools or the ocean, but should be assumed to be present in any freshwater river, pond, lake or similar habitat, even those advertised as 'bilharzia free'. The most risky shores will be within 200m of villages or other places where infected people use water, wash clothes, etc. Ideally, however, you should avoid swimming in any fresh water other than an artificial pool. If you do swim, you'll reduce the risk by applying DEET insect repellent first, staying in the water for under 10 minutes, and drying off vigorously with a towel. Bilharzia is often asymptomatic in its early stages, but some people experience an intense immune reaction, including fever, cough, abdominal pain and an itching rash, around four to six weeks after infection. Later symptoms vary but often include a general feeling of tiredness and lethargy. Bilharzia is difficult to diagnose, but it can be tested for at specialist travel clinics, ideally at least six weeks after likely exposure. Fortunately, it is easy to treat at present.

Rabies This deadly disease can be carried by any mammal and is usually transmitted to humans via a bite or a scratch that breaks the skin. In particular, beware of village dogs and monkeys habituated to people, but assume that any mammal that bites or scratches you (or even licks) might be rabid, even if it looks healthy. First, scrub the wound with soap under a running tap for a good 10–15 minutes, or while pouring water from a jug, then pour on a strong iodine or alcohol solution, which will guard against infections and might reduce the risk of the rabies virus entering the body. Pre-exposure vaccination for rabies is ideally advised for everyone, but is particularly important if you intend to have contact with animals and/or are likely to be more than 24 hours away from medical help. Ideally three doses should be taken over a minimum of 21 days; however, there is now a more rapid course of three doses over seven days when time is short. This super-accelerated schedule requires an additional dose after a year to complete the primary course. All three doses are needed in order to change the treatment needed following an exposure.

If you are bitten, scratched or even licked by a mammal, post-exposure prophylaxis should be given as soon as possible, although it is never too late to seek help, as the incubation period for rabies can be very long. Those who have not been immunised before will need four/five doses of rabies vaccine given over 28–30 days and should also receive a product called Human Rabies Immunoglobulin (HRIG), particularly if they have been bitten or deeply scratched. The HRIG is injected round the wound to try to neutralise any rabies virus present and is a key part of the treatment in higher-risk exposures if you have not had pre-exposure vaccine. HRIG is expensive and is not readily available as there is a global shortage, so it is important to insist on getting to a place that has it. This is another reason for having good insurance. As a last resort, equine RIG (horse serum) can be used and is definitely better than nothing.

Tell the doctor if you have had pre-exposure vaccine, as this will change the treatment you receive. You will no longer need to have RIG and will only need a couple of doses of vaccine, ideally given three days apart. And remember that, if you do contract rabies, mortality is 100% and death from rabies is probably one of the worst ways to go.

Tetanus Tetanus is caught through deep dirty wounds, including animal bites, so ensure that such wounds are thoroughly cleaned. Immunisation protects for ten years, provided you don't have an overwhelming number of tetanus bacteria on board. If you haven't had a tetanus shot in ten years, or you are unsure, get a booster immediately.

TICK REMOVAL

Ticks should ideally be removed complete, and as soon as possible, to reduce the chance of infection. You can use special tick tweezers, which can be bought in good travel shops, or failing this with your finger nails, grasping the tick as close to your body as possible, and pulling it away steadily and firmly at right angles to your skin without jerking or twisting. Irritants (eg: Olbas oil) or lit cigarettes are to be discouraged since they can cause the ticks to regurgitate and therefore increase the risk of disease. Once the tick is removed, if possible douse the wound with alcohol (any spirit will do), soap and water, or iodine. If you are travelling with small children, remember to check their heads, and particularly behind the ears, for ticks. Spreading redness around the bite and/or fever and/or aching joints after a tick bite imply that you have an infection that requires antibiotic treatment. In this case seek medical advice.

HIV/AIDS Rates of HIV/AIDS infection are high in most parts of Africa, and other sexually transmitted diseases are rife. Condoms (or femidoms) greatly reduce the risk of transmission.

Tick bites Ticks in Africa are not the rampant disease transmitters that they are in the Americas, but they may spread tick-bite fever along with a few dangerous rarities.

Skin infections Any mosquito bite or small nick is an opportunity for a skin infection in warm humid climates, so clean and cover the slightest wound in a good drying antiseptic such as dilute iodine, potassium permanganate or crystal (or gentian) violet. Fungal infections also get a hold easily in hot moist climates so wear 100%-cotton socks and underwear and shower frequently.

Eye problems Bacterial conjunctivitis (pink eye) is a common infection in Africa, particularly for contact-lens wearers. Symptoms are sore, gritty eyelids that often stick closed in the morning. They will need treatment with antibiotic drops or ointment. Lesser eye irritation should settle with bathing in salt water and keeping the eyes shaded. If an insect flies into your eye, extract it with great care, ensuring you do not crush or damage it, otherwise you may get a nastily inflamed eye from toxins secreted by the creature. Small elongated red-and-black blister beetles carry warning colouration to tell you not to crush them anywhere against your skin.

Sunstroke and dehydration Overexposure to the sun can lead to short-term sunburn or sunstroke, and increases the long-term risk of skin cancer. Wear a T-shirt and waterproof sunscreen when swimming. On safari or walking in the direct sun, cover up with long, loose clothes, wear a hat, and use sunscreen. The glare and the dust can be hard on the eyes, so bring UV-protecting sunglasses. A less direct effect of the tropical heat is dehydration, so drink more fluids than you would at home.

Other insect-borne diseases Although malaria is the insect-borne disease that attracts the most attention in Africa, and rightly so, there are others, most too uncommon to be a significant concern to short-stay travellers. These include dengue fever and other arboviruses (spread by day-biting mosquitoes), sleeping sickness (tsetse flies), and river blindness (blackflies). Bearing this in mind, however, it is clearly sensible, and makes for a more pleasant trip, to avoid insect bites as far as possible. Two nasty (though ultimately relatively harmless) flesh-eating insects associated with tropical Africa are tumbu or putsi flies, which lay eggs, often on drying laundry, that hatch and bury themselves under the skin when they come into contact with humans, and jiggers, which latch on to bare feet and set up home, usually at the side of a toenail, where they cause a painful boil-like swelling. Drying laundry indoors and wearing shoes are good ways of deterring this pair of flesh-eaters. Symptoms and treatment of these afflictions are described in detail on Bradt's website (*www.bradtguides.com*).

Prickly heat A fine pimply rash on the trunk is likely to be heat rash; cool showers, dabbing dry, and talc will help. Treat the problem by slowing down to a relaxed schedule, wearing only loose, baggy, 100%-cotton clothes and sleeping naked under a fan; if it's bad you may need to check into an air-conditioned hotel room for a while.

Hepatatis This is a group of viral diseases which generally start with Coca-Cola-coloured urine and light-coloured stools. It progresses to fevers, weakness, jaundice (yellow skin and eyeballs) and abdominal pains caused by a severe inflammation of the liver. There are several forms, of which the two most common are typical of the rest: hepatitis A (or infectious hepatitis) and hepatitis B (or serum hepatitis).

Hepatitis A and hepatitis E are spread by the faecal–oral route, that is by ingesting food or drink contaminated by excrement. They are avoided in the same ways you normally avoid stomach problems: by careful preparation of food and by drinking only clean water. But as there are now excellent vaccines against hepatitis A it is certainly worth getting inoculated before you travel (page 123). In contrast, the more serious but rarer hepatitis B is spread in the same way as HIV (by blood or body secretions), and is avoided the same way as one avoids HIV.

There is also a vaccine against hepatitis B. In most cases, with lots of bed rest and a good low-fat, no-alcohol diet, most people recover within six months. If you are unlucky enough to contract hepatitis of any form, use your travel insurance to fly straight home.

Sleeping sickness or trypanosomiasis This is really a cattle disease, which is rarely caught by people. It is spread by bites from the distinctive tsetse fly – which is slightly larger than a housefly, and has pointed mouth-parts designed for sucking blood. The bite is painful. These flies are easily spotted as they bite during the day, and have distinctive wings which cross into a scissor shape when they are resting. They are not common in Namibia, but do occur occasionally in Bushmanland and the Caprivi. Note that not all tsetses carry the disease. Prevention is easier than cure, so avoid being bitten by covering up. Chemical insect repellents are also helpful. Dark colours, especially blue, are favoured by the flies, so avoid wearing these if possible.

Tsetse bites are nasty, so expect them to swell up and turn red – that is a normal allergic reaction to any bite. The vast majority of tsetse bites will do only this. However, if the bite develops into a boil-like swelling after five or more days, and a fever starts two or three weeks later, then seek immediate medical treatment to avert permanent damage to your central nervous system. The name 'sleeping sickness' refers to a daytime drowsiness which is characteristic of the later stages of the disease.

Because this is a rare complaint, most doctors in the West are unfamiliar with it. If you think that you may have been infected, draw their attention to the possibility. Treatment is straightforward, once a correct diagnosis has been made.

RETURNING HOME Many tropical diseases have a long incubation period, and it is possible to develop symptoms weeks or months after returning home (so it is vital that you keep taking antimalaria prophylaxis for the prescribed duration after you leave a malarial zone). If you do get ill after your return, tell your doctor where you have been. Alert him/her to any diseases that you may have been exposed to. Several people die from malaria in the UK every year because victims do not seek medical help promptly or their doctors are not familiar with the symptoms and are slow to make a correct diagnosis. Milder forms of malaria may take up to a year to reveal themselves, but serious (falciparum) malaria will usually become apparent within four months. If problems persist, get a check-up at a hospital that specialises in tropical diseases.

SAFETY

WILD ANIMALS Don't confuse habituation with domestication. Most wildlife in Africa is genuinely wild, and widespread species such as hippo or hyena might attack a person given the right set of circumstances. Such attacks are rare, however, and they almost always stem from a combination of poor judgement and poorer luck. A few rules of thumb: never approach potentially dangerous wildlife on foot except in the company of a trustworthy guide; never swim in lakes or rivers without first seeking local advice about the presence of crocodiles or hippos; never get between a hippo and water; and never leave food (particularly meat or fruit) in the tent where you'll sleep.

SNAKE AND OTHER BITES Snakes are secretive and bites are a real rarity, but certain spiders and scorpions can also deliver nasty bites. In all cases, the risk is minimised by wearing closed shoes and trousers when walking in the bush, and watching where you put your hands and feet, especially in rocky areas or when gathering firewood. Only a fraction of snakebites deliver enough venom to be life-threatening, but it is important to keep the victim calm and inactive, and to seek urgent medical attention.

CAR ACCIDENTS Dangerous driving is probably the biggest threat to life and limb in most parts of Africa. On a self-drive visit, drive defensively, being especially wary of stray livestock, gaping pot-holes, and imbecilic or bullying overtaking manoeuvres. Many vehicles lack headlights and most local drivers are reluctant headlight users, so avoid driving at night and pull over in heavy storms. On a chauffeured tour, don't be afraid to tell the driver to slow or calm down if you think he is too fast or reckless.

CRIME Namibia is not a dangerous country, and is generally surprisingly crime-free. Outside of the main cities, crime against visitors, however minor, is exceedingly rare. Even if you are travelling on local transport on a low budget, you are likely to experience numerous acts of random kindness, but not crime. It is certainly no more dangerous for visitors than most of the UK, USA or Europe.

That said, there are increasing reports of theft and muggings, in particular from visitors to Windhoek, so here as in any other city it is important not to flaunt your possessions, and to take common-sense precautions against crime. A

SAFETY FOR WOMEN TRAVELLERS   *Janice Booth*

When attention becomes intrusive, it can help if you are wearing a wedding ring and have photos of 'your' husband and children, even if they are someone else's. A good reason to give for not being with them is that you have to travel in connection with your job – biology, zoology, geography or whatever. (But not journalism; that's risky.)

Pay attention to local etiquette, and to speaking, dressing and moving reasonably decorously. Look at how the local women dress, and try not to expose parts of the body that they keep covered. Think about body language. In much of southern Africa direct eye contact with a man will be seen as a 'come-on'; sunglasses are helpful here.

Don't be afraid to explain clearly – but pleasantly rather than as a put-down – that you aren't in the market for whatever distractions are on offer. Remember that you are probably as much of a novelty to the local people as they are to you; and the fact that you are travelling abroad alone gives them the message that you are free and adventurous. But don't imagine that a Lothario lurks under every bush: many approaches stem from genuine friendliness or curiosity, and a brush-off in such cases doesn't do much for the image of travellers in general.

Take sensible precautions against theft and attack – try to cover all the risks before you encounter them – and then relax and enjoy your trip. You'll meet far more kindness than villainy.

large rucksack, for example, is a prime target for thieves who may be expecting to find cameras, cash and credit cards tucked away in the pockets. Provided you are sensible, you are most unlikely to ever see any crime.

Most towns in Namibia have townships, often home to many of the poorer sections of society. Generally they are perfectly safe to visit during the day, but tourists should avoid wandering around with valuables. If you have friends or contacts who are local and know the area well, then take the opportunity to explore with them a little. Wander around during the day, or go off to a nightclub together. You'll find that they show you a very different facet of Namibian life from that seen in the more affluent areas. For women travellers, especially those travelling alone, it is important to learn the local attitudes about how to behave acceptably. This takes some practice, and a certain confidence. You will often be the centre of attention, but by developing conversational techniques to avert overenthusiastic male attention, you should be perfectly safe. Making friends of the local women is one way to help avoid such problems.

Theft Theft is rarely a problem in Namibia – which is surprising given the poverty levels among much of the population. However, there are a couple of exceptions to this rule. First, theft from unattended vehicles is common in Windhoek (especially), and other larger towns. If you leave your vehicle (for any length of time) with anything valuable on view or the doors unlocked, then you will probably return to find a window smashed and items stolen. Similarly, be wary of groups approaching a vehicle with open windows; there are occasional reports of theft while someone distracts the driver.

Sadly, in recent years there has been an increase in opportunistic muggings, particularly in Windhoek. Take extra care with your valuables and personal belongings – driving in the city is usually fine, but don't get out of your car in quiet areas or areas with thick vegetation. Viewpoints around the city are a hotspot for this kind of opportunistic theft, and it is easily avoided – just admire the view from your car!

If you are the victim of a theft then report it to the police – they ought to know. Also try to get a copy of the report, or at least a reference number on an official-looking piece of paper, as this will help you to claim on your insurance policy when you return home. However, reporting anything in a police station can take a long time, and do not expect any speedy arrests for a small case of theft.

Arrest To get arrested in Namibia, a foreigner will normally have to try quite hard. However, even though most Namibians are not paranoid about spies, it is always wise to ask for permission to photograph near bridges or military installations. This simple courtesy costs you nothing, and may avoid a problem later.

One excellent way to get arrested in Namibia is to try to smuggle drugs across its borders, or to try to buy them from 'pushers'. Drug offences carry penalties at least as stiff as those you will find at home – and the jails are worse. Namibia's police are not forbidden to use entrapment techniques or 'sting' operations to catch criminals. Buying, selling or using drugs in Namibia is just not worth the risk.

Failing this, argue with a policeman or army official – and get angry into the bargain – and you may manage to be arrested. It is *essential* to control your temper, and to stay relaxed when dealing with officials. Not only will you gain respect, and hence help your cause, but you will avoid being forced to cool off for a night in the cells.

If you are careless enough to be arrested, you will often only be asked a few questions. If the police are suspicious of you, then how you handle the situation will determine whether you are kept for a matter of hours or days. Be patient, helpful, good-humoured and as truthful as possible. Avoid any hint of arrogance. If things are going badly after half a day or so, then start firmly, but politely, to insist on seeing someone in higher authority. As a last resort you do, at least in theory, have the right to contact your embassy or consulate, though the finer points of your civil liberties may end up being overlooked by an irate local police chief.

Bribery Bribery may be a fact of life in some parts of Africa, but in Namibia it is very rare. Certainly no normal visitor should ever be asked for, or offer, a bribe. It would be just as illegal as offering someone a bribe back home.

7

Getting Around Namibia

DRIVING

Driving yourself around Namibia is, for most visitors, by far the best way to see the country. It is generally much easier than driving around Europe or the USA: many of the roads are excellent, the traffic is light and the signposts are usually clear, unambiguous and written in English.

Driving yourself gives you freedom to explore and to stop where you wish across the country, but it doesn't restrict you to your car every day. When visiting private camps or concession areas, you can often leave your hire car for a few days, joining daily 4x4 excursions into more rugged country, led by resident safari guides.

If possible, I'd recommend hiring a vehicle for your whole time in Namibia, collecting it at the airport when you arrive, and returning it there when you depart. This also removes any worries that you may have about bringing too much luggage (whatever you bring is simply thrown in the boot on arrival).

However, if your budget is very tight then you may only be able to afford to take a vehicle for just a few days, perhaps from Windhoek to Swakopmund via the Sesriem area, or to drive around Etosha. However long you keep the vehicle, the type you choose and the company you hire from can make an enormous difference to your trip.

HIRING A VEHICLE Think carefully about what kind of vehicle to hire, and where to get it from, well before arriving in the country. It is almost always better to organise this in advance. Similarly, check out the deals offered by overseas operators *before* you buy your flights. Arranging flights, car and accommodation with one operator, based in your home country, will usually be cheaper and easier than making all the bookings separately.

The normal minimum age to hire a car is 21, though many operators will accept drivers between the ages of 18 and 20 for an additional and often costly young-driver surcharge.

If time is not in short supply but money is, then you could consider hiring for just a few days at a time to see specific sights – which would not be too expensive if you are planning on sitting by waterholes in Etosha all day.

Hiring a car in one city and dropping it off elsewhere (even in another country) is perfectly possible with the major car-hire companies; just factor the relevant drop-off fee into your budget. Although these vary widely, depending on the distance and location, you'll probably be looking at a figure of approximately N$1,800 from Windhoek to Swakopmund, rising to about N$6,300 from Windhoek to the far north or south.

No matter where you hire your vehicle, do give yourself plenty of time when collecting and dropping it off. On collection you need to ensure that it's all in good order, including the spare wheel and tool kit, and that any existing damage is recorded;

then dropping it off, you need the car-hire company to sign off to confirm if there's any damage or not. Make sure that, if possible, you get the *final* invoice before you leave the vehicle, or you may return home to an unexpected credit-card bill. Do also note that companies will expect your vehicle to be in a reasonable state, and may charge for cleaning, particularly if the inside is unacceptably dirty.

Rates Typical current 'per day' on-the-road prices from the more reputable companies, based upon seven–13 days' rental in high season with unlimited mileage and their maximum insurance (see opposite) are:

Medium saloon eg: Toyota Corolla 1.6 or similar	£45/US$60
High-clearance AWD eg: Renault Duster or similar	£80/US$105
High-clearance rugged 4x4 eg: Toyota Hilux 4x4 D/cab	£100/US$130

The cheapest deals are usually available from local firms. Typically these have smaller fleets, often of older vehicles, and they seldom have the back-up support of the big companies. That's fine if you don't have problems, but you'll find that good support makes a massive difference if you have an accident or breakdown in a remote location. You will pay more for an automatic.

There's usually a cost for adding in a second driver, typically around N$350 per rental, plus an extra surcharge for drivers under 21 of around N$320 per day. In addition, a carbon emission tax of N$150 for all hire vehicles was imposed in September 2018.

2WD or 4x4? The type of vehicle you need depends on where you want to go. For virtually all of the country's main sights and attractions, and many of the more offbeat ones, a normal saloon 2WD car is adequate.

The only real exception to this advice is if you're travelling during the rains, around January to March, when you might consider taking a 4x4, just in case you need to ford any shallow rivers that block the road. Additional advantages of a 4x4 vehicle are:

* You relax more on gravel roads, knowing the vehicle is sturdier.
* You may be higher up, giving a slightly better view in game parks.
* It's easier to cross shallow rivers or sand patches if you encounter them.

However, the main disadvantages are:

* The cost of hiring a 4x4 is much higher than hiring a 2WD.
* 4x4s can be heavier to handle, and more tiring to drive.
* A 4x4's fuel consumption is much higher.
* 4x4s have higher centres of gravity, so tend to roll more easily.
* 4x4s sometimes lack a secure boot (trunk), so you can't safely leave bags in an unattended vehicle.

Between the two there is now a middle ground: the AWD. Broadly, these have replaced the old high-clearance 2WD vehicles, the main difference being that they have all-wheel rather than two-wheel drive. For the purposes of car hire, their key advantage is high clearance (which also gives you a better vantage point for wildlife watching). If you need a 4x4 to cope with the road conditions indicated below, this would not be a good substitute.

Regardless of any disadvantages, if you want to explore the northern Kunene Region, further than Tsumkwe in Bushmanland, or any of the really offbeat areas in the Caprivi – then you'll *need* a rugged 4x4. The main point is that in most of these more remote areas, just one 4x4 vehicle simply isn't enough. Your party needs to have a *minimum* of two vehicles for safety (a minimum of two vehicles is a condition of entry for Khaudum National Park), and you should have a couple of experienced bush drivers. These areas can be very dangerous if you drive into them alone or ill-equipped.

What kind of 2WD? This is really a question of budget. A small 2WD vehicle – the most basic typically being something like a Toyota Corolla – is adequate for two adults and most trips. If you've any flexibility in your budget, then it's usually worth stepping up to something larger to give you more power and comfort given the long drives involved in most trips. All but the most basic cars come with air conditioning, power steering and a radio/CD player.

High-clearance 2WDs, like the Nissan Qashqai or X-Trail (or similar), are gradually being phased out in favour of SUV crossovers, or AWDs (see opposite). In both cases, their higher wheelbase can be particularly useful, giving you some of the advantages of 4x4s mentioned above, but without the full cost. If you have three or four people in your party, then these are probably a better choice than any 2WD vehicle.

For a larger group, consider either two small cars or a VW Kombi (which seats eight). Two cars will give more flexibility if the group wants to split up on occasions. Conversely, the combis have lots of space to move around, and six window seats for game viewing. Their main disadvantage is that they lack a secure, hidden boot, so – as with most 4x4s – you can't safely leave the vehicle alone with any luggage in it.

What kind of 4x4? In order of increasing cost, the choice normally boils down to an SUV crossover (eg: Renault Duster), a single-cab or double-cab pick-up, known locally as a backie (eg: Toyota Hilux), or a larger 4x4 SUV (eg: Toyota Fortuner). Occasionally companies also offer more rugged vehicles still, such as the Land Rover Defender or Toyota Landcruiser 70 series, which are particularly useful for expeditions into the more remote corners of the country but do come at a premium. Makes and models change regularly but design and limits are very similar. The only relevant difference is that Toyotas and Nissans are generally more common, and hence their spares are easier to obtain. Conversely, spares – including tyres – for the SUV crossovers can be harder to find away from urban areas.

For two people, the single-cab pick-up is fine. This has just two seats (sometimes a bench seat) in the front and a fibreglass or aluminium canopy over the pick-up section at the back. This is generally lockable and good for keeping the rain off your luggage, but it many not deter theft and generally they aren't so good at keeping out dust. A double-cab will afford you a lot more space to move around and enable you to store cameras and drinks within easy reach.

For three or four people, you'll need the double-cab or the larger SUV type vehicle. The double-cabs are lighter vehicles, generally more comfortable and faster on tar. However, the Land Rovers (TDi or earlier models) and Landcruisers are mechanically simpler, and easier to mend in the bush – *if* you know what you're doing. Further, your luggage is inside the main cab, and so slightly safer, easier to access, and will remain a little less dusty. Five or more people will need the flexibility of two vehicles – more than four people with luggage in either of these is really quite squashed.

Insurance, CDWs and gravel roads Wherever you hire your vehicle, you must read the fine print of the hire agreement very carefully. The insurance and the collision

Distances between towns are only one part of the equation when calculating travelling times. More important are the type of road (tar, gravel, salt) and the terrain, both of which must be taken into consideration.

The distance chart is a triangular matrix. Each row lists the distances (in km) from the named town to each of the towns listed above it, in the column order of the diagonal labels.

Town	Distances to preceding towns
Aus	—
Buitepos	989
Epupa	1544 1171
Gobabis	898 115 1439
Grootfontein	1145 777 729 657
Henties Bay	798 786 733 630 645
Kamanjab	1156 783 388 688 425 345
Karasburg	346 1010 1541 895 1142 1115 1153
Karibib	876 501 802 388 403 242 414 873
Katima Mulilo	1422 1533 1470 1418 767 1404 1156 1901 1252
Keetmanshoop	211 802 1261 687 945 208 665 1693 208 1533
Khorixas	1149 777 501 662 419 234 113 1147 317 1150 982
Lüderitz	125 1136 1667 1021 1268 923 1273 471 999 2027 334 1273
Maltahöhe	249 692 1223 498 824 549 835 540 555 1583 332 829 374
Mariental	432 381 1112 466 713 686 724 429 444 1472 221 718 555 111
Namutoni	1226 863 791 738 167 677 506 1223 484 926 1015 500 1349 905 794
Noordoewer	442 1101 1637 991 1238 1211 1249 147 969 1997 304 1286 609 636 555 1319
Okahandja	764 393 780 276 381 395 392 761 112 1140 553 430 889 443 332 487 857
Okaukuejo	1128 753 650 640 397 579 256 1125 386 1128 917 256 1253 807 696 123 1221 364
Omaruru	937 562 741 339 342 254 453 934 61 726 505 448 1030 173 325 505 1461 173 474
Opuwo	1368 995 176 1263 637 557 212 1365 626 1085 1157 325 1491 936 604 615 565 604 1461 565
Oshakati	1401 708 387 913 342 852 681 1398 659 989 1190 675 1524 969 245 494 1080 245 368 969 320 598
Otavi	1174 683 732 568 87 507 336 1053 404 846 845 330 1080 524 170 190 1031 170 253 524 308 253 345 548
Otjiwarongo	938 565 706 450 207 389 218 935 197 946 727 121 1179 735 190 135 1174 174 190 135 345 191 73
Outjo	1011 638 533 523 280 462 145 1008 269 1011 800 139 1134 690 247 117 1104 208 357 436 191 208 357
Rehoboth	606 407 938 292 539 512 550 603 270 1298 395 544 729 285 174 620 699 158 522 331 762 795 450 332 405
Ruacana	1553 1180 235 1065 494 1143 272 1550 686 1253 1342 121 1676 1061 469 646 798 534 469 253 548 497 615 688 876
Rundu	1393 1020 977 905 248 893 645 1390 741 511 1182 639 1516 961 415 1486 629 617 590 135 430 463 500 787 742
Sesfontein	1389 1016 465 921 658 578 233 1386 647 1389 1178 346 1512 1068 625 1482 957 495 586 289 489 569 451 378 500 783 878
Sesriem	434 877 709 683 771 356 709 725 472 1530 517 615 559 185 296 852 821 390 754 533 992 682 564 637 261 878 1019 1015
Swakopmund	1051 676 802 563 60 412 175 1048 67 709 840 318 731 482 236 1494 619 287 561 236 624 834 489 371 445 323 261 297
Tsumeb	1237 746 670 631 399 570 377 1242 377 907 907 367 1242 798 687 107 1241 355 345 316 602 282 63 181 228 434 513 308 632 745
Tsumkwe	700 709 831 594 690 98 443 1079 206 1458 814 349 938 451 650 691 1175 318 593 655 866 521 403 476 715 750 545 550 795 914 1027 316
Walvis Bay	700 709 831 594 690 98 443 1079 206 1458 814 349 938 451 650 691 1175 318 593 655 866 521 403 476 715 947 947 676 673 946
Windhoek	693 320 851 205 452 466 463 690 181 1211 482 457 816 372 261 533 786 71 435 242 675 708 363 245 318 87 860 700 696 319 356 426 708 389

damage waiver (CDW) clauses are worth studying closely. These spell out the 'excess' or 'deductible' that you will pay in the event of an accident. The CDW excesses vary widely, and often explain the difference between cheap rental deals and better but more costly options.

Namibia has long proved to be a very bad country for accidents; paradoxically the problem is that the gravel roads are too *good*. If they were consistently poor and pot-holed, then people would go slowly. But instead they are often smooth, even and empty – tempting drivers to speed. This results in an enormous damage and write-off rate among the car-hire fleets. Generally this isn't due to collisions, but to drivers who are unfamiliar with the conditions going too fast on gravel roads and losing control on a bend, or losing concentration and falling asleep on a long, straight road. This phenomenon affects 2WDs and 4x4s equally.

Because of this, car-hire companies will sometimes have high excesses. A maximum 80% CDW is not unknown – which would mean that you will always pay 20% of the cost of any damage. With this level of cover, the bill for a major accident, even in a small vehicle, can easily run into thousands of pounds or US dollars.

Always check the fine print of the rental agreement, as some will have quite extreme clauses, stating for example that you are liable for *all* of the damage if you have an accident where no other vehicles are involved and you are driving on a gravel road. Do also check that all the areas you are planning to visit are covered; some policies specifically exclude places such as Kaokoland, Khaudum and the Sperrgebiet.

Driving over borders and one-way hire
Few car-hire companies will allow vehicles to be driven into Angola, Zimbabwe or Zambia. However, if a car-hire company has offices in Botswana and South Africa, you can *usually* take cars into these countries. Then you will need to advise the company in advance, as they need a few days to apply for the right permits and insurances – which is likely to cost an extra N$1,600 or so depending on the company. There's also usually an additional one-way fee; for example expect about N$5,000 from Namibia to South Africa or Botswana. Note that such fees, as well as car-hire rates, are usually asymmetrical: your car hire may be much cheaper from South Africa to Namibia than vice versa.

If you are planning to drive into Botswana from Namibia in a South African-registered vehicle, you will have to surrender any cross-border permit at the border post, or pay for a new one (which is immediately surrendered). Then as you enter Botswana you will pay for a short-term permit and road safety levy fee. On your return, you will need to buy a new cross-border permit.

One-way hire is usually possible, and it's usually easier to arrange with the larger companies, which have a more widespread network of offices, but expect fairly substantial amounts for larger distances from Windhoek. Similarly, for pickups/drop-offs that are not from/to an airport, there will usually be an additional delivery or collection charge, which often increases out of hours, over weekends and on public holidays, as well as in line with distance.

Car-hire companies
Most of the big car-hire companies, including Avis, Budget, Europcar and Hertz, have franchises in Namibia. Their prices tend to be similar, as do their conditions of hire, which leaves quality and availability as appropriate criteria for choosing between them. These vary in cycles depending on the competence of the general manager.

Aside from these large firms, there is a plethora of others, including smaller, local car-hire companies in Windhoek, some of which are good. Others have more dubious reputations, and even buy their cars from the big companies, which dispose of their vehicles after one or two years. This makes their rates cheaper, but compromising on the quality of your vehicle is crazy when you rely upon it so completely. Economise on accommodation or meals – but rent the best vehicle you can.

The following companies are based in Windhoek, though many also have offices in other Namibian towns. All the local companies, and international companies marked *, are members of the Car Rental Association of Namibia (CARAN; m 081 417 3797; www.caran.com.na), a voluntary grouping of the more responsible members of the trade. This lays down guidelines for standards and provides an informal arbitration service if things go wrong.

International companies

🚗 **Avis*** Hosea Kutako Airport \062 540271; Safari Hotel \061 233166; www.avis.co.za

🚗 **Bidvest*** Hosea Kutako Airport \062 540225; Eros Airport \062 228720; e reservations@bidvestcarrental.co.za; www.bidvestcarrental.co.za

🚗 **Britz** Hosea Kutako Airport \062 540242; www.britz.co.za

🚗 **Budget*** Hosea Kutako Airport \062 540271; Aviation Rd \061 233166; www.budget.co.za

🚗 **Europcar*** Hosea Kutako Airport \062 543700; 24 Bismarck St \061 385100; www.europcar.co.za

🚗 **Hertz*** Hosea Kutako Airport \062 540116; BRB Bldg, cnr A B May & Garten St \061 256274; e res@hertz.co.za; www.hertz.co.za

🚗 **Thrifty** Hosea Kutako Airport \062 540004; cnr Stein St & Sam Nujoma Dr \061 220738; Hilton Hotel \061 221165; e resnam@thrifty.com.na; www.thrifty.com.na

Smaller local companies

🚗 **Africa 4x4 Rentals** 16 Church St; \061 244266; m 081 125 2445; www.namibia4x4rentals.com

🚗 **African Sun** 22 Acacia St; \061 223388; m 081 148 4712/3; www.smiling-africansun.com

🚗 **African Tracks** 10 Pettenkofer St; \061 245072; e info@africantracks.com, tracks@iafrica.com.na; www.africantracks.com

🚗 **Asco** 195 Mandume Ndemufayo Av; \061 377200; e info@ascocarhire.com; www.ascocarhire.com

🚗 **Camel** 38 Jasper St; \061 248818; e info@camel-carhire.com; www.camel-carhire.com

🚗 **Camping Car Hire** 36 Joule St; \061 237756; e carhire@africaonline.com.na; www.camping-carhire.com

🚗 **Caprivi** Bessemer St; \061 256323; m 081 162 5791; e info@caprivicarhire.com; www.caprivicarhire.com

🚗 **Namibia Car Rental** Hosea Kutako Dr; \061 249239; m 081 122 2500; www.namibiacarrental.net; see ad, 4th colour section

🚗 **Odyssey** Bessemer St; \061 223269; m 081 127 2222; e odyssey@iway.na; www.odysseycarhire.com

🚗 **Okavango Car Hire** 124 Andimba Toivo Ya Toivo St; \061 306553; m 081124 1282; e info@okavango-carhire.com; www.okavango-carhire.com

🚗 **Pegasus** 81 Daan Bekker St; \061 251451; m 081 124 4375; e pegasus.carhire@gmail.com; www.pegasuscar-namibia.com

🚗 **Savanna** 80 Trift St; \061 229272; m 081 129 9978, 081 278 5222; www.savannacarhire.com.na

A warning Before signing up for a hire car, see the section on insurance on page 137. There is often fine print in these agreements which may mislead the unwary.

ON THE ROAD Almost all Namibia's major highways – usually B roads – are tarred, with dual carriageways designated as A roads. They are usually wide and well signposted, and the small amount of traffic on them makes journeys easy. Less important roads are often gravel, but even these tend to be well maintained and easily passable. The most important of these are C roads, with others usually classified as D, or the newer M classification (short for 'main') which sits between C and D roads.

You may also find minor roads classed as P or F; these are generally single-track farm roads and are not maintained by the Namibian roads authority. Confusion arises because many gravel roads have two or even three numbers – which is why in this guide you will sometimes find more than one number given for a particular road.

Many sights, with the exception of Sandwich Harbour, are accessible with an ordinary saloon car (referred to in this guide as 2WD). Only those going off the beaten track – into Khaudum, Bushmanland or northern parts of the Kaokoveld – need to join an organised group. The only safe alternative to such a group trip is a convoy of at least two 4x4s with at least as many experienced bush drivers. Don't be fooled into thinking that a 4x4 will get you everywhere and solve all your problems. Without extensive experience of using one on rough terrain, it will simply get you into dangerous situations which you have neither the skill nor the experience to cope with. See also page 143.

Some sources advise that you require an international driving permit in order to drive in Namibia, but a normal overseas driving licence with the requisite passport generally seems to be fine, if the licence is written in English. You'll be asked to produce documentation at roadblocks, so keep these to hand. British licence holders can obtain an international driving permit in the UK from post offices, the AA or the RAC; for the US counterpart, contact the AAA.

The speed limit in urban areas is generally 60km/h, and 120km/h on tar roads, but on gravel roads – where it is often clearly marked – it varies from 50 to 80km/h (see also page 142 for more on appropriate speeds). Driving is on the left.

EQUIPMENT AND PREPARATION Driving around Namibia is usually very easy; much easier than driving in most developed, industrialised countries. But because the distances are long, and some areas remote, a little more preparation is wise.

Fuel Petrol and diesel are available in all the major towns, and many more rural areas too. That said, do fill up whenever you have the opportunity. In an emergency, many farms will be able to help you – but you shouldn't need such charity if you think ahead a little. Prices will depend to a certain extent on where you are, but in October 2018 unleaded petrol in Windhoek cost around N$13.80 a litre, and diesel N$14.20. Debit and credit cards are an increasingly accepted means of payment, but don't rely on it.

If you are taking a small expedition into the northern Kaokoveld/Kunene Region, Bushmanland or the more obscure corners of the Caprivi/Zambezi Region, you will need long-range fuel tanks and/or a large stock of filled jerrycans, though for safety reasons, the latter should always be carried on the outside of the vehicle. It is essential to plan your fuel requirements well in advance, and to carry more than you expect to need. Using a vehicle's 4x4 capability, especially in low ratio gears, will greatly increase your fuel consumption. Similarly, the cool comfort of a vehicle's air conditioning will burn your fuel reserves swiftly.

It's worth knowing that if you need to transfer petrol from a jerrycan to the petrol tank, and you haven't a proper funnel, an alternative is to roll up a piece of paper into a funnel shape – it will work just as well.

Spares and repairs Namibia's garages are generally very good, and most larger towns have a comprehensive stock of spares for most vehicles. (Expect to pay over £50/US$65 for a new tyre for a small 2WD saloon, or around £9/US$14.50 for a repair in towns, but significantly more in rural areas and for both SUV and 4x4 vehicles.) You'll often find several garages specialising in different makes of vehicle.

In the bush you'll find that farm mechanics can effect the most amazing short-term repairs with remarkably basic tools and raw materials.

In an emergency, some of the better garages and tyre companies offer a call-out service based on a rate per kilometre.

Navigation The TASA map of the country, readily available in Namibia, is among the best for driving – but there are others. Note that many road numbers have changed in recent years, and continue to change, with several D roads being upgraded to C or M roads with entirely different numbers. The current TASA map indicates many of these changes and often gives multiple names for the same road, but local signposts may not match, so it's wise to take particular care in out-of-the-way places, and to seek local knowledge before setting off.

Those mounting expeditions may want to think about buying more detailed maps from the Surveyor General's office (page 172). If you are heading to the sand tracks of Bushmanland or the wilds of eastern Caprivi, then consider taking a GPS system. See page 111 for further comments.

DRIVING AT NIGHT Never plan to drive at night; this should be considered only as a last resort. Both wild and domestic animals frequently spend the night by the side of busy roads, and will even sleep on quieter ones. Tar roads are especially bad as the surface absorbs all the sun's heat by day, and then radiates it at night – making it a warm bed for passing animals. A high-speed collision with any animal, even a small one like a goat, will not only kill the animal, but will cause very severe damage to a vehicle, and have potentially fatal consequences for the occupants.

2WD DRIVING

Tar roads The vast majority of Namibia's tar roads are excellent. These already link most of Namibia's larger towns and the network is gradually extending. Most are single carriageways (one lane in either direction), and it's an effort to rein back the accelerator to remain within the speed limit of 120km/h. Even so, don't be tempted to speed. These roads are not as insulated from the surrounding countryside as the motorways, freeways and autobahns back home, and you will find hazards like animals crossing, as well as both mobile and fixed speed traps.

On main roads, regular picnic sites with a shaded table and benches (but no toilets) give the opportunity to stop for a break on long journeys. However, always exercise care; there are reports of these being used as ambush places by thieves.

Strip roads Very occasionally there are roads where the sealed tar surface is wide enough for only one vehicle. When you meet another vehicle travelling in the opposite direction on the same stretch of tar, the local practice is to wait until the last possible moment before you steer left, driving with two wheels on the gravel adjacent to the tar, and two on the tar. Usually, the vehicle coming in the opposite direction will do the same, and after passing each other both vehicles veer back on to the tar. It is wise to slow right down before you steer on to the gravel to avoid any nasty surprises.

Gravel roads Most roads in Namibia are gravel, and most of these are very good. Virtually all are fine for 2WD vehicles. They don't normally suffer from pot-holes, although there may be slight ruts where others have driven before you.

You will occasionally put the car into small skids, and with practice at slower speeds you will learn how to deal with them. Gravel is a less forgiving surface on which to drive than tar. The techniques for driving well are the same for both, but on tar you can get away with sloppy braking and cornering that would prove dangerous on gravel.

The main problem with Namibia's gravel roads is that they are too good. Drivers are lulled into a false sense of security; they believe that it is safe to go faster, and faster. Don't fall for this; it isn't safe at all (see the *Insurance, CDWs and gravel roads* section on page 137). Always drive at a speed appropriate for the conditions and your experience, keep your headlights on, and promise that you'll never drive faster than 80km/h on gravel. That way you'll return from a self-drive trip still believing how safe and good the roads are! A few hints for gravel driving in a 2WD vehicle may be helpful:

- **Slowing down** If in any doubt about what lies ahead, always slow down. Road surfaces can vary enormously, so keep a constant lookout for pot-holes, ruts or patches of soft sand which could put you into an unexpected slide.
- **Passing vehicles** When passing other vehicles travelling in the opposite direction, always slow down and give them a wide berth to minimise both the damage that stone chippings will do to your windscreen, and the danger in driving through the other vehicle's dust cloud. If the dust cloud is thick, don't return to the centre of the road too fast, as there may be another vehicle behind the first.
- **Using your gears** In normal driving, a lower gear will give you more control over the car – so keep out of high 'cruising' gears. Rather stick with third or fourth, and accept that your revs will be slightly higher than they might normally be.
- **Cornering and braking** Under ideal conditions, the brakes should only be applied when the car is travelling in a straight line. Braking while negotiating a corner is dangerous, so it is vital to slow down before you reach corners. Equally, it is better to slow down gradually, using a combination of gears and brakes, than to use the brakes alone. You are less likely to skid.

4X4 DRIVING Having a high-clearance 4x4 can extend your options considerably. However, no vehicle can make up for an inexperienced driver, so ensure that you are confident of your vehicle's capabilities before you venture into the wilds. You need lots of practice, guided by an expert, before you'll be able to handle the vehicle in difficult terrain. Driving in convoy is essential in the more remote areas, in case one vehicle gets stuck or breaks down. Some of the key techniques are outlined below.

Driving in sand If you start to lose traction in deep sand, then stop on the next piece of solid ground that you come to. Lower your tyre pressure until there is a distinct bulge in the tyre walls (having first made sure that you have the means to reinflate them when you reach solid roads again). A lower pressure will help your traction greatly, but it will also increase the wear on your tyres. Pump them up again before you drive on a hard surface at speed, or the tyres will be badly damaged.

Where there are clear, deep-rutted tracks in the sand, don't fight the steering wheel – just relax and let your vehicle steer itself. Driving in the cool of the morning is easier than later in the day because when sand is cool it compacts better and is firmer. (When hot, the pockets of air between the sand grains expand and the sand becomes looser.)

If you do get stuck, despite these precautions, don't panic. Don't just rev the engine and spin the wheels – you'll only dig deeper. Instead stop. Relax and assess the situation. Now dig shallow ramps in front of all the wheels, reinforcing them with pieces of wood, vegetation, stones, material or anything else which will give the wheels better traction. Lighten the vehicle load (passengers out) and push. You might consider reversing to get out of the hole you're in. When pulling away, don't

DRIVING NEAR ELEPHANTS

AVOIDING PROBLEMS Elephants are the only animals that pose a real danger to vehicles. Everything else will get out of your way, or at least not actively go after you, but if you treat elephants wrongly there's a chance that you might have problems.

To put this in perspective, most drivers who are new to Africa will naturally (and wisely) treat elephants with enormous respect, keeping their distance – simply out of fear. Also, in the more popular areas of Etosha, where the elephants are habituated to vehicles, you'd have to really annoy an already grumpy elephant for it to give you trouble.

To give specific advice is difficult, as every elephant is different. Each is an individual, with real moods and feelings – and there's no substitute for years of experience to tell you what mood they're in. However, a few basics are worth noting.

First, keep your eyes open and don't drive too fast. Surprising an elephant on the road is utterly terrifying, and dangerous for both you and the elephant. Always drive slowly in the bush.

Secondly, think of each animal as having an invisible 'comfort zone' around it. (Some experts talk of three concentric zones: the fright, flight and fight zones – each with a smaller radius, and each more dangerous.) If you actively approach then you breach that zone, and will upset it. So don't approach too closely: keep your distance. How close depends entirely on the elephants and the area. More relaxed elephants having a good day will allow you to get within 25m of them; bad-tempered ones that aren't used to cars may charge at 250m. You can often approach more closely in open areas than in thick bush. That said, if your vehicle is stationary and a relaxed, peaceful elephant approaches you, then you should not have problems if you simply stay still.

Thirdly, never beep your horn or flash your lights at an elephant (and if at night, you shouldn't be driving yourself anyhow). Either is guaranteed to annoy it. If there's an elephant in your way, just sit back, relax and wait; elephants always have right of way in Africa! The more sound and fury – like wheel spins and engine revving – the more likely that the elephant will assume that you are attacking it, and this is especially the case with a breeding herd.

Finally, look carefully at the elephant(s):

- Are there any small calves around in the herd? If so, expect the older females to be easily annoyed and very protective; keep your distance.
- Are there any males in 'musth' around? These are fairly easy to spot because of a heavy secretion from the penis and the temporal glands (on the sides of their heads), and a very musty smell. Generally they will be alone, unless they are with a cow on heat. Such males will be excitable; you must spot them and give them a wide berth.
- Are there any elephants with a lot of seepage from their temporal glands? If so, beware: expect them to be stressed and easily irritable. This is likely to have a long-term cause – perhaps lack of good water, predator pressure or something as random as toothache – but whatever the cause that animal is under stress, and should be given an extra-wide berth.

let the engine revs die as you engage a low ratio gear, and use the clutch to ensure that the wheels don't spin wildly and dig themselves further into the sand.

Sometimes rocking the vehicle backwards and forwards will build up momentum to break you free. This can be done by intermittently applying the clutch and/or by getting helpers who can push and pull the vehicle at the same

FACING A CHARGE If you do get into a hair-raising situation with elephants, then you've probably not kept your distance. The key was prevention, and you failed. Now you must keep cool, with your logic ruling your fear. A few words here are inadequate – you need experience – but I'll outline some basics.

If you are unexpectedly surrounded by peaceful elephants when your vehicle is stationary and switched off, don't panic. Don't even start the engine, as that would startle them. Just sit there and enjoy it; there's no real cause for concern. Only when they've passed and are a distance away should you start up. When you do start: never start and move off simultaneously, which will be interpreted as the vehicle being very aggressive. Instead start up quietly, wait a little and then move.

More often a situation occurs when one member of the herd will be upset with you. In that case you've approached too closely. (The key was to keep your distance – remember?) Then an annoyed elephant will usually first mock charge. This normally first involves a lot of ear flapping, head shaking and loud trumpeting – mock charges are often preceded by 'displacement activities', and the animals often show uncertainty about charging. The individual then runs towards you with ears spread out, head held high, and trumpeting loudly. This is terrifying, especially if you're not used to it. But be impressed, not surprised; elephants weigh up to 6,000kg and have had several million years to refine this into a really frightening spectacle.

However terrifying, if you stand your ground then almost all such encounters will end with the elephant stopping in its tracks. It will then move away at an angle, with its head held high and turned, its back arched, its tail raised, and the occasional head-shake. Often you'll find the 'teenagers' of the herd doing this – testing you and showing off a bit.

If you flee or back off rapidly during such a mock charge, however, the elephant will probably chase your vehicle, perhaps turning a mock charge into a full charge. So, before you move, make very certain that you have a swift escape route, and that you can drive faster than the elephant can run. (In deep sand, you can forget this.) As a fairly desperate measure, not normally needed, if the elephant is really getting too close, then increasing the revs of your engine – commensurate with the threat – will encourage the animal to stop and back down. Don't beep your horn, don't rev up and down, but do steadily press your accelerator further down as the elephant gets closer. (I've never needed to do this; it's overkill for most mock charges.)

However, if you're really unfortunate you may come across an upset or traumatised animal, or one that really perceives you as a threat and makes a full charge. This is rare – expected only from injured elephants, cows protecting calves, males in musth and the like. Then the individual will fold its ears back, put its head down, and run full speed at your vehicle. I've never faced one of these, but if you do, your only option is to drive as fast as you can. If you can't get away then I'd try revving, as above, matching its threat with your engine's noise. But I'd also start praying – this is a seriously dangerous place to be.

frequency. Once the vehicle is moving, the golden rule of sand driving is to keep up the momentum: if you pause, you will sink and stop.

Driving in mud This is difficult, though the theory is the same as for sand: keep going and don't stop. That said, even the most experienced drivers get stuck.

Some areas of Namibia (like the *omurambas* in Khaudum National Park) have very fine soil known as 'black-cotton' soil, which can become totally impassable when wet.

If you are unlucky enough to need to push-start your vehicle while it is stuck in sand or mud, then there is a remedy. Raise up the drive wheels, and take off one of the wheels. Then wrap a length of rope around the hub and treat it like a spinning top: one person (or more) pulls the rope to make the axle spin, while the driver lifts the clutch, turns the ignition on, and engages a low gear to turn the engine over. This is a difficult equivalent of a push-start, but it may be your only option.

Rocky terrain Have your tyre pressure higher than normal and move very slowly. If necessary passengers should get out and guide you along the track to avoid scraping the undercarriage on the ground. This can be a very slow business, and is often the case in the highlands of the northern Kaokoveld.

Crossing rivers The first thing to do is to stop and check the river. You must assess its depth, its substrate (type of river-bed) and its current flow; and determine the best route to drive across it. This is best done by wading across the river (while watching for hippos and crocodiles, if necessary). Beware of water that's too deep for your vehicle (bearing in mind that it may still be rising), or the very real possibility of being swept away by a fast current and a slippery substrate.

If everything is OK then select your lowest gear ratio and drive through the water slowly but steadily. Your vehicle's air intake must be above the level of the water to avoid your engine filling with water. It's not worth taking risks, (not least as water damage is rarely covered by your insurance), so remember that a flooded river will often subside to much safer levels by the next morning.

Overheating If the engine has overheated, the only option is to stop and turn it off. Stop and let it cool. Don't open the radiator cap to refill it until the radiator is no longer hot to the touch. Keep the engine running and the water circulating while you refill the radiator – otherwise you run the risk of cracking the hot metal by suddenly cooling it. Flicking droplets of water on to the outside of a running engine will cool it. When driving away, switch off the air-con (as it puts more strain on the engine). Open the windows and turn the heater and fan full on. This won't be pleasant in the midday heat, but it'll help to cool the engine. Keep watching the engine temperature gauge.

Grass stems and seeds will get caught in the radiator grill and block the flow of air, causing the engine to overheat and the grass to catch fire. You should stop and remove the grass seeds every few kilometres or so, depending on the conditions.

DRIVING NEAR BIG GAME The only animals which are likely to pose a threat to vehicles are elephants (see box, page 144, for details) or possibly black rhino. So treat them with the greatest respect and don't 'push' them by trying to move ever closer. Letting them approach you is much safer, and they will feel far less threatened and more relaxed. Then, if the animals are calm, you can safely turn the engine off, sit quietly, and watch as they pass you by.

If you are unlucky, or foolish enough to unexpectedly drive into the middle of a herd, don't panic. Keep your movements, and those of the vehicle, slow and measured. Back off steadily. Don't be panicked, or overly intimidated, by a mock charge – this is just their way of frightening you away.

SUGGESTED ITINERARIES If you're organising a small 4x4 expedition, then it is assumed that you know exactly what you're doing, and where you want to go, and hence no 4x4 itineraries have been included here.

The suggested itineraries here, for 2WDs, are intended as a framework only, and the time spent at places is the *minimum* which is reasonable – if you have less time, then cut places out rather than quicken the pace. With more time to spare, consider taking the same routes, and exploring each area in greater detail.

When planning your own itinerary, try to intersperse the longer drives between more restful days. Avoid spending each night in a new place, as shifting your base can become tiring. Try to book hire cars and accommodation as far in advance as you can; that way you'll get the places you want, exactly when you want them.

Included here are two very loose categories: 'budget' and 'indulgent'. These reflect the cost of the choices – although even our 'budget' suggestions are designed as places where a good experience is possible, at a good-value rate, rather than being simply the cheapest places to sleep. Where campsites are suggested, it's because of the experience and location offered, not simply because they offer a good way to reduce costs.

Two weeks
Southern–central Namibia

Night		Budget	Indulgent
1	Fly overnight to Namibia		
2	In/near Windhoek	Hilltop Guesthouse	Eningu Clayhouse Lodge
3–4	Mariental area	Bastion Farmyard	Kalahari Red Dunes
5–6	Fish River Canyon area	Canon Roadhouse	Fish River Lodge
7–8	Lüderitz	Kairos Cottage	Lüderitz Nest Hotel
9	Helmeringhausen area	Hotel Helmeringhausen	Namtib Desert Lodge
10–11	Namib-Naukluft area	Sesriem Campsite	Wolwedans Dunes Lodge
12–13	Namib-Naukluft area	Tsauchab River Camp	Desert Homestead Outpost
14	Fly overnight out of Namibia		

This itinerary, focused on the southern part of Namibia, offers the chance to hike in the world's second-biggest canyon, explore the deserted mining town of Kolmanskop just outside Lüderitz, see the sun rise over the world's biggest sand dunes and enjoy walking among the stunning scenery of the Namib-Naukluft area.

Highlights of Namibia

Night		Budget	Indulgent
1	Overnight flight to Namibia		
2	In/near Windhoek	Vineyard Country B&B	Olive Exclusive/Hilton
3–4	Namib-Naukluft area	Büllsport Guestfarm	Wolwedans Boulders Camp
5–6	Namib-Naukluft area	Desert Camp	Little Kulala
7–8	Swakopmund	Organic Square	Strand Hotel
9–10	Damaraland	Tywfelfontein Country Lodge	Mowani Mountain Camp
11–12	Etosha	Toshari Lodge	Ongava Lodge
13–14	Etosha	Campsite at Etosha Safari Camp	Onguma Tented Camp
15	En route south	Campsite at Okonjima	Okonjima Bush Camp
16	Fly overnight out of Namibia		

This kind of circular two-week trip from Windhoek, visiting the desert in the Sesriem area, the coast around Swakopmund, a glance at Damaraland and some serious game viewing in Etosha in the north, is probably the most common route for self-driving around the main highlights of Namibia. There are endless options, but the key to success is to avoid trying to 'speed up' this route. Two-and-a-half weeks around this rough route, staying in some of these areas longer, would be a real improvement; but try to squash this driving into ten days and it would seem like an endurance test.

During your trip, you can climb the stunning rusty red sand dunes at Sossusvlei, kayak with hundreds of Cape fur seals at Walvis Bay, or get the adrenalin pumping with some adventure activities in Swakopmund. Admire the ancient Bushman rock art in Damaraland, and of course, explore Namibia's famous Etosha National Park.

Three weeks
Southern–central–Etosha

Night		Budget	Indulgent
1	Overnight flight to Namibia		
2–3	Mariental area	Bastion Farmyard	Bagatelle Game Ranch
4–5	Fish River Canyon	Ai-Ais Restcamp	Fish River Lodge
6–7	Lüderitz	Hansa Haus	The Nest
8	Namib-Naukluft area	Hotel Helmeringhausen	Wolwedans Dune Camp
9	Namib-Naukluft area	Desert Homestead	Wolwedans Dune Camp
10–11	Namib-Naukluft area	Desert Homestead	Hoodia Desert Lodge
12–13	Swakopmund	Sam's Giardino	Villa Margarita
14–15	Damaraland	Damra Mopane Lodge	Damaraland Camp
16–17	Etosha	Okaukuejo Restcamp	Safarihoek Lodge
18–19	Etosha	Halali Restcamp	Mushara Outpost
20	En route to Windhoek	Camping at Omandumba Farm	Erongo Wilderness Lodge
21	Fly overnight out of Namibia		

Three weeks allows you to combine the highlights of both northern and southern Namibia, as above. Okaukuejo Restcamp is a highlight of this itinerary, with one of the best floodlit waterholes in southern Africa.

Trans-Caprivi Strip (Zambezi/Kavango regions)

Night		Budget	Indulgent
1	Overnight flight to Victoria Falls or Livingstone		
2–3	Victoria Falls area	Victoria Falls Waterfront	Tongabezi Lodge
4–6	Chobe River area	Camping in Kasane	Chobe Water Villas
7–8	Mudumu area	Mavunje Campsite	Nambwa Tented Lodge
9–10	Popa Falls area	Shametu River Lodge camping	RiverDance Lodge
11	Rundu	N'Kwazi camping	Hakusembe River Lodge
12–13	Etosha	Onguma Tamboti Campsite	Onguma Tree Top Camp
14–15	Etosha	Okaukuejo Restcamp	Ongava Tented Camp
16–17	Damaraland	Hoada Campsite	Grootberg Lodge
18–19	Damaraland	Brandberg Restcamp	Camp Kipwe
20	North of Windhoek	Elegant Farmstead	Okonjima Bush Camp
21	Fly overnight out of Namibia		

This trans-Caprivi route, through the present-day Zambezi and Kavango regions, is intrinsically more expensive than spending the same length of time just in Namibia. Victoria Falls and the Chobe/Kasane are both relatively costly, Botswana's national park fees are relatively high, and there would also be a one-way drop-off fee levied on the car hire. Such a trip is much better suited to a second or third visit to Namibia, rather than the first.

It offers a completely different experience from the rest of Namibia. Hear the roar of the famous Victoria Falls, cruise the waters of the Kwando and Kavango rivers keeping your eyes peeled for hippos and crocodiles, and keep a pair of binoculars handy – the birdlife here is exceptional.

BY AIR

Namibia's internal air links are good and reasonably priced, and internal flights can be a practical way to hop huge distances swiftly. The scheduled internals are sufficiently infrequent that you need to plan your trip around them, and not vice versa. This needs to be done far in advance to be sure of getting seats, but does run the risk of your trip being thrown into disarray if the airline's schedule changes. Sadly, this isn't as uncommon as you might hope. See page 197 for the contact details of airline head offices in Windhoek.

Increasingly, light aircraft flights, both scheduled and private charter, are being used for short camp-to-camp flights. These are pretty expensive compared with driving but are great if you are short on time, do not want to drive or want to visit areas that are otherwise confined to experienced off-road drivers.

REGIONAL FLIGHTS The main regional airports (with their international city codes) are Cape Town (CPT), Johannesburg (JNB), Livingstone, Zambia (LVI), Luanda, Angola (LAD), Maun, Botswana (MUB), Victoria Falls, Zimbabwe (VFA) and Windhoek International (WDH).

Air Namibia (*www.airnamibia.com.na*) operates regular and relatively reliable flights around the region. These include daily flights from Windhoek to Cape Town and Johannesburg, from about N$2,000 one-way. Other destinations include Victoria Falls, Luanda, Lusaka, Lagos, Durban, Harare and Accra. In general, you will find these to be the same price if you buy them locally or overseas. However, if you travel between Europe and Namibia with Air Namibia, and book your regional flights at the same time, then these routes become much cheaper. Prices and timetables of internal flights change regularly.

Both **South African Airways** (*www.flysaa.com*), and **Comair** (a subsidiary of **British Airways**; *www.comair.co.za*) link Windhoek with Johannesburg, while Comair also has flights to Cape Town.

INTERNAL FLIGHTS
Scheduled internal flights Namibia has a reasonable network of scheduled internal flights, run by Air Namibia, and mostly from Windhoek's Eros (ERS) Airport. While timetables and prices change regularly, these flights are not generally too expensive. As an example, Katima Mulilo to Windhoek, a distance of 1,950km, costs on average N$1,400 one-way. Currently, regular flights link Windhoek with:

Katima Mulilo (M'Pacha; MPA)   Oranjemund (OMD)
Lüderitz (LUD)   Rundu (NDU)
Ondangwa (OND)   Walvis Bay (WVB)

Chartered internal flights
✈ **Desert Air** ✆061 228101; m 081 128 4228;   ✈ **Scenic Air** ✆061 249268; m 081 129 9981;
e info@desertair.com.na; http://desertair.com.na   http://scenic-air.com

✈ **Westair Aviation** m 083 937 8247;
e reservations@westair.com.na; http://westair.
com.na
✈ **Wilderness Air** www.wilderness-air.com.
Linked to Wilderness Safaris, & bookable only
through a tour operator, they offer both private

charters & more economical rates, where you
share the cost with others travelling on the same
scheduled route.
✈ **Wings over Africa** \061 255001/2; m 081
129 3673; e info@wings.na; http://wingscharters.
com

Flexible fly-in trips In the last few years, there have been an increasing number of light aircraft flights around Namibia, arranged by small companies using small four- and six-seater planes as well as larger 16-seater 'caravans'. These are particularly convenient for linking farms and lodges which have their own bush airstrips. If you have the money, and want to make the most of a short time in the country, then perhaps a fly-in trip would suit you. Now it's possible to visit Namibia in the same way that you'd see Botswana's Okavango Delta, by flying from camp to camp. This is still the only way to see one or two of the private concessions in the extreme northwest. Any good tailor-made specialist tour operator (page 104) could put together such a trip for you – but expect it to cost at least £520/US$680 per person per night.

One particularly popular option is to take one of the scheduled flights that link Windhoek and Swakopmund with the properties around Sesriem and Wolwedans. This is usually arranged as part of a package through a tour operator, or one of the lodges. It's not cheap, but is a fast way to get into the dunes if time is limited. One company organising such trips is DuneHopper (*www.dunehopper. com*), which offers scheduled packages ranging from two to five nights to the NamibRand and Sossusvlei, with daily departures from Windhoek and Swakopmund. As an indication of costs, a return three-day, two-night trip from Windhoek or Swakopmund to Wolwedans Dunes Lodge is around N$25,500 per person, based on a minimum of two passengers, and including full board and activities.

Of course, if you've a private pilot's licence and an adventurous streak, then Namibia's skies are marvellously open and free of hassles – but you'll have to source a self-fly hire aircraft, then spend a day in Windhoek sorting out the paperwork and taking a test flight.

BY RAIL

TRANSNAMIB Although an extensive railway network connects Namibia's main towns, most trains carry freight rather than passengers. StarLine passenger trains, operated by TransNamib (*www.transnamib.com.na*), are limited to the line between Windhoek and Swakopmund/Walvis Bay and the north–south service between Windhoek and Keetmanshoop, with onward connections to Karasburg, along with trains to Tsumeb and further north.

Trains are rarely full, but they are exceptionally slow and stop frequently, so are not for those in a hurry; most visitors without their own vehicle prefer long-distance coaches or hitchhiking. However, travelling by train affords the chance to meet local people and, as journeys are overnight (there's no chance of enjoying the view), it allows travellers to get a night's sleep while in transit, saving on accommodation costs and perhaps 'gaining' a day at their destination.

TICKETS AND BOOKING Carriages are divided into 'economy' and 'business' sections, some with sleeper compartments that convert to seating in the daytime, and tickets come with a numbered seat reservation. **Fares** are low (the 1,050km journey between Swakopmund and Windhoek, for instance, costs N$160 in business class, one-way). Travellers over the age of 60 are entitled to a 33% discount on production of suitable proof of age. For those travelling with children, one child under the age of six can travel free; others are charged at half price.

Tickets may be booked at any station, ideally in person, but telephone numbers of the **main stations** are as follows:

Karasburg ↘063 271 1110
Keetmanshoop ↘063 229202
Mariental ↘063 249202
Okahandja ↘062 503315

Swakopmund ↘064 463187
Walvis Bay ↘064 208504
Windhoek ↘061 298 2032/2175

ROUTES AND SCHEDULES
The following routes are of most interest to visitors:

Windhoek–Swakopmund & Walvis Bay via Okahandja, Karibib & Usakos (departs Tue, Thu, Fri & Sun at 19.15)

Walvis Bay & Swakopmund–Windhoek via Usakos, Karibib & Okahandja (departs Tue, Thu, Fri & Sun at 19.00)

Windhoek–Keetmanshoop via Rehoboth, Kalkrand, Mariental, Gibeon, Asab & Tses (departs Wed & Sat at 19.40)

Keetmanshoop–Windhoek via Tses, Asab, Gibeon, Mariental, Kalkrand & Rehoboth (departs Thu & Sun at 19.00)

Keetmanshoop–Karasburg via Grünau (departs Wed & Sat at 09.00)

Karasburg– Keetmanshoop via Grünau (departs Thu & Sun at 11.25)

Passengers need to check in half an hour before the train departs. Only two pieces of luggage may be carried free of charge; bicycles are not allowed.

LUXURY TRAINS
Rovos Rail (↘ +27 (0)12 315 8242; e reservations@rovos.co.za; www.rovos.com/journeys/namibia-safari; FBA R102,900–205,800/137,200–274,400 sgl/dbl; rates in South African rand – on par with Namibian dollar) The introduction of Rovos Rail's new route between Pretoria and Walvis Bay has brought rail services in Namibia to a whole new level of luxury.

Passengers have the choice of three types of suite: Pullman, Deluxe and Royal, which vary in size and splendour. The style may be of yesteryear, but all are en suite, with proper hot showers and plenty of plug points. In keeping with the tone of the trip, though, mobile phones, laptops and the like may not be used outside your suite, and there's a smart casual dress code, with formal attire expected at dinner.

The train leaves Pretoria on its 2,110-mile, nine-day journey in mid afternoon, travelling via the diamond town of Kimberley and on to Upington (with time to explore both on foot) before crossing the border into Namibia close to midnight on day 3. A short morning visit to the Fish River Canyon is next on the itinerary, with the afternoon devoted to the Quiver Tree Forest and Giant's Playground. Day 5 will see you exploring the city of Windhoek, before a light aircraft flight to Sossusvlei, where you'll spend the night at Sossusvlei Lodge, giving ample time to take in the Namib's iconic red dunes. After a return flight to Windhoek, the train travels north to Etosha National Park for a wildlife safari at the famous Etosha Pan and a night in a nearby lodge. The final leg of the journey to the Atlantic Ocean brings you to Swakopmund and your final destination, Walvis Bay. Or if you prefer, you can do the whole trip in reverse…

The *Desert Express* *After a 20-year run, TransNamib's luxury* Desert Express *was withdrawn for 'repairs' in 2018, and there is no indication of when – or indeed if – it will return to service. In the hope that this will be in the lifetime of this guide, we have retained the information – but don't hold your breath.*

The result of years of planning and work, the *Desert Express* was introduced in 1998, having been designed, built and fitted for the journey between Windhoek and Swakopmund. It offers a luxurious overnight trip, with a couple of stops along the way in each direction for game viewing and walks.

The train's 24 air-conditioned cabins are small but ingeniously fitted out, with beds that pull down from the walls, washbasins that move, and various switches hidden away. Each has its own en-suite facilities and will sleep up to three people, though two in a cabin is ideal. It's a unique way to be whisked between Windhoek and Swakopmund in comfort, ideally at the start or end of a trip.

Westbound, the train leaves Windhoek at noon on Friday afternoon (or 13.00 between September and March). After about 3 hours it reaches Okapuka Ranch, where travellers disembark for a short game drive. Back on board, a sundowner drink and nibbles are served before an impressive dinner, after which you'll stop in a siding for the night. Early the following morning, you'll move off, catching the sunrise over the desert and passing through the Khan Valley before stopping in the dunes between Swakopmund and Walvis Bay, for a short walk in the desert. It arrives in Swakopmund at 10.00 after a good breakfast.

Eastbound, it departs from Swakopmund on Saturday afternoon at 15.00, winter and summer. After a few hours it stops at a siding from where passengers are taken for a late-afternoon sundowner drink before dinner. The following morning, at 08.00, the train stops once more at Okapuka Ranch for a short activity, before continuing with breakfast and arriving at Windhoek station by 10.30.

BY BUS

In comparison with Zimbabwe, East Africa or even South Africa, Namibia has few cheap local buses that are useful for travellers. That said, small Volkswagen **combis** (minibuses) do ferry people between towns, usually from townships, providing a good fast service, but they operate only on the busier routes between centres of population. Visitors usually want to see the more remote areas – where local people just hitch if they need transport. As an indication of fares, you could expect to pay around N\$300 (£16.50/US\$20) between Windhoek and Ondangwa, one-way.

COACHES
Intercape The South African coach company, Intercape (☏ *+27 21 380 4400;* e *info@intercape.co.za; www.intercape.co.za*), operates its luxury Mainliner vehicles on long-distance routes covering many of the main towns. These are comfortable, with refreshments, as well as music, videos, toilets and air conditioning.

Reservations for all coaches should be made at least 72 hours in advance. Tickets are most easily bought online, but are also available through Intercape's reservations office in Bahnhof Street in Windhoek, next to the railway station (☏ *061 227847*). Alternatively, get in touch with one of their **booking agents**:

Katima Mulilo Caprivi Adventures; ☏ 066 252739	www.sureritztravel.com
Lüderitz Lüderitz Safari & Tours; ☏ 063 202719	**Walvis Bay** Ultra Travel Centre; ☏ 064 207997;
Swakopmund Sure Ritz Travel; ☏ 064 405151;	www.ultratravel.net

Intercape schedules have changed little over the years, but they do vary slightly from time to time so it's as well to check the latest timetables online before planning a trip. Buses are run on the following routes:

Windhoek–Swakopmund & Walvis Bay
via Okahandja, Karibib & Usakos (2 weekly, departing Thu & Sat, returning Fri & Sun)
Windhoek–Victoria Falls/Livingstone
via Okahandja, Otjiwarongo, Otavi, Tsumeb, Grootfontein, Rundu & Katima Mulilo (3 weekly, departing northbound Mon, Wed, Fri, returning Mon, Thu, Sat)

Windhoek–Cape Town via Rehoboth, Mariental, Keetmanshoop, Grünau & Karasburg (4 weekly, departing southbound Mon, Wed, Fri, Sun, returning Tue, Thu, Fri, Sun)
Windhoek–Upington (South Africa) via Rehoboth, Mariental, Keetmanshoop & Grünau (3 weekly, departing southbound Wed, Fri, Sun, returning Thu, Fri, Sun)

Fares Intercape's fares, like airline fares, are no longer charged at a fixed rate, but vary according to factors such as the date of travel, seat availability and, one assumes, profitability of the route. Most fares quoted in this guide are based on the cost of a one-way 'Full Flexi' ticket on a weekday in late 2018, but cheaper 'Flexi' and 'Saver' tickets are available. Note that booking agents usually charge a handling fee on each ticket of around N$25.

Up-to-date schedules and fares may be obtained online (*www.intercape.co.za*), but the following gives an indication of one-way fares from Windhoek:

International
Cape Town N$1,080
Johannesburg (via Upington: Windhoek–Upington N$650, Upington–Johannesburg N$820) N$1,470
Livingstone, Zambia N$680
Victoria Falls, Zimbabwe N$720

Internal
Grootfontein N$490
Grünau N$410

Katima Mulilo N$660
Keetmanshoop N$380
Mariental N$350
Okahandja N$320
Ondangwa N$460
Otjiwarongo N$340
Rehoboth N$310
Rundu N$620
Swakopmund N$310
Tsumeb N$520
Walvis Bay N$320

Namib-Naukluft Lodge Shuttle African Extravaganza (✆ 061 372100; e afex@ afex.com.na; www.african-extravaganza.com) runs a useful Sossusvlei Shuttle service linking Windhoek, Swakopmund and Walvis Bay with their two lodges near Solitaire: Namib-Naukluft Lodge or the Soft Adventure Camp (pages 317 and 318). Though in practical terms this limits you to staying at their accommodation, it is a convenient way to see part of the desert if you don't want to drive.

The shuttle, using air-conditioned minibuses, departs daily from Windhoek or Swakopmund at 14.00 (13.00 April–September), arriving at the lodge just before sunset. After an early morning trip to Sossusvlei, with breakfast in the dunes, guests return to their lodge via Sesriem, for lunch and a sundowner on the property. The return shuttle leaves the lodge early in the morning to reach Windhoek or Swakopmund at around 12.30. Rates vary, depending on where you start/end and where you stay, but the round trip from Windhoek costs N$7,500/8,100 per person sharing/single for the Soft Adventure Camp, rising to N$8,500/9,250 for the Namib-Naukluft Lodge. It's also possible, for an additional N$1,000 per person, to start from Windhoek and end in Swakopmund, or vice versa. Rates include accommodation and meals, drinking water during the journey, Sossusvlei excursion, sunset drive and park entrance fees.

LOCAL TRANSPORT

Private **taxis** operate in the larger towns, and are useful for getting around Windhoek, Swakopmund and Walvis Bay. They are normally summoned by phoning, rather than being hailed from the street.

Minibuses serve the routes between the townships and the centre, usually leaving only when (very!) full. Unless you know where you are going, and have detailed local advice about which ones to take, you're unlikely to find these very useful.

HITCHHIKING

Hitchhiking is still an essential mode of transport for many rural Namibians. For visitors from overseas, it's only feasible provided that they're patient and fairly hardy. It can be a great way to meet people, speedy and cheap – but obviously there are safety concerns, particularly for female travellers, or anyone travelling on their own. How fast you get lifts is determined by how much traffic goes your way, where you stand, and how you look. Some of the gravel roads have very little traffic, and you will wait days for even a single car to pass. So do set off with enough food and water to be able to wait for this long, and choose very carefully the lifts that you take, and where they leave you.

For the sake of courtesy, and those who come after you, don't abuse people's kindness: offer to help with the cost of fuel (most people will refuse anyhow) or pay for some cold drinks on the way. Listen patiently to your host's views and, if you differ, do so courteously – after all, you came to Namibia to learn about a different country.

8

Camping and Walking in the Bush

BUSH CAMPING

Many boy scout-type manuals have been written on survival in the bush, usually by military veterans. If you are stranded with a convenient multi-purpose knife, then these useful tomes will describe how you can build a shelter from branches, catch passing animals for food, and signal to the inevitable rescue planes which are combing the globe looking for you – all while avoiding the attentions of hostile forces.

In Namibia, bush camping is usually less about survival than about being comfortable. You're likely to have much more than the knife: probably at least a bulging backpack, if not a loaded 4x4. Thus the challenge is not to camp and survive, it is to camp and be as comfortable as possible. With practice you'll learn how, but a few hints might be useful for the less experienced African campers.

WHERE YOU CAN CAMP In national parks and areas that get frequent visitors, there are designated camping sites, usually at restcamps. Most people never need to use any sites other than these.

Outside the parks, there are a number of private campsites, as well as a smattering of community ones. In default of either of these, ask the local landowner or village head if they are happy for you to camp on their property. If you explain patiently and politely what you want, then you are unlikely to meet anything but warm hospitality from most rural Namibians. They will normally be as fascinated with your way of life as you are with theirs. Company by your campfire is virtually assured.

CHOOSING A SITE Only experience will teach you how to choose a good site for pitching a tent, but a few general points, applicable to any wild areas of Africa, may help you avoid problems:

- Avoid camping on what looks like a path through the bush, however indistinct. It may be a well-used game trail.
- Beware of camping in dry river-beds: dangerous flash floods can arrive with little or no warning.
- Near the coast, and in marshy areas, camp on higher ground to avoid cold, damp mists in the morning and evening.
- Camp a reasonable distance from water: near enough to walk to it, but far enough to avoid animals which arrive to drink.
- Give yourself plenty of time before it gets dark to familiarise yourself with your surroundings.
- If a storm with lightning is likely, make sure that your tent is not the highest thing around.
- Finally, choose a site that is as flat as possible; it will make sleeping much easier.

CAMPFIRES Campfires can create a great atmosphere and warm you on a cold evening, but they can also be damaging to the environment and leave unsightly piles of ash and blackened stones. Deforestation is a cause for major concern in much of the developing world, including parts of Namibia, so if you do light a fire then use wood as the locals do: sparingly. If you have a vehicle, then consider buying firewood in advance from people who sell it at the roadside in the more verdant areas.

If you collect it yourself, then take only dead wood, nothing living. Never just pick up a log: always roll it over first, checking carefully for snakes or scorpions.

Experienced campers build small, highly efficient fires by using a few large stones to absorb, contain and reflect the heat, and gradually feeding just a few thick logs into the centre to burn. Cooking pots can be balanced on the stones, or the point where the logs meet and burn. Others will use a small trench, lined with rocks, to similar effect. Either technique takes practice, but is worth perfecting. Whichever you do, bury the ashes, take any rubbish with you when you leave, and make the site look as if you had never been there. (See page 577 for details of Christina Dodwell's excellent *Explorer's Handbook – Travel, Survival and Bush Cookery*.) Finally, a practical warning: cooking after dark, especially in the rainy season, by any form of artificial light poses its own hazards in the form of flying insects. Unless you want mopane moths in with the stir-fry, it's best avoided.

Don't expect an unattended fire to frighten away wild animals – that works in Hollywood, but not in Africa. A campfire may help your feelings of insecurity, but lion and hyena will disregard it with stupefying nonchalance.

Finally, do be hospitable to any locals who appear – despite your efforts to seek permission for your camp, you may effectively be staying in their back gardens.

USING A TENT (OR NOT) Whether to use a tent or to sleep in the open is a personal choice, dependent upon where you are. In an area where there are predators around (specifically lion and hyena) then you should use a tent – and sleep *completely* inside it, as a protruding leg may seem like a tasty take-away to a hungry hyena. This is especially true at organised campsites, where the local animals have got so used to humans that they have lost much of their inherent fear of man. At least one person has been eaten while in a sleeping bag next to Okaukuejo's floodlit waterhole, so always use a tent in these restcamps.

Outside game areas, you will be fine sleeping in the open, or preferably under a mosquito net, with just the stars of the African sky above you. On the practical side, sleeping under a tree will reduce the morning dew that settles on your sleeping bag. If your vehicle has a large, flat roof then sleeping on this will provide you with peace of mind, and a star-filled outlook. Hiring a vehicle with a built-in roof tent would seem like a perfect solution, until you want to take a drive while leaving your camp intact.

CAMPING EQUIPMENT If you intend to camp in Namibia, then your choice of equipment will be affected by how you are travelling; you'll have more room in a vehicle than if you just carry a backpack. A few things to consider are:

Tent Mosquito-netting ventilation panels, allowing a good flow of air, are essential. Don't go for a tent that's small; it may feel cosy at home, but will be hot and claustrophobic in the desert. That said, strength and weatherproofing are not so important, unless you're visiting Namibia during the height of the rains.

Mat A ground mat of some sort is essential. It keeps you warm and comfortable, and it protects the tent's ground sheet from rough or stony ground (do put it underneath the tent!). Closed-cell foam mats are widely available outside Namibia, so buy one before you arrive. The better mats cost double or treble the cheaper ones, but are stronger, thicker and warmer – well worth the investment.

Therm-a-Rests, the combination air-mattress and foam mat, are strong, durable and also worth the investment – but take a puncture repair kit with you just in case of problems. Do watch carefully where you site your tent, and try to make camp before dark.

Sleeping bag
For most purposes, a three-season down sleeping bag is ideal, being the smallest and lightest bag that is still warm enough for winter nights. Synthetic fillings are cheaper, but for the same warmth are heavier and bulkier. They do have the advantage that they keep their warmth when wet, unlike down, but clearly this is not so vital in Namibia's dry climate.

Sheet sleeping bag
Thin pure-cotton or silk sleeping-bag liners are good protection for your main sleeping bag, keeping it cleaner. They can, of course, be used on their own when your main sleeping bag is too hot.

Stove
'Trangia'-type stoves, which burn methylated spirits, are simple to light and use, and cheap to run. They come complete with a set of light aluminium pans and a very useful all-purpose handle. Often you'll be able to cook on a fire with the pans, but it's nice to have the option of making a brew in a few minutes while you set up camp. Canisters for gas stoves are available in the main towns if you prefer to use these, but are expensive and bulky. Petrol- and kerosene-burning stoves are undoubtedly efficient on fuel and powerful – but invariably temperamental, messy and unreliable in the dusty desert. If you're going on a long hike then take a stove and fuel, as firewood may not always be available in the drier areas.

Torch (flashlight)
This should be on every visitor's packing list – whether you're staying in upmarket camps or backpacking. Find one that's small and tough, and preferably water- and dust-proof. Head torches leave your hands free (useful when cooking or mending the car) and the latest designs are relatively light and comfortable to wear. Consider one of the new generation of superbright LED torches; the LED Lenser range is excellent.

Those with vehicles will find that a strong spotlight, powered by the car's battery (perhaps through the socket for the cigarette lighter), is invaluable for impromptu lighting.

Water containers
For everyday use, a small two-litre water bottle is invaluable, however you are travelling. If you're thinking of camping, you should also consider a strong, collapsible water-bag – perhaps five to ten litres in size – which will reduce the number of trips that you need to make from your camp to the water source (ten litres of water weighs 10kg). To be sure of safe drinking water, consider taking a bottle with a filter (page 126).

Drivers will want to be self-sufficient for water when venturing into the bush, and so carry several large, sturdy containers of water. If you're driving a vehicle specially kitted out for camping, ensure that the water tank is full at the outset.

See page 110 for a memory-jogging list of other useful items to pack.

DANGERS FROM WILDLIFE Camping in Africa is really very safe, though you may not think so from reading this. If you have a major problem while camping, it will probably be because you did something stupid, or because you forgot to take a few simple precautions. Here are a few general basics, applicable to anywhere in Africa and not just Namibia.

Large animals Big game will not bother you if you are in a tent – provided that you do not attract their attention or panic them. Elephants will gently tiptoe through your guy ropes while you sleep, without even nudging your tent. However, if you wake up and make a noise, startling them, they are far more likely to panic and step on your tent. Similarly, scavengers will quietly wander round, smelling your evening meal in the air, without any intention of harming you.

- Remember to use the toilet before going to bed, and avoid getting up in the night if possible.
- Scrupulously clean everything used for food that might smell good to scavengers. If possible, put these utensils in a vehicle; if not, suspend them from a tree, or pack them away in a rucksack inside the tent.
- Do not keep any smelly foodstuffs, like meat or citrus fruit, in your tent. Their smells may attract unwanted attention.
- Do not leave anything outside that could be picked up – like bags, pots, pans, etc. Hyenas, among others, will take anything. (They have been known to crunch a camera's lens, and eat it.)
- If you are likely to wake in the night, then leave the tent's zips a few centimetres open at the top, enabling you to take a quiet peek outside.

Creepy crawlies As you set up camp, clear stones or logs out of your way with extreme caution: underneath will be great hiding places for snakes and scorpions. Long, moist grass is ideal territory for snakes and Namibia's many dry, rocky places are classic sites for scorpions.

If you are sleeping in the open, note that it is not unknown to wake and find a snake lying next to you in the morning. Don't panic; it has just been attracted to you by your warmth. You will not be bitten if you gently edge away without making any sudden movements. (This is one good argument for using at least a mosquito net!)

Before you put on your shoes, shake them out. Similarly, check the back of your backpack before you slip it on. A spider, in either, could inflict a painful bite.

WALKING

Walking in the African bush is a totally different sensation from driving through it. You may start off a little unready – perhaps even sleepy for an early morning walk – but swiftly your mind will awake. There are no noises except the wildlife's, and your own. So every noise that isn't caused by you must be an animal; or a bird; or an insect. Every smell and every rustle has a story to tell, if you can understand it.

With time, patience and a good guide you can learn to smell the presence of elephants, and hear when impala are alarmed by a predator. You can use ox-peckers to lead you to buffalo, or vultures to help you locate a kill. Tracks will record the passage of animals in the sand, telling what passed by, how long ago, and in which direction.

Eventually your gaze becomes alert to the slightest movement, your ears aware of every sound. This is safari at its best. A live, sharp, spine-tingling experience that's hard to beat and very addictive. Be careful: watching animals from a vehicle will never be the same for you again.

WALKING TRAILS Namibia has several long hikes suited to those who are both fit and experienced in Africa. These include unaccompanied trails along the Fish River Canyon, in the Naukluft Mountains and on Waterberg Plateau, and guided trails on Waterberg, at Tok Tokkie Trails in the Namib, and in the private areas of Fish River Canyon, north of the national park.

There are also hundreds of shorter hikes, and many areas which cry out to be explored on foot. None involve much big game, though you may come across larger animals; all are more about spending time in the environments to increase your understanding of them. Perhaps prime among these are the guided walks at Mundulea.

SAFETY OF GUIDED WALKS In many areas where guided game walks are undertaken, your chances of being in a compromising situation with seriously dangerous game – namely lion, buffalo or elephant – are almost zero. There are many first-class guided walks in the desert and the mountains, showing you superb scenery and fascinating areas, which don't have these risks to contend with.

Generally Namibia isn't the place for a walking safari that concentrates on big game (as always, there are exceptions, such as Desert Rhino Camp and Ongava). Hence many guides don't need to carry a gun, or know how to use one. This is fine for most of Namibia.

However, in areas where you may meet lion, buffalo or elephant, you need extra vigilance. A few lodges will take chances, and send you out walking with a guide who doesn't have big game experience. Don't let them. If lion, buffalo or elephant are present, then you need a professional guide who carries a loaded gun and knows how to use it.

This applies especially in Mahango, Nkasa Rupara and Mudumu, which have thick vegetation cover and healthy game populations. Don't accept the logic that 'experience and large stick' will be good enough. It will be for 99.9% of the time… but you don't want it to become the 0.1%. Don't walk in such areas unless your guide has experience of both big game and firearms.

Further east, in Zambia and Zimbabwe where walking safaris have been refined, the guides must pass stringent exams and practical tests before they are licensed to walk with clients.

GUIDED WALKING SAFARIS If you plan to do much walking, and want to blend in, try to avoid wearing any bright or unnatural colours, including white. Muted shades are best; greens, browns and khaki are ideal. Hats are essential, as are sunblock and water. Even a short walk will last for 2 hours, and there's often no vehicle to which you can retreat if you get too hot.

Cameras and binoculars should be immediately accessible – ideally in dust-proof cases strapped to your belt. They are of much less use if buried at the bottom of a camera bag.

With regard to safety, your guide will always brief you in detail before you set off. S/he will outline possible dangers, and what to do if they materialise. Listen carefully: this is vital.

FACE-TO-FACE ANIMAL ENCOUNTERS Whether you are on an organised walking safari, on your own hike, or just walking from the car to your tent in the bush, it is possible that you will come across some of Africa's larger animals at close quarters. Invariably, the danger is much less than you imagine, and a few basic guidelines will enable you to cope effectively with most situations.

First, don't panic. Console yourself with the fact that animals are not normally interested in people. You are not their normal food, or their predator. If you do not annoy or threaten them, you will be left alone.

If you are walking to look for animals, then remember that this is their environment, not yours. Animals have been 'designed' for the bush, and their senses are far better attuned to it than yours are. To be on less unequal terms, remain alert and try to spot them from a distance. This gives you the option of approaching carefully, or staying well clear.

Finally, the advice of a good guide is more valuable than the simplistic comments noted here. Animals, like people, are all different. So while we can generalise here and say how the 'average' animal will behave – the one that's glaring over a small bush at you may have had a really bad day, and be feeling much more grumpy than average.

Below are a few general comments on how to deal with some potentially dangerous situations.

Buffalo This is probably the continent's most dangerous animal to hikers, but there is a difference between the old males, often encountered on their own or in small groups, and large breeding herds.

Lone male buffalo are easily surprised. If they hear or smell anything amiss, they will charge without provocation – motivated by a fear that something is sneaking up on them. Buffalo have an excellent sense of smell, but fortunately they are short-sighted. Avoid a charge by quickly climbing the nearest tree, or by side-stepping at the last minute. If adopting the latter, riskier, technique then stand motionless until the last possible moment, as the buffalo may well miss you anyhow.

The large breeding herds can be treated in a totally different manner. If you approach them in the open, they will often flee. Occasionally though, they will stand and watch, moving aside to allow you to pass through the middle of the herd. Neither encounter is for the faint-hearted or inexperienced, so steer clear of these dangerous animals wherever possible.

Black rhino The Kunene Region has one of the world's best populations of black rhino – a real success story for Namibian conservation. However, if you are lucky enough to find one, and then unlucky enough to be charged by it, use the same tactics as you would for a buffalo: tree-climbing or dodging at the last second. (It is amazing how fast even the least athletic walker will scale the nearest tree when faced with a charging rhino.) If there are no trees in the vicinity, you have a problem. Your best line of defence is probably to crouch very low, so you don't break the skyline, and remain motionless.

When tracking black rhino in Namibia, you'll almost always be in the company of two or three professional guides/trackers, usually staff of Save the Rhino Trust. I've often been out with them, and the experience can be amazing. On one occasion, we were joined by visitors sporting bright outdoor clothing, who proved disastrously poor at listening to instructions. Having been told to remain dead still because a rhino with a calf was close, one of the group ignored this, stood up and clicked a camera.

The rhino charged. It was so fast: this was a very dangerous situation. Seconds later, as it approached, the trackers all jumped up in unison, shouting and clapping. The rhino changed direction almost instantly, and carried on running into the distance with its calf for miles. It was a tense situation and we were lucky. The one most harmed was the rhino – running for its life, followed by its calf, in 35° heat. We'd put the calf's life in danger, because one visitor couldn't listen to his guide.

Elephant Normally elephants are only a problem if you disturb a mother with a calf, or approach a male in musth (state of arousal). So give these elephants a very wide berth.

Normally, if you get too close to an elephant, it will first scare you with a 'mock charge': head up, perhaps shaking; ears flapping; trumpeting. Lots of sound and fury. This is intended to be frightening, and it is. But it is just a warning and no cause for panic. Just freeze to assess the elephant's intentions, then back off slowly.

When elephants really mean business, they will put their ears back, their head down, and charge directly at you without stopping. This is known as a 'full charge'. There is no easy way to avoid the charge of an angry elephant, so take a hint from the warning and back off slowly as soon as you encounter a mock charge. Don't run. If you are the object of a full charge, then you have no choice but to run – preferably round an anthill, up a tall tree, or wherever.

Lion Tracking lion can be one of the most exhilarating parts of a good walking safari, although sadly they will normally flee before you get close to them. However, it can be a problem if you come across a large pride unexpectedly. Lion are well camouflaged; it is easy to find yourself next to one before you realise it. If you had been listening, you would probably have heard a warning growl about 20m ago. Now it is too late.

The best plan is to stop, and back off slowly, but confidently. If you are in a small group, then stick together. *Never* run from a big cat. First, they are always faster than you are. Second, running will just convince them that you are frightened prey worth chasing. As a last resort, if they seem too inquisitive and follow as you back off, then stop. Call their bluff. Pretend that you are not afraid and make loud, deep, confident noises: shout at them, bang something. But do not run.

John Coppinger, one of Africa's most experienced guides, adds that every single compromising experience that he has had with lion on foot has been either with a female with cubs, or with a mating pair, when the males can get very aggressive. You have been warned.

Leopard Leopard are very seldom seen, and would normally flee from the most timid of lone hikers. However, if injured or surprised, they are very powerful, dangerous cats. Conventional wisdom is scarce, but never stare straight into the leopard's eyes, or it will regard this as a threat display. (The same is said, by some, to be true with lion.) Better to look away slightly, at a nearby bush, or even at its tail. Then back off slowly, facing the direction of the cat and showing as little terror as you can. As with lion – loud, deep, confident noises are a last line of defence. Never run from a leopard.

Hippo Hippo are fabled to account for more deaths in Africa than any other animal (ignoring the mosquito). Having been attacked and capsized by a hippo while in a dugout canoe on the Okavango, I find this very easy to believe. Visitors are most likely to encounter hippo in the water, when paddling a canoe or fishing. However, as they spend half their time grazing ashore, you'll sometimes come across them on land. Out of their comforting lagoons, hippos are even more dangerous. If they see you, they will flee towards the deepest channel nearby – so the golden rule is never to get between a hippo and its escape route to deep water. Given that a hippo will outrun you on land, standing motionless is probably your best line of defence.

Snakes These are really not the great danger that people imagine. Most flee when they feel the vibrations of footsteps; only a few will stay still. The puff adder is responsible for more cases of snakebite than most other venomous snakes because, when approached, it will simply puff itself up and hiss as a warning, rather than slither away. This makes it essential always to watch where you place your feet when walking in the bush.

Similarly, there are a couple of arboreal (tree-dwelling) species which may be taken by surprise if you carelessly grab vegetation as you walk. So don't.

Spitting cobras are also encountered occasionally; they will aim for your eyes and spit with accuracy. If the spittle reaches your eyes, you must wash them out *immediately* and thoroughly with whatever liquid comes to hand: water, milk, even urine if that's the only liquid that can be quickly produced.

CANOEING

There is comparatively little canoeing done in Namibia, though operations do run on the country's borders: down the Orange River, on the eastern side of the Kunene, and occasionally on the Kwando, the Chobe and the Zambezi. The main dangers for canoeists are:

HIPPO Hippos are strictly vegetarians, and will attack a canoe only if they feel threatened. The technique for avoiding hippo problems is first of all to let them know that you are there. Bang your paddle on the side of the canoe a few times (most novice canoeists will do this constantly anyhow).

During the day, hippopotami congregate in the deeper areas of the river. The odd ones in shallow water, where they feel less secure, will head for the deeper places as soon as they are aware of a nearby canoe. Avoiding hippos then becomes a simple case of steering around the deeper areas. This is where experience and knowing the river become useful.

Trouble starts when canoes inadvertently stray over a pod of hippos, or when a canoe cuts a hippo off from its path of retreat. Either situation is dangerous, as hippos will overturn canoes without a second thought, biting them and their occupants.

CROCODILES Crocodiles may have sharp teeth and look prehistoric, but are of little danger to a canoeist… unless you are in the water. Then the more you struggle and the more waves you create, the more you will attract their unwelcome attentions. They become a major threat when canoes are overturned by hippos – making it essential to get out of the water as soon as possible, either into another canoe or on to the bank.

When a crocodile attacks an animal, it will try to disable it. It does this by getting a firm, biting grip, submerging and performing a long, fast barrel-roll. This disorients the prey, drowns it, and probably twists off the bitten limb. In this dire situation, your best line of defence is to stab the reptile in its eyes with anything sharp that you have. Alternatively, if you can lift up its tongue and let the water into its lungs while it is underwater, then a crocodile will start to drown and will release its prey.

There is one very reliable report of a man surviving an attack in the Zambezi. The crocodile first grabbed his arm and started to spin backwards into deep water. The man wrapped his legs around the crocodile, to spin with it and avoid having his arm twisted off. As it spun, he tried to poke his thumb into its eyes, but this had no effect. Finally he put his free arm into the crocodile's mouth, and opened up the beast's throat. This worked. The crocodile left him and he survived with only a damaged arm. Understandably, anecdotes about tried and tested methods of escape are rare.

MINIMUM IMPACT

When you visit, drive through, or camp in an area and have 'minimum impact', this means that the area is left in the same condition as – or better than – when you entered it. While most visitors view minimum impact as being desirable, spend time to consider the ways in which we contribute to environmental degradation, and how these can be avoided.

DRIVING Use your vehicle responsibly. If there's a road, or a track, then don't go off it – the environment will suffer. Driving off-road leaves unsightly tracks which detract from the 'wilderness' feeling for subsequent visitors. In the drier western areas these tracks can also crush fragile desert plants and scar the desert for decades.

HYGIENE Use toilets if they are provided, even if they are basic long-drop loos with questionable cleanliness. If there are no toilets, then human excrement should always be buried well away from paths, or groundwater, and any tissue used should be burnt and then buried.

If you use rivers or lakes to wash, then soap yourself near the bank, using a pan for scooping water from the river – making sure that no soap finds its way back into the water. Use biodegradable soap. Sand makes an excellent pan-scrub, even if you have no water to spare.

RUBBISH Biodegradable rubbish can be burnt and buried with the campfire ashes. Don't just leave it lying around: it will look very unsightly and spoil the place for those who come after you.

Bring along some plastic bags in which to remove the rest of your rubbish, and dump it at the next town. Items which will not burn, like tin cans, are best cleaned and squashed for easy carrying. If there are bins, then use them, but also consider when they will next be emptied, and if local animals will rummage through them first. Carrying out all your own rubbish may still be the sensible option.

HOST COMMUNITIES While the rules for reducing impact on the environment have been understood and followed by responsible travellers for years, the effects of tourism on local people have only recently been considered. Many tourists believe it is their right, for example, to take intrusive photos of local people – and even become angry if the local people object. They refer to higher prices being charged to tourists as a rip-off, without considering the hand-to-mouth existence of those selling these products or services. They deplore child beggars, then hand out sweets or pens to local children with outstretched hands.

Our behaviour towards 'the locals' needs to be considered in terms of their culture, with the knowledge that we are the uninvited visitors. We visit to enjoy ourselves, but this should not be at the expense of local people. Read the box on page 90 and aim to leave the local communities better off after your visit.

LOCAL PAYMENTS If you spend time with any of Namibia's poorer local people, perhaps staying at one of the community campsites, then take great care with any payments that you make.

First, note that most people like to spend their earnings on what *they* choose. This means that trying to pay for services with beads, food, old clothes or anything else instead of money isn't appreciated. Ask yourself how you'd like to be paid, and you'll understand this point.

Secondly, find out the normal cost of what you are buying. Most community campsites will have a standard price for a campsite, an hour's guided activity, or whatever. Find this out before you sleep there, or accept the offer of a walk. It is then important that you pay about that amount for the service rendered – no less, and not too much more.

As most people realise, if you try to pay less you'll get into trouble – as you would at home. However, many do not realise that if they generously pay a lot more, this can be equally damaging. Local rates of pay in rural areas can be very low, and a careless visitor can easily pay disproportionately large sums. Where this happens, local jobs can lose their value overnight. (Imagine working hard to become a game scout, only to learn that a tourist has given your friend the equivalent of your whole month's wages for just a few hours' guiding. What incentive is there for you to carry on with your regular job?)

If you want to give more – for good service, a super guide, or just because you want to help – then either buy some locally made produce (at the going rate), or donate money to one of the organisations working to improve the lot of Namibia's most disadvantaged. For suggestions, see page 121.

UPDATES WEBSITE

You can post your comments and recommendations, and read feedback and updates from other readers online at www.bradtupdates.com/namibia.

Part Two

THE GUIDE

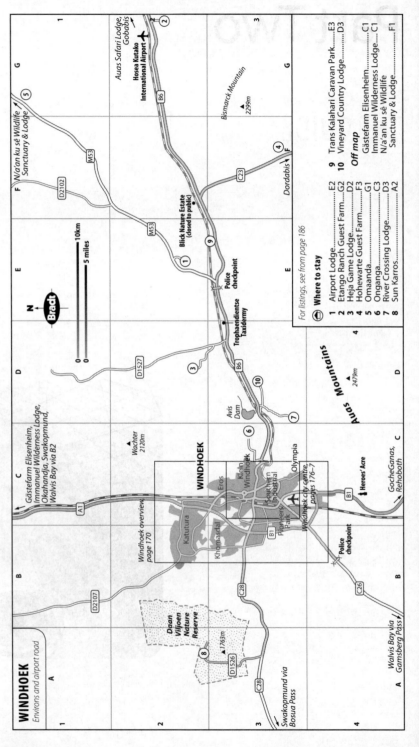

WINDHOEK
Environs and airport road

Where to stay

For listings, see from page 186

1 Airport Lodge...................E2
2 Etango Ranch Guest Farm....G2
3 Heja Game Lodge................D2
4 Hohewarte Guest Farm.........F3
5 Omaanda...........................G1
6 Onganga...........................C3
7 River Crossing Lodge...........D3
8 Sun Karros.........................A2

9 Trans Kalahari Caravan Park....E3
10 Vineyard Country Lodge.........D3

Off map

Gästefarm Elisenheim.............C1
Immanuel Wilderness Lodge....C1
N/a'an ku sê Wildlife
Sanctuary & Lodge.................F1

9

Windhoek

Namibia's capital spreads out in a wide valley between bush-covered hills and appears, at first sight, to be quite small. Driving from the international airport, you pass quickly through the suburbs and, reaching the crest of a hill, find yourself suddenly descending into the city centre.

As you stroll through this centre, the pavement cafés and picturesque old German architecture conspire to give an airy, European feel, while street vendors remind you that this is Africa. Look upwards! The office blocks are tall, but not skyscraping. Around you the pace is busy, but seldom as frantic as Western capitals seem to be.

Leading off Independence Avenue, the city's main street, is the open-air Post Street Mall, centre of a modern shopping complex. Wandering through here, between the pastel-coloured buildings, you'll find shops selling everything from fast food to fashion. In front of these, street vendors crouch beside blankets spread with jewellery, crafts and curios for sale. Nearby, the city's more affluent residents step from their cars in shaded parking bays to shop in air-conditioned department stores. The atmosphere is relaxed, to the extent that visitors tend to forget that this is a capital city. Yet as in any city, it is important to remember that tourists tend to stand out, and as such are potentially vulnerable to crime. So it makes sense to keep any valuables well hidden, and to keep a watchful eye on bags or rucksacks. Similarly, if you're in your own vehicle, keep the doors locked – even when you're just getting out to open a gate – and be aware of what's going on around you.

Like many capitals, Windhoek is full of contrasts, especially between the richer and poorer areas, even if it lacks any major attractions. For casual visitors the city is pleasant; many stop for a day or two, as they arrive or leave, though few stay much longer. It is worth noting that much of the city all but closes down on Saturday afternoons (although some shops open on a Sunday morning), so be aware of this if you plan to be in town over a weekend. Note, too, that during the holiday season, from Christmas to around 10 January, large numbers of locals head for the coast, leaving many shops, restaurants and tourist attractions closed. That said, this is the centre of Namibia's administration, and the hub of the country's roads, railways and communications. If you need an embassy, good communications or an efficient bank, then Windhoek is the right place for you. And to prepare for a trip into the bush, Windhoek is by far the best place in Namibia to get organised and buy supplies.

HISTORY

At an altitude of about 1,650m, in the middle of Namibia's central highlands, Windhoek stands at the head of the valley of one of the Swakop River's tributaries. The Nama people named this place Ai-gams ('fire-water') and the Herero called it Otjomuise ('place of steam'), after the group of hot (23–27°C) springs, now situated in the suburb of Klein Windhoek.

The springs were long used by the original Khoisan hunter-gatherer inhabitants. However, the first recorded settlement here was that of the important chief Jonker Afrikaner and his followers, around 1840. (Jonker had gradually moved north from the Cape, establishing himself as the dominant power in the centre of the country, between Nama groups in the south and Herero to the north.) Many think that the name Windhoek was bestowed on the area by him, perhaps after Winterhoek, his birthplace in the Cape. Others suggest that Windhoek is simply a corruption of the German name for 'windy corner'. Jonker Afrikaner certainly used the name 'Wind Hoock' in a letter to the Wesleyan Mission Society in August 1844, and by 1850 the name 'Windhoek' was in general use.

By December 1842, Rhenish missionaries Hans Kleinschmidt and Carl Hahn had established a church and there were about 1,000 of Jonker's followers living in this valley. The settlement was trading with the coast, and launching occasional cattle-rustling raids on the Herero groups to the north. These raids eventually led to the death of Jonker, after which his followers dispersed and the settlement was abandoned.

The Germans arrived in 1890, under Major Curt von François. They completed the building of their fort, now known as the Alte Feste – Windhoek's oldest building. This became the headquarters of the Schutztruppe, the German colonial troops. Gradually German colonists arrived, and the growth of the settlement accelerated with the completion of the railway from Swakopmund in 1902.

In 1909 Windhoek became a municipality. The early years of the 20th century saw many beautiful buildings constructed, including the landmark Christus Kirche, constructed between 1907 and 1910. Development continued naturally until the late 1950s and 1960s, when the South African administration started implementing policies for racial separation: the townships began to develop, and many of Windhoek's black population were forced to move. This continued into the 1970s and 1980s, by which time rigid separation by skin colour had largely been implemented. The privileged 'whites' lived in the spacious leafy suburbs surrounding the centre; black residents in Katutura (see box, page 205); and those designated as 'coloured' in Khomasdal. Even today, these divisions are largely still in place.

The 1990s, following independence, saw the construction of new office buildings in the centre of town. More recently, impressive government buildings such as the Supreme Court building have been constructed on the east side of Independence Avenue, while the open spaces between the old townships and the inner suburbs are gradually being developed as modest, middle-income housing.

GETTING THERE AND AWAY

Most visitors passing through Windhoek are either driving themselves around or are members of a group trip. Relatively few will need to rely on the local bus, coach or train services detailed here, despite their efficiency.

BY AIR Windhoek has two small but modern airports: Hosea Kutako International Airport (*www.airports.com.na*), which is generally used for international flights, and Eros, which caters mostly for internal flights and a few international flights. Be sure to check which one is to be used for each of your flights. For international air links, see page 107; for internal air travel, see page 149.

Hosea Kutako International Airport [166 G2] The international arrivals airport is located 42km east of the city, along the B6 towards Gobabis. The arrivals

area has ATMs beside the men's toilets and outside the arrivals hall as you head to the car park, and four small bureaux de change, including Magnet (⊕ *05.00–19.00 daily*), Bank Windhoek (⊕ *08.30–14.30 Mon–Fri, 08.30–11.30 Sat*) and Thomas Cook (⊕ *daily for all incoming & outgoing flights*). You can buy SIM cards (*N$7/6 months*) from MTC and Telecom Namibia (⊕ *06.00–20.00 daily*). There are also a few gift shops, and an office for Wilderness Safaris and their affiliates.

For a quick meal before you clear immigration, there's Ilamo, a coffee shop cum bar (⊕ *06.00–21.00 daily;* $$), though more convivial is Delta Café, on the lawn outside the terminal building. A container converted into a small coffee bar, it is wheelchair friendly and accepts Visa.

In the departure lounge, beyond customs, there's plenty of seating, the basic Premium Bistro (more of a café-bar), a couple of souvenir shops, and a larger duty-free shop that also has a range of souvenirs, safari clothes and books. This last accepts Namibian dollars, credit cards and some foreign currency. You will probably get your change in South African rand, and the staff here will also exchange N$100 notes for the equivalent in rand, if asked. Economy-class passengers can pay to use the rather shabby business lounge, but it is perhaps not worth it.

Airport transfers Avis, Budget, Dollar/Thrifty, Bidvest, Europcar and Hertz car-hire companies (page 140) all have desks at the airport, and others will meet you there on request, so picking up a hired car on arrival is straightforward.

If you don't plan to have your own vehicle, and have made no other arrangements, you can prebook one of the services run by local companies. Operators include:

Dunmar Transfers ☏061 244949; m 081 122 0584
Shuttle Namibia ☏061 302007; m 081 122 8888, 081 240 6788; www.shuttlenamibia.com.na

Windhoek Airport Transfers, Tours & Rentals ☏061 258792; m 081 245 0081; www.namibiatours.com.na
Windhoek City Cab & Transfers m 081 257 2188, 081 608 4247

Alternatively, a taxi to/from the airport should cost from around N$350–400, depending on the number of passengers. The ETEA Authorised Airport Shuttle/Taxi counter in the arrivals hall will refer you to a reliable shuttle/taxi driver. If you've asked a porter to carry your bags to your car or taxi, a tip of around N$1–2 is about right.

Eros Airport [177 C7] Windhoek's second airport stands near the main B1 on the way south to Rehoboth, about 500m from the Safari Hotel. It is even smaller than the international airport – positively bijou. Eros is used for most of Air Namibia's internal flights, a few regional services (and sometimes Cape Town flights) and a steady stream of light aircraft traffic. It has a few car-rental desks, including Avis (but there is hardly ever anyone there), and a small café, and is usually refreshingly informal.

Airport transfers There's no public transport to/from here, but as it's relatively close (4km) to the centre of town, taxis (page 172) are easily summoned by phone. Failing that, the Safari Court Hotel and its cheaper partner, the Safari Hotel, are just a few minutes' walk away, and can be reached via Shuttle Namibia (see above).

BY BUS/COACH In addition to Town Hoppers (page 171), several other operators now run shuttle services between Windhoek and the coast; for details, see pages 327 and 348.

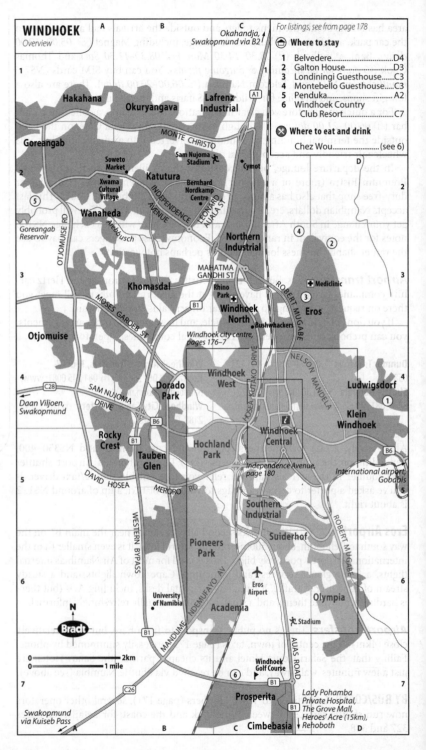

Intercape Mainliner [180 D7] \061 227847; www.intercape.co.za. Coaches depart from opposite the Intercape office in Bahnhof St by Windhoek's railway station. These head south for Upington (with connections to Jo'burg) on Sun, Wed & Fri. Buses between Windhoek & Cape Town operate on Mon, Wed, Fri & Sun. Westbound coaches head to Walvis Bay via Okahandja, Karibib, Usakos & Swakopmund on Thu & Sat only. There is also a service between Windhoek & Victoria Falls

(Zimbabwe) on Mon, Wed & Fri. See page 152 for more details.

Town Hoppers \064 407223; m 081 210 3062; www.namibiashuttle.com. Operates a daily shuttle service between Windhoek & Walvis Bay with stops in Okahandja, Wilhelmstal, Karibib, Usakos & Swakopmund. Buses leave daily from the parking area opposite the railway station at 14.00, arriving in Walvis Bay at 19.30. Fares start at N$250.

BY TRAIN Windhoek is at the hub of TransNamib's (*www.transnamib.com.na*) exceptionally slow network of passenger trains around a limited area of the country, with regular if infrequent services from the city's railway station (*off Bahnhof St;* \061 298 2032/2175). Trains to Keetmanshoop depart on Wednesday and Saturday at 19.40, and to Swakopmund and Walvis Bay on Tuesday, Thursday, Friday and Sunday at 19.15. See also page 150.

ORIENTATION

Under South African rule, Windhoek grew like most large South African cities, forming an 'atomic' structure. Its nucleus was the central business district and shopping areas, surrounded by leafy, spacious suburbs designed for whites with cars. Beyond these, the sprawling, high-density townships housed Windhoek's non-white population.

In modern Windhoek, almost three decades after independence, this basic structure is still in place, though the colour divisions have blurred. The leafy suburbs are still affluent, though are now more mixed, and new suburbs have sprung up in the southern parts of the city. Meanwhile, however, the districts of Khomasdal and Katutura remain crowded, poorer and with very few white residents.

The rapid growth in traffic within Windhoek has resulted in considerable development in the road infrastructure, with flyovers now carrying through traffic over the city's more congested areas and development ongoing. This can make orientation for the driver – particularly someone who has visited the city on a previous occasion – quite a challenge, so do get an up-to-date map and keep an eye on the signposts.

In common with other towns in Namibia, Windhoek undergoes occasional road name changes to reflect the prominence of local or international figures. Changes in the past decade include the following, though it is likely that both names will remain in use for a considerable period of time:

Bach Street *now* Dr Kuaima Riruako Street
Bülow Street *now* Frans Indongo Street
Gloudina Street *now* Joseph Mukwayu Ithana Street
Hochland Road *now* David Hosea Meroro Road
Malcolm Spence Street *now* Mose Tjitendero Street
Mission Street and Gever Street *now* Dr Kwame Nkrumah Road
Omuramba Road *now* General Murtala Mohammed Road
Peter Müller Street *now* Fidel Castro Street
Stübel Street *now* Werner List Street
Uhland Street *now* Dr Kenneth David Kaunda Street

MAPS For most visitors, the TASA map available from several tour operators is one of the best around. Overall, it is good and reasonably accurate. Less detailed maps issued by the Namibia Tourism Board are available free from the tourist information offices (see below).

For detailed maps, head for the Surveyor General's office at 45 Robert Mugabe Avenue (061 296 5036; ⊕ closed lunchtime), between Dr May and Lazarett streets. Ordnance Survey maps are around N$50 each. The 1:1,000,000 map of the whole country is wall-size and shows all commercial farms and their names. The 1:250,000 maps are good for vehicle navigation in the wilder areas, while the 1:50,000 series suits walkers. Most of the surveys were originally made in 1979, so despite being recently printed these maps are old. However, they are the best available.

GETTING AROUND

PRIVATE TAXIS In and around Windhoek it's usually best to walk, as everything is central and close together. It's not a good idea to hail a taxi on the street, particularly for women on their own, so prebook from a reliable source, or try one of those below. In general, agree the fare before you take the taxi.

🚕 **A Kasera Dial-a-Cab** 061 223531; m 081 127 0557

🚕 **Danmar Transfers** 061 244949; m 081 122 0584

🚕 **Shuttle & Taxi 2000** m 081 222 8294, 081 230 6755

🚕 **Windhoek City Cab & Transfers** m 081 257 2188, 081 608 4247

HIRED CAR Windhoek is fairly easy to navigate, with just a few main roads, good signposting and surprisingly little traffic, even at so-called 'peak' times of the day. Parking for a short period is straightforward, too: there are meters along Independence Avenue and some side roads, costing N$0.50 for 20 minutes near the Thüringer Hof Hotel, rising to N$0.50 for just 10 minutes as you get nearer to the post office. Parking is free after 18.00 Monday to Friday, or after 13.00 on Saturday and all day Sunday. Car guards – easily recognised by their orange or yellow vests – are regularly on duty on main roads. Ask them to keep an eye on your car in return for a tip of around N$2–5 for half a day, or up to N$10 in the evening. How vigilant they are is a matter for guesswork, of course, but their presence affords some sense of protection for your vehicle.

If you're shopping in the centre of town, secure and shaded parking is available in the multi-storey car park behind the Avani Hotel (turn down Fidel Castro Street off Independence Avenue, then left again into Werner List Street; the entrance to the car park is on the left). For details of car-hire companies, see page 140.

SHARED TAXIS AND MINIBUSES Shared minibuses and taxis do shuttle runs between the centre of town and both Katutura and Khomasdal. These are primarily for workers from the townships, and as such are mostly at the beginning and end of the working day, though some do run at other times. They are crowded and inflexible, but very cheap. If you want to take one, ask locally exactly where the taxi you need stops in town.

TOURIST INFORMATION

ℹ️ **Namibia Tourism Board** [180 B3] 1st Floor Channel Life Towers, 39 Post St Mall; 061 290 6000; e info@namibiatourism.com.na; www.namibiatourism.com.na; ⊕ 08.00–17.00 Mon–Fri

ℹ Namibia Wildlife Resorts [180 C4] Erkraths Bldg, 189 Independence Av; 📞061 285 7200; e reservations@nwr.com.na; www.nwr.com. na; ⏰ 08.00–17.00 Mon–Fri. NWR is where you book accommodation in the national parks, & get (limited) information about them, either in person or by fax, email or phone. Credit cards are accepted. To book a campsite, you need to pay a deposit of 10%, with the balance payable 60 days before arrival. Alternatively, you can take a chance & turn up at campsites – if there's space, you can pay direct. This is also the place for any dealings with the Ministry of Environment & Tourism (MET;

www.met.gov.na), who have a desk in the same office.

ℹ Windhoek Tourist Information Office [180 B3] Post St Mall; 📞061 290 2690; www. cityofwindhoek.org.na, www.windhoek.my.na; ⏰ 07.30–13.00 & 14.00–16.30 Mon–Fri. For information on Windhoek itself & the surrounding area, or to find a guide to take you off the beaten track, this is the place. The bureau also operates a temporary small pop-up information kiosk (📞061 290 2596) during the same hours on the corner of Fidel Castro St & Independence Av next to the newly completed Freedom Plaza.

TRAVEL AGENTS AND TOUR OPERATORS

Most arrangements are best made as far in advance as possible. Unless you are travelling independently and camping everywhere, this usually means booking with a good specialist operator before you leave (page 104), which will also give you added consumer protection, and recourse from home if things go wrong. However, if you are in Windhoek, and want to arrange something on the spot, then try one of the following. For companies operating local excursions, see overleaf.

UPMARKET
African Extravaganza 316 Sam Nujoma Dr; 📞061 372100; e afex@afex.com.na; www.african-extravaganza.com. Good for guided lodge tours.
ATI Holiday 📞061 228717; e info@infotour-africa.com; www.infotour-africa.com. Tailor-made trips or group safaris to Namibia & neighbouring countries to suit all budgets.
Blue Sky Namibia Tours 📞061 229279; e info@ blueskynamibia.com; www.blueskynamibia.com. Tailor-made trips for small groups.
Chameleon Safaris [180 B7] 5–7 Voigt St N; 📞061 247668; e info@chameleon.com.na; www.chameleonsafaris.com. From budget trips to guided tailor-made & special-interest safaris. Scheduled camping & lodge safaris have weekly departures to Sossusvlei, Etosha & elsewhere.
Ondese Travel & Safaris 📞061 220876; e info@ ondese.com; www.ondese.com. A well-established safari operator covering Namibia, Botswana, South Africa & the Victoria Falls.
Sense of Africa 41 Nickel St, Prosperita; 📞061 275300; e info@sense-of-africa.com.na; www. senseofafrica-namibia.com. Namibia specialist tour operator that offers everything from day tours to fly-in safaris.
SWA Safaris 43 Independence Av; 📞061 221193; e swasaf@swasafaris.com.na; www.swasafaris.

com. A family-owned operator offering self-drive & guided tours of Namibia, Botswana & the Victoria Falls.
Ultimate Safaris 5 Brandberg St, Eros Park; 📞061 248137; m 081 141 2275; e info@ ultimatesafaris.na; www.ultimatesafaris.na. Not to be confused with the British tour operator, Ultimate Travel, this established Namibian operation focuses on upmarket tailor-made trips with its own guides & vehicles. It also operates both Huab under Canvas & Sossus under Canvas.

BUDGET
Cardboard Box Travel Shop 15 Bismarck St; 📞061 256580; e info@namibian.org; www. namibian.org. General agents, ideal for short-notice trips.
Uakii Wilderness 📞062 564743; e info@uakii. com; www.uakii.com. Culture tours of 3–5 days with the Bushmen & various day tours in the Windhoek & Gobabis areas.
Wild Dog Safaris 📞061 257642; e info@ wilddog-safaris.com; www.wilddog-safaris. com. Recommended small-group guided trips – camping & accommodation. Quotes for privately guided trips & self-drive tours on request. Online availability & booking.

A visit to the Bernhard Nordkamp Centre in Katutura (*Hans Uirab St, Katutura;* ✆*061 269572;* m *081 3296526;* e *programcafo@iway.na* or *marybeth_gallagher@ yahoo.com; www.thebncnamibia.com*) may rank as one of the highlights of your trip. Run with boundless energy for many years by MaryBeth Gallagher, it is now in the hands of the Church Alliance for Orphans (CAFO), who strive to improve the lives of children who live in the township.

Initially the centre's aim was to provide after-school facilities for deprived youngsters, but these days there are literacy and numeracy classes to help children to thrive at school. They particularly welcome visitors who want to help out in the afternoons. You don't have to be an experienced teacher, but you must love kids and be willing to teach the basics to small groups. They have all the materials; they just need people to help. They also have a dance group and football teams, and they love to do puzzles and play board games. Even if you can only spare an afternoon it is worth getting in touch to see if you can help – they are always in need of basic school supplies: pencils, erasers, glue sticks, sharpeners, scissors, etc.

When I first went there, my group of eight brought footballs and much-needed stationery. We spent the afternoon with the children, talking, playing games, taking photos and generally learning about an aspect of Namibia that we would never have seen otherwise.

SPECIALIST
DuneHopper ✆061 234793; e info@ dunehopper.com; www.dunehopper.com. 2–5-night fly-in trips from Eros Airport to Sossusvlei & the NamibRand Nature Reserve.

The Trail Hopper ✆061 264521; e hiking@ trailhopper.com; www.trailhopper.com. Specialises in hiking, including Brandberg & Naukluft Mountains & Fish River Canyon.

LOCAL TOURS Various small agencies offer tours of the city, some on foot, some by vehicle. Often an afternoon tour will be combined with driving out to the mountains overlooking Windhoek for a sundowner drink. It is also possible to visit the township of Katutura as part of a Windhoek city tour, though these aren't as popular as Johannesburg's tours of Soweto. Other options include half- or full-day trips to one of the outlying game farms, or 4x4 trail driving.

If you prefer to drive yourself, and want to head off the beaten track, it is worth contacting the tourist information office in Post Street Mall (page 173), who can arrange for a community guide accredited by the City of Windhoek to accompany you.

Companies running day trips seem to change often, but current favourites are:

Oshana Tours & Transfers ✆061 224834; m 081 146 1424; e reservations1@ oshanatransferandtours.com; www. oshanatransferandtours.com. Windhoek City & township tours as well as day trips to nearby lodges.

Red Earth Sunny Tours & Transfers m 081 233 7647; e alexandra@redearthsafaris.com; www. redearthsafaris.com. Along with airport/road transfers, they do Windhoek City tours & ½- & full-day tours to nearby lodges for game viewing.

 WHERE TO STAY

Windhoek has accommodation to suit all budgets, from four-star hotels to backpackers' dorms, and hardly any are run down or seedy. Prices range upwards from about N$900 for a double room with en-suite bathroom, with single travellers usually paying about 30–50% more. Dormitory beds at backpackers' lodges cost around N$200.

The dividing line between hotels and pensions/guesthouses used here is somewhat artificial: one of atmosphere rather than title or price. Hotels tend to be larger and more expensive, but often have more amenities: you can be more anonymous and blend into the scenery. Windhoek's pensions and guesthouses are smaller, often family-run, and usually friendlier and more personal (see also page 115). The larger hotels invariably put on extensive spreads for their meals. Eat-as-much-as-you-can buffet meals, especially breakfasts, are the norm.

HOTELS IN WINDHOEK

✳ 🏠 **Olive Exclusive** [176 D1] (7 suites) 22 Promenaden Weg, Klein Windhoek; ☏ 061 383890; e info@theolive-namibia.com; www. theolive-namibia.com. Independent of the neighbouring Olive Grove since 2014, this seriously stylish boutique hotel just 10mins' walk from the city centre has strong eco-friendly credentials. Stunning photographic works & individual furnishings & fittings grace its deceptively simple & very spacious suites, each designed with natural materials to represent different regions of Namibia. Junior suites share a communal pool shaded by olive trees, while 4 premier suites have private plunge pools on terraces overlooking an olive grove. Indoors, all feature a relaxing lounge area with contemporary gas fire; a big bedroom with hairdryer, robes & slippers; & a bathroom with free-standing bath, & separate shower. There's AC, underfloor heating, TV, Wi-Fi (& a laptop), too; & a Nespresso machine, proper teapot, minibar

& even complimentary port & sherry to help you feel at home. And to complete the destress package, there's the option of an in-room massage. Olive's restaurant (page 190) is among the best in Windhoek, serving an imaginative à la carte lunch menu; if the weather is kind, dine out on the terrace, with gorgeous views over the olive grove to the mountains. The service throughout is an effortless combination of friendliness & efficiency. Secure parking. N$3,765–4,720/6,680–8,360 sgl/ dbl. **$$$$$**

🏠 **Hotel Heinitzburg** [176 D4] (16 rooms) 22 Heinitzburg St; ☏ 061 249597; e heinitzburg@ heinitzburg.com; www.heinitzburg.com. This distinctive white turreted fort was built in 1914 for German Count von Schwenn, who gave it to Countess Margarethe von Heinitz as a wedding gift. Both lived in separate parts of the fort before marriage, though legend has it that a secret tunnel connected their 2 bedchambers. A luxury hotel since 1996, the castle is owned by mother-&-son

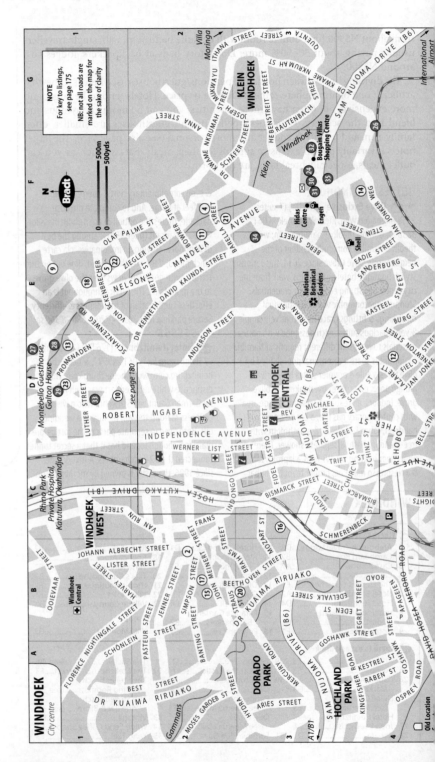

WINDHOEK
City centre

NOTE
For key to listings,
see page 175
NB: not all roads are
marked on the map for
the sake of clarity

N

Bradt

0   500m
0   500yds

KLEIN WINDHOEK

WINDHOEK WEST

WINDHOEK CENTRAL

DORADO PARK

HOCHLAND PARK

National Botanical Gardens

Windhoek Central

Montebello Guesthouse,
Galton House

Rhino Park
Private Hospital,
Katutura, Okahandja

Bougain Villas
Shopping Centre

Hidas Centre

Engen

Shell

Villa Moringa

International Airport

Old Location

see page 180

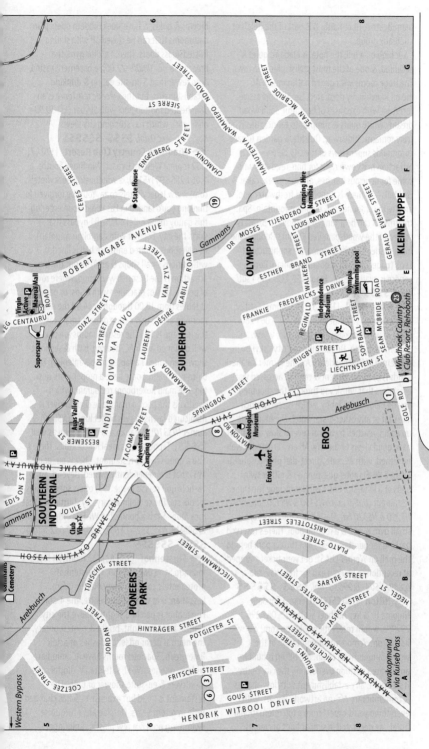

Windhoek WHERE TO STAY

team Beate & Tibor Raith, & is part of the Relais et Châteaux group.

Set high on a hill, the hotel is elegant, quiet & secluded, & one of the most stylish places in town. The huge rooms with gilded bathrooms & AC are all individually decorated. Expect impressive furniture with expanses of beautiful, solid wood, dreamy white quilts & sumptuous fabrics; this is a truly romantic hideaway. Outside, a garden terrace commands super views of the city below – an attraction in its own right for non-residents who come for delicious lunches, afternoon tea, cakes & cocktails – & there is a sheltered freshwater pool area with sunloungers & elephant fountain. Spa treatments can be arranged on request. B/fast is served in the wood-panelled Knight's Room in the main castle, & in the evening the sophisticated Leo's (page 190) offers gourmet dining. Room service is available too. From N$2,137/3,154 sgl/dbl. **$$$$$**

🏠 **Avani Hotel** [180 C5] (173 rooms) Gustav Voigts Centre, 129 Independence Av; ✆061 280 0000; e windhoek@avanihotels.com; www.minorhotels.com. Dominating the city's skyline in the centre of Independence Av, the former Kalahari Sands is both convenient & central, accessed via escalators that whisk you through the shopping arcade below to its lobby, which is pretty much like that of any other 4-star hotel. The rooms are up again, reached by one of several slow lifts; most have good views of the city. All are carpeted & well furnished, with AC, safe, direct-dial phone, satellite TV, free Wi-Fi (hotel guests only) & either twin beds or a king-size dbl. Facilities include the Dunes restaurant (*buffet lunch N$190 & N$320 Sun; dinner N$290 & N$320 Fri*), Oasis bar, Sands Casino, a small gym & spa, & a rooftop pool. There's reserved parking for guests on level 4 of the car park behind the mall on Werner List St; get your ticket stamped at reception so you can exit for free. *N$2,348–6,839/2,504–6,996 sgl/dbl.* **$$$$–$$$$$$**

🏠 **Hilton** [180 C5] (150 rooms) Cnr Sam Nujoma Dr & Rev Michael Scott St; ✆061 296 2929; e wdhhi.reservations@hilton.com; www3.hilton.com. A modern interpretation of the world-famous hotel chain, the Hilton is built in an elevated position overlooking the city centre. It's a bright, airy establishment with lots of glass & contemporary African artwork. Rooms, with everything you'd expect from a top international hotel, are decorated in similar hues of creams,

browns & golds, & have sleek modern open-plan bathrooms that can be closed off with sliding frosted-glass doors. There's a 24hr gym, the Breeze spa (⏰ 08.00–22.00), a basement casino, & no fewer than 5 on-site eating & drinking establishments, but the *pièce de résistance* is an 18m heated rooftop pool with Skybar (⏰ *10.00–midnight*), which has stunning city views. *N$2,150–9,650 dbl.* **$$$$–$$$$$$**

🏠 **Windhoek Country Club Resort** [170 C7] (152 rooms) Western Bypass, Windhoek South; ✆061 205 5911/5109; e windhoek@legacyhotels.com; www.legacyhotels.co.za. You'd be forgiven for thinking you'd landed in Las Vegas upon entering this gaudy mega hotel on the B1 bypass that skirts the city. Popular with gambling Angolans, its cavernous, vaulted entrance hall is lined with various small shops & an ATM, but the big attraction is the Desert Jewel casino, where rows of people fill slot machines with coins, or gamble at tables from 10.00 through to 04.00 the next morning. (Note that casino dress is smart casual & the min age is 18.) The resort's rooms are plush & well designed, with AC, heating, bath & separate shower en suite (1 adapted for paraplegics), & a balcony or patio. Some have a proper work desk too. The main Kokerboom restaurant, which overlooks the pool, a manmade circular river & manicured lawns, serves buffet lunch (*N$260*) & dinner (*N$310*), & has an à la carte menu as well (**$$$$**). Tappers bar is ideal for cocktails. There's also a good Chinese restaurant, Chez Wou (page 191) that is independently owned. Beyond, an 18-hole golf course (page 197) offers special rates for guests. The complimentary city shuttle bus that runs Mon–Sat is a bonus, but Wi-Fi is only free up to 500MB. *N$2,552–12,052/3,002–12,052 sgl/dbl.* **$$$$–$$$$$$**

🏠 **Fürstenhof** [180 A3] (33 rooms) 4 Frans Indongo St; ✆061 237380; e furstenhof@proteahotels.com.na; www.marriott.com. Less than 1km west of the centre, the 4-star Fürstenhof is perched slightly above the city. Central areas are light, bright & contemporary, the neutral décor offset by dashes of acidic lime green. Spacious rooms have AC, minibar/fridges, phones, Wi-Fi, satellite TV, digital safes, hairdryers & en-suite shower or bath. The restaurant is good but expensive, & has changed little in recent years. Outside are a turquoise swimming pool & a few plastic sunloungers, with a nearby spa that opens on to a small garden, sadly next to a noisy road. *N$1,880– 2,180/2,170–2,470 sgl/dbl.* **$$$$**

🏠 **Roof of Africa** [176 E1] (27 rooms) 124 Nelson Mandela Av, Klein Windhoek; ☎061 254708; m 081 124 4930; e info@roofofafrica. com; www.roofofafrica.com. Clearly visible as you're entering Windhoek on Nelson Mandela Av, Roof of Africa has its main entrance in Gusinde St. This well-equipped hotel with a lively atmosphere & helpful staff has a popular bar & huge but relaxed restaurant that's open to the public for b/ fast, lunch & dinner daily, serving freshly cooked buffets daily (*from N$189 pp*) & an à la carte menu that specialises in game steaks. All rooms are en suite, with AC, phone, Wi-Fi, TV & safe, while additional luxuries are a solar-heated swimming pool & private sauna. The on-site travel office is a useful extra, as is the shuttle service to the airport (*N$270 pp*) & the city centre (*N$30 pp*); prices are based on 2 people min. *N$1,028–1,526/1,526– 1,995 sgl/dbl.* **$$$$**

🏠 **Hotel Safari & Safari Court Hotel** [177 C7] Cnr Auas & Aviation rds; ☎061 296 8000; e reservations@safarihotelsnamibia.com; www. safarihotelsnamibia.com. These 2 adjacent hotels are about 3km from the city centre, just off the B1 to Rehoboth, & literally round the corner from Eros Airport. Although they share the same entrance & parking area, each has its own reception & check-in areas. Rooms also have the same facilities: tea/ coffee station, minibar, safe, direct-dial phone, satellite TV & Wi-Fi. All residents have full use of the public areas of each hotel, including the swimming pools, gardens, restaurants & bars. Use of the gym, sauna & steam rooms at the Safari Court is complimentary to guests at both hotels, too, though other spa services & treatments are charged separately. A complimentary shuttle service (🕘 07.00–19.00) operates hourly to the city & the shopping centre at Maerua Park. Transfers to & from Eros Airport are free of charge on request, but those to the international airport are run by private shuttle companies. Catering mainly to businesspeople, it all feels a little generic.

🏠 SAFARI COURT HOTEL (204 rooms) Classed as a 4-star, the Safari Court is the more luxurious of the 2. Modern, elegant rooms are of a high standard, with en-suite baths & powerful showers. Wi-Fi. Along with the Palms Ladies Bar & Terrace Bar there's the Acacia restaurant, whose à la carte

menu (**$$$$**) includes Namibian oysters, ostrich steak & seafood, as well as a fixed-price buffet (*N$195/240 lunch/dinner*). The Oukolele Day Spa has its own juice bar & gym; & shady landscaped gardens enclose a large swimming pool. *From N$1,624/2,182 sgl/dbl.* **$$$$**

🏠 HOTEL SAFARI (197 rooms) This 3-star is less smart & has 2 types of room: standard, laid out motel style, & slightly more expensive 'business class', housed in a separate 2-storey block. There is a lovely big grassy pool area with a café & bar serving snacks & drinks to sunworshippers, making this a popular venue for a mid-afternoon bite to eat. A buffet carvery & à la carte menu are offered at the Welwitschia Restaurant, while Coffee Corner serves cakes & ice creams, & the Skeleton Coast Bar screens sports events on TV. *From N$1,192/1,410 sgl/dbl.* **$$$**

🏠 **Hotel Thule** [176 E1] (25 rooms) 1 Gorges St; ☎061 371950; e reservations@hotelthule.com; www.hotelthule.com. Once an impressive private home, this striking hotel is situated in a prime spot high on the hill above Eros, with sweeping views across the city. To get here from the airport, follow Nelson Mandela Av to the traffic lights after the BP garage, turn right into Metje St; take the 3rd left into Olaf Palme St, then left at the top of the hill into Gorges (later Gutsche) St. At the top of the next hill, turn left again, & the Thule is behind imposing gates on the left. From its flag-festooned entrance past tall palms, the Thule oozes style. Airy, light & very modern, its carpeted rooms are a blend of whitewashed wood furniture & darker, fairly opulent soft furnishings. Rooms, with views across the mountains, or over the central fountain to the city beyond, have dbl or twin beds, AC/ heating & underfloor heating in the bathroom, & plenty of other accoutrements. There are also VIP rooms with a sofa & dressing room, a family room, & 1 designed specifically for travellers with disabilities.

In the main building, & the surrounding grounds, the impact of the hotel's location has been maximised: this is not a place for vertigo sufferers, or for families with young children. Varying levels feature a pool set in a small lawn, a terrace with elegant tables & chairs, a small formal courtyard & a sports bar. The restaurant, appropriately called On the Edge (🕘 b/*fast & dinner;* **$$$–$$$$$**), has sweeping views across the city from its wide curved expanse of

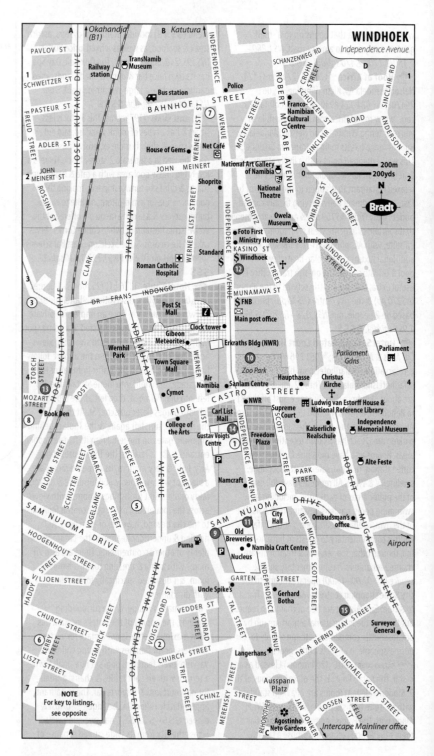

WINDHOEK
Independence Avenue

0 200m
0 200yds

N

Bradt

glass & the terrace beyond. The bar (⏲ *open to public 14.00–21.30 Mon–Fri, noon–21.30 Sat, 16.00–21.00 Sun*) is a great place for a sundowner. And if you look over the edge of the hill at sunset, you may even spot guinea fowl in the trees below. *N\$1,740/2,415 sgl/dbl.* **\$\$\$\$**

🛏 **Thüringer Hof** [180 B1] (26 rooms) Cnr Independence Av & Bahnhof St; ☎ 061 226031; e fom.thuringerhof@proteahotels.com.na; www. marriott.com. A member of the Protea chain, close to the centre of town, this hotel is popular with the German & local business markets & tends to be quite noisy. Dbl or twin rooms are clean & functional, if generally unremarkable; AC/heating, direct-dial phones, tea/coffee stations, safe, Wi-Fi & DSTV come as standard. The hotel's lively beer garden is a greater attraction; with good-value daily specials on the pub-grub menu. The Ivy Grill, with its traditional no-nonsense square tables, white tablecloths & à la carte lunch & dinner menus (**\$\$\$**) is also popular. If you want to stay somewhere that's straightforward & convenient, the Thüringer Hof might fit the bill. *N\$1,540-2,340/1,820–2,620 sgl/dbl.* **\$\$\$\$**

PENSIONS AND B&BS

There has been a proliferation of pensions & guesthouses in recent years. Most are situated in the suburban areas surrounding Windhoek, particularly in Eros, Klein Windhoek & the more affluent Ludwigsdorf, whose neighbourhoods also have plenty of restaurants & bars. In Olympia, to the southeast of the city, pensions are relatively scarce.

Central Windhoek and Windhoek West

🛏 **Hotel Steiner** [180 B5] (17 rooms) 11 Wecke St; ☎ 061 414400; e hotelpensionsteinernamibia@gmail.com. Built on several levels, this quiet pension is a convenient short walk from the centre, squeezed into a cul-de-sac off Trift St, between Sam Nujoma Dr & Fidel Castro St. Its rooms have tiled floors, Mnet & German TV channels, phones, fridges & ceiling fans (with AC in some rooms). Behind the building is a thatched bar overlooking a deep swimming pool. Steiner is a popular & pleasant place to stay & its atmosphere is one of helpful efficiency. *N\$800/990 sgl/dbl.* **\$\$\$\$**

🛏 **Pension Cori** [176 C3] (18 rooms) 8 Puccini St, Windhoek West; ☎ 061 228840; m 081 127 7397; e info@pencori.com. It's not difficult to spot this lilac pension near the corner of Hosea Kutako Dr & Puccini St, a 5min walk from the city centre. Owner Rini lives on the premises & has run her hospitable pension since the late 1990s. Rooms sleeping up to 4 have a private entrance from the garden, & feature a TV, coffee/tea-making facilities, fridge, safe, Wi-Fi & a fan or AC. The attractive garden offers plenty of shady trees, with a swimming pool & a thatched seating area. There are 2 well-equipped outdoor kitchens for guest use, as well as a braai. Airport collection can be arranged (*around N\$280–300 pp*), & there is secure parking. *N\$710/830 sgl/dbl.* **\$\$\$**

🛏 **Rivendell** [176 B2] (12 rooms, flat) 40 Beethoven St; ☎ 061 250006; e rivendell@ infotour-africa.com; www.rivendell-namibia.com. A homely, comfortable, clean & relaxed place to stay to the west of the city, Rivendell is about 15–20mins' walk from the centre. Rooms overlooking the swimming pool are en suite, while those in the main house share bathrooms. Extra beds can be added if required. There is also a self-catering flat for up to 5 people with a bedroom, lounge & kitchenette. Facilities include a communal lounge with honesty bar, free Wi-Fi, TV, metered phone & laundry services. Rates include a full English b/fast, but guests are welcome to use the self-catering kitchen. *N\$670–850/930–1,200 sgl/ dbl.* **\$\$\$**

🏠 **Tamboti** [180 A7] (15 rooms) 9 Kerby St; ☎ 061 235515; e tamboti@afol.com.na; www.guesthouse-tamboti.com. This friendly guesthouse, 15mins' walk from the centre of town, boasts 2 swimming pools, a patio where you can watch the sunset, & secure parking. Each of the varied rooms, including a family room with its own lounge area, has a small shaded area with a bench or chairs & umbrella, & guests also benefit from tea/coffee stations, an honesty bar & complimentary Wi-Fi. Facilities for travellers with disabilities are considered excellent. *N$670/990 sgl/dbl.* **$$$**

🏠 **Tilla's Guesthouse** [176 B3] (9 rooms) 9 Strauss St, cnr Beethoven St, Windhoek West; ☎ 061 259799; m 081 262 4478; e borges@iway. na; www.tillasguesthouse.com. A 15min walk to the town centre, Tilla's is a good-value, no-frills guesthouse with clean, simply furnished en-suite rooms offering AC, DSTV, fridge & tea/coffee facilities. Laundry, free Wi-Fi & secure parking available. *N$700/900 sgl/dbl.* **$$$**

🏠 **Vondelhof** [180 A4] (8 rooms) 2 Puccini St; ☎ 061 248320; e reservations@vondelhof.com; www.vondelhof.com. The friendly Vondelhof, with its tall turret, ochre-washed walls & large pool set in attractive gardens, is close to the centre of town. Each room is individual – with a private patio, or a desk, or interconnecting for families – but all have TV, free Wi-Fi, phone, minibar, safe, fan & coffee/ tea facilities. *N$960/1,360 sgl/dbl.* **$$$**

Eros, Klein Windhoek and Ludwigsdorf

🏠 **Belvedere** [170 D4] (18 rooms) 76–8 Dr Kwame Nkrumah, Ludwigsdorf; ☎ 061 258867; e belvedere@afol.com.na; www.belvedere-boutiquehotel.com. The beautiful colonial-style family home of Herman & Jeanne Davin has been transformed into a guesthouse which sets out to attract both tourists & business travellers. As well as a heated swimming pool surrounded by a wooden deck & a few holes of minigolf, there is a floodlit tennis court, a small-but-smart on-site spa, & private areas within the manicured gardens for individual BBQs. Along with this, each of the tasteful & well-appointed rooms – available in standard or luxury – has all the facilities of a good hotel, including desk with phone & free Wi-Fi, AC & heating, & bath or shower. *N$1,876–2,190/2,602–2,965 sgl/dbl.* **$$$$**

🏠 **The Elegant Guesthouse** [176 E1] (6 rooms) 56 Ziegler & Von Eckenbrecher sts, Klein Windhoek; ☎ 061 301934; m 081 302 8255; e info@the-elegant-collection.com; www.the-elegant-collection.com. Elegant by name & nature, this lovely guesthouse can be reached from the airport by following Nelson Mandela Av to the traffic lights after the BP garage, then turning right into Metje St & left into Ziegler St. Each of the airy, modern rooms combines neutral, earthy tones to create stylish quarters with twin beds, AC, DSTV, Wi-Fi, safe, phone & small courtyard. Central facilities include secure parking, a small pool & a b/ fast room with an honesty bar. *N$1,180/1,990 sgl/ dbl.* **$$$$**

☀🏠 **Galton House** [170 D3] (9 rooms) 72 Amasoniet St, Eros; ☎ 061 230416; m 081 142 6300; e reservations@galtonhouse.com; www. galtonhouse.com. This contemporary & stylish offering with a quiet, relaxed vibe is set high on a hill in leafy suburbia, about 10mins' drive from the city centre. All rooms (inc 1 trpl & 1 family) have slate floors & neutral, minimalist décor with striking aerial photos of African wildlife. Facilities include AC, TV, phone, safe & free Wi-Fi, with tea/ coffee on request. The main house has a bright guest lounge, an open kitchen & dining area, with seating indoors & outdoors, serving a buffet b/fast, à la carte lunches & a set dinner menu (*N$370*) with excellent-quality meals. Outside, the pool is surrounded by loungers & a small covered smoking area. Secure parking available. *N$1,570/2,540 sgl/ dbl.* **$$$$**

🏠 **Montebello Guesthouse** [170 C3] (11 rooms) 30 Akwamaryn St, Eros; ☎ 061 224045; e loni@montebello.com.na; www.montebello. com.na. This contemporary B&B, now under new ownership, might seem stark from the outside but it has a warm, stylish ambience in a quiet residential part of Windhoek. Rooms on the ground floor, some of which open on to the pool area, have neutral décor with splashes of colour, cool tiled floors, AC, TV, free Wi-Fi, minibar, tea/coffee stations, a safe & laundry service. Much more spacious are the 2 rooms on the 1st floor of the main house, which can be combined to create a self-contained apartment with a well-appointed kitchenette & lounge area. Back downstairs, the airy b/fast room & lounge area overlook a small pool with sunloungers & rattan chairs & tables. *N$1,300/1,750–2,000 sgl/dbl.* **$$$$**

🏠 **Olive Grove** [176 D1] (10 rooms, 1 suite) 20 Promenaden Weg, Klein Windhoek; ✆ 061 302640; e info@olivegrove-namibia.com; www. olivegrove-namibia.com. This smart guesthouse on the corner of Ngami St occupies a renovated old house about 10mins' walk from the centre of Windhoek. Friendly yet professional, it boasts excellent service & good food (*3-course dinner N$320 pp*), prepared in an open-plan kitchen that creates an air of informality. Stylish, minimalist décor throughout, including the lounge area, is softened by Moroccan lanterns & old wooden doors of Indonesian origin. Each of the rooms, with AC, minibar, TV, Wi-Fi & plenty of other mod cons, has twin beds set on grey cement plinths, with the same theme running through into large, well-appointed bathrooms (some with bath, others with shower, or even both). In one corner of the courtyard, a small raised terrace incorporates a pool shaded by the signature olive tree, while above, well away from prying eyes, lie a freshwater spa pool & lounging area. *N$1,070– 1,680/1,730–2,720 sgl/dbl.* **$$$$**

🏠 **Palmquell** [176 F4] (16 rooms) 60 Jan Jonker Rd; ✆ 061 234374; e hotel.palmquell@ iafrica.com.na; www.palmquell.com. Owned by Austrians Trude & Fritz Pfaffenthaler, the upmarket Palmquell has a quiet setting among the palm trees that give it its name, with secure parking. If you're coming from the airport, it is clearly signposted to the left off Sam Nujoma Dr. It's a bit too far to walk into Windhoek centre but Maerua Mall is nearby. Relax in the sauna, lounge by the pool or take a cool dip, perhaps followed by a drink at the bar. Dbl & family rooms are simply furnished, but very well equipped, with AC & underfloor heating, phone, TV & safe; paintings by Namibian artists provide an individual touch. A select dinner menu (*N$300*), but not lunch, is available daily except Sat, & there's a good range of South African wines. *N$1,150/1,770 sgl/dbl.* **$$$$**

🏠 **Utopia Boutique** [176 F2] (20 rooms) Cnr Barella St & Nelson Mandela Av, Klein Windhoek; ✆ 085 588 7704, 061 211299; e reservations@ utopiaboutique.com; www.utopiaboutique.com. The former Pension Bougainvilla is about 15mins' walk from the centre of town. Look for the large olive-green building behind a wall draped in bougainvillea; it's not difficult to spot. Modern dbl rooms & suites have queen-size beds & opulent soft furnishings, along with TV, AC, phone, Wi-Fi,

minibar & hairdryer. Outside tranquil, flower-decked gardens & shady pavilions with chairs & tables surround 1 of the 2 pools. Secure parking. *N$1,090/1,620 sgl/dbl.* **$$$$**

🏠 **Villa Violet** [176 E1] (6 rooms) Cnr Ziegler & König sts, Klein Windhoek; ✆ 061 256141; m 081 475 6379; e villaviolet@iway.na; www.villaviolet. net. Heidi & Ben Dassac run a friendly & efficient B&B in a peaceful location, whose rooms open out on to central lawns & a small pool. These are well appointed, with AC, TV, Wi-Fi & safe, & signature splashes of violet in the accessories. It's a relaxed spot, with open kitchen/b/fast room & a pleasant lounge with an honesty bar. *N$1,100/1,900 sgl/ dbl.* **$$$$**

🏠 **The Village Courtyard Suites** [176 D1] (7 suites) Cnr Liliencron St & Robert Mugabe Av; ✆ 061 400510; m 081 767 4254; e reservations@villagecourtyardsuites.com; www. villagecourtyardsuites.com. This collection of suites (2 accommodating 4 people) resembles a yuppie apartment complex. Vast, loft-style rooms fitted with designer furniture, large arty prints, DSTV, Wi-Fi, minibar & well-equipped kitchenette all overlook a central courtyard, where a fish-pond feature is surrounded by boutique shops. B/fast at Lemon Tree Restaurant (page 192; *N$130 pp*) can be included on request. *Room only N$1,675– 2,610/2,560–2,610 sgl/dbl.* **$$$–$$$$$**

🏠 **Casa Piccolo** [176 F2] (16 rooms) 6 Barella St, Klein Windhoek; ✆ 061 221155; e casapiccolo@ iafrica.com.na; www. casa-piccolo.com. Claudia Horn has run Casa Piccolo since 2000, & has expanded into the neighbouring property. The bright yellow walls remain, their sunny feel permeating through the tiled floors & simple white décor of its twin-bed (& 1 family) rooms. It caters mostly for the South African business market, but holidaymakers would be just at home with the bright, clean facilities that include fan, AC/heater, DSTV, Wi-Fi & a central pool. Off-street parking will add peace of mind if you have a vehicle. *N$950/1,450 sgl/dbl.* **$$$**

🏠 **Hotel Uhland** [176 D1] (24 rooms) 147 Dr Kenneth David Kaunda St; ✆ 061 389700; e info@hoteluhland.com; www.hoteluhland.com. Northeast of Windhoek, off Independence Av, this friendly, pink-painted pension stands on the side of a hill, making it an airy spot when it's hot. The city centre is a 10–15min walk, but Uhland has plenty of secure parking if you have a car. Cane furniture complements the carpeted rooms, which each have TV, Wi-Fi, clock/radio, phone, mosquito nets, ceiling fans, tea/coffee-making facilities & minibar. Superior rooms also have AC; some have safes; & 2 family rooms sleep 3–4 people. A comfortable living room with TV & stereo adjoins the b/fast room, & there's a light menu for evening meals, while outside is a patio with a pool & a thatched bar area. *N$840–990/990–1,140 sgl/ dbl.* **$$$**

🏠 **Klein Windhoek Guesthouse** [176 E2] (65 rooms) 2 Hofmeyer St, Klein Windhoek; ☎061 239401; e kwgh@iway.na; www. kleinwindhoekguesthouse.com. Situated in a quiet cul-de-sac next to the Klein Windhoek River, this guesthouse has grown tremendously in recent years, almost taking over both sides of Hofmeyer St. Rooms vary from budget to luxury, plus self-catering units sleeping up to 6 people. AC, fridge, TV & tea/coffee facilities are standard, with some also having Wi-Fi access. Seating areas are dotted throughout the gardens, where there's a decidedly small swimming pool. An Italian-influenced restaurant & bar complete the amenities. If you're after an intimate B&B, this isn't the place for you, but it's good value & efficiently run. *N$970– 1,195/1,300–1,500 sgl/dbl.* **$$$**

🏠 **Londininqi Guesthouse** [170 C3] (9 rooms) 11 Winterberg St, Eros Park; ☎061 242378; m 081 128 1017; e londininqi@mweb. com.na; www.londininqi.com. French-speaking Nathalie & Alex have run this relaxed, family-focused guesthouse for over a decade. Spotless rooms feature simple African fabrics, a minibar stocked with soft drinks & beer, DSTV, phone, free Wi-Fi & safe, & some interconnect for family use. The open kitchen enhances the family feel of the place, with b/fast served in a conservatory overlooking the swimming pool. Dinner & packed lunches are available on request. They support a grass-roots preschool project called Peri Naua (*www.peri-naua.com*) & welcome enquiries from guests about bringing teaching aids or old clothes which they sell to benefit the project. *N$826/1,240 sgl/dbl.* **$$$**

🏠 **Villa Moringa** [176 G2] (11 rooms) 111A Joseph Mukwayu Ithana St, Ludwigsdorf; ☎061 224472; e info@villa-moringa.com; www.villa-moringa.com. East of the city, Villa Moringa is a favourite with businesspeople. To find it from the airport, turn right from the B6 into Mission Rd soon after entering the first suburbs. After about 700m this joins Dr Kwame Nkrumah St; Joseph Mukwayu Ithana St is the 3rd right, & the guesthouse is on the 1st bend. Each of the modern rooms has a different colour theme running through the high-quality furnishings. AC, DSTV, free Wi-Fi, tea & coffee & a free minibar come as standard, while central facilities include a restaurant/b/fast room with licensed bar, a pool & sun terrace. *N$1,462/1,775 sgl/dbl.* **$$$**

Olympia and southeast Windhoek

🏠 **Terra Africa** [177 F7] (10 rooms) 6 Kenneth McArthur St, Olympia; ☎061 252100; e info@ terra-africa.com; www.terra-africa.com. Set in a residential road behind a gate adorned with pink bougainvillea, this rather utilitarian square building belies the care that has been lavished on the modern interior. Tastefully decorated rooms feature artwork (for sale) by local artists & have DSTV, a safe, stocked minibar, AC/heating, tea & coffee & free Wi-Fi. Ask for a south-facing room if possible: they're quieter than those overlooking the pool. A spacious homely lounge with dining area & big picture windows overlooks the landscaped, tree-shaded gardens with a pool deck. Residents can BBQ their own food if they wish, or light lunches such as mini pizzas & toasted sandwiches are available noon–14.00 Mon–Fri. There is also a computer terminal that guests can use free of charge, a small gift shop, & secure parking for 10 vehicles. Families are welcome. *N$890/1,656 sgl/dbl.* **$$$$**

🏠 **Moni** [176 D4] (17 rooms) 7 Rieks van der Walt St; ☎061 228350; e reswhk@monihotel. com; http://monihotel.com. Within 20mins' walk of the city centre, & 10mins from Maerua Mall, this quiet, friendly pension is easiest to reach from the Dr Agostinho Neto roundabout, at the south end of Independence Av. From there take Jan Jonker, then 1st left on to Lazarett, 1st right on to Feld, & then 1st left into Rieks van der Walt St. Everything is immaculately kept – from the gardens to the en-suite rooms, which overlook a central pool area. These are bright & cheerful, with original paintings on the walls, free Wi-Fi, fans, DSTV & tea/coffee-making facilities. Trpl & quad rooms make it a good option for families. The on-site restaurant serves lunch, dinner & light snacks. *N$830/1,200 sgl/ dbl.* **$$$**

Pioneers Park and southwest Windhoek

🏠 **Casa Blanca Hotel** [177 A7] (16 rooms) 2 Gous St/cnr Fritsche St, Pioneers Pk; 🖈061 249623; e casablanca@afol.com.na. Just next to Etambi, the turreted Casa Blanca with wrought-iron finishing has a slightly classier atmosphere but is geared to the business market, with a small conference room/bar, though its main-road location means it can be quite noisy at the front. Comfortable, stylish rooms adorned with artwork are grouped round a small, Italian-style courtyard, & have king or twin beds with minibar, a desk, DSTV & AC/heating. Room 17 is classed as luxury & features an open fire & corner bath, while 3 others have pool views. To the front is a mature garden with numerous indigenous plants & areas where guests can relax, while at the side are a small gym, pool & 'Bedouin's Rest' lounge area with firepit. B/fast is a hot-&-cold buffet, with light meals at lunch & dinner à la carte (🕑 *Sun–Fri only*). On-site parking & free Wi-Fi. *N$1,075/1,550 sgl/dbl.* **$$$$**

🏠 **Hotel Etambi Garni** [177 A7] (11 rooms) 6 Gous St, Pioneers Pk; 🖈061 241763; e etambi@ mweb.com.na; www.etambi.com. Owned by Namibian Michael Meyer, Etambi is 10mins' drive from the city centre, so you really need your own vehicle to stay here. To find it, take Marconi St westward, before turning on to Jordan St, following the signs for Pioneers Pk. The road sweeps around to the right, & after about 1km you take the 3rd left on to Hintrager St. After a further 1km, turn right on to Fritsche St, then left after the shopping centre on to Gous St; Etambi is on the right. It's a friendly & efficient little place, catering largely for independent businesspeople – so has phones, free Wi-Fi & DSTV in the large, modern rooms, each of which has its own entrance off the garden. There is an honesty bar, outside braai for guests to use, & small pool, & 9 secure parking places. City transfers are available at additional charge. *N$1,100/1,330 sgl/dbl.* **$$$**

HOSTELS AND CAMPING

Windhoek has a handful of excellent backpackers' hostels. The city's only dedicated campsite, Arebbusch, is just south of town, so of benefit only to those with vehicles. Campers without transport can pitch a tent at some of the backpackers' hostels.

🏠 **Arebbusch Travel Lodge** [177 D8] (2 houses, 23 chalets, 5 tents, 8 rooms, camping) Auas Rd, Olympia; 🖈061 252255; e reservations@ arebbusch.com; www.arebbusch.com. Less than 10km south of the centre, between the Safari Hotel & Windhoek Country Club, Arebbusch has 18 pitches for campers with their own tents/ caravans, each with power, water, kitchen & washing facilities. For those that don't, there are budget rooms sharing ablutions with the campsite, & walk-in, AC tents with en-suite bathrooms, twin beds, BBQ facilities & fridges. There are a host of self-catering options, too: chalets that sleep up to 5 people, 2 3-bedroom villas & a dbl-storey 3-bedroom cottage with a fireplace. The on-site restaurant offers a good range of steaks & salads, some vegetarian options & a kids' menu. Added to this is a bar & a good pool with waiter service for snacks & drinks. The only real snag is that you need a car to get here. *N$1,180-1,620/1,475–2,025 sgl/ dbl; camping N$280 pp.* **$$–$$$$**

🏠 **Chameleon Backpackers & Guesthouse** [180 B7] (13 rooms, 3 dorm beds) 5–7 Voigt St; 🖈061 244347; e chameleonbackpackers@iway.na; www. chameleonbackpackers.com. Relaxed & friendly, yet efficiently run, this lodge is also very central. Bright, cheerful & clean, each dormitory has lockers & its own bathroom. Dbl, twin & family rooms in various styles offer more privacy, & some are en suite. It's a homely complex, with numerous communal 'rooms': a large lounge, various terrace areas with seating, a fully fitted kitchen, & a thatched bar by an inviting pool with sunloungers. Other facilities include TVs & video, internet access, Wi-Fi & payphone, a BBQ area & a secure cage for luggage, not to mention a pool table & book exchange. Secure off-street parking is available, as are airport pickups/drop-offs (*N$310*). Trips can be booked too. *N$450–650/600–750 sgl/dbl; dorm bed N$220.* **$$**

🏠 **Cardboard Box** [177 B2] (3 rooms, 28 dorm beds, camping) 15 Johann Albrecht St; 🖈061 228994; e info@cardboardbox.com.na; www. cardboardbox.com.na. On the corner of John Meinert St, a short uphill walk from town, this is Windhoek's original backpackers' lodge, where independent travellers might meet potential travelling partners, & friendly dogs are welcome. The capital's favourite for many years thanks to its lively atmosphere, Cardboard Box has 4 6–8 bedded dorms, 3 private rooms with shared facilities, & a campsite. Campers without a tent can book a colourful converted combi fitted with a double mattress. A large, open-sided bar with booths, ceiling fans & sports TV & a separate wooden deck both overlook an inviting pool area where braais are served on Fri & Sat. For a break from the communal kitchen, you can get b/fast in the bar & light meals in the restaurant. Washing machines & internet access are available, as is secure parking & free pickup from the Intercape bus station. *Dorm N$170; camping N$110.* **$–$$**

🏠 **Paradise Garden Backpackers** [176 B2] (3 rooms sharing facilities, 22 dorm beds, camping) 5 Roentgen St, Windhoek West; ☏ 061 303494; **m** 081 280 9208; **e** paradisegarden@ iway.na; www.paradisegarden.iway.na. Every city has a homely, quirky, hard-to-find backpackers' lodge that has a vibe all of its own & Windhoek is no exception – with Paradise Garden fitting the bill. Although 'paradise' might be stretching it a bit for the garden, this small, friendly backpackers has a pool with hammocks, Wi-Fi & computer terminal, an airy TV room/lounge with DSTV, an honesty bar, laundry service – & Yellow the cat as part of the family. There is a pleasant outside area with table tennis & a braai & they will organise bookings for tours & shuttles. They even offer b/fast (*N$60*) & dinner by prior arrangement. *N$450/550 sgl/dbl; dorm bed N$190; camping N$130 pp.* **$–$$**

WINDHOEK ENVIRONS

Lodges & guest farms have proliferated around Windhoek, & many make good alternatives to staying in the city, especially on the way to or from the airport.

To the east (towards the airport)

✳ 🏠 **Omaanda** [166 G1] (12 huts) ☏ 063 673 4958; **e** reservations@omaanda.com; www.zannierhotels.com/omaanda. Opened in 2018 above a small dam on the private Zannier Reserve, the luxury Omaanda is 24km along the M53 northeast of Windhoek. The emphasis here is on a comfortable, unpretentious stay, with very high standards of hospitality. The so-called 'huts', gracefully thatched & connected by raised wooden walkways, outwardly echo traditional Ovambo architecture. Inside, they are very stylish & elegantly furnished, with roomy bathrooms,

big, comfortable beds & TVs with bluetooth connectivity. Decks look out across the reserve. Central areas include a heated swimming pool, pool deck & firepit overlooking the dam, a comfy, open-fronted lounge with sofas & fireplaces, a small spa & treatment area, & a dining room featuring the delicious output of the Belgian head chef.

The aim of the reserve is to release animals that have been rehabilitated in the neighbouring N/a'an ku sê Wildlife Sanctuary (page 122). Guided game drives from Omaanda (extra cost) can include sightings of white rhinos, wild dogs (a pack is often seen at the dam) & more rarely other predators, as well as kudu, oryx & springbok. *FB inc all house drinks N$13,620/20,960 sgl/dbl.* **$$$$$$$**

🏠 **N/a'an ku sê (Naankuse) Wildlife Sanctuary & Lodge** [166 G1] (6 chalets) **m** 081 859 4608; ☏ 061 307338; **e** lodge@ naankuse.com; www.naankuselodge.com. Established in 2007, the Naankuse Reserve is home to a wealth of wildlife, mainly due to the work of its charitable foundation (page 122). Nestled within the sanctuary's bush, its en-suite twin chalets with AC are decorated in earthy natural tones. Activities (at extra cost) focus on interacting with habituated wildlife or walks, game drives and riding in the reserve to see animals in a more natural environment. There is also the option to engage with the San Bushmen. *DBB N$2,875/5,200 sgl/dbl.* **$$$$$**

🏠 **River Crossing Lodge** [166 D3] (20 chalets) ☏ 061 401494/246788; **e** reservations@ rivercrossing.com.na; www.rivercrossing.com. na. A smart lodge with superb views designed to offer an alternative to city accommodation, River Crossing is close to both the airport & town amenities. To find it, take the B6 east towards the airport for 6km, pass under the old railway bridge & after 200m there's a sign to the right; follow this along a track for about 6km. Well-spaced chalets have views over the valley & the Moltkeblick Mountains. All have AC/heating, DSTV, tea & coffee, free Wi-Fi & black-slate walk-in showers. The central lodge area has a comfortable lounge, a bar, a large balcony & a pool with spectacular views, & a restaurant offering set-menu lunch (*N$65–175*) & 3-course dinner (*N$325*). Game drives (*N$750 pp/3hrs*) & horseriding in the mountains (page 207) are available on request. Airport transfer N$500 pp. *N$1,445/3,070 sgl/dbl.* **$$$$$**

Etango Ranch Guest Farm [166 G2]
(11 rooms) 062 540423/540451; m 081 129
3007; e etangoranch@afol.com.na. Although just
3.5km from the international airport, all is peaceful
on this family-run cattle & sheep ranch; to get there,
drive just 150m east of the airport on the B6, then
turn right through a gate & continue 2km or so down
a sandy track until you come to the farm. Owned
by Volker & Anke Grellmann & managed by their
son, Robert, it is in the Namatanga Conservancy.
En-suite twin/dbl rooms with their own veranda,
spacious showers, & a tea/coffee station are set in
pairs, with a further 2 family units, with a dbl bed
& a bunk bed for children under 16. A large lounge/
dining room allows for dining *en famille*, with a set
menu (vegetarians welcome) for lunch & dinner & a
wine list. As well as a small pool, there are excellent
opportunities for birdwatching & walks on the
farm, which has a range of endemic wildlife such
as kudu, oryx & hartebeest, & a group of mountain
zebra. With its rural location close to the airport, this
is an ideal spot for the beginning or end of a trip.
N$2,500/room. $$$$

Hohewarte Guest Farm [166 F3]
(7 rooms) m 081 354 5290; e info@hohewarte.
com; www.hohewarte.com. Once a German
colonial police station & post office & still a
working cattle farm owned by Heike, Hohewarte
stands in a beautiful area of some 10,000ha, at
the foot of the 2,299m Bismarck Mountain. To get
there, follow the B6 for about 28km, then turn
right towards Dordabis; after 15km, Hohewarte is
on the left. Simple rooms with safes are either en
suite or with shared facilities, 2 of them housed
in a separate bungalow near the pool. Informal
meals are enjoyed with the family, & tea &
coffee are always available. There is a cellphone
signal, but no internet or TV. There are several
self-guided walking trails, including to the top
of the mountain, as well as nature or farm drives
(*from N$250/2hrs*) & guided walks (*from N$250*),
& interested guests can have a tour of the farm.
N$1,415/2,354 sgl/dbl. $$$$

Heja Game Lodge [166 D2] (50 rooms)
061 257151/2; e info@hejalodge.com; www.
hejalodge.com. Signposted off the B6, 27km from
the airport (*transfers N$200 pp*), this all-singing
all-dancing lodge caters for tourists, day visitors,
weddings & conferences. To find it, take the turning
for Otjihase Mine & follow the tarred road for
3km, then turn left & follow a heavy gravel track

– through land grazed by wildebeest, springbok,
blesbok, oryx, ostrich & warthog, etc – for a further
3km. Rooms, either with AC or ceiling fans, have
DSTV, free Wi-Fi & (most) a phone; 'luxury' rooms are
just a bit larger. Both the bar (⏲ *18.00–late*) & the
plastic-tableclothed à la carte restaurant ($$$–
$$$$) are open daily, but it's especially busy for
the Sun buffet lunch (⏲ *noon–14.00; N$225*),
when you'll need to book. There's a swimming
pool overlooking the dam & a trail around it that
takes about 1hr to walk. Activities include drives
(*from N$300/2–3hrs*) & guided 20min horse rides
(*N$20–30; Sun only*). Paintballing & dragon-boat
trips can also be arranged with nearby operators.
For lovebirds, 2 private churches can host wedding
ceremonies, with 2 reception venues by the dam.
N$570/980 sgl/dbl. $$$

Onganga [166 C3] (10 rooms)
11 Schuckmann St, Avis; 061 241701;
e onganga@mweb.com.na. This simple, modern
pension near Avis Dam is signposted to the left off
the B6, shortly after leaving Windhoek; turn on to
Christa Davids St, then right on to Avisweg & 2nd
left on to Schuckmann. Built on several levels, its
screened doors & windows allow guests to take
advantage of the breeze afforded by its hillside
position. Quiet twin & dbl rooms have AC, DSTV,
phone, free Wi-Fi, minibar/fridge & tea/coffee-
making facilities. The b/fast room is decorated
with cane furniture & a Chinese restaurant reflects
the current ownership. There's also a small craft
shop. Outside, a small pool facing the mountains
is surrounded by a grassy area set with umbrellas,
overlooked by a rustic bar with a BBQ. There are
several walking trails behind the pension, & access
to Avis Dam. Airport collection N$260 pp. *N$1,250/
room.* $$$$

Vineyard Country Lodge [166 D3] (8 rooms,
1 cottage, camping) 061 224144; m 081 588
2029; e info@vineyard.com.na; www.vineyard.
com.na. Situated 1km along the same track as
River Crossing Lodge (see opposite), the Vineyard
caters mainly for conferences, but owners Colin &
Noelene Bassingthwaighte have tried hard to inject
charm into the converted century-old buildings of a
vineyard. Some of the en-suite rooms are modern,
some traditional, but all have fridges, fans & heaters,
safes & DSTV. There is also a 4-bed self-catering
cottage. The campsite at the back of the property has
8 pitches, each with a braai, sink & bathroom with
solar-heated water. The Wi-Fi is dodgy, but there are

nice touches such as homemade rusk biscuits to go with in-room tea/coffee facilities & 2 free-of-use mountain bikes. B/fast is the whole hog, continental & full English combined. There's a small, cold pool & Avis Dam walks are close by. Airport transfer N$280 pp. *N$850/1,200 sgl/dbl; camping N$250 pp.* **$$–$$$$**

⌂ **Trans Kalahari Caravan Park** [166 E3] (9 rooms, camping) 65 Kappsfarm; \ 061 222877; e info@transkalahari-inn.com; www.transkalahari-inn.com. Set back from the B6, just 21km from the airport (*transfers N$160 pp*), this is more than just a caravan park, with large, simply furnished, en-suite rooms of different standards (some with AC & 2 suitable for families), catering mainly to the German market. The campsite's 9 pitches have electricity, water & a grill area, & a toilet block with hot showers. Panoramic views across the Kappsberg Mountains form a spectacular backdrop for the solar-heated swimming pool, & the main building with a rustic bar & TV (⊕ *19.30–21.00 daily*), & a restaurant serving Namibian–German cuisine, with the emphasis on game (**$$$$–$$$$$**). A good range of crafts is for sale – ideal for last-minute souvenirs. Some may be put off by the owner's 3 labradors & 5 cats; others will appreciate the privacy. Also on site is Bobo Campers who rent & offer repairs. *N$680/790 sgl/dbl; camping N$250 per pitch.* **$$–$$$**

⌂ **Airport Lodge** [166 E2] (6 bungalows, 6 tents, camping) \ 061 231491; m 081 122 6101; e reservations@airportlodgenamibia.com; www.airportlodgenamibia.com. Run by Brian & Hermine Black, Airport Lodge is signposted from the B6, halfway between the international airport & the city; it lies 600m along the M53. Set well apart in extensive bush, each of the lodge's ethnic-décor thatched bungalows has 3 sgl beds (children will love the 3rd, set high up in its own loft area) with the option of a 4th, along with a small veranda, kitchenette, minibar, DSTV, phone & mosquito nets. Some have AC, others have fans, & heaters are provided in winter. There's an open fire for winter evenings, bars inside & out, a large swimming pool, a braai, free Wi-Fi in central areas & a conference room. B/fast costs N$110; dinner is served à la carte. With lovely mountain views & plenty of wildlife (oryx, ostrich & numerous bird species) on the property this is a peaceful & convenient stop before or after a flight (*airport transfers N$150 pp*). *Room only N$715/750 sgl/dbl.* **$$**

To the north and west

Additional options in this direction, but within relatively easy reach of Windhoek, are Daan Viljoen Nature Reserve (page 206), Okapuka Ranch (page 216) & Düsternbrook (page 216).

⌂ **Gästefarm Elisenheim** [166 C1] (9 rooms, hut, camping) \ 061 264429; www.natron/net/tour/elisenheim. Set in grounds of some 5,000ha at the foot of the mountains, Elisenheim offers German hospitality & a place to relax under the care of Andreas & Christina Werner. It is signposted to the left of the main A1 as it leaves the city, just 15km north of the centre. Cross over the highway & follow the track – & the signs – for a further 6km through the newly developed Elisenheim Estate before turning right towards the farm. En-suite rooms are comfortable, & outside is a tree-shaded swimming pool surrounded by a grassy area. Weaver birds nest in the bamboo that shelters the house. Close by is a small campsite, with 5 pitches & its own pool. Campers need to be totally self-sufficient, as nothing is available here except firewood. Travellers with a 4x4 can book the self-catering mountain hut built into the rocks. For dinner, light lunches & b/fast, try the new Farmer's Kitchen Restaurant. Visitors may explore the area, which is home to kudu, warthog, steenbok & plenty of baboons, independently. *Room only N$530/1,560 sgl/dbl; hut N$2,600; camping N$150 pp;* ⊕ *closed 15 Dec–15 Jan.* **$$–$$$$**

⌂ **Immanuel Wilderness Lodge** [166 C1] (9 rooms) \ 061 260901; e office@immanuel-lodge.de; www.immanuel-lodge.de. Set in 10ha of land, Immanuel is on the D1474, a turning off the A1 about 20mins north of Windhoek. It's run by Stephan & Sabine Hock, who came to Namibia from Germany with their 2 children. Dogs, rabbits, parrots, ostriches & a vertically challenged springbok (caused by an ear infection in its infancy) are part of this delightful homestead where visitors are proclaimed to be 'part of the family'. Stephan produces a delicious b/fast, afternoon tea & 4-course dinner (*N$295 pp*) for guests. There's a solar-heated slightly salty pool to cool off in, a nature trail & a wellness centre. Dbl & twin rooms are in 3 separate thatched bungalows, with elegant rustic furniture – some of it homemade. Each has a ceiling fan, tea/coffee facilities &, outside, a small patio with chairs. Don't come here expecting luxury, but for genuine hospitality & warmth, it would be hard to beat. *N$790/1,440 sgl/dbl.* **$$$**

🏠 **Penduka** [170 A2] (6 rondavels, 5-bed dorm, villa, camping) Goreangab Dam; ☏061 257210; e hospitality@penduka.org; www. penduka.com. 8km northwest of the city centre, this lakeside co-operative that employs local women to produce a range of crafts (page 196) also offers accommodation. To get there, follow Independence Av north through Katutura, cross over Otjomuise Rd, then bear left on to Green Mountain Dam; the centre is down a dirt track to the left. Stay in en-suite rondavels on the edge of the lake, beds in a small backpacker dorm with a communal bathroom or a fully equipped 2-bedroom villa that sleeps up to 6. There is also a small campsite with a bush kitchen. The restaurant has a terrace overlooking the lake & serves b/fast, lunch & dinner. Excursions to Windhoek townships & visits to Katutura women's homes can be arranged. Airport pickup N$350/pp. *Rondavel N$276.50–385/395–550 sgl/dbl; dorm bed N$200; camping N$95 pp.* **$–$$**

To the south
Other accommodation options south of Windhoek include **Amani Lodge** (page 210), a French-owned lodge 26km southwest of Windhoek on the C26; & **Eningu Clayhouse Lodge** (page 226), a welcoming option within 1hr of the airport.

🏠 **GocheGanas** [208 C3] (16 chalets) ☏061 224909; e info@gocheganas.com; www. gocheganas.com. Set on a hill overlooking a private 6,000ha reserve, GocheGanas – which means 'Place of the Camelthorns' – is reached from the B1 south of Windhoek; after 20km, turn left on to the D1463, & continue for a further 9km; the lodge is on the right. You'll need a high-clearance vehicle as both the D1463 & the lodge drive were in poor condition in 2018.

The lodge aims to combine wildlife with an extensive spa, including outdoor & heated indoor pools, cave sauna (🕐 *on request*), gym, & 3 treatment 'hives'. There's all you could wish for in the pampering stakes, from crystal baths to Vichy showers & massages – even a fruit & juice bar. Above the spa sits the reception & gift shop, & further up again a fine-dining restaurant & the Toko bar – both with wall-to-wall glass windows. Large & smart, the chalets have great views across the reserve, & are kitted out with twin or king-size beds, AC, TV, safe, minibar, sunken bath & shower (10 have outdoor showers as well), & a private deck. There's also a family chalet, its 2 rooms connected by a shared deck.

GocheGanas boasts an impressive range of large game species for a relatively small reserve, affording the opportunity for relaxing game drives (*N$375 pp min 4*), as well as guided (*N$150 pp*) or self-guided walks & mountain biking (*N$150 pp*). Free Wi-Fi in public areas. *DBB N$3,127–3,869/5,400–6,678 sgl/dbl.* **$$$$$–$$$$$$**

🏠 **Auas Safari Lodge** [208 C2] (16 rooms) ☏061 228104; e info@auas-safarilodge.com; www.auas-safarilodge.com. Auas is about 44km southeast of Windhoek into the Kalahari & is managed by Journeys Namibia, who also run Fish River Lodge, Desert Breeze, Shipwreck Lodge & Grootberg Lodge. To reach it, take the B1 or the C23 heading south, then turn left on to the gravel D1463 – the road may not be viable in a 2WD in the rainy season, so check in advance. The lodge is 22km from the B1, or 16km from the C23. Auas is on a game farm whose residents include black wildebeest, giraffe, & a leopard in a separate enclosure. The active will appreciate the swimming pool, game drives (*N$440 pp*) & guided nature walk (*N$220 pp*), while more sedentary guests can relax on their own veranda. *DBB N$1,665/2,500 sgl/dbl.* **$$$$**

GAME LODGES AND GUEST FARMS Even if you're staying in Windhoek, you may like to spend half a day or so visiting a local game lodge or guest farm. Places within easy reach of the city that welcome day visitors include **Midgard Country Estate** (page 216), **Auas Safari Lodge** (see above), **Amani Lodge** (page 210) and **Hohewarte Guest Farm** (page 187).

❮ WHERE TO EAT AND DRINK

Windhoek has lots of cafés and restaurants, though you'll often have more success searching for European cuisine than African specialities. Until the late 1990s, most served fairly similar fare, often with a German bias, but now Italian, Portuguese, Chinese and even Indian specialities have been added to the mix. Many reach a very high standard, and few are expensive in European or American terms. Note that many places are closed on Sundays.

As a spin-off from the burgeoning restaurant scene, there are plenty of fast-food places, particularly in the new shopping malls. Pies, burgers and the like are freely available at points right across the city, including Nando's on Independence Avenue, just up from the station, while in the shopping malls, particularly at Maerua Mall, pizza parlours proliferate. It's often worth picking up a free copy of the monthly *Out & About in Windhoek* booklet from the tourist information office – it lists new bars and restaurants.

Eating at the very best, and without restricting your choices, you would have to try very hard to make a meal cost more than N$250 per person. Here's a selection of favourites.

RESTAURANTS

✕ Bushbar [177 E8] 6347 Tennis St, Olympia; `061 304480; ◷ 16.00–midnight Tue–Thu, noon–midnight Fri–Sun. This trendy watering hole on the outskirts of town sums itself up with the slogan 'Beer, Beef, Bush'. Windhoek's hip crowd comes here for the superb steaks & burgers, & the chilled-out vibe aided by its lovely terrace overlooking flaxen grasses. Has free Wi-Fi & is worth the taxi ride. Not particularly smart, but superb food. $$$$$

✕ Ekipa [180 C5] Hilton hotel (page 178); ◷ lunch: noon–14.30 Mon–Fri, 12.30–15.00 Sat–Sun, dinner: 18.00–22.30 daily. Upmarket restaurant at the Hilton with state-of-the-art open kitchen. Offers an extensive buffet & an à la carte menu of wood-fired pizzas, burgers, freshly grilled meats & Namibian specialities, with regular themed foodie nights, such as Indian. $$$$$

✕ Leo's at the Castle [176 D4] 22 Heinitzburg St; `061 249597; ◷ 18.30–22.00 daily. Small, modern & sophisticated, the Heinitzburg's stylish restaurant is one for special occasions. The carefully selected à la carte menu, masterminded by the hotel's owner/ chef, is based on French international cuisine & is dominated by fish & game (but vegetarians are well catered for on request). Alternatively, try the 4-course gourmet menu. The wine cellar is the largest in Namibia with over 15,000 bottles, so be prepared to linger over the wine list. Leo's is expensive, but you get what you pay for – although the wine is a little overpriced. Bookings essential, hotel guests prioritised. $$$$$

✕ Olive [176 D1] 22 Promenaden Weg, Klein Windhoek; `061 383890; www.theolive-namibia. com; ◷ 07.00–21.30 daily. The restaurant at the

Olive Exclusive (page 175) gives priority bookings to its guests but it's well worth trying to get a table here, if only to get a glimpse of the hotel's stunning décor, with wall-size images of Himba people & clever use of natural resources like huge pieces of granite & wood. The food is exquisite too, with elegantly presented 4-course set dinners & light à la carte lunches served in a relaxed atmosphere either indoors or on the terrace overlooking the city. $$$$$

✕ Peppercorn [177 E5] Maerua Mall; `061 254154; ◷ 11.00–late daily. Once called the Cattle Baron, this grill & steakhouse is relaxed & very family-friendly thanks to its separate kids' menu. It's pricey, but we've been told the chateaubriand is melt-in-the-mouth delicious. $$$$$

✕ Sardinia Blue Olive [176 F3] Cnr Sam Nujoma Dr & Nelson Mandela Av; `061 258183; ◷ 09.30–22.30 daily. Upmarket Italian restaurant that, despite rumours of arrogant staff, is praised by locals for its vegetarian options, perfect pizzas & fresh fish, fast service & freshly baked bread. $$$$$

✕ O Portuga [176 F3] 312 Sam Nujoma Dr, Klein Windhoek; `061 272900; ◷ noon–23.00 daily. This friendly & relaxed Portuguese/Angolan restaurant has a wide-ranging menu that is particularly strong on seafood, with huge portions. South African wines are fairly standard; Portuguese are very expensive. It's popular with a mixed clientele, but service can be very slow when the place is busy. $$$$–$$$$$

✕ The Social [176 D1] Cnr Liliencron St & Robert Mugabe Av; `061 252946; m 081 623 1011; ◷ 11.00–22.00 Mon–Sat. Despite its proximity to the main road, The Social is both intimate & relatively quiet, with dining inside & out & friendly, willing service that can't help but make you smile. The menu is billed as Mediterranean, but if you're offered fresh fish, don't hesitate; the galjoen was superb – & the kingklip pretty good, too. $$$$–$$$$$

✕ **Café Zoo/La Marmite Royale** [180 C4] 129 Independence Av; ☏061 235647; ⏰ 08.00–23.00 daily. At the bottom of Zoo Park, this elegant & central restaurant has a shaded terrace, making it a perfect lunchtime venue. Cameroonian chef, Martial, was poached from the once-popular La Marmite restaurant, so fans of his cooking should head here for African/Western fusion dishes alongside pizzas & seafood. During the day it serves delicious cakes, coffee & light meals, & after dark locals come for the cocktails (happy hour ⏰ 18.00–20.00 daily), Cuban music & cigars. $$$$

✕ **Chez Wou** [170 C7] Windhoek Country Club; ☏061 205591; ⏰ 11.00–14.00 & 17.00–23.00 daily. The very good Chinese restaurant at the Windhoek Country Club attracts a busy trade from outside the hotel. $$$$

✕ **Wine Bar** [180 D6] 3 Garten St; ☏061 226514; www.windmill-wines.com; ⏰ 16.00–23.30 Mon–Thu, 15.00–midnight Fri, 17.00–22.30 Sat. From the top of one of Windhoek's many hills, the Wine Bar has great views over the city & is quite central. With seating inside & out & a covered balcony area, this is a local favourite for a sundowner on the way home from the office. Wine is their trade; the range is extensive & expert advice is available, with a wine shop on the premises too. The small but varied menu is good, with braais on Thu & Fri nights. $$$$

✳✕ **Joe's Beerhouse** [176 D1] 160 Nelson Mandela Av; ☏061 232457; www.joesbeerhouse. com; ⏰ 16.30–late Mon–Thu, 11.00–late Fri–Sun. The cavernous thatched premises that house Joe's Beerhouse seat over 400 people in a rustic environment set around a large bar area: a stalwart of Windhoek's restaurant scene. Although traditionally strictly for serious 'carnivores', with lots of game & huge portions, veggies are now getting a look in, as are some seafood options. Beers & spirits are excellent, but wines are mediocre. Service can be slow & lackadaisical, but there's always a lively vibe here: Joe's reputation goes before it; the place is almost always full & booking usually essential. A small craft shop sells postcards too. $$$–$$$$$

✕ **Nice** [180 A4] 2 Mozart St, cnr Hosea Kotako Dr; ☏061 300710; www.nice.com.na; ⏰ lunch only noon–14.30 Mon–Fri. The Namibian Institute of Culinary Education is a training restaurant for budding Namibian chefs. Situated in a huge old house that has been renovated into a labyrinth of small restaurants, it has outside seating with small pools as a feature. Dishes from the small but imaginative menu, which changes daily, are created in a kitchen that is on full view behind a large glass window. $$$–$$$$$

✳✕ **The Stellenbosch Wine Bar & Bistro** [176 F3] 78 Sam Nujoma Dr; ☏061 309141; www.thestellenboschwinebar.com; ⏰ noon–15.00 & 18.00–22.00 Mon–Sat. Outstanding bistro with a finely honed menu featuring all manner of mouth-watering dishes such as risotto, pork belly, gourmet salads & prime flame-grilled steaks – all paired with top-notch yet affordable South African wines. $$$–$$$$

✕ **The Stellenbosch Tasting Room** Contact via the wine bar, above. Serves an outstanding selection of wines & light meals. Seating is outside in the courtyard, directly opposite the Wine Bar & Bistro. $$$

✕ **Cape Town Fish Market** [176 G4] 13 Jan Jonker Rd, Klein Windhoek; ☏083 331 8101; ⏰ noon–22.00 daily. In a renovated old house on the newly developed Am Weinberg Estate, this is a place for consistently good seafood. There's seating inside & out & a balcony area with good views over the suburbs. $$–$$$$$

✕ **Grand Canyon Spur** [180 C3] 251 Independence Av & Maerua Mall; ☏061 231003; ⏰ 10.00–22.00 daily. Situated above street level, opposite the Bank Windhoek, the Wild West-style Spur offers mediocre American burgers, steaks & a host of side orders. It's all a bit sticky & cheap, but the atmosphere is lively & it's a godsend for parents because of the soft-play kids' area. $$–$$$$$

✕ **Kubata** [176 D1] 151 Nelson Mandela Av, Eros; ☏061 404944; www.kubata.com.na; ⏰ noon–22.00 Mon–Sat, noon–21.00 Sun. A cosy restaurant offering doner kebabs & a good variety of seafood along with the likes of paella. $$–$$$$$

✕ **Yang Tze** [176 F3] 351 Sam Nujoma Dr; ☏061 234779; ⏰ 11.30–14.30 & 17.30–22.00 daily. This large, efficient Chinese restaurant & take-away is on the upper level of a small shopping

centre, near the junction with Nelson Mandela Av.
$$–$$$$$

✕ Andy's [176 F3] 318 Sam Nujoma Dr; ☎061 401516; ⏰ 16.00–23.00 Tue–Thu, noon–23.00 Fri–Sun. German pub (see also right) serving gigantic pizzas, but service can be slow. $$$

CAFÉS

☕ Dulcé Café [177 E5] Upper Mall, Maerua Mall; ☎061 239966; ⏰ 07.30–18.30 Mon–Fri, 08.00–15.30 Sat, 08.00–13.30 Sun. Superb light, modern café serving Continental fare such as pizzas & wraps, as well as all-day b/fasts & gourmet burgers. Very popular with locals. $$$$

☕ Wecke & Voights Kaffee Bar [180 C4] Gustav Voight Centre, Independence Av; ☎061 377000; ⏰ 07.00–17.30 daily. Urban-chic coffee bar to the side of this upmarket interior-design shop. Good sandwiches & 'build your own' b/fasts. $$$–$$$$

☕ Lemon Tree Restaurant [176 D1] Cnr Robert Mugabe Av & Liliencron St; ☎061 240346; ⏰ 07.00–18.00 Mon–Fri, 08.30–14.00 Sat–Sun. Set in a shady courtyard & overlooking a split-level fish-pond, this popular café serves delicious b/fasts, tasty open sandwiches & light lunches, & a variety of well-made coffees & juices. $$$

✳ ☕ Craft Café [180 C5] 40 Tal St, Old Breweries; ☎061 249974; www.craftcafe-namibia. com; ⏰ 08.00–18.30 Mon–Fri, 08.00–15.00 Sat, 09.00–15.30 Sun. A popular café with open-air balcony, this is one of Windhoek's best eateries, even if the view isn't up to much. Frequented by locals & visitors, it serves a great range of homemade quiches, salads, cakes & puddings, not to mention fresh lemonade & all sorts of other goodies. It's on the same premises as the excellent Craft Centre – though open slightly longer hours (if the Craft Centre is closed, take the stairs to the left in what looks like a red steel tower). $$

☕ Vintage [176 D1] Cnr Robert Mugabe Av & Luther St; ☎061 259295; ⏰ 07.15–16.00 Mon–Thu, 07.15–22.00 Fri, 07.00–14.00 Sat. A converted house with large terrace offering b/fasts & light lunches. It's a particularly good spot for families as there are child-size tables & a playground. $–$$

☕ Wilde Eend Coffee Shop [176 E3] 10 Dr Kenneth David Kaunda St, Klein Windhoek; ☎061 272632; ⏰ 08.00–17.00 Mon–Fri, 08.00–13.00 Sat. Enjoy a tasty b/fast, salad, wrap or sandwich accompanied by a fresh juice, smoothie or coffee in tranquil surroundings. $–$$

☕ The Stellenbosch Market [176 F3] 78 Sam Nujoma Dr; ☎061 309141; www. thestellenboschwinebar.com; ⏰ noon–15.00 & 18.00–22.00 Mon–Sat. A boutique wine shop & deli serving premium wine, coffee roasted in-house & fresh deli goods to take away or eat in, either inside or in the courtyard opposite the Stellenbosch Wine Bar & Bistro. $$$

BARS

🍷 Andy's [176 F3] 318 Sam Nujoma Dr; ☎061 401516; ⏰ 16.00–late Tue–Thu, 11.00–late Fri–Sun. A German pub with *Cheers*-style square bar & walls decorated with car licence plates, it's owned by the larger-than-life bald Andy & draws a very loyal drinking crowd. Has a garden out the back, serves food (see above) & usually screens sports as well.

🍷 Boiler Room [180 B5] 46 Tal St; ⏰ 16.00–late Mon–Sat. Good for drinks prior to events at the neighbouring Warehouse Theatre (page 193).

🍷 Bushbar [177 E8] 6347 Tennis St, Olympia; ☎061 304480; ⏰ 16.00–midnight Tue–Thu, noon–midnight Fri–Sun. This cosmopolitan watering hole on the outskirts of town has a chilled-out vibe & a lovely terrace overlooking flaxen grasses – & free Wi-Fi. See also page 190.

🍷 Dvine Wine & Sushi Bar [180 C5] Hilton Hotel (page 178); ⏰ 17.00–22.00 Mon–Sat. In the sleek wine bar inside the Hilton Hotel, fine wines – displayed in glass-fronted fridges that line the room – are served with first-rate sushi platters.

🍷 Hotel Heinitzburg [177 D4] 22 Heinitzburg St; ☎061 249597; www.heinitzburg.com. For a special occasion or a treat, enjoy cocktails on the garden terrace of this upmarket boutique hotel (page 175).

🍷 Joe's Beerhouse [176 D1] 160 Nelson Mandela Av; ☎061 232457; www.joesbeerhouse. com; ⏰ 16.30–late Mon–Thu, 11.00–late Fri–Sun. Best known for its carnivorous menu, Joe's is just as popular as a drinking hole thanks to its lively atmosphere & excellent beers & spirits.

🍷 Que Tapas [177 E5] 16 Liliencron St, 📱 081 861 7797; ⏰ 11.00–midnight Mon–Sat, 11.00–19.00 Sun. Lively corner bar serving tapas & a large selection of cocktails.

🍷 Skybar [180 C5] Cnr Sam Nujoma Dr & Rev Michael Scott St; ☎061 296 2929; ⏰ 10.00–

midnight daily. The Hilton's rooftop bar is unquestionably the hippest place for drinks, no matter the time of day. The views overlooking town are superb & the slimline pool just adds to the glamour.

🍷 **Wine Bar** [180 D6] 3 Garten St; ☎ 061 226514; ⏰ 06.00–23.30 Mon–Thu, 15.00–midnight Fri, 17.00–22.30 Sat. A local favourite for a sundowner, it has great views over the city, with seating inside & out & a covered balcony area. As you'd expect from the name, wine is their trade; the range is extensive & expert advice is available.

ENTERTAINMENT AND NIGHTLIFE

Windhoek is not famous for its nightlife. Most visitors choose to go to a restaurant for a leisurely dinner and perhaps a drink, and then retire for an early start the next day. But if you're after some fun, there are a few cocktail bars (see opposite) and nightclubs, as well as the occasional concert. Friday is usually the best night. Similarly, weekends at the start/end of the month, when people have just been paid, are busier than those in the middle.

A word of note: in the poorer areas, especially in the old townships, there are some illegal *shebeens* (so-called *cuca shops*), geared purely to serious drinking. It's worth noting that here, as in most traditional cultures in southern Africa, respectable women are rarely seen in bars. Furthermore, if you get word of a local club in one of the townships, go with a local or get a reliable taxi that will take you and collect you.

To find out what's on, take a look at the online events calendar www. whatsonwindhoek.com and pick up a free copy of the monthly *Out & About in Windhoek* booklet from the tourist information office – it lists new bars and restaurants. Information is also advertised at the back of newspapers, especially the Friday editions of *The Namibian* and *Windhoek Observer*, which cover the weekend. Otherwise, keep an eye out for posters around the city, try the Windhoek city information office, or ask at your hotel or pension.

NIGHTCLUBS
☆ **Club Vibe** [177 C5] 4 Nasmith St, Southern Industrial; ⏰ 20.30–02.00 Fri–Sat. Formerly La Dee Da's, this club puts on a wide range of parties from foam to hip hop every w/end. No under 18s.
☆ **El Cubano** [180 C5] Basement of the Hilton (page 178); ⏰ 21.00–late Fri–Sat. Accessed via a side entrance in the basement of the Hilton Hotel, this is the place to go if you like salsa. Can be expensive: drinks are bought with tokens that aren't refunded at the end of the night.

CINEMAS AND CASINOS
Cinema ticket prices are low compared with those in Europe or the US, but films shown in both cinemas are very much the latest Hollywood releases. Drinks & snacks are available too. Windhoek's only officially licensed **casinos** are located inside the **Avani Hotel** (page 178), the **Windhoek Country Club Resort** (page 178) & the basement of the **Hilton** (page 178).

🎬 **Maerua Mall Ster Kinekor Cinema** [177 E5] Maerua Mall; ☎ 083 330 0360
🎬 **The Grove Mall Ster Kinekor Cinema** [170 D7] Frankie Fredericks Dr, Kleine Kuppe; ☎ 061 243603

THEATRES AND CONCERTS
🎭 **College of the Arts** [180 B4] 41 Fidel Castro St; ☎ 061 225841. Occasionally hosts classical concerts in its auditorium.
🎭 **Franco-Namibian Cultural Centre (FNCC)** [180 C1] 118 Robert Mugabe Av; ☎ 061 387330; www.fncc.org.na. Showcases a variety of small concerts, exhibitions & cultural events, & screens art-house films in its cinema too.
🎭 **National Theatre of Namibia** [180 C2] 12 John Meinert St; ☎ 061 374400; www.ntn. org.na. Hosts concerts, opera, theatre, ballet & contemporary dance performances.
🎭 **Warehouse Theatre** [180 C5] Old Breweries Bldg, 48 Tal St; ☎ 061 402253; www. warehousetheatre.com.na; ⏰ 16.00–02.00

Mon–Sat. At this relaxed & trendy venue, jazz, reggae, *mbaganga* & pop bands perform on Thu & Fri; upcoming artists showcase their work on Wed. Cover charges vary with the band. Snacks are available, but dine elsewhere before you arrive; the Boiler Room bar (page 192) is next door.

SHOPPING

Shopping in Windhoek was revolutionised several years ago when the **Town Square** shopping mall [180 B4] (⊕ *daily; morning only at w/ends*) was opened right in the centre. It's a top-notch mall with plenty of choice and sets the standard for shops throughout the capital. Around this, most of the area is pedestrianised, incorporating **Post Street Mall** [180 B3], Mutual Platz, Levinson Arcade and the **Wernhil Park** [180 A4] (*www.wernhilpark.com*). At weekends in particular it's a busy, bustling place.

Parking in the city centre is still relatively straightforward, with a couple of car parks clearly marked. Alternatively, if you want to stay for an hour at most, use one of the meters on Independence Avenue.

Beyond the centre is **Maerua Mall** [177 E5] with plenty of free parking. Then to the east of town, in Klein Windhoek, the relatively new **Bougain Villas Shopping Centre** [176 F3] houses various boutique shops focusing on arts and crafts alongside cafés, delis and salons. Then there's the recently completed **Freedom Plaza** [180 C5], near the Hilton Hotel, and **The Grove Mall** (*www.thegrovemallofnamibia.com*), in the southern suburb of Klein Kuppe [177 E8].

Unless otherwise stated, shops listed below are open around 09.00–17.00 Monday–Friday, and on Saturday morning.

BOOKS AND MUSIC Imported books are generally expensive in Namibia, and even those published locally are subject to a heavy sales tax. But if you want something specific on Namibia, then often you'll get titles here which are difficult to find abroad.

CNA [177 E5 & 180 A4] Maerua Mall & Wernhil Park. A large South African book chain with a section on the latest titles. Very mainstream.
Der Neue Bücherkeller [180 C4] Carl List Mall, Fidel Castro St; ℩061 231615. Linked to Swakopmund Buchhandlung, the New Book Cellar has a good choice of travel books, field guides & natural history books in German & English, plus the usual novels & coffee-table books.
Musica [177 E5] Maerua Mall & Wernhil Park. A large range of CDs & DVDs – good for African music.
Onganda Y'Omambo Books [180 B3] North side of Post St Mall; ℩061 235796. New & secondhand books, with a particularly good selection on Namibian history & culture, & by Namibian authors.

Orombonde Books Main entrance of Namibia Craft Centre [180 C6], Tal St; m 081 148 8462. Run by historian Wolfram Hartmann & his dog, this is one of the most diverse bookstores in town with a variety of titles in numerous languages.
The Book Den [180 A4] Cnr Hosea Kutako Dr & Puccini St; ℩061 239976. Namibia's largest privately owned bookshop with friendly staff to boot.
Uncle Spike's Book Exchange [180 C6] Garten St, cnr Tal St; ℩061 226722. Corner den with shelves stuffed with secondhand books, particularly guidebooks. Buzz to be let through the grid gate.

CAMERAS AND OPTICS Most popular cameras can be found here, though they are usually more expensive than they would be in Europe or the US. There are numerous places that will print your snaps – often within the hour – or sell you a film, but Windhoek's best specialists are:

Foto First [180 C3] Independence Av; ⊕ 08.00–17.00 Mon–Sat. Offers 1hr photo service.

Nitzsche-Reiter Front of Sanlam Centre [180 C4], Independence Av; ☏061 231116

CAMPING KIT

To rent It is easy to arrange the hire of camping kit in Windhoek, provided that you can return it at the end of your trip. Both the following companies have a comprehensive range, from tents and portable toilets to full 'kitchenboxes', gaslights and jerry cans. They are best contacted at least a month in advance, and can then arrange for a pack incorporating what you want to be ready when you arrive. The minimum rental period is three days. They usually request a 50% deposit to confirm the order, with full payment due on collection of equipment.

Adventure Camping Hire [177 C6] 33 Tacoma St; ☏061 242478; m 081 129 9135; e adventur@ iway.na; ⊕ 08.00–13.00 & 14.00–17.00 Mon–Fri. Affordable outlet whose owner, Immo Kersten, is usually on hand to provide expert advice.

Camping Hire Namibia [177 F8] 78 Mose Tjitendero St, Olympia; ☏061 252995; m 081 124 4364; e camping@iafrica.com.na; www. orusovo.com/camphire; ⊕ 08.00–13.00 & 14.00–16.00 Mon–Fri; w/ends by appointment. Rents everything from tents to coffee mugs. Cash only.

To buy If you need to buy camping kit in Namibia, then Windhoek has the best choice. Items from South Africa are widely available, but kit from Europe or the US is harder to find.

Bush Beat [177 E5] Upper Mall, Maerua Mall; ☏061 222 219; www.bush-beat.com. Split into 2 stores either side of the aisle: 1 sells safari clothes, the other, brand-name surf clothing such as Quiksilver & Roxy.

Bushwhackers [170 C4] 32 Rhino St, Rhino Park; ☏061 258760. One of the biggest & best outdoor shops, Bushwhackers is north of the city, & a good one-stop option before heading out into the wilds. Follow Hosea Kutako towards the Northern Industrial area, turn left on to Ooievaar St & then right to Rhino St; Bushwhackers is 200m along on the right. Along with a full range of camping/ hiking gear, a huge fishing section & all the 4x4 gadgets & supplies, they also deal in caravans & boats, sales & spares.

Cape Union Mart [177 E5] Maerua Mall & The Grove Mall; ☏061 220424; ⊕ 09.00–17.30 Mon–Fri, 09.00–14.00 Sat, 09.00–13.00 Sun. A wide range of camping equipment, safari clothes & shoes.

Cymot [180 B4 & 170 C5] 60 Mandume Ndemufayo Av ☏061 295 7000; 342 Independence Av ☏061 237759; www.cymot.com.na. With 1 central branch & a 2nd a little way out in northern Windhoek, Cymot has the best range around: everything from tents & outdoor equipment to a good selection of cycles & spares, to spare parts for cars. There are smaller branches throughout the country.

Due South [177 E5] Lower Mall, Maerua Mall & The Grove Mall; ☏061 370445. South African store with selection of upmarket safari clothing, shoes & camping basics.

Safari Den [176 C5] 8 Bessemer St, Auas Valley Shopping Mall; ☏064 290 9294. A plush shop with binoculars, knives (including Swiss Army & Leatherman tools) & a useful range of tents, sleeping bags & other camping kit.

Safariland (Holtz) [180 C5] Gustav Voigts Centre; ☏061 235941; www.safarilandholtz. com; ⊕ 08.00–17.30 Mon–Fri, 08.00–13.00 Sat, 09.00–12.30 Sun. Has a similar variety of safari & bush wear.

CRAFTS AND CURIOS The **Post Street Mall** [180 B3] normally hosts one of the capital's largest craft and curio displays, as street traders set out their wares on blankets in front of the shops.

Off the streets, if you visit only one place for curios and souvenirs, make sure it's the **Old Breweries Complex** [180 C5] on Tal Street. This attractive courtyard has a number of craft shops and cafés, as well as the excellent Namibia Craft Centre.

Bushman Art Gallery Erkraths Bldg [180 C4], 187 Independence Av; \061 228828/229131; www.bushmanart-gallery.com; ⊕ 08.30–17.30 Mon–Fri, 08.30–13.00 Sat, 09.00–13.00 Sun. Despite the name, this is primarily a shop, albeit with an unusually large selection. At the front it is purely a curio/gift shop, with a good selection of books on Namibia (in German & English), as well as T-shirts, jewellery, gemstones, cards, hats & even socks. At the back, however, among artefacts on sale from all over Africa, are small displays of Bushman tools, clothing, etc, various African masks & Karakul carpets.

Casa Anin [177 F3] Bougain Villas Shopping Centre, 78 Sam Nujoma Dr; \061 256410; www. anin.com.na. Built up by Heidi von Hase from a small village embroidery group with the aim of empowering women whose only skill was sewing learned from missionaries, Casa Anin is now a sought-after brand & supplies many of Namibia's top lodges with their linen & soft furnishings. This is their only retail outlet, selling fine handmade bedlinen, embroidered textiles & interesting gifts.

Namcraft [180 C5] Old Breweries complex, Tal St; \061 250342; ⊕ 08.30–18.00 Mon–Fri, 08.30–17.00 Sat–Sun. This Namibian-owned chain sells crafts & a wide array of jewellery made by craftspeople both from Namibia & worldwide –

ideal for presents. Other outlets in Swakopmund, Walvis Bay & Outjo, & at Mokuti Lodge.

Namibia Craft Centre [180 C6] 40 Tal St; \061 242 2222; ⊕ 09.00–17.30 Mon–Fri, 09.00–16.00 Sat, 09.00–13.30 Sun. At the heart of the Old Breweries complex, this remains the capital's best place for arts & crafts. Numerous stalls showcase the full range: paintings, sculptures, designs in copper, hand-painted fabrics, carvings, basketwork, textiles, embroidered linen, jewellery & much else. Many of the exhibitors welcome visitors to their workshops located around the country. The centre also has an excellent café (page 192).

Penduka [170 A2] Goreangab Dam; \061 257210; www.penduka.com; ⊕ 08.00–17.00 Mon–Sat. Out beyond Katutura, overlooking the Goreangab Dam 8km northwest of the city centre, this co-operative employs local women in a village setting to produce a range of crafts, including textiles & baskets. You can buy them in the on-site shop, have a cup of coffee & slice of cake & – with advance notice – book a workshop in basket braiding, batik or recycled-glass jewellery-making from €15. Alternatively, a selection of Penduka crafts is for sale in the Namibia Craft Centre. Overnight accommodation is also available (page 189).

GEMSTONES Given the incredible minerals and precious stones that are mined in Namibia, it's a wonder that there aren't better gemstones for sale as curios. Sadly, many of the agates and semi-precious stones seen in curio shops on Independence Avenue are imported from as far away as Brazil, but there are exceptions to the rule, as below.

House of Gems [180 B2] 131 Werner List St; \061 225202; www.namrocks.com; ⊕ 09.00–13.00 & 14.00–17.00 Mon–Fri, 09.00–noon Sat. Tucked away near John Meinert St, this was established in 1947 by Sid Peters, one of the country's leading gemmologists. It's a real collector's place, packed with original bits & pieces. Even if you're not buying, it is worth visiting, since here you can see the raw stones sorted, cut, faceted & polished on the premises.

The Diamond Works [180 C5] Unit 40, Old Breweries; \061 229049; www.thediamondworks. co.za; ⊕ 09.00–18.00 Mon–Fri, 09.00–14.00 Sat–Sun. Glossy shop selling predesigned diamond, tanzanite & other gemstone jewellery, but more fun is to pick a rock & watch them cut it on site as you sip on a glass of bubbly.

LEATHERWORK AND TAXIDERMY Windhoek is a good place to buy leatherwork, including lots of ostrich, game and karakul leathers. Don't expect any give-aways, but if you know what you want then there are good deals to be had. The standard varies greatly; highest-quality sources in the centre of town are:

Leder Chic [180 C4] Carl List Mall, Fidel Castro St (near Der Neue Bücherkeller); ✆061 234422. For a selection of leather bags, wallets & belts.
Nakara [180 C5] Gustav Voigts Centre, 165 Independence Av; ✆061 224209; www.nakara-namibia.com. For Namibian ostrich & leather goods including zebra, springbok & kudu skins.
Trophäendienste Taxidermy [166 D3] B6, towards the international airport; ✆061 232236; www.trophaendienste.com; ⊕ 06.30–18.00 Mon–Fri, 09.00–17.00 Sat–Sun. 10km from Windhoek on the main road to the airport – look out for the gaudily painted animals standing on each other by the roadside – is a huge souvenir showroom with a coffee shop selling preserved African animals. All a bit macabre, to be honest.

SUPERMARKETS

Checkers [180 C5] Gustav Voigts Centre, Independence Av & Maerua Mall; ✆061 237410; ⊕ 08.00–20.00 daily
Food Lovers' Market Fruit & Veg City [177 E5] Maerua Mall; ✆061 377150; ⊕ 08.30–18.00 Mon–Thu, 08.30–19.00 Fri, 07.00–17.00 Sat, 09.00–13.00 Sun. Healthy living supermarket. Also at Frankie Fredericks St, Klein Kuppe, & new wing of Wernhil Park.
Pick n Pay [180 A4] Basement of Wernhil Park; ✆061 296 4500; ⊕ 09.00–18.00 Mon–Fri, 09.00–14.00 Sat, 09.00–13.00 Sun.
Shoprite [180 C2] Independence Av; ✆061 217237; ⊕ 08.00–18.00 Mon–Thu, 08.00–18.30 Fri, 08.00–16.00 Sat, 09.00–13.00 Sun
Superspar [177 E5] Maerua Mall & The Grove Mall; ✆061 377000; ⊕ 07.30–19.00 Mon–Fri, 07.30–19.30 Sat, 07.30–18.00 Sun

SPORTS

Nucleus [180 C5] Old Breweries, Tal St; ✆061 225493; www.nucleushfc.com; ⊕ 05.00–21.00 Mon–Thu, 05.00–20.00 Fri, 09.00–17.00 Sat–Sun. This centrally located gym has been operating since the early 1990s. It offers full changing facilities, basic running/cycling machines & general fitness apparatus. There's another branch at Baines Shopping Centre, Pioneers Park. N$150/day, N$300/wk.
Olympia Swimming Pool [177 E8] Cnr Sean McBride & Frankie Fredericks sts, Olympia; ✆061 290 3089; ⊕ daily. This aptly named pool has an Olympic-size main pool, children's paddling pool, kiosk & trained lifeguards. A 2nd pool, the Western Suburbs Swimming Pool, also has a 50m pool.
Virgin Active [177 E5] Centaurus Rd, by Maerua Mall; ✆061 234399; ⊕ 05.00–21.00 Mon–Thu, 05.00–20.00 Fri, 06.00–19.00 Sat–Sun. The city's biggest gym has a large indoor pool, plus a big gym with lots of training machines, an aerobics studio, several glass-backed squash courts, & steam & sauna rooms. Day membership as a casual visitor is N$170, so if you need to relax & have a shower in town before travelling, this is the perfect place. Although the car park is patrolled, don't leave your luggage unattended in your vehicle. A 2nd branch is on Frankie Fredericks Dr in Klein Kuppe, next to The Grove Mall.
Windhoek Golf [170 C7] Western Bypass; ✆061 258498; e gm@wccgolf.com.na; www.wccgolf.com.na. The 18-hole golf course next to Windhoek Country Club Resort (page 178) offers upmarket facilities, including a resident professional, motorised caddies, a driving range & a well-equipped pro shop. The clubhouse has a bar area & a restaurant. Next door is the Windhoek Bowls Club, which has its own clubhouse, bar & swimming pool. Hotel residents N$90/180 9/18 holes; non-affiliated N$290/580 9/18 holes; driving range N$30/60 30/60 balls.

OTHER PRACTICALITIES

AIRLINES

✈ **Air Berlin** [180 A4] Middle Level, Wernhil Park; ✆061 302220; e wdh@sisatravel.com; www.airberlin.com; ⊕ 08.30–16.30 Mon–Fri
✈ **Air Namibia** [180 B4] Town Sq opp Standard Bank (access via Post Street Mall), cnr Werner List & Fidel Castro sts ✆061 299 6333; e central.

✈ **KLM** 4th Floor Maerua Mall Office Tower, Jan Jonker Av; ☎061 415262; Garten St ☎061 256601

✈ **Qatar Airways** 3rd Floor Maerua Mall Office Tower, Jan Jonker Av, ☎061 445208

✈ **South African Airways (SAA)** [180 C4] Sanlam Centre, Independence Av; ☎061 273340; www.flysaa.com; ⊕ 07.30–17.00 Mon–Fri, 08.00–noon Sat.

✈ **TAAG Angolan Airlines** [180 C4] Sanlam Centre, Independence Av; ☎061 226625; www.taag.com; ⊕ 09.00–17.00 Mon–Fri

reservations@airnamibia.aero; www.airnamibia.com.na; ⊕ 08.00–17.00 Mon–Fri, 09.00–noon Sat; Eros International Airport ☎061 299 6508 (mostly domestic & regional flights); Hosea Kutako International Airport ☎061 299 6600 (main international airport)

✈ **British Airways/Comair** ☎061 248528; www.britishairways.com. Telephone/internet only.

✈ **Ethiopian Airlines** Independence Av; ☎61 256601; www.ethiopianairlines.com

✈ **Eurowings** ☎+ 27 21 300 3720

BANKS AND MONEY The centre of town has all the major banks in the country. All have ATMs and are generally very efficient; there are also ATMs in the various shopping malls across the city and at many of the petrol stations. If you need anything complex, like an international money transfer, go to the largest branch possible. In any event, remember to take your passport with you.

Rates for exchanging money are the same at most of the banks, though you can expect to get considerably lower rates from a hotel. Outside of normal banking hours, the bureau de change at Nedbank is open on Saturdays and also accepts American Express cards, while the bureaux de change at the airport are opened for incoming flights. Money can also be changed at the main post office (see below).

$ **Bank Windhoek** [180 C3] 262 Independence Av; ☎061 299 1500; www.bankwindhoek.com.na

$ **FNB** [180 C3] 209–11 Independence Av; ☎061 299 2111; www.fnbnamibia.com.na; ⊕ 09.00–15.30 Mon–Fri, 08.30–noon Sat

$ **Nedbank** Main branch: 12–20 Dr Frans Indongo St ☎061 295 2163; Central: Carl List House, 27 Independence Av ☎061 295 2180; www.nedbank.com.na

$ **Standard Bank** [180 C3] 261 Independence Av; ☎061 2944111; www.standardbank.com.na; ⊕ 09.00–15.30 Mon–Fri, 08.30–11.00 Sat

COMMUNICATIONS AND POST By far the most economical means of staying in touch while you're away is to buy a local SIM card on arrival. These are available at Hosea Kutako International Airport (page 169), or from any of the numerous MTC outlets around the city, including Post Street Mall and Maerua Park. Almost every hotel, pension, B&B and backpackers offers Wi-Fi services.

✉ **Post office** [180 C3] Cnr Independence Av & Daniel Munamava St; ☎061 201 3006; www.nampost.com.na; ⊕ 08.00–16.30 Mon, Tue, Thu & Fri, 08.30–16.30 Wed, 08.00–noon Sat. It's cheap & easy to send packages overseas from here, & it also sells phonecards. Aside from this, the office has a foreign-exchange desk, a good philately counter, a place to make international phone calls, plus access to the internet.

🖳 **Net Café** [180 B2] Cnr Robert Mugabe Av & John Meinert St; ☎061 304165; ⊕ 08.00–21.00 daily. Charges N$10 per 30mins & sells drinks.

EMBASSIES AND HIGH COMMISSIONS Namibia's diplomatic missions abroad can be found on page 107. For visa extensions or anything to do with immigration, you need the **Ministry of Home Affairs and Immigration** (*Cohen Bldg, cnr Kasino St & Independence Av;* ☎061 292 2111; ⊕ 08.00–13.00 Mon–Fri).

🇦 **Angola** (embassy) 4th Floor, Angola Hse, 3 Dr Agostinho Neto St; ☎061 227535; e embangola@ mweb.com.na; www.angola.visahq.com; ⊕ 09.00–15.00 Mon–Fri

ⓔ Botswana (high commission) 101 Nelson Mandela Av, Klein Windhoek; ☎ 061 221941/2/7; e botnam@gov.bw; ⏰ 08.00–13.00 & 14.00–16.30 Mon–Fri

ⓔ Brazil (embassy) 52 Bismarck St; ☎ 061 237368; e brasemb@mweb.com.na

ⓔ Canada (consulate) 1st Floor, Office Tower, Maerua Mall; ☎ 061 251254; e canada@mweb. com.na; ⏰ 08.00–13.00 & 14.00–16.00 Mon–Fri

ⓔ China (embassy) 28 Hebenstreit St, Ludwigsdorf; ☎ 061 402598; e chinaemb-na@ mfa.gov.cn; http://na.chineseembassy.org; ⏰ 08.30–noon & 14.30–17.00 Mon–Fri (office), 09.00–11.30 Mon, Wed & Fri (consular)

ⓔ Denmark (consulate) 11 Eland St, Finkenstein Estate; ☎ 085 124 4219, m 081 226 6838; e cfnorgaard@gmail.com; www.namibia.um.dk; ⏰ 08.00–16.30 Mon–Thu, 08.00–15.00 Fri

ⓔ Egypt (embassy) 10 Berg St, Klein Windhoek; ☎ 061 221501; e embassy.windhoek@mfa.gov.eg; ⏰ 08.30–15.00 Mon–Fri

ⓔ Finland (embassy) 2 Crohn St; ☎ 061 221355; e sanomat.win@formin.fi; www.finland.org.na; ⏰ 09.00–noon Mon, Wed, Thu

ⓔ France (embassy) 1 Goethe St; ☎ 061 276700; www.ambafrance-na.org; ⏰ 09.00–noon Mon–Fri

ⓔ Germany (embassy) 6th Floor, Sanlam Centre, 145 Independence Av; ☎ 061 273100; e info@ windhoek.auswaerties-amt.de; www.windhuk. diplo.de; ⏰ 09.00–noon Mon, Tue, Thu & Fri, 14.00–16.00 Wed

ⓔ Ghana (high commission) 5 Nelson Mandela Av, Klein Windhoek; ☎ 061 221341; ⏰ 09.00–15.00 Mon–Fri

ⓔ Italy (consulate) 41 Von Falkenhausen St, Pioneers Park; m 081 147 1250; e rosannareboldi@yahoo.com; ⏰ 09.00–noon Tue & Thu or by appointment

ⓔ Kenya (high commission) 5th Floor, Kenya Hse, 134 Robert Mugabe Av; ☎ 061 226836; e kenyanet@mweb.com.na

ⓔ Nigeria (high commission) 4 General Murtala Mohammed Rd, Eros; ☎ 061 232103; e enquiries@ nhcwindhoek.org; www.nhcwindhoek.org; ⏰ 09.00–17.00 Mon–Fri; visas ⏰ 09.00–noon Mon–Fri

ⓔ Norway & Sweden (consulate) 39 Schanzen Weg; ☎ 061 258278; e klaus@appih-endresen. com; ⏰ 09.00–noon Mon–Fri

ⓔ South Africa (high commission) RSA Hse, 48 Jan Jonker Rd, Klein Windhoek; ☎ 061 205 7111; e windhoek.consular@dirco.gov.za; www.dirco. gov.za; ⏰ 08.00–16.30 Mon–Thu, 08.00–15.00 Fri, consular: 08.15–12.15 Mon–Fri

ⓔ Spain (embassy) 58 Bismarck St; ☎ 061 223066; e embespna@mail.mae.es; www. exteriores.gob.es

ⓔ Switzerland (consulate) 175 Independence Av; ☎ 061 223853; e windhoek@honrep.ch

ⓔ UK (high commission) 116 Robert Mugabe Av; ☎ 061 274800; e general.windhoek@fco.gov. uk; www.gov.uk; ⏰ consular: 08.00–noon & 14.00–15.30 Mon–Thu, 08.00–11.00 Fri

ⓔ USA (embassy) 14 Lossen St; ☎ 061 295 8500; e consularwindho@state.gov; www.windhoek. usembassy.gov; ⏰ Mon & Wed mornings by appointment only

ⓔ Zambia (high commission) 22 Mandume Ndemufayo St; ☎ 061 237610; e zahico@iway. na; www.zahico.iway.na; ⏰ 09.00–13.00 & 14.00–16.00 Mon–Fri

ⓔ Zimbabwe (high commission) Cnr Independence Av & Grimm St; ☎ 061 227738; e info@zimwhk.com; www.zimwhk.com; ⏰ 08.00–16.30 Mon–Fri; consular: 08.00–noon Mon–Fri

HOSPITALS In an emergency, call ☎ 211111, or ☎ 112 from a mobile. You will be put through to an operator who can reach the ambulance or fire services. In case of difficulty getting through, phone ☎ 1199. For an ambulance from the private International SOS, call ☎ 0800 911911 toll free, or ☎ 061 230505. If you're calling from a mobile, the number is m 081 707. The police can be reached on ☎ 10111. If you've a serious problem outside Windhoek, then contact **International SOS** (page 125).

✚ Windhoek Central Hospital [176 B1] Oievaar St; ☎ 061 203 9111; ⏰ 4hrs. Windhoek's main hospital is good, but with huge demands from the local population it can become very busy. If you've

a serious medical condition then it's better to use your medical travel insurance & contact one of the private hospitals (each of which is open 24hrs & has an accident & emergency department).

⊞ **Lady Pohamba Private Hospital** [170 D7]
Cnr Frankie Fredericks & Ombika drives, Kleine
Kuppe (next to The Grove Mall); ☏083 335 9000/40
⊞ **Mediclinic** [170 D3] Heliodoor St, Eros; ☏061
433 1000, emergency ☏061 222687; www.
mediclinic.co.za. Windhoek's most expensive clinic,
reached via Nelson Mandela Av & then General
Murtala Mohammed Rd.

⊞ **Rhino Park Private Hospital** [170 C3] Hosea
Kutako Dr; ☏061 225434; www.hospital.com.na.
Aims to provide affordable health care, but has no
casualty department.
⊞ **Roman Catholic Hospital** [180 B3] 92 Karl
Werner List St; ☏061 237237; www.rcchurch.na.
More central, but not so plush.

PHARMACIES There are numerous pharmacies throughout the city, most with a
range of goods and drugs that is equal to anything in western Europe or the USA.

✚ **Kalahari Pharmacy** [180 C4] 1st Floor,
Gustav Voigts Centre, Independence Av; ☏061
252448; ⊕ 09.00–17.30 Mon–Fri, 09.00–13.00
Sat, closed Sun

✚ **Langerhans Pharmacy** [180 C7]
7 Independence Av; ☏061 222581; ⊕ 08.30–
17.20 Mon–Fri, 08.30–12.50 Sat, closed Sun
✚ **MediSun** [180 A4] Ground Floor, Wernhil
Park; ⊕ 08.30–18.00 Mon–Fri, 08.30–13.30 Sat,
10.00–13.00 Sun

WHAT TO SEE AND DO

Although Windhoek isn't the planet's liveliest capital, there are some beautiful
old buildings, a number of art galleries and museums – including the glitzy new
Independence Memorial Museum – and some tours worth taking.

WINDHOEK'S HISTORICAL BUILDINGS: A WALKING TOUR (*Duration: 2/3hrs*) Most
of Windhoek's historical buildings date from around the turn of the 20th century,
and are close to the centre of town. Walking is the obvious way to see these.

Starting in the Post Street Mall [180 B3], look for the **Gibeon Meteorites** [180
B4] – a series of odd rock clumps displayed on plinths outside Town Square Mall.
In fact, these reddish rocks freckled with holes are pieces of meteor that were
discovered in 1838 near Gibeon, a village some 60km south of Mariental, by
General J E Alexander. He took samples back to London and the iron-rich clumps
were identified by renowned astronomer and chemist Sir John Herschel. They were
part of what is thought to have been the world's heaviest meteorite shower, which
occurred around 600 million years ago. About 150 meteorites – ranging in weight
from 195 to 596kg – have been recovered so far; many of these are in museums
around the globe. At the junction of the mall with Independence Avenue is a replica
of the **clocktower** [180 C3] that was once on the old Deutsche-Afrikabank. The
original was constructed in 1908.

Now turn southeast, towards Christus Kirche, and cross Independence Avenue
into Zoo Park. From here, you can get a good view of three fine buildings on the west
side of Independence Avenue; like many of Windhoek's older landmarks, they were
designed by the German Willi Sander. On the right is the **Erkraths Building** [180
B4], built in 1910: a business downstairs, and a place to live upstairs. **Gathemann
House**, in the middle, was designed for Heinrich Gathemann, the then mayor of
Klein Windhoek, and was built in 1913 to a basically European design, complete
with a steep roof to prevent any accumulation of snow! It, too, originally had living
quarters above the business. Third in line is the old **Kronprinz Hotel**, designed and
built by Sander in 1901 and 1902. It was extended in 1909, and refurbished and
extended in 1920. It is now overshadowed by the Sanlam building, but a plan

has been made to modernise the shops (one of which is Nakara, page 197) while preserving the façades.

Continuing into **Zoo Park** [180 C4], you will find two features of note on green lawns under the palm trees. A sculptured **Elephant Column** more than a metre high marks the place where primitive tools and elephant remains, dated to about 5,000 years ago, were found. Scenes of an imagined elephant-hunt kill are depicted in bas-relief by Namibian sculptress Dörte Berner, and a fossilised elephant skull tops the column. On the south side of the elephant column is the **war memorial**, about a century old, crowned by an eagle and dedicated to German soldiers killed while fighting the Nama people. As yet there is no memorial here for the Nama people, led by Hendrik Witbooi, although they are remembered as part of the newer monument at Heroes' Acre (page 206).

Now head south on Independence Avenue a short way until the first left turn, up Fidel Castro Street. This junction is the site of the new **Freedom Plaza** [180 C5]. On the left, on the far corner of Lüderitz Street, you will see the **Hauptkasse**. Once the house of the Receiver of Revenue, as well as officers' quarters and even a hostel, it is now used by the Ministry of Agriculture. Opposite the Hauptkasse, on the south side of Fidel Castro Street, **Ludwig Van Estorff House** [180 C4] was built in 1891 as a simple canteen. It is named after a commander of the Schutztruppe, the German colonial troops, who lived here in 1902–10, and is now the National Reference Library.

Nearby, in a commanding position on its own roundabout, is **Christus Kirche** [180 D4], a fairy-tale Evangelical Lutheran church and Windhoek's most famous building. It was designed by Gottlieb Redecker in Art Nouveau and Neo-Gothic styles, and built between 1907 and 1910 of local sandstone. Kaiser Wilhelm II donated the stained-glass windows; his wife, Augusta, gave the altar Bible. Originally this church commemorated the peace at the end of various wars between the German colonists and the indigenous people of Namibia, and inside are plaques dedicated to the German soldiers who were killed. (As yet, there's no mention of the losses of the indigenous people.) The church is normally locked, but if you wish to see inside, it should be possible to borrow the key during office hours (⊕ *07.30–13.00 Mon–Fri*) from the church offices, just down the hill at 12 Fidel Castro Street.

On the west side of Robert Mugabe Avenue, near Christus Kirche, the **Kaiserliche Realschule** [180 D4] is now part of the National Museum. When first built, however, in 1907–08, it was a school, becoming Windhoek's first German high school.

Walking further south along Robert Mugabe Avenue, you'll see the new Bank of Namibia building. On your right, just before crossing Sam Nujoma Drive, is the **Office of the Ombudsman** [180 D5]. Built in 1906–07 as a dwelling for the chief justice and his first clerk, this has much decorative work typical of the German 'Putz' style of architecture. The original stables are now a garage and outbuilding.

Now turn around and walk back towards Christus Kirche, on the right (east) side of Robert Mugabe Avenue. The large building on the right is the old fort, **Alte Feste** [180 D5], built by the first Schutztruppe when they arrived here around 1890. It is strategically positioned overlooking the valley, though its battlements were never seriously besieged. A plaque on the front maintains the colonial view that it was built to 'preserve peace and order' between the local warring tribes – which is as poor a justification for colonialism as any. Inside, although much of the main historical section of the National Museum has been moved to its new neighbour, the Independence Memorial Museum, some displays remain (page 203). In front of the building stands a new **statue of a man and woman**

THE MYSTERY OF THE MISSING REITERDENKMAL

Once one of Windhoek's best-known landmarks, the Reiterdenkmal (Equestrian Statue), disappeared under cover of darkness on Christmas Day 2013. For years the subject of controversial debate, it stood proudly opposite Christus Kirche, commemorating German soldiers who fell during the Namibian war of resistance 1903–07. But with no equivalent memorial to the Herero and Nama – whose losses far outnumbered those of the colonialists – it represented to many a distorted and supremacist view of Namibian history.

In 2010, with the building of the new Independence Memorial Museum, the statue was moved to a plinth outside neighbouring Alte Feste. Government plans to declassify it as a national monument required a public consultation period of 60 days, and on 20 December 2013 notice was given to this effect. However, on the evening of 25 December, while the city centre was deserted, the Reiterdenkmal was surreptitiously removed by the authorities and squirrelled away to the yard in the Alte Feste. Its whereabouts were a mystery – even the receptionist at the Alte Feste knew nothing about its relocation until he saw the horse and rider the following morning, ignominiously propped up by scaffolding poles, peering into his office window. A media frenzy ensued, with fierce debate about the significance of the memorial in today's Namibia and the secretive nature of its removal.

Three German groups in Namibia started legal proceedings to reinstate the Reiterdenkmal, but eventually accepted they were fighting a losing battle. At the time of writing, it remains in the Alte Feste courtyard like a stateless refugee with rumours suggesting it might return to Germany.

representing the heroes of the struggle for independence, with words from the Namibian National Anthem written below: 'Their blood waters our freedom.' This controversially replaced the large Equestrian Statue in December 2013 (see box, above), which commemorated the German soldiers killed during the wars to subdue the Nama and Herero groups, around 1903–07 (but with no mention of the Nama or Herero people who died).

To the left of the Alte Feste, on a hill towering over Christus Kirche, you can't help but notice the new **Independence Memorial Museum** [180 D4] (see opposite). The N$60 million triangular building looks like a high-spec glass-fronted office block gleaming in the sun. Inaugurated by President Pohamba on 20 March 2014, it tells the story of Namibia's struggle for independence, with a towering statue of Sam Nujoma, the country's founding father, in front of it.

Once back at the Christus Kirche, turning right (east) leads you to what were originally the administrative offices of the German colonial government, the **Parliament** [180 D4]. The building became known as the Tintenpalast, or Ink Palace, for the amount of bureaucracy that went on there, and has housed successive governments since around 1912. The Germans occupied it for only about a year, before losing the colony to South Africa after World War I. Now this beautiful double-storey building is home to Namibia's parliament, where visitors can take a 1-hour tour of the building (⊕ *09.00–16.00 Mon–Fri; www.parliament.gov.na*); you can either book online, or (in theory) just turn up. Even if you don't take a tour, do make time for the lovely formal gardens and fountain that grace the area in front.

As you continue north along Robert Mugabe Avenue, on the left is the old **State House** [177 F6]. Built in 1958, on the site of the old German governor's residence, it was used by South Africa's administrator general until 1990, when it became the president's official residence. (A new State House has since been constructed.)

It is now a short walk left, down Daniel Munamava Street, back to join Independence Avenue by the main post office.

MUSEUMS, GALLERIES AND LIBRARIES Windhoek has, perhaps after Swakopmund, some of the country's best museums, galleries and libraries, though even these state collections are limited. The South African regime, which controlled the museums until 1990, had a polarised view of the country's history, understandably, and undesirably, slanted towards their involvement in it. It remains difficult to find out much of the history of Namibia's indigenous peoples, although the museums, particularly the new Independence Memorial Museum, are gradually redressing the balance.

Alte Feste and State Museum [180 D5] (*Robert Mugabe Av*) Once the capital's best museum, with fascinating displays on rock art in particular, Alte Feste has been closed for renovations since 2014, with no indication of when – or if – it will reopen. In the meantime, many of the items have been moved to the smart new Independence Memorial Museum next door – among them exhibits relating to independence and the transition to majority rule in 1990.

Independence Memorial Museum [180 D4] (*Robert Mugabe Av;* \061 276800; ⏱ 09.30–17.00 daily; open until 18.00 in summer, Oct–Apr; admission free) Next to Alte Feste, this new museum finally opened on 20 March 2014 to coincide with the 24th anniversary of Namibia's independence. (It had originally been planned for 2010.) Using newspaper archives, military exhibits, personal records and vividly detailed paintings, the first floor depicts the years of colonial repression under the rule of Germany and South Africa, the second covers the Liberation War and the third recounts the events on the road to independence, culminating in a dramatic and enormous mural called the *History Panorama*. It's an interesting, thought-provoking museum focusing on a relatively little-known part of African history that was inextricably linked to yet overshadowed by events in neighbouring South Africa. The glass lifts on the exterior of the building are worth a visit too, providing great views of the city as you ascend – views that run to 360 degrees from the fourth-floor NIMMS restaurant (*http://nimms.com.na*).

Owela Museum [180 C2] (*4 Robert Mugabe Av;* \061 276825; ⏱ 09.00–18.00 Mon–Fri, 10.00–12.30 & 15.00–17.00 Sat–Sun; open until 18.00 in summer, Oct–Apr; admission free) North of State House, almost opposite Conradie Road, Owela Museum houses the natural history sections of the State Museum, with a good section on cheetah conservation, and a little on the country's traditional cultures.

TransNamib Museum [180 B1] (*1st Floor, Windhoek Station, Bahnhof St;* \061 298 2186; ⏱ 08.00–13.00 & 14.00–17.00 Mon–Fri; admission N$5) Housed upstairs in the old railway station building, this museum is run by the parastatal transport company, TransNamib. It shows the development of transport in the country over the last century, with particular emphasis on the rail network. Ring the bell when you arrive; the museum is probably open, even if the gate is locked!

National Art Gallery of Namibia [180 C2] (*Cnr Robert Mugabe Av & John Meinert St;* \061 231160; www.nagn.org.na; ⏱ 08.00–17.00 Tue–Fri, 09.00–

14.00 Sat; admission free, but donations encouraged) Namibia's small National Gallery has a permanent exhibition of Namibian art – some historical, some contemporary – and also hosts a variety of visiting exhibitions. It's well worth checking out.

Geological Museum [177 C7] (*1 Aviation Rd;* \061 284 8111; ⊕ *08.00–13.00 & 14.00–17.00 Mon–Fri; admission free*) Very few tourists know this museum exists or, if they do, bother to make the journey towards Eros Airport to see it, which is a shame. Treasures include 750-year-old stromatolites, fossilised eggshells and reptiles, and the lower jaw of the first fossil ape found in the southern hemisphere that is over 13 million years old.

National Reference Library [180 C4] (*11 Fidel Castro St;* \061 293 4203) Housed in Ludwig Van Estorff House (page 201), this is really of more relevance to serious researchers than casual visitors.

Franco-Namibian Cultural Centre [180 C1] Many of the books and magazines in the centre's **library** are in French, but there is a good selection of French books that have been translated into English, books on Namibia and books by Namibians. The gallery in the building hosts various photography and art exhibitions (page 193).

Also of interest are the **John Muafangejo Art Centre**, which exhibits the work of young Namibian artists, and the **Centre for Visual and Performing Arts**.

NATIONAL BOTANICAL GARDENS [176 E3] (*8 Orban St;* \061 202 2014; *www. nbri.org.na;* ⊕ *08.00–17.00 Mon–Fri, 08.00–11.00 1st Sat of month; admission free*) One of Windhoek's lesser-known attractions is this 12ha garden, in which 99% of the plants are indigenous species. Part of the gardens have been landscaped, with areas representing the different habitats found in Namibia, while the remainder is just natural Windhoek bush dotted with impressive aloes. It's an attractive spot for a picnic, and there are self-guided trails through the garden, with plant and bird lists available from the reception. To find it, turn left on to Hügel Street from Sam Nujoma Drive, then right after about 200m into Orban Street. The gate into the gardens is at the end of the street.

KATUTURA [170 B2] Windhoek's northern township, Katutura (see box, opposite), is becoming more accessible to visitors, in a similar way to Johannesburg's Soweto.

For the visitor, streets in the township are very confusing and it's easy for an outsider to get lost, so it's best to stick to the main thoroughfares. Nevertheless, it's safe enough here in the daytime, though at night it is not advisable to come without a guide. Some of the city tours (page 174) include Katutura on their itineraries.

There are two **markets** in Katutura: Soweto on Independence Avenue, and Kakukaze Mungunda Market on Mungunda Street. To find out about opening times, contact the Windhoek city information office in Post Street Mall (page 173). Beyond the townships is the Penduka co-operative (page 196).

Xwama Cultural Village [170 A2] (*Cnr Independence Av & Omongo St;* \061 210270; e *info@xwama.com; www.xwama.com; admission free*) In the heart of Katutura, Xwama Cultural Village was set up to showcase Namibia's cultures, song, dance and – particularly – its cuisine. There's a restaurant (**$$**), a take-away food

Since 1913, most black people in the city had lived in what is now known as the Old Location, to the west of Independence Avenue around Hochland Park. When, during the 1950s, the authorities decided to build a new location as part of the Union National Party's enforced apartheid, they were met with stiff resistance, culminating in riots on the night of 10 December 1959. The Old Location was duly abolished, and the people forcefully resettled to Katutura and the neighbouring townships of Khomasdal, Wanaheda and Okuryangava.

Although the line dividing the white areas of Windhoek from the black townships was effectively Hosea Kutako Avenue, the real division came earlier, at the point where Independence Avenue crosses the railway line. During the years of apartheid, workers heading into the centre of town needed to show a *kopf* (or 'head') card to be allowed over the bridge; in the evening, the gate was closed at 18.00, preventing further movement in and out of the centre of Windhoek by black Namibians.

In the early days, there was strict segregation in the townships by tribe, with houses labelled 'D' for Damara, 'H' for Herero, 'O' for Owambo, etc. Even now, house numbers indicate tribal affiliations, each in different areas. After the declaration of independence in 1990, the government invited Namibians from the north to come to the capital to work, with promises of a house, a garden, a job and even a car. Thousands of people accepted the invitation, and the population of the townships swelled – even if the reality did not necessarily match up to the promises. Today, the population of Katutura is officially around 40,000, but unofficial estimates place that figure far higher, at up to 200,000.

At first, long houses were built to meet the needs of large, extended families of farm workers. Later, small corrugated-iron 'box' houses formed the second phase of development. The third phase, with the best of intentions, was the construction by various NGOs of modern houses. Most of the people who moved into the area came from traditional kraals in the north of the country, and were ill-equipped to cope with the challenges of urban life. Where there were small houses, families of eight to 12 people would move in, and Western-style kitchens were left empty as the tradition of cooking in the open air was continued in the small yards.

It would be unsurprising if the streets of Katutura were strewn with litter, but by and large the reverse is the case. It is striking that, in spite of the sprawling nature of the township, and the density of housing, it is both orderly and clean. Water pipes are stationed every 300–400m. In some areas, bougainvillea lines the streets, and there are occasional sunflowers in the gardens. Maize, too, is grown, though this is almost exclusively for *tombo* – maize beer – not to eat. There is little in the way of cultivation of food, and malnutrition is rife.

Perhaps unexpectedly, there is no shortage of schools. These are government run, but most were built by donations from overseas charities and governments. Although, in theory, education is compulsory, the reality is not so straightforward. Aside from the cost of schooling, each child must have a uniform. As wages in the black community are significantly lower than those for white workers, many families cannot afford to provide this uniform, and their children remain on the streets. For the post-school generation, there are a number of training opportunities provided by churches, hospitals and schools, as well as the government, in fields that include nursing and waitressing.

outlet and a craft shop. To reach it, drive north along Independence Avenue, cross the junction with the B1 and continue into Katutura for about 4.2km. Turn left into Omongo Street and the cultural village is immediately on your right.

EXCURSIONS OUTSIDE WINDHOEK

AVIS DAM [166 D3] On the road to the international airport, Avis Dam is a manmade lake created by a dam across the Klein Windhoek River. Paths around the lake are mostly frequented by local dog walkers, but guided morning walks can be arranged through the **Namibia Bird Club** (\ *061 225727; www.namibiabirdclub. org*). The lake is also popular with local people for fishing, picnics, canoeing and bike rides, but there's little of any scenic interest to attract visitors.

For those interested in **watersports**, an alternative option would be Lake Oanob (page 228), about an hour's drive south of Windhoek.

DAAN VILJOEN NATURE RESERVE [166 A2] (⊕ *sunrise–sunset daily; admission N$100 pp, N$10/vehicle*) Namibia's smallest game park, some 20km west of the city, is ideal for a 'close to the city' bush experience. Among others, it is home to klipspringer, zebra, giraffe, oryx, blue wildebeest and numerous bird species, including Rüppell's parrot. Happily, visitors are free to walk around the park and there are two marked hiking trails you can follow. Mountain biking is also possible and there's a short 6.5km self-drive game route as well.

🏠 **Where to stay**

🏠 **Sun Karros** Daan Viljoen [166 A2] (9 chalets, camping; \ 061 232393, 083 323 2393; e reservations@sunkarros.com; www.sunkarros. com. The resort in the middle of the Daan Viljoen Reserve offers luxurious & modern en-suite chalets with private patio, as well as 2 campsites: the Suricate Group site with 12 smart, equipped pitches; & the Porcupine, with a further 7 'luxury' pitches. The restaurant serves an à la carte menu & there's a well-stocked kiosk (ideal for self-drivers needing supplies for their journey), an internet café & a large swimming pool. Nature drives & sundowner drives are offered as well as marked walking trails. *B&B chalet N$1,290/2,580 pp; camping N$300/450 pp, both exc park fees (page 103).* **$$–$$$$**

HEROES' ACRE [166 C4] (*B1 towards Rehoboth, left exit; admission free*) About 15km south of the city, to the left of the B1 as you head south from Windhoek, Heroes' Acre scales up the hillside and is dedicated to 'the Namibian peoples' struggle for independence and self-emancipation'. It was completed in 2002 for the annual Heroes' Day, 26 August – a public holiday.

Entering through the soaring square arches, the eye is drawn to the 170 graves that lead in stepped terraces up to a 34m-high obelisk meant to symbolise a sword and the bravery and strength of the fighters who fought for liberation. The enormous bronze mural behind it depicts the various struggles Namibians have faced throughout history; from left to right: the oppression under German rule (1884–1915), the 1960s fight for liberation from South Africa's occupation and apartheid policies, and the Unknown Soldier leading soldiers to victory and raising the flag for an independent Namibia in 1990.

In front of the obelisk stands an 8m-high bronze statue of Namibia's Unknown Soldier, carrying a rifle and a grenade. Beneath him, on a pedestal, is a replica of President Sam Nujoma's handwriting, reading: 'Glory to the fallen heroes and heroines of the motherland Namibia!'

HORSERIDING Several game farms around the city offer horseriding to guests but you'll need to book well in advance.

Equitrails m 081 338 0743; e sam@equitrails. org; www.equitrails.org. Established by Sam McCartney, a qualified British Horse Society instructor with over 10 years' experience of horse safaris in Africa, Equitrails is based at Gästefarm Elisenheim (page 188). As well as rides by the hour (*N$600 pp/hr*), it offers 3hr sundowner rides (*N$850 pp*), 5hr champagne brunch rides in the mountains (*N$1,300 pp*), day rides with a picnic (*N$1,300 pp*) & 1–5-night lodge-based trails (*from N$5,500 pp*). Return transfers from Windhoek can be arranged.

Hohewarte Guest Farm (page 187) Hohewarte mostly offers sunrise/sunset rides for their guests but Heike Koehler will also quote on tailor-made horseback excursions.

River Crossing Lodge (page 186) Set up by local horseriding personality Andrew Gillies, this operation organises various rides in the nearby & spectacular Moltkeblick Mountains (*N$360 pp per hr*). See also page 211.

OTHER POSSIBILITIES Within relatively easy reach of Windhoek are Okahandja (about 1½ hours by car), with its woodcarvers' markets, and the nearby Von Bach Dam and Gross Barmen Hot Springs (page 217). Or if you just want to escape the city for a day, you could try some watersports at Lake Oanob Resort (page 228).

NAMIBIA ONLINE

For additional online content, articles, photos and more on Namibia, why not visit www.bradtguides.com/namibia?

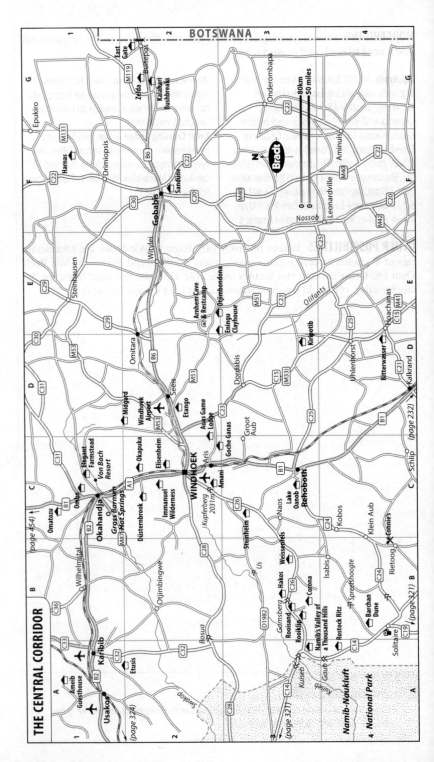

THE CENTRAL CORRIDOR

BOTSWANA

208

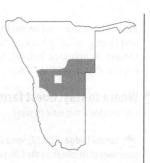

10

The Central Corridor

Despite Windhoek's dominance of the country's central region, it still occupies only a relatively small area; the city doesn't sprawl for miles. Drive just 15km from the centre and you will be on an open highway, whichever direction you choose. The completion of the Trans-Kalahari Highway means that you can drive right across this region from Walvis Bay to South Africa's northern heartland, without leaving tarmac.

This chapter concentrates on this central swathe of Namibia, working outwards from Windhoek – to the edges of the Namib-Naukluft National Park in the west, and to the border with Botswana in the east. Few of the towns in this region warrant more than a refuelling stop: they are generally small and many hardly qualify for the title of 'town'.

WEST FROM WINDHOEK: TO THE COAST

Travelling from Windhoek to the coast, there's a choice of three obvious roads: the main tarred B2, the C28 and the more southerly C26. If speed is important, then take the B2: about 4 hours of very easy driving. Both the 'C' roads are gravel, and will take at least 6 hours to drive, but the trade off is that they are quieter and far more scenic than the B2.

Note that some of the side roads off these three main roads are used very little. The D1412, for example, is a narrow, slow road whose crossing of the Kuiseb is wide and sandy. It would probably be impassable during the rainy season.

THE C28 The shortest of the gravel roads, the C28 goes through beautiful scenery, but is also tortuous, with numerous cattle grids along its route. Around halfway along, you drive (slowly!) through the steep gradients (20%) of the Bosua Pass – where the central Namibian Highlands start to give way to granite kopjes of rounded boulders before the low, flat Namib.

Between the C28 and the B2, Etusis Lodge (page 219) makes a good stop when travelling north–south, as it is somewhat off-piste between Windhoek and Swakopmund.

THE C26 The C26 is much longer than the C28, but just as scenic. Just after its start, it climbs steeply through the Khomas Hochland Mountains to the Kupferberg Pass, then later winds through the remarkable folded mountains of the Gamsberg Pass: 20km of twists and turns, taking about 40 minutes to drive if you go gently (admiring the views). Further on still it merges with the C14 before the Kuiseb

Pass, where the road wend its way down into the river valley, across a small bridge, and then gradually back up to the desert plain (discussed in *Chapter 13*). Rooisand Desert Ranch (see below), near the foot of the Gamsberg Pass, would make an excellent stop on the C26.

🏠 Where to stay: Guest farms and lodges along the C26 *Lodges detailed below are located from east to west.*

🏠 **Amani Lodge** [208 C2] Some 28km southwest of Windhoek on the C26, just before the Kupferberg Pass, Amani lies at an altitude of 2,150m. The lodge was closed at the time of research in 2018, but may well reopen during the lifetime of this book. If so, it will restore its reputation as the highest lodge in Namibia – with attendant views.

🏠 **Steinheim** [208 C3] (studios, house, camping) m 081 855 8744; e barbarasteenkamp@gmail.com. Along a 2km track north of the C26, some 55km west of Windhoek, the Steenkamps were hard at work on their new self-catering venture in late 2018. Along with individual 'eco-cabins' or studios, is a self-catering house: a beautifully designed barn-like structure, with a big porch, 2 en-suite rooms off a large living/dining area, & a further 2 attic rooms. Down by the (normally dry) river are 4 individual & very private camping pitches taking up to 30 campers each. Hiking & 4x4 drives will be possible on the property, with the potential for very experienced riders to go horseriding. Contact them for rates, which are yet to be fixed.

🏠 **Weissenfels Guest Farm** [208 B3] (5 chalets, camping) m 081 124 1818, 081 292 3821; e rowins@iafrica.com.na; www. weissenfelsnamibia.com. About 120km west of Windhoek after the D1265 turn-off, & just east of the Gamsberg Pass, Weissenfels covers 40km² of rolling highlands. Established in 1992, it has been run since 2001 by Winston Retief & Rosi Rohr, who have retained its traditional, homely feel. Guests stay in simple, self-catering chalets with a lounge & bathroom, or at a campsite with 3 pitches – though you could camp out by the dam, too – or at Mama Temba's on the same property, a simple retreat 6km from the farm that also has 5 rondavels. But Weissenfels – underpinned by a deep commitment to natural health – offers far more than a bed for the night. The farm is home to the Vortex Wellness Centre, where Winston has created Namibia's largest labyrinth, wide enough

for a wheelchair; a 2hr walk (*N$450 pp*) includes interpretations. There's a fair amount of game around, too. Explore pleasant hiking trails (with a radio supplied in case you get lost); enjoy a picnic at the farm's rock pools; take a sunset drive into the mountains; or go horseriding (experienced riders only): this is a stud farm, too. *N$1,500/1,300 sgl/dbl; camping N$250 pp.* **$$–$$$**

🏠 **Hakos Guest Farm** [208 B3] (15 rooms, camping) ☎ 062 572111; e info@hakos-astrofarm.com; www.hakos-astrofarm.com. Signposted north of the C26 from the top of the Gamsberg Pass, this small guest farm that specialises in astronomy lies at 1,832m along an exceptionally scenic 7km drive. Simple rooms in 2 blocks come with twin beds, cool stone floors & picture windows, & guests can take in the scenery from the indoor swimming pool. But pride of place goes to the campsite, where each of the 4 pitches has its own beautifully tiled toilet & shower block, a solid dining shelter with braai, & stupendous views.

Hakos is home to the International Amateur Observatory & its equipment is impressive – including 3 small observatories – though amateur astronomers are encouraged to bring their own equipment, & Friedhelm offers guided star tours to the uninitiated (*N$500 up to 4 people*). Popular among the various hiking trails is the 2.25km Planet Way, running to scale from the Sun (or farmhouse) to the farthest reaches of Neptune, or you could set out on a tough 4x4 route into the Hakos Mountains. *DBB N$1,380/2,260 sgl/dbl; camping N$220 pp.* **$$–$$$$**

🏠 **Rooisand Desert Ranch** [208 B3] (9 rooms, observatory chalet, camping) m 081 127 7629; e lifestyle@rooisand.com; www. rooisand.com. At the foot of the Gamsberg Pass, the 120km² Rooisand is about 30km in each direction from the pass itself & the junction of the C14 & C26. The atmosphere is both friendly & informal, with a focus on family-orientated activities. In addition to hiking & drives in the mountains (*from N$175 pp, min 2*), where zebra, oryx & springbok are often spotted, there is a large swimming pool & a floodlit tennis court. Stargazers will appreciate the 2.5km planetary walk, astro tours (N$350/3hrs, min 2) & the well-equipped observatory. Added interest comes from rock paintings on the farm, & a quarry that occasionally throws up some interesting semi-precious stones.

Guests stay in large twin or dbl 'comfort' rooms, much smaller 'budget' rooms by the tennis court, or at the relatively remote campsite. Here, 5 separate pitches with electricity, braais & water share ablutions & a volleyball court with 10 open-sided camping cabins; a swimming/waterhole is planned for 2019. Campers may join activities, & dine in the thatched lapa, but other facilities are for lodge guests only. Note that this is also a low-key hunting farm, but hunting & 'photographic' guests rarely overlap. *DBB N$1,265–1,650/2,530–2,970 sgl/dbl; camping N$200 pp.* **$$–$$$$**

🏠 **Corona Guest Farm** [208 B3] (9 rooms) \061 681045; e corona@iway.na; www.coronaguestfarm.com. Comfortable & efficiently run, Corona is about halfway between Windhoek & Walvis Bay, some 30mins/18km south of the C26 along the tortuous D1438 (the turning is 31km east of the C14/C26 junction), bearing left at the fork; a high-clearance vehicle would be helpful. The imposing old house features shaded terraces, various small lounges, a bar & a reading corner, but it's the huge dining hall, comfortably cluttered with African artefacts, zebra skins & high-backed wing chairs, that steals the show. Big rooms come as family suites, whose balconies overlook a swimming pool with sundeck under jacaranda & palm trees, & twin rooms fronted by lawns. Activities include various farm pursuits plus nature drives & hiking; experienced hikers can tackle the Gamsberg Mountain, though this is unguided and not recommended during the warmer summer months. There is also a shelter containing rock art on the farm. *DBB N$1,500/3,000 sgl/dbl.* **$$$$$**

🏠 **Rooiklip** [208 B3] (6 rooms, 3 chalets, camping) \083 700 0212; e rooiklip@iway.na; www.rooiklip.iway.na. The 7,050ha Rooiklip has been run since 2001 by Franz & Hannelore. To reach it, follow the D1438 as for Corona, but after 10km, take the right-hand fork; a high-clearance vehicle is essential for this bumpy 8km track. Franz's work is in evidence everywhere, from the stone-clad bar & dining area to the sheltered braai with mountain views, the pool with a view, & attractive dbl rooms with stone floors & sliding doors on to their own terrace. There's a 2-bedroom family apartment, too, with a kitchenette & huge dining table, & above the farm you'll find an exceptionally rustic campsite with 3 individual pitches built into the rocks, & the lovingly named Camp Flintstone – complete with Wilma, Fred & Barney on the doors of the stone A-frame chalets! Power is solar generated, the veg home grown, & the welcome warm. Come for the hiking trails, mountain biking (N$50/day), stargazing & 4x4 farm drives (N$350 pp/3hrs), or drive yourself (N$100/vehicle), but most of all come to unwind in natural surroundings. *DBB 1,350/2,500 sgl/dbl; camping N$195 pp.* **$$–$$$$**

🏠 **Namib's Valley of a Thousand Hills** [208 A3] (5 bungalows, camping) reservations \061 250725; m 081 382 2720; e namibsvalley@resdest.com; www.namibsvalley.com. Along a 6km drive south of the C26, just 7km before its junction with the C14, this rustic new venture has sweeping views across the Gaub Valley. Largely constructed of wood & stone, its thatched lapa & simple, en-suite bungalows – twins, dbl & a family – blend into the soft browns & greens of the surrounding landscape. Sharing the views, the 3 pitches at the unfenced campsite have their own simple ablution block, but no power. A pool with a view comes into its own in the hot summer months, while glazing around the lapa helps to keep cold night-time temperatures at bay. *DBB N$1,704/2,664 sgl/dbl; camping N$220 pp.* **$$–$$$$**

Horseriding

Namibia Horse Safari Co m 081 470 3384; e info@namibiahorsesafari.com; www.namibiahorsesafari.com. Owner-guided by Andrew Gillies, this long-established professional operation offers scheduled 10-night mobile riding safaris for experienced riders. From the Fish River Canyon in Namibia's south, across the central Namib Desert to the extremes of the Skeleton Coast and rugged Damaraland, these are billed as some of the most challenging riding safaris on the planet. You'll spend the 1st & last nights in lodges, with 8 nights camping under the stars supported by a professional back-up crew, supplying everything from ice in your gin & tonic to hot showers & delicious meals.

THE MAIN A1/B2 The A1 dual carriageway heads north from Windhoek, merging into the B1 before it turns west at Okahandja – as the B2 – towards the coast. Although the distance to Swakopmund is 358km, the road is flat and the tarred surface means that it is around 4 hours of very easy driving. Several shuttle buses link the towns along this route with Swakopmund and Walvis Bay, as do (very slow) passenger trains; for details, see pages 327 and 348.

Okahandja
The self-styled 'garden town of Namibia' is 71km north of Windhoek, at the junction of the B1 and B2. Along with some reasonable places to stay and eat, banks and 24-hour fuel, it is home to two of the country's best open markets for curios. Add to this a reputation for excellent biltong (dried meat), and quite a lot of old buildings and history, and it's worth breaking your journey here.

History Okahandja is the administrative centre for the Herero people (page 88), despite being considerably southwest of their main settlements. Missionaries first reached the area in the late 1820s, but it wasn't until 1849 that the first of them, Friedrich Kolbe, settled here. He remained for less than a year, driven away by the attacks of the Namas, under Jonker Afrikaner.

He fled with good reason as, on 23 August of the following year, about 700 Herero men, women and children were killed by the Namas at the aptly named Blood Hill. It is said that after the massacre, the women's arms and legs were chopped off in order to take their copper bangles.

The small kopje of Blood Hill can be seen just to the east of the main Windhoek–Swakopmund road. Jonker Afrikaner lies peacefully in his grave, next to several Herero chiefs, opposite the church on Kerk Street.

Getting there and away Most overseas visitors coming through Okahandja are driving, but the town is also served by both coach and train services. Those driving themselves should note that the main B2 bypasses the town, so to go into the centre you'll need to turn off the road at the signposts.

By bus Intercape Mainliner's services between Walvis Bay and Windhoek stop on Friday and Sunday in each direction at Okahandja's Engen and Wimpy Garage on the B1. Buses leave for Windhoek at 13.45, and return at 10.00. Those from Windhoek to Victoria Falls in Zimbabwe reach Okahandja at 13.00 (Wednesday, Friday), with the return journey stopping in Okahandja at 09.30 (Monday, Thursday). There is also a service between Windhoek and Oshakati, stopping in Okahandja every day except Saturday at 18.00 and returning at 19.50 daily except Sunday. Fares are around N$250–400 to Windhoek, and about N$370 to Walvis Bay. See page 153 for more details and information about the various shuttle buses that ply the route between Okahandja and Walvis Bay.

By train Trains – very slow trains – depart from Okahandja for Windhoek at 04.30 on Tuesday, Thursday, Friday and Sunday, and on the same days for Swakopmund and Walvis Bay at 22.00. Tickets to Walvis Bay cost up to N$160 each way. For details, see page 150.

Where to stay Most visitors opt to stay at one of the guest farms surrounding Okahandja (page 216), but there are a few options in town.

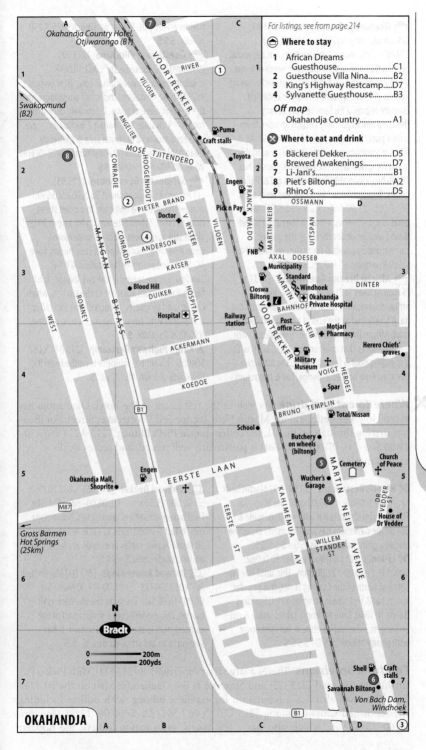

For listings, see from page 214

Where to stay
1 African Dreams
   Guesthouse....................C1
2 Guesthouse Villa Nina............B2
3 King's Highway Restcamp.....D7
4 Sylvanette Guesthouse..........B3
Off map
   Okahandja Country................A1

Where to eat and drink
5 Bäckerei Dekker..................D5
6 Brewed Awakenings.............D7
7 Li-Jani's................................B1
8 Piet's Biltong.......................A2
9 Rhino's................................D5

Okahandja Country Hotel,
Otjiwarongo (B1)

Swakopmund
(B2)

VOORTREKKER
RIVER
VILJOEN
ANGELIER
CONRADIE
MOSE TJITENDERO
HOOGENHOUT
PIETER BRAND
V RYSTER
ANDERSON
CONRADIE
KAISER
MANGAN
BYPASS
ROMNEY
DUIKER
HOSPITAAL
Hospital
WEST
ACKERMANN
KOEDOE

Puma
Craft stalls
Toyota
Engen
FRANCK WALDO
Pick n Pay
Doctor
Blood Hill

OSSMANN
MARTIN NEIB
UITSPAN
DINTER
AXAL DOESEB
Municipality
Standard
Windhoek
Okahandja
Private Hospital
Closwa
Biltong
Railway
station
VOORTREKKER
BAHNHOF
Post
office
Motjari
Pharmacy
Military
Museum
MARTIN NEIB
VOIGT
HEROES
Herero Chiefs'
graves

FNB

School
Butchery
on wheels
(biltong)
Wucher's
Garage
Engen
Okahandja Mall,
Shoprite
EERSTE LAAN
EERSTE ST
KAHIMEMUA AV
MARTIN NEIB AVENUE
Cemetery
Church
of Peace
DR VEDDER ST
House of
Dr Vedder
WILLEM
STANDER
ST

BRUNO TEMPLIN
Spar
Total/Nissan

M87
B1

Gross Barmen
Hot Springs
(25km)

N
Bradt
0   200m
0   200yds

Shell
Craft
stalls
Savannah Biltong
Von Bach Dam,
Windhoek
B1

OKAHANDJA

213

🏠 **Okahandja Country Hotel** [213 A1]
(24 rooms, camping) Voortrekker St; ✆062
504299; e okalodge@africaonline.com.na; www.
okahandjalodge.com. About 2km north of town,
signposted to the east of the B1, this rather smart
hotel is efficient & immaculately maintained.
En-suite rooms, 2 for families, are in large,
thatched blocks partially circling an open lawn
with a pool. They are pleasant inside, with AC &
DSTV, if somewhat unoriginal. Wi-Fi is available
in the reception area. The lawned campsite has
16 pitches, clean ablution facilities & 220V plug
points. Recommended by locals, the restaurant
(🕐 07.00–21.00 daily; $$$–$$$$) offers a
good range of meals, either in the rather bland
dining area, or under thatch in the garden,
surrounded by ponds & fountains. N$840/1,440
sgl/dbl; camping N$160 pp. $$–$$$

🏠 **African Dreams Guesthouse** [213 C1]
(5 rooms) River St; ✆062 500588; e info@
africandreams.com.na; www.africandreams.com.
na. A lovely find at the end of a quiet residential
road, African Dreams has dbl or twin rooms with
wooden floors that open on to a small lawn with
a sparkling pool & firepit. Above, the attractive
thatched lapa houses a lounge, bar & restaurant

(dinner N$190 pp). Secure parking. N$895/1,150
sgl/dbl. $$$

🏠 **Guesthouse Villa Nina** [213 B2]
(9 rooms) 327 Conradie St; ✆062 502497;
e guesthousevillanina@gmail.com. New owners
in 2015 have revitalised this small guesthouse on
the western edge of town. Colourfully decorated
rooms – 5 en suite & 4 sharing 2 bathrooms – are
squeezed around a big braai area & spotlessly
clean pool, with plans for a restaurant in 2019. Free
Wi-Fi. N$400/600 sgl/dbl. $$

🏠 **Sylvanette Guesthouse** [213 B3]
(11 rooms) 311 Hoogenhout St; ✆062 505550;
e areweriaanton@gmail.com. In a quiet street
close to town, Sylvanette was up for sale in 2018,
albeit still open. Twin & dbl en-suite rooms,
decorated with photographs & cute friezes, have
AC, DSTV, fridge, coffee/tea station & Wi-Fi.
Sundowners are served in the airy lounge, & b/
fast in a cosy room adjacent to the kitchen, which
can be used by guests, though dinner (N$150 pp)
is available with advance notice. Secure parking.
N$500/700 sgl/dbl. $$

⛺ **King's Highway Restcamp** [213 D7] ✆062
504086. This simple campsite is on the main B1,
just south of town. N$120 pp. $

✗ **Where to eat and drink** As well as the restaurant at the hotel, Okahandja has
several low-key options along Martin Neib Avenue and Voortrekker Street. For those
just driving through on the B1, the coffee shop at **Piet's Biltong** [213 A2] (🕐 07.30–
19.00 Sun–Fri, 07.00–18.00 Sat) is particularly well placed, and serves steaks as well
as light meals.

✗ **Rhino's Restaurant** [213 D5] 92 Martin Neib
Av; ✆062 500866; 🕐 09.00 until late Mon–Sat.
This lively local sports bar with seating inside &
out on the pavement has a varied menu including
burgers, grills, fish & pizzas. $$–$$$$$

✗ **Li-Jani's** [213 B1] Voortrekker St; ✆062
500013; 🕐 10.00– 21.00 Mon–Thu, until late Fri–
Sat. Just south of the Country Hotel, this popular
sports bar & restaurant occupies a club building
dating to 1880. Dine at simple tables inside & out
on burgers, schnitzels & eisbein, washed down
with plenty of beer. $$$–$$$$

☕ **Bäckerei Dekker** [213 D5] ✆062 501962;
🕐 06.00–15.30 Mon–Fri, 06.00–noon Sat. The
local bakery also offers sandwiches, homemade
pies, b/fast & even steaks to eat in or take away.
Sit inside at pine tables or outside at plastic tables
under a shadecloth. $–$$$

☕ **Brewed Awakenings** [213 D7] Martin Neib
Av; ✆062 500723; 🕐 07.00–17.00 Mon–Sat,
08.00–16.00 Sun. Opposite the southern craft
market, this modern coffee shop is part of the
complex next to the Shell fuel station, & has
seating in an attractive garden. $–$$

Food and provisions There's a large Spar supermarket [213 D4], with Pick n Pay
further up the road [213 C2] and Shoprite at the Okahandja Mall on the B1 [213
B5]. The town also has a reputation for excellent **biltong**, with outlets including
the renowned Closwa Biltong [213 C3] (✆ 062 501123; 🕐 08.00–17.00 Mon–Fri,
08.00–13.00 Sat), which also has a few **tourist information** leaflets, the popular

HERERO PARADE

Okahandja still holds great cultural importance to the Herero, and each year thousands of women in traditional coloured dresses and men in military outfits parade through the town to commemorate their ancestral chiefs – in particular Chief Samuel Maharero, an important figure in the struggle against imperial Germany. The chief died in 1923 while in exile as a refugee of the British in Bechuanaland (present-day Botswana). His body was returned by steam train to Okahandja where he was laid to rest by his father, Chief Maharero, on 23 August 1923. Every year since, on the Sunday nearest that date, the Herero parade gathers near the chiefs' graves at around 09.00 to remember the chieftains.

Piet's Biltong on the B1 junction [213 A2], the Butchery on wheels [213 D5] and Savannah Biltong to the south [213 D7].

Other practicalities Okahandja has a scattering of **fuel stations** alongside its main roads. The town's **post office** is almost opposite the **Motjari Pharmacy** [213 D4], and for **banks** you'll find branches of Standard, FNB and Bank Windhoek on Martin Neib Avenue [213 C3], all with ATMs.

Should you be in need of **vehicle repairs**, try Wucher's Garage [213 D5] (*Martin Neib Av;* \062 501338).

In an **emergency**, the police are reached on \10111, the ambulance/hospital on \062 503030, and the fire service on \062 505100 (*a/h* **m** *081 284 9179*).

What to see and do The large open-air **curio markets** at each end of town [213 B2 and D7] are probably the two best places in the country for wooden carvings (page 94). These include some beautiful thin wooden giraffes (some 2m or more high), huge 'tribal' heads, cute flexible snakes, and wide selections of more ordinary carved hippos and bowls. Do stop for a wander around as you pass, especially if you're on the way to Windhoek Airport – this is the perfect spot for last-minute present shopping, and it's open on Sundays. A word of caution, though: the traders here have become quite aggressive in their sales tactics, and some of the prices quoted appear extortionate. If you're not prepared for the hassle, and to bargain fairly hard (it's not unusual to be 'quoted' a price that's more than ten times the market value), then a curio shop could be a better bet.

Historical sites The town has many historical sites, including the **graves** [213 D4] of a number of influential leaders, such as Jonker Afrikaner, the powerful Oorlam leader; Chief Hosea Kutako, an influential Herero leader who campaigned against South African rule in the 1950s; and Chief Clemens Kapuuo, once president of the DTA, who was assassinated in 1978. Note that casual visitors cannot access these graves.

Close by is the **Church of Peace**, a Lutheran-Evangelistic church built in 1952 and now enclosed by a high fence, and also the **house of Dr Vedder**, one of the oldest in town.

Just south of the post office, on Hoof Street, is a building known as **the old stronghold**, or the old fort. This was the town's old police station, started in 1894, though now it is empty and falling into disrepair. Meanwhile to the west, **Blood Hill** [213 B3], scene of the 1850 massacre, is found between Kaiser and Duiker streets, although there's little to see now. In 2004 a very smart **military museum** [213 C4] was built on Voortrekker Street, though by 2018 it was still not open to the public.

🏠 *Guest farms around Okahandja* Around Okahandja lies some of the best farmland in the country. Some of the local farms accept guests, and some of those are good.

🏠 **Elegant Farmstead** [208 C1] (11 rooms) 📞062 500872; e info@the-elegant-collection.com; www.the-elegant-farmstead.com. Under the same ownership as the Elegant Guesthouse in Windhoek, the former Otjisazu is about an hour's drive from the capital. From the B1, take the D2102 east towards Von Bach Dam about 1km south of Okahandja, then follow the road round some steep bends & across a number of dry river-beds for about 28km to the farm; this isn't a road to drive when it's dark.

The farm stands in an area of rolling acacia scrub/bush – typical of the central plateau around Windhoek. The main building was built as a mission in 1878, & externally retains its old look & feel, though inside, the en-suite rooms are modern & stylish & there is a wine cellar, library & trendy cigar lounge. Pleasant, well-watered gardens offer a variety of seating areas, as does an outside boma & bar, overlooking a campfire & good-size pool. To explore the 2,500ha farm, home to wildlife that includes kudu, springbok, waterbuck, ostrich & giraffe, there are morning & afternoon nature drives (*N$240–385 pp inc drinks & snacks*), sundowners on Signal Hill (*N$225 pp*), champagne brunches in the river-bed & self-guided hiking trails. *DBB N$1,600/2,100 sgl/dbl.* **$$$$**

🏠 **Midgard Country Estate** [208 D2] (46 rooms) 📞062 503888; reservations 📞061 431 8000; e Midgard.res@ol.na; www.midgardcountryestate.com. On a 65km² estate, Midgard is about 85km from Windhoek on the D2102, east of Okahandja. With 2 swimming pools, a tennis court, a gym & sauna, & a skittle alley, as well as a small collection of vintage cars, Midgard is a popular w/end venue, though it is better suited to conferences than casual visitors. This is reflected in the style & layout of its rooms, which have all the accoutrements of a good business hotel. *N$2,528–3,190/room.* **$$$$–$$$$$**

🏠 **Okapuka Ranch** [208 C2] (29 rooms, 1 suite) 📞061 257175/234607; e okapuka@iafrica.com.na; www.okapuka-ranch.com. Equidistant between Okahandja & Windhoek, Okapuka is signposted east of the A1 dual carriageway. The 2km drive to the lodge passes through a 120km² reserve stocked with sable, giraffe, wildebeest, oryx, kudu, springbok, ostrich – & crocodile. The lodge is popular with day visitors, who can join guests on 1½hr game drives & 3hr mountain drives, set out on the 2 walking trails (taking around 2 & 3hrs respectively), & make use of all the facilities, including a chic swimming pool. The lodge itself is built on a rise, with its rooms split across 2 sites. Most are set together under thatch at the edge of the reserve, but an entirely separate mountain lodge has its own 4 rooms & broad views across the bush. All are attractively designed, with warm floor rugs & original artwork on the walls, a private terrace, & a minibar, kettle & phone; some also have AC/heating. The large, thatched bar/lounge area is beautiful, though more imposing than relaxing, & can get busy, especially on Sun when day visitors descend for the 3-course lunchtime buffet. At other times, the restaurant (🕐 *07.15–21.00*) offers an à la carte menu focusing on game. *N$1,221/2,350 sgl/dbl.* **$$$$**

🏠 **Düsternbrook Safari Guest Farm** [208 C2] (8 rooms, 1 suite, 2 safari tents, 4 chalets, camping) 📞061 232572; m 081 864 3000; e info@duesternbrook.net; www.duesternbrook.net. About 30km north of Windhoek, Düsternbrook was Namibia's 1st guest farm, & today offers a broad range of accommodation styles. It is signposted west of the new A1 on to the D1499, near Okapuka Ranch, with clear signs for the remaining 18km to the 14,000ha farm. Its venerable claim to fame is its leopards & cheetah, which are kept in several large enclosures (from 4ha), & can be viewed from a vehicle (*N$360 pp*). It also offers, game & early morning mountain drives, horseriding & well-marked hiking trails from 1hr to several days, with possible sightings including zebra, waterbuck, hartebeest, giraffe, eland, oryx, kudu & hippo, not to mention a rich birdlife.

The main building is a large old colonial farmhouse dating from 1908. Its walls are adorned with paintings & hunting trophies: limited &

sustainable trophy hunting provides meat for the table. There's also a large pool, an information centre & a range of wildlife & natural history books. The owner, Johann, is very into sustainable tourism & has received several Eco awards for his water, energy & waste management. *DBB N$1,241–1,798/2,482–3,596 sgl/dbl; camping N$195–225 pp.* **$$–$$$$**

🏠 **Omatozu Safari Camp** [208 C1] (3 tents, camping) **m** 081 643 7100; **e** info@omatozu. com; www.omatozu.com. Signposted from the B1, 25km north of Okahandja, the intimate Omatozu is along a 4km drive. The large thatched dining area & lounge (with Wi-Fi) has a bar on the deck, & a braai area & campfire offer views over the farm dam. En-suite walk-in tents (2 dbls, 1 family) run to electric lights & even AC, with a laundry service on request. Then about 200m away, 4 pitches at the very clean & well-maintained campsite come with power & their own toilet, hot shower & braai. Campers can buy firewood, & use the bar, with b/fast & dinner available on request. The camp has its own pool, & you can explore on hiking trails & self-drive game loops (*N$300/vehicle*).

DBB N$1,250/2,000 sgl/dbl; camping N$160. **$$–$$$$**

🏠 **Ombo Rest Camp** [208 C1] (4 chalets, 3 rooms, camping) **✆** 062 502003; **m** 081 206 2791; **e** omborestcamp@africaonline.com.na; www.ombo-rest-camp.com. Some 10km north of Okahandja, follow the C31 east for 2km to this great option for campers & backpackers. There's a well set-up campsite with showers, power points, tables, open kitchen, a kiddies' play area & a small farm shop; ablutions are shared with the backpacker rooms. On a different part of the property, the en-suite chalets aren't much to look at from the outside but are comfortable inside with AC, BBQ & kitchenette or fully equipped kitchen. These overlook a small water point that attracts giraffe, ostrich & a variety of antelope. The small pool can be used by campers as well, & the restaurant (⏰ 10.00–14.00 & 18.30–20.30), which is also open to non-residents, offers an à la carte menu (**$$$–$$$$**). Short tours (*N$40 pp*) introduce the farm's ostriches & crocodiles, & hiking trails are a further option. *Chalet N$660/1,110 sgl/dbl; camping N$135 pp.* **$–$$$**

Von Bach Resort and Gross Barmen Hot Springs

These two national recreational resorts, close to Okahandja, have traditionally been used as weekend getaways by local urbanites. In the past, travellers found them relatively cheap places to stay, but with major refurbishment in the last few years, that is no longer the case.

Von Bach Resort

[208 C1] (⏰ *summer 07.00–19.00, winter 06.00–18.00; day visitors N$80 pp, plus N$10 per car; under 16s free*) Although a national protected area, the resort at Von Bach Dam has been run since 2009 by the private Namibian company Tungeni Africa. It is signposted east of the B1 about 1km south of Okahandja, from where it's a further 4km along the gravel D2102 and D2161.

The resort occupies a picturesque site, centred on a large dam that supplies most of the capital's water, and surrounded by a nature reserve backed by mountains. The environment here is thorn-scrub and particularly hilly, supporting some 187 bird species, and wildlife that includes kudu, oryx, warthog, Hartmann's mountain zebra and red hartebeest – though none are easy to spot.

For many visitors, activities focus on the water, with a big lakeside swimming pool, 1-hour boat cruises (*N$260 pp inc drinks*) and canoe rental (*from N$140*), but others opt for the area's hiking trails. Fishing is possible too, but you'll need your own kit.

The resort has its own lakeside restaurant, as well as a boma for less formal dining.

🏠 **Where to stay**

🏠 **Von Bach Dam Tungeni Resort** (22 chalets, camping) **✆** 061 400205; reservations **m** 081 341 9180; **e** info@tungeni.com; www.

tungeni.com. Aim for a lake view at the resort, which comes with only some of the AC but relatively rustic 'deluxe' (cheaper) & 'luxury' chalets

– though there are drawings displayed for a range of new options. Facilities at the 12 campsite pitches include toilets, hot showers & a braai area, but no power. *N$640–840/1,280–1,680 sgl/dbl; camping N$180 pp plus N$150 per pitch.* **$$$–$$$$**

Gross Barmen Hot Springs [208 C1] (⏲ *06.30–18.00 all year; day visitor N$200/100 adult/child 6–12*) Gross Barmen is built around a lake about 25km southwest of Okahandja, on the banks of the Swakop River, and is easily reached from the town's southern side along the M87.

Following extensive (and expensive) renovations by Namibian Wildlife Resorts, the resort was reopened in 2014. Its main attraction is its mineral spring, which wells up at about 65°C, and has been tempered to a bath-like 38°C in the large, indoor spa pool. A sauna, steam room and gym are found in this contemporary indoor complex, too, along with cooling (yes, really!) 'hot' tubs, and big circular rooms where you can book a range of treatments. Outside, the setting really comes into its own, with palm trees around a beautiful big pool and the reed-fringed lake itself, with springbok grazing the surrounding lawns.

The bar and restaurant, serving surprisingly good food (**$$$–$$$$$**), are open to day visitors and residents, with a terrace overlooking the lake so you can watch the waterbirds and terrapins. Set well away is a picnic area, where there are braai stands, a small pool and a bar; note that this is the only place where you can bring your own food. A short hiking trail is a further option.

🏠 Where to stay

🏠 **Gross Barmen Resort** (47 chalets, camping) ☏062 501091; reservations ☏061 285 7200; e reservations@nwr.com.na; www.reservations@ nwr.com.na. Following the renovations, Gross Barmen emerged with neat yet spacious chalets in contemporary shades of grey that – however stylish – afford more than a hint of a soulless housing estate. Most are bush chalets, built in pairs across the site with their own parking area, small garden (some with lake view), comfortable twin beds, & efficient showers. Larger, premier chalets boast a separate lounge area, a bathtub & both inside & outside showers, & a plunge pool with a view. Guests have access to all the spa facilities until 22.00, giving them 4hrs' exclusive use after day visitors have left. For campers, there are 20 pitches sharing 2 ablution blocks; charcoal & drinks can be bought at reception, but little else so do come prepared. *Bush chalet N$1,250/2,200 sgl/dbl; premier N$2,350/4,400; camping N$200 pp. Refundable N$500 deposit payable per chalet, in cash only.* **$$–$$$$$**

Karibib Since 1903, this small town on the railway line from Windhoek to Swakopmund, 112km from Okahandja on the B2, has been known mainly for the very hard, very high-quality marble which comes from the Marmorwerke quarry nearby and is exported worldwide. More recently, in the late 1980s, South Africa's Anglo-American Corporation opened the opencast Navachab Gold Mine on the south side of town, to mine low-grade ore. There's a lot of small-scale mining in the area, too, especially for gemstones; amethyst, tourmaline, aquamarine, quartz, silver topaz, citrine and garnet are just some of the minerals found around Karibib. See the stones on display at the information centre and Karibib Gemstone Centre (see opposite) for an idea of what is around – they all come from the local area.

Slow trains between Windhoek and Walvis Bay call at Karibib four times a week in each direction; for details, see page 151.

Tourist information

ℹ **Henckert Tourist Centre** 38 Hidipo Hamutenya St; ☏064 550700; e bhenckert@ henckert.com; ⏲ 08.00–17.00 Mon–Fri, closed Sat–Sun. This once first-class shop that doubles as an information centre is a shadow of its former self. It began as a small gem shop in 1969, & now has a range of curios, along with a good selection of Namibian semi-precious stones & gemstones. You can still get a coffee here, but the café itself is no longer operating.

Where to stay In town there's the choice of an attractive guesthouse and a backpackers' lodge, but there are also several guest farms nearby (page 216).

🏠 **Angi's Guest House** (10 rooms) 315 Fracht Street; 064 550126; e angis@iway.na. Almost hidden along a gravel street right behind the Engen service station to the east of town, this quiet B&B stands out for the bougainvillea around the entrance, which opens into a pretty, tranquil garden. Its twin rooms – all but 2 en suite – have cool tiled floors & clean lines, & are equipped with AC, TV & kitchenette. There's a pool & a restaurant, open to guests only for b/fast & dinner, with lunch on request. Secure parking. *N$600/900 sgl/dbl.* **$$$**

🏠 **Tommy's Lodge** (8 rooms, 16 dorm beds) 310 Hidipo Hamutenya St; 064 550081; e tommyslodge@gmail.com. At the eastern end of town on the B2, Tommy's is next to the Engen garage. Behind its forbidding entrance is a friendly if rather ramshackle backpackers' lodge. The 3-bed rooms are en-suite, while each of the 4 dorms sleeps 4 & shares facilities. There's also a bar & restaurant, a pool, Wi-Fi, a self-catering kitchen & BBQ area, & secure parking. *Room N$450/600 sgl/ dbl; dorm bed N$210.* **$$**

Where to eat and drink Most of those staying in town in house. If you're passing through, options are limited to the bakery and café inside the OK supermarket, the rather sleazy Club Western Restaurant, or snacks from one of the fuel stations.

Other practicalities Karibib boasts an **OK supermarket** next to Tommy's Lodge, and two **fuel stations**, of which Engen has a bakery and ATM. Along the main road, you'll also find a **pharmacy** (m *081 230 0780*), a **post office**, branches of FNB and Standard **banks**, and a garage where staff can carry out **vehicle repairs**.

In an **emergency**, the police are reached on 064 550088, the ambulance on 064 530067, and the fire service on m 081 422 1805.

What to see and do The town is dotted with several **historic buildings** dating from the early 1900s. Back then, Karibib was an important overnight stop on the railway between Windhoek and Swakopmund, as well as a trade centre. Ask at the information centre for their brief guide to the town.

There are a few **hiking trails** into the rolling landscapes south of town, behind the Klippenberg Country Club. In town itself, the Club Western Gambling and Entertainment Centre, and its adjacent restaurant, seem to be the focus of local excitement although, as an alternative, the town's cemetery is beautifully lit at night!

Karibib Gemstone Centre (*Hidipo Hamutenya Rd;* m *081 321 5113;* e *nkyadavgems@ gmail.com;* ⏱ *07.30–16.30 Mon–Fri or by arrangement*) Should you find yourself with time to spare in Karibib, do pop into this low-key training centre, close to the post office. From the collection of gemstones found in Namibia displayed in the entrance hall, visitors are welcome to continue through to the workshops. where up to 15 students at a time, selected from all over the country, attend a seven-month course in cutting and polishing stones.

Guest farms: Around Karibib
Where to stay

🏠 **Etusis Lodge** [208 A2] (7 bungalows, 5 tents, suite, 2 farmhouses, camping) 064 550826, reservations 061 224712; e etusis@ resdest.com; www.etusis.com. Standing at the foot of the Otjipatera Mountains & surrounded by white marble mountain ridges, Etusis is 16km from the road; the turning is signposted about 19km south of Karibib from the C32.

Central to the lodge is a large thatched building with an open-plan bar & dining area, lounge & small curio shop, with a small swimming pool; Wi-Fi is available. Stay in stone-&-thatch bungalows sleeping up to 4 people, with exposed wooden beams, en-suite bathrooms & AC; walk-in tents, 2 of which share communal facilities; or self-catering farmhouses for 2–7 guests. The campsite, with 5 pitches sharing ablutions, is 22km from the lodge. Activities include scenic drives in search of impala, kudu, mountain zebra, oryx, springbok & klipspringer, as well as horseriding, & unguided hikes in the mountains. *DBB N$1,237–1,375/1,860–2,475 sgl/dbl; camping N$150 pp.* **$$–$$$$**

Usakos
This small town, 147km from Swakopmund, used to be the centre of the country's railway industry. Now it's little more than a stop on the line between Windhoek and Walvis Bay, with banks and fuel to tempt those who might otherwise pass right through. The tourist information centre is useful if you're planning to do much exploration of the local area.

 Where to stay and eat With the sign on the old Bahnhof Hotel stating that it is under renovation (which it has been since 2013), options in Usakos are relatively limited.

Big Brother Guesthouse (10 rooms) m 081 264 7606/7; e bigbrotherguest@gmail. com. Signposted from the Shell garage to the west of town, Big Brother is 1km from the B2, next to the (almost deserted) railway line. It's a welcoming, local guesthouse, opened in 2015 & offering simple but clean rooms, 4 sharing a bathroom & the others en suite. Donkey boilers provide hot water for the small, sandy campsite. The thatched bar & restaurant (⏰ 10.00–18.00 daily) is open to allcomers, but residents have their own separate pool. *N$250–370/500–650 sgl/dbl; camping N$150 pp.* **$$**

X Oasis Food Stall m 081 258 8351; ⏰ 07.00–19.00 daily. A surprising find next to the Shell garage about 1km west of town, this restaurant & take-away is the best place to stop for a good meal. Alongside an uncomplicated menu of burgers, toasties & steaks, they have a selection of jams, honeys & biltong for sale, as well as local crafts. **$$$**

Other practicalities If you need **money** then there's a branch of FNB, and for **supplies** try the minimarket at Engen, Lewis Stores or the Usakos Self-help (which is a shop, not a therapy group). These, like the **fuel stations**, are all on Theo-Ben Gurirab Street – the erstwhile Bahnhof Street.

In an **emergency**, the police are reached on 📞 10111, the ambulance and fire service on 📞 064 530023 (*a/h* m *081 223 6692, 081 141 2395*), and the hospital on 📞 064 530067.

Guest farms: around Usakos
Where to stay

Ameib Guesthouse [208 A1] (7 rooms, 3 bungalows, 2 cabins, camping) Set among rounded granite boulders in the Erongo Mountains, the long-established & idiosyncratic Ameib was closed in 2018, & its future was uncertain. Below is a summary of the information in case it should reopen in the lifetime of this guide.

Approaching on the B2 from the east, turn right towards Swakopmund in the centre of Usakos, then immediately right again, on to the gravel D1935. Follow this for 12km to a signposted right turn on to the D1937 through a beautiful landscape, a little like Damaraland's vegetation, with sparse cover on the hillsides, & lush river valleys. A further 5km brings you to Ameib's gates, then another 11km to the guesthouse.

Visitors come mainly for the excellent rock paintings, many within the large eyelash-shaped

Phillip's Cave that was made famous by Abbé Breuil's *The Rock Paintings of Southern Africa* (page 575). There are also unusual rock formations, like the Bull's Party – a group of large rounded boulders which (allegedly) look like a collection of bulls talking together.

EAST FROM WINDHOEK

The main tarred B6, west to Windhoek and east into Botswana, is part of the Trans-Kalahari Highway that links Walvis Bay with South Africa's Gauteng Province (the area around Johannesburg and Pretoria). There's little of interest to visitors before Gobabis. Even the fuel station at **Witvlei** has closed, though there's still a post office – and perhaps one day the attractive restcamp, Ziegie's, will reopen.

GOBABIS This busy town, standing at the centre of an important cattle-farming area on the western edges of the Kalahari, forms Namibia's gateway into Botswana via the Buitepos border post, about 110km further east. The B6 bypasses the town, which lies on the C20. With its wide, tree-lined avenues and many shops and businesses, it's a prosperous-looking community. As such, it's an ideal place to use the banks, fill up with fuel or get supplies before heading east towards Ghanzi, where most goods aren't so easily available. However, it's less interesting as a stopover.

Getting there and away Most visitors to Gobabis are driving through on the main road. With trains between Windhoek and Gobabis no longer operating, this is the only realistic means of reaching the town.

Tourist information

Uakii Wilderness Survival/Gobabis Information Centre [222 C2] 62 Church St; \062 562324; m 081 728 0494, 081 270 1834; e contact@gobabis.net; www.gobabis.net; ⏰ summer 08.00–17.00, winter 07.30–16.30. Something of a one-stop shop, this offers tourist information, game drives & tours of the region,

& specialises in cultural, historical & community-based tourism, both locally & further afield. There's also a café (page 223), craft shop, cultural centre & even a swimming pool here, along with a guesthouse (*N$600/800 sgl/dbl*, **$$$**), & a campsite, although the last was temporarily closed following a fire in 2018.

Where to stay If you want to stay in the area for a few days, then consider one of the guest farms in the vicinity (page 216). Nearer town are several possibilities, including:

Kalahari Convention Centre [222 B2] (18 rooms, 11 flats) Mark St; \062 564878; m 081 215 7067; e ngoagoses@gmail.com. Formerly known as Horizons, this restaurant/bar offers rooms with en-suite baths, TV & kettle. Outside is a long swimming pool & secure parking. *N$350/600 sgl/dbl*. **$$**

Onze Rust [222 G4] (5 rooms) 95 Rugby St; \062 562214; m 081 128 4669; e onzerust@ iafrica.com.na; www.natron.net/tour/onzerust. An attractive courtyard garden is the focus for a lounge/dining area & purpose-built rooms. Most of these are en suite (sgl, dbl & family permutations) with AC, TV, fridge & private braai facilities; others

share a bathroom. Secure parking. 4x4 track on offer. *N$460–690/520–750 sgl/dbl*. **$$–$$$**

Trans Kalahari End Resort – Die Dam [222 A1] (14 chalets, 2 tents, camping) \062 565656; m 081 470 2311, 081 669 5889; e gobabisdam@afol.com.na. Next to the small Tilda Viljoen Dam, this is an attractive spot just a short drive from town. Approaching from Windhoek, turn right off the C20 before the arch over the road, then right again, past the police station, following the signs. Thatched, brick-built chalets are compact but well designed with a dbl bed & 2 sgls above. There's also a private terrace with BBQ overlooking the dam. At the campsite,

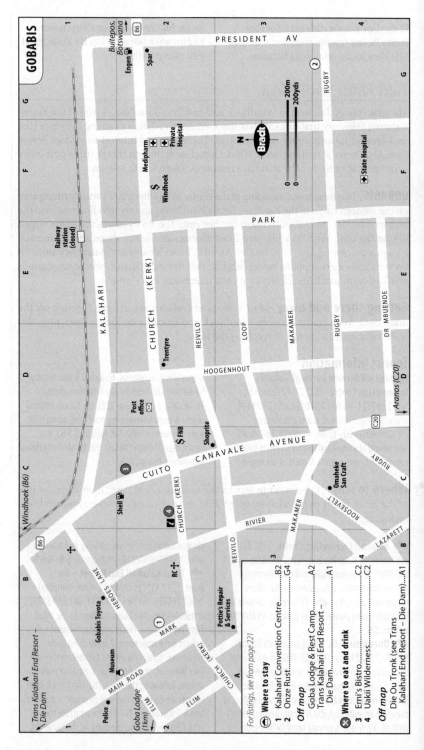

GOBABIS

For listings, see from page 221

Where to stay
1 Kalahari Convention Centre....................B2
2 Onze Rust..G4

Off map
Goba Lodge & Rest Camp.......................A2
Trans Kalahari End Resort –
Die Dam..A1

Where to eat and drink
3 Erni's Bistro....................................C2
4 Uakii Wilderness..............................C2

Off map
Die Ou Tronk (see Trans
Kalahari End Resort – Die Dam)....A1

as well as 7 tree-shaded pitches, there are pre-erected 3-bed tents with a kettle & fan. This is primarily a holiday venue, with paddle boats on the lake, freshwater fishing & minigolf, & there's an interesting restaurant, Die Ou Tronk (see below), as well as a bar. *N$550/990 sgl/dbl; camping N$100 pp.* **$$–$$$**

🏠 **Goba Lodge & Rest Camp** [222 A2] (28 rooms, camping) 062 564499; e goba@iway. na; www.goba.iway.na/. Signposted 1km west of town, this well-maintained site overlooks the Black

Nossob River. Dbl & family rooms at the lodge have all the usual accoutrements – TV, AC, tea-making facilities – & some have safes. The restcamp, next to a small enclosure with ostrich, oryx & blesbok, has both a campsite & simple twin rooms, all sharing an ablution block, kitchen & TV room. Guests can dine inside or out at the à la carte River Restaurant (07.00–21.00 Mon–Fri, 07.00–noon & 16.00–21.00 Sat–Sun). There's also a (fenced) pool. *N$920/1,350 sgl/dbl; camping N$125 pp, plus N$50/vehicle.* **$$–$$$**

✦ Where to eat and drink For snacks during the day there are several take-aways along Church Street, and a Wimpy next to the Engen garage. More substantial are:

✗ Erni's Bistro [222 C2] 29 Cuito Canavale Av; 062 565222; 08.00–22.00 Mon–Sat, closed Sun. Erni has long gone, but you can still have a sandwich lunch or bubblegum milkshake, or dine on 'carpet-bag steak'. **$$–$$$$**

✗ Die Ou Tronk [222 A1] 062 565656; 07.00–22.00 Mon–Fri, 08.00–20.00 Sat, noon–14.00 Sun. The restaurant at Die Dam is a must, if only for the setting: an old German prison, abandoned in 1966. Thick walls & heavy doors

keep the cells cool, but today's inmates benefit from views over the dam, albeit through barred windows. Alongside traditional Afrikaans dishes such as *afval* (tripe) there's a tempting range of pizzas & grills. **$–$$$**

▭ Uakii Wilderness [222 C2] The café at the tourist information office (page 221) is pleasantly located on a shady veranda & offers several local dishes – including the inviting-sounding 'Uakii's dish'. **$**

Other practicalities The main **banks** are all here, as are a couple of 24-hour **fuel stations**. **Garages** include the useful Gobabis Toyota [222 B1] (*062 562081*) on Heroes Lane and Pottie's Repairs and Services [222 B3] (*062 563148;* m *081 122 7402, 081 128 4559*) for Hyundai on Reivilo Street. For **supplies**, start at the Spar [222 G2] at the crossroads of Church Street and President Avenue.

There's a private **hospital** [222 F2] on Church Street with adjacent **pharmacy**, Medipharm (*062 563983*). In an **emergency**, the police can be reached on 10111, the ambulance and hospital on 062 566200, and the fire service on 062 566666.

What to see and do The **museum** (07.30–16.30 *Mon–Fri*), with its collection of agricultural tools and historic artefacts, is supported by the Museum Association of Namibia (MAN). If you're interested in crafts, try the dedicated **Omaheke San Craft Centre** [222 C4] on Roosevelt Street.

Guest farms and lodges: around Gobabis

Where to stay There is an assortment of fairly offbeat guest farms and lodges within reach of Gobabis, and several places geared to people taking overnight stops on the Trans-Kalahari Highway. Next to the border post itself there's also East Gate Rest Camp (page 225).

🏠 **Sandüne Lodge** [208 F2] (12 rooms, 4 cottages) m 081 143 7923; e info@sandune. com.na; www.sandune.com.na. This 3,400ha reserve south of Gobabis is 7.4km off the C22,

down a narrow, sandy track, & is home to blue & black wildebeest, giraffe, zebra & kudu, among others, as well as the Duneside stud. Staff are welcoming, rooms are well appointed & the game is close by in an open Kalahari setting. As well as various hiking trails, there are game drives, Bushman walks, visits to a Bushman village & horseriding. *N$2,000/4,000 sgl/dbl.* **$$$$$**

🏠 **Kalahari Bushbreaks** [208 G2] (8 rooms, 2 chalets, camping) 📞 062 568936/569001; reservations 📞 064 464 144/155; e rbarnard@ iway.com; www.kalaharibushbreaks.com. About 87km east of Gobabis, & 26km west of the Botswana border, Kalahari Bushbreaks is 3km south of the main B6, & clearly signposted. Owned & run by Ronnie & Elsabe Barnard, it's an established lodge on a working farm, with 40km² under game, including eland, oryx, giraffe, kudu, red hartebeest, warthog, zebra (both Burchell's & Hartmann's mountain), & blue & black wildebeest. Several species of antelope that wouldn't normally be found in the Kalahari are here, too, such as waterbuck & blesbok (both normal & albino). Predators include cheetah, leopard & caracal. The farm is occasionally used for hunting – although hunting & photographic guests are kept separate – & there are a few animal trophies on the lodge walls.

The main lodge building consists of a warm, enclosed lounge & bar area with high thatched ceiling. Most of the en-suite bedrooms are centred in this vast structure, with some in the eaves, & 2 set further away with private dining facilities. All are attractively decorated making good use of wood, reeds & leather. Some 2.5km from the lodge are 2 campsites – 1 with power & the other more rustic. Note, though, that campers may no longer visit the lodge without permission from the camp attendant.

A large boma area, ringed with thatch but open to the stars, forms part of a spacious outdoor eating area, with a central fire & canvas 'walls' for cooler evenings. The food is good, & there's an interesting choice of wines, personally selected from independent vineyards.

Many visitors simply stop overnight, but others try out the various walking trails, guided bush walks, or the 20km 4x4 trail, which takes in sites such as rock engravings. *N$1,140/2,060 sgl/dbl; camping N$120–140 pp.* **$$–$$$$**

🏠 **Zelda Game & Guest Farm** [208 G2] (16 rooms, 10 pitches) 📞 062 560427; e bookings@zeldaguestfarm.com, zeldaguestfarm@iway.na; www.zeldaguestfarm. com. About 90km east of Gobabis, & 20km west of

the border, Zelda is 1.3km north of the B6. Half of the 100km² farm is dedicated to game, & the rest to cattle farming. Most people use the farm, with its Baboona bar, restaurant, souvenir stall & leafy, almost tropical garden, as a stopover. For action, there's a cool pool for those hot Kalahari days, or you can watch leopard & cheetah being fed each afternoon. Rather more interesting are farm trails accompanied by a local Bushman tracker, or visits to the !Xhananga village on their 'Be Wild' programme to learn more about the traditions of these people – or indeed to stay overnight. At the farm itself, rooms with AC – some in the house & others in the grounds – are decidedly ornate in décor. There's a good campsite, too, with space for independents & overland groups. *N$675/1,072 sgl/dbl; camping N$140 pp.* **$$–$$$**

🏠 **Harnas Guest Farm** [208 F1] (8 cottages, 3 'igloos', camping) 📞 062 568828/38; m 081 140 3322; e bookings@harnas.org; www.harnas. org. Almost 100km northeast of Gobabis, Harnas probably has the highest profile of any guest farm in the region. To get here, take the B6 east from Gobabis & turn left after about 6km on to the C22. After 12.5km of tar, this reverts to a wide gravel road for about 30km until it reaches a Harnas sign at Drimiopsis, when you take a right. About 7.5km further on, the road branches & you keep left. Continue for a further 38km & the entrance to Harnas is on the left.

Once a cattle farm, Harnas has evolved into a sanctuary for injured & orphaned animals – including wild dogs & cheetah. The Harnas Wildlife Foundation has several projects, which include the rehabilitation & reintroduction of animals wherever possible. Another key element of the farm's activities is a medical outreach project focusing on AIDS prevention & bringing specialist services such as cataract operations to the local people. The foundation runs a volunteer scheme, too; for details, see their website.

Spread around quite a large grassy area are brick-built cottages, overlooking a waterhole, & stone igloo-style bungalows. All are en suite & equipped with AC, kitchenettes & braai areas. Backing this up is a campsite with 3 pitches, each with power, kitchen, braai areas & a central ablution block. Though many self-cater, simple set menus are available with advance notice. There's also a large swimming pool. Activities centre around morning & evening animal feeding tours

(N$165–275 pp), sundowner drives (N$275 pp) & – by prior arrangement – horseriding (N$150 pp/ hr). N$1,520–1,900/2,500–3,100 sgl/dbl; camping N$270 pp; day visitor N$180 pp. **$$–$$$**

CROSSING THE BORDER INTO BOTSWANA The Buitepos border (🕐 *07.00– midnight*) is suitable for 2WD vehicles. There's little on the other side apart from a border post until you reach the small Kalahari cattle-farming town of Ghanzi.

Gobabis is probably the best place for **hitching** from Namibia into Botswana, as many trucks pass this way. Don't accept anything that will stop short of the border at Buitepos, do carry plenty of food and water, and please consider the risk you are taking by getting into a stranger's vehicle.

Where to stay and eat

🏠 **East Gate Rest Camp** [208 G2] (13 bungalows, 6 cabins, camping) ☎ 062 560405; e bookings.eastgate@iway.na; www. eastgate-namibia.com. This well-maintained site, with shady trees & neat paths, is a haven for travellers, offering fuel (🕐 *06.00–midnight*), a shop & a restaurant (*both* 🕐 *06.00–22.00*). Turquoise-&-cream-painted bungalows & cabins & a grassy campsite attract visitors to break a long journey. En-suite bungalows with AC vary in standard & size, from 1 bedroom with kitchen to 2 bedrooms with TV & phone, sleeping 6. Simple twin-bed cabins share facilities. The camp also has a swimming pool. *Bungalow N$950–1,800 (2–6 people); cabin N$220/440 sgl/dbl; camping N$120 pp.* **$$–$$$**

DORDABIS The tiny town of Dordabis, at the end of the tarred C23 to the southeast of Windhoek, is closer to the capital than Gobabis. Set in a beautiful valley covered with tall acacia trees, and between rounded, bush-covered hills, it has a township just outside the centre with few other amenities aside from a post office and a police station.

In recent years the area has attracted attention as the base for several artists and craftspeople, especially weavers, although Dorka Teppiche was closed in 2008 and the equipment donated to the **Dorkambo Co-operative** near Ondangwa (☎ 065 248155; m 081 211 0048; e info@dorkambo.com, sales@dorkambo.com), who continue to produce karakul rugs, among other items.

Where to stay
Many of the guest farms in the area around Dordabis and Gobabis promote hunting rather than just watching game, though there is a handful of exceptions. All are unusual, and worth a visit.

✳ 🏠 **Otjimbondona Kalahari** [208 E2] (4 villas) m 081 243 5478, 081 127 4358; e welcome@otjimbondona.com; www. otjibondona.com. Just off the M51, about 1½hrs' drive southeast of the international airport, this luxurious lodge is in a 3,000ha private reserve fringing the vegetated Kalahari Desert, in an area dominated by pans & grassy scrubland.

No expense has been spared in the design & build of this lodge, which spreads out from an old farmhouse built by the lodge owner's family in 1923. This encompasses a small gym & sauna, library, inside & outside dining areas, sunken firepit & a stunning infinity pool, running almost the length of the main area. The large villas are just as luxurious, each individually decorated to reflect the Namibian people, the local Nguni cattle, Namibia's landscapes or the country's flora & fauna. The set up is open plan, with a bedroom & bathroom on one side of a central walkway & a comfortable living space on the other. Expect lots of glass, plush soft furnishings & bold artwork. Outside, enjoy a dip in your own plunge pool set in the expansive deck or wander down the path to your private sala. Activities include massages, walking, fatbike trails & game drives around the reserve, where you may be surprised by the wildlife you spot.

Owners Anita & Wilfried Slaney have a background in fly-in safaris around Namibia & other countries in southern Africa; they also own & run Profile Safaris, & can organise scenic flights, day trips to Swakopmund or Sossusvlei

Several farms, often driven by kind individuals with the very best of motives, have set up 'orphanage' or 'rehabilitation' programmes in Namibia for injured/unwanted animals. Before visiting, it's perhaps worth considering the logic of some of the arguments for this, and perhaps discussing the issues with your hosts while there.

Some aim just to keep alive damaged or orphaned animals, some of which can be rehabilitated and released, though others can't be. The problems of keeping, say, a small orphaned antelope like a bushbuck are minimal. However, the problems caused by big cats are more major. Keeping such carnivores is difficult, as they need to be in very secure pens. Further, animals need to be killed to feed them. If it's a kindness to keep an injured lion alive, what about the horses, cows or antelope that are slaughtered to feed it? Why is the lion's life more valuable than the herbivores'?

Demand for visitors to see big cats and other 'sexy' species close up makes keeping habituated big cats a potentially lucrative draw for a guest farm. (Note that I don't use the term 'tame' as neither lions nor leopards ever seem to become anything like truly tame.) So is this why it's done?

Cynics claim that it's far from pure compassion. They question why there's a paucity of rescue centres for, say, black-faced impala, a species that is seriously endangered and rare. They're very beautiful and well worth preserving – but are they sexy enough to attract guests? Probably not, the cynics observe.

Most pragmatic conservationists focus on preserving environments and species, believing that individual animals are much less important. They don't see the point in spending time and money keeping a lion alive when the same money could go towards preserving a whole ecosystem elsewhere.

One could argue, however, that when well run, such projects generate large incomes from visitors. This cash can then be used to fund serious, necessary (but perhaps less attractive) research programmes, or education programmes, which really do benefit Africa's wildlife on a much broader scale. That's a fine argument – but if it's the case, and this is their rationale for keeping caged animals as an attraction to raise money, then the cynics argue that it's time such organisations came clean.

for example or longer fly-in safaris, although this should be done with as much advance notice as possible. The lodge's location makes it ideal for a luxurious & relaxing night or 2 at the beginning or end of a trip, although the price may be prohibitive for many. *FBA N$8,440/13,500 sgl/dbl.* **$$$$$$$**

🏠 **Eningu Clayhouse Lodge** [208 E2] (9 chalets) 📞 062 581880 (lodge); 📞 064 464144 (bookings); e info@eningulodge.com; www. eningulodge.com. Just 1hr's drive (65km) south of the international airport, Eningu is 5km from the D1471, close to its junction with the M51. On the fringes of the Kalahari, surrounded by bush-covered dunes on the fringes, it's an environment

of round eroded hills, beloved of masked weaver birds, with perhaps a little Kalahari sand when the grass dies down. It is one of Namibia's most original small lodges, with a strong connection with the arts maintained by owner Bettina Berner.

The semi-detached dbl & family chalets are constructed, as the name suggests, of Kalahari clay bricks, though the apricot adobe effect & boxy design give more than a hint of Mexico. Each has a cool, rustic interior, comfortably furnished with gourd lampshades & colourful cushions, while enchanting portrait photos add a touch of class. Painted floors are dotted with locally woven rugs, & smooth concrete bases ensure the beds

The spectacular scenery of the Namib-Naukluft National Park lends itself to landscape photography (JTP/S) page 295

above The survival of the Bushmen in the harsh environment of the Kalahari is evidence of the supreme adaptability of humans (CM) page 82

left A Herero woman wearing the traditional headdress (SS) page 88

below Thatching the roof of an Ovambo house (TH) page 89

above	Modern-day Windhoek blends the old with the new (SS) page 167
right	Colourfully painted houses brighten up the seaside town of Lüderitz (VA/S) page 272
below left	A guide, as here at Twyfelfontein, can transform your understanding of Namibian culture (TS) page 406
below right	Weighing in at around 60 tonnes, the Hoba Meteorite near Grootfontein crashed to earth some 80,000 years ago (ST/S) page 495

top Some of Namibia's lodges offer breathtaking views (GL/EA)

left Namibia specialises in quirky places to stay, such as this converted harbour-control building near Walvis Bay (SS) page 352

below Camping in a rooftop tent is a real adventure (SS)

above Spend a night among the granite boulders of Damaraland within easy reach of Twyfelfontein (MMC/EA) page 404

right Remote camps abound, such as this one at the foot of the Aus Mountains (TM/EA) page 268

below left Self-catering is a great option for exploring Sossusvlei without breaking the bank (TA/EA) page 309

below right Staying on a private reserve bordering Etosha National Park is a bonus for some visitors (NS/EA) page 440

above   A kayaking trip offers a unique chance for a close encounter with the seals in Walvis Bay (JM) page 362

left   Horseriding is possible at lodges all over Namibia (ET)

below   Get a bird's eye view of the desert on a hot-air balloon ride (CS) page 316

above   Namibia's scenic roads are perfect for independent drivers (SS)

right   Sandboarding is one of many adrenalin sports in the desert near Swakopmund (SS) page 364

below   Mundulea in the Otavi Mountains offers some exceptional walking (TM) page 481

above The play of light on rocks, as here at Spitzkoppe, creates an ever-changing scene (k/S) page 395

left Skeleton trees conjure up an eerie feel at **Dead Vlei** (FL/S) page 315

below The most spectacular route between Windhoek and Sesriem takes you through the steep **Spreetshoogte Pass** (LL/S) page 307

are scorpion- & snake-free. In the summer, fans & gauze windows are effective at catching the cool evening breeze, & in winter, guests are given extra blankets & hot water bottles. A small thatched veranda, mosquito nets, ceiling fans & a tea/coffee station add to the creature comforts.

Eningu's attention to detail stretches to the kitchen, too, where innovative dishes are prepared from fresh (often home-grown) ingredients & served in an intimate dining area. There's also a comfy lounge, & an underground 'cellar' off the attractive boma stocking a range of wines. A bird hide makes a great venue for a sundowner, overlooking a waterhole that's floodlit after dark, with kitchen scraps left out to attract wildlife such as porcupines.

Activities include 3 marked walking trails with information boards & a longer hiking trail, plus archery, volleyball & badminton, though lounging by the swimming pool & hot tub is equally popular. Visits to the workshop & exhibition of internationally renowned sculptor Dorte Burner can be arranged, as can game drives on the adjacent farm, & other local tours, with at least 2 days' notice. This is a tranquil & well-run little lodge, perfect for a 1st/last night in Namibia. *DBB N\$1,740/3,080 sgl/dbl.* **\$\$\$\$**

⌂ **Kiripotib Guest Farm** [208 D3] (14 rooms, 2 chalets, 2 luxury tents) ☎062 581419; e reservations@kiripotib.com; www.kiripotib.com. The engaging Hans Georg & Claudia von Hase run this friendly guest farm on the D1448, just 12km from its junction with the M33 (C15) & about 2hrs' drive from Windhoek Airport. It's also the base for several other ventures: a thriving little arts & crafts business (*day visitors welcome;* ⊕ *all day*), an observatory, & African Kirikara Safaris, which offers mobile safaris around the region.

Kiripotib's spacious accommodation – all en suite with separate WC – is split between pleasant rooms laid out around an attractive garden & pool, brick-built chalets with AC set in open grassland, & 2 'luxury' tents. Meals (*lunch N\$140/325 lunch/ dinner*), including home-grown produce & even freshly squeezed orange juice in season, are served in an extensive thatched lapa, or around the fire under the stars. For winter evenings, a cosy sitting room has a small library.

One of the more unusual aspects of Kiripotib is its craftwork. You can visit the spinning workshop & weavery, where a variety of unique Namibian carpets are made from karakul wool & displayed – along with other arts & crafts – in the gallery. If you're planning to buy one, at around N\$2,200 per m², bring colours & fabric samples to Kiripotib or one of their shops in Swakopmund or Windhoek, so the team can make up one of their designs to match your colours & sizes as closely as possible. (Obviously this takes time, but there is no extra charge, & they send regular shipments to Europe, so delivery is easily arranged.) Also on site, thanks to Claudia's training as a goldsmith, is a small jewellery workshop which, when in full production, makes fascinating viewing.

More traditional are farm & game drives (*from N\$480 pp*) in this classic Kalahari landscape. In 2016 the farm started a collaboration with the Cheetah Conservation Fund (CCF; see box, page 468), under which they look after 4 cheetahs that cannot be released into the wild. You can now watch cheetah feeding (*Mon–Sat; N\$375 pp*), as well as explore walking trails. It's also possible to arrange a drive & ½-day walk in the Karubeams Mountains (*N\$430 pp*), where it takes 1–2hrs to climb on to a lovely plateau, with a fair chance of seeing oryx, kudu & klipspringer. Expert glider pilots with their own craft can make use of the lodge's airstrip; for details, see the website. Finally, the lodge offers stargazing around the new moon throughout the year (*N\$480*), weather permitting, while for the more serious astronomer it has 3 Dobsonian telescopes for hire, as well as an astro-park (⊕ *May–Sep*) with 9 viewing platforms & power points for those with their own telescope. There is even a small kitchen for astronomers to use, with tea & cake provided. *N\$1,235–1,950/2,100– 3,320 sgl/dbl.* **\$\$\$\$**

⌂ **Arnhem Cave Restcamp** [208 E2] (4 chalets, 2 camp chalets, camping) ☎062 581885; m 081 259 6434; e arnhem@afol. com.na; www.arnhemcave.com. The small, self- catering restcamp at Arnhem Cave (see box, page 228) has good, thatched chalets with twin beds, fridges & a couple of mattresses on a platform above. Along with a grassy campsite there are simpler camp chalets, which share an ablution block, & there's also a swimming pool. Wood is for sale & braai facilities are provided, but there is no restaurant. *N\$200–350/400–700 sgl/dbl; camping N\$130 pp.* **\$\$**

Claimed to be the longest cave in Namibia, and the sixth-longest so far discovered in Africa, Arnhem has about 4.5km of passages. It's thought to have been a home for bats for around 9,500 years, and still probably contains about 15,000 tonnes of bat guano, despite it being mined on and off for the last 70 years.

Six species of bat have been identified here, including the giant leaf-nosed bat – the world's largest insectivorous bat. There are also shrews, spiders, beetles, water shrimps and various invertebrates, some of which are endemic to the cave.

Though very dusty, and not at all fun for claustrophobics, there are two guided trails through the cave, departing at 09.00 and 15.00 daily. Times taken vary, with phase 1 (*N$150*) being a little shorter than phase 2 (*N$250*). Dress in old clothes and bring a torch (or hire one).

Arnhem is on the D1808, about 4km south of its junction with the D1506. From the airport take the B6–M51–D1506–D1808; from Gobabis turn left at Witvlei on to the D1800–D1808. Visitors can stay at the restcamp (page 227).

SOUTH FROM WINDHOEK

REHOBOTH Just north of the Tropic of Capricorn and 87km south of Windhoek on the tarred B1, Rehoboth is the centre of the country's Baster community (page 81), which is quite different from any of Namibia's other ethnic groups, and jealously guards its remaining autonomy. Sadly, there are few reasons to stop here; other than the museum, most people pass on through.

Getting there and away If you're without a vehicle and want to visit Rehoboth, it's possible to get there by train or coach.

By bus Intercape's coaches from Windhoek to Cape Town stop at the Shell service station on the corner of Springbok Street and the B1, at 18.05 on Monday, Wednesday, Friday and Sunday, and return at 07.30 on Monday, Friday and Saturday. These cost around N$770 to Cape Town and a rather steep N$330 to Windhoek. Note that seats on buses to Windhoek must be prebooked. See page 152 for more details.

By train Trains depart from Rehoboth for Windhoek at 04.00 on Thursday and Sunday and for Keetmanshoop on Wednesday and Saturday at 21.40. However, not only are the trains very slow (page 150), but the station is too far north of the town to walk, so this is rarely a good option for visitors.

Where to stay, eat and drink In addition to the options below, there are branches of fast-food chains such as the Hungry Lion at Rehoboth shopping mall on the B1.

Lake Oanob Resort [229 A2] (9 rooms, 13 chalets, camping) 062 522370; e reservations@oanob.com.na; www.oanob.com.na. Created in 1994 following construction of the highest dam in Namibia, Lake Oanob Resort is run by a Swiss–Namibian couple, Helena & Christie Benade-Bruhin. To reach it, turn west off the B1 on to the D1280 about 6km north of Rehoboth,

& follow this for around 7km. From the south, take the D1237 as far as the crossroads, then turn left & continue for a further 3km.

En-suite dbl & family rooms have rustic furnishings, & each has a small veranda – ideal for checking out the night sky – while chalets, all overlooking the lake, are extremely well equipped for a longer stay. Campers have a choice of 31 pitches, some on the waterfront, some with shade – & priced accordingly. The resort's facilities, also open to day visitors, include the relaxed à la carte restaurant & bar with free Wi-Fi by the waterfront (⏰ 08.00–20.00 Sun–Thu, 08.00–22.00 Fri–Sat), & a heated pool with pool bar (⏰ Sep–Mar w/ends) & lovely views over the dam. Beside this, another pool & shallow children's pool are open all year & there's a play area too.

Visitors can swim in the lake & take speedboat trips (N$150 pp, min 2), while for watersports enthusiasts there's canoeing (N$30 pp), Aqua-Cycle (N$60 pp) & tubing (N$100 pp). On land, a short walk along the lake is a good chance to spot fish eagles & pelicans, & there are also hikes

(N$30 pp) & 1½hr drives (N$200 pp) in the nature park; look out for springbok, giraffe, zebra, eland, hartebeest, wildebeest, oryx, ostrich & more. As a short stop on the way to or from Windhoek, this is well worth investigating. N$970/1,280 sgl/dbl; chalet N$1,410–1,840 dbl self-catering; camping N$80–150 pp; entrance N$30 pp. **$–$$$$**

🏠 **Hobasen Montana Lodge** [229 B3] (4 rooms) 📞 062 525704; m 081 256 9962; e cloejp@iway.na. A grand name belies this simple lodge, perched above the B1 about 2km south of town. It's run by Vicky Cloete, her son & 4 small dogs. En-suite rooms have twin beds, a fridge, kettle & tea/coffee, & there are 2 grass-surrounded swimming pools, where a restaurant serves meals including b/fast. Wi-Fi is available & they can provide a shuttle to town on request. N$400/ room. **$$**

✗ **Dolphin Fish and Chips** [229 B3] 📞 062 524500; ⏰ 07.00–23.00 daily. Part of the local supplies shop, this greasy take-away does a roaring trade in battered sausage, & fish & chips. Quite the queue at lunchtimes! **$**

Other practicalities Rehoboth has most of the essentials, including branches of the major **banks**, a couple of **fuel stations** and a **post office**. For **supplies**, try Spar or Woermann Brock, or the new shopping mall to the north of town.

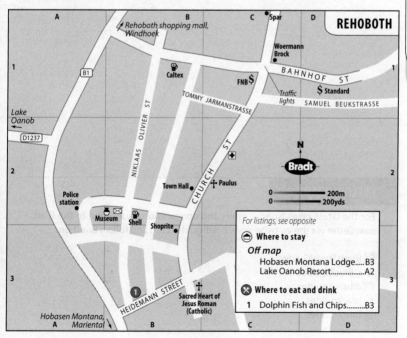

In an **emergency**, the police are reached on ☏ 062 523223, the ambulance on ☏ 062 521900, the hospital on ☏ 062 522006/7, and the fire service on m 081 143 0906, 081 794 9074.

What to see and do Rehoboth's only real attraction for visitors is its small **museum** [229 B2] (☏ 062 522954; www.rehobothmuseum.com; ⊕ 09.00–noon & 14.00–16.00 Mon–Fri, 08.00–noon Sat, Sun & public hols on request; admission N$25) in the old postmaster's building. Good local history exhibits on the origins of the Baster community combine with those on the flora and fauna in the surrounding area, and an unexpected but interesting section on banknotes.

SOUTH OF REHOBOTH South of Rehoboth on the B1, a fuel station with a take-away at the small town of **Kalkrand** is probably the only reason for most drivers to stop.

If you're heading **southwest** towards Sesriem along the C24 (MR47), after about 94km you'll come across a road sign showing a cup and saucer:

✗ **Connie's Restaurant** [208 B4] m 081 360 3400. Connie's warm welcome, larger-than-life personality & home-baked muffins have long made this the perfect place for a break when driving to Sossusvlei. Now, under new ownership, her traditions are maintained by Gunther. With advance warning he offers B&B ($) & will prepare lunch. The place is well signposted, 1km off the road, about a ½hr drive from Klein Aub; you can't miss it. **$–$$$**

The Southern Kalahari and Fish River Canyon

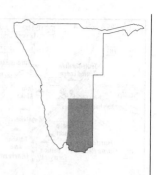

If you have journeyed north from South Africa's vast parched plateau, the Karoo, or come out of the Kalahari from the east, then the arid landscapes and widely separated towns of southern Namibia will be no surprise. Like the towns, the region's main attractions are far apart: the Fish River Canyon, Brukkaros, the Quivertree Forest, and scattered lodges of the Kalahari.

Perhaps because of their separation, they receive fewer visitors than the attractions further north, so if you want to get off the beaten track, go hiking, marvel at ancient landscapes or even raft on the Orange River – then this southern side of the country is the perfect area to do it.

MARIENTAL

Standing on the edge of the Kalahari Desert, in an area which has long been a centre for the Nama people of Namibia, Mariental gained its name from the area's first colonial settler, Herman Brandt, who called it 'Marie's Valley', after his wife.

This area receives virtually no rain some years, so Namibia's successful commercial farmers have diversified in order to survive. The (welcome) current trend towards managing native game rather than farm animals, and earning income directly from tourism, are just two examples of this. Similarly, the shrinking trade in pelts of karakul sheep – once so important to southern Namibia – seems to be concentrating around the town, while an ostrich abattoir has established Mariental as an important centre for the country's ostrich farming.

That said, and despite being the administrative centre of the large Hardap Region, which stretches from the Atlantic coast to Botswana, Mariental itself avoids being a centre of attention by having remarkably few attractions. There are a sprinkling of efficient businesses, ranging from the Desert Optics optometrist to the Spar supermarket on the north side of town, serving the prosperous surrounding farmlands, but like many of Namibia's smaller centres, it's a ghost town on Sundays. Visitors view it as a place to go through, rather than to, often skirting around the town on the main B1 – stopping only for fuel and cold drinks, if they stop at all.

GETTING THERE AND AWAY

By car Approaching by car, you can't miss Mariental. It's set slightly back, adjacent to the main B1, and is very well signposted. There are two main turnings for the town centre: one south of the larger side roads to Stampriet and Hardap Dam,

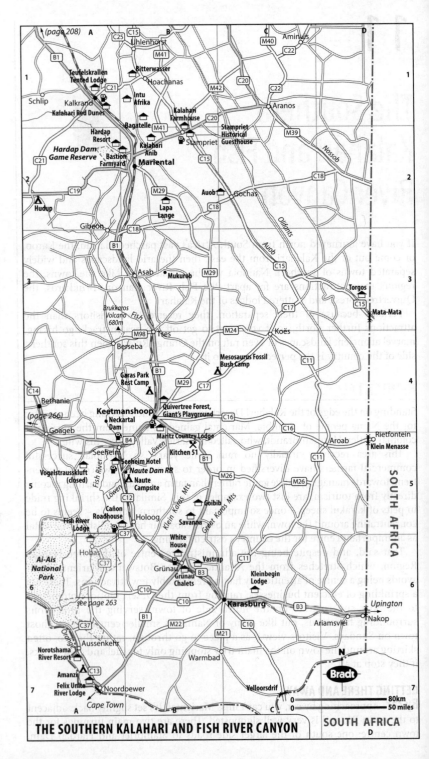

THE SOUTHERN KALAHARI AND FISH RIVER CANYON

and the other just north of the tarred C19 to Maltahöhe. Between the two is the modern, efficient Engen garage, which incorporates a Wimpy restaurant and a small supermarket. The railway line south from Windhoek bisects the town, allowing only one crossing point (on Michael van Niekerk Street).

By bus The Intercape service between Windhoek and Upington stops at the Engen garage [234 A3] at 19.50 on Wednesday, Friday and Sunday heading south, and at 05.45 on Monday, Friday and Sunday going north. Tickets – which must be booked in advance – cost around N$650 to Upington, N$380 to Keetmanshoop and N$320 to Windhoek. See page 153 for details.

By train Mariental is linked to Windhoek and Keetmanshoop by a slow, overnight train service. It departs Wednesday and Saturday for Keetmanshoop at 02.20 and for Windhoek at 00.20. See page 151 for details, or call TransNamib (✆063 249202).

WHERE TO STAY

Bastion Farmyard [234 B1] (5 rooms, camping) ✆063 240827; m 085 701 2093, 081 274 5574; e bastion@iway.na; www. bastionfarmyard.com. Clearly signposted off the B1, this farmstay 10km north of Mariental & 9km from Hardap Dam offers an attractive alternative to in-town accommodation. Pleasant, light rooms are equipped with AC/heating & fans, kettles & hairdryers. B/fast, served in the farmhouse, must be pre-booked, while those who prefer to self-cater will find an excellent kitchen & courtyard braai area. A small shop (⊕ 08.00–13.00 & 14.00–18.00 Mon–Fri, 09.00–noon Sat) sells homemade jams & preserves, drinks, braai packs & bread, as well as a few local crafts. Free Wi-Fi. *Room only N$500–600/700–800 sgl/dbl; camping N$135 pp.* **$$–$$$**

Anandi Guesthouse [234 A3] (9 rooms) 15 River St; ✆063 242220; m 081 241 1822; e anandi@iway.na; www.anandiguesthouse. com. The Anandi stands out with its lilac-painted block building behind high lilac walls. Both dbl & sgl rooms are en suite with DSTV, AC or fan & a small walled balcony, & there's also a self-catering unit. B/fast (*N$75*) is served in a large, pleasant restaurant, with lunch on request. The pool is usually filled during the summer, but if not, just ask. Free Wi-Fi, laundry on request; off-street parking for 10 vehicles. *Room only N$400–550/ N$600–750 sgl/dbl.* **$$**

Tahiti Guesthouse [234 A2] (17 rooms) 66 Michael van Niekerk St; ✆063 240636; e tahitimariental@gmail.com. Looked after by smiley manager, Christa, this simple but good budget guesthouse has small but clean rooms – 6 dbls & 11 twins. All are set around a brick courtyard, & some are self-catering with TV, AC, microwave, fridge, toaster & cutlery/pans. The popular restaurant (✆063 244754; ⊕ 07.00–21.00 Mon–Fri, 08.00–14.00 & 18.00–21.00 Sat, 10.00–14.00 Sun) serves b/fast (*N$89*), good surf 'n' turf, pizzas, burgers & kids' meals. Wi-Fi here stretches to some of the rooms. *N450/800 sgl/ dbl.* **$$**

River Chalets [234 A2] (7 rooms, 6 chalets, camping) ✆063 240515; m 081 128 2601; e garbers@iway.na; www.riverchalets.com. Run by South African Elrien Garbers, & aimed at families & small groups, this well-priced option is on the west side of the main B1 as it bypasses Mariental. Modern dbl or twin rooms have AC, DSTV, fridges & kettles; 3-, 5- or 7-bed self-catering chalets also feature equipped kitchenettes & BBQs on a patio; & there are 10 camping pitches. No meals are served on site. Free Wi-Fi in lounge. *Room only N$590/690 sgl/dbl; camping N$130 pp.* **$–$$**

WHERE TO EAT AND DRINK Options for dining in Mariental are limited. In addition to those listed overleaf, the main garages have facilities to bite-and-run: the Puma garage at the north end of town has the **Bambi** take-away, serving pies and simple meals, while the Engen garage on the B1 has a **Wimpy** (open late into the evening) with tables, and the sort of menu you'd find in any Wimpy across the world.

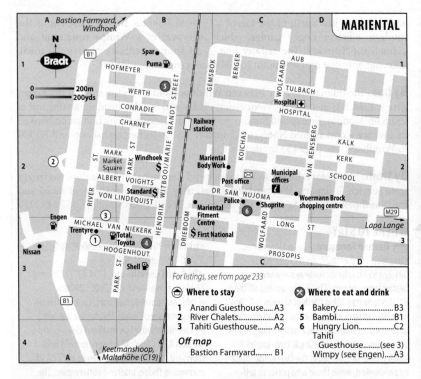

Map labels (within image): A Bastion Farmyard, Windhoek; N; Bradt; B1; 0 200m; 0 200yds; Spar; Puma; HOFMEYER; WERTH; 5; CONRADIE; CHARNEY; BERGER; GEMSBOK; AUB; WOLFAARD; TULBACH; Hospital; HOSPITAL; KOICHAS; VAN RENSBERG; KALK; KERK; SCHOOL; BRANDT STREET; WITBOOI/MARIE STREET; MARK ST; Market Square; PARK ST; Windhoek; ALBERT; VOIGHTS; Standard; DR SAM NUJOMA; Post office; Municipal offices; Mariental Body Work; Police; Shoprite; Woermann Brock shopping centre; RIVER; VON LINDEQUIST; HENDRIK; DRIEBOOM; Mariental Fitment Centre; First National; WOLFAARD; LONG ST; M29; Lapa Lange; Engen; Trentyre; Total, Toyota; MICHAEL VAN NIEKERK; HOOGENHOUT; Nissan; PARK ST; Shell; PROSOPIS; Railway station; Keetmanshoop, Maltahöhe (C19)

For listings, see from page 233

Where to stay
1 Anandi Guesthouse.....A3
2 River Chalets.............A2
3 Tahiti Guesthouse.......A2

Off map
Bastion Farmyard.........B1

Where to eat and drink
4 Bakery......................B3
5 Bambi.......................B1
6 Hungry Lion...............C2
Tahiti Guesthouse.........(see 3)
Wimpy (see Engen)....A3

✕ **Tahiti Guesthouse** See page 233.
✕ **Hungry Lion** [234 C2] Mariental Shopping Centre, Dr Sam Nujoma Av; ⊕ 09.00–20.00 Mon–Fri, 09.00–17.00 Sat, 09.00–14.00 Sun. Part of an African fried chicken chain. *Meals from N$25.* **$**

✕ **Bakery** [234 B3] Cnr Dr Hendrik Witbooi Av & Hoogenhout; ⊕ 07.30–15.30 Mon–Fri, 07.30–noon Sat. Local bakery that prepares sandwiches & sells soft drinks. **$**

SHOPPING
Spar supermarket [234 B1] Dr Hendrik Witbooi Av; ⊕ 08.00–19.00 Mon–Fri, 08.00–15.00 Sat, 08.30–13.00 Sun

Woermann Brock [234 C2] Dr Sam Nujoma Av; ⊕ 08.00–17.00 Mon–Sat. Shopping centre with supermarket, pharmacy & post office.

OTHER PRACTICALITIES
$ Banks [234 B2] Bank Windhoek & Standard on Dr Hendrik Witbooi Av; FNB on Drieboom St. There's an additional ATM at the Engen fuel station on the B1.
✚ Hardap Pharmacy & Clicks Pharmacy Woermann Brock complex [234 C2] Dr Sam Nujoma Av
✚ Hospital [234 C1] Mariental State Hospital, Hospital St; ☏ 063 242092. Has a 24hr admission & emergency department, but it doesn't meet the standard of many of the country's private clinics.
Mariental Fitment Centre [234 B2] Dr Sam Nujoma Av; ☏ 063 240840; a/h m 081 122 3080,

081 148 3441; ⊕ 07.00–17.00 Mon–Fri, 08.00–noon Sat, closed Sun. Offers a call-out service for replacement tyres to anywhere in the country.
Police station [234 C2] Dr Sam Nujoma Av; ☏ 063 10111
✉ Post office [234 C2] Koichas St; ☏ 063 242000
🛈 Tourist information office ⊕ Mon–Fri only. Housed within the municipal offices [234 C2].

HARDAP DAM GAME RESERVE

(*Admission N$40 per adult, under 16s free, plus N$10 per car*) Hardap Game Reserve (incorporating Hardap Dam Recreational Resort) was proclaimed in 1968, covers an area of 25,000ha and is home to Hardap Dam, which provides water for Mariental and various irrigation projects. Situated less than 25km northwest of Mariental on the upper reaches of the Fish River, this dam was until recently Namibia's largest manmade lake – although it was surpassed in late 2018 by the Neckartal Dam, further south on the river.

The dam wall is 39.2m high and 865m long. Covering around 25km², it holds up to about 320 million metres³ of water. In 2006, February rains caused the dam waters to rise so high that the authorities feared that the wall would burst. The decision was taken to open the gates to ease the pressure, but the resulting floods left Mariental under about 1.7m of water, causing significant damage. The Namibian government has since decided that the dam should not be allowed to rise above 70% capacity to prevent further disasters.

The origin of Hardap's name is uncertain. It is probably derived from a Nama name for a big pool that was flooded by the dam, although the word also means 'nipple' (or possibly 'wart') in the Nama language – and one of the rounded hills around the dam is said to resemble a female breast.

FLORA AND FAUNA Hardap stands in the central highlands of Namibia, and its rolling hilly landscape is mostly covered in low-growing bushes and stunted trees. Its river courses tend to be thickly vegetated, often having dense, taller stands of camelthorn (*Vachellia erioloba*) and buffalo-thorn (*Ziziphus mucronata*) trees.

The park is divided by the lake and river. Hilly and thickly bushed, this is classic leopard country – so these are the dominant predators, though they are seldom seen. Hartmann's mountain zebra, oryx, kudu, springbok, eland and red hartebeest are concentrated in the larger, more mountainous southern section of the park, whereas the smaller northern section is home to a small population of black rhino, introduced from Damaraland in 1990. Cheetah used to occur, but they thrived and escaped on to neighbouring farms, so have now been excluded.

Over 280 species of bird have been recorded in the park. Perhaps the most interesting are the Cape species, at the northern edge of their range, such as the cinnamon-breasted warbler, the Karoo eremomela and the uncommon Sclater's lark. You will also find Namibian species towards the southern edge of their ranges, like the delightful rosy-faced lovebirds. The lake and its surrounds are home to plenty of waterbirds, including a strategically important breeding colony of Namibia's great white pelicans, and our glimpse of an osprey in 2018 was a real highlight.

The lake itself also serves an important role, providing breeding stock to fish farms and other state-controlled dams. As a result, it has become popular with anglers, who might expect to catch species including kurper, bass, barbel, carp and yellowfish.

WHERE TO STAY

Hardap Dam Recreational Resort
[232 A2] (50 chalets, 4 dorms, camping) Book via the NWR, page 103; 063 240386/241109; www. nwr.com.na/resorts/hardap-resort. Reopened in late 2015 after an extensive 4yr renovation programme, this aims to be an all-inclusive resort

catering to all. In reality it will attract mainly those on a limited budget & is rarely likely to be full, or even busy.

The main area, perched atop cliffs overlooking the lake & dam wall, includes a restaurant, bar & unique cliff-top pool. Set back from the edge is an open-air theatre/cinema, although its purpose isn't entirely clear. Vouchers can be purchased for Wi-Fi access in the main area.

Simple & functional rather than luxurious, the chalets, dorms & campsite are up to 1.25km from the main area, so most travellers will choose to drive between them. 2-bed bush chalets come with twin beds, a fridge, AC or fan, en-suite shower &

WC. 4-bed VIP rooms with AC are slightly larger & have nicer views of the lake, while the 4-bed family chalets include self-catering facilities. The dormitories, designed with groups in mind, consist of 10 single beds with shared ablutions. At the far end of the resort are the camping pitches. *Chalet N$880–1,650/1,000–1,760 sgl/dbl; dorm bed N$120 pp; camping N$120 pp (max 8 people/pitch).* **$–$$$$**

WHAT TO SEE AND DO Activities include morning and evening game drives and boat trips (*N$350 pp*). Those wanting to fish must bring their own equipment (boathouses can be rented) and obtain a fishing permit (along with a map of the fishing spots, if they have one) from the MET office on entry to the park. You can explore the park's 80km of gravel roads in your own vehicle, while walkers have the choice of two hiking trails.

EAST OF MARIENTAL AND THE B1: THE KALAHARI

The Kalahari Desert often surprises people when they first see it. It is very different from the Namib. First of all, remember that the Kalahari is not a true desert: it receives more rain than a true desert should. The Kalahari is a *fossil* desert. The box on page 3 gives a more complete explanation, but don't expect to find tall Sossusvlei-style dunes devoid of greenery here. The Kalahari's dunes are very different. They are often equally beautiful, but usually greener and less stark, and with this vegetation comes the ability to support more flora and fauna than a true desert – including one of the highlights, the bat-eared fox.

Thus a few days spent in a Kalahari environment adds another dimension to a trip to Namibia, and can provide a smattering of low-density wildlife viewing away from the ever-popular Etosha, or the lush reserves of the Caprivi.

With the reopening of the Namibian–South African border at Mata-Mata (⊕ *08.00–16.30*), opportunities for tourism in the area southeast of Mariental are opening up as more people pass though. Mata-Mata links Namibia with the huge Kgalagadi Transfrontier Park, a truly integrated trans-national wildlife reserve between South Africa and Botswana that was Africa's first 'Peace Park' – although perhaps to the chagrin of the Kalahari gemsbok's small band of existing devotees, who have always regarded this out-of-the-way corner as one of the best national parks on the subcontinent.

GUEST FARMS AND LODGES To the east of the B1, around Bariental, there are several excellent lodges/guest farms. Of these, Bitterwasser (page 238) caters for accomplished glider pilots during the season, between November and February, while Kiripotib Guest Farm, near Dordabis (page 227) should be of interest to those keen on the night sky.

🏠 Where to stay

✱🏠 **Kalahari Red Dunes** [232 A1] (12 chalets) ✆063 264003; e info@redduneslodge. com; www.redduneslodge.com. Some 8km south of Kalkrand & set against the stunning backdrop of the Kalahari's red sands & flaxen grasses, this lovely lodge is accessed via a smooth 3km sand

road from the B1. Blending sympathetically into the surrounding landscape, its spacious chalets are linked via a series of raised wooden walkways & sandy paths. Each has its own shaded terrace with a couch & table, looking across the quiet dunes. The chalets are constructed from canvas tents attached to solid bathroom walls at the back & topped with thatched roofs. All have wooden floors, huge walk-in showers & unique arty basins in the bathroom, & chunky dark wood furniture shipped over from Germany (though note that the twin beds can't be separated). Along with AC/ heater, fridge/minibar with wine & drinks, tea/ coffee station, hairdryer & electronic safe, most also have a real-wood fireplace for cold desert nights. 2 are connected by a central walkway, ideal for a family or friends travelling together, & a larger 'superior' chalet has its own plunge pool.

The main building, which has free Wi-Fi, houses the reception, a cabinet showcasing a small selection of gifts, a circular bar, & a central fireplace surrounded by Moroccan-style couches, while out the back is a small pool with loungers. Activities include a choice of 4 self-guided walking or jogging trails ranging from 5km to 20km, sundowner drives (*N$500 pp*), morning nature drives (*N$390 pp*), mountain bikes that are free to rent, as well as a 2-night, 3-days Trans-Kalahari walk with a nature guide (*N$5,610 pp*). *DBB N$3,590–4,070/6,580–7,540 sgl/dbl.* **$$$$$**

🏠 **Teufelskrallen Tented Lodge** [232 A1] (6 rooms) 📞 063 264288, 061 240020; e teufelskrallenlodge@gmail.com, reservations@teufelskrallenlodge.com; www. teufelskrallenlodge.com. Just 3.5km from the village of Kalkrand, this small lodge is a sister property to Kalahari Red Dunes (see opposite), where all activities take place. Its tented rooms are well spaced for privacy, & with the main area, restaurant & pool at Altes Farmhaus in Kalkrand (a 5–10min drive away), it feels remarkably remote, despite its accessible location. *DBB N$1,730– 1,840/2,860–3,080 sgl/dbl.* **$$$$–$$$$$**

🏠 **Kalahari Anib Lodge** [232 B2] (51 rooms, camping) 📞 063 240529; e info@gondwana-collection.com; https:///store.gondwana-collection.com/accommodation/kalahari-anib-lodge. Set among the Kalahari dunes, down a 3km drive from the C20, this large but well-ordered lodge is on a 10,000ha farm lining the C20 towards Stampriet, about 33km northeast of Mariental. It attracts both tour groups & independent travellers. The reception & a good shop occupy a smart new glass-fronted building, also home to the large restaurant where light lunches (*N$45–100*) & dinner (normally a buffet; *N$360*) are served. A separate bar surrounds a large central fireplace &

large folding windows bring the outside in. Wi-Fi around the main area is free up to 100MB/day.

Arranged around shaded lawns with a large swimming pool are 32 en-suite 'standard' rooms with private verandas & AC; these include a variety of trpl & family rooms. Other 'comfort' rooms are larger, geared more to independent travellers, & set further back with a separate pool that looks out to the open Kalahari savannah. Well away from the lodge are 3 exclusive camping pitches with private bathrooms & BBQs; campers may use all lodge facilities. Both morning & sunset game drives (*N$560 pp*) allow guests to experience the attractions of the Kalahari on the reserve, which is home to giraffe, zebra, red hartebeest & oryx, among others, while for those bent on exploring on foot, there are 3 trail maps covering 5.8/7.3/9.3km. *N$1,679/2,686 sgl/dbl.* **$$$$**

🏠 **Intu Afrika Kalahari Game Reserve** [232 B1] 📞 063 240855; e intu-afrika@exclusive. na; www.intu-afrika.com. The small (10,000ha) private reserve of Intu Afrika is located on the D1268, 86km north of Mariental & just 19km south of the C21, & is clearly signposted from the B1 in both directions. The landscape is classic Kalahari: deep red longitudinal dunes, usually vegetated, separated by lighter clay inter-dune valleys covered in grass, trees & shrubs. The reserve's larger game includes giraffe, oryx, ostrich, blue & black wildebeest, Burchell's zebra & springbok. If you are about on the reserve in early morning or late evening you might also spot bat-eared foxes.

Each of the 3 accommodation options is run individually, with its own facilities, though activities – game drives, guided Bushman walks & quad bikes – are common to all.

🏠 **ZEBRA KALAHARI LODGE & SPA** (13 rooms) 📞 063 240855. Some 5km from the main Intu Afrika gate, this feels perfectly adequate if a bit drab & soulless. Large en-suite rooms with outside showers & AC flank its substantial main building, where a semi-open-air bar, lounge with free Wi-Fi & fireplace, & dining area are furnished with dark wood & leather chairs. The rooms themselves are functional with a minimum of clutter. 8 of these look towards the central L-shaped pool, where 1 wing is much shallower & more suitable for children. A short distance away are a further 5 split-level rooms, each boasting a sitting area & bedroom. The 'spa' is a simple room offering only massages (*N$350–500*). Babysitting is available on request. Activities include quad bikes (N$550/2hrs), nature drive (N$400–450) & Bushman walks (N$300). N$2,622–3,125/4,044–5,050 sgl/dbl. **$$$$$**

🏠 **SURICATE TENTED LODGE** (12 tents) ☏063 240855. Accessed from a separate entrance some 6km further south on the D1268, Suricate is furnished to quite a high but unfussy standard. The wow factor here comes from the lodge's location atop a low red sand dune, overlooking a grassy pan that's popular with wildlife. A large, airy, tented lapa looks out on to an infinity pool, flanked by a gazebo & firepit, & beyond to the pan. Canvas-tented rooms lined up on each side come with wooden decks & plenty of creature comforts, from fans & small plug-in heaters to a safe, minibar, kettle, walk-in mosi nets & phone. Room 9 has the best views of the plains & a waterhole that attracts wildebeest & springbok, while the honeymoon suite has its own private plunge pool & sunloungers. Free Wi-Fi in the main areas. DBB N$2,270–2,675/3,340–4,150 sgl/dbl. **$$$$$**

🏠 **CAMELTHORN KALAHARI LODGE** (12 chalets) ☏063 240855. Not far from the main hub of Zebra, this rustic lodge is the most inviting of the 3 Intu Afrika properties, more remote & with a homely, welcoming feel. The rondavel-style chalets are dotted among camelthorn trees in natural bush. 7 are slightly newer but nearer to the thoroughfare of vehicles going back & forth to Zebra; quieter are the slightly smaller, older chalets at the other side of the main area. All are quite simple in design, decorated in neutral tones, & come with AC, twin beds, & an en-suite shower room with his & hers sinks. A central lapa features a comfortable bar & lounge, & an upper tier housing the restaurant & a small, natural-looking swimming pool. DBB N$1,950–2,270/2,700–3,340 sgl/dbl. **$$$$–$$$$$**

🏠 **Bitterwasser Lodge & Flying Centre** [232 B1] (22 bungalows) ☏063 265300; e info@bitterwasser.com; www.bitterwasser.com. South of Uhlenhorst on the C15, about 59km from the B1, this specialist lodge caters to glider pilots up to world-class level. Note that this is not a school for gliding – it is a place for those who know how. Pilots often stay for weeks, & have broken so many records that along the avenue of palm trees lining the way to the airfield, each palm was planted to commemorate a record. Every year the avenue grows.

Bitterwasser has a range of gliders for hire, but most pilots prefer to ship out their own craft by container for the season, which runs late Nov–Jan. If you're a serious glider, email them for details of their facilities & prices, or check out their website. Gliding aside, the action is limited to swimming, sundowner & nature drives. Out of season, the lodge caters primarily for groups, but could also be an interesting stop for the independent traveller. The extensive restaurant & bar feel rather corporate, but there's a more intimate lounge area. Comfortable accommodation comprises en-suite bungalows, both twin & sleeping up to 4, & all with AC. Wi-Fi is available here & in the main areas. DBB bungalow N$2,204–3,561/3,052–5,088 sgl/dbl. **$$$$–$$$$$**

🏠 **Bagatelle Kalahari Game Ranch** [232 B1] (20 rooms, camping) ☏063 240982; e info@bagatelle-kalahari-gameranch.com; reservations ☏061 224712/217; e reservations@resdes.com.na; www.bagatelle-kalahari-gameranch.com. Relatively new owners Angela & Etienne Carsten continue to make big changes to this 7,000ha former sheep & cattle farm. Set amid rolling, linear dunes 37km north of Mariental, it's a warm & welcoming stopover. The original farmhouse has been converted into a comfortable lounge, restaurant & library area, with a reception, free Wi-Fi & curio shop. Outside there's a bar next to the swimming pool & a boma for lazy afternoons & casual dining. 6 wooden 'dune' chalets are raised on stilts atop a russet sand ridge, 2 of them with their own private plunge pool; 8 others, built of brick & insulated with bales of straw, line the inter-dune 'street'; & another 6 garden & pool rooms are closest to the heart of the lodge, suiting the less mobile. Interiors are similar throughout: white walls with animal-skin rugs, dark wood furniture, African objets d'art, wicker lampshades, comfortable beds, & modern bathrooms separated by a curtain (not door). The only notable difference is that 'dune' chalets have baths as well as showers (& a view!). There is also a campsite with 5 pitches & hot water, but no electricity, & construction is underway of 2 further options, both in the main part of the reserve: **Bagatelle Safari Villa** (8 en-suite rooms), & **Bagatelle Bush Lodge**, an eco-lodge with 12 chalets.

Morning, sundowner & night nature drives (N$450/550/300 pp) offer the opportunity to see kudu, oryx, hartebeest, giraffe, eland, steenbok, wildebeest & ostrich. As part of a Cheetah Conservation Fund project, 2 female cheetahs are housed in a 12ha enclosure beside the main lodge, where guests can watch them being fed in the afternoon, followed by a sundowner in the dunes (N$250 pp). Other activities include massage treatments, horseback safaris (N$650), stargazing & an early morning Bushman-walk tour (N$350). *DBB N$2,195–3,350/3,300–5,080 sgl/dbl; camping N$250 pp.* **$$–$$$$$**

🏠 **Lapa Lange** [232 B2] (1 villa, 4 chalets, 18 suites, camping) 📞063 241801; m 081 129 1085; e lapalange@iway.na; www.gamelodgenamibia. com. 32km southeast of Mariental, on the M29 towards Gochas, Lapa Lange seems to be trying to attract allcomers, from those looking to organise a party or wedding in one of its 3 function rooms to

independent travellers & campers. But while the stuffed lion, leopard & other animals that stalk the walls of the lavish lapa will appeal to some, they'll be a turn-off for others. That said, DSTV above the extensive bar has its aficionados, there's Wi-Fi in the main building, & day visitors are welcome for lunch. All rooms are modern in design, with large windows, thatched roofs & AC. Chalets, set around the camp's waterhole, sleep up to 4 & have a small lounge area & braai facilities; the 2-person villa comes with a hot tub. The campsite has 6 pitches with water, power & ablution facilities, & both tents & beds can be hired. Along with watching captive cheetah being fed, guests can do nature drives, hiking trails & stargazing. *Chalet N$1,980–2,275/3,060–3,280 sgl/dbl; camping N$175 pp.* **$$–$$$$$**

UHLENHORST North of Mariental, this dot on the map seems little more than a large farm today, yet in the 1930s and 1940s there were two hotels, several shops, a post office and a bank here. Uhlenhorst is typical of many small Namibian towns that were once important, but have faded with the advent of communications and good roads into mere shadows of themselves.

STAMPRIET TO GOCHAS Stampriet itself has little of intrinsic interest to drivers except for a couple of banks and a small fuel station – useful should you be running low – and Gochas likewise, but there are some interesting accommodation options. As an added bonus, the C15 between the two small towns makes a pleasant drive, passing through a fertile stretch of farmland parallel to the Auob River. Ground squirrels inhabit the banks lining the road, so it's a great place to observe them as they go about their daily routines. From Gochas, it is a straight drive on the C18, a good, empty road, to rejoin the B1 near Gibeon.

Where to stay: guesthouses and lodges

🏠 **Auob Country Lodge** [232 C2] (25 rooms, camping) 📞063 250101; reservations 📞061 374750; m 081 162 5155; e auob@ncl.com.na; www.auob.com.na. Situated on the C15, about 6km north of Gochas & around 190km from the Mata-Mata border post, the colourful Auob Lodge stands in the Kalahari, close to the dry Auob River, within 80km² of its own land. It also has its own airstrip. Despite the name, the lodge has the atmosphere of a European hotel, with heavy furniture, a bar, pool, lounge & lapa restaurant. The rooms, set around a swimming pool, are comfortable, with AC, ceiling fans, en-suite shower & toilet, but don't expect much in the way of frills. For campers, there are 17 pitches with water & electricity. The lodge offers stargazing, guided hikes & unguided walking trails, & game

drives among typical Kalahari game species, including giraffe, eland, oryx & blue wildebeest. *N$1,690/2,900 sgl/dbl.* **$$$$**

🏠 **Kalahari Farmhouse** [232 B1] (11 rooms) 📞063 260259; e res6@gondwana-collection. com; https://store.gondwana-collection.com/ accommodation/kalahari-farmhouse. Just off the C20, close to the sports ground in Stampriet, & 61km from Mariental, this small lodge is a sister to Kalahari Anib – & at the heart of Gondwana's self-sufficiency project. Central to the lodge is a lovely 1950s farmhouse, incorporating the original kitchen as a dining area. To one side is a large bar & lounge area, leading on to a patio with a good-size pool. To the front, a broad, shaded terrace looks over individual en-suite rooms which are whitewashed inside & out to blend with the farmhouse, with AC/heating for all extremes of temperature, & patchwork quilts adding splashes of colour. Guests may explore the farm, including the Self Sufficiency Centre where they grow all the produce or do a nature drive at Kalahari Anib. Free Wi-Fi around reception. *N$1,844/2,950 sgl/dbl.* **$$$$**

↑ Stampriet Historical Guesthouse
[232 B2] (10 rooms) ☎ 063 260013; e stampriet@ iway.na; www.stamprietguesthouse.com. Neighbouring Kalahari Farmhouse, this

characterful guesthouse – located just before the entrance to Stampriet village sits on a hill offering lovely views. It is run by Irene Zondagh, supported by a veritable menagerie of animals, from parrots, ducks & chickens to dogs, cats & lambs. Rooms are homely & the honeymoon suite has a claw-foot bath. Perks include free Wi-Fi, a pool table, swimming pool, jungle gym for kids, free tea/coffee throughout the day, a lovely arts & crafts souvenirs table, & a restaurant. *DBB N$1,230/2,000 sgl/dbl.* **$$$$**

THE B1 FROM MARIENTAL TO KEETMANSHOOP

Between Mariental and Keetmanshoop is a 221km stretch of tar road that most visitors see at speed. However, a few places are worth knowing about as you hurry past, and Brukkaros is worth a detour for those keen on walking.

GIBEON About 6km west of the B1, this sprawling community lies in a valley. Its sole claim to fame is as the site of what is thought to be the world's heaviest shower of meteorites, some 600 million years ago. Many of these are now displayed outside Windhoek's Town Square Mall (page 200), while a smaller specimen may be seen at the museum in Rehoboth.

Just off the main B1 itself, opposite the bright red station building, is a small cemetery maintained by the Commonwealth War Graves Commission, commemorating both German and South African troops who fell during the Battle of Gibeon on 27 April 1915. The battle itself proved to be decisive in the South African campaign against German colonial occupation of what was then South West Africa.

MUKUROB Known as 'the Finger of God', Mukurob was once an immense rock pinnacle, which balanced on a narrow neck of rock and towered 34m above the surrounding plains. When it collapsed around 8 December 1988, leaving a sizeable pile of rubble, its demise caused much speculation, as the finger's existence was linked to divine approval – and the country was in the process of becoming independent. Initially it was claimed that God was displeased with contemporary developments in this independence process. Later, right-wing extremists were blamed rather than God. Eventually, though, theories linked its fall firmly with the shock waves from the large Armenian earthquake of 7 December. To drive to where it stood, turn east off the B1 on to the D3919, just south of Asab, and follow the road for about 23km. To see it as it once was, drop into the museum in Keetmanshoop and have a look at the replica.

TSES Two-thirds of the way towards Keetmanshoop, almost opposite the turning to Berseba and Brukkaros, Tses is a small township to the east of the B1. As in any poor country township, visitors passing through are treated as something of a curiosity, but made welcome. Across the railway there's a post office, a small trading store, a Catholic school and a fuel station – which occasionally runs out, so don't let your fuel supply run too low in this area.

BRUKKAROS Rising to 650m, the volcanic crater of Brukkaros – or Bruckaros – towers over the expanse of bare, flat plains that surround it. It's a classic volcano shape, clearly visible west of the B1. In the 1900s the Germans used the eastern side of the crater as the base for a heliograph. Then in the early 1930s, the Smithsonian Institute built a solar observatory on the western side, taking advantage of the clear air and lack of artificial lights nearby. Both the Germans and the observatory have now gone, and the skies are as clear as ever – so it's a great place to explore and possibly camp, though the community campsite here has been closed for some years.

Getting there and away About 80km north of Keetmanshoop, and just south of the turning to Tses, turn west on to the M98 (signposted simply 'Berseba'). The road crosses the Fish River after about 19km, and it's worth a short stop to check out the waterbirds, including sacred ibis, that congregate here. In late afternoon you may even spot a family of baboons crossing the river. After a further 19km, just before you reach Berseba, turn north towards the volcano on to the D3904. Though this looks like a short distance, it'll be 9km or so on a flat road before you reach the gates and start to climb the volcano.

Where to stay

Ⓧ **Brukkaros Campsite** [232 A3] In theory it's still possible to use this discontinued community campsite. There are 2 camping spots at the base with drop toilets & bucket showers. Above this, you need a 4x4 and the skill of knowing how to use it to reach the 2nd camping area. With just 3 pitches this should be treated as virtually wild camping with no facilities. Neither fuel, firewood nor water are available so come fully equipped; there's a small store in Berseba if you're out of the basics.

What to see and do From the old 4x4 campsite, a footpath leads to the eroded edge of the crater's southern lip. The path here was made while the observatory was being constructed, and it goes over the lip and into the crater, taking about 40 minutes, then continues up to the old observatory just below the western rim after an hour or so. The rim itself is a very short scramble away.

You can hike around here, or just sit and watch the dust-devils twist their way for miles around as the sun goes down. It is a superb place to sleep out under the stars, which you will probably never see more clearly.

BERSEBA The nearest town to Brukkaros, Berseba is one of the region's oldest settlements – notable for having had a Rhenish missionary, Samuel Hahn, based here as early as 1850. Now it remains a large though poor settlement, surviving by subsistence farming. This area often receives very little rain, and agriculture of any kind is difficult. There are a couple of shops for essentials and a fuel pump at the end of the road, though don't rely on the latter.

Continuing south on the B1, the road remains level and straight. If you're hoping to stop before Keetmanshoop, it may be worth considering the campsite along this road.

Where to stay

Ⓧ **Garas Park Rest Camp** [232 B4] (camping) `\`063 223217; m 081 491 3863; e marian.hulme.z@gmail.com. 20km north of Keetmanshoop, & just west of the B1, this makes a pleasant stop for passing motorists, with basic but clean facilities. The campsite is owned by artist Marian Hulme, whose sculptures are dotted along the road. However, the real appeal is the small stand of quivertrees dotted among giant boulders like a child's building bricks. A rather eclectic mix of traditional huts & other artefacts are displayed around the place. Wood & water are available, but otherwise campers need to be entirely self-sufficient. *Camping N$100 pp.* **$**

Pronounced 'Keet-mans-verp', which is often shortened in slang to just 'Keetmans', Keetmanshoop lies about 480km south of Windhoek at an altitude of 1,000m. It's a bustling little town, and the administrative centre of this region.

Originally there was a Nama settlement on the banks of the seasonal Swartmodder River here, also known as just Swartmodder. Then, in 1866, the Rhenish Missionary Society sent Johan Schröder here from their established station at Berseba. He organised the building of a church and named it Keetmanshoop (which means 'Keetman's hope'), after Johan Keetman, one of the rich benefactors who had paid for the building.

In 1890 that church was swept away by a freak flood, but a new one, built on higher ground, was completed five years later. This was disused for years, but restored and declared a monument in 1978. Now it shelters the town's museum, so at least visit this, even if you see nothing else here.

GETTING THERE AND AWAY

By car Keetmanshoop is situated at the hub of the road network in southern Namibia, linked to Windhoek, Lüderitz and South Africa by good tar roads.

By bus Intercape runs a good service linking Windhoek and Cape Town, via Keetmanshoop. Buses leave the local office at the Engen garage on Lafenis (Fifth) Avenue at 23.05 on Monday, Wednesday, Friday and Sunday heading south, and at 03.35 on Monday, Friday and Saturday going north. For further details, see page 153.

The Starline bus that once connected Keetmanshoop with towns throughout the south is no longer operational, but occasional minibuses run between here and Lüderitz (page 275).

By train Keetmanshoop's 1928 railway station [243 C1] is linked to Windhoek by slow TransNamib passenger trains. These leave the capital on Wednesday and Saturday at 19.40, arriving at 07.00 the next morning, with an onward connection to Karasburg at 09.00. In the other direction, trains leave Karasburg at 11.25 on Thursday and Sunday, connecting with the Keetmanshoop to Windhoek service which departs at 19.00, and arrives in Windhoek at 07.00 the following morning.

TOURIST INFORMATION

ℹ️ Tourist office [243 B2] Cnr Hampie Plichta & Fifth Av; ☎ 063 221266; e stfkeet@iway. na; ⏰ 07.30–12.30 & 13.30–16.30 Mon–Fri, but closes 16.00 Fri. The tourist office resides in perhaps the town's most historic building, the Kaiserliches Postamt – or imperial post office; built in 1910, it is now a national monument. They aim to promote the whole region & will help book accommodation.

🏠 WHERE TO STAY

🏠 Bird's Mansions Hotel [243 B2] (24 rooms, 2 apts) 90 Sixth Av; ☎ 063 221711; e hotel@birdsaccommodation.com; www. birdsaccommodation.com. In the centre of town, Bird's Mansions is linked to Bird's Nest B&B, & friendly service is the hallmark. The self-catering apartments are found off the courtyard at the back, while other rooms are in the main building. All share the same facilities: DSTV, phone, free Wi-Fi & AC, & apartments also have kitchenettes with a fridge/freezer, small hob, b/fast bar & washing machine. The restaurant, with tables inside & on a quiet courtyard, offers a varied menu of fish, game, steak & pasta, while at the rear of the hotel

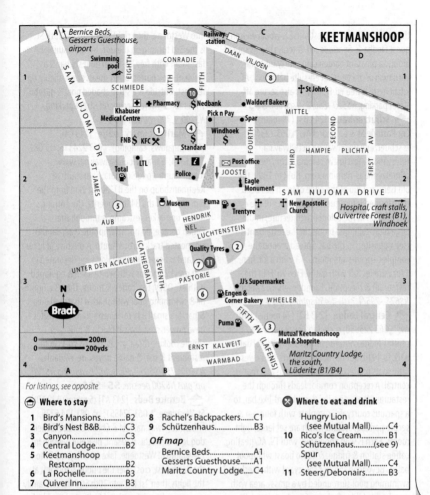

The Southern Kalahari and Fish River Canyon   KEETMANSHOOP

11

For listings, see opposite

🛌 Where to stay

1	Bird's Mansions	B2
2	Bird's Nest B&B	C3
3	Canyon	C3
4	Central Lodge	B2
5	Keetmanshoop Restcamp	B2
6	La Rochelle	B3
7	Quiver Inn	B3
8	Rachel's Backpackers	C1
9	Schützenhaus	B3

Off map

Bernice Beds	A1
Gesserts Guesthouse	A1
Maritz Country Lodge	C4

🍴 Where to eat and drink

	Hungry Lion (see Mutual Mall)	C4
10	Rico's Ice Cream	B1
	Schützenhaus	(see 9)
	Spur (see Mutual Mall)	C4
11	Steers/Debonairs	B3

is a lapa with a pool, braai & eating area – usually used for functions. Plenty of off-street parking on Seventh St, behind the hotel, completes the package. *N$800/1,200 sgl/dbl.* **$$$**

🏠 **Bird's Nest B&B** [243 C3] (10 rooms) 16 Pastorie St; ✆ 063 222906/223344; e guesthouse@birdsaccommodation.com; www.birdsaccommodation.com. This good little B&B close to the centre of Keet is under the same ownership as Bird's Mansions. Rooms, arranged around a quiet courtyard, are fairly small, but light & modern, with attractive fabrics, AC/heating, ceiling fans, DSTV, phone & facilities for making hot drinks. 1 is suitable for families. Outside, the gardens are well tended, underlying the care that goes into this place. There's a small bar & free Wi-Fi. *N$700/1,000 sgl/dbl.* **$$$**

🏠 **Canyon Hotel** [243 C3] (70 rooms) Fifth Av; ✆ 063 223361; e canyonhotel@iway.na; www.canyon-namibia.com. Keetmanshoop's largest 3-star hotel feels in need of a little love & attention, & the rooms are looking pretty tired. That said, they are comfortable, with twin beds, TVs, direct-dial phones & AC, & en-suite bathrooms with showers & hairdryers. Room service is available with N$50 charge, too. Around the complex you'll find a restaurant, bar, pool & gym. Free Wi-Fi is available, plus there's a handy postbox outside. Plenty of parking. *N$605/880 sgl/ dbl.* **$$$**

🏠 **Quiver Inn** [243 B3] (10 rooms) Pastorie St; m 081 855 3835; e info@quiverinnguesthouse. com, quiverinn@gmail.com; www. quiverinnguesthouse.com. We have heard positive things about this new guesthouse & would welcome guest feedback. Spacious self-catering rooms spread around a pleasant garden cum courtyard come with twin or dbl beds, an en-suite bathroom, AC, kitchenette & free Wi-Fi. There is also secure off-street parking. *N$520–850/850 sgl/dbl.* **$$$**

⌂ **Schützenhaus** [243 B3] (19 rooms) Cnr Pastorie St & Cathedral Av; ✆ 063 223400; e schuetzenhaus@iway.na,nct@iway.na, reservations@exclusive.com.na, http://www. schuetzenhaus-namibia.com. Built in 1899, the old German Club at the edge of town has been transformed into a guesthouse. Relics of the past remain in the colonial architecture; in the large high-ceilinged rooms; in the restaurant (see opposite) & in the bar. Spread around the complex are en-suite rooms – 1 with a kitchen, 1 for families & 3 with baths. Free Wi-Fi in the restaurant & reception. Laundry service available. *N$675–795/1,230–1,450 sgl/dbl.* **$$$**

⌂ **Central Lodge** [243 B2] (24 rooms) Fifth Av; ✆ 063 225850; e clodge@iway.na; www. central-lodge.com. The former Hansa Hotel dates back to 1910, but its modern incarnation owes little to its predecessor. The Central is just that – central. A reception corridor leads through the restaurant (see opposite) & cupboard-like bar, to a spacious courtyard, complete with fountain & secure parking, around which are set large, light rooms. Each is well appointed, with TV, AC/heating, coffee station & fridge, & 4 also boast whirlpool baths. Beyond is another courtyard with a secluded swimming pool surrounded by a grassy area with ramshackle tables & chairs. Standards have slipped a little, but the Central remains popular with locals & visitors & has Wi-Fi in the main areas. Associated with the lodge are a new sushi bar & coffee shop, convenient for lunches & light bites. *N$450–670/ 700–900 sgl/dbl.* **$$–$$$**

⌂ **Gesserts Guesthouse** [243 A1] (7 rooms) 138 13th St, Westdene; ✆ 063 223892; e gesserts@ iafrica.com.na; www.natron.net/gessert. This welcoming B&B is a homely place, decked out with crafts made by the owner Hendrik's previous wife. Today, he & his new spouse Zelna Knouwds offer attractive country-style rooms – with AC, & some with fridges or TVs – set around a pretty floral garden including a small pool that is candlelit by night. 2 of the rooms link to make a family unit. To reach it, head northwest on Sam Nujoma Dr, across the railway line. Turn left at the lights

into Westdene, then right into 19th Av; 13th St is the 3rd turning on the left. There's a sunny b/ fast room with free Wi-Fi, an honesty bar & a resident grey parrot; other meals are available on request. Outside is a small shaded pool & gazebo with tables. There's secure off-street parking. *N$700/1,300 sgl/dbl.* **$$$**

⌂ **Maritz Country Lodge** [243 C4] (19 bungalows, camping) ✆ 063 224316; m 081 394 1414; e maritzlodge@iway.na; www. maritzcountrylodge.com.na. 5km south of Keetmanshoop on the B1, about 2km from the junction with the B4 for Lüderitz, the entrance to this upmarket restcamp is through the Engen garage; do not attempt the (very sandy) signposted track further south. A mixture of luxury & standard en-suite bungalows are decorated in soft greys & greens with white linen & equipped with AC, DSTV, tea/coffee & fridge. There's a figure-of-8 swimming pool with shaded thatched area & bar, & a small à la carte restaurant. Campsites have power, smart wash blocks & toilets, & simple cooking/braai areas. There's Wi-Fi in the restaurant & bar, & game drives are available. *N$600–750/950–1,300 sgl/dbl; camping N$120 pp, plus N$200 per site.* **$$–$$$**

⌂ **Bernice Beds** [243 A1] (5 rooms) 129 10th St, Westdene; ✆ 063 224851; m 081 124 6278; e bernice@iway.na. Stef & Christi Coetzee & their dog Jolena run this pleasant, peaceful pension in the suburb of Westdene. Take Sam Nujoma Dr to the northwest, cross over the bridge & turn left at the lights, then 1st left into 10th St. 3 dbl & 2 family rooms are clean & functional & situated in a block at one side; each is equipped with TV, AC/heating, fridge, free Wi-Fi & a safe parking place. It all adds up to good-value accommodation, although they don't provide lunch/dinner. *N$660 dbl.* **$$**

⌂ **La Rochelle** [243 B3] (7 rooms) 12 Sixth Av; ✆ 063 223845; m 081 278 2383; www.keetmans. com. Set on a hill & catching the breeze, this century-old house is owned by Joubert & Annalein de Witt. Splashes of vivid colour add style to the modern dining room. Bedrooms, including 2 for families, vary in size, but all have remote TV, tea/ coffee facilities, fridge & AC. On the roof is a small pool with views over town & next to the secure parking area on a lower level is a pleasant rocky cactus garden. Also on site is Annalein's beauty salon offering manicures, waxing, etc, but no massages. Joubert keeps a variety of budgies & diamond doves

& you can hear their pleasant chirrups while eating b/fast (*N$100*). Not suitable for travellers with disabilities. *N$380–440/600–660 sgl/dbl.* **$$**

🏠 **Rachel's Backpackers** [243 C1] (12 rooms, 30 dorm beds) Schmiede St. Rachel's is central, very simple & cheap – so fine for a night if those are your priorities. The dbl rooms are en suite & there is a large, well-equipped kitchen for guests' use. **$**

🅰 **Keetmanshoop Restcamp** [243 B2] (16 pitches) Eighth Av; ✆063 221265. This was long

one of Namibia's best municipal sites, but these days things aren't up to the standards of many of Namibia's privately owned sites. Inside protective coils of razor wire lie tired-looking but functional ablution blocks with hot water, surrounded by grass lawns. Though it's one of the few places to camp in town & there's lots of space for cars & caravans on the gravel drives, there are better options in the area if you don't need to be in Keet itself. *N$90 pp & N$30/vehicle.* **$**

✖ **WHERE TO EAT AND DRINK** Historically there's been a dearth of places to eat in Keetmanshoop although the recent addition of some larger fast-food chains has increased variety. Still, the best bets remain the hotels, which have their own restaurants – including a new sushi bar. Some of the garages have cafés serving pies, burgers and cold drinks, and Engen has a Wimpy – useful if you're pushed for time. There are also branches of **Spur** and **Hungry Lion** in Mutual Mall [243 C4] on Fifth Avenue, near the Canyon Hotel.

✖ **Schützenhaus** [243 B3] Cnr Pastorie St & Cathedral Av; ✆063 223400; ⏱ lunch & dinner Mon–Fri, dinner only Sat–Sun. Old German trophies displayed in the large, rather formal, very quiet, restaurant hint at the history of the former German Club. At lunch, come for a toasted sandwich, but in the evenings it's a place for committed carnivores, with an à la carte menu offering *eisbein* & schnitzel among others. **$$$–$$$$**

✖ **Central Lodge** [243 B2] Fifth Av; ✆063 225850; ⏱ 11.00–16.00 & 18.30–21.30 daily. Although the Central is widely considered Keetmanshoop's best restaurant, don't raise your hopes too high: the plastic tablecloths set the tone. We're told the steak, stew & burgers are good,

but it's best to steer clear of the pizzas. A kids' menu is also available. There's a cupboard-like bar alongside with a sad-looking stuffed oryx head & a few cursory bar stools. The wine list isn't up to much either. Adding some variety to Keet's culinary scene are a new sushi bar & coffee shop associated with the hotel. **$$–$$$$**

✖ **Steers/Debonairs** [243 B3] Cnr Fifth Av & Pastorie St; ✆063 226763; ⏱ 09.00–22.00 daily. The South African equivalent of McDonald's, this fast-food take-away chain offers pizzas, burgers & chips. **$$**

🍨 **Rico's Ice Cream** [243 B1] Schmiede St; 📱 081 127 2669; ⏱ 09.00–17.00 Mon–Fri, 09.00–13.00 Sat. Treat the kids or yourself to a scoop of soft-whip ice cream from the little sweet shop. **$**

OTHER PRACTICALITIES Keetmanshoop could well be vying for the record for the greatest number of **fuel stations** per head of population; there are plenty. If you're after **souvenirs**, it may be worth checking out the craft stalls by the side of the B1, near the junction with the C16. In an **emergency**, the main hospital [243 B2] (✆*063 220 9000*) is on the main road as you're heading out of town, while the ambulance is on ✆063 223388 and the police on ✆063 10111.

$ Banks [243 B2] Standard: Hampie Plichta Av; Nedbank: Mittel St
Camping supplies & vehicle repairs LTL [243 B2]: Hampie Plichta St; ✆063 223351; e lombaardlouis@iway.na
➕ **Khabuser Medical Centre** [243 B1] Mittel St; ✆063 225687/8; a/h 📱 081 202 2313

➕ **Pharmacy** [243 B1] Mittel St; ✆063 223300/9; a/h 📱 081 124 9369; ⏱ 08.00–17.00 Mon–Fri, 08.00–12.30 Sat
Supermarkets JJ's [243 C3]: Fifth Av; ⏱ 06.00–22.00 daily; Shoprite: Mutual Keetmanshoop Mall [243 C4]
Tyres Trentyre [243 C2] ✆063 223357; Quality Tyres [243 C2] ✆063 224413

WHAT TO SEE AND DO Like many of Namibia's provincial towns, Keetmanshoop doesn't have a wealth of attractions, but you can while away a couple of lazy hours visiting the museum.

Keetmanshoop Museum [243 B2] (*Sam Nujoma Dr;* ✎ *061 302230;* ☉ *07.30–12.30 & 13.30–16.30 Mon–Thu, 07.30–12.30 & 13.30–16.00 Fri; admission free, but donations welcome*) This centrally located old Rhenish Mission Church was built in 1895 to replace the original one that the floods destroyed. Now it is surrounded by rockeries and used as the town's museum. Don't ignore these rockeries, however, as they are dotted with native plants, as well as old wagons, machinery and even a Nama hut. If you're not visiting the Quivertree Forest, then take a close look at the small trees in the museum's garden.

Inside the church is a beautiful pulpit and an interesting collection of local memorabilia, including an elephant's skull, fossils, gemstones, early cameras, photographs, and various implements that were used by past townspeople. Upstairs is a replica of Mukurob, the Finger of God (page 240).

AROUND KEETMANSHOOP The two obvious excursions from town, the Quivertree Forest and the Giant's Playground, are almost adjacent. A little further afield, on the way to the Fish River Canyon via Seeheim, is Naute Dam Recreational Resort (page 248). Both the Fish River Canyon and Brukkaros are possible day trips from Keetmanshoop, although the former is a lengthy drive and well worth a longer visit.

Quivertree Forest and Giant's Playground [232 B4] (☉ *sunrise–sunset, other hours by arrangement only; admission N$60 pp & N$50 per car*) Also known as the 'Kokerboomwoud', the Quivertree Forest is a relatively dense stand of quivertrees (*Aloe dichotoma*), just 14km from Keetmanshoop on the privately owned Gariganus Farm. To find it, take the B1 north for about 1km, then turn right on to the C16 towards Koës, then left on to the M29 shortly after.

These trees are found all over southern Namibia and the northern Cape, but in few places are so many seen together. (A second is a few kilometres south of Kenhardt, on the R27 in South Africa.) Ideally drop in close to sunset or sunrise, when the light is at its best. These skeletal 'trees' make particularly striking photographs when the lighting of a fill-in flash is balanced against a flaming sunset behind.

QUIVERTREES

The quivertree or kokerboom (*Aloe dichotoma*), a type of tree aloe, occurs sporadically over a large area of southern Namibia and the northern Cape, usually on steep rocky slopes. Its name refers to its supposed use by the Bushmen for making the quivers for their arrows – the inside of a dead branch consists of only a light, fibrous heart which is easily gouged out to leave a hollow tube.

The quivertree is specially adapted to survive in extremely arid conditions: its fibrous branches and trunk are used for water storage, as are its thick, succulent leaves, while water lost through transpiration is reduced by waxy coatings on the tree's outside surfaces. Roots, though, are shallow, making the tree vulnerable to high winds and, in common with most desert-adapted flora, its growth rate is very slow. Its beautiful yellow flowers bloom in winter.

Just 5km further down the M29 are some marvellous balancing basalt rocks known as the Giant's Playground. Reminiscent of formations in Zimbabwe's Matobo Hills, these are more limited but still interesting.

Where to stay

🏠 **Quivertree Forest Restcamp** (2 houses, 8 igloos, 1 family room, camping) m 083 768 3421; e quiver@iafrica.com.na; www.quivertreeforest. com. From Keetmanshoop, veer left on to the C16, look for signs, & drive 13km along a dirt track: the camp is on the left. Run by Coenie & Ingrid Nolte, plus an assortment of dogs, they offer an assortment of accommodation. As well as 2 guesthouses, each with its own lounge, & 1 with a kitchen, there are en-suite Star Wars-style 'igloos' with a kitchenette, AC & fridge, though blacked-out windows make these a bit gloomy inside. There is also a tree-shaded campsite adjacent to the Quivertree Forest, with BBQ facilities & electricity. Free Wi-Fi in the main areas. Don't be put off by the cages to the left of, & behind, the farm buildings; this is a holding area for orphaned cheetahs, which are permanently housed in separate enclosures of 15ha & 37ha respectively; you can watch them being fed at 17.00 or go on a supervised cheetah walk (*N$200 pp, or N$300 for non-guests*). Staying here is an alternative to Keetmanshoop, & makes it easier to see the forest & the rocks around dawn & dusk, when the light is at its best for photography. *DBB N$1,050/1,620 sgl/dbl; camping N$140 pp.* **$–$$$$**

Mesosaurus Fossil Site

Some 42km from Keetmanshoop on the C17 towards Koës, this is the place to see the fossils of the huge mesosaurus that inhabited the freshwater lakes of Gondwanaland 270 million years ago. Stands of quivertrees are also a feature of the landscape, as are the giant dolorite rock formations. It's also possible to visit the graves of two German Schutztruppers who died in a 1904 battle between the Germans and the Namas. For visitors, there are guided tours of the site (*N$130 pp*), as well as – for overnight guests – 3–10km hiking trails and a 16km off-road trail for high-clearance vehicles.

Where to stay

🛖 **Mesosaurus Fossil Bush Camp** [232 B4] (4 chalets, camping) m 083 700 0012; e mesosaurus.camp@gmail.com; www. mesosaurus.com. This simple camp some 3km from the road has rustic, en-suite chalets (3 twins, 1 family), 6 pitches for camping, & an isolated bush camp in the river-bed. Each pitch has a table, hot water & braai, with ablution blocks close by & wood available on site, though you will need to bring all other provisions with you. Do note that the famous mesosaurus fossils are not at the camp; to visit you need to join a guided tour. Cash only. *Chalet N$330/660 sgl/dbl; camping N$140 pp.* **$–$$**

Seeheim

About 45km from Keetmanshoop, just south of the modern B4, Seeheim offers access along the C12 to the Fish River Canyon. That said, the roads in this area are in the process of being reclassified and these days the D545 is considered the better route, passing Naute Dam on the way. In its heyday, in the late 19th century, Seeheim was on the old east–west road and was larger than Keetmanshoop, supporting three hotels. Now, marooned by the side of the railway, just one hotel remains.

Where to stay

🏠 **Seeheim Hotel** [232 A5] (36 rooms, camping) ☎ 063 683643; m 081 128 0349; e seeheim@iway.na; www.seeheimhotel.com. Dating back to 1896, the stone-built Seeheim is hidden away in a quarry of sorts. It's one of those quirky finds that defies categorisation. Owned & run by Zirkie Kloppers & family, it is something of a one-stop shop, with an emergency fuel supply, a shop selling souvenirs, safari clothes, meat & other basics, a pub-like bar (selling grapes in summer;

Construction of the controversial Neckartal Dam across the Fish River, north of Seeheim, has been underway since 2013, but has been fraught with problems. Although designed to sustain a 5,000ha irrigation project, the irrigation potential at the smaller and nearby Naute Dam (see below) is still under utilised, prompting questions as to the necessity of Neckartal in the first place. In addition, a legal dispute, labour issues and construction delays have all taken their toll, causing the project to overrun the proposed completion date of 2017. In October 2018, however, it was reported to be finally complete.

It is thought that the resulting reservoir will also afford the opportunity for recreational use, perhaps similar to that at Hardap (page 235), but time will tell. Either way, Neckartal will replace Hardap as Namibia's largest dam, with a projected capacity of around 960 million m³ – though it will take around two years to fill.

oranges in winter), a games room with table tennis, darts & a pool table, a simple restaurant & outside dining area (🕐 *all day, à la carte* **$–$$$**; *large group buffet N$170 pp*) overlooking a swimming pool (*non-residents N$10*). Not to mention a thriving furniture business & even a taxidermy practice, evidenced by the bizarre optics (which will alienate some). All the non-AC en-suite rooms – some in the original building, others added at various levels around the complex – are different & individually furnished with pieces the Kloppers have designed & made themselves from 'kiaat' wood. Rooms 19–36 are newer/more modern with open-plan bathrooms & zebra-print cushions. Around the buildings are pitches for up to 100 campers. Guests can relax in the games room, hike around the lodge or visit the oryx & chicken pens, while Zirkie's organic garden & farm, 50km away, offers the opportunity for game drives (*N$400 pp, min 4*) if booked in advance. There are always offers on, so email for rates. *N$790/1,300 sgl/dbl; camping N$160 pp.* **$$–$$$**

Naute Dam Recreational Resort [232 B5] The resort was closed at the time of research in 2018, though it was still possible to visit the lakeshore, dam and viewpoint. Surrounded by low hills, and overlooked by the Klein Karas Mountains, the lake created by Naute Dam is about 26km long and, at its widest, some 7km. The 470m-long dam was opened in 1972. Standing 37m above the river-bed, it holds back the water from the Löwen River as it feeds into the Fish River to the southwest. From what used to be the main entrance, obvious from the large unmissable buoy on the D545, there is a good vantage point over both the dam itself and the lake beyond with its cluster of small islands.

Despite the lake's obvious attractions, investment in tourist facilities has been almost non-existent and the campsite is in a bad state of repair. Instead, efforts have been concentrated on an irrigation project fed by water from the dam, leading to the production of dates, grapes, prickly pears and pomegranates for export (you can see the date palms just west of the causeway as you drive to the viewpoint).

Flora and fauna The lake has become a focus for numerous birds. There are opportunities for birdwatching from the viewpoint, but it is the reed-fringed sandy lakeshore to the south of the main entrance that is the real haven for waterbirds, with pelicans, herons, kingfishers, cormorants, African darters and sacred ibis all in evidence. Walking, fishing and boating are also permitted in this area, though you will need to obtain a permit in advance from the MET (page 276). The 23,000ha game park protects springbok, klipspringer, oryx, kudu and ostrich, but is not open to the public.

Getting there and away In 2018, the C12 between Seeheim and the intersection to the D545 was in an extremely bad state of repair and was almost undriveable, so we'd recommend using the D545 off the B4, which has been reclassified as the C12, From Keetmanshoop, take the B4 west towards Seeheim and follow the signs to Naute Dam by turning south on to the old D545 (new C12). What's left of the campsite is marked by a large black-and-white buoy off the D545, just before you head down the steep track and cross the Löwen River. If you drive through the reed-lined river bed you have gone too far. To reach the banks of the river if coming from the north, cross the Löwen River, and drive past the Naute Kristal distillery before turning on to the D570, then follow this for 5km, keeping left to avoid the restricted game park area. There are numerous unmarked trails that also lead to the lakeshore, but if you keep following this road you will eventually reach the old, disused, lakeshore campsite that was disappointingly strewn with rubbish when we visited.

Where to stay

Ⓐ Naute Campsite [232 B5] ✆063 250533. The area by the lake is no longer designated for camping. Instead, campers can pitch up at the level, purpose-built site that looks over the lake — though it does feel a bit like a car park. Facilities here were in a real state of disrepair at the time of research, & the kiosk wasn't functioning either, so make sure that you stock up before arriving.

Where to eat and drink

✲✕ Naute Kristall ✆063 683810; m 081 284 5107; www.naute-kristall.com; ⏰ 07.30–16.00 Mon–Fri, 08.00–14.00 w/ends. Twinned with Kristall Kellerei (page 457), Naute Kristall is an unusual combination of distillery & café. The brightly coloured building beside the D545 is hard to miss & makes a great stop to grab a cup of coffee, a bottle of fresh pomegranate juice & a piece of cake, or to indulge in a cocktail or spot of spirit tasting (N$50 pp; groups must book ahead). The spirits are all made on site, predominantly from produce of the Naute Dam irrigation project, & include the award-winning NamGin, Dandy (date brandy), Granate (pomegranate fine spirit) & Matisa (prickly-pear fine spirit). All are for sale & make excellent gifts. **$**

THE DEEP SOUTH

South and east of Keetmanshoop, Namibia's central highlands start to flatten out towards South Africa's Karoo, and the great sand sheet of the Kalahari to the east. Many of the roads here are spectacular: vast and empty with enormous vistas. The C10 between Karasburg and the B1, and the D608, are particular favourites.

The towns here seem to have changed little in years. They vary from small to minute, and remind the outsider of a typical South African *dorp* (a small town). Expect some of them to be on the conservative side.

KOËS This small outpost about 124km northeast of Keetmanshoop lies deep in the Kalahari Desert. It is the centre for the local Afrikaans farming community, and has a few small shops and a basic hotel.

Where to stay

🏠 Torgos Safari Camp [232 D3] (8 tents, 2 chalets) ✆063 252019; m 081 146 0421, 081 302 1236; e info@torgoslodgenam.com; www. torgoslodgenam.com. Bordering the Kgalagadi

Transfrontier Park (🕐 08.00–16.30 daily), Torgos is well located for those crossing into South Africa using the Mata-Mata Gate, just 7km to the east. The 11,000ha private reserve has a good variety of plains wildlife. Both chalets & tents are en suite, but chalets have AC while the tents have fans. A high-ceilinged thatched lapa incorporates a bar, restaurant & lounge, with a boma for evening BBQs, & there's a pool. Dawn & sundowner drives are offered. *Tent N$1,020–1,400/2,040–2,400 sgl/dbl.* **$$$$**

🏠 **Hotel Koës** (8 rooms, 1 chalet) 2 Fontein St; ☎063 252716. Some of the rooms at this small, basic hotel are en suite; others share facilities. It's perhaps not going to be the highlight of your holiday, but it might be useful in an emergency. *N$110/220 sgl/dbl.* **$**

BETWEEN KEETMANSHOOP AND GRÜNAU
The long straight B1 between the two towns is characterised by farmland, backed to the east by the Karas Mountains. Among a number of guest farms along this road, the most established is the White House, but others are worth considering – as is the excellent café at Kitchen 51. The following are listed in order of distance from Keetmanshoop.

🏠 **Where to stay and eat**

🏠 **Kitchen 51** [232 B5] (7 chalets) m 081 255 1556 (WhatsApp calls only); e bookings@ mykitchen51.com; www.mykitchen51.com. Primarily a café/farmstall (🕐 summer 07.00–18.00, winter 07.30–17.30 daily), Kitchen 51 added guest chalets in response to popular demand. Some 50km south of Keetmanshoop on the B1, it has gained a reputation as a great place to break the drive to or from Fish River Canyon, with a delicious selection of homemade bread, excellent coffee & a well-stocked deli. The open-plan self-catering chalets – 4 with an extra twin room for families – are functional with clean modern lines, a small kitchenette (bring your own utensils), AC, en-suite shower room, access to a communal braai area & private parking. B/fast & lunch can be taken at the farmstall & there is the option to pre-order a 2-course dinner as well (N$180 pp). *N$1,000 per chalet.* **$$$**

🏠 **Goibib Mountain Lodge** [232 B5] (8 rooms, camping) ☎063 683131; m 85 693 8476, 085 376 6299 (also on WhatsApp); e goibib@mweb.com.na, goibib@resdest.com; www.goibibmountainlodge.com. This working farm sits close to the road at the base of the Great Karas Mountains, west of the B1 & some 112km south of Keetmanshoop/48km north of Grünau. All its traditional but tasteful en-suite rooms come with AC, radio, minibar, Wi-Fi, tea/coffee facilities & safe. In the lounge, there's a big-screen TV & a range of reference books, while the linked dining area has tables both inside & on a shaded veranda. There's an attractive walled pool area, backed by hills, & behind this a campsite with 5 pitches, each with its own braai, plus a central wood stove & ablution block; campers may use the swimming pool. As well as hiking on the surrounding 8,400ha farm, guests can hire mountain bikes, go stargazing, or take a 2–3hr game drive. While it lacks the personality of a guest farm, Goibib is comfortable & efficiently run. *DBB N$1,441/2,290 sgl/dbl; camping N$160 pp.* **$–$$$$**

🏠 **Savanna Guest Farm** [232 B5] (6 rooms); m 081 124 5269; e savannaf@gmail.com; www.savanna-guestfarm.com. This 22,000ha farm has a pleasant, quiet spot at the foot of the Great Karas Mountains; 42km north of Grünau, it is just off the B1, opposite the D203. In the 1900s the German Army billeted their troops here, with a kraal for the horses, rooms for their officers & a watchtower – now part of the farmhouse – to keep an eye on heliograph communications from stations in the mountains. Today it is a working sheep farm owned & run by Erich von Schauroth, who is also involved in training Arab horses for endurance racing. En-suite rooms with AC are comfortable, though not luxurious; 3 have self-catering facilities & some are suitable for families. Don't come expecting to be entertained, but for walkers or those interested in the farm, this could be a good location, with a pool for added relaxation & a 4x4 trail. There's an honesty bar in the b/fast room (b/fast N$80), & a 3-course dinner with traditional farm cooking is available by arrangement (N$160). *Room only N$550/800 sgl/dbl.* **$$$**

🏠 **White House Guest Farm** [232 B6] (5 rooms, 3 chalets, camping) ☎063 262061; m 081 285 6484; e withuis@iway.na; www.

250

withuis.iway.na. On a working 15,000ha sheep farm which stretches to the distant mountains, the White House is off the B1, about 11km north of Grünau, & some 4km from the main road. The distinct old farmhouse has Oregon pine floors, high wooden ceilings, wide verandas, a huge kitchen & even an old radiogram. It was built in 1912 for £2,500, & bought by the present owner's grandfather in 1926 for £3,500. After use as a school, among other things, it fell into disuse until bought by Dolf & Kinna De Wet, who began to renovate it in 1995. They have done a great job. Just sit down quietly to soak up the atmosphere & journey back to the early 20th century. In the main house are 4 en-suite family rooms, each with its own unique antique features, & a separate 'student' room with its own fridge, dining table, & a little shower-toilet adjacent. The kitchen, with a large fridge, stove, crockery & utensils, isn't luxurious (though it would have been 70 years ago), but it

is comfortable & very authentic with a stocked drinks fridge. Nearer to the family's home are well-equipped self-catering chalets with AC, heaters, a stocked fridge, cutlery, toaster & kettle with tea/coffee. Braai packs (*N$150 pp*) can be ordered with 2 weeks' notice, but an excellent dinner (*N$150*) may be ordered in advance: come with a good appetite! For campers, there are 4 pitches. The White House is a beautiful old place, which is excellent value & well worth a visit (though the historical aspect will pass you by if you're not in the main house). Birders have the choice of 2 hides close to the house, & there are a few walking or biking trails, too, while those with an interest in geology should pre-book a guided tour to the rose-quartz mine on the farm (*N$300 pp*). You can buy various quartz products at reception, along with a small selection of supplies such as rusks & firewood. *Room only N$400/740 sgl/dbl; camping N$100 pp; b/fast N$80.* **$–$$**

GRÜNAU With a fuel station, but no shops, Grünau is at a crossroads, where the railway from Upington in South Africa crosses the main B1. The little town also, more or less, marks the spot where the main tarred B3 from the central and eastern parts of South Africa meets with the B1 coming from the Cape. Thus it is strategically positioned for overnight stops between South Africa and Namibia – but isn't a destination of note in its own right. Though if you have vehicle problems, the branch of Rassies breakdown service here (**m** *081 127 8582, 081 715 2574*) might be useful.

Getting there and away The Intercape bus between Upington and Windhoek departs from the Shell truck stop in Grünau on Monday, Friday and Saturday at 01.15, returning from Windhoek at 16.30 on Wednesday, Friday and Sunday. Fares between Grünau and Windhoek or Grünau and Upington are around N$380 one-way.

Where to stay

Vastrap Guest Farm [232 B6] (9 rooms, 4 chalets, 1 flat) \063 262063; **m** 081 127 7142; **e** vastrap@afol.com.na; www.vastrapguestfarm.com. Around 5km southeast of Grünau on the B3 is a sign to the attractive & welcoming Vastrap Guest Farm, which is about 2km from the road, on a 6,000ha sheep farm belonging to Rean & Hettie Steenkamp. GPS users please note that this is the only road in! Simple but cheerful rooms with en-suite showers & AC have been created within old farmstead buildings that are linked together, & there are also en-suite self-catering chalets. Home-cooked meals (*b/fast N$150, dinner N$185*) are served on request in the dining room, & guests can

make use of both braai & freezer facilities. Outside is a swimming pool, & there's the opportunity for day trips on the farm & guided hunting safaris. Vastrap could also be used as a base to drive to Fish River Canyon, as it is only 120km from the viewpoints on the western side. *Room only N$850; chalet N$1,200 (max 4 pp); flat N$1,600 (max 6 pp).* **$$$**

Grünau Country Hotel (20 rooms, camping) Old Main Rd; \063 262001; **m** 081 124 9162; **e** grunauch@iway.na; www.grunaucountryhotel.com. The hotel with its distinctive tower was rebuilt following a fire, restoring this well-run, traditional hotel, with a 'ladies' bar' (no swearing allowed) & an à la carte restaurant (⏲ *daily for b/fast N$80 & dinner N$120–150*). It is signposted to the west off the B3, just south of the junction with the B1. The 10 standard rooms (6 twins, 4 family) are all en suite, but 10 budget rooms share an outside ablution block with the campsite, where there are electricity & water points, & trees for shade. *Room only N$400–450/450–650 sgl/dbl; camping N$150 pp.* **$$**

🏠 **Grünau Chalets** [232 B6] (12 chalets, camping) ☎ 063 262026; m 081 783 1313;

e willa@iafrica.com.na; www.grunauchalets.com. Just north of Grünau is a Shell fuel station (with ATM), with a simple restcamp. The surroundings are flat & characterless, but the small 1–6-bed bungalows are clean & well appointed, with Wi-Fi, AC, en-suite bathroom, TV, kitchenette & secure parking. 4 camping pitches have their own private ablution facilities, plus power point. The shop sells snacks, firewood & basic foodstuffs, including braai packs, & there's also a kiosk. Animals welcome (*N$40/50 small/large dog*). *N$440/660 sgl/dbl; camping N$140 per pitch, plus N$30 pp.* **$–$$**

KARASBURG

Karasburg is really just a bigger version of Grünau – a busy but convenient overnight stop on a long journey.

Getting there and away Intercape **buses** between Upington and Windhoek head north from the BP garage (XL Motors) next to Spar at 00.10 on Monday, Friday and Saturday, returning south at 01.10 on Monday, Thursday and Sunday. Slow TransNamib **trains** link the town with Grünau and Keetmanshoop twice a week; for details, see page 151.

🏠 **Where to stay and eat** The one hotel in town – Kalkfontein Hotel – has been closed for some time, so you'll have to pick from the meagre handful of B&Bs. For dining, you could try the Pizza Den, opposite the Engen garage on Main Street. Alternatively, there are several take-aways.

🏠 **Kleinbegin Lodge** [232 C6] (7 rooms) m 081 124 9186; e kleinbeginlodge@webmail. co.za. This homely guesthouse, some 30km north of Karasburg on the B3, has traditional dbl en-suite rooms of varying sizes, all with minibars. Guests may use the swimming pool, pool table & table tennis, & kids the small playground. Note that hunting safaris are also possible here. *N$590/890 sgl/dbl.* **$$$**

🏠 **Karas Cottages** (6 rooms) 88 Kalkfontein St; ☎ 063 270349; e jswartz@iway.na. 4 en-suite rooms in the main house have tea/coffee facilities, DSTV, while 2 self-catering 1-bedroom cottages have a lounge & kitchen with fridge, 2-plate stove, cutlery & crockery. Outside is a small pool, & a BBQ area under lots of shady trees. A restaurant & supermarket are located nearby. *N$205/370 sgl/ dbl.* **$–$$**

Other practicalities The town has several 24-hour **fuel stations**, while for **supermarkets** there is Spar next to the Total garage and USave next to BP. Robb's Motors (☎ 063 270189; m 081 275 0022) could be handy if you're in need of tyres or **vehicle repairs**. There's a **post office** on Park Street, and a couple of **banks**: Bank Windhoek on 9th Avenue and FNB on Main Street. The state **hospital** can be contacted on ☎ 063 270167. Signposts to Lordsville and Westerville point the way to Karasburg's old-style satellite townships.

WARMBAD

About 48km south of Karasburg, sleepy Warmbad (the name means 'hot bath' in German) is known for its hot springs, a small museum, and a lovely old stone church, built in 1877. The town was the location of the first Christian mission in 1806, and the centre of the Nama–German war in the early 19th century. Sadly, it's a bit of a depressing place. The discovery of uranium deposits in 2009 brought hope that investment would improve the area, but changes appear to be slow. Visitors have reported that the springs – which had been smartened up in 2006 – are not looked after, a bit unsanitary and unswimmable in winter. There's also a lack of accommodation, with the only community campsite said to be closed, but we understand that guests can still get the key from the village council office and stay overnight (we'd welcome further details). For now, we suggest just stopping by to visit the museum.

What to see and do

Warmbad Museum (⊕ *09.00–17.00 Mon–Fri, 09.00–13.00 Sat, or collect key from lodge; admission N\$10/5 adult/child*) Warmbad's old German prison makes a thought-provoking base for this small museum, which encapsulates the history of the Bondelswarts. A group of mixed origin, they fell foul of the German colonisers, who in 1906 stripped them of their lands and forced their leader, Abraham Morris, into exile. After World War I, far from redressing the situation, the new South African occupiers placed added restrictions on the people. When Morris attempted to return across the Orange River in 1922, a warrant was issued for his arrest, but the Bondelswarts refused to hand him over. In retaliation, the full might of the South African military was mobilised, crushing the Bondelswarts with the loss of over 100 men, women and children, and resulting in the death of their leader. Surrender was inevitable. The remaining guerrillas were taken prisoner and marched to Warmbad, where they were imprisoned – in the building that now houses the museum.

NOORDOEWER This small settlement on the Orange River stands about 3.5km from the main crossing point for Namibia–Cape traffic at Vioolsdrif. If you're crossing into Namibia from that point, you're advised to get there early; the border post is open 24 hours but tends to get busy after about 10.00.

Noordoewer is just 43km from the edge of the Ai-Ais Richtersveld Transfrontier Park. It is also one of the embarkation points for canoeing and rafting trips down the Orange (page 255). A final point of interest is that, thanks to a ready supply of water, there are several large-scale irrigation projects in the area, some producing table-quality grapes like those on the Orange further east in South Africa.

Tourist information used to be available from Noordoewer Guesthouse. Although they still have a number of maps and leaflets available, note that it is not their primary focus.

⬆ Where to stay and eat

⌂ **Noordoewer Guesthouse** (14 rooms) 📞063 297108; m 081 379 5958; e bookings@ noordoewerguesthouse.com; www. noordoewerguesthouse.com. On the C13 close to the Engen garage, this pleasant guesthouse has modern en-suite rooms with Wi-Fi, AC, kettle & fridge, & tables set out on their terraces. There's a small pool in a well-maintained garden & braai facilities are on offer – with dinner also available on request. *N\$755/1,170 sgl/dbl.* **\$\$\$**

⌂ **Orange River Lodge** (12 rooms) 📞067 297012; e orlodge@iway.na; www.orlodge. iway.na. About 3km from the border, next to the Shell petrol station, this small lodge has dbl, twin & family rooms (3 of them self-catering), all set around well-watered lawns with a small pool. Each has a private bathroom, fridge, Wi-Fi, AC & tea/coffee facilities. It's a good place for an overnight stop, with b/fast (*N\$65*) & à la carte meals served in a thatched lapa, where there's a TV & bar, or on an umbrella-shaded terrace. *N\$600/1,200 sgl/dbl.* **\$\$**

Other practicalities The town itself has a couple of 24-hour **fuel stations**, a **supermarket** and a branch of **Bank Windhoek**, which could be useful for changing

Namibian dollars before crossing into South Africa. Next to the bank is a small shop with a bottle store and a post office.

ALONG THE ORANGE RIVER Forming the border between Namibia and South Africa, the Orange River tends to be overlooked by visitors. However, with South Africa's wild Richtersveld National Park (now amalgamated with Ai-Ais National Park as one of the first 'Peace Parks' in the region, Ai-Ais Richtersveld Transfrontier Park) on its southern side, and very little access to its northern banks, it makes a perfect wilderness destination. Against this backdrop, the largely seasonal settlement at **Aussenkehr**, whose population fluctuates from 5,000 or so to 21,000 in tune with the pruning and harvesting of grapes in the reserve, comes as quite a surprise. It may not be the most salubrious place, but from a practical point of view, it supports a branch of both Standard and FNB banks, a couple of ATMs, a post office, and a large Spar with separate Tops off-licence.

Flora and fauna The flora in this area of the Namib is particularly unusual, because its proximity to the Cape leads it to receive some winter rainfall. This seems to promote the growth of succulents, including various *Lithops* and *Mesembryanthemum* species, several of which are endemic to this area. Visit in July, August or September and you may find whole areas in bloom, like Namaqualand just over the border to the south.

There are some fascinating larger plants here too, including *Aloe pillansii*, a close relative of the quivertree, which grows to 6–7m in the shape of a candelabra, and the rare, protected *Pachypodium namaquanum*, or halfman, a curious succulent which grows to 2m tall with a great girth. Its head always faces north.

With the presence of permanent water, expect to see several kingfishers among the birds along the river, including the tiny but beautiful malachite. Look out, too, for the locally common Orange River white-eye – aptly named for its white eye ring.

Where to stay In addition to the places to stay in Noordoewer itself, there are a few more attractive options along the river – listed below from east to west. All are accessed from the C13/D212, which is tarred until just west of Norotshore, and all except Norotshama are linked to one of the canoeing operators. As well as being popular with canoeists, these lodges make excellent spots for birdwatching or fishing – if you have your own equipment.

Felix Unite River Lodge [232 A7] (20 chalets, tents) **m** +27 87 354 0578; www. felixunite.com. The former Provenance Camp has a beautiful setting overlooking a bend in the river & beyond to South Africa. It's a well-run camp, geared largely to canoeists & overlanders, though others are welcome. Varied accommodation includes 10 'cabanas' beside the river, 7 higher up overlooking the river, 2 family 'cabanas', whose 2 rooms share a bathroom & a large honeymoon suite on the river. All have a kettle, fridge & AC – crucial in the summer months when the mercury tops 40°C – as well as sliding doors leading on to a veranda with a view. If – & only if – the cabanas are fully booked there is a group of green canvas

tents sleeping 1–2 people with shared ablution facilities, towels & sheets. High above the river is an extensive restaurant with an à la carte menu for b/fast, lunch & dinner, overlooking a pool & the river below. There's laundry, Wi-Fi throughout & an internet café in the shop, which also has an ATM & stocks everything from snacks to camping equipment & clothes. Although many guests are booked on longer trips, there is the option of full-day canoeing too. *Cabana N$1,150; family cabana & honeymoon suite N$1,975; all room only.* **$$$–$$$$**

Amanzi Trails River Camp [232 A7] (camping) **** 063 297255; www.amanzitrails.co.za. This pleasant grassy campsite just 3km off the

C13 is 16km downstream from the Noordoewer border post & has a friendly, relaxed atmosphere. With reed shelters, screens, braai areas & their own basins, the 24 pitches are shaded by trees & share good ablution blocks. There's also a thatched lapa and separate bar, & electricity, wood & ice are available. *Camping N$150/100 adult/child.* **$$**

🏠 **Norotshama River Resort** [232 A7] (36 rooms, camping) Aussenkehr; 063 297215/6; m 081 128 6247; e norotshama@africaonline. com.na; www.norotshamaresort.com. The 2km avenue of grapevines that leads from the C13, 50km west of Noordoewer, heralds something a little different. In the heart of the Aussenkehr Reserve, the lodge is making a stab at being all things to all people, with 4 luxury chalets, 2 honeymoon chalets, 6 family chalets, 10 river-facing rooms, 10 twin rooms & 4 lake-view rooms, not to mention 15 camping pitches either on the riverbank or little further back near a manmade lake. Facing the river itself is a cavernous restaurant, with outside seating on a vine-shaded terrace, & an à la carte menu that majors on steaks. Wi-Fi across the resort is a plus, as are a pool set among lawns, a curio shop & a friendly bar with a TV – which seems to be particularly popular with locals watching sport. Aside from a couple of fairly dilapidated canoes to rent, activities are limited, though with your own equipment & know-how there are opportunities for fishing or climbing. For groups of 10 or more the lodge can organise trips to Aussenkehr & its nature park, or a visit to a local canyon. *N$935–1,020/1,720–2,448 sgl/ dbl; camping N$170/75 adult/child, inc entry fees to Aussenkehr Nature Park.* **$$–$$$$**

Canoeing

Several companies run canoeing and/or river-rafting trips along the Orange River, most of them based around Cape Town. Many are geared towards South African visitors, and work well for those driving across the border who want to stop for a few days' canoeing. Unlike the Victoria Falls, this isn't a white-water experience, and neither is it a wildlife experience, though you may catch glimpses of game as you paddle. Instead, it is a gentle trip through a stunningly beautiful wilderness area that is notable for its scenery and lack of people.

Prices vary, but for a four-day trip you can expect to pay from N$3,950 per person (minimum six people), including meals, or less for those who are self-catering. For a trip of this length, you'll cover around 65km as far as Aussenkehr, spending about 6 hours each day on the river and camping on the riverbank at night. A six-day trip reaches the Fish River. Such trips can also cater for those with limited mobility.

Rafting companies

Amanzi Trails (Namibia) 063 297 255; (SA) +27 21 559 1573; e info@amanzitrails.co.za; www.amanzitrails.co.za
Aquatrails +27 21 782 7982; e info@ aquatrails.co.za; www.aquatrails.co.za

Felix Unite m +27 87 354 0578; e reservations@felixunite.co.za; www.felixunite. com. The most experienced & probably the largest of the companies currently running this river.
The River Rafters +27 21 975 9727; e info@ riverrafters.co.za; www.riverrafters.co.za

What to take The arrangements with each canoeing company are different, but most will supply two-person Mohawk canoes, paddles, life jackets, all meals and cool boxes for your own drinks (soft, alcoholic and bottled water – but note that glass bottles are not allowed on the river, so you'll need to decant liquids beforehand). They will also have watertight containers to keep limited luggage dry.

As well as drinks, you must bring a sleeping bag, personal toiletries (preferably biodegradable), a set of clothes for the river and one for when you're away from the water. A hat, long cotton trousers and long-sleeved cotton blouse/shirt, as well as a bathing costume, are fine for the river, plus trainers and warm tracksuit (the temperatures can drop!) for wearing off the river.

Some companies advise that you will also need your own knife, fork, spoon, mug, plate, torch, toilet paper and sleeping mat. Participants sometimes take small tents and even folding chairs along, and often you'll be requested to bring large, strong plastic bin liners. The better companies, like Felix Unite, have stocks of all this kit available to hire for their trips. As you're traversing an international boundary, you should also remember to bring your passport and – if you're travelling with children under the age of 18 – you may need an unabridged birth certificate (but check these details with your operator).

FISH RIVER CANYON

At 161km long, up to 27km wide, and almost 550m at its deepest, the Fish River Canyon is arguably second in size only to Arizona's Grand Canyon – and is certainly one of Africa's least-visited wonders. This means that, as you sit dangling your legs over the edge, drinking in the spectacle, you're unlikely to have your visit spoiled by a coachload of tourists – at least, as long as you walk away from the main viewpoint. In fact, away from the busier seasons you may not see anyone around here at all!

The canyon itself starts about 7km south of Seeheim, winding its way south to Ai-Ais. From Hobas through to Ai-Ais it is protected within the Ai-Ais Richtersveld Transfrontier Park, while immediately to the north, protection continues through private reserves on both sides of the river.

GEOLOGY The base rocks of the Fish River Canyon, now at the bottom nearest the river, are shales, sandstones and lavas that were deposited about 1,800 million years ago. Later, from 1,300 to 1,000 million years ago, these were heated and strongly compressed, forming a metamorphic rock complex, which includes intrusive granites and, later, the dolerite dykes that appear as clear, dark streaks on the canyon.

A period of erosion then followed, removing the overlying rocks and levelling this complex to be the floor of a vast shallow sea, covering most of what is now southern Namibia. From about 650 to 500 million years ago various sediments, limestones and conglomerates were deposited by the sea on to this floor, building up into what is now referred to as the Nama Group of rocks.

About 500 million years ago, the beginnings of the canyon started when a fracture in this crust formed a broad valley, running north–south. Southward-moving glaciers deepened this during the Dwyka Ice Age, around 300 million years ago. Later faults and more erosion added to the effect, creating canyons within each other, until a mere 50 million years ago, when the Fish River started to cut its meandering way along the floor of the most recent valley.

HISTORY Situated in a very arid region of Namibia, the Fish River is the only river within the country that usually has pools of water in its middle reaches during the dry season. Because of this, it was known to the peoples of the area during the early, middle and late Stone Ages. Numerous sites dating from as early as 50,000 years ago have been found within the canyon – mostly beside bends in the river.

Around the beginning of this century, the Ai-Ais area was used as a base by the Germans in their war against the Namas. It was finally declared a national monument in 1962. Ai-Ais Restcamp was opened in 1971, though it has been fully rebuilt since then.

FLORA AND FAUNA Driving around you will probably see few larger animals, though there are many if you look hard. These include herds of Hartmann's

AFRICA'S LARGEST CANYON?

Pedants cite Ethiopia's Blue Nile Gorge as being Africa's largest canyon. It is certainly deeper than the Fish River Canyon, at about 1,000m, but it is also narrower (about 20km at its widest), and probably shorter as well. Like many vague superlatives, 'largest' is difficult to define. In this case, we would have to measure the volume of the canyon – and even then there would be questions about exactly where it begins and ends. Suffice to say that both are too large to take in at one sight, and both are well worth visiting.

mountain zebra, small groups of kudu and the smaller klipspringer antelope, which are usually seen in pairs. Baboon make no secret of their presence if around, and dassies (alias rock rabbits) are common, but leopard, though certainly present, are very rarely seen. It's not unusual to drive for a few hours and see no mammals at all.

Birds, too, are around but often not obvious. This isn't a centre for birdwatching, as only about 60 species are thought to live here, but look out for the majestic black eagle, as well as the rock kestrel and rock pigeon, and especially for the localised yellow-rumped eremomela which occur near Ai-Ais. Karoo bustards and ostrich are the highlights of the open plains above the canyon. In the canyon itself, herons, cormorants and kingfishers take advantage of the river's bounty, while both martins and mountain wheatear keep the hiker company from above.

Vegetation is sparse. Both on the top and on the canyon's slopes, the larger species are mostly euphorbias, with the odd quivertree and occasional deep red aloe (*Aloe gariepensis*). However, parts of the canyon's base where there is water are quite lush – like the Sulphur Springs with its palm trees and further south towards Ai-Ais. There you can expect camelthorn, wild tamarisk and ebony trees, among others.

GETTING THERE AND AWAY Detailed routes to the various lodges and camps are given below, but note that you can't drive quickly between the west and the east sides of the canyon. If you are approaching the east side from the north, you're best to take the D545 which passes Naute Dam and has been reclassified at the C12, as the old C12 road that meets the B4 at Seeheim is poorly maintained and almost unusable. If during the rainy season this road is blocked, seek advice locally or take the longer but more secure tar route on the B1 and C10.

WHERE TO STAY Seeing the canyon as a day trip from a base some way off is practical, particularly as the diagonal rays of early morning or late evening light do little for photographers' hopes of capturing the depths of the canyon. Thus Keetmanshoop is one possibility, while for a less urban setting you could opt for somewhere around Karasburg or Grünau to the east, or Seeheim to the north. However, if only to minimise your driving, stay closer if you can – at Hobas Camp (page 260) or Ai-Ais Hot Springs Spa (page 260) within the national park, or at one of the private lodges on either side of the canyon.

Private lodges
East of the Fish River
⌂ **Gondwana Canyon Park** ☏061 427200; a/h m 081 129 2424; e info@gondwana-collection.com; www.gondwana-collection.com. Several places to stay lie within the 1,260km²

Gondwana Canyon Park, which borders Ai-Ais Richtersveld Transfrontier Park. It was established in 1996 by Manni Goldbeck from 7 commercial sheep farms, with the aim of reclaiming the land from overgrazing & returning it to its natural state. Today it is grazed by springbok, oryx, red

11

hartebeest, blue wildebeest, ostrich & both Burchell's & mountain zebra, as well as black rhino. A hallmark of Gondwana is its self-sufficiency project: a hefty proportion of the fresh food served at their properties, including meat, cheese, herbs & vegetables, comes from its own farm in Stampriet, next to Kalahari Farmhouse (page 239). Of the 4 Gondwana accommodation options here, 3 are clustered close together, just 2km off the C37 & 7km south of the turn-off to the canyon's main viewpoint; the 4th, Canyon Roadhouse, stands alone. The properties share & host a variety of activities, such as free sundowner walks (⊕ *16.30; just pay for drinks*), 2hr sundowner drives (⊕ *15.30; N$560 pp*) & guided 3hr morning hikes (⊕ *08.00; 6km; N$330 pp*).

🏠 **CANYON ROADHOUSE** [232 A5] (22 rooms, camping) ✆ 063 683111. North of Canyon Lodge, the Roadhouse is signposted about 17km off the C12 near Holoog, along the C37. Don't be deterred by the name: this quirky outback-style inn rarely fails to charm. It's also a popular stop for overland adventure-travel trucks & visitors drawn to its reliable fuel station (⊕ *07.00–22.00*) & tyre repairs. For others, this oasis is known for the rusting old vehicles displayed in the garden & – more ostentatiously – in the restaurant, where an old truck becomes a reception desk; others are commissioned as offbeat fireplaces, & a huge central *pompstasie* (filling station) serves as the bar. Look out for the saucy paintings in the female & male toilets, & beware: if curiosity gets the better of you, a bell will ring & you'll owe a round of drinks to everyone in the bar! The à la carte lunch menu features pasta, salads & juicy burgers (*N$60–190*), with more substantial fare, including game, in the evening. Next door is an information centre with internet terminal, rock displays & boards explaining the history & conservation of both Fish River Canyon & the wider environment. There's also free Wi-Fi throughout.

At the back around a couple of courtyards are attractive en-suite rooms, their décor picking out the rich reds & yellows of the surrounding landscape. All are thoughtfully kitted out with AC/ heating & international plugs. Further back, over a wooden bridge leading from the pool is a campsite with 12 pitches. *N$1,857/2,970 sgl/dbl; camping N$215 pp.* **$$–$$$$**

🏠 **CANYON LODGE** [263 D3] (30 chalets) ✆ 063 693014. As you approach the lodge, do watch out for the steep sleeping policemen. Once you've negotiated them, you'll be met with a restored old farmhouse, built in 1904, which now houses the lodge reception, a gift shop, a bar with free Wi-Fi & papered with old smoking adverts, & adjoining restaurant, which in summer spills out on to the terrace, but on chilly winter evenings is warmed by blazing open fires. Both guests & day visitors are welcome here (⊕ *b/fast 06.30–09.00, lunch noon–14.00, dinner 18.00–20.30, N$360 pp*) to partake of standard but tasty buffets offering considerable choice.

Spaced among the surrounding kopjes – low hills of bare stone boulders – the chalets are rustic in concept but comfortably appointed. Dbl or twin beds under, mosquito nets, AC/heating & fans, a safe, en-suite showers & a terrace overlooking the rocks sit within raw-stone walls under a thatched roof; rooms 21 & 28 have corner baths. Adding to the area's other attractions is an impressive swimming pool with great views & an honesty bar, though you'll have to summon up the energy to wander the 500m or so from the rest of the lodge. *N$2,442/3,906 sgl/dbl.* **$$$$$**

🏠 **CANYON VILLAGE** [263 D3] (42 rooms) ✆ 063 693025. Just 2km before Canyon Lodge, at the foot of the surrounding mountains, the 'village' is used often for groups. Thatched, en-suite cottages of stone, each with AC, fan & mosquito nets, form a semicircle overlooking the plains. Original artwork on the walls of both the rooms & the long, thatched lapa gives a glimpse of the history of the Nama people in the area. Meals (*dinner N$360*) are served buffet-style in the restaurant, where there's a central fireplace, & there's a large separate bar, as well as a large swimming pool & terrace. *N$1,717/2,746 sgl/dbl.* **$$$$**

🏠 **CANYON MOUNTAIN CAMP** [263 D3] (8 rooms) This simple converted green & white farmhouse is 6km beyond Canyon Lodge, where visitors should book in. The accommodation is only for use by small groups or families who are self-catering, although dinner can be taken at the lodge (*N$360 pp*). Basic but comfortable en-suite rooms enclose a stone-paved courtyard with an equipped communal kitchen with fireplace & a large braai area overlooking the plains. This is a secluded spot with few mod cons (though there's now electricity, but still no phone reception), offering the opportunity to explore independently for a day or 2. *N$450/900 sgl/dbl.* **$$$**

West of the Fish River

Access to the private lodges along the western side of the river is via the D463, a turning off the B4 that is signposted 'Canyon Nature Park' & 'Feldschuhorn'. It's a scenic drive, taking in pans, rolling red dunes & rocks eroded into sometimes extraordinary shapes & formations. Be careful, though, as patches of soft sand can make driving hazardous, & note that the more westerly D462 crosses several river-beds with thick patches of sand, so is not recommended as an alternative.

✳ 🏠 **Fish River Lodge** [263 A1] (20 chalets) 📞063 683005, reservations 📞061 228104; e fishriver@journeysnamibia.com; www. fishriverlodge-namibia.com. The only lodge right on the rim of Fish River Canyon, & set within the 45,000ha private Canyon Nature Park, this is one of Namibia's most spectacularly sited lodges. Sparsely dotted with quivertrees & strewn with irregular chunks of rock, the undulating terrain above the canyon boasts considerable clumps of *Euphorbia gregaria*, & is home to dassies, oryx, klipspringer & ostrich. To find the lodge, follow the D463 – nice & firm despite its 'D' classification – from the B4 for 84km, then turn left & continue for a further 19km/1hr to the lodge along a very rough road (through a goat farm) for which a high-clearance or 4WD vehicle is advisable.

From a distance, a row of military pillboxes appears to line the ridge, but closer inspection reveals a series of spacious, modern, stone-clad chalets on either side of a large central area of similar design. It's all minimalist in concept, some would say stark, with high ceilings, cool grey paintwork, white bathroom fittings & wide, metal-framed French windows, yet designed both to blend into the environment & to cope with soaring summer temperatures. By contrast, 2 central fires in the main lodge don't entirely take the edge off the chill when the mercury plummets, so bring warm clothes. Yet what transcends all is the breathtaking view across the canyon, shared by the central building, the pool & the individual chalets. (A word of warning: children are welcome, but with sheer cliffs & few barriers, the lodge is definitely not child-friendly.) The extensive main area has a bar (with an inventive cocktail list), a central lounge area adorned with zebra rugs, & a dining area. where you'll find a buffet b/fast, optional afternoon tea & cake & a 3-course set

dinner menu. A packed lunch is normally included in the price of activities or can be paid for locally. A small selection of high-end souvenirs invites perusal, spa treatments are available, & there's intermittent Wi-Fi.

Along with 2 self-guided walking trails along the canyon rim, taking approx 1½hrs & 2½hrs respectively, there are guided walks (*N$385 pp*) & sundowner drives (*N$385*). Most popular, though, are the canyon excursion (around *7hrs; N$1,265*), which combines a very scenic drive to the bottom of the canyon for a dip in a rock pool & a packed lunch, & the day hike, where you'll follow a drive to the sundowner point with an 8km walk to the same rock pool. If there is space in a vehicle it is possible to hitch a lift back to the lodge; otherwise it's at least a 16km round trip. A further option is to organise your own flexible, catered hike into the canyon, with all your gear (including camping equipment) transported ahead. For details, see page 264. *DBB N$2,370/3,630 sgl/ dbl.* **$$$$$**

🏠 **Vogelstrausskluft Lodge** [232 A5] Although this lodge was closed in 2018, there are murmurings that it may reopen in the future. Given its location overlooking some lovely scenery & on a 27,000ha reserve that includes a 54km stretch of the Löwen River, that is a positive prospect.

Inside the national park

The two options below are the only places to stay within the national park. Camping is not permitted anywhere else.

Ai-Ais Hot Springs

(🕐 sunrise–sunset) Ai-Ais is best reached from Keetmanshoop by driving south on the main B1, & then turning west on to the C10. (Try to avoid this in the late afternoon, as the sun is directly in your eyes.) Alternatively, from Lüderitz, pass Seeheim on the B4 & take the D545 (reclassified as the C12), then continue past Naute Dam until it rejoins the old C12 road from Seeheim. From here, turn right on to the C37 towards Hobas & the C10. Coming from the south, you can turn left off the B1 on to the D316 – though this road is quieter & perhaps less well graded than the C10.

However you reach it, the final few km of the C10 spiral down, cutting into the rock layers of the canyon's side, until it reaches the bed of the Fish River. It's a marvellous road, though steep in parts, with some sharp corners – so drive carefully. You can arrive at any time, so do not fear being locked out if you are late.

🏠 Ai-Ais Hot Springs Spa [263 A7]
(36 rooms, 7 chalets, camping) ✆063 683676; reservations ✆061 285 7200; e reservations@ nwr.com.na; www.nwr.com.na/resorts/ai-ais-hotsprings-spa. Sitting at the bottom of the canyon at the end of the C10, towards the southern end of the conservation area, this lodge also marks the finishing point for the 5-day hiking trail. '/Ai/ Ais', which means 'burning water' in the Nama language, is a reference to the hot, sulphurous springs that well up here at a fairly constant 65°C. These feed both a large outdoor pool & an indoor spa, with several pools & a wellness centre offering massages, facials & the like. En-suite dbl rooms lead off from the indoor spa: some facing the river; others – smaller & less expensive – at the back (though the 'mountain view' isn't much of a draw). Dotted around this hub are spacious 2-bedroom chalets with kitchens. For campers, some 100 level, sandy pitches share 3 ablution blocks & 3 kitchens – so in high season don't come expecting peace & quiet. Campers are free to make use of the main facilities. The restcamp has a basic shop & fuel station, as well as a restaurant (🕐 b/fast 06.00–08.30, lunch noon–13.30, dinner 18.00– 20.30), though standards of catering remain in the category of school dinners. Guests can use the spa free of charge; day visitors are charged N$20 & should bring their own towels. The more active might bring tennis racquets to play on the (rather ramshackle) court, or wander off up the canyon, which is beautiful. Hikes along the Fish River trail

cost N$300 pp; guided ½- & full-day excursions from N$650 pp. N$1,050–1,250/1,800–2,400 sgl/ dbl Jul–Oct, N$900–1,050/1,500–2,000 Nov–Jun; camping N$210 pp (max 8); park fees extra.
$$–$$$$

Hobas
Visitors to Fish River Canyon pass through the gate at Hobas, where park fees are payable before continuing on to the viewpoint.

🏠 Hobas Camp [263 C2] (6 rooms, camping)
reservations ✆061 285 7200; e reservations@ nwr.com.na; www.nwr.com.na/resorts/hobas-camp. For many years there was nothing but a busy campsite at Hobas with sandy sites spread out under shady, willowy trees & few facilities. However, in 2017 this changed when NWR added a new restaurant/bar (🕐 b/fast 07.00–10.00, lunch noon–14.00, dinner 18.00–21.00), replaced the pool & built 6 new en-suite rooms. These have twin or dbl beds, a sleeper couch & a small kitchenette, & were looking pretty good at the time of research.

As the only convenient base in the area for overland groups, the campsite still frequently gets busy, so it can become festive at times, making competition for quieter pitches high. Those tackling the 5-day hike often camp here the night before they set off, too. Reception still functions as a sparsely stocked shop selling some food supplies, wood, postcards & clothes. Despite the investment in Hobas, it hasn't brought the camp up to the standard of private camps in the area – but for access to Fish River Canyon, it is hard to beat. N$1,100–1,350/1,940–2,400 sgl/dbl; camping N$250 pp. **$$–$$$$**

AI-AIS RICHTERSVELD TRANSFRONTIER PARK (🕐 Oct–Apr 07.00–19.00, May–Sep 07.00–18.00; admission N$233/117 adult/child per day; additional N$80 pp & N$10 per car for admission to viewpoint & surrounding area, payable only at Hobas Camp) The area around the southern part of Fish River Canyon was proclaimed a conservation area in 1968. The land was as poor in potential for agriculture as it is rich in potential for tourism, and this was a way of protecting the area from uncontrolled development. For many years, the 345,000ha national park encompassed Ai-Ais and Hobas, but in 2003 it was combined with the environmentally similar Richtersveld in South Africa, to form Namibia's first transfrontier or peace park: Ai-Ais Richtersveld Transfrontier Park, spanning around 508,600ha.

Those wishing to cross the Orange River that forms the border between the two parks can now do so at the Sendelingsdrift border post (🕐 08.00–16.00), where a pontoon on cables takes a couple of vehicles and passengers (N$160 per vehicle one-way, N$270 return). Note, however, that operation of the pontoon is often suspended during the rainy season due to high water levels, so it's best to phone ahead to check (↘*South Africa +27 12 428 9111*).

The park's borders are well marked along the main access roads. Other than at the control post south of Rosh Pinah (where you sign in or out), most are simply signboards. Access to the park itself is largely free of charge, with the exception of Fish River Canyon.

What to see and do Once in the area, a day is enough to see the canyon properly, unless you've arranged (in advance) to do the five-day hike (see *Hiking the Fish River Canyon*, below). Note that no other visitors are allowed to descend into the canyon from the lip at any time of year.

Start the morning by driving past Hobas for 10km to the **Main Viewpoint**. This is *the* classic view of Hell's Bend, featured in most of the photographs – and probably the only view that you'll see if you're on a bus tour. A visitors' centre features toilets and information boards about the canyon's geology, as well as a raised, shaded platform from which to look down on the canyon.

To the right, a 3km track leads initially to the **Hikers' Viewpoint**, which lends a different perspective and is worth the short rocky wander from the car park if it is cool. This is also the starting point for the five-day hike; do peer over the edge to see the precarious pathway that leads to the foot of the canyon.

Then take the road that leads to the left of the Main Viewpoint. This is a continuation of the D324, which doubles back to run roughly parallel to the canyon, generally keeping within a few hundred yards. There are several stops for viewpoints along its length, perhaps the best being the **Sulphur Springs Viewpoint** (Palm Springs), which has a picnic table and a stunning view of another tight switchback in the river's course.

This road is little used and graded less, so it's bumpy in parts but suitable for a 2WD car driven slowly and carefully. The scenery is so spectacular that you won't want to rush. If you have a 4x4, you can continue past the Sulphur Springs Viewpoint to the southernmost viewpoint at Eagle's Rock – a further 12km of very rough, stony road, but offering a good view of the canyon further south. Either way, you'll eventually have to retrace your tracks to return on the D324, back past the Hobas gate and south.

At the southern end of the canyon, **Ai-Ais** makes a great afternoon stop, giving you time to relax in a mineral pool or to take a gentle walk up the canyon for a taste of what the hikers experience near the end of the route.

HIKING THE FISH RIVER CANYON
Within the national park For fit, experienced and self-sufficient backpackers, the Fish River Canyon is the venue for one of southern Africa's greatest hikes: a chance to follow the river within the national park where vehicles never venture, a distance of about 80–90km from Hikers' Viewpoint to Ai-Ais. However, numbers are limited and hikes must be arranged months in advance with the NWR (pages 103 and 173), so you need to work out your logistics carefully long before you get here.

Regulations and costs Hiking trips within the national park are allowed from 1 May to 15 September, and limited to a maximum of 30 hikers per day. The NWR insists on each group being a minimum of three people for safety, with no children under the age of 12. Each hiker needs to bring a medical certificate (supplied by the NWR) that has been issued within 40 days of the hike and is signed by their doctor, stating that they are fit to do the hike.

The hike costs N$500 per person, which must be paid in advance to the NWR, plus park fees of N$80. Hikers are responsible for all their own food, equipment, safety and transport to/from the canyon. They must also stay at least one night in the national park, either at Hobas Camp or at Ai-Ais Hot Springs Spa.

Preparations and equipment This is a four- or five-day hike covering 80–90km in what can be some of the subcontinent's most extreme temperatures. There's no easy way out once you start; no chance to stop. So this isn't for the faint-hearted, or those without experience of long-distance hiking, but for those who come prepared, it's excellent.

Your own large, comfortable backpack with your normal hiking equipment (page 156) should include:

- 2-litre water bottle, with some method of purifying water
- Sleeping roll and bag to –8°C (though a tent is not needed)
- Cooking utensils and food for at least six days, plus a stove and fuel (wood for fires is generally available on the second half of the hike)
- Waterproof shoes or sandals for river crossings
- Light rainproof jacket, in the unlikely event of a shower
- Good map. One rough route-plan with pretty colour pictures and lots of advice is usually available at Hobas, though it is best used in conjunction with a more 'serious' version from the Surveyor General's office in Windhoek (page 172).

In addition, each group should have a comprehensive medical kit, as help may be days away if there is an accident.

Transport If you're driving yourself, leave your vehicle at either Ai-Ais or Hobas. A shuttle bus (*N$270 pp one-way, min 3 people*) covers the 62km trip between the two points, officially leaving Ai-Ais at various times after 06.00, but check this the day before, when you arrive at Ai-Ais. From Hobas, there is a second shuttle, which transports hikers to the start for a further small fee.

The hike The descent into the canyon is very steep in parts, taking between 45 minutes and 2 hours to reach the river – a distance of just 1.5km, but a descent of around 430m from the Hikers' Viewpoint. Chains are provided on the more difficult sections near the top. Even beyond this, the first stretch remains taxing, with expanses of loose river-sand between areas of large boulders, though at this stage the trail stays mostly on the eastern side of the river. It can be slow going.

After around 14km there is an 'emergency exit' up to the Sulphur (Palm) Springs Viewpoint, but most people eventually reach the area around Sulphur Springs and spend their first or second night there, 18km into the walk. The springs themselves are fast-flowing, hot (57°C) and apparently rich in fluorides, chlorides and sulphates.

The terrain gradually gets easier after Sulphur Springs, traversing fewer stretches of boulders, and more sand and rounded river-stones – but it remains challenging. River crossings become a feature of the hike as the Fish zigzags through the canyon. As the canyon widens out, the vegetation increases and landmarks appear in the canyon walls: Table Mountain, Three Sisters and Four Fingers Rock. Towards the end, the route options increase, some heading away from the river across the mountains, and it's surprisingly easy to get lost. Finally, 80–90km from the start (depending on how many times you cross the river and whether or not you cut corners) you arrive at Ai-Ais.

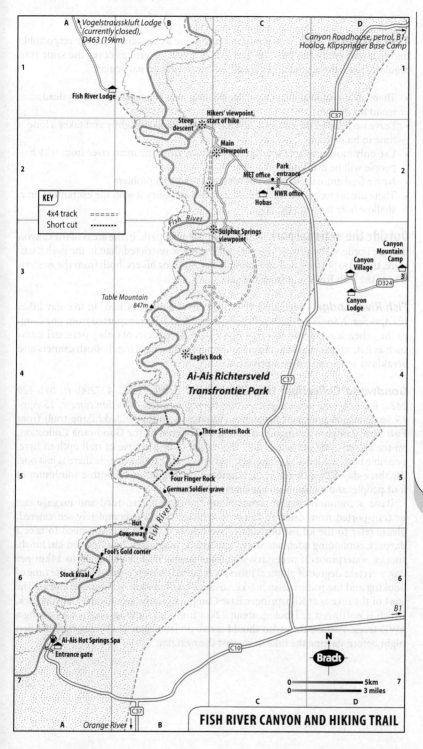

KEY

4x4 track	======
Short cut	--------

A   B   C   D

Vogelstrausskluft Lodge (currently closed), D463 (19km)

Canyon Roadhouse, petrol, B1, Hoolog, Klipspringer Base Camp

Fish River Lodge

C37

Hikers' viewpoint, start of hike

Steep descent

Main viewpoint

MET office

Park entrance

NWR office

Hobas

Fish River

Sulphur Springs viewpoint

Canyon Village

Canyon Mountain Camp

Canyon Lodge

D324

Table Mountain 847m

Eagle's Rock

Ai-Ais Richtersveld Transfrontier Park

C37

Three Sisters Rock

Four Finger Rock

German Soldier grave

Hut

Causeway

Fish River

Fool's Gold corner

Stock kraal

B1

Ai-Ais Hot Springs Spa

Entrance gate

C10

N

Bradt

0 ——— 5km
0 ——— 3 miles

C37

Orange River

A   B   C   D

FISH RIVER CANYON AND HIKING TRAIL

Trail etiquette Trail etiquette here is the same as sensible rules for responsible hiking anywhere in the bush (page 163). However, as groups cover the same trail regularly here, these guidelines are all the more vital. In particular:

- There are no 'official' fireplaces; use existing ones if possible. Use only dead wood for fires.
- Leave no litter in the canyon – even fruit peel looks unsightly and takes a long time to biodegrade.
- Use only biodegradable soap, and wash away from the main river from which people will be drinking.
- Never feed animals; baboons in particular can be a problem.
- There are no toilets, so burn all toilet paper and bury it with the excrement, in a shallow hole far from the river.

Outside the national park
North of the national park, in the areas of the canyon that are bordered by private reserves, hiking is less restricted than in the park itself. Here, there are both guided and unguided options for hikers, both from the western side of the Fish River and from the east.

Fish River Lodge (page 259) The lodge offers a range of two- to five-day hikes (⊕ *Apr–Sep; N\$6,050–15,400 pp*). Your overnight kit is transported from one camp to the other, leaving you to carry just a light daypack containing personal items such as hat, sunglasses, suncream and camera, plus a light lunch. Bush dinners and breakfasts are prepared by a private chef.

Gondwana Collection: the Klipspringer Trail (✆ *061 427200;* m *081 129 2424;* e *info@gondwana-collection.com; www.gondwana-collection.com;* ⊕ *15 Apr–15 Sep; N\$2,500 pp; min 4 people*). An alternative to the guided hiking trails from Fish River Lodge is an unguided hiking trail offered by the Gondwana Collection, on the eastern side of the canyon. There used to be a couple of trail options here, available both guided and unguided, and also a mule trail, but now there is just one: the three-day Klipspringer Trail. Numbers are limited to 12, with a minimum of four people, and a minimum age limit of 12 years.

Basic accommodation in camps along the route is provided and luggage can be transported from camp to camp by vehicle. As this is completely self-catered, please refer to the kit list on page 156 and bear in mind that you need to take a daypack containing adequate water, suncream, sunglasses, hat, first-aid kit, lunch, snacks, waterproofs if necessary, and toilet paper. With walks of up to 14km per day, a certain degree of physical fitness is required. A map is provided at the time of booking and the route is also marked using a combination of signs and cairns. The start of the hike is at Klipspringer Base Camp within the Gondwana Canyon Park, which is northwest of Hoolog, about 22km from the signpost on the C12, along a 4WD track. Participants, who should arrive no later than 15.00, stay here the first night before starting the hike in earnest the next day.

12

Lüderitz and the Southwest

Though the European colonisation of Namibia started in this southwestern corner, it remains perhaps the country's least-known area for visitors. At the end of a long road, Lüderitz now attracts a trickle of visitors seeking out its wonderful turn-of-the-20th-century architecture, desolate beaches, and position as the springboard for trips into the once-forbidden area that is now the Sperrgebiet National Park.

But there is more than Lüderitz in this region. Early historical sites from the 1900s are dotted throughout the area – and though places to stay are often far apart, most of the hotels and guest farms are excellent value. Best of all are the amazing landscapes. Rugged mountains and flowing desert sands make the empty roads spectacular – with the D707, the southern sections of the C13, and even the main B4 across the Koichab Pan ranking among the country's more dramatic drives.

THE ROADS TO LÜDERITZ

FROM KEETMANSHOOP As you drive east from Keetmanshoop to Lüderitz, the main B4 is now all tarred. After about 44km the C12 turns off left to the Fish River Canyon. A kilometre or so afterwards the B4 crosses the Fish River itself, which meanders down a broad, shallow, vegetated valley with few hints of the amazing canyon to the south.

To the north of the road are some spectacular flat-topped hills, capped by hard dolorite, which erodes slowly. One of these has been named Kaiserkrone, the 'Kaiser's crown', as it is an unusual conical shape capped by a symmetrical dolorite crown.

There are several small towns along this road, including Seeheim (page 247). Most can supply fuel and essentials, but none is comparable in size to Lüderitz or Keetmanshoop, so – except increasingly at Aus – few visitors stop at any for long.

Goageb Once a stop on the railway, this tiny town still appears on maps but today is totally derelict – a ghost town. It sits to the left of a new white bridge, just past the exit for Bethanie.

A more uplifting spot is **Kuibis Restaurant** (m *081 335 3523;* ⊕ *07.00–17.00 Mon–Sat (18.30 in summer), 09.00/10.00–17.00 Sun;* $), some 55km to the west, run by Mrs Greef. It serves light meals such as toasted sandwiches and has a small shop selling kudu and oryx biltong for which it seems to have quite a name.

Bethanie About 30km north of Goageb, Bethanie (or Bethanien) is a centre for local administration. The main road into town from the B4 is the tarred C14, but if you're coming from Lüderitz turn on to the D435 about 20km further west. There is no longer any public transport here.

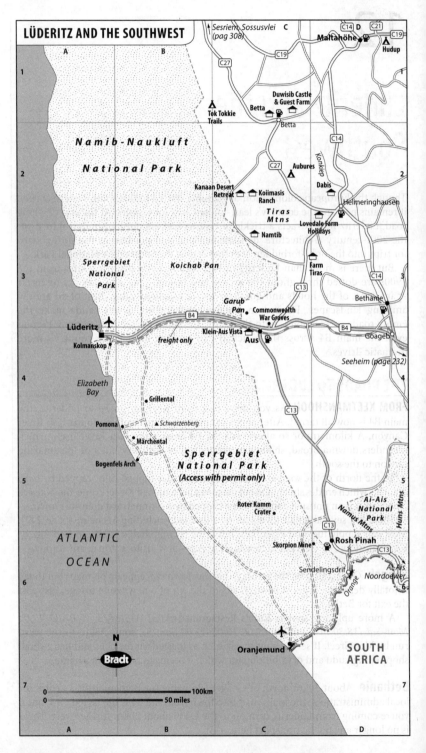

LÜDERITZ AND THE SOUTHWEST

↑ Sesriem, Sossusvlei (pag 308)

C14 **D** **C21**

Maltahöhe

C19

Hudup

C19

C27

Duwisib Castle & Guest Farm

Betta

Tok Tokkie Trails

Betta

Namib-Naukluft

National Park

C14

C27

Aubures

Dabis

Kanaan Desert Retreat

Koiimasis Ranch

Tiras Mtns

Helmeringhausen

Lovedale farm Holidays

Namtib

Farm Tiras

Sperrgebiet National Park

Koichab Pan

C14

C13

Bethanie

Garub Pan

Commonwealth War Graves

Lüderitz ✈

B4

Klein-Aus Vista

B4

Goageb

Kolmanskop

freight only

Aus

Seeheim (page 232)

Elizabeth Bay

Grillental

▲ *Schwarzenberg*

C13

Pomona

Märchental

Sperrgebiet National Park
(Access with permit only)

Ai-Ais National Park

Bogenfels Arch

Namus Mtns

Huns Mtns

Roter Kamm Crater

C13

ATLANTIC

Skorpion Mine

Rosh Pinah

C13

OCEAN

Sendelingsdrif

Ai-Ais Noordoewer

Orange

N

Bradt

✈

Oranjemund

SOUTH AFRICA

0 ——————— 100km
0 ——————— 50 miles

The town is dominated by the apparently modern Lutheran church, which was actually one of the first churches in Namibia. Originally built in 1859, it was restored by American evangelists in 1998.

Where to stay and eat

Bethanie Guesthouse (13 rooms, camping) 270 Chief C Fredericks Av; 063 283013; m 081 344 7252; e info@bethaniehotel.com; www.bethaniehotel.com. One of the country's oldest hotels, built around 1880, the Bethanie is located on the right as you enter town & owned by the rather serious Wessel Esterhuysen. Character remains in the form of a huge lapa at the rear encompassing dining, seating, TV, swimming pool & BBQ areas, all under thatch with a firepit & outside heaters for added comfort. En-suite rooms – 7 with AC, others with fans – are off to the side, while campers have fenced pitches & an ablution block. *N$550/1,000 sgl/dbl; camping N$150 pp.* **$$–$$$**

Coffee Shop Beside the Puma petrol station; 07.00–16.00 Mon–Fri, 07.00–13.00 Sat. Cheery café with a pleasant terrace decorated with cacti & a few tables. Along with sausage rolls, pies, pastries, chips, sandwiches, crisps, penny sweets & super slices of cake, they also have a Bank Windhoek ATM & very clean toilets – ask for the key at the till. **$**

Other practicalities There's a rather empty **grocery store** (08.00–17.00 Mon–Fri, 08.00–13.00 Sat, closed every 3rd Sat), a basic **restaurant** (08.00–17.00 Mon–Fri) and a **fuel station** (08.00–18.00 daily).

Aus About 211km west of Keetmanshoop a slip road turns left off the B4 to Aus, notable for its unpredictable weather and its history as a POW camp. Just after the turning off the B4, you'll see a smart **tourist information centre**, but don't get your hopes up – after opening in 2006, it sadly closed a few years later due to 'funding issues'. Today, this small hillside town is mostly used as a stopover by truckers and motorcyclists who come to refuel at the 24-hour **fuel station** in the heart of the village. Just down the road from the tourist centre, on the left, is a **police post** (063 258005), and near the petrol station is the **post office** (08.00–16.30 Mon–Fri, 08.00–11.30 Sat).

Weather and flora Aus's weather can be extreme, very cold in winter and hot in the summer. It is also unpredictable – which stems from its proximity to the Cape – although the winter rain, and its associated flora, is more pronounced in the area around Rosh Pinah (page 271). (The Cape has a different weather pattern from anywhere else in southern Africa, with winter rainfall from May to September, and gloriously warm, dry summer weather from November to February.)

Sometimes Aus's weather will follow a typically Namibian pattern; at others it will have the Cape's weather, with showers in winter, and occasionally even snow. If heavy or prolonged, this rain can cause a sudden flush of sprouting plants and blooms, rather like the 'flower season' in Namaqualand, south of the border. Many unusual plants have been catalogued here, including a rather magnificent species of bulb whose flowers form a large globe, the size of a football. When these seed, the globe breaks off and rolls about like tumbleweed. Endemic to this small area is the yellow-flowered Aus daisy (*Arctotis fastiosa*), which grows only within a 30km radius of the town; a slightly more orange subspecies is found at Rosh Pinah. In winter, the yellow *kuibi* or butterflower (*Papia capensis*) brightens up the plains at the foot of the mountains, interspersed with the blue sporry (*Felicia namaquana*) and the bright purple fig bush. Higher up, the mountain butterflower holds sway, the western slopes are scented by wild rosemary, and the Bushman's candle is to be found – although here it is yellow or, rarely, white, unlike its bushier pink cousin in the desert to the west.

History When the German colonial troops surrendered to the South African forces in 1915, a camp for the prisoners of war was set up a few kilometres outside what is now Aus, just off the C13 about 1km south of the B4. At one point 1,552 German POWs were held by 600 guards. It seems that the German prisoners worked hard to make their conditions more comfortable by manufacturing bricks, building houses and stoves, and cultivating gardens. They eventually even sold bricks to their South African guards. The camp closed shortly after the end of the war, and little remains of the buildings bar a few earth mounds where the walls once stood, although a memorial marks the spot. On a hill 1.3km to the east of town, however, behind the local cemetery, is a small **cemetery** maintained by the Commonwealth War Graves Commission. Here lie 61 prisoners of war, and a further 60 members of the garrison, most of them victims of a flu epidemic in 1918. If you're driving up here, keep to the right-hand track.

Getting there and away Nowadays, visitors to Aus have little choice but to arrive by car. The railway through town is being upgraded for freight traffic (an ongoing process that seems to be progressing glacially slowly), but it is unlikely to be reopened for passenger trains.

Where to stay and eat

Klein-Aus Vista [266 C4] (30 rooms, 8 chalets, hikers' cabin, camping) 063 258116; e info@klein-aus-vista.com; www.klein-aus-vista.com. Nestled against the Aus Mountains, 1,400m above sea level, Klein-Aus Vista is 3km west of Aus to the south of the main B4. It's a family business, owned & run by brothers Piet & Willem Swiegers, who grew up here & have amalgamated 5 farms to form the privately owned 51,000ha Gondwana Sperrgebiet Rand Park. This is an evocative landscape, defined by granite outcrops & mountains, dry river-beds scattered with rocks & vast rose-hued desert plains. After winter rain, from Jul to Sep, the plains explode into an expansive carpet of yellow & violet flowers. To the north, the park borders the Namib-Naukluft National Park, home of the Namib desert horses.

Hiking is a major attraction, with a number of circular trails of varying distances & levels of difficulty (4–20km; 1½–5hrs); they're very well marked in one direction, but don't attempt them in reverse! Alternatively, there is plenty of scope for striking out on your own to seek out wild flowers or choose a vantage point to watch the sunset. Guided trips include sunset drives (N$415 pp) in the reserve. Piet is also a keen mountain-biker (he organises the annual 2-day MTB Challenge (www.klein-aus-vista-mtb-challenge.com) at the start of May), so 5 bikes & helmets are available for intermediate & advanced riders (N$400 pp/ day) who can follow a series of trails marked in the booklet you are given on payment of park fees for hiking & riding on the reserve (N$45).

Sundecks & a horseshoe-shaped pool are the newest additions, with the latter providing welcome relief in the hotter months. It all adds up to a super spot to spend a day or 3 unwinding during a long trip, with good service & diverse accommodation.

DESERT HORSE INN (30 rooms) The focus here is the main reception, bar & restaurant – where an excellent 3-course dinner (N$350) is served with a reasonable selection of wines. There's a superb little gift shop kept by Piet's wife, & – beneath the restaurant – a cosy lounge with fast free Wi-Fi, TV, bar & fireplace. Around this hub are smart en-suite rooms, built in pairs, & kitted out with fan heaters & hot water bottles as they can be chilly. N$1,560/2,520 sgl/dbl. **$$$$**

EAGLE'S NEST (7 chalets) Those seeking to enjoy the solitude & beauty of the mountains may be better served by these highly individual en-suite chalets, some 7km from the main reception. Built around gigantic granite boulders, with private verandas, these combine the best of rustic design – stone walls, heavy wooden furniture &

a traditional fireplace – with electricity, modern bathroom fittings & a well-equipped kitchenette, minibar stocked with wine & beer, & dining table. You'll also find reference books covering the history, flora & fauna of the area. Guests can arrange take-away BBQ packs & b/fast platters, or eat in the main restaurant. *N$2,135/3,440 sgl/dbl.* **$$$$$**

🏠 GEISTERSCHLUCHT (hikers' cabin) Formerly used for groups but now open to individuals & families, this simple self-catering cabin has been revamped & is now more similar to the chalets at Eagle's Nest. The name translates roughly to 'ghost canyon' after a group of diamond thieves who were shot by detectives trying to escape in a Hudson Terraplane in 1934, & are said to return for their lost treasure at full moon. Inside are a kitchen/bar & living area & 2 rooms sharing a bathroom, each with 2 ¾ beds & a bunk bed, so sleeping up to 8 guests. Braai packs can be arranged or meals can be taken at the restaurant, 6km away. *Room only N$380/760 sgl/dbl.* **$$$**

⛺ CAMPSITE (10 pitches) Well-spaced pitches are situated in a peaceful, narrow valley with shade from camelthorn trees, & good ablution blocks with hot water. Braai, tables & benches are available, but pitches don't have power. *N$140 pp.* **$**

🏠 **Bahnhof Hotel** (27 rooms) 📞063 258091; m 081 235 6737, 081 127 6391; e bahnhof-hotel-aus@iway.na; www.hotel-aus.com. This modern hotel in the centre of Aus itself has large, twin rooms with en-suite showers (1 with wheelchair access) & a further 14 new rooms built to the side with fans, small radiators & African art above the beds. Between them is a courtyard with a beer garden & fountain. À la carte meals (*N$55–275*) with freshly baked bread are available to guests & non-residents alike – while those on the move can order b/fast & lunch packs. A raised wooden terrace at the front makes a pleasant place to eat, or to while away an hour with a cool drink. Gated parking is available at the back of the property & there's free Wi-Fi for guests. They offer a number of tours, including ½- or full-day tours of Huib Park (*N$965 pp*), a 1½hr history tour of Aus (*N$250 pp*), sundowner tours (*N$300 pp*) and a Sperrgebiet tour (*N$695 pp*). *N$978/1,668 sgl/dbl.* **$$$$**

🏠 **Namib Garage** (19 rooms, camping) 📞063 258029; e namibaus@afol.com.na; www.ausnamibia.com. The self-catering rooms at Aus's garage, hosted by friendly Karin & Steve, are divided between 3 separate houses. All are simple, clean & equipped with a TV, AC & a kitchenette, making them ideal for longer stays. Opposite the garage itself, a wall encloses the campsite, with 7 pitches & hot water in the ablution blocks. Accommodation enquiries should be made at the garage (🕐 *fuel 24hrs*), which also has a well-stocked mini supermarket (🕐 *07.00–19.00 Mon–Sat*), postbox, & ATM. The garage also offers recovery services & tyre repair/replacement. *Rooms from N$600 dbl; camping from N$100 pp.* **$$**

What to see and do
Feral horses at Garub At the foot of the Aus Mountains, about 20km west of Aus, a sign 'feral horses' points north off the road. Follow the track for 1.5km and you'll come to Garub 'pan', an artificial waterhole that sustains the desert horses and is popular with the local oryx and ostrich as well.

A wooden observation shelter is a good spot to watch the horses and take photographs, with the added bonus of an information panel about their origins. It is likely that during the lifetime of this book that the precarious existence of the feral horses will change. As it stands, at the time of research a sustained drought and heavy predation by the local hyena population has seen the horses' numbers decline significantly. In the face of indifference from the Namibian authorities the locals have been raising funds to feed them as a temporary measure until other more permanent solutions can be found. It seems that in the long term the horses may well be moved out of the Namib-Naukluft National Park on to a private reserve or farm.

Koichab Pan to Lüderitz
Driving west from Garub, you enter the flat, gravel plains of the huge Koichab Pan, ringed by mountains in the distance. It's a vast and spectacular place where you'll be able to see any oncoming traffic on the straight road for perhaps 20km before you pass it.

On the edge of the Koichab Pan, around Garub, are perhaps the only desert-dwelling horses in the world. On average, the numbers fluctuate between 90 and 300 at any one time, depending on the annual rainfall. In 1996, for example, there were about 134 horses, and the following year at least ten new foals were born, but 1999 saw a sharp drop to just 89 animals. The current number stands at around 80, so the situation is looking precarious.

Their origins have fuelled considerable controversy over the years. Some considered that they were descended from farm animals that had escaped, or horses that the German Schutztruppe abandoned at the start of World War I. Others, that they came from Duwisib Castle, near Maltahöhe. By October 1908 Captain Von Wolf, Duwisib's owner, had assembled a herd of about 33 animals, namely '2 imported stallions, 17 imported mares, 8 Afrikaner mares, 6 year-old fillies'. He was a fanatical horseman, and by November 1909 he had expanded this collection to '72 horses. Mares: 15 Australians, 23 others, 9 thoroughbreds. Rest: Afrikaners and foals. 2 imported thoroughbred stallions'. Von Wolf left Duwisib in 1914 and was later killed at the Battle of the Somme. Yet there were reports of wild horses near Garub in the 1920s, ten years before Von Wolf's farm manager reported the loss of any horses.

Research conducted by biologist Telané Greyling in 2005, with the support of the MET, as well as Klein-Aus Vista and the Gondwana Desert Collection, suggests that the herd was drawn together from all of these sources, as well as those of the South African Army. As a result of this research, plans have been drawn up to protect the welfare of these animals that are neither domestic nor natural game, with resources to be raised in part by improving tourist options. For more information, see www.wild-horses-namibia.com.

Observe the horses in March, surrounded by a wavy sea of fine green grass, and their situation seems idyllic. But see them on the same desolate gravel plains on an October afternoon, and you'll appreciate their remarkable survival.

As you draw nearer to Lüderitz, the last 20km or so of the road cross a coastal dune-belt of marching barchan dunes – which are constantly being blown across the road from south to north. Ever-present bulldozers battle to clear these, but sometimes you will still encounter low ramps of sand on the tar. Drive very slowly for this last section, as hitting even a small mound of sand can easily wreck a vehicle's suspension.

FROM AI-AIS OR NOORDOEWER VIA ROSH PINAH Noordoewer (page 253) is one of the main access points into Namibia from South Africa. But while most drivers head north on the fast B1 towards Keetmanshoop, there is a second road, the C13, that travels northwest, running along the boundary of the Ai-Ais Richtersveld Transfrontier Park then on to Rosh Pinah, along the border of the Sperrgebiet National Park. Much of the road runs through spectacular mountain scenery, often alongside the Orange River, offering some excellent picnic spots and opportunities for birdwatching. (For details of accommodation and canoeing expeditions along the river, see page 254.) There are few settlements along the C13 – except at Aussenkehr – so you should take more than the usual emergency rations of food and water.

For those coming from Ai-Ais, it is well worth considering taking this southerly route to Lüderitz, too. The erstwhile 4x4 track to the southwest has been upgraded to the C37/D207, with ongoing work to improve the infrastructure along this stretch of road. Note, however, that west of the C37 there are some sharp twists and turns, and hidden inclines that may be unexpectedly steep, so exercise considerable caution on this stretch. And a final word of warning: after heavy rain, usually in the early months of the year, the Fish River can flood. Even with a 4x4 the road is often impassable, so do check this before you set out.

ROSH PINAH About 165km south of Aus, and a similar distance from Ai-Ais (165km) or Noordoewer (154km), the mining town of Rosh Pinah lies in a very remote corner of Namibia, almost on the eastern border of the Sperrgebiet National Park. Yet the combination of a tarred toad through to Aus, and the border post at Sendelingsdrift (⏲ *08.00–16.30 when river not flooded*), has already led to an increased trickle of visitors. If – or perhaps when – access to the new national park is improved, the town's importance for visitors is likely to grow significantly.

For now, there is a palpable air of prosperity about the town, a reflection of the success of the Skorpion mine. The road between Rosh Pinah and Aus has been tarred to facilitate the heavy goods vehicles that trundle regularly between here and the port at Lüderitz, cutting the drive from Ai-Ais to Aus from around 6 hours to just 4 hours or so.

History A deposit of copper was discovered just south of here by a Prussian Jew, Mose Eli Kahan, who had fled Europe to escape persecution. By the 1920s this was being worked, but was abandoned when the price slumped in the 1930s. Thirty years later, in 1968, Kahan found a zinc deposit in the mountains, which he named Rosh Pinah. Though he died soon afterwards, his son eventually joined forces with the large South African mining company Iscor to develop it.

Production began in 1969, and by the end of the century the mine was producing around 72,000 tonnes of zinc per year, as well as a lead concentrate, and also a little silver. More recently, the discovery of better-quality zinc led to the development of the nearby Skorpion mine, which opened in 2003 at a cost of U$54 million, representing the largest investment in Namibia since independence. The mine was expected to last around 15 years but it is still going strong, and a some now anticipate it continuing into 2028.

Where to stay and eat

🏠 **Amica Guesthouse** (10 rooms, 4 houses) 304 Roterkam St; \063 274043/978; e amicaguesthouse.com. The en-suite rooms at the main house are fairly simple but clean & pleasant, each equipped with DSTV, AC, safe & phone. Away from here are 4 separate 3-bedroom, self-catering houses with a similar feel & style but offering more privacy; these are largely aimed at longer-stay mine employees but would be perfectly nice for a night or 2. There's a swimming pool in the courtyard, which is overlooked by a double-storey outdoor dining area (food is described as 'gourmet') & giant chess set, while inside are a cocktail bar & coffee shop. Free Wi-Fi is available throughout, & a laundry service is available. *N$930/1,200 sgl/dbl; self-catering N$2,000/house.* **$$$**

🏠 **Four Seasons Lodge** (28 rooms, 10 chalets) \063 274416; m 081 270 6040; e fourseasons@ iway.na; www.roshpinahinfo.co.za. The white-painted buildings of this lodge, with green roofs & canopied carports, are clearly visible next to the Engen fuel station beside the C13. All rooms have AC, fridge & TV, with the carports belonging to self-catering chalets, which are aimed more at longer stays. In the centre, surrounded by a low wall, are a good pool, a large bar & a restaurant serving the usual steaks & grills. Safe on-site parking. *B&B room N$715/1,050 sgl/dbl; self-catering chalet N$1,150.* **$$$**

✗ **Kokerboom Restaurant** Spar shopping centre; m 081 366 9414; e kokerboom2@ gmail.com. Opened in Nov 2017, & one of 2 establishments in Rosh Pinah to claim 'restaurant' status, this seemed to be the talk of the (rather small) town in 2018, & certainly seems to be a better prospect than the Four Seasons. Expect the usual offering of grilled meats, burgers & pizza; they will even deliver. $$

Other practicalities A new shopping mall, branches of FNB and Standard **banks**, a couple of **supermarkets**, a **post office**, a **private clinic**, and a 24-hour **fuel station** smack of a town on the up. There are also a couple of **tyre-repair** places and a branch of Cymot.

LÜDERITZ

Lüderitz is a fascinating old German town, full of character, with relaxed locals who often have time to talk, but the recession has bitten hard here, with high unemployment and ensuing social problems. 'A small drinking town with a fishing problem' is the motto emblazoned across T-shirts worn by the locals. All the same, around the centre of town, houses are painted in improbable pastel shades, which makes Lüderitz feel like a delightful toy town at times.

The air here is tangibly clean, even on the foggiest of mornings. Locals say that Lüderitz can have all four seasons in a day, as the weather can change in hours from bright, hot and sunny, to strong winds, to dark, cold and foggy – and then back to sunshine again. This variation, together with a cold sea and the prevailing southwest wind, rule out Lüderitz as a beach destination, though brave souls still take brief dips from the beach near the Nest Hotel or round on the peninsula.

In the evenings, there are a few lively bars, and a handful of quiet restaurants, notable for the seafood brought in by the freezing waters of the South Atlantic Benguela Current that sweeps up the coast. But the entertainment here pales in comparison with that of Swakopmund.

Lüderitz is not somewhere to 'drop in on' – you need to make a special journey to come here – but it's worth visiting for its architecture, its peninsula, and to see a part of Namibia that seems almost unaware of the outside world. If you do choose to visit the area, allow a minimum of two nights to appreciate both the town and its surroundings. Try to avoid Sundays and public holidays, though, when almost everything closes down and the town is empty.

Tourism is having an impact here, but only gradually. Although several new hotels and guesthouses opened their doors in the years following independence, there's been a marked downturn in the town's economy, offset only partly by visiting cruise ships. Even the trendy new waterfront development near the harbour is looking a little tired. On the plus side, use of the harbour as the export base for the Skorpion zinc mine near Rosh Pinah has brought

LÜDERITZ
For listings, see from page 277

🛏 **Where to stay**
1 Backpackers Lodge..............C4
2 Cormorant House................A2
3 Element Riders....................B5
4 Hansa Haus..........................C5
5 Haus Sandrose.....................B5
6 Island Cottage.....................A1
7 Kairos Cottage.....................A1
8 Krabbenhöft & Lampe........B6
9 Kratzplatz............................A5
10 Lüderitz Nest......................A6
11 Obelix Guesthouse.............C6
12 Sea-View Zum
     Sperrgebiet......................D3
13 Shark Island Resort............A1

Off map
    Timo's Lodge.......................D2

❌ **Where to eat and drink**
14 Barrels.................................A4
15 Captain Macarena..............C3
    Crayfish Bar................(see 10)
16 Diaz Coffee Shop/
     Beer Garden.....................B5
17 Essenzeit Waterfront..........C3
18 Garden Café.........................C3
    Penguin........................(see 10)
19 Ritzi's..................................B5

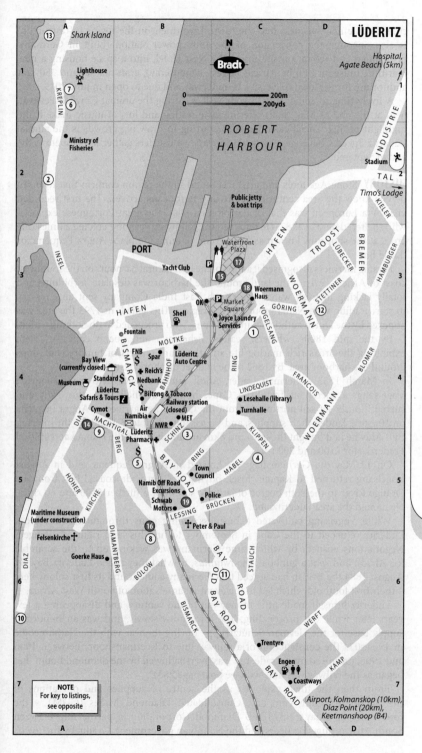

LÜDERITZ

A — Shark Island ⑬
B
C
D

Hospital,
Agate Beach (5km)

N
Bradt

0 —— 200m
0 —— 200yds

Lighthouse ⑦
⑥

KREPLIN

Ministry of
Fisheries

*ROBERT
HARBOUR*

INDUSTRIE

Stadium

②

INSEL

TAL

KIELER

Timo's Lodge

Public jetty
& boat trips

PORT

Waterfront
Plaza ⑰

Yacht Club
P
⑮

HAFEN

WOERMANN

TROOST

LÜBECKER

BREMER

HAMBURGER

⑱ Woermann
Haus

OK
P   Market
Square
Joyce Laundry
Services ①

GÖRING

VOGELSANG

⑫

HAFEN

Shell

Fountain

BISMARCK

MOLTKE

FNB   Spar
Bay View $
(currently closed)   Standard $

Lüderitz
Auto Centre

BAHNHOF

RING

Reich's
Nedbank $
Museum
Lüderitz   Biltong & Tobacco
Safaris & Tours ℹ   Railway station
Air   (closed)
Cymot   Namibia
⑭   MET
⑨   *NACHTIGAL*   NWR
③
Lüderitz
Pharmacy
$
⑤

DIAZ

BERG

SCHINZ

LINDEQUIST

Lesehalle (library)
Turnhalle

FRANCOIS

KLIPPEN

MABEL

④

WOERMANN

BLOMER

Maritime Museum
(under construction)

Felsenkirche ✝

⑩

HOHER

KIRCHE

DIAMANTBERG

BAY ROAD

RING

Town
Council

Namib Off Road
Excursions
Schwab ⑲   Police
Motors
⑯   *LESSING*   *BRÜCKEN*
⑧
✝ Peter & Paul

Goerke Haus

BÜLOW

BISMARCK

BAY

OLD BAY ROAD

⑪

STAUCH

WERFT

KAMP

Trentyre
Engen
BAY   Coastways

ROAD

Airport, Kolmanskop (10km),
Diaz Point (20km),
Keetmanshoop (B4)

NOTE
For key to listings,
see opposite

A   **B**   **C**   **D**

considerable new business into the town. Investment in the town's infrastructure is also ongoing: the conversion of the 1909 power station (built in Germany, dismantled and rebuilt on site), near the Nest Hotel, into a space housing a new maritime museum (it'll be Africa's largest, supposedly), craft market and 350-seat auditorium for the local university, is underway and due to open in June 2019.

A lively time to coincide with your visit is during the annual Crayfish Festival, held at the end of May. Stalls offering taste testing and lots of music make it the highlight of their social calendar. Also starting to draw big crowds is the annual Lüderitz Speed Challenge, where world-class windsurfers gather to compete at the end of September.

HISTORY Stone Age tools and artefacts found in the region confirm that Khoisan people knew the area centuries before any Europeans arrived. The first recorded visit by a European was that of Bartolomeu Dias, the great Portuguese explorer, who sheltered here in 1487. He returned the following year and erected a limestone cross at the spot now known as Diaz Point, naming the place Angra Pequena, or 'Little Bay'.

Passing mariners recognised it as one of the best natural harbours on the southwest coast of Africa – even if the land around the harbour was desolate, forbidding and totally lacking in fresh water. The Dutch East India Company sent an emissary to start trading with Nama groups in the region. This failed. In 1793 the area was annexed by the Dutch authorities in the Cape – who proceeded to do nothing with it.

By the mid 1800s, whalers, sealers, fishermen and guano collectors were exploiting the area's rich marine life and there are reports of hundreds of ships around the harbour area. By 1862 some had set up shore bases here.

In March 1883 a German trader, Adolf Lüderitz, with help from Heinrich Vogelsang, a merchant from the Cape, bought a small ship, the *Tilly*, and surreptitiously set sail northward from the Cape. They arrived at Angra Pequena on 10 April, landed their supplies, and Vogelsang set off to Bethanie in the interior. By 1 May he had bought the bay (and 8km around it) from the Nama *kaptein* Josef Frederiks for £100 and 200 rifles.

On 12 May the German flag was hoisted in Angra Pequena, and in August Vogelsang returned to Kaptein Josef, buying a 32km-wide coastal belt from the Orange River to the 26th degree of latitude south for a further £100 and 60 rifles. He named the area Lüderitzland.

While Vogelsang cultivated a business selling guns throughout the region, Lüderitz returned to the Cape in September to find his land rights challenged. Negotiations ensued, by which time Germany was waking up to the scramble for Africa, and sent a gunboat, the *Nautilus*, to what they called Lüderitz Bay. By August 1884 the British had agreed that Germany could found its first colony here – their first foothold which led to the eventual annexation of South West Africa.

Lüderitz himself made little money out of the venture, and disappeared a few years later while out prospecting. The town grew slowly, and was an important supply base for the German Schutztruppe during the war with the Nama people in 1904–07. The construction of a railway line to Keetmanshoop, between 1906 and 1908, promised more trade, but was overshadowed by the diamond boom that began as the railway was finished (see box, page 288).

From then the town exploded as the centre of supplies and operations of the diamond-mining company, Consolidated Diamond Mines (CDM) – the forerunner of today's NAMDEB Diamond Corporation, a partnership between South Africa's huge De Beers and the Namibian government. Gradually the town's fishing industries developed, and an important export trade of rock lobster was established. However, the CDM headquarters moved to Oranjemund in 1943, precipitating the start of the town's slow decline.

Only in the last few years, through tourism and fishing, has Lüderitz's economy started to look up again. There is still some diamond diving here, too (see box, page 276), and NAMDEB continues to have a considerable stake in the town. Ironically tourism has been helped by the lack of development between the 1940s and the 1990s, which preserved many of the beautiful buildings of the early 20th century.

GETTING THERE AND AWAY Lüderitz is out on a limb, and the drive, across an empty sandy plain punctuated by telephone poles, takes time. Most visitors drive here between visiting the Namib-Naukluft National Park and the Fish River Canyon. Passenger trains have not run for several years; although the town is bisected by a railway, the ongoing but very slow work on upgrading the track is geared only to freight.

By car See *The roads to Lüderitz* (page 265) for comments on the whole journey, but note that for the last 20km there is a 60km/h speed limit. This is because the fast tarmac road cuts through a field of shifting barchan dunes, which constantly march across it. Go slowly. Even a small pile of sand is hard when hit at speed.

By air Air Namibia operates direct flights from Windhoek to Lüderitz departing on Tuesdays and Thursdays. The return flight goes via Oranjemund on the same days, whereas on Saturday it goes to Oranjemund before Lüderitz, then returns direct to Windhoek. The airport is about 11km east of the town, opposite Kolmanskop.

By bus There have been no bus services linking Lüderitz with the rest of Namibia for some years, increasing the town's isolation. However, local minibus operator 'Aunty Anna' (m 081 390 9210) runs transfers to Keetmanshoop (N$170 pp) and sometimes to Windhoek; rates vary. Book through Lüderitz Safaris and Tours (page 276), who also act as booking agents for Intercape, so you can plan onward journeys here even though the coaches don't operate in this area.

Hitchhiking Compared with many of Namibia's attractions, Lüderitz is relatively easy to reach by hitching. The tar road from Keetmanshoop has a steady trickle of traffic along it, and intrepid hitchhikers have even made it from Walvis Bay along the C14 via Sesriem – though taking food and water with you is essential on this route.

By sea Although Lüderitz is a port of call for a number of cruise ships throughout the year, no regular passenger boats call here.

GETTING AROUND If you don't have your own car, there are two options – hire a car or use the service of one of the town's tour operators (page 276). Transport from the airport or to Kolmanskop with one of the tour operators costs at least N$700 for two people, and a further N$350 for each additional passenger. Again, you can arrange this through Lüderitz Safaris and Tours (page 276).

Car hire Two of the big car-hire companies have offices in Lüderitz – but be aware that you should book ahead in order to ensure availability.

The wealth of southwestern Namibia may have been built on diamonds from the Sperrgebiet, but today the greatest proportion of the diamonds found in the area around Lüderitz are mined from under the sea rather than in the Sperrgebiet itself. These alluvial diamonds are found all along the Orange River and at its mouth, but over the years many have been swept farther north by the Benguela Current, with significant deposits now to be found in the seas around Lüderitz harbour.

The leading company in this field is Namibian Minerals Corporation (NAMCO), which has been operational since 1994. Following the company's estimates that around 2.6 million carats of diamonds were to be found in these waters, large-scale operations went live in 1998, with some 650,000 carats now produced each year. Boats put out to sea regularly from the harbour in Lüderitz. On the larger diamond boats, robotic machines trawl in waters up to 150m deep, digging a trench in the sea bed then sucking up the material from depths of 10–16m, up to 25m, ready for processing on board. While the first bags collected contain little except sand, beneath this layer is gravel; it is among the gravel that diamonds are most likely to be found. NAMDEB, too, has considerable resources devoted to this sector within an area that extends 200km out into the Atlantic.

Smaller boats are owned and operated by diamond divers under licence to NAMDEB. Each boat is allocated a specific area, not more than 5km from the coast, in which to search. Theirs is a dangerous job, in unforgiving conditions, but the potential rewards have in the past been high: in 1999, 60,000 carats of diamonds were collected in this way. Nowadays, though, hauls are decreasing – and most boats have ceased operating since the recession, and the attendant fall in the value of diamonds.

When the boats return to port, the sacks are taken by officials from NAMDEB to their processing plant, where the contents are classified. All boats, including any personal luggage on board, are thoroughly checked and inspected for any gravel that may have been overlooked before they are declared 'clean'.

Avis 25 Bismarck St; 063 203968; m 081 124 1829

Budget 25 Bismarck St; 063 202777; m 081 251 5835

TOURIST INFORMATION

Lüderitz Safaris & Tours [273 B4] Bismarck St; 063 202719; m 081 129 7236; e ludsaf@ africaonline.com.na; ☉ 08.00–12.30 & 13.30–17.00 Mon–Fri, 08.00–noon Sat, 08.30–10.00 Sun. Owned & run by the all-knowing Marion Schelkle, this convenient & very efficient tour operator doubles as an excellent tourist information office & is also the booking agent for Intercape buses (though there is no service to Lüderitz). They issue permits & book tours for Kolmanskop, & run a range of day excursions to ensure that the visitor can make the most of a limited stay in the town.

A large selection of books & crafts is on sale in the office.

MET [273 B4] Schinz St; 063 202 8111; ☉ 08.00–17.00 Mon–Fri. Next door to the NWR office (see opposite) is the Ministry of Environment & Tourism office, where you can purchase permits for the Namib-Naukluft National Park. It is also anticipated that permits for the Sperrgebiet National Park will be available here once park rules & fees have been finalised – although this process has been ongoing for some time.

NWR [273 B4] Schinz St; ☎063 202752; e reservations@nwr.com.na; www.nwr.com.na; ⏰ 08.00–17.00 Mon–Fri. Housed in the old post office building dating back to 1907, the NWR office is the place to book the campsite at Shark Island.

TOUR OPERATORS

Coastways Tours [273 C7] Bay Rd; ☎063 202002; m 081 122 9336; e lewiscwt@iway.na; www.coastways.com.na. Operators of self-drive 4x4 trips to Walvis Bay, & Saddle Hill & Spencer Bay in the Namib-Naukluft Park (*N$980 pp, min 4*), Coastways also runs trips to Bogenfels in the Sperrgebiet (page 289).

Ghost Town Tours Although this operator is still looking after tours to Kolmanskop, their office seems exceptionally elusive & there are rumours that the system is going to change. For now, you can book these tours either at the gate or through Lüderitz Safaris & Tours (see opposite).

Namib Off Road Excursions [273 B5] Bay Rd; m 081 128 8050; e noextours@gmail.com; www.noextours.weebly.com. Formerly Mukorob Tours, this operator runs ½-day trips into the Sperrgebiet, visiting Elizabeth Bay & Kolmanskop, ½-day peninsula tours & longer guided self-drive camping tours into the Namib-Naukluft National Park (page 295).

🏠 **WHERE TO STAY** Lüderitz has several hotels varying from the upmarket Nest and slightly less corporate Zum Sperrgebiet to several more personal establishments. A proliferation of self-catering guesthouses reflects the long-term nature of many visitors to the town, but there's also a backpackers' lodge and a windswept campsite (complete with super lighthouse). It is best to book most of them in advance, as the town's rooms quickly fill up during the busier times of year (page 97).

🏠 **Lüderitz Nest Hotel** [273 A6] (73 rooms) 820 Diaz St; ☎063 204000; e reservations@ nesthotel.com; www.nesthotel.com. Set on its own right on the sea to the southwest of town, with its own beach, the 4-star Nest is Lüderitz's largest hotel. Rooms, all with sea views, are built around a sheltered courtyard enclosing a good-size swimming pool. Along with en-suite shower or bath, they have twin or dbl beds, flat-screen TV, phone, AC/heating, coffee/tea-making facilities & hairdryer. 3 are adapted for travellers with disabilities: 1 with shower, 2 with bath. There is a large reception area, the lovely waterfront Penguin restaurant serving an excellent buffet b/fast, the chic new Crayfish Bar (page 280), a children's play area on the beach, & free Wi-Fi throughout. Outside is a guarded parking area. Staff can arrange airport transfers & book tours. *N$1,630/2,600 sgl/dbl.* $$$$

🏠 **Sea-View Zum Sperrgebiet** [273 D3] (22 rooms) Cnr Woermann & Stettiner sts; ☎063 203411; e cro@united.com.na; www. unitedafricagroup.com.na/page/sea-view- zum-sperrgebiet. Sitting on a low hill above the harbour, up a steep, narrow drive, this old hotel was looking tired when we visited, despite a management change, but renovations were underway. For now, the older compact rooms are a bit faded & dark, but come with TV, safe, coffee/tea-maker, hairdryer, en-suite facilities that include a good shower (some also have baths), & a small balcony with a view over either the harbour or the courtyard. Newer rooms are lighter & feel refreshed, although we wouldn't go as far as to say they feel modern. The à la carte restaurant itself is rather soulless, but there are balcony tables above a small (but impressive) unheated indoor swimming pool that's surrounded by banana trees & shaded glass walls, & overlooking the harbour in the distance. A small sauna in the basement can be heated on request. Free Wi-Fi everywhere. *N$885–1,500/1,115–1,740 sgl/dbl.* $$$

🏠 **Bay View** [273 A4] Diaz St. Although this was closed at the time of research, there is talk of a simple B&B reopening here in the future.

❋ 🏠 **Cormorant House** [273 A2] (8 rooms) Insel St; ☎063 202264; m 081 128 8625; e cormorant@iway.na; www.thecormoranthouse. com. Perched on the edge of the rocky shore at the southern end of Shark Island, this smart guesthouse, which opened in Jan 2017, is one of our favourites in Lüderitz. Bright rooms, decorated in whites & blues to reflect the coastal location, have lovely uninterrupted sea views. 6 of them have the added bonus of a balcony to revel in the sea air further, & room no 6 sleeps up to 5 people. Full self-catering facilities are provided in each room as well as Wi-Fi & flat-screen TV. There is also a communal braai room, sheltered from Lüderitz's sometimes questionable weather, & secure parking. *N$900–1,350 per room.* **$$$**

🏠 **Haus Sandrose** [273 B5] (2 rooms, flat) 15 Bismarck St; ☎ 063 202630; **m** 081 323 1111; **e** haussandrose@iway.na; www.haussandrose. com. Linda & Erich Looser's central accommodation is guaranteed to make visitors feel individual. Entirely distinct styles mark out their 3 self-catering units, each with private facilities: the roomy Grosse Bucht flat (which has a connecting door with Klein Bucht & is ideal for a family of 4) & the twin Bogenfels & Halifax rooms all have their own kitchens. Outside, there's a quiet, shady courtyard with braai facilities. *Room only N$450/900 sgl/dbl.* **$$$**

🏠 **Island Cottage** [273 A1] (3 rooms) Kreplin St, Shark Island; ☎ 063 203626; **m** 081 292 2984; **e** retha.c@afol.com.na. The small red-walled B&B situated on the windswept Shark Island peninsula has en-suite rooms (1 dbl, 2 twins with a couch) that are modern, classy & well equipped. A kitchen area, TV, phone & – optimistically – fan are standard, & there's an outside braai area, but the big plus of the 2 larger rooms is a superb west-facing sea view from the veranda. The owner, Retha, also runs a spa on site. *Room only N$560/820 sgl/dbl.* **$$$**

🏠 **Kairos Cottage** [273 A1] (5 rooms) Kreplin St, Shark Island; ☎ 063 203080; **m** 081 650 5598, 081 818 6727; **e** christo.b@iway.na; www. kairoscottage.com. This smart, family-owned B&B has 3 dbl & 2 twin en-suite rooms, all with ocean views, kitchenette with fridge & coffee station, heaters, flat-screen TV & free Wi-Fi. The wraparound terrace has stunning uninterrupted sea views. In short it offers superb value for money. *N$500/950 sgl/dbl.* **$$$**

🏠 **Kratzplatz** [273 A5] (12 rooms) 5 Nachtigal St; ☎ 063 202458; **m** 081 129 2458; **e** kratzmr@ iway.na; www.kratzplatz.info. On the right side of Barrels (see opposite), this friendly & comfortable B&B run by Manfred & Monica Kratz is painted bright red, so you can't miss it! The main building, a converted church, features whitewashed, high-ceilinged rooms, all en suite, & all kitted out with TVs, coffee facilities & fridges; there are also 4 self-

catering rooms. The style & furnishings are modern & simple: this is a pleasant place, with secure parking & free Wi-Fi throughout. *N$630/760 sgl/dbl; self-catering from N$380 pp.* **$$$**

🏠 **Obelix Guesthouse** [273 C6] (15 rooms, 1 dorm) ☎ 063 203456; **m** 081 227 7735; **e** obelixvillage@iway.na. Named after the *Asterix* comic strip, this quirky guesthouse has dbl, twin & family en-suite rooms & a dormitory arranged around a central courtyard. Where they are simple, the central lapa is ostentatiously over the top: lined with animal skins, trophies & stuffed wild animals. Guests may use the kitchen & braai facilities, & there's a bar, but b/fast is usually included, with lunch & dinner (both N$150) available on request – it's best to book in advance. Free Wi-Fi & safe parking. *N$570/880 sgl/dbl; dorm bed N$250 pp.* **$$–$$$**

🏠 **Hansa Haus** [273 C5] (4 rooms) Mabel St; **m** 081 128 4336, 081 203 4458; **e** hansahaus@ iway.na; www.hansahausluderitz.co.za. Right at the top of Mabel St, this imposing blue house was built in 1909 with a commanding view of the town & harbour, including from the front balcony. Run by Cicely Burgers, it accommodates self-catering guests (no b/fast available) in dbl & twin rooms – 3 with sea views – with lovely wooden floors & high ceilings. These 3 share a shower room, whereas the 4th – a family room – has its own bath. A separate lounge with flat-screen TV & free Wi-Fi, & a modern, well-equipped kitchen are bonuses; the only snag is the location – on the 2nd floor of the building up steep steps, so not suitable for travellers with disabilities or families with very young children. *Room only from N$340/680 sgl/dbl.* **$$**

🏠 **Krabbenhöft & Lampe** [273 B6] (2 apts, 5 rooms) 25 Bismarck St; **m** 081 206 6562; **e** info@ klguesthouse.com; www.klguesthouse.com. This imposing place at the top of the town houses some unexpected guest accommodation. Constructed in 1910, & proclaimed a national monument in 1992, the building used to be home to a carpet-weaving factory but is now simply a shop. Upstairs, however, the large, spotless rooms retain many architectural features, with high ceilings & old wooden floors, albeit now with modern kitchens, bathrooms & beds. 2 flats on the 1st floor are fully self-catering, while 1 flight further up ('Oberdeck') are 5 twin rooms with shared ablutions, kitchen facilities & a TV. Free Wi-Fi throughout. It's certainly distinctive, & represents good value for money.

The entrance is the brown gate on the right of the main building; if no-one is there ask for Katrina, the supervisor of the premises, inside the shop or in the courtyard at the back. *Room only from N$350/550 sgl/dbl.* **$$**

⛺ Shark Island Resort [273 A1] (20 pitches, lighthouse) Kreplin St; book via NWR, page 103. The campsite here has a superb location, with power, functional washblocks & toilets, & braai facilities, but it is amazingly windy; make sure your tent is well anchored. If there's nobody on the gate then just pitch your tent – but try to find a site sheltered by the rocks; the attendants will come over to collect money. The sites are overlooked by a sparsely furnished lighthouse, with 2 twin bedrooms, kitchen, DSTV, 2 bathrooms & living area, which must be Lüderitz's most imposing place to stay. *Camping N$250 pp; lighthouse N$360 pp.* **$$**

🏠 Timo's Lodge [273 D2] (22 rooms) Tal St, Township; m 081 124 8812, 081 128 0946; e info@timoslodge.com.na, bookings@ timoslodge.com.na; www.timoslodge.com.na. A superb budget option run by township resident, Timo. Full of smiles, he offers homely, very clean, en-suite, self-catering rooms of varying sizes arranged around a gated courtyard; there's a security guard on post at night, so it's very safe. The entrance is round the back, in front of the yellow Rotary Club. *Room only N$400/550 sgl/dbl.* **$$**

🏠 Backpackers Lodge [273 C4] (5 rooms, 2 cabins, camping) 2 Ring St; ☏ 063 202000; m 081 261 2174; e luderitzbackpackers@hotmail. com. Lüderitz's original backpackers offers very simple twin or family rooms that share facilities with the dormitories. Its large main room with TV has lots of space, albeit surrounded by beds as it doubles as an overflow dormitory for overland groups. There's also an equipped kitchen with free Wi-Fi & a laundry service. A yard at the back is a good spot for a braai & 3 or 4 camping cars (it's not level enough for tents), & a couple of converted boat cabins here do service as self-catering rooms. *N$240/350 sgl/dbl; dorm bed N$140; camping N$110 pp.* **$–$$**

🏠 Element Riders [273 B5] (8 rooms) 7 Schinz St; m 081 666 6599; e info@element-riders.com; www.element-riders.com. Look out for the surfboard sign outside this budget option, which is slightly better than Backpackers Lodge. They have 1 dorm room, a shed-like family room that can sleep 5 & dbl rooms dotted around a concrete courtyard sharing communal showers. There's a bright, sunny, self-catering kitchen with hotplates (no ovens), free Wi-Fi, & laundry (chargeable per load); they also rent bikes & can organise numerous sports activities, from surfing to land-boarding. *N$250–350/360–460 sgl/dbl; dorm bed N$125 pp.* **$–$$**

✘ WHERE TO EAT AND DRINK There's not an endless choice of cuisine in Lüderitz, but seafood (and particularly crayfish – or rock lobster – in season (November– April) is a speciality. If seafood is above your budget (you can expect to pay around N$300 for a seafood platter) then fish, steaks and more usual Namibian fare are also available, while some good smaller take-aways serve burgers and bar food, which can be excellent value.

Lüderitz doesn't major on nightlife, but locals congregate frequently at Barrels (see below).

✘ Penguin [273 A6] Nest Hotel, page 277; ☏ 063 204000; ⊕ b/fast 07.00–10.00, light meals 11.00–18.00, lunch 12.30–14.00, dinner 18.30– 22.00, all daily. The Nest Hotel's smart restaurant serves up lovely sea views & has the best crayfish in town. Their buffet b/fast, 3-course set lunch & à la carte dinner are all open to non-guests as well. For dessert, the house speciality is crêpe suzette, prepared & flambéed at your table – quite a show! Reservations advised. **$$$$$**

✘ Barrels [273 A4] 5 Nachtigal St; ☏ 063 202651; ⊕ 18.00–21.30 Mon–Fri. With a lapa-style roof above the bar, walls festooned with candles dripping wax, & barrels serving as tables, this lively joint at Kratzplatz (see opposite) is hugely popular with the backpacking fraternity & beyond, & hosts occasional live music. Alongside its pizza menu (*from N$115*) is a substantial dinner buffet (*N$160*) – usually either *eisbein* (pork knuckle) or chicken with salad & vegetables – served informally around the fire. **$$$$–$$$$$**

✗ **Ritzi's** [273 B5] Cnr Lessing & Bay Rd; ☎ 063 202818; ⏰ 10.00–22.00 Mon–Sat, 16.00–22.00 Sun. Friendly staff & generally good food are the hallmarks of this popular eatery, though service can be slow. Despite a move from its Waterfront location to a rather less appealing spot in town, the menu still majors on seafood, but alternatives include a range of pizzas & several specials. Prices come as a pleasant surprise, including a seafood platter at N$220, & the wine list is unusually good value. Booking is advisable in the evenings. **$$$$–$$$$$**

✗ **Essenzeit Waterfront** [273 C3] **m** 081 401 4337; **e** bookings@essenzeit-luderitz.com; ⏰ 09.00–22.00 Mon–Sat. Taking the place of Ritzi's on the Waterfront, Essenzeit has arguably the best location of the restaurants in Lüderitz & is often full. If service isn't always as attentive as it could be, the menu is extensive & the food generally tasty. Booking ahead recommended. **$$–$$$$$**

Diaz Coffee Shop/Beer Garden [273 B5] Bismarck St; **m** 081 700 0475; ⏰ 08.00–21.00 daily. This long-term favourite in Lüderitz continues to thrive in its new location beside Krabbenhöft & Lampe. The café offers free Wi-Fi (ask for access code) & is a good place to take the chill off a Lüderitz morning, with b/fast, snacks & delicious cakes, or to relax over lunch or dinner from the extensive menu. **$–$$$$**

✱ **Garden Café** [273 C3] 17 Hafen St; **m** 081 124 8317; ⏰ 07.00–17.00 daily. It doesn't look like much from the outside but this quirky café set just a street back from the Waterfront is well worth a visit. Inside it is filled with antiquities & black-&-white photos from times gone by. But perhaps the best bit is the lush garden with plenty of shaded seating areas, a bathtub full of strawberry plants & even a resident tortoise. The homemade cakes are fantastic & it is also a good choice for b/fast or a light lunch. **$–$$**

✗ **Captain Macarena** [273 C3] Waterfront; ☎ 063 203958; ⏰ 09.00–18.00 Mon–Fri, 09.00–13.00 Sat. Serves fish & chips, & good calamari to take away from premises in the modern Waterfront development. **$**

Crayfish Bar [273 A6] Nest Hotel, page 277; ⏰ noon–22.00 daily. Thanks to its superb sea views, chic décor with surfer photographs & underlit bar, the Nest's renovated bar is the ideal spot for a coffee mid morning, or a sundowner. You can also order from the Penguin restaurant's à la carte menu (page 279) if you get peckish while sampling the large choice of cocktails here.

SHOPPING

Biltong & Tobacco [273 B4] Bismarck St; ☎ 063 203776; ⏰ 07.30–17.30 Mon–Fri, 09.00–13.00 Sat. Stock up on biltong nibbles at this small store with lime-green front entrance.

Cymot [273 A4] 4 Nachtigal St; ☎ 063 203855; ⏰ 08.00–13.00 & 14.00–17.00 Mon–Fri, 08.00–noon Sat. Handy in case you need any camping equipment before heading north into the Namib-Naukluft.

OK Grocer [273 B3] Hafen St; ⏰ 08.00–18.00 Mon–Fri, 08.00–13.00 Sat–Sun

Spar [273 B4] Cnr Bahnhof & Moltke sts; ⏰ 08.00–18.00 Mon–Fri, 08.00–13.00 Sat, 09.00–13.00 Sun

OTHER PRACTICALITIES All the major Namibian **banks** – Standard, FNB, Bank Windhoek and Nedbank – have branches and ATM facilities in Lüderitz. The **post office** [273 B4] is on Bismarck Street and it's worth looking out for the town's monthly **newspaper**, *Buchter News*; with event listings.

Emergencies Police [273 B5] ☎ 063 202255; ambulance & hospital [273 D1] ☎ 063 202446; fire service ☎ 063 202255

Joyce Laundry Services [273 C3] Hafen St; **m** 081 291 1306; ⏰ 07.00–18.00 Mon–Fri, 08.00–14.00 Sat–Sun

✚ **Reich's pharmacy** [273 B4] Bismarck St; ☎ 063 202806; **m** 081 788 5807; ⏰ 08.00–17.30 Mon–Fri, 08.00–13.00 Sat

Fuel and vehicle repairs There's an Engen **fuel station** [273 C7] (⏰ *06.00–21.00 Mon–Fri, 06.00–18.00 Sat–Sun*) on the edge of town, and **Shell** in the centre

[273 B3]. For tyres, there's **Trentyre** [273 C7] (☎ *063 202137;* m *081 122 3482, 081 144 3001*) on Bay Road, but for more serious vehicle repairs try **Lüderitz Auto Centre** [273 B4] (*Bahnhof St;* ☎*063 204052;* m *081 250 7251;* ⊕ *07.30–17.00 Mon-Fri, 07.30–12.30 Sat*), which also offers a recovery service.

WHAT TO SEE AND DO Even visitors with a limited attention span find enough to occupy themselves around Lüderitz for a day, while those who enjoy a more leisurely pace will take three or four to see the area's main attractions.

For many visitors, the focus of the town is the new **Waterfront** [273 C3]. With a small tower that affords a good overview of the town, and a public jetty, it is a pleasant place to while away an hour or so watching the boats in the harbour. There is a good seafood restaurant, a café and public toilets (with a nominal charge – if they're open).

Walking tour The best way to explore Lüderitz is on foot. The following suggested route takes in a selection of the highlights, but if you'd like to know more, including about the town's architectural heritage, ask at Lüderitz Safaris and Tours (page 276).

Start at the **fountain** [273 B4] opposite the port, at the junction of Diaz and Bismarck streets. This was built in 1967 to mark the advent of a permanent water supply from the Koichab Pan. Continue up Bismarck Street, cross over the railway tracks (still in use) on Bay Road and turn left into Schinz Street. On the left you'll pass the **old post office** [273 B4], built close enough to the railway station to transfer mailbags to and from the train, but now housing the offices of the NWR and MET. At the end of this road, on the corner, are the brightly painted **Lesehalle** [273 C4] or library, and the adjacent **Turnhalle** [273 C4], or gymnastics hall, which dates to 1909 and is still used for public functions – though no longer as a gym. From here, turn right along Ring Street, then left on Bay Road to find the **Town Council** [273 B5] on your left. Built as a school in 1908, its function was soon switched to that of town hall, a purpose which it still fulfils. On the wall in front, the large **blue-and-white tiled mural** was presented to the town by the Portuguese community in 1988 to celebrate the landing of Bartolomeu Dias in 1488. A short detour to the left from here takes you up **Mabel Street** [273 C5], where the houses on the right were built in 1908 for the Imperial German Railway commissioners. Now in private hands, these represent some of Lüderitz's most attractive buildings, and include the Hansa Haus guesthouse (page 278).

Back on Bay Road, continue a little way before turning right across the railway – currently being restored. Almost in front of you is the **Krabbenhöft und Lampe building** [273 B6], constructed in 1910 as a fashionable store trading everything from fancy foodstuffs to fashion. Guesthouse accommodation is now offered on the upper floors (page 278).

Leaving the best until almost last, turn left here up Zeppelin Street and on to Diamantberg to the **Goerke Haus** [273 A6] (page 282), undoubtedly one of the town's architectural highlights and well worth a visit in its own right. From here, walk downhill then back up to another Lüderitz landmark, **Felsenkirche** [273 A6] (page 282), built high on **Diamantberg** and with views across the bay. Finally, make your way back down Berg and Nachtigal streets, passing the striking **bright red building** that started life as a greengrocery before becoming a church, and is now Barrels restaurant. At the end, turn right into Diaz Street, where you'll find the **museum** [273 A4] (page 282). If you've timed it right, and you're here during the afternoon, you may be able to visit at least one of these last three attractions – though opening hours are very limited.

If you've still time (and energy) you could continue to **Shark Island** [273 A1], now joined to the mainland by a causeway and the relatively new harbour development. Most people visit only if they're staying here, but it's a pleasant – if windy – walk past the harbour and boatyard, and gives a hint of the town's maritime heritage – though there is little to hint at the island's darker past (page 73).

Felsenkirche [273 A6] (⊕ *Apr–Aug 16.00–17.00 Mon–Sat; donations welcome*)
From almost every angle on land and sea, this small, rather stark Lutheran church, whose name translates as 'Church of the Rock', is clearly visible. Located close to the Goerke Haus, it was built in 1912 and has some stunning stained-glass windows; the altar window was a gift from German Chancellor Bismarck.

Museum [273 A4] (✆ *063 202532;* ⊕ *15.30–17.00 Mon–Fri except hols; admission N\$15 pp*)
Built by German schoolchildren in 1968, this small museum opposite the Bay View Hotel on Diaz Street has exhibits on the diamond-mining industry (including fake diamonds), an egg collection, a good section on the Bushmen, a variety of small exhibits on other indigenous cultures, and assorted cases of local flora and fauna.

Goerke Haus [273 A6] (*Zeppelin St;* ⊕ *14.00–16.00 Mon–Fri, 16.00–17.00 Sat–Sun, closed public hols; admission N\$25 pp*)
High up on Diamantberg, Goerke Haus is the beautiful cream building with a blue roof that is built into the rocks above the level of the road. The town's best-preserved historical building, visible from afar, it is one of Lüderitz's so-called 'diamond palaces', thought to have been designed by a German architect, Otto Ertl.

The original owner, Hans Goerke, was born in Germany in 1874 and arrived in German South West Africa with the Schutztruppe in 1904. In 1907 he became provisions inspector for the German forces – just before diamonds were discovered near Kolmanskop. By the end of 1909 he had resigned from the army and was making a fortune in the diamond rush, which enabled him to have this house built. When completed in 1910, it was valued at 70,000 Deutschmarks (£3,500/US\$5,250).

Goerke himself returned to Germany in 1912. In 1920 the house was bought by CDM, but in 1944 they sold it back to the government of South West Africa for £2,404 (US\$3,606), and the house became the residence of the local magistrate. When, in 1981, the magistrate was recalled to Keetmanshoop – Lüderitz just didn't have enough crime – the CDM repurchased the house and restored it for use by their visitors.

Although the house was built during the Art Nouveau period (Jugendstil in German), it isn't typical of that style. Nevertheless, an informative leaflet notes some of the relevant details to look out for, including the flamingo motifs on the stained-glass windows and the decorative detail on either side of the hat-and-coat stand in the hall, resembling Egyptian papyrus bells. Typical of Art Nouveau, too, is the mix of artistic styles, seen in the Roman arches over the stairwell, supported by an Egyptian lotus column, and capped by a Grecian Doric capital, while the posts at the foot of the stairs resemble dentilled Gothic spires.

The house retains many original features, and others – such as the carpets, curtains and friezes – have been restored or replicated. Although there have been moves to have the original furniture returned from South Africa, the current furniture is beautiful, from the piano with ivory keys to marble-topped dressing tables in the bedrooms and oak furniture around the lounge. Don't miss it.

Diamantberg [273 B6] Behind Goerke Haus, Diamantberg is the highest land around town. With a pair of stout shoes you can easily scramble up for a good view of the town and harbour beyond. Standing in the cool sea breeze, under desert sun, much about the landscape seems extreme. There is little vegetation to soften the parched land, while the sea beyond seems cold and uninviting. However, as if to compensate, the townspeople have painted many of their buildings in soft pastel shades. Quaintly shaped wooden buildings, just a few storeys high and painted baby-blue, pink and green, all give Lüderitz the air of a pleasant, gentle town.

EXCURSIONS FROM LÜDERITZ

If you have your own transport then Lüderitz Peninsula, Agate Beach and Kolmanskop are well worth visiting. To see some of the area to the south of Lüderitz, in the Sperrgebiet – the restricted diamond area – you must join an organised tour. There is also an excellent boat trip from the harbour.

BOAT TRIPS Weather permitting, boat trips leave the harbour [273 C2] at around 08.00 for a 2-hour trip (*N$450 pp*) past the whaling station at Sturmvogel Bucht, around Diaz Point and on to Halifax Island in search of African penguins, seals and the endemic Heaviside's dolphin. While visitors are almost guaranteed to see these creatures, keep your eyes open and you'll spot plenty of birds as well, from scoters and various species of cormorant to oystercatchers and flamingos. Sadly, the traditional schooner, *Sedina*, is no longer in service, but you can still set sail in a motorised catamaran; both services operate on near-identical routes.

◢◣ **Penguin Catamaran Tours** m 081 200 0978; e penguincatamaran@gmail.com; www. penguincatamarantours.com

◢◣ **Zeepaard** ☏063 202173; m 081 604 2805; e zeepaardboattours@gmail.com. This long-standing operation is run by the knowledgeable Heiko Metzger, with considerable respect for the wildlife.

AGATE BEACH This windswept beach is a 5km drive north of Lüderitz, alongside fenced-off areas of the Sperrgebiet National Park that add to the air of desolation, particularly in winter. To get there, follow the signs out of Lüderitz along the coast road from the corner of Tal and Hamburger streets, pass Lüderitz Secondary School on the right and the town sewage works, then just keep going. On the way, you'll pass a pond to the right of the road which attracts small numbers of flamingos and other waterbirds, while nearby the odd springbok or oryx takes advantage of a patch of green around the water-treatment plant.

The beach stretches a long way and is fun for beachcombers. The sand is sprinkled with fragments of shining mica and the occasional agate – whose occurrence depends on the winds and the swell. Sometimes you will find nothing; at others – especially at low tide – you can pick up a handful in a few hours. The beach's braai spots and picnic tables make it a popular place at weekends, and swimming, too, is an (albeit chilly) option.

LÜDERITZ PENINSULA To the southwest of the town lies the Lüderitz Peninsula, bordered by the sea on three sides yet a rocky desert within. Here, the lower slopes are dotted with a surprising variety of salt-tolerant succulent plants. In winter, if there's been some good rain, many of these are in flower, affording scope for hours of plant spotting. Around the coast there are some rocky beaches and some sandy

12

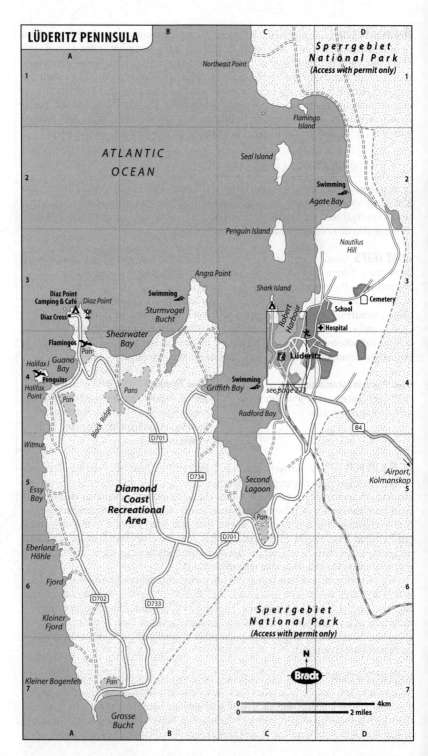

LÜDERITZ PENINSULA

A   **B**   **C**   **D**

Sperrgebiet National Park (Access with permit only)

Northeast Point

ATLANTIC OCEAN

Flamingo Island

Seal Island

Swimming
Agate Bay

Penguin Island

Nautilus Hill

Angra Point

Shark Island

Swimming

Diaz Point Camping & Café
Diaz Point
Diaz Cross
Sturmvogel Bucht
Robert Harbour

Cemetery
School
Hospital

Shearwater Bay

Flamingos
Pan

Lüderitz

Halifax I
Guano Bay
Penguins
Halifax Point
Pan

Pans

Swimming
Griffith Bay
see page 273

Witmun
Black Ridge

D701

Radford Bay

B4

Essy Bay

D734

Diamond Coast Recreational Area

Second Lagoon
Pan

Airport, Kolmanskop

Eberlanz Höhle

Fjord

D701

D702

Kleiner Fjord

D733

Sperrgebiet National Park (Access with permit only)

N

Bradt

Kleiner Bogenfels
Pan

Grosse Bucht

0   4km
0   2 miles

ones; all are worth exploring. Note that while the roads here are fine for 2WD cars, don't be tempted to follow tracks across soft sand made by local 4x4 enthusiasts, or you'll need their help to pull your vehicle out. Note, too, that the pans in this area are favourite nesting spots for the rare Damara tern, which is another important reason to stay on the tracks. Easier to spot are flamingos, swift terns and the occasional African black oystercatcher.

To reach the peninsula, simply follow the B4 out of town for about 2km, where there's a turning clearly signposted to the right. If you'd prefer a tour, this can be arranged through Lüderitz Safaris and Tours (page 276) from around N$500 for 2 hours. Aside from at Diaz Point, there are no facilities except a few old toilet blocks.

The most interesting parts of the peninsula are:

Radford Bay [284 C4] This is reached shortly after leaving the town, and is often home to a flock of flamingos.

Second Lagoon [284 C5] Also popular with visiting flamingos, and sometimes the odd stranded motorist. Continuing to the right, you'll come to…

Griffith Bay [284 B4] Excellent views of the town across the cold, misty sea, plus a few crystal-clear rock pools to dabble in. It is named after an American officer who sheltered here and was later killed during the American Civil War.

Sturmvogel Bucht [284 B3] The whaling station here can no longer be visited by boat, but is visible from the sea as part of a boat trip.

Diaz Point [284 A3] Reached by a short wooden bridge is a granite cross, a replica of the one erected by Bartolomeu Dias, the first European explorer to enter the bay. He sheltered here on 25 July 1488, referring to the bay as Angra Pequena, or 'Little Bay'. There are often seals sunning themselves on the rocks here. Just south of Diaz Point is a grave bearing a stark reminder: 'George Pond of London, died here of hunger and thirst 1906'. Today a small café saves visitors from the same fate.

⌐ Where to stay and eat

⋀ **Diaz Point Campsite** [284 A3] (camping) **m** 081 239 8055. After a 20km drive from Lüderitz across a lunar landscape, it's easy to feel you've got lost on the way to this campsite at the tip of the peninsula – but keep going! Though nowadays it may not be worth your while. This once well-run & pleasant if slightly quirky campsite & café has become something of a drinking den for locals now that the delightful Regina Korff no longer runs it. Despite the unusual bunkhouses made of boats, it feels more like a bar than a campsite, yet it does have a unique location & if you choose a quiet spot & cater for yourself it might still be an interesting stop for a night. *N$80 pp.* **$**

Guano Bay [284 A4] Another good place to spot flamingos, either from land or from the sea.

Halifax Island [284 A4] The large African penguin colony here can be viewed with a good pair of binoculars from the cliffs and beaches on the western side of Guano Bay, or – closer up – from the deck of a boat (page 283). The empty houses you can see belonged to guano collectors.

Essy Bay [284 A5] A number of very rocky little bays, each with a place for a braai. All are linked by a network of good sand roads.

Eberlanz Höhle [284 A6] A cave cut deeply into the rock, about 10 minutes' walk from the road; there's a path marked over the rocks.

Kleiner Fjord [284 A6] A small sandy beach with deep water and lots of kelp, unsuitable for swimming.

Grosse Bucht [284 A7] A wide sandy beach with dark sand, long stranded pieces of kelp, plenty of kelp flies, and several turn-off points for stopping. The sand is dotted with mounds of salt-tolerant succulent plants in beautiful greens and reds, and the bay is perfect for accomplished windsurfers and kiteboarders, with very strong winds.

SPERRGEBIET NATIONAL PARK The Sperrgebiet, or 'forbidden zone', was first declared in 1908. Then mining was confined to within a few kilometres of the coast, while a coastal belt 100km wide was declared 'out of bounds' as a precaution to prevent unauthorised people from reaching the diamond fields. At the height of restrictions there were two diamond areas: No 1 from the Orange River to 26°S, and No 2 from 26°S northward to the Kuiseb, incorporating most of Namibia's great dune sea. Over the years these areas have shrunk, leaving – until recently – only parts of No 1 as forbidden. Then, in 2009, the whole area, as far south as the Orange River and north to Lüderitz and beyond, was designated a national park. Covering 26,000km², the new park is in its infancy and it will take some time before NAMDEB has restored much of the damage caused by mining. In the meantime, security remains tight. Signs by the roadside threatening fines or imprisonment for entering these areas unaccompanied remain serious.

History and archaeology Archaeologists estimate that early Stone Age people inhabited the area around the Orange River at least 300,000 years ago, while the presence of rock art indicates that their descendants made their way inland. It wasn't until the 15th century that the first Europeans – Portuguese sailors – arrived here. As trading in international waters increased, so did the value of the ships' cargo – borne out by the discovery in 2008 of a 16th-century Portuguese ship beneath the sands. Carrying a cargo of over 2,000 heavy gold coins, as well as ivory, astrolabes and a veritable arsenal of weapons, the *Bom Jesus* was part of a fleet that left Lisbon in early 1533 in search of fortune. That it sank in foul weather off a coast where diamonds were for the taking is a cruel irony.

Later sailors, the whalers and sealers of the 19th century, sought less glamorous bounty, trading with the small Khoi communities they found along the coast. The discovery in the 20th century of diamonds – riches beyond the wildest dreams of the early traders and prospectors – was almost by chance.

Flora and fauna Lack of human intervention within most of the Sperrgebiet for almost a century has left a remarkable diversity of wildlife. Plants, in particular, have thrived, with over a thousand species identified: almost a quarter of Namibia's total, qualifying the Sperrgebiet as one of the world's top 34 biodiversity hotspots. Many of these are succulents that bring bursts of colour to the desert during the rainy season.

A total of 215 bird species has been identified within the park as a whole, many of them congregating at its southern edge, in the wetlands at the mouth of the Orange River. The authorities claim that 80 species of mammal live within the park confines, too, including the solitary brown hyena, and a further 38 marine mammal species offshore.

Getting there and permits The most readily accessible area within the new national park is Kolmanskop, which you can visit in your own car, provided that you buy a permit in advance (page 276). Trips to Elizabeth Bay or Bogenfels, however, must be booked well in advance. In order to obtain a permit, you will need to give a copy of your passport with your full name, ID number and nationality to the relevant tour operator (page 277) *at least* two working days before the trip. Note that visitors may not take anything out of the area, including rock samples – take note, all amateur geologists. Vehicles coming from the Sperrgebiet remain subject to random searches by NAMDEB officials.

Kolmanskop (↖ 063 204031; ☉ 08.00–13.00 *daily, or longer with photographer's pass; admission N$90/55 adult/child; photographer's pass N$200*) In truth, most travellers come to Lüderitz just to visit this now-famous ghost town. Once the principal town of the local diamond industry, it was abandoned in 1956 – with the final three families admitting defeat in 1959 – and now gives a fascinating insight into the area's great diamond boom. In its heyday, the town was home to over 300 adults and 44 children, and luxuries included a bowling alley, iced refrigerators and even a swimming pool. A few of the buildings, including the imposing concert hall, have been restored, but many are left exactly as they were deserted, and are gradually being buried by the surrounding dunes.

In a room adjacent to the concert hall, there is a simple café-style restaurant (☉ 09.00–13.00 *Mon–Sat*). Do make time to look at the photographs that adorn the walls, from early mining pictures to some chilling reminders of the far-reaching effects of Nazi Germany.

A century since diamonds were first discovered here, it's now possible to buy diamonds in the 'Diamond Room', with prices upwards from N$500. There's also a display charting the history of the diamond boom and the people with whom it is inextricably linked.

Getting there and other practicalities Kolmanskop is just beside the main B4 road, 9km east of Lüderitz. At present, you can buy a permit in advance from Lüderitz Safaris and Tours (page 276); or at the entrance gate – which is particularly useful if you're travelling from Aus along the B4, but note that the system may change if/when the MET takes back ownership of the concession in the future. The N$90 permit includes a 45-minute guided tour departing from the main hall at 09.30 and 11.00; travellers are split into English- and German-speaking groups. If you'd like to be there earlier or later, buy a photographer's pass. This also includes a guided tour, but allows you to park outside the gate and visit at any time between sunrise and sunset, for as long as you like, giving the chance to absorb the eerie atmosphere without other visitors. Because the town faces east, the best photographs are taken in the morning. Arrive early, take your photographs without other visitors around, and have a quick snack in the on-site café before joining the first guided tour. And note that all visitors are permitted to take photographs; a photographer's pass simply buys you more time.

Elizabeth Bay This south-facing bay, 40km south of Lüderitz, has a band of diamond-bearing coarse grits and sands measuring about 3km by 5km. It was mined from 1911 to 1948, and then reopened in about 1991. Despite a projected minimum lifespan of ten years, the owners announced in 2018 that they were seeking a buyer to extend its lifespan beyond its projected closure in 2019.

Guided tours pass into the Sperrgebiet through the Kolmanskop gate, and from there to Elizabeth Bay. The scenery on the way is mostly flat gravel plains, with

Kolmanskop, or 'Kolman's hill', was originally a small hill named after a delivery rider, Kolman, who used to rest his horses there.

In April 1908, Zacharias Lewala was working nearby when he picked a rough diamond from the ground. He took this to his German foreman, August Stauch, who posted a claim to the area, and then got the backing of several of the railway's directors to start prospecting. Stauch exhibited some of his finds in June 1908, prompting an immediate response: virtually everybody who could rushed into the desert to look for diamonds. Famously, in some places they could be picked up by the handful in the moonlight.

T V Bulpin (page 576) records the story of one resident, Dr Scheibe, going prospecting:

> While he plotted his position on a map, he told his servants to look for diamonds. One of them simply went down on his knees, filled both hands with diamonds, and even stuffed some into his mouth. Dr Scheibe stared at the scene in amazement, repeating over and over again, *'Ein Märchen, ein Märchen'* ('A fairytale, a fairytale').

This first large deposit at Kolmanskop lay in the gravel of a dry river-bed, so soon a mine and a boom town developed there. Deposits were found all over the coastal region and around Lüderitz. Quickly, in September 1908, the German colonial government proclaimed a *Sperrgebiet* – a forbidden zone – to restrict further prospecting, and to license what was already happening.

Between 1908 and the start of World War I over five million carats of diamonds were found, but the war disrupted production badly. At the end of it, Sir Ernest Oppenheimer obtained options on many of the German mining companies for South Africa's huge Anglo-American Corporation, joining ten of them into Consolidated Diamond Mines (CDM) of South West Africa. In 1922–23, CDM obtained exclusive diamond rights for 50 years over a coastal belt 95km wide, stretching 350km north of the Orange River, from the new South African administrators of South West Africa. These were later extended to the year 2010, allowing NAMDEB to control the country's diamond production for 20 years following independence. Although these rights have now theoretically lapsed, the government is a 50% shareholder in the business, and little has changed.

Meanwhile many small towns like Kolmanskop were flush with money. It had a butcher's, a baker's and a general shop; a large theatre, community hall and school; factories for furniture, ice, lemonade and soda water; a hospital with the region's first X-ray machine; comfortable staff quarters, elaborate homes for the managers – and a seawater pool fed by water pumped from 35km away. Yet Kolmanskop was fortunate: it was next to the main railway line. Other deposits were less accessible, far from water or transport – and many such early mines still lie half-buried in the Namib.

some dunes as you approach the coast. This is a chance to see the working diamond mine, albeit from a distance.

Getting there and away Namib Off Road Excursions (page 277) runs half-day trips (⏲ *08.30–about 13.00, Mon–Fri, 4–8 people; N$700 pp based on 4 people*), including a light snack. No children under 14 are permitted. It's important to book in advance as it takes at least 24 hours to get the requisite permits – and it's far safer to allow at least two working days.

Pomona/Bogenfels

A day trip into the Sperrgebiet as far as Bogenfels covers some 265km on mostly good gravel roads, passing through areas of considerable historical, geological and botanical interest. On the way you'll visit the ghost town of Pomona and the Idatel or Märchental ('fairytale valley'), famous for the diamonds that were collected here by moonlight.

Where it has been untouched by diamond mining, much of the environment is pristine, but many of the diamond areas have been ravaged by the industry, leaving behind expanses of bare rock devoid of sand and without a hint of vegetation. In some areas there is shining dolomite rock, its colours varying in the sun from blue or pink to pure white. In the occasional winter, if there has been some rain, other areas are alight with colour from numerous plants, many of them seen only once every ten years or so, taking advantage of nature's brief bounty. Here, in among grey scrubby plants, are the soft green of new grasses, the bright pink Bushman's candle, and the milk bush, favoured by oryx; here too are the so-called 'window' plants, whose leaf tips feature tiny windows that allow light through to the main plant buried below, so that photosynthesis can take place inside the plant.

Pomona itself once housed over a thousand people, of whom some 300–400 were German, and the rest black Namibian workers, the latter living in huts that accommodated up to 50 people. While the black workers were on fixed-term contracts, away from their families, whole clans of Germans lived here, with their own school, church, hotel and even a bowling alley. Water was brought in by narrow-gauge railway from Grillen Tal, several kilometres away, where the crumbling ruins of the main pump station can still be explored.

In the early years, a claim could be bought for 60 Deutschmarks, rising to a staggering 6,000DM by 1917–18. Diamonds were not mined, but were sifted by hand with great trommel sieves, their rusting frames now good only for photographers.

The third mining town in the area was at Bogenfels, where a small desalination plant is still to be seen right on the beach. The main attraction for visitors, though, is the spectacular rock arch that stands about 55m high beside the sea. Despite its inaccessibility, photographs have made it one of the south's better-known landmarks.

Getting there and away Full-day guided tours are run by Coastways Tours (page 277), departing from Lüderitz at around 08.30 and returning around 17.00. Costs are N$1,950 per person, including national park fees and lunch, based on a minimum of four people. As with Elizabeth Bay, you need to book at least two working days in advance in order to get the permits.

Future possibilities

Several options for opening more of the park to visitors are under consideration, along with the establishment of some basic restcamps. Guided hiking trails and drives are strong contenders, as are visits to various fossil and archaeological sites, diamond mines, shipwrecks and seal and seabird colonies. One significant attraction in its own right is the **Roter Kamm Crater**, west of Rosh Pinah. Said to be the fourth-largest meteorite crater in the world, it can be viewed from the Aurusberg Mountain, which itself has a botanical hiking trail.

Oranjemund

This prosperous mining town in the far southwest corner of Namibia is the headquarters of NAMDEB, who for many years have owned all the property – hence daily Air Namibia flights linking the town with Windhoek.

Without an invitation from a resident, and the permission of NAMDEB, visitors have usually been forbidden entrance. Even then, those leaving the mining area have had to pass strict X-ray checks, which search for hidden diamonds. According to the MET, the town will 'soon' be open to visitors, with opportunities for exploring the new national park, and the mouth of the Orange River, from its southern boundary. However, this has been the case for more than a decade while the authorities are tangling with various legal issues, so don't hold your breath.

NORTH OF THE B4

HELMERINGHAUSEN Despite being a large dot on the map, Helmeringhausen is little more than a homestead with a shop and fuel station in the middle of some very scenic roads. Just to the north are flat plains with little hills of balancing rocks – rather like the cairns found on Scottish mountains, only somewhat bigger.

Heading southwest on the C13 towards Lüderitz, the road winds down and opens out into an immense valley – a huge plain lined by mountains with a clear escarpment on the east, and a more ragged array – the Tiras Mountains – to the west. It is spectacular, especially at sunset.

Helmeringhausen itself feels like an oasis. There is the well-stocked **Helmering Winkel shop** (⊕ *08.00–17.00 Mon–Fri*) for basics and a vital **fuel station** (⊕ *08.00–17.00 Mon–Fri*) beside it.

🏠 **Where to stay and eat** In addition to the local hotel, there are a handful of excellent small guest farms around here. Dabis makes a natural overnight stop when driving between the Fish River Canyon and the Sesriem area, while Namtib (and others in the Tiras Mountains; see opposite) is also a candidate if you are travelling between Lüderitz or Aus and Sesriem. It seems like a large area, but the community is, in fact, very close-knit and most of the guest-farm owners socialise together regularly.

🏠 **Helmeringhausen Hotel & Guest Farm** (22 rooms, camping, house) 📞063 283307; e helmering@iway.na; www. helmeringhausennamibia.com. A classic example of an original, rustic Namibian guest farm, the hotel was founded in 1938 but has expanded considerably in recent years. It continues to offer simple en-suite rooms with twin beds curtained by mosquito nets. There is safe parking at the back (though it's difficult to imagine a crime problem here), & a few tables & chairs around a small pool with a braai area. For winter evenings, there's a separate lounge with a fireplace & even a piano, while for the more energetic, hikes or farm drives can be arranged.

Lunch & a set 3-course dinner are available in the restaurant, which is open for afternoon tea & snacks too. The adjacent coffee shop is a magnet for passing drivers, drawn to light lunches or fresh apple crumble in a shady garden with lawns & picnic tables. A row of vines separates this from a campsite with 6 neat pitches, & opposite is a self-

catering house for up to 6 people. Sadly there have been reports of the owners behaving very rudely, so do bear this in mind – and report back to Bradt. *N$835/1,350 sgl/dbl; camping N$250 pp.* **$$$**

Nearby guest farms

🏠 **Dabis Guest Farm** [266 D2] (11 rooms) 📞063 283300; e gaugler@farmdabis.com; www. farmdabis.com. Owned by the Gaugler family for 4 generations, since 1926, Dabis is currently run by Jörg & Michelle Gaugler (& their 4 children!). From its entrance on the C14, 10km north of Helmeringhausen, it's a further 7km down a track with some steep dips & humps (still manageable in a 2WD) to the old farmhouse, in a valley surrounded by hills.

Dabis has achieved an effective balance between welcoming guests – including day visitors with advance notice – & operating as a farm. It's a personal place, & near to self-sufficiency, with home-grown vegetables & fruits, homemade jam (which you can buy), & farm-reared sheep bred for lamb production & leather, using advanced rotation techniques to survive on the meagre rainfall. Be sure to sample their homemade smoked meats.

Accommodation is in comfortable en-suite twin rooms, 2 with outside bathrooms & 1 with a bath. Guests benefit from a swimming pool & tennis court in very good condition (racquets available), but one of the main attractions of staying here is learning about the farm. Most guests arrive in time for coffee & cake at 16.00, then go out on a complimentary farm drive for an hour or 2, when Jörg will explain his techniques in depth, as well as ecology & sustainability issues, considerably enriching a visit. If you're lucky, you may spot one of the small animals on the farm, such as bat-eared foxes. *DBB N$1,990/3,330 sgl/dbl.* **$$$$**

🏠 **Lovedale Farm Holidays** [266 D2] (3 self-catering units, camping) 14km along the C27 from Helmeringhausen, just off road; m 081 281 9074; e stay@lovedale-namibia.com; www.lovedale-namibia.com. Malcolm & Louisa Campbell run this Jersey stud & Swakara sheep farm, whose fully equipped self-catering units sleeping 2–7 people have their own braai areas; braai packs (*N$230*), eggs, butter & cream are all available. Furnishings are simple & rustic. The soft-sand shady campsite has hot showers, electricity & toilets. Activities include a self-guided 45min 2km walking trail, birdwatching & stargazing. *From N$400/690 sgl/ dbl.* **$$**

⚐ **Farm Aubures** [266 C2] 🕿 063 683314; e amiller@iway.na. 51km up the C27 from Helmeringhausen, along a 5km driveway, this working sheep farm is run by Adrienne & Jörn Miller. Their campsite, with 6 pitches, is 1km from the farmhouse, & has flushing toilets & hot-water geysers but no electricity. *Camping N$150/100 adult/child.* **$$**

TIRAS MOUNTAINS
Dominating the skyline southwest of Helmeringhausen, and fringing the Namib's red dunes, the jagged Tiras Mountains are increasingly attracting visitors. This little-visited area is characterised by vegetated apricot dunes, rugged hills and gravel plains. Don't expect lots of wildlife; all the desert favourites are here, but in low numbers.

Linking the C13 in the south to the C27/D407 is the scenic D707 which, although gaining a reputation for being quite dangerous, takes in the beauty of both mountains and dunes.

🛏 **Where to stay** The pick of the accommodation options here is Namtib Biosphere Reserve. Others fall within an area of 125,000ha that has been loosely designated by a group of local farmers as the Tiras Berge Conservancy. Accommodation listed below is roughly clockwise from the south.

🏠 **Farm Tiras** [266 D3] (chalet, hut, camping) 🕿 063 283350; m (WhatsApp) 081 314 2375. Just off the main C13, 42km south of Helmeringhausen, this cattle farm run by Anita Koch is an oasis of green among flaxen grasses. On the farm itself there's a smart self-catering chalet, while across the road are a campsite, & a 1-room hut with outdoor bathroom & good views. You're welcome to charge your phone at the house, but there's no internet. *Chalet N$590/1,000 sgl/dbl; hut N$390/640; camping N$180 pp.* **$$–$$$**

✳🏠 **Kanaan Desert Retreat** [266 C2] (8 tents, camping) 🕿 063 683119; e kanaan@ naankuse.com; www.kanaannamibia.com. The newest addition to the N/a'an ku sê collection (page 122), Kanaan sits in a 33,000ha private reserve bordering the Namib-Naukluft National Park (page 295). The scenery is beautiful & as a place to stop for a night on the journey north from Aus/Lüderitz it is probably our favourite option. Or stay for a couple of nights & enjoy scenic drives, horseriding or the opportunity to watch the 2 rescued, unreleasable cheetah that are kept in a large enclosure. The lodge itself is relatively simple & blends nicely into the surroundings. The stylish main area is perched on top of a hill, with stilted tents on a lower contour of the same hill. These have twin beds with mosquito nets, a fan, wardrobe, desk & en-suite bathroom with a shower, toilet & washbasin. There are also 8 shaded camping pitches, each with its own private ablutions. *DBB N$2,500/4,520 sgl/dbl; camping N$175 pp.* **$$–$$$$$**

Namtib Biosphere Reserve [266 C3]
063 683055; e stay@namtib.net; www.namtib.
net. Nestled in an isolated valley surrounded by
mountains, & overlooking the edge of the desert
plain, Namtib lies 12km east of the scenic D707.
It is clearly signposted (as Namtib Desert Lodge)
from the C27/D407 (76km) & the C13 (47km).

Don't be put off by the name: this is not a
scientific project, but a welcoming lodge &
campsite with a personal feel, run on strongly
ecological lines by Thorsten & Linn Theile. Theirs
is a working farm, with klipspringer, oryx &
springbok roaming the plains. It is also favoured
by Rüppell's korhaan & the rare endemic dune lark.
The evasive kudu inhabits the gorges & mountains,
where black eagles nest & leopard, cheetah &
caracal are hidden. There are some rock hyraxes
around as well, not to mention bat-eared fox,
aardwolf & porcupine. Visitors can explore on foot,
perhaps on the waymarked botanical trail in the
kopjes, which are also suitable for mountain bikes
(bring your own), or go on guided nature drives
(N$400/3hrs) to gain a deeper insight into life at
the edge of the desert. It all adds up to a good
stopover, or a place to relax for several days.

NAMTIB DESERT LODGE (8 rooms) The
original simple chalets are unusually designed,
comfortable & clean, with twin or dbl beds, & a
private bathroom separated from the room by a
small open-air quadrangle, where many guests
choose to sleep in the heat of the summer. A
further 3 rooms (2 sgl, 1 family) are in a separate
building. Electricity is from a generator & lights
are battery powered but, for those who have long
appreciated the simplicity at Namtib, candles are
still provided in the rooms. Candlelight plays a part
in the extensive lounge & dining area, too, where
guests can relax in front of the fire or drink a cool
beer, & where delicious home-cooked 3-course
meals are served *en famille* (lunch N$130, dinner
N$260). There's a small book exchange & Wi-Fi.
N$1,440/1,920 sgl/dbl. $$$$

LITTLE HUNTER'S REST (5 pitches) About 2.5km
from the lodge is a separate campsite, in a
beautiful location backed by mountains &
overlooking the plains & the desert beyond.
Pitches are widely spread under camelthorn trees
& there's a central ablution block, but no electricity.
Provisions such as firewood & meat are available;
alternatively, campers may have dinner at the
lodge, space permitting. N$170 pp. $$

Koiimasis Ranch [266 C2] (6 chalets,
camping) 063 683052; e koiimasis@yahoo.com;
www.namibia-farm-lodge.com. Located along a
20km 4x4 track east of the D707, this ranch is run
by Wolf & Anke Izko, who offer 6 chalets – 2 of
them self-catering & camping. DBB N$2,530/4,100
sgl/dbl; self-catering N$800/1,600 sgl/dbl; camping
N$200 pp. $$–$$$$$

MALTAHÖHE This small town is an important crossroads, as it is linked by the
tarred C19 to the main north–south B1. Although it is sometimes used by budget
travellers as a base to visit Sossusvlei, the round-trip distance of over 340km is off-
putting. For most visitors, the town and its immediate environs are too far from
the desert to be of major interest. The most interesting attraction locally is virtually
unknown. About 30km north of here, on the farm Sandfeld, is a fascinating valley
which, when the rains are good, fills with water to a depth of about 30cm. This
doesn't happen every year, but when it does – normally between mid-February and
mid-March – the shallow lake quickly becomes covered in a spectacular bloom of
red, pink and white lilies, *Crinum crinum paludosum*. These last about a week, and
are said to be endemic to the valley, which is known as the 'lily-veld'.

Where to stay and eat There's accommodation in Maltahöhe itself, and Duwisib
Castle is within easy reach. Those going west from the B1 along the C19 might be
interested in Hudup Campsite.

Maltahöhe Hotel (27 rooms, dormitory)
063 293013, 067 240901; e info@maltahoehe-
hotel.com; www.maltahoehe-hotel.com. The
smartest option in town has a glass veranda where
the predominantly German clientele sit at tables
adorned with fresh flowers & sip filter coffee.
There is a well-stocked bar, an à la carte restaurant
serving lunch & dinner, a pool at the rear & a small

internet café. The en-suite dbl & family rooms are clean & cool: tiled floors, good walk-in showers, & fans. There is also an 18-bed dormitory across the road for backpackers & budget travellers. If you're not staying, it's worth popping in for a drink, if only to study the large old map mounted in the bar that shows the allocation of Namibia's farmland. *N$995/1,700 sgl/dbl.* **$$$$**

🏠 **Ôa Hera** (5 dorm rooms, camping) 📞 063 293028; **m** 081 215 2595; **e** oaheraa@iway.na. Ôa Hera, meaning 'that which is sought after', started life as a warehouse-style art gallery & craft centre (🕐 *08.00–17.00 daily*). Affiliated to the Red Stone restaurant, & located at the western end of town, it is now increasingly popular with backpackers. Affordable accommodation is in small rooms with a dbl or bunk beds, sharing a bathroom. There's free (slow) Wi-Fi.

In the funky, semicircular restaurant, orange poles support swathes of hessian, affording shade, while succulent plants in terracotta pots, unusual sculptures & brightly painted concrete tables & benches rest on the gravel floor. It's a cool, pleasant place for a good bite to eat – from toasted sandwiches to more substantial fare such as game goulash; most of the veg come from their own garden. *Dorm bed N$160 pp; camping N$70 pp.* **$–$$**

⛺ **Hudup Campsite** [266 D1] 📞 063 293512; **e** ottohunt@mweb.com.na. Signposted around 300m from the C19, this rustic site is idyllically sited on a tributary of the Fish River about 13km east of Maltahöhe. There are BBQ areas & clean ablution facilities, but often you'll have just ground squirrels, lizards & the wind in the trees for company. In theory, hiking trails & game drives can be organised. *N$160 per vehicle (2–4 people).* **$**

Other practicalities The town has a **fuel station** (with an ATM), a **Standard Bank** (🕐 *Mon & Fri only*), and a useful **information office** at the Maltahöhe Hotel. There are also a few **shops**, including **Pappot** (📞 *063 293 397;* **e** *pappot@mweb.com. na;* 🕐 *06.00–19.00 Mon–Sat*), which stocks most of the essentials, including bread, meat and eggs, and has a small **campsite** (*N$120 pp;* **$**).

DUWISIB CASTLE [266 C1] (📞 *063 295030/1;* **m** *081 291 5280;* 🕐 *08.00–13.00 & 14.00–17.00 daily; admission N$70 pp*) Standing solidly amid the rolling hills beside the D826, 72km southwest of Maltahöhe, the sandstone fortress of Duwisib Castle is another of those anachronisms in which Namibia seems to specialise. Look from a distance and you won't believe it: a small, square castle with fortified battlements and high turrets in the middle of the African bush.

The castle (now incorporating some guest rooms) is built around an open central quadrangle, where there is now a small lawn and fountain, shaded by a couple of beautiful jacaranda trees. Its rooms are sparsely furnished, though there are some excellent original pieces dating back to around the turn of the 20th century, and interesting paintings and prints on the walls – many equestrian in theme. Above the entrance hall is a steep set of stairs (easily missed) up to a small gallery overlooking the entrance, and there is also a cellar, which has been converted into a rather dingy bar.

History The castle's history has been documented in an excellent booklet by Dr N Mossolow (page 573), available at the castle. It tells how Hansheinrich von Wolf was born in 1873 into a military family in Saxony and served with the Royal Saxon Artillery near Dresden. He came to South West Africa as a captain in the Schutztruppe, when he volunteered after the outbreak of the Herero War. He was decorated in 1905, and returned to Germany where he married Miss Jayta Humphrey in 1907.

Later that year he and his wife returned to German South West Africa, and over the next few years bought up farming land in the area. By October 1908 he had '33 horses, 68 head of large stock and 35 head of small stock' on his farm, and two wells. An 'extravagant residence of undressed stone, with 22 rooms and a cellar' had reached

2m above its foundations. He bought up more farmland, up to 50,000ha, and by 1909 the castle was complete, with furnishings and paintings imported from Germany.

Von Wolf proceeded to enlarge the area under his control by buying more land. A fanatical horseman and breeder of horses, he spent much time and energy developing his stable (see box, page 270).

In 1914 he set off with his wife to England, to purchase another thoroughbred stallion, but on the way war broke out. The ship diverted to South America, where they were briefly interned before he arranged a secret passage back to Europe. Eventually they arrived back in Germany where von Wolf reported for duty as an officer. On 4 September 1916 he was killed at the Battle of the Somme.

🏠 Where to stay

🏠 **Duwisib Castle** [266 C1] (5 rooms, camping) \061 725 4800; e reservations@nwr. com.na; www.nwr.com.na. Now under NWR ownership, the castle fell into a poor state of repair before being renovated in 2014, when the rooms around the courtyard were converted into guest rooms. There is also a small informal restaurant ($) with tables under cover around the quad. *N$970/1,940 sgl/dbl; camping N$150 pp.* **$$–$$$$**

🏠 **Duwisib Guest Farm** [266 C1] (8 rooms, 1 bungalow, camping) \063 293344; e duwisib@ iway.na; www.farmduwisib.com. On the D826 within walking distance of Duwisib Castle, this working cattle & goat farm is owned & run by Christian Frank-Schultz. Choose from castle-view en-suite rooms, a fully equipped self-catering family room & the twin-bed self-catering Springbok bungalow. There are also 5 camping pitches nestling in a picturesque valley below, & sharing ablutions. Excellent farmhouse cooking makes it worth prebooking meals (*b/fast N$140, dinner N$220*), & wood is available. The reception/shop/dining area doubles as a café during the day for visitors to the castle. *DBB room 1,180/2,080 sgl/dbl; self-catering bungalow N$930 per night; camping N$130 pp.* **$–$$$$**

BETTA The small settlement of Betta, 20km west of Duwisib Castle at the crossroads of the D826 and C27, is a veritable oasis for those travelling between Sesriem and Aus. Notable for the presence of a cash-only fuel station (⊕ *24hrs*) that carries out tyre repairs, it also boasts a campsite with self-catering chalets as well, and a small restaurant with a well-stocked shop that usually sells fresh vegetables and fruit, ice creams, wine, firewood, gifts – and homemade cakes.

🏠 Where to stay

🏠 **Betta Camp** [266 C1] (13 chalets, camping) \067 224 0901/3/4; m 081 477 3992; e reservations.betta@travel-weaver.com; www. bettacamp.com. Surrounded by mountains, this spacious level, sandy site is ideal for individuals or groups. Pitches have electricity, a sink area with lockable cupboard stocked with plates, pots, etc, & their own shelter for a car, with the option of sleeping on the roof above if you're after a snake-free zone. If you don't fancy camping, there are fully equipped self-catering chalets with 2 or 4 beds & lovely private bathrooms, all modern & cool with walled verandas – & a welcome lollipop! The restaurant overlooking the pool serves cold drinks, toasted sandwiches, burgers & pies, as well as dinner (*N$120*), available on request. No Wi-Fi. *N$600/950 sgl/dbl; camping N$130 pp.* **$–$$$**

13

The Namib-Naukluft National Park

People have different reactions when they encounter a desert for the first time. A few find it threatening, too arid and empty, so they rush from city to city, through the desert, to avoid spending any time there at all. Some try hard to like it for those same reasons, but ultimately find little which holds their attention. Finally there are those who stop and give the place their time, delighting in the stillness, strange beauty and sheer uniqueness of the environment. The desert's changing patterns and subtly adapted life forms fascinate them, drawing them back time after time.

Covering almost 50,000km², the Namib-Naukluft National Park is one of the largest national parks in Africa, protecting the oldest deserts in the world. The Namib Desert's scenery is stunning, and its wildlife fascinating; you just need to make the time to stop and observe it.

The sections in this chapter run roughly south to north. Note that the NamibRand, Sesriem, the Naukluft and Solitaire are very close together.

HISTORY

The park has grown gradually to its present size. In 1907 the area between the Kuiseb and Swakop rivers was proclaimed as 'Game Reserve No 3'. It was augmented by the addition of Sandwich Harbour in 1941.

In 1956 the Kuiseb Canyon and Swakop River Valley were added, along with the Welwitschia Plains, and in 1968 the park was renamed the Namib Desert Park. In 1979 a large area of what was the protected 'Diamond Area No 2' was added, including Sesriem and Sossusvlei, and the park was officially joined to the Naukluft Park, creating the Namib-Naukluft National Park.

Most recently, in 1986, the rest of 'Diamond Area No 2' was added, taking the park's southern boundary as far south as the main road to Lüderitz, and increasing its area to its present size of 49,768km² – larger than Switzerland, or about the same as Maryland and New Jersey combined.

FLORA AND FAUNA

With a wide variety of fascinating species and unique adaptations, the Namib's community of animals and plants may not be as obviously appealing as those on Africa's grasslands, but it is equally impressive to the informed and observant visitor.

Though the Naukluft's wildlife is discussed separately, the flora and fauna elsewhere in the Namib-Naukluft are similar, dependent more on the landscape than on precise location. (Dr Mary Seely's book, *The Namib*, is a superb and simple guide to this area, widely available in Windhoek and Swakopmund. See page 574) The four basic types of environment found here, and some of their highlights are:

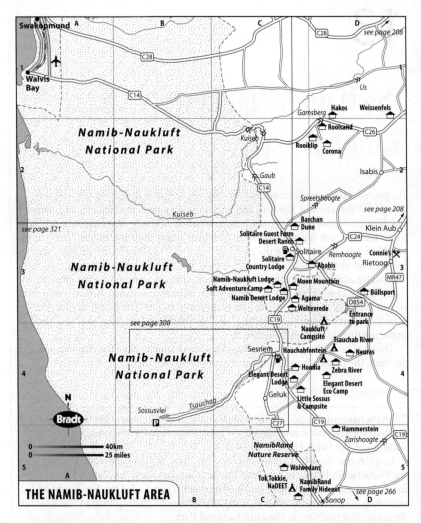

THE NAMIB-NAUKLUFT AREA

SAND DUNES Dunes are everybody's idea of a desert, and generally thought of as being bare and lifeless. While this is not inaccurate for many deserts, the Namib is sufficiently old for endemic species to have evolved.

Various grasses grow on some of the more stable dunes, but most of the vegetable matter comes from wind-blown detritus. This collects at the bottom of the dunes, to be eaten by fish-moths (silverfish), crickets and the many tenebrionid beetles – or *tok tokkies*, as they are known – near the base of the food chain. Particular tenebrionid species occur in specific environments, with those in the coastal fog belt adapting in ingenious ways in order to harness the available moisture.

These then provide food for spiders, geckos, lizards and chameleons which, in turn, fall prey to sidewinder snakes. Rare Grant's golden moles eat any small beetles or larvae that they can catch, and birds are mobile enough to move in and out of the dunes in search of the smaller animals. Endemic to this region is the dune lark, which is seldom found outside the dune areas.

RIVER VALLEYS AND PANS The river valleys that run through the Namib are linear oases. Though dry on the surface, their permanent underground water sustains trees and bushes, like the camelthorn (*Vachellia erioloba*) and nara melon (*Acanthosicyos horrida*), found in the middle of the great dune sea at Sossusvlei.

Other common river-valley trees include the ana or anaboom tree (*Faidherbia albida*); the shepherd's tree (*Boscia albitrunca*), easily identified by its white trunk; the wild green-hair tree (*Parkinsonia africana*) and the marvellously weeping false ebony (*Euclea pseudebenus*).

The lush vegetation found in these valleys makes them a favourite for numerous insects and birds, as well as larger mammals like oryx, kudu and springbok. These are the most likely areas to find nocturnal cats, from leopard to caracal, especially where the rivers cut through mountains rather than dunes.

GRAVEL PLAINS Throughout the desert, and especially north of the Kuiseb River, the Namib has many expansive, flat plains of rock and stone. These come alive during the rains, when they will quickly be covered with tall thin grass and creeping yellow flowers, attracting herds of oryx, springbok and even Hartmann's mountain zebra. During drier times there are fewer large mammals around, but still at night black-backed jackal, aardwolf and the occasional aardvark forage for termites, while bat-eared and Cape foxes scavenge for insects, reptiles, and anything else edible.

Spotted hyena and even the rare brown hyena are sometimes recorded here. Both leave distinctive white droppings, but only the sociable spotted hyenas make such eerie, mournful calls.

Resident larger birds include ostrich, secretary birds, Rüppell's korhaan and Ludwig's bustard, while enthusiastic 'twitchers' will seek the pale, apparently insignificant Gray's lark (among other larks), which is endemic to the gravel plains of the Namib.

INSELBERGS AND MOUNTAIN OUTCROPS Throughout the Namib there are mountains, often of granite or limestone. Some, like many between Sesriem and Sossusvlei, have become submerged beneath the great dune sea. Others, especially north of the Kuiseb River, jut up through the flat desert floor like giant worm casts on a well-kept lawn. These isolated mountains surrounded by gravel plains are inselbergs (from the German for 'island-mountain') – and they have their own flora and fauna. Euphorbia, acacia, commiphora, zygophyllum and aloe species are common, while the succulent lithops (often called living rocks, for their pebble-like shape) occur here, though less frequently.

Many inselbergs are high enough to collect moisture from morning fogs, which sustain succulents and aloes, and with them whole communities of invertebrates. Temporary pools in crevices can be particularly interesting, and there's a whole microcosm of small water creatures that lay drought-resistant eggs. These survive years of desiccation, to hatch when the pools do finally fill.

Being open land, these make perfect perches for raptors: lappet-faced vultures, greater kestrels and red-necked falcons are typical of this environment. Also watch for sandgrouse, which congregate at water around dusk and dawn, and other well-camouflaged foraging birds.

NAMIBRAND NATURE RESERVE

Covering about 2,100km², an area almost the same size as Luxembourg, the NamibRand Nature Reserve is one of the largest private reserves in Africa. Lying south of Sesriem, it borders on to the main Namib-Naukluft National Park in the west, a boundary of about 100km, and in the east its extent is generally defined by the Nubib Mountains. Within this is a wide variety of different desert landscapes and environments, from huge red sand dunes to vegetated inter-dune valleys, sand and gravel plains, and some particularly imposing mountains. It's a spectacular area of desert.

There are several ways to visit the reserve, all utilising small lodges and camps as bases for expert-led guided trips. If you want a detailed look at the central Namib, with guides who understand it, this is an excellent complement to a day or two of driving yourself around Sesriem and Sossusvlei.

HISTORY The reserve was formed from a number of separate farms established in the 1950s to eke out an existence farming in the desert. Several severe drought years in the 1980s demonstrated that farming domestic stock here just wasn't viable. There were allegations of farmers opening their fences to game from the Namib-Naukluft National Park, only to kill the animals for their meat once they left the park.

Game was the only option, and this survived well on the farm Gorrasis, owned by Albi Brückner (a businessman, rather than a farmer, who'd bought the farm for its landscapes).

In 1988 Brückner bought out two neighbouring farms, Die Duine and Stellarine, and gradually the reserve was broadened from that base. Now various shareholders have contributed money to the reserve, and different operators hold 'concession' areas which they utilise for tourism.

FLORA AND FAUNA The NamibRand's flora and fauna are the same as that in the western areas of the Namib-Naukluft. However, there are also red hartebeest, which

SUSTAINABLE LIVING IN THE NAMIB DESERT

Many people wonder how anything survives in the Namib Desert which, at 55 million years old, is the oldest desert in the world, and one of the driest. Enter NaDEET (the Namib Desert Environmental Education Trust), which from its base in the NamibRand Nature Reserve teaches Namibia's youth about this harsh environment, and how it is possible not only to survive here, but also to live in a sustainable manner.

NaDEET has hosted thousands of youngsters on its sustainable living programme, which focuses on energy, water, waste and biodiversity, while also encouraging teamwork and co-operation. Practical, experimental learning allows participants, many of whom have never visited the desert before, to see first hand the importance of looking after their environment and the benefits to themselves and Namibia of sustainable living. The children are expected to look after their own living space, do their own cleaning and cook their own food using fuel-efficient stoves, self-constructed solar ovens and handmade fire bricks of recycled paper.

Guests at Wolwedans, or even passers-by, can arrange a visit (*between 08.00 & 17.00*) to find out more and perhaps to join in with the activities. For those willing to make a greater contribution, NaDEET occasionally accepts short-term volunteers for a minimum of three months. To arrange this, contact their new office in Swakopmund (*Green Centre, 5 Libertina Amathila Av;* m *081 367 5310;* e *admin@nadeet.org; www.nadeet.org*).

aren't usually found in the national park, and blesbok which have been introduced from South Africa.

WHERE TO STAY/WHAT TO SEE AND DO What you see and do here depends entirely on where you stay, as many of the camps in the concession have a different emphasis.

🏠 **Sossusvlei Desert Lodge** [308 F1] (10 chalets) ☎ +27 11 809 4300; e contactus@ andbeyond.com; www.andbeyond.com. One of Namibia's most stylish modern lodges, this lies down a rather rocky 4km driveway off the C27 in the north of the NamibRand Reserve, about 97km from Betta & 40km south of Sesriem. Spacious split-level chalets, made largely of stone & glass, are built into the rocks overlooking a desert plain, their graceful interiors a mix of bright chrome & earthy, desert colours. These personal cocoons have minibars, coffee stations & AC. Most of their glass walls slide or fold away, opening up the room to the desert, & at night a skylight above your bed can slide back, allowing you to stargaze: telescopes provided!

The main lodge is similarly luxurious, with a lovely terrace with sweeping views & a small observatory with computer-controlled telescope. The food is excellent, the wine cellar impressive – & there's a slightly surreal pool. Activities focus on Sossusvlei walking & driving trips, while hot-air balloon trips are an unusual & fun addition to the normal trips. *FBA N$6,975/11,200 sgl low/high season; N$13,950/22,400 dbl.* **$$$$$$$**

🏠 **Wolwedans** [296 C5] ☎ 061 230616; e info@wolwedans.com; www.wolwedans.com. Wolwedans comprises 4 separate accommodation choices, each a considerable distance from the others across the reserve. While all cater for the top end of the market, they have a range of styles to suit different visitors. Particularly special is the possibility of arranging a wedding, from a religious service to a civil ceremony.

The turning to the main farmhouse, west off the C27, is about 32km of bumpy road to the north of the junction of the D827 & C27. Coming from the north, it is 50km south of the C27/D845 junction. If you are approaching from Sesriem, that's about 40km south of the 1st NamibRand signboard south of Sesriem on the C27. The camp has its own airstrip as well. Once on the 'drive' to Wolwedans, ignore the small house on the left & continue about 20km from the gate to the Wolwedans farmhouse, or basecamp, from where transfers

into the various camps are arranged. Beware of turning off this track, as you may become stuck in the sand. All rates below include the NamibRand entrance fee.

Activities usually consist of afternoon & full-day drives into the reserve with a professional guide, including a picnic lunch, & guided walks. Scenic flights to the Diamond Coast & Sossusvlei can also be arranged.

🏠 **WOLWEDANS DUNE CAMP** (8 tents) The flagship of the reserve since it opened, Dune Camp is built on wooden decks raised above the sand. Each tent has an en-suite hot shower & toilet, twin beds & solar-powered lights, with a veranda set to the side for uninterrupted views of the landscape. The lodge's central open dining area & sundeck are furnished with soft leather-seat chairs so you can sit enjoying the views with a glass of wine. An open kitchen allows you to chat to the chef while your meal is being prepared (the standard of food is excellent). This camp is more suited to the adventurous traveller who will appreciate its quiet atmosphere & old-style feel. *FBA N$10,200/15,100 sgl/dbl.* **$$$$$$$**

✳ 🏠 **WOLWEDANS DUNES LODGE** (9 chalets, 1 suite) Since 1998, Dunes Lodge has been run with all the courtesy & attention to detail of a country house, with an atmosphere of relaxed gentility. More luxurious than the Dune Camp, it sits atop one of the red dunes. Purpose-built wooden chalets are built on stilts with their own secluded verandas & en-suite showers & toilets. The real coup is the bedrooms. Solid wooden twin beds, draped with nets that give all the allure of a dreamy 4-poster, face directly east through a canvas 'wall' that, when rolled up, affords unparalleled stargazing & a front-row view of sunrise over the mountains.

Simple walkways over the dunes lead to the hub of the camp, where a comfortable bar with leather armchairs, a separate library & 2 lounges all share the view. There are also 2 dining rooms where meals are taken at individual tables or around a large table, depending on individual preference. Dinner is a relatively formal affair, with some of the best food to be had in Namibia,

& good wines to match from a chilled wine cellar. And after dinner, what better than to while away the evening around the campfire on the deck? This is a place to relax, unwind & get a real feel for the surroundings. Guided activities usually return in time for a civilised afternoon tea, or perhaps a leisurely dip in the pool before lounging on the surrounding deck. *FBA N$9,600/6,950 sgl/dbl; suite supp't N$4,000/6,000.* **$$$$$$$**

⌂ **WOLWEDANS PRIVATE CAMP** (suite) Tucked away in a secluded valley, the Private Camp caters for just 6 guests: ideal for honeymooners or anyone seeking the ultimate in privacy. It has 3 spacious bedrooms with verandas & en-suite bathrooms, while an adjoining sala with a day bed makes an inspired place for children to sleep. The camp boasts its own lounge, dining area, library & a fully equipped kitchen. But forget the washing up – all this comes with a dedicated chef & housekeeper, so total relaxation is the order of the day. *FBA N$9,250 pp based on min 3 people, inc private drives.* **$$$$$$$**

⌂ **BOULDERS SAFARI CAMP** (5 chalets) ⊕ Closed 1 Dec–28 Feb. Nestled among the massive granite boulders that give the camp its name, Boulders is 40km south of the base camp & is reached by a leisurely 2hr scenic drive through the reserve. Staying here gives a true feeling of peace & isolation, with only the sound of the wind to break the silence. The canvas-&-wood en-suite chalets are decorated in natural tones, with 4-poster beds draped in flowing white nets, & canvas sides that can be rolled up for seemingly endless views over the plains & the distant mountains, or for watching the sunrise from the comfort of your bed.

The lounge & dining area is tastefully decorated with dark wooden furniture & old German bookcases full of leather-bound books. Meals can be eaten around the large wooden dining table or, for a more personal touch, private dinners can be arranged on the veranda by lantern-light. But wherever you eat, you cannot fail to be impressed by the skilfully created food & quality wines. Activities also include hikes up the kopjes & sundowners on top of the boulders. *Min 3-night stay. FBA N$10,050/14,700 sgl/dbl.* **$$$$$$$**

⋀ **Tok Tokkie Trails** [296 C5] ✆061 264521; e toktokkie@toktokkietrails.com; www. toktokkietrails.com. As the name suggests, this place is about walking. It is signposted 400m or so north of the C27/D827 junction, from where it's a further 11km to the base, through a couple of gates.

The Tok Tokkie Trail, named for the specially adapted beetles that are found in the Namib, is designed to offer a really close-up look at the Namib Desert environment, concentrating not only on the flora & fauna but also on how the whole desert ecosystem works. The landscape is beautiful: small vegetated sand dunes, mountains, dry rivers, open plains & the huge African sky. The 22km trail, accompanied by a specialist desert guide, is run over 2 nights & 3 days, starting at around noon on day 1, & finishing at about 11.00 on day 3. While you need to be reasonably fit, the group travels at the pace of the slowest; this is no route march. You carry only a daypack with water, picnic lunch & personal items; your luggage is delivered to the camp by a support crew, who prepare a 3-course dinner under the stars. At night, you'll sleep out on comfortable camp beds with mattress, duvet & pillow, laid out in separate dbl or twin 'dune bedrooms'. There are long-drop toilets & a hot-water bucket shower is available.

A sunhat, sunscreen & sunglasses are essential, but water bottles & all bedding are provided. Hiking boots are a good idea but comfortable closed walking shoes are fine. In the winter, Jun–Sep, the desert nights can be cold, & warm clothing, including a woolly hat, is recommended. *FBA N$3,490 pp per night; min age 8.* **$$$$$$**

⌂ **NamibRand Family Hideout** [296 C5] ✆061 226803; m 081 127 2957; www.nrfhideout. com. Once the home of Karakul sheep farmers, this truly isolated rustic farmhouse is available on a self-catering basis for families or private groups of up to 10 people sharing 4 bedrooms, a kitchen, living room & dining room. To find it, take the turn-off for Tok Tokkie Trails (400m north of the C27/D827 intersection), then continue for 16km down the track. With views over the open plains of the NamibRand Reserve towards the mountains in the distance, with limited phone signal & Wi-Fi available only at the base camp 5km away, it's a great place to truly appreciate the isolation & emptiness of the desert. Though as the nearest shop with basic supplies is 42km south of the C27 turn-off, make sure that you are properly stocked up for the duration of your stay.

There are several activities here you can enjoy independently, such as unguided walking trails & scenic drives through the desert, & fatbikes can be borrowed from the farmhouse. For those who don't have their own 4x4 vehicle, a driver & vehicle are available so you can explore the dunes & the mountains on 1–3hr drives. *N$2,000/night 1–4 people, N$2,400/night 5–10 people.* **$$$**

🏠 **Sonop** [296 D5] (10 rooms) e contact@ zannier.com; www.zannierhotels.com. Due to open in 2019 in the NamibRand Reserve, this luxury hotel is from Zannier Hotels, who have also opened Omaanda, outside Windhoek (page 186). Based on this we are expecting Sonop to be a small 1920s-style camp with a retro-explorer style. As well as the main camp, a luxury mobile option is also planned.

SOUTH OF THE RESERVE If you're heading south of the NamibRand, you'll come across some of the most scenic routes in the country: the D826, C27 and D707 (see *Chapter 12*). Sand dunes line the west of these roads, and mountains overlook the east – spectacular stuff. However, they do tend to be quite slow-going, and the gravel is sometimes not as good or as wide as the faster C19 or C14, so allow plenty of time for your journey (an average of about 50km/h is realistic).

NAUKLUFT MOUNTAINS

An hour's drive northeast of Sesriem, the main escarpment juts out into the desert forming a range known as the Naukluft Mountains. In 1968 these were protected within the Naukluft Mountain Zebra Park – to conserve a rare breeding population of Hartmann's mountain zebra. Shortly afterwards, land was bought to the west of the mountains and added to the park, forming a corridor linking these mountains into the Namib National Park. This allowed oryx, zebra and other game to migrate between the two, and in 1979 the two areas were formally combined into the Namib-Naukluft National Park.

GEOLOGY The uniqueness of the area stems from its geology as much as its geographical position. Separated from the rest of the highlands by steep, spectacular cliffs, the Naukluft Mountains form a plateau. Underneath this, to a height of about 1,100m, is mostly granite. Above this base are alternating layers of dolomites and shales, with extensive deposits of dark limestone, rising to about 1,995m. Over the millennia, rainwater has gradually cut into this massif, dissolving the rock and forming steep kloofs, or ravines, and a network of watercourses and reservoirs – many of which are subterranean. The name Naukluft, which means 'narrow ravine', is apt for the landscape.

Where these waters surface, in the deeper valleys, there are crystal-clear springs and pools – ideal for cooling dips. Often these are decorated by impressive formations of smooth tufa – limestone that has been redeposited by the water over waterfalls.

FLORA AND FAUNA Receiving occasional heavy rainstorms in summer that feed its network of springs and streams in its deeper kloofs, the Naukluft supports a surprisingly varied flora and fauna.

The high plateau and mountainsides tend to be rocky with poor, if any, soil. Here are distinctive euphorbia, acacia, commiphora and aloe plants (including quivertrees, which are found in a dense stand in Quivertree Gorge). Most are low, slow-growing species, adapted to conserving water during the dry season. The variations of slope and situation result in many different niches suiting a wide variety of species.

Down in the deeper kloofs, where there are permanent springs, the vegetation is totally different, with many more lush, broad-leaf species. Wild, cluster and sycamore figs are particularly prevalent, while you should also be able to spot camelthorn, buffalo-thorn, wild olive and shepherd's trees.

13

The Naukluft has many animals, including large mammals, though all are elusive and difficult to spot. Hartmann's mountain zebra, oryx, kudu and klipspringer are occasionally seen fleeing over the horizon (usually in the far distance). Steenbok and the odd sunbathing dassie are equally common, and springbok, warthog and ostrich occur, but are more often found on the plains around the mountains. The mountains should be a classic place for leopard, and the smaller cats – as there are many small mammals found here – though these are almost never seen.

Over 200 species of birds have been recorded here, and a useful annotated checklist is available from the park office. The Naukluft Mountains are at the southern limit of the range of many species of the northern Namib – Rüppell's parrot, rosy-faced lovebirds and Monteiro's hornbill all occur here, as do species typical of the south like the Karoo robin and chat. In the wetter kloofs, watch for species that you wouldn't find in the drier parts of the park, like the water-loving hamerkop, brubru and even African black ducks. Raptors are usually seen soaring above. Black eagles, lanner falcons, augur buzzards and pale chanting goshawks are common.

GETTING THERE AND AWAY The national park's entrance is on the D854, about 10km southwest of the C14, which links Solitaire and Maltahöhe. Approaching from Windhoek, pass Büllsport and take the D854 towards Sesriem.

Alternatively, Büllsport Guest Farm owns a section of the Naukluft Mountains, accessible from the farm without going into the national park, and Ababis borders on to the mountains.

WHERE TO STAY The options are to camp at the basic national park's site, or to use one of these guest farms as a base. The mountains are also within a few hours' drive from most of the lodges in the Solitaire and Sesriem areas.

Büllsport Guest Farm [296 D3] (14 rooms, 2 campsites) \063 693371; e info@buellsport. com; www.buellsport.com. Run by Johanna & Ernst Sauber, this is one of the best traditional guest farms in the country, attracting a wide range of nationalities to stay. You can expect excellent food & wonderful 3-course dinners with wine. The 8 standard rooms are en suite, while the 6 luxury rooms behind the main house all have toilets separate from the bathroom, underfloor heating & cooling, & spacious patios where guests can relax after a hard day's hiking. There is an indoor dining area with a large sliding glass door that opens on to a patio with views of the garden, while the lovely swimming pool has picturesque views of the surrounding mountains.

Alternatively, there are 2 campsites, both tucked away in the mountains 3km from the farm: 1 for private groups, the other for general use. Both have 2 flush toilets, 2 sinks, a shaded lapa & 2 showers – you'll have to buy wood from the farm shop for the 'donkey' water heater. The general campsite doesn't have electricity.

Many visitors use this as a base for visiting the Naukluft Mountains, as Büllsport owns a section of them. There are a number of trails varying in length & difficulty, & Johanna also offers short horseriding trails into the mountains. For 2 or more experienced riders, she can arrange a 2-day trail, including meals & an overnight bushcamp in the Naukluft. A short drive from the farmhouse is an old German Schutztruppe post, & a few hrs' walk from that is a large natural rock arch – dubbed the 'Bogenfels of the Naukluft', after the original in the Sperrgebiet. Alternatively, the farm is just under 2hrs' drive (115km) from Sesriem, so makes a practical base for day trips there if closer accommodation is full. 4x4 excursions to Sossusvlei are available by arrangement. *DBB standard N$1,958/3,470 pp sgl/dbl; private campsite N$1,350 per group; general campsite N$250 pp.* **$$–$$$$$**

Zebra River Lodge [296 D4] (17 rooms) \061 234342; e eden@africanonline.com,na; www.zebra-river-lodge.com. Owned by Louis & Geraldine Fourie, this renovated farmhouse is set in 12,500ha in its own canyon in the Tsaris Mountains. To find it, turn south from the D850, between the D854 & the D855; note that the driveway is several kilometres long & crosses a sand river which – in exceptional years – flows across the road.

The standard rooms lead off a wide veranda around a fish-pond, while quieter rock chalets further away from the main building afford extra privacy. All are en suite with plenty of space & lovely old-fashioned German furniture – & the 'honeymoon' suite has a large stand-alone bath, a king-size bed, & even more space. In the lodge's main area, there's a swimming pool surrounded by green lawns, a dining room, & a terrace where home-cooked 3-course dinners are served, weather permitting.

ZRL can be used as a base for driving yourself to Sesriem or the Naukluft, but don't ignore the lodge's own area, which is home to the world's oldest examples of stromatolite fossils; a tour costs N$280 pp. Other activities include a sundowner drive (*N$275 pp*), guided walk to natural spring (*N$324 pp*), ½-day Sossusvlei excursion (*N$2,000 pp*) & various guided walking trails (*N$150 pp*). *DBB standard room N$1,900–2,180/2,600–3,200 sgl/dbl.* **$$$$**

Å Tsauchab River Camp [296 D4] (14 chalets, camping) 063 293416; reservations 064 464144; e reservations@logufa.com; www. tsauchab.com. Johan & Nicky Steyn offer a very warm welcome & well-priced accommodation across their quirky & highly original camps. The entrance is on the D850, very close to the junction with the D854. They operate 12 different campsites, each very individual in feel, and accommodating approx 2–50 guests. In addition there are en-suite chalets (with 12v power, water & BBQ).

Facilities are spread across this huge farm. Walking in the wild fig forest (detailed trail maps available), tackling the 4x4 drives, chilling out in the springs & water pools, & taking time to admire Johan's inspired, homemade metal sculptures that line the entrance are all great pastimes. Nicky will do any meals on request, from picnic lunches to tasty braais, or there's a wide selection of fresh food & cold drinks available in the farm shop. *N$1,200/2,100 sgl/dbl; camping N$120 pp, plus N$160 per pitch.* **$–$$$$**

Å Hauchabfontein Camping [296 D4] (camping) 063 293433; e irmi@mweb.com. na. Part of Immo & Irmi Foerster's farm, this neat,

scenic campsite lies beside the Tsauchab river-bed & close to a lovely quivertree forest. It's located on the D854, between the D850 & C19, about 5km southwest of the Naukluft View, 59km from Sesriem & 44km from Naukluft. Facilities are clean & reliable with stone-built hot-water showers & toilets, & peaceful acacia-shaded pitches. Occasionally fresh fruit & vegetables are available from the farm, as are trips to the nearby natural springs & sundowner trips. *N$120 pp, children under 10 free.* **$**

⌂ Elegant Desert Lodge [296 C4] (29 rooms) 061 301934; e info@the-elegant-collection. com; www.elegant-desert-lodge.com. Now part of the Elegant Collection, the former Betesda Lodge is at the junction of the C19 & D854. Change of ownership has triggered renovation in the main building of the traditional farmhouse, which now has a modern, fashionable style. Rooms, however, have retained their crazy-paving-style stone floor, large tiled en-suite shower, mosi net & solar heating, while in the huge family rooms, a half-height partition wall separates the dbl & 2 sgl beds. The main stone-&-thatch building is very lodgelike, with a wide check-in area, & a huge dining area (*dinner N$160 pp*) with large leaded patio doors & a long buffet counter. Shaded loungers surround a lovely stone pool, & there's a stepped-down rectangular boma with fixed tables, chairs, a built-in BBQ & bar. Free Wi-Fi in reception. Activities, including 2hr sundowner drives (*N$415 pp*), 2hr quadbiking trips (*N$550 pp*) & Sossusvlei excursions (*N$900 pp*) must be prebooked. *DBB N$1,665/2,500 sgl/dbl.* **$$$$**

⌂ Elegant Desert Eco Camp [296 D4] (10 tents) 061 301934; e info@the-elegant-collection.com; www.the-elegant-collection.com. This rustic tented camp, a simpler option than its nearby sister camp, Elegant Desert Lodge, is accessed along a track from the D854, about 50m from the junction with the C19. Built around the base of a large rocky hill, each of its tents looks over the alternating gravel plains & savannah of the Namib Desert. From the outside they look simple in style, with timber frames & green canvas, & the outdoor shower is rustic, but inside they're smartly furnished with dbl or twin beds, wooden wardrobes & en-suite bathrooms with modern showers. From this circle of rooms, steep wooden steps lead to the top of the hill, with sweeping views across the desert. Here you'll find a wooden deck, perfect for sundowners (a good reward after you've expended the energy getting up there), & a small swimming pool. It's advisable to prebook activities, which are as at Elegant Desert Lodge. *N$1,535/2,300 sgl/dbl.* **$$$$**

🏠 **Ababis Guest Farm** [296 D3] (5 dbl rooms, 2 houses, camping) ☎ 063 293362; e info2@ababis-gaestefarm.de; www.ababis-gaestefarm.de. Ababis stands on the west side of the C14, opposite the junction with the C24, on the northern edge of the Naukluft Mountains. The 160-year-old colonial farmhouse, owned by Kathrin & Uwe Schulze Neuhoff, has been a guest farm since 1993, offering large en-suite standard rooms that are simply furnished, with a desert-inspired colour scheme. Former interior designer Kathrin has added her own touches to the main areas, with a strange mixture of colonial artefacts, modern art & sculptured lighting in the lounge & dining room. There's also a stone-clad swimming pool & tanning deck. In addition to the rooms at the main house, guests can rent a twin-bed honeymoon suite, or 1 of 2 'comfort' rooms that sleeps up to 4, & have an outdoor toilet, solar-heated shower & small kitchen; you can buy supplies at their farm shop.

The farm has around 50 cattle, as well as areas devoted purely to wildlife, including oryx, springbok, blesbok, occasional zebra, a few kudu & some bat-eared foxes. It is a good base for long hikes, but there's also a gentle walking trail down to a (usually) dry river, which takes a few hours, & a more energetic 1½hr hike to the summit of a nearby mountain for panoramic views over the farm. If you reserve 3 days in advance, they can arrange a 4x4 trip to Sesriem Canyon & Sossusvlei (*approx N$2,915 per vehicle*). Uwe also offers training courses for off-road drivers. *DBB N$1,400–1,700/2,800–3,400 sgl/dbl; camping N$180 pp.* **$–$$$$**

🏕 **Naukluft Campsite** [296 D3] (6 chalets, 21 pitches) ☎ 063 683791; reservations ☎ 061 285 7200; e reservations@nwr.com.na; www.nwr.com.na. About 8km southwest of Büllsport, on the D854, is the ornate entrance to the Naukluft section of the Namib-Naukluft National Park. Through the gates, a road winds up northwest into the Naukluft for about 12km before the campsite.

The site has some beautifully situated camping spots, surrounded by mountains & trees. Of these, 5 are about 100m away from the others,

in a peaceful area by the river-bed. Water, firewood & toilets/showers are provided. There are also 6 pleasantly furnished en-suite chalets, for which b/fast is included. Other meals can be cooked on the communal braais or bought from the small restaurant on site – though the range of food can be limited, & is fairly basic. The campsite can get busy, so it's wise to book in advance. *N$1,100/1,350 pp sgl Nov–Jun/Jul–Oct; N$1,940/2,400 pp dbl Nov–Jun/Jul–Oct; camping N$250 pp.* **$$–$$$**

🏠 **Hammerstein Lodge & Camp** [296 D5] (5 bungalows, 51 rooms, camping) ☎ 063 693111; e hammerst@hammerstein.com.na; www.hammerstein.com.na. Situated on the C19, the turn-off north to Hammerstein has a clear signpost between the D845 (which goes past the Naukluft Mountains) & the D827. Run by the same people as Hoodia Desert Lodge, & yet poles apart, this well-established private restcamp caters predominantly to large German groups. As well as en-suite twin rooms in staggered rows, there are self-catering bungalows, each with 2–4 beds. Clean & bright rooms feature pine furniture & an outside bench overlooking a wide gravel pathway, but seek out the more pleasant grassy area beside the pool where garden tables are shaded by lovely camelthorn trees. Buffet meals are served in either the cavernous restaurant or at a long banqueting table, & there's a bar, complete with wall-mounted animal skins, for after-dinner drinks. Some game is kept here (including caracal, cheetah & leopard in unimpressive 1ha enclosures), & you're encouraged to join their Wild Cat Walk. *B&B room N$1,160/1,360 sgl/dbl; bungalow N$290/580; camping N$140 pp.* **$–$$$**

🏠 **Sossus Under Canvas** (8 tents) ☎ 061 248137; e info@ultimatesafaris.na; www.ultimatesafaris.com. Set up in a range of locations on the private Neuhof Nature Reserve, about 30mins' drive south of Sesriem, this semi-permanent camp opened in 2018. Its walk-in tents have open-air en-suite bathrooms with flush toilet & bucket shower, & – as protection from the prevailing winds – a natural stone wall on the eastern side. Sossus under Canvas aims to focus on a wilderness experience & guiding rather than luxury. It can be booked only as part of a longer private trip through Ultimate Safaris, so daily rates are not available.

WHAT TO SEE AND DO Animals are seldom seen in this mountainous area, so hiking is the main activity, but there's also an off-road driving trail, which takes two days and is aimed at local enthusiasts testing their vehicles to the limits.

Hiking
Naukluft has two circular day hikes: the Waterkloof and Olive trails. Both can be started from the Naukluft Campsite, and neither needs booking ahead, or any special equipment. That said, at least a day's water, snacks and a medical kit should be taken along, as rescue would be difficult if there was an accident. Walkers should be fit and acclimatised, and strong hiking boots are essential as the terrain is very rocky.

There is also one long eight-day Naukluft Trail, rated as one of Africa's toughest hikes – though it can be shortened to four days. Like the others, this is unguided, but simple diagrammatic maps are available from the park warden's office.

Waterkloof Trail The Waterkloof is 17km long and starts near the campsite. It takes 6–7 hours to walk comfortably, and is marked by yellow-painted footprints on the rocks. At first the trail follows the Naukluft River upstream, through some beautiful gorges, and in the early months of the year you'll often find pools here, complete with tadpoles and frogs.

After a gentle 2 hours you reach a painted rock marking the last water point (though bring water, don't rely on this), beyond which the canyon opens out. After about 2 hours more there's a marked halfway point, from where a steep climb leads you to the trail's highest point: a 600m peak with fine views all around.

From there the trail winds down through a stand of euphorbia into a large valley, to follow the course of the (usually dry) river. It cuts off several of the bends, and keeps left to avoid some steep shelves, which form waterfalls in the rainy season. In this area some large cairns mark the route of the old German cannon road, which also follows the river valley for a while, before climbing steeply up to the main southern ridge of the plateau. Below those waterfalls, you meet the Naukluft River, and turn left to follow the trail for a few kilometres back to camp.

Olive Trail This starts about 4km from the park office – clearly signposted off the track from the entrance gate. You can walk here, or drive and park in the small parking area.

The Olive Trail is 10km long and takes about 4 hours to complete. From the parking area it gradually climbs to the top of a small plateau, before descending through a series of river valleys and gorges (using chains in places), to meet a rough 4x4 track which leads back to the parking area.

Naukluft Trail (⏱ *1 Mar–31 Oct; hikes start every Tue, Thu & Sat for first 3 weeks of each month; book in advance at the NWR in Windhoek; group limit 3–12 people; N$330 pp, inc space at Hiker's Haven for nights before & after trail, excluding park fees, paid separately; medical certificate required*) This 120km, circular seven- to eight-day trail starts from the park office, where there's a bunkhouse known as Hiker's Haven. Hikers can use this on their first and last nights. Initially the trail follows the (usually dry) Naukluft River south as it flows out of the mountains, before climbing up to the edge of the escarpment, with excellent views to the left over the plains. The Putte shelter is reached about 14km (6 hours) after starting.

On the second day the route covers 15km (6 hours), crossing a rolling plateau to the Bergpos junction, before dropping down the narrow Ubusis Kloof to reach Ubusis Hut. Day three starts by retracing your steps to Bergpos, and turning left across the plateau to Alderhost shelter (12km, taking 6 hours).

On day four the trail is level, before dropping down to a shelter at Tsams Ost for the evening – 17km later (6 hours). There's a rough 4x4 track from here down and west to the main C19, so hikers doing only a four-day trip can be collected here.

Day five is steep and then undulating, though it levels out towards the end where it follows a tributary of the Die Valle River, to reach the Die Valle shelter about 17km (6 hours) later. Day six is a tough one, climbing up a narrow gorge to reach a high point called Quartz Valley, before dropping down the Arbeid Adelt Valley to the Tufa shelter, 16km and about 6 hours later.

On day seven the trail climbs steeply, using chains in places, back up to the plateau and some excellent views, to reach Kapokvlakte shelter after 14km (5 hours). Finally, on the last day, the trail descends gradually, then steeply, to meet the Waterkloof Trail and follow the Naukluft River back to camp. Energetic hikers could combine the last two days into a 30km walk which would take about 11 hours to complete. An early start from Tufa shelter is essential, and if there are less than 5 hours of daylight, then you should stop at Kapokvlakte shelter.

4x4 trail (⊕ *Closed at time of research in 2018. Normally open all year, weather permitting; book in advance at the NWR in Windhoek; groups of 1–4 vehicles, with max 4 people per vehicle; N$290 per vehicle, excluding park fees, which are paid separately*) This 73km two-day trail was designed for those with their own 4x4 and the experience to use it properly, though at the time of research in 2018 the trail was closed so do check and book prior to arrival.

After the first 28km there is an overnight camp, where four stone-walled, partially open, A-frame shelters have built-in bunk-beds. There are toilets here, water, a solar-heated shower and a braai area. Bring your own firewood, camping kit and supplies.

Neuras Winery ✳ [296 D4] (✆ 063 293417; e *neuras@naankuse.com; www. neuraswines.com;* ⊕ *all year; wine tour & tasting N$390 pp; wine & cheese tasting N$255*) In a delightful setting surrounded by trees and inviting blue pools, this organic winery is on a 14,400ha farm just off the D850 between Tsauchab River Camp and Zebra River Lodge, producing 3,000 bottles of wine a year. Although you might not expect to find wine-producing vineyards in a country as dry as Namibia (it's the second-driest vineyard in the world), Neuras offers wine tasting and, with advance notice, 1-hour tours of the winery, including the historic garden, which dates back to the 1890s. Crystal-clear natural springs irrigate the vines, which produce a high-quality grape due to the unique microclimate. The farm is also home to mountain zebra, springbok, oryx, ostrich and a wide variety of birds.

While it's possible to visit just for the afternoon to sample the wines, it's also possible to stay overnight in the rustic chalets (*B&B N$1,400/2,800 sgl/dbl; DBB N$1,480/2,960;* **$$$$**), and to join the cheetah-feeding tour (*N$335 pp*).

SESRIEM AND SOSSUSVLEI AREA

When people speak of visiting the Namib Desert, this is often the area they mean. The classic desert scenery around Sesriem and Sossusvlei is the stuff that postcards are made of – enormous apricot dunes with gracefully curving ridges, invariably pictured in the sharp light of dawn with a photogenic oryx or feathery acacia adjacent.

Sesriem and Sossusvlei lie on the Tsauchab River, one of two large rivers (the other being the Tsondab, further north) that flow westward into the great dune field of the central Namib, but never reach the ocean. Both end by forming flat white pans dotted with green trees, surrounded by spectacular dunes – islands of life within a sea of sand.

GETTING THERE AND AWAY Sesriem is clearly signposted 12km southwest along the C27 from its junction with the C19. The best, easiest and cheapest way to see the area is with your own car – so the vast majority of visitors drive. There is no public transport, and while hitching is possible it is difficult, as there are many possible routes here. (This also makes it easier to get away than to arrive.)

If you don't have your own transport, you have several choices. Various tour groups run trips to Sossusvlei from both Windhoek and Swakopmund (pages 173 and 369). Alternatively, there's a private shuttle bus that links Namib-Naukluft Lodge with Windhoek and Swakopmund (page 153). This lodge runs day trips into Sesriem and Sossusvlei which cost about N$1,250 per person. The third option is to fly in by light aircraft with one of the pleasure flight companies (page 149). These drop visitors at either Sossusvlei Lodge or Wolwedans, from which there are guided tours around the area – though neither is a cheap option.

Best routes
Quickest The quickest route from Windhoek is normally south on the B1, then west on the C47 just after Rehoboth to Rietoog, right on to the D1206 to Büllsport (where the guest farm makes a good overnight stop if you're just off a plane). Then continue on the D854, almost in the shadow of the Naukluft Mountains, right on to the C19 and then left for 12km to Sesriem. This takes about 4½ hours.

Most spectacular The most spectacular route from Windhoek is via the C26, followed by the steep Spreetshoogte Pass on the D1275; this can easily be a 6-hour drive.

From Keetmanshoop Approaching from Keetmanshoop, taking the main tar road to Maltahöhe is best, followed by the obvious C19.

From Lüderitz From here Sesriem is really too far for comfort in one day, and a stopover would be wise. This approach does allow you to take the D707 and the C27, which can both be slow going, but are certainly among the most spectacular roads in the subcontinent – with desert sands to their west, and mountain ranges to the east.

From Swakopmund From Swakop it is quickest to drive south to Walvis Bay and then take the C14, via the Kuiseb River canyon. Allow at least 4 hours for this – more if you want to drive at a leisurely pace and stop for a picnic.

Rainy season access For a few days each year, rain causes rivers to wash across certain roads – making them difficult, or impossible, to cross. (See advice on crossing rivers, page 146.)

The D854 is often badly affected, having three or more rivers flowing across it, fed by rains that fall on the Naukluft Mountains. The third of these, nearest Sesriem, usually seems the deepest – though this does depend on where the rain falls in the mountains.

Similarly, the Tsauchab River (which flows through Sesriem Canyon, and on to Sossusvlei) crosses the C19 between its junctions with the D854 and C27. It also crosses the C27 south of Sesriem (but north of the turn-off to Kulala). Both these river crossings look very wide, but are usually shallow and can be crossed with care in a normal 2WD.

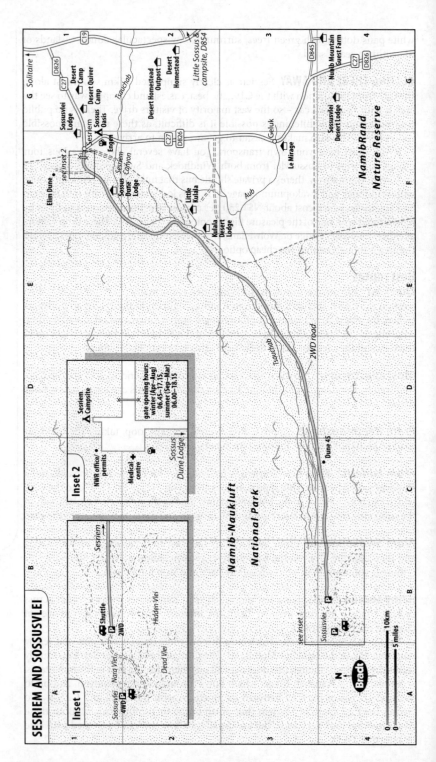

SESRIEM AND SOSSUSVLEI

Inset 1

Sossusvlei
4WD
Sossusvlei · Nara Vlei
Shuttle
2WD
Sesriem →
Hidden Vlei
Dead Vlei

Inset 2

Sesriem Campsite
NWR office/ permits
Medical + centre
gate opening hours:
winter (Apr–Aug): 06.45–17.15,
summer (Sep–Mar) 06.00–18.15
Sossus Dune Lodge

Namib-Naukluft National Park

Dune 45

see inset 1
Sossusvlei

Tsauchab
2WD road

Elim Dune
see inset 2
Sossus Dune Lodge
Sesriem
Sesriem Canyon
Little Kulala
Kulala Desert Lodge
Aub
Le Mirage
Geluk

Solitaire ↑
C19
D826
C27
Desert Camp
Desert Quiver Camp
Sossusvlei Lodge
Sesriem
Sossus Oasis
Engen
Tsauchab

Desert Homestead Outpost
Desert Homestead
Little Sossus & campsite, D854
D845

C27
D826
Nubib Mountain Guest Farm
C27
D826
Sossusvlei Desert Lodge

NamibRand Nature Reserve

N
Bradt

0   10km
0   5 miles

308

If you anticipate problems, then approaching from Maltahöhe, on the C19, is probably the safest route – though it's a long way around from Windhoek. It is vital to ask reliable local advice before you set off.

Other practicalities There is a reliable Engen **fuel station** [308 F1], the Sossus Oasis (⊕ *05.30–18.00 daily*), at the junction along the C27, opposite Sesriem Campsite. It sells almost anything you could possibly need for your journey, including fuel, fresh sandwiches, cold drinks, car parts and tyre repairs, hot and cold food, souvenirs and clothes; there is also an ATM, Wi-Fi and a luxury campsite (page 313).

WHERE TO STAY The only accommodation option inside the gates, and the only one that allows visitors to access the park before sunrise, is Sossus Dune Lodge (page 310). However, Sesriem campsite (page 313) which sits just outside the gate, has one entrance that opens 1 hour before the main gates (see times on map opposite).

Alternatively, you can broaden your choice and stay at one of the nearby lodges. None of these is cheap, but some lower-cost lodges such as Desert Homestead may require you to drive more than 35km to the gate. However, Desert Quiver Camp is a reasonable price and just 5 minutes' drive away. Realistically, though, anywhere in the Naukluft, Solitaire or even northern NamibRand also makes a practical base for visits to the Sossusvlei area, provided that you don't insist on being at Sesriem for sunrise. In fact, as tourism to this corner of the desert increases, brighter visitors are starting to move away from the busy Sesriem and Sossusvlei area, to find superb desert experiences in the private areas of desert that lie to the north and south – like Wolwedans. For the present, however, this remains an area where you must book well in advance in order to have any hope of finding good accommodation when you arrive.

✴ 🏠 **Little Kulala** [308 F2] (11 kulalas) \063 683022; reservations \061 274500; e lkc@iway. na; www.wilderness-safaris.com. Little Kulala is unlike any other property in Namibia: a stunning, über-chic, modernist take on a safari lodge. Its striking interior design is characterised by bleached timber decks, architectural objets d'art & textured fabrics in muted desert tones.

There are 11 *kulalas* (meaning 'to sleep' in the Oshivambo language), including 1 family room that sleeps 4. These are light, bright & airy, with 2 sides being entirely glassed to ensure maximum views across to the dunes. Shaggy rugs, felt pebble cushions, fabulous beds & candles aplenty make them a great place to retreat to, while the large private deck, curved wicker loungers & plunge pool make the space beyond the room equally appealing. Bathrooms are en suite with an indoor power shower & an equally lovely, pebble-strewn outdoor shower. All rooms have AC, fully stocked fridge, tea/coffee station & a digital safe. Rooftop 'skybeds' (with waterproof-covered duvet & mattress) can also be arranged for romantic

stargazing, but be aware of the cold night air when selecting this option.

The central dining area offers excellent cuisine under dramatic makuti thatch. There are suspended swinging chairs on the deck for casual daydreaming; a library & wine cellar for connoisseurs; a pool for a cooling dip & a friendly bar for fireside drinks at the end of the evening. Early morning guided game drives to the dunes use the reserve's private access, & local walks, sunset drives & ballooning can be arranged. *FBA inc local drinks N$10,600–17,403/16,330–26,860 sgl/dbl.* **$$$$$$$**

✴ 🏠 **Hoodia Desert Lodge** [296 C4] (12 rooms) \063 293298; reservations \061 237294; e hoodia@exclusive.com.na; www. hoodiadesertlodge.com. Run by Thomas & Henreza Becker, Hoodia is located halfway between the junction with the C27 & the D854 along the C19, 22km from Sesriem; it has a 7km driveway. The setting is stunning – on the banks of the dry Tsauchab River, with mountains in all directions – & the lodge itself is equally attractive. The spaced-out, lovingly looked-after thatched bungalows all have AC, an empty fridge for your own supplies & en-suite terracotta-coloured bathrooms, with an outside bath & shower for lingering under the stars. Rooms are clean & bright with cool cream curtains, white bedlinen & lots of windows, & a terrace that looks out over the mountains. Handily, guests are also provided with battery-operated mini lanterns to guide them between their room & the main lodge after dark.

In the main lodge, modern portraits of African women painted by a local artist hang in the lounge decorated with deep sofas, a coffee table littered with nature books, a chessboard & other games, a TV quietly playing & a small cupboard selling T-shirts & fleeces. Leading off from this, on a lower level, is the round dining room, which has floor-to-ceiling windows on 3 sides & a central fireplace used as a braai in good weather. Food is delicious, influenced by dishes from all over the world, & is complemented by a range of South African wines; complimentary tea/coffee & rusk biscuits are available all day in the dining room. The wooden deck over the river is a good spot to watch birds & appreciate the peace & quiet with a sundowner. The mountain views are also visible from the small, raised turquoise swimming pool off to the right-hand side. Sundowner drives (*N$275 pp; book before 15.30 on day*) & excursions to Sossusvlei (*N$1,250 pp; min 2 people, inc entrance fee & food*) are available. A stay here is topped off by great service from attentive hosts. *DBB N$4,175/8,100 sgl/dbl.* **$$$$$$**

🏠 **Kulala Desert Lodge** [308 F2] (23 chalets) 📞+27 11 257 5000; e enquiry@wilderness.co.za; www.wilderness-safaris.com. Signposted off the C27, some 13km south of Sesriem (but north of the junction with the D845), & then about 14km from the road, Kulala sits against the red glow of the dunes, overlooking the national park from the southern banks of the Tsauchab River. With a private entrance to the park, guests have a much shorter & quicker route to the dunes than through the main gate. However, if you are self-driving, access to the vlei remains limited to the C27 & the park entrance at Sesriem, so Sossus Dune Lodge, the Sesriem campsite & Sossusvlei Lodge are effectively a shorter drive from the vlei.

Inspiration for Kulala's clay construction came from North African designs, & inside, the light & airy décor is refreshingly cool. Neutral-coloured sofas with

fluffy cushions sit at heavy wooden tables; light pine furniture & yet more cushions in the lounge area encourage relaxation; earthy-toned sofas surround a blazing fire; & rich mahogany-leather footstools add to the cosy charm of the place. A wraparound deck provides lovely views across the dunes, while a large pool & shaded loungers are welcome relief from the midday heat. Wi-Fi is available in these main areas.

The chalets, or *kulalas*, are large tents built on wooden platforms overlooking the river-bed, topped with thatched roofs, & some of the chalets have interconnecting doors or walkways for families. Each incorporates an en-suite stone-tiled bathroom with toilet & shower (use the bucket provided to collect cold water that runs off until hot water comes through the pipes). Gnarled & polished wood furniture is lovely, & grey bedcovers add to the room's natural tones. Outdoors enthusiasts can have their mattresses placed on the chalet's solid roof for a night under the stars – a fun & free option, if chilly in winter.

Sandwiched between the national park to the northwest, & the private NamibRand Nature Reserve to the south, Kulala has 32,000ha of its own land on which it operates nature drives & balloon safaris (page 316), a truly wondrous experience which is well worth the cost. Sossusvlei excursions & eco quadbiking are offered, though many guests drive themselves around the area using Kulala as merely a stylish base. *FBA N$3,420–6,390/5,310–9,380 sgl/dbl.* **$$$$$– $$$$$$**

✳ 🏠 **Sossus Dune Lodge** [308 F1] (25 chalets) 📞063 693258; e reservations@nwr. com.na; www.nwr.com.na. Run by the NWR, Sossus Dune Lodge has a great location just 4km inside the Sesriem Gate, so visitors can access the park before sunrise & after sunset. This is a good choice for photographers who wish to capture the sunrise or Sossusvlei without the crowds. Identical rondavel-style chalets in yellow canvas & thatch are lined up in a row, linked by wooden walkways; a quick tip: room numbers are posted on the floor of the walkway entrance to your chalet. Chalets are large & bright, with floor-to-ceiling glass panels so you can take in the mountain views while lying in bed, or from the curved sunloungers in front of the window. Dark wood furniture contrasts with brightly coloured mosquito nets, & there are fans instead of AC, plus wooden chairs on a private veranda which offers superb stargazing at night.

Bathrooms have open-plan showers & his 'n' hers sinks. Room 13 has the best view of the waterhole.

The central chalet has a large open-plan bar & separate dining room looking out over the mountains. Next to this is a glittering pool with a shady sunbathing area where you can cool off from the afternoon heat. There's no Wi-Fi, & the mobile signal is patchy. You can drive yourself to Sossusvlei as long as you return by 1hr after sunset; if you plan to set off before b/fast (*from 06.30/07.00 winter/summer*) b/fast bags can be provided at no extra cost. To reach the dunes, turn right out of the car park, then left when you reach the tar road. Guests can also take advantage of the lodge's guided sunset & nature drives, & trips to Sesriem Canyon & Elim Dune (*all N$400 pp*). *DBB N$2,200/3,800 sgl Nov–Jun/Jul–Oct; N$4,000/7,200 dbl Nov–Jun/Jul–Oct; inc park fees.* $$$$$–$$$$$$

Le Mirage Desert Lodge & Spa [308 F3] (29 rooms) ☏063 683019; reservations ☏061 224712; e info@mirage-lodge.com; www.mirage-lodge.com. Forget hazy images in the desert heat: Le Mirage is a collection of sizeable buildings merging little with the desert surroundings. It's a curious fusion of a grand Arthurian castle – cathedral-style windows, trefoil turrets, monogrammed linen – & a Moroccan riad, with inner courtyards, palm trees, antique chests & sapphire-blue mosaic bathrooms. Rooms are divided between 2 buildings: the smaller (8 rooms) characterised by its cool, galleried courtyard, complete with gushing waterfall & cascading bougainvillea. All are spacious & tastefully furnished with antiques & good-quality, modern amenities: AC, safe, minibar & coffee/tea station. Stone walls, sand-blasted room dividers, high, beamed ceilings & 4-poster beds add to the grandeur. In the new building each room boasts a small balcony, & 2 have access to 'star decks' where guests can sleep under the night sky on top of the turret. At ground level, a decadent spa offers all types of massage, facials & aromatherapy baths in 5 treatment rooms. There's also an outdoor pool & a colonial-style, open-sided bar & lounge. The last of the buildings contains the restaurant & wine cellar. Here, heavy wooden tables are interspersed with gas patio heaters, as the central atrium can make this a chilly dining option. Activities include ½-day Sossusvlei drive (*N$925 pp*), 2hr quadbiking trip (*N$475 pp*), sundowner (*N$500 pp*) & night game

drive (*N$300 pp*). *DBB from N$2,505/3,065 sgl Dec–Jun/Jul–Oct; N$3,770/4,660 dbl.* $$$$$

The Desert Homestead & Horse Trails [308 G2] (26 bungalows) ☏063 293301; reservations ☏061 240020; e reservations@homestead.com.na; www.deserthomesteadlodge.com. Well signposted from the C19, 3km northwest of the D854 junction, Desert Homestead sits in a wide grassy valley, sheltered by the Nubib, Tsaris & Naukluft mountains. It has sensational views shared by both the elevated central area & the sweeping curve of well-spaced bungalows. The large terrace, between the thatched entrance & the rock garden & crystal-clear swimming pool, is an idyllic spot for lunch or sundowners. Thatched, whitewashed pole bungalows are set below the main area & make for excellent retreats in the midday sun. The interiors are simple but stylish with elegant dark wood furniture, crisp white linen, mosquito net, a few interesting objets d'art & a long shower room, with rustic brass pipes & a pleasing lack of general clutter. Ceiling fans keep the rooms cool by day & thick fur blankets counter the winter chill. Outside, a pair of wooden chairs on the concrete terrace make a great spot for solitary reading or simply admiring the view – & the sunset.

Horseriding, for both beginners & experienced riders, is a core activity, with well-trained horses for trips lasting from 1hr to a 2-night sleep-out ride (*N$4,620–7,865 pp*). Free Wi-Fi in main areas. *B&B N$2,290/3,980 sgl/dbl Jan–Mar, N$2,440/4,280 Mar–Dec.* $$$$$

Desert Homestead Outpost [308 G2] (12 houses) ☏061 240020, after hours ☏063 293301; e info@deserthomesteadoutpost.com; www.deserthomesteadoutpost.com. Accessed from the C19, the 9km track leading to Desert Homestead Outpost is 4km northwest of the D854 junction. The lodge has been constructed around the lower section of one of the area's rocky mountains, with enough elevation to afford excellent views across the gravel plains to the Namib's dunes in the distance. The main area is spread across 3 levels, housing the reception, indoor & outdoor dining areas, & a swimming pool. A steep trail leads to the top of the mountain, where the views are spectacular; it's one of the best spots for a sundowner in the area worth the tough climb over a loose surface,

Partially set up on stilts, the houses (& 1 suite) are each decorated in neutral greens & browns, offering a modern style with a classic safari lodge feel. Spacious en-suite bathrooms feature a loo with a view, & the newer houses away from the main area also have outdoor showers. If arranged in advance you can sleep on the roof of your room: a sometimes chilly option but with incredible views of the stars.

Along with hiking & jogging trails, there are 2hr nature/sundowner drives (*N$430*), while other activities – including horseriding – are run from Outpost's sister property, Desert Homestead, about 10km away (page 311). *DBB N$3,520/5,960/sgl/ dbl Jan–15 Mar, N$3,280/6,440 16 Mar–Dec.* **$$$$$–$$$$$$**

🏠 **Desert Quiver Camp** [308 G1] (24 chalets) 063 293611; e info@desertquivercamp.com; www.desertquivercamp.com. A sister property to Sossusvlei Lodge, 4km down the road, the simple, modern, self-catering chalets here are arranged in a semicircle either side of the main area. Each has twin beds, a fold-out sleeper couch, en-suite shower room, & AC/heating, with a patio in front containing a small kitchen & free-standing BBQ. The nearest place to stock up on provisions is the garage at Sesriem, 5km away, but braai packs can be ordered for evening delivery, & utensil boxes can be borrowed from reception for a N$300 deposit. The main area incorporates a bar with a large TV, & a swimming pool overlooking a small manmade waterhole, often drawing springbok & oryx in front of the camp. Those not wishing to self-cater can book into the restaurant at Sossusvlei Lodge. Excursions & other activities in the area can be booked through the lodge, too, but you will need to drive yourself there. Desert Quiver is only 5km from the park entrance though, so it's a good base for those looking to drive themselves to the dunes. *Self-catering N$1,326/1,770 sgl/dbl Dec–Jun, N$1,582/2,110 Nov, Jul–Oct.* **$$$$**

🏠 **Nubib Mountain Guest Farm** [308 G4] (5 rooms) 063 293240; m 081 129 3573; e hbaumann@nubibmountain.com; www. nubibmountain.com. A little gem 10km southwest of the C19 & D854 road junction, along a 5km driveway, this quiet oasis is set amid a 30,000ha farm run by Germans Horst & Irmelien Baumann, who inherited the land from her parents. There are just 5 dbl rooms: 2 classic rooms in the main house & 3 modern ones in a separate block at the back, all with French doors overlooking a waterhole & the Tiras Mountains. These outer rooms have

solar-heated hot water. The house is surrounded by luscious cacti gardens & there's a circular pool with astounding views. Meals are taken with your hosts under a covered open-air porch. *DBB N$880/1,560 sgl/dbl.* **$$$$**

🏠 **Sossusvlei Lodge** [308 F1] (51 rooms) 063 293636; reservations +27 21 930 4564; e reservations@sossusvleilodge.com; www. sossusvleilodge.com. Immediately on the right of the park entrance at Sesriem, the comfortable Sossusvlei Lodge is convenient for those wanting to drive to Sossusvlei at first light, or leave the park late in the day. It's an innovative mix of materials & colours: concrete, ironwork, canvas & leather; reds, apricots, greens & whites. The twin 'tents' are elaborate, permanent constructions; each has an en-suite shower, toilet & basin built as part of the solid base, which supports the canvas walls of the bedrooms. Inside is fairly spacious, with adjoining large sgl beds, bedside tables, lamps, easy chairs, a dressing table, etc – so banish any thoughts of camping when you read of 'tents' here.

A shaded bar & beer garden with views of the plains sit near a swimming pool surrounded by grass & sunloungers. The restaurant serves help-yourself b/fast & lunch, while dinner is buffet-style, with various meats (often including game) cooked to order & served on the open-air terrace. A book exchange, 24hr coffee station with juice & cookies, Wi-Fi (strongest in reception) & a big curio shop add to the amenities.

The atmosphere is that of a hotel, as you will be left to organise yourself, though morning & afternoon trips into the park can be organised through the on-site Adventure Lodge (e *adventure@sossusvleilodge.com*) – the area's main operator for helicopter, hot-air balloon & scenic flights over the dunes, as well as quad-buggy nature drives & Elim Dune walks. It also has a reasonably reliable ATM. That said, it's best to prebook your activities at the same time as your accommodation. And as the sky at Sesriem is clear for about 300 days per year, why not climb their water tower to see the stars at their best or for aerial photos? *DBB from N$3,245/4,624 sgl/dbl Nov, Jul–Oct, N$2,335/3,408 Dec–Jun.* **$$$$**

🏠 **Desert Camp** [308 G1] (28 chalets) 063 683205; e info@desertcamp.com; www. desertcamp.com. Owned by the same team behind Sossus Oasis & Sossusvlei Lodge, Desert Camp is 8km from the C19 & D826 junction, with a 2km driveway. Here, rather smart chalets blend into the surrounding desert scenery with views across to the mountains. Inside, each has twin beds, en-suite bathroom & granite-tiled floors. The surprise is on the outside, where – along with a BBQ & shaded parking spot – there's a compact lock-up kitchen compartment, complete with 2-plate stove, fridge/freezer & washing facilities, & a picnic table. Guests can rent boxes of cooking utensils, but those who prefer to let someone else do the cooking can eat dinner & b/fast at Sossusvlei Lodge. For groups, 2 bomas with self-catering facilities are available, with a fully stocked & serviced bar whose flat-screen TV keeps you abreast of the latest sports event. There's also a small pool that is very tempting in the heat; collect towels from reception. Free Wi-Fi can be picked up in the central bomas & in the 1st, closest, chalets. *Room only N$1,088/1,382 sgl/dbl; DBB (meals at Sossusvlei Lodge) N$1,853/2,746 sgl/dbl Jul–Nov, N$1,621/2,438 Dec–Jun.* **$$$–$$$$**

🏠 **Little Sossus Lodge & Campsite** [296 C4] (20 chalets, camping) ☏064 464144; m 081 155 5512; e littlesossus@live.com; www.littlesossus. com.na. Overlook the waterhole with sweeping views of the distant Nubib Mountains, the well-spaced chalets here – 12 twin & 4 with 4 beds – all have cool stone walls, polished wood furniture, mosquito nets, & a large en-suite shower. The main area, with Wi-Fi, offers outside dining on the veranda & a long dining room with 2 fires built into the stone walls for winter evenings, a curved bar & a small pool area with sunloungers. Sundowner trips & guided Sossusvlei trips can be arranged, plus you can drive to a nearby natural spring to swim in 3m-deep rock pools.

Opposite the lodge is a campsite with 10 pitches – 7 dbls & 3 family pitches. Each is built on a concrete base with brick walls & high tin roof, designed to take a roof tent, & has its own basic 'en-suite' bathroom with a shower, basin, hot & cold water & flush toilet. (Family pitches have 2 bathrooms & a simple kitchenette.) As well as a small lounge & a large seating area, there's a shop (ring the bell) that stocks most camping essentials, including wood, food, ice & cold drinks, a wide range of foodstuffs, & produce

from the vegetable garden. This is a peaceful place to camp, with mountain views on all sides & the occasional springbok & oryx wandering past. *B&B N$1,520/2,500 sgl/dbl; camping N$150 pp.* **$$–$$$$**

⛺ **Sesriem Campsite** [308 D1] (44 campsites, 6 overflow) ☏063 293652; central reservations ☏061 285 7200; e reservations@nwr.com.na; www.nwr.com.na. In 1989, Sesriem campsite had just 10 pitches, & was the only place in the area. Each was shaded by an old camelthorn tree, which boasted a tap sprouting beside its trunk, & was protected by a low, circular wall. It was stunning. Times have changed, but the bonus is the gates into the park from the campsite open 1hr earlier than the main gates, giving you a head start to reach Sossusvlei.

Today there are 44 pitches, an overflow field (on the left) – which is often busy – & 4 ablution blocks, which can be none too clean. But it's still a marvellous place to camp, especially if you get one of the original pitches, on the edge of the campground. Fuel & wood are available & the campsite shop has a large selection of basic foods, drinks & souvenirs, as well as useful items such as matches – though it's better to bring food with you. Sossus Dune Lodge welcomes campers to dinner, provided they book a table before midday. There's no Wi-Fi, but free tea/coffee are available in the bar & there's a swimming pool.

To guarantee camping space, especially in the high season, you should book at the NWR in Windhoek before arriving, although it's always worth checking on arrival to see if there's a space available. *N$220 pp & park fees (N$80 pp & N$10 per vehicle).* **$$**

⛺ **Sossus Oasis** [308 F1] (camping) ☏063 293632; e reservations@sossus-oasis.com; www. sossus-oasis.com. Owned by the same people as Sossusvlei Lodge & Desert Camp, Sossus Oasis sits at the entrance gate to Sesriem & Sossusvlei. It offers 2 options for campers: simple sites with shared washing & cooking facilities, or private shaded sites with extended tin roofs, en-suite bathroom areas inside log cabins with solar-heated showers, & electricity. There's also a swimming pool. *Camping N$210 pp.* **$$**

GETTING ORGANISED Sesriem is the gateway to this part of the park, and the hub of the area. Park opening times vary depending on sunrise and sunset, but as a general guideline are ⊕ 06.00–18.15 in summer (September–March), and ⊕ 06.45–

17.15 in winter (April–August). The NWR office, where everybody stops to buy their entry permits – is located here and you can fill up with fuel and supplies of cold drinks at Sossus Oasis (page 313). From here a short road leads left to Sesriem Canyon, and another heads straight on, through a second gate, towards Elim Dune, Sesriem's small airfield, and Sossusvlei.

WHAT TO SEE AND DO

Sesriem Canyon About 4km from Sesriem, following the signs left as you enter the gates, is Sesriem Canyon. This is a narrow fissure in the sandstone, 30m deep in places, carved by the Tsauchab River. It was used by the early settlers, who drew water from it by knotting together six lengths of hide rope (called *riems*). Hence it became known as *ses riems*.

For some of the year, the river's bed is marked by pools of blissfully cool water, reached via an easy path of steps cut into the rock. It's a place to swim and relax – perfect for the heat of the day. At other times, though, the water can be almost stagnant and definitely not a place to bathe – except for the large frogs that are marooned in these pools. It's also worth following the watercourse 500m upriver from the steps, where you'll find it before it descends into the canyon – another great place to bathe at times.

Beware of flash floods in the canyon itself. Heavy rain in the Naukluft Mountains occasionally causes these, trapping and drowning visitors.

Sossusvlei area The road from Sesriem to Sossusvlei is soon confined into a corridor, flanked by huge dunes. Gradually this narrows, becoming a few kilometres wide. This unique parting of the southern Namib's great sand sea has probably been maintained over the millennia by the action of the Tsauchab River and the wind.

Although the river seldom flows, note the green camelthorn (*Vachellia erioloba*) which thrives here, clearly indicating permanent underground water. Continuing westward, the present course of the river is easy to spot parallel with the road. Look around for the many dead acacia trees that mark old courses of the river, now dried up. Some of these have been dated at over 500 years old.

For an overview of the natural history of the dunes, see page 296.

Access (☉ *sunrise–sunset; admission N$80, under 16s free, N$20 per car*) To protect the area the Namibian government has closed several vleis over the years that have been damaged by excessive numbers of visitors, and in theory only a certain number of vehicles are allowed to start along the road during three periods each day (sunrise, midday and the afternoon). Even with the rapid increase in tourism to the area, though, the number of visitors rarely, if ever, exceeds each quota.

About 24km after leaving Sesriem, you cross the Tsauchab River and then, after a further 36km, low sand dunes apparently form a final barrier to the progress of the river or the road. Nowadays, this is as far as you can drive yourself, and is where you park – currently free of charge. A large group of acacias shades a couple of picnic tables. Nearby are a few toilets of dubious cleanliness.

From the parking area to Sossusvlei itself, you must either walk or take the shuttle bus. The exception is if you are staying at a nearby lodge and taking a guided excursion, in which case your guide will usually be able to drive closer.

The first pan is only about 500m over the sandbar, but it'll take an hour or more to cover the 5km to the farthest pan, Sossusvlei itself, on foot. Around five shuttle 4x4s are run by NWR from 06.00 until 16.00 (*N$50 pp one-way, N$100 return*). The driver will collect you from Sossusvlei or Dead Vlei at a prearranged time; if you don't want to be rushed, allow around 2–3 hours. Most visitors choose a leisurely walk into the pan when it's relatively cool, returning by bus as the heat intensifies.

Elim Dune As you drive towards Sossusvlei, Elim Dune is about 5km from Sesriem. The turning off to the right is shortly after the entrance into the park, leading to a shady parking spot. It is the nearest sand dune to Sesriem, and if you arrive late in the afternoon, then you might, like me, mistake it for a mountain.

From the parking spot you can climb it, though this takes longer than you might expect – allow at least an hour to get to the top. The views over plains towards the Naukluft Mountains on the east, and dune crests to the west, are remarkable. It is especially worth the long climb at sunset, and conveniently close to the gate at Sesriem.

Numbered dunes Along the final stretch of road towards the parking area are a few side-tracks leading to the feet of some of the dunes, numbered according to their distance along the road from the office. **Dune 45**, on the south side, is particularly photogenic. It is also closest to the road, with a small parking area, and makes a popular climb; you'll often see a black line of human ants slogging up in the early morning sun to catch the views.

Hidden Vlei On the left of the parking area, you'll see signs to Hidden Vlei – which is reached by climbing over the dunes for about 2km. As at Dead Vlei, here you'll find old, dead acacia trees, which were deprived of water when the river changed course, but still stand to tell the tale.

Dead Vlei Like Hidden Vlei, but perhaps more accessible, Dead Vlei is an old pan with merely the skeletons of trees left – some over 500 years old. Many consider it to be more starkly beautiful than Sossusvlei and, if time is short, we suggest that you spend your time here.

From the parking area, walk 1km over the sandbar following the track that will lead you into the large main pan. Keep to the left-hand side, and you'll soon find the old parking area for Dead Vlei. From here, it's a 500m hike over the dunes into Dead Vlei.

Sossusvlei and Nara Vlei After about 4–5km the track bends round to the right, and ends in front of Sossusvlei. This is as far as the pans extend. Beyond here, only tall sand dunes separate you from the Atlantic Ocean.

Most years, the ground here is a flat silvery-white pan of fine mud that has dried into a crazy-paving pattern. Upon this are huge sand mounds collected by nara bushes, and periodic feathery camelthorn trees drooping gracefully. All around the sinuous shapes of the Namib's (and some claim the world's) largest sand dunes stretch up to 300m high. It's a stunning, surreal environment.

Perhaps once every decade, Namibia receives really torrential rain. Storms deluge the Naukluft's ravines and the Tsauchab sweeps out towards the Atlantic in a flash flood, surging into the desert and pausing only briefly to fill its canyon.

Floods so powerful are rare, and Sossusvlei can fill overnight. Though the Tsauchab will subside quickly, the vlei remains full. Miraculous lilies emerge to bloom, and bright yellow devil thorn flowers (*Tribulus* species) carpet the water's edge. Surreal scenes reflect in the lake, as dragonflies hover above its polished surface. Birds arrive and luxuriant growth flourishes, making the most of this ephemeral treat.

These waters recede from most of the pan rapidly, concentrating in Sossusvlei, where they can remain for months. While they are there, the area's birdlife changes radically, as waterbirds and waders will often arrive, along with opportunist insectivores. Meanwhile, less than a kilometre east, over a dune, the main pan is as dry as dust, and looks as if it hasn't seen water in decades.

Individual dunes afford superb views across this landscape, with some of the best from 'Big Daddy'. It's a strenuous climb to the top, looking out across to 'Big Mama', but the climb, followed by a long walk, is rewarded by the spectacle of Dead Vlei laid out below – and the fun of running down the slip-face to reach it.

Ballooning Namib Sky Balloon Safaris (◊ *063 683188;* m *081 304 2205;* e *info@ namibsky.com; www.namibsky.com*) run early morning balloon trips over the desert – which are expensive but superb. You start from Sossusvlei Lodge, Kulala or Sossusvlei Desert Lodge before dawn, and are driven to a take-off site, which varies with the winds and conditions – though if it's too windy, the flight may be cancelled.

The crew gradually unfurl the balloon, and inflate it with propane burners. When ready, everybody climbs into the basket, and the balloon is inflated to take off. Gradually, it sails higher over a rolling vision of mountains, plains and iridescent sand dunes, observing the silent dawn as it rises over one of the earth's most beautiful landscapes. Floating at wind speed is travelling in still air – with only the occasional burst of gas interrupting the silence while you sip on champagne. It's an eerie experience, and an excellent platform for landscape photography.

Beneath the balloon a support vehicle follows as best it can, carrying a table, chairs and full supplies for a champagne breakfast – which is set up wherever the balloon lands. Eventually, everything is loaded on to the support vehicle and its trailer, and guests are returned to where they started, usually a little before midday.

Though a morning's ballooning costs N$6,500 per passenger for a flight lasting between 45 minutes and 1¼ hours, it is such an unusual and exhilarating experience that it is not only highly recommended, but also (arguably) quite good value.

SOLITAIRE AREA

North of the Sesriem area, the C19 leads into the equally beautiful, but pot-holed C14, often with dunes on one side and mountains on the other. These are the main routes from Sesriem to Swakopmund, so are relatively busy (typically a few cars per hour).

SOLITAIRE Solitaire is a large dot on the map, but it is just a few buildings, run by the helpful, if idiosyncratic, Moose. Yet it is so atmospheric, so typical of a middle-of-nowhere stop in the desert, that it's been the location for several film and advert scenes.

There is a fuel station here that is pretty reliable, and it is still the best place for miles to have punctures mended. The Solitaire General Dealer behind the garage opens all hours, selling quite a wide range of supplies (the best around, though that's no great praise). Shopping here, with the wooden counters, old-fashioned weighing scales and jars of sweets, feels like stepping back in time. Buy anything from tinned food and cold drinks to ostrich egg necklaces, kudu leather shoes, cold beer, firewood and basic medicines. They even offer reasonably accurate tourist information. Opposite the General Dealer is a bakery, selling superb fresh bread as well as a wide range of muffins, cakes and pastries and their legendary apple pie, all baked on the premises. Most people stop for a drink and a snack either here or at the neighbouring Café Van Der Lee (⊕ *noon–15.00*), which serves a selection of sausages, steaks and chips for N$90–120.

Where to stay Around Solitaire are several good places to stay while visiting the desert, several of them frequented by group trips. Many of these establishments can be used as bases from which to explore the Sesriem area, while those further north have spectacular mountainous scenery of their own worth seeing, and are useful stopovers on the way to/from Sesriem.

🏠 **Moon Mountain Lodge** [296 C3] (17 rooms) ☎ 067 240901/3/4; m 081 150 2677; e reservations@travel-weaver.com; www. moonmountain.biz. Along the C19, about 50km north of Sesriem, with a 3km driveway, you'll find this impressively situated & privately owned lodge. The last section of the driveway is very steep; best to park at the bottom in the shaded area & be collected by the camp managers. All rooms have private plunge pools, & the 6 suites come with mini kitchenette, bathrobes & particularly palatial bathrooms; camping mattresses & cots are available for kids, & there's also a TV lounge & bar. Excursions to Sossusvlei are the main attraction, but sunset drives (N$500 pp), nature drives & walks, & stargazing are also on offer; they can also book ballooning & scenic flights, & arrange airport pickups from Naukluft (N$166). DBB N$1,813– 2,163/3,154 –3,860 sgl/dbl. $$$$$

🏠 **KuanguKuangu** [296 C3] Contact via Barchan Dune, page 318; e filanciu@ kuangukuangu.com; www.kuangukuangu.com. The answer to every romantic city-dweller's dream lies on the farm owned by Willem & Hannetjie, who also run Barchan Dune Retreat. A hideaway cabin built of natural materials (with kitchen & bathroom, hot water, electricity & – for those who simply can't escape – mobile phone coverage) for just 2 people, it's in an isolated setting northeast of Solitaire. But it's easy to miss – follow the directions to Barchan Dune, but as you approach the farm building, turn left away from the farm towards the grazing horses, & continue down a winding sandy track to KuanguKuangu. If total solitude palls, help is at hand: meals or braai packs are available at the farm. Dinner €23 pp; b/fast €7 pp; braai pack €7 pp), & a farm drive (€13) can also be organised. €120 or N$1,900/night. $$$$

🏠 **Namib Desert Lodge** [296 C3] (72 rooms) ☎ 063 293665; e info@gondwana-collection. com; www.gondwana-collection.com. Directly opposite Moon Mountain (see above), this large lodge sits at the foot of a red sandstone cliff – the 'fossilised' dunes of the protomorphic Namib – within the private Gondwana Namib Park. The

10,000ha reserve incorporates a range of these petrified dunes, & is frequented by oryx, springbok & ostrich. With its location just 60km north of Sesriem, & a mere 5km from the main C19, the lodge is a good starting point for an excursion to Sossusvlei. Expect a warm welcome at reception, which is also an enormous souvenir shop, selling everything from postcards to fluffy toys, including unique Matukondjo dolls handmade by unemployed local women, & it has free Wi-Fi. Set among trees & palms are en-suite rooms (inc 3 family rooms) with AC: neat & functional if a little uninspired. Attractive murals & cow-skin rugs decorate the main area, with its raised, hexagonal fireplace; the large central dining area has several long tables to accommodate the many bus groups that stay here, & there's a well-stocked wine cellar & a bar with a long cocktail list. Outside, 2 swimming pools are fronted by an illuminated waterhole. Visitors may take drives through the park with its magnificent scenery; recommended are the 2hr sunset drives (N$510 pp), which explain the fossilisation & fairy circles (see box, page 320) occurring in the desert. They can also arrange guided hikes customised to travellers' requests. B&B N$1,689/2,706 sgl/dbl. $$$$

🏠 **Namib-Naukluft Lodge** [296 C3] (16 rooms) ☎ 061 372100; e trixim@afex.com. na; www.namib-naukluft-lodge.com. On the C19, south of Solitaire & 60km from Sesriem Gate, this is outwardly rather uninspiring, despite being designed by a well-known Namibian architect. Inside, though, it is plush, with 'normal' modern rooms built in a row. If these, rather than trendy tents, appeal, perhaps this is the place for you.

Each room has adjacent twin beds, en-suite toilet & (powerful) shower, with sliding glass doors leading on to a veranda facing a huge desert plain. There's a large lounge bar & dining room, though meals are often eaten on the veranda, where you can watch the antics of ground squirrels against the desert backdrop. Alternatively, a braai area in the shade of a large kopje offers sociable moonlit dining. At the far end of the row of rooms is a small, popular & sparklingly clean swimming pool & a shaded area for relaxing. There's even a 9-hole golf course – best in the winter months. You can take short walks on the lodge's own land, & – if you don't have a car – reserve a seat on their daily 4x4 trips to Sossusvlei (N$1,250 pp). B&B N$1,400/2,400 sgl/dbl. $$$$

🏠 **Soft Adventure Camp** [296 C3] (15 chalets) 🐾 061 372100; e afex@afex.com.na; www.namib-naukluft-lodge.com. A sister property to Namib Naukluft Lodge, this camp is reached from the C19, south of Solitaire & 60km from the Sesriem Gate; take the same track as for Namib-Naukluft Lodge, but turn left just before you get to the lodge. Its simple, en-suite chalets, constructed around the foot a rocky, granite hill, are sparsely furnished, but come with ceiling fans & AC. The open-sided main area is a small way up the hill, overlooking the chalets & the gravel plains beyond. A small swimming pool nestled among the boulders makes a wonderful spot from which to watch the sunset.

Most visitors spend the mornings visiting Sossusvlei; if you don't have your own vehicle you can arrange a ½-day visit to the dunes (N$1,250 pp). Guests can also take short walks on the land around the lodge, longer guided hiking trails around the mountains & nearby waterhole (N$300 pp), or scenic sundowner drives (N$225). N$1,400/2,400 sgl/dbl. $$$$

🏠 **Rostock Ritz** [321 F4] (20 'igloos', camping) 🐾 064 694000; reservations m 081 258 5722; e reservations@rostock-ritz-desert-lodge.com; www.rostock-ritz-desert-lodge.com. Run by Kücki, of Kücki's in Swakopmund, this unusual lodge is about 5km off the C14, around 20mins' drive south of the C26, passing through the Tropic of Capricorn. Low, stone-built individual 'igloos' with en-suite facilities are designed to keep cool. Each sleeps 2 people & has magnificent views of the surrounding desert. 3 units are suitable for wheelchairs & 2 are luxury. The main area continues the igloo style, with 3 of them linked to create a restaurant, bar & reception area. Outside, the pool has its own commanding views from the unusual hanging sunloungers. Day visitors are welcome to take advantage of the lodge's à la carte restaurant (🕐 lunch noon–14.30, dinner 18.00–late), which is a good spot to break for lunch on a long drive.

7km from the lodge is their campsite with 4 spots, epic views, electric lights, kitchen & solar-heated hot showers. Check in at the lodge, where wood can be bought; campers can dine here, too,

but may not use the pool. Attractions include 10 self-guided hiking trails, ranging from easy to moderately difficult, leading through dunes, canyons & mountains, while for the less energetic there are scenic drives, scenic flights & 4x4 trips to see Bushman cave paintings. N$1,896 /2,892 sgl/ dbl; camping N$128 pp. $–$$$$

🏠 **Solitaire Guest Farm Desert Ranch** [296 C3] (16 rooms, camping) 🐾 062 572024; reservations 🐾 061 305173; e reservations@ solitaireguestfarm.com; www.solitaireguestfarm. com. Off the C14, 500m east of the fuel station at Solitaire, this small guest farm on 5,000ha has been beautifully renovated while retaining its original charm. The en-suite dbl rooms & self-catering house are decorated with wooden carvings & African art, with bright animal-print bedspreads & elephant-print curtains adding a unique touch. In the large dining room, with a fireplace in the corner for winter evenings, owner Walter often eats with the guests around dining tables fashioned from tree trunks. The pool is a favourite with children, & walking, hiking & game drives, including sunset drives & night drives, ensure that the visitor can see something of the area, returning to the option of farm-cooked meals. DBB N$1,375/2,490/3,100 sgl/dbl/trpl; camping N$120 pp. $$$$

🏠 **Barchan Dune Retreat** [296 C3] (3 bungalows, 2 rooms) 🐾 062 682031; e barchan@iway.na; www.barchandunes.com. This friendly little guest farm, owned by Willem & Hannetjie, is about 3km off the D1275; coming from Rehoboth, take the C24 to Nauchas, turn right on to the D1275, then about 20km beyond the Spreetshoogte Pass you'll reach a sign on the left to the farm. Well-camouflaged bungalows, built into the hillside & barely visible from the main house, are bright & airy. Each has 3 beds, a sofa, fresh flowers & a huge en-suite bathroom which bizarrely contains a desk. Dbl rooms are smaller with AC & a shower. At the foot of a kopje, the main area has a lovely carved table for indoor dining, or, in warmer weather, home-cooked meals are served on the porch. It's a peaceful setting with gorgeous views & attracts numerous birds, which you can watch while relaxing on the terrace. For those who want to see something of the area, hiking trails & scenic drives are available. Cash only. DBB N$1,300/2,600 sgl/dbl. $$$$

🏠 **Agama River Camp** [296 C3] (10 chalets, 8 pitches) 🐾 063 293262; e agama@resdest.com;

www.agamarivercamp.com. This peaceful camp is 50km north of Sesriem on the C19 – look out for the international flags blowing outside the gate – makes a good stop off on the way to or from Sossusvlei, & there are a few walks in the area for those who wish to linger. On its russet-coloured chalets, ladders lead up to white-painted roofs where travellers can sleep & stargaze on warm nights. Inside they're cool & spacious with AC, towels for the swimming pools, polished concrete floors, rustic en-suite bathrooms with copper piping & a small terrace. The campsite has its own larger & deeper pool, while pitches have their own washing-up facilities & braai. There's the added bonus of a soft sand base, while the arty ablution facilities are open-topped with stone walls & donkey boilers to heat the water in the evenings.

The communal space has a restaurant, viewing deck & a bar with Wi-Fi. There's shaded parking for cars &, with a 10-day warning, prearranged meals & b/fast packs are available. If you have no tent then these, along with bedding, crockery & cutlery, can be rented in advance (*N$280 pp*). *DBB N$1,330/2,660 sgl/dbl; camping N180 pp.* **$$–$$$$**

🏠 **Solitaire Country Lodge** [296 C3] (25 rooms, camping) 📞 063 293621; reservations 📞 064 062024; e reception@solitairenamibia.com; www.solitairecountrylodge.com. Immediately next to the bustling petrol station, bakery & general store, behind a pole fence neatly planted with aloes & cacti, the single-storey, flat-roofed buildings of this lodge are painted apricot & have a wide, inward-looking veranda area that continues around the quad. A glass-fronted restaurant overlooking a lush central quad of grass & a large swimming pool make this a pleasant outpost. The 23 twins & 2 family rooms are very clean & spacious, with free-standing fans, wrought-iron beds, & en-suite, tiled shower rooms (hot water all day). At the campsite, behind the lodge, there's a hot & cold water ablution block & electricity at all plots. Next door is the Solitaire Moose McGregor Bakery, famed for its apple pie, but there is quite a lot of noise from the petrol station traffic & nearby airstrip. For walkers, the 8km Sunset Hill trail is signposted from the lodge. *N$1,320/2,340 sgl/dbl; camping N$100 pp.* **$–$$$$**

🏠 **Weltevrede Guest Farm** [296 C3] (17 rooms, camping) 📞 063 293208; e info@weltevredeguestfarm.com; www.weltevredeguestfarm.com. Signposted east of the C14, Weltevrede is about 47km from Sesriem, 37km from Solitaire, with a 1km driveway. Next to the farm's main buildings, en-suite rooms are motel-style, simple structures with 24hr electricity, a good-size private terrace & parking. Clean & spacious, they're furnished with a wardrobe, carved table, & cream linens, & have a small patio for sunset. Rooms 1–13 have views of the plains & a small waterhole. A small bridge beside the papyrus-filled pond leads to the large thatched dining area, where meals are served, an honesty bar operates & there's free tea & coffee. Weltevrede also has 4 tent pitches under shady trees, best booked in advance. Pitches have water & electricity, & there are showers, flush toilets & a firepit (wood & ice can be bought). Both campers & farm guests can use the circular swimming pool. The reception area doubles as a curio shop selling postcards & souvenirs. Wi-Fi is available in the bar (*N$20/day*). *DBB N$1,200/1,550 sgl/dbl; camping N$150 pp.* **$–$$$$**

THE PARK'S NORTHERN SECTION

Between the normally dry beds of the Swakop and Kuiseb rivers, the desert is largely rock and stone. Though the area has few classic desert scenes of shifting dunes, the landscapes are still striking and certainly no less memorable. They range from the deeply incised canyons of the Swakop River Valley to the open plains around Ganab, flat and featureless but for the occasional isolated inselberg.

WHEN TO VISIT The prime time to visit this section of the park is towards the end of the rains, when the vegetation is at its most lush and, if you are lucky, you'll find scattered herds of oryx, springbok and zebra. During this time the best campsites to go to are the more open ones, like Ganab, on the plains.

For the rest of the year it is still spectacular, but you'll find fewer animals around. Then perhaps it's better to visit Homeb, or one of the inselbergs, as the flora and fauna there remain a little more constant than on the plains – not shrivelling up so much in the dryness of winter.

ACCESS TO THE PARK (*N$80 per adult, plus N$10 per vehicle, under 16s free*) To drive off the main roads in this area (that is anywhere *except* the C14, C28, D1982 and D198), you need a permit, which must be obtained in advance from the NWR in Windhoek (page 173) or the park office at Sesriem. These permits allow you to venture on to the park's smaller roads and to camp in any of the area's sites for an additional fee. Most of the roads are navigable by 2WD, with only a few around Oryxwater and Groot Tinkas classed as 4x4. Even these are probably negotiable with a high-clearance 2WD and a skilled driver, though you'd be waiting a very long time indeed for anyone to pass by if you became stuck.

Few of the maps of Namibia show these roads clearly, with the notable exception of the Globetrotter map, published by Struik.

WHERE TO STAY

Namib-Naukluft campsites (*No advance reservations: permits available from the MET, who have an office in Swakopmund; N$80 per site plus N$20/10 adult/child, excluding park fees*) Basic campsites are situated at Kuiseb Bridge, Homeb, Mirabib, Groot Tinkas, Kriess-se-Rus, Vogelfederberg, Bloedkoppie, Ganab and Swakop River. They have no facilities to speak of, except for communal ablution facilities, but there is plenty of variety for you to choose from. To spend a night or two camping here – which is the only way to do this part of the desert justice – you must be fully independent in terms of fuel, food, water and firewood.

Ⱥ Bloedkoppie [321 D1] (or Blutkopje) Literally 'blood hill', for its colour in the light of sunset, this large, smooth granite inselberg rises out of the Tinkas Flats near the Swakop River. It can provide some challenging scrambles if the heat has not drained your energy. Do not approach any birds' nests, as some of the raptors in the park are very sensitive to disturbance; they may even abandon them if you go too close. Look out for the temporary pools after the rains, filled with life. Sadly, there have been reports that facilities here are not maintained as well as they could be, & that the bins are not changed often enough.

Ⱥ Ganab [321 E2] Right next to a dry watercourse, which winds like a thin green snake through the middle of a large gravel plain, this open site has a wind-powered water pump nearby. Around Mar, if the rains have been good, then it can be an excellent spot for herds of springbok & oryx – & you can see for miles.

Ⱥ Groot Tinkas [321 E1] Hidden away in a valley amid a maze of small kopjes, there is a small dam with sheer walls of rock & some fairly challenging rough driving too. Look out for frogs in the pool, & turn over a few stones to find scorpions & their harmless mimics, pseudo-scorpions.

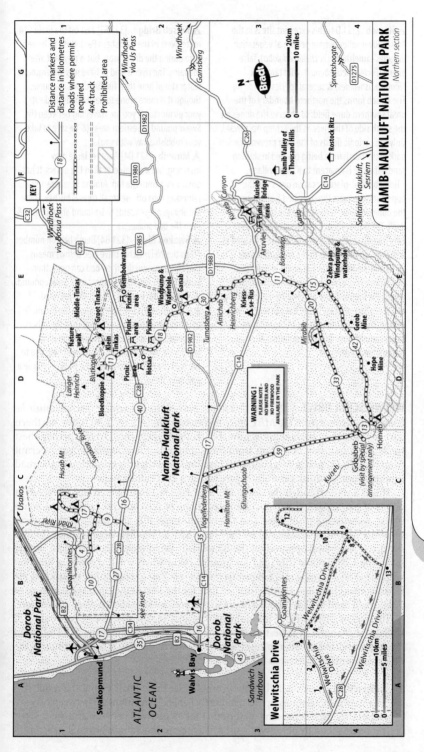

NAMIB-NAUKLUFT NATIONAL PARK
Northern section

KEY

	Distance markers and distance in kilometres
	Roads where permit required
	4x4 track
	Prohibited area

0   20km
0   10 miles

N

Bradt

WARNING !
PLEASE NOTE –
NO WATER AND
NO FIREWOOD
AVAILABLE IN THE PARK

Welwitschia Drive

0   10km
0   5 miles

Goanikontes

Welwitschia Drive

Dorob National Park

Swakopmund

ATLANTIC OCEAN

Walvis Bay

Sandwich Harbour

Namib-Naukluft National Park

Windhoek via Bosua Pass

Windhoek via Us Pass

Windhoek

Gamsberg

Spreetshoogte

Rostock Ritz

Namib Valley of a Thousand Hills

Kuiseb Canyon

Kuiseb Bridge

Picnic areas

Solitaire, Naukluft, Sesriem

Gaub

Aruvlei

Bakenkop

Zebra pan Windpump & waterhole

Gorob Mine

Hope Mine

Mirabib

Kriess-se-Rus

Heinrichberg

Amichab

Tsamsberg

Windpump & Waterhole

Ganab

Gemsbokwater

Picnic area

Middle Tinkas

Groot Tinkas

Nature walk

Klein Tinkas

Blutkoppie

Bloedkoppie

Picnic area

Hotsas

Langer Heinrich

Husab Mt

Khan River

Swakop River

Goanikontes

Usakos

Vogelfederberg

Hamilton Mt

Ghaubchaob

Gobabeb (visit by special arrangement only)

Homeb

Kuiseb

321

Ⓧ Homeb [321 D4] This excellent site is in the Kuiseb River valley, where perennial vegetation includes camelthorn (*Vachellia erioloba*), false ebony (*Euclea pseudebenus*), wild tamarisk (*Tamarix usneoides*) & several species of wild fig. The Kuiseb forms the northern boundary of the great southern dune field, so observe the dunes on the south side of the river as they creep northward. Only the periodic floods of the river prevent the park to the north from being covered in shifting sands. The site is adjacent to a small village.

Homeb's well-placed location gives you the opportunity to cross the river-bed & climb among the dunes, as well as to explore the river valley itself. The proximity of 3 different environments is why Namibia's Desert Research Centre is located at Gobabeb, on the Kuiseb to the west of Homeb.

Ⓧ Kriess-se-Rus [321 E3] Again in a dry river-bed, Kriess-se-Rus lies below a bank of exposed schist. The layers of rock are clear to see, providing an interesting contrast to the flat calcrete plains nearby. You'll find quivertrees (*Aloe dichotoma*), many camelthorns, & some euphorbia & commiphora bushes.

Ⓧ Kuiseb Bridge [321 F3] Just off the main C14 route, west of the Gamsberg Pass, this can be very bare during the dry season, but is pleasant after the rains. The river is said to have less underground water stored here than further down its course, though it is more prone to flash floods. Make it your picnic stop if you are travelling between the Swakopmund & Sesriem areas (& be sure to take your rubbish away with you).

Ⓧ Mirabib [321 D4] Another large grey inselberg, but even quieter than the others. It has great views from the top. Around it, where any rainwater runs off, are small trees & bushes. There are always a few lizards to be found around here, & even the odd snake.

Ⓧ Swakop River [321 B4] Being beacon number 10 on the Welwitschia Drive (see below) means that this beautiful dry river-bed can get rather busy at times with day trippers from Swakopmund.

Ⓧ Vogelfederberg [321 C3] This rounded granite outcrop is the closest site to the ocean, & gets more moisture from the fog than the others. Its shape helps form a number of fascinating temporary pools. Polaroid glasses will help you to see past the reflections & into the pools; if you've a pair, take them.

WELWITSCHIA DRIVE [321 A3] (*N$40 pp, plus N$10 per vehicle; permits must be bought in advance from the MET office in Swakopmund – page 329*) In the northern corner of the Namib-Naukluft National Park, the Welwitschia Drive is perhaps best treated as a half-day excursion from Swakopmund. It is essential to get a permit from the MET office in Swakopmund first, and note that the condition of the road is pretty poor, so think carefully before taking a 2WD along here.

This is a route through the desert along which are 13 numbered stone beacons at points of particular interest. It culminates at one of the country's largest, and hence oldest, welwitschia plants (see also the box on page 408, and take a look at www.plantzafrica.com, a website run by the South African Biodiversity Institute). To find the drive, leave Swakopmund on the B2 towards Windhoek, then turn right shortly on to the C28. Follow this road for around 16km when you'll come to a junction with the D1991 – you could follow this north for 4.5km to have coffee or lunch at the Goanikontes Oasis Rest Camp. Turn left here for the start of the circuit (see map, page 321). You'll need to allow about 4 hours so that you can stop at each place and explore.

The recent discovery of uranium in this area means that the drive route will shortly be changed. It is best to check the latest information at the MET office in Swakopmund before attempting the trip. However, here is a brief outline of the different points of interest at the beacons:

1   **Lichen field** Look carefully at the ground to see these small 'plants', the result of a symbiotic relationship (ie: a mutually beneficial relationship between two organisms, each depending on the other for its survival) between an alga, producing food by photosynthesis, and a fungus, providing a physical structure.

Look closely, and you'll see many different types of lichen. Some are thought to be hundreds of years old, and all are exceedingly fragile and vulnerable.

2 **Drought-resistant bushes** Two types of bush found all over the Namib are the dollar bush, so called because its leaves are the size of a dollar coin, and the ink bush. Both can survive without rain for years. Despite the sign here, there are few drought-resistant bushes to be seen!

3 **Tracks of ox wagons** Although made decades ago, these are still visible, showing the damage that can so easily be done to the lichen fields by driving over them.

4 **The moonscape** This is an unusual and spectacular view, usually called the moonscape, looking over a landscape formed by the valleys of the Swakop River. It is best seen in the slanting light of early morning or late afternoon.

5 **More lichen fields** These remarkable plants can extract all their moisture requirements from the air. To simulate the dramatic effect of a morning fog, simply sprinkle a little water on one and watch carefully for a few minutes.

6 This is another impressive view of the endless moonscape.

7 **Old South African camp** This is the site of an old military camp, occupied for just a few days during World War I.

8 Turn left at this marker to visit the next few beacons.

9 **A dolerite dyke** These dark strips of rock, common in this part of the Namib, were formed when molten lava welled up through cracks in the existing grey granite. After cooling it formed dark bands of rock which resisted erosion more than the granite – and thus has formed the spine of many ridges in the area.

10 **The Swakop River Valley** Picnicking in the river-bed, with a profusion of tall trees around, you might find it difficult to believe that you are in a desert. It could be said that you're not – after all, this rich vegetation is not made up of desert-adapted species. It includes wild tamarisk (*Tamarix usurious*) and anaboom (*Faidherbia albida*), better known for its occurrence in the humid Zambezi Valley almost 1,600km east – sustained by underground water percolating through the sands beneath your feet.

11 **Welwitschia Flats** This open expanse of gravel and sand is home to the Namib's most celebrated plant, the endemic *Welwitschia mirabilis*. These are found only in the Namib, and at just a few locations which suit their highly adapted biology.

12 **The big welwitschia** This beacon marks the end of the trail, and one of the largest *Welwitschia mirabilis* known – estimated at over 1,500 years old. Visitors are asked not to walk inside the ring of stones placed here to protect the plant.

13 **Old mine workings** On the way back to Swakopmund, continue straight past beacon 8, without turning right. Where the road joins route C28 to Swakopmund, marked by this final beacon, is one of the desert's old mine workings. In the 1950s, iron ore was mined by hand here. Now it is just another reminder of the park's chequered past.

SEND US YOUR SNAPS!

We'd love to follow your adventures using our *Namibia* guide – why not tag us in your photos and stories via Twitter (🐦 *@BradtGuides*) and Instagram (📷 *@bradtguides*)? Alternatively, you can upload your photos directly to the gallery on the Namibia destination page via our website (*www.bradtguides. com/namibia*).

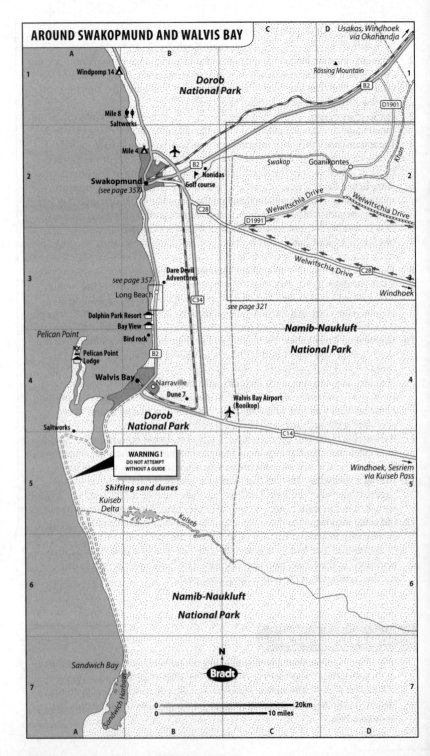

AROUND SWAKOPMUND AND WALVIS BAY

Usakos, Windhoek via Okahandja

Rössing Mountain

Dorob National Park

Windpomp 14

Mile 8 Saltworks

Mile 4

Swakopmund
(see page 357)

Nonidas
Golf course

Swakop

Goanikontes

Khan

Welwitschia Drive

Welwitschia Drive

Welwitschia Drive

Windhoek

see page 357

Dare Devil Adventures

Long Beach

Dolphin Park Resort
Bay View
Bird rock

see page 321

Namib-Naukluft National Park

Pelican Point

Pelican Point Lodge

Walvis Bay

Narraville

Dune 7

Walvis Bay Airport (Rooikop)

Saltworks

Dorob National Park

WARNING !
DO NOT ATTEMPT
WITHOUT A GUIDE

Windhoek, Sesriem via Kuiseb Pass

Shifting sand dunes

Kuiseb Delta

Kuiseb

Namib-Naukluft National Park

N

Brad†

Sandwich Bay

Sandwich Harbour

0 ————— 20km
0 ————— 10 miles

14

Swakopmund and Walvis Bay Area

Flying low over Namibia's coastline is probably the best way to get a sense of perspective about it. You see how it divides the South Atlantic Ocean from the baking desert. Both seem harsh and unforgiving.

Clinging to the boundary, often under a blanket of morning fog, are Swakopmund and Walvis Bay. Politically, Walvis Bay has always been vital. It has the only deepwater harbour between Lüderitz and Angola. Historically, Swakopmund is probably the more interesting, with old German architecture to rival that in Lüderitz.

Most visitors stay in Swakopmund, which tends to be the livelier of the two, though birders in particular may prefer Walvis Bay. Both have a good choice of small hotels and restaurants, making them obvious stops when driving between the Namib-Naukluft National Park and the Skeleton Coast or Damaraland.

HISTORY

In 1884, the whole of present-day Namibia was declared a protectorate of Germany – except the region's only large natural harbour, Walvis Bay, which remained under British control. Thus, in order to develop their interests in the area, the German authorities decided to make their own harbour on the northern banks of the Swakop River, and beacons were planted in 1892 to mark the spot, where The Mole is today (page 345). Following this, the German authorities made several (largely unsuccessful) attempts to develop landing facilities. A quay was built, although it subsequently silted up, followed by a wooden, and later an iron, jetty. Finally in 1915, when Germany's control of the country was surrendered to South Africa, all maritime trade reverted to Walvis Bay.

During the South African administration of Namibia, before independence, there was a deliberate policy of developing no other ports to compete with Walvis Bay – as South Africa anticipated keeping hold of the Walvis Bay enclave, even if it was forced into giving most of Namibia independence.

As planned, South Africa kept the Walvis Bay enclave as part of the Cape Colony even after Namibian independence in 1990, though it agreed to a joint administration in 1992, and finally relented in February 1994, when Walvis Bay officially became part of Namibia.

SWAKOPMUND

Considered by most Namibians to be the country's only real holiday resort, this old German town spreads from the mouth of the Swakop River out into the surrounding desert plain, and is climatically more temperate than the interior. The palm-lined streets, immaculate old buildings and well-kept gardens of the centre give Swakop (as the locals call it) a unique atmosphere, and make it a hugely pleasant oasis in which to spend a few days.

Unlike much of Namibia, Swakopmund is used to tourists, and has a wide choice of places to stay and eat, and many things to do. The town has also established a name for itself as a centre for adventure travel, attracting visitors seeking 'adrenalin' trips to take part in options ranging from free-fall parachuting to dune-bike riding and sandboarding. This is still too small to change the town's character, but is enough to ensure that you'll never be bored. On the other hand, visit on a Monday during one of the quieter months, and you could be forgiven for thinking that the town had partially closed down!

To a certain extent, Swakopmund is a victim of its own success, with more and more people seeking to buy property on the coast, which in turn has put pressure on its infrastructure. While the increasing diversity of shops is for some a positive result, it also means that you'll have to book a table at the town's most popular restaurants, even

out of season. Rather more importantly, there is now enormous pressure on the already overstretched water supply, which is currently piped in from elsewhere in Namibia. Talk of building desalination plants so that the town can be self-sufficient has been partially realised, with one completed and another under construction. This, however, has only been triggered by the massive water demand made by new uranium mines in the coastal desert: uranium has provided the cash and therefore uranium gets the water. But there is light at the end of the tunnel. Uranium mines have a lifespan of around ten–15 years and thereafter the water should become available to the public. It is hoped that this will eventually become a lasting and positive legacy of the current, highly controversial mining policy.

GETTING THERE AND AWAY

By air There are currently no scheduled flights into Swakopmund, so visitors need to fly to Walvis Bay (page 348). A pre-booked transfer from Walvis Bay Airport into Swakopmund costs around N$300–400, or N$90 per person by local taxi. Air Namibia on Sam Nujoma Avenue [331 D4] (\064 405123; ⏱ 08.00–13.00 & 14.00–17.00 Mon–Fri) is a useful office for reconfirming onward flights and other airline business.

By train Swakopmund is linked to Windhoek and Walvis Bay by the normal, slow TransNamib train services. These run from and to Windhoek every day

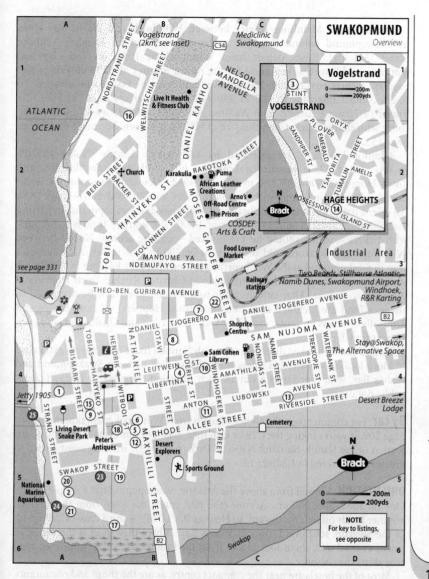

Vogelstrand

VOGELSTRAND

HAGE HEIGHTS

ATLANTIC
OCEAN

Industrial Area

Two Beards, Stillhouse Atlantic,
Namib Dunes, Swakopmund Airport,
Windhoek,
R&R Karting

Stay@Swakop,
The Alternative Space

Desert Breeze
Lodge

see page 331

Railway
station

NOTE
For key to listings,
see opposite

except Saturday, Monday and Wednesday arriving into Swakopmund at 05.02, and thence to Walvis Bay for 07.15. Trains depart from Walvis Bay at 19.15, arriving in Swakopmund at 20.30, and Windhoek at 07.00 the next day. See page 151 for details, or call the station in Swakopmund (\064 463187).

The *Desert Express* (page 152) is a completely different, high-end service aimed primarily at tourists – though following an increasingly sporadic service, all trains were withdrawn for repairs in 2018, and its future seems very uncertain.

Street name changes A number of street names changes have recently been

By bus Several bus services link Swakopmund and Windhoek, with stops at Usakos, Karibib and Okahandja. Note that times for all buses will be an hour earlier between April and October.

The Intercape Mainliner service between Windhoek and Walvis Bay stops in Swakopmund behind the Pick n Pay supermarket on Hendrik Witbooi Street [331 E4]. Buses depart from Windhoek at 10.00 on Thursday and Saturday, and leave Swakopmund for the return journey at 10.35 on Friday and Sunday. Tickets cost N$200–280 one-way and must be booked in advance. To book, contact Intercape (\ +27 21 380 4400; www.intercape.co.za) or Sure Ritz Travel (4 Hewepa Arcade, Sam Nujoma Av; \ 064 405151; www.sureritztravel. com), who charge a ticket-handling fee of N$25 per person. For more details, see page 153.

Additional options are operated by Welwitschia Shuttle (\ 064 405105; m 081 263 1433; e mandie@afol.com.na; http://welwitschiashuttle.com), and Town Hoppers (\ 064 407223; m 081 210 3062; e townhoppers@iway.na; www. namibiashuttle.com), along with Carlo's and McClune's in Walvis Bay (page 348). All offer a daily minibus service between Windhoek and Swakopmund, departing Swakopmund at 07.00 and Windhoek at 14.00. The journey time is 4–5 hours, with tickets – which should be pre-booked – costing around N$260 between Windhoek and Swakopmund one-way, or N$300 to Walvis Bay. All minibuses stop in Swakopmund at the Woolworth's parking area [331 E4], but in Windhoek the stops are different: Welwitschia buses at Christus Kirche; Town Hoppers at the railway station. Alternatively, door-to-door collection can be organised in advance (and are included in the cost for Town Hoppers), as can pickups and drop-offs at towns en route, including Usakos, Karibib and Okahandja, and even airport transfers.

Tickets can be booked directly or through Namib i (page 330), for no extra cost.

More locally, Welwitschia offers a regular service between Swakopmund and Walvis Bay, with four buses a day in each direction, Monday to Friday (except public holidays).

By car For comments on the choice of roads from Windhoek to Swakopmund, see page 209. If you're taking the C28 or C26 then also see comments on the northern section of the Namib-Naukluft National Park (page 319). The long coastal road to the north is covered in *Chapter 15*.

ORIENTATION Viewed from above the Atlantic, Swakopmund has a simple layout. One tar road, Sam Nujoma Avenue (the B2), enters the town from the interior; another heads off left, northward, to Henties Bay (C34). A third crosses the mouth of the Swakop, southward towards Walvis Bay. Where they meet is the centre of town, a raised area about four blocks from the Promenade – the palm-lined road that skirts the seashore.

Most of the hotels are near the compact centre, as are the shops and restaurants, so it's an easy town to walk around. In recent years, though, an explosion of development has hit this small resort, obliterating sea views almost overnight in the scramble to build ever closer to the shore. Whereas once the campsite at 'Mile 4' was quite literally four miles from Swakopmund, today the town's suburban sprawl has crept up to meet it. While this has had little impact on the centre of town in itself, it has certainly changed the picture from above.

Street name changes A number of street name changes have recently been introduced in Swakopmund, replacing the familiar German names with others to honour local and national dignitaries. Inevitably, many of the former names are still used, as follows:

- Bahnhof Street *is now* Theo-Ben Gurirab Avenue
- Breite Street *is now* Nathaniel Maxuilili Street
- Brücken Street *is now* Libertina Amathila Avenue
- Kaiser Wilhelm Street *is now* Sam Nujoma Avenue
- Knobloch/Kolonnen *is now* Rakotoka
- Lazarett Street *is now* Anton Lubowski Avenue
- Moltke Street *is now* Tobias Hainyeko Street
- Nordring/Sudring *is now* Moses Garoëb Street
- Post Street *is now* Daniel Tjongarero Avenue
- Promenade *is now* Molen Street
- Roon Street *is now* Hendrik Witbooi
- Schlacter *is now* Welwitschia
- Woermann St *is now* Leutwein Street

GETTING AROUND Swakopmund's centre is so small that most visitors walk around it, although obviously you'll need a car to get out of the centre.

By bike The Cycle Clinic [331 E3] (*10 Hendrik Witbooi St;* \064 402530), between the Hansa Hotel and Sam Nujoma Avenue, hires out bicycles (*N$20/hr, N$100/day*). These range from mountain bikes to touring models, and come complete with (compulsory) cycle helmets. A deposit of N$200 is required. It's also possible to hire bikes from the Strand Hotel [331 B2] (*N$200/½ day*). Alternatively, Swakopmund Cycle Tours (page 371) can drop off rental bikes at your hotel.

By car If you're hiring a car on arrival, then any of the local **car-hire** companies will meet you at Walvis Bay Airport (there are currently no direct flights into Swakopmund). Some have offices in both towns; others are just in Walvis Bay (page 352).

🚗 **Avis** Swakopmund Hotel & Entertainment Centre; \064 402527
🚗 **Bidvest** \+27 11 398 0383; e reservations@bidvestcarrental.co.za
🚗 **Budget** Swakopmund Hotel & Entertainment Centre; \064 402527/204128

🚗 **Crossroads 4x4 Hire** 3 Henties Bay Rd/ Nordring St; \064 403777; e crossroads@iway.na; www.crossroads4x4hire.com. 4x4 specialist.
🚗 **Europcar** See *Walvis Bay*, page 352
🚗 **Hertz** See *Walvis Bay*, page 352

A word of warning for drivers It is not advisable to drive between Swakopmund and Walvis Bay late in the evening. Although the distance is short and both the B2 and the parallel C34 roads are good, the B2 in particular tends to be used as a race track by drink-drivers, and there are frequent accidents.

Taxis There is no organised taxi service in Swakopmund, but during the day taxis frequent the town centre, where it's likely that they will find you before you find them. Do exercise caution when getting into any unbooked taxi; rather, organise one through your hotel or pension.

TOURIST INFORMATION
ℹ️ **Henckert Tourist Centre** Cnr Sam Nujoma Av & Nathaniel Maxuilili Av
Ministry of Environment & Tourism (MET) [331 D4] Cnr Sam Nujoma Av & Bismarck St; \064

404576; ⏲ 08.00–13.00 & 14.00–17.00 Mon–Fri, 08.00–13.00 Sat. Upstairs from NWR you can obtain permits for entry to national parks here, including the new Dorob National Park.

Namibia Wildlife Resorts (NWR) Cnr Sam Nujoma Av & Bismarck St; \064 402172; ⏲ 08.00–17.00 Mon–Fri. Travellers make reservations for NWR accommodation, including campsites in some of the parks.

ℹ Namib i [331 E3] Cnr Sam Nujoma Av & Hendrik Witbooi St; \064 404827; e namibi@ iway.na; ⏲ 08.30–13.00 & 14.00–17.00 Mon–Fri (opens & closes ½hr earlier in winter), 09.00–13.00 Sat–Sun. The superb tourist information bureau in the centre of town has an extensive selection of pamphlets & information on Namibia, with a special emphasis on the local area, & it also sells postcards & stamps – don't miss it.

 WHERE TO STAY When thinking about visiting Swakopmund, note that from about mid-December to mid-January, the whole population of Windhoek seems to decamp to the relative cool of this coastal town for their 'summer break'. As a result, hotels and guesthouses get fully booked, and the town is filled to bursting, so reservations are essential. At other times, Swakopmund is not so frantic, though the better (and better value) hotels usually need reserving before you arrive. As the town is well used to families, many establishments offer a special rate for children, so it's well worth asking.

Because of Swakopmund's cooling morning fogs, and the moderating maritime influence on its temperatures, air conditioning is seldom needed here and few of the hotels provide it, though several do have heating. For the same reason, camping on the large, open sites by the sea can be very cold and uncomfortable, while the cheaper bed and breakfasts and guesthouses are very reasonably priced. So even if you're camping for most of your trip, this may be a good place to treat yourself to a bed for the night. Below, the various establishments are divided into hotels, pensions and bed and breakfasts, backpackers' lodges, restcamps and camping.

Hotels

Along with some large, international-style hotels, Swakopmund has many other small hotels full of character, & a few gems.

⌂ The Strand Hotel [331 B2] (125 rooms) The Mole; \064 411 4000/4308; e strand.res@ol.na; www.strandhotelswakopmund.com. On the site of the old Strand Hotel, this modern building on the historic Mole is one of the newer international-style hotels, just a few mins' walk from the beach & with views of the Atlantic from some of its AC rooms. These are modern & smartly decorated, their black-&-white photos & paintings preventing them from feeling too sterile. Each is en suite & kitted out with a tea & coffee station, minibar, satellite TV & free Wi-Fi, while 'luxury' rooms & the suites have their own balconies with guaranteed beach or sea views.

The main foyer is bright & airy, with a number of comfortable sofas, & direct access to the hotel's 4 restaurants: Ocean Cellar, Farmhouse Deli, Brew & Butcher & Café Mole, as well as an

SWAKOPMUND *Town centre*
For listings, see left

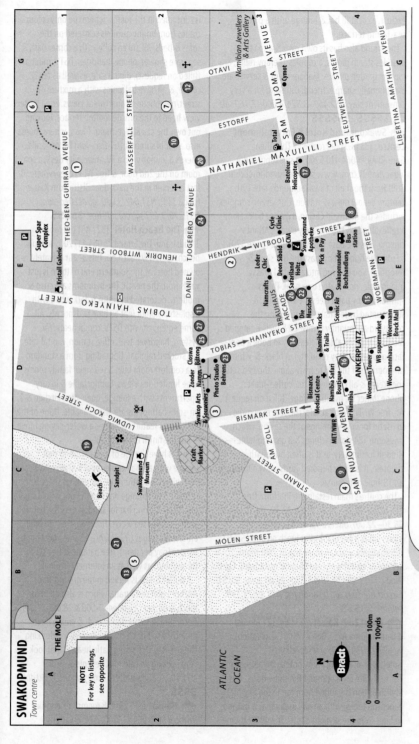

SWAKOPMUND

Town centre

NOTE
For key to listings, see opposite

THE MOLE

ATLANTIC
OCEAN

MOLEN STREET

Beach

Sandpit

Swakopmund
Museum

Craft
Market

Super Spar
Complex

Kristall Galerie

TOBIAS HAINYEKO STREET

LUDWIG KOCH STREET

THEO-BEN GURIRAB AVENUE

WASSERFALL STREET

HENDRIK WITBOOI STREET

DANIEL TJOGERERO AVENUE

STRAND STREET

SAM ZOLL STREET

BISMARK STREET

SAM NUJOMA AVENUE

TOBIAS HAINYEKO STREET

HENDRIK WITBOOI STREET

NATHANIEL MAXUILILI STREET

SAM NUJOMA AVENUE

OTAVI STREET

ESTORFF

LEUTWEIN STREET

WOERMANN STREET

LIBERTINA AMATHILA AVENUE

Namibian Jewellers
& Arts Gallery

Lymot

Total

Bateleur
Helicopters

Cycle
Clinic

Swakopmund
Apotheke

CNA

Pick n Pay

Bus
station

Leder
Chic

Deon Sibold

Holtz

Safariland

Namcrafts

BRAUHAUS
ARCADE

Die
Muschel

Swakopmunder
Buchhandlung

Scenic Air

Namibia Tracks
& Trails

ANKERPLATZ

WB supermarket

Woermann
Brock Mall

Woermann Tower

Woermannhaus

Bismarck
Medical Centre

Namibia Safari
Boutique

MET/NWR

Air Namibia

Swakop Arts
& Souvenirs

Zonder
Nanny

Closwa
Biltong

Photo Studio
Behrens

Swakopmund
Museum

Namibian

0 100m
0 100yds

N
Bradt

1
2
3
4

A B C D E F G

exclusive cocktail bar & lounge with a private sea-facing terrace.

The Strand also has its own gym & a spa that includes steam rooms, a couples' therapy room, & a rooftop garden terrace. Management & service are exceptionally sharp & friendly, making for a very convenient stay. *N$2,460–3,826/4,000–7,160 sgl/ dbl.* **$$$$$–$$$$$$**

🏠 **Swakopmund Hotel & Entertainment Centre** [331 G1] (90 rooms) 2 Theo-Ben Gurirab Av; 📞 064 410 5200; e swakopmund@ legacyhotels.com; www.swakopmundhotel.com. Built from the shell of Swakopmund's late 19th-century yellow railway station, this leisure complex includes the Mermaid Casino, a gym, a hair salon, a reflexologist & the privately owned Atlanta cinema, & is the base for Avis car hire (page 329).

From the huge lobby, past the gift shop & reception, you emerge into a central grassy quadrangle, dominated by a pool. This is surrounded by palm trees & easy chairs, & surmounted by fountains. Overlooking the courtyard are brightly furnished & well-equipped rooms, 1 with disabled access; try to book a pool-facing room, as they're quieter. A black-&-white photograph of the old railway above the bed sets the scene, & all come with tea/coffee-maker, phone, Mnet TV, minibar/fridge (filled on request), AC, free Wi-Fi & digital safe. The safe may come in useful for your winnings at the casino, which has some 184 slot machines & 8 gaming tables – though fortunately, as it is often busy with local clientele, it is a few hundred yards away. Close by is an 18-hole golf course.

The centre's main restaurant, Platform One (🕐 *b/fast 06.30–10.00, lunch 12.30–14.30, dinner 18.30–22.00*), offers a varied à la carte menu Mon–Sat & a popular buffet lunch on Sun (*$$$*). Alternatively, you can make use of 24hr room service or visit the on-site Chinese restaurant, Chez Wou (🕐 *13.00–14.30 & 17.30–22.00 daily; $$$*). *Airport transfers can be arranged. N$2,495/3,590 sgl/dbl.* **$$$$$**

🏠 **Hotel Zum Kaiser** [331 C4] (21 rooms) 4 Sam Nujoma Av; 📞 064 417100; reservations 📞 +27 21 930 4564; e reservations@ hotelzumkaiser.com; www.hotelzumkaiser.com. Formerly the Swakopmund Boutique Hotel, this stylish option is painted from top to toe in white & neutral tones, with an airy lobby that is bathed in light from the skylight above. The white theme

is continued in the rooms, where the only colour comes from bright cushions scattered on the sofas & beds. All are en suite with a corner bath & separate shower, phone, hairdryer, DSTV, minibar (filled on request), digital safe, as well as tea & coffee, & all have balconies with a mixture of street/neighbouring apartment views. For a better view head to the private rooftop terrace, looking out over the sea & Woermann Tower, where there's also a bar in summer (🕐 *Dec–Jan*) for cocktails. There's a lounge with a TV, an activity desk, a spa room on the 2nd floor, & free Wi-Fi everywhere. B/ fast is served in the next-door Bistro Zum Kaiser (page 339). *N$1,047/3,020 sgl/dbl Dec–Jun; N$1,270/3,692 sgl/dbl Jul–Nov.* **$$$$$**

🏠 **The Beach Hotel** [327 A5] (33 rooms) 1 Südstrand/The Strand; 📞 064 417700; e info@ beach.na; www.beach.na. This 3-star privately owned hotel at the southern end of town is just yards from the beach. The bedrooms are crisp & modern, decorated in white & dark wood with a splash of colour lent by blue bedspreads. All come equipped with DSTV, combi heater/AC system, hairdryer, tea/coffee station, digital safe & a stocked minibar. Upgrading from a standard to a comfort room buys a sea view; family rooms have limited sea views. Comfortable & luxury apartments with a lounge, open-plan kitchen & 2 en-suite bathrooms are also available. None of the bathrooms features a bath – a water-saving move – but the finish is high quality.

Guests have the use of a wraparound roof terrace with a small corner pool & superlative 360° views, but otherwise communal space is restricted to a lounge on the 4th floor with a small, unofficial-looking bar for sundowners & a balcony with pleasant sea views. However, they do offer on-site massages (*N$315/hr*), a same-day laundry service (pay per item), free parking & free Wi-Fi throughout, as well as an internet terminal.

A buffet b/fast is served in the ground-floor Anchor Point restaurant, which is also open for lunch & dinner (🕐 *noon–14.00 & 18.00–21.30*). Decorated in smart dark woods & cream linen tablecloths, it has a covered terrace overlooking the street with flaming patio heaters that look very inviting on cold misty evenings. *From N$1,100/1,800 sgl/dbl to luxury apt N$3,000 dbl.* **$$$$**

🏠 **Hansa** [331 E3] (58 rooms) 3 Hendrik Witbooi St; 📞 064 414200; e reservations@

hansahotel.com.na; www.hansahotel.com.na. One of the oldest hotels in Swakopmund, the Hansa is privately owned & fairly large – though it has a private residents' lounge with a small library & a separate wood-panelled bar (with a fireplace for the winter). Light lunches (*about N$140*) can be eaten on the terrace next to a lush tropical garden, as well as in the award-winning restaurant (page 339). Its good-size rooms with solid furnishings were gradually being updated in 2018. All are heated, have AC, direct-dial phones, digital safes, well-stocked minibars & 15-channel TVs with CNN, BBC & Mnet. Rooms 5 & 6 are adapted for guests in wheelchairs. There's free Wi-Fi & 2 terminals for guests. The Hansa's management is sharp & the service good: they provide courtesy transport around town. *N$1,160/2,260 sgl/dbl.* **$$$$**

✴ 🏠 **The Delight** [331 F1] (54 rooms) Theo-Ben Gurirab Av; ☎ 061 427200; e thedelight@ gondwana-collection.com; www.gondwana-collection.com. Opposite the Swakopmund Hotel & Entertainment Centre, The Delight is another of Swakopmund's new, international-style hotels. As soon as you walk in the glass-fronted entrance you get a feeling for the hotel, whose quirky bright red & blue décor runs from the open-plan reception, bar & lounge area right through the hotel.

The rooms, though, are built around a tranquil central courtyard, where creative gardening – including hanging pallets planted with local succulents – provides the rooms with a peaceful atmosphere & a surprising amount of privacy. Inside they are well furnished with en-suite bathrooms & showers, tea & coffee stations, satellite TV, minibar & free Wi-Fi, although this can be slow at times.

Only b/fast is served in the large dining room, but The Delight is just 3 blocks away from The Mole, home to several of Swakopmund's best restaurants. Friendly reception staff can easily make dinner reservations for you, as well as book activities & tours. *N$1,700/2,700 sgl/dbl.* **$$$$**

🏠 **Hotel Eberwein** [327 B4] (17 rooms) Sam Nujoma Av (cnr Otavi St); ☎ 064 414450; e eberwein@iafrica.com.na; www.hotel-eberwein.com. This former family house, built in 1909 & close to the centre of town, has been a privately owned hotel since 1999. Its rooms (*16 dbl, 1 sgl*) all have en-suite shower, flat-screen TV, tea/coffee, phone & underfloor heating. They are clean & bright & some have Victorian-style

high ceilings & sculpted drapes. It is very German in character, efficiently run & with friendly staff. There's a cosy bar & b/fast area, but no restaurant. Secure parking is available at the back. Free Wi-Fi can be picked up in the bar & reception, & there is also a fixed computer terminal for guest use. *From N$1,258/1,900 sgl/dbl to N$2,430 dbl.* **$$$$**

🏠 **Hotel Europa Hof** [327 A4] (35 rooms) Cnr Bismarck & Anton Lubowski sts; ☎ 064 405061/2; e info@europahof.com; www.europahof.com. Opened in 2017, Hotel Europa Hof stands out due to its incongruous European design & exposed wooden beams. The hotel boasts 5 sgl, 26 dbl and 4 family rooms, with facilities that include a large restaurant/bar area, secure parking & free Wi-Fi throughout. *N$1,140/1,740 sgl/dbl.* **$$$$**

🏠 **Hotel Schweizerhaus** [331 D3] (24 rooms) 1 Bismarck St; ☎ 064 400331–3; e schweizerhaus@ mweb.com.na; www.schweizerhaus.net. Above the genteel & popular Café Anton (page 340), the 2-star Schweizerhaus is the grandfather of Swakopmund's hotels, having been around since 1965. Its ocean views still make it popular & en-suite rooms – updated in recent years – come with TV & direct-dial phone. Most rooms also have a balcony, including all the 'luxury' rooms, which face the sea; others overlook a courtyard at the back. The staff are normally very friendly, & there's a night porter on duty should you arrive late. *N$998–1,470/1,700–2,200 sgl/dbl.* **$$$$**

🏠 **Swakopmund Sands** [327 A5] (21 rooms) 3 The Strand; ☎ 064 405045; e swakopsands@ iway.na; www.swakopsandshotel.com. This beachside hotel with a large open car park to the side has been given a facelift. It now offers a very smart variety of luxury, sgl, dbl & family rooms with high padded headboards, DSTV, fridge, tea/coffee & small digital safe; some come with corner baths, others with rain showers. The only public areas are a lounge with deep sofas & a fireplace, & the b/fast room. It caters mainly to businesspeople, but is attractive & you can't fault the standard of furnishings & the beach location. *N$1,080/1,775 sgl/dbl.* **$$$$**

Lodges, pensions and B&Bs
Swakopmund excels at the B&B &, if you don't need the facilities of a larger hotel, there are numerous high-quality options offering more personalised service & local insights. Almost all are within walking distance of the town centre.

Close to the centre

Central Guesthouse [327 B4] (8 rooms) Cnr Leutwein & Lüderitz sts; 064 407189; e info@guesthouse.com.na. Monica & Jockle Grüttemeyer run this boutique guesthouse, whose bright & comfortable en-suite rooms are equipped with mahogany furniture, contrasting with clean white linen. Little touches in the rooms such as extra-length beds, hairdryers & sewing kits are in addition to flat-screen TVs & safes. Well-stocked minibars with tea/coffee facilities & snacks are shared between rooms. The lounge has free Wi-Fi, cosy deep sofas, board games & lots of books on Namibia; the b/fast area has an open fire in winter; & there's a covered area with a braai. Secure guarded parking. This is a lovely, friendly place to stay. *N$1,600/1,960 sgl/dbl.* **$$$$**

✱ **Cornerstone Guesthouse** [327 B5] (7 rooms) 40 Hendrik Witbooi St; 064 462468; m 081 129 0026; e info@cornerstoneguesthouse. com; www.cornerstoneguesthouse.com. With friendly welcome, Peter & Margo Bassingthwaighte are on hand to look after you at this charming & intimate guesthouse within walking distance of the town centre; you can't fail to spot the yellow building, surrounded by pretty gardens. Rooms are bright, clean & comfortable with whitewashed bedsteads & wooden floors. All are en suite with their own patio, as well as satellite TV, fridge, safe, hairdryer, international wall sockets & free Wi-Fi, with details such as sprigs of lavender & personal toiletries. A delicious b/fast is served to a background of classical music, & laundry & off-street parking add to the facilities. Margo & Peter also own 2 luxury self-catering apts on the beach & 1 in town (*N$1,500–2,550*). The most special is **An der Mole**, an immaculate, fully furnished & extremely homely 3-bedroom apartment, with fully equipped kitchen & laundry, a large balcony with ocean views, a BBQ, dbl underground garage & DSTV – you'll want to stay forever. With personal attention & homely extras, the Cornerstone is good value for money. *Room N$1,090/1,800 sgl/dbl.* **$$$$**

Namib Guesthouse [327 B4] (8 rooms) 61 Anton Lubowski St; 064 407 171; e info@ namibguesthouse.com; www.namibguesthouse. com. A serene, privately owned guesthouse about 15mins' walk from Swakopmund centre & beach. Run by Nicoletta Betts, the compound sits behind a large electric gate & rooms are arranged around

a small astroturf-laden 'garden' with a few palm trees. Rooms 1 & 2, designated 'luxury', are decked out with red imitation-leather headboards, black cushions & white linens, & their black-&-white tiled en-suite bathrooms fitted with a bath & roomy walk-in shower. Standard rooms are spacious with cool blue walls stencilled with gold floral patterns, high-up panoramic windows on the back wall & a large window at the front looking on to the courtyard. Rooms 1–4 are wheelchair friendly; there are no rails, but they're open plan & spacious. Rooms 4 & 5 can function as family rooms. All have a laptop safe, flat-screen TV with DSTV, tea/coffee station, hairdryer & free Wi-Fi. A laundry service is available.

In the b/fast room – where the b/fast buffet receives many compliments from guests – artwork by local artists hangs on the walls & is for sale. There's no gated parking, but a security guard is posted at night. The owner arranges all manner of Swakopmund-based activities for guests, from fishing to desert tours. *From N$990–1,090/1,560–1,800 sgl/dbl.* **$$$$**

Organic Square Guesthouse [327 B5] (20 rooms) 29 Rhode Allee; 064 463979; e info@ guesthouse-swakopmund.com; www.guesthouse-swakopmund.com. This privately owned, luxury guesthouse in central Swakopmund is now spread across 2 houses within easy walking distance of each other. Both are decorated with a vibrant mix of rustic wood, modern artwork, polished concrete floors & cool grey walls interspersed with bright pops of lime paint. The colour scheme continues in the spotless, open-plan bedrooms where walk-though bathrooms (most with showers, but 1 with a bath) are positioned behind a wall & the bed. All rooms face on to the inner courtyard, which has a trickling fountain & planters filled with lavender, & all are equipped with flat-screen TV with DSTV, hairdryer, minibar, & a tea/coffee station, but no AC, to save energy. Nice touches include complimentary snacks, including welcome Ferrero Rocher chocolates. 4 family rooms can each sleep 4. B/fast is organic continental, & complimentary tea/coffee are available all day, with an espresso machine in the b/fast room. There's free Wi-Fi everywhere, but It's slower in the rooms. A laundry service is available. Lovely. *N$1,700/2,090 sgl/dbl.* **$$$$**

Sam's Giardino [327 C4] (9 rooms) 89 Anton Lubowski Av, Kramersdorf; 064

403210; e request@giardinonamibia.com; www.
giardinonamibia.com. If you want somewhere
quiet with personalised service, try this kooky
Swiss-run B&B, just 10–15mins' walk east of the
town centre. Sam Egger, the owner, doesn't accept
groups & loves to chat with guests. The rooms are
simple & airy, with pine-clad ceilings & wicker
furniture to match, plus en-suite shower, phone
& hairdryer. Almost all overlook the well-kept
garden that gives the pension its name, complete
with sunloungers & a mini bridge spanning a carp
pond. There's secure parking; laundry is available &
there's free Wi-Fi in the main areas.

At b/fast expect candles & Wagner, with real
Swiss muesli & the warmth of an open fire to offset
Swakopmund's famed morning mists. There are
books aplenty, & a TV lounge with a selection of
natural history videos. In the evenings, Sam will
lay on a 5-course set meal (*N$400 pp*) at 19.30 –
you can choose to have fewer courses, if you want
– with the help of local staff whom he has trained
in European cuisine & service; the small restaurant
makes a surprisingly romantic setting for dinner.
But his real passion is for wine – he offers tastings
if you book ahead (*min 2 people*). This is a highly
individual pension that is a little tired around
the edges, but would appeal to anyone seeking
privacy. *N$1,200/1,800 sgl/dbl; family/honeymoon
room N$2,700/room.* **$$$$**

🏠 **The Stiltz** [327 B5] (9 rooms, 2 villas)
Strand St; 📞 064 400771; e info@thestiltz.com;
www.thestiltz.com. The Stiltz combines a great
location at the edge of town, within easy reach
of restaurants & shops, with a flair for design,
resulting in a place that defies conventional
categorisation. Accommodation consists of a
series of rustic wooden chalets, built (as the name
suggests) high on stilts, & linked by wooden
walkways. Zany colours adorn the insides, giving
the place a bright feel on the days when the sun
shines, & compensating for those when the sea is
shrouded in mist. Views from the chalet balconies
vary – some look out over the dunes, some out to
sea (rooms 4, 6, 7 & 8), & others over the Swakop
River bed & its resident birdlife or the lagoon at its
mouth. Typically, each has twin beds or a large dbl,
en-suite bathroom, an honesty minibar, heating,
& the odd idiosyncratic design feature that serves
to accentuate the individuality of the place. The
only niggle is a distinct lack of plugs in the rooms,
but the free Wi-Fi connection is very good. A

superb b/fast (but no other meals) is served in
a large purpose-built chalet set on its own with
panoramic views; it's definitely a place to linger. A
small car park off the road is guarded overnight.
*Room N$1,540–2,090/1,980–2,520 sgl/dbl; villa
N$3,430/4,260.* **$$$$**

🏠 **Swakopmund Guesthouse** [327 B5]
(15 rooms) 35 Hendrik Witbooi St; 📞 064 462008;
e reservations@swakopmundguesthouse.com;
www.swakopmundguesthouse.com. Fresh, light
& modern, this guesthouse is directly opposite
Cornerstone, just 5mins from the beach &
shopping area. The seaside theme running through
the décor is highlighted by scattered beach
pebbles & seashells, crisp white linen, & bright
turquoise waves painted carefully on the walls. All
rooms are en suite with a minibar, fridge, TV, safe,
hairdryer & Wi-Fi, with 7 luxury rooms, 7 standard
& a suite. The outside courtyard makes a pleasant
place to sit, in unusual hanging pod chairs. *From
N$1,200/1,960 sgl/dbl to N$3,000 dbl.* **$$$$**

🏠 **Villa Margherita** [331 G2] (10 rooms,
1 apt) 34 Daniel Tjongarero St; m 081 332
4293; e info@villamargherita.com.na; www.
villamargherita.com.na. Dubbed 'the charming
house' by its Italian owners, Villa Margherita lives
up to its name: a beautiful colonial house built in
1913 & lovingly looked after. Its stylish en-suite
rooms are all slightly different, with 3 upstairs
in the main house itself, & 5 others in a newer
wing outside. Large block-colour paintings adorn
the walls, with a mix of antique & contemporary
artwork. Rooms have king- or queen-size beds,
flat-screen DSTV, safe, hairdryer & free Wi-Fi. Most
rooms have a private lounge area, too, or you can
curl up in the communal living room, with a large
fireplace & a selection of books. Alternatively,
there's Il Tulipano apartment at the back with
living room & modern kitchen. In the summer,
b/fast is served in the small leafy garden with
fountain; at other times it's in the intimate b/
fast/dining room, where you can also have lunch
(🕐 12.30–14.00) & dinner (🕐 18.00–20.00) from
an organic à la carte menu (**$$$$**). Massages
are available at the on-site spa room. A stay here
will give you quality & professional service in a
beautifully designed setting. *N$1,700/2,260 sgl/
dbl.* **$$$$**

🏠 **A La Mer** [327 A4] (46 rooms) 4 Libertina
Amathila Av; 📞 064 404130; e alamer@iway.
na; www.pension-a-la-mer.com. Just across the

road from the Tug (page 339) & 50m from the Promenade, the hard-to-miss orange exterior of A La Mer makes it look more like a motel than a hotel. Following refurbishment, the rooms are really quite stylish, with white linens set against red walls, & chunky stone basins, copper towel rails & underfloor heating in the bathrooms. Rooms 25–27 have sea views from their balconies, while rooms 28–30 overlook the gated car park. Downstairs, there's a small bar for guests & the high-ceilinged restaurant serves b/fast, which can also be eaten outside. It all adds up to a very good budget option. *N$875–1,155/1,250–1,650 sgl/dbl.* **$$$–$$$$**

🏠 **Meike's Guesthouse** [327 B4] (8 rooms, 1 apt) 23 Windhoeker St; ☎064 405863; e meike@ africaonline.com.na; www.meikes-guesthouse.net. It's easy to spot this eco-friendly guesthouse thanks to the guinea fowl painted on the outer wall – Meike is a fan of the bird & you'll see her devotion stretches all the way to the napkin rings! This bright, modern guesthouse is about 5mins' walk from the centre of town & has 5 dbls & 3 family rooms. All are simple & tastefully decorated, with en-suite shower, flat-screen TV, fridge & a small terrace in front. There's also a seaside-themed self-catering apartment sleeping 4. B/fast is a generous German buffet. This is very much a personal B&B run on traditional lines. Free Wi-Fi & 1 computer terminal for guest use. *N$950/1,450 sgl/dbl.* **$$$**

🏠 **Secret Garden Guesthouse** [327 A4] (9 rooms, 2 suites) 36 Bismarck St; ☎064 404037; e sgg@iway.na; www.secretgarden.com.na. Just 500m from the beach, & close to the centre of town, this attractive, terracotta-painted guesthouse is run by the slow-to-warm-up Peter Odendall. Most of its en-suite rooms – 6 dbls & 2 suites – look over the lush palm-shaded garden courtyard that gives the guesthouse its name; a further 3 'comfort' rooms are set in a private garden. Modern & well appointed, with soft blue-&-white furnishings reminiscent of the seaside, each has tiled or wooden flooring, coffee/tea facilities & hairdryer, & underfloor heating in the bathroom. 2 suites have a kitchenette, 4 beds, TV, free Wi-Fi & AC. Laundry costs N$70/5kg. In addition to a spacious lounge with DSTV, there's a b/fast room with honesty bar. The adjacent bistro serves guests with a huge choice of wood-fired pizzas in the evenings (🕐 *17.00–22.00 Mon–Sat;* **$$$**). 9 secure parking spaces are available &

airport/station transfers are free of charge. *From N$700/960 to N$1,100/1,400 sgl/dbl.* **$$$**

North and east of town

☀️ 🏠 **Beach Lodge** [327 C1] (19 rooms) 1 Stint St; ☎064 414500; e reservations@beachlodge. com.na; www.beachlodge.com.na. The architects have excelled themselves here! Each room forms part of a boat-shaped building that occupies a stunning site right on the beach, 5km from town in the Vogelstrand neighbourhood. Rooms, named after shipwrecks on the Namibian coast, are light, airy & stylish with en-suite shower &/or bath, floor-to-ceiling sliding doors on to a patio or a private balcony area with sweeping sea views, a desk with glass strip filled with sand & shells, DSTV & direct-dial phone. All rooms have heaters (very useful in winter) & 9 have fireplaces, while 'luxury' rooms have free-standing baths & 2 family rooms have small kitchenettes. The atmosphere is one of shipshape efficiency rather than personal care, so it's well suited to those seeking absolute privacy & relaxation. Gated parking is allocated to each room. Free Wi-Fi. The b/fast room doubles as The Wreck restaurant (page 339). *N$1,300–1,485/1,700–2,560 sgl/dbl.* **$$$$**

🏠 **Desert Breeze Lodge** [327 D4] (13 rooms, 1 villa) Riverside Av; ☎064 406236; e info@desertbreezeswakopmund.com; www. desertbreezeswakopmund.com. Owned by the creators of The Stiltz (page 335), Desert Breeze is a collection of eco-chalets spread along the granite cliffs, overlooking the dunes, on an (as yet) unnamed road in the eastern suburbs of Swakopmund. The town centre feels a million miles away as you enter grounds that are dotted with cacti & carved statues, & the earth-coloured walls of the chalets are almost camouflaged against the sandy desert backdrop – save for 1 blue, orange or lime-green wall to set them apart. Standard rooms feature dbl or twin beds on a slightly raised level & angled to look out over the dunes through a large corner window: the views from the bed are stunning. On a lower level is a sofa, rustic wooden coffee table & wood-burning stove, & an en-suite walk-in glass-block shower with open-plan toilet & sink. Each chalet also has a small, private terrace & comes with a minibar, tea/coffee station, fan, digital safe, solar-heated water reserve on the roof & an in-room Wi-Fi booster. In the villa, 2 rooms (1 en suite) lead off from a large open-plan lounge/dining room with wood-burning stove & L-shaped wicker sofa.

From the spacious reception area, stairs lead up to an open-plan lounge & b/fast room whose *pièce de résistance* is panoramic windows overlooking the dunes & a viewing deck with stove for colder nights. Activities can be organised via Living Desert Adventures (page 370) & airport transfers. *N$1,650/1,850–2,250 sgl/dbl; villa N$8,220 dbl.* **$$$$**

🏠 **Sea Breeze** [327 D2] (14 rooms, 5 self-catering flats) 48 Turmalin St; 📞 064 463348; e seabreeze@seabreeze.com.na; www.seabreeze.com.na. Sadly, the sea views that originally gave this guesthouse its name have been obscured by construction of other properties, but the warm welcome offered by owners Bennie & Charlot more than compensate. Lovingly looked-after en-suite rooms are named after precious stones & decorated tastefully & smartly with corresponding colour schemes. Flats have a bedroom, lounge/kitchenette with TV, international-style plugs, bathroom & balcony; some have up to 5 beds, & all have heating. Paintings by local artists adorn the walls, & Charlot runs a small curio shop supporting the Tsumkwe Bushmen community. And if you feel like splashing out, a champagne b/fast is available on request.

There's free Wi-Fi throughout, & outside is secure parking & garage space for up to 15 vehicles at no extra charge. To get here, follow the beach road north towards Veneta along the Strand. The road becomes First Av, then eventually Fischreier; turn left into Turmalin St & Sea Breeze is on the left by the beach. It's about 4.5km from the centre of town, which represents a 45min stroll along the beach, or a 10min (*N$30*) taxi ride. *N$1,100/1,600 sgl/dbl.* **$$$$**

🏠 **The Alternative Space** [327 D4] (5 rooms) 167 Anton Lubowski Av (cnr Alfons Weber St); 📞 064 402713; m 081 300 9352; e sibylle@thealternativespace.com; www.thealternativespace.com. One of a kind, this Greek-style boutique guesthouse in a quiet neighbourhood 15mins' walk east of the town centre is owned (& was built) by your hosts Sibylle & Frenus. Having started life as an 'off-the-wall' backpackers' lodge, it now has luxury en-suite rooms with off-street parking – yet the atmosphere remains as relaxed as ever. Rooms are minimalist, simple & clean with exposed wooden beams, lots of white, & en-suite shower & toilet;

3 feature romantic antique free-standing baths, of which 1 sits outside beneath the bougainvillea. Complimentary wine & chocolate bars are a nice touch. B/fast is semi-self-service (you can boil your own eggs to perfection) & guests can use the kitchen to prepare other meals – or slink upstairs to the library. Namibian art adorns the walls, braais in the central courtyard are a regular occurrence &, in the evening, you can gather in the communal lounge for a game of chess beside the open fire while reclining on one of the large Moroccan-style sofa beds or swaying in the hammock. The TV only plays 1 channel & the free Wi-Fi only works in the main areas, so the focus here is on enjoying the simple things in life: good conversation, a drink from the ice-box honesty bar, & access to a wide-ranging music collection. It's certainly one of the quirkiest & coolest locations in Swakopmund. *N$699/1,000 sgl/dbl.* **$$$**

🏠 **Stay @ Swakop** [327 D4] (12 rooms) 173 Anton Lubowski St; 📞 064 403138; m 081 634 5212; e info@stay-at-swakop.com; www.stay-at-swakop.com. This large house in the peaceful eastern suburbs is a 3min drive from town. Clean, functional rooms configured as sgls, dbls & trpls come with flat-screen TV, tea/coffee, safe, but no AC. There's a roof terrace, but the views aren't very inspiring. *N$810/1,200 sgl/dbl.* **$$$**

Backpackers' lodges

🏠 **Dunedin Star** [327 B3] (27 rooms) 50 Daniel Tjongarero St (cnr Windhoeker St); 📞 064 403437; e bookings@dunedinstar.com; www.dunedinstar.com. Named after the ship involved in the Skeleton Coast's most famous wreck in 1942 – & the same rust red colour – the Dunedin Star is just 5mins' walk from the centre of town. It has simple, no-frills en-suite sgl, dbl & trpl rooms with safes on the wall. There is a small garden, a bar & a laundry service (*N$80/bag*), & massages on request at reasonable prices. Given the main road location, it's fortunate that most rooms are at the back, so reasonably quiet, & that there's secure parking. There's free Wi-Fi in the main areas & a book exchange in the b/fast room, too. *N$430/620 sgl/dbl.* **$$**

🏠 **Villa Wiese** [327 C3] (36 dorm beds, 8 rooms) Cnr Theo-Ben Gurirab Av & Windhoeker St (entrance on Windhoeker St); 📞 064 407105; e bookings@villawiese.com; www.villawiese.com. This colourful old building on the outskirts of town is named after the German who built it in 1905. A friendly option with plenty of atmosphere, its facilities include a lounge with white piano & a book exchange, a rather dirty & dark self-catering kitchen (⊕ *11.00–23.00*), a large & lively upstairs bar (⊕ *15.00–23.00*) with free Wi-Fi & board games, laundry service (*N$80/bag*) & lockers in the rooms. A bacon & egg b/fast costs N$60. Each dormitory has 4–5 beds (with bedding but no towels) on 2 levels, & its own passably clean shower & separate toilet, while dbl rooms (fully equipped) are all en suite. Outside there's a BBQ in a pleasant courtyard, & secure parking. Trips can be arranged. *Dorm bed N$220.* **$$**

🏠 **Desert Sky** [327 B4] (7 rooms, 15 dorm beds, camping) 35 Anton Lubowski Av; ☏064 402339; **m** 081 210 6779; **e** info@ desertskylodging.com; www.desertskylodging. com. This centrally located backpackers' hostel not far from the beach is one of the most popular in town, & it is easy to see why. It's welcoming & helpful, the atmosphere is friendly, & facilities are good. As well as clean, cheerful 3-, 4- & 8-bed dormitories & both dbl & family private rooms, there's a fully equipped kitchen, storage lockers & safe, plus central coffee & tea area, & a TV lounge. Outside is safe parking & a small grassed area for 2/3 tents. Phonecards are sold at reception, unlimited Wi-Fi costs N$30, & laundry costs N$25/ kg. If you're after action, this is also a pretty good place to come for advice. *Dorm bed N$220 pp; private room N$700; camping N$170 pp.* **$$**

🏠 **Skeleton Beach Backpackers** [327 B1] (9 rooms, 18 dorm beds, camping) 14 Moses Garoëb St;☏061 259485; **m** 081 287 7420; **e** magicbus@ iafrica.com.na. Newest backpackers with 6 dbls & 3 dorm rooms (*1 8-bed, 1 6-bed, 1 4-bed*) with fresh décor, low beds & lovely en-suite showers with stone tiles. There's a small communal kitchen, a lounge with big flat-screen TV & free Wi-Fi that looks on to a garden with a brick-built braai & a few plastic tables & chairs, & lots of gated parking. There are 4 shaded camping spots for small tents. Laundry N$50/kg. *Dorm bed N$170; camping N$120 pp.* **$–$$**

Restcamps and campsites

🏠 **Swakopmund Municipal Restcamp** [327 B5] (200 chalets) ☏064 410 4618/9, 4621; **e** restcamp@swkmun.com.na; www.swakopmund-restcamp.com; ⊕ office 07.30–22.00 daily. On the north side of the road that crosses the Swakop River to Walvis Bay, this huge old restcamp is quite an institution. Packed closely together inside a large electric fence, its chalets & bungalows vary from tiny fishermen's cabins, whose cramped beds in minute rooms have changed little over the years, to luxury VIP flats with modern décor & bright pastel colours. The flats are fine & simple, with 'luxury' flats being larger, but otherwise similar. A-frame chalets have a much more interesting design, & their wooden construction is warmer in the winter than the others – though all the beds in these are sgls. All are good value, provided you don't mind getting lost in the maze of other identical chalets while you search for your own. Dinner is served in the camp's restaurant from 16.00 to 22.00. At present the restcamp supplies linen but not towels; pans & cutlery can be borrowed from the storage hut (⊕ *07.30–16.30 Mon–Fri, 08.00–11.00 Sat–Sun*) for free, & room safes can be hired for N$10/day. No Wi-Fi. Credit cards accepted. *2-bed N$475–521; 4-bed N$801; 'A' frame to resthouses N$851–1,000; key deposit N$200–300.* **$$**

⚠ **Tiger Reef Campsite** [327 A5] (23 sites) Strand;☏064 400935; **m** 081 791 0134; **e** campsite@lighthousegroup.com.na; www. goingwhere.co.za/tiger-reef. In the south of town, close to the beach, this revitalised campsite has 23 lapa-style covered camping areas, each with its own private ablution block. These are arranged around a circular lawn with a plant-lined brick path running the circumference. There's a pool, free Wi-Fi picked up by the chalets closest to reception The popular Tiger Reef Beach Bar (page 341) is a great place to while away afternoons & evenings. Alternatively, the manager can arrange a host of activities, from skydiving & paragliding to sandboarding & fishing. *N$160 pp + N$290 site, N$90/car.* **$$**

✗ **WHERE TO EAT AND DRINK** Alongside Swakopmund's selection of more traditional restaurants, the town's café culture has exploded in recent years, with plenty of innovative, high-quality options acting as fuel stops during sightseeing.

✗ **Cosmopolitan** [331 G2] 37 Daniel Tjongarero Av;☏064 400133; ⊕ 16.00–late Mon–Sat. This luxury restaurant/lounge bar claims to have the best sushi in town, plus a very good cocktail bar (page 341). **$$$$$**

✹ ✕ **Jetty 1905** [331 A4] ☏064 405664;
✉ jetty1905@lighthousegroup.com.na; www.
jetty1905.com; ⏲ 17.00–22.00 Tue–Thu,
noon–15.00 & 17.00–22.00 Fri, noon–15.00 &
18.00–22.00 Sat–Sun. Perched at the end of the
jetty above the often stormy Atlantic Ocean, Jetty
1905 has a unique location, & is the best restaurant
from which to watch the sunset. Suitably enough
the cuisine is mostly seafood, including excellent
sushi & fresh oysters, but the steaks are also highly
rated. Reservations are essential, often a day or 2 in
advance to avoid disappointment. $$$$$

✹ ✕ **Kücki's Pub** [331 E4] 22 Tobias Hainyeko
St; ☏064 402407; www.kuckispub.com;
⏲ 17.00–late daily. A bit of an institution, this
spit & sawdust-style pub has a lively atmosphere &
serves very good food despite the motto: 'Hot beer,
lousy food, bad service – welcome'. The shellfish
is excellent & the service friendly, & there are kids'
options. It has a busy, backpackers' atmosphere but
without being too noisy or rowdy, & we enjoyed
several meals here on our last visit. Tables are
situated both on the ground floor & upstairs. They
have a good range of draught beers on tap, & an
interesting selection of bottled South African &
Namibian craft beer. Do book in advance, as it's
often full. $$$$$

✕ **Ocean Cellar** [331 B2] The Mole; ☏064 411
4308; ✉ strand.res@ol.na; ⏲ noon–22.00 daily.
Connected to the Strand Hotel, Ocean Cellar makes
the most of its seafront location with sweeping
glass windows, & ample outside seating on the
Promenade. The menu consists mainly of seafood,
with fresh oysters from Walvis Bay & the sushi
being particular highlights. $$$$$

✕ **The Tug** [327 A4] The Strand; ☏064 402356;
⏲ dinner 18.00–22.00 (sundowners from
17.00) daily, lunch noon–15.00 Sat–Sun only.
Without doubt the most interesting place to eat
in Swakopmund, The Tug is just that – an old tug
raised up above the seafront next to the jetty. The
terrace is a great place to watch the surf as the
sun goes down. The menu is among the best in
town & majors on seafood, in a style that's lighter
& less traditional than at the Hansa. The wines are
undistinguished & a little expensive, but the place
is always full & booking – sometimes weeks ahead
– is essential. $$$$$

✕ **Hansa** [331 E3] 3 Hendrik Witbooi St; ☏064
414200; ⏲ noon–14.00 daily, 18.30–21.00
winter, 19.00–21.30 summer. The award-winning

European restaurant at the Hansa serves stylish,
elaborate & quite heavy cuisine – using lots of
sauces – in quite formal surroundings. It majors on
seafood, but also has a good range of steaks & a
couple of vegetarian dishes. Its selection of South
African wines is impressive, with bottles averaging
around N$150–180 each, from some good
vineyards. Reservations essential. $$$$

✕ **Bistro Zum Kaiser** [331 C4] 4 Sam Nujoma
Av; ☏064 417100; ⏲ 06.30–21.00 Mon–Fri,
06.30–11.00 Sat–Sun. The restaurant of the Hotel
Zum Kaiser (page 332) sits beside it as a separate
building. Decked out in calming dark woods & with
a portrait of the Kaiser above the fireplace, it serves
a continental & English buffet b/fast until 10.00
that's open to non-guests as well. After that, it's
posh pub fare such as gourmet sandwiches, game
steaks, seafood & salads; be sure to try their Malva
pudding for dessert. $$$$

✕ **Lighthouse Pub & Restaurant** [331 C1]
The Mole; ☏064 400894; ⏲ noon–21.30 Mon,
Wed & Thu, noon–22.00 Fri–Sat, noon–21.00
Sun. Good for sundowners overlooking the sea,
the large restaurant here adjoins an equally large
bar. You can eat outside on the wooden terrace
with magnificent sea views, or there are tables
inside for cooler periods. With everything from a
seafood platter & wood-fired pizzas (available to
take away) to charcoal grills & burgers, prices vary
considerably. $$$$

✕ **Swakopmund Brauhaus** [331 E3] The
Arcade; ☏064 402214; ⏲ 10.00–15.00 & 17.00–
21.30 Mon–Fri, 10.00–15.00 & 18.00–21.30
Sat, closed Sun & public hols. Authentic German
tavern-style bar & restaurant dishing up German
classics. $$$$

✕ **The Wreck** [327 C1] 1 Stint St; ☏064 414528;
www.the-wreck.com; ⏲ 17.30–23.00 Mon–Sat,
noon–15.00 Sun. The restaurant at Beach Lodge
(page 336) continues the ship theme that defines
the lodge, with floor-to-ceiling windows looking
out to sea, from which you can spot the occasional
surfer. With excellent, friendly service & candlelit
tables, the atmosphere is suited to couples, but
families & groups eat here too. The reasonably
priced menu has a range of delicious game,
seafood, pasta & curry dishes, plus a children's
menu. Beautifully presented food features quality
ingredients with interesting flavour combinations.
It may be a short drive from the town centre, but
this place is worth it. $$$$

✕ Bits 'n' Pizzas [331 F2] 30 Daniel Tjongarero Av; m 081 726 3126; ☺ noon–14.00 & 16.00–21.00 Tue–Thu, 11.00–14.00 & 16.00–22.00 Fri–Sat, 16.00–21.00 Sun. Take-away or sit-in pizzeria with very good wood-fired pizzas (with the option of gluten-free bases when the flour is available), pastas, salads & a few meat & fish dishes. $$$

✕ Royal Bull [331 E2] 21 Daniel Tjongarero Av; ✆064 405141; ☺ 16.00–late Mon–Sat. Despite various changes in management, & now under a new name, the former Erich's has stood here for nearly 30 years, thanks to its reputation for well-presented fish & Namibian game dishes, & a generally innovative menu. $$$

✕ N'Amigos [331 F2] Cnr Nathaniel Maxuilili St & Daniel Tjongarero Av; ✆064 406711; ☺ 17.00–late Mon–Sat. Cheap & cheerful Mexican offering nachos, burritos, chimichangas & steaks. $$$

✕ Pizzeria & Western Saloon [331 E3] 8 Tobias Hainyeko St; ✆064 403925; ☺ 17.00–late Mon–Sat, 17.00–21.00 Sun. With 2 separate shopfronts, but run by the same team, the Western Saloon – despite the name – serves neither burgers nor hotdogs, but classic German fare. $$$

✕ Garnish [331 E4] 1 Tobias Hainyeko St; ✆064 405401; www.garnish-restaurant.com; ☺ 11.30–21.30 Wed–Mon. Curry may not be the first cuisine that you'd associate with a coastal Namibian town, but if you fancy something different then take the lead from many locals. With an extensive menu, this relatively new Indian restaurant is busy from opening to closing, with an open-plan kitchen that allows you to watch curries being prepared throughout the day. $–$$

Cafés and light meals

☕ Krisjans Bistro [331 F3] Sam Nujoma Av; m 081 861 4614; ☺ 07.00–18.00 Mon–Fri, 08.00–14.00 Sat–Sun. A recent addition to Swakopmund's café scene, this trendy, modern bistro is slightly more expensive than other cafés in town, but serves excellent coffee, along with b/fasts & lunches in tune with international food trends, but with a local flair. Main course N$40–170. $$$$

☕ Garden Café [331 D3] 11 Tobias Hainyeko St; ✆064 403444; ☺ 08.00–18.00 Mon–Fri, 08.00–15.00 Sat–Sun & public hols. A grassy knoll – albeit astroturf – tucked away behind the Art Africa shop with palm trees, a sandpit for kids & a lovely light menu of all-day b/fasts,

salads, ciabatta sandwiches & Italian coffee – try their 'Red Cappuccino' made from Rooibos tea, cinnamon & honey. To access it walk through the shop, or go down the graffitied alleyway to the left-hand side, where local artists display their work. Great for families. $$$

☕ Farmhouse Deli [331 B2] The Mole; ✆064 411 4308; e strand.res@ol.na; ☺ 06.00–21.00 daily. Easily reached through the lobby of the Strand Hotel or along the seafront at The Mole, the Farmhouse Deli is decorated in a style reminiscent of a Namibian farmhouse. Italian food often comes with a Namibian twist, such as their oryx ragu. They also serve a good b/fast, & it's an excellent spot for a coffee overlooking the Atlantic. $$–$$$

☕ Beryl's [331 F4] Cnr Hendrik Witbooi St & Woermann; ✆064 403963; ☺ 06.30–18.00 Mon–Thu, 06.30–18.30 Fri, 06.30–17.00 Sat, 07.30–15.00 Sun. Need a fast-food fix? This greasy spoon is frequented by local office workers who come for the cheap burgers. $$

☕ Bojo's [331 E2] 13 Daniel Tongarero Av; ✆064 400771; ☺ 07.00–17.00 Mon–Fri, 08.00–16.00 Sat, 09.00–15.00 Sun. Friendly eco-friendly café whose walls are festooned with black-&-white photos, paintings, quotes & coffee-related sayings. Locals come for the delicious cakes made with organic stoneground flour, very good coffee & filled bagels, pancakes & croissants, with some gluten-free options. There's free Wi-Fi, but a donation to their sponsored charities is the decent thing to do. $$

☕ Café Anton [331 D3] Schweizerhaus Hotel, 1 Bismarck St; ✆064 400331; ☺ 06.30–19.00 daily. In comparison with Swakopmund's trendy slew of new cafés, this classic is looking a little dated. However, the views of The Mole & the ocean, genteel atmosphere & excellent range of cakes & pastries – the cheesecake is delectable – make this a pleasant place for morning coffee or afternoon tea. There are also tables outside, under the palm trees. $$

✳ ☕ Two Beards & a Saint [327 D3] 5 Einstein St; m 081 441 0255; e bistro@2beardscoffee.com.na; www.2beardscoffee.com.na; ☺ 08.00–17.00 daily. Despite its unusual location, behind a furniture warehouse on the outskirts of town, this small but trendy café serves some of the best coffee in Swakopmund. With the beans roasted on site, and the father & son team's obvious passion for the drink, the coffee here is incredibly good; drink it on site, along with a great selection of cakes or the lunch menu, or take it away as beans. Although the café is some distance from the town centre, it is next door to the area's only craft brewery & gin distillery (page 342), so a visit here can easily be combined with an afternoon experiencing Swakopmund's emerging craft drinks scene. $$

☕ **The Village Café** [331 E4] 23 Sam Nujoma Av; ☎064 404723; ⊕ 07.00–17.00 Mon–Fri, 07.00–13.30 Sat. Next door to Café Treff, this popular & chilled-out place states that 'we open when we get here & we close when we go home'. Frequented by locals & with garden seating, it offers a range of coffees, sandwiches, milkshakes, cakes, waffles & pancakes to the sounds of Bob Marley. Free Wi-Fi. $$

✳ ☕ **Wild Rocket** [331 F3] 37 Sam Nujoma Av; ☎064 461046; ⊕ 07.30–16.30 Mon–Fri, 08.00–14.00 Sat. Tucked behind the Autohaus Swakopmund, to the right of the Puma fuel station, this oasis decorated in lavenders & greens specialises in healthy wraps, sandwiches & the only veggie b/fast in town – using organic products whenever possible. Homemade wholewheat breads, freshly squeezed juices & smoothies feature too. They also sell farmers' cheese, juices & jams, & every Wed from noon you can buy freshly delivered farm vegetables. There are a few tables outside. Cash only. $$

☕ **Ice & Spice** [331 D4] 11 Sam Nujoma Av; m 081 695 7750; ⊕ 08.00–17.00 daily. German owners Friedrich & Liesl offer homemade ice creams & light lunches. A bougainvillea-covered outdoor terrace has patio heaters, & they offer cocktails here in the evening. Free Wi-Fi. $

☕ **Raith's Gelateria** [331 D3] Tobias Hainyeko St; ☎064 404454; ⊕ 07.00–21.00 Mon–Thu & Sat, 07.00–14.00 Fri & Sun. Handy for a coffee, light lunch &/or ice cream after visiting the Swakopmund Museum (page 345). $

☕ **Slow Town** [331 D2] 9 Altona Haus, Daniel Tjongarero Av; m 081 127 7681; www. slowtowncoffee.com; ⊕ 08.00–17.00 Mon–Fri, 09.00–13.00 Sat. For those in need of a caffeine fix, this place roasts its own beans in a warehouse in Swakopmund. Along with varieties from Costa Rica, Ethiopia & Guatemala, it has its own house blend, & a selection of cakes. The rustic interior is ideal for chillaxing thanks to the laid-back music, free newspapers & chessboard. Free Wi-Fi is available, although can be slow. $

☕ **Tea Time** [331 D2] 9 Tobias Hainyeko St; ☎064 406769; ⊕ 10.00–17.00 Mon–Sat. This classy, tiny teahouse has over 85 varieties from across the globe. Owner Brigitte Hartz makes cakes & soup to serve with them & you can browse the shelves lined with books. On the 1st Fri of the month she hosts screenings of French movies with English subtitles; tickets cost N$35 & include wine & snacks. $

Bars

♀ **Cosmopolitan** [331 G2] 37 Daniel Tjongarero Av; ☎064 400133; ⊕ 16.00–late Mon–Sat. Upmarket cocktail bar also serving fine wines & cigars. On w/ends they have live music. They also have a good restaurant (page 338).

♀ **Tiger Reef Beach Bar** [327 A5] Strand St; ⊕ 13.00–midnight Tue–Fri, 11.00–midnight Sat–Sun. On the beach, just beyond the aquarium, this is a popular spot for sundowners. Attracting a predominantly younger crowd, it still makes a great place to sit with your toes in the sand & watch the sunset.

♀ **Desert Tavern** [327 A5] Swakop St; ☎064 404204; ⊕ 16.30–02.00 Mon–Sat, 16.30–22.00 Sun. On the left as you walk in, there's a large bar that is often propped up by locals. On the right is a fire which is often lit, creating some atmosphere & a lot of smoke.

ENTERTAINMENT AND NIGHTLIFE Swakopmund has a surprisingly lively nightlife, especially in the summer holiday season, although many travellers just have a few drinks in their hotel bar before retiring to bed. Then, around Christmas and New Year, many of Windhoek's more affluent residents arrive at their cool seaside cottages, intent on fishing by day and partying by night. For listings of all events, check the Namib i information board (page 330) outside the entrance.

The two-screen city cinema, **Atlanta** (☎064 402743), inside the Swakopmund Hotel and Entertainment Centre (page 332), shows the latest Hollywood films, including those in 3D. You'll find a shop selling sweets and hot and cold drinks in the foyer.

The annual 'Kuska' **carnival** is held on the last weekend of June with a parade of flotillas and lots of parties.

SHOPPING
Food and drink
Large stores

Pick n Pay supermarket [331 E4] Sam Nujoma Av, opposite tourist information office

Shoprite Centre [327 C4] On the main B2 out of town, at its intersection with Windhoeker St, this houses an FNB ATM, a fast-food take-away & Shoprite supermarket.

Super Spar Complex [331 E1] Cnr Tobias Hainyeko & Mandume ya Ndemufayo sts; ⊕ 07.00–20.00 Mon–Sat, 08.00–20.00 Sun & public hols. One of the town's most recent shopping complexes, it has a large Spar supermarket & a range of other shops offering everything from mobile phones to shoes.

WB supermarket [331 D4] Woermann Brock Mall on Sam Nujoma Av, near Bismarck St

Speciality outlets

Closwa Biltong [331 D2] 2 Tobias Hainyeko St; ☎ 064 407273; ⊕ 09.00–17.00 Mon–Fri, 09.00–13.00 Sat. Specialist biltong shop selling a huge variety, from chilli beef to eland & oryx.

Namibia Dunes Craft Brewery 5 Einstein St [327 D3]; m 081 124 7647; e dup@namibdunes. com; ⊕ 09.00–17.00 daily. The explosive trend for craft brewing has made its way up from South Africa. One of Namibia's first craft breweries, this offers tours, tastings & a chance to pick up some bottles of locally made beer.

Stillhouse Atlantic [327 D3] 5 Einstein St; m 081 252 8876; e info@stillhouseatlantic.com; www.stillhouseatlantic.com; ⊕ noon–17.00 daily. A craft distillery, this small family business opened in 2017 & produces Namibian dry-blend gins distilled with botanicals such as Nara melon, hand-picked seaweeds & other plants endemic to the coast. It's possible to taste their gin here, as well as pick up a few bottles at their distillery on the outskirts of town.

Clothes and equipment

African Leather Creations [327 B2] ⊕ 08.00–17.00 Mon–Fri, 08.00–noon Sat. Traditional Kudu Veldskoens (Vellies) & other leather items.

Cymot [331 G3] 43 Sam Nujoma Av; ☎ 064 400318; www.cymot.com.na; ⊕ 08.00–17.00 Mon–Fri, 08.00–noon Sat. Camping equipment, car spares & cycling gear.

Namibia Safari Boutique [331 D4] Sam Nujoma Av; ☎ 064 403391; ⊕ 08.00–13.00 & 14.00–17.00 Mon–Fri, 08.30–13.00 Sat. All manner of safari clothing & accessories, including binoculars, knives, flasks, torches, etc.

Photo Studio Behrens [331 D3] 7 Tobias Hainyeko St; ☎ 064 404711. Sells batteries & a range of binoculars, does 1hr photo processing & will also carry out minor camera repairs.

Safariland Holtz [331 E3] 21 Sam Nujoma Av; ☎ 064 402387; ⊕ summer 08.00–18.00 Mon–Fri, 08.00–13.00 Sat, 09.00–13.00 Sun, winter 08.30–17.30 Mon–Fri, 08.30–13.00 Sat, 09.00–13.00 Sun. Safari clothes & equipment.

Books and music

CNA [331 E3] Hendrik Witbooi St, next to Namib i. A branch of the South African chain; more mainstream than Swakopmunder Buchhandlung.

Die Muschel [331 E3] Brauhaus Arcade; ☎ 064 402874; www.muschel.iway.na; ⊕ 08.30–17.30 Mon–Fri, 08.30–13.00 & 15.00–17.00 Sat, 10.00–13.00 & 15.00–17.00 Sun. A good selection of books & fine art, as well as the on-site Art Café offering coffee & cakes.

Swakopmunder Buchhandlung [331 E4] 22 Sam Nujoma Av; ☎ 064 402613; ⊕ 08.30–17.30 Mon–Fri, 08.00–13.00 Sat. Open since 1900, this oasis of peace has a reasonable selection of English-language books on Namibia, & some novels too, as well as stationery.

Young Ones 32 Sam Nujoma Av; ☎ 064 405795. African music specialist.

Arts, crafts and souvenirs Swakopmund is filled with commercial art galleries and curio shops, particularly in the centre of town around Brauhaus Arcade [331 E3] off Sam Nujoma Avenue, and in the attractive Ankerplatz complex [331 D4] further down the road near the sea. Some of the best of these include The Art Gallery (☎ 064 404312) in Brauhaus Arcade, which specialises in Namibian (as against African) art, and in the same complex, **African Curiotique** (℡ *064 462732*) and **Okaporo Curio Shop** (℡ *064 405795;* ⊕ *daily*). There is also a **curio market** around the lighthouse area [331 D2], with a good range of crafts on sale, though some are more authentic than others.

African Kirikara Arts & Crafts [331 D4] Ankerplatz, Sam Nujoma Av & Brauhaus Arcade; ℡064 463146; www.kirikara.com; ⊕ 09.00–13.00 & 14.30–17.30 Mon–Fri, 09.00–13.00 & 16.00–18.00 Sat, 10.00–noon Sun (Brauhaus Arcade 13.00–16.00 Sat–Sun). This is a first-class place to look for hand-woven rugs, made on the owner's farm Kiripotib (page 227). It also has a range of crafts & gemstones, & makes jewellery.

Amber Moon [331 E3] Inside Namib i tourist office (page 330). An independent craft shop which supports local industries & various non-profit organisations by providing a platform for local people to sell their own handmade crafts.

COSDEF Arts & Craft [327 C2] New Industrial Area, cnr Einstein & Newton sts; ℡064 406122; www.cosdef.org.na. This non-profit organisation offers community members a place to sell their crafts, such as beaded jewellery, leather purses & crochet. There's a restaurant, small Namibian food stalls, live shows on the stage & amphitheatre, & production units where you can see the crafts being made.

Deon Sibold [331 E3] Brauhaus Arcade; ℡064 404790; ⊕ 08.00–18.00 Mon–Fri, 08.00–13.00 Sat. Specialises in shoes, bags & belts.

Karakulia [327 B2] 2 Rakotoka St; ℡064 461415; www.karakulia.com.na. Karakulia has a shop in Brauhaus Arcade [331 E3], but its workshop is just off the main road as you head north from Swakopmund, opposite the junction of Tobias

Hainyeko & Moses Garoëb streets. It's a very long walk, so transport would be useful! Here you can watch the whole art of spinning & weaving karakul wool (see box, page 95) into carpets & wall-hangings, as well as buy the finished products. You can even have designs made to order & then reliably shipped home for you. Karakulia has grown considerably since its inception in 1979 & now has around 50 employees, who also benefit from a programme of adult education.

Leder Chic [331 E3] Brauhaus Arcade; ℡064 404778; ⊕ 09.00–17.00 Mon–Fri, 09.00–13.00 Sat. Leather suitcases & bags.

Namcrafts [331 E3] Brauhaus Arcade; ℡061 222614; www.namcrafts.com; ⊕ 08.00–18.00 Mon–Fri, 08.30–14.00 Sat–Sun. Beautifully crafted wooden carvings sold here come from local sources.

Namibian Jewellers & Arts Gallery [331 G3] 55 Sam Nujoma Av; ℡064 404525; www. namibian.jewellers.online.ms; ⊕ 08.00–13.00 & 14.30–17.30 Mon–Fri, 09.00–13.00 Sat. To the east of the centre, Michael Engelhard's modern shop & gallery features contemporary Namibian art & jewellery, with exhibitions changing every 6 weeks or so.

Swakop Arts & Souvenirs [331 D2] Next to Café Anton (page 340); ℡064 402942; ⊕ 10.00–18.00 daily. Fairly cheap & cheerful souvenir shop selling carvings, postcards, batik, magnets & jewellery.

Semi-precious stones These are much in evidence in this part of Namibia, but two places stand out: **Kristall Galerie** (page 346) and **Stonetique** (*27 Libertina Amathila Av;* ℡*064 405403*).

Antiques

Peter's Antiques [327 A4] 24 Tobias Hainyeko St; ℡064 405624; e petersantiques@yahoo.com; www.peters-antiques.com; ⊕ 09.00–13.00 & 15.00–18.00 Mon–Fri, 09.00–13.00 & 17.00–18.00 Sat, 17.00–18.00 Sun. Perhaps the best antique shop in Africa, Peter's is a most comprehensive & eclectic collection. The owner, an intense Namibian of German origin, started the shop in the early 1980s as an extension of his

hobby, & since then his collection, his reputation & the shop have gradually grown. Now he has a network of collectors all over sub-Saharan Africa, who buy & ship old African artefacts to Swakopmund. (Purchasers should carefully consider the ethics of such a collection before even considering making a purchase.) He also sells some new, cheaper arts & crafts that are produced specifically for tourists.

The shop is now quite large, & densely packed with all sorts of things. The smells of wood, skins & dyes that go to make the pieces pervade the place, making it instantly fascinating & slightly revolting. As well as tribal artefacts, Peter's has an extensive collection of antique books, many in German, concerned with Namibia's history. He is also involved with commissioning & distributing facsimile reprints of old books & maps, reproducing these manuscripts for future generations.

SPORTS

Swimming The city's municipal swimming pool near The Mole has closed and now all the action takes place at **Live It Health and Fitness Club** [327 B1] (*Nathaniel Maxuilili St;* ✆ *064 401084; www.liveit.com.na;* ⊕ *06.00–20.00 Mon–Thu, 06.00–19.00 Fri, 07.00–13.00 Sat, closed Sun*), north of the city centre. Facilities include a heated swimming pool and saunas, gym, two squash courts, and a number of fitness classes. There's also the Fusion Health Café on site with free Wi-Fi.

Golf About 7km west of Swakopmund, on the main B2 road from Windhoek, Rossmund golf course (✆ *064 405644;* e *golf@rossmund.com*) is set on the northern banks of the Swakop River, backed by the dunes. The 18-hole, par-72 course is open to day members, who occasionally find themselves playing alongside the local springboks. The club has its own restaurant overlooking the greens, and the unremarkable **Rossmund Lodge** (✆ *064 414600;* e *lodge@rossmund.com; www. rossmund.com; $$*), which is mainly aimed towards the business crowd, but does have an inviting sculpted swimming pool.

OTHER PRACTICALITIES

Banks There are plenty of banks in the centre of town, many with ATMs. You will find FNB, Nedbank, Standard Bank and others clustered around the junction of Hainyeko Street and Sam Nujoma Avenue [331 D4].

Communications The majority of cafés and hotels in Swakopmund offer free Wi-Fi, and while it can be slow at times it's reliable enough to make calls and send messages. If you want a local SIM card, or indeed a whole handset, try Coastal Cellular at the Super Spar Complex [331 E1] (✆ *064 405936;* m *081 128 3283*), or their other branch in Woermann Brock Mall.

The **Nampost post office** is on the corner of Tobias Hainyeko Street [331 E2] (⊕ *08.00–16.30 Mon, Tue, Thu & Fri, 08.30–16.30 Wed, 08.00–noon Sat*).

Emergency and health In an emergency, the police can be reached on ✆ *064 10111*, the ambulance and former Cottage Hospital (now Mediclinic Swakopmund) on ✆ *064 412205*, and the fire service on ✆ *064 410411*. For sea rescue services, call m *081 129 6295* or the police – which is also the emergency number to use if you can't get through anywhere else.

✚ **Bismarck Medical Centre** [331 D4] 17 Sam Nujoma Av; ✆ 064 405000; ⊕ 08.00–noon & 17.00–18.00 Sat, 10.00–11.00 & 17.00–18.00 Sun. For less serious illnesses. Has a pharmacy that's also open at w/ends.
✚ **Mediclinic Swakopmund** [327 C1] Cnr Haupt Av & Franziska van Neel St; ✆ 064 412200; emergency ✆ 064 412205; www.mediclinic.co.za.
Located north of the town, this is probably the 1st port of call for overseas visitors in need of urgent health care.
✚ **Swakopmund Apotheek** [331 E3] Sam Nujoma Av; ✆ 064 400772, a/h ✆ 064 463610; ⊕ 08.00–18.30 Mon–Fri, 08.00–13.00 & 17.00–18.00 Sat, 10.00–13.00 & 17.00–18.00 Sun, 09.00–13.00 & 17.00–18.30 public hols.

Fuel and vehicle repair Twenty-four-hour fuel stations abound in Swakopmund. The best garage is Arno's Off-Road Centre on Hidipo Hamutenya Street [327 C2] (📞 *064 400300*).

WHAT TO SEE AND DO Unlike most Namibian towns, there's plenty to do in Swakopmund. Attractions in the town itself are covered below, but see also page 364 for further ideas in the area surrounding Swakopmund and Walvis Bay.

The Mole [331 A1] If you only have a little time to spare, then wander down to The Mole. This was to be a harbour wall when first built, but the ocean currents continually shifted the sandbanks and effectively blocked the harbour before it was even completed. A similar 'longshore drift' effect can be seen all along the coast, at inlets like Sandwich Harbour. Partially because of this sandbank's protection, the beach by The Mole is pleasant (though watch out for jellyfish) and generally safe to swim from, if small and surprisingly busy at times.

Historical buildings Central Swakopmund is full of amazing old German architecture in perfect condition, some of the buildings now housing museums, art galleries or libraries.

Pre-eminent among these is the beautiful **Woermannhaus Building** [331 D4], in the centre of town just off Sam Nujoma Avenue, dating from 1894. For an overview of the town and its setting, you could do worse than climb the 93 steps up the **Woermann Tower** [331 D4]. The door to the tower is labelled as 'No Unauthorised Access', but you can get the key from the travel agency in the Woermannhaus Building, for a charge of N$20 per person; climb the dusty stairs to the top for 360° views over town.

Also of note are the old **railway station** [331 G2], completed in 1901 and now the home of Swakopmund Hotel and Entertainment Centre, and the **old prison** [327 B2], on Moses Garoëb Street as it heads north out of town.

Guided 2½-hour walking tours of the individual buildings can be arranged in English and German with Frau Angelika Flamm-Schneeweiss (📞 *064 461647; 📱 081 272 6693*); prebook one at the Namib i tourist office (page 330).

Alternatively, both the handout from the municipality itself, and the short book entitled *Swakopmund – A Chronicle of the Town's People, Places and Progress*, available at the museum, give descriptions and brief histories for some of the buildings.

For guided city tours, see page 347.

Museums, galleries and libraries
Swakopmund Museum [331 C2] (*Strand St;* 📞 *064 402695; www. scientificsocietyswakopmund.com;* ⊕ *10.00–17.00 daily, inc public hols; admission N$30/10 adult/child, N$25 student*) Situated in the old customs building, the museum was founded by Dr Alfons Weber in 1951. Something of a British Museum of yesteryear, it has exhibits on life in the Namib Desert and the South Atlantic, huge collections of insects and birds' eggs, an excellent section on rocks and minerals, and lots of information on the colonial German history in the region.

The main hall is dominated by a long row of taxidermy animals, such as zebra, cheetah, hyena and ostrich, with elephant and hippo skulls sitting to the side. Also in the entrance, on the left, is a section showing the history of the Hansa Brewery.

In the museum's newest wing, the 'People of Namibia' exhibition covers Namibia's indigenous cultures and, in the same section, there's a permanent exhibition about

Devil's Claw – a plant with anti-inflammatory healing properties used by the San Bushmen – with interactive video screens. There's also a re-creation of what old doctors' and dentists' surgeries must have been like. Frightening stuff.

Upstairs are archaeology exhibits, including a plaster cast of the skull of Otjisewa Man, thought to be 100,000 years old; the original sits in Windhoek's State Museum (page 203).

Attached is Raith's Museum Café (⊕ *09.30–Mon–Fri, 09.00–18.00 Sat–Sun*) selling ice creams and overlooking the beach.

Finally, on the first Friday of the month the museum arranges tours of **Rössing Mine** – the largest opencast uranium mine in the world. Tours cost N$40/30 adult/child and the proceeds go to the museum.

Sam Cohen Library [327 B4] (*Cnr Sam Nujoma Av & Windhoeker St;* ☎ *061 402695;* ⊕ *08.00–13.00 & 15.00–17.00 Mon–Fri, 09.00–13.30 2nd Sat of month; admission free, research N$75/hr*) Built in the 1970s to accommodate over 2,000 volumes of the Africana collection belonging to the estate of Ferdinand Stich, a local bookshop owner and collector, this private and peaceful library also houses a further 8,000-plus volumes encompassing most of the literature on Swakopmund, and has a huge archive of newspapers from 1898 to the present day (some in German, some in English). There's also a collection of old photographs and maps. In the past you could just pop in for free, but nowadays they feel quite strongly that you should offer a donation. The entrance is on the left-hand side of the building.

Living Desert Snake Park [327 A4] (*Libertina Amathila Av;* ☎ *064 405100;* ⊕ *09.00–17.00 Mon–Fri, 09.00–13.00 Sat; admission N$100/50 adult/child 4–16yrs*) This privately owned snake park belonging to Stuart Hebbard has been open more than 20 years. It boasts more than 25 species of Namibian snakes, along with lizards, chameleons, scorpions and other creatures, which is enough to satisfy even the most inquisitive child – or adult. The animals are kept under glass in two small rooms, where snake feeding takes place on Saturdays from 10.00 to 13.00 and, for N$60, you can have your photo take with Dodo the python draped around your neck.

National Marine Aquarium [327 A5] (*Strand St;* ☎ *064 410 1214;* ⊕ *10.00–16.00 Tue–Sun & hols; admission N$40/20 adult/child, student or pensioner*) It's a cold fish indeed that isn't impressed by Swakopmund's gleaming new aquarium. Everything centres around the main tank that holds a staggering 320,000 litres of water pumped directly from the ocean and housing fish found in Namibian waters. The highlight is a walk-through tunnel with perspex ceiling, so you can watch massive dusky kobs, garrick, spotted gulley sharks and Atlantic spotted grunter swim overhead. Raised cabins with portholes, where kids – big and small – can lounge while watching the fish are inventive too. Feeding time at the main tank takes place daily at 15.00, and on Tuesdays, Saturdays and Sundays a diver goes into the tank to hand-feed the fish. The upper floor gives open views of the top of the main tank and has a small games area featuring giant fish where children can sit and answer quizzes on embedded computer screens.

Kristall Galerie [331 E1] (*Cnr Tobias Hainyeko St & Theo-Ben Gurirab Av;* ☎ *064 406080; www.namibiangemstones.com;* ⊕ *09.00–17.00 Mon–Sat; admission N$20/12 adult/child*) This ultra-modern building houses what is claimed to be the largest-known crystal cluster in the world, estimated to be around 520 million years old and weighing over 14 tonnes. Displays include a 'scratch pit' (a fake outdoor rockery) where visitors – mainly children – can rummage among the piles of semi-precious stones and pick their favourites to take home (parents, you'll need to collect an empty bag from reception; small ones cost N$20, medium N$40 and large N$60). There's also an exact replica of the original Otjua tourmaline mine, where the huge crystal was discovered, and a craft area with windows where you can watch jewellery makers at work: from sorting and drilling to designing and beading. And there's a shop, of course, selling expensive and glittering semi-precious stones in various guises. It's fun for families, and well worth a visit for anyone fascinated by geology.

Activities

Birding tours Batis Birding (page 369) offers half- or full-day tours; their qualified guides can help with special requests. Rates start from N$650 per person.

Camel rides See page 368.

Guided city tours

Historical walk around Swakopmund The walk starts at the Swakopmund Museum at a prearranged time and lasts 2 hours. The guide will enlighten you on the early days on the Namibian coast, with plenty of anecdotes. It costs between N$250 and N$300 depending on the number of people.
Operators: Historische Stadtfuehrungen, Panorama Cycle Tours; page 370.

Tour of Swakopmund Yesterday, Today and Tomorrow A 1½-hour guided tour by car. It needs to be prebooked and requires at least two people. N$300 per person.
Operators: Charly's Desert Tours, Kallisto Tours; page 369.

Township tours If you'd like to visit the townships of Mondesa and DRC, you'll be picked up at 09.00 or 15.00 from your accommodation to visit the market, traditional elders and the kindergarten. You will then take tea at a private DRC home, and have lunch at a *shebeen* with traditional foods including *mahangu*, mopane worms and wild spinach. The 4-hour tour costs N$420 per person including snacks and drinks.
Operators: Hafeni Cultural Tours, Hata Angu Cultural Tours, Panorama Cycle Tours; page 369.

WALVIS BAY

Walvis Bay (meaning 'whale bay') seems larger and more spaced out than Swakopmund, and has a very different character. Perhaps Afrikaans was the dominant influence here, whereas German was clearly the driving force in shaping Swakopmund's architecture and style. Yet the town has grown fast in recent years, reflecting an expanding population based on industrial and commercial development, and its increasing popularity with visitors keen to stay near the lagoon. Construction by the Chinese of a big new tanker jetty and container terminal in 2018 is transforming Walvis Bay into a much busier port, attracting more and bigger ships into the harbour. For visitors, there are new places to stay, but the most notable change is at the Waterfront, which is now an attractive place to eat – or simply to watch the boats.

In spite of this, most visitors still stay in Swakopmund, venturing down to Walvis Bay for boat trips or to go **birdwatching** on the lagoon or beyond. Here, the shallow, sheltered waters attract huge flocks of seabirds and migrant waders, including the famous flamingos and pelicans.

HISTORY The first Europeans at Walvis Bay came with the Portuguese navigator Bartolomeu Dias on the ship *São Cristóvã* in 1487, although at that time no formal Portuguese claim was made. Over the ensuing years, the territory passed through Dutch, British and South African hands until finally it became part of Namibia.

Although Namibia became independent in 1990, the port of Walvis Bay, and the enclave that surrounds it, remained part of South Africa from 1990 until 1994 – despite being surrounded by the newly independent country of Namibia. However, at midnight on 28 February 1994 the South African flag was taken down, and 5 minutes later the Namibian flag was raised here. This transferred the enclave to Namibian control and ended a point of contention between the two countries. Walvis Bay is strategically important as the coast's only deepwater port, and ceding control of it to Windhoek was a very significant step for South African politicians to make.

GETTING THERE AND AWAY

By air Air Namibia has daily flights from both Cape Town and Windhoek to Walvis Bay International Airport. From Cape Town, flights depart at 10.25, arriving in Walvis Bay at 12.35, then continuing on to Windhoek at 13.10, to arrive at 13.50. The return flight leaves Windhoek at 14.30, touching down in Walvis Bay at 15.10, then departing for Cape Town at 15.45. There are no flights between Walvis Bay and Swakopmund.

Flights between Walvis Bay and Johannesburg are handled by Airlink and South African Express Airways.

The **airport**, with a smart new terminal opened in 2014, lies 11km to the east of town off the C14, on the northern edge of the desert. In addition to offices for Air Namibia (\ *064 202867*), South African Express (\ *064 207428; www.flyexpress. aero*) and Airlink (\ *064 220906; www.flyairlink.com*), the terminal building has desks for the major car-hire companies, along with a small souvenir shop, a Standard Bank ATM, and a couple of cafés on the first floor. A shuttle into the centre of Walvis Bay can be prebooked through the tourist information office in Swakopmund (page 330) for around N$300–400 per person.

By train Walvis Bay is linked to Windhoek via Swakopmund and Okahandja by the normal, slow train services. These run to and from Windhoek on Tuesday, Thursday, Friday and Sunday, arriving in Walvis Bay at 07.15 and departing at 19.00. An economy ticket costs N$118. See page 151 for details, or call TransNamib in Walvis Bay (\ *064 208504*) – though you'd be better to go to the station [351 E2] in person.

Walvis Bay is also the final port of call for the nine-day luxury Rovos Rail journey from Pretoria; for details, see page 151.

By bus Intercape Mainliner (\ *061 227847*) runs a good service linking Windhoek and Walvis Bay, which stops next to Pick n Pay on the corner of Theo-Ben Gurirab Street and 11th Road [351 E3]. This departs from Windhoek at 10.00 on Thursday and Saturday, arriving in Walvis Bay at 14.50, and returns Friday and Sunday at 10.00, arriving in Windhoek at 14.50. Tickets cost around N$250 one-way, and must be booked in advance, either direct with Intercape (page 153), or in Walvis Bay with Ultra Travel (page 352).

Scheduled minibus shuttle services between Windhoek, Swakopmund and Walvis Bay are run by several companies, including Walvis Bay's Carlo's Shuttle & Tours [350 D5] (*65 Union St, next to tourist office;* \ *064 205537;* m *081 270*

4395; **e** *carloshuttle@iway.na; www.carloshuttlenamibia.com*) and McClune's (*Theo-Ben Gurirab St;* ☏ *064 221713;* **m** *081 128 7916;* **e** *mcclunes@mweb.com.na*), and two in Swakopmund (page 328). The journey takes 4 hours to Swakopmund, or 5 hours to Walvis Bay, with tickets costing N$250 per person, one-way, or N$90 between Walvis Bay and Swakopmund. Buses depart from Walvis Bay at 07.00 and 14.00, or from Swakopmund at 08.00 and 15.00, every day except Saturday, when they are morning only. The same applies to return buses, which leave Windhoek at 07.00 and 14.00. Both outfits offer private hire, too, either between Walvis Bay and Swakopmund or further afield.

ORIENTATION For today's visitor, the focus of Walvis Bay is firmly on the lagoon and the adjacent waterfront. Originally, however, the town was built for its harbour, and its streets were until recently numbered from there: 1st Street nearest the harbour, parallel to the sea, and 16th Street furthest from it. Similarly its roads were perpendicular to the harbour, starting with 1st Road in the south and continuing to 18th Road in the north.

These somewhat unexciting thoroughfares form a grid that is the city, and are easily navigable. Or at least were until most of the street numbers were changed to names. To add to the entertainment, Tom Swemmer Street and Civic Centre Street were both at one time called 12th Street. And 13th Street, 14th Street, Simon Luanda Street and Piet/Heibeb Street were all, at one time, called Hidipo Hamutenya Avenue. (Even with four sections of this street now renamed, there is still one section of Hidipo Hamutenya Avenue remaining!)

Since many people still refer to the original street names, the following may be useful:

- 6th Road *is now* Robert Forbes Street
- 10th Road *is now* Cyril Fernandez Street
- 12th Road *is now* Sport Road
- 13th Road *is now* Rikumbi Kandanga Street
- 18th Road *is now* Ana Mupentami Road
- 2nd Street West *is now* J J Cleverly Street
- 4th Street West *is now* Paul Vincent Street
- 5th Street West *is now* Frank Guthrie Street
- 6th Street *is now* Peter Dixon Street
- 7th Street *is now* Sam Nujoma Avenue
- 8th Street *is now* Hage G Geingob Street
- 8th Street West *is now* Fritz Lange Street
- 9th Street *is now* Theo-Ben Gurirab Street
- 9th Street West *is now* Thomas Morris Street
- 10th Street *is now* Nangolo Mbumba Drive
- 11th Street *is now* John Muafangejo Street
- 15th Street *is now* Peter Mueshihange Street
- Kuiseb Street *is now* Nathaniel Maxuilili Avenue
- Oceana Street *is now* Ben Amathila Drive

GETTING AROUND Walvis Bay is quite spread out and there's little in the way of local public transport. If you've no vehicle then walking is usually pleasant, and hitching is occasionally successful, even in town. Should you wish to take a taxi, ask your hotel or guesthouse to organise this for you rather than hailing one on the street.

A　　B　　C　　D

1

TANKER
JETTY

2

Walvis Bay
Harbour

PORT AREA

21

Walvis Bay
Pharmacy

Shoprite

14

OK

3

Namcrafts &
Art Gallery

22　19　Jetty Shoppe

WATERFRONT

P

Spar

5TH STREET WEST

PETER

DIXON STREET

9TH

ROAD

NUJOMA AVENUE

8TH

ROAD

HAGE GEINGOB ST.

17

THEO-BEN

GURIRAB

ATLANTIC STREET

13

1ST ST WEST

6

8

3RD STREET

2ND STREET

CLEVERLY ROAD

THE ESPLANADE

24

12

PAUL VINCENT STREET

ROAD

GUTHRIE

5TH ROAD

SAM

6TH ROAD

Walvis Bay
Private
High School

FRANK

BR. NUJOMA ST.

SAM

1

ST

TOM SWEMMER ST.

FREDERIK

ERSKINE ST

FRITZ

LANGE ST

MORRIS

LAGOON ROAD

STREET

NANGOLO

MBUMBA

DRIVE

4

11

THOMAS

LAGOON ROAD

5TH ROAD

ROBERT FORBES RD

Walvis Bay

MUNGANDA STREET

PROTEA

STREET

Carlo's
Shuttle

Lagoon

5

FAIRVIEW AVENUE

10

1ST

ROAD

2ND ROAD WEST

MAIN

4TH ROAD NORTH

18

6

KAVAMBO NUJOMA DRIVE
aka MILLIONAIRES' ROW

5

1ST STREET NORTH

2ND STREET NORTH

RCAD

4TH STREET NORTH

6TH ROAD WEST

7

2ND ROAD WEST

15TH STREET NORTH

TEMPLE

15

HARMONY STREET

8TH ROAD WEST

PIONEER STREET

9

*Pelican Point
Lodge*

7

4

ARIZONA STREET

7TH ROAD EAST

A　　B　　C　　D

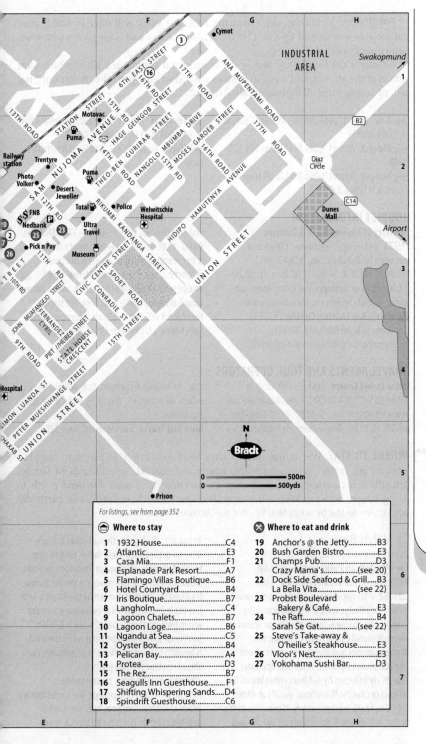

For listings, see from page 352

Where to stay

1	1932 House....................................C4
2	Atlantic...E3
3	Casa Mia...F1
4	Esplanade Park Resort..............A7
5	Flamingo Villas Boutique.........B6
6	Hotel Countyard..........................B4
7	Iris Boutique.................................B7
8	Langholm.......................................C4
9	Lagoon Chalets............................B7
10	Lagoon Loge.................................B6
11	Ngandu at Sea.............................C5
12	Oyster Box.....................................B4
13	Pelican Bay....................................A4
14	Protea..D3
15	The Rez...B7
16	Seagulls Inn Guesthouse.........F1
17	Shifting Whispering Sands.....D4
18	Spindrift Guesthouse................C6

Where to eat and drink

19	Anchor's @ the Jetty.................B3
20	Bush Garden Bistro....................E3
21	Champs Pub...................................D3
	Crazy Mama's.....................(see 20)
22	Dock Side Seafood & Grill.....B3
	La Bella Vita.......................(see 22)
23	Probst Boulevard
	Bakery & Café............................E3
24	The Raft..B4
	Sarah Se Gat......................(see 22)
25	Steve's Take-away &
	O'heilie's Steakhouse............E3
26	Vlooi's Nest...................................E3
27	Yokohama Sushi Bar.................D3

Swakopmund and Walvis Bay Area WALVIS BAY

14

For drivers, local boys, often wearing reflective vests, will offer to watch your car for you; you should tip them N$3–5 during the day and N$5–10 at night when returning to your vehicle.

To hire a car locally, try one of the main rental companies, all of which have offices at the airport, and some in town as well. Most are open office hours only, but will of course meet all flights. See also page 329.

Avis Airport ☏064 209487; 89 Hage Geingob St ☏064 209633

Bidvest Airport ☏064 204128; m 081 128 6900

Budget Airport ☏064 204128; 89 Hage Geingob St ☏064 209633

Europcar Airport ☏064 202317; Pelican Bay Hotel ☏064 207391; m 081 127 8110

Hertz Airport ☏064 200853; e res@hertz. co.za

TOURIST INFORMATION
Ministry of Environment & Tourism
(MET) 643 Heinrich Baumann St (port area, between 1st & 2nd sts East; ☏064 205971; ⏱ 08.00–13.00 & 14.00–17.00 Mon–Fri, 08.00–13.00 Sat. As in Swakopmund, this is where you obtain permits for entry to the national parks.

i Walvis Bay Tourism Centre [350 D5] Cnr Union St & 5th Rd; ☏064 207444; e tourismbookingoffice@gmail.com; www.

walvisbaytourism.com; ⏱ 08.00–17.00 Mon–Fri, 09.00–13.00 Sat. Along with a variety of leaflets & free maps, they sell souvenirs & can book accommodation. There are also toilets here (*N$5*) & an extensive secondhand bookshop, with a biltong shop & drinks available next door. Out the back they have 3 self-catering Dune Chalets, each with twin beds & a kitchenette (*N$650 per chalet*).

TRAVEL AGENTS AND TOUR OPERATORS
Ultra Travel Centre [351 E3] 199 Nangolo Mbumba Dr; ☏064 207997; e res@ultratravel.net; www.ultratravel.net; ⏱ 08.00–17.30 Mon–Fri, 08.30–12.30 Sat. An exceptionally helpful agency

that can arrange accommodation, dolphin tours, safaris, air tickets, etc, & is an agent for Intercape bus tickets.
Sure Ritz Travel Swakopmund; page 328

WHERE TO STAY Walvis Bay doesn't have Swakop's variety of places to stay, but options are many, from comfortable hotels and intimate guesthouses to family-friendly self-catering units, and even a converted lighthouse. Or head north to Long Beach, between Walvis Bay and Swakopmund, where families in particular are drawn to the beaches that border the Atlantic Ocean.

In Walvis Bay
Hotels and lodges
☀ 🏠 **Pelican Point Lodge** [324 A4] (10 rooms) Pelican Point Peninsula; ☏064 221282; e info@pelicanpointlodge.com; www. pelicanpointlodge.com. Marooned across the lagoon, this unique & fascinating lodge within Dorob National Park is converted from the harbour-control building that for years served the peninsula's lighthouse (see box, opposite). Guests are collected by 4x4 from either Walvis Bay Airport or near the Waterfront, usually at either 14.00 or 17.00, for the leisurely 45min drive to the lodge; self-drivers & day visitors are not allowed.

As you pass the lagoon, the saltworks & finally drive on to the beach itself, there's time to stop for photographs – perhaps of flamingos, pelicans, jackals or seals – before you reach the lighthouse. It's a spectacular spot, fringed by the Atlantic with just the lights of Walvis Bay twinkling across the water. Even on a sunny day, the black-&-white lighthouse looks forbidding, but when the wind is howling or the mist rolls in, it accentuates the sheer remoteness of the place.

Inside the old harbour-control building, though, all is calm & shipshape. The contemporary beach-chic décor combines teak wood, white polished concrete floors & cool blue-&-green

THE STORY OF A LIGHTHOUSE

Look across the water from Walvis Bay and you may spot a black-and-white lighthouse, sometimes clear against the sky, at others, looming out of the fog. Although there has been a 'post light' on this spot since 1916, the secondhand lighthouse didn't materialise until 1932. Built in Hamburg in 1915, it stood guard over the South African port of Durban for 17 years, until the authorities decreed that it should be moved to Pelican Point, just 200m from the tip of the peninsula. Shipwrecks litter the Namibian coast, here as further north, and the need for a lighthouse was urgent to warn seamen of the very real dangers of these treacherous waters. Later, in the 1960s, a jetty and railway were installed to bring in materials for the construction of a harbour-control centre to support the lighthouse. This remained in service until Namibia gained independence from South Africa in 1990. Although still owned by the port authorities, the building became increasingly dilapidated until it was rescued and transformed into the present-day Pelican Point Lodge (see opposite). While the lighthouse itself remains in active service, its eerie foghorn echoing across the water on many a misty morning, the sands beneath have shifted. Now, with the spit growing relentlessly at around 50m a year, it's at least 2.4km from the end of the peninsula. And the sands march on.

walls, offset by simple but stunning photographs. Sea-themed bedrooms (including 2 family rooms) feature floor-to-ceiling windows with panoramic views of either the Atlantic or the lagoon; those on the ground floor have direct access on to the beach, while those upstairs arguably have better views. Open-plan bathrooms with his 'n' hers sinks have good hot showers, & free-standing bio-fuel fires are a welcome addition to counter Walvis Bay's infamous fogs. But the best is saved for the top, where the breathtaking Captain's Cove boasts 360° views, a wraparound terrace with wicker sunloungers, a free-standing 2-person oval bath with candelabra for romantic nights, a dbl bed & its own mezzanine lounge.

From the spacious open-plan lounge/restaurant/bar, squashy sofas are fronted by huge windows overlooking the beach, with more bio-fuel fires providing warmth. There's Wi-Fi throughout, but this is a place to chat over a drink before dinner, from a succinct 3-course menu that changes daily, & majors on seafood. Walking along the windswept beach, past colonies of fur seals, is arguably the best way to explore the peninsula, but fatbikes add a different perspective, or consider a sunset drive to Donkey Bay, or a sunset boat cruise. Kayaking with seals & trips to Sandwich Harbour can also be arranged. At the end of your stay, you'll be ferried back to Walvis Bay aboard

the lodge's boat, with sparkling wine & oysters to speed you on your way. The boat leaves at 08.30 to be the first on the water, passing close to seals cavorting in the waves & – if you're lucky – the occasional dolphin or even whale, before docking in town at 10.30. *DBB N$6,200–9,200/10,200– 15,000 sgl/dbl; min 2-night stay.* $$$$$$– $$$$$$$

⌂ **Flamingo Villas Boutique Hotel**
[350 B6] (28 rooms) 30 Kavambo Nujoma Dr; 📞 064 205631; m 081 296 3436; e reservations@flamingovillana.com; www.flamingovillana.com. Opposite the lagoon, & built with the Chinese market in mind, this traditional hotel was new to the scene in 2016, & was already being enlarged in 2018. Photos of Namibia add a sense of place to its fairly corporate but comfortable & spacious rooms, which all have AC/heating & carpeted floors. Only the 'luxury' ones face the lagoon (& also boast a bath & king-size bed); all others have twin ¾ beds. The bar is popular with allcomers, & the rather formal restaurant serves a cosmopolitan menu ($$$$–$$$$$) with regular specials. *N$2,020–2,805/2,693–4,182 sgl/dbl.* $$$$– $$$$$

⌂ **Iris Boutique Hotel & Restaurant**
[350 B7] 42 Kovambo Nujoma Dr; 📞 064 207700; e operations@irisgroup.com.na; www.irisgroup.com.na. Opposite the lagoon, the former Egumbo

is now under new ownership & in 2018 was the subject of large-scale renovation work. The aim is to turn it into something of an evening venue, but for the moment it's a case of wait & see.

🏠 **Pelican Bay Hotel** [350 A4] (48 rooms, 2 suites) The Esplanade; ✆064 214000; reservations ✆+27 21 430 5300; e res. pelicanbay@proteahotels.com.na; www. proteahotels.com. This imposing Protea hotel has an enviable location by the lagoon, its light, lofty lobby, with fountains either side of the entrance, reinforcing the architect's vision of sun, sea & sand. Facing the water, the rooms, each with a small terrace or balcony, are furnished using a light lime-washed wood, but are somewhat lacking in individuality. All have AC, en-suite bathroom/ shower, TV, phone & coffee-making facilities; some are interconnecting to make family suites, & there's 1 with wheelchair access. The elegant blue-themed Aquarius restaurant looks out across the bay, while for light snacks, head for the Neptune coffee shop which serves until 23.00 every day. There's also a hair salon on site, secure parking & free Wi-Fi throughout. *N$1,620/1,970 sgl/dbl, but rates vary*. **$$$$**

🏠 **Protea Hotel** [350 D3] (58 rooms) Cnr Sam Nujoma Av & Cyril Fernandez St; ✆064 213700; e info@proteawalvis.com.na; www.proteahotels. com. The original Protea has been significantly enlarged over the years, but still caters more to businesspeople than tourists. Fairly standard rooms – 4 adapted for wheelchairs – are modern & carpeted, with twin beds, AC, DSTV, facilities to make tea & coffee, direct-dial phones, & en-suite bath with a powerful overhead shower. You'll also find the Oasis restaurant, which serves both buffet & à la carte meals, a lounge, free Wi-Fi, & an enormous car park. In short, this is an efficient & comfortable if rather soulless hotel, in the centre of town. *N$1,355/1,630 sgl/dbl; variable rates*. **$$$$**

🏠 **Langholm Hotel** [350 C4] (15 rooms, 3 suites) 18–20 J J Cleverly St; ✆064 209230; m 081 687 6633; e desk@langholmhotel.com; www.langholmhotel.com. This friendly, green-&-white-painted hotel with secure parking is owned by the welcoming Nic Adams, & is very near to the lagoon. Well-appointed lime-green dbl & twin rooms come with white linens, a fridge (stocked on request), safe, tea/coffee station, DSTV, direct-dial phone & free Wi-Fi, & 5 of the en-suite rooms

have baths instead of corner showers. The 2 luxury suites, one of them suitable for a wheelchair user, are lovely. There's a relaxing lounge with a bar (🕓 *until 23.00 every evening*), whose ceiling is festooned with a huge assortment of hats (1,800 at the last count!) donated by visitors. Don't sleep in so late that you miss the extensive b/fast. An à la carte dinner is available Mon–Sat. *N$1,170–1,425/1,350–1,640 sgl/dbl*. **$$$–$$$$**

🏠 **Atlantic Hotel** [351 E3] (32 rooms) 128 Sam Nujoma Av; ✆064 213000; m 081 128 4501; e reservations@atlantichotel.com.na. Walvis Bay's 1st hotel dates back to 1920, when the railway used to stop right here. Fast forward almost a century to find it extensively renovated in 2017, from the light, tiled lobby to large bedrooms with AC, dark wood furnishings, tiled floors – & a real sense of space. The fittings are stylish, the bathrooms come with big oval baths & separate showers, & king-size beds (as well as a fridge & DSTV) are standard. Downstairs, aerial photos of the town adorn the restaurant, there's a separate bar area, & secure parking. If a proper hotel is what you are looking for, this might be just the place. *N$700/900 sgl/dbl*. **$$$**

🏠 **Casa Mia Hotel** [351 F1] (23 rooms) 224–228 Sam Nujoma Av; ✆064 205975; e info@ casamiahotel.com; www.casamiahotel.com. Behind the smart navy-blue walls of this town-centre hotel, light wood & grey-&-white décor give a relatively contemporary feel. Smallish en-suite rooms have DSTV, phone, tea/coffee-maker & AC. The restaurant (🕓 *07.00–21.30 daily*) has a good reputation but the menu is limited (**$$–$$$**); don't expect modern cuisine. You'll find a pool table & TV in the bar, & there's even a casino. Free Wi-Fi. *N$650/850 sgl/dbl*. **$$$**

🏠 **Hotel Countyard** [350 B4] (18 rooms) Cnr 16 3rd Rd & J J Cleverly St; ✆064 213600; http:// ecountyardbirdwatchinghotel.com. With new ownership comes a bizarre new name for this old hotel, in a residential road near the lagoon. Despite the name, everything is set around 2 grassy courtyards, shaded by a couple of sturdy palm trees. En-suite sgl, dbl & family rooms have satellite TV & a phone, while some have a small lounge, & others a kitchenette. It's a clean, functional option, with dinner available on request & secure parking. *N$750/850 sgl/dbl*. **$$$**

🏠 **Ngandu at Sea** [350 C5] (18 rooms, 1 apt) Cnr 1st Rd & Thomas Morris St; ✆064 207327;

e theart@iafrica.com.na. Just a stone's throw from the lagoon, Ngandu's colourful murals & paintings by local artists lift the otherwise rather sombre feel. Every room – dbl, twin, sgl & family – has an en-suite shower, & some have views of the lagoon. Dbls have DSTV, phone, tea/coffee facilities, fridge & fan; 1 room is self-catering, & a self-catering apartment is a short walk from the main building. Lunch & dinner (on request) are served in the large, angular dining area with bar, & outside is a pleasant courtyard festooned with pot plants. With free Wi-Fi throughout & 2 conference rooms for up to 40, this is a place that would suit businesspeople as well as holidaymakers. *N$660/770 sgl/dbl.* **$$$**

Guesthouse, B&Bs and restcamps

🏠 **Lagoon Loge** [350 B6] (9 rooms) 88 Kavambo Nujoma Dr; 064 200850; m 081 129 7953; e french@lagoonloge.com.na; www.lagoonloge.com.na. Using the French spelling of 'lodge', much to the puzzlement of the locals, this distinctive yellow building decked with flowers was the brainchild of Helen & Wilfred Meiller. A must for bird lovers, it is situated right opposite the lagoon, with daily entertainment provided by flocks of flamingos (in season!) & other waterbirds. Wilfred's skills as a wood-turner are evident in the individually decorated rooms, each with a different theme. If you're into the seaside, then a large mural of Walvis Bay may suit your style, & if birds are your passion, ask for their bird room. There are also 3 family rooms. All are en suite, with a balcony or terrace facing the lagoon, but it's the new 'penthouse' suite that steals the best views of the bay. Facilities include an unheated swimming pool in the secluded rear garden, & a sun room at the front that doubles as a b/fast room. *N$1,190/2,040 sgl/dbl.* **$$$$**

🏠 **Oyster Box** [350 B4] (12 rooms) Cnr Esplanade & J J Cleverly St; 064 202247; m 081 160 0600; e info@oysterboxguesthouse.com; www.oysterboxguesthouse.com. Standards of maintenance may have slipped in the rooms of this guesthouse, owned by the proprietors of Hotel Heinitzburg in Windhoek (page 175), but service is reasonably efficient, & the location, on a quiet road across from the lagoon & near the Raft restaurant. is one of the best in Walvis Bay. The entire property follows a beach-chic theme, with lots of whites & paintings of shells hanging on the walls. Stone-floored bedrooms are modest in size, their grey walls softening white wooden furniture & crisp white linens on comfortable beds. All have flat-screen TVs, AC & combi international plug sockets, but only 4 – which also boast large corner baths – look over the lagoon. The best seats, though, are in the 2nd-floor b/fast room, where big picture windows give cinematic views over the lagoon, & a wraparound terrace allows guests to eat outside on warmer mornings. A small lunch/dinner menu featuring quiches, steaks, etc (**$$$–$$$$$**) is available every day until 20.30, & downstairs is an open-plan lounge where you can enjoy a drink from the bar until 21.00. Gated parking & free Wi-Fi throughout. *N$1,008–1,293/1,608–2,025 sgl/dbl.* **$$$$**

☀ 🏠 **The Rez** [350 B7] 16 Mandume Ndemufayo Circle; 064 221725; m 081 837 1224/1230; e hugo@therez.com.na; www.therez.com.na. Personable South African owner/managers Hugo & Jason's new venture, opened in 2017, has shaken up the B&B scene in Walvis Bay. Hugo's photos on the walls vie with distressed wood mirrors, 1950s furniture, classy lamps & Moroccan artefacts in an eclectic fusion of styles that affords an unexpectedly contemporary yet homely feel. Help yourself to coffee all day in the simple b/fast room, settle down around the funky firepit on the enclosed terrace, & unwind. Then retire for the night to a classy dbl room, most of which have a private patio. The Wi-Fi is free, the welcome is warm, & it's all just 500m from the lagoon. *N$1,095–1,430/1,870–2,310 sgl/dbl.* **$$$$**

🏠 **1932 House** [350 C4] (7 rooms, 2 apts) 26 Fritz Lange St; 064 274850; m 081 331 3267; e info@1932house.com.na; www.1932house.com.na. Restored in 2011 to create a guesthouse near the lagoon, 1932 is an interesting mix of contemporary & 1930s style, sometimes bordering on the kitsch. En-suite rooms – 6 dbl, 1 family – are light & airy & there are 2 self-catering apartments for longer stays. All have access to the cactus-studded garden with small plunge pool, outdoor lounge & braai area. Lunch & dinner can be prepared on request. Free Wi-Fi. *N$900–950/1,000–1,200 sgl/dbl.* **$$$**

🏠 **Shifting Whispering Sands** [350 D4] (7 rooms) 82 Sam Nujoma Av; 064 205348; e shiftwhispsands@iway.na; www.shiftingwhisperingsands.com. Efficiency is the watchword at this central guesthouse in immaculately maintained gardens. Largely geared to the business market, it has 3 dbl & 4 twin rooms with Wi-Fi, DSTV & kitchenette, & secure parking. *N$700/950 sgl/dbl.* **$$$**

🏠 **Spindrift Guesthouse** [350 C6] (8 rooms) 22 Main Rd; 📞 064 206723; **m** 081 129 3940; **e** spindrift@iway.na. Run by Kees & Liz Visser, this delightful home-from-home option makes a lovely first impression thanks to its lush gardens, mature palms & the small wooden bridge, spanning a carp pond, that you cross to get to the property. Colourful rooms – 4 dbls, 1 twin, 3 family rooms – with DSTV, tea/coffee & (some) with baths, are decorated with paintings by Liz, whose work is also on display in the art gallery at the back. B/fast at the communal table; lunch & dinner available on request. There's free Wi-Fi, an L-shaped swimming pool & a couple of secure parking spots too. *N$700/920 sgl/dbl.* **$$$**

🏠 **Lagoon Chalets** [350 B7] (33 chalets, 7 rooms, camping) 8th Rd W; 📞 064 217900; **m** 081 128 7151; **e** info@lagoonchaletswb.com; www. lagoonchaletswb.com. A family business of 30yrs' standing, Lagoon Chalets provides well-thought-out rooms & chalets sleeping from 2 to 8 people, in various configurations, along with 14 neat camping pitches. Cool tiled floors, white linen, neutral décor & immaculate kitchenettes attract allcomers, from backpackers & overlanders to families & groups of friends, not least as the rates include 'fixing' – not just cleaning, but even your washing up. Wi-Fi is free; fans & heaters are available should the temperature soar (or drop), & there's a self-service laundry. Add in a play park for children & the Bush Café (🕐 *07.00–11.00 & 17.00–21.00 Mon–Sat; also open to outsiders*) & it's a very appealing package, especially for families, groups of friends & backpackers. *Room or chalet N$440–1,320; camping N$165 pp & N$110/pitch.* **$$–$$$**

🏠 **Seagulls Inn Guesthouse** [351 F1] (10 rooms) 199 Sam Nujoma Av; 📞 064 202775. The turquoise walls of this central guesthouse give no hint of the simple rooms behind, arranged around an inner courtyard studded with palms. It's not terribly well organised when the owner Andreas Soldan is not there, but the staff are friendly & it's good value, so perhaps worth checking out. Note that it's not to be confused with the excellent B&B of the same name in Swakopmund. *Room only N$440–60.* **$$**

🏠 **Esplanade Park Resort** [350 A7] (27 bungalows) Esplanade; 📞 064 206145; **e** esplanadepark@iway.na; www.walvisbaycc.org. na; 🕐 office 08.00–13.00 & 14.00–17.00 daily. At the western end of town, on the left past Hesko St & opposite the lagoon, the former municipal bungalows look quite smart nowadays with their cream-washed walls. Configurations differ, with 1- & 2-bedroom options (sleeping 3 or 5 people respectively), family bungalows & the VIP one (sleeping 6), but all have a living room, toilet & separate bathroom, & a proper, well-equipped kitchen with stove, fridge/freezer, etc. They also have outside braais (but no grids), sinks & a private garage. Bedding is provided, but towels & soap are not. While it's good-value accommodation, it still feels like a restcamp & is not at all cosy. From *N$495–660/825–990 1/2 bedrooms.* **$$**

Long Beach (Langstrand)

Some 19km north of Walvis Bay, along the B2 from Swakopmund, is the area known as Long Beach, or Langstrand. Once scarcely more than a handful of houses, Long Beach has become the focus of property developers, with houses of all styles joining up the once-isolated resorts that flank the beach. It remains very quiet out of season, but expect the whole atmosphere to go up a few notches in the main holiday periods, especially around Christmas & New Year. With the development have come a couple of places to eat, with a choice of the classy Salt at the Bay View, or the more down-to-earth cuisine of Erik's Cove at Long Beach Resort.

🏠 **Bay View** [324 B3] (44 suites) 136 Damara Tern; 📞 064 273 4200; **m** 081 707 0764; **e** info@ bayview.com.na; www.bayview.com.na. A big departure for Langstrand, the 6-storey Bay View has a prime beachside position with an ocean view from each of its cool, classy suites. These have lots of space for king-size or twin beds, a sleeper couch, huge TV & even a kitchenette. The adjoining Salt Restaurant (🕐 *06.30–10.00, noon–15.00 & 18.00–21.30 daily;* **$$$$–$$$$$**) shares the views from both inside & a big terrace with umbrella-shaded tables. With a spa, a 2nd-floor heated pool & a bar on the top floor (& a lift!), it's a tasteful place to unwind, if slightly corporate. Fatbikes help to explore the beach, & there's free Wi-Fi. *Variable rates, around N$1,860/2,200 sgl/dbl.* **$$$$**

🏠 **Hotel Longbeach** [357 A5] (17 rooms) Longbeach Circle; 📞 064 218820; **m** 081 738 8567;

e res.longbeachlodge@united.com.na. Following a takeover from Protea by United Hotels in 2017, standards have slipped at the Longbeach, though the beachside setting remains a big plus. In the restaurant & bar, looking out to sea, terracotta tiles & ochre-patterned fabrics reflect the warmth of the surrounding desert. Above, dbl or twin en-suite rooms are light & open, with small ocean-facing terraces & carpets that have seen better days. There is free Wi-Fi, a small pool & a braai area for guests' use. *N$810/1,130 sgl/dbl.* **$$$**

🏠 **Burning Shore** [357 A3] (9 rooms, 1 suite) 152 4th St, Long Beach. This established & very personal beachfront lodge was closed in 2018. Let's hope that it is soon restored to its former glory.

🏠 **Dolphin Park** [324 B3] (20 chalets, 1 house) 📞064 204343; **m** 081 143 1291; **e** dolphinpark@iway.na; ⏲ office Oct–May 08.00–13.00 & 14.00–17.00 daily. This purpose-built seaside resort is popular with Namibians & South Africans, especially during the summer holidays, but can be almost deserted at other times. It was designed around a swimming pool complex that's also open to day visitors (⏲ *10.00–17.00 daily; admission N$30/15 adult/child; slide N$15/ride*). Self-catering 2- & 4-bed brick chalets topped with rounded roofs have hotplate, pots, crockery & utensils & a braai drum, while the 6-bed VIP cottage has a proper stove, deep freezer & DSTV. Bedding is provided, but no towels or braai grid, & you'll need to bring all your own food as even the snacks & drinks from the kiosk are available only at w/ends & during the holidays. *Chalet from N$495–605 2 people; house N$1,500–1,980.* **$$**

⛺ **Long Beach Resort** [357 B1] (120 campsites) 📞064 200163; **e** longbeachresort@iway.na; ⏲ office 08.00–13.00 & 14.00–17.00 daily. At the northern end of the Long Beach development, this rather barren campsite has pitches with water & electricity for both caravans & tents. The location – squeezed between the desert dunes & the Atlantic – is lovely, & while it all feels rather barren, the ablutions are acceptable, the sheltered salt-water 'pool' by the jetty is a great place to cool off in the Atlantic & there's a braai area on the beach with jaunty yellow-&-blue picnic tables. Restaurant & bar facilities are now privatised, with Erik's Cove (see right) & the Jetty Bar (⏲ *11.00–late daily*) – aptly at the end of the jetty. *N$30–40 pp plus N$90–130/pitch.* **$–$$**

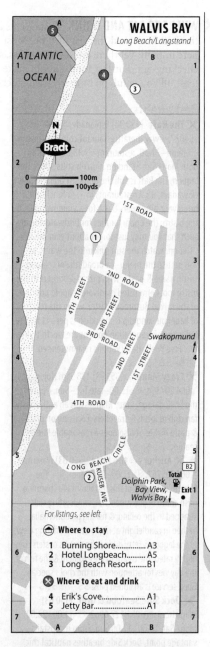

For listings, see left

🏠 **Where to stay**
1 Burning Shore..............A3
2 Hotel Longbeach..........A5
3 Long Beach Resort........B1

✖ **Where to eat and drink**
4 Erik's Cove.....................A1
5 Jetty Bar.........................A1

✖ **Erik's Cove** [357 A1] 1st St; **m** 081 496 0422; bar ⏲ 15.00–21.00 Tue–Fri, 11.00–21.00 Sat, 10.30–16.00 Sun; kitchen ⏲ from 16.00 Tue–Sat. Enjoy great views of the Atlantic from basic wooden tables inside & out as you tuck into toasties, pizzas, ribs & steaks, & there's a proper bar, too. **$$–$$$$**

WHERE TO EAT AND DRINK

✕ **WHERE TO EAT AND DRINK** Restaurants and cafés in Walvis Bay come and go, but the Raft has stood the test of time. Most first-time and regular visitors are drawn here initially, yet there are several others, smaller or less well known, that are worth checking out. For fast food, simply make your way to Dunes Mall, where you can feast till you're full on burgers, fried chicken, at one of several chain restaurants.

Restaurants

✕ **The Raft** [350 B4] Esplanade; ☏ 064 204877; www.theraftrestaurant.com; bar/bistro ⊕ noon–21.30, restaurant ⊕ 18.00–21.30, both Mon–Sat. Standing high on stilts above the lagoon, The Raft is still the quirkiest place in town. Nowadays, it's 2 restaurants in 1. At lunchtime, bring your binoculars & ask for a window table in the bistro; the opportunities for birdwatching are such that you may just forget about your meal. Later on, watch the sun sink into the waves as you peruse the menu – a broad mix of seafood, sushi, game & pasta, with pizzas & burgers in the bistro too. Committed carnivores should approve of the mixed Bushman Platter, while the fish trio of kabeljou, kingklip & monkfish is perfect for the indecisive, & vegetarian options are worth trying, too. Free Wi-Fi. Reservations recommended. $$$–$$$$$

✕ **Crazy Mama's** [351 E3] 138 Sam Nujoma Av; ☏ 064 207364; ⊕ 15.00–late Tue–Sun. Opposite the Shell garage, Crazy Mama's has an enthusiastic fan club of locals & travellers. Focusing on pizza & pasta dishes, it also does a reasonable line in seafood. $$$–$$$$$

✱ ✕ **Anchor's @ the Jetty** [350 B3] Waterfront; ☏ 064 205762; ⊕ 11.00–22.00 Tue–Sun. The fisherman interior of this restaurant is a charming mish-mash of picnic benches, windsurfing sails strapped to the ceiling, & fishing paraphernalia, bathed in candlelight at night-time & offering views of the lagoon & jetty during the day. Its oysters come highly rated, the calamari are excellent & the fish of the day vies for attention with the chef's specials. Good service is an added plus. $$–$$$$$

✕ **Dock Side Seafood & Grill** [350 B3] Waterfront; m 081 127 6062; ⊕ 11.00–23.00 Mon–Sat, 10.00–17.00 Sun. From its upstairs vantage point, Dock Side breathes nautical chic, with 180° views of the harbour from big picture windows & a sheltered terrace. Seafood is the obvious accompaniment from a very varied menu that also includes pizzas. $$–$$$

✕ **La Bella Vita** [350 B3] Waterfront; ☏ 064 206959; ⊕ 08.00–late daily. On the ground floor of a 2-storey building, this rather dark, low-key place with bright painted tables & chairs & a big bar has a relaxed vibe, & there are high tables outside if you prefer. On the menu, specials such as springbok stroganoff make a refreshing change from the grills & seafood. $$–$$$

✕ **Steve's Take-away & O'heilie's Steakhouse** [351 E3] 89 Theo-Ben Gurirab St; ☏ 064 205384; ⊕ 08.00–22.00 Mon–Sat. A locals' hangout with gargantuan portions from a surprisingly varied menu, from pies to T-bone steak. $$–$$$

✕ **Yokohama Sushi Bar** [350 D3] 122 Sam Nujoma Dr; m 081 489 4264; ⊕ 11.00–19.00 Mon–Thu; 11.00–20.00 Fri–Sat. If you're craving sushi, help is at hand at this simple restaurant right next to the pharmacy. For 2 people, try the 30-piece platter (N$200). $$–$$$

Cafés and light meals

☕ **Probst Boulevard Bakery & Café** [351 E3] 148 Theo-Ben Gurirab St (near 12th Rd); ☏ 064 202744; ⊕ 06.30–17.45 Mon–Fri, 06.30–14.00 Sat. Open since 1957, this licensed café & bakery is very popular with the locals, with seating inside & out, & a reasonably priced menu for b/fast & lunch. $$–$$$

✕ **Vlooi's Nest** [351 E3] Hage G Geingob St; ☏ 064 220157; ⊕ 07.00–17.00 Mon–Fri, 07.00–14.00 Sat. Tucked off the road in a small arcade, this friendly & relaxed venue feels a world away from town. Enjoy b/fast, lunch specials, good grills & their popular salads at pine tables inside, or out by the carp pond – & try the genuine Italian ice cream for dessert. $$–$$$

☕ **Bush Garden Bistro** [351 E3] Sam Nujoma Av; ☏ 064 203753, 085 693 3692; ⊕ 08.00–17.00 Mon–Fri, 08.00–14.00 Sat. Do pop into this aptly named café, shielded from the road by shrubs & flowers. New in 2018, its menu includes yoghurt jars, tramezzini & pittas, as well as the usual coffee & cake, salads & soups, etc. $–$$$

Bars

🍷 **Champs Pub** [350 D3] Cnr Peter Dixon & Cyril Fernandez sts; ☏ 064 209884; ⊕ Mon–Sat. DJ on

Wed, Fri & Sat. A sports bar with a dance floor & a strong local following, Champs is popular both early evening & post-dinner.

♀ **Sarah Se Gat** [350 B3] Waterfront; m 081 122 0181; ⏲ 10.00–02.00 Mon–Sat, 10.00–18.00 Sun. The best bar in town for sundowners, Sarah's has great views of the lagoon – especially from the roof terrace. Inside, it's dark, cosy &

totally relaxed, with good beer & cocktail specials from their Cheers-style square bar. There's karaoke on Sat nights, & most Sun evenings live bands play a mixture of rock, 80s & 60s music. If you get peckish, you can order in food from La Bella Vita or Dock Side (see opposite); just keep buying their beers!

NIGHTLIFE AND ENTERTAINMENT Walvis Bay is quieter than Swakopmund. Try the bars listed above or ask local advice as to what's good, and take care if you're thinking of a club in one of the townships. Along Sam Nujoma Avenue, numerous seedy gambling houses feature banks of slot machines and little else.

SHOPPING With your own car, you are close enough to drive easily to Swakopmund, where the choice of shops of visitor interest is usually greater. However, with the opening in 2017 of Dunes Mall [351 H2] on the edge of town, Walvis Bay now has a pretty good range of outlets in its own right.

Clothes and equipment
For safari & hiking gear, try Old Khaki & Cape Union Mart at Dunes Mall [351 H2].

Cymot [351 G1] Cnr Sam Nujoma Av & Ana Mupentami Rd; ☎ 064 202241; www.cymot.com. na; ⏲ 08.00–17.00 Mon–Fri, 08.00–noon Sat. For camping equipment, car spares & cycling gear.
Anglers Kiosk [351 E2] Cnr 8th & 13th sts; ☎ 064 206373. Behind Puma fuel station. Fishing equipment galore.
Photo Volker [351 E2] 141 Sam Nujoma Av; ☎ 064 203015; www.photovolker.com; ⏲ 08.00–13.00 & 14.00–17.00 Mon–Fri, 08.00–12.30 Sat; Waterfront [350 B3] ⏲ 09.00–15.00 daily. Has some camera equipment & can print digital images as well as processing film. The gallery next to their town-centre shop sells large photo prints, most taken in Namibia.

Food and provisions
Opening hours for supermarkets in Walvis Bay are typically around 08.00–21.00 Mon–Sat, with slightly shorter hours on Sun.

Dunes Mall [351 H2] Checkers, Pick n Pay
Sam Nujoma Av [350 D3] Shoprite, OK Grocer, Spar

Souvenirs and gifts
Most shops catering for the tourist market are at the Waterfront, but there are also a few on the main Sam Nujoma Av.

AfriGold Hage G Geingob St; m 081 278 3144; e sharleenfranken@gmail.com. For stylish, personally designed leather belts & jewellery – from beads to silver & gold – seek out this owner-run shop almost hidden opposite Vlooi's Nest café (see opposite).
Jetty Shoppe [350 B3] Waterfront; m 081 147 3633; ⏲ 07.30–17.00 daily. Sells souvenirs, gifts, rugs, T-shirts & more.
Namcraft [350 B3] Waterfront; ☎ 064 221390; ⏲ 08.00–19.00 Mon–Fri, 08.00–17.00 Sat–Sun. Store of the famous chain selling lovely jewellery & other shiny knick-knacks, along with bags & scarves.
Spindrift Art Gallery [350 C6] 22 Main Rd; ⏲ 07.00–17.00 Mon–Fri, or by arrangement. Pick up something for the walls back home at the guesthouse of the same name (page 356).

OTHER PRACTICALITIES Most of the **banks** have premises with ATMs along the main Sam Nujoma Avenue, with several more at Dunes Mall [351 H2]. The **post office** [351 F2] is on the corner of Sam Nujoma Avenue and 14th Road.

Car repairs and spares There's a branch of the parts specialist, Motovac, at 173 Sam Nujoma Avenue [351 F2] (↘ 064 202314). Several outlets can help if you're unlucky enough to have a flat tyre. Most are open ⊕ 7.30–17.00 Monday–Friday, and 08.00–noon Saturday, but Pieter Els at BestDrive in particular will respond to a call out at any time.

BestDrive/Maxiprest 91 Circumferential St; ↘ 064 204234, 204220/4; m 081 129 4531; ⊕ 07.30–17.00 Mon–Fri, 08.00–noon Sat. A real find!

Trentyre [351 E2] Peter Dixon St; ↘ 064 209511; ⊕ 07.30–17.00 Mon–Fri, 08.00–noon Sat

Health and safety Although there's a state hospital in Walvis Bay [351 E4] (↘ 064 216300), visitors in need of treatment would be better advised to contact the private Welwitschia Hospital [351 F3] (↘ 064 218911), which brought Namibia to worldwide attention following the birth of Angelina Jolie and Brad Pitt's baby, Shiloh, in 2006. Should you need a pharmacy, try the ABC Chemist at the Welwitschia Hospital (↘ 064 202271), or the central Walvis Bay Pharmacy [350 D3] (*Sam Nujoma Av;* ↘ 064 202117), opposite Crazy Mamas.

In an **emergency**, the police are reached on ↘ 10111, the fire service on m 081 122 0833/0888 or m 081 922 from a mobile phone, and the ambulance on m 081 924 from a mobile. For sea rescue services, call Namport control (↘ 064 208 2263–5), or contact the police – which is also the emergency number to use if you can't get through anywhere else.

SPORTS FACILITIES Walvis Bay Golf Club [350 C6] has a nine-hole course off Fairview Avenue, just before the lagoon. For details of fees for visitors, contact them on ↘ 064 200526.

WHAT TO SEE AND DO Most of the town's activities centre around the lagoon. There are some superb birdwatching opportunities both here and in the surrounding area (see box, page 362), and highly recommended kayak trips on the lagoon from Pelican Point (page 362).

Boat trips from the Waterfront take visitors out to see dolphins in the lagoon and beyond (see opposite). Alternatively, if you have a 4x4 you can drive out towards Pelican Point around the lagoon, past the salt-works: a desolate track lined with salt ponds that have been reclaimed from the sea, inhabited only by seabirds and the occasional brown hyena. Note, though, that to drive yourself beyond the end of the obvious track is – quite simply – dangerous, not least because quicksand is an ever-present risk. If you want to go further, treat yourself to a trip to Sandwich Harbour (page 368) with one of the experienced operators.

Off the water, options are more limited, although you could pop into the small **museum** [351 E3] (↘ 064 201 3273; ⊕ 09.00–16.30 Mon–Fri) next to the Civic Centre, which has a collection that includes photographs, maps and natural history exhibits.

Walvis Bay Lagoon The lagoon dates back some 5,000 years, making it the oldest lagoon on the Namibian coast. A safe haven for over 150,000 birds, including avocets and black-winged stilts, it also acts as a feeding station for a further 200,000 shorebirds and terns on their biannual migration to and from the Arctic; in all, more than 50 species of bird have been identified here. Up to 90% of all South African flamingos spend the winter here, while 70% of the world's chestnut-banded plovers depend on the lagoon for their survival.

WALVIS BAY LAGOON: A BLEAK FUTURE

Pressure on the lagoon in recent years has built up from a number of areas: construction of housing to the southeast, salt-pans to the south and west, and a road dyke to the east and south. All these factors have served to reduce flooding, which would naturally keep up the water levels. Added to this is the knock-on effect of the diversion of the Kuiseb River in 1967, since when the dunes have effectively 'marched round' and headed straight for Walvis Bay. The sand blown from the desert contributes significantly to the silting up of the lagoon.

The salt-works that surround the edge of the lagoon in Walvis Bay are South African-owned on a very long lease; salt is exported raw from Namibia, then processed in South Africa for industrial use (as against that from Swakopmund, which is for human consumption). The salt-pans in Walvis Bay are entirely manmade, with the company now owning as far as Pelican Point and expansion ongoing; it is estimated that they cover some 80% of the area that was once lagoon. As salt extraction increases, it is forecast that the entrance to the lagoon will eventually close up and the lagoon itself will dry up. Initiatives to re-establish the natural flow of water include the construction of culverts under the road leading to the salt-works, but there are no guarantees; on the basis of current information, the lagoon could one day disappear completely. And this in spite of the fact that it has been protected as a wetland of international importance under the Ramsar Convention since 1995.

Visit during the summer, and you could be forgiven for wondering what the fuss is about, not least as this is when the flamingos leave for their breeding spots at Etosha Pan and beyond. But come between the end of September and April, at low tide, and the scene is transformed. Then, flocks of greater and lesser flamingos (see box, page 64) are busily searching in the muddy shallows for algae and other food. Here they may be joined by the occasional pelican, while a little further out you may be lucky enough to see bottlenose dolphins leaping above the water. To enjoy the spectacle, simply take a stroll along the path that runs from the Waterfront almost to the end of the tar road. It can be magical.

Boat trips (*from N$750 pp*) A few companies run excellent boat trips from the Waterfront or Tanker Jetty to Pelican Point and Bird Island. Trips, often in motorised catamarans but occasionally under sail, usually start at around 08.30 and last about 3–4 hours. Collection and return to Swakopmund may be included in the rates. Most operators offer drinks on board, and some, such as Mola Mola, serve sparkling wine and oysters. Several also offer a half-day 4x4 excursion to Sandwich Harbour, or a combination of the two (*from N$2,000 pp*) – though Sandwich Harbour (page 368) is far better as a full-day excursion in its own right. For details of boat operators, see page 363.

Dolphins – both the bottlenose and the endemic Benguela (heavysides) – are present all year round, as are Cape fur seals, which may often cavort around the boats. In October and November, whales frequent these waters, with possible sightings of humpback, southern right, Minke and even killer whales, while from then until April there is the chance of seeing the leatherback turtle. You may even be lucky enough to spot the giant sunfish, or mola. Note, though, that these are popular excursions, so don't be surprised to see several other boats on the water.

There is some excellent birdlife in the vicinity; just take a walk on the southwest side of Walvis Bay, around the lagoon (page 360). The flock of feeding flamingos and pelicans that I often find there usually allows me to get much closer than others that I come across in the area. Birdwatchers might also want to stop at one of the guano platforms in the sea between Walvis and Swakopmund.

SWAKOP RIVER DELTA Here small tidal lagoons surrounded by reeds are very good for birding. Expect whimbrels, curlews, the odd flamingo and pelican, white-breasted cormorants, Cape cormorants, black-winged stilts, avocets and more.

The remains of the old railway bridge lie here, washed down in 1934 when the Swakop River performed its flood-of-the-century stunt. On the pillars there are often crowned and bank cormorants, while along the river-bed, between the tamarisk trees, kestrels swoop around catching mice.

The local Wildlife Society has laid out a pleasant 4km trail starting next to the cemetery. This takes you downstream into the river mouth, and back to the beach. Walkers should beware of quadbikes that move pretty fast through this area.

KUISEB DELTA This area is criss-crossed by a labyrinth of tracks in which even experienced guides can get lost. Unmarked archaeological sites dot the area, where pottery shards, beads, shell middens and stone tools can be seen. Wildlife includes springbok, ostrich, jackal and brown hyena, and birds such as the endemic dune lark.

Look out for the nara bushes (*Acanthosicyos horridus*) – their spiky green (and hence photosynthesising) stems have allowed them to dispense with leaves completely. This is an advantage given the propensity of leaves to lose water. Naras are perhaps not truly desert plants, as their roots go down many metres to reach underground water, which they need in order to survive. From February to April and August to September the local Topnaar people harvest nara melons here.

The area is accessible only by 4x4 and you'll only appreciate it with a good guide. To approach on your own, take the Esplanade by the lagoon southwest from Walvis Bay, and after about 4km ignore the sign to Paaltjies (where the road divides) and keep left. The track splits and you take the left fork marked Rooibank via Wortels.

SANDWICH HARBOUR This small area about 45km south of Walvis Bay has a large saltwater lagoon, extensive tidal mudflats and a band of reed-lined pools fed by freshwater springs, together forming one of the most important birdlife refuges in southern Africa. Typically you'll find about 30 species of birds at Sandwich. It offers food and shelter to thousands of migrants every year and some of Namibia's most

Kayak trips (*N$650 for a 5hr trip*) The brainchild of Jeanne Meintjes, who runs Eco Marine Kayak Tours, this guided excursion starts with a Land Rover trip from Walvis Bay to Pelican Point, which is very much part of the fun. From here, you'll set off in single or double kayaks among the seal colonies, and perhaps out to the point where there is also the possibility of seeing dolphins. No experience is necessary. Trips are run in the mornings only, when winds are light and the sea is generally calm. Warm jackets or spray-resistant waterproofs and dry bags for cameras are provided, and a light snack is served afterwards with coffee. The tour can be combined with an afternoon trip to Sandwich Harbour with Sandwich Harbour 4x4.

Operators: Eco Marine Kayak Tours, Pelican Point Kayaking; see opposite.

spectacular scenery – for those lucky enough to see it. Where else can you walk along a pelican-covered beach while pink flamingos glide above the sand dunes?

Guided trips Several operators offer half-day trips to the harbour, but it deserves a full day, so pick your operator accordingly. This is not a place for inexperienced drivers, and several vehicles have been lost to the sea in recent years. However, the track to the harbour between the dunes and the sea is increasingly narrow, and there are sometimes access problems due to fog or flooding, which can lead even the experts to cancel or curtail a trip.

The most experienced operator doing regular trips here is Turnstone Tours (page 371). These are best booked far in advance, and are highly recommended. For other operators, see page 369. Technically it is still permissible to drive yourself to Sandwich Harbour, but it's exceptionally dangerous to go without a local expert, and is likely to be forbidden in future.

Once you've organised your trip, do take windproof clothes and something to drink, as well as binoculars, camera and lots of memory card space/film; you're bound to need them!

What to see and do Once you reach the bay, you continue on foot. The northern part consists of a number of almost enclosed reed-lined pools at the top of the beach, which back directly on to huge dunes. These are fed partly by the sea via narrow channels which fill at high tide, and partly with fresh water which seeps from a subterranean watercourse under the dunes and enables reeds (albeit salt-tolerant ones) to grow. These in turn provide food and nesting sites for a number of resident waterbirds. On my last visit I managed to spot dabchicks, moorhens, shelducks, common and marsh sandpipers, several species of tern (Caspian, swift, white-winged and whiskered all visit) and even avocets and African spoonbills – as well as pelicans and flamingos.

As you continue along the beach, the 'harbour' itself comes into view. During the early 18th century it was used by whalers for its deep, sheltered anchorage and ready supply of fresh water. Subsequently a small station was established here to trade in seal pelts, fish and guano. Then, in the early part of the 20th century, it was used as a source of guano but, after the mouth of the harbour silted up, this ground to a halt in 1947, leaving only a few bits of rusting machinery to be seen today.

It's worth climbing up one of the dunes, as from there you can see the deep lagoon, protected from the ocean's pounding by a sandspit, and the extensive mudflats to the south, which are often covered by the tide.

Fishing trips See page 367.

Boat-trip and kayak operators

⚠ **Catamaran Charters** Waterfront [350 B3]; 📞 064 200798; m 081 129 5393; e seawolf@iway. na; www.namibiancharters.com. Sail aboard one of 3 15m motorised catamarans (new boats due in 2019) with plenty of snacks & sparkling wine. When conditions are suitable the sails are hoisted for a more exhilarating ride. Private charters are available, as are seafood beach braais & Sandwich Harbour combo trips.

⚓ **Eco Marine Kayak Tours** 📞 064 203144; m 081 129 3144; e emkayak@iway.na; www. emkayak.iway.na; see ad, page 371. Specialist operator run by Jeanne Meintjes, who established the original kayak tours on the lagoon.

⚠ Laramon Tours m 081 124 0635, 081 128 0635; e bookings@laramontours.com; www. laramontours.com. With 3 motorised catamarans, they offer ½-day dolphin & sightseeing cruises (*N$750 pp*).

⚓ Levo Tours ☎064 207555; m 081 291 6270; e bookings@levotours.com; www.levotours. com. This established company offers seal & dolphin cruises in one of 5 ski-boats, departing from the Tanker Jetty at 08.30. You can also combine a cruise with a visit to Sandwich Harbour, returning at 17.30.

⚓ Mola Mola Waterfront [350 B3] ; ☎064 205511; m 081 127 2522; e info@mola-namibia. com; www.mola-namibia.com; see ad, page 371. The well-respected Mola Mola organises 3½hr bird- & dolphin-watching cruises from their 3 boats, which take up to 18, 24 & 26 passengers

respectively. They also have 4x4 trips into the dunes, & a combo that includes both options.

⚠ Ocean Adventures ☎064 402377; m 081 240 6290, 081 627 1440; e info@ swakopadventures.com; www.swakopadventures. com. 2 catamarans.

⚓ Pelican Point Kayaking Waterfront [350 B3]; m 081 149 7377; e naude@pelican-point-kayaking.com; www.pelican-point-kayaking.com. Specialists in kayaking trips on Walvis Bay Lagoon, with a combo to Sandwich Harbour also possible.

⚠ Sun Sail Catamarans Waterfront [350 B3]; m 081 788 6800, 081 978 6786; e bookings@ sunsailnamibia.com; www.sunsailnamibia. com. 3–4hr cruises aboard one of 3 catamarans, sometimes under sail, come with oysters & sparkling wine. Sandwich Harbour trips also available.

AROUND THE TOWNS

Because the towns of Swakopmund and Walvis Bay are just 30km apart (about 25 minutes' drive, on a good tar road), this section covers attractions and activities in the areas outside both of the towns.

ACTIVITIES AROUND THE TOWNS There are numerous activities in the desert and coastal areas around Swakopmund and Walvis Bay, from sandboarding to nature tours. Because there's a lot of crossover between tour operators and the tours they run, we've listed the individual activities and the relevant operators first, followed by contact details for all the tour operators on page 369.

Desert-based tours New activities in the dunes are constantly being dreamed up to add to the existing range. Some, such as quadbiking, skydiving and sandboarding, may be combined in one trip. Current options include:

Sandboarding (*About N$500 pp lying down, N$600 for stand-up boarding*) Typically, trips leave from Swakopmund in the morning around 09.30, collecting you from your accommodation and returning around 13.30. The idea is to push off the top of a dune and lie on the board as it slides down. Speeds easily reach 70km/h or more, though at first you'll do a few training rides on lower dunes, where you won't go much faster than 40km/h. Finally, they take you to a couple of the larger dunes, for longer, faster runs, before lunch in the desert, and the return drive to Swakopmund. As a spin-off from sandboarding, offered by all operators, stand-up boarding, also known as dune-boarding, uses a modified snowboard. Participants stand on a small surfboard which shoots down the side of dunes – rather like skiing, only on sand. It may have more finesse, and certainly requires more skill.
    Operators: Alter-Action, DareDevil, Dune 7, Ultimate Sandboarding; page 369.

Quadbiking (*Around N$550 pp for 2hrs; longer & shorter trips available, departing through the day*) Ride four-wheel motorcycles through the dunes, although note that quadbikes are not allowed into the Namib-Naukluft National Park. Manual, semi-automatic and automatic bikes are available, with helmets, goggles and gloves provided. If you're setting off on your own, please consider the harmful effect on the environment (see box, page 366).

Historical quadbike tour (*N$1,050 pp*) Drive through the dunes and Kuiseb Delta (see box, page 362), to see fauna, flora, fossils and petrified elephant footprints. Starts at 08.30 from Lagoon Chalets in Walvis Bay and returns at 12.30; cold drinks included.
Operators: Kuiseb Delta Adventures, Photo Ventures; page 370.

Quadbike tours through the dunes (*N$450–600 pp*) Guided 1-hour tour from N$450, 90-minute tour from N$550, 2-hour tour from N$650, 90-minute sundowner tours N$600 (all prices per person). Participants should be over 16; younger children may accompany parents on their quad, but there might be an additional charge.
Operators: DareDevil, Desert Explorers, Dune 7, Element Riders; page 369.

Desert ecosystem tours While many local companies offer half-day or even full-day tours covering a relatively well-beaten trail that includes the Welwitschia Drive (see box, page 367), a really attractive alternative is to discover less well-known areas of the desert in the company of a specialist, such as Turnstone Tours. One such trip might take you inland near the old railway, then over rolling dune fields towards the moonscape, from where you can see Rössing Mountain in the distance. Down below, mining claims have been staked out here and there on the gravel plains. While most of the material mined is granite, many other minerals are to be found, including small quantities of yellowish-green uranium oxide, or purpurite; this is the raw material that is processed into yellowcake, and eventually refined into plutonium and other substances. Look out, too, for the cellophane-like hornblend, or the pinky-orange of titanium.

There's a lot more to this apparently barren plain than minerals, however. Individual welwitschia plants and quivertrees form an integral part of the landscape, as do the tiny stone plants (*Lithops karasmontana*) that may be found hidden beneath a quartz outcrop. Lichens cling to the rocks, small holes tell of hairy-footed gerbils, and day geckos scurry past. Across the plain is the linear oasis of Goanikontes on the Khan River. Built by the Germans, Goanikontes was once used as a staging post for horse-carts from Swakopmund, since food for horses and cattle could be grown. Here and along the huge plain of the Swakop River numerous plants can be identified clinging to life, and klipspringers eke out a precarious existence along the rocks.

Dune 7 Past the Bird Sanctuary in Walvis Bay, just off the C14 on the way to the airport and Sesriem, this is one of the highest dunes in the area and has a small picnic site near its base, among a few shady palms. It's a popular spot for both energetic dune-climbers and sundowners.
No operator required; self visit

Little Five Desert Tour (*N$700 pp*) Highly recommended, this guided 4x4 drive into the dunes explores the incredible landscape and its living creatures. Starts at 08.00 from Swakopmund; returns by 13.30. Pickup from your accommodation; cold drinks included.
Operators: Batis Birding, Living Desert Adventures, Tommy's Living Desert Tours; page 369.

Welwitschia Tours (*From N$700/1,400 pp ½/full day*) Offered on a half-day, ¾-day or full-day basis with some departing at 09.00, others at 14.00. Rates vary, and usually include pickup within Swakopmund and drinks. (See also box, opposite.)

Operators: Batis Birding, Charly's Desert Tours, Kallisto Tours, Loubster's Tours, Swakop Tour Company; page 369.

Air-based tours

Scenic flights (*Conception Bay from N$2,980; Sossusvlei from N$4,200, based on 5 participants per plane*) Of the flights offered from Swakopmund, the most popular are the 2¼-hour Sossusvlei flight and the 1½-hour Conception Bay flight. You'll fly south via the Kuiseb and the dune landscape, returning over the coastline where you can see shipwrecks and Sandwich Harbour (see box, page 362). For photographers, Bateleur Helicopters offers specialist flights with removable doors on their helicopters, allowing clear views for photos.

Operators: Bateleur Helicopters, Pleasure Flights & Safaris, Scenic Air, Sossusfly, Wings over Africa; page 369.

PROTECTION OF THE DESERT

Many companies around Swakopmund have taken advantage of the unique environment to introduce adventure sports. Quadbiking, sandboarding, sand-skiing and other activities are growing in popularity, but they could have serious consequences for the sand dunes and other desert areas on which they depend.

While most operators take this issue seriously, confining their sports to a specific area and spelling out to participants the harm that can be caused by thoughtless manoeuvres, individuals may not be so careful. Even then, sandboarding and sand-skiing have a weight-to-surface relationship that is unlikely to cause significant damage. Sadly, though, serious harm is being caused by individuals on privately owned bikes setting off across the dunes and gravel plains without any understanding of the nature of the area.

Broadly, the low-impact part of the dunes is the area on the top, with the greatest potential for danger to the habitat being on the lee side. Most of the life in the dunes is found in the top 10cm, so a thoughtless biker can cause untold damage in just a few seconds. Beyond the dunes, slow-growing lichens form an integral part of the region's ecology, but they are very fragile. Trample them underfoot or ride over them and they are unlikely to survive, depriving many forms of wildlife of food and shelter. The gravel plains of the Namib Desert are the nesting area of the endemic Damara tern, one of the rarest terns in the world, yet – with a quick twist of the handlebars – a nest can be crushed in seconds.

In 2010 the Dorob National Park was created, filling in the unprotected gaps between the northern Skeleton Coast and southern Namib-Naukluft parks. The basic objective behind this was to implement conservation measures, and many tourist activities are now banned within the borders of the park without a permit from the Ministry of Environment and Tourism. This means that visitors to the area must visit with a guide who knows the ecological and conservation concerns in the area, significantly increasing protection for this sensitive area of desert.

N$40 pp, plus N$10 per vehicle; permits must be bought in advance from the MET in Swakopmund; page 329.

In the northern corner of the Namib-Naukluft National Park, an afternoon's excursion from Swakopmund or Walvis Bay, the Welwitschia Drive (see page 322 for a full description) is a route through the desert with numbered beacons at points of interest, culminating in one of the country's oldest welwitschia plants. Part of the drive is the 'moon landscape', or 'moonscape' – a rolling, barren area of rocky desert formed by the valleys around the course of the Swakop River. It's a spectacular sight, often spoken of, and best viewed by the slanting light of mid morning or late afternoon. However, be warned that the discovery of uranium close to the route means that the MET are in the process of changing it, so check with them when you buy your permit, and before attempting the drive.

Skydiving (*Tandem from N$2,500 pp, static from N$1,400 pp*) With clear air and a starkly beautiful coastline, Swakopmund is a natural space to learn to fly or even skydive. Jumps can normally only be booked at short notice because they're weather-dependent. After a basic safety chat and a scenic flight over Swakopmund and the surrounding area, you are strapped to an experienced instructor to throw yourselves out of a plane at 10,000ft. Your free fall lasts for about half a minute before, hopefully, your parachute opens and there's a further 5-minute 'canopy ride' before landing. There is no age limit, but participants must be large enough to fit the equipment. A tandem jump takes about 3 hours, with static line jumps also available.
Operators: Ground Rush Adventures, Swakopmund Sky Diving Club; page 369.

Water-based tours

Fishing Long popular all along this coastline with South African visitors, fishing is good all year round, although the best times are October to April. The turn of the year is particularly busy, with anglers arriving in search of big-game fish such as copper sharks and other similar species, which can weigh as much as 180kg. Other species that may be caught include kabeljou, steenbras, barber, galjoen and garrick.

The area is good for crayfish, too, although the catch is limited to a maximum of seven per person, or 14 per vehicle. Permits are required for all types of fishing.

Fishing trips (*From N$1,500 pp*) Trips aboard a boat or on shore are offered from Swakopmund daily, on a full-day basis only, departing at 08.00 and returning by 16.00. Rates include tackle and bait, equipment, fishing licence, lunch and drinks.
Operators: Aquanaut Tours, Ocean Adventures Angling Tours; page 369.

Inter-tidal drive at Walvis Bay (*N$625/450 adult/child*) A 2½-hour trip at low tide with expert guide to discover molluscs, anemones, seaweeds, crustaceans interacting with birdlife, and remnants of shipwrecks.
Operator: Aquanaut Tours; page 369.

Kayaking on Walvis Bay Lagoon (*N$700 pp*) Start at 07.30 from the lagoon with a 4x4 ride towards Pelican Point. Kayak close alongside seal colonies near the point, then return to Walvis Bay by midday. Light breakfast, coffee and all equipment included. See also page 362.

Operators: Eco Marine Kayak Tours, Pelican Point Kayaking; page 363; Sandwich Harbour 4x4; page 370.

Dolphin and seal cruise on Walvis Bay Lagoon (*From N$750 pp, inc transfers to/from Swakopmund*) Boats leave Walvis Bay around 09.00, returning around midday, and cruise through the harbour, visiting guano islands and Pelican Point (home to more than 60,000 seals), with the chance of seeing dolphins. See also page 361.

Operators: Catamaran Charters, Laramon Tours, Levo Tours, Mola Mola, Ocean Adventures, Sun Sail Catamarans; page 363.

Sandwich Harbour Tour (*From N$1,700 pp*) Departs Swakopmund by 4x4 at 08.30 via the salt-pans and lower Kuiseb Delta to the lagoon at Sandwich Harbour, returning at 17.00 and including a delicious lunch. Encounter fauna, flora, quicksand and hummock dunes. Includes a delicious lunch. See also page 362.

This tour is also available as a combo, incorporating a half-day boat cruise and half-day Sandwich Harbour tour (*from N$2,000*).

Operators: Photo Ventures, Sandwich Harbour 4x4, Turnstone Tours; page 370.

Cape Cross Tours (*N$1,300 pp, inc drinks*) Includes a tour of the salt-pans, lichen fields and Henties Bay. Departs Swakopmund at 09.00; return by 14.00.

Operators: Charly's Desert Tours, Kallisto Tours; page 369.

Riding

Horseriding (*From N$550 pp/hr, min 2 participants; inc transfers to/from Swakopmund; singles pay more*) Ride through the Swakop Valley, with rides planned to suit the experience of the participants. Weight limit 80kg for inexperienced riders; 90kg for experienced riders. A 1½-hour late-afternoon ride costs N$650 per person, minimum two participants.

Operator: Okakambe Trails; page 370.

Camel riding (*N$200/100 adult/child*) The Camel Farm (*east of Swakopmund, down the D1901;* ✆ *064 400363;* e *erbelke@mweb.com.na*) offers a 20-minute ride between 14.00 and 17.00 Monday to Saturday.

EXCURSIONS BEYOND THE TOWNS

Rössing Mine (⊕ *1st Fri of month; tickets via Swakopmund Museum, page 345; N$40/30 adult/student or child*) Rössing is remarkable, particularly if you're interested in engineering, mining or geology. It's a vast opencast uranium mine. For children (especially the sort that never grow up) there are the biggest lorries in the world.

The opencast mine is awesome, so deep that the same vehicles working at the bottom of the pit look like Dinky toys. You certainly get an alternative view of the desert, and the viewpoints Rössing has set up (with information plaques) provide interesting photo opportunities. There's a video charting the mines and the uranium production process, with the requisite emphasis on safety, and a tour of the whole site.

Visiting Rössing is probably the sort of thing that I would have done when I was a child, on holiday with my family, to fill in a rainy day. Then I'd look back on it, and be glad that I'd done it. It certainly appeals to those already interested, but many will feel they see enough of this kind of industrial development at home. Trips leave from outside Café Anton on Bismarck Street in Swakopmund on the first and third Fridays of each month. Reservations should be made at Swakopmund Museum.

Minerals Tours (*N$1,100/1,700 pp 4/7hrs, min 2 participants*) Tours are offered either just to Rössing Mountain (*4hrs*), or including the canyons (*7hrs*). Pickup in Swakopmund. Prices include drinks, but bring your own snacks and/or lunch.
    Operators: Charly's Desert Tours, Kallisto Tours; see below.

Dorob National Park
(*Permit required from MET office; page 329*) Namibia's newest national park stretches from the Swakop River to the Ugab River bordering the Skeleton Coast Park. It was created in 2010 to protect the fragile desert ecosystem – which acts as a breeding ground for Damara terns and other seabirds – from quadbikers that have been tearing across the landscape. Within its perimeter is a 'dead sea' salt-pan litter with old mining equipment and tracks, and the Messum Crater, the result of a volcano implosion slowly filled in with sand – the crater impression can be seen in the sand. Permits are required to enter the area with your own car; they can be collected from the MET office, are free, and are valid for three months.

Spitzkoppe Day Tour
(*N$1,700 pp, min 3 people*) Guided tour to the Namibian 'Matterhorn' with explanations of fauna/flora, Bushman paintings and geology. Pickup in Swakopmund at 09.00; return at 18.00. Tours, which include cold drinks, can also be run for two people, but at a higher rate.
    Operator: Charly's Desert Tours, Kallisto Tours; see below.

TOUR OPERATORS For boat-cruise and kayak operators based in Walvis Bay, see page 363.

Alter-Action Sandboarding \064 402737; m 081 128 2737; www.alter-action.info/web. The original sandboarding company.

Aquanaut Tours \064 405969; e info@ aquanauttours.com; www.aquanauttours.com. Fishing trips & beach drives.

Bateleur Helicopters m 081 150 3234, 081 301 9631; e swakop@bateleurhelicopters.com; www. bateleurhelicopters.com. Set routes to Sossusvlei, Dead Vlei & along the Namib coastline, as well as custom routes.

Batis Birding \064 404908; m 081 639 1775; www.batisbirdingsafaris.com

Charly's Desert Tours \064 404341; e info@ charlysdeserttours.com; www.charlysdeserttours. com. One of Swakopmund's longest-running operators, established in 1966. ½-day trips include sightseeing tours of Swakopmund & Walvis Bay, plus trips into the desert & to Cape Cross; full days go further into the desert, to Spitzkoppe or down to the Kuiseb Delta.

DareDevil Adventures \064 220158; m 081 755 3589; e daredev@iway.na; www. daredeviladventures.com. Based opposite Long Beach. Offer quadbiking, sandboarding & combos of the 2.

Desert Explorers Adventure Centre [327 B5] Nathaniel Maxuilili St, Swakopmund; m 081 124 1386; e info@namibiadesertexplorers.com. The booking office for Desert Explorers' quadbike trips also acts as agent for many of Swakopmund's adventure operators, with activities like duneboarding, skydiving & kayaking.

Dune 7 Adventures m 081 626 1714, 081 624 9665; e info@dune7adventures.com; www. dune7adventures.com

Element Riders m 081 666 6599; e info@ element-riders.com; www.element-riders.com

Ground Rush Adventures \064 402841; m 081 124 5167; e info@skydiveswakop.com.na; www.skydiveswakop.com.na

Hafeni Cultural Tours \064 400731; m 081 146 6222; e hafenictours@gmail.com, info@ hafenitourism.com; hafenitourism.com. Tours of Mondesa township, township dinners, walking tours, & visits to Damara, Namas & Oshiwambo people. A portion of the proceeds go to supporting Hope Orphanage & Hanganeni Primary School.

Hata Angu Cultural Tours m 081 124 6111; e info@culturalactivities-namibia.com; www. culturalactivities-namibia.com. As well as 4hr tours of the township (*depart 10.00 & 15.00*) they can

Namibia may boast some of the best examples of on-land shipwrecks, but most remain a well-kept secret. Of those in the Skeleton Coast Park there is very little left other than a few bits of wood and scrap metal.

But it was the *Eduard Bohlen*, a 100m hulk apparently rotting in the desert south of Walvis Bay, that was the inspiration for my quest. For a skilled 4x4 driver it's relatively accessible, passing the wreck of the *Shawnee* (a small tug) on the way, but you do need a guide and a decent vehicle. The tide must be out, too, and beware the salt-pans around Sandwich Harbour.

The *Eduard Bohlen* ran aground in 1909 and now lies about 300m from the beach. The first sight of this rusting behemoth plays tricks with your head. How could such a massive ship get so far inland? In truth, it hasn't moved; it still lies at sea level but is now partially buried by the shifting sands.

Harder to access is the *Otavi*, deep in the desert north of Lüderitz, and the true belt-holder of the best land-shipwreck title. We were driven by Lewis Druker at Coastway Tours, accompanied by a mining company official in another vehicle.

A full day's drive across some quite terrifyingly large dunes leads to a camp. The next day, an hour's easy desert driving and some light scrambling brings you to the top of a cliff, and a scene that looks like a film set from the *Pirates of the Caribbean*. The *Otavi* ran aground in 1945 in a crescent bay. Protected first by miles and miles of the Namib Desert, then by high cliffs, its final guardians are 8,000 Cape fur seals frolicking with their young in the wreck itself. Of all the places I've been in the world for just 30 minutes, it remains my favourite!

A longer version of this article by Nick Molley is available on the Bradt website: www.bradtguides.com/namibiashipwrecks.

organise lessons in the Damara click language, & visits to a local herbalist or HIV centre & orphanage.

Kallisto Tours & Services ☎ 064 402473; e info@kallisto.com; www.kallisto.com. A full range of town tours, excursions & longer trips, as well as transfers.

Kuiseb Delta Adventures m 081 128 2580; e fanie@kuisebonline.com; www.kuisebonline. com. Historical & educational desert tours.

Living Desert Adventures ☎ 064 405070; m 081 127 5070; e nature@iafrica.com.na; www. livingdesertnamibia.com. A highly respected company offering superb 4–5hr & full-day trips (*N$700 pp ½ day, min 2*) into the desert, departing at 08.00, that both locals & travellers rave about. Tailor-made options are also available.

Namibia Tracks & Trails ☎ 064 416820; m 081 269 7271; e travel@namibia-tracks-and-trails. com; www.namibia-tracks-and-trails.com. An efficient one-stop shop that acts as agent for many of Swakopmund's adventure operators.

Ocean Adventures Angling Tours ☎ 064 463123; m 081 124 0208; e info@

fishingtoursnamibia.com; www. fishingtoursnamibia.com

Okakambe Trails ☎ 064 402799; e okakambe@ gmail.com; www.okakambe.iway.na. Short rides & multi-day tours of the desert on horseback.

Panorama Cycle Tours Contact tourist information centre Namib i (page 330).

Photo Ventures m 081 426 1200, 081 128 6713; www.photoventuresnamibia.com. Seal & dolphin tours, Sandwich Harbour & kayaking, as well as special photographic tours around Namibia.

Pleasure Flights & Safaris ☎ 064 404500; m 081 129 4545; e redbaron@iafrica.com.na; www.pleasureflights.com.na

Sandwich Harbour 4x4 Atlantic St, Waterfront, Walvis Bay; ☎ 064 200958; m 081 147 3933; e info@ sandwich-harbour.com; www.sandwich-harbour.com

Scenic Air ☎ 064 403575; m 081 127 0534; www.scenic-air.com

Sossusfly ☎ 064 404071; m 081 250 7171; www.sossusfly.com

Swakop Tour Company Daniel Tjongarero St; m 081 124 2906; e proverb@afol.com.na;

www.swakoptour.com. This well-recommended company, run by Georg Erb, offers set tours for small groups that are of particular appeal for geologists & botanists. These include the 5hr Klipspringer Canyon Tour into the desert (*N$1,200 pp*) & a shorter Dunes of the Namib Tour, around sunset (*N$900*). Also customised itineraries.

Swakopmund Cycle Tours m 081 251 5916, 085 222 1667; www.swakopmundcycletours. com. 3½hr cycling tours around the township (*N$450 pp*), with departures at 09.00 & 14.00, & 2½hr walking tours of the town (*N$350 pp*), with departures at 09.30 & 14.30. They also rent bikes & will deliver them to town-centre hotels at no extra cost (*N$195/265 pp ½/full day*).

Swakopmund Sky Diving Club 064 405671; m 081 343 1843; e info@skydiveswakopmund. com; www.skydiveswakopmund.com

Tommy's Living Desert Tours m 081 128 1038; e tommys@iway.na; www.tommys. iway.na. Tommy Collard's expertly guided tours (*N$700/1,350 pp ½/full day, under 12½ price*) offer a comprehensive insight into the desert & dunes, & the creatures that live there.

Turnstone Tours 064 403123; e turn@ iafrica.com.na; www.turnstone-tours.com. For an informative day in the desert with a first-rate guide, try Turnstone Tours, pioneer of trips to Sandwich Harbour. You might pay a bit more than for other tours, but full-day trips (*N$1,900/1,800 pp 3 people/4 or more*) to Sandwich Harbour & the 'Sheltering Desert' come with a delicious picnic & more than 20 years' experience on these spectacular but demanding routes. For those with more time, there are short camping tours into Damaraland, the Erongo Mountains & the Namib Desert, with private tours available on request.

Ultimate Sandboarding m 081 421 6021; e ultimateboarding@gmail.com; www. ultimatesandboarding.com

Wings over Africa 064 403720; m 081 129 1554; e info@wings.na; http://wingscharters.com

15

The Skeleton Coast

By the end of the 17th century, the long stretch of coast north of Swakopmund had attracted the attention of the Dutch East India Company. They sent several exploratory missions, but after finding only barren shores and impenetrable fogs, their journeys ceased. Later, in the 19th century, British and American whalers operated out of Lüderitz, but they gave this northern coast a wide berth – it was gaining a formidable reputation.

Today, driving north from Swakopmund, it's easy to see how this coast earned its names of the Coast of Skulls or the Skeleton Coast. Treacherous fogs and strong currents forced many ships on to the uncharted sandbanks that shift underwater like the desert's sands. Even if the sailors survived the shipwreck, their problems had only just begun. The coast here is a barren line between an icy, pounding ocean and the Namib Desert. The present road, the C34, runs parallel to the ocean, and often feels like a drive along an enormous beach – with the sea on one side, and the sand – or gravel – continuing forever on the other. It's testament to the power of the ocean that, despite the havoc wreaked on passing ships, very few wrecks remain visible.

This fragile coast is divided into three narrow, protected areas. North of Swakopmund up to the Ugab River, covering about 200km of coast, is Dorob National Park. Beyond this lies the Skeleton Coast Park, the southern part of which – as far as Terrace Bay – is freely accessible to the public, while access to the northern section is restricted to fly-in visitors.

For the first 250km or so, from Swakopmund to about Torra Bay, there are almost no dunes. This is desert of gravel and rock. Then, around Torra Bay, the northern dune sea of the Namib starts, with an increasingly wide belt of coastal dunes stretching north to the Kunene River. But nowhere are these as tall, or continuous, as the Namib's great southern dune sea, south of the Kuiseb River.

At first sight it all seems very barren, but watch the amazing wildlife documentaries made by the famous film-makers of the Skeleton Coast, Des and Jen Bartlett, to realise that some of the most remarkable wildlife on earth has evolved here. Better still, drive yourself up the coast road, through this fascinating stretch of the world's oldest desert. You won't see a fraction of the action that they have filmed, but with careful observation you will spot plenty to captivate you.

FLORA AND FAUNA

SAND RIVERS A shipwrecked sailor's only hope on this coast would have been to find one of the desert's linear oases – sand rivers that wind through the desert to reach the coast. The Omaruru, the Ugab, the Huab, the Koichab, the Uniab and the Hoanib are the main ones. They are few and far between. Each starts in the highlands, far inland, and, although normally dry, they flood briefly in years of good rains. For most of the time their waters filter westward to the sea through their sandy beds. Shrubs and trees thrive, supporting whole ecosystems: green ribbons which snake across seemingly lifeless plains.

Even in the driest times, if an impervious layer of rock forces the water to surface, then the river will flow overland for a few hundred metres, only to vanish into the sand again as swiftly as it appeared. Such watering places are rare, but of vital importance to the inhabitants of the area. They have allowed isolated groups of Himba people to stay in these parts, while also sustaining the famous desert populations of elephant and – in the past – black rhino.

In many of these river valleys there are thriving populations of oryx, kudu, springbok, steenbok, jackals, genets, small wild cats and even giraffe. The shy and secretive brown hyena is common, though seldom seen. Zebra are scarce residents, and even lion or cheetah will sometimes appear, using the sand rivers as alleys for hunting forays. Desert-adapted elephants, although seasonal, are surviving well along the perennial river systems into the Skeleton Coast. Lion used to penetrate the desert right to the coast to prey on seals. Although it is many years since the last such coastal lion was seen, rising game populations in the interior are encouraging a greater population of lion in the region, so perhaps we'll see individuals on the beaches again before too long.

BESIDE THE SEA Outside the river valleys, the scenery changes dramatically, with an outstanding variety of colours and forms. The gravel plains – in all hues of brown and red – are bases for occasional coloured mountains, and belts of shifting barchan sand dunes.

Yet despite their barren appearance, even the flattest of the gravel plains here is full of life. Immediately next to the sea, high levels of humidity sustain highly specialised vegetation, succulents like lithops, and the famous lichens – which

THE SKELETON COAST

are, in fact, not plants at all but a symbiotic partnership of algae and fungi, the fungi providing the physical structure, while the algae photosynthesise to produce the food. They use the moisture in humid air, without needing either rain or even fog. That said, frequent coastal fogs and relatively undisturbed plains account for their conspicuous success here.

In some places lichens carpet the gravel desert. Take a close look at one of these gardens of lichen, and you'll find many different species, varying in colour from bright reds and oranges, through vivid greens to darker browns, greys and black. Most cling to the rocks or the crust of the gypsum soil, but a few species stand up like the skeletons of small leafless bushes, and one species, *Xanthomaculina convoluta*, is even wind-blown, a minute version of the tumbleweed famous in old Western films.

All come alive, looking their best, early on damp, foggy mornings. Sections appear like green fields of wispy vegetation. But if you pass on a hot, dry afternoon, they will seem less interesting. Then stop and leave your car. Walk to the edge of a field with a bottle of water, pour a little on to a small patch of lichens, and stay to watch. Within just a few minutes you'll see them brighten and unfurl.

Less obvious is their age: lichens grow exceedingly slowly. Once disturbed, they take decades and even centuries to regenerate. On some lichen fields you will see vehicle tracks. These are sometimes 40 or 50 years old – and still the lichens briefly crushed by one set of wheels have not regrown. This is one of the main reasons why you should *never* drive off the roads on the Skeleton Coast.

Next to the sea, small flocks of sanderlings may descend on beachfront lagoons, along with white-fronted plovers, while higher up, lappet-faced vultures circle in search of carrion. You may even spot Ludwig's bustard as it rises up, an untidy bundle of white and yellow.

FURTHER INLAND East of the coastal strip, between about 30km and 60km inland, the nights can be very cold, and many mornings are cool and foggy. However, after about midday the temperatures rocket and the humidity disappears. This is the harshest of the Namib's climatic zones, but even here an ecosystem has evolved, relying on occasional early morning fogs for moisture.

This is home to various scorpions, lizards and tenebrionid beetles, living from wind-blown detritus and vegetation including dune-creating dollar bushes (*Zygophyllum stapffii*) and perhaps the Namib's most fascinating plant, the remarkable *Welwitschia mirabilis*.

This is the terrain favoured by Rüppell's korhaan. Several species of lark are at home here, too, though few – except perhaps the red-capped – are easy to distinguish. Birds of prey include the lanner falcon and brown snake eagle, while smaller species include the familiar chat.

GETTING THERE AND AWAY

It is even more vital here than in the rest of Namibia: you need a vehicle to see the Skeleton Coast – at least as far north as Terrace Bay. Although hitchhiking is not restricted, vehicles are few and far between, and – with often bitterly cold mornings and desiccating afternoons – heat exhaustion would be a real danger. An alternative is to join an organised tour. A few tour companies in Swakopmund run excursions to Cape Cross, about 120km or 1½ hours' drive to the north, stopping at one of the lichen fields and some of the more obvious sites of interest on the way. Tours can also be arranged from Henties Bay.

By far the best option is to drive yourself, equipped with plenty of water and a picnic lunch, and stop where and when you wish to explore. Set off north as early as possible, catching the southern sections of the road in the fog, and prebook overnight accommodation if you plan to go as far north as Terrace Bay. The drive here takes about 5 hours, though most people stop to explore and have refreshments, and so make a whole day of it.

Until recently, the first stretches of the main C34 were what is known locally as a salt road, but the road has now been tarred as far as Henties Bay. Continuing north from here, the road reverts primarily to the more normal gravel.

North of Terrace Bay, visitor access to the national park is restricted to those on fly-in safaris. For details, see page 387.

Note Beware of driving on the salt-pans anywhere along this coast, as they can be very treacherous.

DOROB NATIONAL PARK

You can drive on the main roads through this southernmost section of the Skeleton Coast, which has long been popular with fishing parties, but to drive off road to the beach (other than along access roads), or inland, you need a permit, which can be obtained from the MET office in Swakopmund (page 329) or Walvis Bay (page 352), or at the Henties Bay tourist office (page 376). Several access points to the beach line the road, and campsites, some of them seasonal, dot the coastline. This area is also home to Cape Cross Seal Reserve, and the rapidly growing town of Henties Bay.

SWAKOPMUND TO HENTIES BAY
Sea ponds About 7km north of Swakopmund lie a number of large, shallow ponds. These are mostly natural ponds used for salt production by the Salt Company. Some are filled with sea water, which is then left to evaporate, while others are used for farming oysters. Sometimes you'll see one coloured bright red or green by algae, or pink by a flock of feeding flamingos!

Nobody lives here, but workers from Swakopmund manage the site. Both the salt and the oysters are sold within Namibia, and most restaurants in Swakopmund will offer you both.

Wlotzkasbaken This small settlement, about 31km north of Swakopmund, looks like a colony on the moon. It was named after Paul Wlotzka, a keen Swakopmund fisherman who first built a hut here, and guided visitors to this rich fishing area. For the most part, Wlotzkasbaken is simply a collection of colourful holiday homes, used mainly by Namibians who love sea fishing and come here for their annual summer breaks around December and January. Its houses are spread out along the desert coast, each overshadowed by its own long-legged water tower (which rely on tankers driving the water from inland). To the east are a few apparently barren hills and boulders, but get out of the car to take a closer look, and you'll find many small plants and shrubs there. The Namib's fogs are densest (and so deliver more moisture) at higher elevations, so even these relatively small hills catch much more water from the fog than the flat plains.

Among the boulders there are also small land snails, beetles and small vertebrates. These include what is thought to be the world's only lizard that actually mimics an invertebrate for protection. The juveniles of the *Eremias lugubris* species have the same coloration and style of movement as a beetle known locally as the 'oogpister' – which protects itself like a skunk by expelling a foul-smelling liquid.

Wreck of the *Zeila* About 13km south of Henties Bay [373 A7], the rusting hulk of the *Zeila* lies in shallow waters, very close to the C34. It's a sobering sight, all that remains of a fishing trawler, the *Zeila*, which ran aground on 25 August 2008 – though fortunately no lives were lost: the ship was being towed to India for scrap when it became parted from the towing line. It is easy to pull off the road to take a closer look, but be prepared for some serious hassle from people selling rocks, here, and don't leave anything unattended.

Where to stay and eat Government-owned campsites are positioned regularly along this coastline, used mainly in high summer when Namibian and South African families and those on fishing trips descend for the holidays. Otherwise, you can expect these sites to be totally empty.

Pitches are spread along the beach at intervals of 100m or so, each with toilets and running water. Central ablution blocks are perfectly adequate, with showers and fresh water available. There is usually also a basic shop selling soft drinks and tinned goods, and – more importantly – fuel, though as supplies rely on generator power, it's not wise to bank on availability. Each campsite also has a freezer available for campers to freeze the day's catch.

Following a brief period under private management, these campsites are back in the hands of the **NWR** (\ *061 285 7200;* e *reservations@nwr.com.na; www.nwr.com. na*), which has now renovated them all, and most are now open all year. South of Henties Bay, you'll find the following:

⋏ Jakkalsputz Campsite [373 A7] (67 pitches) This is about 9km south of Henties Bay – small plots of desert beside the beach, with pitches marked off as campsites & shared ablution blocks. *N$180–200 pp*. **$$**

⋏ Windpomp 14 Camp [373 A7] (30 pitches) \ *083 700 4414;* e *camp@windpomp14.com; www.sunkarros.com*. Having been closed for almost a decade, the old Mile 14 Campsite was rebuilt in partnership with NWR & Sun Karros Lifestyle in 2015. With electricity & water for each pitch, & new ablution facilities with hot showers & flush toilets, as well as the Barnard pub & restaurant, it has once again become a popular hangout with both fishermen & campers. There is even an airstrip close to the entrance. For those driving past, the restaurant makes a welcome stop. *N$160–230 pp*. **$$**

HENTIES BAY About 76km from Swakopmund, this windswept town is set immediately above the shore, around a stream (normally dry and sandy) of the Omaruru Delta. A surge in property development in recent years reflects the town's increasing popularity with Namibians and South Africans, who flock here during their annual holidays in December and January to escape the interior's heat and to go fishing. Brightly coloured bungalows penetrate the morning mists, while down in the river-bed surreal patches of green herald the local golf club. Perhaps the pair who erected the town's gallows in 1978 – as an appeal to residents to keep the place clean – are winning the battle.

Tourist information

⛿ Henties Bay Tourism [377 C2] Cnr Jakkalsputz Rd & Nickey Iyambo Av; \ *064 501142;* e *priscilla.noarises@hbaymun.com.na; www. hentiesbaytourism.com;* ⊕ *08.00–17.00 Mon–Fri.* From its smart new premises, the tourist office offers helpful leaflets & maps, the Giggling Coffee Pot café & a clean visitors' toilet, so it's worth a stop on your way out of town. In peak season (*Dec/Jan*) community members sell curios here, along with homemade goods & biltong.

The building is also home to Tao's Hut (⏰ *08.00–17.00 daily;* $$$$–$$$$$), a restaurant serving traditional Namibian cuisine, but reservations are essential. The related Sari-Ma Tours & Travel (m *081 140 1157*) organises farmstays all over Namibia.

🏠 **Where to stay**   Along with the property boom in Henties Bay goes a rise in tourist accommodation, though much of it is self-catering and outside the town. In town itself there are still a few reliable options.

🏠 **De Duine Hotel** [377 B2] (20 rooms) 34 Duine Rd; 📞 064 500001; e reservation@ deduinehotel.com; www.deduinehotel.com. Originally owned by Namibia Country Lodges,

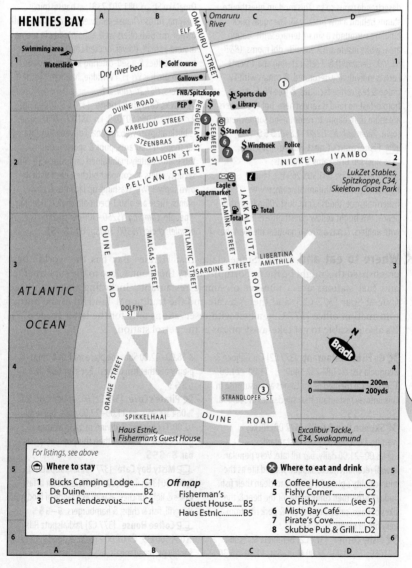

HENTIES BAY

Omaruru River

ELF

OMARURU STREET

Swimming area
Waterslide ●

Dry river bed   ▶ Golf course

Gallows ●

DUINE ROAD

FNB/Spitzkoppe
PEP $ ✝ Sports club
● Library

BENGUELA ST

KABELJOU STREET   ⑤
                   Ⓔ $ Standard
STEENBRAS ST   Spar   ⑥ $ Windhoek   Police ●
                SEEMEEU ST   ⑦   ④
GALJOEN ST

PELICAN STREET   NICKEY IYAMBO   ②
                  ⑧   LukZet Stables,
                       Spitzkoppe, C34,
Eagle ●   ✉ Ⓔ   *i*   Skeleton Coast Park
Supermarket

DUINE ROAD   MALGAS STREET   ATLANTIC STREET   FLAMINK STREET   JAKKALSPUTZ ROAD

🅿 Total
🅿 Total

LIBERTINA
AMATHILA

ATLANTIC   SARDINE STREET

OCEAN   DOLFYN ST

N

0 ———— 200m
0 ———— 200yds

ORANGE STREET   ③   STRANDLOPER ST

SPIKKELHAAI   DUINE ROAD

↓ Haus Estnic,
Fisherman's Guest House

Excalibur Tackle,
↓ C34, Swakopmund

For listings, see above

🛏 **Where to stay**

1 Bucks Camping Lodge.....C1
2 De Duine.............................B2
3 Desert Rendezvous..........C4

Off map
Fisherman's
  Guest House..... B5
Haus Estnic.......... B5

🍴 **Where to eat and drink**

4 Coffee House...............C2
5 Fishy Corner................C2
  Go Fishy..................(see 5)
6 Misty Bay Café............C2
7 Pirate's Cove...............C2
8 Skubbe Pub & Grill.....D2

& then Protea, De Duine is now in private hands. Its staff are friendly & helpful, & its en-suite rooms comfortable, with TV, fridge, kettle & safe. Old newspapers adorn the walls of the restaurant (⏲ *07.00–22.00*) which serves everything from burgers to fish & pasta: simple but good. A separate bar has a cosy wood-burning stove. *N$695/1,120 sgl/dbl.* **$$$**

🏠 **Desert Rendezvous** [377 C4] (2 rooms, 2 apts) 238 Strandloper St; 📞 064 500281; m 081 255 3751; e desertrendezvous@iway.na; www. desertrendezvous.co.za. This modern guesthouse stands behind a low brick wall. The squat brick building surrounds a smart terrace with seating area, while inside are 2 en-suite dbl rooms, (*B&B N$1035 per night*) & 2 self-catering apartments. Each is individually decorated, & comes with TV, fridge & tea/coffee facilities, & free Wi-Fi. Apart from b/fast no food is served here, but the owners are more than happy to recommend somewhere in town. *Room only N$1,380–1,840.* **$$$**

🏠 **Fisherman's Guest House** [377 B5] (9 rooms) Cnr Brukkaros & Auas sts; 📞 064 501111; m 081 303 2694; e louis. fenaux@huntandfishnamibia.com; www. fishermansguesthouse.com. Just 200m from the beach, this bright yellow guesthouse is popular with anglers, & has a strong nautical theme. It has a large lounge, bar & restaurant area, with meals available by arrangement (*N$220*). Dbl & twin rooms are all en suite, with minibar, TV & phone; there's also an attractive family room. Public rooms & 3 of the bedrooms are accessible by wheelchair. Outside, a sheltered garden overlooks the sea, & there's secure parking. Deep-sea fishing, rock & surf angling, & dolphin- & seal-viewing trips can be organised, as can various other shore-based activities. *N$904/1,349 sgl/dbl.* **$$$**

☀ 🏠 **Haus Estnic** [377 B5] (3 rooms) 1417 Omatako St; m 081 201 2381; e hausestnic@ iway.na; https://hausestnic.weebly.com. This small owner-run B&B offers well-appointed twin rooms around a small, flower-decked courtyard with braai facilities & a self-catering kitchen. Each en-suite room has Wi-Fi, TV, fridge, hairdryer, kettle & cafetiere. *N$1,200 dbl.* **$$**

⚒ **Bucks Camping Lodge** [377 C1] (camping, 2 chalets) 📞 064 501039; m 081 827 7087; e buckcamp@mweb.com.na. Conveniently located for shops, restaurants, pubs & sports facilities, this immaculately maintained campsite with 24hr security offers 45 compact pitches, each with its own shower, WC, washing-up facilities & power points. There are also 1-bedroom chalets sleeping 4 people. *Camping N$250–300 per pitch (max 4 people); chalet N$300/360 sgl/dbl.* **$–$$**

✖ **Where to eat and drink** Some claim that Henties Bay has the world's best crayfish, so this might be the opportunity to try them out. Close to the supermarket and fuel stations are a number of simple restaurants, including the Bean Tree Café at Spar [377 C2], and there's a café and the traditional Tao Hut at the tourist information office [377 C2], albeit with reservations only for the latter (page 377). It's also possible to get take-away pizzas at the petrol station.

✖ **Go Fishy Restaurant** [377 C2] Cnr Galjoen & Benguela sts; m 081 252 5400; ⏲ 11.00– 21.00. The nautical themed décor comes as no surprise in this unfussy restaurant that specialises in seafood. **$$$–$$$$$**

✖ **Skubbe Pub & Grill** [377 D2] Nickey Iyambo Av; 📞 064 501373; restaurant ⏲ 08.00–21.00 daily, bar till late. Very popular & well recommended, Skubbe started life as the municipality's place for anglers to clean their fish. Today's fishermen come more for the beer & the likes of hake, calamari, eisbein & pork ribs from a very broad menu. **$–$$$$$**

✖ **Fishy Corner** [377 C2] Benguela St; 📞 064 501059; ⏲ 10.00–22.00 Mon–Sat, 11.30–15.30 & 18.00–22.00 Sun. *The* place for fish & chips (& plenty of other fish dishes). Eat in or take away. **$$$$**

✖ **Pirate's Cove** [377 C2] 602 Jakkalsputz Rd; 📞 064 500960; ⏲ 11.00–22.00 daily, bar until 02.00. For burgers & 'divine' pizza in a range of guises, look no further than this popular sports bar. **$–$$$**

☕ **Misty Bay Café** [377 C2] Jakkalsputz Rd; 📞 064 501336; ⏲ 08.00–16.00. Come for b/fast, cakes & light lunches, as well as a range of food from the grill, fish & chips, & hamburgers. **$–$$$**

☕ **Coffee House** [377 C2] Jakkalsputz Rd; 📞 064 500139; ⏲ 07.00–16.00. A good variety of freshly prepared meals. **$$**

Shopping The town has three reasonable **supermarkets**, a couple of bottle stores, and a few general shops. Some are centred on the Eagle complex, in the middle of town, but carry on up the road and bear left, and you'll come to a branch of Spar. For fresh fruit and vegetables, there's also the National Youth Service Garden Project (drive straight past the 'Welcome to Henties Bay' sign, turn right in the direction of Spitzkoppe, and the Garden Project is immediately on your right).

For **curios**, try the tourist information office, or the curio shops by Pirate's Cove sports bar [377 C2].

Other practicalities Do fill up with **fuel** in Henties Bay if you're heading north or east. **Fuel stations** are rare in either direction, but there are several here, including one on the main road that slightly bypasses town, and two in the town itself. For **vehicle repairs**, try Grobler Motors (`064 501211`), at the Total fuel station. There are several **banks** with ATMs.

There's free **Wi-Fi** during office hours at the tourist information office, and more facilities at the Namtel office, next to the **post office** [377 C2].

Should you need a **doctor**, make your way to the Benguela Health Centre in the Spar complex [377 C2], which also has a **pharmacy** (`064 500423`; m *081 128 2230*).

What to see and do

Fishing If you'd like to join the locals fishing, you'll need a permit (*N$14/day*), obtainable from one of the tour operators. Sought-after fish include kabeljou (carp), the galjoen (blackfish), steenbras and stompneus, as well as the now-scarce dassie, or – when the waters are very warm – shad. Angling equipment is available from various outlets, including Excalibur Tackle [377 C5] on Jakkalsputz Road (`064 501959`), and Leon's Tackle Shop (m *081 208 7659*) at the Spar supermarket [377 C2].

Access to fishing spots by 4x4 is designated at regular intervals along the coast north of Henties Bay. Alternatively, contact one of the operators specialising in angling tours, which include:

Henties Angling Tours m 081 251 1489
Rock & Surf Angling m 081 240 3219

Sea Ace Fishing Adventures `064 500545`; m 081 233 9242; e info@seaace.com.na; www. seaace.com.na. Options include deep-sea fishing.

Other sports While keen fishermen delight in declaring their catches, ardent **golfers** can have a game at the Henties Bay Golf Course (m *081 129 1963*). This resides in a section of the original Omaruru Delta, and doesn't suffer from a shortage of sandy bunkers. If that doesn't appeal, there are **tennis** courts (`064 500751`), and **horseriding** at LukZet Equestrian Stables (page 380).

Hiking and birding Non-fishing visitors might like to take a short wander up the Omaruru's course, while fit, acclimatised hikers can choose from three circular but unmarked trails, taking in some of the desert scenery around the town. The 20km Omaruru River Walking Trail takes you north along the coast, then inland along the riverbed, returning to the centre of town, or there's a significantly longer option – at 70km – leading inland to the Omdel Dam on the Omaruru River. There's also the 18km Jakkalsputz Walking Trail, which runs south along the coast to Jakkalsputz Campsite, returning on a parallel track just inland. Maps are available from the tourist board.

Omdel Dam itself attracts numerous bird species when it's holding water, and makes a good picnic spot. To get there, take the C35 towards Uis for about 27km, then turn right for a further 14km before reaching the dam wall.

4x4 trails The tourist board has route maps with GPS co-ordinates, route descriptions and pictures (*N$100 each*) for a series of 4x4 trails from the town. The routes vary in length from 246km to 312km, and take in some of the region's most spectacular scenery, including the Omaruru and Ugab rivers, and Messum Crater (page 402).

Quadbiking Since the creation of the Dorob National Park, quadbiking has been restricted in order to prevent environmental damage, and is now limited to the coastal area west of the C34, and south of the Omaruru River down to Swakopmund (except in front of the campsites). Ask for details at the tourist information centre.

Horseriding **LukZet Equestrian Stables** [377 D2] (*1925 Sand St;* m *081 680 1064;* e *info@lukzet.com; www.lukzet.com*) James and Penny Jones offer pony and horse rides, and also have a petting zoo. Refreshments are available at their Horseshoe Pub & Café, and accommodation too, in one of two large self-catering houses with sea views, sleeping eight and 12 people respectively. They can also organise car rentals, flights and 4x4 excursions.

HENTIES BAY TO SKELETON COAST PARK
The C34 continues north along the coast from Henties Bay as far as the national park entrance gate – and beyond. Near Henties Bay, two roads break away to the right. The D1918 heads almost due east for about 121km, passing within 30km of Spitzkoppe (page 395) before joining the main tarred B2 about 23km west of Usakos. The more popular C35 heads northeast across an amazingly flat, barren plain: certainly one of the country's most desolate roads, although enlivened on each side by views of Brandberg to the north, and Spitzkoppe to the south. This is the main route to Uis, the Brandberg and Khorixas, as well as to southern Damaraland – although if you are planning to stop for the night somewhere like Terrace Bay, Damaraland is best accessed along the C39 further north.

Where to stay and eat

Å **Mile 72 Campsite** [373 A7] (5 chalets, 230 pitches) Book via NWR (page 103); ☺ all year. Some 35km north of Henties Bay along the C34, & 20km south of Cape Cross, this is yet another desolate row of ablution blocks – desolate, that is, unless you're here in the summer. Then the renovated campsite with improved facilities comes into its own. Chalets have 2 sgl beds & a sleeper couch, with an en-suite shower & WC. An on-site kiosk sells snacks & cool drinks. Camping N$180–200 pp. **$$**

Å **Mile 108** [373 A6] (160 pitches) Book via NWR (page 103); ☺ all year. 80km north of Henties Bay, & 64km from Mile 72, could this be more desolate? Even so, it's still smarter than in recent years, & has a kiosk selling snacks & cool drinks. N$180–200 pp. **$$**

Omaruru River Driving north past Henties Bay, note all the vegetated depressions (indicating watercourses) that you pass through, spread out along 10–15km around the town. These are all part of the Omaruru River delta. Because of the high rainfall in its catchment area, in the mountains around Omaruru, this flows regularly and the sandy river-bed usually supports quite a luxurious growth of vegetation.

The vegetation includes a variety of desert flora, native to the Namib's many river-beds, as well as some exotics like wild tobacco (*Nicotiana glauca*), jimson weed (*Datura stramonium*) and the castor oil plant (*Ricinus communis*). These are found both here and in many of the other river valleys further north. Dr Mary Seely, in her excellent book *The Namib Desert* (page 574), suggests that the seeds for the first such plants might have been imported with fodder for horses during the South African War. As they are hardy plants, eaten by few animals, they have been very successful.

Gemstones With so little precipitation, even unobservant visitors notice that the basic geology of the Namib often lies right on its surface, just waiting to be discovered. Don't miss the chance to stop somewhere on the C34 or C35 around here. Wander a few hundred metres from it, and do some gem hunting. Even if you're not an expert, you should find some beautiful crystals.

It was while staying at Mile 72 in 1972 that a Namibian mineralogist, Sid Peters (founder of the House of Gems in Windhoek; page 196), went hunting for minerals. He found several aquamarines and then a long light-blue crystal that he couldn't identify. Eventually the Smithsonian Institute in Washington DC confirmed that this was jeremejebite, a very rare, hard mineral containing boron, first discovered in its white form over 80 years ago in Siberia.

Cape Cross The Portuguese captain and navigator Diego Cão landed in 1485. He was the first European of his time to reach this far south down the coast of Africa, and to mark the achievement he erected a stone cross on the bleak headland, inscribed in Latin and Portuguese with:

Since the creation of the world 6684 years have passed and since the birth of Christ 1484 years and so the illustrious King John has ordered this pillar to be erected here by Diego Cão, his knight.

Diego Cão died for his daring, and was buried on a rock outcrop nearby, which they called Serra Parda. His cross remained in place until the 1890s, when it was taken to the Oceanographical Museum in Berlin. In 1974 the whole area was landscaped and a replica cross erected, which stands there today.

David Coulson, in his book *Namib* (page 576), relates that an old slate was found half-buried in the sand around here, with a message dated 1860 reading:

I am proceeding to a river sixty miles north, and should anyone find this and follow me, God will help him.

It is not known who wrote the message, or what became of them.

Cape Cross Seal Reserve [373 A6] (⊕ *Jul–mid-Nov 10.00–17.00 daily, mid-Nov–Jun 08.00–17.00 daily; admission N$250, plus N$50 per car; no motorcycles*) All along the Namibian coast there are colonies of Cape fur seals (*Arctocephalus pusillus pusillus*), though the one at Cape Cross is one of the easiest to access. Occupied all year round, it numbers up to 100,000 animals. The amazing sight of tens of thousands of heads bobbing on land and in the water is matched only by the overpowering stench of the colony that greets you. The noise, too, is unexpected – a positive cacophony of sound that resembles an entire farmyard of animals at full volume. Today's visitors can watch the seals from boardwalks rather than the beach, which is a plus for the seals – if not for photographers. Other facilities include toilets and a picnic area.

THE SEALS

In mid- to late October the large males, or bulls, arrive, their massive body weight of around 360kg far exceeding that of the 75kg females. They stake their territorial claims and try to defend them from other males. Shortly afterwards, in late November or early December, each of the pregnant females gives birth to a single pup. These will remain in and around the colony, and continue suckling for the next ten or 11 months.

Not long after giving birth, each female mates with the male that controls the harem, and so the cycle continues, with the pups born about a year later. Once all the pups are born, and the females have mated, most of the males will leave to break their fast and replenish the enormous amounts of body fat burned while defending their territories. In the last few months of the year, the scene can be quite disturbing, with many pups squashed by the weighty adults, or killed by the area's resident populations of jackal and brown hyena.

🏠 Where to stay and eat

🏠 **Cape Cross Lodge** [373 A6] (18 rooms, 2 suites, camping) ☏ 064 694012/7; reservations m 081 169 2186; e bookings@capecross.org; www.capecross.org. Just 4km from the seal colony, this modern lodge – now more of a small hotel – is a beacon for visitors. This is where the desert meets the sea, the vast, open spaces reflected in light, airy rooms (4 suitable for families, 6 with wheelchair access), with panoramic sea views from individual balconies or verandas. Solid, limed-wood furniture & pastel décor complement the maritime setting.

Downstairs is a cavernous restaurant, split by a central fire from a small lounge area & a bar. The restaurant (⊕ 07.00–10.00, noon–15.00 & 18.00–20.30), adorned with paintings that are for sale, serves both light meals such as pizzas & sandwiches, & main meals (set lunch N$270), but non-residents must book for dinner, either à la carte, or a 4-course set menu; a candlelit meal on the beach can be organised on request. A rather quirky wine cellar affords a good selection of wines, & (with pre-booking) doubles as a cosy private dining area. There's even a small museum relating to the early sailors & settlers along these shores.

The lodge also has a comfortable & fairly well-equipped campsite. High wooden fences protect your tent from the elements, while allowing some privacy. Each of the 21 pitches has a light, power points, braai area & a cold-water sink,

with flushing toilets & hot showers in a central ablutions block. There's also a common room for campers with a pool table & DSTV; a shop selling basic foodstuffs, as well as some angling bits & pieces, & a separate bar close to the campsite.

Aside from the seal colony itself, visitors are attracted by the sheer beauty of the setting. Just to sit on the screened terrace & watch baby seals cavorting in the waves can occupy half the afternoon, though for the more energetic there are plenty of walks & opportunities for birdwatching. Those planning to discover 'some of the best surfing in Namibia' should bring their own equipment. A word of warning though: don't even think of swimming without taking local advice; the water is cold, currents are very strong & riptides can be extremely dangerous. Advance notice is required for fishing trips as well as for various tours: to the seal reserve &, further afield, Messum Crater, the wreck of the *Winston*, & the 'Dead Sea' – a saline lake south of the lodge. *DBB N$2,045/3,140 sgl/dbl; camping N$200 pp.* **$$–$$$$$**

⚠ **Cape Cross Campsite** (5 pitches) The small, simple campsite at the seal reserve [373 A6] has just 5 pitches & basic ablutions. Although it provides some shelter from the cold winds, note that the campsite at Cape Cross Lodge is more comfortable & sheltered, albeit not nearly as wild & exciting. *N$30 pp, plus N$10/vehicle.* **$**

Wreck of the *Winston* Just 12km south of the Ugab River Gate to the Skeleton Coast Park is a signpost west to the first of the coast's wrecks that – until recently – remained visible: the *Winston*, a fishing boat that grounded here in 1970. For years visited only by seals, terns and Cape gulls, it has finally been buried by the sands a couple of kilometres from the road, along a rutted track [373 A6]. Don't be tempted to drive on the salt-pans here (or anywhere else on this coast); they can be very treacherous.

SKELETON COAST PARK: THE SOUTH

(⏱ *07.00–15.00 daily, last exit 19.00; admission N\$250 plus N\$50 per car; under 16s free*) From the Ugab to the Kunene, the Skeleton Coast Park protects about a third of the country's coastline. The southern part of this, as far as Terrace Bay, is easily accessible to anyone with a car and some forward planning. It's a fascinating area and, surprisingly, is often omitted from scheduled tours and safaris – perhaps because the accommodation is relatively basic. This is a shame, though it does mean that from July to September – when some of the rest of the country is busy with overseas visitors – it is still blissfully quiet.

Imagining the Skeleton Coast, most people think that it's littered with dozens of picturesque wrecks – but that's really no longer the case. Shipwrecks do gradually disintegrate. They're pounded by the waves, corroded by the salt water, and eventually what's left of them washes out to sea or vanishes into the sands. Further, modern navigation techniques, using accurate charts and most recently GPS receivers, have greatly reduced the accident rate on this coast. Thus while a few decades ago the coast probably was littered with wrecks, now they're few and far between – so take the opportunity to wander down to the few that remain while you can!

PARK ACCESS Access to the park is via one of two gates: the Ugab River Gate [373 A6] on the C34, to the south, or the Springbokwasser Gate on the C39, to the east. Because the climate here is harsh, and the area quite remote, the Ministry of Environment and Tourism has fairly strict regulations about entry, which must be followed.

Entry permits may be bought at either gate, though note that you must reach your gate of entry before it closes at 15.00 to be allowed into the park – otherwise you will simply be turned away. If you're planning to stay at Torra Bay or Terrace Bay, it is strongly advised to book well in advance through the NWR (page 103), and bring your confirmation slip with you. If you've left it too late, try calling ahead (📞064 694007) to see if there's space. You cannot just turn up without any form of reservation.

The coast road inside the Skeleton Coast Park is mostly just normal gravel, so keep your speed below 80km/h to be safe. No driving is permitted within the park boundary after 19.00.

Ugab River (Ugabmund) Gate Some 126km from Henties Bay, or 166km from Terrace Bay, this is the park entrance for those driving along the coast road [373 A6]. Inside, dusty displays of *Onymacris* spp beetles and other insects are rather more interesting than the rather macabre collection of animal skulls that adorn the building.

Springbokwasser Gate There's a small, privately owned **campsite** just outside the gate [373 A5] catering to those who arrive too late to access the park.

THE UGAB RIVER The catchment area for the Ugab (or Uchab) River stretches as far as Otavi, making this a long and important river for the Namib. It flows at least once most years, and you drive across its bed just after the southern gate into the park. Although much of the visible vegetation is the exotic wild tobacco (*Nicotiana*

15

glauca), there are still some stunted acacia trees and other indigenous plants, like the nara bushes (*Acanthosicyos horridus*) with their (almost leafless) spiky green stems, and improbably large melons.

Shortly after crossing the Ugab, look east to see the view becoming more majestic, as the escarpment looms into view above the mirages, which play on the gravel plains. Near the mouth of the Ugab is the wreck of the *Girdleness*, though it is difficult to see.

WRECK OF THE *SOUTH WEST SEAL* Near the road, about 15km north of the Ugab River [373 A6], this is clearly signposted (though not by name) and very easy to visit. It is one of the coast's most convenient wrecks (for the visitors, not the sailors), so if you're looking for a picnic stop, it is ideal. The *South West Seal* itself was a small vessel that ran aground in 1976.

THE HUAB RIVER North of the Ugab, the next river crossed is the Huab. This rises in the escarpment around Kamanjab, and is one of the coast's most important corridors for desert-adapted elephants and rhinos – though you're highly unlikely to see either so far from the mountains.

Immediately north of the river, if you look to the east of the road, you can see the beginnings of barchan dunes standing on the gravel plains. Here sand is blowing out of the bed of the Huab, and actually forming a dune field (see page 7 for the origins of barchan dunes).

It's much easier to spot the rusting hulk of an old oil rig, c1960, with a turn-off to a small parking area adjacent. This was originally part of a grand scheme to extract oil from the coast, organised by a prospector called Ben du Preez, which ran up huge debts before his banks foreclosed. Amy Schoeman's superb coffee-table book, *The Skeleton Coast* (page 576), relates this story in detail. As a postscript, she notes that some of Terrace Bay was originally built by du Preez as his base.

Now the old framework provides a perfect breeding spot for Cape cormorants, so be careful not to disturb the birds by getting out of your car between around September and March.

TOSCANINI For such a significant dot on the map, this minute outpost will seem a great disappointment, especially if you miss it! Despite sounding like another campsite, it is in fact the site of a disused old diamond mine: more rusting hulks and decaying buildings.

Elsewhere this kind of dereliction would be bulldozed, landscaped and erased in the name of conserving the scenery, but here it's preserved for posterity, and the visiting seabirds.

North of Toscanini, before the Koigab River, you pass the wrecks of the *Atlantic Pride*, the *Luanda* (1969) and the *Montrose* (1973), though they're not easy to spot, and the road is far enough from the sea for what's left of them to be obscured.

THE KOIGAB RIVER Squeezed between the larger Huab and Uniab rivers, the Koigab (or Koichab – not to be confused with Koichab Pan near Lüderitz) has quite a small catchment area and floods relatively rarely. Thus it seems more of a depression than a major river-bed. For fishing visitors, the Koigab is the southern boundary of the Torra Bay fishing area.

TORRA BAY Shortly before Torra Bay, the C39 splits off from the main coastal C34 and heads east, leaving the park (39km later) at the Springbokwasser Gate and proceeding into Damaraland. Watch the vegetation change quite quickly on this route, as the road passes the distinctive Sugar Loaf Hill on the right, through ecosystems that are increasingly less arid, before finally entering Damaraland's distinctive flat-topped mountains dotted with huge *Euphorbia damarana* bushes.

Just north of this C34/C39 junction is a section of road that stands in the path of barchan dunes that are marching *across* it. Stop here to take a close look at how these dunes gradually move, grain by grain, in the prevailing southwest wind. Then turn your attention to the build-up of detritus on the leeward side of the dunes, and you may be lucky enough to spot some of the area's residents. Look carefully for the famous white beetles (*Onymacris bicolor*) which are endemic to the area and have been the subject of much study. White beetles are very uncommon, and here it is thought they have evolved their coloration to keep cool, enabling them to forage for longer in the heat.

Many of the plants on this gravel plain around the barchan dunes build up their own small sand dunes. The dollar bushes (*Zygophyllum stapffii*), with their succulent dollar-shaped leaves, and the coastal ganna (*Salsola aphylla*) are obvious examples. Big enough to act as small windbreaks, these bushes tend to collect wind-blown sand. These small mounds of sand, being raised a little off the desert's floor, tend to have more fog condense on them than the surrounding ground. Thus the plant gets a little more moisture. You will normally see a few beetles, too, which survive on the detritus that collects, and add their own faeces to fertilise the plant.

Just inland from Torra Bay is a fascinating area of grey-white rocks, sculpted into interesting curves by the wind and the sand grains.

Where to stay

Å **Torra Bay Campsite** [373 A5] Book via the NWR, page 103; www.sunkarros.com. The seasonal campsite at Torra Bay comes to life in Dec & Jan, when it plays host to a plethora of fishing parties. It's absolutely no frills, with small, square pitches marked out by rows of stone, & no shade, yet it's hugely popular – & booked up months ahead. Facilities include 5 ablution blocks with WC & 1 with a shower, a shop & a filling station. *Camping N$230 pp;* ☉ *Dec–Jan only.* **$$**

THE UNIAB RIVER Perhaps the most accessible river for the passing visitor is the Uniab Delta, between Torra Bay and Terrace Bay. If you stop in only one river for a good look around, stop here. Not only is it quite scenic, but its headwaters come from around the huge Palmwag concession, home to many of the region's larger mammals, so it offers your best chance of spotting the park's scarce bigger game.

In ancient times, the river formed a wide delta by the sea, but that has been raised up, and cut into by about five different channels of water. When the river floods now, the water comes down the fourth channel reached from the south, though the old channels still support much vegetation.

Throughout this delta you'll find dense thickets of reeds and sedges and small streams flowing over the ground towards the sea. Some 10km from Torra Bay (20°12.953'S, 13°12.603'E) there's a pond just 5 minutes' walk east of the road, then 5km further north there's another by the road itself. Sometimes these will attract large numbers of birds – plovers, turnstones and various sandpipers are very common, as are ducks such as the Hottentot teal and Cape shoveler. Palaearctic migrants make up the bulk of the species.

Close to the first pond, a clear path leads east to the remains of an ancient 6th-century nomadic pastoral settlement. Several ruined stone structures hint at a small, Himba-style community, but little else is visible, although there is an interpretive signboard. A further 3km beyond this (20°11.358'S, 13°12.025'E), between the two ponds, there is a small waterfall about 1.5km west of the road.

Here a gentle trickle of water (supplemented by an occasional rainy-season torrent) has eroded a narrow canyon into the sandstone and calcrete layers of the river-bed, before trickling to the sea.

Keep quiet while you are walking and you should manage to spot at least some of the area's wildlife, including springbok, oryx and black-backed jackal, which are all common here. Elephant, lion and cheetah have also been sighted, but very rarely. Slightly elusive are the brown hyena, whose presence can be confirmed by the existence of their distinctive white droppings (coloured white, as hyenas will crunch and eat bones). Their local name, *strandwolf*, is an indication that they often scavenge on the beaches for carrion, especially near seal colonies. While these animals look fearsome, with their powerful forequarters and a thick, shaggy coat, they are solitary scavengers posing no danger to walkers unless cornered or deliberately harassed.

TERRACE BAY About 287km from Henties Bay, 8km beyond the sign to Dekka Bay, Terrace Bay is the furthest north that visitors can drive on the coast. It's a desolate spot, slightly surreal with its neat street-lighting and lone palm tree looming out of the mist. Originally built as a mining venture, it now functions solely as a restcamp for visitors. It makes an excellent short stop between Swakopmund and Damaraland, offering the opportunity to extend your time in the park, and thus get to know the desert better.

Fishermen, though, come here all year, and even the former president, Sam Nujoma, often took his holidays at Terrace Bay. His phalanx of bodyguards used to make fun company for the unsuspecting visitors he met there, though in later years he booked the whole place for himself and his entourage.

In the evening, take a look at the big shed behind the beach. On it you'll see (and smell) hundreds of cormorants which roost there every night – attracted by the warmth from the generator within. Though rarely seen, the occasional brown hyena patrols this area at night, looking for hapless cormorants that have fallen from the roof, or along the waterfront, where the day's catch is gutted.

The only supplies are limited to a small shop in the restcamp offering drinks and souvenirs, and a vital fuel station/garage (⊕ *07.30–19.30 daily*) tucked rather obscurely behind the beach.

⌂ Where to stay

⌂ **Terrace Bay Camp** [373 A4] (20 rooms, 2 beach chalets) Book via the NWR (page 103). The restcamp at Terrace Bay is the resort's *raison d'être*, built originally for the mine staff, & inherited by the government in 1977 when that failed. Now there's nothing here apart from this small camp & its staff accommodation. Although you can in theory just turn up, pre-booking is close to essential as space is limited, there's no campsite, & it's a long way to come only to be turned away.

The entire camp has been upgraded in recent years, & while it's still not luxurious, it feels so isolated that it can be fun for a day or 2. The bungalows remain functional in construction, with twin beds, a fridge, a shower & WC, & double-glazed windows. For groups, the VIP suite, with its own kitchen & lounge with TV, now hosts less imposing guests than the president, sleeping up to 8 people in 4 bedrooms. A surprising bonus is the bar & restaurant, with friendly service, good food & walls that serve as a large-scale visitors' book completed by enthusiastic guests.

Fishing permits can be obtained here, as can hooks, line & bait. If time allows, one of the staff might be persuaded to take you fishing; although as government employees they may not charge for such expeditions, they do appreciate a reasonable tip for their time & help. *DBB N$920/1,070 Jul–Oct sgl/dbl, N$1,210/1,360 Nov–Jun; self-catering chalet from N$1,080 pp, min 4 people; credit cards accepted, but slow.* **$$$**

MÖWE BAY Around 80km north of Terrace Bay, this is the administrative centre for the national park and acts as a base for a few researchers who are allowed to work here. It is not open to the general public, except as a place to park for visitors to the new Shipwreck Lodge (page 391).

SKELETON COAST PARK: THE NORTH

Unlike the southern section of the Skeleton Coast Park, access to the north – formerly the 'wilderness area' – is restricted to visitors on a fly-in safari. No self-drivers are permitted into this area.

The visitor looking to see this remarkable northern area of the park currently has two choices. Both are fairly costly and packed full of activities, but they're very different in style. Both rank among the best trips on the subcontinent.

The only caveat to this eulogy is that, while this region appears harsh and 'in your face', it actually offers some of Africa's most subtle attractions. Endless savannah covered with wildebeest is enthralling; gravel plains dotted with welwitschia may seem less so. Most appreciate leopards, but the lichens' appeal is less obvious. Hence in some ways these trips are better suited to visitors who have been on safari to Africa before. Often it seems that the trips are praised most highly by the most experienced safari-goers. Much of the credit here is due to the calibre of the guides: the area's subtle attractions require top guiding skills to bring them to life – and both operations have this.

TRIPS AND WHERE TO STAY *Map, page 394*
Skeleton Coast Fly-In Safaris (✆ 061 224248; e info@skeletoncoastsafaris.com; www.skeletoncoastsafaris.com) Even from the outset, the original fly-in safaris to the Skeleton Coast spent much time outside the concession – in the adjacent Kaokoveld, for example, and visiting Purros and the Kunene – as well as time in it. Thus although being excluded from the concession in 1992 was a blow, they were able to adapt their trips to use similar, adjacent areas and offer trips which were just as good, if not better, than the original ones. The flying and guiding ability of the Schoemans is such that they could organise a fly-in safari to an industrial wasteland… and end up making it one of the most fascinating places you've ever been.

Getting there and away Skeleton Coast Safaris use light aircraft (typically six-seater Cessnas) like most safaris use Land Rovers: exploring areas from the sky, flying low-level over dune fields, and periodically turning back for better views. So there's a lot of flying in small aircraft – generally short 30–40-minute hops which most people find fascinating.

Trips and costs There are four main trips, Safaris A, B, C and D respectively, though the last three are really variations of the core trip, Safari A. Trips operate all year, and normally require a minimum of two people. Prices include all meals, drinks and activities. As with most upmarket options in Africa, you should find it slightly cheaper to book this through an overseas tour operator who specialises in the region.

Safari A: Skeleton Coast *(4 days/3 nights; US$8,336/16,670 sgl/dbl; $$$$$$)*
This starts at 10.00 at Eros Airport in Windhoek, before flying west over the escarpment to Conception Bay, south of Sandwich Harbour, and north to refuel at Swakopmund. It stops again for a beach picnic lunch and a visit to a seal colony,

To understand the current situation in these northern concessions, it's helpful to know the history of the park, as well as some of the politics.

The Skeleton Coast Park was initially part of Etosha National Park, proclaimed in 1906. Then in 1967, South Africa's Odendal Commission cut Etosha down to 25% of its original size, making in the process several 'homelands' for the existing communities. Included among these were parts of what became known as Damaraland and Kaokoland, and also the Skeleton Coast.

During the late 1950s and 1960s various private companies, including the Sarusas Mining Corporation, were granted the rights for mining and fishing on the Skeleton Coast. In the late 1960s, the corporation assembled a project team to build a brand-new harbour at Cape Frio. They did all the research and got backing from investors, but at the last moment the South African government pulled the plug on the project. After all, a new Namibian port would reduce the stranglehold on the country held by Walvis Bay, which had historically belonged to South Africa even before it took over the administration of German South West Africa.

The corporation took the case to court and, as part of an out-of-court settlement, the South African government agreed that the Skeleton Coast should be reproclaimed as a national park, a status that was confirmed in 1971. Instrumental in this case was the young lawyer on the corporation's team, Louw Schoeman.

In order to preserve part of the area in totally pristine condition, the northern part was designated as a 'wilderness area' – to be conserved and remain largely untouched. Strictly controlled rights to bring tourists into one part of this area were given to just one operator. Rules were laid down to minimise the operator's impact, including a complete ban on any permanent structures, a maximum number of visitors per year, and stipulations that *all* rubbish must be removed (no easy task) and that visitors must be flown in.

During the course of his research into the case, Louw had fallen in love with the amazing scenery and solitude of the area. He had already started to bring friends up to the area for short exploratory safaris; as word spread, he started taking paying passengers too. When he won the tender for this concession, giving him the sole right to operate in one section of the area, he started to put his new company, Skeleton Coast Fly-in Safaris, on a more commercial footing. The logistics of such a remote operation were difficult and it remained a very exclusive operation. Its camps took a maximum of 12 visitors, with much of the travel by light aircraft. The whole operation was 'minimum impact' by any standard. Louw was one of the first operators to support Namibia's pioneering Community Game Guard schemes (see box, page 15), and he maintained a very ecologically sensitive approach long before it was fashionable.

I travelled to the coast with Louw in 1990. It was spellbinding: one of the most fascinating four days that I've spent anywhere. Partly this was the area's magic, but much was down to Louw's enthusiasm, and the sheer professionalism of his operation. Gradually, Skeleton Coast Fly-in Safaris had become a textbook example of an environmentally friendly operation, as well as one of the best safari operations in Africa. Louw's wife, Amy, added to this with the stunning photographs in her book, *The Skeleton Coast* (still the definitive work on the area; see page 576), and his sons, André and Bertus, joined as pilot/guides, making it a family operation. In many ways, it put the area, and even the country, on the map as a top-class destination for visitors. Largely due to Louw's passion for the area, fly-in safaris to the Skeleton Coast had become one of Africa's ultimate trips.

POST-INDEPENDENCE POLITICS In 1992, the new government put the wilderness area concession up for tender, to maximise its revenue from the area. No Namibian operator bid against Louw; it was clear that he was conducting an excellent, efficient operation in a very difficult area. However, a competing bid was entered by a German company, Olympia Reisen, which has extensive political connections in Namibia and Germany. They offered significantly more money, and won the concession.

Local operators were uniformly aghast, and Louw, somewhat inevitably given his legal background, started legal proceedings to challenge the bid. Tragically, the stress of the situation took its toll and he died of a heart attack before the case was heard. Although his challenge succeeded, the decision was overturned by the cabinet, and Olympia Reisen was awarded the concession for an unprecedented ten years.

The monthly 'rent' that Skeleton Coast Safaris had paid was abolished. In its place, Olympia Reisen paid the government N$1,000 for every visitor taken into the concession. However, with no 'rent' and no minimum number of visitors, the government's income from the concession dropped drastically.

By the mid 1990s it was clear that Olympia Reisen was never going to make a commercial success of the operation. Finally, in 1999, Wilderness Safaris – a major player in southern Africa with a good reputation for sensitive development and responsible operations – made a deal with Olympia Reisen to take control of tourism in the area. They ripped down the poor structures that Olympia Reisen had erected, removed from the area truckloads of accumulated rubbish, and set about a series of ecological impact assessments prior to opening a totally new camp in 2000. As part of their ecological management, Wilderness continued to monitor the area, providing a base for a number of wildlife researchers.

They won the long-term concession here in 2003, but when this came up for renewal in 2010, and again in 2011, it was extended for only a year at a time. Then in December 2011, a fire burned down the kitchen and main area of Wilderness's Skeleton Coast Camp, and with no long-term commitment on the table, they broke down what was left of the camp and pulled out of the concession completely. In 2014 they opened the carefully named Hoanib Skeleton Coast Camp (page 391), in the northwest corner of the Palmwag concession, just outside the Skeleton Coast National Park, which promises some of the same kind of experiences that their old Skeleton Coast Camp used to offer.

Meanwhile, the Schoeman family continued to operate their own fly-in safaris by using remote areas of the Skeleton Coast just south of the wilderness area, and parts of western Kaokoland and Damaraland just east of the park's boundary. Although these are slightly different areas of the coast and its hinterland, their style and guiding skills remained as strong as ever – and their trips remained superb. On several occasions I've spoken with travellers whom I've sent on these trips who have been full of praise and described them as 'life-changing experiences'.

The situation continues to evolve, and in 2018, a partnership including Journeys Namibia and the community was granted permission for the brand-new Shipwreck Lodge, right on the coast.

before flying north and inland to the first of their three main camps, **Kuidas Camp**, in the Huab River valley. Kuidas is the base for the next morning's exploration of the Huab River valley and huge gravel plains dotted with *Welwitschia mirabilis*.

After lunch you'll hop to Terrace Bay for a short Land Rover trip to explore the beach and nearby roaring dunes (totally surreal), before flying out to **Leylandsdrift Camp**, in the heart of the Kaokoveld near the Himba community at Purros (page 429). From here the early morning is spent exploring the river valley, which has a thriving population of desert-adapted elephants, among other game, and visiting some of the local Himba people.

Continuing up the coast there are the remains of the *Kaiu Maru* shipwreck to be seen before the northwestern corner of Namibia is reached: the mouth of the Kunene River. Further inland, east of the dunes (which cover most of the park in this northern area), you'll land at the north end of Hartmann's Valley. The afternoon is spent exploring this beautiful and very remote area, before finally reaching **Kunene Camp**. The last morning of the trip is usually spent on a boat on the Kunene, before lunch and a long scenic flight back to Windhoek, arriving in the late afternoon.

Safari B (*4 days/3 nights; US$9,042/18,084 sgl/dbl;* **$$$$$$$**) Starts earlier than Safari A, and includes a stop at Sesriem, a drive into Sossusvlei, and a scenic flight over the vlei before flying on to Conception Bay, and continuing with Safari A.

Safari C (*5 days/4 nights; US$10,395/20,790 sgl/dbl;* **$$$$$$$**) Starts off like Safari B, but then after Kunene Camp includes a final night at one of the lodges on the eastern side of Etosha National Park, with time spent exploring the park by private 4x4.

Safari D (*6 days/5 nights; US$14,407/28,814 sgl/dbl;* **$$$$$$$**) Starts off at 07.00, with a flight to Sesriem and a trip into Sossusvlei, before flying on to Wolwedans Dune Camp (page 299) for two nights. An afternoon exploring the NamibRand Reserve is followed the next day by a flying day trip south to Lüderitz for a 4x4 excursion into the Sperrgebiet, ending up at Elizabeth Bay (page 287). This has big advantages over doing the same excursion on your own from Lüderitz, as you'll have one of Skeleton Coast Safaris' excellent guides with you, who will bring this amazing area to life. After your second night at Wolwedans, this trip continues as Safari A.

The camps All the camps have small but comfortable igloo tents containing twin beds separated by a bedside table, an en-suite bucket shower and a chemical toilet (so you don't need to go outside your tent after dark to use the camp's flushing toilets).

Kuidas Camp [394 B4] In the Huab River valley, east of the national park boundary, Kuidas lies in a dry, rocky landscape that's typical of western Damaraland, & there are some rock engravings within walking distance of the camp.

Leylandsdrift Camp Under a broken canopy of camelthorns (*Vachellia erioloba*)

& makalani palms (*Hyphaene petersiana*), Leylandsdrift is near the (almost invariably dry) Hoarusib River.

Kunene Camp [420 A1] Overlooks the Kunene River at the north end of Hartmann's Valley (page 430).

Wilderness Safaris (\ *061 274500;* e *info@wilderness.com.na*; *www.wilderness-safaris.com*) Wilderness Safaris' Hoanib Skeleton Coast Camp lies just outside the national park. Note that they normally prefer travellers to make arrangements through a good overseas tour operator (page 104) in their own country, rather than directly with them in Namibia.

Getting there and away Light-aircraft flights with Wilderness Air operate daily to Hoanib, usually leaving Windhoek in the morning with a change of plane or refuelling stop at Doro !Nawas, and arriving at the Skeleton Coast in time for lunch. The return journey usually departs mid morning from Hoanib and will have you back in Windhoek in the early afternoon. Flights, which are not included in the rates (*N$13,446 pp, one-way*) are from Windhoek's International Airport in comfortable twin-engine 13-seater Cessna 'caravans' or similar.

Trips There's a minimum two-night stay at Hoanib, but staying for three nights is strongly advised, not least as that gives time for their full-day trip to the coast. Taking in highlights such as the roaring dunes, the Clay Castles and a seal colony, you'll have a leisurely lunch in the dunes before – weather permitting – a scenic light-aircraft flight back to Hoanib. Stay longer if funds allow – or consider combining a trip here with Serra Cafema Camp (page 431), on the northern edge of Hartmann's Valley, northeast of Hoanib Skeleton Coast Camp.

The camp

✳ 🏠 **Hoanib Skeleton Coast Camp** [420 C4] (8 tented chalets) www.wilderness-safaris.com. A successor to Skeleton Coast Camp, Hoanib opened in 2014 & is accessible only by light aircraft.

From its remote base in the Hoanib River bed, it offers the opportunity to explore on foot, by 4x4 & (weather permitting) by air, with chances of seeing desert-adapted elephant & some of the elusive predators found in the area. The camp itself is exclusive & very comfortable, with en-suite tents (inc 1 family) that have en-suite bathrooms & shaded decks. While you'll be based at camp for b/fast & dinner, you'll usually spend the whole of each day on a 4x4 safari exploring some of the area's many attractions. These can be long days, but are always varied – & punctuated by regular stops for drinks & picnics. *FBA N$15,410–25,390/23,750–39,132/sgl/dbl, exc transfer flights.* **$$$$$$$**

Journeys Namibia In partnership with Natural Selection, Trip Travel and the Purros and Sesfontein conservancies, Journeys Namibia was granted permission to open a new lodge right on the coast, at the mouth of the Hoarusib River, 45km north of Möwe Bay. The result is Shipwreck Lodge, opened in 2018.

Getting there and away Guests at Shipwreck Lodge either fly in to the airstrip at Möwe Bay, or leave their vehicles. They are then collected at pre-agreed times, usually either 11.00 or 15.00, and transferred the 45km to the lodge in a closed 4x4. At the end of your stay, you'll leave the lodge at 09.00 for the return journey to Möwe Bay.

The camp

🏠 **Shipwreck Lodge** [420 B4] (10 cabins) 📞 061 228104; m 081 260 0830; e shipwreck@ journeysnamibia.com; www.shipwrecklodge. com.na. An entirely new departure within the Skeleton Coast National Park, Shipwreck Lodge has not only a stunning location but an intriguingly clever design. Nestled among the dunes with a view of the Atlantic are extraordinary, shipwreck-shaped cabins (twin/dbl, & 2 family), their wood-burning stoves staving off the maritime chill, & private decks giving the maximum opportunity to enjoy this wild landscape. The design runs through to the light, open-plan hub of the lodge, where you'll dine in understated comfort at individual tables.

From this windswept base, guests spend their time on full-day excursions to the seal colony at Möwe Bay, taking in shipwrecks & abandoned mines, or inland to the Hoarusib River, with the possibility of seeing desert-adapted elephants.

There are also sundowner drives to the roaring dunes & – weather permitting – the possibility of fishing & beach lunches. *FBA N$16,300–19,900/24,400–29,800 sgl/dbl, exc flights.* **$$$$$$$**

THE SIGHTS Although there are some specific 'sights' along the Skeleton Coast, and each of the operators has its own focus, these are almost incidental. Visiting this whole region is about experiencing the solitude and the beauty of a variety of landscapes, each with its own fragile ecosystem, existing side-by-side. While on safari, you'll frequently stop to study the plants and smaller animals, or perhaps to capture landscapes on film. A few of the better-known places in the area include:

The coast Along the coast's misty, desolate beaches there is always something of interest to inspect more closely, or to photograph. Ghost crabs scuttle among the flotsam and jetsam of the centuries, while rare Damara terns fly overhead. Colonies of Cape fur seals line the beaches, backed by patrolling jackals in search of an easy meal. Tree skeletons dot the sands, weathered by wind and sea, and bleached whale bones testify to a once-profitable whaling industry in these waters.

Inland Strandloper rock circles are found in several areas of higher moisture near the coast. Probably made by Khoisan people, some of these are simply circles, the remains of shelters used by hunter-gatherers (Strandlopers, or beachcombers) who lived near the shore. Others are more elaborate, covering larger areas and laid out in lines, and it's speculated that perhaps they were hunting blinds – which suggests that the area had a denser population of game in relatively recent (in geological terms) times.

Lichen fields and welwitschia plants These are widespread on gravel plains throughout the Namib. However, here they are at their most extensive and usually in pristine condition. In several places there are clearly visible vehicle tracks which have left a lasting impression on the lichens. These can be precisely dated by historical records.

The roaring dunes are one of the most amazing experiences on the coast. If you slide down one of the steep lee sides, the sand makes an amazing and unexpected loud noise which reverberates through the whole dune. It really has to be felt to be believed, and gets even louder when you slide a whole vehicle down the dune! One theory links the 'roar' with electrostatic discharges between the individual grains of sand when they are caused to rub against each other. Why some dunes 'roar' and others don't remains a mystery – but there are other roaring dunes: some in the Namib south of the Hoanib River, and in Witsand Nature Reserve in South Africa's northern Cape.

16

The Kunene Region

The huge region of Kunene is Namibia's least densely populated area and comprises one of Africa's last wildernesses. Stretching from the coastal desert plain in the northwest it rises into a wild and rugged landscape in the interior. Slow-growing, drought-resistant trees cling to rocky mountains, and wild grass seeds wait dormant on the dust plains for showers of rain.

Because of the low population in the northern parts of this region, and the spectacularly successful Community Game Guard scheme (see box, page 15), there are relatively good populations of wildlife here, living beyond the boundaries of any national park. This is one of the last refuges for Namibia's black rhinos, which survive and thrive in this region by ranging far and wide and instinctively knowing where the seasonal plants grow.

Kunene is also home to Namibia's famous desert-adapted elephants. Some naturalists have previously cited their long legs and proven ability to withstand drought as evidence that they are in fact a subspecies of the African elephant. Though this is not now thought to be the case, these remarkable animals are certainly adept at surviving in the driest of areas, using their astonishing knowledge of the few water sources that exist.

Historically the Kunene region has been split into two areas: Damaraland in the south, and Kaokoland in the north. Together these used to be known as the Kaokoveld. However, more recently the use of the term Kaokoveld has become blurred and it is now sometimes used to mean just Kaokoland, in the north. Although the whole of the region covered in this chapter is now officially known as Kunene Region, we have retained the old names as they are still commonly in use. This chapter divides Damaraland into southern and northern parts because, for the visitor, the north of Kunene is very different from the south.

Southern Damaraland's most interesting places are easily accessible in your own 2WD vehicle. This is an area that is easy to explore for yourself, based at one of the camps or lodges. The main attractions are the mountains of Spitzkoppe and Brandberg, the wealth of San rock art at Twyfelfontein, the Petrified Forest, and various rock formations.

Northern Damaraland attracts visitors to its scenery, landscapes and more numerous animals – and is best visited by driving yourself to one of the huge, private or community conservancies: Palmwag, Etendeka, Torra or Khoadi-Hoas (properly spelled ≠Khoadi-//Hôas). Joining a guided 4x4 safari starting from one of these bases is the best way to appreciate the area.

Kaokoland is different. North of Sesfontein and the Hoanib River, there are few campsites and only a handful of very remote lodges. This is the land of the Himba (page 88), a traditional, pastoral people whose homelands push up into Angola, relying on their herds of drought-resistant cattle for a livelihood. Their villages are situated by springs that gush out from otherwise dry riverbeds.

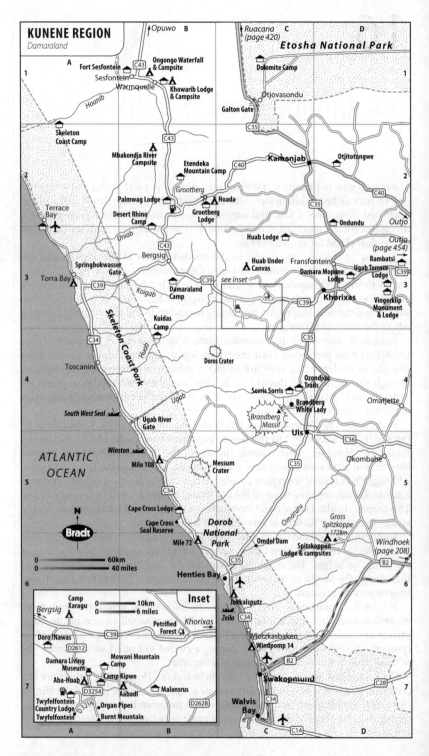

KUNENE REGION
Damaraland

Opuwo

Fort Sesfontein

Ongongo Waterfall & Campsite

Sesfontein

Warmquelle

Khowarib Lodge & Campsite

Hoanib

Skeleton Coast Camp

Mbakondja River Campsite

Etendeka Mountain Camp

Grootberg

Palmwag Lodge

Hoada

Terrace Bay

Desert Rhino Camp

Grootberg Lodge

Uniab

Bergsig

Huab Lodge

Huab Under Canvas

see inset

Springbokwasser Gate

Torra Bay

Koigab

Damaraland Camp

Kuidas Camp

Doros Crater

Toscanini

Skeleton Coast Park

Huab

Ugab

South West Seal

Ugab River Gate

ATLANTIC OCEAN

Winston

Mile 108

N

Bradt

0   60km
0   40 miles

Cape Cross Lodge

Cape Cross Seal Reserve

Messum Crater

Ruacana (page 420)

Etosha National Park

Dolomite Camp

Otjovasondu

Galton Gate

Kamanjab

Otjitotongwe

Ondundu

Outjo

Outjo (page 454)

Fransfontein

Damara Mopane Lodge

Huab Under Canvas

Bambatsi

Ugab Terrace Lodge

Khorixas

Vingerklip Monument & Lodge

Ozondjou Trails

Sorris Sorris

Brandberg White Lady

Brandberg Massif

Uis

Omatjette

Okombahe

Omaruru

Gross Spitzkoppe 1728m

Windhoek (page 208)

Dorob National Park

Mile 72

Omdel Dam

Spitzkoppen Lodge & campsites

Henties Bay

Jakkalsputz

Zeila

Wlotzkasbaken

Windpomp 14

Swakopmund

Walvis Bay

Inset

Bergsig

Camp Xaragu

0   10km
0   6 miles

Khorixas

Doro !Nawas

Petrified Forest

Damara Living Museum

Mowani Mountain Camp

Aba-Huab

Camp Kipwe

Aabadi

Malansrus

Twyfelfontein Country Lodge

Twyfelfontein

Organ Pipes

Burnt Mountain

Most of Kaokoland's remote roads need high-clearance 4x4 vehicles and are dangerous for unprepared visitors. Although the main C43 that runs north to Epupa on the Angolan border, and the D3701, which links the C43 to the Kunene River, are both now graded, they should still be treated with respect; graders scarcely cope with the C43, never mind the D road. If you're an independent driver planning to explore further afield you will need to organise your own expedition: two or more fully equipped 4x4s, with experienced drivers and enough fuel and supplies for a week or more. This isn't a place for casual or inexperienced visitors.

For less intrepid travellers, the best way to visit is by air, or with one of the more experienced local operators who know the area well – and understand the potential dangers.

Throughout the Kaokoland area, if you're driving yourself and see local people hitchhiking, bear in mind there is no public transport up here. In such a remote, rural area, Namibians will often stop to help if there is a chance to cram an extra body into their vehicle. It is up to you whether you give local people lifts, but your insurance will not cover them, so make sure you consider the risk you're taking.

SOUTHERN DAMARALAND

With several very accessible attractions, including the UNESCO World Heritage Site at Twyfelfontein, southern Damaraland is an easy area to visit yourself. Because of the region's sparse population, it's wise to travel with at least some basic supplies of food and water. If you plan to explore the area's great mountains – Brandberg and Spitzkoppe – then coming fully equipped to camp and look after yourself will give you the greatest flexibility.

SPITZKOPPE (*Day visit N$60 pp, plus N$80 per vehicle; permits obtainable from the campsite*) At the far southern end of the Kunene Region lies a small cluster of sculpted red granite mountains, rising from the flat gravel plains that make up the desert floor. These include Spitzkoppe, Klein Spitzkoppe and the Pondok Mountains, of which the highest – at 1,728m – is Spitzkoppe. Its resemblance to the famous Swiss mountain earned it the name of the Matterhorn of Africa, while the extreme conditions found on its faces, towering more than 600m above the surrounding plains, ensured that it remained unclimbed until 1946.

Soaring above the craggy rocks are falcons, buzzards and eagles, while lower down you may be lucky enough to spot the two endemics that inhabit the mountains: the white-tailed shrike, and Monteiro's hornbill. Rock hyrax are visibly at home in the caves and crevices, but rather more secretive are leopard, though occasionally you may look up to find yourself being watched from a high vantage point.

Getting there and away Spitzkoppe – along with the campsite and both lodges – is reached along the D3716. From Henties Bay, take the D1918 (also signed as the M43) eastward for 103km, then turn left on to the D3716. Coming from Usakos, take the Henties Bay turn-off after 23km on the B2 and follow it for about 18km before taking a right turn on to the D3716. From Uis, leave on the C36 to Omaruru, but turn right on to the D1930 after only 1km. It's then about 75km to the right turn on to the D3716.

Where to stay The established campsite at Spitzkoppe was joined by an upmarket lodge in 2016, with the tented lodge to be brought into the fold in 2019. All are on a 500ha tract of community-owned land, and are run in partnership with the local community.

Spitzkoppen Lodge [394 D6]
(15 chalets) m 081 850 2566; reservations 064
464144; e reservations@logufa.com; www.
spitzkoppenlodge.com. Some 7km from the
campsite, & tucked between giant boulders on
its own 32ha reserve, the lodge is dwarfed by the
looming presence of Spitzkoppe itself. Its chalets,
raised on low stilts, are not unlike mobile homes
in construction, but canvas roofs, soft turquoise
fabrics, zebra-skin rugs & superb photographs give
another feel entirely, & private verandas take in the
extensive views. Golf buggies are on hand if you
can't face the trek of up to 10mins to the hub. Here,
a walkway spirals up, linking the reception & curio
shop with the restaurant, bar & a cooling pool set
into the rocks – & with a great sundowner view.
Guests are free to explore on foot, & – in addition
to other activities in the area (see below) – can go
on guided bicycle tours, try a spot of horseriding,
or take a 2hr guided drive (N$250 pp), which
encompasses attractions such as Bushman art in
the main reserve & areas such as the Zebra Pool
within the lodge's own reserve. With excellent food
& attentive service, it adds up to a well-thought-
out & very well-run lodge in a dramatic location.
DBB N$4,280/6,960 sgl/dbl. **$$$$$$**

Spitzkoppe Bush Camps [394 D6]
(10 tents) Contact via Spitzkoppe Campsites (see
below). Coming into the same fold as the campsite
in 2019, this is to be redeveloped with a simpler
focus than the lodge, with tented accommodation
& meals cooked over open fires.
Å Spitzkoppe Campsites [394 D6] m 081
270 5533; e pg@spitzkoppe.com, accounts@
spitzkoppe.com, reservations@logufa.com; www.
spitzkoppe.com. Beyond the gauntlet of villagers
selling jewellery, crafts & stones, this extensive
but quiet campsite has a spectacular location
surrounding Spitzkoppe itself. Dotted across a wide
area at the foot of the rocks, its numerous secluded
pitches, each for up to 8 campers, have private
braai facilities & long-drop toilets. Hot showers
& flushing toilets are found in an ablution block
close to the site entrance, along with a restaurant
(⏰ 07.30–21.00 daily; book on arrival). Here
you can also purchase drinks, provisions such as
firewood & braai packs, & a few souvenirs. With a
strong emphasis on sustainability, & all proceeds
going back into the local community, this campsite
is well worth supporting. Camping N$170 pp. **$$**

What to see and do Nowadays, to explore the mountains you must have a guide, who can be organised from the campsite. A guided tour (N$60 pp/2hrs up to 4 people) takes in some of the rock-art sites that litter the mountains – including Small Bushman's Paradise. Those in the verdant valley known as Bushman's Paradise, at the extreme eastern end of the hills, are usually reached via a leisurely walk or a steep 30m climb using chain 'ropes' – and sadly have been vandalised (yes, even here).

Because of their height and proximity to the ocean, these mountains receive more fog and precipitation than most, much of which runs off their smooth granite sides to form small pools. These are ideal places to search for the shrimps and invertebrates that have adapted to the environment's extremes by laying drought-resistant eggs.

Hiking and climbing Spitzkoppe's lower slopes provide some challenging scrambles. There are several hiking trails of varying distances, for which a guide (1 for up to 10 participants) is compulsory; this can be booked on arrival.

For experienced and very fit walkers, there are three designated longer hikes: the Pondok, Matterhorn and Bushman Circle routes, taking approximately 4½ hours, 6–8 hours and around 7 hours respectively. Though no specialist climbing gear is required, these involve some steep ascents and a certain amount of scrambling. Gross Spitzkoppe itself, however, is exclusively for experienced climbers with their own gear. To find out about this, contact the Namibia Mountain Club (www.mcnam.org).

UIS Once known as Uis Mine, this small town was effectively an extension of the tin mine which dominated it until 1990. When the mine closed, much of the town's

The discovery of tin deposits in the Uis area was made in the early 20th century, but it was not until 1924 that small-scale extraction was carried out. This continued until the end of the 1950s, when the South African state-owned company, ISCOR, set out to realise the commercial potential of the mine.

Full-scale production started in the early 1960s. This was an opencast mine, for several years the world's largest hard-rock tin-mining operation. Materials were transported from the pits by truck and the waste dumped in huge white heaps, which continue to dominate the town. Some 84,000 tonnes of tin were extracted over the years, much of it low-grade ore. This, however, was expensive to process, and by 1990 the business was rapidly losing money. The cost of production, together with a downward spiral in the market price of tin, finally led to the closure of the mine in 1990. Around 2,000 jobs were lost, and the small town that had grown up to support the workers was left destitute.

In recent years, a little artisanal tin mining has started again and local people hope that the mine will once again bring wealth to the area. Meanwhile, the white slag hills of mined and crushed rock are used as a playground for hikers and trail bikers, while the groundwater lake in the middle of the mine area is used as a fish farm.

population left, but for those who remained, tourism has become an important source of income.

The tourist information office at the eastern entrance to the village comes courtesy of a government grant. While practical information is in short supply, more rewarding are the display panels about the mine and local rock art, as well as the adjacent coffee shop, some clean toilets, and a small selection of curios. For something more individual, try the UIDAGO Weaving Centre.

Where to stay and eat In addition to the following places in Uis town itself, relatively nearby options include Brandberg White Lady Lodge and Campsite, Ozondjou Trails and the high-end Sorris Sorris Lodge (page 399).

Brandberg Restcamp (5 self-catering flats, 4 poolside rooms, 2 backpacker dorms, camping) 064 504038; e brandberg@ africaonline.com.na; www.brandbergrestcamp. com. Under the management of the enthusiastic, if somewhat eccentric, Basil Calitz, the Brandberg Restcamp is an unusual, no-frills complex. It was once the tin mine's recreation centre – which explains the badminton court, table tennis & 25m pool. Spilling out from the restaurant & bar is a shaded poolside terrace with dining tables. B/fast, a light lunch (served à la carte) & dinner (*3-course set menu N$180*) are open to non-residents, as is the Old Prospectors' Pub – complete with dartboard & an unusual L-shaped pool table. There's free Wi-Fi, a TV room & even occasional live music.

Guests choose from en-suite twin or backpackers' rooms (both with fans, the former with AC & the latter with 2 sets of bunks), 2-bedroom flats (each sleeping 6, with en-suite bathrooms, living area & kitchenette), poolside twin rooms where b/fast is included & a campsite with electric points & ablution block.

Basil's enthusiasm for the region & its geology makes him a fascinating guide. A sundowner tour (*N$150 pp*), especially to the old Uis tin mine, is a must. Other trips (*all min 2 people*) include desert elephant tracking (*May onward; N$1,500 pp*), '360 degrees around the Brandberg' (*N$2,500 pp*) & an excursion to Spitzkoppe. Geological tours of 1–2 days with a qualified geologist need to be organised well in advance. If you pitch up here, do take a beer bottle or beer mat to add to

Basil's collection in the bar. *Self-catering N$300 pp (max 6); B&B poolside room N$700/1,200 sgl/ dbl; backpacker N$300 pp; camping N$150 pp.* **$$-$$$**

🏠 **Uis White Lady B&B & Camping** (13 rooms, camping) 📞 064 504102; m 081 128 0876; e whitelady@iway.na; www.namibweb. com/whiteladyuis.htm. Clearly signposted from the entrance to town, this is the original White Lady guesthouse, built in 2001 & restored in 2006 by Namibian-born owner Analene van Dyk. Tile-floored rooms with high, thatched roofs & ceiling fans/AC are designed to keep cool; each has dbl or twin beds, a fridge & coffee/tea facilities. Alongside is a swimming pool surrounded by artificial lawn (drought put paid to their grass),

with b/fast served in the thatched lapa with its own kitchen. The shaded campsite is spotlessly clean with neatly separated pitches, electrical points & a separate braai area. Wi-Fi is available. *N$994.50/1,404 sgl/dbl; camping N$160 pp.* **$$-$$$**

✖ **Montis Usti Restaurant** Cnr Uis & Sports sts; m 081 257 1307. Named after the Brandberg acacia tree (*Senegalia montis-usti*), which is endemic to this area, the Montis Usti is owned & managed by Wilma De Klerk, whose sister owns the White Lady B&B. In the whitewashed, barn-like restaurant they serve b/fast, light lunches & steaks in the evening (*N$150*). There's a separate take-away area next door & a small terrace with BBQ at the back. **$$$**

Other practicalities Uis **fuel station**, which also handles punctures and basic repairs, may not excel in visitor amenities but it can help with the essentials. Almost opposite is the Brandberg Restcamp (⏰ *06.00–21.00 daily*). Adjacent to this is the Brandberg **supermarket** (⏰ *07.30–17.30 Mon–Fri, 08.00–16.00 Sat–Sun*), selling basic foodstuffs.

What to see and do Although many visitors to Uis are en route to somewhere else, the area has two strong draws. For most people, the nearby Brandberg Massif (see below), now a national monument in recognition of the importance of the wealth of San art secreted among its rocks, is the greatest attraction.

Rather less obvious as an excursion is a visit to the opencast tin mines themselves. There are no organised tours as such, but Basil Calitz at Brandberg Restcamp regularly takes visitors up in the evening for a sundowner. With their combination of desolation and stunning scenery, the old mines would make a great film set. Should you visit alone, don't attempt to swim in the water, however tempting. Its mineral content is high, and the depth, as well as the near impossibility of access, makes it unsafe for swimming.

If you're interested in **geology**, Uis and the surrounding area is well worth exploring, with even the shortest walk in the hills likely to throw up something of interest. It's straightforward enough to set out on foot from Uis, but for guided tours contact Basil at Brandberg Restcamp.

BRANDBERG Measuring about 30km by 23km at its base and 2,573m at its highest point, this ravine-split massif of granite – Namibia's highest mountain – totally dominates the surrounding desert plains. The dome was formed by volcanic activity in the Cretaceous period 130 million years ago, when the South Atlantic Ocean was being formed. The region remains a minor earthquake zone, with a harmless quake of 5.6 magnitude recorded in 2009 (Nambia's largest on record), and a series of small tremors felt in 2018.

Designated a national monument in 1951, and now under consideration for UNESCO World Heritage Site status, the mountain contains one of the world's richest galleries of rock art, executed between 1,000 and 6,000 years ago. The most famous of the art works – and fortunately for visitors among the most accessible – is the White Lady.

Getting there and away Though you cannot miss seeing it while driving in the vicinity, getting to Brandberg without driving over the fragile lichen plains needs thought. Its eastern side, around the Tsisab Ravine, is easily reached in an ordinary car via the D2359, a turning west off the C35 about 14km north of Uis on the way to Khorixas. This is the location of a ranger post where guides are on hand to take visitors into the hills, and it is from this point that visitors can see the famous White Lady (Witvrou in Afrikaans) rock painting.

If you have a 4x4 vehicle you can also use the rough tracks that turn towards the massif from the north, west and south, off the D2342, starting some 14km southwest of Uis on the Henties Bay road.

If you are heading out to the coast, then the D2342 and D2303 are passable in a 2WD. The D2342 has some sharp turns, though the spectacular scenery and a profusion of welwitschia plants make it worth the journey. In the past, these roads, particularly the D2303 as it approaches the Ugab River, have been in poor shape, but they are now graded a couple of times a year, so should usually be more accessible.

Where to stay In addition to several places to stay in nearby Uis, the Ugab Valley has its own lodge and campsite (also known as the Ugab Campsite), close to the mountains. Two newer, more luxurious camps are located further up the valley.

Brandberg White Lady Lodge [394 C4] (15 rooms, 8 chalets, 6 tents, camping) 064 684004; m 081 791 3117; e ugab@iway.na; www.brandbergwllodge.com. Beautifully situated at the foot of the Brandberg, this lodge is clearly signposted from the D2359, from where it's a further 11km along a sandy but easily navigable track.

This is a joint venture with the Tsiseb Conservancy, & most staff come from the local community. The central garden & pond are overlooked by a terrace with chairs & tables, shaded by passion fruit & an Angolan bean climber. Behind, there's a thatched, brick-built dining area, & a separate bar & lounge with soft sofas, all decked out in dark wood. The 2 swimming pools provide a welcome chance to cool off.

Guest accommodation is mostly scattered away from the central areas, so it's very quiet. There are 2 blocks of rather small en-suite twin or family rooms with bamboo ceilings & roof fans, but well-spaced individual stone-built chalets are cooler & offer greater privacy at the same price. Dotted further out across the large property are pre-erected, 2-bed 'Sahara Deluxe' tents on stone platforms, each with open-air ablution facilities & BBQ area. Finally, there's self-camping on a level, sandy site under camelthorn shade with 6 shared, simple, clean ablutions. Each pitch has water, BBQ & a rubbish bin, with firewood available. Overlanders have a separate site & their own ablutions.

While for many visitors this is a base from which to explore the Brandberg, various drives are on offer for a min of 5 people: sundowner (N$250 pp), scenic drive (N$350 pp) & elephant drive (N$450 pp). DBB N$1,550/2,650 sgl/dbl; tent N$1,310/2,150 sgl/dbl; camping N$150 pp, plus vehicle N$40. $$–$$$$

Sorris Sorris Lodge [394 C4] (9 chalets, inc 1 suite) m 081 100 6677; e reservations@ namibia-exclusive.com; www.namibia-exclusive. com. This desert designer lodge, opened in 2015 on the private concession of the same name, hugs the rocky landscape above the Ugab River, near the D2319. It is signposted off the C35 north of Uis, but you will need a 4x4 to reach it via the rough track. You can also drive to Sorris Sorris up the Ugab riverbed: it's about 12km from Brandberg White Lady Lodge. In keeping with the exclusive style of Sorris Sorris & the nature of its design & architecture (multiple unprotected edges & drop-offs), they don't accept children under 10.

The dominating central area consists of a partly open-sided, roofed terrace with folding glass windows & an outside deck & firepit area, all built to exploit the views to the max. The meals & drinks served are of a very high standard, with a 6-course tasting menu for dinner & lots of creative ideas emerging from the kitchen. A good-sized, unheated pool is built into the deck near the main lounge, & Wi-Fi is available up here in the common areas.

The guest chalets are reached by wooden walkways & flights of steps that zigzag across the boulder-strewn hillside. Externally the rooms look like pre-fab garages, but the interiors are beautifully designed in an elegant style somewhat reminiscent of a sauna, with plenty of washed, lightwood timber, pale colours & minimal clutter. The very large beds face the striking Ugab Valley landscape through full-height glass. Behind them, & raised above bedroom level, is a fully open bathroom, with a washbasin in the plinth behind the bed, & a freestanding bathtub by the glazed back wall. A partially glazed shower cubicle occupies a back corner of the bathroom area (beware: you need to be close friends to share one of these rooms as privacy is not guaranteed while showering), while a toilet (thankfully with a door) occupies the other corner. At the front of each chalet is a delightful, shaded deck, furnished with recliners & cushioned bench seating.

Activities focus on wildlife & landscape drives in search of the area's black rhinos (seen roughly twice a month) and less elusive elephants, which are usually tracked down eventually somewhere along the sandy Ugab River course. *FBA N$17,210/27,758 sgl/dbl.* **$$$$$$**

🏠 **Ozondjou Trails** [394 C4] (9 tents) 📞083 700 0063; e travel@namibia-tracks-and-trails; www. namibia-tracks-and-trails.com. Ozondjou Trails opened in 2016 on the north bank of the Ugab. To reach the camp, turn left (west) just north of the C35 bridge over the Ugab & follow the signs about 4.5km to the southwest. It's also possible to reach the camp by driving northeast along the Ugab riverbed from Brandberg White Lady Lodge (32km away) or Sorris Sorris (24km).

Sited above the usually dry river, & facing impressive cliffs, this is a rustic-luxury bush camp in a remote location. Its decent-sized en-suite tents – 2 twins, 1 trpl – are mounted on platforms, with plumbed bathrooms. The central area consist of a shady lounge & dining area where meals are eaten communally, & a nearby firepit area overlooking the ephemeral river. Power is solar-generated & water comes from a solar-powered borehole.

Bush walks & sundowners, game drives in search of desert-adapted elephants & other mammals, & excursions to visit a local farm & school are all part of the stay, which is for a min of 2 nights. The camp has a good link with the Elephant Human Relations Aid (EHRA) organisation, whose base camp is close by. *FBA 2 nights N$13,057/17,410 sgl/dbl, inc most drinks, exc spirits.* **$$$$$**

What to see and do Two attractions – the area's rock art, and the opportunities for climbing in the mountains – are drawing increasing numbers of visitors to the Brandberg. Walking alone into the mountains is no longer permitted, so you'll need to take a guide from the Dâureb Mountain Guide Centre (m *081 203 0537*) – contact on the day is fine for guided day trips, but for multi-day excursions on the Brandberg you will need to plan further in advance, and obtain a permit from the National Heritage Council (see opposite).

Rock paintings This area has been occupied by San Bushmen for thousands of years and still holds a wealth of their artefacts and rock paintings. Only a fraction of these have been studied in detail, and some are undoubtedly still to be found. The richest section discovered so far is the Tsisab Ravine, on the northeastern side of the massif. Here one painting has been the subject of much scholarly debate since its discovery by the outside world in 1918: the famous White Lady of Brandberg (see box, opposite). Further up the Tsisab Ravine there are many other sites, including the friezes within the 'Girls' School', 'Pyramid' and 'Ostrich shelters'.

Guided walks to see the paintings (*2hr White Lady N$50 pp, N$20 per vehicle*) are organised at the Dâureb Mountain Guide Centre. Initially these follow the riverbed, taking in some of the area's flora and fauna on the way, including the tall endemic Brandberg acacia (*Senegalia montis-usti*) with its red trunk, and the khori or mustard bush (*Salvadora persica*). Families of rock hyraxes, or dassies, make their homes among the rocks, while colourful lizards dart in and out of the

THE WHITE LADY OF BRANDBERG

The figure of the 'White Lady' stands about 40cm tall and is central to a large frieze which apparently depicts some sort of procession, in which one or two of the figures have animal features. In her right hand is a flower, or perhaps an ostrich egg-cup, while in her left she holds a bow and some arrows. Unlike the other figures, this one has been painted white from below the chest. The coloration and form of the figure are reminiscent of some early Mediterranean styles and, together with points gleaned from a more detailed analysis of the pictures, this led early scholars to credit the painters as having links with Europe. Among the site's first visitors was the Abbé Henri Breuil, a world authority on rock art who studied these paintings and others nearby in the late 1940s, and subsequently published four classic volumes entitled *The Rock Paintings of Southern Africa* (page 575). He concluded that the Lady had elements of ancient Mediterranean origin.

More recent scholars consider that the people represented are indigenous, with no European links, and they regard the White Lady as being a boy, covered with white clay while undergoing an initiation ceremony. Yet others suggest that the painting is of a medicine man. Whichever school of thought you prefer, the White Lady is well signposted and – though somewhat faded – worth the 40-minute walk needed to reach the site.

If you wish to get more out of the rock art, then Breuil's books cannot be recommended too highly – though as beautifully illustrated antique Africana they are difficult to find, and expensive to buy. More accessible, but well worth a visit, is the exhibition on rock paintings at the Alte Feste and State Museum in Windhoek (page 203).

shrubby vegetation. The walk to the White Lady is relatively flat and not particularly challenging, with just a few rocky areas and a short climb at the end, but even in the early morning the heat is intense, so go prepared with a hat and plenty of water. The site itself is fenced, and to prevent further damage to the painting, flash photography is not permitted.

Climbing With the highest point in Namibia and some good technical routes in a very demanding environment, the Brandberg massif attracts serious mountaineers as well as those in search of a few days' interesting scrambling. Regardless of your climbing experience, an official guide must accompany you on your excursion, and you'll need to get a permit (*N$150*) well in advance. These can be obtained either in person from the National Heritage Council (NHC) offices in Windhoek (*52 Robert Mugabe Av;* 061 244375; 08.00–17.00 Mon–Fri), or by emailing Bertold Karipi at the NHC (e *bkaripi@nhc-nam.org*). While in theory a permit takes one–two days to prepare, allow plenty of time to avoid disappointment. Once your permit is issued, a guide will be organised for you at the Brandberg and you'll be supplied with their contact details. The costs of a typical climb will be N$600 for you and your guide, and you'll need to be fully self-sufficient with tents, sleeping bags, food and drink. Adequate safety precautions are crucial, too, as the temperatures can be extreme and the mountain is very isolated.

If you'd prefer to let someone else do the organising, contact Basil Calitz at Brandberg Restcamp in Uis (page 397), but do note that it's essential to contact him at least a month in advance, to allow time to organise a permit.

TWO CRATERS In the remote west of southern Damaraland, the Messum and Doros craters are relatively close to accessible areas, yet are themselves very remote. The only practical way to get in here is with a guide who knows the area – as for safety's sake you need back-up in case of problems.

Messum Crater
Southwest of Brandberg, straddling the boundary of the Dorob National Park, Messum Crater is an amphitheatre of desert where once there was an ancient volcano, more than 22km across. Now two concentric circles of mountains ring the gravel plains here. Messum was named by the man who first described it, Captain W Messum, who explored the coast of southwest Africa from the sea, in around 1846–48, and ventured as far inland as what later became known as the Brandberg. It's possible to climb down to the salt-pan at the bottom of the crater, where there are also rock engravings. If you want to visit the area you will need to be self-sufficient and have a fully supplied 4x4 expedition of at least two vehicles.

Doros Crater
Some 35km northwest of Brandberg, and 15km southwest of Twyfelfontein, is the remote Doros Crater (or Doros Craters, as the joined pair are sometimes called). The geology is interesting here, and there's evidence of early human habitation. Once again, you'll need a full 4x4 expedition to get into this area.

KHORIXAS
Khorixas used to be the administrative capital of the old 'homeland' of Damaraland. Now it is less important, but it is conveniently placed between Swakopmund and Etosha. Because of this, and its accessibility by tarred road from the east, Khorixas makes a good base for visiting southern Damaraland, with several good lodges within striking distance. If you stop in town, keep an eye on your things, and be ready for persistent pestering from impoverished locals trying to sell you souvenirs – such as a key ring with your name magically carved on it.

⌂ Where to stay
There are a few accommodation options in Khorixas town, and several others in the surrounding area (see opposite).

⌂ **iGowati Country Hotel** (29 rooms, camping) 📞067 331592; e igowati@mweb.com. na; www.igowatilodge.com. Right in the centre of Khorixas, opposite the fuel station, iGowati Country Hotel is something of a peaceful oasis, with its well-kept grounds & cool fountains, & it makes a good overnight or lunch stop. Efficient & welcoming, it has a comfortable restaurant (⊕ *all day*), with more tables by the pool, serving b/fast, lunch & dinner (*N$100/150/200*). There's also a bar & curio shop. Uncluttered en-suite rooms run in a curved thatched block overlooking a central lawn. Each has twin beds, or a dbl bed with twin loft room. Camping is at the back, with power & braai facilities, & some pitches with private ablutions. *Room N$500; camping N$150 pp.* **$$**

⌂ **Khorixas Restcamp** (28 chalets, 10 rooms, camping) reservations 📞061 285 7200; e reservations@nwr.com.na; www.nwr.com.na/ resorts/khorixas-camp. In a convenient position, just 1km west of town along the D2625, this old restcamp was significantly upgraded in 2009 & undergoing further work in 2018. The modern en-suite chalets have AC, linen, kitchenette & BBQ. The campsite has 20 pitches with electricity, BBQ & tables under thatch. The restaurant with bar offers an à la carte menu of grills & steaks with tables both inside & around a large pool. A shop in the reception area sells the basics. *Chalet N$620–800/940–1,300 sgl/dbl; sgl room N$410–450; camping N$250 pp.* **$$$**

Other practicalities
The town has a reliable 24-hour Engen **fuel station** with an ATM, and several shops – including a **pharmacy**, an outlet for Camping Gaz, and a branch of OK Value (⊕ *daily*), which offers cashback. Opposite the fuel station and

close to iGowati Country Hotel is a **craft shop**, where a sign proclaims 'Crafts for Conservation' (⊕ *08.00–17.00 Mon–Fri*).

EAST OF KHORIXAS This area of Damaraland is the location of the Vingerklip rock pinnacle, and plenty of similarly striking Wild West-style scenery, but it's quite a way from the main attractions of southern Damaraland. For most visitors, it is best considered as a stopover en route between Etosha and the Twyfelfontein area, rather than as a destination in its own right.

Where to stay

🏠 **Damara Mopane Lodge** [394 D3] (60 chalets) reservations ☏ 061 427200, lodge ☏ 067 687185; e info@gondwana-collection.com; www.gondwana-collection.com. Situated on the C39, 20km east of Khorixas, the promising central areas & gardens of this stopover lodge are rather spoiled on first glance by utilitarian guest chalets radiating in rows beneath the mopane trees. It's all supposed to resemble a local village, & while that's rather a stretch, the place is totally redeemed by the quaint but virtuous feature of every guest bungalow having its own walled vegetable, herb & fruit garden, watered by the lodge's filtered waste water & providing produce for the kitchen that ends up on your plate in the dining room. Inside, each neatly furnished, en-suite chalet has AC & mosquito net. Set amid the lawns, & plentiful birdlife, is a very large swimming pool. *N$1,717/2,746 sgl/dbl.* **$$$$**

🏠 **Ugab Terrace Lodge** [394 D3] (16 bungalows, camping) reservations m 081 149 1488, lodge m 081 140 0179; e info@ ugabterracelodge.com; www.ugabterracelodge. com. Located on the D2743, about 14km south of the main Khorixas–Outjo rd (C39), Ugab Terrace Lodge is perched at the end of a ridge, surrounded by a stunning landscape of flat-topped mountains. The 1km access track from the D2743 is very steep in parts (though it has been paved at strategic points) so you're advised to park at the campsite & call for a lift.

The main dining area/lounge has panoramic views, with a large patio on 2 sides. The 3 linked swimming pools (2 baby pools & 1 large) are built into the stone surroundings, with great views down the valley towards the Vingerklip & nearby mesas. Comfortable, if slightly dated, bungalows are spaced out along the sides of the hill, 8 facing the sunrise & 8 the sunset. Each has twin beds, an en-suite bathroom with a shower, ceiling fans & a small balcony. Activities focus on walking, as well as nature drives & stargazing – & the only 2

ziplines in Kunene (650m & 880m; *N$270 pp for the 880m zip; N$400 for both*). *DBB N$2,000/3,000 sgl/dbl; camping N$190 pp.* **$$–$$$$$**

🏠 **Vingerklip Lodge** [394 D3] (24 bungalows, honeymoon suite) ☏ 067 290319; reservations m 081 786 2310; e reservations@vingerklip.com. na; www.vingerklip.com.na. Just 1km south of the Vingerklip itself, on the D2743 east of Khorixas, this lodge has been designed to take advantage of the scenery. From the top, a thatched seating area with 360° views looks down over a series of terraces, where 2 swimming pools, a spa pool, bars, a braai area & sunloungers share the equally breathtaking views, many of them overlooking the lodge's waterholes.

Vingerklip's small bungalows, spread out along the hillside, are modern & attempt to be stylish, but are not particularly luxurious. On the ground floor, each bungalow has 2 twin/dbl en-suite rooms, with a digital safe & private terrace. In addition, the left room has a 1st-floor loft sleeping 2 children.

The bungalows' strongest point is a stunning view – though for the best panoramas you'll have to climb up to the plateau behind the lodge, where the Heaven's Gate honeymoon suite has unbeatable views across the plains – shared with the adjacent Eagle's Nest restaurant with its eyrie-like lookout bar. If you'd like to have your dinner up here, do book in advance.

Back at ground level, the main lounge/dining area is large, & the food is buffet-style, so don't leave dinner too late, or you may find little left. Vingerklip makes a useful overnight stop, with some excellent waymarked & guided walks in the immediate area. It's also possible to organise a range of day trips, including a sundowner drive (*N$250 pp*). *DBB N$1,100/2,800 sgl/dbl; suite N$3,040/4,120 sgl/dbl.* **$$$$–$$$$$**

🏠 **Bambatsi Guest Farm** [394 D3] (7 chalets, camping) m 081 245 8803; e bambatsi@iway.

na; www.bambatsi.com. Bambatsi is off the C39 about 58km east of Khorixas, & 75km from Outjo. A 5km bumpy track leads to a plateau overlooking mopane woodlands & this pretty, owner-run establishment with a couple of affectionate dogs & wonderful views. Each chalet has en-suite shower & toilet, with a private terrace at the back overlooking the plains. Meals are served on a broad terrace (*dinner N$200*), & facilities include a large, sparkling pool. *DBB N$2,000 dbl; camping N$160 pp.* **$$$$**

Vingerklip [394 D3] (⊕ *08.00–17.00; admission N$10 pp, free to lodge guests*)

For years now the Vingerklip ('Finger Rock'), has been a well-known landmark in this area, some 61km to the east of Khorixas. Around it are the flat-topped mesas, so typical of much of Damaraland, that resemble a scaled-down version of the southwest United States' Monument Valley. They are the remains of an ancient lava flow which has largely now been eroded away.

Amid this beautiful scenery, Vingerklip is a striking, vertically balanced natural obelisk. It's an impressive sight, and similar to the once-impressive 'Finger of God' near Asab that collapsed in 1988 (page 240). You can walk to the base of the Vingergklip in 20 minutes from the lodge, or reach it from the D2743 which runs right past it. From the base, it's a 3-minute stiff hike up to the foot of the pinnacle itself.

WEST OF KHORIXAS With stunning scenery and attractions that include both the world-renowned Twyfelfontein rock engravings and the opportunity to see desert-adapted elephants, this is arguably the most popular part of Damaraland for visitors. That said, apart from the welcome bases of the various lodges, there is little in the way of facilities in this area, although a small kiosk at the junction of the C39 and the D2612 offers snacks, cold drinks and basic dried foods.

🏠 **Where to stay** Options below are listed roughly from east to west, with Huab Under Canvas further north.

⋏ Malansrus Tented Camp [394 B7] (9 twin tents) `064 416820; m 081 269 7271; e travel@ namibia-tracks-and-trails.com. Opened in 2018, 16km east of the Twyfelfontein turn-off on to the D2612, Malansrus lies on the banks of the often dry Aba Huab River. It combines a classic safari feel of green canvas tents, with a more modern & luxurious interior design featuring pale wooden furniture & copper light fittings. Both the en-suite tents & the open-sided main area are built in a shady mopane grove with views on to a set of granite kopjes close by. Half-day game drives in search of the area's desert-adapted elephants (*N$880*) & a guided excursion to the rock carvings at Twyfelfontein, Burnt Mountain & the organ pipes (*N$400*) can be combined into a full-day activity (*N$1,480*) during a stay here, with a min 2-night stay required. *FBA N$3,250/5,000 sgl/dbl, inc most drinks.* **$$$$$**

⋏ Aabadi Mountain Camp [394 B7] (16 tents, camping) m 081 368 4192; e aabadi@face2facenamibia.com; www.aabadi-mountaincamp.com. Aabadi is a no-frills place, eschewing the luxuries of many of Namibia's camps, located 300m south of the D2612, almost 8km east of the turn-off to Twyfelfontein. Well spaced around the grassy site, which is dotted with mopane trees, are plain safari tents erected on concrete plinths with a couple of chairs in front. Inside are twin beds, with a battery cum wind-up torch for light. A zipped door leads to an open-air shower & flush toilet, with a donkey boiler for hot water. Campers (max 14 per group) have 13 pitches well away from the tents, sharing bucket showers & flush toilets. At the heart of the camp is a bar & dining area under canvas (*b/fast N$120, lunch N$180, dinner N$275*) & the firepit is the focus of conversation under the stars. During May–Oct, elephants are frequent visitors to camp. *Tent N$650 pp; camping N$150 pp.* **$$–$$$**

✳🏠 Camp Kipwe [394 A7] (9 rooms, 1 suite) lodge m 081 122 2072; reservations `061 232009; e reservations@cbt.com.na; www.kipwe.com. Camp Kipwe is signposted from the D2612, almost opposite the approach to Mowani. It's a tribute to Francesca Mattei & the late Wolfgang Rapp, who initially built the camp, that their design of airy, igloo-shaped *epondoks* – Oshivambo for rooms, cooled by AC – has been retained by co-owners Mowani. Set among the kopjes with stunning views west across the surrounding plains, each room is constructed of stone with a private veranda shaded by rustic poles. The interiors are simple & modern, with twin beds & rush matting enlivened by splashes of lime green. A door leads to an open-air shower, WC & basin, artfully arranged among the rocks. The family room incorporates a children's tent with camp beds, ideal for the over 3s, & there's a suite with private lounge.

The harmonious circular theme continues into the linked lounge & dining areas, with umbrellas on a wooden deck & a firepit to the side. Kipwe appeals to a slightly younger clientele & has a greater sense of freedom, but is slightly pricier than Mowani. Climb to the top of a well-placed kopje for a sundowner, cool off in the small pool tucked among the rocks, or stretch your legs on the plains. Longer, guided walks can sometimes be organised, along with other activities at Mowani. *FBA (2 nights) N$15,220–18,240/25,440–30,480 sgl/dbl, inc 2 activities/day.* **$$$$$$$**

🏠 **Mowani Mountain Camp** [394 A7] (13 tented rooms, 2 suites) lodge m 081 142 4582; reservations 📞 061 232009; e reservations@cbt. com.na; www.mowani.com. Well signposted on the D2612, about 3km east of the junction with the D3254, Mowani is nestled between the boulders of a kopje & is reached up a sandy track 3km north of the road.

The rounded, thatched domes of its main buildings, with views across to the surrounding mountains, give the impression of a rather fine village, blending beautifully with the giant granite boulders that surround them. There's a pool hidden among the rocks, & a stunning sundowner bar to make the most of the view. Then, in the evening, the candlelit restaurant takes on a special-occasion feel, backed up by an extensive wine list – with coffee served in the lounge or around the firepit.

Dotted among the boulders are large thatch-&-canvas tented rooms; from their private verandas, 6 share the views, & the others face east. The tents are comfortable though not large, with dbl or twin beds, table fans, tea/coffee stations, safes & en-suite

showers & toilets. Of the suites, the honeymoon suite is truly special, combining colonial design with a high standard of 21st-century luxury, including a lounge area with DSTV, indoor/outdoor bath & shower, & a private pool set into the rocks.

Activities – included for those on FBA rates – take in nature drives in search of desert elephants (N$800 pp), guided walks & excursions to the attractions around Twyfelfontein (N$415 pp) – although, as elsewhere in this area, many people use the lodge as a base for driving around themselves. Mowani is far from cheap, but you get both good service & good design for your money. *DBB N$4,720–10,920/7,340–17,140 sgl/dbl; FBA (2 nights) N$11,670–14,385/19,140–23,770 sgl/ dbl.* **$$$$$$**

⛺ **Aba-Huab Community Campsite** [394 A7] 📞 067 687120; e eliasxoagub@gmail.com. Aba-Huab is owned by the entrepreneurial Elias Xoagub. Well signposted on the D3254, about 11km north of Twyfelfontein, it stands on a large site beside the (usually) dry riverbed. Shady pitches for independent travellers & groups have water, BBQ & electricity points. If you don't have your own tent, there are simple pre-erected tents (supply your own sleeping bag & mat or rent theirs) & basic rooms with en-suite facilities. As well as 3 ablution blocks with solar-heated showers & flushing toilets, there's a communal firepit, pool table & a bar where meals (b/fast N$120, lunch N$150, dinner N$180) can be prepared with advance warning. Firewood & ice are available too. *Camping own equipment N$150 pp; tent or room N$350/660 sgl/dbl.* **$$**

🏠 **Twyfelfontein Country Lodge** [394 A7] (56 rooms, 1 suite) 📞 061 374750; e twyfelfontein@com.na; www.twyfelfontein. com.na. This large, well-staffed lodge is set in a picturesque, boulder-strewn valley near the Aba-Huab River, 10km from the world-renowned rock art site of Twyfelfontein along the D3214. Indeed, close to the lodge entrance it has its own 2,000-year-old rock engravings.

The en-suite thatched rooms are built in blocks of 8, with 4 that will convert into family units. They're quite small inside (in contrast to the completely over-the-top VIP suite) with twin/dbl beds, ceiling fan & digital safe, & traditional, heavy décor with dark wood & African-print fabrics.

A very large, open-plan, thatched central area, built on 2 floors with open sides, backs on to a rocky hillside. On the 1st floor is a pleasant bar area with comfy seating, & a rather utilitarian dining hall where buffet meals are served. Below, in the grounds at the front, there's a good-sized swimming pool & small lawn area with loungers & sunshades.

While most people use the lodge as a base to drive themselves around the area, or as a stopover that's conveniently close to Twyfelfontein, walks can be arranged, as can drives in large, trucklike 4x4s holding up to 18 passengers down the Huab River in search of elephants & other wildlife (*N$600*). Stargazing is another option. The lodge has a small fuel station offering petrol & diesel & a workshop for basic repairs & punctures. *DBB N$2,490/4,140 sgl/dbl.* **$$$$$**

🏠 **Doro !Nawas** [394 A7] (17 chalets) ✆ 061 274500; e info@wilderness.com.na; www. wilderness-safaris.com. Clearly signposted, 5km from the C39, & brooding on the crest of a low hill like a dark Moorish castle, Doro !Nawas sits between the Etendeka Mountains in the north & Twyfelfontein in the south. With its exposed location & 360° panoramic views of the Damaraland plains it looks at first glance like it might have been based around an old fort. In fact it was built from scratch as a joint venture between Wilderness Safaris & the local Doro !Nawas community.

A moody darkness prevails in the natural stone walls of the guest chalets, with dark wood for the roof & heavy, stone-effect bedhead, though the cave-like feel is lightened by sliding doors leading out to a wide, secluded veranda, which – courtesy of beds that can be rolled out – makes a great place to spend a night under the stars. A roomy ablutions area incorporates 2 washbasins, separate toilet, & inside & outside showers. While the dark style won't appeal to everyone, the chalets are a good size,

individually spaced around the foot of the hill, their thatch merging into the surrounding landscape, & 2 of them combine to form a family unit. Note that Doro !Nawas has neither Wi-Fi nor AC.

Up in the 'castle', the dining room cum bar dominates the whole of one side, while stairs lead up to an open-air rooftop area that lends itself to sundowners or taking in the night sky. There's a small pool with a view, too, ensuring that you're never divorced from the beauty of the location. Attentive & well-trained staff, 70% from the local area, set out to ensure that your visit is enjoyable – even on the rare occasions when activities are on hold & lashing rain serves to intensify the brooding atmosphere.

In addition to trips in search of desert elephants, which are regularly spotted quite close to the lodge, there are guided walks, & visits to Twyfelfontein, the Organ Pipes, Burnt Mountain & the Petrified Forest, although many guests drive themselves to these attractions. *FBA N$5,810–8,860/8,950–13,560 sgl/dbl.* **$$$$$$–$$$$$$$**

⛺ **Huab Under Canvas** [394 C3] (8 tents) ✆ 061 248137; e info@ultimatesafaris.na; www. ultimatesafaris.na. Nestled deep within the Huab Conservancy, this semi-permanent camp has walk-in tents with open-air en-suite bucket showers & flush toilets. The focus here is on the remote wilderness of Damaraland within their private concession, & – with 2 dedicated rhino rangers – particularly on tracking black rhino as well as desert-adapted elephants. 'Stellar escapes' sleep outs & a multi-day walking trail are an added bonus, but you cannot visit Twyfelfontein from here. The camp can be booked only on an exclusive basis (*min 2-night stay*) as part of a longer private trip through Ultimate Safaris (page 173).

What to see and do

Twyfelfontein rock engravings [394 A7] (🕐 *08.00–17.00 daily; last booking 15.30 in winter); admission N$100 pp inc guided tour of 30–45min*) Twyfelfontein (Doubtful Spring) was named by the first European farmer to occupy the land – a reference to the failings of a spring of water which wells up near the base of the valley. The valley is also known as Uri-Ais, and seems to have been occupied for thousands of years. At one time the spring, on the desert's margins, would have attracted huge herds of wildlife from the sparse plains around, making this uninviting valley an excellent base for early hunters. This probably explains why the slopes of Twyfelfontein, amid flat-topped mountains typical of Damaraland, conceal one of Africa's greatest concentrations of rock art. The boulders that litter these slopes are dotted with thousands of paintings and ancient engravings, only a fraction of which have been recorded.

Declared a UNESCO World Heritage Site in 2007, Twyfelfontein was unusual among African rock art sites in having both engravings and paintings, though today only the engravings can be seen. Many are of animals – rhino, giraffe, lion and zebra are all identifiable – or consist of geometric motifs, which may have been maps to water sources. It is not yet known why the animal images were made: perhaps they were part of the people's spiritual ceremonies, perhaps the area was an ancient school nursery, or perhaps they were simply doodling or expressing the creative urge.

You have to be accompanied by a guide along one of two demarcated trails, which take around 30 minutes or 45 minutes (the cost is the same, whichever tour you take, and that is determined by your fitness or enthusiasm). The paths are quite uneven, and the longer route includes a little light scrambling, so you'll need stout shoes. Don't forget a hat and some water. The best time to visit is first thing in the morning or in the early evening, which is also the best time for photographs. Evening is the busiest time at the site, so try to get there before the tour buses descend. The visitor centre provides fairly comprehensive information, and is well worth a little more of your time. There's also a shaded picnic area with cold drinks for sale.

Getting there and away To reach the valley, which is well signposted, take the C39 west from Khorixas for 73km. From here, turn left on to the D2612 for almost 15km, then right on the D3254 for 6km and then left again on to the D3214 for a further 4km to reach the ticket office and museum.

Organ Pipes [394 A7] (⏲ *daily; no charge, though the man on security duty may request a tip*) If you have half an hour spare, then retrace your tracks from Twyfelfontein, and turn right (south) at the junction on to the D3254, signposted to Burnt Mountain. After 4.5km there's a flat area above a small gorge on the left. Park here and take one of the paths down, where you'll find hundreds of polyhedral columns of grey dolerite in an unusual formation resembling a small and much less impressive version of the Giant's Causeway in Northern Ireland. The columns are thought to have formed about 120 million years ago when dolerite shrank as it cooled, producing these geometric formations. Most of the columns are around half a metre to 1m in height, but some are up to 5m high.

Burnt Mountain [394 A7] (⏲ *daily; no charge*) Continuing just 1km beyond the Organ Pipes, you'll see Burnt Mountain. In the midday sun this is little more than a disappointing heap of black shale amid the dominant sandstone. But when the rocks catch the early morning or late afternoon light, the mountainside glows with a rainbow of colours, as if it's on fire.

Damara Living Museum [394 A7] (e *contact@lcfn.info;* ⏲ *daily; admission: village experience N\$90 pp, bush walk N\$70 pp; both experiences N\$150 pp*) North of the Aba-Huab River, the local Damara people have constructed a small village to showcase their culture. It is clearly signposted to the east of the D3254, just near the junction of the D2612. From the neatly demarcated parking area, two huge boulders mark the entrance to the compound, which incorporates traditional Damara houses for the chief and his wife. Visitors may have the opportunity to see how weapons, tools, jewellery and crafts are made, as well as experiencing dancing, singing and traditional games. Bush walks offer the chance to see how the Damara people foraged and hunted in the past.

16

Petrified Forest [394 B6] (⏱ *08.00–18.00 daily; admission N$100 pp inc guide*)
Signposted beside the C39, about 44km west of Khorixas, lie a number of petrified trees on a bed of sandstone. Although there are several petrified forests signposted from the C39, this site has been declared a national monument and is well worth your support. Crafts and drinks are for sale in the shop and there are toilets.

Demarcated paths lead around the site, and a tour normally takes around 30 minutes. The helpful and well-trained guides (you can't wander unaccompanied) point out some of the highlights of the petrified forest, including some ancient welwitschia plants growing among the remains. The fossil trunks are extraordinary, many of them resembling recently felled logs, complete with stone bark, and areas of gouged wood that look as if they should be soft. Some are partially buried, while others are completely exposed because the sandstone surrounding them has eroded away. It is thought the trunks were carried here by a flood or major river some 260 million years ago, and washed up on a sandbank. Subsequently sand was deposited around them, creating ideal conditions for the cells of the wood to be replaced by silica, and thus become petrified.

Desert-adapted elephants and local birdlife Most of the lodges in the area run nature drives in search of desert-adapted elephants, which are regularly seen between May and October. It is worth noting that once the rains start, the elephants

WELWITSCHIA MIRABILIS

Welwitschia, Namibia's most famous plant, is usually found growing in groups on the harsh gravel plains of the central Namib and western Kunene Region. Each plant has two, long, shredded leaves and is separated from other welwitschia plants by some distance. Individual plants appear as a tangle of foliage (some green, but mostly desiccated grey) emerging from a stubby wooden base. There is a very large example by the swimming pool at Twyfelfontein Country Lodge.

Friedrich Welwitsch, an Austrian botanist first described the plant in 1859. Since then botanists have been fascinated by the species, the only member of the *Welwitschia* genus, hence the species name *Welwitschia mirabilis* – Latin for marvellous.

Research suggests that welwitschia can live for more than 1,000 years and are members of the same group of plants that includes conifers and cycads. Although their leaves can spread for several metres and their roots more than a metre underground, it is still a mystery how they obtain water. One theory suggests that dew condenses on the leaves, and then drips to be absorbed by fine roots near the surface of the ground.

Welwitschia rely on the wind to distribute their seeds, but young plants are rare. They germinate only when the conditions are perfect, in years of exceptional rain. I was once shown one on the Skeleton Coast that was eight years old. It was minute: consisting of just two seedling leaves and no more than 2cm tall.

Their ability to thrive in such a harsh environment is extraordinary, and their adaptations are still being studied. There has even been a recent suggestion that older welwitschia plants may change the chemical constitution of the soil around them, making it harder for young plants to establish themselves nearby and compete for water and space.

retreat up the Huab River, and at the end of the season drives from some lodges can be very long, with significant stretches of time on the road. Fortunately the riverbed itself, lined with tamarisk and reeds, is an attraction in its own right. Pools attract birds from the hamerkop to the blue-cheeked bee-eater, while away from the river, keep an eye out on the plains for Rüppell's korhaan and birds of prey such as black-breasted snake eagles and lappet-faced vultures.

NORTHERN DAMARALAND

Approaching northern Damaraland from the west, along the C39, is perhaps the most interesting way to enter this region north of the Huab River. After the flat coast, you soon find the gravel plains dotted first with inselbergs, then with low chains of weathered hills. The land begins to rise rapidly: you are coming on to the escarpment, around 50km from the coast, which lies at the edge of one of the largest ancient lava sheets in the world. Some 300 million years ago, slow-motion torrents of molten lava poured over the land here in successive layers. Now these formations, the **Etendeka lavas**, dominate the scenery, with huge flat-topped mountains of a characteristic red-brown-purplish colour.

The rainfall here is very low, and the sparse covering of grasses is dotted with the large Damara milk-bush (*Euphorbia damarana*). This plant, which is endemic to this region, grows in round, spiky, clumps, perhaps 3m in diameter and 2m tall. If you break off a stem you'll reveal the poisonous milky-white latex, which protects the bushes from most herbivores, except black rhino and kudu, both of which happily eat the plant. (A tale is told of a group of local people who roasted meat over a fire of dead milk-bush stems – only to die as a result.)

If you could continue as the crow flies, northeast towards Etosha, then the land below you would become progressively less dry. Flying over the Hobatere area, you'd notice that the higher rainfall promotes richer vegetation. In the northern areas you would see an undulating patchwork of mopane scrub and open grassy plains, dotted with various trees, including the distinctive flat-topped umbrella thorn or acacia (*Vachellia tortilis*). You would have left the desert.

FAUNA Generally the wildlife populations increase as the vegetation becomes lusher in the east. In the mountains around Palmwag, Etendeka and Damaraland Camp there are resident steenbok, baboon, kudu, porcupine and the occasional klipspringer and warthog, joined by wide-ranging herds of Hartmann's mountain zebra, gemsbok and springbok. Equally nomadic but less common are the giraffe and desert-adapted elephant.

An enduring memory from here is the sight of a herd of giraffe. We watched them for almost an hour, as they skittishly grazed their way across a rocky hillside beside what is now the main C43. Their height seemed so out of place in the landscape of rocks and low trees.

Black rhino are present throughout the region, but spend most of their days sleeping under shady bushes, and so are rarely seen, even by those who live here. (Strenuous rhino-tracking trips are run by Desert Rhino Camp and Grootberg Lodge, as well as – with advance notice – by Khowarib Lodge.)

Leopard occur here, and cheetah and lion are seen periodically – it is thought there are only around 120 desert lion left in the region, as they range over huge areas in search of suitable prey resulting in significant human–wildlife conflict.

The birdlife is interesting, as several of the Kaokoveld's ten endemic species are found here. Perhaps the most obvious, and certainly the most vocal, are Rüppell's korhaan – whose early morning duets would wake the soundest sleeper. The ground-feeding Monteiro's hornbill is another endemic, not to be confused with the local red-billed hornbills. There is also the endemic Herero chat, which occurs along with its more common cousins, the ant-eating tractrac and other, more familiar chats. While not endemic, black eagles are often seen around the rockier hillsides: surely one of Africa's most majestic raptors.

Looking further east, to Hobatere and Huab, there is more vegetation, making a classic environment for big game animals. These areas can support more large mammals, and elephants are certainly more common, and more easily spotted. The desert-adapted species seen to the west are joined in Hobatere by eland, black-faced impala and Damara dik-dik. The latter two subspecies are endemic to the region. Similarly, the variety of birds becomes wider as you move east, with species that occur in Etosha often overlapping into Hobatere.

KAMANJAB On the eastern side of Damaraland, Kamanjab is a tiny town at the junction of the main C40 and C35, effectively a link between Damaraland and both Etosha and eastern Namibia. Its all-important 24-hour Shell and Total garages are the last certain fuel stop before Ruacana if you're heading north – and come as a relief to those driving south. The best shop is the MultiSave, just down the road from the Total fuel station where you can also find an unreliable ATM. The Northwest Garage also has a selection of curios and snacks and offers tyre repairs. Most people are just passing through, but the rock engravings at Peet Albert's Kopje could be worth a stop.

Where to stay and eat

Melissa's Guest House (19 rooms) \067 330055; e mgkananjab@gmail.com; www. melissasguesthouse.com. This small hotel right in the centre of town is popular for an overnight stop with both local businesspeople & tourists. Its rooms are at the back: clean & comfortable, with fans, mosi nets, a kettle for hot drinks, & en-suite shower & toilet. Dark wood lends to a cosy atmosphere to the bar & restaurant (⊕ 07.00–22.00 daily), where meals – from steaks & pizza to occasional African dishes – are available to allcomers. Massages are available from the resident beautician, & in the relaxing beer garden, a swimming pool was under construction in 2018. *N$630/1,100 sgl/dbl.* **$$$**

Kamanjab Rest Camp & Game Park Lodge (4 chalets, camping) \067 330290; m 081 823 2234; e kjbrestcamp@gmail.com; www.kamanjabrestcamp.com. 3km west of Kamanjab off the C40, this well-run restcamp is privately owned & very welcoming. Spotless twin-bed rooms are en suite, while campers share

ablutions in the large, well-designed campsite with 8 pitches. Of these, 3 have power, & all have a water tap & BBQ area. Guests can visit the small game park, home to species including oryx, kudu & springbok, or enjoy the small pool. This also makes an excellent lunch stop with the plus of home-grown salad. *N$440/660 sgl/dbl; camping N$100 pp; no credit cards.* **$$–$$$**

Oppi Koppi (15 bungalows, camping) \067 330040; e info@oppi-koppi-kamanjab.com; www.oppi-koppi-kamanjab.com. Up a side road from Melissa's Guest House, & accessed through a rather grand thatched gateway, this peaceful Belgian/Dutch-owned spot has been redeveloped to include a smart restaurant, bar & pool area. 12 'luxury' rooms have AC & an outside terrace, whereas 3 standard rooms just have fans. Pitches at the campsite are each equipped with a braai, power & drinking water, & share well maintained ablution blocks. The restaurant is open to all guests (⊕ 07.00–20.30 daily). *N$700–890/1,240–1,620 sgl/dbl; camping N$150 pp.* **$$–$$$**

Peet Albert's Kopje Set among the granite hills, some 5km east of Kamanjab to the left of the C40, this is the site of a large number of 2,000-year-old rock engravings. Many of these, including those depicting animals, were created by the

San people, while the more geometric designs were the work of the Khoi. A further attraction is the 'gong rock', a granite boulder which resounds when struck, thus gaining the name.

Although designated a national monument, the site is quite overgrown. To visit independently, you'll need to pick up the key from Oppi Koppi in Kamanjab (⏰ 07.00–22.00 daily). This is also where you pay the admission fee (N$60 pp; N$100 deposit for the key). From the gate to the entrance is a further 1.5km. There's a pamphlet entitled *The Rock-engravings at the Peet Alberts Koppie near Kamanjab*, but unfortunately getting hold of a copy is exceptionally difficult.

NORTH OF THE HUAB RIVER North of the Huab River lie a number of large **concession areas** that are set aside for tourism. These are chunks of land that the government has allocated to one operator, who has the sole use of the land for tourism purposes. Local people can live and even keep animals within some of these tourism concessions, but development is limited. With Namibia's increasing emphasis on **community conservancies**, considerable change is afoot in this area. Yet, while this is very significant for local people, the impact on visitors is likely to be less noticeable, not least because all the operators in this area have long worked closely with their local communities and to the benefit of the environment. The more upmarket lodges in these areas are not places that you can drop into for a day and expect to fully appreciate (even assuming they have space), and a visit of two or three nights is best arranged in advance.

Where to stay around Palmwag

C39 south of Palmwag

🏠 **Damaraland Camp** [394 B3] (10 chalets) Contact via Wilderness Safaris; 📞 061 247500; e info@wilderness.com.na; www.wilderness-safaris.com; advance reservations essential.

Damaraland Camp lies close to the ephemeral Huab River, along a 12km track south of the C39. The turning (✥ 20°19.464'S, 14°04.969'E) is next to a smallholding, some 33km west of the junction with the D2612 to Twyfelfontein. Although an experienced driver going slowly could negotiate the track to the camp in a 2WD that's not overloaded, a rendezvous is normally arranged at the junction. From here you'll be taken to the camp by 4x4, leaving your vehicle under the watchful eyes of a local family.

The camp consists, of square, thatched chalets on wooden platforms, some of them on high stilts to ensure a view & others lower down. Creative use of wooden poles, canvas walls, zip-up doors & reed screening has been combined with plenty of space to provide light, airy & cool accommodation. Floors are of natural wood, the lighting is subtle but effective & there are plenty of thoughtful touches, including a sensible desk, tea- & coffee-making (with water on request),

ceiling fans & a roll-down door to the bathroom for privacy. Batteries can be charged in the office.

The camp's décor, a mix of creams & soft browns, continues into the extensive main area, where a 22-seater dining table lines one side & a large pool with umbrella-shaded chairs the other, with decking at the front. With simple, almost minimalist seating, the effect is soft & uncluttered.

The area around the camp is dry & vegetation is sparse; even milk-bushes aren't present to any great extent except along the riverbed. However, there are some good welwitschia specimens on the way to the Huab River valley, which makes a good venue for drives in search of desert-adapted elephant & other wildlife. A couple of 3km trails, the Damarana & the Shepherd's trail, allow you to explore the mountains on foot, while closer at hand you can visit a local village. For longer stays, rhino tracking may be possible on request, although as the animals move freely in a vast, unfenced area, there is no guarantee of finding them.

Damaraland Camp's brand of community involvement has attracted numerous accolades & it is one of Namibia's best camps, now 40% owned & largely run by the local community. Visitors often comment on how positive & happy the atmosphere is here, so it is well worth booking 2–3 nights (an overnight stop is too short). *FBA N$6,960–13,200/10,730–20,340 sgl/dbl.* **$$$$$$–$$$$$$$**

C40 east of Palmwag

✴ 🏠 **Grootberg Lodge** [394 B2] (14 twin & 2 family chalets) \067 333212; reservations \061 228104; e reservations@grootberg.com; www. grootberg.com. Perched at the top of the Grootberg Pass, between Palmwag & Kamanjab, this lodge in the ≠Khoadi-/Hôas Conservancy was opened in 2005 & is owned by the local community. Local staff are being trained to run the lodge, with the aim of managing it themselves by 2020.

To get there, simply follow the C40 from Palmwag towards Kamanjab & you'll find the lodge entrance at the very top of the Grootberg Pass, at a commanding 1,645m. Don't attempt the extremely steep, narrow track up to the lodge: just park at the pass & the warden will arrange for you to be collected; somebody will be down to pick you up very quickly, as it's only a 5min ride in their 4x4.

Grootberg's combined attractions are a stunning location, with breathtaking views south towards the Brandberg, and excellent activities, which include regular rhino tracking with very frequent sightings.

The lodge buildings, clad in the local lava stone, are whitewashed inside, with an uncluttered, cool, relaxing décor – think comfy, neutral sofas with casual throws, classic wooden tables & chairs in the dining area, classy photographs on the walls, & a small range of well-chosen books. Outside, a wide veranda with tables & umbrellas makes the most of the view, though the vertiginous drop makes this less than relaxing for parents with young children.

Each of the twin or dbl chalets faces south, with sliding doors leading to en-suite bedrooms with handmade furniture of unpolished pine. Power is supplied from a generator: there are no sockets in the rooms but guests are welcome to charge electrical appliances in the main area.

In addition to guided walks (*from N$180*) & scenic sundowner drives (*N$570*), guests can track elephants (*N$1,370*) or rhinos (*N$1,925*), or do a Damara cultural tour (*N$750*) – all pp for 2 people min. *DBB N$2,483/3,732 sgl/dbl.* **$$$$$**

▲ **Hoada Campsite** [394 B2] (8 pitches, 4 tents) m 081 425 7141; e hoada@journeysnamibia. com; www.grootberg.com/hoada-campsite. Under the same management as Grootberg Lodge

(25km east of Grootberg Lodge on the C40), this small community campsite lies at the foot of a kopje about 200m from the road. This beautiful & secluded spot offers shady & private camping areas, & a small swimming pool cleverly built into the boulders. Each spacious campsite has its own kitchen area with running water & BBQ facilities, as well as its own outside shower with warm water & a flush toilet. The nicely put-together 'comfort' tents, on platforms, have electricity, but the self-camping pitches have no electricity or power points – and note that the only supplies available are firewood bundles (*N$90*). Hoada guests are welcome to drive to Grootberg Lodge to participate in their activities, though you have to be staying at the lodge to do their rhino tracking. *N$700/tent; camping N$205 pp.* **$$**

C35 south of Kamanjab

🏠 **Huab Lodge** [394 C3] (8 bungalows) \ 067 312070; e info@huab.com; www.huab.com; reservations \061 224712; e reservations@resdest. com.na. Huab is owned & run by Jan & Suzi van de Reep, who have worked in tourism in Namibia for years. Together with friends, they bought up a number of adjacent farms in a hilly area, around the headwaters of the Huab River. Although this land was of significance as a refuge for some of the Huab River's desert-adapted elephants, farmers had fenced the land, & didn't enjoy the elephants' feeding forays on to their farms, causing much human–wildlife conflict. With the fences down, antelope have returned, the ecosystem has reverted to its natural state & elephants are seen around the lodge more. This is a textbook demonstration of how tourism can be used to finance conservation initiatives, & is a compelling argument for encouraging ecotourism to Namibia.

The lodge is situated on the banks of the Huab (beware: if the rivers are in flood, reaching it can be difficult). It is along the D2670, well signposted from the C35 between Kamanjab & Khorixas. The approach road is 36km long, with 4 farm gates, & becomes increasingly scenic, so don't expect a quick arrival.

Huab boasts classic thatch-on-brick design, tasteful décor, a little landscaping, & lots of quality. Light, spacious bungalows, with a wide frontage & private veranda, all have 2 queen-size, extra-long beds & en-suite bathrooms with separate shower & toilet. Electricity & hot water are mostly solar & there are sockets in the bungalows. Solid, handmade Zimbabwean teak railway sleeper furniture is offset by soft furnishings that are made up at the lodge from locally designed fabrics, which are also on sale in the curio shop.

If you're in luck, Jan himself will be available to guide you for an activity. He is one of the country's best guides, so even if there's no wildlife around (& that's unusual now that the animals have repopulated the land), you'll still find the drives & walks fascinating, & have plenty to spot from the bird hide.

Huab's hospitality is excellent, with communal meals becoming relaxed, social occasions in the thatched central hub, where it's easy to feel completely at home. For total relaxation, you can bathe away the day's aches under thatch in natural hot springs, alongside a cooler tub for contrast, or treat yourself to a wellness therapy (the only extra cost). To keep in touch, there's Wi-Fi in the rooms & central area. *DBB N$2,720/5,540 sgl/ dbl Dec–Jun, N$4,586/7,240 Jul–Oct.* ☺ *All year.* **$$$$$–$$$$$$**

Palmwag to Sesfontein A veterinary fence on the C43 marks the road north towards the Palmwag and Etendeka concessions, and on to Sesfontein. The main controls at the veterinary gate are applied on your way south, when you leave the stock disease-control area to the north and have to declare any raw meat (which they will confiscate). Just north of the gate is a small fuel station owned by Palmwag Lodge (⊕ *24hrs*). Everybody seems to fill up here (note that payment for fuel is accepted only in cash). This is also the location of the airstrip.

Near here, you may come across people selling carved vegetable ivory trinkets (made from the hard, ivory-coloured seed of the makalani palm tree – *Hyphaene petersiana*), but it's as well to be suspicious of those offering you tours. They are very unlikely to be licensed guides.

North of the veterinary fence, the road grading is rougher than to the south, so it's even more important than usual to watch your speed. There are also several steep descents into riverbeds, which make this road especially challenging during the rains.

Palmwag Concession (*Admission N$70 pp/day, N$130 pp overnight, plus N$110/vehicle*) The huge Palmwag (pronounced 'Palumvag') Concession occupies an area of 5,500km² to the north of the junction of the C43 and the C40, immediately after the veterinary fence, and stretches west as far as the Skeleton Coast. It is bordered on the eastern side of the C43 by the Etendeka Concession and the ≠Khoadi-//Hôas Conservancy.

You can buy a day permit around the Palmwag Conservancy from Palmwag Lodge itself, and Twee Palms Gate (5km north of the vet fence) or the Aub Gate, further north also on the C43. However, unless you are an experienced 4x4 enthusiast, used to the terrain, and with good navigational skills (and preferably a GPS), this is not practical. One trainee guide based at Palmwag got lost in his vehicle, became disoriented, and was found severely dehydrated in the Skeleton Coast Park. It is a difficult area. The best way to see the area is to leave your car at the lodge and take one of the guided game drives. The area's ecosystem is too fragile to withstand the impact of many vehicles, and the animals are still wary of people.

Where to stay

Palmwag Lodge [394 B2] (10 tented chalets, 2 family rooms, 13 bungalows, 4 safari tents, camping) \067 333214; reservations: \061 234342; e eden@africaonline.com.na; www. palmwaglodge.com. Palmwag is the oldest lodge in the area, beautifully situated at the edge of the concession, 500m north of the veterinary fence on the west side of the road, & next to a palm-lined tributary of the Uniab River. The river often flows above ground here, & the presence of scarce water frequently draws elephants close to camp.

Something of a crossroads for travellers in the area, Palmwag attracts all sorts: South African families on camping trips, shady mineral prospectors, upmarket visitors on fly-in safaris, plus local game guards back from the bush & staying at the adjacent base of the Save the Rhino Trust (see box, below). Most people are here to relax & unwind, or to get a transfer into one of the more upmarket camps on a neighbouring concession. The 'just-passing-through' nature of much of the lodge's trade explains the proliferation of rules & notices that decorate the menus & public areas: 'No separate billing! One table, one group, one bill, one payment'; 'Wi-Fi NO – we encourage you to talk to each other.'

There's a wide range of accommodation, with all rooms being en suite, & all camp pitches have lights, power points & water. A pool bar & à la carte restaurant pump out the usual meals & snacks, & the 2 clean swimming pools have shade & loungers.

The lodge offers a good programme of activities: morning & afternoon game drives (*N$810 pp; max 6 people*), morning & afternoon guided walks (*N$230 pp*), all-day rhino tracking (*N$2,335 pp*), a Damaraland Tour (*N$2,080 pp inc lunch & drinks*) & an under-canvas sleep-out (*N$4,725 pp, min 2 people*). *Concession fees are extra. DBB N$2,840/4,540 sgl/dbl; camping N$270 pp.* **$$–$$$$$**

Desert Rhino Camp [394 B2] (8 tents) Contact via Wilderness Safaris; 061 274500; e info@wilderness.com.na; www.wilderness-safaris.com. A smart tented camp in the Palmwag Concession, taking up to 16 guests in large, Meru-style tents. Each tent is built on a low wooden platform, with large mesh windows, Velcro canvas flaps, & a good measure of style. Expect very comfortable twin beds with high-quality linen, & an en-suite bathroom with flush toilet, twin washbasins & a good hot shower.

The food is good, & activities major on rhino-tracking – usually with a guide from camp & trackers from the Save the Rhino Trust. Typically you're likely to drive around looking for tracks from the vehicle. Then, when a promising set is found, you'll get out to follow them on foot, led by the trackers. It's an excellent option if you are moderately fit & want to try to get close to one of these extraordinary beasts.

However, note that the dangers inherent in approaching big game at close quarters can be thrown into sharp contrast on such a trip. No trip to Africa (or indeed anywhere) can be guaranteed as totally safe; this is no different. If you don't follow your guide's instructions precisely, then you're likely to have 1,000kg of nimble-footed,

SAVE THE RHINO TRUST

This excellent local charity (*064 403829;* e *srt@rhino-trust.org.na; www. savetherhinotrust.org*), founded by the late Blythe and Rudi Loutit in 1982, emerged in response to the slaughter of the region's wildlife that took place in the 1970s and 1980s, when some 95% of Africa's rhinos were lost to poaching. As rhino populations shrank to near extinction, Blythe and Rudi started a pressure group to stop indiscriminate hunting in the area.

Once the worst of the hunting was stopped, SRT pioneered conservation and protection in the area, even employing convicted poachers as game scouts. Who would know better the habits of rhino, and the tricks of the hunters? Eventually, they were able to reverse the extermination of the rhino from the communal areas of the Kaokoveld – a process that has been enthusiastically supported by the chiefs and headmen, as well as by the neighbouring farming community.

This work laid the foundations for the successful community conservation programmes that now operate in Kunene. SRT's close work with local communities and the Ministry of Environment and Tourism (MET) has brought benefits to the communities through tourism revenues, as well as security for the black rhino, whose population has significantly increased since the 1980s.

SRT operates numerous daily rhino patrols, including patrols from Desert Rhino Camp, which with prior arrangement guests can join.

sharp-horned rhino heading at you very rapidly. These activities are not for the faint-hearted, so don't book in here unless you fully accept that you may be placing yourself far out of your comfort zone – & potentially in some danger. *FBA N$6,500–13,400/10,020–20,600 sgl/dbl.* **$$$$$$–$$$$$$$**

Å Campsites In addition to the lodges, there are 6 campsites dotted along the main track through the concession. These are very basic areas, with a tree for shade, & no toilet or shower facilities. It really is wild camping. Details of these, together with a map & GPS co-ordinates, are available from Palmwag Lodge or the staff at each gate. For those looking to camp outside the concession, there are several campsites close to the road between the veterinary fence & Sesfontein (page 417).

Etendeka Concession This conservancy is the location of the long-established Etendeka Mountain Camp and its new sibling, Etendeka River Camp.

Where to stay

🏠 Etendeka Mountain Camp [394 B2] (10 tents) \061 239199; e info@etendeka-namibia.com; www.etendeka-namibia.com. Etendeka is an excellent tented camp, 15km north of Palmwag (as the crow flies), on the open, rolling Etendeka lava plains. A model of sustainability, it was established by Dennis Liebenberg, who still runs it & who takes a no-frills approach to giving his guests a real experience of the Kaokoveld.

Etendeka is remote & you can't drop in here: you need to have pre-booked. Most visitors self-drive to Palmwag Lodge, where you can leave your car safely & meet the Etendeka driver for the 1½hr 4x4 transfer to the camp (normally at 16.00 – but check when you book).

Etendeka doesn't aim at luxury, but it does what it does very well. Guests are put up in decent-sized, twin-bed tents, each with a private bathroom, just outside the tent. Bathrooms are equipped with a plumbed-in hot & cold water basin, DIY bush shower (filled from your tap), flush toilet & electric light. The main dining & bar areas are under canvas, & meals are a social occasion when all the guests, plus normally Dennis & the guides, eat together around the fire (it gets chilly here in the winter), upon which much of the food is cooked. Such bush cooking has been refined to an art form, so the cuisine from the embers is impressive. An inviting, small unheated swimming pool is tucked in next to the main area, in a sheltered spot complete with sunloungers.

Activities – guided walks, scenic drives & game drives – are tailored to your interests & abilities. After an early b/fast, a normal day might include a 2–4hr walk, lunch, a few hours to relax, & perhaps a long afternoon game drive, incorporating a short hike to one of the area's mountains for a sundowner. This is a great place to come walking, though walks are usually at a fairly gentle pace.The conservancy's wildlife includes good populations of giraffe, Hartmann's mountain zebra, oryx & springbok, as well as desert-adapted elephant, & very occasionally black rhino. The striking Damara milk-bush sprouts prolifically from the stony, brown landscape all around this area, & Etendeka's guides are excellent on their plants & birds, as well as mammal identification.

The lodge is closely involved with the region's Community Game Guard scheme, & gives a proportion of its revenue to the local communities, so that they too can benefit from the income generated by visitors, & have an incentive to help preserve the region's wild game. *FBA inc transfer to camp & all drinks N$4,750/7,570 sgl/dbl.* **$$$$$$**

🏠 Etendeka River Camp (5 sleep-out platforms) \061 239199; e info@etendeka-namibia.com; www.etendeka-namibia.com. Also known as the 'Etendeka Walking Trail', for which this camp acts as the principal overnight location when you do an expertly guided 3–4 day hiking trail through the concession, Etendeka River Camp is a junior satellite camp a few km south of the main camp. Bush cooking over a fire & simple ablution arrangements are the hallmarks of an overnight stay here, but you'll sleep in comfort on camp beds mounted on sheltered platforms. Other details are as for the main Etendeka Mountain Camp. **$$$$$$**

Anabeb Conservancy Bordering the Palmwag Conservancy to the east, this narrow conservancy straddles the C43 north to Sesfontein, with animals such as giraffe, springbok, kudu and ostrich frequently seen from the road. There's a good campsite along this road between the vet fence and Khowarib:

⌂ Where to stay

⋏ Mbakondja River Campsite [394 B2] (8 pitches) There are 2 access tracks signposted from the C43 to this private campsite. The first, a distance of 6km, is 47km from the veterinary fence; the second, 8km further north, is 10km from the road. Both are rocky, with a high-clearance vehicle strongly advisable on the southern route. The site has very little shade, but each neatly demarcated pitch has its own traditionally built block housing a flush toilet & shower, supplied with water heated in an old oil drum, & firewood (N$10/bundle) is available.

This is a place to come for the people more than the location. It's owned & run by a welcoming Damara family (the Kuvares), who will take visitors by donkey cart to see wildlife such as ostrich, zebra, oryx, kudu & springbok, in return for a donation. *Day visit N$50 pp; camping N$100 pp.* **$**

Khowarib and Warmquelle

Consisting of little more than a handful of homesteads and a couple of tyre-repair places, Khowarib lies on the perennial Hoanib River, some 73km north of the Palmwag veterinary fence, and 31km southeast of Sesfontein.

About 10km further north of Khowarib, at the site of a spring, is the even tinier settlement of Warmquelle, situated on the site of a spring. In the early years of the 20th century the spring was used in an irrigation project, for which an aqueduct was constructed. Now only a few parts of the old aqueduct remain, together with a small Damara settlement, which supports a basic shop, a baker and a puncture-repair outlet.

The main attraction at Warmquelle is the **Ongongo Waterfall** (*day visit N$50 pp*), where a seasonally deep, clear pool, fed by a small waterfall, is sheltered by an overhang of rock. Few can resist the temptation to strip off and swim here, which isn't surprising given the temperature, although it's considerably less inviting when the water is low. Access is as for Ongongo Campsite (see opposite).

⌂ *Where to stay*

The lodge at Khowarib (opened in 2009), and a sprinkling of relatively recently opened campsites in the area, increase the options for those heading even further north. Of the campsites, some are just a patch of ground where camping is shared with donkeys, cattle and the odd rusting vehicle, but two of the community campsites are worth a mention: Khowarib and Ongongo. Both were originally set up with the help of the Save the Rhino Trust and the Endangered Wildlife Society, and both channel most of their income back into the local community. If they're full, you can camp at Khowarib Lodge itself. And basic camping is also possible at Anmire Cultural Village, signposted just 300m to the south of Khowarib, at Okondju Herero Traditional Village, 8.5km to the north of Khowarib, and at Red Rocks Campsite at Warmquelle junction. There are also a couple of good choices in Sesfontein itself.

✳ ⌂ Khowarib Lodge [394 B1] (14 tented chalets, camping) ✆ 064 402779; m 081 219 3291; e reservations@khowarib.com; www. khowarib.com. After a long, dusty drive, there are plenty of surprises at this scenic lodge, 75km north of the Palmwag veterinary fence, & 25km from Sesfontein. Set 1km east of the C43, it has an enviable location on the Hoanib River, framed by the craggy mountains of the Khowarib Gorge. Giant iron masks guard the entrance to a trio of thatched buildings comprising the reception, bar & dining area. While meals are often served alfresco under the starlit sky, by attentive & friendly staff from the nearby village, the thatched dining area is screened for windy evenings or the occasional burst of rain. Black eagles nest in the surrounding rocks, & the rare short-toed thrush is occasionally spotted, but you might not expect such common waterbirds as the blacksmith plover or Egyptian goose. Steps descend to a row of individual chalets raised on piles. Nestling among mopane trees, each has a private balcony in a canopy of acacia, leadwood & jackalberry trees, where cicadas fail to drown out the soft gurgle of the river a few metres below. The chalets themselves are simple, rustic affairs, built of solid poles & canvas, with wooden doors, screen-panelled windows & – another surprise – mains electricity (a mini fridge is a welcome feature). Behind each chalet, & open to the stars, is a good-sized, stone-walled enclosure with toilet, shower & twin basins. There are 2 family chalets (one sleeping 3 & one 4), but the chalet balconies make them unsuitable for young children. Khowarib Lodge's own campsite just 500m to the east provides 4 pitches along the river, & 4 behind, each with electric points, braai & water, though it's a shame that their campsite competes with the established community campsite nearby (see below). The small, sparkling swimming pool, surrounded by lawn, is a welcome reprieve from the afternoon heat. It has shading & sunloungers, as well as a shower & separate toilet. It's the little details that make Khowarib extra-special, like beer glasses taken from the freezer for each order.

Full-day elephant- & rhino-tracking trips (*N$1,595 & N$1,760 pp*) must be organised in advance. Other activities include ½-day visits to a Himba village (*N$660 pp*) or to see Bushman rock engravings 24km away (*N$770 pp*), birding & nature walks (*N$330 pp*) & nature drives (*N$450–660 pp*). *DBB N$2,181/3,490 sgl/dbl Jan–May, N$2,780–4,428 Jun–Dec; camping N$150 pp.* **$$–$$$$$**

⚊ Khowarib Community Campsite [394 B1] (4 pitches, 5 tents) **m** 081 407 9539; **e** maxi@

nasco.org.na; www.nasco.org.na. 1km past Khowarib Lodge along the same track (suitable for 2WD vehicles), this established campsite run by the local community is set on the edge of the sandy cliffs overlooking a bend in the river. It's a spotless site with private hot & cold showers, flush toilets, dining shelters & braai facilities. One of the pitches, with 5 pre-erected tents, is designed for groups – so be aware of that if you're in search of peace & quiet. Aside from water, you'll need to come fully equipped. Guides are sometimes available for walks around the area. *Camping N$100 pp.* **$**

⚊ Ongongo Campsite [394 B1] (10 pitches) **** 061 239643; **m** 081 473 2926; **e** ongongo@ naturefriendsafais.com; www.ongongo.com. About 11km north of Khowarib along the C43 is the turn-off for another community campsite, signposted from Warmquelle itself. The track follows a water pipeline for about 6km, heading roughly northward. The road is rough & very rocky in parts, sandy in others, & at one point you cross the dry bed of the river, before turning right to reach the site's office. 2WDs are not recommended; it is more sensible to park in a designated area at the top & carry equipment down to the campsite. Each pitch (max 8 people) has private ablutions with hot showers & flush toilets, & a shaded area with basin for cooking & washing. Bring all your food & equipment as there is no shop on site.

The site's main attraction is the Ongongo Waterfall, which is open to day visitors (*N$50 pp*) as well as campers. Keep an eye out, too, for rosy-faced lovebirds chattering in the trees. *N$550 per pitch.* **$$**

SESFONTEIN Named after the 'six springs' that surface nearby, the small town of Sesfontein marks the northern edge of Damaraland – and the gateway to Kaokoland. It is a dusty but photogenic spot, set between mountains in the Hoanib Valley.

The local vegetation is dominated by umbrella thorns (*Vachellia tortilis*), the adaptable mopane (*Colophospermum mopane*), recognised by its butterfly-shaped leaves, and the beautiful, feathery real fan palms (*Hyphaene petersiana*). You will often be offered the 'vegetable ivory' seeds of these palms, carved into various designs, as souvenirs by the local people. These are highly recommended, as often the sellers are the carvers, and it is far less destructive than buying woodcarvings – though note that sellers can occasionally be quite pushy.

In the early 20th century, the German administrators made Sesfontein into an important military outpost. Following the severe rinderpest epidemic in 1896, they wanted to control movement of stock around the country, so in 1901 they built a fort here, complete with running water and extensive gardens to grow their own supplies. However, by the start of World War I this had been abandoned, and it was only much later that it was renovated into a picturesque lodge.

Sesfontein still feels like an outpost in many ways, despite being an important centre for the local people, who live by farming goats and the occasional field of maize. The efficiency of the foraging goats is shown by the lack of vegetation lower than the trees, and hence the clouds of fine dust which often hang in the valley's air. A jumble of signs offering everything from Himba tours and desert excursions to tyre repairs and internet cafés suggests that tourism is on the rise, but so far it's all very low key.

Sesfontein still offers the adventurous an interesting view of a real small town, not sanitised by the colonial designs of townships. It is spread out and very relaxed, home largely to Himba and Herero people. If you're staying here, then try to rise early to watch the village come to life. Sometimes the national anthem will drift across the cool air, beautifully sung by children at the school within earshot of the fort. Watch as farmers drive their cattle to water, and smartly dressed workers head for town. In the afternoon there are always a few people about, and there's no better way to watch village life than sitting with a cold drink on the steps of one of the shops – though you may attract a crowd of playful children, or the odd sideways glance from the local youths who hang out here at weekends to listen to music.

Getting there and away The C43 from Palmwag makes an interesting drive in a normal 2WD vehicle, passing through a narrow gap in the mountains just east of the town. Whereas continuing north to Opuwo is relatively straightforward, the going gets much tougher northwest of Sesfontein.

Where to stay For years the only lodge in town, Fort Sesfontein has now been joined by Sesfontein Guesthouse. Sesfontein's increasing popularity as a springboard for Kaokoland is also reflected in a proliferation of campsites, which include – in addition to those listed here – Zebra campsites, just to the west.

Fort Sesfontein [394 B1] (22 rooms)
065 685034/32; m 081 129 2377; e info@ fort-sesfontein.com; www.fort-sesfontein.com. When it opened in 1995, Fort Sesfontein was one of the most original & imaginative places to appear following independence. Rebuilt more or less to the old plans, it is set around a lush central courtyard full of palm trees alive with masked weaver birds. The rooms (including 2 for families) are mostly in the old fort, but some are upstairs, & the tower is home to the suite. All are large en suite & rustically furnished, with fans & AC, which is as essential as the large swimming pool: Sesfontein can get very hot. If you need a TV, though, you are in the wrong place. The old officers' mess is now an extensive bar/lounge with dining tables that spill out by the pool. Lunch (N$135) is available to all comers, & there's a set dinner menu (N$280). Guided 4x4 day trips can

be organised & they'll provide a guide, lunch & drinks for a self-drive safari. If you're arriving by air, the lodge will collect you at Sesfontein's airstrip. *N$1,710/2,750 sgl/dbl.* **$$$$$**

Sesfontein Guesthouse (6 rooms)
m 081 627 4118; reservations 061 239643; www.sesfontein-guesthouse.com. Promising budget B&B accommodation with shared ablutions, the new guesthouse is run by the same team as Ongongo Campsite (page 417). Lunch & dinner can be booked in advance. N$1,100/1,500 sgl/dbl. **$$$**

Camel Top Campsite (6 pitches) 065 275513. With large pitches, private toilets, hot showers & firewood available, this is a perfectly acceptable site, if nothing special. It lies west of the town, just over 1km off the D3707 along one of 2 clearly signposted tracks, & is accessible in a 2WD. *N$80 pp.* **$**

Other practicalities That the number of outlets offering **tours** is matched only by the number of **tyre-repair** outlets is an indication of the increasing popularity of this isolated spot – and the severity of the roads further west. For **tours**, drop in to Sesfontein Conservancy (065 275502; ⊕ 08.00–17.00 Mon–Fri), which organises

full-day trips to a Himba village or in search of desert-adapted elephants. They can also arrange village visits within Sesfontein in return for a donation. Do note, however, that the conservancy is almost impossible to contact by phone, so visiting the office in person is likely to be more successful.

If you are just passing through, you'll find the supplies in the small **shops** useful, and the **fuel station** here (*summer* ☉ *07.30–18.00*) is particularly valuable as little other fuel is available between Sesfontein and the Kunene, except at Opuwo.

What to see and do For most people, the best way to see the area is on an organised trip: either one prearranged with a specialist before you arrive, or a day trip arranged locally to Himba villages, rock paintings and in search of desert elephants. To explore further into Kaokoland is difficult (see below).

KAOKOLAND

This vast tract of land is Namibia at its most enticing – and yet most inhospitable. Kaokoland appeals to the adventurer and explorer in us, keeping quiet about the dangers involved. On the eastern side, hilly tracks become mudslides as they get washed away by the rains, while the baking desert in the west affords no comfort for those who get stranded. Even dry riverbeds hide soft traps of deep sand, while the few which seem damp and hard may turn to quicksand within metres. Having struggled to free a Land Rover with just one wheel stuck in quicksand, it is easy to believe tales of vehicles vanishing within an hour.

One road on the eastern side was particularly memorable for me – it started favourably as a good gravel track. After 20km, it had deteriorated into a series of rocky ruts, shaking us to our bones and forcing us to slow down to 10km/h. After a while, when we'd come too far to think of returning, the track descended into a sandy riverbed, strewn with boulders and enclosed by walls of rock. The only way was for passengers to walk and guide the driver, watching as the tyres lurched from boulder to boulder.

Hours later we emerged – on to another difficult track. Gradually it flattened and the driving eased: we were happy to be travelling faster. Then the pace was interrupted. Streams crossed the road. Someone would wade across to check the depth, and then the 4x4 would swiftly follow, its momentum carrying it across the muddy bed. The third stream stopped us: more than thigh-high, fast flowing – a river in flood. We slept dry in our tents, thankful that the floods hadn't reached that first rocky riverbed while we were there.

In recent years, the region's main arteries have been improved, making it more accessible to independent drivers. Two graded roads – the C43 and the D3701 – are generally safe enough in the dry season, though even then it's important to stay alert as some riverbed crossings are both steep and occasionally rocky, and the graders get here only infrequently. The rest of the D roads, however, are another matter. For these you should ideally still have a two-vehicle 4x4 expedition, all your supplies, an experienced navigator, detailed maps and good local advice on routes. Even then you'll probably get lost a few times. This is not a trip to undertake lightly: if things go wrong you will be hundreds of kilometres from help, and days from a hospital.

If you can get an expedition together then, in contrast to Damaraland's regulated conservancy and private concession areas, you'll find that Kaokoland has yet to adopt any formal system of control, and you are free to travel where you can. However, this freedom is causing lasting damage to the region. The drier areas, especially to the west, have a very fragile ecosystem: driving a vehicle off the tracks

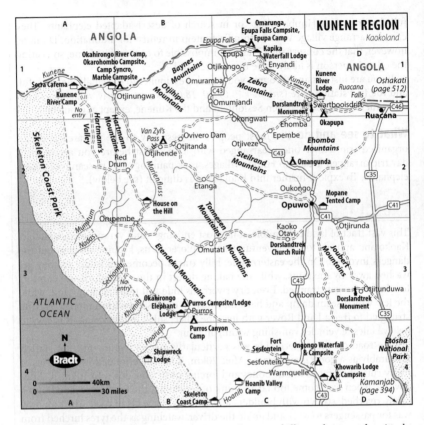

and 'across country' can cause permanent damage, killing plants and animals, and leaving marks that last for centuries. Vehicle trails made 40 years ago can still be seen, as the crushed plants and lichens haven't yet recovered. So you must be responsible and treat the environment with care – and *never* drive off the tracks.

In addition to a handful of upmarket lodges, there are several demarcated campsites, some run directly by the community. These cater for self-sufficient expeditions in 4x4s, and travellers are urged to support them. Where there is no such provision, you can choose your own site, provided that you obtain permission from the head of the local village, and show due respect to the area's inhabitants (page 155). Here, more than anywhere else, there is a need to be responsible.

HOW TO VISIT KAOKOLAND Although the main arteries through Kaokoland have opened up in recent years, much of it remains remote; touring this area independently is not an option for most people. The few camps here tend to be either very basic or very organised. The basic ones are simple campsites, often run by the local communities with the backing of one of the conservation/development organisations. The organised camps are expensive, most linked with small, specialist, fly-in operators.

Specialist Kaokoland operators Kaokoland is rugged and remote. When planning a visit to this area, consider who is taking you, rather than exactly where you're staying. Choose the most knowledgeable operator with whom you feel comfortable, and then go with them. Trusting your arrangements to anyone who does not know the area intimately is foolish.

Do satisfy yourself that your operator values the fragility of the area and its culture. Among other things, consider:

- How (if at all) they ensure that the local people benefit from your visit. Do they charge an automatic bed-night levy which is then paid into local community funds?
- How sensitive they are to the local cultures. Do their staff speak the local languages?
- Whether their staff are from the local community, creating local employment prospects.

Such operations may use their own fixed camps, or mobile camps, which can be moved when necessary. This is both the best and the most comfortable way to see Kaokoland. Among many that run occasional trips are three excellent specialists, listed below: two well established, and a third, newer venture under the auspices of Namibian Conservancy Safaris.

Also worth considering in this region is the more general operator **Namibia Tracks and Trails** (\ *064 416820;* m *081 269 7271;* e *travel@namibia-tracks-and-trails.com; www.namibia-tracks-and-trails.com*).

Conservancy Safaris Namibia \ 064 406136; m 081 149 7611; e info@kcs-namibia.com.na; www.kcs-namibia.com.na. This conservancy-owned venture, linked to IRDNC (see box, page 15) has excellent credentials & offers guided mobile safaris around the region. Tours for up to 9 participants start from 6 nights/7 days, mainly in Damaraland but as far north as Purros depending on where the wildlife is, to the longest – 14 nights/15 days – which includes a couple of nights camping on the banks of the Kunene River. In addition, there are specialist safaris led by acknowledged experts in their fields, covering topics from desert lions to conservation & culture. Not surprisingly, these trips aren't cheap – but then they're far removed from the norm, are relatively flexible (with the option of adding time in Etosha & even the Caprivi), & all profits go to a group of 5 conservancies in the far northwest, which host the safaris.

Kunene Tours & Safaris \ 064 402779; e info@kunenetours.com; www.kunenetours.com. Run by Caesar Zandberg, this established specialist organises overland trips in the Kunene Region, based out of Khowarib Lodge (page 416). You can choose from set trips ranging from 4 to 8 nights or plan your own custom trip with no limitation. In either case, your days are spent exploring – in either their vehicle or your own 4x4 – & evenings are spent in pre set-up mobile camps.

Skeleton Coast Fly-in Safaris See page 387. Though you might not immediately associate the experts on the Skeleton Cost with the Kaokoveld, most of their trip to the Skeleton Coast is, in fact, spent just inland in the Kaokoveld. They normally visit the Purros area, & the region around the Kunene River, at the north end of the Hartmann's Mountains.

OPUWO This rough-and-ready frontier town is the hub of Kaokoland and – with improved access from the north and south – it's becoming increasingly important for visitors too. Most come to learn more about the Himba people who inhabit the surrounding area, but some are en route to Epupa Falls.

While the town is the Himba 'capital', it does not provide the photographic opportunities to match the preconceived images of many visitors, and it isn't an attractive place in its own right; the proliferation of bars tells its own tale. It does, however, attract an eclectic mix of people. Even if you're just waiting to fill up, take a look around. Herero women in their Victorian-style dresses contrast with traditional rural Himba, who come into town to trade or buy supplies, with their decorated goatskin dress and ochre-stained skins. Strong, powerful faces speak clearly of people who have yet to trade their own culture for what little is being offered to them here. As with any frontier post, the place abounds with shady local traders. These mix with occasional businessmen, and the eccentric characters who emerge from the bush to replenish supplies, and then disappear again with equal speed.

Getting there and away Opuwo is at the junction of the tarred C41 and the gravel C43, some 54km west of the main C35 between Kamanjab and Ruacana. As you approach, large, irrigated maize fields give way to the dry, dusty town, sprawling over a low hillside with no apparent centre. Its buildings are functional rather than attractive, and the outskirts fade into ramshackle groups of Himba and Herero huts.

Where to stay Despite its frontier-town appearance, Opuwo has a surprisingly large range of accommodation, topped by Opuwo Country Lodge.

Opuwo Country Lodge [422 A1] (40 rooms, camping) \065 481661; m 081 149 1435, 081 239 3299; e reservations@opuwolodge.com; www. opuwolodge.com. Situated on a hilltop overlooking the valleys & mountains, this privately owned hotel, originally opened in 2005, was taken over by Wouter & Lientjie Smith in 2012. The impressive main building incorporates the reception, lounge & dining areas (buffet dinner N$325), a curio shop, wine cellar & bar. Running the whole length of the building is an extensive terrace-with-a-view, fronted by an infinity pool. Rooms (including 3 family units) have AC, a balcony & plenty of mod cons, but only the larger 'luxury' ones have a scenic view. The campsite, with 12 pitches, is located well away from the main hotel.

Excursions include a 3hr Himba village trip (N$710 pp), which can feel rather commercialised,

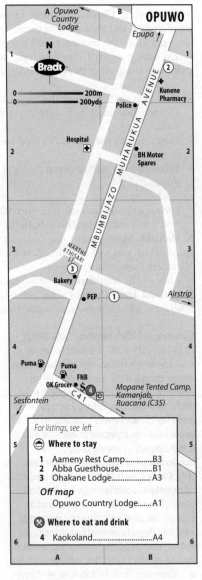

For listings, see left

Where to stay
1 Aameny Rest Camp..............B3
2 Abba Guesthouse................B1
3 Ohakane Lodge..................... A3
Off map
Opuwo Country Lodge........ A1

Where to eat and drink
4 Kaokoland..............................A4

& day trips to Epupa or Ruacana Falls (*weather permitting; N$1,870 pp*). Closer to home, a good 2.5km self-guided walking trail leads down into the valley, with the potential to spot some of the area's flora & birdlife. N$2,035/2,860 sgl/dbl; camping N$175 pp. **$$–$$$$**

Ohakane Lodge [422 A3] (13 rooms) Marthi Athisari St; \065 273031, 061 401593; m 081 295 9024; e ohakane@gmail.com. This small lodge, named after the local word for 'wild dog', is

Read the camping advice on page 155, and remember the following:

- Never camp in a riverbed; flash floods often claim lives.
- Never camp close to a water point. Desert-adapted animals will often travel for days to get to one of these. They may die of thirst if you keep them from the water with your presence.
- Gather any firewood you will need in the highlands before you get to this area, and keep its use to a minimum.
- In such a dry landscape be very careful not to cause bush fires.
- Take home everything that you bring in. No rubbish should be buried: it may take centuries to decay, and will almost certainly be dug up before then by scavengers.
- Water is very limited, so bring in all you need. Use sparingly any that you find.
- The few streams and springs in the area are used for drinking by animals and people. Do not contaminate them, and be sure to wash well away from them.

well signposted just behind the Shell fuel station. An unprepossessing entrance belies an attractive lodge, with secure parking. Light, spacious rooms, all en suite with AC & TV, are set around lawns & a small pool with a bar. Lunch (*N$105*) & dinner (*N$185*) are served under thatch or outside beneath the trees, & there's a small selection of curios for sale. Unfortunately, the proximity to a local bar can mean loud music over the w/ends. Both Himba village trips (*N$695 pp, ½-day; min 4*) & trips to Epupa Falls (*N$5,800 per vehicle*) can be organised. *N$715/1,190 sgl/dbl.* **$$$**

🏠 **Abba Guesthouse** [422 B1] (15 rooms) Mbumbijazo Muharukua Av; 065 273155; m 081 234 6810; e abbaguest@gmail.com, info@ abbaguesthouse.com; www.abbaguesthouse.com. This unexpected find has a strong Christian ethos – & the bonus of internet access (*N$10/30mins*). Dbl & twin rooms, all en suite & some with microwave, are pleasant, & there's a small garden

but, other than b/fast (*N$59 pp*), no food is served. *N$350/500 sgl/dbl.* **$$**

⚐ **Aameny Rest Camp** [422 B3] (8 bungalows, 10 rooms, camping) 065 273572; m 081 275 0156, 081 260 2089; e aamenylodge@yahoo.com. Taken over by Western Tjiposa, a Himba man, in 2009, Aameny is quietly situated just off the main road, with secure parking. Trees shade the small, grassy pitches with picnic tables & electric light, & 2 ablution blocks (with hot water). Traditional-style twin rooms offer accommodation under thatch, from simple rondavels with electric light & fan to others that are en suite with kettle & TV. Meals (*b/fast N$60, dinner N$120 pp*), including local dishes on request, are served in a simple dining area, where internet & Wi-Fi is also available. Western also offers visits to various Himba villages, which alternates to spread tourist money & minimise impact. *Camping N$180, rooms from N$200/340 sgl/dbl.* **$$**

🍽 **Where to eat and drink** As in many Namibian towns, most tourists eat in their hotels, but the **Kaokoland Restaurant** [422 A4] (⊕ 08.00–21.00 w/days, 10.00–21.00 w/ends) is good for those passing through. It's actually a coffee shop, next to OK Grocer, and is unexpectedly pleasant, with Wi-Fi. Stop here for breakfast, light meals, grills and burgers, and a range of drinks.

Shopping Opuwo now has both Spar and OK Grocer [422 A4] supermarkets; the latter, located next to the BP garage, opens an hour earlier (⊕ 07.00–19.00 daily), and has its own bakery that is probably the best place to buy **curios**. Otherwise, have a browse through the wares displayed on the pavement in front of the supermarket. Here and elsewhere in town you can usually find someone selling little piles of ochre, used by the Himba women to colour their skin.

Other practicalities Approaching from the C41, the town's main facilities are on the right, just before the T-junction. In Opuwo, several places vie to sell you **fuel**, including the 24-hour Puma station, and Caltex, just right of the T-junction [422 A4]. From a logistical point of view, this is the only fuel north of Sesfontein and west of Ruacana, so it's an important place to top up.

In the complex adjacent to the Puma garage is a branch of **FNB bank**, with an ATM and a foreign-exchange bureau, making Opuwo more traveller-friendly than in previous years, and the **internet café** here should ease any communication problems while in the vicinity. If you're in need of **tyres** or vehicle repairs, try B H Motor Spares [422 B2] (↖065 273101) or Wesstech Autorepairs (m 081 467 0040).

In an **emergency**, the police can be contacted on ↖065 273359, 065 273148/04, and the ambulance or hospital [422 A2] on ↖065 272800. For minor medical needs, try the **Kunene Pharmacy** [422 B1] (↖065 273221; m 081 128 5140; ⊕ 08.00–17.00 Mon–Fri, 08.00–noon Sat), next to Abba Guesthouse.

KUNENE RIVER From the hydro-electric dam near Ruacana, the Kunene River threads west through the Baynes Mountains to the Atlantic, meandering between arid hills and wild, rough-looking mountains on both sides. Angola lies to its north, Namibia to its south; both look identical. Along its way, photogenic, feathery fronds of green makalani palms line its path. This narrow strip extends for perhaps only 30m from the river itself. Further from the water than that, the land reverts to its parched, dry state: the preserve of Kaokoland's semi-desert flora and fauna.

Note that water levels in the river itself are largely controlled by the dam rather than the seasons, and can vary considerably, even during one day.

Flora and fauna The flora and fauna along the Kunene are representative of the ecosystem found in the palm forest which lines the river for most of its length.

Hippos have been exterminated from much of the river, although some have been reintroduced upstream. Crocodiles are still common, though (bathing is safe only immediately beside the falls at Epupa), and small mammals are a feature of the palm forest. Few large wild mammals are regularly seen around here, although spotted impala and kudu are resident, and both mountain zebra and giraffe have been reintroduced into the Kunene River Conservancy.

Away from the river, mopane scrub reclaims the land, spotting the arid landscape with patches of dusty green. To relieve the monotony, you're rarely out of sight of the mountains, layered against the horizon in darkening shades of grey.

Birdlife Ornithologists will find a fascinating variety of birds, including various bee-eaters, kingfishers ranging from the giant to the tiny malachite kingfisher, louries, bulbuls and hornbills, as well as rollers (purple, lilac breasted and European), golden and lesser masked weavers, scarlet-breasted sunbirds, and perhaps the odd, lost, great white egret. The rare rufous-tailed palm thrush and the Cinderella waxbill also occur in this riverine palm forest, which is typical of their highly restricted habitat; both are resident around Epupa Falls and close to Kunene River Lodge. Equally unusual is the yellow-breasted shrike, a morph of the more common crimson-breasted shrike. Easier to see, though, are the colonies of rosy-faced lovebirds that colonise the trees along the river, and Rüppell's parrot, with its flashy yellow shoulder stripe. Distinctive among the birds of prey are Verreaux's or black eagle, the bateleur or short-tailed eagle, and the gymnogene, as well as the inevitable fish eagles.

Getting there and away From the south, access to the Kunene River has been dramatically improved following the grading of the C43 (also signposted as the D3700) north of Opuwo. While you should still exercise considerable care along this road, it's perfectly passable during the dry season, although a high-clearance vehicle is essential to negotiate the steepest riverbed crossings.

Driving from the east is more challenging. The D3700 runs directly from Ruacana along the Kunene for about 145km as far as Epupa Falls. However, although the first 65km or so, as far as Kunene River Lodge, is reasonable driving (though a high-clearance 4x4 is strongly advised), the latter stages remain very rough – taking me three days of painstaking driving on one occasion – and should not be taken lightly. Thus the best – and by far the quickest – route is to follow the road along the river between Ruacana and Swartbooisdrift, then to cut inland along the D3701 (technically graded but with generally erratic maintenance), before joining the C43 near Epembe. From here, it's a further 103km to Epupa. I strongly suggest that nothing west of the lodge along the river should be attempted without a self-sufficient two-vehicle party of rugged 4x4s.

Where to stay

Λ Omungunda Campsite m 081 838 2556; e tjipuruaj@yahoo.com; Some 40km north of Opuwo, on the C43, there's a signpost for this pretty, quiet campsite. It's very simple & rustic, but provides hot showers & flush toilets. *N$110 pp.* **$**

Epupa Falls
Though visitors go to Kaokoland more for the whole experience than any individual sight, Epupa Falls [420 B1] is one of its highlights.

Here at Epupa the river widens to accommodate a few small islands, before plunging into a geological fault. This is 35m deep in places and, as the river is sizeable – at least in the early months of the year – it makes a lot of noise and some spray. The falls don't compare with Victoria Falls in scale, but they are all the more beautiful for occurring in such an arid region. Add to the scene a phalanx of watchful baobabs, many balancing improbably on precarious rocks above the chasms, or standing forlornly on the small islands in the stream. It's a magical spot.

Central to the small community around the falls is a Himba settlement with a shop from which music emanates for much of the day. The increase in the number of visitors has led to the establishment of a small craft stall near the falls, but most Himba visits concentrate on more traditional communities a short distance away.

With generally dry vegetation, and strong winds, the area is particularly susceptible to bush fires. One of these, in 2009, jumped the river from Angola, blackening the trees, destroying one of the campsites, and leaving a general trail of destruction in its wake.

Where to stay

⌂ Epupa Camp [420 C1] (10 tents, camping) \ 061 237294; m 081 366 4003; e reservations@epupa.com.na; www.epupa.com.na. On the palm-fringed banks of the Kunene, 700m east of the main falls, this established camp occupies a tranquil, compact site opposite a small island. As well as a campsite with 12 pitches, guests can stay in safari tents, each with a shaded balcony, mosquito-netted doors & windows, camp-style beds & a simple en-suite shower & toilet at the

For several years the Namibian and Angolan governments have been considering the construction of a hydro-electric dam across the Kunene. It's a highly controversial project, and after considerable opposition the original site, at Epupa, was discounted in favour of one 40km downstream, in the Baynes Mountains. Here, it is proposed to construct a 200m-high dam, flooding some 57km² of Himba tribal lands.

Advocates of the scheme have pointed to Namibia's rising power consumption, the apparent 'waste' of the Kunene's huge potential, and the lack of employment opportunities in the northern Kunene Region; critics regard it as a 'prestige project' for the government, arguing that its power will be expensive and unnecessary, and that it will do immense damage to the Kunene's ecosystems and the culture of the Himba people who live near the river. That the Epupa site has been taken out of the equation is thanks to considerable efforts from local and international groups since the project's inception in 1998. On the environmental side, the California-based International Rivers (*www.internationalrivers.org*) concluded that the original report was 'riddled with incorrect conclusions, false assumptions and missing data', and continues to campaign against a dam at the Baynes site. Socially, several organisations, including Namibia's nonprofit law firm Legal Assistance Centre (LAC; *www.lac.org.na*) and the London-based Survival International (*www.survival-international.org*), have helped the Himba communities to put their case forward, and to campaign against the dam. In 1998, leaders in the Kunene Region submitted 11 major objections to the proposed site at Epupa, many of which will pertain to the new site. These include loss of land and riverine resources (the narrow palm forest beside the river is a vital source of food for both people and livestock); disappearance of wildlife; inundation of ancestral grave sites; health threats brought about by a large lake; overcrowding through the construction period; increased crime; loss of ecotourism potential; and the creation of a barrier, putting a stop to regular river crossings by Himba communities on opposite sides of the river.

Now, despite the years of legal turmoil, it seems that the newly titled Baynes Hydropower Project is to go ahead. The Namibian and Angolan authorities are planning to build a 200m dam wall downstream of Epupa Falls, which will hold a projected 2,650 million m³ of water, and generate an estimated average 1,610 GWh per annum for an estimated investment of US$1.2 billion. At its fullest, the waters of the newly created lake will lap at the foot of Epupa Falls so while their days aren't quite numbered it seems there is change in the air.

Perhaps as a glimmer of hope the project was due to have started in mid 2017, but by the end of 2018 construction had still not begun.

back. 7 of the tents face the river, as do the dining area & terrace, a firepit & a tiny plunge pool. Behind sits the reception area with a small library. Lights are powered by a generator or batteries.

Key to the success of this camp is a welcoming & attentive team of staff, largely drawn from the local community. Activities include sundowner trips to the hills & falls, guided visits to a local Himba village, & gentle ½-day rafting trips on the Kunene. The falls themselves are an easy walk away. *DBB N$2,260/3,700 sgl/dbl; camping N$180 pp.* **$$–$$$$$**

🏠 **Omarunga Camp** [420 C1] (14 chalets; camping) m 081 620 6887; e bookings@ damaraland-namibia.com; www.omarungalodge. com. This immaculately maintained lodge is spread out along the river, with a riverside bar & restaurant. Tented chalets (1 suitable for a family) under light thatch are set on stone plinths interspersed with patches of grass; 5 directly face the river, & a further 5 have a river view. Gauzed windows allow the circulation of air, while inside are tiled floors, smart mosi nets & stone bathrooms with flush toilets. Camping chairs on a narrow veranda complete the picture. To one side, adjacent to Epupa Falls Campsite, is a spotless campsite with 10 pitches & central ablution blocks; campers can use the bar & have dinner (*3 courses for N$410*) by prior reservation.

Activities range from Himba tours with a local guide (*N$820 pp*) to guided walking trails (*N$230*) & sunset excursions (*N$290 pp*). *DBB N$2,840/4,540 sgl/dbl; camping N$195 pp; airstrip transfer N$875 per vehicle return.* **$$–$$$$$**

☀ 🏠 **Epupa Falls Lodge & Campsite** [420 C1] (5 chalets, camping) m lodge 081 250 8225, campsite 081 361 1799; e bookings@ epupafallslodge.com; www.epupafallslodge.com. As Epupa became more of a Mecca for visitors to Kaokoland, a site next to the falls was set up to benefit from these visitors, & in order to protect the fragile palm forest from being ruined by those in search of virgin camping sites. Owned by Koos Verwey, who used to operate the highly respected Kaokohimba Safaris, it's got an excellent location

on the banks of the river, right above the falls. En-suite chalets, built on stilts & boasting excellent views, & a rustic but spotlessly clean campsite, its stone-built ablution blocks with flush toilets & water heated by donkey boilers. High up on stilts is a kitchen (*dinner N$300*) & bar, with tables overlooking the rapids. Campers, who have 7 pitches, can often buy vegetables & even a few crafts from the local villagers, & there's a small curio shop on site, with firewood, fresh *boerewors* (sausage) & chicken & ice when available.

In the river just upstream of the camp are hot springs. When the water is low, these are accessible. Koos himself now specialises in taking small-groups hiking, cycling & on guided tours of the Kunene Region. These are tailored for the individual, & not scheduled. *DBB chalets N$1,773/3,076 sgl/dbl; camping N$150 pp.* **$$–$$$$$**

🏠 **Kapika Waterfall Lodge** [420 C1] (10 chalets, camping) \ 065 685111; e kapika. epupa@gmail.com; www.epupalodge.com. Kapika offers en-suite twin chalets overlooking the river & a campsite. The restaurant is open for b/fast, lunch & dinner, & there's a bar & pool. Activity options cover a range of scenic drives, nature walks, Himba village tours, sundowners & ½-day rafting trips. *B&B N$1,945/3,090 sgl/dbl; camping N$275 pp.* **$$–$$$$$**

Other attractions Sunrise bathes the nearby hills in clear red light, and this is a good time to explore. The hills have an uneven surface of loose rock, so wear a stout pair of shoes and watch out for snakes. Temperatures are cold at first, but it warms up very rapidly, so take water, a sunhat and suncream. As with exploring anywhere near this border, seek local advice. Some areas were mined during the liberation struggle, and injuries still occur, albeit not in the last ten years or so.

Most lodges and campsites in the area can arrange trips to visit a Himba village. For comments on these, see box, page 428.

Gemmologists should keep their eyes on the ground for the rose quartz crystals that abound. You may also find the chipped stone implements of past inhabitants.

Canoeing Several of the lodges along the river have canoes available for their guests, usually offering a haul upstream followed by a gentle drift back with the current. For those in search of more exciting waters, the specialist operator Felix Unite (page 255) may be able to arrange itineraries up to ten days for groups of at least 16, incorporating a couple of days in Etosha, and six days paddling the Kunene from Hippo Pools to Epupa. Although there is some white water along this stretch, the appeal is more in the environment, with plenty of birdlife and a diversity of habitats. This is a participation-based expedition, but a back-up crew carries the heavy kit by vehicle. The best time to go is in the winter months, between late June and August.

East of Epupa: Swartbooisdrift With little in the way of tourist infrastructure, this isolated spot retains much of the magic of the Kunene River, its water levels regulated by the dam some 50km upstream at Ruacana. When river levels are high, rafting through the canyon upstream can be arranged at Kunene River Lodge.

Just west of the lodge is the Dorslandtrek Monument, which marks the spot where in 1928 a group of the original Dorslandtrekkers from South Africa crossed back over the border from Angola into what was then South West Africa.

Where to stay There are a few simple campsites along the river in the area around Swartbooisdrift. Of these, **Okapupa Camp** lies about 12km east of Kunene River Lodge. All are basic, and you can expect to pay around N$80 per person to camp. If you're after something more comfortable, the lodge has its own camping area. For campsites near Ruacana Falls, see page 521.

Kunene River Lodge [420 D1]
(8 rooms, 4 chalets, camping) 061 228104/7;
e kuneneriverlodge@journeysnamibia.com;
www.kuneneriverlodge.com. This private lodge within the Kunene River Conservancy is owned & run by Peter & Hillary Morgan. It lies on the D3700, about 65km west of Ruacana, just east of the junction with the D3701. During the rainy season, a 4x4 is essential.

It's a well-vegetated spot, with mature leadwood & jackalberry trees, 1 entwined with an increasingly rare snake vine. At one end of the site, an attractive pool is screened by banana trees,

beloved of the local monkeys, while at the other, a bar & restaurant overlook the river.

Set along the river are 12 grassy, tree-shaded camping pitches, with flush toilets & hot water in a stone ablution block. Sharing this, & set behind the campsite, are small, rustic chalets, while further back is a row of 8 bungalows which are more upmarket, 1 suitable for families & all en suite. There is mains power available.

This is a great place for water-based activities, including white-water rafting through the Onduroso Gorge (N$530 ½-day), canoeing (N$220 per 2-person canoe) & fishing – with rods available at N$145/day. Note, however, that these are subject to water levels, which fluctuate according to flow levels determined at Ruacana. Motorboat trips are on offer, too (*sundowner N$365 pp*).

Peter is an enthusiastic & knowledgeable birder, happy to lead guests along a usually dry tributary in search of rarities such as the Cinderella waxbill (*N$365 pp*), & the newly discovered Angola cave chat in the Zebra Mountains (*N$990 pp*) – just 2 of the 285 species recorded here. There are also trips to a Himba village (*N$330 pp*). With this range of options, Kunene River Lodge suits adventurous travellers as well as those in search of more leisurely activities – &, of course, keen birders. *N$1,663/2,500 sgl/dbl; camping N$190 pp.* **$$–$$$$**

THE WESTERN VALLEYS

In the west, Hartmann's Valley and the Marienfluss are often visited by the Kaokoveld's specialists. Both valleys run north–south, bounded in the north by the Kunene, which flows all year. The main approach road is the D3707, a 4x4 track heading northwest from Sesfontein.

Purros

Some 106km west of Sesfontein (and a similar distance from Orupembe), you'll come to the village of Purros, located on the Hoarusib River. Largely a Himba area, Purros is increasingly popular with visitors to its traditional Himba village, as well as to see the wildlife that congregates along the river.

Getting there and away Purros has its own airstrip, used by most of the visitors to the new lodge; the flight from Windhoek takes 2¼ hours. Those planning to drive in should do so only with a fully equipped 4x4 vehicle – and preferably two. The D3707 from Sesfontein may be deceptively good for the first few kilometres, but then deteriorates significantly as it crosses increasingly hostile terrain with no shade. Boneshaking surfaces do nothing for even the hardiest of tyres, and numerous river crossings make losing the road altogether a real possibility. This is not a trip to be taken lightly.

Where to stay The village's community campsite also has a separate 'bush lodge', both of which are worth visiting. Entirely differerent is the upmarket **Okahirongo Elephant Lodge**, just across the river from the village.

Okahirongo Elephant Lodge [420 B1] (8 chalets) \065 685018/20; e info@okahirongo. com; www.okahirongolodge.com. From a distance the collection of dark-brown boxes lined up on a ridge against the hills is a bit of an anticlimax, but appearances can be deceptive: contemporary style at this joint Italian–South African venture is serious business.

Between each pair of 'boxes', heavy pole doors pivot on a central axis to reveal a day bed on a shaded platform looking across to the mountains. To one side is a spacious bathroom with twin basins, large clay bath, showers inside & out, & a separate toilet; to the other, dark wood chairs & desk complement a rather grand dbl bed with 4-poster mosquito nets. At one end, 2 units combine into a family suite.

In the centre of the ridge, a Himba-inspired domed entrance leads to more boxes – a reception area, 2 lounges, 2 dining areas, curio shop, a library & even a sunlounger cube – all decorated in rich earthy tones & grouped around an azure infinity pool. It's open & airy to make the most of any breeze, but curtains & blinds are there for colder nights, as is a welcoming firepit. Food – claimed as a fusion of Italian & African cuisine – is generally a cut above the average, well prepared & well presented.

For all its luxury, the lodge's greatest draw is a truly panoramic view of the mountains across the plains. Activities focus on nature drives along the Hoarusib River in search of elephant & lion, & trips to a Himba village near Purros. Other possibilities are scenic drives to the Skeleton Coast, fly-in fishing trips, & scenic flights. Rather bizarrely, there's also a golf driving range, with clubs available, & cookery classes are under consideration.

Although some guests drive themselves in, most arrive at the airstrip, a 5min drive away. A 2-night stay is a minimum, & if you're after a spot of R&R, a 3rd wouldn't go amiss – it's a long way to go. *DBB N$6,650/9,000 sgl/dbl.* **$$$$$$**

Purros Bush Lodge [420 B3] (7 rooms) Contact as for the campsite (see below); failing that, try Purros Canyon Camp (see right), who may be able to assist. Close to the campsite, but signposted along a separate track, this self-catering community lodge opened in 2009. Thatched, stone-built rooms, including 1 for families, are en suite & nicely laid out, with cream curtains at screened windows & solar-powered lights, though there's no fan. Outside each is a washing-up area & a parking shelter. Commanding views across the landscape are to be had from a lookout tower. Activities can be arranged as at the campsite, & here, too, you'll need to be entirely self-sufficient except for firewood. *N$385 pp.* **$$**

Purros Campsite [420 B3] (6 pitches) Reservations m 081 716 2066; e robbinuatokuja@hotmail.com. Managed by the charismatic Robbin Uatokuja, the community-run Ngatutunge Pamue site, meaning 'We build together', is 2km north of Purros, on the D3707. The approach road has patches of sand, so drive with care. Large pitches, set on a sandy, wooded site on the bank of the Hoarusib River, each have their own flush toilet, hot & cold shower, fireplace (no grid), sink with tap, & bin. Firewood is available (though use

sparingly; it's in short supply), but in all other respects you'll need to be entirely self-sufficient.

A major purpose of the camp, & its sister lodge, is to provide employment for the Himba from Purros village. Full-day drives (*N$400 pp*), & expeditions to visit the Himba people or see local elephants (*N$250 pp*), can be arranged with a local guide, an effective way to put some money directly into the local economy. Note that elephants occur frequently in the area & around the campsite, & should not be harassed in any way; they are dangerous & unpredictable animals, & have killed people. *Camping N$110 pp.* **$**

Purros Canyon Camp [420 B3] (6 pitches) Reservations 081 716 2066, 081 700 1933; e robbinuatokuja@hotmail.com; www. purroscanyoncamp.com. This new campsite about 2km south of Purros itself opened in 2018 & is owned & also managed by Robbin Uatokuja, in conjunction with the local community. The camp's pitches promise to be well spaced for privacy, & have their own flush toilets, hot & cold water & braai. Robbin is a veteran guide of the area of some repute & offers the same activities from Canyon Camp as he does from the community campsite (see left). Furthermore, he is a key member of the Kaokoland Guides (*www.kaokolandguides.com*), who may also be able to assist with bookings in the Purros area. *Camping N$110 pp.* **$**

What to see and do Close to Purros is a traditional **Himba village** where visitors are welcome. While the village is used to visitors, it's worth remembering that it is their home; this is in no way a show village. It may be possible to visit the village on foot, which is a more leisurely and satisfying way to meet these pastoral people, allowing plenty of time for an exchange of views and questions through your guide. After all, how would you like it if a group of strangers drove up to your house, came in and took pictures of your family and then departed within just a few minutes? So do greet the villagers, and spend time talking with them, and learning a little of how they live. Many now are helped by the income made from selling jewellery, or guiding visitors around their local area – they deserve your support.

The area's other attraction is the **Hoarusib River**, whose pools of permanent water attract both desert-adapted elephant and a small pride of desert-adapted lion. Baboons cavort along the edge, and high in the rocks are the tell-tale white marks of rock dassies. Birds, too, are drawn to the river. Vivid flashes of colour signal the olive (Madagascar) bee-eater, the dusky sunbird or the common waxbill, while at the water's edge congregate plovers, lapwings, Egyptian geese and the occasional hamerkop.

Hartmann's Valley As you enter the valley, a small weather-worn sign stresses the ecologically important things you must do, and includes a diagram of how to turn a vehicle around to minimise damage to the environment. Take time to read and memorise it, or perhaps take a photograph as a reminder.

Hartmann's Valley itself is very arid, though its weather can vary dramatically. As well as searing heat, the valley receives sea mists which creep up from the coast, making it an eerie place to visit.

It is 70km from end to end, a minimum of 2½ hours' drive one-way, and the condition of the track along it varies. In the south, the road starts by crossing a number of steep-sided river valleys. It soon changes to compacted, corrugated sand, which shakes your vehicle violently. Finally, this becomes soft before high dunes prevent you reaching the Kunene by vehicle. Despite the harsh conditions, it is very beautiful. Drive through at sunrise if possible; then it's cooler than later and shows off the surrounding hills at their finest.

Where to stay There are two private camps at the end of the valley:

✳ 🏠 Serra Cafema Camp [420 A1] (8 chalets) Contact via Wilderness Safaris; ☏061 274500; e info@wilderness.com.na; www. wilderness-safaris.com. This exclusive camp beside the Kunene has been reinvented several times over the last decade, often due to flooding in the off season. With each reincarnation comes a grander & more luxurious feel to add to the palpable air of remote relaxation. With a pool, sunken bar & lounge, it is certainly a haven on the edge of the harsh wilderness of the Kaokoveld, & possibly the most remote camp in Namibia.

Large elevated chalets linked by decking are spread out in a fringe of riverine vegetation. Each has canvas walls & a thatched roof, but any similarity to a tent stops there. A large set of sliding glass doors forms one long side of each chalet, opening on to a vast wooden deck with spectacular views over the river. Inside are a bedroom with canopied bed, writing table & several fans; a small lounge area, with sofa & coffee tables; & a large dressing area cum bathroom, with bath, shower &

dbl sinks. Soft lighting & natural wood aplenty are offset by cream-coloured fabrics.

While some just relax at camp, it is a great place from which to explore this remote area – home to springbok, ostrich & oryx, but very few people. Guests can walk in the mountains & along the river valley, but most prefer the guided quadbike or 4WD excursions among the dunes & to visit local villages. There's also a full-day outing to the Marienfluss Valley, complete with a delicious picnic lunch, & boat trips promise relative cool in the afternoons. The cost of flying in & the high quality of the camp itself make this one of Namibia's most expensive camps. *FBA N$11,560–22,523/17,810–34,720 sgl/dbl.* **$$$$$$$**

🏠 Kunene River Camp [420 A1] Run by Skeleton Coast Safaris, this very small & simple camp is usually used for a final night as part of their fly-in trips to the Skeleton Coast & the Kaokoveld. See page 387 for details & costs of these trips, & please note that the camp is always booked as part of their packages; you cannot just drop in.

The Marienfluss

The next valley inland from Hartmann's is the Marienfluss. If you are driving, this is reached via the Himba settlement at Red Drum – a crossroads marked by a red oil can.

The Marienfluss has more soft sand and is greener than Hartmann's Valley. It is covered with light scrub and the odd tree marks an underground river. A most noticeable feature of the Marienfluss is its 'fairy circles' (see box, page 320), although they are also found, to a lesser extent, in Hartmann's Valley.

Where to stay At the northern end of the Marienfluss there is a nice selection of simple campsites, and one very luxury lodge. Campsites – where for the most part you can just turn up rather than pre-booking – are set mainly under the shade of camelthorn trees (*Vachellia erioloba*) on the banks of the Kunene River. There are also a couple of community-run campsites further south.

🏠 **Okahirongo River Camp** [420 B1] (6 chalets) ☎065 685018/20; e info@okahirongo. com; www.okahirongolodge.com. Set up by the team behind Okahirongo Elephant Lodge (page 429), this small eco-friendly camp in the Marienfluss Conservancy relies 100% on solar energy to keep pollution to a minimum. From its vantage point on a low hill overlooking the Otupambua rapids, you can see across the Kunene River to dramatic mountain scenery in Angola. For birders, this is a potential place to spot the Cinderella waxbill or the grey kestrel, while limited game includes oryx, giraffe, springbok & ostrich.

Standards here are as high as at its sister lodge, although here the chalets are large safari tents (1 suitable for a family) with inside & outside showers. Activities, too, are similar, focusing on Himba trips, river trips, fishing & guided walks. Most guests fly in to the nearby airstrip. *DBB N$6,650/9,000 sgl/dbl.* **$$$$$**

🏠 **House on the Hill** [420 B2] (3 cottages) m 081 124 6826, 081 229 3383; e houseonthehill. nott@gmail.com; www.houseonthehillnam. com. This small self-catering lodge in the remote northwest of the Kunene Region was set up in 2009 in a joint venture between the Orupembe Conservancy & local artist Trevor Nott. The original house was abandoned by the manager of a local marble mine when it shut down in 1999. Today 3 fairly basic cottages (1 sleeping 4, 2 sleeping 2) are perched on the hill with magnificent views of the surrounding landscape. Each contains a fridge, basic utensils, crockery, cutlery & a gas cooker, with solar hot water & electricity. Guests should expect to be fully self-sufficient but there are staff on site who may be able to provide laundry & car-washing services along with fresh bread & firewood on request (& at a price to be agreed). *N$1,100 per chalet.* **$$$**

🏠 **Camp Syncro** [420 B1] (3 bungalows, 4 pitches). Camp Syncro was up for sale in 2018 & the owners had relocated to Switzerland. While the camp is still open, it is not possible to book & pay in advance, so it seems its future is uncertain.

Å **Marble Campsite** [420 B1] (5 pitches) This community-owned campsite in the Orupembe Conservancy is on the site of an abandoned marble mine, between Orupembe & Red Drum. Each of the pitches has a braai & food preparation area, but they share communal ablutions. There is supposed to be hot & cold running water & solar-powered lights but this is by no means reliable. From the camp there are 2 self-guided walking trails & it is also possible to arrange a visit to a Himba village. *N$120 pp.* **$**

Å **Okarohombo Campsite** [420 B1] (9 pitches) ☎065 658993; e maxi@nasco.org.na; www.nacso. org.na. This simple, remote campsite under ana trees (*Faidherbia albida*) is run by the local Himba community, who speak little English. Contact the Marienfluss Conservancy Office (☎*065 685993*; *www.nacso.org.na/conservancies/marienfluss-conservancy*) for reservations. It offers 4 private sites, each with private hot shower (from solar panels), toilet & kitchen area, & a further 5 sharing ablution & cooking facilities. Like most community campsites, it is worth your support. *N$120 pp.* **$**

Å **Van Zyl's Pass Campsite** [420 B2] (6 pitches) m 081 211 6291; e maxi@nasco.org.na; www. nacso.org.na. On the banks of a sandy river-bed, this community campsite is 20km east of Van Zyl's Pass. 3 pitches have private flush toilets, hot showers, basins, braais & sinks, & there's a 4th 'overflow' pitch. Advance booking is likely to be tricky & there is little need to do so; simply turn up, but beware: do not attempt the pass without at least 2 4x4 vehicles, sufficient supplies & adequate back-up plan; see page 141 for planning an expedition. *N$120 pp.* **$**

What to see and do The track that goes past these camps leads after about 3km to three options. The left fork goes to an excellent viewing point, over some rapids in the river. The centre and right turns are both blocked to vehicles. If you walk up the middle track, you'll find a small beach on the Kunene. The right track leads off to some trees, which may have been a campsite once.

In the morning and evening you'll see many Himba people going about their business, often with their cattle. There is also some wildlife around, including springbok, ostrich, bat-eared fox, bustards, korhaans and many other birds.

17

Etosha National Park

Translated as the 'Place of Mirages', 'Land of Dry Water' or the 'Great White Place', Etosha is an apparently endless pan of silvery-white sand, upon which dust-devils play and mirages blur the horizon. As a game park, it excels during the dry season when huge herds of animals can be seen amid some of the most startling and photogenic scenery in Africa.

The roads are all navigable in a normal 2WD car, and the park was designed for visitors to drive themselves around. However, if you would prefer guided trips – or want an introductory guided tour in a safari vehicle – these can be organised both at camps and lodges within the park, and by the private lodges just outside (or consider instead one of the concession areas in Damaraland).

For most people, though, Etosha is a park to explore by yourself. Put a few drinks, a camera, extra memory cards and a pair of binoculars in your own car and go for a slow drive, stopping at the waterholes – it's amazing.

There are now five lodges and camps (confusingly all now known by NWR as 'resorts') within the park, as well as an ever-increasing number of lodges outside its boundaries.

BACKGROUND INFORMATION

HISTORY Europeans first knew Etosha in the early 1850s when Charles Andersson and Francis Galton visited it. They recorded their early impressions:

> … we traversed an immense hollow, called Etosha, covered with saline encrustations, and having wooded and well-defined borders. Such places are in Africa designated 'salt pans'… In some rainy seasons, the Ovambo informed us, the locality was flooded and had all the appearance of a lake; but now it was quite dry, and the soil strongly impregnated with salt. Indeed, close in shore, the commodity was to be had of a very pure quality.

They were among the first explorers and traders who relentlessly hunted the area's huge herds of game. In 1876 an American trader, McKiernan, came through the area and wrote of a visit to Etosha:

> All the menageries in the world turned loose would not compare to the sight that I saw that day.

The slaughter became worse as time progressed and more Europeans came until, in 1907, Dr F von Lindequist, the Governor of German South West Africa (as Namibia was then), proclaimed three reserves. These covered all of the current park and most of Kaokoland – between the Kunene and Hoarusib rivers. The aim was to stem the

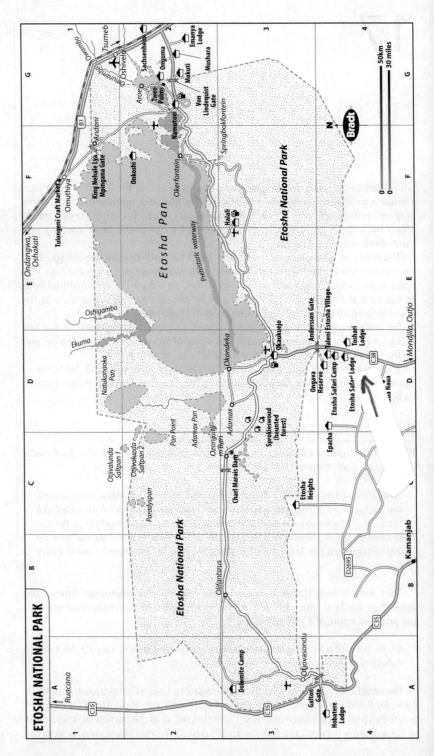

ETOSHA NATIONAL PARK

434

rapid depletion of the animals in the area, and protect all of the land through which the seasonal migrations passed. It was an excellent plan for conserving the wildlife – though perhaps not so perfect for the people who lived in these areas.

This protected area remained largely intact until the 1950s and 1960s. Then, just as a nature conservation unit and several tourist camps were set up, the reserves were redefined and Etosha shrank to its present size.

In the last decade, there has been much talk of developing a 'people's park' – designed to link Etosha with the Skeleton Coast. If this were to come to fruition, it would cross the concessions currently held by Hobatere, Etendeka and Palmwag, creating a 20km-wide corridor to allow free movement of wildlife between the two national parks.

While this is still on the agenda for some interested parties, including some in the Ministry of Environment and Tourism (MET), it's a complex issue with many political ramifications, and the topic has recently gone quiet. Behind the scenes, however, local advocates are already strengthening the ties between them, as well as trying to harmonise their approach to environmental and conservation issues, which has to be a step forward, whether or not any type of formalised park ever comes to fruition.

GEOGRAPHY, LANDSCAPE AND FLORA The defining feature of the 23,000km² national park is the huge Etosha Pan, which appears to be the remnant of a large inland lake that was fed by rivers from the north and east. One of these was probably the Kunene, which flowed southeast from the Angolan highlands and into the pan. However, some 12 million years ago continental uplift changed the slope of the land and the course of these tributaries. The Kunene now flows west from the Ruacana Falls and into the Atlantic. Thus deprived, the lake slowly vanished in the scorching sun, leaving behind only a salty residue. Few plants can grow on this and so wind erosion is easy, allowing the pan to be gradually hollowed out.

The pan has probably changed little over time. It is roughly 110km from east to west and 60km from north to south, covering an area of 6,133km² (around a quarter of the park's surface) with flat, silvery sand and shimmering heat. If the rains to the north and east have been good, then the pan will hold water for a few months at the start of the year, thanks mainly to the Ekuma River and the Omuramba Ovambo. Only very rarely does it fill completely.

In the rest of the park, beyond the sides of the pan, the terrain is generally flat with a variety of habitats ranging from mopane woodland to wide, open, virtually treeless plains. In the east of the park, around Namutoni, the attractive makalani palms (*Hyphaene petersiana*) are found, often in picturesque groups around waterholes. The small, round fruit of these palms, a favourite food of elephants, is sometimes called vegetable ivory because of its hard white kernel. In the west, one of the more unusual areas is the Haunted Forest, Sprokieswoud in Afrikaans, where the contorted forms of strange moringa trees (*Moringa ovalifolia*) form a weird woodland scene. Further west still, the environment becomes hillier, with mopane woodlands dotting the open savannah: very pretty but with few obvious centres for the game to congregate.

Etosha is so special because of the concentration of waterholes that occur around the southern edges of the pan and which, as the dry season progresses, increasingly draw wildlife. In fact, the best way to watch animals in Etosha is often just to sit in your vehicle by a waterhole and wait.

Three types of spring create these waterholes, which differ in both appearance and geology:

Contact springs These occur in situations where two adjacent layers of rock have very different permeabilities. There are many to be seen just on the edge of the pan. Here the water-bearing calcrete comes to an end and the water flows out on to the surface because the underlying layers of clay are impermeable. Okerfontein is the best example of this type of spring, which is generally weak in water supply.

Water-level springs These are found in hollows where the surface of the ground actually cuts below the level of the water table, often in large depressions in the limestone formations. They are inevitably dependent on the level of the water table, and hence vary greatly from year to year. Typical of this type are Ngobib, Groot Okevi and Klein Okevi.

Artesian springs Formed when pressure from overlying rocks forces water up to the surface from deeper aquifers (water-bearing rocks), these normally occur on limestone hillocks, forming deep pools that often have clumps of reeds in the centre. These springs are usually very reliable and include Namutoni, Klein Namutoni and Chudob.

MAMMALS The mammals found here are typical of the savannah plains of southern Africa, but include several species endemic to this western side of the continent, adjacent to the Namib Desert.

The more common herbivores include elephant, giraffe, eland, blue wildebeest, kudu, gemsbok, springbok, impala, steenbok and zebra. The most numerous of these are the springbok, which can often be seen in herds numbering thousands, spread out over the most barren of plains. These finely marked antelope have a marvellous habit of pronking, either (it appears) for fun or to avoid predators. It has been suggested that pronking is intended to put predators off in the first place by showing the animal's strength and stamina; the weakest pronkers are the ones predators are seen to go for. The early explorer Andersson described these elegant leaps:

> This animal bounds without an effort to a height of 10 or 12 feet at one spring, clearing from 12 to 14 feet of ground. It appears to soar, to be suspended for a moment in the air, then, touching the ground, to make another dart, or another flight, aloft, without the aid of wings, by the elastic springiness of its legs.

Elephant number around 2,000 across the entire park and are mostly seen in the dry season when large family groups troop down to the waterholes to drink, wallow and bathe, whereas during the rains they disperse across the park. Although it was once thought that digging for water below the sand wore down their tusks, this is in fact only the case for the desert elephants found in Damaraland and the Skeleton Coast. In Etosha, where many elephants have broken tusks and big tuskers are rare, the damage probably results from a lack of essential minerals. As an aside, the park's elephant population has been under scientific scrutiny for the infrasonic noises (below the range of human hearing) which they make. It is thought that groups communicate over long distances in this way.

Among the rarer species, black rhino continue to thrive here, with the floodlit waterholes at Okaukuejo, and to a lesser extent Halali, providing two of the continent's best chances to observe this aggressive and secretive species. On one visit here, I watched as a herd of 20 or so elephants, silently drinking in the cool of the night, were frightened away from the water, and kept at bay, by the arrival of a single black rhino. It returned several times in the space of an hour or so, each time causing the larger elephants to flee, before settling down to enjoy a drink from the pool on its own. Conversely, white rhino are rarely seen in the park, though Springbokfontein seems to be the best place for a sighting

Black-faced impala are restricted to Namibia and southern Angola, occurring here as well as in parts of the Kunene Region to the west. With only isolated populations, numbering under a thousand or so, they are one of the rarest animals in the region. The Damara dik-dik is the park's smallest antelope. Endemic to Namibia, it is common here in areas of dense bush.

Roan antelope, sable and red hartebeest occur all over the subcontinent, though they are common nowhere, with Etosha no exception. Hartebeest are seen more frequently than either roan or sable.

All of the larger felines are found in Etosha, with good numbers of lion, leopard, cheetah and caracal. The lion tend to prey mainly upon zebra and wildebeest, while the cheetah rely largely upon springbok. The seldom-seen leopard take a varied diet, including antelope and small mammals, while the equally elusive caracal go for similar but smaller prey.

There have been several attempts to introduce wild dog here, but so far with no success. Among other problems, the dogs don't know to avoid lion, which have subsequently killed them for no apparent reason. In addition, the dogs tend to be affected by canine diseases carried by animals from farms surrounding the park.

Also found in the park are both spotted and brown hyenas, together with silver jackal (or Cape fox), and the more common black-backed jackal – many of which can be seen in the late evening, skulking around the camps in search of scraps of food.

BIRDS Some 340 species of birds have been recorded in Etosha, including many uncommon members of the hawk and vulture families.

Among the birds of prey, bateleur, martial, tawny and Wahlberg's eagles are fairly common, as are black-breasted and brown snake eagles. Pale chanting goshawks are more often seen than the similar Gabar or the smaller little banded goshawk. The list of harriers, falcons and kestrels occurring here is even longer, and worthy of a special mention are the very common rock kestrels, and the unusual red-necked and particularly cute pygmy falcons, which are less readily seen. The impressive peregrine falcon and Montagu's harrier are two of the rarer summer migrants.

Lappet-faced and white-backed vultures are common here, outnumbering the odd pair of white-headed or hooded vultures. Palmnut vultures are occasionally seen in the east of the park.

The number of large birds stalking around the plains can strike visitors as unusual: invariably during the day you will see groups of ostriches or pairs of secretary birds. Equally, it is easy to drive within metres of many kori bustards and black korhaans, which will just sit by the roadside and watch the vehicles pass. In the wet season, blue cranes, both beautiful and endangered, are common here: Etosha is worth visiting in January and February for them alone. Other specialities of the park include violet wood hoopoe, white-tailed shrike, bare-cheeked and black-faced babblers, short-toed rock thrush, and a pale race of the pink-bellied lark.

PRACTICAL INFORMATION

WHEN TO VISIT To decide when to visit, think about the weather, consider the number of other visitors around, and work out if your main reason for coming is to see the animals or the birds.

Weather Etosha's weather is typical of Namibia, so see page 3 for a general overview. At the beginning of the year, it's hot and fairly damp with average temperatures around 27°C and cloud cover for some of the time. If the rains have been good, then the pan will have some standing water in it.

The clouds gradually disperse as the rains cease, around March–April. Many of Etosha's plants are bright green during this time but, with some cloud cover, the park's stark beauty isn't at its most photogenic.

From April to July the park dries out, and nights become progressively cooler. In August they are normally above freezing, and by the end of September they are warm again. October is hot, and gets hotter as the month progresses, but the humidity remains very low.

Even the game seems to await the coming of the rains – traditionally in late November, or perhaps December, but now tending to arrive earlier. When these do materialise, the tropical downpours last only for a few hours each afternoon, but they clear the air, revive the vegetation, and give everything a new lease of life.

Photography From a photographic point of view, Etosha can be stunning in any month. A personal favourite is late April to June, when the vegetation is green, yet the skies are clear blue and there's little dust in the rain-washed air.

Other visitors Etosha can get very busy, particularly around Easter and in high season (July–October). Then advance bookings are *essential*; you may not even get a camping site without a prior reservation, and in August, accommodation inside the park can be full over a year in advance.

The dates of the South African school holidays are a lot less relevant than they used to be, as Namibia is no longer the only foreign country where South African passport holders are welcomed. However, ideally try to avoid Namibian school holidays. February to mid-April, late May to June, and November are probably the quietest months, though with availability increasingly tight in the peak months, even May, June and November are now busier than in previous years.

Game viewing Etosha's dry season is certainly the best time to see big game. As the small bush pools dry up and the green vegetation shrivels, the animals move closer to the springs on the pan's edge. Before the game fences were erected (these now surround the park completely), many of the larger animals would have migrated between Etosha and the Kaokoveld – returning here during the dry season to the region's best permanent waterholes. Now most are forced to stay within the park and only bull elephants commonly break out of their confines to cause problems for the surrounding farmers.

Hence the months between July and late October are the best for wildlife. Though the idea of sitting in a car at 40°C may seem unpleasant, October is normally the best month for game viewing and the heat is very dry. Park under a shady tree and be grateful that the humidity is so low. During and after the rains, you won't see much wildlife, partly because the lush vegetation hides the animals, and partly because most of them will have moved away from the waterholes (where most of the roads are) and gone deeper into the bush. However, often the animals you see will have young, as food (animal or vegetable) is at its most plentiful then.

Birdwatching The start of the rainy season witnesses the arrival of the summer migrants and, if the rains have been good, the aquatic species that come for the water in the pan itself. In exceptional years thousands of flamingos will come to breed, building their nests on the eastern side of the main Etosha Pan, or in Fischer's Pan. This is an amazing spectacle (see box, page 64). However, bear in mind that Etosha's ordinary feathered residents can be seen more easily during the dry season, when there is less vegetation to hide them.

GETTING THERE AND AWAY

By road Hiring your own vehicle is best done in Windhoek (page 140). However, if you are travelling through, and hiring a car just for Etosha, then consider doing so from Tsumeb. This is normally best organised in advance, through a tour operator (page 104) or a car-hire company in Windhoek (page 140), some of which will let you pick up and drop off cars at Mokuti or Ongava.

Many operators organise guided trips around Namibia, including a few days in Etosha, often staying in the national park's accommodation. However, you only need to see one air-conditioned 75-seater coach driving through the park to convince you that this is not the best way to visit either Etosha or Namibia. Most have their bases in Windhoek; see page 173 for details.

By air Scenic Air run flights between Windhoek and either Ongava or Mokuti (*1½–2hrs; from N$8,760/10,500 respectively*), though there is no fixed schedule for these. Wilderness Air runs daily flights from Ongava airstrip, just south of the park's Andersson Gate, back to Windhoek (*about 1½hrs; from N$9,177 pp*).

PARK ACCESS (⊙ *sunrise–sunset; admission N$80 per adult, plus N$10 per vehicle, under 16s free*) There are four gates into the national park, although the majority of visitors use either the Von Lindequist Gate, near Namutoni, which is 106km from Tsumeb, or the Andersson Gate, south of Okaukuejo, 120km from Outjo. A less well-known option, introduced in 2003, glories in the name of King Nehale lya Mpingana Gate. This is in the northeast corner of the park, near Andoni, with access 17km from the B1 north of Tsumeb. The fourth access point, the Galton Gate, lies at the western end of the park. Until March 2014, this whole western region was closed to the public, with the exception of guests at Dolomite Camp, but since then it has been open to the general public.

Entry permits are issued at the gates. From there, you must proceed to the nearest camp/resort office and settle the costs of your permit and any accommodation within the park. With the exception of Onkoshi Camp, rates for accommodation within the park exclude entrance fees, so be aware that even if you are staying overnight, fees are still payable.

It is possible to leave and re-enter the park during the validity of a permit as long as you make your intentions clear at the gate on arrival, and inform them where you are staying, and then also notify the camp when you pay.

The gates open around sunrise and close about 20 minutes before sunset. For the precise times on any given day, see the notice next to the entry gates of each camp. Driving through the park in the dark is not allowed, and the gates do close on time.

GETTING AROUND To see Etosha you need to drive around the park. There is no way to walk within it, or to fly just above it. If you do not have your own vehicle then you must either hire one (page 140), or book an organised trip.

Etosha was designed for visitors to drive themselves around. The roads are good; a normal 2WD car is fine for all of them. The landscapes are generally open, as the vegetation is sparse, so you don't need eyes like a hawk to spot most of the larger animals. That said, some people still prefer organised tours to visit the park.

Organising your own safari Most of Etosha's roads are made of calcrete and gravel, which gives a good driving surface without the unnatural appearance of tar, but they can be slippery when wet. The speed limit within the park is 60km/h. Be warned that most of the park's accidents occur near sunset, as people try to dash back to camp before the gates close.

An excellent map of the park and the more colourful 'Honeyguide' publication, with colour sketches of most of the common birds and animals, are normally for sale in the resort shops.

For details of planning your day, and the main waterholes to visit, see page 451.

Organised tour Some visitors really don't want to drive themselves around. Others appreciate the benefit of a local guide or the height of a safari vehicle – though a higher viewpoint isn't necessarily better for photographs, which often are best at eye level for realism.

Many organised trips to the park emanate from the surrounding private lodges. See page 443 for ideas about what is possible from each. Alternatively, you could try one of the tour operators in Windhoek.

 WHERE TO STAY AND EAT

INSIDE ETOSHA In addition to the three long-established national park restcamps (or 'resorts') inside Etosha, there is the smaller, smarter Onkoshi Resort, and Dolomite Resort in the previously private western side of the park. All these accommodation options within the park are operated by Namibia Wildlife Resorts (NWR; page 103).

Aim to spend a minimum of two nights at any camp/resort you visit. Remember that, with a speed limit of 60km/h, it will take you at least 2 hours to drive between Namutoni and Halali, or Halali and Okaukuejo. To get to Onkoshi, you'll need to allow around 1½ hours from Namutoni, and Dolomite Camp is around 180km from Okaukuejo, taking around 4–5 hours once you've factored in some game viewing on the way.

Reservations Booking accommodation in advance with the NWR (\ *061 285 7200; e reservations@nwr.com.na; www.nwr.com.na*) is wise, but you need to be organised and stick to your itinerary. The alternative is to plan on camping, while hoping for spaces or cancellations in the chalets and bungalows. For this you'll need to ask at the camp office just before it closes at sunset. This is often successful outside the main holiday months, but you need a tent in case it is not.

Note that during the main holiday seasons, especially around Easter and August, even Etosha's campsites are fully booked in advance. If you haven't a reservation, you must stay outside the park and drive in for day trips.

The original restcamps The reception office at each of the three restcamps, or resorts (⊙ *dawn–dusk*) is where you pay for your stay, as well as any park fees due. Don't forget to pay all your park fees before you try to leave the park. You can't pay them at the gate.

Facilities Each of the erstwhile restcamps has a range of accommodation, including bungalows and a campsite and a restaurant where most visitors take at least one of their meals. At the time of research, meal prices (*b/fast N$150, lunch N$230, dinner N$280*) were common to all camps. Outside prescribed mealtimes, there's usually a kiosk that sells drinks and snacks (⊕ *10.00–17.00 daily; Namutoni*

⌚ *08.30–noon & 13.30–18.00*). After dinner, the bar normally stays open until about midnight.

The camp shops (⌚ *06.00–19.00 daily*) sell a good range of tinned and packet foods as well as bread, cheese and cured meats. Frozen meat, sausages and firewood (with braais in mind) are sometimes stocked, but can sell out quickly in busy months. Beer, lots of cold drinks, and a limited selection of wine are also found here. Take your own cooking equipment. Aside from food, there is also the usual mix of tourist needs, from curios, T-shirts, and wildlife books to postcards and even stamps. You can normally buy phonecards at the shop for the payphone, and Wi-Fi vouchers (*N$50 for 300MB, N$100 for 700MB*) are sold both here and at the restaurant.

Each camp also has a swimming pool and – importantly – a **fuel station** (⌚ *sunrise–sunset*), but don't run it too close; you wouldn't want to run out of fuel in the middle of the park.

Lodges

🏠 **Onkoshi Resort** [434 F2] (15 chalets)
Opened in 2008, this was envisaged as the jewel in the crown of NWR's Etosha resorts. It lies 42km north of Namutoni, in an area previously closed to all but lodge guests. The road to Onkoshi was graded in 2017, so it's now possible to drive direct to the lodge.

Approached down a wooden walkway, the stone-&-thatch central building has a comfortable lounge & bar area which, together with a restaurant (*lunch/dinner N$210/230*) & terrace, a small pool & loungers, allows guests to gaze over the vast open space of Etosha Pan.

Spread out on either side of the main areas, the chalets are designed to make the most of their location overlooking the pan. While the setting is stunning, the rooms are looking a little dated, though they remain spotless. Folding glass doors open on 2 sides, & twin beds, inside their mosquito net, face the pan. The slightly larger 'honeymoon chalet' has a queen bed & ostrich-leather covered furniture; others are more plain, with wooden bedside tables & a sleeper couch. You'll also find a freestanding bath tub, inside & outside showers (though be aware of the limited privacy of the outside shower) & separate WC.

Although Onkoshi isn't in a wildlife-rich area, they offer morning, evening & night drives (*N$650/750 pp*), but the beauty here is the pan: between Jul & Oct you may be lucky enough to see flamingos that come here to nest. On the downside, as the pan dries out prolific insect life may occur; while this affects the whole park, the camp's proximity to the pan makes it particularly susceptible. *B&B from N$2,020/3,640 sgl/dbl.* **$$$$$**

🏠 **Dolomite Resort** [434 A3] (20 rooms)
Opened in 2011, Dolomite brought the previously off-limits area of western Etosha into the public domain, with access through the Galton Gate. The land in this part of the park is hilly with much bush: very pretty but with few obvious centres for game to congregate. Set among dolomite outcrops, the camp has views to east & west over the surrounding savannah from the reception, lounge, bar, infinity pool & restaurants. The chalets, constructed of thatch & canvas with wooden decking, are comfortable & stylish, if a little cramped. They are, though, private & widely spaced, but note that there are many steps along the wooden walkways, & some of the stone paths are long & uneven, so access may be unsuitable for the less agile. Morning & afternoon game drives (*N$650/750 pp day/night drives*) are offered in the surrounding areas of the park, & at the time of research a licence for night driving was in the pipeline. *B&B N$2,020–2,740/3,640–5,080 sgl/dbl.* **$$$$$**

Restcamps

☀ 🏠 **Okaukuejo Resort** [434 D3] (45 rooms, 59 chalets, camping) 📞 067 229800. Etosha's oldest restcamp is the administrative hub of the park & the centre of the Etosha Ecological Institute. It occupies a level, grassy site at the western end of the pan, about 120km north of Outjo. We found the waiting staff very friendly, but standards of service & cleanliness are highly variable.

Okaukuejo's big attraction is that it overlooks a permanent waterhole that is floodlit at night, giving you a chance to see some of the shy, nocturnal animals that come to drink – oblivious to the noise, the bright lights & the people sitting on benches just behind a low stone wall. The light doesn't penetrate into the dark surrounding bush, but it illuminates the waterhole like a stage – focusing all attention on the animals. During the dry season you would be unlucky not to spot something of interest by just sitting here for a few hours in the evening, so bring a couple of drinks, binoculars & some warm clothes to settle down & watch. You are virtually guaranteed to see elephant & jackal, while lion & black rhino are very regular visitors. The main annoyance is noise from the bungalows beside the waterhole, or from the many people sitting around.

The well-spaced dbl rooms & chalets (including 2 for families & 2 suitable for guests with a disability) are smartly fitted out but with a rustic feel. Configurations vary, but all are en suite, with AC & seating areas, plus fridge & kettle. 20 bush chalets have a lounge & a braai area; 45 dbl rooms are similar without the lounge; 30 waterhole chalets also have a view of the waterhole; & 5 premier waterhole chalets are built on 2 storeys, with a large bedroom & terrace above, & a combined sitting room & 2nd bedroom below. The campsite's 37 pitches have BBQ facilities & power points, but no grass & little shade. Good food (a buffet in season) is served at reasonable prices in the modern restaurant, which has AC. Laundry is in theory possible (*around N$20–30 per item*), but the washing machines are unreliable.

Okaukuejo's shop is well stocked, with sweets & drinks available from the kiosk by the large circular swimming pools. Along with the park's only post office (⏱ *08.30–13.00 & 14.00–16.30 Mon–Fri, 08.00–11.00 Sat*), there's a tourist information office & a curio shop (⏱ *08.00–17.00 daily*). Nearby, a spiral staircase inside a castle-like tower can be climbed for a good view of the surrounding area. Day/night game drives (*N$650/750 pp*). *B&B room N$1,570/3,140 sgl/dbl, bush chalet N$1,620/2,940, waterhole chalet N$2,100/4,000; camping N$300 pp (max 8 per pitch).* **$$–$$$$$**

🏠 **Halali Resort** [434 F3] (40 rooms, 31 chalets, camping) 📞 067 229400. The smallest, & usually the quietest, of the old restcamps, Halali is 75km from Namutoni, 70km from Okaukuejo, & just northwest of the landmark Tweekoppies. There's a small dolomite kopje within the camp's boundary, accessible on a short self-guided trail signposted as 'Tsumasa'. The Moringa waterhole on

its boundary, which can be viewed from a natural rock seating area a few hundred metres beyond the campsite, regularly attracts elephant, black rhino & other game. It isn't as busy as Okaukuejo's waterhole, but as it is set apart from the camp, it usually has fewer disturbances & a more natural ambience.

Close to the entrance are the shop & restaurant, with a kiosk by the large pool. Meals are served buffet style in season, or à la carte the rest of the year. Accommodation, less extensively refurbished than at the other camps, is smaller & simpler. Twin or dbl en-suite rooms come with AC, fridge & kettle; bush chalets have a kitchenette in the living room; & larger family chalets have a separate kitchen, lounge & big braai area with terrace. There are also honeymoon suites & 4 chalets with disabled access. The 58 camping pitches are very close together but usually with reasonable tree shade. Day/night game drives (*N$650/750 pp*). *B&B room N$1,270/2,240 sgl/dbl, chalet N$1,510–1,680/2,700–3,080; camping N$300 pp (max 8 per pitch).* **$$–$$$$$**

🏠 **Namutoni Resort** [434 G2] (24 rooms, 20 chalets, camping) 📞 067 229300. Situated on the eastern edge of the pan, Namutoni is based around a beautiful old 'Beau Geste' type fort, in an area dotted with graceful makalani palms (*Hyphaene petersiana*). It dates back to a German police post, built before the turn of the 20th century. Later it was used as an army base & then for English prisoners during World War I, before being restored in 1957. Despite refurbishment around 2015, the volume of travellers through this camp has given it a tired look so the long-mooted renovations – to move the accommodation back into the fort, & bring the main areas back outside it – would be well timed.

For now, a museum in the fort gives the history of the park, its flora, fauna & people. For some downtime, there's a shady thatched viewing area for the waterhole, & a swimming pool. Rooms are contemporary in style, with a private entrance patio enclosed by a pole fence, twin or dbl beds, & a good-sized bathroom with sunken bath & shower, 2 basins & outside shower. Chalets are more spacious but similarly appointed. None of the rooms has braai or cooking facilities; for these you'll need to camp on one of 25 grassy & well shaded pitches, each with power, & sharing ablution blocks.

Game drives (*N$650/750 pp day/night*) offer an advantage over self-driving, as morning drives start 1hr before the gates open, & evening ones ends 1hr after they close. *B&B room N$1,200 pp*

Nov–Jun, N$1,650/3,000 sgl/dbl Jul–Oct; chalet N$1,400 pp Nov–Jun, N$1,900/3,500 sgl/dbl Jul–Oct; camping N$300/350 pp Nov–Jun/Jul–Oct (max 8). **$$–$$$$$$**

NEAR ETOSHA Several private lodges are clustered around each of Etosha's entrance gates. Notable among these on the eastern side are Mokuti, and the lodges on the Onguma and Mushara reserves, near Namutoni, with Ongava, Etosha Safari Camp and Lodge and Taleni Etosha Village south of Okaukuejo. Other options lie within 30–45 minutes' drive of the gates in each direction. Many have their own vehicles and guides, but note that all vehicles in the park are subject to the park's strict opening and closing times, and none are allowed off road while inside Etosha.

Traditionally, such lodges have cost more than the public camps and lodges within the park but, following significant investment by the NWR, the gap in terms of both rates and, often, facilities is closing. Places listed below start with those closest to the park gates. For additional accommodation south of Etosha, but within easy distance of the park, see page 455.

South of Etosha (Andersson Gate)

🏠 **Ongava Reserve** [434 D4] `\`083 330 3920; e reservations@ongava.com; www.ongava.com. Down a long drive just by the Andersson Gate, the private Ongava Reserve, abutting Etosha's southern side, covers 30,000ha, & is the base for 4 discrete camps. For costly but quick transfers, you can use small aircraft, operated by Wilderness Air.

The environment & wildlife are similar to those near Okaukuejo, although without the huge salt-pan its scenery is less spectacular. Nevertheless, Ongava offers a greater choice of activities than is possible in the national park. The reserve has over 25 lions & in excess of 2,500 head of game, & is one of the few remaining places in Africa where visitors have a fairly reliable chance of encountering both black & white rhino. To guarantee the chance of tracking rhino on foot you should book this in advance, & never try to walk without a guide.

Activities at each of the camps are conducted independently. They feature escorted walks/drives on Ongava's own reserve & longer game drives into the national park. In summer there is normally a long (*around 5hrs*) activity in the morning. This is followed by lunch & time at leisure before dinner, after which there is a night drive. In winter the morning activities are shorter, about 3–4hrs long, & lunch is normally followed by a late-afternoon game drive which often continues after dark by floodlight.

🏠 ONGAVA LODGE (14 chalets) `\`063 683022. This is the original focus of the reserve, set on a hill

10km from the entrance gate. Centred around a 3-level thatched boma that covers the lounge, bar & restaurant (serving excellent food), it overlooks a waterhole from a well-designed viewing area. There's plenty of space for relaxing & a swimming pool to cool off. Perched on the hillside, the stone-&-thatch chalets have a rustic yet stylish look, nestled among natural vegetation with views over the reserve from their wooden decks. Rooms are large & luxurious, with AC, twin queen-size beds (& 1 family chalet), en-suite showers inside & out, 24hr mains electricity & a kettle with tea/coffee. The large curio shop also stocks safari clothes & other souvenirs. *DBB N$5,615–7,487/8,982–11,980 sgl/dbl; FBA N$9,811–13,081/15,696–20,930 sgl/dbl.* **$$$$$$$**

🏠 LITTLE ONGAVA (3 luxury suites) This exclusive hideaway, set on the crest of the hill above Ongava Lodge, operates as an entirely self-contained camp, with dedicated & exceptionally well-trained staff. Wooden walkways link the suites, which have spectacular views across the reserve from each of their 3 rooms, as well as from their extensive decks & private plunge pools. If that's not enough, you can also contemplate the view from a luxurious shaded day bed.

Each suite boasts all the mod cons of a 5-star establishment but manages to combine style with comfort & – crucially – a strong sense of place. A series of sliding doors separate the bedroom from a huge bathroom, & further sliding doors lead outside. All is tastefully furnished, with solid wood & neutral colours bringing an intimacy that is all too often lacking in similar upmarket establishments. *FBA N$17,676–23,568/28,280–37,708 sgl/dbl.* **$$$$$$**

☀ ⌂ ONGAVA TENTED CAMP (9 tents) ☎ 067 687041. Very large Meru-style tents, under shade nets, form the basis of this small, relaxed camp, some 10km north of Ongava Lodge. The tents, erected on timber decks, have twin beds (or 1 family unit), chairs & mosquito nets, plus en-suite indoor & outdoor showers, & a veranda. B/fast & lunch are taken at individual tables, but dinner is eaten as a group in the central boma, set just 20m from the busy waterhole, with a small pool alongside. *FBA N$9,811–13,081/15,695–20,930 sgl/dbl.* **$$$$$$$**

⌂ ANDERSSON'S CAMP (8 suites) ☎ 067 687181. Andersson's Camp was undergoing a complete rebuild during 2018, but once reopened the camp will have a strong focus on environmental & conservation issues. With a close proximity to the Ongava Research Centre you will have a chance to meet & converse with resident scientists, conservationists & rhino security personnel.

The camp's new suites, constructed from natural stone & recycled materials & furnished with scientific tomes & journals, will include mosquito nets, kettle with tea/coffee, & en-suite bathrooms with both indoor & outdoor showers, & each will have a private veranda.

A communal lounge area will surround an infinity pool, looking towards a waterhole, along with an underground hide giving eye-level views of the area's wildlife. *DBB N$5,615–7,487/8,982–11,980 sgl/dbl; FBA N$9,811–13,081/15,692–20,930 sgl/dbl.* **$$$$$$**

⌂ **Taleni Etosha Village** [434 D4] (45 chalets) ☎ 067 333413; **e** reservations@ etosha-village.com; www.etosha-village.com. Just 2km from the Andersson Gate, Taleni is styled loosely on a traditional village, with tented chalets on timber decks well spaced among mopane trees. Bedrooms have AC, kettle, a sleeper couch, a safe & sockets for charging, & there's an en-suite bathroom & shower. There are 3 separate dining areas serving good buffet-style meals, & 3 pools, all in attractive gardens. Activities include ½/full-day game drives (*N$580/825*) into Etosha, sundowner drives & sunrise guided walks (*both N$260*) & stargazing on the property (*N$200*). *DBB N$1,857–2,773/2,110–3,110 sgl/dbl.* **$$$$–$$$$$**

☀ ⌂ **Etosha Safari Camp** [434 D4] (56 chalets, camping) ☎ 067 333404; **e** res6@ gondwana-collection.com; www.gondwana-collection.com. Part of the Gondwana Group, this lodge brings the spirit of a township to life, with a funky 'village' feel. There's a shebeen, a shop in a railway carriage, a games room & a central courtyard with 'wheelbarrow' & 'bathtub' chairs, & the whole place is decorated with 1950s memorabilia. Nearby you'll find the lively 'Down Corruption' bar, & the swimming pool on a raised deck area. Scattered across the hillside are brick-built chalets (inc 10 for families & 3 trpls), all with AC, safes & a fun shower enclosure. There's also a large, open campsite. Popular with small groups, the camp is right by the C38, & just 9km south of Etosha. *B&B chalet N$1,526/2,442 sgl/dbl; camping N$195 pp.* **$$$$**

⌂ **Etosha Safari Lodge** [434 D4] (65 rooms) ☎ 067 333411/9; **e** res6@gondwana-collection.com; www.gondwana-collection.com. This large lodge has a spacious dining area, bar & lounge in a central thatched building with a wraparound terrace & long sunset deck making the best of its spectacular view. Well-appointed individual chalets stretch out along the ridge in either direction (there is a shuttle service for those at the far ends!). Each has twin beds, AC, kettle, internal phone, open shower area & separate WC, & a small terrace taking in that view; 5 are family units. Dinner (*N$360*) is either buffet or a set menu, with sunset cocktails & occasional drumming sessions. A few short walking trails include one to the sister property, Etosha Safari Camp, & guided game drives (*N$1,000/1,480 ½/full day*) into Etosha are also available. Back at the lodge, 3 swimming pools offer further options. *B&B N$2,162/3,460 sgl/dbl.* **$$$$**

⌂ **Toshari Lodge** [434 D4] (44 rooms, camping) ☎ 067 333440/4; **e** info@toshari-namibia.com; www.toshari.com. About 27km from the Andersson Gate, & 71km north of Outjo, Toshari has a large thatched central building housing a reception area with comfy sofas & internet access, a bar & a restaurant (*N$165/295 lunch/dinner*) with tasteful artwork, & a pool with grassy surrounds. All rooms have AC, mosi nets, tea/coffee facilities & deck chairs on the terrace; the 5 luxury rooms also have glass sliding doors overlooking the wilderness, plus a minibar. 3 grassy camping pitches have their own bathrooms, power points &

braai area. Game drives into the park (N$735/1,029 pp ½/full day; min 5 people). B&B standard N$1,275/1,916 sgl/dbl; luxury N$1,410/2,226 sgl/dbl; camping N$160 pp. **$$$$**

🏠 **Epacha Reserve** [434 D4] 📞 067 333423; reservations 📞 +27 10 442 5885; e cro@aha.co.za; www.aha.co.za. The private Epacha Reserve covers 21,000ha of the wonderfully named Ondundonzondandana Valley, but contains just 2 properties: Epacha Lodge & Eagle Tented Lodge, both set on a gentle slope in the surrounding bush. The reserve, whose entrance is 27km along the D2695 from the C38, is stocked with a smattering of antelope species that can be spotted on game drives, & clay pigeon shooting is offered from both lodges.

🏠 EPACHA GAME LODGE **& SPA** (18 chalets, presidential suite) With the large foyer, wooden reception desk & facilities such as a library, billiards room & smoking room, Epacha has the initial feeling of a grand old hotel rather than a game lodge. However, with the abundance of dark colonial-style wooden furniture, dusty taxidermy & unfinished gardens we couldn't help but feel that the grandeur was somewhat faded. The lodge's rooms are scattered across the hillside, with golf-carts available to shuttle guests to the furthest rooms. Each is en suite, with an open-air shower & private balcony. There's also a 5-room presidential suite with its own private pool, although when busy the suite's 3 bedrooms are sold as individual units. The lodge also has a communal pool in the main area, lit up with flashing primary colours at night, & overlooked by a large wooden bar. For further indulgences there's a health spa with a Jacuzzi, steam room & a range of treatments. Morning & afternoon game drives (N$550 pp) are an option, but with species such as rhino, elephant & lion missing from the reserve, a visit to Etosha (N$1,000 pp), 57km away, will yield better game viewing. DBB N$3,505–4,235/5,670–7,120 sgl/dbl. **$$$$$**

🏠 EAGLE TENTED LODGE (16 tents) This lodge offers 2 styles of en-suite accommodation. Each of the 8 safari-style 'standard' tents, built on a 4m-high wooden platform, has an open view with glazed wooden doors leading out to a private balcony. 8 'de luxe' tents, with open-air bath tubs, have been built away from the main areas at ground level under 'carport'-style shade-netting canopies. Constructed from rustic-looking stone, the main

building is reminiscent of a French chateau, and incorporates a restaurant & bar with open windows, as well as a wine cellar. Outside, a couple of small pools look over green gardens & a waterhole. Guests can visit the spa at Epacha. DBB N$2,545–3,015/3,750–4,680 sgl/dbl. **$$$$$**

🏠 **Etosha Heights Reserve** [434 C3] Reservations 📞 067 312521; e resnam@naturalselection.travel; www.etoshaheights.com. While the Etosha Heights Reserve has traditionally permitted hunting, this 60,000ha private reserve, one of the largest in Namibia yet with just 2 lodges, has switched focus to photographic safaris. Sharing a 70km boundary with Etosha, it is well stocked with game, being home to large herds of springbok & eland, black rhino & elephant, with lion making an impressive comeback. The entrance to the reserve is along the D2697, about 13km from the junction with the D2680, & 12km from the D2695 junction.

🏠 SAFARIHOEK LODGE (11 chalets) On a hill overlooking mopane woodland & a floodlit waterhole, this modern lodge's chalets come with twin or king-size beds, AC, minibar, kettle with tea/coffee, a huge but sparse bathroom with indoor & outdoor showers, & a private deck overlooking the reserve. 2 standard chalets closest to the main area are wheelchair friendly; 8 luxury chalets are larger with better views. The dedicated family chalet has a small living area separating the master bedroom from the children's room. Décor is somewhat minimalist, with a collection of rather mismatched furniture. The thatched main area, with pale polished concrete floors, has an open-plan lounge with a chrome-&-glass bar, & a restaurant, although meals are also served on the outside deck. An oval swimming pool is surrounded by sunloungers & neutral-coloured sofas. Safarihoek is too far from Etosha to visit for the day, but you can seek out the reserve's impressive array of wildlife on morning, afternoon & night drives, as well as guided walks through the bush. A real highlight though is the split-level hide, equipped with toilets & charging points, offering ground-level & elevated views of the productive waterhole. DBB standard N$2,530–4,890/7,980–11,400 sgl/dbl; luxury N$3,025–5,520/6,050–7,980; FBA standard N$3,500–6,840/3,500–4,950 sgl/dbl; luxury N$3,900–7,240/8,460–12,080. **$$$$$**

🏠 MOUNTAIN LODGE (8 chalets) Revamped & realigned for photographic tourism in 2018,

Mountain Lodge sits atop a rocky outcrop with panoramic views of the surrounding bush. Compared with the modern Safarihoek, it has a much more rustic, traditional feel. There's plentiful use of varnished wood, & the main area is dominated by the huge trunk of a leadwood tree, around which are the bar, dining room & lounge. A curved wooden deck reaches around the front of the lodge, looking down towards a small waterhole. A small swimming pool is located on a lower section of decking. The thatched chalets are solidly built with tiled stone floors, heavy wooden fittings, en-suite shower & bath, and a varnished wooden deck looking out over the bush. *DBB N$2,440–5,155/4,880–7,360 sgl/dbl; FBA N$3,680–7,085/7,360–10,120 sgl/dbl.* **$$$$$–$$$$$$**

🏠 **Mondjila Safari Camp** [434 D4] (11 tents, camping) ✆067 333446; reservations ✆061 237294; e reservations@exclusive.com.na. Some 47km south of Okaukuejo, just 3km from the C38 along the D2779, Mondjila's walk-in tents with twin beds & en-suite showers are set on a hillside with quite steep slopes. The restaurant, bar & pool have fabulous views, & the campsite, with 8 pitches, has braai areas, power & light. *DBB N$1,170–1,220/2,200–2,440 sgl/dbl; camping N$150 pp.* **$$–$$$$**

West of Etosha (Galton Gate)

🏠 **Hobatere Lodge** [434 A4] (14 rooms) Reservations ✆061 228104; e hobatere@ journeysnamibia.com; www.hobatere-lodge.com. After a period of closure, Hobatere reopened in mid 2015, and is now 100% community owned through the Khoadi-//Hôas Conservancy. It's located on a private reserve about 65km north of Kamanjab, set on the banks of the small Otjovasondu River, just west of Etosha's Galton Gate (which opened to the public in 2014). The environment in this increasingly prolific reserve is similar to that of western Etosha, & can be explored on morning, afternoon (*N$620 pp*) & night drives (*N$685 pp*). As the little-used Galton Gate is so close, you can easily drive yourself around Etosha's western areas, although the lodge also offers full-day drives into the park (*N$950 pp*). The main area has a restaurant, lounge, bar & veranda for viewing game at the waterhole, as well as a swimming pool & curio shop. Journeys Namibia, the team currently managing Hobatere,

also manages Fish River Lodge (page 259) & Grootberg Lodge in northern Damaraland (page 412). Grootberg has particularly impressive levels of community involvement & staff hired from the local area, a style of management that helped the team win this concession & has been successfully repeated here. *DBB N$1,950/3,500 sgl/dbl.* **$$$$$**

East of Etosha (Von Lindequist Gate)

🏠 **Mokuti Etosha Lodge** [434 G2] (118 rooms) ✆067 229084; e mokuti.res@ol.na; www.mokutietoshalodge.com. Situated on the C38, 25km west of the B1, Mokuti is set in its own 4,300ha reserve, immediately next to Etosha's Von Lindequist Gate. More of a hotel than a lodge, it's traditional in design, yet spread out & with up-to-date facilities. In addition to the recently refurbished bar, plus the Boma and Tambuti restaurants, there's a 24hr gym overlooking a waterhole, & a spa offering massages, manicures & aromatherapy. Rather less indulgent are the conference facilities, business centre for guest use & Wi-Fi access throughout, free to residents.

Spacious twin & double en-suite rooms, with high thatched ceilings, stylish interiors & AC, are dotted across the lawns. Family rooms boast extra beds & separate lounges, & 2 twin rooms are modified for guests with disabilities, with handrails & widened doorways.

Mokuti's reserve is fenced, so is generally safe to wander around. A couple of short walking trails are clearly marked, though it is equally easy to spot wandering antelope from the poolside; more elusive on the trails are the snakes that can be seen in the hotel's reptile park. Look out for the bontebok, which are not indigenous, but come from the Cape. Most guests here have their own vehicles (the hotel has useful fuel pumps for diesel & unleaded petrol), & drive themselves around eastern Etosha, but Mokuti does run game drives into Etosha with its own vehicles & guides from sunrise until 11.00, & 14.00 until sunset (*N$720 pp, or N$5,440 for a private vehicle seating 9*). *DBB from N$2,304/3,690 sgl/dbl.* **$$$$$**

🏠 **Onguma Reserve** [434 G2] ✆061 237055; e reservations@onguma.com; www.onguma.com. Right next to Etosha's eastern gate, & accessed through an impressive fortified gate, Onguma Reserve boasts more than 34,000ha of protected land, bordering Fischer's Pan. The easy 9km drive through the reserve feels like eastern Etosha, with its mix of pans, woodland & open plains. Game found here includes lion, leopard & rhino, as well as the widely seen impala, oryx, wildebeest & springbok, & some 300 species of bird have been spotted. Onguma, meaning 'the place you don't want to leave' in the local Herero language, has 7 separate accommodation options, whose activities include bush walks (*N$450 pp, min 16 yrs*), & game drives both in the reserve (*N$450 pp*) & into Etosha (*N$760 pp, min 10 yrs*).

🏠 **ONGUMA BUSH CAMP** (18 rooms) 📞 067 229112. This fully fenced camp is, technically speaking, Onguma's budget option, geared to families, although its stylish main area & comfortable rooms do not come across as 'budget' at all. Rooms are fairly simple but well furnished, & all have AC, mosquito nets & en-suite bathrooms. 3 waterhole & 3 pool-view rooms are bigger than the others, with the waterhole-view rooms notably being outside the camp's perimeter fence, giving you a feeling of being in the bush, with plains game such as black-faced impala often seen at the waterhole. A cool & airy multi-level lounge & dining area is the highlight here. Partially on stilts overlooking the crystal-clear waterhole, it's open & spacious; complete with a downstairs playroom for children, as well as an adjacent pool with sunloungers & umbrellas for shade. *Lunch packs N$150. DBB N$2,550–3,460/3,420–5,240 sgl/dbl Jan–Jun, N$2,640–3,590/3,540–5,440 Jul–Dec.* **$$$$**

⛺ **ONGUMA LEADWOOD CAMPSITE** (6 pitches) Alongside the Bush Camp, but separately fenced, Onguma's Leadwood campsite has shaded pitches each with its own WC, shower & power point. Campers can use the pool & restaurant (with advance reservation; *dinner N$380 pp*) at Bush Camp, but otherwise need to bring all their own food. *Camping N$255/130 pp adult/child.* **$$**

⛺ **ONGUMA TAMBOTI CAMPSITE** (15 pitches) Some 3km from the Onguma entrance gate, Tamboti is a more luxurious, fenced campsite, complete with a restaurant, pool, waterhole & small kiosk selling camping essentials. Each individual campsite has its own kitchenette, private WC & shower, as well as power points, & deep verandas provide shade. Campers (with advance reservation) are welcome for meals at Etosha Aoba or Bush Camp. *Camping N$255/130 pp adult/child.* **$$**

⛺ **ONGUMA TENTED CAMP** (7 tented rooms) 📞 067 229114. Some 2km further on, Onguma's Tented Camp reinvents the term 'tent' with its safari chic approach, but it may not suit the traditionalist. From the tall, brushed-steel vases at the entrance to lime-washed giraffes by the door, the camp has woven an art-gallery style through the more traditional bush lodge theme. In the central area, creamy canvas held aloft by solid light-wood poles hints at a circus tent, but with light & air aplenty. A backdrop of stone-clad walls & a polished concrete floor is balanced by squashy beanbags, comfy sofas & zebra-print armchairs, with bright splashes of colour. Outside, a small infinity pool is just the spot for a cooling plunge, with loungers alongside to relax & watch wildlife at the floodlit waterhole, set among indigenous vegetation.

The big-top effect continues in each of the rooms, where stone combines with wood, polished stone & canvas to create a cosy but smart feel. Rooms have a fan, reading lights, tea & coffee facilities & Wi-Fi; en-suite bathrooms have both shower & bath; & sliding doors lead to a private deck where comfortable chairs afford a great view of the waterhole. *Lunch N$220 pp. DBB N$4,620/7,280 sgl/dbl Jan–Jun, N$5,340/8,000 Jul–Dec. No children under 12.* **$$$$$**

☀ 🏠 **ONGUMA TREE TOP CAMP** (4 tree houses) 📞 067 229114. Reached via timber walkways, this intimate camp is entirely built on stilts facing a beautiful, often productive waterhole. The bar, lounge & dining area are alongside an open kitchen where you can watch the chef prepare your meals. Carefully chosen furnishings use natural materials throughout, giving the lodge & its thatched rooms a real feeling of being in the bush. Dbl/twin rooms are small but neat, with canvas walls that can be rolled up or down, & en suites have basin, WC & outdoor shower. The camp can be booked for exclusive use, ideal for a single group or family. *DBB N$3,280/4,760 sgl/dbl Jan–Jun, N$3,500/5,080 Jul–Oct. No children under 12.* **$$$$**

🏠 **ONGUMA PLAINS: THE FORT** (13 suites) 📞 067 229135. This unique lodge, built to emulate a Moorish fort, with grand tower & beautifully designed separate suites, is different from any other you'll find in Namibia. The terracotta-mud finish to the 60cm-thick walls, the timber ceilings, & pierced bronze lights would not disgrace a riad in Marrakech, but here your large room opens on to timber decking with sunloungers & benches topped with colourful cushions, overlooking Fischer's Pan & the national park beyond. A bathroom is set in the tower of each suite with a shower, 2 basins & WC, & a separate outdoor shower. All have a fireplace, AC, well-stocked minibar, fridge, tea & coffee facilities, internal phone & Wi-Fi, while the Sultan (in the tower of the main building) & honeymoon suites also boast a bath & flat-screen TV. There's Wi-Fi throughout and a curio shop.

Stepping stones across candlelit pools lead to the open dining area & terraces, overlooking the waterhole & serving superb meals. You can view the sunset from a shallow pool set with tables & chairs, so you can cool your feet, or from the adjacent swimming pool. The area is not fenced, so animals roam free & close to your suite. For safety, guests are taken to the main areas from their suites by golf buggy. *Lunch N$220. DBB N$5,910, 8,860 sgl/dbl Jan–Jun, N$7,200/10,800 Jul–Dec; suite from N$7,040/10,800 sgl/dbl Jan–Jun, N$8,600/13,180 Jul–Dec. No children under 7.* **$$$$$$–$$$$$$$**

ONGUMA ETOSHA AOBA (11 bungalows) ✆067 229100. A friendly lodge set in a pretty tamboti forest, Aoba has well-designed thatched bungalows, though some are looking a little dated compared with the other Onguma properties. From a small veranda, a large patio door, which interchanges with a gauze screen, leads to a room with twin beds under a mosquito net & ceiling fan, a kettle & safe, & a door leading to a tiled WC & shower. 4 renovated luxury bungalows have AC & a secluded outside area with loungers & outdoor shower, while 3 family 'Bush Suites' have the same, plus a private veranda with seating & a 'bush' minibar.

Large black-&-white paintings adorn the walls of the oval thatched area with bar & tables for b/fast & dinner, & close by is a pool surrounded by sunloungers for the foolhardy. Free Wi-Fi is available in the rooms & the main area, & a small office doubles as a curio shop.

As well as a guided 2hr morning bush walk into the reserve, morning game drives into Etosha can be organised, & there's a sundowner drive on the Onguma Reserve (*N$450 pp*), but most guests drive themselves into the park from here. Etosha Aoba lacks some of the character and camaraderie of an all-inclusive lodge, but it's comfortable, pleasantly run & with good food (*lunch N$150,*

3-course set dinner N$380), making it a good base for driving around eastern Etosha. *DBB from N$2,320–2,860/3,820–4,900 sgl/dbl Jan–Jun, N$2,400–2,860/3,980–5,060 Jul–Dec. No children under 7.* **$$$$$**

The Mushara Collection [434 G2] ✆061 241880; e reservations@mushara-lodge.com; www.mushara-lodge.com. The only family-run lodge on the eastern side of Etosha occupies a 2,500ha reserve, with game drives (*N$650 pp*) available, & visits to the Ombili Foundation at a nearby San community. Owners Marc & Mariza Pampe offer 4 choices of DBB accommodation, with lunch available (*N$150; lunch pack N$90 pp*).

MUSHARA LODGE (13 rooms, 1 family house) ✆067 229106. Just 8km from the eastern entrance of the national park, Mushara is near a private airstrip, & only 500m from the main road. Despite the name, its style is more that of a hotel, albeit one with a high standard of service & attention to detail.

A cavernous entrance leads through to a split-level bar & smart lounge where wood & seed chandeliers, zebra hides & solid wood are complemented by modern, comfortable chairs & metal tables arranged into intimate seating areas. Outside, more seating surrounds a large pool backed by lawns. Rooms are very attractive & built in pairs in spacious terracotta-painted bungalows. Each is slightly different, but all are decorated in neutral colours, airy & light, with a porch overlooking the pool. Expect AC, all-round mosquito nets, an en-suite bath or shower, fridge, hairdryer & phone. The family house has 2 en-suite rooms (1 twin, 1 dbl), a lounge, a kitchenette, a terrace & a climbing frame in a small fenced garden. *DBB room from N$2,000 pp Jan–Feb, N$2,300 Mar–Dec; family house N$8,000 Jan–Feb, N$9,200 Mar–Dec.* **$$$$$**

VILLA MUSHARA (2 villas) A short walk from the Lodge, Mushara has top-of-the-range accommodation in 2 luxury villas, whose thatched roofs contrast with the glass & monochrome décor of their beautifully kitted out spacious interiors, each with a wealth of accoutrements, a mini patio & a square pool. *DBB villa N$4,200/7,000 sgl/dbl Jan–Feb, N$4,800/8,000 Mar–Dec. FBA available.* **$$$$$$**

MUSHARA BUSH CAMP (16 tents) With a separate turning just 3km further down the road, this is a family-friendly, comfortable & affordable base from which to explore Etosha. From the gravel pathways to the high ceilings of the central lounge & dining area, the feeling is of light & space. The canvas walls of the main building are open on 3 sides, & whitewashed safari chairs, silvered tables & splashes of vibrant colour suggest a stylish boutique hotel rather than a traditional lodge. Large secluded tents have dbl or twin beds, with side ledges as bedside tables, colour co-ordinated mosquito net, basin & open shower with separate WC, & deckchairs on the veranda. The lodge is very child-friendly, evidenced by 4 tents with a sleeper couch & extra single bed taking up to 2 children; a separate play area (complete with tractor, sandpit & slide); toy boxes & even kiddie-size dining tables & deckchairs. A circular swimming pool is set in lush gardens, a curio shop sits next to reception, & there is free Wi-Fi access throughout. *DBB N$2,000/3,000 sgl/dbl Jan–Feb, N$2,300/3,500 Mar–Dec.* **$$$$$**

🏠 MUSHARA OUTPOST (8 tents) The luxurious Outpost has discreet en-suite tents on raised decks with glass sliding doors & windows looking out into the trees. Beautifully furnished, each has AC, a small safe, kettle & cafetiere. The main stone building, housing the reception, lounge & communal dining table, has squashy settees & chairs spilling out on to a large terrace with full-length curtains & 2 fireplaces to ensure warmth on cold winter evenings. Adjacent are a large pool & curio shop, & brick pathways lead to a waterhole & a large, comfortable viewing hide. *DBB from N$2,800/4,500 sgl/dbl Jan–Feb, N$3,200/5,200 Mar–Dec. No children under 12.* **$$$$$**

🏠 **Emanya Lodge** [434 G2] (17 chalets) ✆061 222954; e bookings@emanya.com; www.emanya. com. Off the C38, about a 20min drive from the eastern gate of Etosha, Emanya is a privately owned, chic & luxurious lodge. Each of its thatched chalets has a tea/coffee station, AC, TV, electric safe & en-suite bathroom. The main area includes a large, sparkling blue pool, stylish lounge & dining area overlooking well-maintained gardens, a split-level viewing deck over the lodge's waterhole, & relaxing foot spa treatments. Free Wi-Fi. *Lunch N$100. DBB N$1,732–1,897/2,898–3,174 sgl/dbl.* **$$$$–$$$$$**

🏠 **Sachsenheim Guest Farm** [478 G2] (22 chalets, camping) ✆067 230011; e sachse@ iway.na. Off the B1, 3km north of the C38 turning towards Namutoni, & across the railway line, Sachsenheim is an old-style game farm turned restcamp. Owned by the Sachse family since 1946, it's an oasis of green & colour – with bottlebrush & jacaranda trees – & is the most affordable place in the area. A wide range of spotlessly clean accommodation options brings to mind a model village: neat individual chalets, plus a small central campsite under trees, where new pitches have individual ablutions, shade, power & light. Rooms – all en suite – are nicely appointed with fridge, kettle, fan & mosquito nets. Dotted among lovely gardens with plentiful seating areas are a restaurant with indoor & outdoor seating, a bar & sparkling pool, plus there's a floodlit waterhole, & free Wi-Fi. *B/fast N$180, dinner N$250. B&B from N$990/1,520 sgl/dbl; camping from N$180 pp, plus N$50 per vehicle.* **$–$$$**

WHAT TO SEE AND DO

If you are staying at one of the private lodges then you may have the choice of walking trips on their land. Otherwise, although some will opt for a guided drive (page 440), most visitors come to Etosha to explore the park for themselves by car.

PLANNING YOUR DAY The best times for spotting animals are in the early morning and the late afternoon, when they are at their most active. So, if you can, leave your camp as the gates open at sunrise for a few hours' drive before breakfast. Before you leave, check the book of recent sightings in the park office, as animals are creatures of habit. This record may help you to choose the best areas to visit for that particular day.

Use the middle of the day for either travelling or relaxing back at camp. Dedicated enthusiasts may park beside one of the more remote waterholes. Excellent sightings are occasionally reported in the midday heat – though photographs taken in the glare of day can be disappointing.

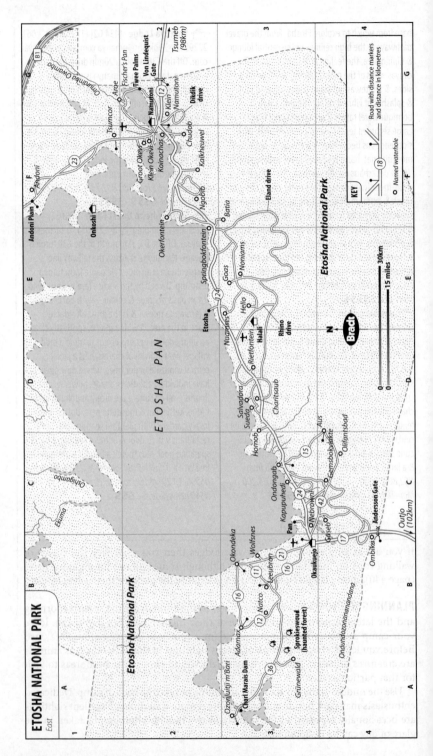

ETOSHA NATIONAL PARK
East

ETOSHA PAN

Etosha National Park

Etosha National Park

KEY

Road with distance markers
and distance in kilometres

Named waterhole

450

Finally, check when the gate to your camp closes, and then leave for a late afternoon drive. Aim to spend the last few hours before sunset at one of the waterholes near your resort, or near the entrance gate if you're staying outside the park. Leave this in time for a leisurely drive back.

THE WATERHOLES The excellent map of Etosha available at the park shows the roads open to visitors, and the names of the waterholes. Obviously the game seen at each varies enormously. One day you can sit for hours watching huge herds; the next day the same place will be deserted. However, some waterholes are usually better (noted by *), or at least more photogenic, than others. Here are a few personal notes on some of the main ones:

Adamax [450 B3] A dry waterhole in acacia thickets, notable more for adjacent social weaver nests than for its game.

Andoni [450 F1] As far north as you can go, close to the King Nehale lya Mpingana Gate, this isolated spot is a manmade waterhole in the middle of an open vlei. Although not hugely busy as a rule, it does on occasion attract a large number of plains game including oryx, springbok and zebra, and the bird species are numerous.

*Aus [450 D4] A natural water-level spring here is supplemented by a solar pump, in the middle of woodlands of stunted mopane. As you look from the parking area, the sun rises directly over the pan. It is said to be a good, busy spot for animals – though I've never had much luck here.

Batia [450 F3] Away from the side of the pan, near Springbokfontein, the road to Batia is often better than the waterhole itself, which is a very flat and almost marshlike collection of reeds with puddles dotted over a large area.

Charitsaub [450 D3] Away from the pan, Charitsaub is in the middle of a huge area of grassy plains. Though often dry, it has a small spring below. Likely game includes zebra, wildebeest and springbok.

*Chudob [450 F2] An excellent artesian waterhole, which usually hosts good concentrations of game, including eland (one of the best for this species), giraffe and, in the late afternoon, black rhino. There's lots of open space around the water, and I've spent many hours here on several occasions. Don't miss it.

Dolomietpunt The nearest waterhole to Dolomite Camp [434 A3] but, unfortunately, not visible from most of the camp itself. However, you can drive down, and the waterhole is often frequented by elephants and other plains game.

Etosha [450 E2] Just north of Halali, this is not a waterhole, but a spectacular lookout place. There's a short drive across the pan where you can stop and admire the shimmering mirages. It is often closed when wet.

Fischer's Pan [450 G2] The road from Namutoni skirts the edges of this small pan, and when there's standing water in the pan it is *the* area for waterbirds. Take care of the road across the pan, between Aroe and Twee Palms, which often floods. When dry there will be fewer birds around, though the palm trees remain picturesque.

*Gemsbokvlakte [450 C4] In the middle of a grassy plain, dotted with the odd stand of acacia, combretum and mopane bushveld, this permanent (with a solar-powered pump) waterhole attracts plains game species like springbok, oryx, zebra, giraffe and ostrich.

*Goas [450 E3] This is a large, flat, natural waterhole and cars can view it from several sides, which is good as there's often a lot of game here, particularly in the dry season. Elephants drinking here can be spectacular, and the waterhole is big enough to attract a constant buzz of bird activity.

Groot Okevi [450 F2] The parking area is a super vantage point, overlooking the waterhole which is about 25m away. There is some thick bush around the water. Black rhino can be seen here, along with predators, and it's conveniently close to Namutoni.

Homob [450 D3] A small spring in a deep depression, quite far from the viewing area. Just a few springbok and oryx were present when last visited. There is also a long-drop WC here; bring your own toilet paper.

*Kalkheuwel [450 F2] A super waterhole which often has lots of game. There's a permanently filled water trough, and usually also a good pan, which is close to the car park.

Kapupuhedi [450 C3] On the edge of the pan, with the parking area above it, this is often dry.

*Klein Namutoni [450 G2] A pretty waterhole, close to Namutoni. It's good for game viewing and the wildlife is relaxed and used to traffic. Dik-dik Drive is nearby, where the tiny Damara dik-dik can often be seen.

Koinachas [450 F2] A very picturesque artesian spring, perhaps 100m in diameter, with a large thicket of reeds in the centre. It's an excellent birding spot, but seldom seems crowded with game.

Moringa Just a short walk from Halali Restcamp [450 E3], this is a productive waterhole with a rocky, raised area that has shade and wooden benches, making it a good spot for photography, albeit a little higher up than would be ideal.

*Nebrowni [450 C3] A small waterhole on the edge of a side channel to the main pan. This is just 200m from the main road, but often omitted from maps. With bush to one side, and grassy plains to the other, it can attract a wide variety of game, and is arguably one of the best waterholes in the park.

Noniams [450 E3] Though it's convenient for Halali, I've never had much luck seeing any game here.

Nuamses [450 E3] A very deep water-level spring with a large clump of tall reeds in the centre. Quite photogenic with lots of rocks around – though the foreground is obscured by a lip of rock in front of the waterhole. Not known for its prolific game.

Okerfontein [450 F2] Right on the edge of the pan. The viewpoint is slightly elevated, and the nearer parts of the water are hidden from view by a lip of rocks.

*Okondeka [450 B3] On the edge of the pan, Okondeka often has streams of game arriving and leaving it, which stretch for miles across the surrounding grasslands. These include large numbers of wildebeest, zebra, oryx, springbok and ostrich, as well as a large pride of lion. The water is a little far from the car-parking area for close-up photos, but shots taken from the road, with vistas of the main pan in the background, can be spectacular.

*Olifantsbad [450 C4] Literally 'elephant's bath', this is another natural water-level spring helped by a solar pump – making two good waterholes in a large arena for wildlife. It is notable for elephant, kudu, red hartebeest and black-faced impala.

*Ombika [450 B4] Despite its proximity to the Andersson Gate, Ombika shouldn't be underestimated as it is often a busy waterhole. Unfortunately for photographers, this water-level spring is far from the viewing area, inside a deep natural rock cavern, allowing even zebra to almost disappear from view when drinking.

Ondongab [450 C3] Like Kapupuhedi, this is on the edge of the pan but has recently been dry. The view of the pan would be spectacular were it not for the thorn bushes surrounding the parking area.

Ozonjuitji m'Bari [450 A3] This is a small waterhole filled by a solar pump. Flat, grassy plains surround it, and the game varies greatly. Sometimes it is deserted, and on other occasions you'll find one of the park's largest gatherings of oryx. In the dry season, likely sights include ostrich, wildebeest, zebra, springbok, perhaps the odd giraffe and lots of dancing dust-devils in the background. Roan have previously been seen here too.

Pan [450 C3] On the edge of the pan, the waterhole is not obvious, and there is often little game. This road becomes a mess of sludge in the wet season.

*Rietfontein [450 D3] A large, busy, water-level spring, with quite a large area of reeds in the water, surrounded by much open ground. There's a wide parking area with plenty of space, and at the waterhole giraffe, zebra and springbok were drinking when last visited. It's also a great spot for birds of prey.

*Salvadora [450 D3] On the edge of the pan, Salvadora attracts columns of zebra, wildebeest and springbok. The viewpoint is higher than the spring, and close to it – so is perfect for photographs, with the main pan stretching off forever behind it.

Springbokfontein [450 E2] A shallow collection of reeds to one side of the road, which often has little game. However, look to your right as you drive to nearby Batia, as there is often game at a spring there.

Sueda [450 D3] Away from the pan, and just west of Salvadora and Charitsaub, Sueda has a large area of reeds, and rocklike clay outcrops, around a spring on the edge of the pan. Again, parking is above the level of the spring.

Wolfsnes [450 B3] A location where you can appreciate the vast expanse of the pan. Just switch off your motor and listen to the silence.

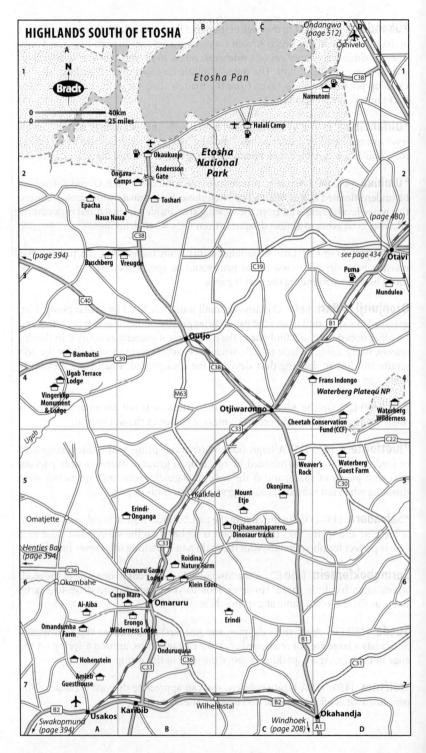

HIGHLANDS SOUTH OF ETOSHA

A · B · C · D

N Bradt

0 — 40km
0 — 25 miles

Etosha Pan

Ondangwa (page 512)

Oshivelo

C38

Namutoni

Halali Camp

Etosha National Park

Okaukuejo

Andersson Gate

Ongava Camps

Epacha

Toshari

Naua Naua

C38

(page 480)

(page 394)

Buschberg

Vreugde

see page 434

Puma

Otavi

C39

B1

Mundulea

C40

Outjo

Bambatsi

C39

Ugab Terrace Lodge

C38

Frans Indongo

Waterberg Plateau NP

Vingerklip Monument & Lodge

M63

Otjiwarongo

Waterberg Wilderness

Ugab

C33

Cheetah Conservation Fund (CCF)

C22

Weaver's Rock

Waterberg Guest Farm

Erindi-Onganga

Kalkfeld

Mount Etjo

Okonjima

C30

Omatjette

Otjihaenamaparero, Dinosaur tracks

Henties Bay (page 394)

C36

C33

Roidina Nature Farm

Omaruru Game Lodge

Klein Eden

Okombahe

Camp Mara

Ai-Aiba

Omaruru

Erindi

B1

Omandumba Farm

Erongo Wilderness Lodge

Onduruquea

C36

Hohenstein

C33

C31

Amieb Guesthouse

Wilhelmstal

B2

B2

Okahandja

Usakos

Karibib

Windhoek (page 208)

A1

Swakopmund (page 394)

A · B · C · D

18

Highlands South of Etosha

While Etosha is the main attraction in the north of Namibia, the region south of it has much of interest. Large farms dominate these hilly, well-watered highlands, and many have forsaken cattle in favour of game to become guest farms that welcome tourists. Okonjima was one of the first of these, and remains a major draw for visitors. Many of the others are less famous, but they still offer visitors insights into a farmer's view of the land, and opportunities to relax. On the eastern side of this area, the Waterberg Plateau is superb, though more for its hiking trails and scenery, and feeling of wilderness, than for its game viewing.

OMARURU

At a crossroads of the tarred C33 and the less-frequented C36, about 60km north of Karibib, Omaruru is a green and picturesque town astride the (usually dry) river of the same name, in a gently hilly area. Many of the farms around it have turned to tourism, which is on the increase, so there is no shortage of lodges or guest farms in the area. The town has also acquired something of a reputation for the creative arts, with many artists settling here to work.

GETTING THERE AND AWAY The demise of the TransNamib train service from Windhoek means that most visitors have no alternative but to reach Omaruru by road.

WHERE TO STAY

🏠 **Central Hotel** [456 C2] (11 rooms) Wilhelm Zeraua Rd; \064 570030; e centralhotel@iway. na; www.centralhotelomaruru.com. On the main street north of the river, this small, traditional hotel has been sensitively restored by owners Alexander & Alma Steyn. Think dark stone floors, original wooden beams & hand-carved doors in the main building, with an attractive bar & cheerful b/fast room. Its modern rooms, each with a private patio as well as AC, TV, fridge & coffee/tea facilities, are in individual rondavels or set in line in a whitewashed block, softened by thatch. It also has a pool, a popular beer garden & restaurant, & secure parking. *N$900/1,200 sgl/dbl.* **$$$**

🏠 **Evening Shade** [456 D1] (5 rooms) 116 Wilhelm Zeraua Rd; \064 570303; m 081 124 6184; e info@evening-shade.com; www.

eveningshade.com. Tucked behind Gallery 116 (page 457), & under the same ownership, Chris Johnston's small B&B is set around a couple of huge trees in a shady garden, where vegetables for the café are grown. Cool & spacious rooms – 3 twins & 2 sleeping 5 or 6 – are simply but stylishly decorated with exposed brickwork, the original high ceramic ceilings & fully equipped kitchens, along with free Wi-Fi, DSTV & a safe. Each has its own secure parking spot, & a laundry service is available. *N$730/950 sgl/dbl.* **$$$**

🏠 **Kashana** [456 C2] (17 rooms) Dr Ian Scheepers Dr; \064 571434; e info@kashana-namibia.com; www.kashana-namibia.com. Just south of the Omaruru River, this substantial guesthouse with an imposing entrance is based around a carefully restored building dating back to

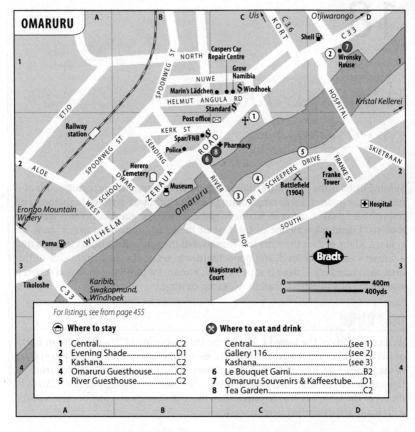

OMARURU

For listings, see from page 455

🛏 Where to stay		🍴 Where to eat and drink	
1 Central.................................C2		Central...............................(see 1)	
2 Evening Shade......................D1		Gallery 116........................(see 2)	
3 Kashana..............................C2		Kashana............................(see 3)	
4 Omaruru Guesthouse.........C2		**6** Le Bouquet Garni..................B2	
5 River Guesthouse................C2		**7** Omaruru Souvenirs & Kaffeestube......D1	
		8 Tea Garden.............................C2	

1907. It offers a large restaurant (⊕ *07.00–22.00 daily;* $$$–$$$$) with a terrace area, a lively bar & a small craft & jewellery shop. Behind this are large thatch-&-brick chalets, a block of smaller rooms, & family rooms on 2 levels. These vary in size & price, but each is spacious & comes with African-print linen, crafted dark furniture, locally made metal sculptures & mosaic floor tiling, as well as AC, DSTV, fridge, safe & Wi-Fi. There's also an L-shaped pool & secure parking. *N$450–870/550–1,155 sgl/dbl.* $$$

Omaruru Guesthouse [456 C2] (20 rooms) 305 Dr Ian Scheepers Dr; ☏ 064 570035; e hello@ omaruru-guesthouse.com; www.omaruru-guesthouse.com. Under the ownership of Christian Hafner, this long-standing B&B remains excellent value with bedrooms (inc 2 family rooms) in a separate block from the main building. All have fridge, fan, DSTV, Wi-Fi & hairdryer. The older main building has a bright dining room & TV lounge, while outside are a small pool, pretty garden & secure parking. *N$550/850 sgl/dbl.* $$

River Guesthouse [456 C2] (6 rooms, camping) Dr Ian Scheepers Dr; ☏ 064 570274; m 081 124 5365; e eckmitt@iway.na; www. river-guesthouse.com. Opposite Franke Tower lies a family home transformed into a quirky, owner-run guesthouse. Set around a central courtyard, almost overgrown by a jungle of palm & banana trees, are 4 dbl & 2 family rooms, all en suite & with fans & coffee/tea facilities, & fridges in some, along with a b/fast room, a small bar & a boma. There's also a pool surrounded by hammocks. The nearby campsite offers 6 pitches, 2 sets of ablutions, plug points & BBQ areas. *N$550/850 sgl/dbl; camping N$160 pp; no credit cards.* $$$

🍴 **WHERE TO EAT AND DRINK** In addition to the restaurants at the Central Hotel and Kashana, Omaruru boasts a clutch of cafés, all along the main Wilhelm Zeraua Road.

✳ 🍴 Omaruru Souvenirs & Kaffeestube
[456 C2] ☏ 064 570230; ⏰ 07.30–17.00 Mon–Sat,
08.30–17.00 Sun. The historical & handsome
Wronsky House (see below) is the setting for a
charming coffee house with a veranda & attractive
garden that serves delicious cakes & light lunches,
including German–Namibian specialities. The
well-stocked souvenir shop here doubles as a small
information centre. $–$$$

🍴 Le Bouquet Garni [456 B2] ⏰ 08.30–
16.00 Mon–Sat. Next to the pharmacy, the pretty
garden with a children's play area is the setting for
some wickedly enticing cakes as well as creative
& fresh salads, soups, sandwiches & plenty more.
$–$$

🍴 Gallery 116 [456 D1] ☏ 064 570544;
m 081 124 6184; e info@johnstonenamibia.com;
⏰ 07.30–17.00 daily. A slimmed-down version of the
former Main Street Café, this popular venue still serves
homemade, natural food from its own garden & local
suppliers wherever possible. Come for b/fast, coffee &
toasties, & do try the cheesecake. Then check out the
adjoining photo gallery & mineral collection. $–$$

🍴 Tea Garden [456 C2] ⏰ 08.30–16.00
Mon–Fri, 08.30–14.00 Sat. Behind the pharmacy,
& under the same ownership, this peaceful garden
café has umbrella-shaded tables. The healthy stuff
– juices, smoothies & salads – is balanced by the
likes of coffee & cake, so guilt isn't entirely off the
menu! $–$$

OTHER PRACTICALITIES There are branches of FNB, Bank Windhoek and Standard **banks** and a **post office** on the main Wilhelm Zeraua Road, as well as several **fuel stations** and **garages** and the Ongwari **pharmacy** (☏ *064 571262;* m *081 234 1270;* e *ongwari@iway.na*). For **vehicle repairs**, Caspers Car Repair Centre (☏ *064 571464;* e *ccrc@iway.na*) is probably the best option in town.

For **food and provisions**, there's a huge Spar supermarket (⏰ *08.00–19.00 Mon–Sat, 09.00–19.00 Sun*) with an ATM on Wilhelm Zeraua Road.

In an **emergency**, the police are reached on ☏ 064 10111 or 064 570010, the ambulance and hospital on ☏ 064 570037, and the fire brigade on ☏ 064 570029/46 or m 081 351 0502.

WHAT TO SEE AND DO The town's main attraction is **Franke Tower**, a monument to Captain Victor Franke, who is said to have heroically relieved the garrison here after they were besieged by the Herero in 1904. The achievement earned him Germany's highest military honour and this monument built by grateful German settlers in 1908. It's normally locked, but to climb up it ask at your hotel if they have the keys.

Don't miss a visit to the historical and handsome **Wronsky House** [456 D1] on the main street, now housing a coffee house and souvenir shop (see above). Built as a general trading store by Wilhelm Wronsky after he settled here from Brazil in the 1890s, the building was completed in 1907. Today many of the original tiles, ceiling wood and fittings remain, all transported by boat from Germany and then by ox wagon from the coast. Ask in the shop to have a look at the small museum upstairs; the signage is in German but to some extent the artefacts speak for themselves.

Out of town, wine lovers have a choice. Head east for 4km along Dr I Scheepers Drive, which soon becomes the good gravel D2328, and after about 4km you'll come to **Kristall Kellerei** (☏ *064 570083;* e *winery@wederpc.com; http://kristallkellerei.com;* ⏰ *09.00–16.30 Mon–Fri, 09.00–12.30 Sat*), a small-scale vineyard and manufacturer of Namibian brandy. Along with wine-tasting they serve an accompanying lunch of cold meats and cheeses. In the opposite direction, about 5km west of town, is the **Erongo Mountain Winery** (m *081 292 2465; www.erongomountainwinery.com;* (⏰ *09.00–17.00 Mon–Sat*), open for tastings by appointment only.

Art and crafts Shops come and go, but Omaruru has developed a reputation as the arts and crafts centre of Namibia, and there remains plenty of interest. On the western side of town, you'll find **Tikoloshe** [456 A3] (📞 *064 570582/571215;* e *tiko@iway.na; www.tikolosheafrika.com*), where craftsmen carve imaginative animals from roots. In town itself, there's **Marin's Lädchen** [456 C1] (📞*064 570203*), displaying a selection of jewellery and gifts.

Mineralogists (and **photographers**) should drop in to see Chris Johnston at Gallery 116 (page 457). The impressive gallery and studio alongside the café features both his own photographs and a fascinating selection of very specialist local minerals which they even send abroad on a mail-order basis.

Finally, if you're visiting Omaruru on the second-last weekend of September, look out for the Artist Trail, a series of events and exhibitions to celebrate the work of local artists.

⌂ AROUND OMARURU: LODGES AND GUEST FARMS

Erongo Mountain Nature Conservancy

The 2,000km² Erongo Conservancy encompasses 30 farms & their lodges over which fences have been taken down in order to create a protected area. As proof of its success, white rhino were released here in 2009 & the first calf born in 2010, although they are rarely spotted. Prime among the lodges within the conservancy is Erongo Wilderness Lodge, but others include Ai-Aiba, Omandumba, Hohenstein and Camp Mara.

✳ ⌂ **Erongo Wilderness Lodge** [454 B6] (10 tents, 1 suite) 📞061 239199, 064 570537; e info@erongowilderness-namibia.com; www. erongowilderness-namibia.com. From Omaruru, take the C33 south for 2km & turn right on to the D2315. You'll soon enter an area littered with kopjes – huge piles of rounded rocks which make up hills that look like piles of giant pebbles, & inselbergs – isolated mountains that rise abruptly from the surrounding plains: these are the Erongo Mountains. At 10km from the junction & soon after passing through the manned gate to the Erongo Conservancy, you'll find the lodge to the south of the road. Unless you have a 4x4 & are confident using it, leave your vehicle in the parking area at the bottom from where you & your luggage will be transferred the 800m to the lodge.

The lodge's spacious tents (inc 1 family tent) are built high on wooden stilts among granite boulders. The rustic feel is deliberate, but with a minibar, kettle, fan & toiletries, guests won't be deprived of mod cons. Various wooden walkways & paths (some of them steep) connect these to the main lounge & dining room area, which has a large terrace overlooking a stunning vista of the mountains. Look out for the rosy-faced lovebirds

that hang around at b/fast. Food here is excellent, accompanied by an extensive wine list. Nearby, a small swimming pool has been built into the rocks.

It's a lovely spot to spend a few days, but Erongo's real attraction is as a base for walking. Guides are on hand for both short walks in the late afternoon (usually to the top of the nearby kopje for a G&T while the sun sets), & longer walks: on the flat, or around the base of the hills, or on steeper routes where short scrambles may be needed. For those wishing to set out unaccompanied, there are 4 marked walking trails of 1½–4½hrs. The rough rock generally grips rubber soles well. There are also nature drives & guided visits to local rock paintings (*N$550*), described by Hilary Bradt as 'wonderfully lively, & the location in a cave with terrific views is superb'.

Pause for a while wherever you are & you'll realise that there's wildlife around, from leopards & klipspringers to dassies & brightly coloured rock agamas, but you'll have to look for it. For birders, this is also a good spot to see some of Namibia's harder-to-find species including Hartlaub's francolin, Montero hornbill, Damara rockrunner & black eagle – there was a nesting pair of these on our last visit. *DBB N$3,565/5,990 sgl/dbl.* **$$$$$**

⌂ **Hohenstein Lodge** [454 A7] (10 rooms) 📞064 530900; e info@hohensteinlodge.com; www.hohensteinlodge.com. To the southwest of the Erongo Mountains, Hohenstein is about 25km north of Usakos on the D1935, set on the edge of Damaraland within the Erongo Mountain Nature Conservancy, & named after the highest mountain in the Erongo chain. The lodge has been carefully built to take advantage of the panoramic views from both the bungalows & the central area, where dinner (*N$350*) is taken inside or out on the veranda, overlooking a waterhole. Simply decorated rooms have twin beds with bright animal-print covers. Visitors may opt for a guided walk to the 'Boulder Forest' & small gemstone mine claims, nature drives, or a sundowner drive. Hohenstein also offers an exclusive 2-day package (*N$4,925/4,325 sgl/pp sharing*) called Absolut Erongo, inc 1 night at the rustic & remote Etemba Wilderness Camp with walking tours to see Etemba's renowned Bushmen paintings. To reach Etemba, by 4x4 only, you drive to Ai-Aiba (see below), turning left at the entrance gate. *DBB N$1,830–1,940/3,060–3,280 sgl/dbl.* **$$$$$**

Ai-Aiba [454 A6] (20 rooms) ☎ 061 239199; e info@aiaiba-namibia.com; www. aiaiba-namibia.com. Self-styled 'the Rock-painting lodge', Ai-Aiba is now under the same ownership as Erongo Wilderness Lodge (see opposite), but here the proliferation & quality of San rock art is the main draw. The lodge is situated about 45km west of Omaruru, just off the D2315, & within the Erongo Mountain Nature Conservancy. From Damaraland, turn south on to the D2306, 56km east of Uis & after 33km turn on to the D2315; Ai-Aiba is shortly on the left. Nestling in the shelter of giant granite boulders, each of its attractive thatched bungalows houses 2 en-suite rooms, their cool tiled floors offset by solid rustic furniture & neutral fabrics. The matching central building, its open beams giving it the feeling of a large barn, overlooks a small pool flanked by palms. As well as visits to the rock art, there are guided & self-guided walking trails, nature drives & visits to a local San living museum (all at extra cost). *N$1,446/2,630 sgl/dbl.* **$$$$**

Omandumba [454 A6] (8 rooms, 12 safari tents, camping) ☎ 064 571086; m 081 245 3713; e omandumba@iway.na; www.omandumba.de. About 45km from Omaruru on the D2315, just after the turn-off to Ai-Aiba (see above), the farm is marked by a sign with figures of an African family walking above a board noting the owner's names: Harald & Deike Rust. Rather than being a guest farm or lodge, the emphasis here is on 'normal' Namibian farm life, where the owners dine with their guests.

Following major refurbishment, guests can choose from the original brick rooms at the farm, each with a private terrace & carport; a newer bushcamp, & a self-catering house on the neighbouring farm, also owned by the Rust family. At the bushcamp, safari tents are erected under corrugated metal roofs with

brick en-suite bathrooms at the back. Communal meals are enjoyed overlooking a small waterhole. The fully equipped self-catering 'farmhouse' is 8km from Omandumba, & sleeps up to 6 in 3 bedrooms. 5 private camping pitches with showers & toilets are also available.

Regardless of where you stay, the key attractions are walking trails in the Erongo Mountains, excellent rock-art drives guided by the owners, who have detailed knowledge of the area's rock paintings & engravings (*N$400 pp*), & a Living Museum of the San People where guests learn about their culture in what was believed to be an outpost of the San communities. *DBB N$1,150pp; self-catering rates on application; camping N$150 pp.* **$$–$$$$**

Camp Mara [454 B6] (5 rooms, camping) ☎ 064 571190; m 081 128 1203; e campmara@ iway.na; www.campmara.com. In a rural setting opposite the entrance to Erongo Wilderness Lodge (see opposite), this traditional, 42ha guest farm is reached down a bumpy 1km track off the same road. The 3 original guest rooms, built in a thatched block by owner Ecki Meyer, differ in size, but all are spacious with French windows & simple, rustic furnishings, & 2 have self-catering facilities too. Others – a dbl & a sgl – are in the main house. Campers have 3 individual pitches near the (normally dry) Omaruru River, each with a private toilet & shower, fireplace & braai. This is an unhurried spot, the sort of place where you can linger after b/fast watching hornbills & rosy-faced lovebirds come to feed before taking time to explore the mountains on a guided walk (*N$600/1,000 pp ½/full day*) or to visit some Bushman paintings & a living museum with Ecki himself (*N$1,600 2pp & N$$500 pp entrance fee*). Home-cooked dinners (*N$250*) – eaten at a convivial communal table – are available on request. *N$1,250/2,500 sgl/dbl; camping N$200 pp.* **$$–$$$$**

Northwest of Omaruru

Erindi-Onganga Guest Farm [454 B5] (5 rooms, camping) ☎ 067 290112; e fnolte@ iway.na; www.natron.net/erindi-onganga/main (in German). This traditional, working guest farm with a German atmosphere is about 62km from Omaruru. To reach it take the C36 towards Uis for about 6km, then branch right on to the D2344 towards Omatjete. Follow this for about 25km, then turn right again on to the D2351 towards Epupa (note this Epupa is closer than the one on the River Kunene!). After about 25km, Erindi-Onganga is signposted to the right, about 6km along a farm road.

Rooms are carpeted throughout & are clean, with en-suite facilities. The main farmhouse, Fritz & Petra Nolte's home, has a dining room (where traditional farm-cooked meals are served), a lounge area with large fire for cool evenings, & even a sauna. About 800m away, you can pitch a tent at the campsite overlooking a large reservoir, or stay in one of 3 pre-erected, equipped tents. Outside are a swimming pool, some marked hiking trails & the working farm which most visitors come to see. Nature & sunset drives (*N$350 pp*) on the farm offer the chance to see a variety of antelope & other small game. Note that bow hunting is also conducted here, so you need to be comfortable with this aspect of the farm if you plan to stay. *DBB N$1,250 dbl, inc farm drive if staying 2 nights; camping N$80/180 own tent/pre-erected tent.* **$$–$$$$**

East and south of Omaruru

Klein Eden Guest Farm [454 B6]
(11 chalets, camping) `064 570620; m 081 291 3790; e kleinedengasteplaas@iway.na; www.kleinedenguestfarm.com. To reach this largely self-catering guest farm, take Hospital Rd east from Omaruru, then left on to the D2328 for 28km & left again on to the D2330 for 500m. Each of the chalets – 2 of them B&B, the others entirely self-catering – has a different layout & furnishings but all are modern & shiny, with indoor braais & well-equipped kitchens, AC, fans, DSTV, safes & Wi-Fi. Facilities include a swimming pool & children's playground on the lawns. The rather bland communal hall/lapa area has cooking facilities & pool tables but no restaurant, bar or shop, so bring all food & drink with you. *B&B N$1,210/1,490 sgl/dbl; self-catering N$1,090/1,250 sgl/dbl; camping N$240 pp.* **$$–$$$**

Omaruru Game Lodge [454 B6]
(13 bungalows) `064 570044; m 081 642 2442; e omlodge@iafrica.com.na; www.omaruru-game-lodge.com. Northeast of Omaruru, about 15km along the D2329, this lodge is owned by a Swiss architect, which explains the impressive design of its bungalows. All are beautifully built of stone, with thatched roofs that reach almost to the ground, AC, heating, & en-suite shower & toilet. Some, designated 'superior', are simply bigger.

The lounge/bar/dining area is equally impressive, & overlooks a dam on one side of the lodge's fenced 'small game park' (150ha in size) complete with giraffe feeding station, which is regularly visited by other wildlife too, including rhino, hartebeest, wildebeest, eland, sable & roan antelope – so can feel more like a zoo than a game park. This is separate from the lodge's 'large game park' which covers a more respectable 3,400ha, & is home to the same range of antelope plus a small family of elephants.

Paths wind around the camp & the figure-of-8 pool among well-watered lawns under beautiful apple-ring acacias (*Faidherbia albida*), which the elephants would relish if only they could get to them. Walk at night, when the paths are lit, & it's hard to escape the feeling that this is Africa at its neatest & tidiest, but not its wildest. *DBB standard N$1,900–2,200/3,300–3,500 sgl/dbl.* **$$$$$**

Erindi [454 C6] `083 330 1111–4; m 081 553 5592, 081 145 0000; e reservations@erindi.com; www.erindi.com. Owned by Gert Joubert & opened in 2008, Erindi is a 710km² private game reserve boasting the only free-roaming lion pride on private land in Namibia. Other species introduced to attract tourists include wild dog, elephant & rhino, all viewed on morning & evening game drives in open 4x4 safari vehicles. At additional cost, a whole raft of activities are available here, including special game drives for children, night & full-day drives, telemetry tracking drives, cheetah & leopard project walks & visits to a San village on the reserve.

There are 4 gates into the reserve, reached from Omaruru (D2328) to the west, Kalkfeld (D2414) to the north & Otjiwarongo (D2187) or Okahandja to the east. Coming from Okahandja, take the B1 north for about 45km, then turn west on to the D2414 &, after 40km, fork left on to the D2328. 4km further on, turn left & follow signs for 20km to the reserve.

Old Traders Lodge (49 suites) In the southern part of the Erindi reserve, suites at the Old Traders Lodge overlook a waterhole. They range from comfortable standard suites to the decadent Livingstone suite with teak & leather furniture, but all have AC, DSTV, fridge, safe & en-suite shower & bath. Buffet meals are served in a large thatched dining area with adjacent lounge & fireplace, or on the terrace. There's also a pool & a children's play area. *DBB from N$2,390/3,980 sgl/dbl; FBA from N$3,490/6,180 sgl/dbl, inc 2 game drives daily.* **$$$$$**

🏠 **Camp Elephant** (15 chalets, camping) Some 30km from the main lodge, but still very much part of Erindi, Camp Elephant has 2-bed self-catering chalets & 30 camping pitches with private ablution blocks & kitchens. There's no restaurant or bar here, but there is a farm shop for provisions. *Chalet from N$3,190 dbl; camping from N$1,290 per pitch.* **$$$–$$$$$**

🏠 **Onduruquea Lodge** [454 B7] (12 rooms) 📞064 570692; m 081 772 8726; e info@onduruquea-lodge.com; www.onduruquea-lodge.com. Owned & run since 2017 by the Harmsen family from the Netherlands, the former Namib Guest Farm – just off the C33 between Omaruru & Karibib – has been given an entirely new lease of life, with a focus on 'fine cuisine & relaxation'. Yoga lessons, & massages in a purpose-built 2-person suite, complement self-guided walks, sunset game drives (*N$700 pp*) & night drives, with guests returning for a convivial chat around the firepit. A

fusion of African & French cuisine underpins the 3-course menu at dinner; the wine list boasts a selection of wines from France & the South African Jordans; & there's a good cocktail menu.

At the heart of the lodge is a large, paved courtyard with thatch-shaded tables that leads to a proper swimming pool & pool bar (*happy hour ⏲ 15.30–17.30*). Most of the rooms are set in pairs in cool, thatched oval 'rondavels' opening on to the courtyard. In each you'll find twin beds & AC, while 'deluxe' rooms have more contemporary styling & their own terraces facing the waterhole. That view is shared from the deck of 2 further tented rooms, in a more natural setting just outside the lodge's low walls. It's an attractive spot, set on a 160km² estate that is home to various antelope, with attendant leopard & cheetah, & is very well managed. *DBB from N$1,440/2,880 sgl/dbl.* **$$$$–$$$$$**

OTJIWARONGO

Originally a staging post on the railway from Tsumeb to Swakopmund, which was completed in 1906, Otjiwarongo is conveniently situated at a crossroads for the road network in an area dominated by commercial cattle ranching. Once a small market town with a mix of people that includes many Herero women in traditional dress, Otjiwarongo is experiencing something of a boom just now due to new industries nearby, including the B2 Gold mine, opened in 2014, and a new cement factory, claimed to be the most modern in the world. Although it has few intrinsic attractions, and most visitors just pass through, there are some decent new hotels that are aiming beyond the local business market, and plenty of shops for provisions.

GETTING THERE AND AWAY Somewhat ironically, given the town's history, there are no longer any passenger trains to Otjiwarongo. If you're driving yourself from Omaruru, note that there's a useful Shell fuel station on the C33 at **Kalkfeld**, though the presence of the enormous Kalkfeld Tourist Centre seems a little excessive.

By bus The Intercape Mainliner bus service linking Windhoek with Victoria Falls drops into Otjiwarongo, stopping at Engen service station on Hage Geingob Street. Going northbound, it stops at 16.45 on Monday, Wednesday and Friday. Heading south, it stops at 06.10 on Monday, Thursday and Saturday. One-way fares are around N$324–380 to Windhoek, and N$480–530 to Victoria Falls. See page 153 for more details.

Hitching Hitching from central Otjiwarongo is difficult. First start walking out in the direction you want to go, and then hitch from there.

TOURIST INFORMATION At 5 St George's Street, **Omaue Namibia** (📞067 303830; ⏲ 08.00–13.00 & 14.00–17.00 Mon–Fri, 08.00–13.00 Sat) doubles as a friendly and useful information centre [462 D2].

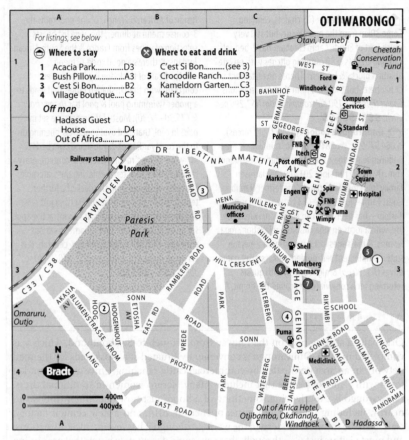

For listings, see below

🛏 **Where to stay**
1 Acacia Park.............D3
2 Bush Pillow.............A3
3 C'est Si Bon...........B2
4 Village Boutique.....C3

Off map
   Hadassa Guest
      House..................D4
   Out of Africa...........D4

✖ **Where to eat and drink**
   C'est Si Bon..........(see 3)
5 Crocodile Ranch........D3
6 Kameldorn Garten.....C3
7 Kari's...................D3

🏠 **WHERE TO STAY** Most visitors in the area stay at one of the guest farms (page 464). However, some of the establishments in town are also worth considering for a stopover.

🏠 **Bush Pillow** [462 A3] (7 rooms) 47 Sonn Rd; m 081 128 5323; e reservations@bushpillow.co.za; www.bushpillow.co.za. This good, trendy guesthouse is just over 1km from the main Hage Geingob St; turn left into Sonn Rd at the 1st Caltex fuel station, & it's on the corner of Hoog St. It has safe parking & a pleasant garden (with pool) behind secure walls, where there's also space for a BBQ. The rooms, each named after a famous (or infamous!) elephant, are clean & bright, with en-suite bathrooms & satellite TV; decorated in rich, warm colours, many also have fun artistic touches. Some have AC. The communal areas include pleasant indoor & outdoor lounges, a dining area (*dinner N$250 with advance notice*) & a well-stocked bar. Laundry & Wi-Fi are also available. Day trips to the Cheetah Conservation Foundation, 40km away, & shorter excursions to nearby Whale

Rock for a sundowner, are worth considering. *N$1,080 dbl.* **$$$**

🏠 **C'est Si Bon Hotel** [462 B2] (56 rooms) Swembad Rd; ☎ 067 301240; e reservation@ cestsibonhotel.com; www.cestsibonhotel.com. Signposted from the main Hage Geingob St between the church & the Puma station, this is one of a growing breed of medium-size hotels/ lodges in Namibia's provincial towns that aim to cater for small groups that stop for the night. It's a thoroughly efficient & comfortable place, though it lacks some of the individuality (& idiosyncrasies) of the smaller establishments. That said, it's one of the best places in town to stay & eat. Thatched rooms are spread around the edges of a large lawn, overlooking a pool. Each is adequate but not huge, with twin beds, AC, DSTV, Wi-Fi, fridge, tea/coffee facilities, & an en-suite shower. 'Luxury' & presidential rooms are more spacious, some sleeping up to 5. *From N$890/1,150 sgl/dbl.* **$$$**

🏠 **Hadassa Guest House** [462 D4] (9 rooms) 36 Lang St, opposite Out of Africa Lodge; ☎ 067 307505; m 081 774 9382; e hadassa@otjiweb. com; www.hadassaguesthouse.com. This deservedly popular boutique guesthouse is now run by French couple Orlane & Emmanuel Bonnin. The décor is chic, with dark wood, neutral tones & splashes of colour, the ambience is peaceful & relaxed; & each room has AC, TV, Wi-Fi, fridge & coffee/tea station. They pride themselves on their dining, emphasising local game with a French twist (advance booking required) & there's a lovely pool in pristine gardens. The guesthouse supports Peri Naua (*www. peri-naua.com*), a local kindergarten project for underprivileged children & guests are encouraged to bring school materials or old clothes, which they pass on. Guests are also entitled to 10% discount on activities at the Cheetah Conservation Fund (see box, page 468). *N$750/950 sgl/dbl.* **$$$**

🏠 **Out of Africa Hotel** [462 D4] (44 rooms) Long St; ☎ 067 302230; e oatlodge@iway.na; www.ooafrica.com. Also signposted on the right as you enter Otjiwarongo, the attractive white building of this hotel houses brightly painted en-suite rooms with AC, TV, phone & fridge. There is secure parking, a pool, conference facilities &

a restaurant with an à la carte menu. *N$885– 985/1,150–1,265 sgl/dbl.* **$$$**

🏠 **Village Boutique Hotel** [462 C3] (28 rooms) Cnr Hage Geingob & School sts; ☎ 067 306679; m 085 600 0911; e infovillage@iway.na; www. villageboutiquehotelnamibia.com. Sister property to Out of Africa Town Lodge, this smart hotel has been converted from 2 old townhouses. Rooms are classed as standard or luxury, the main difference being that the latter are bigger. All are stylishly furnished with tiled floors, AC, DSTV & tea/coffee stations, & are set close together around the gardens, where there's a small pool. The elegant restaurant is spread across various rooms, serving an à la carte menu & fabulous cakes (*booking preferred;* ⊕ *closed evenings Sat– Sun*). *N$1,242/1,392 sgl/dbl.* **$$$**

🏠 **Acacia Park** [462 D3] (2 chalets, 8 rooms, camping) Hindenburg St; ☎ 067 303100; m 081 216 0004; e caciapa@mweb.com.na. Although there are several reasonable B&Bs in Otjiwarongo, those on a shoestring budget might consider this large, noisy restcamp with a pool, pub & restaurant – though the sports bar & karaoke focus won't endear it to many. Recent reports of dirty & dilapidated rooms don't help, so stick to the campsite, whose pitches have BBQ, tap & power point. Unless funds are very tight, you will be better off elsewhere for a bed. A large perimeter fence with manned gate offers reasonable security. *Camping N$80 pp.* **$**

✖ **WHERE TO EAT AND DRINK** Most visitors dine at their hotels or at the C'est Si Bon Hotel. The restaurant at the Crocodile Ranch [462 D3] serves a substantial sit-down lunch, but for something lighter, or a coffee stop, try:

✖ **Kari's Restaurant** [462 D3] Cnr of Hindenburg & Hage Geingob sts; ☎ 067 304310; m 081 298 2077; ⊕ 08.00–21.00 Mon–Fri, 08.00–17.00 Sat. This thatched restaurant has an upstairs terrace & tables scattered around the gardens. Its varied menu includes pizzas, salads, sandwiches & steaks. **$$–$$$$**

🍽 **Kameldorn Garten** [462 C3] 17 Hindenburg St; m 081 244 5967; ⊕ 07.00–18.00

Mon, Tue & Thu, 07.00–22.00 Wed & Fri, 08.00–15.00 Sat. Just off Hage Geingob St & under the arched entrance on the left (there's parking round the back), this coffee shop & bistro is recommended. Run by chefs Eleini & Dieter Radeck, it offers sandwiches, daily specials & the 'biggest burgers in Namibia'. Adjacent is a small craft shop with secondhand books. **$–$$$$**

OTHER PRACTICALITIES The Town Square **shopping** mall [462 D2] on the corner of Rikumbi Kandaga Street and Dr Libertina Amathila Avenue is a good illustration of how the town is growing. Full of smart clothes shops, a pharmacy, ATM, a large Shoprite and fast-food outlets, it also has a large car park with car guards.

There are several **fuel stations** around town (some open 24 hours), and Standard, Bank Windhoek and FNB **banks** are all in the centre. For **food and supplies**, seek out the shops on the main Hage Geingob and St George's streets, including both Spar and Pick n Pay. If you're in need of **vehicle repairs**, there's a Nissan/Toyota dealer (*38 Hage Geingob St;* ✆ *067 302903*) here, too.

In an **emergency**, your first port of call should be the excellent private hospital, **Mediclinic Otjiwarongo** [462 D4] (*Sonn Rd;* ✆ *067 303734; www.mediclinic.co.za*), which handles serious cases, including medical rescue, for much of northern Namibia. A friend of mine needed some serious emergency surgery here, and on returning to London her private consultant told her that the operation had been performed to the highest standards. Otherwise the state ambulance service is on ✆ 067 300900, the fire brigade on ✆ 067 304444, and the main government hospital on ✆ 067 300900. The police [462 C2] are reached on ✆ 067 10111.

WHAT TO SEE AND DO One of the locomotives that first served Otjiwarongo has been preserved and stands in front of the railway station building. It is worth a quick look even if you're not a steam enthusiast.

A visit to the **Crocodile Ranch** [462 D3] (✆ *067 302121;* e *andi@iway.na;* ⊕ *08.00–17.00 Mon–Fri, 08.00–15.00 Sat, 09.00–15.00 Sun; admission N$50*) makes for an interesting hour or so. The ranch has been going for decades now, and has established a small export business for crocodile skins, while the meat is sold locally. There's also a restaurant on site serving light lunches such as toasted sandwiches, burgers and steaks.

Further afield, the **dinosaur footprints** at Otjihaenamaparero (page 467) and the **Cheetah Conservation Fund** (CCF; see box, page 468) are the only excursions suitable from Otjiwarongo. **Waterberg Plateau Park** (page 469) is a destination in its own right, as is **Okonjima** and the **AfriCat Foundation** (see box, page 466), although if you're short of time, the **AfriCat Day Centre** (✆ *067 687032; www.africat.org;* ⊕ *09.00–15.00 daily; admission free*) is well worth a visit and reachable from Otjiwarongo. Here, visitors can go on hiking trails, and take the excellent AfriCat tour (*N$450*) which departs at 11.00 and 13.00 daily. There's a bar and café where light lunches are available, as well as showers, useful if you're heading back to Windhoek for a late flight.

AROUND OTJIWARONGO

⌂ **Where to stay: nearby guest farms** There are several guest farms in the area. Okonjima is well known for its excellent work with big cats, and Mount Etjo has much interesting publicity material, though seems to appeal more to Afrikaans-speaking visitors than those who rely on English. Frans Indongo makes a good base for visits to the CCF – although they now have their own accommodation options.

⌂ **Frans Indongo Lodge** [454 D4] (4 rooms, 8 chalets) ✆ 067 307946/7; e indongo@afol.com. na; www.indongolodge.com. This attractive lodge, situated 43km northeast of Otjiwarongo on the D2433, is owned by businessman Dr Frans Indongo. It is designed to reflect his roots as a farmer's son in northern Namibia, with the tall wooden stakes that typically enclose an Ovambo homestead used to separate & define areas of the lodge.

En-suite rooms & chalets, 1 with wheelchair access, are cool & modern in design. All come with the extras that you would expect in a good-quality lodge: AC, phone, Wi-Fi, TV, hairdryer, fridge & kettle. The central area has a pleasant pool, bar &

restaurant, & is fronted by a large wooden deck which looks out over the 170km² farm. This & an observation tower provide plenty of opportunities for checking out animals at the illuminated waterhole, or birds attracted to the artificial stream.

Guests can take part in game drives on the farm (*N$290 pp*) or 3 hiking trails, while excursions include visits to the Waterberg Plateau & the CCF information centre. Dinner N$300; B&B N$1,400/2,550 sgl/dbl. **$$$**

✳ ⌂ **Okonjima** [454 C5] ✆ 067 314000; m 081 127 6233; e info@okonjimalodge. com; www.okonjima.com. Set amid the rolling Omboroko Mountains & overlooking the plains,

Okonjima is best reached from the B1, about 130km north of Okahandja (7km south of Otjiwarongo). From the turn-off, take the private road that is clearly signposted 'Okonjima 10km', & follow the signs to the main gate for a further 14km drive to the lodge.

Run by the Hanssen family for 3 generations, this relaxed place has, over the years, been one of Namibia's most popular & successful draws for visitors. Much of its appeal has been because this is the base for the AfriCat Foundation (see box, page 466). Income from the lodge helps to support the foundation, as well as funding a critical environmental education programme & the running of the 200km² park, which is home to released cheetah, leopards & other native wildlife. Visitors are virtually guaranteed to get close to at least some of the big cats. That said, levels of hospitality have always been well above the norm, too.

All the camps here operate independently, with their own dining facilities. Meals, served plated or buffet-style, are consistently good, with quality wines at good prices. Children aged 7–12 can stay only at Plains Camp & the Bush Suite, with only the campsite accepting children of all ages; note, however, that there are additional age limits on some activities.

Essentially the camps offer the same activities in the early morning and late afternoon, taking a maximum of 9–12 visitors per vehicle, sometimes from more than 1 camp; night drives are possible too. Alternatively, a private guide & vehicle is available at extra cost. Tracking the radio-collared leopards from a 4x4 takes in the rocky Etjo sandstone outcrops & the reserve's natural wildlife – from wildebeest & giraffe to kudu, eland & Hartmann's mountain zebra, as well as birding 'specials' such as Carp's tit & the Damara rock runner. Leopard tracking can yield superb photographs; many winners of photo competitions have taken their shots at Okonjima! There is also the opportunity to track cheetah, wild dog & hyena on foot, but note that Okonjima does not allow guests into close contact with the animals, or to touch the cheetahs. Further options are self-guided walking trails of 3–8km in a safe area of the reserve; a 'Bushman Trail', when your guide explains how the Bushmen used to live & the uses of some of the plants; and tours of the AfriCat Centre, which provide a fascinating overview of their conservation, cheetah welfare & education projects.

With so much going on, Okonjima has become a destination in itself rather than simply a stopover at the beginning or end of a trip. There's nowhere else quite like it & for some visitors it's a 'must-see'. To get the best out of it, spend at least 2 nights here, ideally arriving around 16.00 in time for tea & the afternoon activities. If you're short of time or not staying overnight, you can call in at the AfriCat Carnivore Care & Information Centre, complete with a café & showers, where visitors can join twice-daily AfriCat tours (*11.00 & 13.00; N$450 pp*).

🏠 **PLAINS CAMP** (28 rooms) This is the hub of Okonjima, previously called Main Camp, but rebuilt in 2014 to create 14 'standard' rooms, & 14 'view' rooms, which simply have more space. All furnishings have been made on site, with the décor cool & fresh rather than rustic bush. Each room has 2 dbl beds, a desk, fridge & sliding doors opening to a veranda shielded by big bamboo poles. 2 rooms are wheelchair accessible with convertible rails in bathrooms & a couple of others are interleading. so ideal for families with older children. The central lapa is designed like a traditional barn with huge glass windows to make the most of the views of the surrounding bush & a small waterhole, & a waterhole pool with a windmill to the side. *DBB N$3,080–4,915/3,960–7,630 sgl/dbl; activities N$550–750 pp per activity. No children under 7.* **$$$$$–$$$$$$**

🏠 **BUSH CAMP** (8 chalets, junior suite) Large, thatched rondavels at this more traditional camp, 3km from Plains Camp, are well separated & more luxurious. Each has 2 dbl beds, Hemingway-style furnishings & an open-sided lapa containing a minibar & daybed with views over the bush – or the night sky. A (wheelchair-accessible) junior suite boasts sliding glass doors, a lounge with fireplace, & a bath & outside shower too. The curved theme continues to the main area & restaurant (serving excellent food), overlooking a firepit, a small pool & a waterhole. Evenings can be particularly fun in the night hide, which looks over a small floodlit waterhole where scraps from the camp attract porcupines, honey badgers & occasionally rarer species such as caracal. *DBB N$6,425/10,650 sgl/dbl; FBA N$8,290/14,380 sgl/dbl. No children under 12.* **$$$$$$–$$$$$$$**

🏠 **OKONJIMA VILLA** (2 rooms, 2 suites) & **BUSH SUITE** (2 rooms) Up there with the best accommodation

Based out of Okonjima, the non-profit AfriCat Foundation (e *info@africat. com; http://africat.org; see ad, 4th colour section*) was founded in the early 1990s. From its initial aim, to rescue, relocate and even rehabilitate both problem and unwanted big cats, today their priority has broadened to encompass all carnivores, raising awareness of the issues involved in carnivore conservation and living with predators, and focusing on environmental education, habitat preservation and animal welfare.

Claimed as the largest rescue-and-release programme in the world, the foundation has rescued more than 1,000 cats since it was founded in the early 1990s, representing a cheetah-to-leopard ratio of around 2:1. Of these, over 90% of the leopards and nearly 80% of the cheetahs have been released into the wild.

Animals being rehabilitated at Okonjima have for many years been protected within a 4,500ha area, but in 2010 fencing was completed around a further 16,000ha, with its own existing leopard population. In May of that year, the first cheetahs, and later hyena and wild dog, were released into this area, learning to hunt for themselves while being closely monitored. The aim now is for the predators to roam freely in this extended park rather than being kept in captivity, and this involves clearing thousands of hectares of encroached bush to create the open spaces that cheetah need. Those animals that cannot hunt for themselves, including several cheetah, are cared for within a smaller reserve dedicated to welfare and outreach projects rather than conservation. Some can occasionally be seen on the excellent AfriCat Tour, which includes a visit to the information centre and clinic and explanations on how the animals are looked after.

Central to the foundation's work is environmental education for all members of the community. This is now the priority for the AfriCat Foundation, with an Environmental Education Centre for children from schools across Namibia, as well as for farmers and teachers.

Guests interested in AfriCat stay at Okonjima, and learn more about the foundation's work from there, or can visit the Day Centre. AfriCat no longer offers their volunteer programme, PAWS.

---

in Namibia, each of these exclusive & secluded options has its own game-drive vehicle & is staffed by a private chef & guide. Tasteful & über-comfortable bedrooms & living rooms under deep thatch are fronted by an extensive veranda with a large pool overlooking a waterhole. In each, there's the option to roll beds out under the stars. This is serious if understated luxury in an open bush setting, ideal for well-heeled families or groups of friends. That said, the villa is located in the main park rather than in the fenced Okonjima 'safe' zone so, with leopards roaming freely, children under 12 are not permitted, whereas children over 7 may stay at the Bush Suite. For those who can't escape reality, there's Wi-Fi internet & mobile phone reception. *FBA villa N$9,365/16,530 sgl/dbl; suite N$12,505/22,810 sgl/dbl.* $$$$$$$

⚕ **OMBOROKO CAMPSITE** At the other end of the scale, the campsite up in the hills features 4 entirely secluded – & exclusive – pitches. Each has electricity, private hot showers, flush toilets, firepit & braai, & there's a pool just for campers, but other than firewood you'll need to be entirely self-sufficient. Booking is essential. *N$440 pp.* $$$

🏠 **Mount Etjo Safari Lodge** [454 C5] (15 rooms, camping) \067 290173–5; e mount. etjo@iway.na; www.mount-etjo.com. The name *etjo*, meaning 'a place of refuge', describes this lodge founded in the early 1970s by Jan Oelofse, now well known in local political circles. (The 'Mount Etjo

Declaration' was signed here on the way to political independence in 1989.) To find it, turn west from the main B1 on to the D2483, about 63km south of Otjiwarongo, then continue for 40km on a gravel & sand road as it heads towards the huge, flat-topped sandstone massif of Mount Etjo, which is often a deep shade of burgundy. The road surface colour changes from white to red in the distance, but watch how it differs from the deeper soil, made into tall termitaria. Approaching from the west, the lodge is about 28km from Kalkfeld: 14km on the D2414 then another 14km on the D2483.

En-suite rooms, some with a jacuzzi & dbl beds, others with twins, balance a rustic feel with a level of luxury. 2 suites have king-size beds, private sitting rooms & private gardens, & the beautifully spacious private villa boasts a pool & waterhole, as well as a private kitchen. A central lapa with a campfire is the focus for evening meals, served with home-grown vegetables, & lunch is available with advance notice. A pool & bar are added bonuses. About 3km from the lodge, the campsite offers 6 individual pitches, each with electricity, private toilet & shower, & shared BBQ facilities. There are usually 2 activities a day, focusing on game drives (*N$350 pp*). As well as elephant, black & white rhino, zebra & giraffe, there are hippo, black wildebeest & nyala, which don't naturally occur in the area. A pride of lion kept in an enclosure are fed regularly & can be observed by guests (*N$170 pp*). Campers may join in activities. *DBB N$1,654–4,494/4,711–8,987 sgl/dbl; camping N$595 per pitch (max 4).* **$$$$$–$$$$$**

Cheetah Ecolodge [454 D4] \067 306225; e bookings@exclusive.com.na; www.

cheetahecolodge.com. Cheetah Ecolodge is the umbrella name for accommodation based at the Cheetah Conservation Fund's (CCF; see box, page 468) research centre 44km east of Otjiwarongo. Both places to stay here generate income to support the fund's work.

BABSON HOUSE (3 rooms) Booked on an exclusive basis, Babson House offers luxurious accommodation for up to 6 people overlooking Chewbaaka's pen (he is one of the CCF's unreleasable ambassador cheetahs). The décor is Africa meets English manor house: large 4-poster beds, rich fabrics & leather furniture that might feel a little dated to some. There are 2 spacious en-suite dbl rooms upstairs & a smaller, less extravagant room with small bathroom downstairs. A private lounge & dining room comes with DSTV, Wi-Fi & binoculars for guests to sit on the veranda watching cheetah, perhaps while the house chef prepares meals. *FBA inc private activities N$9,000/12,000 sgl/dbl.* **$$$$$**

CHEETAH VIEW LODGE (5 suites) Opened in 2017 following the success of Babson House, Cheetah View has brought the CCF to the attention of more visitors, & those looking for something less luxurious. En-suite twin rooms offer simple comfort rather than luxury, each with a view of the bush & the distant Waterberg from a covered veranda. The main area & 1 family suite overlook a small waterhole that promises to draw wildlife from the surrounding bush in the dry season. *DBB N$1,750/3,200 sgl/dbl, inc 15% off CCF cheetah activities.* **$$$$$**

Dinosaur footprints [454 C5] (⊕ *sunrise–sunset daily; admission N$20/10 adult/ under 12*)

Several fossilised animal tracks are preserved in the area's distinctive Etjo sandstone on the farm with the unforgettable name, Otjihaenamaparero. All date from about 150–200 million years ago. The most spectacular is a series of prints about 25m in length, which were made by a large, three-toed, two-legged dinosaur. Just imagine yourself in Jurassic Park.

To get here, take the C33 south for over 60km from Otjiwarongo until Kalkfeld is signposted left, on to the D2414. The farm is 29km from there, signposted 'Dinosaur's Tracks'. Follow the signs which will take you down the D2467, a road not recommended for 2WD vehicles, and then through a farm gate (but note that signs for 'Dinosaur Camp Site' lead to Mount Etjo Safari Lodge, not to Otjihaenamaparero.

Where to stay

Otjihaenamaparero [454 C5] (3 rooms, camping) m 081 462 2983; e dinotracks@afol. com.na, service-team-dino@web.de; www.

dinosaurstracks-guestfarm.com. Otjihaenamaparero Farm began with a campsite, to which owners Adele & Reinhold Strobel added a small whitewashed

The Cheetah Conservation Fund (☏ *067 306225;* e *info@cheetah.org; www. cheetah.org; see ad, 4th colour section*) was started by Larie Marker in 1990 to develop a permanent conservation research centre for cheetah. Today they are based on a 15km² farm northwest of Waterberg Plateau, 44km east of Otjiwarongo (turn right as you head north out of Otjiwarongo, just before the bridge over the railway line). Their aim is to 'secure habitats for the long-term survival of cheetah and their ecosystem through multi-disciplined and integrated programs of conservation, research and education'.

The foundation has a thriving Visitor and Education Centre (⏲ *08.00–17.00 daily except Christmas day, last admission 16.00; N$200/100 adult/child*). To get there, take the B1 north from Otjiwarongo; as you leave the town, the D2440 is on the right, with a brown sign to CCF. Take this road and follow it for about 45 minutes.

Visitors may just turn up during opening hours, but if you time your visit for around 14.00 you should be there for feeding time (though it's as well to phone first to check). With advance booking it's also possible to watch the cheetahs on their morning exercise. This takes place at around 08.00 each morning, when a group is taken out for a run, following a coloured lure that is dragged in front of them around a 'track' (*N$480*). Note, however, that only adults aged 16 and over are allowed in the run area. At all times, you can expect to see some of the orphaned cheetahs living at the centre, and to visit the interactive museum that covers everything from the history of the cheetah to its behaviour and habitat. Conservation issues are prominently covered in the centre, too. There's also a small, well-stocked shop that sells drinks and souvenirs. For those wishing to stay longer, the Visitor Centre sells light lunches and breakfasts can be pre-ordered for those going on the cheetah run.

The museum provides visitors and students with the opportunity to learn more about the behaviour and biology of the cheetah, and the Namibian ecosystem that supports Africa's most endangered cat species. Excellent graphics and interactive displays chart the history of the cheetah from prehistory to modern times, and explain how their range and numbers have diminished. Other exhibits show where the cheetah fits into the cat species family tree, how it differs from the 36 other cat species, how it is adapted for a high-speed sprint and its specialised hunting techniques, and finally its life cycle from cub to adult. A life-size 'playtree' shows the importance of these trees in a cheetah's territory.

The CCF's research programmes include radio-tracking research to understand more about cheetah distribution and ecology; bio-medical research to learn more about overall health, diseases and genetic make-up; habitat and ecosystem research; wildlife and livestock management to reduce predator conflicts; and non-lethal predator control methods. In addition to supporting extensive environmental education programmes, both on site and in schools, CCF also sells 'bushblok': excellent burning firewood made from encroaching bush, which is otherwise a menace to wildlife and especially to a hunting cheetah.

Visitors to the centre can stay at the luxurious Babson House or the simpler Cheetah View Lodge (page 467), but most stay in Waterberg Plateau Park, or at one of the surrounding lodges, and spend half a day visiting the centre from there.

guesthouse in 2003. Alongside simple, en-suite rooms, there's a living area with kitchen that's ideal for self-catering – though home-cooked meals are available on request. The tree-shaded campsite has 5 pitches, each with drinking water & fireplace, 2

toilets/showers & a central sink for dishwashing. Aside from visiting the dinosaur tracks, guests can take nature drives, & guided walking tours can be arranged. *N$490/840 sgl/dbl; camping N$120 pp; no credit cards.* **$–$$$**

WATERBERG PLATEAU PARK

(\067 305001/2; ☼ *sunrise–sunset daily; admission N$80 pp, plus N$10 per vehicle (2WD access), under 16s free*) Historically important during the war between the German forces and the Hereros, Waterberg Plateau was first envisaged as a reserve for eland, Africa's largest species of antelope. In 1972 it was proclaimed a reserve and has since become a sanctuary for several rare animals, including eland and both black and white rhino.

GEOGRAPHY The park centres on a plateau of compacted Etjo sandstone, some 250m high. This lump of rock, formed about 180–200 million years ago, is the remnant of a much larger plateau that once covered the whole area. It is highly permeable (surface water flows through it like a sieve), but the mudstones below it are impermeable. This results in the emergence of several springs at the base of the southern cliffs.

FLORA AND FAUNA For a fairly small park, there are a large number of different environments. The top of the plateau supports a patchwork of wooded areas (mostly broad-leaved deciduous) and open grasslands, while the foothills and flats at the base of the escarpment are dominated by acacia bush, but dotted with evergreen trees and lush undergrowth where the springs well up on the southern side. This diversity gives the park its ability to support a large variety of animals.

Waterberg has become an integral part of a number of conservation projects, seeing the relocation of several endangered species (including black and white rhino, roan and sable antelope) in an attempt to start viable breeding herds. These have added to the game already found here, which ranges from giraffe and kudu to leopard, brown hyena, cheetah and (reports claim) wild dog and lion.

The birdlife is no less impressive, with more than 200 species on record. Most memorable are the spectacular Verreaux's (black) eagles, and Namibia's only breeding colony of Cape vultures. Although REST (page 474) is working to conserve these imposing raptors, numbers have sharply declined in recent years due to both the changing environment and the increasing use of farm poisons (both intentional poisons, and the chemicals in fertilisers and pesticides).

GETTING THERE AND AWAY Waterberg is very clearly signposted, 91km to the east of Otjiwarongo: follow the B1, the C22 and finally the D2512, this last for about 24km. Note that although the park is accessible in a 2WD, the road from the B1 can be very rutted, so allow yourself plenty of time. On the plus side, that gives you a better chance to watch out for wildlife.

WHERE TO STAY

🏠 **Waterberg Camp** [map, page 470] (34 rooms, 35 chalets, camping) Reservations via NWR, Windhoek (page 173) or at the park office (☼ *06.00–18.00 daily*). Established in 1989, the camp is beautifully landscaped over the

escarpment's wooded slopes. In 1910 the Germans built a police station on a plantation here: now it's a restaurant – & the prison cell has become a wine cellar! Much of the original building remains, its history captured in fascinating photographs

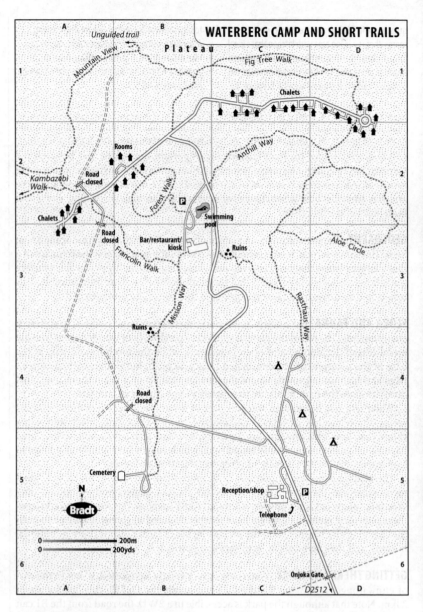

WATERBERG CAMP AND SHORT TRAILS

Unguided trail

Plateau

Mountain View

Fig Tree Walk

Chalets

Anthill Way

Rooms

Road closed

Kambazebi Walk

Forest Walk

Chalets

Road closed

Francolin Walk

Mission Way

Swimming pool

Bar/restaurant/ kiosk

Ruins

Aloe Circle

Ruins

Resthaus Way

Road closed

Cemetery

Bradt

N

Reception/shop

Telephone

0 ————— 200m
0 ————— 200yds

Onjoka Gate

D2512

& memorabilia on the walls. The plantation itself has regenerated into bush, but it is said that the occasional orange tree can still be found. Other amenities include a poorly stocked kiosk (⊕ 06.00–18.00 daily), large swimming pool & conference facilities.

Accommodation ranges from dbl rooms & 'luxury' dbl chalets, to 'standard' 2-room chalets with 4 beds, although we've heard that a little renovation

wouldn't go amiss. The campsite is well shaded, with chairs, lights & good ablutions, but watch out for dawn raids from baboons & ground squirrel burrows pock-marking the road. There's also a fuel station, normally selling both petrol & diesel (though don't rely on it). *Room N$800/1,300 sgl/ dbl; chalet N$940/1,580 sgl/dbl; camping N$250 pp (max 8).* **$$–$$$**

WHAT TO SEE AND DO This park is unusual in that you can't drive yourself around. Instead you must either hike or take one of the park's organised drives with one of their driver/guides.

Organised drives lasting about 3 hours (*N$650 pp*) take place in the morning and late afternoon, and are best booked with the park office as soon as you arrive. They tour around the plateau in search of game, visiting the permanent waterholes and some of the hides. However, although the guiding is usually good, and there are chances of seeing uncommon sable and roan antelope, the bush here is thicker and the game densities appear much lower than, say, Etosha, so many visitors find the game disappointing.

Between the reception and restaurant, a side road leads to a war cemetery where intricate headstones commemorate German soldiers killed in the Waterberg battle during the 1904 Herero uprising led by Chief Samuel Maharero (see box, page 215). Perhaps unsurprisingly, there are no equivalent memorials to the Herero.

Hiking If you come to Waterberg for the walking, then you won't be disappointed. There are nine short trails that you can take all year around from the vicinity of the camp, described in booklets from the office, and designed to give visitors a flavour of the park. The panorama from the end of the trail up to Mountain View is definitely worth the effort and time (about 45 minutes) that it takes to get there.

Guided walks and longer trails, however, have been discontinued, which is a great shame. The latter included an unguided four-day 50km trail in the south of the park which could be done in the dry season, from April to November. There was no better way to experience this park, though reservations had to be made months in advance; please let us know if you manage to book this excellent activity.

Similarly, the park had been gaining a reputation for excellent long guided hikes, particularly the three-day Waterberg Wilderness Trail, a 42km hike to the west of the park, but these have for some years been closed by the Ministry of Environment and Tourism. If resurrected, such hikes would be an excellent way to enjoy the best of Waterberg.

AROUND WATERBERG
Where to stay

Waterberg Wilderness Farm [454 D4] Otjosongombe; ☏ 067 687018; m 081 284 9630; e info@waterberg-wilderness.com; www. waterberg-wilderness.com. Waterberg Wilderness Farm is an excellent & good-value spot for a little relaxed walking & would be perfect for a 2/3-night stay. The farm includes part of the Waterberg Plateau itself, as well as some of the flatter farmland around. It lies 280km north of Windhoek: turn off the B1 on to the C22 (28km south of Otjiwarongo), turn left on to the D2512, & drive past Waterberg Camp & Resort; at Otjosongombe turn left (clearly signposted) towards a small gorge in the plateau, & drive for a further 4km to the reception.

A stay at one of the 3 lodges here includes the option of joining guided hikes of around 3hrs on to & around the plateau in the morning or afternoon (*N$200 pp*). The scenery is stunning, & although getting on to the plateau can be steep at times, walking around the top is relatively flat. You'll see plenty of signs of game although, like walking safaris anywhere, the animals will usually flee before you get too close. Given that both buffalo & rhino live on the property, it's wise to keep your wits about you. There's a series of self-guided walking trails, too, with a map provided to identify the plants along the way. Nature drives (*N$600 pp*) on the flat land below the plateau are more productive for game, & the owners are gradually restocking the property, having converted it from a cattle farm to a game area. It's a good place to spot Damara dik-dik, & along with the usual antelope there are also small numbers of giraffe & rhino. Finally, there's the option (with a day's notice)

18

of spending half a day visiting a local Herero community with a guide.

🏠 **WATERBERG WILDERNESS LODGE** (12 rooms) 2.2km from the main reception, the original farm building has been converted into a lovely lodge by owners Joachim & Caroline Rust. Built from Waterberg's red sandstone & set in a green oasis, surrounded by cliffs, it has 4 family & 8 dbl rooms. All are en suite & are spotlessly clean, fairly spacious & designed traditionally though with an eye for touches of stylish minimalism. B/fast is usually a buffet, often mixing traditional German fare with other European styles. If you arrive by 15.30 on your first afternoon, you'll be in time for tea & cakes on the terrace (also included); later, dinner is served & everyone eats together. There's a fire for winter evenings, while 2 spring-water pools offer a refreshing dip in the hotter months. *DBB N$1,664/3,328 sgl/dbl.* **$$$$$**

🏠 **WATERBERG PLATEAU LODGE** (8 chalets, camping) Up a steep drive, nestled among the rocks along the edge of the plateau, are en-suite chalets, each with a wood-burning fire, private plunge pool & spectacular views. Afternoon tea is served in the restaurant atop a rocky outcrop offering 180° views. *DBB N$2,017/4,034 sgl/dbl.* **$$$$$**

🏠 **WATERBERG VALLEY LODGE** (5 tents) A halfway house between chalets & camping, this tented camp has its own pool & lapa, & beautiful views over the valley. *DBB N$898/1,796 sgl/dbl.* **$$$$**

In the valley below, 2 campsites each have pitches with private BBQ & tap. There are clean ablution facilities & a shared swimming pool, & wood/BBQ meat can be purchased at the office. *Camping N$250 pp.* **$$**

🏠 **Waterberg Guest Farm** [454 D5] (4 rooms, 5 bungalows) ☎ 061 237294; m 081 751 4866; e info@waterbergnamibia.com; www. waterbergnamibia.com. On the south side of the tarred C22, 32km east of the main B1, this guest farm is run by Harry & Sonja Schneider-Waterberg, whose family have owned the 40,000ha farm for over a century. It lies at the centre of the much larger Waterberg Conservancy, which also incorporates the Cheetah Conservation Fund (CCF) & much of the Waterberg Plateau. Its location, a little distance from Waterberg, allows great views of sunrise over the plateau, an experience missing from many of the lodges situated immediately below the plateau.

En-suite, sparsely furnished rooms are either in the original farm buildings, which have been converted with care & quality, or in bungalows just 200m from the main house. Bungalows are built to a traditional Herero design, but with no shortage of mod cons, including indoor & outdoor showers. For families, there are linked dbl & twin rooms with a small sitting area, & 2 bungalows. Outside is a small splash pool &, beside it, a thatched bar. Guests are seated together for b/fast & dinner in the dining room, & the lounge houses an impressive wine collection.

The main activities here are ½-day trips to the CCF, but there are also opportunities for hiking in the mountains behind the farm, which are of a very similar geology & form to the Waterberg. Harry's a good birder, & knows his way around the bush very well, so is a good man to guide you if he's there. Finally, the farm offers a range of wellness treatments, from massage to aromatherapy. Mind you, Harry has 5 dogs, so if you're not a fan, this place probably isn't for you. *Room N$1,359/2,500 sgl/dbl; bungalow N$1,920/3,708; N$100 key deposit.* **$$$$–$$$$$**

🏠 **Weaver's Rock Guest Farm** [454 C5] (4 bungalows, 2 chalets, camping) ☎ 067 304885; m 081 128 4098; e wrgf@iway.na, srtc@iway.na; www.weaversrock.com. The guest farm is situated on Hohenfels ('high rock') Farm, which was purchased from the German colony in 1903 by Earl zu Bentheim Tecklenburg-Rheda after completing his service in Sumatra. Several generations later it is still in the family, run by the lovely Sabine & Alex & their children, Mark & Nadia. After turning on to the C22 towards Waterberg Plateau & driving for 5km, it is signposted up the hill on a farm road for another 5km. Guests are accommodated in en-suite bungalows with great views across the valley or 2 very simple bush chalets, built of stone & wood, with tin roofs & outdoor shower rooms.

There are 11 grassy camping pitches with BBQ, water & electricity border a well-established garden. Fresh home-grown produce is part of the fare with b/fast & dinner (N$250 pp) served in the thatched lapa overlooking a swimming pool; campers can join farm meals on request.

Activities include farm drives, pony rides for children or horseriding for adults, bush dinners & self-guided hikes, including a great 20min walk to a small lake for a refreshing swim. *Bungalow N$785/1,430 sgl/dbl; bush chalet N$420/750, both exc meals; camping N$135 pp.* **$–$$$**

This small ranching town of about 8,500 people is some 65km from Otjiwarongo and 115km south of Etosha's Okaukuejo camp. It stands on a limestone formation in fertile grasslands, dotted with livestock ranches and the odd fruit farm. The name 'Outjo' is variously translated as 'place on the rocks' or 'little hills' – referring to the area's hilly topography.

This territory had long belonged to the Herero people when the first Europeans arrived to stay. The adventurer Tom Lambert settled here with his family in 1880, and few others followed until the Schutztruppe established a control post here in 1897. The following year the first 'stand' of town land was officially given out.

In 1901 the town water tower was completed, and is still easily seen today. Development ground to a halt during the Herero war around 1904–05, and again just before independence, but in the last two decades or so the town seems to have had a new lease of life thanks to tourists en route to Etosha. That said, the town is still small, and keep an eye out for minor hassle in the form of curio sellers who won't take 'no' for an answer.

Outjo is a useful pit stop on the way to or from Etosha, Khorixas or the northern Kaokoveld, but not usually a destination in itself.

TOURIST INFORMATION The town's tourist information office [473 B1] (⏰ 08.00–18.00 Mon–Sat, closed Sun) can be found inside Namibia Gemstones shop, in the corner almost opposite the Outjo Bäckerei. The curio shop opposite the Caltex also has helpful local tourist information.

WHERE TO STAY

Etosha Garden Hotel [473 D2] (20 rooms) 6 Otavi St; ☏ 067 313130; e info@etosha-garden-hotel.com; www.etosha-garden-hotel.com. This is a lovely, established hotel with large rooms overlooking an open courtyard, shaded by jacaranda, palm trees & lush greenery. Most of the rooms have twin beds, simple wooden furniture, & rugs scattered on cool, waxed concrete or tiled

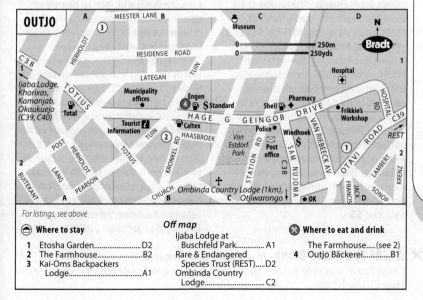

For listings, see above

Where to stay
1 Etosha Garden...................D2
2 The Farmhouse..................B2
3 Kai-Oms Backpackers
   Lodge............................A1

Off map
Ijaba Lodge at
   Buschfeld Park..............A1
Rare & Endangered
   Species Trust (REST).....D2
Ombinda Country
   Lodge............................C2

Where to eat and drink
   The Farmhouse.....(see 2)
4 Outjo Bäckerei..............B1

floors, & an en-suite bath or shower. There is also a small swimming pool. In the à la carte restaurant (SS–$$$$) you can enjoy lunch, tea or coffee with apple strudel, or perhaps the hotel's game specialities for dinner. Popular with groups, this is a good option for a 1-night stop, or even just an extended lunch, on the way to/from Etosha. *N$625/840 sgl/dbl.* **$$$**

⌂ **The Farmhouse** [473 B2] (6 rooms) `067 313444;` m 081 326 3739; e dinnerfarmhouse@ iway.na; www.farmhouse-outjo.com. Above the trendy Farmhouse café is a small guesthouse. Each of its stylish en-suite rooms has Wi-Fi & TV, & some have AC. It's a good option for a small group or family & there is safe parking. *N$770/1,110 sgl/ dbl.* **$$$**

⌂ **Ombinda Country Lodge** [473 C2] (24 rooms, camping) `067 313181;` e bookings@ ombindalodge.com; www.ombindalodge.com. Ombinda rose from the remnants of Outjo's old municipal restcamp in 1995, & has been thriving ever since. It lies about 1km southeast of town, signposted off the main C38 towards Windhoek. The en-suite thatched rooms – 15 twin, 4 trpl & 5 family – are built around a grassy central area with large pool, thatched bar/restaurant with TV & alfresco dining area offering an à la carte menu for lunch & dinner. There's also a small, tree-shaded campsite that's popular with overlanders. Ombinda is pleasant, safe & secure, ideal for families with children, but its rooms are close together so this may not be the place to get away from it all. *From N$480/800 sgl/dbl; camping N$150 pp.* **$$–$$$**

⌂ **Kai-Oms Backpackers Lodge** [473 A1] (6 rooms, dorms, camping) Meester Ln; `067 313597;` m 081 375 0152; e vzyl.deon@yahoo. com. Situated in a quiet Outjo suburb & well signposted off the main street, this backpackers' lodge is full of character considering it's in a small, rural town. The rooms are built around a central courtyard split into various shaded sitting & BBQ areas & decorated with murals, antiques, carvings & plant pots. There's a small camping area, off-street parking, a self-catering kitchen & dining room. *Dorm bed from N$300; camping N$120 pp; b/ fast not inc.* **$$**

Close to Outjo

⌂ **Ijaba Lodge at Buschfeld Park** [473 A1] (6 bungalows, camping) `067 313665;` e ijabalodge@gmail.com; www.ijaba-lodge.com. Almost 2km north of Outjo, just across the Storm River on the left, this relaxed lodge is set in 95ha & makes a pleasant stopover. Lush grounds with mature citrus trees offset cream-painted bungalows with simple but clean rooms. 3 dbls have bathroom, lounge area, fridge & kettle, & a further 3 are set up for families, with adjoining bedrooms. The sloping campsite has level pitches with power & some shade, & a BBQ area; there are tents here too should you not have your own. For entertainment, there's a lovely pool with grassy surrounds; a small waterhole that attracts a range of birds & game such as kudu, Damara dik-dik & duiker; & 2 self-guided walking trails into the mountains. *N$740/1,260; camping N$160 pp.* **$$–$$$**

⌂ **Rare & Endangered Species Trust (REST)** [473 D2] (8 bungalows, camping) m 081 367 9425; e rest@iway.na, bookings@ restnamibia.org; www.restnamibia.org. Previously located near Okonjima (page 464), REST moved to its (hopefully) permanent location 4km east of Outjo toward Otavi in 2016. The new location has allowed them to build a campsite & self-catering bungalows to allow visitors to stay overnight & better understand the trust's work. 2 bungalows should be completed in early 2019, with a further 6 to follow shortly after. There are currently no plans for a restaurant, though, so guests will either need to cook for themselves (there are braai facilities) or venture into Outjo for a meal.

Overnight guests & day visitors alike are welcome to enjoy twice-daily tours of the visitor centre (*11.00 & 15.30 daily; US$55 pp*). These will give travellers the chance to see the animals that the trust is rehabilitating at the time, ready to be released, as well as certain non-releasable animals, including the now-famous pangolin, Honey Bun. That said, they could be out foraging, so there are no guarantees. In the short term, the centre has halted its vulture restaurant programme, but it is hoped to reinstate this once construction of the bungalows is complete. *Self-catering bungalow US$200/300 sgl/dbl; camping US$85 pp.* **$–$$**

✗ **WHERE TO EAT AND DRINK** In addition to the restaurants at various places to stay, Outjo boasts a couple of cafés that would make a good stop; both are on the main Hage Geingob Drive.

✕ The Farmhouse [473 B2] Cnr Hage Geingob Dr & Tuin St; ☎067 313444; **m** 081 326 3739; **e** dinnerfarmhouse@iway.na; www.farmhouse-outjo.com; ⏲ 07.00–21.00 daily. Part of a trendy complex, this is a friendly café with a cosy interior & a well-laid-out beer garden. Come for a cooked b/fast, sandwich, wrap, burger or light lunch, along with internet & good coffee. There is also a small guesthouse (see opposite). **$–$$$$$**

✕ Outjo Bäckerei [473 B1] ☎067 313055; **e** imagesofafrica@iway.na; ⏲ 07.00–17.00 Mon–Fri, 07.00–13.30 Sat, closed Sun. Directly opposite the Caltex garage on the north side of town, this popular bakery has expanded from a small seating area inside to include a welcoming, partly thatched garden restaurant. There's a selection of burgers, some excellent pies & a good range of confectionery & German-style pastries. Picnic lunch packs can be arranged on request & free Wi-Fi is available, although the connection is quite slow. **$–$$$$$**

OTHER PRACTICALITIES Outjo is a good place to get organised. In the centre is an open area, like a village green, near which can be found most of the town's facilities, including fuel stations, supermarkets, several curio shops, a couple of cafés and a post office. (The last was memorable for having an old-style public phone as late as 1994, which accepted 10c or 20c pieces and needed cranking into action.) For **banks**, the FNB is beside the green, with the Standard Bank (and ATM) almost opposite and Bank Windhoek close to the OK supermarket on Sam Nujoma Drive.

For **fuel** there is the Shell station opposite the police station, the Engen garage (with workshop) next to the Standard Bank, and the Total station on the way northwest out of town. All are (in theory) open 24 hours. Frikkie's Workshop [473 D1] (☎*067 313561*; **m** *081 127 8302*), almost opposite the hospital, offers **vehicle repairs**.

In an **emergency**, the police [473 C2] are reached on ☎067 10111 or 067 313005, the ambulance on ☎067 313044, the hospital [473 D1] on ☎067 313250 and the fire brigade on ☎067 313404. Outjo **pharmacy** [473 C1] (☎*067 313276*) is on the main street.

WHAT TO SEE AND DO The town's **museum** [473 C1] (☎*067 313402*; ⏲ *08.00–13.00 & 14.30–17.00 Mon–Fri; admission N$10 pp*) is well worth a visit, with displays of local history and a variety of animal horns, skins and bones, minerals and gemstones. There's also a unique sheep-shearing machine that works with a bicycle chain. If you can't get to it during normal opening hours, it's worth phoning to see if they will open specially.

AROUND OUTJO
Where to stay In addition to the following guest farms nearby, take a look at the accommodation around Etosha's Andersson Gate (page 443).

🏠 Vreugde Guest Farm [454 B3] (7 rooms) **m** 081 418 4865, 081 332 4427; **e** info@ vreugdeguestfarm.com; www.vreugdeguestfarm. com. The delightful Elsie & Danie Brand opened the 3,400ha family farm to guests in 2001, & management has now passed to the next generation, Danie & Rachael Brand. They continue to offer a remarkably warm welcome that reflects their name for the farm: *vreugde* means 'joy'. The farm is signposted 9km along the D2710, a turning to the west off the C38 about halfway between Outjo & Etosha's Andersson Gate. Accommodation is in traditionally decorated rooms or in chalets (1 for families) looking over a carefully tended lawn & flower-beds. These are individually & tastefully decorated in shades of creams & terracotta, with ceiling fans & cool stone floors. Allergy sufferers who struggle with thatch will appreciate the metal roofing of all but 2 of the rooms. Outside, mature trees provide plenty of shade & attract numerous birds, while in the centre, additional shade is afforded by a lapa that feels like an English summerhouse, albeit thatched & open to the breeze. There is a pool to one side & a braai area. Meals are served around a large table, giving guests the chance to find out about the farm, & drives or walks are also on offer. Longer guided day trips into Etosha can be arranged.

With its location just 40km/½hr from Etosha, the award-winning Vreugde is a well-recommended place to stop en route from Kaokoland, or for day trips into the national park. *DBB N$1,270/2,240 sgl/dbl.* **$$$$**

🏠 **Buschberg Guest Farm** [454 A3] (7 rooms, 1 pitch) m 081 279 5667; e info@buschberg.com; www.buschberg.com. Run by close friends of the Brands at Vreugde, this small guest farm lies 10km further west along the D2710, & on occasion takes the overspill from Vreugde. The farmhouse here is also surrounded by well-maintained gardens & there is a campsite. *DBB N$800/1,600 sgl/dbl; camping N$150 pp.* **$$$$**

Nearby mountains The hills of the Ugab Terrace, west of the town, deserve special mention for their unusual shapes. A particularly interesting section, signposted 'Ugab terraces', can be found near the Vingerklip (page 404), west of Outjo, about 9km south from the C39. There, some of the formations have been likened to castles from the Middle Ages. These are made of conglomerate, and stand on the edge of a plateau that stretches for more than 80km and eventually forms the northern boundary of the Ugab River valley. Because of differential erosion, only the harder section now remains – often sculpted rather spectacularly.

19

The Triangle and Bushmanland

The triangle of Otavi, Tsumeb and Grootfontein has long been one of the most prosperous areas of Namibia, rich both minerally and agriculturally. Geologists will find it particularly fascinating because of its interesting underground caverns and the famous Tsumeb mine, while the rolling farmland has a lush, well-watered feel that is seldom found south of here.

From the highlands, the old homelands of Hereroland and Bushmanland extend east to the Botswana border, sloping down from the agricultural plains of the central plateau into the endless, gently undulating Kalahari. This 'desert' is very different from the Namib, in landscape and people, although its population density is almost as low.

This northeastern corner of the country is time-consuming, and even difficult, to visit, but offers a fascinating wilderness experience for those who are well prepared and make the time to reach it. It's also the home of many groups of San people: a draw for a small, but increasing, number of visitors.

OTAVI

Situated in a fertile farming area near one of the country's biggest irrigation schemes, this small town has the 24-hour Fourways Total service station on the main road that skirts around it to the east. Although the region's new gold and copper mines are equidistant between Otjiwarongo and Otavi, the latter has seen little benefit economically compared with Otjiwarongo and it remains quiet and sleepy. Some of the streets are tar, others are gravel.

Near Otavi are several interesting **cave systems** (page 483), though visits to these need to be carefully organised in advance; you cannot just turn up. Just 3km out of town, and exceedingly well signposted, is the **Khorab Memorial**, which marks the spot where the German colonial troops surrendered to the South African forces on 9 July 1915.

GETTING THERE AND AWAY Intercape Mainliner's bus services from Windhoek to Livingstone and Victoria Falls stop at the Fourways Total service station in Otavi at 17.50 on Monday, Wednesday and Friday, and in the opposite direction at 04.55 on Monday, Thursday and Saturday. The one-way trip costs around N$440 to Windhoek, and N$420 to Victoria Falls. See page 153 for more details.

The small local minibuses (normally VW combis) that link Otavi with Tsumeb and Grootfontein usually stop at the main Fourways service station, too, and this is probably also the best place from which to hitchhike.

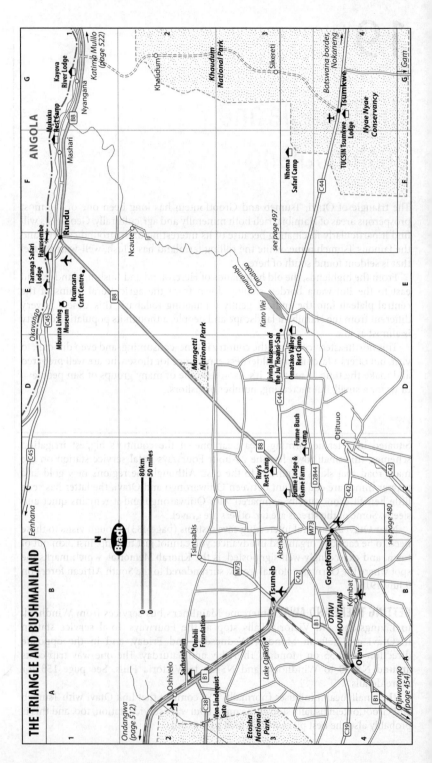

THE TRIANGLE AND BUSHMANLAND

Ondangwa
(page 512)

Katima Mulilo
(page 522)

see page 497

see page 480

Otjiwarongo
(page 454)

ANGOLA

N

80km

50 miles

WHERE TO STAY

In town

Hotel Otavi & Grasdak Restaurant (20 rooms, 8 chalets) 6 Park St; ☎067 234334; m 081 285 4388. The busy bar at the former Otavi Gardens Hotel seems also to act as reception & restaurant, & is a focal point for some of the town in the evening. All rooms are en suite with fans & tea/coffee-making facilities, whereas en-suite chalets have AC, fridges & TV with dbl & twin beds. *N$600/850 sgl/dbl.* **$$$**

Palmenecke Guest House (7 rooms) 96 Hertzog Av; ☎067 234199; m 081 285 8400; e susan@africaonline.com.na; www.palmenecke. co.za. Alexander & Susan du Toit's immaculate & cheery B&B is set among pretty gardens under the palms. Bright, airy rooms are all en suite, with AC, Wi-Fi & DSTV. Guest facilities include a lapa & braai, a bar & a restaurant (*b/fast N$75; dinner N$80*), with a huge fireplace for chilly winter nights. Outside are a swimming pool, & secure parking. *N$540/690 sgl/dbl.* **$$**

Near Otavi

Khorab Lodge [480 B3] (14 chalets, 2 houses, camping) ☎067 234352; m 081 149 2670; e reservations@khorablodge.com; www. khorablodge.com. You can't miss the bright orange walls of Khorab Lodge, set back just off the B1 to Otjiwarongo, about 3km south of Otavi. High thatched ceilings dominate the main building, which houses a large, plush bar area, relaxing couches & a restaurant with a varied à la carte menu including steaks, fish, pasta & salads (*dinner N$230–290*). At the back, set around green lawns, herbaceous borders & even a small artificial stream, are 10 standard chalets, with tiled floors dotted with rugs, twin or dbl beds & airy thatched

ceilings. They are large & well built, using colourful fabrics, with fans & en-suite showers & WC. Newer 'luxury' chalets, built further back facing the bush, are decorated in a very modern style with a leather day bed, & have AC, DSTV, fridge, microwave, iron & even a dinky folding ironing board. Set apart, each within its own walled garden, are 3-bed family houses with fully fitted kitchen, laundry & flat-screen TV. Wi-Fi is available in the central area. There is also a well-equipped campsite, & a large pool with fitness area. Note that some rooms can be noisy at night with traffic on the B1. *N$910–1,110/1,360–1,780 sgl/dbl; camping N$180 pp.* **$$–$$$**

Zum Potjie Restcamp [480 B3] (5 bungalows, camping) ☎067 234300; e info@ zumpotjie.com; www.zumpotjie.com. Signposted from the B1 to Tsumeb, 6km north of Otavi, Zum Potjie is 2km off the main road. In a lovely, unpretentious smallholding, home to Friedrich & Erika Diemer, each of the twin-bed bungalows is clean & simple with a basic, prefabricated design & en-suite shower & WC, while camping pitches have braais, excellent ablution blocks, power & water. A small swimming pool is set in the well-tended garden, food is available in the small restaurant & bar (*dinner N$200*), which is decorated with an amazing collection of African artefacts, & laundry can be arranged.

There is a botanic walking trail, & a quirky & rather fascinating farm museum full of the owners' family memorabilia over the generations. Guests can take short trips guided by Friedrich, & Erika's homemade jams, served at b/fast, are also for sale, as is game for braais. *N$550/900 sgl/dbl; camping N$130 pp & N$45 per pitch.* **$$–$$$**

WHERE TO EAT AND DRINK You'll find fish and chips at the Fruit Store, and drinks at Ot-Quell Bottle Stall or the supermarkets. Alternatively, there's Grasdak Restaurant at Hotel Otavi or the various options at the Fourways service station. Here, you can variously stop at the Camel Inn for steaks and ribs and a drink, or tuck into a pizza at one of the other fast-food joints. Or 3km south of town try Khorab Lodge.

OTHER PRACTICALITIES There are three **fuel stations**, including the substantial Fourways complex next to the main road, Circle in the centre of town and Shell just to the south on the B1. For **food supplies**, there are very good Spar and OK supermarkets, but more interesting are the fresh fruit and vegetable stalls at Fourways fuel station, where there's also a farm shop selling game meat and biltong.

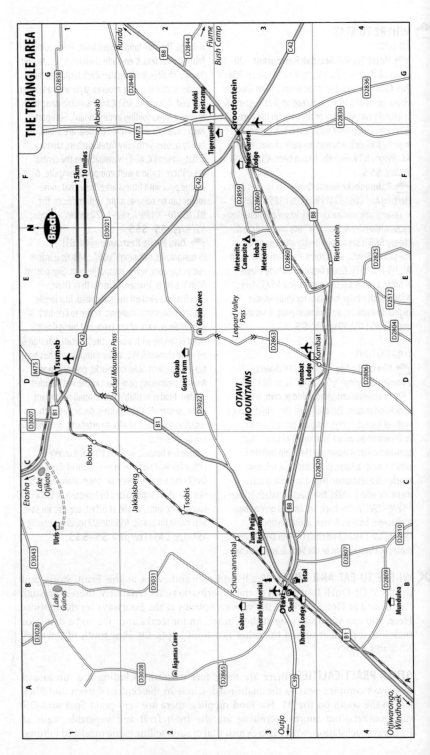

For **vehicle parts**, there's a branch of Cymot on Rheinhold Shilongo Street (↘*067 221161*). Standard, Bank Windhoek and First National **banks** have a presence in the town, with ATMs.

AROUND OTAVI
Nearby guest farms

✳ 🏠 **Mundulea Bush Camp & Walking Trails** [480 B4] (4 tents) ↘064 403123; e turn@ iafrica.com.na; www.turnstone-tours.com. Biodiversity is the watchword for one of the most intriguing & fulfilling back-to-nature experiences in Namibia: Mundulea. A private reserve established in 2001, it covers 120km² of prime bush & mountain savannah in the ancient Otavi karstveldt. This lime & marble landscape spans dolomite ridges, steep gorges & underground caverns. Deep subterranean water feeds spreading trees & the rich soil provides fertile ground for a huge diversity of animal, bird & plant life.

The reserve is easy to find, from a turning off the B1 southwest of Otavi. Guests, who must have a confirmed booking, will be sent precise directions to the old farmhouse, from where they will be transferred to the small camp.

Almost 20 years ago, Mundulea's owner, Bruno Nebe, began reintroducing wildlife, & actively supporting habitats, that used to flourish in this area – a region once known as the heartland of Namibia's game populations (see box, page 482). Guests spend their days exploring the reserve on foot, giving them a chance to connect with the natural environment. For birders, Mundulea has notched up some 267 species, while for the more geologically inclined, it offers a fascinating array of rock formations & fossils, with the chance to explore caves & caverns.

The camp itself, which aims for minimal disturbance to the natural surroundings, has the feel of a traditional bushcamp, but the walk-in tents with shaded porches are spacious, & large, semi-open en-suite showers with solar-heated water & flushing toilets add to creature comforts. Sandy footpaths connect the tents with a couple of hides looking over a well-frequented waterhole, & with the heart of the camp. Here, wholesome meals are cooked on an open fire, accompanied by fresh vegetables & salads grown on the farm. Much of the rustic furniture & fittings were made at Mundulea, often from materials found on the reserve, with attractive & sometimes intriguing results. Do check out the dining table & the bread oven!

Every day here is different, depending on your interests & walking ability, but over 4 days you will explore the reserve's contrasting landscapes, diverse habitat & wildlife, focusing on what occurs naturally. Typically, you'll set out after b/ fast for a slow amble, while your guide helps you to interpret tracks, rocks, plants, wildlife large & small. As with any walking trail, this is not an opportunity to get close to the animals, though it's surprising how invisible you become in a well-constructed hide. After lunch – often a delicious salad – & a well-earned rest, the 2nd walk of the day will take you to a different area, perhaps at a different pace.

Getting acquainted with Mundulea, & with its deliberate, low-impact progress is seriously worthwhile for those who want to look a little deeper into Namibia's environmental issues. This is an ideal 'last stop' on the way back to Windhoek, an opportunity to explore the bush in the company of an outstanding guide. But be warned; guests tend to find themselves drawn back to Mundulea & the ideas it embodies time & time again. *FBA 3 nights/4 days N$17,800 pp sharing (4–8 people); N$20,250 pp sharing (2–3 people).* ⊕ *Closed Dec–Jan.* **$$$$$– $$$$$$$**

🏠 **Gabus Game Ranch** [480 B3] (9 rooms, cottage, 2 tents, camping) ↘067 234291; m 081 127 9278; e office@gabusnamibia.com; www. gabusnamibia.com. Gabus Farm, north of Otavi, has been in the Kuehl family for 4 generations, & has been developed into a comfortable guest farm by its current owners, Heidi & Heinz Kuehl. To get here, take the C39 towards Outjo for 2km, then turn right on to the D3031 for a further 8km. Accommodation is well thought out for everyone from couples & honeymooners to families. Rooms are fresh & spacious, with en-suite bath & WC, AC, tea/coffee facilities & hairdryers. These – & all areas open to guests – overlook a waterhole which is the focus of kudu, eland, waterbuck, impala, springbok & hartebeest, among other wildlife. A couple of new tents have been built for the budget traveller, & there's also a campsite with ablution blocks, power & water.

At the turn of the millennium, top guide Bruno Nebe embarked on a unique new venture: to support the regeneration of land degraded over more than a century by cattle farming and overgrazing in what used to be the heartland of Namibia's game populations.

Before the first fence was taken down, it was important to establish the natural history of the land, and to do this, Bruno turned to one of the mid 19th-century's most prolific travel writers on Namibia: Charles John (Karl Johan) Andersson. Born in 1827, the Swedish explorer first set foot in modern-day Namibia in 1850, and over the next 17 years spent most of his time in the region, hunting and carefully chronicling his finds in three extensive biographies: *Lake Ngami*, *The River Okavango*, and the posthumously published *Notes of Travel in South-western Africa*. Andersson, as was typical of his era, was an inveterate hunter, but his passion was for natural history. Despite being hampered by lack of money, he persevered, eventually setting up home with his wife in the Namibian town of Otjimbingwe, between Windhoek and Walvis Bay. From here, he explored the central highlands extensively, and his detailed accounts bring to the 21st-century reader an understanding of the area's natural riches.

Once the fences from four no-longer-viable farms in the ancient Otavi karstveldt had been painstakingly removed, the next challenge was to clear the dense scrub that made much of the land impenetrable. With everything in its favour in terms of natural habitat, high rainfall and low human impact, Mundulea was named after the purple-flowering shrub, *Mundulea sericea*, which grows throughout the reserve. Its double-edged powers to heal and harm, nourish and poison are based in both local folklore and science: a constant reminder that plans for Mundulea should be carefully considered!

Since 2001, the reserve has made a gradual transition from a heavily fenced cattle ranch to a low-profile but very successful wildlife sanctuary. The animals that have been reintroduced are exclusively those that naturally thrive in this environment, and thus have the best chance of long-term survival. There are good numbers of eland, which thrive in the privacy of the hills and valleys. Kudu, oryx, red hartebeest, tsessebe, wildebeest, duiker, steenbok, dik-dik and warthog are common sights, while giraffe, mountain zebra and roan are becoming easier to spot as their numbers increase. There are also leopard, cheetah, and brown and spotted hyena, as well as rarities like aardvark, bushbabies and the critically endangered pangolin. Doing particularly well is a group of indigenous black-faced impala. Having veered dangerously towards extinction, this Namibian subspecies was the initial *raison d'être* for Mundulea, which was envisaged as a safe haven for Namibia's endemic game species. Working closely with the Ministry of Environment and Tourism (MET) and international researchers, Mundulea is also a long-term member of the MET's black rhino custodianship scheme.

As biodiversity has increased, often through trial and error, so the grasses and other plant life have multiplied. Bird species are on the increase in this varied environment (267 and counting) and the once-vanished oxpecker – nature's alternative to chemical insecticides – has recently been reintroduced. But this is by no means the end. Mundulea is very much work in progress, and for the visitor, time spent at the small bushcamp (page 481) offers an unparalleled opportunity to find out more.

Activities include game drives (N$300 pp) & guided hikes with Heinz. They also offer an adventurous day trip to some stunning caves on a neighbouring farm – but be warned; it's not for the faint-hearted. *Dinner N$330. N$1,522/2,450 sgl/dbl; tent 600/900 sgl/dbl; camping N$145 pp.* **$$–$$$$$**

✳ 🏠 **Ghaub Guest Farm** [480 D2] (10 rooms, camping) 📞 067 240188; e info@ ghaub-namibia.com; www.ghaub.com. Situated in the Otavi Mountains, in the heart of the Triangle, Ghaub was originally founded as a mission station in 1895. It lies some 60km northeast of Otavi, & 50km from Tsumeb, on the south side of the D3022, about 3km west of its junction with the D2863. The 12,000ha reserve is now owned by Joachim & Caroline Rust. As a guest farm, it has successfully retained a lot of character, with high ceilings & plenty of space, especially in the recently upgraded rooms. Each is en suite, clean & well cared for, with twin beds & a large veranda with impressive views of the surrounding land & hills; these include 3 family units sleeping 4. There are also 3 lovely campsite pitches with private ablutions, kitchens, braai, electricity & water, & campers can use the pool & restaurant (*dinner N$300*) if the bungalows aren't busy. There's Wi-Fi access in reception. Tours of the Ghaub Caves (see below), 3.5km away, are organised from here. Other activities include farm drives, nature drives & walking trails. The atmosphere is informal & friendly, thanks to the engaging manager Mika Shapwanale, who has been here for around 20 years.

Ghaub is recommended for a few nights if you want somewhere to relax by the pool, & perhaps do a little gentle walking – provided that you don't mind a lack of must-see attractions in the vicinity. *DBB N$1,870/3,740 sgl/dbl; camping N$250 pp.* **$$–$$$$$**

Cave systems

The area around Otavi doesn't have a wealth of big attractions, unless your passion is caves. In that case, plan to spend quite a lot of time here, as there are many systems to explore – although for some you'll need to plan in advance.

Ghaub Caves [480 D2] (*Guided tour N$400 pp; 2–3hrs*) On the Ghaub Guest Farm (see above), 50km northeast of Otavi, are some caves famous for their stalactites (but no Bushman paintings, as the farm owners are at pains to point out). Designated a national monument, they are signposted from the D2863, from where you can drive to the entrance – and a locked gate. This must be booked in advance by phoning the farm to organise a guide and a heavy-duty torch; you cannot visit independently, and the place is not suitable for a casual visit. From the entrance, after some steep steps for around 20m, it's a scramble over rocks, which get very slippery when wet. The reward, however, is a network of caves extending for some 2.5km, of which around 2km are accessible.

Aigamas Caves [480 A2] Some 33km northwest of Otavi, on a tectonic fault-line, this cave system is about 5km long. It has aroused particular interest as the home of *Clarias cavernicola*, a species of catfish that appears to be endemic to this cave system, although it is now threatened by falling water levels. These fish are a translucent light pink in colour and totally blind, having evolved for life in the perpetual darkness of these caves. Interestingly, their breeding habits are still unknown and no young fish have ever been found.

To visit the cave, make arrangements at the municipal offices in Otavi, next to the restcamp. This may take several days.

Uiseb Caves More extensive than Ghaub, these caves have several different chambers and passages containing some impressive stalactites and stalagmites. With no facilities at all, they are described as 'unspoilt' and arrangements to see these, too, must be made at the municipal offices in Otavi.

Kombat Memorable largely for its name, Kombat is just north of the main road, about halfway between Otavi and Grootfontein, and was for years known in Namibia for its mine. Since the mine closed down due to flooding in 2007, however, Kombat has become close to a ghost town, albeit enhanced by the jacarandas that flower here in late summer. Only a few residents still hang out here, trying to make a living. The place came into the news again when businessman Knowledge Katti bought the town from the mine operators in 2017, then sold it on to the government – presumably at a profit.

 Where to stay

 Kombat Lodge [480 D3] (5 rooms, camping) ☏ 067 231149; m 081 124 0714; e kombatlodge@iway.na. Just off the B8, Kombat Lodge has clean & simple rooms & a campsite,

as well as a pool & restaurant in a thatch-&-brick building. *N$350/600 sgl/dbl; camping N$50 pp.* **$–$$**

TSUMEB

The attractive town of Tsumeb stands in the north of the central plateau, an area of rich farmland and great mineral wealth. Its wide streets are lined with bougainvillea and jacaranda trees, and in the centre of town is a large, green park, a favourite for the townspeople during their lunch break.

Economically the town was dominated by the Tsumeb Corporation which, in the early 1990s, mined a rich ore pipe here for copper, zinc, lead, silver, germanium, cadmium and the variety of unusual crystals for which Tsumeb is world famous. Tsumeb's one pipe has produced about 217 different minerals and gemstones, 40 of which have been found nowhere else on earth. However, in the late 1990s this closed, badly affecting the town. Although the mine has since been reopened for specimen mining, this isn't on a fraction of the scale of the original operation.

Fortunately, Tsumeb still retains some light industries, and is close enough to Etosha to benefit from a steady flow of tourists. It remains a pleasant place to visit, and doesn't have any of the air of depression that you might expect given the erstwhile importance of the mine.

GETTING THERE AND AWAY The largest of the Triangle's towns, Tsumeb once had the best connections. Today, though, although the town has its own airstrip, it is rarely used by visitors, and there are no scheduled flights into the region.

As in the rest of northern Namibia, there are no longer any passenger **trains** to Tsumeb.

By bus Intercape Mainliner's services from Windhoek stop in Tsumeb at the Engen/Wimpy Gateway on Omeg Allee [485 B1]. The bus between Windhoek and Oshakati runs daily except Fridays and Saturdays, departing Windhoek at 18.00 to arrive in Tsumeb at 23.35. The return bus, on the same days, leaves Tsumeb at 00.45, arriving in Windhoek at 06.00. A one-way ticket costs from N$470.

Buses between Victoria Falls and Windhoek also stop here on Monday and Wednesday, leaving Windhoek at 13.00, and Tsumeb at 18.35, for the onward journey to Victoria Falls, where it arrives the next day at 13.00. The return journey is on Sunday and Wednesday, departing from Victoria Falls at 11.50, and reaching Tsumeb at 05.50 the next morning. One-way fares start at N$500. See page 153 for details. For tickets, contact Travel North Namibia (page 487), who also run their own shuttle services to Windhoek three times a week.

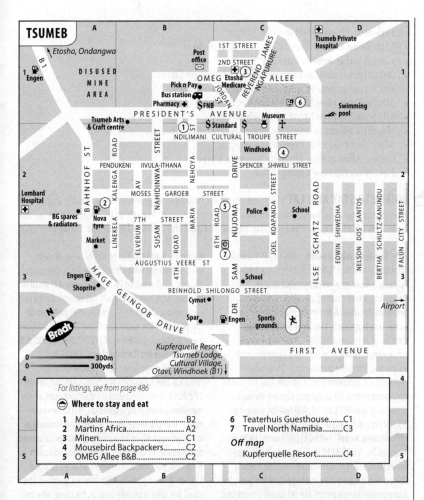

TSUMEB

↖ Etosha, Ondangwa

DISUSED
MINE
AREA

1ST STREET

2ND STREET

Post office ✉

Tsumeb Private Hospital

OMEG Etosha Medicare ALLEE

Pick n Pay

Bus station

Pharmacy ✚ $ FNB

PRESIDENT'S AVENUE

Tsumeb Arts & Craft centre

① $ Standard $

Museum ✝

Swimming pool

NDILIMANI CULTURAL TROUPE STREET

Windhoek ④

PENDUKENI IIVULA-ITHANA

SPENCER SHIWELI STREET

MOSES NAHIDINWA GAROEB STREET

Police ✚

School

Lombard Hospital ✚

BG spares & radiators

Nova tyre ②

7TH STREET

⑤

Market

AUGUSTIUS VEERE ST

⑦

Engen

Shoprite

REINHOLD SHILONGO STREET

Cymot

School

Spar

Engen

Sports grounds

Airport →

FIRST AVENUE

Kupferquelle Resort, Tsumeb Lodge, Cultural Village, Otavi, Windhoek (B1)↓

0 ———— 300m
0 ———— 300yds

For listings, see from page 486

🛏 **Where to stay and eat**

1 Makalani......................................B2
2 Martins Africa.........................A2
3 Minen..C1
4 Mousebird Backpackers............C2
5 OMEG Allee B&B......................C2

6 Teaterhuis Guesthouse........C1
7 Travel North Namibia..........C3

Off map
Kupferquelle Resort..............C4

The Triangle and Bushmanland TSUMEB

19

For more local transport, keep a lookout for the small minibuses (normally VW Combis) that link the Triangle towns. Both south- and northbound Combis arrive and depart at the old Caltex garage on Hage G Geingob Drive.

Hitching Hitching from central Tsumeb is difficult. You must first get yourself to the main junction of the B1 and the C42 (page 484). If you're going south, then hitch on Dr Sam Nujoma Drive, about 500m after leaving town, before the caravan park.

ORIENTATION
Street name changes Various street names have been changed in Tsumeb in the last few years. Although in theory these are now in place, many people still refer to the original names, so the following may be useful:

- 2nd Road *is now* Elverum Avenue
- 3rd Road *is now* Susan Nahidinwa Street
- 8th Road *is now* Joel Koapanda Street
- 10th Road *is now* Edwin Shiwedha

- 11th Road *is now* Nelson dos Santos
- 12th Road *is now* Bertha Schultz-Kanundu
- 13th Road *is now* Falun City Street
- 3rd Street *is now* Ndilimani Cultural Troupe Street
- 4th Street *is now* Pendukeni Iivula-Ithana Street
- 5th Street *is now* Maria Nehoya Street
- 6th Street *is now* Moses Garoëb Street
- Hospital Street *is now* Rev James Ngapurure Street
- Main Street *is now* President's Avenue
- Omeg Allee *is now* Dr Sam Nujoma Drive
- Post Street *is now* Omeg Allee

WHERE TO STAY AND EAT
With established hotels and guesthouses, and a couple of places for backpackers, Tsumeb has plenty of choice. Most visitors eat at one of the hotels, with the restaurants at the Makalani and the Minen being the most popular.

Kupferquelle Resort [485 C4] (50 rooms, 10 suites, camping) \067 220139; e booking@ kupferquelle.com; www.kupferquelle.com. Occupying a tree-shaded site about halfway between the town & the main road intersection, some 1km from each, this large resort boasts a range of accommodation – standard, twin & trpl rooms & suites – as well as a campsite with 25 pitches. With the popular Dros Steakhouse restaurant & swimming pool on site, too, this could be a good option for those just passing through. *Room only from N$1,380/1,900 sgl/dbl; camping N$120 per pitch, plus N$60 pp.* **$$–$$$**

Minen Hotel [485 C1] (49 rooms) Dr Sam Nujoma Dr; \067 221071/2; e contact@minen-hotel.com; www.minen-hotel.com. The friendly Minen is in an attractive spot opposite the park. Its more modern twin rooms are set round a courtyard with a swimming pool & a beautiful lush garden, while older but refurbished dbls overlook a 2nd courtyard. All have AC/heating & fan, en-suite WC & shower or bath, TV & fridge. Rooms are almost out of earshot of the busy bar at the front, which can become quite lively at w/ends, especially at the end of the month when people are paid. To the side of the hotel is a pleasant veranda with umbrella-shaded tables & chairs: a popular spot for lunch or drinks. Inside is a more formal restaurant (⏰ 18.00–21.30 daily). *N$695–805/1,050–2,900 sgl/dbl.* **$$$**

Makalani Hotel [485 B2] (28 rooms) Ndilimani Cultural Troupe St; \067 221051; e makalani2@tsumebnam.com; www. makalanihotel.com. This smart & efficient hotel, distinctively painted in yellow with green windows, is right in the centre of town. Rooms are comfortable with (firm!) twin beds, direct-dial phones, AC & satellite TV. The restaurant is small & friendly, with a reasonable if not adventurous à la carte menu; alternatively, meals may be taken by the pool or in the rustic bar. Other facilities include a private bar & gambling. *N$720/1,060 sgl/dbl.* **$$**

Mousebird Backpackers [485 C2] (4 rooms, 6 dorm beds) Cnr Pendukeni Iivula-Ithana & Joel Koapanda sts; \067 221777; m 081 272 2650; e info@mousebird-namibia.com; www. namibweb.com/mousebird.htm. In the centre of town, near the museum, the colourful Mousebird is aimed squarely at backpackers, with private twin or dbl rooms (1 en suite), dorm accommodation & camping on the lawn. There's a fully equipped kitchen & dining room, with free tea & coffee. The small bar area is usually busy &, for those who miss electronic home comforts, there is a satellite TV, a collection of videos & a PlayStation, with internet access at extra cost. Outside are a braai area & secure parking. *N$230/370 sgl/dbl; dorm bed N$130; camping N$90 pp.* **$$**

OMEG Allee B&B [485 C2] (9 rooms) Dr Sam Nujoma Dr; \067 220631; e omegalle@ gmail.com. This immaculate B&B, named after both a railway company & the town's first mine (Otavi Minen Eisenbahn Gesellschaft), has 7 dbl & 2 sgl rooms, all with AC, en-suite shower, satellite TV, fridge, kettle, hairdryer & safe. *N$550/730 sgl/dbl.* **$$**

Teaterhuis Guesthouse [485 C1] (10 rooms) Cnr Ilse Schatz Rd & President's Av; m 081 148 8133; e teaterhuis@gmail.com. The clue here is in the name: Theo & Surine

Bekker have converted part of a 1960s theatre into a guesthouse, & the foyer is now an eclectic restaurant. Building work in 2018 was in hand to increase the number of rooms to 10 – the newer ones en suite & with AC. The theatre itself remains unchanged, complete with the original retro seats, & shows are still held today. *N$605–900/825–1,265 sgl/dbl.* **$$$**

🏠 **Travel North Namibia** [485 C3] (8 rooms) Dr Sam Nujoma Dr; \067 220728; m 081 299 4214; e info@travelnorthguesthouse.com; www.travelnorthguesthouse.com. Dbl & twin rooms at this friendly guesthouse are mostly en suite, though 1 has a private bathroom across the corridor, & all have AC, Wi-Fi, DSTV, fridge, tea/coffee facilities & braai. There's a pleasant garden & play area for children, plus an excellent coffee

shop serving delicious homemade cakes, & a hair & beauty salon. They are also agents for Europcar. *Room only N$520/900 sgl/dbl.* **$$$**

🏠 **Martins Africa** [485 A2] (16 rooms, 11 dorm beds) Linekela Kalenga; \067 220310; www.marmotrs.iway.na. While the dorms remain at this established self-catering place, there are en-suite rooms too, including 2 for families, & all with AC, TV, fridge & kettle. Cheaper rooms with ceiling fans share several showers & WCs with the 4 dorm rooms. In the central areas you'll find chairs & tables, a TV, a fully equipped kitchen (no meals are available) & laundry facilities, as well as a BBQ area, pool & children's playground. *Room only N$610/760 sgl/dbl (20% discount Fri–Sun); dorm bed N$250.* **$$**

OTHER PRACTICALITIES There are several **fuel stations** around town, many of them open 24 hours. President's Avenue [485 B1] has branches of FNB, Standard and Bank Windhoek **banks**. Travel North Namibia offers **internet** access at N$30 per hour.

The mine has made Tsumeb relatively rich, and its main shopping street is often bustling, with various clothes shops, take-aways and curio outlets. With a branch of Shoprite [485 A3] in the new Le Platz Shopping Centre on Hage G Geingob Drive, as well as the Pick n Pay supermarket [485 B1] at one end of Dr Sam Nujoma Drive (opposite the post office), and Spar in 9th Street [485 B3], food shopping is not a problem either. **Barry Jacobs Apteek** (*067 222190, a/h* *067 220508*) is the place to call if you're in need of medication.

Health and safety There's a recommended doctor at Etosha Medicare on Dr Sam Nujoma Drive [485 C1] (*067 220001*), and right next door is the good **Etosha Pharmacy** [485 B1] (*067 220216*). **In an emergency**, the police [485 C2] are reached on \067 223 5017, the hospital [485 A2] and ambulance service on \067 224 3000, 067 081924, and the fire service on \067 221004 (*a/h* m *081 124 8677*). There is also Tsumeb Private Hospital [485 D1] (*067 221001*) serving the mine, which may be able to help in an emergency.

WHAT TO SEE AND DO
Tsumeb Museum [485 C1] (*President's Av;* ⊕ *09.00–noon & 14.00–17.00 Mon-Fri, 09.00–noon Sat, other times by arrangement; admission N$40 pp*) Facing the park, next to a beautiful Lutheran church, is one of Namibia's best little museums. Appropriately, located in a historic German school dating from 1915, and now a national monument, it has an excellent section on the region's geology and exhibits many of the rare minerals and precious stones that were mined here from 1890. With prior notice, it's even possible to visit the mine itself, including the smelter.

The Khorab Room contains old German weaponry, recovered from Lake Otjikoto, which was dumped there by the retreating German forces in 1915 to prevent the rapidly advancing Union troops from capturing it. Pieces have been recovered periodically, including the Sandfontein cannon that is on display here. You can also see the uniform of the German Schutztruppe (colonial troops), along with the photo album of the notorious General von Trotha, which makes fascinating reading if your German is good.

Train buffs will be drawn to the gleaming steam engines outside the museum, as well as to exhibitions covering the construction of the Otavi railway line from Swakopmund to Otavi – though Otavi itself is no longer served by passenger trains. There is also a small section on the lifestyle of the Bushmen, Ovambo, Herero, Kavango and Himba people.

Helvi Mpingana Kondombolo Cultural Village   [485 C1] (✆ 067 220787; ⊕ 08.00–16.00 Mon–Fri, 08.00–13.00 Sat–Sun & hols by arrangement; admission N$35.50 pp) Facing the park, between the Kupferquelle and the centre of town,

THE GREATEST CRYSTAL-PRODUCING MINE ON EARTH

Mining was started in the place now known as Tsumeb well before historical records were kept. Then it's thought that the San, who were known to have settlements at Lake Otjikoto, 24km away, were probably attracted by the hill's green colour, and perhaps mined malachite here. This they probably then traded with Ovambo people who would smelt it to extract the copper. Perhaps the earliest records of this are from the writings of Francis Galton who, in 1851, met both Bushmen and Ovambos transporting copper near Otjikoto.

In 1893, Matthew Rogers came to the Green Hill here for about a year, sinking test mine shafts and concluding that there was a major deposit of copper and lead, along with quantities of other commodities including gold and silver. Similar tests in 1893 and 1900 quantified this further; all suggested a very rich area for minerals and ore.

To exploit this deposit, a railway was built in 1905 and 1906, linking Tsumeb with Walvis Bay. By 1907 the mine was producing high-grade copper and lead ores. Despite halting production during World War I and World War II, mining expanded steadily. By 1947 the mine extended to 576m below the surface, and most of the higher levels of the mine had been exhausted. Further investigations showed the existence of more reserves.

Various changes in ownership of the mine occurred after the wars. By 1966 the mine had produced over nine million tonnes of ore; its reserves were estimated at eight million tonnes. However, in May 1996 mining ceased in some of the deeper levels (which, by then, were around 1,650m below the surface) because the cost of pumping out water from these levels had finally outweighed the cost of the ore recovered. This was the beginning of the end. In June one of the main shafts was flooded after its pumps were switched off, and a large strike (July/August 1996) finally stopped mining operations, and the mine closed.

As well as producing huge quantities of ore, Tsumeb was described as 'the greatest crystal-producing mine on earth' for its amazing variety of geological specimens, crystals and minerals. Numerous rare minerals had been found here, some completely unique to Tsumeb. Unfortunately, a specialist mining company that started mining the upper levels of the complex in 2000, looking for one-off 'specimens', ceased operations just two years later. Other operations, albeit on a larger scale, have so far met with a similar fate, and now it looks as though tourism will be the latest seam to be mined.

is a relatively new building which was constructed with Norwegian funds and modelled on the fort at Namutoni. Open-air displays on most of the country's main ethnic groupings and their traditional housing make for a worthwhile visit. There's also a small curio shop.

Tsumeb Arts and Crafts Centre [485 B1] (*TACC; 18 President's Av;* ✆ 067 220257; ⏱ 08.45–17.00 & Mon–Fri, 08.45–13.00 Sat; group visits & Sun by prior arrangements with Brigitte, m 081 285 4388) Next to the Etosha Café and Biergarten, the TACC is a charitable trust set up to help develop the skills of Namibian artists and craftspeople. It provides them with a base, training and some help in marketing their produce – including this shop selling their work at a reasonable price, with no haggling or pressure to buy. It's well worth a visit.

AROUND TSUMEB
Nearby lodges

!Uris Safari Lodge [480 C1] (22 rooms, camping) ✆ 067 221818/220248; e gavin.uris@ gmail.com, marketing@uris-safari-lodge-namibia. com; www.uris-safari-lodge-namibia.com. Access to this lodge, which has recently changed hands, is from the B1, 10km west of Tsumeb, from where it's a further 12km through a private 17,000ha game reserve. Dbl & family rooms are laid out in pairs in renovated mine cottages, with these & the central building alike under steep thatch. A Moroccan twist prevails, with coloured glass lanterns, silvered chairs, traditional rugs & deep cushions, while in the en-suite rooms, following the theme, are tasselled mosquito net 'tents', as well as AC, kettle, hairdryer, safe & phone. Family rooms have a loft area for children aged 6–12. At the campsite, 100m from the main building, the 2 pitches have private ablutions, power, light & water, & are very convenient for the restaurant (*b/fast N$110, dinner N$270*). There's an attractive swimming pool with in-water loungers, set in luscious gardens; a function area known as 'the chapel'; & a conference room. Check out the underground wine cellar too. Wi-Fi is available in reception.

Guided walks are offered which include visits to the mines; copper was first mined in Namibia here & guided tours take you underground into a derelict mine with its machinery still in place. Various game drives take in the reserve's wildlife, including eland & kudu. *N$1,495/2,242 sgl/dbl B&B; camping N$195 pp.* **$$$$**

Lake Otjikoto [480 C1] (✆ 067 220253; admission N$50 pp) About 20km north of Tsumeb, just west of the B1, this lake (once thought to be bottomless) was formed when the roof of a huge subterranean cave collapsed, leaving an enormous sinkhole with steep sides. Together with Lake Guinas, the lake is home to a highly coloured population of fish: the southern mouthbrooder (*Pseudocrenilabrus philander*). These have attracted much scientific interest for changes in their colour and behaviour as a result of this restricted environment. Now the lake is also home to some *Tilapia guinasana*, which are endemic to Lake Guinas but have been introduced here to aid their conservation.

Sub-aqua enthusiasts regularly dive in the lake's green waters and have recovered a lot of weaponry that was dumped in 1915 by the retreating German forces. Much is now on display in Tsumeb Museum (page 487), though some is still at the bottom of the lake.

Andersson and Galton passed this way in May 1851, and noted:

After a day and a half travel, we suddenly found ourselves on the brink of Otjikoto, the most extraordinary chasm it was ever my fortune to see. It is scooped, so to say, out of the solid limestone rock… The form of Otjikoto is cylindrical; its diameter upwards of four hundred feet, and its depths, as we ascertained by the lead-line, two hundred and fifteen… To about thirty feet of the brink, it is filled with water.

After commenting that the local residents could remember no variation in its height, and musing on where its supply of water came from, Andersson described how he and Galton:

> standing in need of a bath, plunged head-foremost into the profound abyss. The natives were utterly astounded. Before reaching Otjikoto, they had told us, that if a man or beast was so unfortunate as to fall into the pool, he would inevitably perish.
>
> We attributed this to superstitious notions; but the mystery was now explained. The art of swimming was totally unknown in these regions. The water was very cold, and, from its great depth, the temperature is likely to be the same throughout the year.
>
> We swam into the cavern to which the allusion has just been made. The transparency of the water, which was of the deepest sea-green, was remarkable; and the effect produced in the watery mirror by the reflection of the crystallized walls and roof of the cavern, appeared very striking and beautiful…
>
> Otjikoto contained an abundance of fish, somewhat resembling perch; but those that we caught were not much larger than one's finger. We had several scores of these little creatures for dinner, and very palatable they proved.

The lake has changed little since then, except perhaps for its water level, which has lowered as a reflection of the area's water table: the gradual diminution of the groundwater around here is a threat to the lake's future. For most visitors, though, it represents something of an anticlimax – although experienced divers relish the challenge of exploring the lake's depths.

In terms of practicalities, there are plans to reopen the campsite, but for now there are just drinks and curios available from dawn until dusk, and an on-site craft shop.

Lake Guinas [480 B1] On a private farm with access for visitors, 32km west of Tsumeb, Lake Guinas, with its blue waters, is deeper and more attractive than Otjikoto, though there are no facilities at all. To get there, take the B1 towards Ondangwa, turn left on to the D3043, and then left again after 19km on to the D3031. The lake is about 5km along, near the road. It is home to a colourful species of cichlid fish, *Tilapia guinasana*, which is endemic here. In recent years these fish have been introduced into Otjikoto and several reservoirs to safeguard their future.

Ombili Foundation [478 A2] (☎ 067 230050; e ombili@iway.na, info@ombili.de; www.ombili.de) Established in 1989 by a group of farmers, the Ombili Foundation aims to help the San people to adapt to the demands of the 21st century. It is based on a farm north of Tsumeb, on which areas have been set aside for both foraging and gardening, as well as cattle. The foundation has its own nursery and primary schools, as well as a community centre, workshop and shop for the essentials. Aside from being an interesting project in its own right, Bushman crafts are on sale.

Visitors are welcome to visit by appointment (⊕ 07.00–noon & 14.00–17.00 Mon–Fri). To get there, take the B1 northwest from Tsumeb for around 55km, then turn off right on to the D3004 for a further 20km. The farm is off that road to the right.

GROOTFONTEIN

This small, bustling town is found at the northern end of the central plateau, amid rich farmland. For the visitor, Grootfontein has few intrinsic attractions, but it is the gateway to both Bushmanland and the Caprivi Strip. If you are heading to either, then resting here or in the environs for a night will allow you to tackle the long drive ahead in the cool of the morning.

GETTING THERE AND AWAY

By bus Intercape Mainliner's services between Windhoek and Victoria Falls stop on the main road at Maroela Motors. For Victoria Falls, these depart on Monday and Friday at 19.15. Southbound they depart on Sunday and Wednesday at 23.50. One-way tickets cost around N$450 to Windhoek, and N$740 to Victoria Falls. See page 153 for details.

Hitching Hitching from Grootfontein is relatively easy with a clear sign, as most traffic passes through town. Alternatively, talk to drivers at the fuel stations.

WHERE TO STAY Grootfontein does not have any really impressive places to stay, but both the hotel and guesthouses are adequate for brief stops, and there are a couple more options just a short distance from the town.

In town

Courtyard Guesthouse [492 D2] (8 rooms) 2 Gauss St (top of Hidipo Hamutenya); 067 240215; e kenl@iway.na. Under new management, this popular guesthouse is centred on a small courtyard, with a pool under palms & a sausage tree. Airy en-suite rooms have AC, DSTV, ceiling fan, fridge, kettle & hairdryer, while older-style rooms feature the kiaat-wood furniture typical of the Grootfontein region. There's an atmospheric bar in the thatched lapa & courtyard, & a restaurant serving a huge range of pizzas (inc take-away service) along with lunch specials (N$70) & an à la carte menu. Wi-Fi access payable by voucher. *N$500/750 sgl/dbl.* **$$$**

Meteor Travel Inn [492 D3] (6 rooms) Cnr Okavango Rd & Hage Geingob St; 067 242078/9; e mdcolang@iway.na. Laid out around a courtyard at the back, the Meteor's rooms come with AC or fan, those with AC costing more, & free Wi-Fi. Though it isn't luxurious, the new owner is upgrading it bit by bit. Dinner is available on special request. *N$520/690 sgl/dbl.* **$$**

The Stone House [492 C2] (4 rooms) 10 Toenessen St; 067 242842; e boet@iway.na; www.stonehouse.iway.na. As the name suggests, this small guesthouse on a quiet residential street is clad in stone. It's an attractive place, its stylish rooms featuring large en-suite bathrooms, plus AC, DSTV, Wi-Fi, minibar & coffee/tea facilities, while outside is a small pool. *N$550/750 sgl/dbl.* **$$**

Near Grootfontein

Tigerquelle Vegetable & Guestfarm [480 G2] (6 rooms, camping) 067 243143; m 081 262 1098; e tigerveg@iway.na; www. tigerquelle.com. Signposted from Grootfontein along the B8 towards Rundu, this oddball place is a commercial vegetable farm owned & run by Herr Wander. After 2km, turn left on to the D2885 for 1.8km; alternatively, take the C42 to Tsumeb for 2km, then turn right on to the D2905 (there's no signpost here). The original farmhouse, built around 1904, has a superb dining room & an orangery-style hallway, with later additions such as the sunset tower housing the bar. A large swimming pool set beside ancient fig trees has only natural water. En-suite rooms are very simple, but the real gem is the campsite, set in the bush down a track away from the house with 6 grassy pitches, each with water point, power & braai – & 1 with its own thatched loo! The brick-built ablution block is adjacent, & a self-catering en-suite chalet is nearby. Meals (cooked to order using vegetables from the farm & meat & game from the local butcher) are available at the house, or you can purchase from the farm. Coffee & cake at 15.30 (N$55) is a plus! Reservations essential. *DBB N$90/1,880 sgl/dbl; camping N$140 pp inc firewood.* **$$–$$$$**

Peace Garden Lodge [480 A2] (48 chalets, camping) 067 243648; e peacegardenlodge@iway.na; www. peacegardenlodge.info. Around 5km west of Grootfontein on the B8 towards Otavi, the

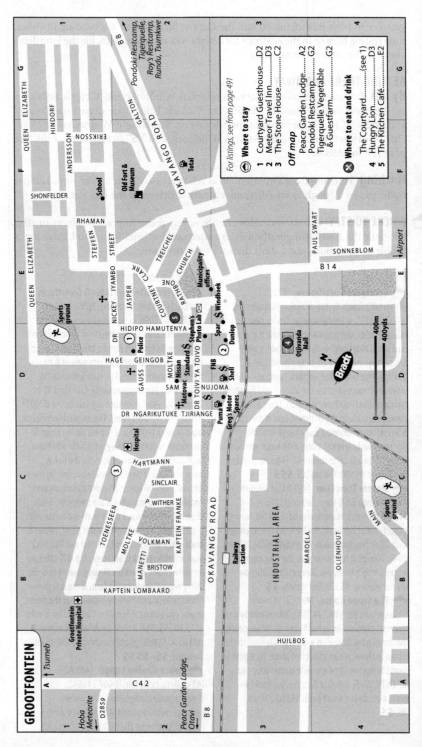

GROOTFONTEIN

For listings, see from page 491

Where to stay
- Courtyard Guesthouse....D2
- Meteor Travel Inn........D3
- The Stone House..........C2

Off map
- Peace Garden Lodge......A2
- Pondoki Restcamp.........G2
- Tigerquelle Vegetable
  & Guestfarm..............G2

Where to eat and drink
- The Courtyard............(see 1)
- Hungry Lion..............D3
- The Kitchen Café........E2

Hoba Meteorite

Pondoki Restcamp,
Tigerquelle,
Roy's Restcamp,
Rundu, Tsumkwe

Old Fort & Museum

Total

School

Peace Garden Lodge, Otavi

Grootfontein Private Hospital

Railway station

INDUSTRIAL AREA

Airport

Otjivanda Mall

Municipality offices

Stephen's Photo Lab

Police

Greg's Motor Spares

Hospital

Sports ground

Sports ground

Tsumeb

substantial Peace Garden Lodge has 13 standard, 20 luxury & 15 VIP chalets, all with AC, tea/coffee stations & fridge. It has a big restaurant & a somewhat soulless bar, with a large pool in the garden & another nearer the chalets. The campsite has few trees, but the 10 pitches each have a seating area shaded by thatch & shade-cloth with power, ablutions, lighting & a braai area. *N$680–860/760–1,880 sgl/dbl; camping N$95 pp.* **$–$$$$**

Pondoki Restcamp [480 G2] (10 rooms; camping) m 081 310 6795; e pondoi1@iway.

na. Perfectly located to break your journey on the eastern outskirts of Grootfontein, Pondoki offers twin & dbl immaculate rooms & a good restaurant that's open to passing visitors (⏰ *07.00–08.00, noon–14.00 & 18.00–20.30 Mon–Sat;* **$$$– $$$$**); note that overnight guests do still get fed on a Sun! For campers, there are 4 pitches for groups, & 3 for smaller parties. The pool is pristine, the shaded bar area cool & the whole place very efficiently run. *N$550/850 sgl/dbl; camping N$120 pp.* **$$–$$$**

✕ **WHERE TO EAT AND DRINK** Grootfontein isn't blessed with much choice for eating out, though the **Courtyard Guesthouse** (page 491) is popular for pizzas and take-aways and there are fast-food chains such as **Hungry Lion** [492 D3] at the new mall, south of the railway.

🍴 **The Kitchen Café** [492 E2] Freemasonry Hall, Hidipo Hamutenya St; ✆067 240111; ⏰ 07.00–17.00 Mon–Fri, 08.00–14.00 Sat.

Close to the town centre, a relaxed venue serving sandwiches, burgers, fish & chips & more. **$$$**

OTHER PRACTICALITIES Grootfontein is a good stop for supplies, with branches of Standard, Bank Windhoek and First National **banks** and a well-stocked Spar **supermarket**, all in the centre of town, with Pick n Pay at the new Otjivanda Mall [492 D3] across the railway. It's not a bad place to sort out vehicle problems, either, with **garages and spares** from Greg's Motor Spares [492 D3] (✆*067 240127*) and a branch of Motovac [492 D2] (✆*067 242314*), as well as Dunlop tyre centre [492 D3] (✆*067 242626*). For photographers, **Stephen's Photolab** [492 D2] (✆ *067 243316*) offers batteries, a small range of cameras and even film. The **post office** [492 E2] is on the triangle of green just behind the municipal centre, between the main Okavango Road and Rathbone Street.

In an **emergency**, the police [492 D2] are reached on ✆067 242111, the ambulance and hospital [492 C2] on ✆067 248150/2 and 081 924, and the fire service on ✆067 243100; m 081 762 7420. Grootfontein also has a private **hospital** [492 B1] (✆*067 260064/6/8*).

WHAT TO SEE AND DO There's not much to do in the town itself, with the museum the only real attraction during the day. Even the outdoor pool by the restcamp has been closed for some years (though should it reopen, that's likely to be between October and May).

In the evenings things are even more limited, although the bars at the Courtyard Guesthouse, Meteor Travel Inn and the Rugby Club are open all week, except Sunday. For excursions from Grootfontein, see page 494.

Old Fort Museum [492 F2] (*Eriksson St;* ✆*067 242456;* ⏰ *09.00–12.30 & 14.00– 16.30 Mon–Fri; admission N$40*) This small, privately run museum close to the centre of town was originally a Schutztruppe fortress. It was built in 1896 and a tower added eight years later. At its heart is the original forge of a local blacksmith, featuring a range of tools and wagon wheels. There are also significant displays focusing on the Himba people, with photos and artefacts.

19

AROROUND GROOTFONTEIN
Where to stay

Fiume Lodge & Game Farm [478 C3]
(9 chalets) 067 240486; e fiumelodge@iway.na;
www.fiume-lodge.com. Set on a private game farm
that is owned & managed by the Gressmann family,
Fiume Lodge is some 35km north of Grootfontein, &
just 3km west of the B8. This makes it a particularly
good spot for the night for those travelling to or from
Rundu & the Caprivi Strip.

Neat brick chalets, which frame lawned gardens
with a central pool & firepit, have twin beds (or
family accommodation), high ceilings, ceiling fans
& AC. Meals are taken in a thatched lapa of similar
style, incorporating a bar & lounge with a pool table
& TV. Along with sundowner drives, potentially
seeing animals such as zebra, hartebeest, giraffe,
eland & Damara dik-dik, comes the opportunity
(with advance notice) to spend a day with a
Namibian farmer, both watching & participating in
activities, as the need arises. *DBB N$1,760/2,800 sgl/
dbl; reservations essential.* **$$$$**

Fiume Bush Camp [478 C3] (8 tents)
Contact via Fiume Lodge, see above. Opened
in 2016, 53km from the D2844 & along a 3km
track, this is effectively a satellite of Fiume Lodge
(above), built to make it easier for guests who
want to learn more about the San culture without
the long drive from the lodge. The rudimentary
camp looking out over a grassy plain seems rather
underwhelming at first, its twin-bedded tents dark
& sparsely furnished, with basic brick-built shower
rooms, but the water is hot courtesy of donkey
boilers, the food is good & plentiful, & most
important, the staff are delightful.

Most guests spend 2 nights here, giving time for a
full day of activities. From the camp, it's just a couple
of mins' walk to where you'll meet members of the
local Ju/'hoansi community, who will accompany
you &, with the aid of a translator, explain some of
their traditional lifestyle. The day starts with a gentle
walk through untamed bush, during which you'll
learn about plants & their uses – for making tools,
for their medicinal properties, for food & water – &
perhaps try some that are edible. You'll watch
simple traps being prepared, & learn a little about
the poison used to tip the arrows for hunting. After
a break for lunch, you'll return in the afternoon for
an arts & crafts session, perhaps helping to make
or thread beads, or to craft a simple bow. Then in
the evening, there's time to watch the medicine or
elephant dance. As part of the lodge's commitment
to the Ju/'hoansi San community, they support a
kindergarten in the village, attended by some of the
camp's staff. *FBA N$4,950/8,280 sgl/dbl.* Closed
mid-Dec–mid-Jan. **$$$$$$**

Roy's Rest Camp [478 C3] (8 rustic chalets
inc 1 disabled access, camping) 067 240302;
e royscamp@iway.na; www.roys-rest-camp.com.
Situated on the main B8 to Rundu, 55km north
of Grootfontein & just past the C44 turn-off to
Tsumkwe, Roy's is a super little lodge built in an
artistic & very rustic style. It was opened on the
established Elandsgate farm in 1995 by Wimple
& Marietjie Otto, whose ancestors were some of
the first European settlers in Namibia. The camp
is named after Wimple's father, Royal; when the
authorities didn't approve of 'Royal Restcamp', it
was cut to Roy's Rest Camp.

Bungalows of different configurations –
including 3 for families – are wonderfully rustic
to the point of being quite offbeat, even down to
the en-suite showers & private braai area. All have
AC & are serviced by electricity, although paraffin
lamps light the way to the bungalows & campsite.
Good home-cooked meals, best arranged in
advance (*dinner N$250 pp*) are served in the bar/
dining area next to the swimming pool & souvenir
shop. Free Wi-Fi.

The campsite's 17 green, well-watered pitches
come with electricity, braai sites (for which braai
packs are available), tree shade, & hot & cold
showers, plus a bush kitchen with stove, fridge, etc.
All of this is set in 28km² of natural bush, which
has been stocked with blue wildebeest, eland,
kudu, zebra, duiker, steenbok & warthog. Through
this are 2 marked walking trails, of 1.5km & 2.5km
respectively, on which many of the trees are labelled.
Visits to the Ju/'Hoansi Living Museum are also
possible. Assuming that you're happy with the
rustic environment, this is an ideal spot to spend a
night en route between the Triangle & the Caprivi.
N$1,050/1,782 sgl/dbl; camping N$130 pp. **$$$**

Excursions from Grootfontein
There are a couple of attractions in the area that
are accessible only if you have a vehicle, although Dragon's Breath Cave is not open
to the general public.

This cave is claimed to contain the world's largest-known underground lake. It is 46km northwest of Grootfontein, just off the C42 to Tsumeb, on the farm Harasib. Although it is not open to casual visitors, it is sometimes visited by specialist cave divers.

The lake has crystal-clear, drinkable water with a surface area of almost 2ha, and lies beneath a dome-shaped roof of solid rock. The water is about 60m below ground level and to get to it currently requires the use of ropes and caving equipment, with a final vertical abseil descent of 25m from the roof down to the surface of the water. This perhaps explains why it is not open to the public.

Hoba Meteorite [480 E3] (⊕ *08.00–17.00 daily; admission N$50 pp*) This famous lump of rock is about 20km west of Grootfontein on the D3002, clearly signposted from both the C42 approach road from Tsumeb, and the B8 between Grootfontein and Otavi. Here, in 1920, the farm's owner discovered the world's largest single metallic meteorite, weighing around 60 tonnes, which crashed to earth some 80,000 years ago. Nearly 3m wide and up to 1.33m high, it is made up mostly of iron (about 82%) and nickel (16.4%), with other trace elements including cobalt.

The meteorite was declared a national monument in 1955 and protection now extends to the area around it, partly to deter souvenir hunters. (The locals became particularly irate when even personnel from the UN's Transition Assistance Group, UNTAG, were found to be chipping bits off for souvenirs as they supervised the country's transition to democracy.) Now the site has a small shop selling souvenirs, sweets and soft drinks, a picnic area (*N$100/group*) with braai stands and numbered trees linked to a leaflet (*N$2*), and clean toilets.

Where to stay You can camp overnight in the car park (*N$50 pp*), but better is the campsite down the road.

⋀ Meteorite Campsite [480 E3] (6 pitches) 📞064 672420; **m** 081 242 5456; **e** malanjn@iway. na. Pitches at this rural campsite, just a couple of km from the meteorite, have electricity & water, & share a pool. *N$100 pp.* **$$**

Mangetti National Park [478 D2] Proclaimed as a national park in 2008, this relatively unknown area lies on community land to the east of the B8, roughly halfway between Grootfontein and Rundu. Covering just 41,990ha, it has been fenced as a game park since 1973.

Wildlife includes large antelope, especially eland, which are at home in the woodlands and bush that characterise the park, as well as the much rarer sable. Elephant and giraffe are also resident, along with leopard, hyena and wild dog. It is hoped that designation as a national park will bring benefits not just to wildlife and the environment but also to the local community.

BUSHMANLAND

To the east of Grootfontein lies the area known as Bushmanland. While it is today in the Otjozondjupa Region, I'll use the old name here for clarity as it is still what most people call the area. This almost rectangular region borders on Botswana and stretches 90km from north to south and about 200km from east to west.

Drive east towards Tsumkwe, and you're driving straight into the Kalahari. However, on their first trip here, people are often struck by just how green and vegetated it is, generally in contrast to their mental image of a 'desert'. In fact, the Kalahari isn't a classic desert at all; it's a *fossil* desert. It is an immense sand sheet which was once a desert, but now gets far too much rainfall to be classed as a desert.

Look around you and you'll realise that most of the Kalahari is covered in a thin, mixed bush with a fairly low canopy height, dotted with occasional larger trees. Beneath this is a fairly sparse ground-covering of smaller bushes, grasses and herbs. There are no spectacular sand dunes; you need to return west to the Namib for those!

This is very poor agricultural land, but in the east of the region, especially south of Tsumkwe, there is a sprinkling of seasonal pans. Straddling the border itself are the Aha Hills (page 505), which rise abruptly from the gently rolling desert. This region, and especially the eastern side of it, is home to a large number of scattered Bushman villages of the Ju/'hoansi !Kung.

WILDLIFE The wildlife is a major attraction, though don't expect to see vast herds like those in Etosha or you will be disappointed. During the late dry season, around September and October, game gathers in small herds around the pans. During and after the rains, from January to March, the place comes alive with greenery and water and the animals disperse. Birds and noisy bullfrogs abound, and travel becomes even more difficult than usual, as whole areas turn into impassable floodplains. From April the land begins to dry out, and during July and August daytime temperatures are at their most moderate and the nights cold.

CULTURE The other reason for visiting is to see the Bushman people. The conventional view is that less than a century ago these people's ancestors were a traditional hunter-gatherer society using Stone Age technology. Yet they possessed a knowledge of their environment that we are only just beginning to understand. Tourism is an increasingly vital source of revenue for these people. In placing a high value on traditional skills and knowledge, it is hoped that it will help to stem the erosion of their cultural heritage.

GETTING THERE AND AWAY The C44 through to Tsumkwe is the main access route into the area. This is long, a total of about 226km to Tsumkwe, before continuing a further 50km east to the border post with Botswana at Dobe (⊕ *08.00–18.00 daily*). From there it's another 150km (a 3-hour drive) of patchy gravel road to the small Botswana town of Nokaneng, on the main tar road that runs down the western side of the Okavango Delta.

Tsumkwe feels remote, but it is easily reached from Grootfontein by ordinary 2WD vehicle. From Nokaneng, travelling west, an experienced driver should be able to get a high-clearance 2WD through to Tsumkwe, but a 4x4 is recommended. Virtually all the other roads in Bushmanland require a sturdy 4x4 and a good guide, or a GPS, and preferably both.

Along the C44, about 31km from the B8, is a police station on the south side of the road. Beyond this, about 88km from the tar, is Omatako Valley Restcamp. Then around 89km before Tsumkwe, one of the turnings to the right is signposted 'Mangetti Duin', marking the way to one of the best stands of mangetti trees in the area – notable because mangetti nuts are one of the staple foods of the Bushmen. Otherwise there are a few turnings to villages, but little else. The area is not densely populated, and travellers coming this way should carry both water and some food, as only a handful of vehicles use the road on any particular day.

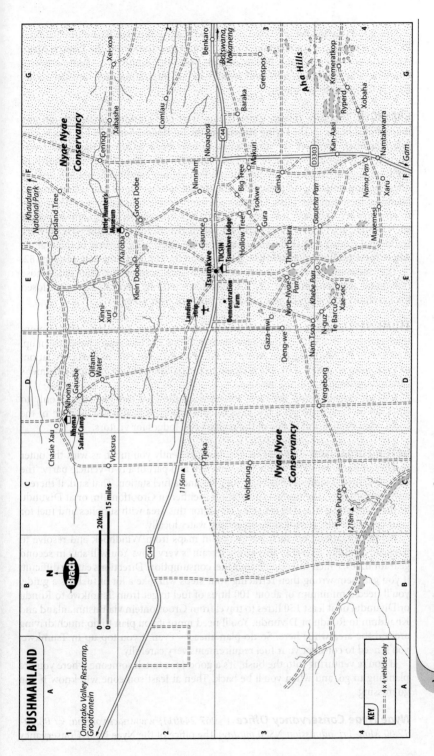

One good way to visit is by combining it with a trip through Khaudum National Park, thus making a roundabout journey from Grootfontein to the Caprivi Strip. Alternatively, approaching Bushmanland from the south, via Summerdown, Otjinene and the old Hereroland, would be an interesting and unusual route. Expect the going to get tough.

GRASHOEK This tiny village, some 150km west of Tsumkwe, is scarcely on any maps, but is home to **The Living Museum of the Ju/'Hoansi-San** [478 E3] (*www.lcfn. info/juhoansi*). The first 'living museum' to have been set up in Namibia, it was opened in 2004 on the edge of the N#a Jaqna Conservancy, about 7km north of the C44. Supported by the Living Culture Foundation Namibia (*www.lcfn.info*), it offers 'an authentic way of presenting traditional culture'. This – and others around Namibia, including the Little Hunter's Museum near Tsumkwe (page 503) – aims to give visitors a chance to share in the culture of previously marginalised people such as the San; to give those people a sound reason to retain and pass on their traditional culture and skills; and to address the underlying poverty of the regions where these traditional people live. For more on the culture of the San, see page 82.

The museum has three pitches at its own small campsite (*N\$50 pp*), whose individual ablutions include 'dry' toilets and beautifully decorated reed-enclosed bucket showers (for which you need to bring your own water).

TSUMKWE Though it is the area's administrative centre, Tsumkwe is little more than a crossroads around which a few houses, shops and businesses have grown up. Apart from the South African Army, it's never had the kind of colonial population, or even sheer number of people, that led to the building of (for example) Tsumeb's carefully planned tree-lined avenues.

It is an essential stop for most travellers in the area though, even if only to stock up on fuel, or to get a few cans of cool drinks. It is also the location of the conservancy office and of one of the region's two lodges for visitors.

Getting organised To visit this area independently you must, as with the outer reaches of Kaokoland, be totally self-sufficient and part of a two-vehicle party. The region's centre, Tsumkwe, has basic supplies and a fuel station. That said, if there is any problem here, the nearest fuel station is either in Grootfontein, or at Divundu in the Caprivi. So it makes sense to set off for this area with supplies and fuel for your complete trip, relying only on getting water locally.

Before embarking on such a trip, obtain maps from Windhoek and resolve to navigate carefully. Travel in this sandy terrain is very slow. You will stay in second gear for miles, which will double your fuel consumption. Directions can be difficult; if you get them wrong then retracing your steps will take a lot of fuel. As a guide, you'll need a minimum of about 100 litres of fuel to get from Tsumkwe to Rundu or Divundu, or at least 150 litres to travel from Grootfontein via Bushmanland and Khaudum to Rundu or Divundu. You'll need more if you plan to do much driving around the area while here. So do plan ahead – even if you top up in Tsumkwe, you'll need to consider your fuel requirements very carefully.

If you're venturing into the bush, it's a good idea to tell someone where you are planning to go, and when you'll be back. Then at least someone will know if you go missing.

Nyae Nyae Conservancy Office (\067 244011; *www.nacso.org.na*; ⊕ 08.00–17.00 Mon–Fri; admission N\$80 pp/day) The office of the Nyae Nyae Conservancy (page 500) is on the right side of the road when travelling east from Grootfontein, just before you reach the main Tsumkwe crossroads. This is the place to find out about campsites within the conservancy and to arrange a local guide (usually from about N$250 per day). If you're planning on camping in the area for a few days and exploring a little, then a guide is highly recommended. He or she can help you get a lot more out of the area – and you will actively be giving a little more back to the local community. For details of the Nyae Nyae headquarters in Windhoek, see box, page 500, but note that it's not possible to make reservations through that office.

Where to stay in and around Tsumkwe
As well as the following, there are several basic campsites within the Nyae Nyae Conservancy (page 501).

TUCSIN Tsumkwe Lodge [497 E3] (22 cabins, camping) \067 687055; reservations \067 240901/3/4, 240975; e reservations. tsumkwe@travel-weaver.com. The established Tsumkwe Lodge is now in the hands of TUCSIN: The University Centre for Studies in Namibia, whose remit is to support the culture of the Ju/'hoansi San. The lodge operates as a hospitality & training centre, & all profits are ploughed back into the community. To find it, turn right at the crossroads in Tsumkwe, then right again opposite Nature Conservation; it's about 2km from the centre. Twin cabins & a family room are constructed of canvas & metal & are all en suite, with twin beds, mosquito nets & private verandas. A small campsite has just 6 pitches, each with electricity & BBQ, & sharing an ablution block. Meals ($$$$$) are available in the deeply thatched lapa, where there's also a bar, & outside is a small pool. Visitors can take drives to Khaudum National Park & Nyae Nyae Pan, or visit one of the local Bushman villages (*from N$508/982 pp ½/full day, min 4). N$952/1,330 sgl/dbl; camping N$146 pp.* $$–$$$

Nhoma Safari Camp [497 D1] (10 tents, camping) m 081 273 4606; e info@nhomasafaricamp.com; www.nhomasafaricamp.com. This remote & fairly simple camp stands beside the Ju/'hoan village of Nhoma, 80km from Tsumkwe. The turn-off to the camp from the C44 is 185km east of the B8, or 41km before you reach Tsumkwe. The road is normally good enough for a 2WD but, before you set off, phone ahead to find out the state of the road & if necessary to arrange to be met.
Walk-in tents with en-suite or private showers or corner baths have twin or dbl beds, or an extra sgl. There's a campsite with 4 pitches, too, & campers are welcome to participate in meals (*b/fast N$180, lunch N$230, dinner N$280) & activities (N$1,850 pp/day)* by arrangement.

Activities centre around the Ju/'hoan community: hunting & veld food gathering, traditional games, ancient crafts & the healing dances – though each day is different. In the winter (*Jul–Oct*), there are day trips to Khaudum National Park, with the possibility to overnight in the park in a mobile camp, & from May to Jan a full-day trip to visit Nyae Nyae Pan is a further option. Advance bookings are essential.
Nhoma's origins lie in the mid 1990s, when Arno & Estelle Oosthuysen built Tsumkwe Lodge. They knew the local people well, had a sensitive attitude to working with them & soon started introducing them to tourists. By 2007, when they sold Tsumkwe Lodge, they'd been working so closely with the Ju/'hoan community at Nhoma that they built this small camp.
At its best, the Ju/'hoan cultural experience at Nhoma can be insightful & truly amazing. It's as interesting for children as for adults, because the local youngsters will relax & start playing with the young visitors very quickly – integrating far more easily than the adults. So if your children are active & not shy, expect to have difficulty dragging them away from Nhoma when it's time to leave. *FBA N$4,400/7,800 sgl/dbl; camping N$250 pp.* $$–$$$$$$

Omatako Valley Rest Camp [478 E3] www.omatakovalley.com. On the way to Tsumkwe, about 88km east of the B8, is a restcamp run by one of the local Bushman communities as part of the Omatako San Community Project. Driving into Bushmanland, it is hard to miss, in a dip immediately on the right of the C44, 13km past the veterinary control. Contacting the restcamp is difficult, but if you want to let them know you're coming, drop an email to cb@indigosafaris.com.
If you are heading for Tsumkwe then stop here for cool drinks. A small shop sells a good selection

of locally made crafts including beads, necklaces, spears, various tools & baskets. For overnight visitors there is a tree-shaded campsite with braai areas & sinks, as well as dubious showers & flush toilets open to the elements. There's firewood for sale (*N$20*), lamps for hire (but no electricity), & sometimes a whole variety of things to do, including guided bush walks & cultural events (*N$80 pp*), with English-speaking guides on hand. Such events might include the opportunity to try bush food or attend a dance evening, but they are dependent on which of the villagers are around when you are, so none is guaranteed. *Camping N$50 pp*. **$**

NYAE NYAE CONSERVANCY Stretching 9,000km² around Tsumkwe is the Nyae Nyae Conservancy area, first gazetted in 1998. Here the communities have been given the right to manage their wildlife and tourism in a sustainable way, for their own benefit. While they have always hunted the wildlife here using traditional methods, now they can also derive income from trophy hunting in the area.

NYAE NYAE DEVELOPMENT FOUNDATION

Based just east of Tsumkwe, the Nyae Nyae Farmers Co-operative was established in 1986 with a charter to support and encourage the Ju/'hoansi of eastern Otjozondjupa to return to their historical lands known as Nyae Nyae.

Historically, this group of Bushmen has been in a difficult position. The South African Army (SADF) moved into what was eastern Bushmanland in 1960, to occupy the region as part of its war against SWAPO and the destabilisation of Angola. It formed a battalion of Bushmen to track down guerrilla fighters – using the Bushmen's tracking ability to lethal effect. Many of these people moved to Tsumkwe; whole families were dependent on the SADF.

This social upheaval, with lifestyles changing from nomadic hunter-gathering to dependence on an army wage, led to social problems among the people, including crime, alcohol and prostitution. Towards the end of the war, it was decided to improve their quality of life by taking them back to the ground they had come from, a move initiated by the Nyae Nyae Development Foundation (*9 Delius St, Windhoek West;* 061 236327; e nndfn@iafrica.com.na; *www.nndfn.org*) and its founder, John Marshall.

So in the late 1980s and early 1990s, the Nyae Nyae Farmers Co-operative focused on grass-roots self-help projects, encouraging the Bushmen to start farming, rearing cattle and growing their own food. Boreholes were provided, but few made a success of these projects. The Bushmen are not natural farmers or pastoralists. They seem to have a different approach to survival from most other ethnic groups in Africa.

The Nyae Nyae Development Foundation continues to run various development programmes such as training conservancy staff, water development in villages and traditional gardens. A craft programme is well established, providing workers with training in production, and buying their products to sell in Tsumkwe and Windhoek. They are also behind G!hunku Crafts (see their website for details).

However, perhaps the most interesting project was initiated by the WWF in 1994. This has aimed to set up a conservancy for sustainable utilisation and management of the wildlife in the eastern area of Bushmanland – which was finally put into place in 1997. This is being administered by the Nyae Nyae Development Foundation.

The Nyae Nyae Conservancy has an office in Tsumkwe (page 498). This should be your first stop in the region and is where you pay conservancy fees, organise guides and sort out campsites (you should pay any camping fees to the village nearest the campsite).

Some of the villages are more accessible than others, with cleared campsites underneath baobab trees and a greater likelihood of finding an English-speaking member of the community to act as guide. //Xa/oba village, 23km north of Tsumkwe, is now home to the Little Hunter's Museum, offering authentic activities linked to the San culture on a daily basis. Almost all are accessible only by 4x4 but, depending on the season, some can be reached with a 2WD with good clearance. There are no vehicles for hire in the area.

Where to stay In the past, campers have set up their sites randomly in Bushmanland, with no permits necessary. Many left litter behind them and caused problems for the local people and the wildlife. They often used to camp close to water, frightening the area's already skittish animals, and even go swimming in reservoirs meant for drinking. Visitors were unaware that they were staying in an area used for hunting or gathering, and didn't realise the effect that their presence was having on the wildlife. This 'free camping' has now been banned. Instead, head for one of the (increasing number of) village sites, where you'll find a place to camp for which you pay the nearby community directly.

In the first edition of this book – in 1998 – I listed three such sites. Now many more villages have simple adjacent sites and welcome visitors. Ask at the conservancy office in Tsumkwe and they'll give you a map of these, or better still, a local guide, and advise you of their costs.

Wherever you camp, you must take great care not to offend local people by your behaviour. It is customary to go first to the village and ask for permission to stay from the traditional leader, but first read the guidelines on cultural etiquette (see box, page 90).

Remember that you are in a wilderness area, where hyena, lion and leopard are not uncommon, so always sleep within a tent. Try not to scare the wildlife, or damage the place in any way. Keep fires to a minimum, and when collecting fuel use only dead wood that is far from any village.

Some local people have been designated as community rangers, with a brief to check on poaching and look out for the wildlife. They may ask what you are doing, and check that you have paid your camping fees.

Guiding and camping fees Payment to the communities should be fair. The camping fee is likely to be around N$70 per day per person, depending on the village. Each of the guides will expect around N$250 per day, plus food if staying out overnight; this must be discussed and agreed beforehand. The Little Hunter's Museum (page 503) provides a range of activities such as tracking, bushwalks and dancing. The cost of these differs from village to village, but expect to pay from N$150 per person for dancing, or N$350 for tracking.

Guidelines for visiting villages The traditional leader (*n!ore kxao*) or headman is usually one of the older men of the village, who will normally make himself known to visitors. Never enter someone's shelter, as this is very rude. Often the headman will be assisted by someone who speaks Afrikaans or even English, and if he or she is not around then somebody else will normally come forward to help you. Unless you have a basic grasp of Afrikaans, you may have to rely upon sign language.

Taking photographs of the people or place is normally fine, provided that you ask in advance, and pay for the privilege.

If you wish to buy crafts from the village, then do not try to barter unless specifically asked for things; most people will expect to be paid with money. Similarly, if one of the villagers has been your guide, pay for this with money. Remember that alcohol has been a problem in the past, and do not give any away.

Water is essential for everybody, and in limited supply for most of the year, so be very careful when using the local waterholes or water pumps. Often there will be someone around who can help you. Never go swimming in a waterhole or reservoir.

Cultural sensitivity and language
Cultural sensitivity isn't something that a guidebook can teach you, though reading the box on cultural guidelines on page 90 may help. Being sensitive to the results of your actions and attitudes on others is especially important in this area.

The Bushmen are often a humble people, who regard arrogance as a vice. It is normal for them to be self-deprecating among themselves, to make sure that everyone is valued and nobody becomes too proud. So the less you are perceived as a loud, arrogant foreigner, the better.

Very few foreigners can pick up much of the local Ju/'hoansi language without living here for a long time. (Readers note that spellings of the same word can vary from text to text, especially on maps.) However, if you want to try to pronounce the words then there are four main clicks to master:

/	is a sucking sound behind the teeth
//	is a sucking sound at the side of the mouth, used to urge a horse
!	a popping sound, like a cork coming out of a bottle
≠	a sharper popping sound (this is the hardest)

Cultural questions
When you see the Bushmen, it's tempting to lament their passing from noble savage to poor, rural underclass: witness the lack of dignified 'traditional' skins and the prevalence of ragged Western clothes, or see the PVC quivers that the occasional hunter now uses for his arrows.

While they clearly need help in the present, part of the problem has been our blinkered view of their past. This view has been propagated by the romantic writings of people like Laurens van der Post and a host of TV documentaries. However, modern ethnographers now challenge many long-cherished beliefs about these 'noble savages'.

Essential reading in this respect is *The Bushman Myth: The Making of a Namibian Underclass*, by Robert J Gordon (page 573). It stands out as an excellent, scholarly attempt to place the Bushmen in an accurate historical context, and to explain and deconstruct many of the myths that we hold about them. In partial summary of some of his themes, he comments:

The old notion of these people as passive victims of European invasion and Bantu expansion is challenged. Bushmen emerge as one of the many indigenous people operating in a mobile landscape, forming and shifting their political and economic alliances to take advantage of circumstances as they perceived them. Instead of toppling helplessly from foraging to begging, they emerge as hotshot traders in the mercantile world market for ivory and skins. They were brokers between competing forces and hired guns in the game business. Rather than being victims of pastoralists and traders who depleted the game, they appear as one of many willing agents of this commercial depletion. Instead of being ignorant of metals, true men of the Stone Age, who knew nothing of iron, they were fierce defenders of rich copper mines that they worked for export and profit. If this selection has a central theme, it is to show how ignorance of archival sources helped to create the Bushmen image that we, as anthropologists, wanted to have and how knowledge of these sources makes sense of the Bushmen we observe today.

Gordon's book isn't a light or swift read, but it will make you think. See also my comments on the wider context, including the modern media's portrayal of the San, on page 82.

What to see and do
The Little Hunter's Museum of the Ju/'Hoansi-San [497 E1] (*www.lcfn. info/hunters*) Linked to the Living Museum of the Ju/'Hoansi-San (page 498), the Little Hunter's Museum lies around 23km north of Tsumkwe. It was opened in 2010, and involves almost the entire population of the village of //Xa/oba. Here, in addition to engaging visitors with the traditional lifestyle of the San, there is the possibility of taking part in a traditional hunt, perhaps including bow hunting or trapping with snares.

Adjacent is the simple, sandy Elephant Song campsite (*N$50 pp*), where each of the two pitches has its own 'dry' toilet, reed-enclosed bucket shower (but bring your own water) and braai facilities.

Cultural activities It's worth being realistic from the outset of your visit – whether to a village or to one of the living museums: if you're looking for 'wild Bushmen' clad in loincloths and spending all day making poison arrows or pursuing antelope, you will be disappointed.

The people in this area have been exposed to the modern world, and often mistreated by it, for decades. None now live a traditional hunter-gatherer lifestyle. Walk into any village and its inhabitants are more likely to be dressed in jeans and T-shirts than loincloths, and their water is more likely to be from a solar-powered borehole pump than a sip-well.

However, many of the older people have maintained their traditional skills and crafts, and often their knowledge of the bush and wildlife is simply breathtaking. Those that I met appeared friendly and interested to show visitors how they live, including how they hunt and gather food in the bush – provided that visitors are polite and ask permission for what they want to do, and pay the right price.

This kind of experience is difficult to arrange without a local guide who is involved in tourism and speaks both your language and theirs. Without such a guide, you won't get very much out of a visit to a local village. So even if you have your own 4x4 transport, start by dropping into Nhoma Safari Camp or, if it is open, the conservancy office in Tsumkwe. Ask for a local guide to help you, who can travel around with you. You can pay them directly, and this will open up many possibilities at the villages.

None of the village activities is artificially staged. They are just normal activities that would probably take place anyhow, though their timings are arranged to fit in with your available time. However, because they are not staged, they will take little account of you. As a visitor you will just tag along, watching as the villagers go about their normal activities. All are relaxed. You can stop and ask questions of the guide and of the villagers when you wish. Most of the local villagers are completely used to photographers and unperturbed by being filmed – provided, of course, that you have agreed a fee for this in advance.

Ideally, for a detailed insight, spend a few days with a guide and stay beside just one village. If they are happy about it, see the same people for an evening or two as well as during the days. This way, you get to know the villagers as individuals, not simply members of an ethnic group. Both you and they will learn more from such an encounter, and so enjoy it a lot more. Typical activities might include:

Food-collecting/hunting trips These trips normally last about 3–4 hours in the bush, which is typical for the living museums. You'll go out with a guide and some villagers and gather, or hunt, whatever they come across. The Bushmen know their landscape, and its flora and fauna, so well that they'll often stop to show you how this plant can be eaten, or that one produces water, or how another fruits in season. They also have a particularly rich tradition of storytelling, and it shows clearly if they also demonstrate how snares are made and set, for example, and give animated re-enactments of how animals are caught.

Even experts on the area comment that after years of going out with the Bushmen, they will still often find something new that they've never seen before. It's an ethnobotanist's dream.

The hunting tends to be for the smaller animals, and in season the Bushmen set up trap-lines of snares to catch the smaller bucks, which need checking regularly and setting or clearing. Springhares are also a favourite quarry, hunted from their burrows using long (typically 5m), flexible poles with a hook on the end.

Don't expect to go tracking eland with bows and arrows in half a day, though do expect to track anything interesting that crosses your path. These trips aren't intended as forced marches, and the pace is generally fairly slow. However, if there's some good food to be had, or promising game to be tracked, then walks through the bush can last for hours. Bring some water and don't forget your hat.

It's usually best to discuss payment in advance, and agree a cost. However, bear in mind that working with money is relatively new to many of these people, so don't expect any sophisticated bargaining techniques. As a quid pro quo, don't use any such ruses yourself, or try to screw the people into a hard bargain; just aim for a fair price (which you learned when you stopped and asked at the conservancy office earlier!).

Traditional craft demonstrations As part of a half-day trip into the bush, or perhaps in the afternoon if you're visiting a living museum, you may stop for a while at the village, and there the people can show you how they make their traditional crafts. For example, bow making could include a demonstration of how to create the string from a particular plant, while for jewellery making, there may be ostrich shells to shape, or seeds to pierce ready for threading.

Evening singing and dancing In the evenings, you can arrange (in advance, with payment agreed first) to visit a local village, and join an evening of traditional dancing. If you are at a living museum, then you will be on site, perhaps staying at the campsite next door. If not, it probably means driving to just outside a village, where those who want to take part will meet you. They will build a fire, around which the women and children will gradually gather. Eventually those sitting will start the singing and clapping, and men will start dancing around the circle sitting in the firelight. They will often have percussion instruments, like shakers, strapped to their ankles.

The singing is beautiful, essentially African, and it comes as no surprise that everybody becomes engrossed in the rhythm and the dancing. On rare occasions, such concentration among the dancers can induce states of trance – the famous 'trance dances' – which are traditionally used as dances to heal, or prevent illness.

As an observer, expect to sit on the ground on the edge of the firelight, outside of the dancers' circle. You will mostly be ignored while the villagers have a good time. They will have been asked to dance for your benefit, for which they will be paid, but everything else about the evening is in their control. This is the kind of dancing that they do for themselves, with nothing added and nothing taken away.

Note that they're used to most visitors just sitting and watching while they dance. If you want to join in it's often not a problem… but expect to be the source of a lot of amusement for the resident professionals.

Nyae Nyae Pan Aside from coming here out of a general curiosity about the area's wildlife and culture, one area stands out: the Nyae Nyae Pan. This is a large complex of beautiful salt-pans, about 18km south of Tsumkwe. During good rains it fills with water and attracts flamingos to breed, as well as dozens of other waterbirds including avocets, pygmy geese, grebes, various pipers and numerous plovers. Forty-six different species of waterbirds have been recorded here when the pan was full. Towards the end of the dry season you can normally expect game to be drinking here, and the regulars include kudu, gemsbok, steenbok, duiker and elephant. Meanwhile black-backed jackals patrol, and the grass grows to 60cm tall around the pan, with a belt of tall trees beyond that.

AHA HILLS Look southeast of Tsumkwe on the maps and you'll find an isolated group of hills straddling the border between Botswana and Namibia: the Aha Hills [497 G3]. Named, it's claimed, after the onomatopoeic call of the barking geckos that are so common in the area, these are remote enough to have a certain mystique about them – like their counterparts in Botswana, the Tsodilo Hills.

However, there the similarity ends. The Aha Hills are much lower and more flattened. Their rock structure is totally different: a series of sharp, angular boulders quite unlike the smooth, solid massifs of Tsodilo. So they are quite tricky to climb, and have no known rock art or convenient natural springs. All of this means that though they're interesting, and worth a visit if you're in the area, they do not have the attraction of Botswana's Tsodilo Hills.

With a guide, the track past Xobaha village does lead on to the hills, and it's possible to climb up Kremetartkop (which has some lovely baobabs on the top) in an hour or so. The view from the top – across into Botswana and 360° around – is pure Africa.

Do leave at least a whole afternoon for this trip, though. I didn't, and ended up driving back to Tsumkwe in the half-light, which wasn't ideal. However, I caught a rare glimpse of a caracal bounding through the long grass in the headlights.

KHAUDUM NATIONAL PARK (*Min 2 4x4 vehicles per party; admission N$50 pp per day, plus N$10 per vehicle*) Immediately north of Bushmanland on the Botswana border, Khaudum is a wild, seldom-visited area of dry woodland savannah growing on old stabilised Kalahari sand dunes. These are interspersed with flat clay pans and the whole area is laced with a life-giving network of *omurambas*.

Omuramba is a Herero word meaning 'vague riverbed', which is used to describe a drainage line that rarely, if ever, actually flows above ground but often gives rise to a number of waterholes along its course. In Khaudum, the *omurambas* generally lie along east–west lines and ultimately link into the Okavango's river system, flowing underground into the delta when the rains come. However, during the dry season the flood in the Okavango Delta helps to raise the level of the water table in these

'I hope someone in the village remembers me from last year.'

'*Ja, ja.*' Arno, my guide, was certain they would. 'You should have seen the excitement when they shared out the beads you sent. You remembered them: they won't have forgotten you.'

I walked through the circle of yellow, beehive-shaped huts to where the headman was sitting, the only one on a chair, a concession to his age. As he clasped my hand my translator, Steve, explained, 'My father says he is very pleased you have come back to see us.' From across the village Javid stared at me briefly and then dashed across to shake my hand. People smiled spontaneously as they recognised me: I didn't know who to say hello to first.

My stay at Nhoma the previous year had been brief. A Ju/'hoan village in remote northeast Namibia, it is one of about 30 villages at the edge of the Nyae Nyae Conservancy. I was persuaded that visitors provided vital revenue to the villagers, but had also read about marginalised people with problems of poverty, unemployment and ill health. I anticipated that a visit would be at best a glum affair, and perhaps even a voyeuristic intrusion on a suffering people. Instead I found fun. Women sat by small fires in front of their huts with tall wooden mortars and pounded protein-rich mangettis that tasted pleasantly nutty, if a little gritty. Some boiled vivid scarlet beans: after the flesh is eaten, the kernel is roasted. Waste nothing: sometimes there is only nothing. While the women prepared food the men made hunting necessities. With his chop-chop, the Bushman's axe, Sao scraped fibres from mother-in-law's-tongue; these are twisted to make rope for a bird trap. Abel cleaned a dried steenbok skin to make a kit bag for the hunt. With great concentration Joseph squeezed the grub of a beetle cocoon to put poison on some arrows. Care is needed, as there is no known antidote and to avoid an accidental scratch it is not put on the tip. Even with all this work going on, it was never quiet: all around was talking and laughter.

The previous year N!hunkxa made ostrich-egg beads, painstakingly filing them to the same size with a stone. These, along with pieces of leather, wood and porcupine quills, were threaded into necklaces and bracelets, all brown and white. But what the women really wanted, they told me, were small glass beads, especially red and yellow ones. A few of them already had brightly coloured glass-bead necklaces and bracelets. Some, mainly the older ones, had bead medallions fixed through their hair so that they hung down on to their foreheads. The beads I had sent had all been used. Not only were the women wearing more necklaces and bracelets than last year, but also rings. Some of the men too wore ornate beaded belts or had circles of beads embroidered on their shonas, leather loincloths.

This time I had brought more beads and I was going to learn how to make something. As N!hunkxa unwrapped the beads a dozen or so women stopped work to see what I had brought. We sat on the sand in a circle under the shade of

omurambas – ensuring that the waterholes don't dry up, and do attract game into Khaudum. The vegetation here can be thick in comparison with Namibia's drier parks to the west. Zambezi teak and wild syringa dominate the dunes, while acacias and leadwoods are found in the clay pans.

Flora and fauna The bush in and around Khaudum is quite complex. Different areas have totally different types of vegetation; biologists say that there are nine different 'biotypes' in Bushmanland.

a large tree. Pleasantly warm now; it would soon be too hot to be in the sun. In the middle of the group was a large canvas sheet and we made indentations in it to stop the beads rolling away. N!hunkxa chose an easy style for me to make, two parallel lines which crossed over at intervals. Other women made elaborately decorated coils or wide headbands with zigzag patterns. Steve kept my pattern correct by calling out the numbers and colours of beads, 'Two blue, one red…'. Jewellery-making was obviously the chance for a good gossip. Though I couldn't understand the words I could absorb the rhythms of the conversation, quick one-line repartee, and long stories with a punchline.

Everyone was generous in praise of my necklace when it was finished. As I tried it on I thought, 'When I get home this will always remind me of Nhoma.' This was followed by the realisation that I had brought the beads because the women liked them: it seemed pointless to take them away. Did I really need an object to remind me of that morning? It was better if N!hunkxa had it.

'Steve, please can you tell N!hunkxa that I would like her to have this so that she always remembers me.'

'Kaja' ('Good'), several of the women said, knowing this was one of the words I understood. The approval in their expressions too told me that inadvertently or instinctively I had done just the right thing. I was later to find out that in Ju/'hoan society, gift exchange, *xaro*, is important in bonding people together. What is significant is the act of exchanging of gifts, not their value: beadwork is often a preferred offering for exchange.

N!hunkxa disappeared, to return a few moments later with an ostrich-bead necklace with a leather medallion, which she fastened round my neck.

'N!hunkxa would like to give you a name,' Steve said.

'What is it?' I wondered, knowing that visitors are often very accurately if not always flatteringly likened to animals, for example 'Elephant man' for someone with a big nose.

'No, no, you don't understand. She wants to give you her name.'

'Mi wi a (thank you),' I said, sensing that an honour had been conferred, but not quite understanding.

I now know that by taking N!hunkxa's name I had essentially taken on her relationships and obligations. Any customs governing her behaviour towards other Ju/'hoan would apply to me also: thus I would have obligations of care towards those she did. Those who would look after her would look after me too. I had become one of her kin. However, we live so many miles apart that it is difficult to nurture this relationship, to help in difficult times or take pleasure at the good things. So I send beads because I know how much pleasure they give, because beads to me represent the connections made that morning.

Towards the southern end of the park, and between Tsumkwe and Sikereti, the bush is thick. Umbrella thorn, leadwood and cluster-leafed terminalia (also known as silver-leaf terminalia) are the dominant vegetation. The dune crests often have stands of mangetti and marula trees and, although spectacular baobab trees are dotted around the whole region, there is a particularly high density of them in the Chokwe area.

Inside the national park, Khaudum has spectacular forests of teak (especially prevalent in the southeast) and false mopane trees, which form a shady canopy

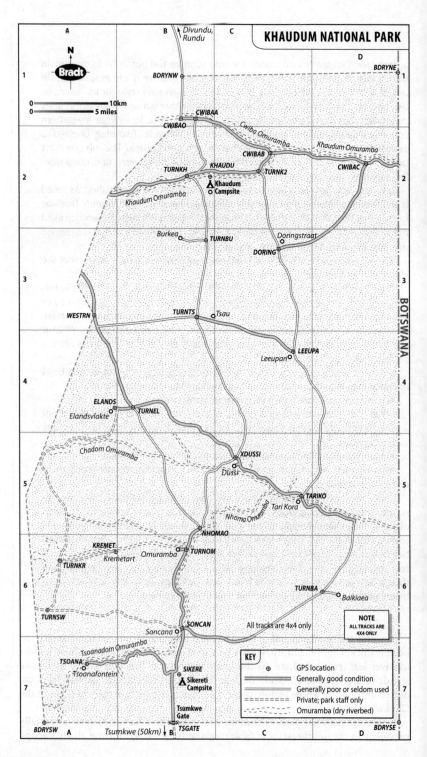

KHAUDUM NATIONAL PARK

↑ Divundu, Rundu

N
Bradt

0 ———————— 10km
0 ———————— 5 miles

BOTSWANA

BDRYNW
BDRYNE

CWIBAA
CWIBAO
Cwiba Omuramba
Khaudum Omuramba
CWIBAB
CWIBAC
TURNKH   KHAUDU   TURNK2
⛺ Khaudum
○ Campsite
Khaudum Omuramba

Burkea ○ TURNBU
Doringstraat
DORING

WESTRN   TURNTS ○ Tsau

LEEUPA
Leeupan ○

ELANDS   TURNEL
Elandsvlakte

Chadom Omuramba

XDUSSI
○ Dussi

TARIKO
○ Tari Kora
Nhoma Omuramba

NHOMAO
KREMET   TURNOM
TURNKR   Kremetart   Omuramba

TURNBA
○ Baikiaea

TURNSW

SONCAN
Soncana ○   All tracks are 4x4 only

NOTE
ALL TRACKS ARE
4x4 ONLY

Tsoanadom Omuramba
TSOANA   **SIKERE**
Tsoanafontein   ⛺ Sikereti
Campsite

Tsumkwe
Gate
BDRYSW   ✕ TSGATE   BDRYSE
Tsumkwe (50km) ↓

KEY
⊕ GPS location
——— Generally good condition
——— Generally poor or seldom used
====== Private; park staff only
- - - - Omuramba (dry riverbed)

508

above low-growing herbs and grasses. All over the park, where the dunes are wooded you'll often find open expanses of grassland growing between them.

Though seldom occurring in numbers to rival Etosha's vast herds, there is some good wildlife here and Khaudum has a much wilder feel than any of Namibia's other parks. Its game includes the uncommon tsessebe and roan antelope, the latter noted for their penchant for lots of space, and areas with low densities of other antelope. Most of the subcontinent's usual big-game species (excluding rhino and buffalo) are also represented – blue wildebeest, red hartebeest, kudu, oryx, giraffe, steenbok, duiker – as well as smaller animals typical of the Kalahari. In the dry season there are often large herds of elephants that travel from Botswana.

Leopard, lion, cheetah and spotted hyena are the main predators and, though there are good populations of these, they are seldom seen through the dense bush. Khaudum is certainly Namibia's best park for wild dog, which range over vast areas and probably criss-cross the Botswana border. That said, because of the dense bush and relative lack of game-drive loops, they are very rarely seen by visitors here.

Getting organised Within the reserve, tracks either follow *omurambas* or link the dozen or so waterholes together. Even the distinct tracks are slow going, so a good detailed map of the area is invaluable. Try the Surveyor General's office in Windhoek (page 172) before you arrive. Map number 1820 MUKWE is only a 1:250,000 scale, but it is the best available and worth having – especially when used in conjunction with the one opposite.

The map with GPS locations is included here by kind courtesy of Estelle Oosthuysen, of Nhoma Safari Camp, who personally mapped it out and noted the GPS co-ordinates in late 2002 (in UTM format – so any translation errors are entirely mine!).

Water is available but nothing else, so come self-sufficient in fuel and supplies. Because of the reserve's remote nature, entry is limited to parties with two or more 4x4 vehicles and each needs about 120 litres of fuel simply to get through the park from Tsumkwe to the fuel station at Mukwe, on the Rundu–Bagani road. This doesn't include any diversions while there. You'll need to use 4x4 almost constantly,

GPS REFERENCES FOR KHAUDUM NATIONAL PARK

BDRYNE	18°22.961'S	21°00.015'E	SONCAN	19°03.211'S	20°43.010'E
BDRYNW	18°23.289'S	20°43.050'E	TARIKO	18°53.661'S	20°52.332'E
BDRYSE	19°09.833'S	21°00.016'E	TSGATE	19°09.903'S	20°42.310'E
BDRYSW	19°09.922'S	20°32.244'E	TSOANA	19°05.648'S	20°35.583'E
CWIBAA	18°26.320'S	20°44.118'E	TURNBA	19°00.440'S	20°53.954'E
CWIBAB	18°28.740'S	20°49.967'E	TURNBU	18°35.032'S	20°44.909'E
CWIBAC	18°29.555'S	20°57.510'E	TURNEL	18°47.192'S	20°39.125'E
CWIBAO	18°26.331'S	20°42.964'E	TURNK2	18°30.143'S	20°49.099'E
DORING	18°35.705'S	20°50.677'E	TURNKH	18°30.479'S	20°43.618'E
ELANDS	18°47.212'S	20°38.052'E	TURNKR	18°57.932'S	20°33.451'E
KHAUDU	18°30.131'S	20°45.253'E	TURNOM	18°57.342'S	20°43.314'E
KHAUNO	18°23.289'S	20°43.050'E	TURNSW	19°01.720'S	20°32.222'E
KREMET	18°57.459'S	20°37.721'E	TURNTS	18°40.630'S	20°44.159'E
LEEUPA	18°43.157'S	20°51.693'E	WESTRN	18°40.484'S	20°36.094'E
NHOMAO	18°55.898'S	20°44.347'E	XDUSSI	18°50.825'S	20°47.092'E
SIKERE	19°06.157'S	20°42.399'E			

even in the dry season, making travel slow and heavy on fuel. In the wet, wheel chains might be useful, though black-cotton soil, especially towards the south of the park, can be totally impassable.

Game viewing is better here during the dry season, although most of the classic Kalahari game species found here are not strictly dependent on the presence of waterholes. Elephants are a notable exception to this rule, and they usually migrate away from sources of permanent water when it rains.

Getting there and away

From the north Turn off the main road 115km east of Rundu at Katere, where the park is signposted. Then Khaudum Camp is about 75km of slow, soft sand away.

From the south Khaudum is easily reached via Tsumkwe and Klein Dobe. Entering Tsumkwe, turn left at the crossroads (✇ *19°35.514'S, 20°30.199'E*), just beyond the schoolhouse. This rapidly becomes a small track, and splits after about 400m. Take the right fork to Sikereti (✇ *19°6.318'S, 20°42.325'E*), which is about 60km from Tsumkwe and 77km south of the camp at Khaudum.

Where to stay Khaudum National Park's two campsites have been neglected for many years, but one at least has been refurbished. Note that neither camp is fenced, so leave nothing outside that can be picked up or eaten, and beware of things that go bump in the night. In an emergency, the park staff at Sikereti and Khaudum may have radios. If you can find them, they can usually help you. A far more attractive alternative would be to organise a trip into the national park through Nhoma Safari Camp or Tsumkwe Lodge (page 499).

In late 2018, a new lodge was under construction in Khaudum National Park. For now, you can still just turn up and pay park (and if necessary campsite) fees, but you'll need to arrive with an absolute minimum of three days' food and water.

Å Khaudum Campsite [508 B2] (6 pitches)
e reservations@khaudumcamping.com. Located in a lovely spot atop a dune, overlooking an *omuramba*, this is a great place to watch the sunset. Now in private hands, it was upgraded in 2015. N$330 pp, plus N$110 per vehicle. **$$$**

Å Sikereti Campsite [508 B7] (9 pitches)
Sikereti stands in a grove of purple-pod terminalia trees, one of several such dense stands in the park. *No charge.*

20

Ovamboland

This verdant strip of land between Etosha and the Kunene and Okavango rivers is largely blank on Namibia's normal tourist map. However, it is highly populated and home to the Ovambo people, who formed the backbone of SWAPO's support during the struggle for independence. The region was something of a battleground before 1990, and now the map's blank spaces hide a high concentration of rural people practising subsistence farming of maize, sorghum and millet.

Before independence this area was known as Ovamboland, but since then it has been split into four regions: Omusati, Oshana, Ohangwena and Oshikoto. Here, for simplicity, I will refer to the whole area as Ovamboland. During the summer Ovamboland appears quite unlike the rest of Namibia. It receives over 500mm of rain annually, and supports a thick cover of vegetation and extensive arable farming.

The Ovambo people are Namibia's most numerous ethnic group, and since independence and free elections their party, SWAPO, has dominated the government. Much effort continues to go into the improvement of services here.

There are two main arteries through Ovamboland: the B1/C46, and the more northerly B10, which links the region to Rundu and is tarred throughout. The small towns that line these roads, like trading posts along a Wild West railroad, are growing rapidly.

You often see people hitching between the rural towns, and the small, tightly packed combi vans which stop for them: the local bus service. If you want to offer a lift to a hitchhiker who has waved you down, it is up to you, but make sure you consider the risk that you're taking – your insurance will not cover anyone you give a lift to.

Ovamboland has three major towns – Ondangwa, Ongwediva and Oshakati, while further west is the very different town of Ruacana, which was built solely to service the big hydro-electric power station there. Other, smaller towns vary surprisingly little and have a very similar atmosphere. There is usually a petrol station, a take-away or two, a few basic food shops, a couple of bottle stalls (alias bars) and maybe a beer hall. The fuel is cheaper at the larger 24-hour stations, in the bigger towns, and you can also stock up on cold drinks there. The take-aways and bars trade under some marvellous names, such as Never Return Bar and Gangsters' Paradise. They can be lively, friendly places to share a beer, but a word of warning: they are not recommended for lone women visitors.

Away from the towns, the land seems to go on forever. There are no mountains or hills or even kopjes; only isolated clumps of feathery palm trees and the odd baobab break the even horizon. After a year of good rains, the wide flat fields are full of water, like Far Eastern rice paddies, complete with cattle wading like water buffalo. Locally known as *oshanas*, these shallow lakes are also desirable fishing spots, drying out towards the end of the year into extensive flat pans beneath which African bullfrogs and small catfish live out the dry season in the mud.

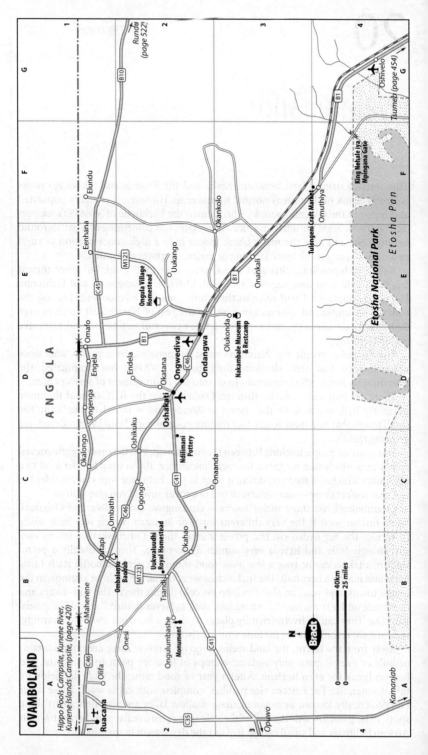

OVAMBOLAND

A Hippo Pools Campsite, Kunene River, Kunene Islands Campsite, (page 420)

ANGOLA

Etosha National Park

Etosha Pan

Runda (page 522)

Tsumeb (page 454)

The main B1 is a fast, tar road, running through several villages as it eats up the miles to the larger towns further north. Here and elsewhere in this area, watch out for cattle, goats and donkeys, as well as children, wandering across the road, and note that the speed limit in residential areas can be as slow as 40km/h.

Travelling north from Tsumeb, notice how the population density increases as the land becomes wetter, and the dominant maize crop gradually gives way to open fields where cattle graze. Where the land is not in agricultural use, greener mopane bushes gradually replace the acacia scrub by the roadside. Keep your eyes open for raptors – especially the distinctive bateleur eagles that are common in this southern area.

Some 110km north of Tsumeb, or 169km from Ondangwa, there's a turning west on to the C38 towards Etosha's Von Lindequist Gate, then a further 19km brings you to **Oshivelo**, where you must stop to pass through a police post and veterinary cordon fence. The small town is just a kilometre north of the bed of the Omuramba Ovambo, which feeds into Etosha Pan, but for most visitors it's more notable as a source of fuel. There's also an ATM at the garage, as well as a small supermarket.

After a further 65km, you'll come to a turning west clearly signposted to Etosha's northeastern King Nehale lya Mpingana Gate (formerly the Andoni Gate), which is just 17km from the B1. The opening of this gate, in 2003, has broadened the options for those wishing to combine a visit to Etosha (page 433) with a trip along the country's northern border.

North of here, along the B1, are two of the region's small **craft projects** (see box, below), but if you miss these, don't despair: alongside the road are stallholders selling handmade baskets, varying in size up to the huge and highly decorative

CRAFT PROJECTS

Several small community craft projects have been set up in the north-central region, which broadly encompasses the area of Ovamboland. Such projects add an extra dimension for visitors into a region that has hitherto seen little of Namibia's tourist boom, and in the process bring much-needed income to small, rural communities.

Coming from Tsumeb, the first of these outlets, on the right-hand side of the road at Omuthiya, is the small **Tulongeni Craft Market** [512 F4], where you'll find a selection of locally made baskets, pottery and woodcarvings. Some 28km further north, on the left of the B1 and 55km from Ondangwa, is the **Onankali Mahungu Paper-Making Project** (m 081 291 6235; ⏰ 08.00–17.00 Mon–Fri, 09.00–noon Sat–Sun, but pre-booking essential Sun). As the name suggests, it specialises in handmade paper and paper products, made from the stalks and leaves of *mahangu* – the millet staple grown throughout the area.

Closer to the heart of Ovamboland is the **Ndilimani Pottery**, poorly signposted on the C41, about 18km west of Oshakati, while north of Ondangwa, at Engela village, a group of basket-weavers around a Lutheran mission make baskets and hats under the name **Nghuoyepongo**. If you can't get to the individual projects themselves, then many of the crafts are available at the **Ombalantu Baobab Tree and Heritage Centre** in Outapi, where specialist wire-makers ply their trade, as well as at **Nakambale Museum** and **Uukwaluudhi Royal Homestead**, and in Windhoek at the Namibia Craft Centre.

Ovamboland TSUMEB TO ONDANGWA

20

grain-storage containers. From a practical standpoint, the rapidly growing linear town of **Omuthiya**, just 6km from the turning to Etosha, or 83km from Ondangwa, boasts a Standard Bank and a post office, as well as a fuel station.

ONDANGWA

Spread out along the main B1, Ondangwa is the first main town you come to in Ovamboland if approaching from Tsumeb, and is just 91km from Etosha's northern gate. Typical of the region, it is largely linear, spanning a distance of over 4km to the junction with the C46. Despite its proximity to the Angolan border (⊕ 08.00–18.00), the town itself is relatively hassle free. A lack of tourist attractions is balanced by the proximity of Nakambale Museum, just a few kilometres to the south.

GETTING THERE AND AWAY

By air The airport is on the C46, 3km west of the B1 turning north to Angola. Air Namibia (*reservations* ☏ 061 299 6111/6333; www.airnamibia.com.na) operates three return flights a day, Monday to Thursday, between here and Windhoek's Eros Airport, and two a day Friday to Sunday (*from N$1,153 one-way*).

By road Long-distance combis connect Ondangwa (as well as Ongwediva and Oshakati) with Windhoek (*around N$280 one-way*). More locally, you'll find numerous local combi vans, or taxis, stopping along the main roads to pick up and drop off passengers. Expect to pay around N$35 between Ondangwa and Oshakati. Note that these prices will fluctuate with supply and demand – holiday periods will be particularly costly!

Car hire
🚗 **Avis** ☏ 065 241281 　　🚗 **Europcar** ☏ 065 240261
🚗 **Bidvest** m 081 124 8262

By train TransNamib's passenger service between Windhoek and Ondangwa hasn't run for many years, and there is no sign of this being reinstated.

🏠 **WHERE TO STAY** Ondangwa's hotels are geared primarily to businesspeople, mostly aid workers and visiting government employees, although a trickle of tourists is making its way up here. If you're after somewhere more traditional, try Nakambale (page 516). Either way, you shouldn't need to sample the none-too-inviting 'day and night accommodation' offered to the south of town.

🏠 **Ondangwa Town Lodge** [515 B2] (15 rooms) Brian Simataa St; ☏ 065 241715; e ondangwatl@iway.na. Signposted north of the B1, the distinctive apricot walls & lilac trim of this modern hotel are clearly visible from the road. En-suite rooms have AC, fan, TV, kettle & fridge. The restaurant is separate from the bar, which has a thatched seating area in front. There's also a small pool & secure parking. *N$650/850 sgl/dbl.* **$$$**

🏠 **Protea** [515 B1] (67 rooms) Main St; ☏ 065 241900; e res.ondangwa@proteahotels.com.na; www.proteahotels.com.na. This 4-star hotel,

typical of business hotels throughout the world, sits on the corner where the B1 turns off towards Angola; follow the signs for Protea Hotel. En-suite twin or dbl rooms, which include 2 adapted for guests with a disability, have AC, kettle & satellite TV, with a fridge in the 2 suites. Facilities include a large swimming pool, restaurant with intercontinental menu, & bar, business centre & casino. There's free Wi-Fi throughout & airport transfers with a local taxi service (*N$60 pp each way*). *N$995/1,195 sgl/dbl.* **$$$**

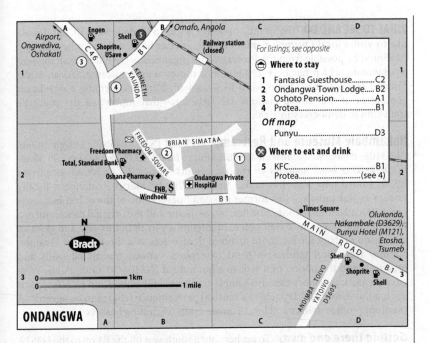

ONDANGWA

For listings, see opposite

Where to stay
1 Fantasia Guesthouse............C2
2 Ondangwa Town Lodge.....B2
3 Oshoto Pension....................A1
4 Protea..................................B1

Off map
Punyu..................................D3

Where to eat and drink
5 KFC......................................B1
Protea...............................(see 4)

Fantasia Guesthouse [515 C2] (17 rooms, camping) Off Brian Simataa St; \065 240528; m 081 379 6406; e fantasiaguesthouse@gmail. com. North of the B1, this simple guesthouse offers twin or dbl en-suite rooms & secure parking. Outside is a bar with covered terrace, & a restaurant that is open to both guests & the public. *N$500/750 sgl/dbl*; camping N$150 2pp. **$–$$$**

Oshoto Pension Hotel [515 A1] (15 rooms) Main Rd; \065 240157; e oshotoht@iway.na. On the B1 just beyond the traffic lights towards Oshikango. Imposing twin staircases lead up to the larger 'luxury' rooms, while others are in a block outside. All are en suite with AC, TV, kettle & fridge.

There's a restaurant with a separate bar, & outside seating under thatch, while lawned gardens shelter a pool. *N$550/700 sgl/dbl*. **$$**

Punyu Hotel [515 D3] (30 rooms) \065 240556; e tangeni.shikale@gmail.com. One of the oldest hotels in the area, the Punyu is 200m along the M121 towards Eenhana. It's a rather congested complex, but clean. Dotted around are a large restaurant, bar, swimming pool (albeit not in use during 2018) & thatched gazebos for outdoor drinks; the casino has been undergoing renovations for some years. Elaborately decorated rooms have TV, phone, AC & bath with shower, & some have complimentary Wi-Fi. *N$450/580 sgl/dbl*. **$$**

WHERE TO EAT AND DRINK The modern restaurant at the Protea (see opposite) serves a broad international menu, with everything from pizzas to steaks. If you're passing through and in a hurry, there's a branch of **KFC** [515 B1] on the B1, just after the turning towards the Angolan border.

OTHER PRACTICALITIES There are 24-hour BP, Shell, Caltex and Engen **fuel stations**, a couple of big **supermarkets** [515 B1] and even an outdoor market. Try the last for fresh vegetables, and perhaps a cob of maize to snack on.

On Main Road are branches of the major **banks** [515 B2] with ATMs, and a **post office** [515 B2]. Here you'll also find **BZ Truck Repairs** (\ 065 241324). There are several **pharmacies**, including two on Freedom Square Street [515 B2], behind FNB.

In an **emergency**, contact the police on \065 242663, the ambulance/Onandjokwe State Hospital on \065 240111, or Ondangwa Private Hospital on \065 283100.

WHAT TO SEE AND DO There's little to delay visitors in Ondangwa itself, but if you'd like to visit a local Ovambo homestead, ask at your hotel if this can be arranged (it should be possible from the Protea). More organised is the old Finnish mission at **Olukonda**, which has been restored as a museum and restcamp. (As an aside, Finland seems to have maintained its links with Namibia, forming a significant contingent of the United Nations' UNTAG force that supervised the country's transition to democracy in 1990.)

Nakambale Museum and Restcamp [512 E3] (§ *065 245668; Maggie* m *081 249 3108;* e *nakambalemuseum@gmail.com;* ☉ *08.00–13.00 &* 14.00–17.00 *Mon-Fri, w/ends & bank holidays on request; contact Maggie 2 days ahead; admission N$30; guided tour N$50)* Founded in the 1870s by Martti Rautanen – locally known as Nakambale – this former mission boasts some of the oldest buildings in northern Namibia. Today, the Rautanens' home and the original church form a museum that traces the development of missionary work in this area and gives an indication of daily life for those involved. It also acts as a showcase for Ovambo culture, with local guides on hand to explain various traditional skills and practices, and the option of a visit to a homestead (*N$100/30 adult/child*). With advance notice, visitors can also sample traditional Ovambo food (*N$100 pp*) or during the school holidays enjoy a musical performance (charge to be agreed). A small shop offers drinks and locally made crafts, including baskets.

Getting there and away To get here, turn southwest off the B1 on to the D3629, signposted 'Olukonda Mission'; it's just after the Shell garage and some 20km south of Ondangwa. Follow this road for about 5.5km to a church on your left, where you turn towards the museum.

🏠 **Where to stay**
⋏ **Nakambale Restcamp** [512 E3] (camping) m 081 249 3108. The huge shared camping area here can accommodate up to 30 campers sharing toilets & showers, though individuals can choose their own pitch. There are power points, a small kiosk selling drinks only & a craft shop. In late 2018, there were plans to build guest accommodation, but no completion date has been confirmed. *Camping N$100 pp.* **$$**

🏠 **AROUND ONDANGWA**
Where to stay
🏠 **Ongula Village Homestead Lodge** [512 E2] (5 huts) § 085 625 6551; e hilya@ongula. com; reservations § 061 250725; e ongula@resdest. com; www.ongula.com. 8km before Ondangwa on the B1, take the M121 & follow this to the end of the tar, then continue another 6km on the dirt road & the homestead is signposted from Oshigambo. 'Luxury' rondavels offer a comfortable stay in a secure compound, opposite a working Owambo homestead. During the day, guests can join in with the traditional chores at the homestead such as pounding *mahangu*, basket-weaving & clay-pot making, & there are day trips to nearby attractions. *DBB N$1,330/2,660 sgl/dbl pp.* **$$$$**

ONGWEDIVA

Just 22km west of Ondangwa, the small town of Ongwediva is, with Oshakati, home to the northern campus of the University of Namibia, and – at least on the surface – displays an air of relative affluence. It's probably only a matter of time before it merges with the larger town of Oshakati, just a few kilometres further along the C46.

WHERE TO STAY AND EAT

🏠 **Afrika Stadt Haus** (45 rooms) Marula
St; 065 233600; e afrikastadt@mweb.com.
na, jschmidt@mweb.com.na. Despite the clear
signpost from the C46 opposite the Engen garage,
this hotel isn't obvious – until you know that it's
the striking green & brown building to the left of
the street. Red glass panels in the dining area &
colourful wall paintings continue the theme, but
the barnlike beer garden & bar, complete with
big-screen TV, is decidedly functional. Rooms – in
standard & luxury categories – are all en suite,
with AC, TV & free Wi-Fi. *N$775/875 sgl/dbl*. **$$$**

🏠 **Bennie's Entertainment Park &
Lodge** (124 rooms) Cnr Auguste Tanyanda &
Mandume Ndemufayo sts, opposite Maroela
Mall; 065 231100; e benniesparkreception@
gmail.com. The eponymous owner of Bennie's
has certainly made his mark on the area with this
highly popular complex (see below). The lodge

is set behind the entertainment park, just off the
C46 by the Shell garage. En-suite dbl rooms are
thoughtfully decorated with dark wood furniture,
all with AC & DSTV. Some are in neat rows, their
wooden balconies lining narrow walkways; others
are larger with tiled verandas; & suites overlook
the park. Guests have their own pool & the use of
computers in the lobby; there's also Wi-Fi access.
Other facilities are in the park, which is open to
guests. *N$550/650 sgl/dbl*. **$$**

🏠 **Etuna Guest House** (36 rooms) 5544 Valley
of the Leopard St; 065 231177; e bookings@
etunaguesthouse.com; www.etunaguesthouse.
com. To get here, turn right off the C46 as you head
towards Oshakati, just before Shoprite; Etuna is
100m down on the left. Simply furnished rooms in
chalets or rondavels are en suite with AC & fridges,
& meals are available in the restaurant from an à la
carte menu. *N$600/650 sgl/dbl*. **$$**

OTHER PRACTICALITIES Aside from the usual run of **fuel stations** and **banks**, there
are a couple of **supermarkets**: Spar next to the Engen garage, and Shoprite, as well as
an open-air market. There is also a Pick n Pay in the Oshana Regional Mall.

For medical matters, the private **Ongwediva Medipark hospital** (*Auguste
Tanyanda St; 065 232911*) is close to Bennie's, with its own **pharmacy** and
another nearby.

WHAT TO SEE AND DO Many visitors to Ongwediva are here because of the
university, but **Bennie's Entertainment Park** (see above; ⏰ *07.00–late daily;
admission N$20 pp, children N$10*) draws allcomers looking for a spot of R&R.
Peacocks patrol the landscaped gardens and springbok graze on the lawns. A rather
formal restaurant serves salads, grills, pizzas and Portuguese dishes, and there's
an upstairs bar. Outside, sunloungers surround a large swimming pool, while a
separate pool has a water slide. An ice-cream kiosk and bar, individual braai areas,
a children's playground, minigolf and an aviary add to the package.

OSHAKATI

By Namibian standards, this is a large, sprawling town, more commercialised than
Ondangwa yet similar in character. That said, finding your way around is not as
straightforward as in the more linear Ondangwa, and it's surprisingly easy to get
lost in the streets off the main C46. There are no tourist attractions, but the town
acts as the centre for several government departments.

GETTING THERE AND AWAY The town is located some 40km northwest of
Ondangwa along the C46. As yet no commercial flights operate from the small
airport; the nearest commercial airport is at Ondangwa.

WHERE TO STAY Oshakati's hotels, as those in Ondangwa, cater mainly for
businesspeople, although the choice here is wider.

Oshakati Country Hotel [518 A1] (46 rooms) Robert Mugabe Av; 065 222380; e res. osh@united.com.na. Great carved doors open into a thatched lobby where giant masks & tall wooden giraffes ooze a sense of Africa. Here you'll find a substantial sports bar, a restaurant (with tables outside on the terrace too) & a conference centre. Normally meals are à la carte, but a buffet dinner is served when it's busy. Rooms, set at the back around lawns & a pool, are spacious if uninspiring. All have AC, TV, free Wi-Fi & phone. Sadly, reports have been rather negative, mentioning poor service, & calling into question the cleanliness of the hotel. *N$650/880 sgl/dbl*. **$$$**

Oshakati Guest House [518 C3] (22 rooms) Cnr Sam Nujoma Rd & Leo Shoopala St; 065 224659; e bookings@oshakati-guesthouse. com; www.oshakati-guesthouse.com. Opened in 2008, this pleasant guesthouse has cool en-suite dbl rooms with TV, AC, fridge & kettle. Set at the back of a brick-paved yard, they're well cushioned from any noise from the large sports bar & restaurant, where you can order dinner à la carte. *N$895/1,295 sgl/dbl*. **$$$**

Oshandira Lodge [518 A3] (22 rooms) 065 220443; e oshandira@iway.na. Close to the airport, with secure parking, Oshandira is convenient for business users. Since being taken over in 2008, it has seen the addition of an upstairs restaurant & a sundowner area. Rooms come with AC, DSTV, a phone & some have fridges; free Wi-Fi for guests. The restaurant is one of the best in town, so often gets busy; its menu incorporates traditional Ovambo food, with Portuguese dishes on request. Alongside the swimming pool is a popular sports bar with large-screen TV (noon–22.00). *N$650/850 sgl/dbl*. **$$$**

Rocha's Hotel [518 D1] (38 rooms) Main Rd; 065 222038; m 081 470 4636. Next to Rocha's restaurant, which is the main draw, this is the simplest of the bunch. Rooms are built in a block around a central courtyard, garden & pool, with free Wi-Fi for guests. *N$520/770 sgl/dbl*. **$$$**

✕ WHERE TO EAT AND DRINK Oshandira Lodge offers a good menu, but **Rocha's** (*Main Rd;* 065 222038; 06.00–22.00 daily) is a favourite. By all means drop in for a burger or a beer at this relaxed bar/restaurant, but it's the Portuguese specialities (**$$–$$$$$**) that are highly rated. Fast food comes courtesy of **KFC** [518 C1] in the Yetu Complex, and a **Wimpy** [518 C1] at the Engen garage.

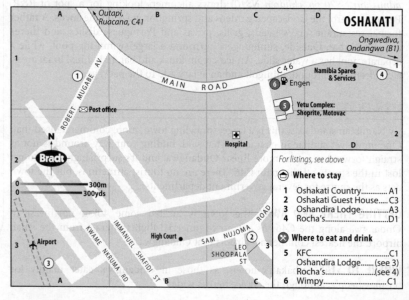

OSHAKATI

For listings, see above

Where to stay
1 Oshakati Country.............A1
2 Oshakati Guest House.....C3
3 Oshandira Lodge.............A3
4 Rocha's.............................D1

Where to eat and drink
5 KFC.......................................C1
   Oshandira Lodge........(see 3)
   Rocha's...........................(see 4)
6 Wimpy.................................C1

For an evening out, Oshakati can be excellent – provided that you enjoy joining in with the locals and don't demand anything too posh. Venues come and go so ask around for the current 'in' places.

OTHER PRACTICALITIES Oshakati has all the major services that you might need, including lots of 24-hour **fuel stations**, and several **banks** and ATMs. It's well served for **vehicle spares**, too, with a Nissan and Toyota dealer, Ozzy's (❄ *065 222132*), across the road from Namibia Breweries on Okatana Road, and – for Land Rovers – Northern Auto Repairs (❄ *065 221802*) behind Oshakati Spar along the C46. Motovac (❄ *065 225672*) has a branch in the Yetu Complex [518 C1], and Cymot (❄ *065 220916*) is next to Old Mutual, west along the C46, along with smaller outfits such as Trentyre.

For **food** shopping, there's the Spar complex on the C46, and a branch of Shoprite in the Yetu Complex. More interesting is the large African market on Main Road (⊕ *daily except Sun*).

If you need medicine there are several **pharmacies**, including Oshakati Pharmacy (❄ *065 220964*) on the main road, which has good basic supplies.

In an **emergency**, the police are reached on ❄ 065 223 6000, the ambulance on ❄ 065 223 3222, and the fire service on m 081 144 8222. If you're in need of a **hospital**, the best option is Ongwediva Medipark (page 517).

OSHAKATI TO RUACANA

The tarred C46 continues northwest from Oshakati to Outapi (also known as Ombalantu), some 86km away. Alongside the road is a canal – a vital water supply for Oshakati during the dry season. Driving by, you pass women carrying water back to their houses, while others wash and children splash around to cool off. Along the banks, piles of clay bricks lie drying in the sun. Occasionally there are groups meeting in the shade of canalside trees, and boys fishing in the murky water. Some have just a string tied to the end of a long stick, but others use tall conical traps, perhaps a metre high, made of sticks. The successful will spend their afternoon by the roadside, selling fresh fish from the shade of small stalls.

If you're not in a hurry, consider taking the C41 west to Okahao and Tsandi, before continuing north on the gravel M123 to Outapi. Some 18km from Oshakati, you'll pass a roadside sign indicating **Ndilimani Pottery** (see box, page 513) to the left.

OKAHAO While the small town of Okahao has all the essentials – a couple of fuel stations, a market, various shops including a pharmacy, a police station and even a hospital – it's not a place where you'd particularly want to linger.

⌐ **Where to stay** Should you need somewhere to stop for the night, there are a few guesthouses that could fit the bill, including Mika Ilonga Guesthouse next to the church, and King Uushona B&B a few kilometres to the west. Just east of town, the fairly large **Ongozi Guesthouse** looks promising, with rooms built in a semicircle at the back overlooking a huge baobab, but it was deserted when we visited.

TSANDI Some 25km from Okahao you'll come to Tsandi, a rural town with a fuel station but where donkey carts are still in regular use. It's worth stopping at the **Uukwaluudhi Royal Homestead** [512 B2] (⊕ *08.00–17.00 Mon–Fri; admission N$40 pp*), on your right just east of the town. Built in 1960 for the royal family of

Uukwaluudhi, one of seven traditional kingdoms in the region, it was home to King Taapoopi and his family. Although clearly designed with a view to protecting royalty, the reception areas, kitchens and bedrooms are similar to those of more humble Ovambo homesteads. Helpful guides explain what each room is for, and the uses of the various household items displayed, but to see traditional dancing, try the local food, or be presented to the king, you'll need to book in advance. For the visitor, there are toilets, a kiosk selling curios, cold drinks and an interesting – if overpriced – book: *A Journey Through Uukwaluudhi History*. It's worth mentioning that when researching this book, it was exceedingly difficult to get in touch with the Royal Homestead, and we've heard that they can be unreliable in terms of their opening.

This area of northern Namibia is the heartland of SWAPO. A monument at **Ongulumbashe**, a 15-minute drive from the Royal Homestead, marks the spot where in 1966 the guerrillas first clashed with South African police, thus effectively launching Namibia's struggle for independence. To find it, take the left turning just 2km from the homestead, and follow the road. Ask at the homestead if you'd like a guide.

OUTAPI Approaching Outapi from the south, about a kilometre before the town behind the open market, is the **Ombalantu Baobab Tree and Heritage Centre** [512 B1]. A locally renowned hollow tree, it has served variously as a church, a post office and – in the war years – a hideaway, but is today the site of a community-run venture that incorporates a campsite, heritage centre and craft market.

From Outapi, it's an easy 70km of tar road to Ruacana. West of the border post with Angola, the flat plains give way to a more undulating landscape dotted with scrubby vegetation, culminating in views across to a large dam on the Angolan side of the border.

⌂ Where to stay and eat

⌂ **Outapi Town Hotel** (30 rooms) ☎ 065 251029; e outapith@iway.na; www.outapith. iway.na. This brick-built hotel on the main C46 to Ruacana is traditional in style & deceptively spacious. Brown & cream walls are enlivened by occasional murals, & rooms – complete with frilly bedding – have AC, TV, kettle, fridge, free Wi-Fi & phone. There's a formal restaurant, serving local & international dishes, & a separate bar, while

outside is a pool set in grassy surrounds. Secure parking. *N$450/690 sgl/dbl.* **$$**

⋀ **Ombalantu Baobab Tree** [512 B1] (4 pitches) e obthc@iway.na. In theory, the Heritage Centre has its own campsite, but don't bank on it. Along with braai facilities & an ablution block with WC & warm showers, each pitch has its own power & water points. *N$80 pp.* **$**

Other practicalities Outapi is a good source of **supplies**, with a branch of Shoprite as well as a market. There are **banks** and a **pharmacy** here, too, and the town is also the location of the district **hospital**. Most of these facilities are located on the M123, but the **fuel stations** are on the main C46.

RUACANA

The small town of Ruacana perches on the border with Angola, about 291km north of Kamanjab and about 200km west of Oshakati. It owes its existence to the big hydro-electric dam that is built at a narrow gorge in the river some 20km downstream, and supplies over half of the country's electric power. This is of major economic and strategic importance, so the road from Tsumeb via Ondangwa has long been good tar all the way, and that from Kamanjab is now also tarred. The town itself is located 4km south of the C46 along the D3618.

Few visitors stop in Ruacana, and facilities – aside from the lodge – are limited to the supermarket, a large school and a BP fuel station with its own minimarket. This is the only source of fuel for miles, so do stock up if you're heading west.

WHERE TO STAY

Ruacana Eha Lodge (21 rooms, 6 huts, camping) 065 271500; e info@ ruacanaehalodge.com.na; www.ruacanaehalodge. com.na. This unexpected find was originally built for those working on the dam, which explains the presence of a gym & volleyball, as well as a good swimming pool. Set in attractive gardens, it has en-suite twin rooms that are slightly institutional in layout, but are modern & nicely appointed with AC, TV, phone, kettle, fridge & a private veranda. More fun – if more basic (albeit with AC & kettles!)

– are traditional Himba-style huts with twin beds. A tree-shaded campsite has 16 pitches with individual braais, water & electricity. Both share the ablution block, with hot water, which also has facilities for people with limited mobility. There's a spacious restaurant (N$220/250 lunch/dinner) & separate bar. Excursions to the falls & a Himba village can be arranged with 48hrs' notice; you must take your own transport but the lodge will arrange a guide for you (N$185 pp). N$800/1,000 sgl/dbl. **$$$**

RUACANA FALLS Just 20km west of Ruacana, the falls used to be an attraction for visitors, but now the water flows over them only when the dam upstream in Angola allows it to, and even then much is diverted through a series of sluices to the hydro-electric station on the border. Between June and December, they are usually dry.

The falls are well signposted from the C46, 2.5km east of Hippo Pools. The viewpoint is in no-man's-land, so technically you have to exit the country to see them. However, at the large and underused border post (08.00–19.00) you can do so temporarily, without going through the full emigration procedures; at most you'll be asked to sign a book. Be careful when taking photographs: ask permission and don't take pictures of anything apart from the falls. This border area is still very sensitive.

Where to stay

Hippo Pools Campsite [512 A1] (10 pitches) No contact details, but we're assured it's still open. Located on the Kunene River just west of the falls, at the junction of the D3700 & the C46, this community campsite is also known as Otjipahuriro Campsite, & is a great place for birdwatchers. It's an attractive site at the foot of the valley, with pitches set out under trees overlooking the river, each with its own fireplace & water tap. The eco-friendly ablution block has WC & showers, but there's no power, you'll need to be totally self-sufficient except for firewood. Trips can be arranged (from N$25 pp), including guided walks to the falls & visits to local villages. N$50 pp. **$**

Kunene Islands Campsite [512 A1] (2 tents, camping) m 081 127 3931, 081 129 3931; e unicorn@iway.na. Just 8km west of Hippo Pools, this attractive campsite with 21 pitches occupies

an idyllic riverside spot within the Uukolonkadhi Ruacana Conservancy, overlooking small islands & the hills of Angola. A variety of birds & the occasional monkey share the site with campers, who have pitches with braai facilities, taps & LED lighting. If you don't have your own tent, there are twin ones here. A stone ablution block incorporates flush WC & hot/cold showers. Water is pumped directly from the Kunene, but it's best to bring your own drinking water – & everything else you need, although firewood is available. You can swim in the clear natural pool, which is kept clean by plants & fish, & 4WD visits to river springs 4km upstream can be arranged. Fishing is also possible from designated spots, although the camp is otherwise fenced off from the riverbank. No day visitors. Tent N$250; camping N$100 pp. **$$**

WEST OF RUACANA West of Ruacana is the Kunene Region, covered in *Chapter 16*. The road in this direction, as far as Kunene River Lodge, is relatively accessible (though a 4x4 is essential during the rains), but beyond that requires considerable care at all times; for details, see page 424.

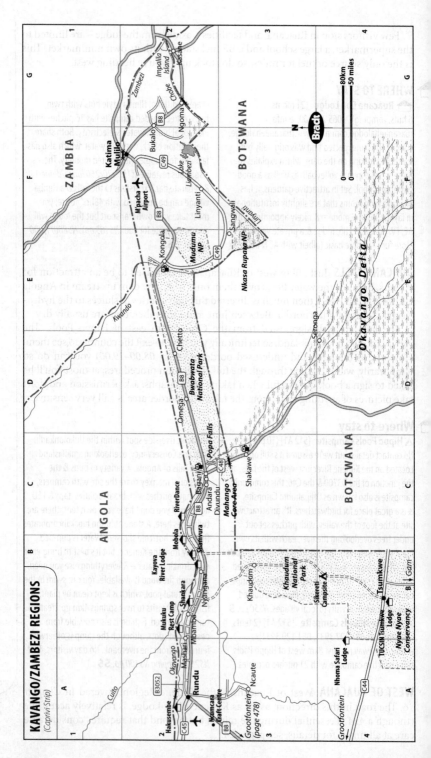

KAVANGO/ZAMBEZI REGIONS
(Caprivi Strip)

21

Rundu and the Kavango/Zambezi Regions (The Caprivi Strip)

The north of Namibia is generally very lush, watered by a generous annual rainfall. East of Ovamboland – which means northeast of Grootfontein – lie the regions of Kavango East and West and Zambezi (formerly known as the Caprivi Strip).

These support a large population, and a surprising amount of wildlife. The wildlife has visibly increased in the national parks here in the last few years, helped enormously by various successful community-based game-guard and conservation/development programmes (see box, page 15).

The main B8 road across the strip, or the Golden Highway as it has sometimes been called, is an important artery for trade with Zimbabwe and Zambia, and has become increasingly busy in recent years. Now fully tarred, it has come a long way since the dusty gravel road that I first crossed in 1989, when many viewed the region as *terra incognita*.

Unlike much of the rest of Namibia, the Kavango and Zambezi regions feel like most Westerners' image of Africa. You'll see lots of circular huts, small kraals, animals, and people carrying water on their heads. These areas are probably what you imagined Africa to be like before you first arrived. By the roadside you'll find stalls selling vegetables, fruit or woodcarvings, and in the parks you'll find buffalo hiding in the thick vegetation. This area is much more like Botswana, Zimbabwe or Zambia than the rest of Namibia, which is only what you would expect if you look at a map of the subcontinent, or read the history of the area: it really is very different from the rest of the country.

THE KAVANGO REGIONS

Sandwiched between Ovamboland to the west, and Zambezi to the east, the Kavango Regions broadly correspond to the old region of Kavangoland. Although divided for administrative purposes into Kavango East and West in 2013, this has little impact on travel.

Within both regions, the main town is Rundu – a useful stopover for most visitors, but an end in itself for few. Further east is Popa Falls, a set of rapids on the Kavango River (called the Okavango in Botswana). These falls mark an important geological fault, where the river starts to spread out across the Kalahari's sands to form the remarkable Okavango Delta in Botswana.

Just downstream from Popa, tucked into a corner of the country on the border with Botswana, is Mahango Core Area (formerly Mahango National Park); officially part of the bigger Bwabwata National Park, it is often still referred to as a national park in its own right. Bounded on one side by the broadening Kavango, it encompasses a very wide range of environments in its small area, and its game has improved vastly since the 1990s. With its expansive reed-beds, tall trees and lush vegetation, Mahango is typical of the game parks further east.

DRIVING FROM GROOTFONTEIN TO RUNDU
The road between Grootfontein and Rundu is about 250km of good tar. Initially the only variation in the tree and bush thorn-scrub is an occasional picnic site by the roadside, or band of feathery makalani palms towering above the bush. About halfway to Rundu, however, you stop at a veterinary control post: a gap in the veterinary fence now known as the Mururani Gate. (The fence is there to stop the movement of cattle, and the transmission of foot-and-mouth and rinderpest disease.) This is the line where land-use changes drastically: from large commercial ranches to small subsistence farms. The difference is striking; the landscape changes drastically, becoming more like the stereotypical Western view of rural Africa. Drivers should take care, as with more settlements there are now many more animals and people wandering across the road.

Gradually shops and roadside bars appear, and eventually stalls selling woodcarvings and pots. About 30km before Rundu, to the west of the road, is the **Ncumcara/Mile 20 Community Craft Centre** [522 A2] (m 081 294 7986, 081 285 6594) selling woodcarvings, baskets, jewellery, and jams made from indigenous fruits, all at very reasonable prices and all under the Hambera trademark, denoting goods from the Kavango regions. Such products originate solely from community forests and are harvested, processed and produced under controlled conditions by local people in the villages.

Closer to the town, especially during the wet season, stalls appear piled high with pyramids of tomatoes and exotic fruits – evidence of the agricultural potential in the rich alluvial soils and heavy rainfall.

Where to stay For a good place to stop along this road, try Roy's Rest Camp [478 C3], some 55km north of Grootfontein, Fiume Lodge [478 C3], about 20km further south, or Fiume Bush Camp or Lodge [478 C3], a little way to the east (page 494).

RUNDU Northeast of Grootfontein and about 520km west of Katima Mulilo, Rundu sits just above the beautiful Kavango floodplain and comes as a relief after the long, hot journey to reach it. Perhaps because of this distance, it feels like an outpost; it certainly has few specific attractions although it has seen something of a boom in recent years, with bright new shopping malls and businesses. But these distances also make it a prudent stopover, and most of the lodges expect visitors to spend just one night with them. Indicative of its proximity to Angola, just across the river, Rundu has a relaxed, slightly Portuguese atmosphere.

RUNDU
For listings, see from page 526

Where to stay
1 Beaufort Guesthouse........................C1
2 Glory Backpackers.............................C1
3 Kavango River Lodge.........................B1
4 Tambuti Lodge....................................C1

Off map
Hakusembe River Lodge..................A3
Hotel Rundu...E4
Kaisosi River Lodge............................F1
Ngandu Safari Lodge.........................E1
n'Kwazi Lodge.....................................E4
Samsitu Camping...............................A3
Sarasungu River Lodge.....................E1
Taranga Safari Lodge.........................A3

Where to eat and drink
5 Debonairs..D3
6 Gino's Bakery Take-away................. D2
   KFC (see Rundu Mall).......................D2
   Hungry Lion (see Rundu Mall)........D2
7 Portuguese Take-away and bar.....G4
   Steers...(see 5)
   Tambuti Lodge..............................(see 4)

Off map
Sarasungu (see Sarasungu
   River Lodge)...................................... E1

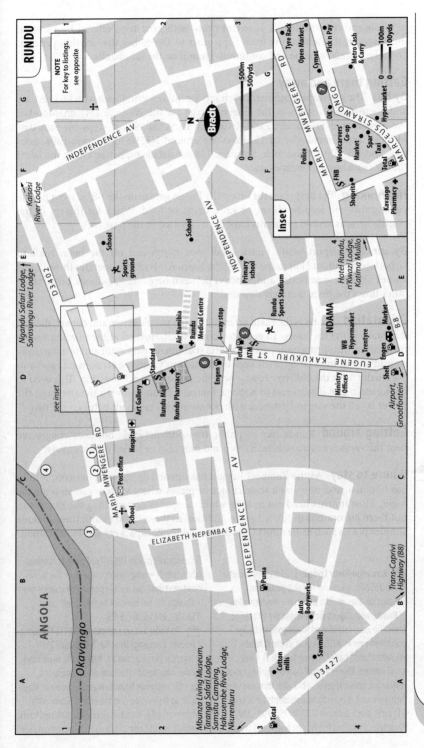

RUNDU

NOTE
For key to listings, see opposite

Inset

ANGOLA

Okavango

Ngandu Safari Lodge,
Sarasungu River Lodge

Kaisosi
River Lodge

D3402

see inset

School

School

Sports
ground

Primary
school

INDEPENDENCE AV

INDEPENDENCE AV

MARIA MWENGERE RD

Post office

School

ELIZABETH NEPEMBA ST

INDEPENDENCE AV

Hospital

Art Gallery

Standard

Rundu Mall

Rundu Pharmacy

Engen

Air Namibia

Rundu
Medical Centre

4-way stop

Total
ATM

Rundu
Sports Stadium

Ministry
Offices

Puma

Auto
Bodyworks

Cotton
mills

Sawmills

D3427

EUGENE KAKUKURU ST

NDAMA

WB
Hypermarket

Trentyre

Engen

Market

Shell

B8

Hotel Rundu,
n'Kwazi Lodge,
Katima Mulilo

Airport,
Grootfontein

Trans-Caprivi
Highway (B8)

Mbunza Living Museum,
Taranga Safari Lodge,
Samsitu Camping,
Hakusembe River Lodge,
Nkurenkuru

Total

Inset

MARIA MWENGERE RD

MARCUS SIRAWO

SONGO

Police

FNB

Shoprite

Woodcarvers'
Co-op

Market

Kavango
Pharmacy

Spar

Taxi

Total

OK

Cymot

Open Market

Tyre Rack

Pick n Pay

Metro Cash
& Carry

Hypermarket

While the river itself is a powerful draw, with boat trips offered by many of the lodges, it is often so low from September to December that anything except, possibly, a shallow canoe will constantly ground on the sandbanks.

Getting there and away

By bus The Intercape Mainliner coach service linking Windhoek with Livingstone and Victoria Falls stops at the Engen garage on the B8 [525 D4] on Monday, Wednesday and Friday at 22.05. Returning to Windhoek, it stops on Saturday, Monday and Thursday at 01.15. Fares are around N$580 to Victoria Falls, one-way, and N$790 to Windhoek. See page 153 for details or, better, check the latest timetable on www.intercape.co.za.

Hitchhiking The best place for lifts is the Engen garage on the B8, as most people passing this will stop to fill up, or get a drink or food. Watch for thieves in the crowds here, as several problems have been reported in the past.

By air The 'airport' – it's pretty small – is signposted off the main road to Grootfontein, about 6km to the west of the town. Air Namibia operates three flights a week (Wednesday, Friday and Sunday) between here and Windhoek Eros, but at other times the place is largely deserted.

Orientation
The B8 is the main artery on which people arrive and depart, though it actually skirts the town. To get into Rundu itself, turn off at the buzzing Engen fuel station. This brings you past the sports stadium on your right and to a four-way stop junction, marked by Shell and Total garages. Continue straight on, and you eventually meet the old river road – now the D3402 – at a T-junction. This used to be the main gravel road east to Katima, but now it runs between the river and the newer B8 all the way to Divundu, with occasional access roads between the two.

Getting around
Rundu has no public transport network, but taxis congregate near the various supermarkets in town and may also be hailed on the streets.

Where to stay
As the Zambezi Region has opened up more to tourism, Rundu has boomed, and now has a wide choice of places where visitors can stop for the night. Most tourists head out to lodges and campsites dotted along the riverfront, but there are options in town, too. In addition to those listed below, these include simpler places such as Beaufort Guesthouse, Glory Backpackers and Hotel Rundu.

In town

Kavango River Lodge [525 B1] (19 chalets) 066 255244; e kavangolodge@gmail.com. Situated on a secure 3ha site on the western edge of Rundu, with superb views across the Okavango River, the long-established Kavango River Lodge was taken over in 2016. Each of its dbl & family en-suite chalets has AC/ceiling fan, Wi-Fi, TV & small kitchen. There's a small pool by the Riverview restaurant, which is set on a hill with stunning west-facing views & is open to non-residents for b/fast, à la carte lunch & dinner (N$100/250/200–280). River trips, including fishing (for tigerfish & bream)

& sundowner cruises (N$170 pp) can be organised when there's enough water in the river. The tennis court next door can usually be used by arrangement – though the net may not be there! *Self-catering N$802/1,304 sgl/dbl.* **$$$**

Ngandu Safari Lodge [525 E1] (41 rooms, 4 houses, camping) Usivi Rd; 066 256723; e ngandu@iafrica.com.na. Just off the main road by the river, beside the turn-off to Sarasungu, the efficiently run Ngandu was taken over in May 2018, so renovation is in the offing. Along with whitewashed A-frame chalets with thatched roofs, reminiscent of Cape Dutch style, there are smaller rooms in various configurations, clustered close together. For now, both 'deluxe' & 4 family rooms have AC, DSTV, fridge & kettle; standard rooms are slightly smaller, without TV; & 7 budget rooms are pretty simple. Wi-Fi is available throughout. There's also a campsite with 2 ablution blocks & 20 pitches, each with its own kitchen.

The lodge has a separate restaurant, braai areas, a curio shop, 2 swimming pools, conference facilities, a laundry, shaded parking & 24hr security. *N$867/1,240 sgl/dbl; camping N$60 pp.* **$–$$$**

✳ 🏠 **Tambuti Lodge** [525 C1] (8 bungalows, camping) ◊066 255711; e tambuti@iway.na; www.tambuti.com.na. This small, eco-friendly Luxembourg/locally owned guesthouse on the western edge of Rundu, is perched above the river, about 300m from the road leading to the river & the tiny Rundu Beach, yet near the centre of town. Its whitewashed bungalows with tin roofs are scattered around lush gardens & are clean, light & airy, with AC, stone floors, minibar, DSTV, & either roll-top baths or showers en suite. At the back is a tree-shaded pool, a braai area for guest use, & a bar overlooking the river. There is Wi-Fi in reception. With a strong emphasis on supporting local businesses, the restaurant specialises in traditional food, & the lodge arranges village visits & river activities, the latter through Samsitu Camp (see right). *N$750/1,000 sgl/dbl; camping N$60 pp.* **$–$$$**

Further west along the river

🏠 **Hakusembe River Lodge** [478 A3] (20 chalets, camping) ◊066 257010; e info@gondwana-collection.com; www.gondwana-collection.com. On the opposite side of town to most other lodges, Hakusembe is about 14km west of Rundu, off the main road to Nkurenkuru. To reach it, turn northwest off the main B8 on to the B10 about 4km southwest of Rundu. Follow this towards Nkurenkuru for about 10km, where the lodge is signposted towards the river.

Hakusembe's riverside location is enhanced by a beautiful flower garden, complete with carefully tended roses . Its en-suite chalets – some set amid green lawns & others with river views – have AC & mosquito nets. Behind these are 4 camp pitches taking 8 people each, with private ablution blocks, power points & water. Each of the 2 2-storey family chalets has a lounge, bathroom & kitchen, plus a

loft bedroom that opens on to a terrace – ideal for sundowners. There is a swimming pool, & nearby, under thatch, a popular bar & dining area (with Wi-Fi) – though meals are often served on the terrace overlooking the Kavango River (*dinner N$330*).

Boat trips (prices vary depending on numbers) are available Jan–Oct for sightseeing, birdwatching, fishing (*N$180 pp/1½ hrs, min 2 people*), & popular sunset champagne cruises (*N$240 pp*). *N$1,958/3,134 sgl/dbl; camping N$195 pp.* **$$–$$$$$**

🏠 **Taranga Safari Lodge** [478 A3] (10 rooms, camping) ◊066 257236; m 081 277 6000; e info@taranganamibia.com; www.taranganamibia.com. This bush lodge, 35km west of Rundu & just off the B10, is one of the best in the area & has the potential to be a really great lodge if maintenance & service were stepped up. Overlooking the river, all its tents have private decks, dark wood furniture & flooring, animal-skin rugs & cream interiors, along with fans, fridges & tea/coffee facilities. Much bigger are 2 'deluxe' tents, their open-plan bathrooms featuring roll-top baths & his 'n' hers sinks; opt for these if you can. Walkways lead to a tented dining room/bar area in similar style to the rooms, passing a small pool & the lovely Kingfisher Bar on a small pontoon over the river (*lunch N$125*). The 6 campsites have power, water, braai & tented ablution blocks. Activities include walks around the 12ha grounds where steenbok & springbok have been reintroduced, fishing (*N$200 pp/hr*), self-guided birding walks, birding river cruises (*N$200 pp/hr*), sunrise/sunset cruises (*N$250/450*), & both guided village & river walks (*N$275*). *DBB N$1,750/1,950 luxury/deluxe sgl, N$3,500/3,900 dbl; camping N$250 pp.* **$$–$$$$$**

⚑ **Samsitu Camping** [478 A3] (5 pitches) ◊066 257023/255602; m 081 129 3290; e kavpharm@iafrica.com.na. Right next door to Hakusembe River Lodge, Andrew Fudge's campsite can accommodate 10–30 campers, with lovely pitches right on the river, each with braai & fireplace, water, power, light & shared ablution blocks. The central area has a bar & pool under deep thatch with a kiosk selling snacks. There are several boating options, from morning safaris & sunset cruises (*N$190*) to unguided canoeing (*no charge*). This is a relaxed place with lots of opportunities for activities, though it is not really suitable for small children. *N$100 pp.* **$**

Further east along the river

🏠 **Kaisosi River Lodge** [525 F1] (16 rooms, camping) ☎066 267125; m 081 249 5090; e kaisosi@iway.na; www.kaisosiriverlodge.com; ✪ 17°52.477'S, 19°49.954'E. Right on the river to the east of Rundu (signposted; take the 1st turning to the left as you head east out of town), Kaisosi is a comfortable, well-maintained place for a stopover, if somewhat lacking in atmosphere. Carpeted rooms, in deep-red, 2-storey chalets, are clean & tidy, with AC, direct-dial phone, & sliding doors opening on to a patio or balcony with river views. Standard rooms have twin beds, a fan & shower; 'luxury' rooms are larger, with dbl bed & combined bath & shower. Sound-proofing isn't great, so ask for an upstairs room if you're averse to noisy neighbours. There's also an excellent campsite with 16 pitches, all with private shower & WC. The brick-built, thatched main building includes the bar & dining area (b/fast N$110, lunch & dinner à la carte). Just outside are a couple of pools overlooking the river & a large area of wooden decking. Activities range from a champagne b/fast (N$210) or sunset cruise (N$135 exc drinks), to fishing (N$250 pp/hr, min 4 people, licence can be purchased in advance). N$850/1,310 sgl/dbl; camping N$150 pp. **$$–$$$**

🏠 **Sarasungu River Lodge** [525 E1] (26 bungalows, camping) ☎066 255161; m 081 367 9141/9132; e sarasungu@nawa.com.na. One of the oldest lodges around Rundu, Sarasungu is by the river, just outside town. The well-signposted turn-off from the main road leads down a hill, passing Ngandu on your left, before reaching the lodge a kilometre or so down a rutted, sandy track.

Local fabrics & African artefacts bring an individual touch to large, comfortable en-suite bungalows spread out on green lawns, adjacent to a large pool. Constructed of brick under thatch, they come with AC, a veranda & river view, twin or dbl beds beneath mosquito nets, & most have a small sitting area with chairs & coffee table, DSTV, fridge & kettle. 'Luxury' rooms are larger & smarter. Dotted around the grounds & on the original shady site by the river are 26 camp pitches, each with its own ablution block.

The Fish Trap restaurant & bar, with its TV loft area & rustic décor, is the focal point of the lodge, & its menu is extensive. Alongside pizzas, pastas & more traditional grills, African dishes are added to buffet selections to tempt you to try, with the most popular featuring on the regular menu too (lunch $$$– $$$$; buffet dinner N$250). Excursions include boat trips, fishing trips & champagne sunset cruises (all N$200 pp/hr). Wi-Fi is available at reception. N$500/750 sgl/dbl; camping N$70 pp. **$–$$$**

🏠 **n'Kwazi Lodge** [525 E4] (18 chalets, camping) m 081 242 4897, 081 718 5371; e reservations@nkwazilodge.com; www. nkwazilodge.com; ✪ 17°52.063'S, 19°54.502'E. About 22km east of Rundu, n'Kwazi is well signposted (with fish eagle logos) from the main Rundu–Katima road. Take the tar road for 10km, then the 3rd turning left (✪ 18°03.308'S, 19°52.071'E); 5km later, turn right on to the D3402, the old gravel Rundu–Katima road, then left after a further 3km. The lodge is about 4km along this road.

N'Kwazi was built in 1995 by Wynand & Valerie Peypers, & is now managed by their son, Pieter. It's a relaxed, friendly place, with families particularly welcome. At the heart of the lodge are a couple of large thatched areas – 1 a sunken dining room & central fire, the other a bar, with ample comfortable seating & Wi-Fi – with the river beyond. A small pool lies in the gardens. Decent, home-cooked meals are available, with excellent, fresh buffets in the evenings (lunch $$$$, buffet dinner N$295).

Of the chalets, 13 are large, comfortable, wood & stone structures, with high thatched ceilings, large meshed windows, warm fabrics & solar lights for when the generator stops at 22.00. The others, with similar interiors, are set further from the main area. The adjacent campsite has ample space, showers & power.

The Peypers have for many years supported the local community through villages, schools & churches, which guests may visit on request (N$60 pp). As part of this, they run a scholarship project enabling children to progress to high school (150 so far); 5 have completed university & more are now attending. They have also set up their own preschool whose 40–50 children aged 4–6 are supported by guest donations. Local dancers perform at the lodge (N$50 pp), too, & there are also sunset cruises (N$150 pp). N$813/1,368 sgl/dbl; camping N$125 pp. **$–$$$**

✕ **Where to eat and drink** Rundu has a few choices for eating out but don't expect top-class restaurants; most people eat at their hotel or lodge. Of these, **Tambuti Lodge** (page 527) is by far the most interesting, with an emphasis on local foods

– think Kalahari truffles, baobab ice cream and marula oil – in a charming setting under a shady acacia tree. **Sarasungu** is also fairly close, serving pizzas or more substantial mains from around N$70. Further afield, Hakusembe, n'Kwazi and Kaisosi also have good tables.

Close to the centre, near the Woodcarving Co-op, there's the **Portuguese Take-away and bar** [525 G4] (\ *066 255240/255792*), which has a very local feel and is more of a pool bar than an obvious take-away. There's also **Gino's Bakery Take-away Restaurant** [525 D2] – a bakery/café with sandwiches, pastries etc, almost next to the Rundu Mall. Fast-food chains are on the increase with both **KFC** and **Hungry Lion** in Rundu Mall [525 D2], plus **Debonairs** pizza [525 D3] and **Steers** steakhouse [525 D3] close by on Independence Avenue.

Shopping
Rundu Mall [525 D2] on Eugene Kakakuru Street has expanded considerably in recent years and now has a plethora of shops for provisions, clothes, and IT requirements, as well as pharmacies (see below). There's also a branch of cycle/outdoor specialists **Cymot** (\ *066 255668*).

Food and supplies
In town, try the Pick n Pay, Spar, WB Hypermarket or large Shoprite supermarkets, which all have a good selection of produce. Close to the Shell garage, stallholders sell a range of fresh fruit and vegetables. Then heading east on the old gravel road, 2km past the turning to Kaisosi River Lodge, is the **Uvhungu Vhungu Green Scheme Irrigation Project** (\ *066 256440;* m *081 167 2258;* e *vungu@iway.na*). For those with a sophisticated line in camp cooking, this is a useful source of juices and fresh dairy produce such as milk, butter and cream.

Crafts or curios
Mbangura Woodcarvers' Co-op [525 F4]\ 066 256170; m 081 278 5667. With a retail outlet in the centre of town (hidden behind market stalls opposite Spar), this large, thriving co-operative supplies many of the curio markets further south, including in Okahandja. It is worth a visit, although most of the carvings on display are larger items such as tables & chairs.

Ncumcara Community Forestry Craft Centre [522 A2] m 081 294 7986, 081 285 6594. 30km south of Rundu; for further details, see page 524.

Other practicalities
There are several 24-hour **fuel stations** in town, including the main Shell, Engen and Total stations, all of which have shops, and a number of **garages**, including Auto Body Works [525 B4] in the industrial area (\ *066 256841*), Dunlop Tyre Services, and the more local TrenTyre [525 D4] and Tyre Rack [525 G3]. For **banks**, there are branches of Bank Windhoek, Standard and FNB.

Health and safety
For **medical** needs, Rundu Pharmacy (\ *066 255849*) is in the centre of Rundu Mall [525 D2], with another, Kavango Pharmacy [525 F4] (\ *066 255602*) further along. Along with a medical practice, Rundu Medical Centre [525 D2] (*3 Eugene Kakakuru St;* \ *066 267233;* m *081 434 4004*) houses Riverside Pharmacy (\ *066 267225*), and a dentist (\ *066 267664*). The **hospital** [525 D2] and **ambulance** services are on \ *066 265500*, and the police [525 F4] on \ *066 266300*.

What to see and do
While Rundu itself lacks any obvious attraction, the Kavango River more than makes up for it, so if the water is high enough (usually January to October), it's worth making time for a river trip.

On the Angolan bank, which at this point is generally steeper and more densely vegetated than its Namibian counterpart, numerous small villages line the river, with men, women and children constantly up and down the tracks to bathe and wash clothes. Tall reeds line the banks on the Namibian side, with villagers crossing between the two countries in mokoros.

In excess of 400 species of birds have been recorded along this part of the river, making it a haven for birders. The African fish eagle is now breeding well since being hunted during the Angolan war. From its vantage point in the tall trees overlooking the river, it looks down on a domain that boasts several species of kingfisher (including the pied, giant, malachite and woodland), and two of jacana, as well as the swamp oboe, the wire-tailed swallow and a range of colourful bee-eaters. One evening boat trip here in March yielded all of these, as well as Senegal coucal, black-crowned night heron, common sandpiper, wagtails, black-headed heron, little bittern and pygmy geese.

Hippos, too, have returned, though are less welcome to the villagers than to visitors seeking out the region's wildlife.

Sunset cruises are run by several of the lodges, with birdwatching trips a speciality of some. Typically, a trip will involve a slow meander against the current, then a leisurely drift back. For the more active, fishing for tigerfish or bream draws plenty of hopeful anglers.

Mbunza Living Museum [525 A3] (**m** *081 215 2496;* **e** *contact@lcfn.info; www.lcfn.info/mbunza;* ☉ *08.00–17.00 daily; admission N$150–280 pp*) Many lodges in the area support this museum, about 14km west of Rundu on the road

THE CAPRIVI STRIP

Although, administratively, the boundary between the Kavango and Zambezi (formerly Caprivi) regions lies halfway across Bwabwata National Park (formerly the Caprivi National Park), the term 'Caprivi Strip' refers to the entire 450km strip of land that thrusts east between Angola and Botswana from Namibia's northeast corner, and continues to the Zambian border to the east of Katima Mulilo. While the Zambezi Region, lying at the eastern half of the Strip, was named as such in 2013 in a continuing drive to reclaim places evoking an unhappy colonial history, it's likely that the Caprivi Strip itself will be known as such for some time yet.

HISTORY OF THE STRIP On the map, the Caprivi Strip appears to be a strange appendage of Namibia rather than a part of it. It forms a strategic corridor of land linking Namibia to Zimbabwe and Zambia, but seems somehow detached from the rest of the country. The region's history explains why.

When Germany annexed South West Africa (now Namibia) in 1884, it prompted British fears that they might try to link up with the Boers, in the Transvaal, thus driving a wedge between these territories and cutting off the Cape from Rhodesia. Out of fear, the British negotiated an alliance with Khama, a powerful Tswana king, and proclaimed the Protectorate of Bechuanaland – the forerunner of modern Botswana. At that time, this included the present-day Caprivi Strip. Geographically this made sense if the main reason for Britain's claim was to block Germany's expansion into central Africa.

Meanwhile, off Africa's east coast, Germany laid claim to Zanzibar. This was the end game of the colonial 'scramble for Africa', which set the stage for the Berlin Conference of July 1890. Then these two colonial powers sat down in Europe to reorganise their African possessions with strokes of a pen.

to Hakusembe River Lodge (page 527). Its interactive programmes show visitors traditional Kavango culture, from arts and crafts to fishing, bushwalking and singing and dancing, and has received excellent feedback – and there's no need to book.

RUNDU TO DIVUNDU: 204KM While the tarred B8 is straight, it has a lot of potholes on extended stretches, plus livestock wandering across it, so you'll need to remain alert and drive particularly carefully. The equivalent section of the old road makes a pleasant if considerably slower drive, much of it surrounded by green, irrigated fields with the Kavango River as a backdrop. Again, do watch out for goats and cattle on the road.

Where to stay Should you wish to break the journey, there are a few places not far from the main road and close to the river, listed below from west to east. Others in this area are Muramba River Lodge, Kavango Bush Camp, Tatella Guesthouse and Moyo's Guesthouse.

Mukuku Rest Camp [522 B2] (3 chalets, camping) m 085 574 1520, 081 245 6633; e mukuku11@gmail.com. Roughly 58km east of Rundu, turn left off the B8 towards Mupapama, then right at the T-junction on to the D3403, & left again at the signpost for the restcamp, following the track to the river. This small owner-run camp has just 3 rustic, brick-&-thatch self-catering chalets, each with twin beds & a private veranda, plus a kitchen with fridge; 1 is a larger family chalet. There are also shaded campsites with hot showers & a pool. Meals & drinks are served in the

Britain agreed to sever the Caprivi from Bechuanaland and give control of it to Germany, to add to their province of South West Africa. Germany hoped to use it to access the Zambezi's trade routes to the east, and named it after the German Chancellor of the time, Count George Leo von Caprivi, who apparently never set foot in Namibia (making the later name change even more understandable). In return for this (and also the territory of Heligoland in the North Sea), Germany ceded control of Zanzibar to Britain, and agreed to redefine South West Africa's eastern border with Britain's Bechuanaland.

At the end of World War I the Caprivi was reincorporated into Bechuanaland, but in 1929 it was again returned to South West Africa, then under South African rule. Hence it became part of Namibia.

More recently, during the late 1990s, cross-border skirmishes between Angolans and Namibians destabilised this whole area. Problems arose when Namibia's ruling SWAPO party went to the aid of Angola's MPLA (Popular Movement for the Liberation of Angola), in their civil conflict against the rebel UNITA party. An agreement between the Namibian government and the MPLA allowed Angolan troops to attack their rivals from Namibian soil, thus bringing the conflict over the border into Namibia. In 1999, the situation came to a head when members of a French family travelling through the Caprivi Region unwittingly became caught up in the conflict and were killed. As a result, the decision was taken that any traffic crossing the Caprivi Strip could proceed only in armed convoy. Thus, for the next few years, two armed convoys a day escorted all vehicles travelling between Kongola and Rundu.

Although the road across the Caprivi Strip is now safe, travellers are still advised to stick to well-travelled routes and not to venture off-road to the north where, in certain areas that are barred to public access, unexploded ordnance is still being cleared.

21

main area by convivial hosts. *N$870/900 sgl/dbl; camping N$100 pp.* **$–$$$**

🏠 **Shankara Lodge** [522 B2] (6 bungalows, camping) 📞066 258616; m 085 554 8051; e shankara@gmail.com. About 85km east of Rundu, this would make a reasonable stopover to break a journey. To get there, turn left off the B8 at ✪ 17°59.791'S, 20°30.202'E (there is no sign), follow the tarred road about 3km to the T-junction, then turn left again on to the D3402; the entrance is about 1km on your right. Simple but clean 6-bed family bungalows are set in well-kept gardens. Each has a kitchen with fridge/freezer & braai facilities, or meals are available at the lodge by prior arrangement. 2-bed bungalows are closer to the river, & there are also 15 camping pitches with ablutions & power. There is a large pool, & a small boat with outboard engine can be hired (*N$350/hr*). *Bungalow N$550–2,150 (2/6 people); camping N$100 pp.* **$–$$$**

🏠 **Kayova River Lodge** [522 B2] (8 chalets, 12 tents, camping) 📞066 258212; e bookings@kayovariverlodge.com; www.kayovariverlodge.com. This pleasant lodge owned by the Kayova Community Development Foundation lies 110km east of Rundu, following the signposts on to the D3411 & the D3024. The chalets are spread in a row in simple gardens & river views. With wood floors & high thatched ceilings, they all have DSTV, fridges, tea/coffee facilities & twin or dbl beds with mosquito nets. 2 inter-leading chalets work well for a family. Overlooking the river are large safari tents, simply but well furnished with stone floors, en-suite bathrooms & AC, & a big open space features 12 camping pitches (with power, water & braai, & shared ablution blocks) that were being renovated in 2018. The bar &, à la carte restaurant, with Wi-Fi, are near a small pool. Fishing & birdwatching trips are available, & – more unusually – yoga. *Bungalow N$605–663/1,210–1,326 sgl/dbl.* **$–$$$**

🏠 **Shamvura Camp** [522 B2] (1 cottage, 4 tents, camping) 📞066 264007; m 081 241 7473; e shamvura@iway.na; www.shamvuracamp.blogspot.com. Set high above the river, Shamvura is 120km from Rundu. From the B8, turn left on to the D3411 opposite the Khaudum turn-off (✪ *18°03.152'S, 20°46.346'E*), or – if coming from Divundu – turn right after 80km on to the D3438 (✪ *18°03.305'S, 20°53.518'E*), then follow the signs for 12km. The central bar with DSTV & pool

are home to both a goat & occasionally orphaned otters, as well as owners Mark & Charlie Paxton. Accommodation is modest, either a timber-&-reed family cottage on a raised platform sleeping up to 6, with fridge/freezer, small cooker, crockery & cutlery, or well-spaced 2–4-bed Meru tents, each named for its own private area under a tree with WC/shower & braai; 1 also has a freezer/stove, etc, like the cottage. Meals are available at the lodge. Campers have 6 pitches sharing a double ablution block. Free firewood & water are provided, along with free Wi-Fi by reception. Activities include guided walks & birding (412 species recorded to date), small-boat fishing (*from N$400/hr*), canoeing & mokoro trips (high water only) & microlight flights. Day drives with a specialist guide can be organised to Mahango (*from N$4,000*) & occasionally Khaudum (*from N$2,400*) national parks. *Cottage/tent from N$550/400 pp; camping N$120 pp.* **$–$$$**

🏠 **Mobola Island Lodge** [522 B2] (5 bungalows, camping) m 081 230 3281; e mobolalodge@gmail.com; www.mobola-lodge.com. Owned & run by Alexander Both, this lovely self-catering lodge lies 175km east of Rundu. From the B8, turn left on the D3415 for 4km, right at the T-junction on to the D3402 for a further 11km, then follow the signs down a sandy track to the lodge. The 3 dbl & 2 family bungalows (sleeping 4) are well equipped, with kitchenette & outdoor braai. Each has a terrace overlooking the Kavango River & beautiful gardens full of bougainvillea. There are also 6 camping pitches with shared ablutions, power, water & light. The pretty pool has a waterfall pumped from the river & there's an island bar reached by a small bridge, perfect for sundowners. There's no restaurant, but pre-ordered b/fasts (*N$150 pp*) can be brought to your room & braai packs are available. Boat trips, fishing & village visits can be arranged. *Bungalow from N$1,300 dbl; family from N$2,600; camping N$150 pp.* **$$–$$$**

☀ 🏠 **RiverDance** [522 C2] (6 rooms, camping) 📞066 258401; m 081 124 3255; e reservations@riverdance.com.na; www.riverdance.com.na. RiverDance is 180km east of Rundu, 4km further along the D3402 from Mobola. Stylishly elegant & relaxing, this lovely lodge changed hands in mid 2018 & is now owned & managed by Pascale & Chris, who aim to continue ensuring that the local people benefit from the lodge's success. All staff are from the nearby village of Mamono & 20% of lodge profits go to community projects. The bar & restaurant area is located on decking high above the river, with vast cream sofas & a small pool nearby. Most rooms are on stilts above the river, with wood panelling & glass interiors, & private decked terraces. Imaginatively designed, 2 can be converted to family rooms & 3 have separate private bathrooms on the deck with showers & free-standing baths. Another 2-room family unit is being added. The 4 grass campsites all have private facilities including kitchenettes & bathrooms. Campers can order pizzas or, along with non-residents, can book excellent meals in the restaurant, although lodge guests have priority (*lunch/3-course dinner N$115/325*). Activities include game drives to Bwabwata National Park (*N$550 pp*), sunrise & sunset cruises (*N$400/350*), fishing (*N$300/hr for 2 people*), island walks (*N$250*) & village visits (*N$200*) that give a real insight into local life. *DBB N$1,530/2,550 sgl/dbl; camping N$150 pp (max 4 per site).* **$$–$$$$**

DIVUNDU/BAGANI As the main B8 approaches Divundu and Bagani, which are really little more than road junctions, it passes through several villages before reaching a 24-hour Engen garage, which also has a surprisingly well-stocked supermarket that sells made-up rolls and cold drinks. The local bakery is just around the corner. The Intercape bus between Windhoek and Victoria Falls stops here northbound at 13.00 on Monday, Wednesday and Friday, with southbound buses at 22.40 on Wednesday, Friday and Sunday.

DRIVING ACROSS THE STRIP AND OPEN AFRICA ROUTES

The main B8 from Rundu to Katima is a tarred road that runs parallel to the old gravel highway. While the old road is scenic in parts, it is rutted and dusty: not for those in a hurry. A word of warning about the tar road, though: don't underestimate the distances. Driving in one day from Rundu to Mudumu, from Popa Falls to Katima Mulilo, or from Mudumu to Kasane or Victoria Falls, are the maximum distances that you should attempt as part of a normal holiday trip:

Rundu to Divundu: 204km (page 531)
Divundu to Kongola and the Kwando River: 198km (page 544)
Kongola to Katima Mulilo: 110km (page 552)

The South African initiative Open Africa has established almost 70 routes across the continent to encourage tourism and development in rural regions. Member lodges, businesses and conservancies work together on common conservation and development aims, and all have a strong ethos of responsible, sustainable tourism.

Crossing the Kavango/Zambezi regions is the Four Rivers Route (named for the Zambezi, Okavango, Kwando and Chobe river systems), which is subdivided into three. The Kavango Open Africa Route runs roughly from Mpungu in the west to Divundu in the east, incorporating Mahango and, to the south, Khaudum National Park. This continues as the Caprivi Wetlands Paradise Route east to the Ngoma border. Here it links up with the Four Corners Experience, which stretches from Ngoma, through Botswana's Chobe National Park to Kasane (south of Impalila Island) and on to the Victoria Falls. An excellent map of the route, with information on its members and the area, is available in local lodges, or contact Mark Paxton, owner of Shamvura Camp (see opposite; m *081 167 0747*; e *mw.paxton@gmail.com*); or Simone Micheletti (m *081 147 7798*). Also check www.openafrica.org for further information.

DIVUNDU TO POPA FALLS AND THE BOTSWANA BORDER A few hundred yards before the bridge over the Kavango, where the new road meets the old, there's a junction. The road to the right – the C48/D3430 – leads to Botswana, via Popa Falls and the Mahango Core Area of Bwabwata National Park. Note that the only fuel in this area is on the west side of the bridge. Most travellers wouldn't choose to stay in Divundu, but if you find yourself short of a place for the night, then try the **Divundu Guest House** (m *081 148 5324;* e *Peter@divundu-gh.com.na;* **$$$**), which has en-suite rooms and a restaurant.

Popa Falls Game Park (☉ *sunrise–sunset; 2WD access; admission N$20 pp; no charge if dining/drinking at restaurant*) Popa Falls lie at a point where the Kavango River breaks up and drops 2.5m over a rocky section, caused by the first of five geological faults. Essentially they are a series of rapids, pretty rather than spectacular; even the warden at the entrance admits that many visitors are disappointed. Beyond the falls, the Kavango begins gradually to spread out across the Kalahari's sands until eventually, as the Okavango River in Botswana, it forms its remarkable inland delta.

The area by the riverside at Popa Falls is thickly vegetated with tall riverine trees and lush green shrubs, which encourage waterbirds and a variety of small reptiles. Footbridges have been built between some of the islands, and it's worth spending a morning island-hopping among the rushing channels, or walking upstream a little where there's a good view of the river before it flows over the rapids. In a few hours you can see all of this tiny reserve, and have a good chance of spotting a leguvaan (water monitor), a snake or two, and many different frogs. The various birds include cormorants with a captivating technique of underwater fishing.

Getting there and away The falls are right on the Kavango's western bank, south of the Divundu Bridge, near Bagani. From the main B8, take the road signposted to Botswana just west of the Bwabwata National Park; the reserve is on the left after about 3.5km, immediately beside the road. Note that the gates usually close at sunset, so if you're planning on staying the night make sure you arrive before dark.

Where to stay and eat Popa Falls Resort sits directly beside the falls, but there are several options nearby, all clearly signposted. They are listed below from north to south.

Popa Falls Resort [535 B2] (20 cabins, camping) Book via the NWR (page 103); lodge ☎066 259023, or take pot luck. This neat, organised camp right next to the falls has been substantially refurbished, costing some N$40 million. The result is contemporary & stylish: very different in character from most NWR camps . The à la carte restaurant & bar (☉ 07.00–09.00, noon–14.00 & 18.00–21.00 daily; lunch/dinner N$210/230) close to the river & swimming pool looks smart & modern, though feedback suggests that the service & food don't quite live up to the ambience. Right by the falls but quite a walk from the main camp is the trendy Jetty Bar on stilts, although opening times are vague. Wi-Fi is in the main area.

Popa's excellent accommodation – 10 river cabins & 10 chalets (4 dubbed 'luxury') are similar in style, all with thatched roofs, private terraces, &

AC, TV, safe, fridge, tea/coffee facilities, minibar & kitchenettes. Campers have the choice of 7 individual pitches with power, light, water & shared ablutions, while for overlanders there are 3 separate, larger camping areas a healthy distance away. Activities include boat trips to the rapids (from N$300 pp) & game drives to Mahango (am/pm N$450 pp; night drive N$550). Beware of the mosquitoes, which are numerous. From N$1,130/2,260 sgl/dbl; camping N$140 pp. **$–$$$$**

Divava Okavango Lodge & Spa [535 C2] (20 chalets) ☎066 259005; e info@divava.com; www.divava.com. High on the bank of a bend in the river, some 2km downstream of Popa Falls, Divava has a stunning location. Each of its thatched chalets, some built high in the trees close to the river, & others further back with open river views, has a split-level bedroom with a large terrace. Furnished

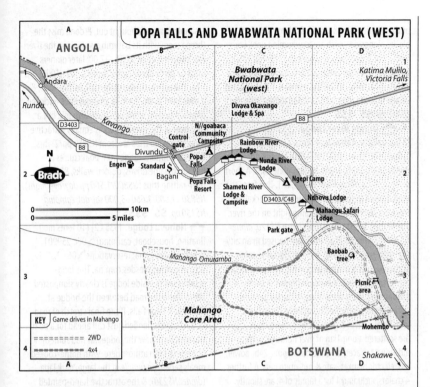

ANGOLA

Bwabwata
National Park
(west)

Katima Mulilo,
Victoria Falls

Andara

Runda

Kavango

D3403

B8

Divava Okavango
Lodge & Spa

B8

N//goabaca
Community
Campsite

Control
gate

Divundu

Rainbow River
Lodge

Engen

Standard

Popa
Falls

Nunda River
Lodge

N

Bradt

Bagani

Popa Falls
Resort

Shametu River
Lodge &
Campsite

Ngepi Camp

D3403/C48

Ndhovu Lodge

0 ————— 10km
0 ————— 5 miles

Mahango Omuramba

Park gate

Mahangu Safari
Lodge

Baobab
tree

Picnic
area

KEY

Game drives in Mahango

========== 2WD
■■■■■■■■■■ 4x4

Mahango
Core Area

Mohembo

BOTSWANA

Shakawe

in contemporary style with extremely comfortable beds & luxurious linen, they are equipped with AC, minibar, safe & tea/coffee-making facilities. Bathrooms have both a free-standing bath with a view & indoor & outdoor showers. Rooms have direct-dial phones & mobile coverage, & there is Wi-Fi in reception. The bar & restaurant (serving a 5-course dinner) are further down the bank, on a long terrace in the trees – or you can arrange a private meal on board their safari boat).

Next to the swimming pool (with plans to be heated) is The Spa, offering facials, massages & manicures: the treatment rondavels, sauna & steam room probably have the best views at the lodge. Activities include boat trips, fishing, game drives in Mahango & a traditional village tour. Staff are friendly & professional, but the many steps at this lodge may make it difficult for those with limited mobility. *DBB from N$2,800/4,300 sgl/dbl Dec–Jun, to N$3,720/5,800 Jul–Oct.* **$$$$$**

🏠 Shametu River Lodge & Campsite [535 C2] (15 rooms, camping) ↘066 259035; m 081 653 1901; e shameturiverlodge@iway. na; www.shameturiverlodge.com. Next to Divava Okavango Lodge (see opposite), just 7km from

Divundu off the C48/D3403, Shametu has 5 'luxury' tents on stilts & 4 slightly larger, more secluded 'luxury' chalets right on the river's edge, overlooking Popa Falls. Further back, 7 standard chalets (2 creating a family chalet) look over the gardens. All have en-suite showers, tea & coffee facilities & mosi nets over twin/dbl beds, but the 'luxury' are lighter & have better views. 6 immaculate campsites have private, thatch-&-cane ablution areas & hot showers, kitchenette, braai, firepit, power & water.

By the river & pool is a large deck, then up the hill is the bar, lounge & restaurant, furnished with dark wood & local carvings. Attentive owners Louis & Amori Gerber grow their own organic vegetables for use in their restaurant. Activities include boat & mokoro trips, fishing, birding walks, village visits & game drives. *N$1,100–1,310/1,740–1,970 sgl/dbl; DBB N$1,410–1,620/2,360–2,590; camping N$205 pp.* **$$–$$$$**

🏠 Rainbow River Lodge [535 C2] (24 chalets, camping) ↘066 259067; m 081 210 6678; e info@ rainbowriverlodgenamibia.com. About 1km from Divava, this simple lodge has basic but neat en-suite chalets, each with standing fan & mosi nets. Beautifully sited on the riverbank are 13 camping

21

pitches (with power & water) & 2 large ablution blocks, alongside which are a swimming pool, bar, restaurant & deck (*lunch/dinner N$$115/130–250*). Overlanders are welcome, & Wi-Fi is available. There are 2hr boat trips (*N$290 pp, min 6*) & a 1½hr guided village tour (*N$100*). *N$770/1,380 sgl/dbl; camping N$150 pp.* **$$–$$$**

❋ 🏠 **Nunda River Lodge** [535 C2] (8 bungalows, 4 chalets, 7 tents, camping) 📞066 259093; m 081 310 1730; e bookings@ nundaonline.com; www.nundaonline.com. A short drive from Rainbow River Lodge, & 1.4km from the road, Nunda (named for the fruit of the jackalberry tree) is a lovely owner-run camp right on the river. The lounge & restaurant/bar (*lunch N$120, dinner N$260*) – with Wi-Fi access – are housed in an airy, thatched stone building with comfortable sofas, scattered rugs & a large deck with sweeping views across the river – & attendant hippos. A pretty swimming pool is set among colourful gardens.

Comfortably furnished bungalows (thatched with brick, canvas & glass) & large Meru tents are scattered along 1km of river frontage, with individual terraces, en-suite bathrooms, 24hr power, fan, electric blanket, safe & mosquito nets. A further 4 chalets, including 1 for a family of 4, are slightly smaller & not river-facing. Sharing ablutions, each camping pitch has a braai area, water & electricity; subject to availability, campers may dine in the restaurant. As well as boat cruises (*N$255–275 pp*), game drives (*N$490–550*) & village walks (*N$155*), traditional dancing, mokoro trips & bird walks can be arranged. *DBB N$1,600–1,890/2,620–2,900 sgl/dbl; camping N$150 pp.* **$$–$$$$**

❋ 🏠 **Ngepi Camp** [535 C2] (12 tree houses, 3 bush huts, 2 tents, camping) 📞066 259903; m 081 202 8200; e bookings@ngepicamp.com; www.ngepicamp.com. Ngepi is 4km off the road, signposted between Divava & Ndhovu. From its inception as a sprawling, grassy campsite by the river under some shady trees, Ngepi seems to have grown in line with the enthusiasm of its owner Mark Adcock, its managers & staff, with some quirky touches that add colour & humour to the place. It's fun & lively, with something of a party atmosphere. Aside from the campsite, with 21 pitches & various ablution blocks, there are en-suite bush huts with their own braai areas, & colourful if pricier dbl, twin & family tree houses with roll-down reed walls, mosi nets & open-air showers with great river views. It's all very eco-friendly

– simple, but well thought out; & don't miss the throne room with its bathtub overlooking the river! The kitchen is open 07.30–17.00; later dinners must be prebooked (*lunch/dinner N$65–100/210*).

For the active, there's volleyball, frisbee-golf, & a river 'pool' in the form of an innovative enclosed pontoon tied up alongside the riverbank, but a cool beer at the riverside bar is equally attractive. Guided mokoro trips are from N$250 pp/2½hrs, & further options range from boat cruises & fishing to game drives, guided walks, & dragon river-rafting trips (*N$800/1,500 pp day/overnight*). *N$830–1,500/1,660–3,000 sgl/dbl; camping N$150 pp.* **$$–$$$$**

🏠 **Ndhovu Lodge** [535 C2] (10 tents inc 1 floating, houseboat, camping) 📞066 259901; e ndhovu@iway.na; reservations 📞061 224712; e reservations@resdes.com.na. This long-established riverside lodge is clearly signposted 20km along the road between the bridge at Divundu & Popa Falls. If the final stretch of road to the lodge is flooded, just call ahead for a boat transfer. Until now the lodge has had something of a guest-farm atmosphere, with home-cooked meals served *en famille* in the large, dark lapa (*dinner N$230*), & the attractive hand-painted crockery on sale in the curio shop. But with new owners in Jun 2018, changes may well be afoot.

Simple Meru-style walk-in tents, facing the river, have twin or dbl beds, & an en-suite bath or shower at the back. Rather different is a tent on a floating pontoon, its large dbl bed encased in a lace mosquito net, & the shower & chemical loo en suite. Mains electricity is backed up by solar power. Camping, limited to 1 group at a time (*max 10 people*), must be prebooked. There's a small pool shaded by trees, while a wooden deck over the river is a good place to chill. Activities include boat trips (*N$285 pp*) & 4x4 excursions into the nearby Bwabwata NP, predominantly to the Mahango area. *N$545/840 sgl/dbl (plus park fees). DBB N$1,360–1,540/2,720–3,080 sgl/dbl; camping N$200 pp.* **$$–$$$$**

🏠 **Mahangu Safari Lodge** [535 C2] (15 bungalows, 6 tents, camping) 📞066 259037; e mahangulodge@iway.na; www.mahangu.com. na. The approach across a neat grassy lawn gives a slightly suburban feel to this thatched lodge, with its lime-green walls & reed fences. Situated adjacent to Ndhovu (bear right rather than left at the entrance), it was opened at the end of the

1990s, with German owner Ralf Walter aiming to make even the most nervous visitor feel entirely secure. Green-painted brick-built bungalows – including 3 for families – face the river; each is en suite, with animal-print fabrics, AC, safe & 24hr electricity. Camping is on the riverfront, with power, water & shared ablution blocks. Meru-style tents are backed by brick-built bathrooms with solid doors to keep out creepy crawlies.

Inside, numerous game trophies adorn the walls, so it's not to everyone's taste, but most meals (*lunch/dinner N$130–190/290*) are served outside beneath mature jackalberry trees, where the riverside bar has draught beer on tap. Wi-Fi is available in central areas. Nearby, a high tower affords views across the river, while below, a couple of decks shelter under thatch, & the 2 pools (including a floating river pool) are shaded by a marula tree. Activities include game drives to the Mahango area of Bwabwata NP (*N$535–580 pp*), boat trips (*N$250 pp*) & fishing (*N$500/hr up to 3 people*). DBB N$1,270–1,460/2,280–2,600 sgl/dbl; camping N$190 pp. **$$–$$$$**

⚐ N//goabaca Community Campsite
[535 B2] (4 pitches) The turn-off for N//goabaca (see page 502 for explanation of obliques) is 1km east of the bridge, & the campsite is 4km from the road – the last 500m along a sandy track. There are no reliable contact details, so would-be campers simply turn up & hope for space. Each of the private pitches has flush WC, hot shower & a water tap; 2 have viewing decks, & all overlook Popa Falls from the eastern bank. The site is run by Kxoe Bushmen, many of whom worked as trackers & scouts for the South African Army during the war, but have subsequently been economically & politically marginalised. Tourism cannot only pay them, but also encourages them to put a higher value on their traditional skills & bushcraft, so support them if you can. N$120 pp. **$**

MAHANGO CORE AREA (⏲ *sunrise–sunset; 2WD/4x4; N$40 pp, plus N$10 per vehicle; no charge if you're driving straight through on the main road*) This small reserve, formerly Mahango National Park and now part of Bwabwata National Park, is tucked away in a corner of the Caprivi Strip, bounded to the south by the Botswana border. It is bisected by one of the main roads between Namibia and Botswana, a wide gravel artery from which two game drives explore the area.

Though forming its eastern boundary, the Kavango River is also the focus of this reserve. The eastern loop road passes beside the river and is normally the better one for game. Here the river forms channels between huge, permanent papyrus reed-beds. Adjacent are extensive floodplain areas, where you're quite likely to spot red lechwe or even sable, a relatively scarce but beautiful antelope which seems to thrive here.

Beside the floodplain, on the higher and drier land of the bank, are wide belts of wild date palm-forest, as well as the lush riverine vegetation that you'd expect. Further from the river are dry woodlands and acacia thickets, dotted with a few large baobabs. This rich variety of greenery attracts an impressive range of animals, including the water-loving buffalo, elephant, sable, reedbuck, bushbuck and waterbuck, and the more specialist red lechwe and sitatunga. Good numbers of hippo and crocodile are also present.

Mahango is a great favourite with birdwatchers; more species can be found here than in any other park in Namibia. This variation should come as no surprise, as the reserve has one of Namibia's few wetland habitats, adjacent to large stretches of pristine Kalahari sandveld. Thus, many water-loving ducks, geese, herons, plovers, egrets, kingfishers and various waders occur here, along with the dry-country birds that you'll find in the rest of Namibia. Okavango specialities like the slaty egret can sometimes be spotted, and for many birds – including the lesser jacana, coppery-tailed coucal and racket-tailed roller – Mahango marks the western limit of their distributions. Among the larger species, the uncommon western banded snake eagles occur, though black-chested and brown snake eagles are more frequently seen. Similarly, the park's Pel's fishing owls are rare compared with its marsh, giant eagle and spotted owls.

When to visit As with most parks, the game varies with the season. The dry season, July to October, tends to be better as the riverfront is at its busiest with animals drinking. Sometimes the park is inundated with elephants and buffalo. During the summer rains (from November to April) the big game here can be disappointing and, as the vegetation is still thick, other animals can be elusive. However, summer migrants like the exquisite carmine bee-eaters are then in residence, making this the perfect time for birdwatching here.

Where to stay There are no facilities in Mahango itself, so most people stay in one of the lodges or restcamps between the park and Popa Falls (page 534).

Game drives There are two game-drive loops to explore, both branching from the main road about 800m south of the northern entrance to the park. The better, eastern road, which is good gravel, soon overlooks the floodplain, passing a picnic spot before returning to the main road farther south. The western course, which can offer good sightings of plains game, is suitable for high-clearance 4x4s only. It follows a sandy *omuramba* away from the river, before splitting after about 10.7km, where the right fork continues along the *omuramba*, terminating at a waterhole, while the left rejoins the main road 19km later.

EXCURSIONS INTO BOTSWANA

As you drive across the Caprivi Strip, Botswana's Okavango Delta can feel so near, and yet so far. However, just south of Mahango, within Botswana, are several small camps which are close enough to reach while crossing the Caprivi Strip. They offer a taste of the Okavango Delta, within easy reach of Namibia.

At the southern end of Mahango lies Namibia's Mohembo border post (⏰ 06.00–18.00 *daily*), followed by the Botswana customs and immigration post. These are generally quiet posts, and staff on both sides seem pleasant and efficient, but you'll still need to allow around half an hour to clear the formalities in each direction. There are various forms to be filled out on both sides, so it's worth collecting these as you drive into Botswana, to save time on the return trip. In addition to the standard information required at border posts (passport details, vehicle registration, etc), you'll need to know your vehicle engine and chassis numbers, which are usually shown on the tax disk on the front windscreen and on the cross-border document you should have with a rental vehicle; if it's not clear, the longest number is probably the chassis number. The same information is required separately by the police, who rather unexpectedly may not be in uniform. On the Botswana side, there's a road levy of N$200/P12. When returning to Namibia, you may be charged for a CBC (cross-border charges) permit (*N$180 for a private car*), depending on where your vehicle was registered, and whether the rental company originally purchased a single- or multiple-entry permit.

Note that prices in this section are in either Botswana pula (£1 = P13.69; US$1 = P10.83; €1 = P12.08 in May 2019), or US dollars; many places will not accept Namibian dollars.

MOHEMBO BORDER AND FERRY From the border, the road leads shortly to a T-junction, about 13km north of Shakawe. To continue to Shakawe, turn right at the junction. A left turn takes you to the (free) Mohembo ferry which crosses the Okavango, and usually takes a few vehicles at a time. Expect to find a lot of people waiting around here – some to cross, others to meet those who have crossed, or to

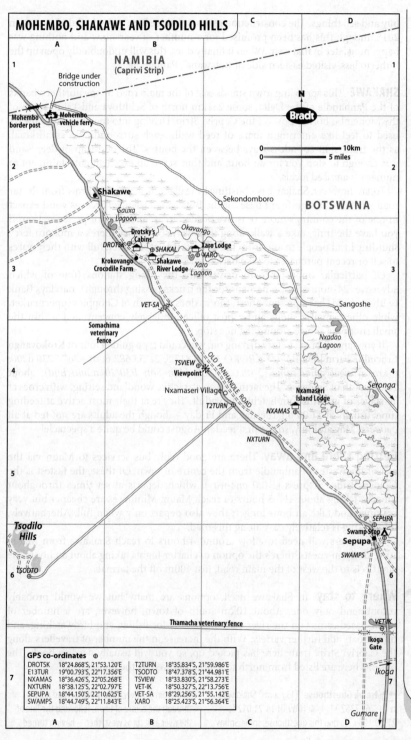

MOHEMBO, SHAKAWE AND TSODILO HILLS

NAMIBIA
(Caprivi Strip)

BOTSWANA

Bridge under
construction

Mohembo
border post

Mohembo
vehicle ferry

Shakawe

Sekondomboro

Gauxa
Lagoon

Drotsky's
Cabins

DROTSK

Okavango

Xaro Lodge

XARO

SHAKAL

Krokovango
Crocodile Farm

Shakawe
River Lodge

Xaro
Lagoon

Sangoshe

VET-SA

Somachima
veterinary
fence

Nxadao
Lagoon

TSVIEW
Viewpoint

OLD PANHANDLE ROAD

Seronga

Nxamaseri Village

Nxamaseri
Island Lodge

T2TURN

NXAMAS

NXTURN

**Tsodilo
Hills**

SEPUPA

Swamp Stop

Sepupa

TSODTO

SWAMPS

VET-IK

Ikoga
Gate

Thamacha veterinary fence

Ikoga

GPS co-ordinates ⊕

DROTSK	18°24.868'S, 21°53.120'E	T2TURN	18°35.834'S, 21°59.986'E
E13TUR	19°00.793'S, 22°17.356'E	TSODTO	18°47.378'S, 21°44.981'E
NXAMAS	18°36.426'S, 22°05.268'E	TSVIEW	18°33.830'S, 21°58.273'E
NXTURN	18°38.125'S, 22°02.797'E	VET-IK	18°50.327'S, 22°13.756'E
SEPUPA	18°44.150'S, 22°10.625'E	VET-SA	18°29.256'S, 21°55.142'E
SWAMPS	18°44.749'S, 22°11.843'E	XARO	18°25.423'S, 21°56.364'E

Gumare

0 ——————— 10km
0 ——————— 5 miles

N

Bradt

21

buy and sell things. The construction of a new bridge here was scheduled to start in 2018, though this has been promised for a number of years now and nothing was happening later in that year. When it finally does, this will undoubtedly open up the hitherto less-visited eastern side of Botswana's Panhandle.

SHAKAWE This sprawling town stands east of the main road on the northern banks of the Panhandle of the Delta, some 281km north of Sehithwa and 13km south of the Mohembo border post on the Caprivi Strip. Driving into the old village always used to feel like entering a maze of reed walls, each surrounding a small kraal, as the track split countless ways between the houses. The odd trap of deep sand was enough to stop you for an hour, and thus serve up excellent entertainment to numerous amused locals.

Today, however, Shakawe is a bustling little place. Just a stone's throw from the tar road you'll find a significant base for the Botswana Defence Force, as you'd expect in one of the country's more sensitive border areas, and a major police station. If you have the time, take a walk along the river; sometimes there's a mokoro ferry shuttling local people to and from the eastern side of the river, full with their wares to sell or recent purchases to take back home.

Of particular importance to drivers are the filling stations (one of which advertises 24-hour service, perhaps for the trucks passing through). Barclays Bank (with an ATM) has a presence here, too, as does a branch of Choppies supermarket, while other, smaller shops and a post office are largely concentrated within the small shopping centre around the bus stop.

If you fancy a break before driving on, you could try a guided tour of **Krokovango Crocodile Farm** [539 B3] (⊕ *KROKO 18°25.817'S, 21°53.682'E;* m *+267 7230 6200;* e *krokovango@gmail.com;* ⊕ *08.00–17.00 Mon–Sat; P30/20 adult/child*), about 10km south of Shakawe. The farm is in an attractive woodland setting, with crocs at all stages of growth from hatchling to adult. They're at their most active at feeding time, usually at 11.00 on Tuesday and Friday – though the adults are not fed at all between May and July, so the first feed in August could be quite a spectacle!

Getting there and away There are good daily bus services to Maun via the rest of the western Panhandle from the centre of town. Of these, the fastest is the Golden Bridge Express (*P100 one-way*), which departs at set times throughout the day, taking about 4½–5 hours to reach Maun. Minibuses are cheaper but very cramped and take an hour longer; they also depart only when full. Alternatively, hitchhiking is relatively easy along this road.

Self-drivers will need to allow around 4 hours to reach Shakawe from Maun. And for fly-in guests, there's the option of charter flights taking about an hour. The airstrip is to the west of the main road, just 400m off the tarmac.

Where to stay In Shakawe itself, options are many but we would probably recommend only one. About 10km south of town, however, are a number of water-based camps on the river catering mainly for fishing and birdwatching, and houseboats add further variety. With the increase in the number of travellers along the Caprivi Strip, trade here has picked up, so you will usually need to book. The options here are listed from north to south, followed by the houseboats.

Hawk Guesthouse (13 rooms) Shakawe; m + 267 7352 3114; ⊕ HAWKH 18°21.012'S, 21°50.108'E. To find this guesthouse, some 5mins' walk from the river, follow the tar road north through the centre of town, following the line of the river as it turns west, then – having turned away from the river – it's on the left after another 1.5km. En-suite sgl & dbl rooms are arranged on 3 sides of a small courtyard with a walled enclosure. It's hardly picturesque, but they're clean & come with mosi nets, a kettle & satellite TV, plus 6 have AC, satellite TV & a fridge. You can pitch a tent here if you need (though there's no designated site), & there's also a pool & restaurant. *P364/460 sgl/dbl; camping P100 pp.* **$–$$**

🏠 **Drotsky's Cabins** [539 B3] (10 chalets, camping) 📞+ 267 683 0226, +267 496 8638; e drotsky@btcmail.co.bw, drotskys@info.bw; www. drotskys.com; ✷ DROTSK 18°24.868'S, 21°53.120'E. Almost 8km south of Shakawe you'll find a left turn off the tar road on to a sandy track. This leads east, crossing the old road up the Panhandle for about 3km to reach the extensively remodelled Drotsky's Cabins. You should be able to drive this track in a normal 2WD car, though the sand can be very thick so some driving skill is needed.

This once-small fishing camp is still run by Jan & Eileen Drotsky & their family, who have seen Shakawe change from a remote outpost to a thriving little town. The central area is designed like a vast log cabin on high stilts, under a thatched roof, & is approached by an almost palatial series of steps & walkways. Adorned with wrought-iron chandeliers & woodcarvings, & with a separate bar under whirling fans, it may sound rather grand, but the effect is homely rather than ostentatious. Wi-Fi is available in this main area, which is entirely wheelchair accessible (as is one of the chalets).

The log-cabin theme continues in the large, twin-bedded en-suite chalets, also raised up on stilts; space is clearly not an issue here! AC, fans & flat-screen TVs are standard, while old-fashioned armchairs add a touch of traditional comfort, & we loved the ornate ceramic basins. Outside, perfectly manicured lawns sweep around a pool to the river beyond. Campers enjoy a shaded but sandy campsite with 20 pitches on the site of the original cabins, each with lights, electric points & a firepit – but watch out for the local monkey population! There are ablution blocks here, & meals can be arranged at the main camp with advance notice.

The river at this point is several km wide, a network of deepwater channels & large beds of papyrus. It's excellent for birdwatching or fishing – with several boats with a driver/guide for hire by the hour or day, & fishing tackle available too

– but there's little game around except for hippos & crocodiles. It is also possible for self-drivers to use this as a base for the Tsodilo Hills, 65km away, although this is a long round trip.

Drotsky's is a genuine old camp, where hospitality hasn't been learned from a manual. It can be a super lodge, & offer you fascinating insights into the area, its history & its ecosystems. *Room only P1,725 per room; camping P200 pp.* **$$–$$$$**

🏠 **Shakawe River Lodge** [539 B3] (10 chalets, 4 dome tents, camping) 📞+267 684 0403; e info@ shakawelodge.com; www.shakawelodge.com; ✷ SHAKAL 18°26.059'S, 21°54.326'E. Known for decades as Shakawe Fishing Camp, this opened in 2013 in a new guise. Gone is the simple fishing camp of yore, its expansive river frontage now hosting a stylish yet very open lodge that's all neutral colours beneath a topping of smart thatch. From the entrance, you're greeted by a riverside vista of palm trees & papyrus, where basket chairs hang enticingly in the breeze. Sunloungers on a raised pool deck catch the river view, too, as do the smart restaurant & lounge. Most of the twin & king-size dbl en-suite chalets with sliding glass doors are lined up along a rather reedy section of the river, their contemporary décor enhanced by AC, TV & a bar fridge.

Downstream, the shady old riverside campsite has had a make-over, but remains relaxed & unpretentious, with 10 clearly demarcated pitches, its own bar, & spotless if well-worn showers & WC. Campers are welcome to dine at the lodge, where an à la carte menu (**$$$$**) features a good selection of pizzas. Beside the slipway, look out for the rusting hulk of an old houseboat, a relic of the Angolan war from the late 1970s. Apparently it was used by 32 Battalion of the South African forces, who were stationed in the Caprivi Strip, but it broke loose & drifted south, & has been gently rusting in Botswana ever since!

The lodge is clearly signposted some 2.5km east of the main road, about 5.5km north of the Somachima Veterinary Fence (✷ *VET-SA 18°29.256'S, 21°55.142'E*), or 11km south of Shakawe, & is accessible by 2WD. Guests have always come here to fish, especially during the peak season of Jun–Aug, & fishing is still a focus; boats can be hired by the hour or day (*from P300/1,500 exc fuel*), but birdwatching, as well as day trips to the Tsodilo Hills & Mahango (*P900 pp, min 4 people*) add another dimension. *DBB P2,040–2,710/2,680–2,720 sgl/dbl; camping P150 pp.* **$$–$$$$**

🏠 **Xaro Lodge** [539 B3] (10 tents) m +267 7280 7476; e reservations@xaro-lodge.com; www.xaro-lodge.com; ✥ XARO 18°25.423'S, 21°56.364'E. About 14km downstream from Shakawe, Xaro is reached by a 15min boat trip from Samochama village. It is set in 30ha on an outcrop from the mainland, amid an old, established grove of knobthorn (*Senegalia nigrescens*), mangosteen (*Garcinia livingstonei*) & jackalberry (*Diospyros mespiliformis*) trees, while in the garden you'll find a host of succulents & cacti, banana trees & even a small baobab (*Adansonia digitata*). Originally built in the mid 1980s by Hartley's Safaris, Xaro passed through several hands until it was bought by the current owners in Apr 2018. We understand that they have since rebuilt the main area, refurbished the tents & added both a honeymoon tent & a 5-person family tent. The tents, raised on wooden decks, have large, glass sliding doors that open on to a veranda affording beautiful views over the Okavango. The main area has a bar, lounge & dining space & there is a swimming pool in the gardens. Historically the lodge was a favourite for fishing, but they are now focusing on birdwatching & photography from motorboats. They also offer a 2-night option including a full-day trip to the Tsodilo Hills (*US$525/room*). *FBA US$395/room, exc alcoholic drinks.* **$$$$$**

Houseboats

Moored on the river near Shakawe, several houseboats offer the opportunity to explore the western fringes of the Delta from a base on the river itself. It's an entirely different approach, & may well appeal to those seeking a more relaxing trip with less of an emphasis on fishing (although fishing is still an option!). For a general overview & other options, contact Okavango Houseboats

(*www.okavangohouseboats.com*), or consider one of the following:

⛴ **//Kabbo Houseboat** (8 cabins) Contact Wilderness Dawning; ☎ +267 7230 8855; e reservations@wildernessdawning.com; www. wildernessdawning.com; ⏰ Apr–Oct. This 2-storey 'floating lodge', moored on the river near the Hawk Guesthouse (page 540), is designed to make the most of its location. On the lower deck, each comfortable en-suite cabin has sliding glass doors just above water level, while above are the dining area, bar & – for those who want to brave the African sun – sundecks. Tender boats assist with activities – boating, birdwatching & fishing trips (catch & release) are available or – if you tire of the water – there are guided walks on smaller islands & visits to the Tsodilo Hills (*all US$80 pp, min 2*). *FB US$1,920/night, min 8 people, inc 1 water-based activity/day; exc drinks, transfers.* **$$$$$**

⛴ **Kubu Queen** (2 cabins) m +267 7230 6821/2; e oldafricasafaris@ngami.net; www. kubuqueen.com; ⏰ all year. From its base at Shakawe, the old-style, wooden *Kubu Queen* is moored at a different spot each night, with tender boats so that guests can explore the river & its channels, & go fishing (except in the closed season, Jan–Feb). Nature walks on some of the larger islands are a further option. Inside, there's a lounge, bar & dining area. Both cabins have a dbl bed, while a further 2 guests can sleep under the stars on the upper deck, where simple twin beds are set up under mosquito nets. The shower & WC are shared, but groups are not mixed, so you won't be sharing with strangers. Another alternative for up to 12 people is to camp on one of the islands.

The boat is owned by Greg & Kate Thompson, who have worked in the safari industry in the Okavango for almost 20 years; Greg is a professional guide. *FB US$280 pp (min 4), inc fishing, airstrip transfers; exc VAT, drinks, fuel for tender boats.* **$$$$$**

NXAMASERI Though the small village of Nxamaseri is not a stop for most visitors, I've included it in this section because the surrounding area is very interesting, offering an insight into the attractions of the Okavango Delta that put it on a par with most of the reserves further east. It's also fairly accessible due to the presence of a lodge.

The Nxamaseri Channel is a side channel of the main Okavango River. When water levels are high, there are plenty of open marshy floodplains covered with an apparently unblemished carpet of grass, and dotted with tiny palm islands. It's very like the Jao Flats, and is one of the Okavango's most beautiful corners.

If you want a real delta experience in the Panhandle, then this should be high on your list of places to visit – though getting here requires either your own vehicle or a flight.

Flora and fauna highlights The Nxamaseri Channel is north of the point where the main Okavango River divides at the base of the Panhandle, and is a stretch of open, clear water up to about 30m wide in places. Beside the edges you'll find stands of papyrus and common reeds, while its quieter edges are lined by patches of waterlilies, including many night lilies (*Nymphaea lotus*; aka lotus lilies), as well as the more common day lilies (*N. nouchali caerulea*). Look out also for the heart-shaped floating leaves, and star-shaped white or yellow flowers, of the water gentian (*Nymphoides indica*).

As with the rest of the Panhandle, this isn't a prime area for game viewing. You may catch glimpses of the odd lechwe or the shy sitatunga, and you're almost bound to see hippo and crocodile, but big game is scarce. However, the channel is a super waterway for birdwatching; home to a tremendous variety of waterbirds. Without trying too hard, my sightings included many pygmy geese, greater and lesser jacanas, lesser gallinules, colonies of reed cormorants, darters, several species of bee-eater and kingfisher, green-backed herons, a relaxed black crake, numerous red-shouldered widows and even (on a cloudy morning in February) a pair of Pel's fishing owls. Beside the channel are pockets of tall riverine trees and various real fan and wild date palms, whose overhanging branches house colonies of weavers (masked, spotted-backed and brown-throated). Upstream of the lodge, on the main Okavango River, there's a colony of carmine bee-eaters at a location known locally as 'the red cliffs'. This is occupied from around early September to the end of December, but is probably at its best in late September/early October (the best time for most migrant species here). While watching for birds, keep an eye out for the elusive spotted-necked otter (*Lutra maculicollis*) which also frequents these waters.

Getting there and away Nxamaseri village lies about 37km south of Shakawe. Follow the tar road to the Somachima Veterinary Fence (⊕ *VET-SA 18°29.256'S, 21°55.142'E*), then after 10km you'll pass a slight rise, marked by a sign as 'Tsodilo View' (⊕ *TSVIEW 18°33.830'S, 21°58.273'E*). From here, on a clear day, you should be able to see the Tsodilo Hills to the southwest, but thick vegetation has obscured the view, and sand sprinkled with broken glass makes it a far from attractive place for a break. Less than 3km south of this viewpoint you'll pass a sign to Nxamaseri, which leads to the village of the same name. The turning to Nxamaseri Island Lodge (⊕ *NXTURN 18°38.125'S, 22°2.797'E*) is clearly signposted almost 9km south of the village turn-off. Advanced reservations are essential; this is not a place to try to drop into unannounced. Most visitors are transferred to the lodge (⊕ *NXAMAS 18°36.426'S, 22°5.268'E*) from the airstrip, but self-drivers leave their vehicle in the guarded parking spot by the turning, and are transferred by 4x4 vehicle and boat for the final few kilometres.

🔼 Where to stay

✳ 🔼 **Nxamaseri Island Lodge** [539 C4] (7 chalets) **m** +267 713 26619; **e** info@ nxamaseri.com; www.nxamaseri.com. Started as a fishing camp in about 1980, Nxamaseri is now back in the hands of the original owners, P J & Barney Bestelink, & remains a wonderful all-round

lodge justifying a stay of at least 2 days. It has been built within a thick & tropical patch of riverine vegetation. All around are knobthorn (*Senegalia nigrescens*), waterberry (*Syzygium cordatum*), sycamore fig (*Ficus sycomorus*), mangosteen (*Garcinia livingstonei*), jackalberries (*Diospyros* mespiliformis), sausage trees (*Kigelia africana*) & some of the most wonderfully contorting python vines (*Cocculus hirsutus*) that you'll see anywhere.

Ongoing refurbishment means that the strong sense of place has been retained, but with higher standards of accommodation & food. Its wide, thatched lounge/dining area is built around a couple of lofty old jackalberry trees, with an open frontage to the river: it's comfortable & well thought out, but not ornate. Wooden walkways lead to large chalets & a 2-bedroom family room sharing a bathroom. The chalets are built of brick beneath high thatched roofs, but the newer rooms & the family room are predominantly canvas structures. Each chalet has 4-poster-style mosi nets, bedside lights powered by a generator or batteries, an en-suite shower & WC, & a wooden deck above the river. More secluded is the new, spacious 'Tsodilo room', which has a private deck overlooking a small channel. This is also used as a honeymoon suite & for guests spending a day at the Tsodilo Hills.

It is claimed that fly-fishing in the Delta was pioneered at Nxamaseri, & certainly it remains an attraction for people who fish seriously, but to this have now been added first-class boat trips for birdwatching, visits to a local village to watch basket-making, & day trips to the Tsodilo Hills. There tends to be less emphasis on mokoro excursions, but these are also possible (& magical) when the water levels are high & there are suitable areas of shallow water nearby. Fly-fishing & lure/spinning fishing with top-quality equipment under expert guidance are possible throughout the year. That said, the very best tigerfishing months are Aug–Nov, while the best times for bream are Mar–Jun. During the first 3 months of the year the rain & new floodwaters are said to disturb the fish, which move out to the floodplains, so fishing in the channels can be more difficult. Nxamaseri's record tigerfish catch is about 10kg, though in a normal season they'd expect to have 10–15 catches over the 6kg mark. Like most Okavango lodges, Nxamaseri operates a 'catch & release' system, except for the occasional bream that has been damaged. They have a large, flat, bargelike boat which provides a particularly stable platform for several people fishing, & is also ideal for photography, plus a fleet of aluminium-hulled craft. *FBA US$900/1,200 sgl/dbl Jul–Oct, US$475/950 sgl/ dbl Nov–Jun, exc alcoholic drinks, lost tackle; day trip to Tsodilo Hills & full-day fishing.* **$$$$$$**

ZAMBEZI (CAPRIVI) REGION

The Zambezi (formerly Caprivi) Region's nerve centre, Katima Mulilo, is closer to Lusaka, Harare or Gaborone than it is to Windhoek, and in many ways this region is more like the countries that surround it than like the rest of Namibia. For example, note the different designs of the rondavels and villages as you travel through. Some are identical to those in eastern Zimbabwe, while others resemble the fenced-in kraals in Botswana. Even the local language used in the schools, the region's lingua franca, is the Lozi language – as spoken by the Lozi people of Zambia.

Situated on the banks of the Zambezi, Katima Mulilo is a bustling town with a busy local market and most of the facilities that you are likely to need. Away from the main town, the region has two established national parks: Nkasa Rupara (previously called Mamili) and Mudumu. These are both lush, riverside reserves with increasing numbers of animals. Bwabwata National Park (formerly Caprivi Game Park) is also seeing a boom in wildlife, having been badly abused during the war of independence, and it is now benefiting from the restocking of animals and closer involvement of communal conservancies. Right on the area's eastern tip, relying mainly on the riverside attractions of Botswana's Chobe National Park, several new lodges are springing up, as indeed they are throughout the region.

For a history of the Caprivi Strip, see box, page 530.

DIVUNDU TO KONGOLA AND THE KWANDO RIVER: 198KM Because it borders Angola, this area was very sensitive and was controlled by the military for many years (see box, page 531). Now, only two control posts remain to remind you of Caprivi's past troubles: one at Divundu and another at Kongola. You do not need

ZAMBEZI'S COMMUNAL CONSERVANCIES

Communal conservancies such as those in Kunene are becoming the linchpin of sustainable tourism in the Zambezi Region. Of more than 80 conservancies across the country, around a dozen can be found on this relatively tiny strip of land. Many are involved in joint ventures with lodges listed on the following pages (including Lianshulu, Nambwa, Nkasa Lupala and Mavunje) and/or have their own campsites (like Salambala and Rupara). Essentially, conservancies give local people ownership of their land, its natural resources and crucially its revenue, ensuring that they see a tangible benefit from tourism. Consequently, conservation becomes increasingly important, wildlife thrives and local economies improve, while tourists get more interesting and often more authentic travel opportunities. It's a win–win situation and the Namibian model is gaining worldwide recognition, informing development in destinations as varied as Nepal and Mexico. For further information, visit www. namibiawildlifesafaris.com and www.nacso.org.na.

any permits to cross the strip and the people staffing the control posts will usually just ask where you are going and wave you on with a smile; alternatively, you may occasionally be asked to provide information about you and your trip, including your vehicle's engine and chassis number.

Bwabwata National Park
(☼ *sunrise–sunset*; *2WD access*; *N$80 pp, plus N$10 per vehicle*) A large chunk of the Caprivi Strip is taken up by the Bwabwata National Park (frequently pronounced 'Babatwa'). It is bordered to the east and west by the Kavango and Kwando rivers, and is divided into three 'core areas'. The B8 bisects this currently undeveloped park which, while it is home to much wildlife, has few facilities and little in the way of marked game-viewing side roads. This is changing, however, with development planned over the next few years to include new gravel roads, improved infrastructure and new lodges and camps opening on the riverbanks. All that you can usually see from the main road are a few raptors aloft and the occasional elephant dropping on the road – but drive carefully in case something does appear unexpectedly.

Bwabwata's three 'core conservation' areas are Mahango and Buffalo (both to the west) and Kwando in the east; although sometimes referred to as parks in their own right, they are all now part of Bwabwata. In between is a 'multiple-use' area with villages and farming land. Measures aimed at helping these communities to coexist with wildlife include ensuring that they benefit from a share of tourism profits and compensation payments for crops or livestock lost to elephants and predators. There are also, of course, new employment opportunities through tourism: most of the new lodges work hand in hand with their local community conservancies.

The western entry point to the park is technically at the checkpoint on the bridge at Divundu, just before the fuel station – which is the only reliable source of fuel for hundreds of kilometres in each direction. For visitors who are simply driving through the park in transit across the strip, there is no charge. Those planning to explore further, however, must purchase a permit. For the western entry point into Bwabwata, permits are obtainable at Buffalo (stressed on the 'a', as Buffalo), a few kilometres east of the bridge at Divundu. There is nowhere to stay, but there is a map of the game drives in the vicinity. For permits for the eastern end of the park, visitors must go to Susuwe (page 547).

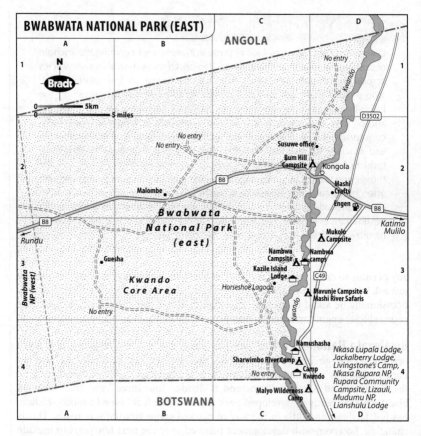

The park is very sparsely populated by humans, with only a few larger settlements: Omega, 70km from Divundu, then Chetto, 40km further on, and Omega III, 60km to the east. Few visitors stop at any of these but they might be helpful in an emergency.

Kwando River area

The southern border of the eastern Zambezi Region is defined rather indistinctly along the line of the Kwando, the Linyanti and the Chobe rivers. These are actually the same river in different stages. The Kwando comes south from Angola, meets the Kalahari's sands, and forms a swampy region of reed-beds and waterways called the Linyanti swamps. (To confuse names further, locals refer to sections of the Kwando above Lianshulu as 'the Mashi'.)

These swamps form the core of Nkasa Rupara National Park (page 551). In good years the Linyanti River emerges from here and flows northeast into Lake Liambezi, from where it flows out from the eastern side as the Chobe River. This beautiful river has a short course before it in turn is swallowed into the mighty Zambezi, which continues over the Victoria Falls, through Lake Kariba, and eventually discharges into the Indian Ocean in Mozambique.

To explore any of these areas on your own, ensure that you have the relevant 1:250,000 maps from the Surveyor General (numbers 1723, 1724, 1823 and 1824), and a good road map of Namibia; see also page 111. Combine these with local guidance and you will find some interesting areas. If you are heading off into Nkasa Rupara, you should also have some back-up (eg: a second 4x4 vehicle), and both a GPS and a downloaded map app that is accessible offline would be useful.

Kongola and environs
Though a large dot on most maps, Kongola is just a small settlement, about 7km east of the impressive new bridge that carries the B8 over the Kwando – tangible proof, in tar and concrete, that the Caprivi Strip is regarded as a major trade artery. Its centre, at the main road's junction with the C49, is a fuel station. Fuel here, particularly unleaded, isn't entirely reliable so do fill up earlier if you have a chance. There's also a shop on site selling freshly made bread, and a separate post office. On the opposite corner is **Mashi Crafts** (⏁ *Mon–Fri & Sun*), a community craft centre selling curios made by the local Kxoe community. It specialises in traditional baskets, beadwork and east Caprivian reed mats and carvings, each clearly labelled with the name of the maker, and his or her village.

Getting there and around The Intercape Mainliner bus between Windhoek and Victoria Falls stops at Kongola on Saturday and Thursday at 02.45, with southbound buses stopping at 20.30 on Wednesday and Friday. One-way tickets cost N$500 to Victoria Falls, or N$750 to Windhoek.

Orientation From Kongola, the main B8 continues straight to Katima Mulilo. Heading south, the tarred C49 heads south towards Linyanti and eventually loops round to come out near Katima Mulilo. Initially, it passes a number of lodges that line the eastern banks of the Kwando River, before going deep inside Mudumu National Park, and skirting Nkasa Rupara. About 126km from the B8 turn-off is the village of Linyanti, where there may be fuel available; it is then a further 90km or so to Katima.

Susuwe Triangle
To the west of the Kwando River, inside Bwabwata National Park's Kwando Core Area, is a narrow tract of land that is wide in the north, but becomes narrower towards the Botswana border. Known variously as 'the Triangle', 'the Susuwe Triangle' or 'the Golden Triangle', it is rich in wildlife.

To explore this area you'll need a 4x4 and some detailed maps; you'll also need a permit from the MET rangers' station (✦ *17°51.703'S, 23°19.159'E;* ⏁ *06.00–18.00 daily; N$40 pp per day, plus N$10 per vehicle*). To find this, turn south from the western end of the Kongola Bridge and you'll find the Susuwe Gate just off the main road. This is where you should buy your permit and ask for a useful map; it's also wise to ask their advice on what you plan to do.

Well worth visiting is Horseshoe Lagoon, about 5km south of Nambwa Tented Lodge. This stunning oxbow lake set in riverine woodland attracts excellent game and numerous birds. Elephant are in abundance near here during the dry months (July–October), their presence evident both in the damage to trees and in the cleared sandy area lining the shore: even if you see nothing, you can't miss the prints of various animals in the sand. The overhanging trees have been colonised by a large family of baboons, which makes for entertaining viewing. A word of caution, though: driving alone in this area during or just after the rainy season is ill-advised. It's all too easy to get bogged down in the black-cotton soil, and there are few people around to help out should you get stuck.

Where to stay There are several places to stay on the eastern bank of the Kwando River. Some are just campsites, others are much more comfortable, and there is talk of more new lodges being planned. Of interest are two community campsites on the western bank: Nambwa Campsite (now part of Nambwa Tented Lodge), and Bum Hill Camp. Both were developed and are managed by communities adjacent to Bwabwata National Park, with the income derived used for conservation and the benefit of the communities. This is the result of an agreement between the MET and these communities, the first time in Namibian history that such a venture has been allowed within a national park. The conservancy management is also in charge of wildlife in the areas next to the park, as well as having responsibility for making sure that income from these campsites is used for conservation and benefits the local communities.

If you're driving yourself, be aware that the road south from Kongola, now marked as the C49, was previously known as the D3501 and the MR125.

In the park

Nambwa Tented Lodge [546 D3] (10 tents) \066 250410; reservations \061 400510; e reservations@africanmonarchlodges. com; www.africanmonarchlodges.com. South of the B8, the turn-off to Nambwa (⊕ *17°47.039'S, 23°20.141'E*) is the same as for the new Susuwe Gate & rangers' station: take the track parallel to the river, following the signposts to the camp. Note that many sections of this are through thick sand, so a 4x4 is essential: the 14km can take up to 1hr. Alternatively, you can get a transfer from the park gate (*N$325*).

Nambwa is in a beautiful island location on the site of a former community campsite, & is still very much involved with the local Mayuni Conservancy, who own a share of the lodge & benefit from a percentage of its turnover. Huge, individually styled luxury tents are raised (some up to 5m high) into the trees with views over the river or floodplain. These are roomy & relaxing with pale wood & cream interiors, a comfortable lounge area & en-suite bathroom with free-standing bath & separate shower. The décor is opulent but the impact on the environment minimal, with the spacious, tented lapa built on wooden decks around marula & sausage trees (Wi-Fi is available only here). Viewing decks overlook a waterhole & floodplain, well frequented by wildlife (including Oliver, the resident hippo), while just behind camp is a small pool with swing loungers. As well as game drives, activities include mokoro & boat trips, fishing, bush walks with armed rangers, night drives & visits to a cultural centre, as well as time with researchers on local lion & hyena projects & with birding experts. *DBB N$3,450–6,605/6,900– 10,160 sgl/dbl, exc park fees; FBA N$4,970– 9,035/9,940–13,900 sgl/dbl, inc transfers from gate, park fees, laundry.* **$$$$$**

Nambwa Lagoon Camp (5 tents) Contact Nambwa Tented Lodge (see left). Right next to the Tented Lodge, Lagoon is billed as a separate camp, but guests here share the restaurant, bar & pool at the lodge & it is only the en-suite canvas tents that differ. These are raised on decks overlooking the floodplain, & are clean & simple, with twin beds, mosi nets & whitewashed furniture. *DBB N$2,750–5,220/5,000–8,030 sgl/dbl, exc park fees.* **$$$$$–$$$$$$**

✱ **Kazile Island Lodge** [546 C3] (10 tented rooms) \066 252315; m 081 145 6799; e kazile@africanmonarchlodges.com; www.africanmonarchlodges.com. Sister camp to Nambwa Tented Lodge, Kazile is accessible only by boat. It is raised on decking within a mangosteen forest, allowing animals to pass through – which they do on a regular basis. Cream canvas & linens complement light, airy en-suite rooms & whitewashed furniture. These are well appointed, with twin/dbl beds under mosi nets, fans, plug points & safes, plus a small balcony with wicker chairs overlooking the river. The open-sided main lounge & dining area is similarly bright & spacious, with a contemporary take on the traditional safari style, leading down to a split-level deck & firepit. Wi-Fi is available here. Activities focus on boat cruises on the Kwando River, guided bushwalks (with the chance of seeing sitatunga) & game drives into the park. *DBB N$2,085–3,410/4,170– 5,250 sgl/dbl, exc park fees.* **$$$$$**

Å **Nambwa Campsite** [546 D3] (4 pitches) m 081 428 0512; e reservations@ africanmonarchlodges.com. Near to the lodge, this community site has 2 ablution blocks with showers & hot water all day, & a braai area, but no power. Campers can use the bar at the Tented Lodge when it's not busy. New plans are being mooted for the campsite, so do check the website for updates. *N$250 pp, plus park fees.* **$$**

▲ Bum Hill Campsite [546 D2] (6 pitches) There are no reliable contact numbers or booking offices in place, so just turn up & hope they have space. Built to be ecologically sustainable, Bum Hill offers 3 pitches that share ablutions & a kitchen (no power), & a further 3 exclusive sites, each on a 3m-high deck overlooking the river, with private hot shower, toilet & washbasin, & a private braai area. **$**

East of the park

Lodges in this section are listed as if driving south along the road.

✳ ▲ Mavunje Campsite & Mashi River Safaris [546 C3] (3 tents, camping) **m** 081 461 9608; **e** mashiriversafaris@gmail.com; www.mashiriversafaris.com. Signposted off the C49, 12km south of Kongola, this is a joint venture between Mashi communal conservancy & British guide Dan Stephens. The emphasis is on private river-based & walking safaris with bush camping in undisturbed locations. It's not luxury: Dan provides the things you need but nothing you don't & you're expected to muck in with setting up camp, etc, but it's a great adventure for those who want to get that bit closer to the bush. Mavunje is the main base, opposite the Horseshoe Lagoon & near the release boma for relocated animals; it's also on an elephant corridor, so there's plenty of wildlife around!

The small camp is for exclusive use only, rustic & simple in design but well thought out & incredibly well presented. The twin-bedded tents, with linen, share a bathroom made of cane & thatch & a fully equipped kitchen with dining area; meals can be provided with advance notice. There are also 4 individual, immaculate campsites, well spaced out, & each with a private toilet hut & (hot) shower, plus a private kitchen & dining area. Dan has an excellent knowledge of the area & its wildlife, he guides & cooks on the river safaris, & has exclusive use of campsites on islands where you'll stay. Safaris can be 1–3 nights or tailored to your plans, with activities including walking & birding. Day trips on the river are also available. All staff are local & the community benefits from a percentage of the income received. *Day river safari from N$1,250, pp inc lunch, drinks & activities; 1–2-night river safari from N$2,350/4,700 sgl/dbl (min 3 people), inc meals, drinks & activities; tented camp N$400/800 sgl/dbl; camping N$220 pp.* **$$–$$$$$**

⌂ Namushasha Lodge [546 C4] (29 chalets, camping) **** 066 686024; **e** namu@iway.na, info@gondwana-collection.com; www.gondwana-collection.com. Standing above the Kwando River, Namushasha overlooks Bwabwata National Park. To get there, take the C49 off the B8, then turn west at the signpost for a further 4km along the lodge's well-maintained drive (though the final kilometre is over a sandy ridge, so 2WD vehicles need to be driven carefully).

A baobab tree guards the arched entrance, leading to solid, brick-&-thatch chalets with dark floors & furniture, slightly offset by cream-painted walls & toning fabrics. Some are adjacent, others detached, with twin or dbl beds under 4-poster mosquito nets, en-suite bathrooms & private balconies, most looking over the river. 'VIP' & family suites have interleading bedrooms, living/dining room & kitchenette, & en suites with a huge shower & a basin set into solid wood.

Overlooking the river to the national park, the central building features a reception, curio shop & lofty bar/lounge area under thatch, & a separate dining room (*dinner N$330*) with netting to protect from mosquitoes. Steps lead down to a deck fronting the water, with a firepit for chilly winter evenings. Nearby is a swimming pool, where a dugout canoe modified into a poolside bench is surrounded by green lawns. Activities include boat trips (*from N$300 pp*), game drives (*N$510*) and fishing (*from N$150 pp*). There's also a 2.5km self-guided walking trail along the riverbank near camp, & the **Namushasha Heritage Centre**, a community-run initiative that allows guests to see how local tribes used to live (*N$80 pp*). The lodge is open to day visitors for lunch & activities. *N$2,160/3,460 sgl/dbl.* **$$$$**

▲ Sharwimbo River Camp [546 C4] (4 chalets, camping) **m** 081 124 0489; **e** book@sharwimbo.com; www.sharwimbo.com. Set down a track off the C49, for which you'll need a 4x4, the simple but comfortable Sharwimbo was refurbished in early 2018. Pole-&-canvas self-catering chalets, all en suite, overlook the river, with 6 camping pitches & shared ablution blocks adjacent. Boat trips can be booked (*from N$200 pp*), & guests can drive themselves to the nearby national parks. *N$900/1,600 sgl/dbl; camping N$150 pp.* **$$–$$$$**

Camp Kwando [546 C4] (6 tree houses, 14 chalets, camping) m 081 149 1435; e reservations@campkwando.com; www. campkwando.com. Camp Kwando lies 26km south of Kongola, along the C49, & then a further 3km west from that, past the 'traditional village' of Kwando, where visitors are welcome. Right by the river, the camp makes good use of traditional design, its central area comprising a series of rondavels interlinked in circles that include the lounge, dining & bar areas, plus a deck & firepit. Simply furnished in solid wood & cream canvas, & decorated with local artefacts, it's stylish & comfortable. Tented chalets with a small veranda sit on low stilted decks under thatch above the marshes; each has twin beds, mosi nets & 24hr solar-powered electricity, with en-suite shower & toilet. Overlooking the river across to Botswana are more spacious, tree-house-style chalets, with wide stepped access & a higher specification that includes solid-wood furniture & floors. The circular campsite has 4 tree-shaded pitches with

private ablutions & power, & there's a nearby pool. Activities include boat trips (*from N$445 pp*), fishing trips (*N$2,175/boat, max 4 people*), visits to a traditional village & school, & game drives to Mudumu & Bwabwata (*from N$625 pp*). Unusually, Camp Kwando offers activities designed specifically with children in mind, including traditional fishing (*N$150 pp*). DBB N$1,480–2,260/2,640–3,600 sgl/dbl; camping N$275 pp. **$$–$$$$$**

⚑ Malyo Wilderness Camp [546 C4] (4 tents, camping) m 081 124 1436; e deon@karambareservations.com; www.caprivi.biz/malyo. Approx 3km after the turning for Camp Kwando is the turn for this campsite, at ⊕ 18°02.157'S, 23°21.048'E. It has permanent self-catering tents (just bring food & bedding) & a large communal area with shared ablution blocks for camping with your own equipment, right on the river. Be warned; it's only accessible with a 4x4 because of thick sand en route. N$280/560 sgl/dbl; camping N$130 pp. **$–$$**

Mudumu National Park
(*Admission N$40 pp, plus N$10 per vehicle; permits for day visitors can be bought from Nakatwa Camp, Lianshulu Lodge, or the rangers' station as you enter the park*) The more northerly of the region's two reserves, Mudumu covers 850km² of riverine forest south of Kongola, either side of the C49, and is bordered by the Kwando River on the west. The reserve has good populations of a large variety of animals and, together with Nkasa Rupara and the Susuwe Triangle, is notable for its buffalo (otherwise uncommon in Namibia), roan and sable antelope (both generally uncommon species), the water-loving lechwe and sitatunga, and often large herds of elephant, mainly between July and October.

Mudumu can be explored on foot or by 4x4, though don't expect much organisation or many clearly marked game drives.

Where to stay To stay in the park, the choice is either an unfenced campsite with river water and basic sanitation, Nakatwa Nature Conservation Camp, or Lianshulu Lodge, by the river. If you opt to camp, then follow the signs to the camp and note that the reserve, which is not fenced or clearly demarcated, borders on to hunting areas. Some of the camps beside the Susuwe Triangle also run trips into Mudumu.

Lianshulu Lodge [546 D4] (7 chalets, 3 suites) m 081 127 4584; e reservations@caprivicollection.com; www.caprivicollection.com. The owner-run Lianshulu was one of the first private lodges to be built inside a Namibian national park, in 1989. It stands in a private 404ha concession on the banks of a backwater of the Kwando River, about 5km down a good bush track off the C49, & 40km from the B8 turn-off. Though there are sandy sections, it's usually

accessible with care in a 2WD vehicle, but there is also a private airstrip.

The lodge shelters beneath a canopy of mature jackalberry & mangosteen trees, giving an air of seclusion & ensuring that it blends into the surrounding bush. Wildlife can come & go freely, (with daily visits made by a large crocodile, Nandi). An imposing entrance leads into a huge central area with an integral viewing platform looking west over the Lianshulu Lagoon, complete with firepit, & a 2nd fire right at the back, well away from chilly night breezes. Despite the size, the layout of solid wood furniture & ethnic fabrics combines to create a more intimate series of 'rooms', with lounge, bar & dining areas, while various brunch spots include islands on the lagoon. Painted chalets (with en-suite shower) & suites (larger, with bath, & capacious open-air shower) are well spaced along the river, affording a high standard of accommodation & privacy. Each is under thatch, with 2 dbl beds, mosquito nets, colourful rugs on the tiled floors, a safe & a veranda overlooking the river. 1 room is designed for families, & is also wheelchair-adapted.

Under the eye of a team of 6 guides, visitors explore the river's channels afloat, go on game drives (including at night) & take guided bush walks through Mudumu, these last in an area that is exclusive to the lodge (though do be aware that the guides are unarmed). Fishing & fly-fishing trips are also available. Lianshulu is an efficiently run operation that maintains close links with the community, & is heavily involved with education at several levels. They are closely involved with the primary school at Lianshulu, having built toilets, repainted school buildings & installed power & solar pumps. *DBB N$4,565–5,460/7,020–8,860 sgl/dbl; FBA N$7,030–7,980/10,800–12,700; all inc laundry, exc park fees.* **$$$$$$–$$$$$$$**

🏠 **Bush Lodge** (12 chalets) Some 3km downstream from the main Lianshulu Lodge, this is essentially a slightly simpler version, with more rustic chalets suited to (slightly) more budget-conscious travellers. *DBB N$2,650– 3,135/4,500–5,460 sgl/dbl, exc park fees; FBA N$3,865–4,335/6,920–7,870 sgl/dbl; all exc park fees.* **$$$$$–$$$$$$**

Lizauli Traditional Village This small village is signposted from the C49, just to the north of Lianshulu, and is an interesting attraction for visitors. For a nominal entrance fee, visitors are guided around the village where traditional arts and crafts are being practised. Aside from the fascination of the actual attractions – an iron forge, a grain store, and various carvers and basket-weavers – a visit here gives a good opportunity to sit down and talk to some local people about their way of life. This is just one of several important community projects in this area.

Sangwali Museum In 1999, Stella Kilby, a distant relative of some British missionaries, founded a small museum at Sangwali in memory of her ancestors. To find the museum, continue along the C49 from Lianshulu until you reach a sign indicating Sangwali, then a second pointing to Sangwali Health Clinic (this is about 50km south of the turning to Namushasha). Take this road for about 5km, passing the clinic, and continuing towards Rupara as indicated by some rough handmade signs. About 500m before the log bridge, you'll see the museum on the left.

Inside, large wall maps trace the route of Livingstone's travels from South Africa through the Botswana desert until he reached the Linyanti River at Sangwali in 1855. Here, he persuaded the London Mission Society to open a mission station. But four years later when two missionaries, Holloway Hellmore and Roger Price, arrived with their families, the local Makololo tribe weren't overjoyed. When eight of the travellers died after eating meat that had apparently been poisoned, the survivors turned their backs on the nascent mission and trekked all the way back to South Africa. The story is recorded in Stella's book, *No Cross Marks the Spot* (Galamena Press, Southend on Sea, 2001).

Nkasa Rupara (formerly Mamili) National Park (⊕ *sunrise–sunset; N$80 pp, plus N$10 per vehicle*) This unfenced swampland reserve of about 350km² was created shortly before independence. Consisting largely of marshland, veined by a network of reed-lined channels, it incorporates two large islands: Nkasa and Lupala, also called Rupara – hence the new name for the park in 2013. Together with Mudumu National Park, it has the vast majority of Namibia's population of sitatunga, red lechwe and puku, as well as large herds of buffalo and a recorded 430 bird species.

The park is located in the southwest corner of the eastern Caprivi, where the Kwando River sharply changes direction to become the Linyanti. Driving here is challenging, to say the least. Even during the normal rains, most of the park is flooded, but some roads have improved, with bridges to ease access. Two remote lodges have been built and are well worth the bumpy road to reach them.

Approaching along the D3501, the turn-off to Nkasa Rupara National Park is at Sangwali village. This community, together with the nearby villages of Samudono and Nongozi, has set up a conservancy in the area just outside the park, where they have a simple campsite. There is a small craft stall, Sheshe Crafts, about 4km from the D3501 as you head into Nkasa Rupara. This sells locally produced baskets, carvings, reed mats and some very authentic fishing traps.

Where to stay

Nkasa Lupala Tented Lodge [546 D4] (10 rooms) 066 686101; m 081 160 1740; e info@nkasalupalalodge.com; www. nkasalupalalodge.com. Just outside Nkasa Rupara NP & 75km from Kongola, the lodge is reached by taking the C49 then the D3518 to Sangwali village. Either leave your car there (safe parking is available at the conservancy offices) & be picked up by the lodge, or follow the road to Nkasa Rupara/ Mamili National Park for 11km then, at Shisintze rangers' station, turn east for 1km. The route is well signposted but don't attempt it without a 4x4.

Opened in 2011 by Italian Simone Micheletti, the lodge has fairly simple en-suite tents on stilts overlooking a channel of the Linyanti swamps. It was designed to be as eco-friendly as possible, & runs on solar power, with innovative design features created from recycled tin drums & locally sourced materials. The central lapa is on 3 floors, with great views from the relaxing lounge & bar up top, & a small pool & curio shop below. Despite its many comforts (including Wi-Fi), you know you're deep in the bush, with no other lodges around. Birdlife is prolific here, with over 430 species, & elephants are frequent visitors to camp. Activities (N$380–1,000 pp) include game drives, walks, village visits & boat trips, or a combination of them. This is another lodge that works closely with its local communal conservancy, Wuparo, with local staff, & a proportion of income going to community projects. DBB from N$2,625/4,450 sgl/ dbl. **$$$$$**

Jackalberry Camp [546 D4] (4 tents) 066 686101; m 081 147 7798; e jackalberry@ resdest.com; www.jbcamp.com. Some 14km south

of its sister camp, Nkasa Lupala, Jackalberry sits within the national park, so if you're not using the lodge's transfer you'll need to stop at the park gate for a permit. It's a small, beautifully simple camp, its spacious tents set around a cosy, multi-level main area with restaurant, lounge & bar. Dubbed Jackalberry Tower, this seems to snake up & around a large jackalberry tree. The tents themselves are basic but comfortable, with twin or dbl beds, mosi nets, high-sided gauze windows to allow a decent breeze through, plugpoints, tea/coffee facilities & a fridge (a nod to the days when Jackalberry was a self-catering camp). Solar-powered hot showers are en suite, & outdoor showers are in the offing. DBB from N$3,490/5,800 sgl/dbl. **$$$$$**

Livingstone's Camp [546 D4] (5 pitches) 066 686208; e info@livingstonescamp.com; www.livingstonescamp.com. The campsite has changed ownership a couple of times in the last few years, with varying degress of success. Private campsites sit along the river, each with a private ablution block & thatched kitchen/lapa area. From N$340 pp. **$$**

Rupara Community Campsite [546 D4] (7 pitches, 4 self-catering chalets) m 081 469 2558, 081 406 7579. Owned & run by the team at Nkasa Lupala, this is on the way to Nkasa Lupala lodge, about 6–7km south of Sangwali (page 551) & 1.5km north of the Nkasa Lupala Tented Lodge (see left). It's a basic but pretty campsite with a small bar where each of the pitches has its own water tap & firepit, but shares ablutions with hot showers. All proceeds get ploughed back into the local community. N$80 pp. **$**

KATIMA MULILO Established by the British in 1935, Katima is the capital of the Zambezi Region. It's a large town, beautifully placed on the banks of the Zambezi.

In a bold new initiative, the Kavango-Zambezi Transfrontier Conservation Area (TFCA), arguably one of the world's largest conservation areas, was officially launched in Katima on 15 March 2012. Known locally as KAZA, the new 'peace park' (*www.peaceparks.org*) covers around 287,132km^2, a total of 26 protected areas in five countries, connecting the national parks of the Kavango/Zambezi regions and Khaudum with those in neighbouring Botswana, Zambia, Zimbabwe and Angola – and notably including the Okavango Delta and Victoria Falls. As with all the peace parks, the primary aim is to create corridors to allow migratory animals, in this case elephants, zebra and buffalo, to move freely between the various reserves, unencumbered by manmade boundaries. It focuses on sustainable development, in particular relating to tourism, to ensure that local communities themselves get value from protecting their wildlife. KAZA's website (*www.kavangozambezi.org*) is full of information on the project.

Leafy outskirts lead to an open central square, from where it's a short stroll to the town's main street. Recently, as western Zambia has started to open up, Katima has taken on the role of frontier town: a base for supplies and communication for the new camps on the Upper Zambezi River in Zambia. It has just a little of the Wild West air that Maun used to have a decade ago, when it was remote and the hub of the Okavango's safari industry.

History When Katima became capital of the original Caprivi Region, it replaced the old German centre of Schuckmannsburg, which was named after the then governor of German South West Africa. It was, though, formerly called Luhonono, after a tree prevalent in the area, and this name was reinstated in 2013. Today's Luhonono, however, consists of just a police post, a clinic and a few huts. Collectors of trivia, note that the taking of Schuckmannsburg on 22 September 1914 was the first Allied occupation of German territory during World War I.

Getting there and away

By air Katima's M'Pacha Airport lies about 18km west of town, towards Rundu, and doubles as the military airbase. There are four Air Namibia services a week between Windhoek Eros and Katima Mulilo, on Monday, Wednesday, Friday and Sunday, returning the same day. A one-way ticket costs around N$1,600. The ever-helpful Caprivi Adventures (page 554) can arrange transfers to and from the airport.

At other times, aside from the odd private flight for Lianshulu or Namushasha, the airport is deserted, with no facilities whatsoever apart from toilets. The **Air Namibia** office (\ *066 253191; reservations* \ *061 299 6111/333;* ⊕ *08.00–17.00 Mon–Fri*) is on Hage Geingob Road.

By road Katima is about 69km from the Ngoma border post with Botswana, and with only one road through the Caprivi Strip, **hitching**, at least as far as Grootfontein or Kasane in Botswana, is relatively easy. Lifts to Victoria Falls and Etosha have also been reported.

The Intercape Mainliner **bus** from Victoria Falls and Livingstone to Windhoek stops at the Engen garage on Hage Geingob Road [555 A4]. Buses for Windhoek leave Katima on Sunday, Wednesday and Friday at 18.50, arriving back on Tuesday, Thursday and Saturday at 04.50. Victoria Falls-bound buses leave Katima on Tuesday, Thursday and Saturday at 05.00. That said, departure times are subject to change so do check the website (*www.intercapeco.za*). Tickets, which may be purchased through Caprivi Adventures (see below), cost around N$630 through to Windhoek, and around N$350 to Livingstone.

In addition, **minibuses** ply between Katima Mulilo and Windhoek, via Rundu, while others go to Livingstone or into Botswana.

To and from Zambia
To reach the Zambian border, drive west past the Protea Hotel Zambezi River until the tarred B8 turns left towards Rundu. Instead of following it, continue straight on to a gravel road for about 4km, passing the (unpleasant) rubbish dump, until you reach the border post at Wenela (⊕ *06.00–18.00 daily*).

Sesheke, the small Zambian settlement near the border, is split in half by the Zambezi. Either side makes Katima look like a thriving metropolis in comparison. Namibian dollars can usually be changed into Zambian kwacha here, before continuing on the long gravel road north to Ngonye Falls and ultimately to Mongu.

Tourist information

Caprivi Adventures [555 A3] ✆ 066 252739; m 081 206 1514; e capriviadventures@gmail.com; www.capriviadventures.com. Just before the Zambia–Ndola T-junction on the B8, this is a mine of useful information. Having taken over management in 2017 of the popular local transfers & tours operated by Tutwa Tourism & Travel, including tailor-made river cruises, specialist birding excursions, fishing trips & camping adventures, they now also arrange safaris & local day trips. They also act as an agent for Intercape Mainliner, & offer free Wi-Fi for customers.

Where to stay

In town

Protea Hotel Zambezi River [555 D1] (42 rooms) ✆ 066 251500; e gm-zambezi@ proteahotels.com.na; www.proteahotels.com. Just a few hundred metres off the main road as it enters Katima from Ngoma, the Protea caters mainly for business visitors & tourists stopping for just a night, & it lacks the style, character or activities to entice them to stay longer. Large, en-suite twin or dbl rooms are set in a row along the river, most with wide patio doors with a view – but with a footpath right along the river, there's little privacy. The rooms themselves, though clean & tidy, are a little dated & corporate. Dark wood furniture & carpets set the tone, but they do have AC, satellite TV, direct-dial phone, hairdryer & tea/coffee facilities. Though reception staff are attentive, restaurant service can be slow & the food far from outstanding, but there's always a swim in the pool to make you feel better. Limited Wi-Fi is available in public areas. Activities are limited to fishing trips & 1½hr cruises on the river. *From N$1,345–1,755/1,640–2,206 sgl/dbl, depending on availability.* **$$$$**

Fish Eagle's Nest [555 D1] (14 rooms) ✆ 066 254287; m 081 291 7791; e fisheaglesnest@afol.com.na; www.caprivi.biz/ fisheaglesnest. This pleasant B&B, opened in 2009

KATIMA MULILO
For listings, see below

⊖ **Where to stay**

1 3Palms Eco Guesthouse....................B1
2 Fish Eagle's Nest................................D1
3 Protea Hotel Zambezi River...........D1

Off map
  Caprivi Houseboat Safari Lodge.....D1
  Caprivi Mutoya Lodge......................D1
  Caprivi River Lodge...........................D1
  Hippo Lodge & Photo
    Club Zambezi..................................D1
  Muchenje Houseboat Safaris
    & River Lodge.................................D1
  Namwi Island.....................................D1
  Shamwari Houseboat
    Adventures..................................... D1
  Zambezi Mubala Camp..................... D1
  Zambezi Mubala Lodge.................... D1

✖ **Where to eat and drink**

4 Passione Portuguese......................... A3
  Wiesenhof Coffee Shop
    (see Caprivi Adventures)............... A3

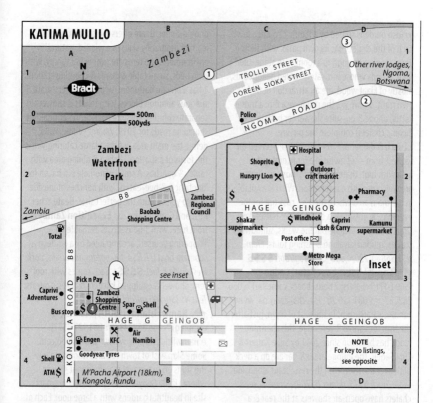

KATIMA MULILO

Zambezi

Trollip Street
Doreen Sioka Street
Ngoma Road
Police

Zambezi
Waterfront
Park

B8

Zambia

Total

Zambezi
Regional
Council

Baobab
Shopping Centre

Caprivi
Adventures

Pick n Pay

Zambezi
Shopping
Centre

Spar   Shell

Bus stop

Engen   KFC   Air
Namibia

Goodyear Tyres

Shell

ATM

M'Pacha Airport (18km),
Kongola, Rundu

see inset

HAGE   G   GEINGOB

HAGE   G   GEINGOB

Other river lodges,
Ngoma,
Botswana

NOTE
For key to listings,
see opposite

Inset

Hospital

Shoprite

Hungry Lion

Outdoor
craft market

Pharmacy

HAGE G GEINGOB

Shakar
supermarket

Windhoek

Caprivi
Cash & Carry

Kamunu
supermarket

Post office

Metro Mega
Store

by Martmarie Strauss, is situated just opposite
the turning for the Protea (formerly Zambezi
River Lodge). Its 12 en-suite dbl/twin rooms & 2
self-catering rooms are set around a small pool in
a peaceful garden with secure courtyard parking.
All have AC, 4-channel DSTV, free Wi-Fi, fridge
& kettle. A set-menu dinner is served Mon–Thu
(N$100). *N$860/1,180 sgl/dbl.* **$$$**

🏠 **3Palms Eco Guesthouse** [555 B1]
(6 rooms, inc 1 wheelchair accessible) ☏066
252850; e info@3palms.com.na; www.3palms.
com.na. Formerly 3 Palms B&B, this delightful
boutique guesthouse opened in 2013 & is the
best place to stay in town. Rooms are individually
decorated in neutral tones with splashes of colour
& mosquito screens, AC, DSTV, fridge, tea/coffee
facilities, safe, Wi-Fi & private terraces. Some of the
bathrooms lack a bit of privacy, so if you're after a
twin, ask for one with a separate bathroom. Of the
2 family rooms, 1 has been designed specifically for
wheelchair users, with plenty of space & rails, & all
areas of the guesthouse are wheelchair accessible.
The gardens are immaculate with a swimming
pool, a raised deck overlooking the river, a pretty

lapa with an honesty bar, & masses of birds. The
b/fast menu changes daily, & you can choose from
a set 3-course dinner menu (N$210); otherwise
Passione Restaurant (page 558) will deliver dinner
for guests. *From N$900/1,300 sgl/dbl.* **$$$**

Out of town

Several lodges of different styles lie along the
river east of town, as do various houseboats.
These are listed here broadly in order of distance
from Katima Mulilo. The first 4 are reached from a
signposted turn-off on the B8, about 2–3km east
of Katima Mulilo. For the others, turn off the B8
about 11km east of Katima on to the gravel road
towards Kazimbela.

🏠 **Caprivi River Lodge** [560 D1] (8 chalets)
Ngoma Rd; ☏066 252288/95; e hakumata@
iway.na; www.capririverlodge.com.na;
⊕ 17°29.280'S, 24°18.575'E. Some 5km east of
town, & about 800m down a wide sandy track, this
compact, spotlessly clean lodge is looked after by
owners Mary & Keith Rooken-Smith. River-facing
chalets, including 1 luxury family unit, are fronted

by lush gardens shared by a family of guinea fowl. Each of the chalets has its own patio, with sliding doors leading through to a room with stone-tiled floor, & beds whose intricately carved headboards, mostly of kiaat wood, are an attraction in their own right. 5 have AC, the rest have a fan; a fridge, kettle, phone & en-suite shower (or bath in the 'luxury' chalets) complete the picture.

Lunch & dinner (*N$70–120/230*) are served on request from a set menu in a large dining/bar area with high thatched ceiling; non-residents are welcome with a reservation. Wi-Fi is available in the main area where there's a cosy fire for the evenings, & outside is a cool pool for hotter days. Organised trips include birding walks, sundowner cruises, guided kayaking & fishing tours. *From N$1,568–1,720/1,936–2,294 sgl/dbl.* **$$$$**

🏠 **Caprivi Houseboat Safari Lodge**
[560 D1] (5 chalets, 2 houseboats, camping) ☎066 252287; **m** 081 129 2811; **e** chs@iway.na; www.zambezisafaris.com. To the east of town, just after the turn for Caprivi River Lodge, this charming lodge has been run since 2011 by Silke Kauert & Curt Sagell. The lounge areas & bar are on a deck high over the river, with the restaurant alongside (*light lunch N$75, dinner N$200*). Stone-&-reed chalets have open-air showers at the rear & a canvas curtain at the front on to a terrace with beautiful river views. For campers, 2 pitches with shared ablution blocks, small kitchenettes & braai facilities share the views. Full of character are 2 aluminium-sided boats, more like caravans than houseboats, with kitchen, shower & WC, & 2 roof tents on top; to allow for another 2 people you can collapse the dining table to form a bed. Tailor-made itineraries allow fun excursions such as 2–4 nights into Chobe & 1–2 nights at the lodge (*from N$3,900–5,100/boat per night self-catering, plus fuel*). More local are boat cruises (*sunset N$150–300; ½-day N$300–750*) & fishing (*½/full-day with skipper N$1,000/1,700, inc tackle*). *From N$1,125/1,250 sgl/dbl.* **$$$**

✳ 🏠 **Hippo Lodge & Photo Club Zambezi** [560 D1] (14 tents, 8 bungalows, 3 houseboats) **m** 081 124 3060; **e** info@photo-club-zambezi.com; www.photo-club-zambezi.com. A dream brought to fruition by owner Beate Schwippert in 2017, Photo Club Zambezi runs from the bright & cheerful Hippo Lodge, set amongst camelthorn & fig trees on a 12ha site overlooking the Zambezi. An experienced wildlife photographer, Beate offers the opportunity to learn photography skills in a relaxed, natural environment. The tents are simple but roomy, with twin beds, small table & chairs & charging station. 1 has a private bathroom, while the others share 6 spacious ablution blocks, with toilets & showers in separate cubicles. En-suite river-facing bungalows should be ready for 2019. Vibrant yellow walls define the main area, where a large catering van is the focus of a spotless kitchen & dining area with tables & benches. A small waterhole is a haven for kingfishers & bee-eaters, with benches alongside to help you capture the perfect shot. Beate & her husband Gunther also run **Expedition Zambezi** from here, with 3 houseboats available for skippering yourself, accompanied by a guide in a separate boat (*FB N$4,400 pp/day, inc drinks, park fees, guide & fuel,* **$$$$**). Each comes with roof tent, shower & equipped kitchen, & takes 2 guests. *Tent N$350/700 sgl/dbl.* **$$**

🏠 **Namwi Island** [560 D1] (12 chalets, camping) ☎066 252243; **m** 081 127 4572; **e** namwiisl@iway.na; www.namwiisland.com. Some 5km east of town towards Ngoma, follow the signs on to a gravel road for about 4km to where Lizelle Booysen has created a very smart site in beautiful gardens with a large pool. Each of the 24 grassy pitches has its own paved parking area & power. The central ablution block boasts single-sex toilets & showers, & scullery & laundry facilities. Sharing these are 4 budget chalets of brick & thatch, with just 2 beds, desk & light, & a braai area, while a further 8 self-catering 'luxury' chalets have AC, bathroom & kitchen. *Chalet only N$475/1,080 luxury/budget dbl; camping N$200 pp.* **$$–$$$**

🏠 **Caprivi Mutoya Lodge** [560 D1] (8 tents, 5 chalets, camping) ☎066 253553; **m** 081 287 5438; **e** info@caprivimutoyalodge.com; www.caprivimutoyalodge.com. On the site of the old Mvuvu Tented Camp, this is approx 24km east of Katima Mulilo; from the B8, take the dirt road for 12km, turn left after Lisikile Fish Farm & the lodge is 300m from the road. Overlooking a lagoon, the pretty accommodation blocks are sheltered by waterberry & jackalberry trees (from the local name for the former, the lodge takes its name), surrounding a sparkling swimming pool. The main area with restaurant (*dinner N$190*), reception & gift shop splits self-catering, en-suite chalets from the standard & 'luxury' tents. Set further back from the water is a campsite with tidy shared ablution blocks, BBQ, light & power points. You can rent both bicycles & mekoro, though be aware that there are hippos in the river. Fishing, boat cruises & village walks, plus trips further afield, are further options. *Chalet from N$560–1,060/900–1,900 sgl/dbl; camping N$160 pp; all exc tourism levy, laundry.* **$$–$$$$**

🏠 **Zambezi Mubala Camp** [560 D1] (8 tents, camping) 📞 066 252801; m 081 165 1241; e mubalacamp@gondwana-collection.com; www. gondwana-collection.com. Primarily a fishing camp, although the birding is considered to be an attraction too, the former Island View Lodge is a sister property to Mubala Lodge (see below). To get there, take the B8 towards Ngoma for 13km (about 56km from Ngoma) to the D3508, where the camp is signposted to the left. Follow this gravel road (which was being tarmacked in 2018) for 20km, then turn left & follow the arrows. Transfers can be arranged from Livingstone, Victoria Falls & Kasane.

Both the safari tents & 12 shady camping pitches are spaced out along the Zambezi River, the latter with water points, braai & shared ablutions. Much of the original camp's *raison d'être* was tigerfishing, & this is still a feature; boats & equipment can be hired with a guide on a ½- or full-day basis (*from N$250/hr pp, plus fuel*). There's a pool set amid lawns & the central bar area has a pool table; there's also a small shop selling fishing tackle. *N$563/900 sgl/dbl; camping N$195 pp.* **$$–$$$**

☀🏠 **Zambezi Mubala Lodge** [560 D1] (21 cabins) 📞 066 253521; m 081 165 1740; e mubalamanager@gondwana-collection.com; www.gondwana-collection.com; ✪ 17°32.414'S, 24°34.000'E. One of the newest additions to the Gondwana Collection, Mubala Lodge stands on the banks of the Zambezi, downstream from Katima. Guests leave their cars at Mubala Camp (see above), & are transferred to the lodge by boat; you must arrive at least 1hr before sunset; return transfers from the lodge run hourly from 07.30 to 10.30.

Mubala means 'colourful' in the local Silozi language, & the lodge doesn't disappoint. Set along the river are stylish, spacious cabins with mellow green & cream tones on the outside, & an explosion of turquoise & jade within. Accentuating the nautical theme are wave & ripple textures on walls, & porthole-style windows. In each twin, dbl & family cabin, a small lobby & kitchenette leads to a spacious en-suite bathroom, & all have fans, fridges, mosquito nets & tea/coffee facilities.

A capacious, open-sided dining area beneath upcycled metal roofing from the old lodge houses solid wood tables & wicker chairs, with weighted canvas curtains for cooler evenings. The outdoor bar overlooks the river, adjacent to a large swimming pool shaded by canvas partitions in different shades of green & blue, & with plenty of comfortable sunloungers. The birdlife is prolific here, reflected in watercolour prints throughout.

Though river-based activities are the main draw (*sundowner cruise N$240 pp; fishing N$250/hr pp or N$1,000/boat ½ day, inc b/fast & drinks*), the lodge is also popular with photographers & birders (especially for the massive carmine bee-eater colony that migrates here in Sep), with added interest provided by nature walks. Trips to Chobe & Victoria Falls can be organised, too. *N$2,416/3,866 sgl/dbl, inc transfers, exc laundry.* **$$$$$**

🚤 **Muchenje Houseboat Safaris & River Lodge** [560 D1] (4 chalets, houseboat) 📞 +27 82 820 2949, +27 81 258 5220, +27 81 143 9477; e muchenjehouseboatsafaris@gmail. com, muchenje.riverlodge@gmail.com; www. muchenjehouseboatsafaris.co.za. Follow the signs from Zambezi Mubala Camp (see left), & you'll come to this, small self-catering lodge, whose functional chalets were nearing completion in Jun 2018 following flooding. The houseboat, with 2 dbl beds sleeping up to 4, has AC & a small braai, & a kitchen with 2-plate gas stove, fridge & freezer. Various packages from 3 nights/4 days focus on either fishing or Chobe National Park, always accompanied by a tender boat. *3-night fishing trip self-catering from N$7,000 pp (min 4); 4-night Chobe trip from N$13,500 pp.* **$$$$–$$$$$**

🚤 **Shamwari Houseboat Adventures** [560 D1] (5 cabins) m 081 128 5637, 081 147 4253; e shamwari@mweb.com.na; www. shamwarihouseboat.com. To reach Shamwari, head towards Zambezi Mubala Camp (see left), taking a right turn at the signpost for Kalambezi Rest Camp & Rice Project. Renovated in 2014, Shamwari has 2 twin cabins (only 1 en suite), with AC & large glass-panelled sliding doors. A spacious lounge/dining area leads to an open-air braai deck with jacuzzi, & DSTV is on board for those who can't leave it behind. Tender boats accompany the Shamwari for fishing, birding or game viewing – with trips to Chobe National Park possible via the Kasai Channel. Meals are provided but all drinks – beer, wine, bottled water, juices, etc – are extra; guests can provide their own or advise their requirements & they will be prepurchased accordingly. *FB/self-catering from N$3,500/2,100 dbl, inc tender boats, exc fuel.* **$$$$-$$$$$**

✗ Where to eat and drink
If you are staying in Katima Mulilo or the surrounding areas, you'll probably eat at your lodge. Alternative options are at present limited to just:

✗ Passione Portuguese Restaurant [555 A3] Kongole Rd, above Bank Windhoek in Zambezi Shopping Centre; 066 252282; m 081 221 2906; ⏰ 08.30–22.00 Mon–Sat, 10.00–22.00 Sun. A popular restaurant serving pizzas, fish & grills, it also does take-aways. **$$$**

☕ Wiesenhof Coffee Shop [555 A3] Zambezi Shopping Centre; ⏰ 08.00–17.00 Mon–Fri. Inside Pick n Pay, this franchise serves b/fast & light meals. **$$**

Other practicalities
Katima has branches of Bank Windhoek, FNB, Nedbank and Standard **banks**, all with ATMs. Note that changing Zambian currency here is likely to be a problem, so if you have kwacha you may need to cross the border and exchange currency with local traders on the Zambian side.

For **food and provisions**, start just behind the square at the Zambezi Shopping Centre [555 A3]. Supermarkets are well covered, with Pick n Pay in the central area, but for something more colourful, head for the busy market in the centre of town, near the craft centre.

Should you be in need of **car repairs**, try Tractor and Truck Repairs on the main road in from Rundu. **Car hire** is available from the Budget Rent-a-Car office at the Engen garage on Hage Geingob/Kongola Road.

Emergency and health
The police can be contacted on 066 10111. Should you be in need of medical treatment, the number for the ambulance/hospital is 066 251400, but you'd be better advised to contact one of the town's doctors.

➕ Dr Sitengu Next to Shoprite; 066 252083
➕ Katima Medical Practice (Dr Ward) Next to Caprivi Pharmacy; 066 252418; m 081 128 0985

➕ Katima Dental Practice Hage Geingob Rd; 066 252083; ⏰ 08.00–17.00 Mon–Fri, 08.00–noon Sat
➕ Zambezi Pharmacy [555 D2] Zambezi Shopping Centre, Hage Geingob Rd; 066 253446; ⏰ 08.00–13.00 & 14.00–17.00 Mon–Fri, 08.30–noon Sat, closed Sun

What to see and do
Katima has few intrinsic attractions, although the lodges along the Zambezi are very pleasant places to stay. For those interested in local crafts, the outdoor craft market on Olifant Street is a good outlet and well worth a visit.

If you have more time, then use it for trips on the river, or as a base for longer expeditions into Mudumu, Nkasa Rupara, the Upper Zambezi and Lake Liambezi.

Zambezi Waterfront Tourism Park
A new development in Katima is likely to have a considerable impact on the local economy and tourist infrastructure, if and when it finally opens. Located on a 21.66ha site along the B8 Ngoma Road, just past the T-junction, it is an ambitious public–private partnership which, when complete, is expected to have various levels of accommodation, a campsite, restaurants and conferencing, plus an aquarium, museum and theatre, and even water-based sports and activities. Despite an original completion date of December 2009, the place was

still not open in 2018 (although it looked complete), and there was no indication of an opening date.

LAKE LIAMBEZI This large, shallow lake is located between the Linyanti and Chobe rivers, about 60km south of Katima Mulilo. When full it covers some 10,000ha, although since 1985 it has been much drier, and frequently something of a dust bowl – until the exceptional rains of 2009. Thus, for many years, people and cattle have populated its bed rather than hippos and crocodiles.

Lake Liambezi's main source of water used to be the Linyanti River, but after many years of poor rainfall, water has failed to fill the lake after filtering through the Linyanti Swamps (which themselves are pretty dry much of the time). As a result, there has been a trend towards less and less water in the lake and the marshes around it, and more villages have emerged. Despite good water levels in the Kwando–Linyanti system in the 2011/12 rainy season, the water didn't even break through as far as the Linyanti River. By 2014, however, for the first time in many years, Lake Liambezi had a few inches of water, due to some good rains, a recovery of the Bukalo Channel from the northeast, and possibly some flow-back from the Chobe River. It has since become a popular fishing area for local fishermen, sustained by good rains in 2018.

Where to stay A community campsite has been established in the nearby Salambala Conservancy (page 564).

ZAMBEZI–CHOBE CONFLUENCE Two rivers bound the eastern end of the Zambezi Region: the Chobe to the south, and the Zambezi to the north. Their confluence is at the end of Impalila Island, at the eastern tip of Namibia. The Zambezi flows relentlessly to the sea but, depending on their relative heights, the Chobe either contributes to that, or may even reverse its flow and draw water from the Zambezi. Between the two rivers is a triangle of land, of about 700km², which is a mixture of floodplains, islands and channels that link the two rivers.

This swampy, riverine area is home to several thousand local people, mostly members of Zambia's Lozi tribe. (The main local languages here are Lozi and Sobia.) Most have a seasonal lifestyle, living next to the river channels, fishing, keeping cattle, and farming maize, sorghum and pumpkins. They move with the water levels, transferring on to higher, drier ground as the waters rise.

Flora and fauna The area's ecosystems are similar to those in the upper reaches of the Okavango Delta: deepwater channels lined by wide reedbeds and rafts of papyrus. Some of the larger islands are still forested with baobabs, water figs, knobthorn, umbrella thorn, mopane, pod mahogany, star chestnut and sickle-leafed albizia, while jackalberry and Chobe waterberry overhang the rivers, festooned with creepers and vines.

Large mammals are scarce here, but most that do occur swim over from Botswana's Chobe National Park. These include elephants and buffalo, and even lions have been known to take to the river in search of the tasty-but-dim domestic cattle on the other side.

Even when there are no large mammals here, the birdlife is spectacular. Large flocks of white-faced ducks congregate on islands in the rivers, African skimmers nest on exposed sandbanks, and both reed cormorants and darters are seen fishing or perching while they dry their feathers. Kingfishers are numerous, from the giant to the tiny pygmy, as are herons and egrets. However, the area's most unusual bird is

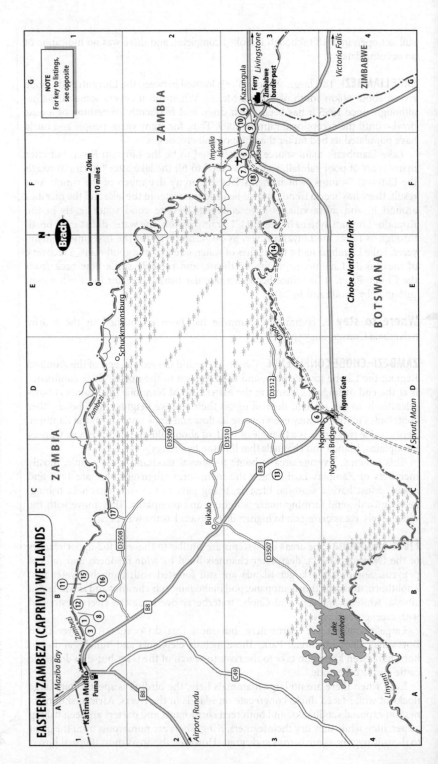

EASTERN ZAMBEZI (CAPRIVI) WETLANDS

NOTE
For key to listings,
see opposite

ZAMBIA

ZAMBIA

BOTSWANA

ZIMBABWE

Chobe National Park

Zambezi

Zambezi

Chobe

Lake Liambezi

Linyanti

Maziba Bay

Katima Mulilo

Puma

Airport, Rundu

Bukalo

Schuckmannsburg

Impalila Island

Kasane

Kazungula

Ferry Livingstone

Zimbabwe border post

Victoria Falls

Ngoma

Ngoma Bridge

Ngoma Gate

Savuti, Maun

B8

B8

B8

C49

D3507

D3508

D3509

D3510

D3512

① ③ ⑧ ⑫ ⑪ ⑮ ⑯ ② ⑰ ⑬ ⑭ ⑥ ⑤ ⑦ ⑱ ⑨ ⑩ ④

N

Bradt

0   10 miles
0   20km

the unassuming rock pratincole with its black, white and grey body, which perches on rocks within the rapids and hawks for insects in the spray.

⌂ **Where to stay** The largest island in this area, Impalila, is at the very tip of Namibia and is home to a select group of lodges, while in the last few years others have popped up in the Caprivi Wetlands, west of Impalila Island, and a couple of safari boats add further interest.

Impalila gained notoriety during the 1980s as a military base for the South African Defence Forces (SADF), as it was strategically positioned within sight of Botswana, Zambia and Zimbabwe. It still boasts a 1,300m-long runway, used occasionally by charter airlines to bring visitors to the lodges, but the barracks are now a school, serving most of the older children in the area. Visitors to the island arrive either by air, or by boat from Kasane. You'll have to clear customs and immigration for both Botswana and Namibia on arrival and departure, but fortunately, as borders go, the **customs and immigration post** on Impalila (⊕ 07.30–16.30) is fairly informal and quick.

⌂ **Chobe Water Villas** [560 F3] (16 chalets) ☏ +264 66 253602; reservations ☏ +264 61 431 8001/2; e chobe.res@ol.na; www.chobeatervillas. com. Looking across to Sedudu Island from Namibia's Kasika Conservancy, & nearer to the park than any of Impalila Island's lodges, Chobe Water Villas opened in 2017 on the site of the old King's Den. Guests usually arrive by boat from Kasane, clearing Namibian immigration at Kasika. Almost all the staff are from one of the local villages.

Subtle greys & orange highlights underpin a design inspired by aspects of Namibian culture, giving the feel of a contemporary art installation: seemingly every part of the main structure is symbolic. In the classy restaurant, for example, 'rain' chimes sound like thunder when stirred by the breeze. There's plenty of practical input, too, from the library (with steps) & the cleverly screened buffet area to 2 bars – 1 for those included in the rates, & 1 for premium drinks. For the warmer months, there's an infinity pool mirroring the Chobe River, & a table (just one!) set in a shallow pool of water. For cooler evenings, tables morph into gas fireboxes & firepits materialise riverside. With Wi-Fi throughout & sports TV in a small meeting room, the outside world isn't far away either. There's even a 'conversation pit'!

The impressive thatched chalets stand on stilts at the water's edge, their balconies (with telescopes) offering almost unbroken views from wooden sunloungers, as if from the prow of a ship. To add to the sense of seclusion, 4 of them are on the 'honeymoon island', reached across a bouncy suspension bridge. Inside, all is calm & orderly, with the same contemporary styling, a king-size bed & comfortable sofa, ceiling fan (no AC), Nespresso machine, complimentary minibar, & a great big bathroom with a separate shower & bath. Power is supplied by a combination of solar panels & generator, with inverters for lights at night.

Game drives & river cruises in & around Chobe National Park are included in the rates; other options, such as village tours & trips to Victoria Falls, can be organised at extra cost. *FBA from US$630/1,050 sgl/dbl Dec–Jun to US$1,050/1,686*

Rundu and the Kavango/Zambezi Regions (The Caprivi Strip)   ZAMBEZI (CAPRIVI) REGION   **21**

Jul–Nov, inc transfers from Kasane Immigration Office; exc laundry. No children under 13. ☺ *All year.* $$$$$$$

🏠 **Cascade Island Lodge** [560 G3] (8 suites) Ntwala Island; contact as for Kaza Safari Lodge (see below). The former Ntwala Island Lodge was extended & substantially rebuilt in 2017, but is now available only for group tours. The location is beautifully secluded, a cluster of islands within the Mambova Rapids, reached from a natural reed-fringed harbour. Long wooden walkways lead to the main area, facing the rapids, & on to the chalets. The newer chalets are more contemporary in construction & style, & closer together than the older ones. That said, they're all pretty spacious, & all have a bath, inside & open-air showers & separate toilet, & a private plunge pool set into a deck extending over the water. The calm colour scheme continues into the main area, where oversize wildlife photos dominate the décor & wooden & cane chairs invite relaxation by the river. A fleet of aluminium boats is at the ready for guests to explore the quiet backwaters, indulge in a spot of fishing, or take in a sunset cruise. $$$$$$–$$$$$$$

🏠 **Kaza Safari Lodge** [560 G3] (8 chalets) Contact Flame of Africa; ☎ +27 31 762 2424; e sales@flameofafrica.com; www.anthology. co.za. Situated on the northwest of Impalila Island, overlooking the Zambezi's Mambova Rapids, the former Impalila Island Lodge served in many ways to bring the island to people's attention. Now under new ownership, it was refurbished in late 2017, but retains much of the appeal of the original. Though it caters mainly to group bookings, they do occasionally have space for ad hoc stays.

Kaza has a peaceful location, about 45min by boat from Kasane (or a shorter boat trip to the south of Impalila Island followed by a 10min drive). The large thatched bar/dining area & comfortable lounge, built around a huge baobab, is open to the breeze, though can be sheltered when it's cold. The pool deck has reclining loungers, umbrellas, & a great view of the river.

Each of the en-suite wooden chalets has glass & gauze sliding doors on to a veranda, overlooking the rapids. Inside, much is made of polished local mukwa wood, with its natural yellow & brown colours, alongside twin beds or a king-size dbl. Each room has AC, & there's Wi-Fi in the main area.

Along with game drives into Chobe there are

boat cruises taking in lunch at their own floating restaurant, the Raft, sunset cruises & fishing excursions, as well as walks to a local village or to the ancient baobab. $$$$$$–$$$$$$$

🏠 **Ichingo Chobe River Lodge** [560 G3] (8 Meru tents) m +267 7130 2439 (on island); m +267 7134 8435, +27 83 431 7399 (reservations); e enquiry@zqcollection.com; www. zqcollection.com. Originally the brainchild of Dawn & Ralph Oxenham, Ichingo occupies a secluded site on the south of Impalila Island, overlooking the quiet backwaters of some of the Chobe River's rapids, a world away from busy Kasane just across the water. Now within the same fold as the *Zambezi Queen* & *Chobe Princess* riverboats (see opposite), it has seen some changes, but fortunately the new owners have retained the atmosphere of this lovely old lodge. Instead, they have focused on improving creature comforts such as AC, king-size beds (or large twins) & larger bathrooms in the walk-in tents, along with a plunge pool & loungers overlooking the rapids.

Each of the tents is set high above the flood levels – important in a location where the rise & fall of water is up to 2m – & there's a balcony at the front, with views of the water through the vegetation, dominated by water-tolerant waterberry trees (*Syzygium guineese*), & the orange-fruited mangosteen (*Garcinia livingstonei*). Meals are taken around a large wooden table in the thatched dining area/bar/lounge that fronts on to the river.

The lodge makes a super base for birdwatching, fishing (popular with families) & game viewing from their fleet of little boats along the Chobe River, & offers some excellent fly-fishing in the rapids. There are also visits to a local village & walks to a giant baobab. Game drives into Chobe can be arranged, usually on departure day as part of the transfer back to Kasane. *FBA N$6,435–6,950/9,900–10,692 sgl/dbl, inc boat transfer from Kasane Immigration Post. No children under 6.* $$$$$

🏠 **Zovu Elephant Lodge** [560 F3] (10 rooms) m 081 128 2116; e bookings2@ zovuelephantlodge.na. Just metres from the boundary with Chobe Water Villas, Zovu's green- & cream-coloured chalets dot the grounds, surrounded by well-tended gardens, in the centre of which is a large pool. All are en suite, if a little dated, with fans, fridge, Wi-Fi & tea & coffee facilities. The large, glass-fronted main area &

restaurant have beautiful views out across the Chobe River, with elephant crossing points visible. Excursions include boat trips, game drives & trips to Chobe & Vic Falls. *FB N$3,920/6,460 sgl/dbl, inc most drinks, transfers from Kasane Immigration Post.* **$$$$$$**

✴ 🏠 **Serondela** [560 E3] (8 rooms) 📞066 252677; m 081 147 7798; e info@serondelalodge. com; www.serondelalodge.com. Sister camp to Nkasa Lupala & Jackalberry (page 552), Serondela is 45mins by boat from Kasane, & opened in Mar 2018. It's a lovely, relaxed lodge that prides itself on its eco-friendly & low-impact design, using recycled materials throughout: driftwood, cattle yokes & upcycled PVC features; it sounds bizarre, but fits beautifully into the surrounding landscape. If you're dropping off your rental car in Kasane, you'll need to be there at least 1hr before sunset for the transfer from the immigration office. As well as fishing trips & boat cruises, a game drive in Chobe NP is included, usually on check-out day to facilitate getting to & from Kasane. *FBA N$4,895/7,800 sgl/dbl, inc transfers, exc laundry. No children under 13.* ⊕ *All year.* **$$$$$$**

Safari boats

Several safari boats cruise on the Zambezi & Chobe rivers, as well as into the contiguous wetlands of the Caprivi Strip. These Namibian-registered vessels, part of the same group as Impalila Island's Ichingo River Lodge, are permitted to cruise the waters of the Chobe when the national park is closed & all Botswana-registered vessels must leave, so offer a unique opportunity to watch game & experience the tranquillity of the river after dark & at sunrise. Most passengers take the time to relax, but from all the boats, smaller tender boats are available for fishing (in season), game viewing or birdwatching with an experienced guide, & there is the opportunity to visit a Namibian village.

🚤 **Zambezi Queen** [560 F3] (14 suites) 📞+267 7130 2439, +27 21 715 412; e enquiry@zqcollection.com; www. zqcollection.com; ⊕ all year. The *grande dame* of Chobe's riverboats, the 42m *Zambezi Queen* moves slowly between 2 mooring points on the Chobe River over 2 or 3 nights – with cruises departing from Kasane on set departure dates throughout the week. Up on deck there's a pool & various areas for relaxing in the shade or soaking up the sun, & at night a telescope beckons guests to explore the heavens. In the lounge areas, AC assures cool comfort, while from the adjacent restaurant you can spot animals at dusk as they approach the water. A well-stocked bar is popular, too! There's mosquito screening throughout, including in the individual suites which feature sliding doors to private balconies & river views from the beds. *2 nights (dep Mon & Wed) FBA R21,021–32,340/30,066–46,256 sgl/dbl (2 nights), inc transfer from Kasane, exc community levy R95 pp/night; rates in South African rand (on a par with Namibian dollar).* **$$$$$$$**

🚤 **Chobe Princess** [560 F3] (4–5 cabins) Contact as for *Zambezi Queen* (see above). More intimate & more wide-ranging than the *Zambezi Queen*, the 3 *Chobe Princesses* – with 4 or 5 cabins – cruise some 50km of the Chobe River, mooring at points as far west as Serondela over 2 or 3 nights. The en-suite cabins are smaller than on the *Queen*, but similarly well appointed, with AC & big picture windows, so you can sit & watch wildlife from your cabin, as well as on deck. This is the chance for total relaxation with a drink, or in the on-board plunge pool, but for more involvement, various activites are available. *FBA R15,015–23,100/19,963–30,712 sgl/dbl (2 nights), inc transfer from Kasane, exc community levy R65 pp/night; rates in South African rand.* **$$$$$$– $$$$$$$**

Ngoma border The road from Katima to Ngoma is now fully tarred. At Ngoma itself there's little apart from the border post, a smart office next to the bridge by the Chobe River. About 2km further on, over the river, Botswana's border post is a newer building perched high above the water. Both seem efficient, pleasant and generally quiet. This crossing (⊕ *07.00–18.00*) is fine for 2WD vehicles.

Beyond, you have a choice of routes: the fully tarred road to Kasane, cutting through Chobe National Park, or much slower, but more scenic routes. Of these, one leads to Kasane, taking in game viewing along the Chobe riverfront; the other heads through forested and communal lands towards Savuti and Maun. Both these scenic options require park permits and a 4x4 vehicle.

Chobe River Camp [560 D3] (20 tented chalets) \066 250614; e res6@gondwana-collection.com; www. gondwana-collection. com. The former Camp Chobe was taken over & refurbished by Gondwana in early 2017. Looking across the river to Chobe National Park in Botswana, its stylish tented chalets have en-suite bathrooms & solar power, & are elegantly furnished with mopane timber & cream canvas. The split-level central lapa has a raised bar with large sofas & dining area below, again making the most of the river views, with a swimming pool on the lawn nearby. Wi-Fi is available in central areas. Activities include sunset cruises, nature walks & game drives. N$1,399/2,238 sgl/dbl. **$$$**

Λ Salambala Community Campsite & Restcamp [560 C3] (4 pitches) m 081 418 5760. The turn-off for Salambala from the main B8 is about 15km north of Ngoma or 46km south of Katima Mulilo. Another of the Caprivi's excellent community campsites (page 16), it has 3 separate pitches for tents & another suited to larger groups. Each has a kitchen area, firepit, private flush WC & a shower with hot water. A small waterhole attracts local game, & guided walks, fishing, game drives & village visits can be arranged. All profits from the camp go back to the community. From N$80 pp. **$**

Appendix 1

TRACKS AND SIGNS

An extract from Southern African Wildlife: A Visitor's Guide *by Mike Unwin*

Animals seldom parade across the bush the way they do across a TV screen. In fact, the untamed wilderness, far from teeming with wall-to-wall wildlife, can sometimes seem a disappointingly empty place. But there is much more to see than simply the animals themselves, and the trained eye will find the land littered with evidence of their presence or passing: tracks and trails, pellets and droppings, diggings and rubbings, torn branches, flattened grass, feathers, nests and bones. These clues, often known by the Afrikaans word *spoor*, tell the story of what happened when nobody was looking.

Some awareness of tracks and signs will greatly enrich your own understanding of wildlife. Trackers, like forensic detectives, combine acute eyesight and vigilance with great patience, a photographic memory and the imagination to reconstruct a complete picture from a few scattered fragments. It is a humbling experience to watch an expert in action: a mere scratch in the soil can not only identify the animal responsible, but also reveal its age, sex, size, where it was heading, how it was moving, when it passed by and why.

MAKING TRACKS Every animal that touches the ground leaves tracks. Some are easily recognised; others are more puzzling. Most small creatures, such as lizards, can only be identified to a broad generic level, but many larger mammal species have unique signatures. No two individuals of any species are identical, and the tracks of many show marked differences of size and shape between forefeet and hindfeet or between male and female. Conditions underfoot are critical to tracking. The clearest tracks are laid on surfaces that hold an impression, such as firm mud or damp sand. Hard, baked soil is too resistant, while soft sand allows slippage that distorts the shape.

Weather is also important: wind and rain can help to date tracks, but may erode or completely obliterate them. Neither overcast weather nor a midday sun are very helpful to trackers. Early morning is the best time to look – partly because tracks are still fresh, but also because the low light and slanting shadows throw any imprint into sharper relief.

The heavy brigade The bigger the animal, the harder its footfall. Elephants leave huge, round tracks, up to half a metre across, with the hindfeet smaller and more oval than the forefeet. In soft mud they create knee-deep craters that become sunbaked into a treacherous pitted moonscape. On hard ground, the latticework of cracks on their soles leaves a distinct, mosaic-like impression, even though the circular track outline may be invisible. A small heap of soil in front of each print indicates the elephant's direction (the rear of each track shows a clean edge). Rhino tracks have a cloverleaf shape, with each foot showing three distinct toes. On hard ground only the curved outer rim of each toenail may be visible. White rhinos have larger tracks (up to 30cm long) than black rhinos (about 24cm), with relatively broader toe

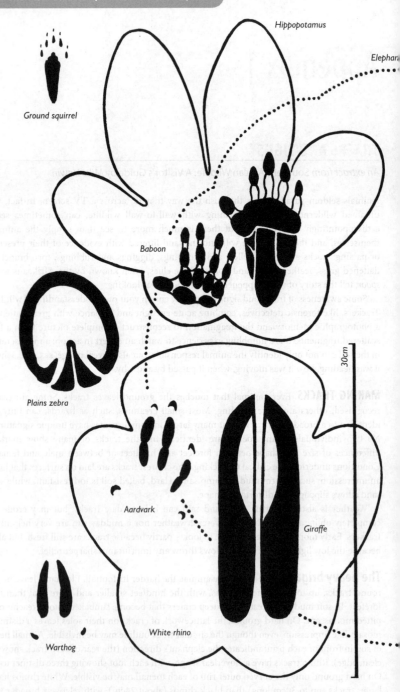

ANIMAL TRACKS (DRAWN TO SCALE)

Ground squirrel

Hippopotamus

Elephant

Baboon

Plains zebra

Aardvark

Giraffe

White rhino

Warthog

30cm

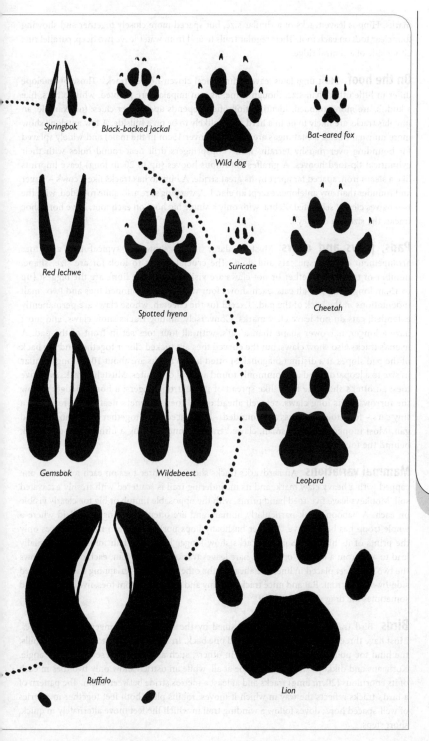

Springbok

Black-backed jackal

Wild dog

Bat-eared fox

Red lechwe

Suricate

Spotted hyena

Cheetah

Gemsbok

Wildebeest

Leopard

Buffalo

Lion

marks. Hippos leave tracks of a similar size, but spaced more closely together and showing four clear toes on each foot. Their regular trails to and from water leave two deep, parallel ruts either side of a central ridge.

On the hoof

Most ungulates leave symmetrical cloven-hoofed tracks. Those of antelope differ in little other than size, though some, like an impala's, are pointed, while others, like a kudu's, are more rounded. Identification often depends upon other clues: for example, an impala's tracks are likely to be in a herd and unlikely to be on a hillside. A few antelope show more unusual tracks: a sitatunga's are very long (over 15cm in the male) and widely splayed for bounding over marshy terrain, while klipspringers drill neat round holes with their cylindrical tip-toed hooves. A giraffe's enormous hooves (up to 20cm long) leave imprints like a steam iron, spaced far apart by its great stride. A buffalo has tracks like a cow's – larger and rounder than any antelope's except an eland. A warthog's are also quite rounded, with the two halves clearly separated. Zebra, with only a single big hoof on each foot, leave horseshoe tracks, the size of a donkey's.

Pads, paws and claws

Most predator tracks show the typical pad and toes arrangement of domestic cats and dogs. The crucial things to look for are size, shape, number of toes and whether or not claws are visible. The male lion's are the biggest (up to 15cm long) and, like all cats, each shows four well-spaced, rounded toes and two small indentations in the back of the pad. Except for the cheetah, whose claws are permanently extended, cats do not leave claw marks. Conversely, all dog tracks show claws, and most have a longer, narrower shape than a cat's, with all four toes set in front of the pad. A hyena's tracks also show claws, but the curved toes are tucked closer together and the back of the pad slopes at a distinct diagonal. Spotted hyena tracks are about 10cm long, similar in size to a leopard's, and are commonly found around campsites. Mustelid tracks have five toes: an otter's show the hand-like spread of its dextrous fingers; a honey badger's show the furrows of its long claws, set well ahead of the toes. A genet's neat tracks resemble a tiny cat's – four-toed, clawless and rounded – but spaced close together by its short-legged gait. Most mongooses leave small, clawed tracks, some showing a fifth hind toe set back behind the four in front.

Mammal variations

An aardvark's tracks show only three toes on each foot, each one capped with a heavy claw mark, and its meandering trail is scattered with freshly excavated soil. Monkeys leave five-toed hand prints, with the opposable thumb or big toe clearly visible on each. A baboon's look particularly human, and are often confusingly overlaid where a whole troop has been active. A lesser bushbaby hops upright between trees, so leaves only the prints of its hindfeet. Squirrel tracks show longer hind feet than forefeet, and usually lead to and from a burrow or tree. A hare leaves tracks in sets of four, each of which shows the two front feet placed in line, one ahead of the other, and the overlapping back feet placed side-by-side in front. Rat and mice tracks are tiny and show four front toes, five hind toes and sometimes the drag mark of the tail.

Birds

Bird tracks can be roughly classified by the shape and arrangement of the toes. Most have three toes pointing forward and one back. In some, such as starlings or hornbills, the hind toe points straight back, while in others, such as doves, it is set at a slight angle. Korhaans and dikkops show no hind toe at all, while an ostrich show only two toes in each of its enormous (20cm long) tracks and at least a metre's stride between them. The pattern of a bird's tracks reflects the way in which it moves: robins place both feet together in a series of well-spaced hops; doves follow a winding trail in which the feet move alternately in quick, short steps.

Scale trails The undulating motion of a typical snake leaves a series of S-shaped ripples, where each curve has pushed against surface irregularities to propel the body forward. A few heavy-bodied snakes, such as pythons and puff adders, can also grip the ground with their belly to push themselves along caterpillar-fashion, leaving a broad, straight furrow, stamped with the impression of belly scales and bisected by the thin drag-line of the tail tip. The sidewinding Peringuey's adder leaves a strange sequence of disconnected bracket marks where each violent undulation has flung its body off the hot sand.

Other distinctive reptile tracks include the riverbank mud-chute of a crocodile – whose tracks show five splayed toes on the forefeet, four toes on the longer back feet, and a heavy furrow gouged by the tail – and the large, long-clawed prints of a monitor lizard, spaced either side of its wavy tail drag line. Smaller lizards inscribe neat, winding tramlines of closely spaced prints which, in soft surfaces such as sand, can be hard to distinguish from those of beetles and other larger invertebrates.

DROPPINGS Unsavoury as they may seem, droppings can speak volumes about the whereabouts and behaviour of animals. Many male mammals delineate their territory using the strategically placed whiff of dung. Some, such as rhino and civet, build up big middens with regular deposits; others, such as hyena and many antelope, roll in theirs to soak up the scent and spread it around. Some droppings are visible from a great distance: a splash of white often reveals the nest or roost of birds such as vultures or cormorants, while dassie colonies stain the rocks yellow and brown with their viscous urine.

Depositing a load An elephant scatters its fibrous, football-sized droppings anywhere, and elephant country remains littered with dung long after the herds have moved on. When fresh, these droppings are full of goodies, and a host of foragers, from baboons to francolins, pick through the steaming contents in search of seeds, fruits and pods. White rhino dung is fine in texture, consisting entirely of grass, whereas black rhino dung is full of twigs and other woody matter. Over time, a bull rhino builds up a waist-deep midden, spread over several square metres, into which he scrapes deep grooves with his hind feet to pick up the scent. In areas where both rhino species occur, one may deposit its dung on the midden of the other. Hippo scatter their dung with their tail, plastering it messily over vegetation beside their trails. Buffalo droppings are black and loose, falling in folded 'pats' like domestic cattle's, and are often left trampled and smeared by the traffic of the herd.

Piles of pellets Antelope leave neat piles of dark pellets, each pointed at one end and indented at the other. Many, such as impala, use communal dung heaps. Antelope are so efficient at deriving moisture and sustenance from their food that even the largest species have remarkably small, dry droppings – though a wildebeest's may congeal in sticky clumps. A giraffe's droppings, also amazingly small, are widely scattered by their great drop. Zebras deposit their dark, kidney-shaped droppings in neat mounds, which grow paler with age and break down into heaps of fine, dry grass.

Smelly scats Carnivore droppings – or scats – are cylindrical sausages, often pointed or twisted at one end – as any dog-owner will confirm. Because of their meat content, they tend to be smellier than those of herbivores. Hyena droppings are green when fresh, but turn to a conspicuous chalky white because of their high bone content. A lion's may also whiten with age, but can be black with blood, and are usually full of fur. Civet droppings are surprisingly large, and often contain the hard undigested exoskeletons of millipedes, as well as berries and insect husks. Otter droppings, or spraints, consist mostly of crushed crab shell and are deposited at the water's edge.

WHO'S AT HOME? Many animals can be detected by the homes they build. Bird nests are the best known, and some, such as the enormous thatches of sociable weavers or hamerkops often provide shelter for a whole community of other animals. Tree holes offer a desirable residence to anything from hornbills and hoopoes to bushbabies and squirrels, and a promising-looking cavity is always worth watching during the breeding season. Burrows should be checked for signs of life: a complex of small holes may indicate a mongoose or ground squirrel colony, while a big burrow may house either the aardvark that dug it, or more recent tenants such as warthogs, wild cats or porcupines – so look out for signs of occupation, such as a snake skin or porcupine quill.

The state of an area's vegetation can also betray local residents with no permanent home. A flattened depression in long grass might be where a waterbuck bedded down for the night, while tattered bushes could be the work of a territorial bull sable, who thrashes them with his horns. Deep parallel gashes gouged into a tree trunk are the calling card of the local leopard, and a shiny tree stump beside a mud wallow is a 'rubbing post', polished to a smooth finish by generations of itchy rhinos.

FEEDING SIGNS A good look at the landscape soon reveals who had what for dinner. Elephant are the messiest of eaters: freshly broken branches, peeled strips of bark and tussocks of grass tossed across the track are all sure signs of their presence, as are deep holes dug in sandy riverbeds for fresh water. Big grazers such as hippo or rhino trim clearly defined and well-managed lawns. Giraffe prune thorn trees up to a height of six metres, creating a visible browse line, and leave glistening strings of saliva in overhead branches. Kudu leave bushes frayed and nibbled at head height, while black rhino will even munch thorny, poisonous euphorbias, sometimes demolishing them entirely. Many smaller animals also refashion the landscape in their search for food: bark stripped from the foot of a tree trunk is probably the work of porcupines; excavations at the base of an anthill show where an aardvark dug for termites; a hillside littered with overturned stones shows the methodical foraging of baboons for lizards and scorpions.

Predators usually leave evidence of their kills, though even a large carcass quickly disappears beneath an army of scavengers, as hyenas scatter the bones, vultures strip the skin, blowfly maggots consume the final shreds of flesh and ants clean the last drops of blood from the soil. Even the keratin of an antelope horn is food for the larvae of the horn-boring moth, which leaves strange tubular casts along its length. Leopards often cheat scavengers, at least for a while, by hoisting their kill into a tree, so look out for hooves overhead. A scattering of feathers may reveal the regular plucking post of a raptor – which tears out tough flight feathers individually, leaving small, V-shaped punctures on the shafts, whereas a mammalian predator rips them out in clumps, shearing right through the quills with its teeth. Owls and other birds of prey regurgitate pellets of undigested bones and fur, often found beneath their roosts, while some shrikes impale prey such as lizards and grasshoppers on acacia thorns and barbed-wire fences.

Appendix 2

LANGUAGE

There isn't the space here to include a guide to Namibia's many languages, although, if you are staying in a community for longer than a few days, then do try to learn a few local greetings from your hosts. To get you started, here are the essentials in the major languages that you'll come across. Note, too, that the Afrikaans *moro* has been widely adopted to say 'hello' to tourists – especially among the Himba.

	Damara/Nama	**Herero/Himba**	**Ovambo**
Hello; How are you? (to older man/woman)	*Matisa*	*Perivi*	*Wa le lepo (tate/meme)*
Answer 'Fine' ('Khaingya')	*!Gâi-i-a*	*Nawa*	*Ondili nawa*
Thank you	*Kai-aios, Kai-gangans*	*Okuhepa*	*Ndagi, Ondapandula*
Goodbye	*!Gâitses* *Karee nawa* (stay well)	*Gainga nawa*	*Bye bye*, or *Kalapo nawa*

Do note, too, the cultural guidelines in the box on page 90, and notes on pronunciation of the 'click' languages on page 502. For background details on language, see *Chapter 4*.

While travelling, you are likely to come across unfamiliar words that are in common use in southern African English, many of Afrikaans origin. These include:

apteek	chemist or pharmacy (most towns have one)
bakkie	pick-up truck, with open back
berg	mountain, or mountain range
boerewors (or *wors*)	sausage – an essential component of any *braai*
boma	traditional enclosure, often used at safari camps to mean the area around the fire where everyone gathers
braaivleis (*braai*)	barbecue
the bush	generic term for any wild area, usually implying some thick vegetation cover
bundu	the bush (see above) – more often used in Zimbabwe
cuca shop	bar
dam	manmade lake
donga	small ravine, sometimes caused by water erosion
donkey boiler	system of heating water in a drum over a wood-burning fire
dorp	small rural town, though often implies a place with small-minded, reactionary attitudes
kantoor	an office
klippe	rock or stone (as used in *klip*springer)

kloof	ravine, often with a small river at the bottom
kopje (or *koppie*)	rocky hill, often alone in an otherwise flat area
kraal	cattle enclosure or group of African huts (Owambo)
lapa	Traditionally, an enclosed area within a homestead; often used to mean a large, thatched area for dining etc
lekker	good, nice – now slang, typically used to describe food
mielie	corn or maize, the staple for most of the subcontinent
mieliepap	maize flour porridge, often eaten for breakfast
mokoro	dugout canoe (plural *mekoro*)
ompad	diversion, often used on road signs
omuramba	dry river-bed
orlag	war
pad	road or track
rivier	river
robot	traffic lights (ie: '*robot* ahead', or 'turn left at the *robot*, then…')
rondavel	traditional African hut (usually round)
tackies	running shoes or trainers
veld	grassland – like 'the bush', this term is used for wide, open wilderness areas, but implies mostly low vegetation cover
vlei	depression, valley, lake or low-lying place where water gathers; this term is used throughout the subcontinent
wato	type of dugout canoe
werft	traditional settlement (often Herero)

Appendix 3

FURTHER INFORMATION

BOOKS AND JOURNALS Many of these books are quite widely available, including online, while others may be found only in Namibia.

History

Andersson, Charles John *Lake Ngami* and *The River Okavango* Originally published in the late 1850s; republished as facsimile reprints by Struik, Cape Town, 1967. These two fascinating books record Namibia in the 1850s through the eyes of one of the first traders and hunters in the area.

Baines, Thomas *Explorations in South-West Africa* London, 1864. Although linked more with the countries further east, the travels of Baines, as he accompanied Livingstone and others, make fascinating reading.

Camby, Robert *The History of Rehoboth* A very useful pamphlet for understanding Rehoboth's history.

Cocker, Mark *Rivers of Blood, Rivers of Gold: Europe's Conflict with Tribal Peoples* Jonathan Cape, London, 1998. This highly readable book explores four colonial episodes: the conquest of Mexico, the British onslaught in Tasmania, the uprooting of the Apache in North America, and the German campaign in South West Africa during the early 20th century. It gives an excellent, detailed account of the 1904–07 war, and examines the conflict, and the main characters, in the context of contemporary world politics.

Davis, Ronald, PhD and researchers at Stanford University 'Y chromosome sequence variation and the history of human populations' *Nature Genetics*, November 2000.

Dunbar, R I M 'Why gossip is good for you' *New Scientist*, 21 November 1992.

Gordon, Robert J *The Bushman Myth: The Making of a Namibian Underclass* Westview Press Inc, Colorado and Oxford, 1992. If you, like me, had accepted the received wisdom that Bushmen are the last descendants of Stone Age man, pushed to living in splendid isolation in the Kalahari, then you must read this. It places the Bushmen in an accurate historical context and deconstructs many of the myths we have created about them.

Katjavivi, Peter H *History of Resistance in Namibia* Co-published James Currey, London; OAU in Addis Ababa; UNESCO Press in Paris. Rather more scholarly than *Namibia – The Facts*, it's impressive in its detail.

Mossolow, Dr N *Hansheinrich von Wolf and Duwisib Castle* Society for Scientific Development, Swakopmund, 1995. This neat 20-page account of the castle and its founder is half in German and half in English, and often available from the castle itself. The middle eight pages are black-and-white photographs of the castle and its characters. Worth buying while you are there.

Olusoga, David, and Erichsen, Casper W *The Kaiser's Holocaust* Faber and Faber, London, 2010. While the title of this new history may be seen as inappropriate, there is no doubt that – in the pursuit of land – the colonial German powers were responsible for the deaths of countless Nama and Herero people in the early years of the 20th century. Whether the parallels drawn between their atrocities and the Nazi policies of later years are justified is a matter for considerable debate.

Parsons, Q N 'Franz or Klikko, the Wild Dancing Bushmen: A Case Study in Khoisan Stereotyping' *Botswana Notes & Records*, vol 20 (1989), pp 71–6.

Reader, John *Africa: A Biography of the Continent* Penguin Books, London, 1997. Over 700 pages of highly readable history, interwoven with facts and statistics, to make a remarkable overview of Africa's past. Given that Namibia's boundaries were imposed from Europe, its history *must* be looked at from a pan-African context to be understood. This book can show you that wider view; it is compelling and essential reading.

Natural history

Burke, Antje *Wild Flowers of the Central Namib* Namibia Scientific Society, 2003.

Carruthers, Vincent *Wildlife of Southern Africa* Random House Struik, 2008. Features more than 2,000 plants and animals likely to be encountered by a visitor.

Craven, Patricia, and Marais, Christine *Namib Flora* Gamsberg Macmillan, Windhoek, 1986. This delightful hardback covers a small area 'from Swakopmund to the giant *welwitschia* via Goanikontes', though many of the plants that it beautifully illustrates will be found elsewhere. Similar in style, and equally well illustrated, is *Damaraland Flora* Gamsberg Macmillan, Windhoek, 1992. This volume covers Spitzkoppe, Brandberg and Twyfelfontein, but is invaluable anywhere in the Kaokoveld.

Grunert, Nicole *Fascination of Geology* Klaus Hess Publishers, Namibia. With good illustrations and diagrams, this is a welcome starting point to the complexities and fascination of Namibia's geology.

Le Roux, Piet, and Muller, Mike *Field Guide to the Trees and Shrubs of Namibia* revised and expanded by Coleen Mannheimer and Barbara Curtis, Macmillan Education, Windhoek, 2009. A comprehensive and very well-illustrated guide.

Lovegrove, Dr Barry *The Living Deserts of Southern Africa* Fernwood Press, South Africa, 1993. A beautifully illustrated book with a scholarly text that is both informative and accessible.

Main, Michael *Kalahari: Life's Variety in Dune and Delta* Southern Books, Johannesburg, 1987. Though primarily concerned with Botswana, this is a superb, highly readable treatise on the Kalahari. It covers the origins and ecology of this thirstland and even tackles some of the more sticky political and human questions facing the region. The many marvellous details in the book, and Main's general clarity on the issues, come from personal experience – he's lived in Botswana and travelled there very extensively. But even if you're heading for Namibia's Kalahari, it's still worth getting a copy. The only problem is that it will, of course, captivate you and make a subsequent visit to Botswana essential.

Newman, Kenneth *Birds of Southern Africa* Southern Books, South Africa; published in numerous editions from 1983. One of the best identification field guides to birds in southern Africa, including Namibia.

Rothmann, Sakkie and Theresa *The Harsh and Forbidden Sperrgebiet Rediscovered* Swakopmund ST Promotions, Namibia, 1999.

Seely, Dr Mary *The Namib Desert* Research Foundation of Namibia, Windhoek, 3rd edn 2004. A detailed work on the desert's origins, with descriptions of many sites and the animals and plants that live there. This paperback is well worth getting when you arrive in Namibia. Also in this series is *Waterberg*.

'Shipwreck in the Forbidden Zone' *National Geographic*, October 2009. An absorbing article about the discovery in 2008 of the oldest shipwreck to be found in sub-Saharan Africa.

Sinclair, Ian, Hockey, Phil, Ryan, Peter, and Tarboton, Warwick *Sasol Birds of Southern Africa* Struik, Southern Africa, 2011. First published in 1993, this is particularly useful for the illustrations of birds at different stages of their development, and in flight.

Stuart, Chris and Tilde *Field Guide to Mammals of Southern Africa* Struik Publishers, South Africa, revised 2015.

Unwin, Mike *Southern African Wildlife: A Visitor's Guide* Bradt Travel Guides, UK, 2011. A compact, single-volume guide to the habitats, identification and behavioural characteristics of the region's wildlife. The well-written text, which includes sections on tracks and signs, is matched by exceptionally good photographs.

Van der Walt, Pieter, and le Riche, Elias *The Kalahari & its Plants* Pretoria, 1999.

Children's field guides

SASOL *'My first' guides* Penguin Random House, South Africa. I highly recommend this series of A4 paperback books for young children (aged three–seven) on safari. They are accurate, clearly organised, well illustrated and concisely written. The layout is good and the use of a graphic key means that even children who cannot read are able to decipher the pertinent points for each creature. Accompanying colouring books are available for many of the guides.

My First Book of Southern African Mammals 2008. 58 of the most common and popular African mammals with large colour illustrations, simple text and a key to the animals' size, tracks and diet.

My First Book of Southern African Animal Tracks 2014. A good tracking book with clear illustrations of the animal and its tracks, plus a child-friendly scale to show the size of the tracks.

My First Book of Southern African Birds: Volume 1 2006. An excellent first reference book featuring the 56 most striking and commonly seen southern African bird species. Each page features a large illustration of each bird, with a small paragraph of information and a clear key to the food eaten, nesting style and the bird's track.

My First Book of Southern African Birds: Volume 2 2009. A further 58 birds introduced in identical style to Volume 1.

My First Book of Southern African Insects 2009. Features 58 of the most common, colourful and unusual insects, from ants and dragonflies to beetles and bees.

My First Book of Southern African Creepy-Crawlies 2010. A companion to *Southern African Insects*, this showcases 58 spiders, snails, millipedes and other creepy crawlies. The key shows the creatures' size, diet and when it is active.

My First Book of Southern African Snakes and Other Reptiles 2007. As well as 56 snakes, this covers other reptiles, from lizards to tortoises. It illustrates the reptile itself, with information about its home, diet, size, reproduction – and danger rating.

Newman, Kenneth *What's That Bird? A Starter's Guide to Birds of Southern Africa* Struik, South Africa, 3rd edition 2004. Written by the famous birder, Kenneth Newman, this is an excellent bird book for older children and adults new to African birdwatching.

Art and culture

Breuil, Abbé Henri *The Rock Paintings of Southern Africa* Trianon Press Ltd, Paris, 1955–60. These large volumes cover some of Namibia's major rock-art sites, including the controversial 'White Lady' of Brandberg.

Lilienthal, Adelheid *Art in Namibia* National Art Gallery of Namibia.

Malan, Professor J S *Peoples of Namibia* Rhino Press, Pretoria, 1995.

Mans, Minette *Ongoma! – Notes on Namibian Musical Instruments* Gamsberg Macmillan, Windhoek, 2000. This resource book for teachers on traditional instruments deserves a wider readership.

Rural Art in Namibia Rössing Foundation of Namibia, 1993. A 25-page colour booklet, categorised by region, illustrating traditional Namibian arts and crafts, including interviews with artists about their work.

Photography

Bannister, Anthony, and Johnson, Peter *Namibia – Africa's Harsh Paradise* New Holland, London, 1990. One for the coffee table, this covers the whole country but concentrates on the Bushman and Himba people.

Coulson, David *Namib* Sidgwick & Jackson, London, 1991. This stunning coffee-table book doubles as a readable travelogue. Published 18 years after Coulson's first visit, its insight tells much of his love for Namibia's wilderness.

Marais, Chris, and du Toit, Julienne *Namibia Space* Struik, 2006. One of several coffee-table books showcasing the beauty of Namibia's landscapes.

Schoeman, Amy *The Skeleton Coast* Struik, Cape Town, 2003. Involving, well-informed text and superb photographs make this an excellent read, and *the* definitive work on the coast. Amy's late husband was the legendary Louw Schoeman, and she remains involved with Skeleton Coast Fly-in Safaris, though she now concentrates on travel writing and photography.

Biography and travelogues

Martin, Henno *Sheltering Desert* First English edition published William Kimber, London, 1957. The story of two German geologists who lived out World War II by hiding in the Kuiseb Canyon; good holiday reading if you're visiting the Namib-Naukluft National Park.

Namhila, Ellen Ndeshi *The Price of Freedom* New Namibia Books, Windhoek, 1997. A biographical account by a young Namibian woman of 19 years spent in exile prior to the country's independence.

van der Post, Laurens *The Lost World of the Kalahari* First published Hogarth Press, 1958, subsequently many reprints by Penguin. Laurens van der Post's classic account of how he journeyed into the heart of the Kalahari Desert in search of a 'pure' Bushman group – eventually found at the Tsodilo Hills. His almost mystical description of the Bushmen is fascinating, so long as you can cope with the rather dated turgid prose. You then need to read Robert J Gordon's very different book (page 573) to put it in perspective.

Guidebooks

Bulpin, T V *Discovering Southern Africa* Discovering Southern Africa Productions, South Africa, 1970. In this part guidebook, part history book, Bulpin covers mainly South Africa but also extends into Namibia and Zimbabwe. A weighty tome with useful background views and information, written from a South African perspective.

Travel narratives from Bradt

Jackman, Brian and Scott, Jonathan and Angela *The Marsh Lions: The Story of an African Pride* Bradt, 2012. A wildlife classic, this is a compelling and fascinating account of the daily drama of life and death in Kenya's finest big-game country.

Kent, Princess Michael of *A Cheetah's Tale* Bradt, 2017. A wonderful story of a vanished Africa, of a girl growing up and of the incredible bond that can exist between humans and animals.

Scott, Jonathan and Angela *The Leopard's Tale* Bradt, 2013. A unique and moving portrait of Africa, and the most intimate record ever written about the secretive lives of leopards.

Other Bradt Africa guides For a full list of Bradt's Africa guides, see www.bradtguides.com/shop.

Briggs, Philip *South Africa Highlights* Bradt, 2011.

McIntyre, Chris *Botswana Safari Guide: Okavango Delta, Chobe, Northern Kalahari* Bradt, 2018.

McIntyre, Chris *Zambia* Bradt, 2016.

Murray, Paul *Zimbabwe* Bradt, 2019.
Stead, Mike, Scafidi, Oscar and Rorison, Sean *Angola* Bradt, 2019.

Health/reference

Dodwell, Christina *An Explorer's Handbook – Travel, Survival and Bush Cookery* Hodder & Stoughton, London, 1984. Over 170 pages of both practical and amusing anecdotes, including chapters on 'unusual eatables', 'building an open fire' and 'tested exits from tight corners'. Practical advice for both plausible and most unlikely eventualities – and it's a great read.

Wilson-Howarth, Dr Jane *The Essential Guide to Travel Health: Don't Let Bugs Bites and Bowels Spoil Your Trip* Cadogan Books, London, 2009. Formerly simply *Bugs, Bites and Bowels*, this amusing and erudite overview of the hazards of tropical travel is small enough to take with you.

Wilson-Howarth, Dr Jane, and Ellis, Dr Matthew *Your Child Abroad: A Travel Health Guide* Bradt Travel Guides, UK, 3rd edn ebook 2014. Full of practical first-hand advice from two leading medical experts. An indispensable guide if you plan to travel abroad with young children.

Fiction

Andreas, Neshani *The Purple Violet of Oshaantu* Heinemann, London, 2001. A Namibian woman's perspective on love and marriage in the context of traditional values and beliefs.

Brink, André *The Other Side of Silence* Vintage, London, 2003. The story of Hanna X, who joined a group of women sent to German South West Africa in the late 19th century to service the needs of the new colony's men. By turns brutal and uplifting.

Hiyalwa, Kaleni *Meekulu's Children* New Namibia Books, Windhoek, 2000. Reads more like a biography of a child growing up during Namibia's struggle for independence than a novel. Powerful stuff.

WEBSITES

www.airnamibia.com Air Namibia's site includes schedules and fares.
www.gov.na The official website of the Namibian government.
www.met.gov.na Ministry of Environment and Tourism website.
www.namibian.com.na *The Namibian* newspaper online.
www.namibiatourism.na Namibia Tourism Board's official site.
www.namibweb.com A rather ramshackle site focused on travel around Namibia.
www.nbc.com.na The government-sponsored Namibia Broadcasting Corporation (NBC).
www.nwr.com.na Namibia Wildlife Resorts (NWR). Essential for booking accommodation in national parks.
www.swakop.com Details useful information for tourists to Swakopmund and Walvis Bay.

FOLLOW BRADT

For the latest news, special offers and competitions, subscribe to the Bradt newsletter via the website www.bradtguides.com and follow Bradt on:

f BradtTravelGuides
🐦 @BradtGuides
📷 @bradtguides
P bradtguides
▶ bradtguides

Index

Page numbers in **bold** indicate major entries; those in *italics* indicate maps

INDEX OF ADVERTISERS